Abnormal Psychology
Current Perspectives
SECOND EDITION

Contributing Authors

George J. Allen
University of Connecticut

James E. Birren
University of Southern California

James P. Curran
Purdue University

Karen K. Evans
Institute for Behavioral Services

Michael B. Evans
*Institute for Juvenile Research,
Illinois Department of Mental Health*

Louis R. Franzini
San Diego State University

Leonard D. Goodstein
Arizona State University

Richard L. Hagen
Florida State University

Ella Lasky
*Manhattan Community College,
The City University of New York*

Alan J. Litrownik
San Diego State University

Robert W. Lundin
University of the South

Willard A. Mainord
University of Louisville

Robert G. Meyer
University of Louisville

C. Scott Moss
Federal Correctional Institution, Lompoc, California

Robert C. Neubeck
Institute for Behavioral Services

Oakley S. Ray
Vanderbilt University

Robert L. Solnick
University of Southern California

Bonnie R. Strickland
University of Massachusetts at Amherst

Fredric Weizmann
York University

Reviewers

Gilbert W. Derath
Michigan State University

Juris G. Draguns
Pennsylvania State University

Michael Gazzaniga
State University of New York at Stony Brook

Richard Hirschman
Kent State University

Allen C. Israel
State University of New York at Albany

Rosemary O. Nelson
University of North Carolina at Greensboro

Jacob Orlofsky
University of Missouri at St. Louis

David Pomerantz
State University of New York at Stony Brook

Coordinating Author
JAMES F. CALHOUN
State University of New York at Stony Brook

Writer
Joan Ross Acocella

Adviser
Leonard D. Goodstein
Arizona State University

Abnormal Psychology
Current Perspectives
SECOND EDITION

CRM / RANDOM HOUSE

Second Edition

987654321

Copyright© 1972, 1977 by Random House, Inc.

All rights reserved under International and Pan-American Copyright Conventions. No part of this book may be reproduced in any form or by any means, electronic or mechanical, including photocopying, without permission in writing from the publisher. All inquiries should be addressed to Random House, Inc., 201 East 50th Street, New York, N.Y. 10022. Published in the United States by Random House, Inc., and simultaneously in Canada by Random House of Canada Limited, Toronto.

Library of Congress Cataloging in Publication Data
Main entry under title:
Abnormal psychology.
Includes bibliographies and index.
1. Psychiatry. 2. Psychology, Pathological.
I. Calhoun, James F. II Acocella, Joan Ross.
III. Goodstein, Leonard David.
RC454.A25 1976 616.8'9 76-18948
ISBN 0-394-31062-4

Manufactured in the United States of America

Cover sculpture by Rodelinde Albrecht

Design by Leon Bolognese

Preface

In presenting the second edition of this book, we have been guided by the same hope that generated the first edition: the hope of furthering the current effort to view abnormal behavior from the two seemingly opposite poles of scientific precision and human understanding. For centuries the traditional approach to abnormal psychology has been a sort of obscure middle path between these two poles—a combination of mistrust, inference, and superstition. Much has been lost in the process. Those regarded as abnormal have been swept into a dark and forgotten corner of our social consciousness, there to suffer without help or understanding, while society itself, by clinging to a pinched vision of the "normal," has forfeited breadth, courage, and sympathy. Happily, this traditional attitude now shows signs of undergoing some revision. And for whatever this book can contribute to such change, we shall be grateful.

Introduction

In the second edition of *Abnormal Psychology: Current Perspectives*, we have sought to retain the strengths of the first edition. At the same time, however, the text has been reorganized and thoroughly rewritten, both to bring it up to date and to increase its pedagogical value.

The central theme of the first edition—that normal and abnormal behavior must be viewed as a continuum rather than a dichotomy—has been firmly restated. In chapter after chapter we have reiterated the caution against regarding abnormal behavior as something absolute, as something easily identifiable, or as something freakish and strange, from which most of us are safely insulated. In the view of this book, abnormal behavior develops according to the same principles as normal behavior. Indeed, abnormality is such only in the eye of the beholder, for it is, after all, the society's norms that determine what we will view as "normal" and "abnormal."

Just as the general philosophy of the first edition has been retained, so also has the organizational framework. This edition, like the last, utilizes the classificatory system of DSM-II. Though this system has severe limitations (which are discussed in detail within the text), it is still the most comprehensive system available and one with which the student should be familiar, if only because it is so widely used by diagnosticians. Nevertheless, in an attempt to compensate for the shortcomings of the system, both editions have deviated from it, the second more so than the first. Thus, in some chapters disorders classified separately in DSM-II have been presented together (as in Chapter 5, which deals with the neuroses, the personality disorders, and transient situational disorders); in other chapters classifications have split off from their DSM-II grouping (as in Chapter 8, where sociopathy is treated separately from the other personality disorders).

One unique feature of the first edition was its attempt to give the student the broadest possible view of abnormal behavior by studying the various behavioral deviations from the viewpoint of the three major theoretical perspectives: the psychodynamic, the behavioral, and the humanistic-existential. The second edition has retained this tripartite approach.

Indeed, it has improved upon it by devoting to each perspective a full introductory chapter, by stating each perspective's thinking on the origins and treatment of the various types of abnormal behavior in the chapters which form the central section of the book, and by examining in the final chapters each perspective's general approach to diagnosis and treatment. In addition, three other psychological perspectives—the interpersonal, the psychosocial, and the cognitive—along with the two major nonpsychological perspectives—the physiological and biological—are clearly introduced in Chapter 4; these, like the other major perspectives, are integrated with discussion of various disorders wherever relevant.

After providing these theoretical tools in the introductory chapters, the text proceeds to examine the various psychological disorders in Chapters 5 through 17. In all these chapters the number of case studies has been expanded. The reporting of research, the foundation on which our understanding is based, has been completely updated. Furthermore, the coverage of various topics has been expanded to reflect current concerns in psychology. Schizophrenia, a vastly inclusive and controversial category of abnormal behavior, is given two chapters: one to describe the problem in its various manifestations and a second to report on the wide range of current theories and research. Childhood psychosis, including both autism and childhood schizophrenia, is covered in a separate chapter, where it receives a more thorough treatment than in any other textbook on abnormal psychology. The sociopathic, sexual, and addictive disorders are each treated in a separate chapter and are reconsidered not only in light of the most current research but also in view of our shifting social attitudes toward these problems. Finally, the unit on the developmental disorders is the most thorough coverage available. Not only is a separate chapter devoted to the developmental problems of childhood, so that such matters as enuresis, night terrors, and stuttering can be considered in detail as *developmental* disorders (not to be confused with the more grave problems of childhood psychosis), a second chapter considers in careful detail a category of developmental disorder that is very much with us but too often ignored: the disorders of aging.

As for the supports to our text, the full-color graphics program that distinguished the first edition has been retained. At the same time, however, the captions for the illustrations have been thoroughly revised to enhance their pedagogical value, and many new photographs have been added. Also new is the series of boxed inserts appearing throughout the book. Many of these boxes summarize important concepts for the student. Others are designed to give the student something extra—for example, a description of a particularly fascinating research project or of a particularly vivid case.

Finally, there has been a complete revision of the textbook's ancillary materials, including a new *Readings, Cases, and Study Guide*, which provides a reading, a research report, a case study, and self-test items for each chapter.

By juggling these many balls at once, we have attempted to achieve three main objectives. First, through the description of the various types of abnormal behavior and through the reporting of theory and research, we have sought to provide the soundest possible information on abnormal psychology. Second, through the use of illustrations, boxes, and studies, we have made an effort to tie theory and research to concrete human reality, for otherwise it is unlikely to be valued or remembered. Finally, through repeated discussion of the slippery problems surrounding classification, diagnosis, and treatment, we have attempted to drive home the point that dealing with abnormalities in human behavior is not as clear-cut as dealing, for example, with abnormalities in the coloration of sweet peas. The study of abnormal behavior is both vaguer and more highly charged than any other area of scientific study. For while one behavioral abnormality may be caused by a misplaced molecule, another by misguided parents, another by infelicitous conditioning, another by a combination of these three factors and several others besides, they all have this in common—that they pierce to the core of our lives. Indeed, what we are examining when we study abnormal behavior is, at bottom, the obscure network of feeling—joy and sorrow, hope and despair, intimacy and isolation, mastery and terror—in which all of us, normal and abnormal, grope for the meaning of our lives.

Contents

VII
Dealing with Disorder

Boxed Inserts

I Historical and Theoretical Influences

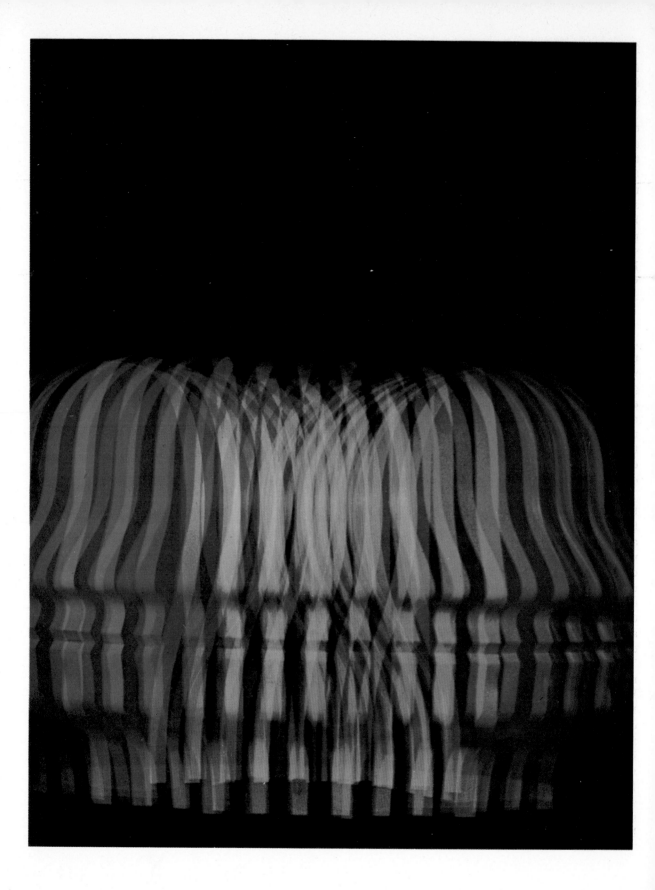

NORMS AND DEVIANCE

If in the 1970s a man stood on a busy streetcorner flagellating himself with a whip equipped with iron spokes at its tip, what would happen? It is likely that a concerned bystander would call the police and that the police would come and take the man to a psychiatric emergency ward, where he would be admitted to the ranks of the mentally disturbed. In the fourteenth century, however, when bubonic plague was raging across Europe, killing off scores of people, such flagellants stood in marketplaces throughout France, Italy, Germany, and eastern Europe, whipping themselves to atone for the sins that were presumed to have provoked God to send the so-called Black Death. And these flagellants were regarded with awe and reverence by the people through whose towns they passed on their penitential journey.

Such a difference in outlook is easily explained. The medieval mind had no inkling of the scientific rationalism of the twentieth century—the kind of thinking that could lead one to believe that anyone whipping himself should be treated for a mental disturbance or that plagues are more likely to emanate from rats than from divine wrath. Submerged as it was in a religion that transcended reason, the medieval mind could understand ecstasy, trance, and passionate self-sacrifice much more easily than it could have understood modern notions of common sense.

In short, the way we define madness changes with time and depends on the rules by which we live our lives, the behavioral norms that determine what we can and cannot do, and where and when and with whom. Such norms circumscribe every aspect of our existence, from our most far-reaching decisions down to our most prosaic daily routines. Let us examine, for example, the rather ordinary process of eating. Do we eat whatever we want, wherever and whenever we want it? We decidedly do not. Our eating behavior is governed by norms as to what is "good for us" to eat, how often we should eat, how much we should eat, and where we should eat. Eating at a football game or at a rock concert is fine, but eating in church, in a seminar, or at a symphony concert is not. Furthermore, there are rules as to when and where certain things can be eaten. Drinking wine with dinner is accepted practice; drinking wine with breakfast would be considered rather odd. Likewise, if a man lunches on shrimp cocktail and stuffed squab in the bleachers at the ball park, his sanity or at least his virility may well be questioned by the fans seated around him; he is expected to

1
Abnormality: Yesterday and Today

eat a ball-park lunch—hot dogs and beer. Conversely, if his wife serves hot dogs and beer at a candlelit dinner party, her guests, who are expecting something closer to, shrimp cocktail and stuffed squab, will consider her either very daring or very ignorant.

Some cultures even have strict taboos governing the question of whom one can eat with. Certain tribes, for instance, prohibit eating in the presence of blood relatives on the maternal side, since eating makes one vulnerable to being possessed by a devil and such devils are more likely to appear when one is in the presence of one's maternal relatives.

To the outsider, such norms may seem odd and unnecessarily complicated, but an adult who has been raised in the culture and who has assimilated its norms through the gradual process of socialization simply takes them for granted. Far from regarding them merely as folkways, he learns to regard them as what is "right." But what happens when a person deviates from these norms? How is this deviance regarded? This will depend essentially on three factors: how the society defines deviance, how it explains deviance, and how it handles deviance.

The Definition of Deviance

When we ask how a society defines deviance, what we are asking is how wide a range of behavior it will allow as acceptable. In many large university towns in the United States, for instance, a young person running a block or two across a university campus in the nude is not something that would cause a great concern either on the part of one's neighbors or on the part of the police. In other communities considerably more modest deviations are regarded with alarm. Thus there are many towns in Italy where a woman wearing a sleeveless dress is not allowed to enter a church. This question of how deviance is defined can cause considerable friction among various groups within a society. For example, the Gay Liberation movement now under way in some large cities in the United States may be conceptualized as an effort to convince American society to adjust its definition of normal behavior so that homosexuality will fall inside rather than outside the limits. And it may in fact be said that American society is in the process of broadening its definition of normalcy, so that fewer and fewer types of behavior are being classed as abnormal.

The Explanation of Deviance

But no matter how broad the definition of normal behavior, there will still be some behaviors that are considered abnormal. Murder, incest, and rape, for example, are not likely to be welcomed into most societies' "normal" range in the near future. And yet there will always be people who will commit these acts, along with a wide variety of other seemingly incomprehensible behaviors such as declaring oneself to be God, talking to nonexistent people, smearing feces on walls, and even biting off one's own fingers. This, then, brings us to our second question: How is a society to explain such deviant behavior? The answer is that a society will explain deviance according to its own prevailing beliefs. Indeed, the intellectual history of mankind can be read in the history of man's attempts to explain deviance: as possession by evil spirits, as a loss of divine grace, as the result of an early and severe toilet training, as a function of biochemical imbalances in the brain, and so on. Some societies attempt to subsume all deviant behavior under a single theory. In contrast, Western society has, since the eighteenth century, developed multiple theories of abnormal behavior. For example, it has drawn a distinction between criminality and "mental illness," a distinction that is based more on arbitrary legal definitions than on any clear evidence of an essential difference between the two forms of deviance.

The Handling of Deviance

Our final question—how a society handles deviance—will again be answered according to the nature of the society. In a small, traditional culture where the deviant person can be watched over, he may remain in the community, and his odd ways will be seen as a problem for the family rather than for the society. A large technological society, on the other hand, will tend to isolate the deviant so as to prevent him from disrupting the functioning of the family and the community and so as to prevent his behavior from influencing that of others. Where specific treatment procedures are used, these treatments will depend entirely on what we have just discussed: the way in which the society explains deviance. If bizarre behavior is interpreted as resulting from possession by devils, then the logical treatment is anything that is recognized as an efficient means of drawing out devils. Since devils are thought to be fearful of snakes, the deviant person can be placed in a pit of snakes. Likewise, since devils are known to be sensitive to insults, obscenities can be hurled at the deviant. Similarly, if deviance is seen as the fruit of deep-seated psychological conflicts, then the appropriate treatment is talking, so as to draw up into the consciousness whatever psychic calamity is responsible and then proceed to resolve it. Or if biochemical imbalances are thought to be the source of deviance, then the appropriate treatment is the administration of drugs to correct the imbalance. In short, the treatment of deviance will follow the explanation of deviance, and the explanation of deviance will follow the nature of the society.

How modern society defines, explains, and handles deviant behavior is the subject of this book. However, our modern conceptions of abnormal psychology are not a new birth. Rather, they are the result of centuries of trial and error in dealing with what each century has defined as abnormal. Accordingly, this chapter will present first a brief history of Western man's interpretation of deviance. We will then proceed to examine three modern interpretations of deviance: the statistical model, the medical model, and the psychological model.

CONCEPTIONS OF ABNORMALITY: A SHORT HISTORY

Ancient Demonology

Just as early man attributed all the movements of nature—health and sickness, sunshine and storm, good harvests and bad harvests—to the action of supernatural forces, so deviant behavior was explained as the result of possession by spirits. Archeological evidence indicates that Stone Age people had a rather direct way of dealing with these spirits, through a crude surgical technique called *trephining*. Trephining involved chipping a hole or *trephine* into the skull of the possessed person in order to allow the evil spirit to escape. Interestingly enough, certain skulls found in Peru show evidence of healing around the trephine, indicating that some of our ancestors actually survived the operation.

The idea that abnormal behavior was due to the body's being invaded by an evil spirit seems to have endured for many centuries. References to possession may be found in the ancient records of the Chinese, the Egyptians, the Greeks, and the Hebrews. The Bible itself mentions demonic possession in a number of places. King Saul is said to have had an "evil spirit" of which he could be relieved only by the sound of David's harp (1 Samuel 16). Leviticus deals straightforwardly with the subject of possession: "A man also or a woman that hath a familiar spirit, or that is a wizard, shall surely be put to death: they shall stone him with stones; their blood shall be upon them" (Leviticus 20:27)—a text that was to be invoked often during the witch hunts of later centuries. In the New Testament, Jesus himself is reported to have drawn out devils from the possessed. In one case he coaxed an entire legion of evil spirits out of a man and transferred them to a herd of swine, whereupon the swine flung themselves into the sea (Mark 5:1–13).

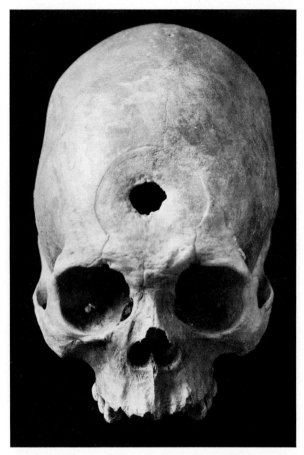

Fig. 1.1 *The technique of trephining involved chipping a hole in the skull of the disturbed person through which the evil spirit, believed to be the source of the person's abnormal behavior, might escape. That some individuals actually survived the operation is shown by this skull; the bone had had time to heal considerably before the individual died.*

However, not all spirits were regarded as evil. A person could be invaded by a divine spirit as well, in which case the person's irrational utterances were reverently regarded as cryptic fragments of divine truth, spoken not so much by the possessed person as by the divine spirit within him. Such, for example, seems to have been the case in ancient Greece with the priestesses of the oracle of Apollo at Delphi. When questioned by a suppliant, they would utter their replies in the lyrical and mysterious language

Handling Mental Illness in Traditional Societies

When someone living in a mobile, technological society cannot handle the demands and stresses of everyday life and reacts by becoming withdrawn or by exhibiting bizarre behavior, along with his other problems he finds himself unwelcome in that society. No one is free to take care of him; everyone is too busy. And no one really wants to see him; he has become not only a disturbed person but a disturbing presence. As Harry Truman said, "If you can't take the heat, get out of the kitchen." The mentally disturbed are ushered out of the "kitchen," placed in mental hospitals, and labeled as "sick," "crazy," or at least "different from the rest of us." In the eyes of society, they have failed.

Traditional societies offer a striking contrast to this manner of dealing with the psychologically disturbed. We shall look at two examples, the Hutterites of the American Midwest and the Gururumba of New Guinea.

The Hutterites are a small, cohesive religious sect occupying an isolated cluster of farm villages in Montana and the Dakotas. Their lives are governed by their strict Anabaptist religious principles: pacifism, austerity, moral self-examination, and above all, the welfare of the community. The Hutterites dress the same, worship daily in the same churches, hold all property communally, eat at communal tables, and know each other's business. Their world is stable and secure in a way that outsiders can scarcely understand. (For example, since 1875 only five Hutterite marriages have been dissolved.) While such a society demands a high price in conformity, it also yields many benefits in terms of community support. The orphaned, the disabled, and the aged are well taken care of. And so too are the mentally ill.

As structured and predictable as their lives are, the Hutterites are not immune to mental illness. One study (Eaton and Weil, 1953) found that of the present population, 1 out of 43 was either suffering from, or had recovered from, a mental disorder. However, the Hutterites' treatment of the mentally ill is quite unique in American society. At the first signal that a member of the

of the god who inhabited their bodies, often to the great confusion of the questioner.

The records that have survived, however, indicate that most possessions were held to be possessions by devils, in which case the evil spirit had to be drawn out of the person. This practice, called *exorcism*, involved a wide variety of techniques, ranging from the mild to the brutal. Prayer, noisemaking, and the drinking of various unsavory brews appeared to suffice in some cases. In other, more difficult cases, the possessed person was submerged in water, whipped, and starved in order to make the body a less comfortable habitation for the devil. Of course, many people died from such "cures"—an unfortunate result that was to be attributed to the strength of the evil spirit rather than to the incompetence of the healer.

The Greeks and the Rise of Rationalism

Among the many achievements for which ancient Greek civilization is so highly valued by Western culture, perhaps the most formidable is what has been called the Greeks' "discovery of the mind." To the Greeks of the fifth century B.C. we owe the birth of rationalism, the belief that human reason is equal to the task of understanding nature. And through the application of this new belief to psychological problems, abnormal behavior was for the first time in history studied as a natural rather than a supernatural phenomenon.

This latter innovation was essentially the work of one man, the Greek physician Hippocrates (c. 460– c. 360 B.C.). While most of his contemporaries still clung to the belief that madness was a punishment sent by the gods, Hippocrates set about to prove that all illness, including mental illness, was due to natural causes. He had little patience with mystical explanations. For example, in his treatise on epilepsy, known at the time as the "sacred disease," he noted: "If you cut open the head, you will find the brain humid, full of sweat and smelling badly. And in this way you may see that it is not a god

community is losing his grip, all the other members surround him and his family with sympathy and support. No stigma whatsoever is attached to mental illness; instead, the person is regarded as "sick," just as if he had the flu. He is taken care of at home (hospitals are shunned), and while he is permitted the rest and comfort usually accorded the ill, he is encouraged to do whatever work he can and to take part in whatever family and community activities he can handle. To the Hutterites, then, mental illness is no terror but a part of life, and a part that can be handled with sympathy and common sense.

The Gururumba of New Guinea differ from the Hutterites as widely as any primitive tribe could possibly differ from an austere Christian sect. But like the Hutterites, the Gururumba have reserved a place in their social structure for mental breakdown. Like other tribes of New Guinea, Malaya, and Indonesia, the Gururumba have a somewhat ritualistic way of breaking down, called "running amok" (Honigman, 1967). Amok occurs in three stages—depression, withdrawal, and finally a frenzied excitement in which the "wild man" goes berserk and runs through the village destroying whatever he lays his hands on. Among the Gururumba, amok occurs exclusively among young men who are just beginning to assume the prestige and the complicated economic responsibilities of adulthood. When a young man cannot handle this new burden, he runs amok, thus venting his fury and frustration. And while his fellow tribesmen assume that his frenzy is caused by ghosts, they take it as a signal that the man's role and responsibilities must be adjusted. They do not punish him for the damage he has caused, nor do they deprive him of comradeship. Rather, they simply expect less of him. They do not pressure him to pay his debts on time or to contribute his share of food for the tribal feasts. He is still very much a part of the tribe, but it is understood that he cannot pay the price of becoming one of its most powerful or respected members. He is willing to take a back seat, and they let him do so.

Thus in a sense the Gururumba react to the phenomenon of psychological breakdown somewhat differently from the Hutterites, who use care and compassion in the effort to restore the distressed individual to his former social role. There is, however, one important similarity, and it is typical of traditional societies in general—neither society withdraws its support from the individual, to say nothing of banishing him from their sight. The banishment approach, it might be said, is one of the costs of "civilization." Unfortunately, it is the helpless who pay.

which injures the body, but disease" (cited in Zilboorg and Henry, 1941, p. 44).

Hippocrates' achievement was threefold. First, he set himself the novel task of actually *observing* cases of mental disturbance and of recording his observations in as objective a manner as possible. Consequently, it is in his writings that we have our first truly scientific descriptions of mental disorders such as phobia, epilepsy, and postpartum psychosis. In short, Hippocrates was the first empirical clinician.

Second, Hippocrates developed the first *organic* theory of abnormal behavior—that is, a theory attributing abnormal behavior to physical disorders. Though he recognized that external stress could have a damaging psychological effect, it was primarily internal processes that he held responsible for mental disturbance. To modern science some of his organic theories appear rather crude. Hysteria, for example, he attributed to a wandering uterus. (The uterus at that time was thought to be unanchored in the female body and thus free to float about.)

Likewise, he believed that various personality disorders were due to an imbalance among four *humors*, or vital fluids, in the body: phlegm, blood, black bile, and yellow bile. An excess of phlegm rendered the person phlegmatic—that is, indifferent and sluggish. An excess of blood gave rise to rapid shifts in mood. Too much black bile made the individual melancholic, and too much yellow bile made him choleric—irritable and aggressive. However primitive some of these theories may seem, they foreshadowed and in many ways made possible today's physiological and biochemical research in abnormal psychology.

Third, Hippocrates was the first to attempt a unified system of abnormal mental states. He classified mental disorders into three categories: mania (abnormal excitement), melancholia (abnormal dejection), and phrenitis (brain fever).

Hippocrates' great contributions were in the areas of theory and methodology. He made no important advances specifically in the cure of mental disorder.

However, his treatment methods were considerably more humane than those of the exorcistic tradition, and this in itself was of course a significant advance. His treatment for melancholia, for example, involved rest, exercise, a bland diet, and abstinence from sex and alcohol. Since such a regimen could be most easily followed under supervision, he often moved patients into his home, where he could watch them.

This trend toward a gentler and more dignified treatment was supported by Hippocrates' younger contemporary, the philosopher Plato (429–347 B.C.). Though still adhering to a quasi-supernatural theory of mental disorder, Plato insisted that the mentally disturbed should be regarded as a family responsibility and that they should not be held accountable or be punished in any way for their irrational acts. Such thinking led to the establishment, in later Greek civilization, of retreats for the mentally ill. In Alexandria, for example, special temples dedicated to the god Saturn were set aside as asylums where the mentally ill could recover with the help of rest, exercise, music, and other therapeutic activities.

The Middle Ages and Renaissance: The Return to Demonology

With the fall of Greek civilization and the transfer of empire to Rome, the enlightened Hippocratic approach to mental disorder survived for yet a few more centuries. In the first century B.C., Asclepiades, a Greek physician practicing in Rome, was the first to differentiate between chronic and acute mental illness; furthermore, he described the differences among hallucination, delusion, and illusion and explained how each of these could be used as a diagnostic sign. Galen (129–c. 199 A.D.), another Greek physician who practiced in Rome, codified the organic theories of his predecessors and made significant advances in anatomical research. (It was Galen, for example, who first showed that the arteries contained blood—not air, as was commonly thought.) After the death of Galen, however, there was little progress. And eventually, with the fall of Rome to the barbarians in the fifth century, naturalistic psychology gave way to a resurgence of ancient superstition. Demonology was reborn and quietly received into the arms of the new Christian church.

Madness in the Middle Ages The literature and art of the period indicate that during the Middle Ages there seems to have been an alarming rise in the incidence of mental illness. Furthermore, peculiar

episodes of mass madness developed. At the beginning of this chapter we have mentioned the *flagellants*, who roamed Europe in bands, ecstatically whipping themselves. In Italy, and later throughout Europe, there were also numerous outbreaks of *tarantism* or dancing frenzy. Presumably because they had been bitten by a tarantula, people would rush out of their houses and begin dancing frenetically in the streets, much to the amazement of their neighbors. Soon the neighbors too were "infected," and the entire mob would dance itself to exhaustion. Elsewhere there were episodes of *lycanthropy*, in which groups of people, particularly in rural villages, got the notion that they were wolves and began behaving accordingly.

Apparently even small children were not immune to mass madness. Contemporary accounts relate episodes in which groups of children would go into seizures, and in response to exorcistic treatments, would vomit up various exotic items such as feathers, spangles, and pieces of cloth (Goshen, 1967).

Such epidemics of mass hysteria are less difficult to understand when we consider the lives that ordinary people led in the Middle Ages. In the first place, the Roman Catholic religion, which touched every corner of their lives, consistently deemphasized reason in favor of the miraculous, the ecstatic, and the irrational. Second, daily existence for these people was in no way easy. Particularly in the late Middle Ages, when mass madness reached its peak, Europe was festering with war, social revolutions, famine, and plagues and thus provided a fertile ground for the growth of a general emotional uneasiness.

Demonology and Exorcism The treatment of the mentally ill in the Middle Ages must, like everything else medieval, be viewed within the context of the Christian church. Just as religion was the foundation for the glorious artistic achievements of the period, so also was Christian doctrine often used as justification for the abuse of the mentally ill during the Middle Ages and Renaissance. Unlike the religion of the Greeks, which glorified the human body and its earthly existence, the early Christian church held that earthly life was simply a proving ground for the *true* life—that is, life after death, which would last unto eternity. In this scheme the individual mattered very little; his body was simply the squalid prison of his eternal soul, and that soul belonged to God. Thus it is no surprise that the naturalistic psychology of the ancient Greeks, which looked to the human body and the vicissitudes of human life for the

Fig. 1.2   In this sixteenth-century drawing by Brueghel, men are shown restraining women afflicted with tarantism or dancing frenzy.

causes of mental disorder, was eclipsed as the church slowly gained power. Its place was taken by super-naturalism, the belief that all things in nature must be explained in terms of a divine will beyond the reach of human reason. And this attitude held sway as long as the church retained its power.

So early science was replaced by ancient demon-ology. In the early Middle Ages the possessed were generally subjected to rather gentle exorcistic treat-ments. They were prayed over, sprinkled with holy water, taken to various shrines, and given the usual potions to drink. As time passed, however, theolog-ical doctrine regarding possession was refined, and treatments accordingly became less mild. The possessed were starved, dunked in hot water, chained, and flogged. One pious healer recorded the following prescription: "In case a man be lunatic, take a skin of mere-swine [porpoise], work it into a whip, and swinge [whip] the man forthwith; soon he will be well. Amen" (cited in Zilboorg and Henry, 1941, p. 140). Another popular technique was to yell a long litany of insults and curses at the possessed. Devils were known to be very proud; it was Satan's

pride, after all, that had caused his fall from Heaven. Thus it was hoped that a barrage of insults, by wounding the devil's pride, would drive him out of the possessed. A priest who wearied of making up his own curses could simply read from the popular *Treasury of Exorcisms*, which contained hundreds of pages of violent curses anthologized for use on such occasions (Deutsch, 1949).

It should by no means be assumed that either the belief in demons or the faith in exorcistic treatments was confined to the ignorant and the violent. Martin Luther himself was convinced that Satan followed him around and inflicted various illnesses on his body to keep him from his holy work. And the wise and mild-mannered Sir Thomas More, after seeing to the treatment of a lunatic, wrote to a friend as follows: "I caused him to be taken by the constables and bound to a tree in the street before the whole

town, and there striped [whipped] him until he waxed weary. Verily, God be thanked, I hear no more of him now" (cited in Deutsch, 1949, p. 13). Indeed, almost everyone believed, and those who did not generally kept their silence.

The Witch Hunts Early in the fifteenth century the church tended to distinguish between voluntary possession, in which a person deliberately made a pact with the devil, and involuntary possession, in which the unfortunate individual, against his will, was simply invaded by a devil. Accordingly, the latter type was originally treated less harshly. However, by the end of the fifteenth century, such distinctions had faded. All persons who were deranged were held totally responsible for their actions. In short, they were considered to be witches and sorcerers. Floods, pestilence, bad crops, miscarriages, lamed horses—any event that was distressing and inexplicable was blamed on whatever hapless individual in the village happened to be acting queerly. And since the mentally disturbed often imagine that they have committed heinous sins or have engaged in all manner of exotic forbidden practices, it is not surprising to find that many of the accused freely confessed to whatever crimes they were charged with. When they did not confess freely, they were tortured until they did confess—and often

Fig. 1.3 *In medieval times abnormal behavior was taken as evidence of the devil's work, and the detection and treatment of the disturbed was the responsibility of the religious establishment. This late-fifteenth-century painting portrays St. Catherine of Siena casting the devil out of a possessed woman. The devil is pictured as a tiny imp fleeing from the woman's head, apparently to escape the forces of prayer and goodness.*

until they implicated others as well. Once the confession had been extracted, they were summarily tried and then strangled, hanged, beheaded, or burned alive.

Thus the witch hunts began. Ironically enough, this dark period in the treatment of mental illness spans the three centuries of the Renaissance, the period that has been venerated by later ages as the rebirth of ancient wisdom—of learning, of science, of curiosity about man and nature, and of reverence for earthly existence. It is conservatively estimated that from the middle of the fifteenth century to the end of the seventeenth, 100,000 people were executed as witches. During the seventeenth century twenty thousand witches were put to death in Scotland alone. In England, France, Italy, and Germany, thousands more were hanged and burned in town squares. In Geneva in 1515, two hundred witches were burned alive in a period of only three months

Modern Exorcism

To many modern readers, living in a scientific age, the ancient practice of exorcism appears crude, bizarre, and shockingly naïve. The fact is, however, that exorcisms are still performed today—and not just by "free-lance" Pentecostal preachers or Jesus freaks, but also by Roman Catholic, Greek Orthodox, Anglican, and Lutheran clergymen. This fact, which came to light amid the excitement generated by the popular theological horror movie *The Exorcist*, has been consistently played down by the churches involved. Most Christian clergymen take a very dim view of demonology. Cases of "possession," they point out, are routinely referred to psychiatrists, and exorcism is reserved as a rite of very last resort, to be attempted only in extraordinary cases and only after psychiatrists and physicians, our latter-day secular exorcists, have given up the case.

Nevertheless, this last resort has been used and is still being used. Monsignor Luigi Novarese, the official Roman Catholic exorcist of the Pope's own diocese of Rome, reports that he has performed about sixty exorcisms, always without harm to himself or the possessed. American clergymen are a bit more reluctant both to perform the ancient rite and to discuss it. Episcopal Archdeacon John Weaver of San Francisco claims that during one exorcism, "I saw something black go out of a person and dive into a lake. What happened was so shaking that I didn't do another exorcism" (cited in Woodward, 1974). Others, however, continue to perform exorcisms despite their own qualms and despite criticism and ridicule from their fellow clergymen. Recently, for example, Father Karl Patzelt, a Jesuit priest who directs the Russian Catholic Center of San Francisco, managed, with the approval of his archbishop, to dispose of a group of "demons" who for two years had been setting fires, moving furniture, throwing knives, and pulling other tricks in the home of a suburban family.

Many psychiatrists and religious thinkers attribute the current fascination with exorcism, and what appears to be the current rise in the number of exorcisms being performed, to the spiritual impoverishment of our age: cut off from God by technology, science, and rationalism, our spiritual yearnings, they claim, have issued into the perverse channel of demonology. Others, including Father Patzelt, feel that anything that affirms the reality of the devil also affirms the reality of God and is thus of spiritual value. Whatever the reason, demonology—along with witchcraft, astrology, and other occult sciences—has captured the imagination of a large sector of the American public within the last few years. And the primitive rite of exorcism, though its rarity would not seem to justify the recent publicity, is still with us.

Fig. 1.4   In the fifteenth and sixteenth centuries, mass disorder was believed to be caused by witchcraft, and bizarre behavior was evidence that the "afflicted" individual had either been seized by or was in league with the devil. This sixteenth-century woodcut depicts the devil carrying off a witch.

Approaches to Abnormal Behavior:
A Historical Sketch

Ancient Greece, China, Middle East	Demonology and exorcism
Greece: fifth century B.C.	Hippocrates: scientific study of abnormal behavior as a natural phenomenon
Europe: fifth–fifteenth centuries A.D.	Demonology and exorcism
Europe and American colonies: late fifteenth–seventeenth centuries	Publication of *Malleus Maleficarum*; witch hunts; establishment of first mental hospitals
Europe: eighteenth century	Pinel: unchaining of patients at La Bicêtre; reform of mental hospitals
	Pinel and Tuke: introduction of moral therapy
	Mesmer: discovery of hypnosis
United States: eighteenth century	Rush: advancement of cause of mental health in United States
United States: nineteenth century	Dix: campaign for widespread establishment of mental hospitals
Europe: nineteenth century	Rise of biogenic theory: Kraepelin's classification of mental illnesses; linking of general paresis to syphilis
	Rise of psychogenic theory: Liébault and Bernheim's success with hypnosis; Breuer and Freud, *Studies in Hysteria*; Freud's development of psychoanalysis

(Deutsch, 1949). The hunting down of witches ceased to be simply a reaction to some natural calamity; instead, it became a day-to-day social and religious duty. Neighbors reported neighbors. Priests turned in their own parishioners. Everyone was suspect. And the best defense against suspicion was to show a pious zeal in reporting others.

In 1484 Pope Innocent VIII, alarmed at the rise in the incidence of demonic possession, issued a papal bull formally endorsing the witch hunts. The pope began:

It has indeed lately come to Our ears, not without afflict-ing Us with bitter sorrow, that ... many persons of both sexes, unmindful of their own salvation and straying from the Catholic Faith, have abandoned themselves to devils, ... and by their incantations, spells, conjurations, and other accursed charms and crafts, enormities and horrid offences, have slain infants yet in the mother's womb, as also the offspring of cattle, have blasted the produce of the earth, the grapes of the vine, the fruits of trees, nay, men and women, beasts of burthen, herd-beasts, as well as animals of other kinds, vineyards, or-chards, meadows, pasture-land, corn, wheat, and all other cereals; these wretches furthermore afflict and torment men and women, beasts of burthen, herd-beasts, as well

as animals of other kinds, with terrible and piteous pains and sore diseases, both internal and external; they hinder men from performing the sexual act and women from conceiving, whence husbands cannot know their wives nor wives receive their husbands; over and above this, they blasphemously renounce that Faith which is theirs by the Sacrament of Baptism, and at the instigation of the Enemy of Mankind they do not shrink from commit-ting and perpetrating the foulest abominations and filth-iest excesses to the deadly peril of their own souls, whereby they outrage the Divine Majesty and are a cause of scandal and danger to very many (cited in Zilboorg and Henry, 1941, pp. 147–148).

The document went on to say that two Dominican monks, Heinrich Kraemer and Johann Sprenger, had been appointed by the Holy See to lead the inquisition against the evildoers.

To aid themselves and other inquisitors, Kraemer and Sprenger put together a manual, entitled *Malleus Maleficarum* ("The Witches' Hammer"). The *Malleus* had three parts. The first affirmed em-phatically the existence of witches and the duty of all Christians to recognize their existence. The second part detailed the symptoms by which witches could be recognized. (A reliable sign, for example, was the presence of red or insensitive spots on the skin; these were the marks made by the devil's claw when he touched the witch to seal the pact.) The third part of the manual described the proper procedures for examining and sentencing witches. The *Malleus* went into numerous printings. Believed by many to have been divinely inspired, it became the bible of three centuries of witch-hunting.

Witch-hunting in America Witch-hunting came late to the American colonies, but when it came, in the seventeenth century, it spread quickly, fanned by the simultaneously repressive and naïve religion of the Puritans. The American witch hunt reached its peak in the famous witchcraft craze of Salem, Massachusetts, in 1692. This ignominious episode is described as follows by Deutsch:

The witchcraft mania in Salem grew out of the quite innocent frolics of a group of young girls who used to gather at the village minister's house. Here they were wont to play at fortune-telling and palm-reading and to discuss the supernatural. Ghosts, devils and witches were favorite subjects of their discussions. In the tense, repressed atmosphere of Salem, where the "invisible world" seemed even to the soberest adults as immanent and real as the visible world, the over-wrought imaginations of these sternly repressed children began to break through the bounds of sanity. They started to see strange things, hear preternatural voices, and dream strange dreams. Their condition soon came to the attention of the village elders, who investigated and solemnly concluded that the girls were "afflicted," or bewitched.

Stimulated and excited by the attention they had attracted, . . . the children began to manifest in heightened degrees all sorts of hysterical symptoms; they barked and mewed, they went into frequent "fits" of catalepsy and convulsions, they jumped and screamed, uttered wild gibberish . . . leaped on tables and crawled under them, and cried out that they were being choked, weighed down, pricked and slashed by the devil and his witches.

Pressed for the names of those who were casting evil spells over them, they named first one, then another, of the inhabitants of Salem until it seemed that fully half the village had signed their souls over to the devil. Terror seized the villagers. The hysteria became contagious, and others were soon exhibiting the same symptoms and hurling wild accusations against their neighbors. In that one year (1691–92), 250 persons were arrested and tried in Salem on witchcraft charges: fifty were condemned; nineteen were executed; two died in prison; and one died of torture.

The type of testimony that was accepted as truth by the unbelievably credulous judges, and that was instrumental in sending a score of innocents to their death, is exemplified in the interrogation of Sarah Carrier, eight. . . :

"How long hast thou been a witch?"
"Ever since I was six years old."
"How old are you now?"
"Near eight years old."
"Who made you a witch?"
"My mother. She made me set my hand to the book."
"You said you saw a cat once. What did the cat say to you?"
"It said it would tear me to pieces if I would not set my hand to the book." [that is, the "Devil's Book"]
"How did you know that it was your mother?"
"The cat told me so, that she was my mother" (1949, pp. 34–35).

Thus Sarah Carrier's mother, Martha, was hanged as a witch.

In the face of such gruesome and irrational proceedings, influential people at last began to object. In 1693 the governor of Massachusetts Colony ordered the release of all those imprisoned on witchcraft charges. And though trials did recur occasionally, the witch hunts soon died out. In 1722 one final witch was burned in Scotland. Thereafter the treatment of the mentally ill in Europe and America gradually entered a more rational phase.

The Eighteenth and Nineteenth Centuries: The Return to Science

There had in fact been a number of lonely voices raised in protest while the witchcraft frenzy was still raging. The Swiss physician Paracelsus (1493–1541) objected openly and adamantly to demonology. Paracelsus' theory of mental illness was hardly more scientific than that of the witch-burners; he was convinced that madness was caused by movements of the moon and the stars. Yet for the time, Paracelsus' attitude toward the mentally disturbed was truly revolutionary. He vehemently rejected the notion that the mentally ill were to blame for their aberrations. Instead, he saw them as unfortunate souls in need of help. "The insane and the sick are our brothers," he declared. "Let us give them treatment to cure them, for nobody knows whom among our friends or relatives this misfortune may strike" (cited in Zilboorg, 1935, p. 93).

Another courageous opponent of demonology was Johann Weyer (1515–1588), a German physician who appears to have been the first medical practitioner to specialize in mental illness. Strictly concerned with empirical evidence, the humane, commonsensical Weyer in 1563 published a massive treatise declaring that those who were being tortured and burned as witches were actually mentally ill. Weyer argued that demonology was an offense

Fig. 1.5 *A full moon was believed to cause madness, from which the terms "lunacy" and "lunatic" were derived. This seventeenth-century French engraving depicts moonstruck women dancing in the town square.*

against God and that the only pious course was for men to use the equipment that God had given them, their brains, to discover the natural causes of mental illness. Weyer's lead was soon followed by an Englishman named Reginald Scot, who in 1584 published his *Discovery of Witchcraft*, a scholarly work pointing out in painstaking detail the overwhelming evidence of mental illness in those who were being persecuted and the overwhelming lack of evidence of their diabolical powers. The response of church and state to such writings was swift and unequivocal. Weyer was denounced from the pulpit, and his writings were banned by the church. Scot's book was ordered seized and burned by King James I, who then proceeded himself to write a refutation, entitled *Demonology*.

The skeptical French philosopher Michel de Montaigne (1533–1592) also spoke out, arguing as usual for caution, tolerance, and a healthy doubt:

The lives of the witches in my neighborhood are in danger whenever a new writer appears who takes their dreams for fact. . . . One should not always respect the confessions of persons involved in a crime, for there have been too many cases in which people accused themselves of having killed others who were afterwards found alive and in good health. Those extravagant accusations! I think it suffices to deem an individual, whatever his reputation, capable of what is human. . . . Is it not far more natural to think that our mind is deranged by the volubility of our crazed spirits than to believe that a mere mortal with the help of strange spirits could in person fly out through the chimney on a broomstick? (cited in Zilboorg and Henry, 1941, pp. 169–170)

Protests came from within the church as well. St. Vincent de Paul placed himself in great danger by declaring openly that the so-called possessed were simply ill and that the duty of Christians was to help them rather than to persecute them.

Such protests, as we have seen, had little effect in their own time. Eventually, however, with the advent of the eighteenth century—the period that we call the Enlightenment—passion gave way to reason, and mental illness was given back into the hands of science.

The Reform of the Asylums During the Renaissance a number of hospitals for the mentally ill had been founded in various cities. Such hospitals appeared first in Moslem Spain during the fifteenth century. Then in the following centuries Christian Europe and America followed the example. Mental hospitals were opened in London, Paris, Vienna, Moscow, Philadelphia, and other cities. However, the dreadful conditions which the mentally ill endured in such "asylums" made the quick death meted out by the witch-hunters seem almost merciful in comparison. In the first mental hospital to be founded in Christian Europe, the hospital of St. Mary at Bethlehem in London, patients lay howling in chains while the curious public bought tickets to go in and watch them perform. (Eventually the hospital's contracted name, "Bedlam," became a synonym for any wild mob scene.) In other hospitals patients were chained, caged, starved, preyed upon by rats, left for years lying naked in their own excrement, and, as at Bedlam, displayed in their misery for the amusement

Fig. 1.6 Two well-dressed English matrons tour the wards of Bedlam. For many years anyone who paid the admission fee could view the inmates there.

of the public (Foucault, 1965). In Vienna, the architects of the new mental hospital managed to create an ingenious structure, the so-called Lunatics' Tower, in which the mentally ill were housed along the outer walls of a round tower so that they could be viewed by interested passers-by.

The first change in this system came in the late eighteenth century, through the work of Philippe Pinel (1745–1826), chief physician at La Bicêtre, a large asylum in Paris, during the French Revolution. Pinel's position was simple: that the mentally ill were simply ordinary human beings who had been deprived of their reason by severe personal problems and that to treat them like animals was not only inhumane but also obstructive to recovery. Pinel managed to convince the revolutionary government to allow him to unchain a group of patients at La Bicêtre, many of whom had not seen the light of day for thirty or forty years. The story of the unchaining has become quite famous. Their legs lame from disuse, their lungs unaccustomed to fresh air, their eyes dazzled by the sunlight, the patients hobbled out onto the grounds, awe-struck by a world whose existence they had forgotten (Selling, 1940). Pinel's experiment, which could easily have backfired, succeeded far beyond his hopes. Not only did the patients become more manageable, but many of them recovered and were released.

The unchaining was only the first of Pinel's reforms. He replaced the foul dungeons in which the patients had lived with airy, sunny rooms. He did away with such violent treatments as bleeding, purging, and cupping (blistering the skin by placing

Fig. 1.7 Chaotic and inhumane conditions in the asylums of the eighteenth and nineteenth centuries undoubtedly perpetuated and intensified the disordered behavior of persons condemned to them. An eighteenth-century engraving portrays the infamous London robber Jack Sheppard, visiting his mother in her cell in the Bedlam asylum.

Fig. 1.8   Philippe Pinel supervises the unchaining of the inmates at La Salpêtrière, the hospital he directed after his work at La Bicêtre.

small hot cups on it). Furthermore, he spent long hours talking with the patients, listening to their problems and giving them comfort and advice. He also kept records of these conversations and began developing a case history for each patient.*

Later Pinel reorganized Paris' other large mental hospital, La Salpêtrière, along the same lines. And after his retirement, his student and successor Jean Esquirol (1772–1840) extended his reforms, founding ten new mental hospitals in various parts of France, all based on the humane, rational treatment developed by Pinel.

At the same time that Pinel was instituting the first changes at La Bicêtre, a Quaker by the name of William Tuke was attempting similar reforms in northern England. Convinced that the most therapeutic environment for the mentally ill would be a quiet and supportive religious setting, Tuke moved a group of mental patients to a peaceful rural estate which he called York Retreat. There they talked out their problems, worked, prayed, rested, and took walks through the countryside. Not surprisingly, York Retreat's recovery rate was high.

---

*It is important to keep in mind the significance of Pinel's record-keeping. The characteristic patterns that emerge in the course of various disorders can only be determined if records are kept. Prior to Pinel, progress in the identification of such patterns—necessary for classification, research into the etiology of disease, and, most important of all, treatment—was not possible.

Though vigorously resisted by Pinel's and Tuke's contemporaries, these new techniques eventually became widespread, under the name of *moral therapy*. Based on the idea that the mentally ill were simply ordinary people with extraordinary numbers of problems, moral therapy aimed at restoring their "moral" balance by providing a pleasant and relaxed environment in which they could discuss their difficulties, live peacefully, and engage in some useful employment. More than anything else, moral therapy aimed at treating patients like human beings. And apparently this approach was stupendously successful. Contemporary records show that during the first half of the nineteenth century, when moral therapy was the only treatment provided by mental hospitals in Europe and America, at least 70 percent of those hospitalized for a year or less either improved or actually recovered.

The Reform Movement in America   The foremost figure in the development of the American mental health system was Benjamin Rush (1745–1813), born in the same year as Pinel and known as the "father of American psychiatry." A very famous doctor—as well as a signer of the Declaration of Independence, a member of the Continental Congress, surgeon general to the Continental army, treasurer of the United States Mint, and founder of the first free medical dispensary and the first antislavery society

Fig. 1.9 A technique for treating depression in the nineteenth century: the unhappy individual was spun in a rotating chair.

Fig. 1.10 Unlike the punitive devices of the seventeenth and eighteenth centuries, this nineteenth-century crib was used only for restraining violent patients.

in America—Rush advanced the cause of mental health by writing the first American treatise on mental problems (*Medical Inquiries and Observations upon the Diseases of the Mind*, 1812), by organizing the first medical course in psychiatry, and by devoting his attention, as the foremost physician at Philadelphia Hospital, exclusively to mental problems. In retrospect, Rush's theories seem rather primitive: he believed that mental illness was due to the blood vessels' in the brain being overloaded with blood as the result of excitement. And the treatments to which this theory led him seem even more primitive. To relieve the pressure in the blood vessels, he relied very heavily on bleeding. Furthermore, he held that terrifying patients by such methods as strapping them into a gruesome-looking device called the "tranquilizer" or dropping them suddenly into ice-cold baths was also useful in slowing down the flow of blood to the brain. However, these procedures were clearly intended not to torture but to cure, and were accompanied by a number of very humane practices. For example, Rush recommended that doctors regularly bring little presents such as fruit or cake to their patients. He also insisted that Philadelphia Hospital hire intelligent and kind attendants such as would be fit companions for the patients—to read to them, to talk to them, and to share in their activities. In sum, Rush contributed a great deal to American psychiatry, lending it his

prestige and turning it in the direction of a humane therapy.

The job of extending these reforms was taken up by an unknown Boston schoolteacher named Dorothea Dix (1802–1887). At the age of forty Dix took a job teaching Sunday school in a prison. There she had her first contact with the gruesome conditions suffered by the mentally ill. Soon she was traveling across the country visiting the squalid jails and poorhouses in which the mentally ill were confined and lecturing the state legislatures on their duty to these miserable and forgotten people. To the Massachusetts legislature she spoke as follows:

I come to place before the Legislature of Massachusetts the condition of the miserable, the desolate, the outcast. I come as the advocate of helpless, forgotten, insane and idiotic men and women . . . of beings wretched in our prisons, and more wretched in our Alms-Houses.

I proceed, Gentlemen, briefly to call your attention to the state of Insane Persons confined within this Commonwealth, in *cages, closets, cellars, stalls, pens: Chained, naked, beaten with rods,* and lashed into obedience (cited in Deutsch, 1941, p. 165).

Dix carried her campaign across the United States, to Canada, and to Scotland. Not only was she directly responsible for the founding and funding of thirty-two mental hospitals, but she also established the care of the mentally disturbed as a primary public obligation.

The Mental Hygiene Movement

While Dorothea Dix was able to move thousands of the mentally disturbed out of prisons and alms-houses and into the new mental hospitals, they were often treated no better in their new homes than in their old. Indeed, many of them were gradually beaten to death by the attendants assigned to care for them. In 1908, Clifford Beers, an educated man who had recently recovered from a four-year bout with psychosis, published *A Mind That Found Itself*, a book documenting the abuse inflicted on him and his fellow patients in three different institutions. The following is a typical vignette:

Of all the patients known to me, the one who was assaulted with the greatest frequency was an incoherent and irresponsible man of sixty years. . . . He was profoundly convinced that one of the patients had stolen his stomach—an idea inspired perhaps by the remarkable corpulency of the person he accused. His loss he would wofully voice even while eating. Of course, argument to the contrary had no effect; and his monotonous recital of his imaginary troubles made him unpopular with those whose business it was to care for him. They showed him no mercy. Each day—including the hours of the night, when the night watch took a hand—he was belabored with fists, broom handles, and frequently with the heavy bunch of keys which attendants usually carry on a long chain. He was kicked and choked. . . . An exception to the general rule (for such continued abuse often causes death), this man lived a long time—five years, as I learned later ([1908] 1970, p. 169).

Soon after his recovery, Beers founded the National Committee for Mental Hygiene, dedicated to teaching the public that the mentally ill should be treated rather than punished for their unusual behaviors and to raising money for the improvement of the state institutions. Beers' campaign, supported by the famous psychologist William James, was one more milestone in the centuries-old struggle to convince the average citizen that the mentally disturbed are still human beings. The struggle continues today.

However, Dix's reforms had one unfortunate result that she could not have anticipated, and that is that they contributed to the decline of moral therapy (Foucault, 1965). The new hospitals Dix inspired became overcrowded almost immediately, thus dispelling the calm, tranquil atmosphere necessary to moral therapy. Walled off in somber isolation in rural areas, these institutions also helped the public to unlearn the lesson that Pinel and Tuke had worked so hard to teach: that the mentally ill were simply ordinary people. To the public mind, these huge fortresses seemed to conceal some dark horror, and the mentally disturbed were once again seen as freakish, dangerous, and alien.

But the major factor in the decline of moral therapy was the increasing popularity of the organic theory of mental illness, the so-called *medical model*. The development of the medical model (which will be discussed in the next section) convinced those working with the mentally disturbed that their efforts should be directed toward biological research rather than toward the creating of the total therapeutic environments typical of moral therapy. Thus the money that had been going to pay attendants who knew how to read to the patients and play chess with them was now redirected toward equipping laboratories. The effect of the medical model on the public mind was equally decisive. It simply confirmed whatever suspicions the public had that the mentally disturbed were *not* like other people. They were "sick," and therefore, unlike other human beings, they could not profit from comfort and rest in order to pull themselves back together. Furthermore, their sickness made them "different," so they did not have to be shown the same consideration that one would extend to an ordinary human being.

Thus moral therapy fell into disuse. Recovery rates dropped considerably and have not increased to any significant degree ever since (Bockoven, 1963; Dain, 1964). Indeed, it is only recently that these recovery rates have been pointed to in criticism of the medical model and that efforts have been made to revive moral therapy under the name of "milieu therapy" (Chapter 19).

Biogenic vs. Psychogenic Theory

In the later chapters of this book it will become clear that for almost every type of mental disturbance there is a lively dispute between proponents of a *biogenic* theory (i.e., the medical model), claiming that the disturbance is due to an organic disorder, and proponents of a *psychogenic* theory, claiming that the disturbance is due primarily to emotional stress. This schism, which often lends a certain live-liness to psychological journals, first became pronounced in the nineteenth century.

The Rise of the Medical Model Biogenic theory, as we have seen, had its start with Hippocrates. Then, after centuries of demonology, the biogenic viewpoint began to surface once again in the late eighteenth and early nineteenth centuries, when medical research was making rapid advances. The first systematic presentation of the biogenic theory of mental disturbance was made by a German psychiatrist, Wilhelm Griesinger, in the middle nineteenth century. But it was Emil Kraepelin (1865–1926), a follower of Griesinger's, who first placed the medical model in the forefront of European psychiatric theory. In his *Textbook of Psychiatry* (1883), Kraepelin not only argued for the central role of brain pathology in mental disturbance but furnished psychiatry with its first comprehensive classification system, based on the biogenic viewpoint. He contended that mental illness, like physical illness, was divisible into separate pathologies, each of which had a different organic cause and each of which could be recognized by a distinct cluster of symptoms, called a *syndrome*. Once the symptoms appeared, the mental disturbance could be classified. And once classified, its course and outcome could be expected to resemble those seen in other cases of the same illness, just as one case of the mumps can be expected to develop and turn out like other cases of mumps.

Kraepelin's organic theory and his classification system received wide publicity and generated high hopes that the hitherto impenetrable mysteries of mental illness might be shown to have concrete, chemically manageable organic causes. At the same time the neurological and genetic components of psychopathology were gaining attention through the writings of another famous follower of Griesinger's, Richard von Krafft-Ebing (1840–1902), who emphasized organic and hereditary causation in his *Textbook of Psychiatry* (1886) and in his pioneering encyclopedia of sexual disorders, *Psychopathia Sexualis* (1892).

At the turn of the century neurological research was progressing so rapidly that it seemed that the hopes raised by Kraepelin might at last be in the process of fulfillment. The senile psychoses, the toxic psychoses, cerebral arteriosclerosis, mental retardation—one mental syndrome after another was tied down to a specific brain pathology. The most stunning success of all, however, was the discovery,

through the work of Krafft-Ebing and other scientists, that *general paresis*, a mysterious mental syndrome involving the gradual and irreversible breakdown of physical and mental functioning, was simply an advanced case of syphilis, in which the syphilitic spirochetes had passed through the bloodstream and into the central nervous system and the brain.

This discovery had an immense impact on the mental health profession and helped to establish the medical model of mental disturbance in the unshakable position it still occupies today. However, at the same time that neurological research was nourishing biogenic theory, other findings were laying the foundation for a comprehensive psychogenic theory of mental disturbance.

Mesmer and Hypnosis The history of modern psychogenic theory begins with a colorful and controversial figure, Friedrich Anton Mesmer (1733–1815). Mesmer, an Austrian physician, subscribed to Paracelsus' notion that heavenly bodies influenced psychological states. According to Mesmer, the movement of the planets controlled the distribution of a universal magnetic fluid, and the shiftings of this magnetic fluid were responsible for the health or sickness of mind and body. Furthermore, he was convinced that this principle of "animal magnetism" could be taken advantage of in the treatment of a rather common complaint at the time, *hysteria*—the appearance of a physical disability, such as deafness or paralysis, for which no organic cause can be found.

Mesmer's therapy for his hysterical patients was truly exotic. In solemn ceremony, the patients would enter a room and seat themselves around a huge vat containing bottles of various fluids from which iron rods protruded. The lights were dimmed and soft music was played. Then Mesmer himself appeared, "magnetic" wand in his hand and lavender cape flowing behind him. He passed from patient to patient, touching various parts of their bodies with his hands, with his wand, and with the rods protruding from the vat, in order to readjust the distribution of their magnetic fluids.

The most astonishing aspect of this treatment is that it seems in many cases to have worked. Nonetheless, Mesmer was investigated and barred from practice in both Vienna and Paris. Yet even the investigating physicians cited in their reports what since has been recognized as Mesmer's great contribution to psychiatry: the discovery of the power of suggestion in curing mental disorder. Mesmer is

Fig. 1.11 A "mesmerist" demonstrating the principle of "animal magnetism."

Fig. 1.12 Soft music and dim light were used to create an air of mystery and enhance the effect of "mesmerism."

now acknowledged to have been the first practitioner of *hypnosis* (earlier known as "mesmerism"), an artificially induced sleeplike state in which the subject becomes highly susceptible to suggestion.

The Nancy School Some years after Mesmer died an obscure death in Switzerland, his findings were taken up once again by two enterprising French physicians, Ambrose Auguste Liébault (1823–1904) and Hippolyte-Marie Bernheim (1840–1919), who were both practicing in Nancy, a city in eastern France. For four years Bernheim had been treating a patient with no success whatsoever. Finally, after hearing that a certain Dr. Liébault was having considerable success with unconventional methods, Bernheim sent the patient to Liébault. And when the patient returned shortly afterwards completely cured, Bernheim naturally called on Liébault to ask him what he had done. What Liébault had done was simple: he had hypnotized the patient and then had told him, while he was under hypnosis, that when he awakened his symptoms would be gone (Selling, 1940).

Bernheim was won over, and thereafter the two physicians worked as a team. Together they discovered that hysterical complaints could not only be cured by hypnosis but could also be induced through hypnosis. For example, if a hypnotized subject were told that he had no feeling in his hand—as is the case in *glove anesthesia*, a form of hysteria—the hand could then be pricked with a needle without the subject's showing any response. On the basis of such findings, Liébault and Bernheim evolved the theory that hysteria was actually a form of self-hypnosis and that other mental disorders might also be due entirely to psychological causes.

This view eventually drew a number of adherents, who became known as the "Nancy school." And the Nancy school soon came under direct attack by a formidable challenger, Jean-Martin Charcot (1825–1893), a famous Parisian neurologist who at that time was director of La Salpêtrière Hospital. Charcot had also experimented with hypnosis but had eventually abandoned it and was convinced that actual organic damage to the nervous system was the cause of hysteria. The bitter debate between the Paris school, consisting of Charcot and his supporters, and the Nancy school was one of the earliest major academic debates in the history of psychology. Eventually the insurgent Nancy school triumphed, and Charcot himself was won over to the psychogenic theory of hysteria. However, the ramifications of this debate extended far beyond the specific problem of hysteria, for it raised the possibility that any number of psychological disorders might in fact be due to emotional states rather than to organic causes.

Breuer and Freud: The Beginnings of Psychoanalysis One of the many students of Charcot was Sigmund Freud (1856–1939), a young Viennese physician who had come to Paris to study under the great neurologist. Later Freud became acquainted with the methods of Liébault and Bernheim as well, and when he returned to Vienna, he went to work with a physician named Josef Breuer (1842–1925), who at that time was also experimenting with the use of hypnosis. A few years earlier Breuer had treated a woman, later known to medical history as

Fig. 1.13 Freud's now-famous couch on which his patients relaxed as they poured out their dreams and free associations.

Anna O., who was troubled by hysterical paralysis, inability to eat, and various disturbances of sight and speech. Somewhat by chance, Breuer discovered that under hypnosis the patient was able to discuss her frustrations and problems quite freely and uninhibitedly, and that after doing so, she obtained some relief from her symptoms. Breuer, quick to recognize the therapeutic value of this emotional purging, called it the "cathartic method" or "talking cure" (Jones, 1953).

Together Breuer and Freud experimented extensively with "talking cures" and soon became convinced that hysteria and other disorders were caused by "unconscious" conflicts which could be drawn out under hypnosis and which, once aired, would lose their power to maintain the symptoms. In 1895 Breuer and Freud published their findings and put forth their theory of the unconscious in a volume entitled *Studies in Hysteria*, which has since become a milestone in the history of psychology.

Later, working independently, Freud found that he no longer had to use hypnosis to draw out unconscious material. (He apparently was not good at hypnosis and did not like the technique [Selling, 1940].) Instead, he relied on a method which he called *free association*, in which the patient was asked to relax on a couch and simply to pour out whatever came to his mind. The patient was also encouraged to talk about his dreams and his childhood. Freud then interpreted this material to the patient on the basis of the theories he was gradually building up as to the nature of the unconscious mind. To this form of therapy, in which the patient is cured through the gradual understanding of his unconscious conflicts, Freud gave the name *psychoanalysis*.

The development of his theories of the unconscious (which will be explained in Chapter 2) occupied the remainder of Freud's long and fruitful career. These theories, at first laughed at by his contemporaries, have not only become the basis for the psychodynamic perspective on mental illness but have also exerted a massive influence on all aspects of twentieth-century thought.

CURRENT MODELS OF ABNORMAL BEHAVIOR

The history that we have just detailed, combined with modern advances in medicine and mathematics, has yielded three major models* of abnormal behavior: the statistical model, the medical model, and a third broad approach that we will call the psychological model. How each of these models, along with a few less comprehensive models, approaches abnormality—and what implications each of these approaches has for the individual and the

---

*In this section, the word "model" is used in its informal, nontechnical sense—to provide an analogy for the conceptualization of a point of view. Another example of such use occurs when we use the word "games" to understand various interpersonal interactions, or the model of "acting" to describe the way people may relate to their world.

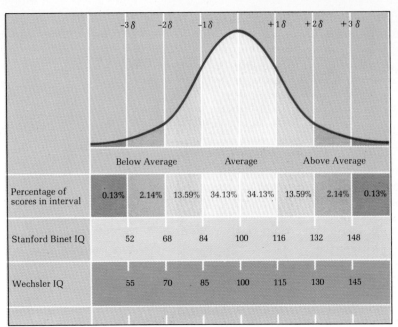

	−3δ	−2δ	−1δ		+1δ	+2δ	+3δ
	Below Average			Average		Above Average	
Percentage of scores in interval	0.13%	2.14%	13.59%	34.13%	34.13%	13.59%	2.14%	0.13%
Stanford Binet IQ		52	68	84	100	116	132	148
Wechsler IQ		55	70	85	100	115	130	145

Fig. 1.14   The statistical method of measuring psychological traits, though useful for such areas as intelligence, has serious weaknesses when applied to the determination of abnormality. Calling statistically rare behavior "abnormal" creates the following consequences: normality becomes equivalent to conformity, and many adaptive and creative though unusual ways of living are therefore viewed as abnormal; deviations that are of obvious positive social and personal value (for example, heroism or genius) are considered abnormal, with the implication that they should be ameliorated; and some frequently occurring behavior, such as anxiety, is defined as normal and thus escapes detection and study.

society—is the subject of the final section of this chapter.

The Statistical Model

Derived more from mathematics than from psychology, the *statistical model* concentrates on the definition of abnormality. According to this approach, abnormality is any substantial deviation from a statistically calculated average. Those who fall within the "golden mean"—those, in short, who do what most other people do—are normal, while those whose behavior differs from that of the majority are abnormal. Thus a psychologist working within the statistical model may be compared to a college professor who grades exams "on the curve," giving Cs to students who score within close range of the class average, no matter how high or low that average, and distributing As and Fs to those who deviate substantially from this "norm." (The difference between the two is that while the professor considers one extreme deviation to be good and accordingly gives it an A, the psychologist working within the statistical model tends to place the highest value on the average—a problem we will discuss shortly.)

In the area of abnormal psychology, the statistical model is the basis of many evaluations of abnormality. The diagnosis of mental retardation, for instance, is based on statistical accounting: those whose tested intelligence falls below an average range for the population are labeled retarded. However, careful statistical calculations are not always considered necessary in order to locate deviance. Any behavior which is simply unusual or infrequently seen can, according to the statistical model, be judged abnormal. For example, in communities where homosexuality (or at least the acknowledgment of homosexuality) is rare, it is commonly considered abnormal, whereas in larger metropolises where homosexuality is both more common and more commonly acknowledged, professionals are less likely to consider it deviant; this differential labeling would be in accordance with the statistical perspective. Furthermore, any behavior that seems "extreme" would fall under the heading of pathological. Thus a person who is mildly depressed is likely to be labeled as simply neurotic, whereas an extreme depression will be classed in the more serious category of psychosis.*

Such a cut-and-dried definition of abnormality of course makes psychological assessment a relatively easy matter. In the first place, anyone looking for deviance is sure to find it, since in any population there will always be deviations from the norm.

Neurosis and *psychosis* will be dealt with fully in Chapters 5, 7, and 11. For the moment neurosis may be defined as a pattern of maladaptive behaviors stemming from anxiety. Psychosis, on the other hand, is a condition of personality disorganization so severe that the individual loses contact with reality. Neurotics are not usually hospitalized, whereas psychotics generally are.

Second, locating deviance is a simple task. One has only to study a random sample of people, calculate their average performance with regard to the behavior in question, and then label as deviant those whose performance falls outside the average range. Thus if a sexologist was to determine that American adults engage in sexual intercourse on an average of once a week, then both a particularly active couple, averaging once a day, and a particularly chaste couple, averaging once every six weeks, would be considered outside the "normal" range.

Just as the statistical model makes psychological assessment rather uncomplicated, so also does it render treatment relatively simple, at least in the sense that the goal of treatment is never in question. If abnormality is defined as a deviation from the norm, then the goal of treatment is a return to the norm. Such a treatment philosophy has rather profound social implications, since it enthrones conformity as the major criterion for mental health. Thus the function of mental health professionals would be the maintenance of the status quo—a system which, according to some reports, is now operating in the Soviet Union, where political dissenters are often silenced by confinement in mental hospitals. Many homosexuals have argued that such a system is operating in the United States as well, as evidenced by the psychological treatment of homosexuals, which is usually aimed at redirecting the individual toward heterosexuality rather than helping him to establish satisfactory homosexual relations.

In sum, the central problem with the statistical model is that it lacks any system for differentiating between desirable and undesirable behaviors. And in the absence of such a system, it is the average behavior that tends to be considered the ideal. Such a point of view is potentially very dangerous, since it discourages and denigrates even valuable deviations from the norm. Thus not only mentally retarded people but also geniuses might be considered candidates for psychological treatment. Cultural and artistic movements that strike out in new directions could be squelched and their proponents classified as deviants. Likewise, anyone who deviated from mankind's semi-selfish norm to perform an act of great self-sacrifice could be judged insane.

Hence there is serious question as to how much emphasis can be safely placed on the norm. Indeed, there is also some question as to whether the actual norm is what we would think of as "normal." In the 1950s, for example, one of the findings of a project called the Midtown Manhattan Study was that in a large random sample of the population of New York City's East Side, fewer than 25 percent of the people could be considered psychologically "well," while nearly 20 percent could be judged to be "incapacitated" by psychological disturbance (Srole et al., 1962). Thus it appears that neurosis may be the norm rather than the deviation, in which case, according to the statistical model, those who are symptom-free would have to be labeled as deviant.

Such embarrassments are not uncommon in working with the statistical model. Yet there are many professionals who still hold to it. And as we have seen, a number of our diagnostic categories are based on the statistical approach. One reason for the endurance of this model is probably the simple fact that it never has to look far for empirical support. Human beings do tend to behave in similar ways; hence in the measurement of any behavior there will always be two extremes, with a vast majority in the middle. The question of how this distribution relates to our ideals regarding human behavior is the major problem of the statistical model.

The Medical Model

The *medical model*, as we have noted earlier, interprets abnormal behavior as the result of an organic dysfunction. This dysfunction may originate in a virus or germ, or in an inborn organ defect (perhaps genetically transmitted), or in some form of physical trauma, such as a blow on the head. Some psychologists have even extended the definition of the medical model to include illnesses caused by psychic trauma, such as parental rejection. In any case, the medical model rests on the three basic assumptions: (1) that the patient suffers from a disease, (2) that this disease is recognizable by a specific syndrome or set of symptoms, and (3) that each disease has its own separate and specific cause.

As we have seen, the discipline of modern psychology grew up under the auspices of the medical model in the late eighteenth and early nineteenth century. When the mentally ill were rescued from the witch-hunters, it was to *hospitals* that they were taken. And there they were treated by *doctors*. Pinel, Rush, Kraepelin, Freud, even Mesmer—all the founders of modern psychology, no matter what their persuasion, were medical doctors. And most of the nineteenth century's greatest advances in the field of psychology—the conquest of general paresis, for example—were medical advances.

Today the medical model is still pervasive. Even those who sternly reject this model still find themselves using such terms as "symptom," "syndrome,"

DSM-II DIAGNOSTIC NOMENCLATURE*

I. MENTAL RETARDATION
Borderline
Mild
Moderate
Severe
Profound
Unspecified
With each: Following or associated with
Infection or intoxication
Trauma or physical agent
Disorders of metabolism, growth, or nutrition
Gross brain disease (postnatal)
Unknown prenatal influence
Chromosomal abnormality
Prematurity
+ Major psychiatric disorder
+ Psychosocial (environmental) deprivation
Other condition

II. ORGANIC BRAIN SYNDROMES (OBS)
A. Psychoses
SENILE AND PRESENILE DEMENTIA
Senile dementia
Presenile dementia
ALCOHOLIC PSYCHOSIS
+ Delirium tremens
+ Korsakoff's psychosis
+ Other alcoholic hallucinosis
+ Alcohol paranoid state
+ Acute alcohol intoxication
+ Alcoholic deterioration
+ Pathological intoxication
Other alcoholic psychosis
PSYCHOSIS ASSOCIATED WITH INTRACRANIAL INFECTION
General paralysis
Syphilis of CNS
Epidemic encephalitis
Other and unspecified encephalitis
Other intracranial infection
PSYCHOSIS ASSOCIATED WITH OTHER CEREBRAL CONDITION
Cerebral arteriosclerosis
Other cerebrovascular disturbance
Epilepsy
Intracranial neoplasm
Degenerative disease of the CNS
Brain trauma
Other cerebral condition
PSYCHOSIS ASSOCIATED WITH OTHER PHYSICAL CONDITION
Endocrine disorder
Metabolic and nutritional disorder
Systemic infection
Drug or poison intoxication (other than alcohol)
+ Childbirth
Other and unspecified physical condition
B. Nonpsychotic OBS
Intracranial infection
+ Alcohol (simple drunkenness)
+ Other drug, poison, or systemic intoxication
Brain trauma
Circulatory disturbance
Epilepsy
Disturbance of metabolism, growth, or nutrition
Senile or presenile brain disease
Intracranial neoplasm
Degenerative disease of the CNS
Other physical condition

III. PSYCHOSES NOT ATTRIBUTED TO PHYSICAL CONDITIONS LISTED PREVIOUSLY
SCHIZOPHRENIA
Simple
Hebephrenic
Catatonic
+ Catatonic type, excited
+ Catatonic type, withdrawn
Paranoid
+ Acute schizophrenic episode
+ Latent
Residual
Schizo-affective
+ Schizo-affective, excited
+ Schizo-affective, depressed
Childhood
Chronic undifferentiated
Other schizophrenia
MAJOR AFFECTIVE DISORDERS
Involutional melancholia
Manic-depressive illness, manic
Manic-depressive illness, depressed
Manic-depressive illness, circular
+ Manic-depressive, circular, manic
+ Manic-depressive, circular, depressed
Other major affective disorder
PARANOID STATES
Paranoia
+ Involutional paranoid state
Other paranoid state
OTHER PSYCHOSES
Psychotic depressive reaction

IV. NEUROSES
Anxiety
Hysterical
+ Hysterical, conversion type
+ Hysterical, dissociative type

Phobic
Obsessive-compulsive
Depressive
+Neurasthenic
+Depersonalization
+Hypochondriacal
Other neurosis

V. PERSONALITY DISORDERS AND CERTAIN OTHER NONPSYCHOTIC MENTAL DISORDERS

PERSONALITY DISORDERS

Paranoid
Cyclothymic
Schizoid
+Explosive
Obsessive-compulsive
+Hysterical
+Asthenic
Antisocial
Passive-aggressive
Inadequate
Other specified types

SEXUAL DEVIATION

+Homosexuality
+Fetishism
+Pedophilia
+Transvestism
+Exhibitionism
+Voyeurism
+Sadism
+Masochism
Other sexual deviation

ALCOHOLISM

+Episodic excessive drinking
+Habitual excessive drinking
+Alcohol addiction
Other alcoholism

DRUG DEPENDENCE

+Opium, opium alkaloids and their derivatives
+Synthetic analgesics with morphinelike effects
+Barbiturates
+Other hypnotics and sedatives or "tranquilizers"
+Cocaine
+Cannabis sativa (hashish, marihuana)
+Other psychostimulants
+Hallucinogens
Other drug dependence

VI. PSYCHOPHYSIOLOGIC DISORDERS

Skin
Musculoskeletal
Respiratory
Cardiovascular
Hemic and lymphatic
Gastrointestinal
Genitourinary
Endocrine

Organ of special sense
Other type

VII. SPECIAL SYMPTOMS

Speech disturbance
Specific learning disturbance
+Tic
+Other psychomotor disorder
+Disorders of sleep
+Feeding disturbance
Enuresis
+Encopresis
+Cephalalgia
Other special symptom

VIII. TRANSIENT SITUATIONAL DISTURBANCES

Adjustment reaction of infancy
Adjustment reaction of childhood
Adjustment reaction of adolescence
Adjustment reaction of adult life
Adjustment reaction of late life

IX. BEHAVIOR DISORDERS OF CHILDHOOD AND ADOLESCENCE

+Hyperkinetic reaction
+Withdrawing reaction
+Overanxious reaction
+Runaway reaction
+Unsocialized aggressive reaction
+Group delinquent reaction
Other reaction

X. CONDITIONS WITHOUT MANIFEST PSYCHIATRIC DISORDER AND NONSPECIFIC CONDITIONS

SOCIAL MALADJUSTMENT WITHOUT MANIFEST PSYCHIATRIC DISORDER

+Marital maladjustment
+Social maladjustment
+Occupational maladjustment
Dyssocial behavior
+Other social maladjustment

NONSPECIFIC CONDITIONS

+Nonspecific conditions

NO MENTAL DISORDER

+No mental disorder

XI. NONDIAGNOSTIC TERMS FOR ADMINISTRATIVE USE

Diagnosis deferred
Boarder
Experiment only
Other

*Many of the titles listed here are in abbreviated form.

+These diagnoses are new and do not appear in DSM-I.

"pathology," "mental illness," "mental disorder," "patient," "therapy," "treatment," and "cure," all of which are derived from the medical analogy. In this book, though it is not based on the medical model, such terms will occur repeatedly. They are almost unavoidable.

Furthermore, most professionals in the field, regardless of their orientation, tend to rely on the medically based classification system contained in the American Psychiatric Association's *Diagnostic and Statistical Manual of Mental Disorders*, second edition (1968), commonly referred to as DSM-II (see pp. 24–25). This diagnostic system, the descendant of Kraepelin's early classification scheme, is a vast listing of descriptive terms covering just about every behavioral deviation known to man. Under each term is a list of symptoms, and these symptoms are assumed to add up to a disease, for which the descriptive term is the name. Thus if one has an irrational fear of some particular thing—cats, for example—and any encounter with cats brings on heart palpitations, trembling, nausea, and other physical symptoms of fear, then these symptoms add up to a syndrome called a "phobic neurosis," and that "phobic neurosis" is assumed to be one's disease.

Like any model, the medical model has its own implications with regard to the handling of abnormal behavior. In the first place, a professional working according to this model naturally has no hesitation about labeling patients. Indeed, the medical model places enormous emphasis on diagnosis, since the diagnosis—the determination of what "disease" category the patient fits into—determines the treatment, each disease having its own specific treatment. Treatment itself is relatively clear-cut, since it deals not with the patient's behavior (now relegated to the status of mere "symptoms") nor with his environment—both of which can be frustratingly complex and intractable—but with the presumed organic dysfunction. This dysfunction is treated with drugs, with hospitalized rest, with other physical regimens, and possibly even with surgery.

Working according to such guidelines, the medical model has had a number of successes. We have already discussed earlier in this chapter the discovery, at the turn of the century, of the physical origin of such syndromes as the senile psychoses, the toxic psychoses, and cerebral arteriosclerosis. And today a large number of mental problems are being relieved through the use of drugs developed within the medical model. However, as a comprehensive interpretation of abnormal behavior, the medical model has been bitterly criticized in recent years.

One of its most eloquent and relentless critics is Thomas Szasz, who in a book entitled *The Myth of Mental Illness* (1961) claims that what the medical model calls mental illnesses are not illnesses at all, but rather "problems in living" manifested in deviations from moral, legal, and social norms. To label these deviations "sick" is, according to Szasz, not only a blatant falsification of the conflict between the individual and the society but also a dangerous sanctification of the society's norms.

Furthermore, Szasz and a number of other critics have called attention to the medical model's effects on the patient. Even if we do feel that people who deviate from social norms should be "treated," what kind of success can we expect from a treatment which places the patient in a hospital, thus removing him from the realm of normal life to which he is supposed to be adjusting; designates him as "sick," thereby relieving him of any responsibility for his past or future behavior; makes him the passive and helpless recipient of whatever treatment his "healthy" medical caretakers choose to prescribe; and affixes to him a label that may continue to haunt him long after he is "well" again? Time and again studies have shown that when you call a person sick and expect him to act in a "sick" fashion, he will not disappoint you. According to the critics of the medical model, hospitals everywhere are filled with patients who have settled back, comfortably or uncomfortably, into the "sick" role.

In sum, the major criticism of the medical model, in spite of its achievements, is that there is simply no evidence that most mental problems can be accurately compared to physical problems. Hence such a comparison—applied, as it is in the medical model, on a comprehensive scale—is a distortion of a rather complex human problem and an impediment to any solution to that problem.

Absolute Models

There are three other models of abnormal behavior which, while less common than the statistical and medical models, still exert considerable influence in setting criteria for the diagnosis of abnormality and in determining goals for treatment. Unlike the statistical and medical models, each of these three models assumes a certain absolute standard for mental health.

The *personal discomfort model* is important in that it is the one model that gives primary importance to the individual's perception of his own mental functioning. Here the criterion for the judgment of disorder is the person's own unhappiness with his life. It is this personal discomfort that brings him into treatment, and it is the relief of this discomfort that is the goal of treatment. It is not difficult, however, to see the weakness in this model: a pathological murderer may report no distress whatsoever and yet still, in the eyes of others, stand in need of treatment.

Considerably more conservative is the *adequacy model*, which judges normalcy on the basis of a person's ability to interact successfully with his environment—to get along with his family, to make friends, to hold down a job, to adapt to the demands placed on him by his society, and so forth. While the criterion of adequacy is useful in many ways and is taken for granted by many professionals, it should be noted that such a model tends to assume the "rightness" of the social environment, such that anyone who finds it impossible to adapt to that environment is abnormal. Thus, according to this model, a woman who, in defiance of the standards of her family and her social class, chooses to go out and work rather than stay home and keep house for her family could be considered abnormal.

Somewhat similar to the adequacy model is the *cultural model*, according to which the standard for normalcy is a person's ability to conform to the norms of his culture. A great virtue of this model is that it acknowledges the importance of differential social expectations—the fact that the norms which guide a teenager in an urban ghetto may differ from the norms to which a middle-class suburban adult is responding. However, as with the statistical model, the failing of the cultural model is that it holds out no ideals of behavior other than adherence to accepted practices.

The Psychological Model

In this book we will attempt to take a broad perspective which may be called by the equally broad term *psychological model*. This model rests on four basic assumptions. The first is that abnormal behavior is to some extent the result of *psychological* processes—that is, those intangible entities that we call our attitudes, desires, thoughts, memories, and so forth. The behavior that issues from these processes may be measured in comparison with the behavior of a group, as in the statistical model, and it may also be accurately related to biological functioning, as in the medical model. But it is assumed that these relations to society and biology are complementary to the reality of the psychological processes. And if these processes must be described in subjective terms—terms such as grief or love or loneliness—the

fact remains that the reality that such terms describe is as substantial to most individuals as their statistical relation to a group or the biological correlates of their emotions.

Second, this book will proceed on the assumption that human behavior can be studied scientifically. That is, scientists can observe objectively both behavior and the environment in which it occurs. From these observations they can draw conclusions as to the causes of behavior, and knowing these causes, they can predict and control behavior.

A third assumption of this book is the integrity of the individual. In contrast to the statistical model, which tends to deprive the individual of his uniqueness and autonomy, and in contrast to the medical model, which tends to relieve the individual of any responsibility for his actions, the psychological perspective attempts to discern, against a background of social and biological necessities, a human being with his own unique set of memories, expectations, and behaviors, and with the ability to change his behavior.

Finally, the psychological perspective assumes that human behavior is highly complex and that allowance must be made for this complexity. Thus the individual's feelings must be taken into account along with his physical makeup, his cultural environment, and his personal history. Furthermore, the individual must be seen not as either normal or abnormal (as is the case with the statistical and medical models), but as a more complicated being with a wide range of behaviors, each of which may fall in a different spot on a continuum ranging from the most adaptive and fulfilling to the most defeating and distressing. Finally, to add to the complexity, those behaviors that are the most defeating—the most "abnormal"—must be seen as issuing from the same causes and as following the same principles as the most normal behaviors. In short, everyone has reasons for the things that they do, and though their actions may vary widely, their reasons are usually quite similar. We all experience such feelings as attraction and loathing, hope and despair, self-love and self-contempt. And though these feelings may be translated into an infinitely wide variety of behaviors, we still cannot afford to isolate any one of these behaviors as freakish or alien.

Working within this comprehensive psychological model, we shall stress in the following chapters three current perspectives on human behavior: the psychodynamic perspective, the behaviorist perspective, and the humanistic-existential perspective. Each of these models is narrower and more specific than the

MAJOR MODELS OF ABNORMAL BEHAVIOR

Statistical model	Abnormality is any substantial deviation from the average; treatment involves restoring average behavior.
Medical model	Abnormal behavior results from organic dysfunction and is to be treated through organic methods (e.g., drugs).
Absolute models	Abnormal behavior is defined as the lack of some absolute (e.g., personal satisfaction, adequacy within society, conformity to social norms); treatment aims at adjusting behavior to supply the missing absolute.
Psychological model	Abnormal behavior results primarily from intangible intrapsychic processes; treatment aims at adjusting these processes.

broad model that we have just defined, and more often than not they disagree with one another. But taken together, they provide an ample and many-faceted view of human psychology. Chapters 2, 3, and 4 will introduce these three perspectives, along with a few less comprehensive viewpoints included in Chapter 4. Then Chapters 5 through 17 will describe the most common categories of abnormal psychology and will discuss the psychodynamic, behavioristic, and humanistic-existential views as to the cause and treatment of these disorders, as well as views from other perspectives when appropriate. Chapters 18 and 19 will review the general methods of assessment and treatment developed by the major perspectives. Finally, Chapter 20 will examine the current theoretical problems in the field of psychology and will discuss the various new directions in which modern psychology is moving, in an attempt to do greater justice to the richness and intricacy of the human mind.

SUMMARY

Mental disorder may be conceptualized as deviance from a society's norms, and how a society defines, explains, and handles such deviance will determine that society's approach to mental disorder.

For many centuries, deviant behavior was seen as the result of possession by supernatural forces, either good or evil. To drive out evil spirits, ancient man developed various exorcistic techniques, including incantations, noisemaking, and the drinking of special potions. With the rise of Greek civilization, science at last entered the realm of mental disturbance. In the fifth and fourth centuries B.C. Hippocrates worked out an organic theory of mental

disorder and developed scientific methods for observing and classifying such disorders. Hippocrates' organic theory was further advanced during the Roman Empire. However, when Rome fell, science fell with it, and ancient demonology was once again invoked to explain abnormal behavior.

In conformity with the antirational tendencies of medieval and Renaissance Christianity, mental illness was seen as a supernatural visitation—and eventually as a diabolical visitation. Accordingly, the "possessed" were exposed to various forms of punishment—whipping, starvation, curses, and so on—in order to drive out the devil. Soon even these techniques were considered too mild, and as Europe entered the Renaissance, exorcism was replaced by witch hunts. This new brutality toward the mentally ill was ushered in by a papal bull issued by Pope Innocent VIII and by the publication of a church-approved manual, *Malleus Maleficarum*, on the proper procedures for identifying and dealing with witches. Eventually the witchcraft frenzy made its way to the American colonies, and there it culminated in the Salem witchcraft craze of the late seventeenth century.

In the eighteenth and nineteenth centuries, science once again took over the handling of mental disorder. Through the pioneering efforts of Pinel in France and Tuke in England, the abusive treatment of the mentally ill in the asylums of the day was replaced by moral therapy, an approach that stressed the fact that the mentally disturbed were ordinary human beings and attempted to create a restful and supportive environment in which they could work out their problems. Through the work of Rush and Dix, the treatment of mental disorder in America underwent similar reforms. However, the concomitant rise of the medical model and the proliferation of mental hospitals contributed to the decline of moral therapy.

Psychological theory in the nineteenth century was divided between the biogenic view and the psychogenic view. Biogenic theory, advanced by such scientists as Kraepelin and Krafft-Ebing, received substantial confirmation from medical breakthroughs at the turn of the century, especially the discovery that general paresis was the result of syphilis. Meanwhile, the development of hypnosis, in the hands of Mesmer, Liébault, and Bernheim, led eventually to Breuer and Freud's discovery of the unconscious and thus laid the foundations for Freud's comprehensive psychogenic theory of mental disorder.

Current models of abnormal behavior include the statistical model, the medical model, a number of absolute models, and finally, the psychological model. The statistical model defines abnormality as a substantial deviation from average behavior. The problem with a model is that instead of defining any standards of desirable and undesirable behavior, it simply glorifies the majority behavior, to the disadvantage of originality and individuality.

The medical model, which is quite common, interprets abnormal behavior as the result of organic dysfunction and thus relies on organic treatment. The weaknesses of this model are that it oversimplifies the complex matter of abnormal behavior and that it tends to encourage patients to adopt a passive "sick" role.

Three absolute models of abnormal behavior are the personal discomfort model, which defines normality in terms of personal satisfaction with one's life; the adequacy model, which defines normality as the ability to adapt to one's environment; and the cultural model, which defines normality as conformity to the norms of one's culture.

The psychological model, on which this book is based, assumes that abnormal behavior is the result of psychological problems, that behavior can be studied scientifically, that a human being is both unique in his psychological equipment and responsible for his actions, and that human behavior is highly complex. Included within the psychological model are the psychodynamic, behaviorist, and humanistic-existential perspectives on abnormal behavior, and it is these three viewpoints that will be stressed in the chapters that follow.

In Chapter 1 we have discussed the specific origins of the psychodynamic perspective: Mesmer's seemingly accidental discovery of hypnosis, Liébault and Bernheim's theory of hysteria as self-hypnosis, the quarrel between the Nancy school and the Paris school, and finally, the collaboration of Breuer and the young Sigmund Freud in the development of the "cathartic" method. It is possible to say, however, that psychodynamic theory was a logical culmination of nineteenth-century thought in general. In the intellectual life of the nineteenth century we can trace two basic strands of thinking. On the one hand, there was determinism, which saw human life as externally controlled behavior, behavior that fit into a larger system and was determined by that system, whether it was society or the new tide of industry or the evolutionary theory formulated by Darwin in the middle of the century. On the other hand, there was subjectivism, focusing entirely on the inner life, which was considered dark, passionate, irrational, and rebellious to any externally imposed system. And just as the scientific advances of the age supported and furthered deterministic thought, so the artistic life of the nineteenth century was devoted to subjectivism, the rescue of the interior self.

In the last quarter of the century, against this divided intellectual backdrop, Freud came of age in Vienna, at that time one of the most exciting cultural centers of Europe. And what Freud did was to tie the two strands of nineteenth-century thought together, creating a system—a deterministic system—of the irrational inner life.

In this chapter we will first outline Freud's theories on the structure of the mind, the structure of consciousness, the dynamics of the mind, the stages of development, and the components of normal and abnormal behavior.* We will then discuss the ways in which Freud's followers modified his theories. Finally, we will assess the psychodynamic perspective in relation to other models of human behavior, and we will attempt to draw some conclusions regarding the strengths and shortcomings of this perspective.

2
The
Psychodynamic
Perspective

---

*Freud was an extraordinarily prolific writer throughout his long life; it is impossible to do full justice to his views in one short chapter. The reader should be aware that what is presented here is a condensation of his extensive theoretical perspective.

Fig. 2.1 Sigmund Freud, father of the psychodynamic model.

BASIC CONCEPTS OF PSYCHODYNAMIC THEORY

The Structural Hypothesis: Id, Ego, and Superego

Basic to psychodynamic theory is what is called Freud's *structural hypothesis*, his conceptualization of the human psyche as an interaction of three forces: the id, the ego, and the superego. Each of these three forces has its own origin and its own highly specific role in maintaining normal personality functioning (Freud, 1920).

The Id According to the Freudian system, each individual is endowed with a specific amount of psychic energy, which can be neither increased nor decreased. In the newborn infant, psychic energy is bound up entirely in the *id*, the mass of biological drives with which the individual is born. Thus the id is the foundation of the psychic structure and the source from which the later developments of ego and superego are forced to borrow their energy.

The energy of the id is divided between two types of instincts. The first type is *Eros* (the Greek word for "love"), the constructive life instinct aimed at survival, self-propagation, and creativity. In this category are included the needs for food, warmth, and—above all—sex. (In Freud's broad use of the term, "sex" covers a wide range of life-giving and

life-sustaining activities, all the way from genital intercourse to artistic creation.) The energy of the life instinct, the *libido*, Freud saw as a driving force permeating the entire personality and propelling it through life.

Opposed to Eros is the second type of instinct, *Thanatos* (the Greek word for "death"), the death instinct. Discussions of the death instinct, including Freud's, tend to have a quality of vagueness about them (Sarnoff, 1971). It is clear, however, that Freud saw the human organism as instinctively drawn back to the original inanimate state from which it arose, a state in which all tension would be dissipated—in short, the state of death (Freud, 1932). This instinctive attraction toward death gives rise to self-directed aggressive tendencies. However, since self-destruction is opposed by the life-preserving energy of the libido, the individual's aggression is generally redirected outward, against the world, motivating him to compete, to conquer, and to kill.

The instincts of the id are essentially biological and take no account of logic or reason, reality or morality. They are concerned only with the reduction of whatever tensions the organism feels: the need for warmth, food, tactile stimulation, and so forth. This tendency of the id to devote itself exclusively to immediate tension reduction is called the *pleasure principle*. In its pursuit of the pleasure principle, the id has only two methods at its disposal (Freud, 1920). The first is *reflex action*—that is, instinctive and automatic behavior such as sucking or rooting (the automatic response by which the infant finds the nipple when his cheek is placed against the mother's breast) that immediately reduces the biological tension involved. The id's second method of self-gratification, *primary process thinking*, involves the conjuring up of a mental image of the source of satisfaction. Thus the hungry baby will create a mental picture of the bottle or breast, an imaginary wish-fulfillment.

The Ego While the id can imagine what it needs, it has no way of going out and getting what it needs. Nor does it have any way of determining which means of tension reduction are safe and which are not. To fulfill these functions, the mind develops a new psychic component, the *ego*, after the first six months of life. The ego takes for itself part of the energy of the id and proceeds to serve as the mediator between the id and reality. Through what is called *secondary process thinking*—that is, remembering, reasoning, and evaluating, all on the basis of the child's prior contacts with reality—the ego

Freud's Structural Hypothesis

Psychic component	Age when developed	Principle of operation	Function
Id	Present at birth	Pleasure principle	Gratification of life and death instincts through reflex action and primary process thinking
Ego	Six months	Reality principle	Mediation, through secondary process thinking, between the demands of the id and the demands of reality and of the superego
Superego	Five to six years		Restraint of sexual and aggressive impulses in accordance with the moral standards of the parents and the society

locates in reality the counterpart of the id's desires, anticipates the consequences of using that means of self-gratification, and then either reaches out for that means or else delays gratification until a more appropriate means can be found (Freud, 1920, 1932).

Let us imagine, for example, a three-year-old boy playing in his room. The id signals that aggressive impulses seek release, and the boy reaches for his toy hammer. The ego then goes into action, scanning the environment for the appropriate outlet. The boy's baby sister is playing near him. Should he clobber her over the head with his hammer? The ego, which knows from experience that this will result in the painful consequence of a spanking, says no and continues the scanning process. Also nearby is a big lump of clay. The ego determines that no harm will come from pounding the clay, and so the boy proceeds to bang away at it.

Thus, in contrast to the id's pleasure principle, the ego operates on what is called the *reality principle*, the foundation of which is the concern for safety. And it is through this basic ego function of finding realistic means to satisfy the id that the mind develops and refines all of its higher cognitive functions: perception, learning, discrimination, memory, judgment, and planning.

The Superego Imagine that three years later the same boy once again sits with hammer in hand looking for something to pound. Again he considers his sister's head, but this time he rejects that outlet not because it would result in a spanking but because it would be "wrong." What this means is that the boy has developed a *superego*.

The superego is that part of the mind that represents the moral standards of the society as interpreted by the parents. As a consequence of the resolution of the Oedipus complex, which we will discuss shortly, the child internalizes his parents' standards, and these standards come together to form the third psychic component, which like the ego takes its energy from the id. This new superego, which is approximately equivalent to what we call "conscience," takes no more account of reality than the id does. Instead of considering what is realistic or possible, it embraces an abstract moral ideal—an ideal which constantly demands that the sexual and aggressive impulses of the id be stifled and that moral goals be substituted instead. The superego, then, is the great nay-sayer. Its function is to prohibit. And it is up to the ego to find a way to satisfy the id without giving pain (experienced as "remorse" or "guilt") to the superego.

Thus in the fully developed psychic structure the ego has three fairly intransigent parties to deal with: the id, which seeks only the satisfaction of its irrational and amoral demands; the superego, which seeks only the satisfaction of its impractical ideals; and reality, which offers only a limited range of objects for satisfying the id and which metes out stern punishment for unwise choices (Blum, 1953).

The Topographical Approach: Levels of Consciousness

Freud originally conceptualized the organization of the mind according to what is called the *topographical approach*—that is, in terms of levels of consciousness (Freud, 1920). And though he later replaced this organizational principle with the structural hypothesis of id, ego, and superego, he continued to believe that the mind was divided into three levels of consciousness (Freud, 1948). The first level, the *perceptual conscious*, contains whatever requires no act of recall—that is, whatever narrow range of mental events the individual is concentrating on at a given moment. Beneath the perceptual conscious lies the second level, the *preconscious*, consisting of whatever the person can remember without great difficulty. Thus the preconscious is the storage bin for those facts, events, images, and ideas that are readily available to the perceptual conscious but that are simply not being attended to at the moment. Beneath the preconscious extends the vast pool of the *unconscious*, the third and largest level. The unconscious contains all those memories that are not readily available to the perceptual conscious, either because the individual has completely forgotten them or because he has actively "repressed" them—that is, forced them out of consciousness—in order to avoid conflict. Such repressed material, however, does not disappear. It surfaces again whenever ego controls are loosened—in fantasies, in dreams, in slips of the tongue, under anesthesia, under hypnosis. Furthermore, it acts as a hidden motivating factor for "conscious" behavior.

While there is no exact congruence between these three levels of consciousness and the three parts of the structural hypothesis, there is a rough correspondence between the two systems. As Fig. 2.2 indicates, id, ego, and superego all have roots in the unconscious. However, id impulses are totally confined to the unconscious; superego processes take place at a higher level of consciousness; and ego functioning is even closer to the perceptual conscious.

The Dynamics of the Mind

As we have seen, each of the three structural components of the psyche has its own exclusive interests. Hence these three forces are constantly at war with one another, the id forever insisting on gratification while the pragmatic ego, the idealistic superego, and reality all strive to curb the id's hedonistic demands. The superego too is likely to become overinsistent, demanding that the id be

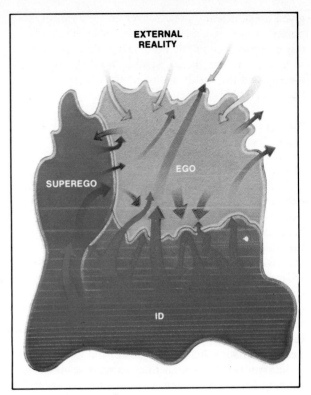

Fig. 2.2   A representation of Freud's conception of adult personality. The id, the ego, and the superego are seen as structural divisions of the psyche. The arrows represent the interactions and conflicts continually taking place between these structures. The increased shading toward the lower part of the figure represents levels of decreasing consciousness: the id is wholly unconscious; both ego and superego function at all levels of consciousness. The id is represented as the primary source of psychic energy. Both the ego and superego, which do not have energy of their own, are derived or differentiated from the id during childhood in response to the demands of external reality. The ego is the structure differentiated first; it is the only structure that has direct contact with external reality and it uses energy derived from the id to cope with reality and to meet (or control) the demands of the id. The superego, differentiated somewhat later than the ego, is represented as only partially independent of the id because it shares with the id a tendency toward irrationality and blind force. The superego helps to control the id, but only by placing additional demands on the ego.

given no satisfaction whatsoever and that all id impulses be sternly repressed. Thus, according to traditional psychodynamic theory, the life of the mind is a state of continual conflict among opposing forces. And the result of this conflict is a condition that Freud (1932) called *anxiety*.

Anxiety Anxiety, akin to what most of us call "fear," is a state of psychic pain which acts as a signal to the ego that danger is at hand. Freud (1932) distinguished three types of anxiety, each based on a different source of danger. In *reality anxiety* the person is threatened by something in the outside world; a person who sees a rattlesnake an inch from his foot experiences reality anxiety. In *moral anxiety* the source of the danger is the superego, which threatens to overwhelm the person with guilt and shame over something that he has done or even something that he has thought of doing. In *neurotic anxiety* the danger comes from id impulses that threaten to burst through ego controls and cause the individual to do things that will bring punishment down on him.

Anxiety can be dealt with in a number of ways, ranging from the eminently reasonable to the most unrealistic. If, for example, a pregnant woman is afraid of childbirth, she can alleviate her fears by going to childbirth classes and learning how to control labor pains. But in cases where the anxiety is particularly acute, or where there appears to be no reasonable way of dealing with it, or where the source of anxiety remains totally unconscious, the ego will resort to what are called *defense mechanisms*.

Defense Mechanisms Defense mechanisms are psychic stratagems that reduce anxiety by concealing the source of the anxiety both from the self and from the world. We all use defense mechanisms—and use them unconsciously. The problem with them, however, is that they are "stop-gap" measures. They protect the individual from awareness of whatever threat it is he is experiencing, but they generally do so at the cost of falsifying reality and of impeding personality growth. Furthermore, if the anxiety is particularly strong, the defenses will become proportionately stronger, eventually usurping most of the time and energy that the person should be using for adaptive functioning.

We shall list below some of the most common defense mechanisms. It should be kept in mind, however, that each of these defenses can range from the imperfectly adaptive to the most maladaptive—that is, they may be used by a reasonably mature person simply to "get over a hump," or they may appear as symptoms of a serious mental problem.

Repression In *repression*, as we have already seen, unacceptable id impulses are pushed down into the unconscious and thereby forgotten. Thus, for example, a girl who is sexually attracted to her father will simply remove this intolerable incestuous thought from her consciousness. It may come up again in her dreams, but upon awakening these too will be repressed.

One of the earliest of Freud's conceptualizations, repression is the most fundamental mechanism of psychodynamic theory (Blum, 1953). It is on the basis of this mechanism that Freud constructed his symbolic interpretation of human behavior, whereby a person's actions are viewed as masked representations of the contents of his unconscious. And Freud evolved his technique of psychoanalysis expressly for the purpose of dredging up this repressed material, in the belief that once the person faced his banished memories and desires, these forbidden thoughts would then cease to cause him anxiety and thus would lose their power to force him into maladaptive behaviors in the effort to relieve that anxiety (Freud, 1937).

Projection Projection is the mechanism whereby internal threats are transformed into external threats. Like all defense mechanisms, it is based on repression. For example, a person who is terrified of his own aggressive impulses may repress these impulses and then project them onto others. He will then proceed to complain that these other people are abusing him—stealing his pencils, talking behind his back, telling lies about him, or what have you. This stratagem relieves anxiety by allowing the person to express his fear and at the same time to pose as the innocent party.

Displacement Displacement, like projection, involves a transfer of emotion. Here, however, it is not the source of the emotion that is falsified, but the object of the emotion. Afraid to display or even to experience certain feelings (usually hostile ones) against whoever has aroused them, the person represses the feelings. Then, when the opportunity arises, he transfers them to a safer object and releases them in full force on this new object. A good example of projection may be found in a story by James Joyce entitled "Counterparts." In it, a man who has been subjected to various defeats and humiliations all day long goes home and beats his young son on the pretext that the boy let the fire go out.

Denial Denial is the refusal to acknowledge a source of distress. A person may deny his feelings about something, or in an extreme case, he may deny the memory or even the actual existence of whatever it is that is causing his anxiety. For example, a soldier who has undergone horrifying experiences in a prison camp may upon his release convince himself that his captors treated him kindly, since the memory of what he actually endured arouses too much anxiety. Or a woman whose husband has died may persist in the belief that he is alive, insisting that he will return home.

Reaction Formation In *reaction formation* a person represses whatever feelings are arousing his anxiety and then vehemently professes the exact opposite of these feelings. Thus a man who professes to be disgusted by homosexuals and who claims that they should all be locked up may be engaging in a reaction formation to his own homosexual impulses.

Intellectualization Intellectualization is the avoidance of unacceptable feelings by the repression of these feelings and then the replacement of them with an abstract intellectual analysis of the problem. Intellectualization is a common refuge of patients in psychotherapy. Eager to convince the therapist that they have some insight into their feelings but unwilling to confront these feelings in their disturbing actuality, patients will produce elaborate abstract self-analyses in order to "detoxify" their true impulses and avoid any direct discussion of them.

Fixation In *fixation* an individual who experiences anxiety at a certain stage of his development refuses to progress beyond that stage, for fear that even greater conflicts may await him at the next level. Such fixations generally result in immature behavior in limited areas of the individual's functioning. (The subject of fixation will be enlarged upon in the section dealing with developmental stages, below.)

Regression Related to fixation, *regression* involves the return to a developmental stage that one has already passed through. Unable to deal with its anxiety, the ego simply abandons the scene of the conflict, reverting to an earlier, less threatening stage where gratification was easier to come by. Regression is a good example of the fact, stated earlier, that defense mechanisms can vary from relatively harmless means of self-comfort to signs of severe personality disorganization. In its extreme aspect, regression can involve a total breakdown of physical and mental functioning: the regressed adult may be reduced to a babbling helpless creature who has to be fed and toileted like a baby. On the other hand, well-adjusted people, both children and adults, will often resort to minor regressive behaviors simply to take the edge off whatever pressures they are ex-

DEFENSE MECHANISMS

Repression	Forcing unacceptable id impulses back into the unconscious
Projection	Transferring one's own feared impulses onto an external agent
Displacement	Venting emotions on a substitute object, out of fear of directing them toward the original object
Denial	Refusal to acknowledge an anxiety-producing feeling, fact, or memory
Reaction formation	Expressing or acting out the opposite of one's unacceptable feelings
Intellectualization	Indulging in intellectual analysis of one's problems in order to avoid direct confrontation of anxiety-producing impulses
Fixation	Refusal to progress beyond a conflict-ridden stage of development
Regression	Returning mentally to an earlier stage of development in order to avoid conflict at one's actual stage
Sublimation	Redirecting libidinal or destructive impulses away from unacceptable objects and toward acceptable substitute objects

fixation

projection

WHAT LION?

denial

displacement

reaction *formation*

Repression

Fig. 2.3 *Defense mechanisms are associated with the psychodynamic theory of neurotic behaviors. Defense mechanisms protect the
individual from anxiety by concealing the source of the threats he
encounters. Unfortunately, they do so by distorting reality and interfering with the individual's adjustment.* Repression, *which is the
unconscious burying of anxiety-causing impulses, is shown by a
woman who is not only concealing and restraining a monstrous impulse but also trying to conceal from herself the fact that she is doing
so. The hands pointing in all directions illustrate the mechanism of*
projection, *in which the individual accuses others of possessing attributes he finds unacceptable in himself.* Fixation *at a certain stage
of development is represented by Orphan Annie, who never progressed beyond the dependency needs of childhood. The refusal to
face a threatening reality can be seen in the* denial *of the lion's existence. In* displacement, *hostile feelings are transferred to a safe
object. In* reaction formation, *the individual will profess feelings
opposite to what he is experiencing.*

periencing. Hall gives an admirable catalog of "normal" regressive behavior used by adults:

They smoke, get drunk, eat too much, lose their tempers, bite their nails, pick their noses, break laws, talk baby talk, destroy property, masturbate, . . . chew gum and tobacco, dress up as children, drive fast and recklessly, believe in good and evil spirits, take naps, fight and kill one another, bet on the horses, daydream, rebel against or submit to authority, gamble, preen before the mirror, act out their impulses, pick on scapegoats, and do a thousand and one other childish things. Some of these regressions are so commonplace that they are taken to be signs of maturity (1955, pp. 95-96).

Sublimation Sublimation differs from all the other defense mechanisms in that it may be truly constructive. Sublimation involves the rechanneling of impulses away from forbidden outlets and toward socially acceptable outlets. Freud hypothesized that many of the gorgeous male and female nudes created by Renaissance painters and sculptors were sublimations of repressed sexual impulses. Forbidden to gratify directly the sexual demands of the id, these artists transferred their libido to a mental image of the desired object and then proceeded to bring that image to life in marble or on canvas. Indeed, Freud saw civilization itself as resting on the act of sublimation (Lindzey et al., 1973).

The Stages of Psychosexual Development

The adjective "psychosexual" is itself an introduction to Freud's theory of personality development. Freud saw this development as progressing through a series of stages, in each of which the psyche directs its libidinal energy toward a different zone of sexual pleasure. In each stage the child's primary interest is the attainment of stimulation of whatever zone he is concentrating on at that stage: the mouth, the anus, or the genitals. Hence Freud (1932) saw the child as motivated primarily by sexual impulses. (Of all Freud's theories, this was the one that was the most profoundly shocking and repulsive to the Victorian society in which he lived.) And he viewed the adult personality as the consequence of the ways in which these sexual impulses were satisfied at each stage of development. For at each stage the child must deal with the conflict between the demands of the id and the amount of gratification available within the limits imposed by reality. Both undergratification and overgratification can lead to conflict. And this conflict can in turn lead to fixation, in which the adult personality is "frozen" at the stage

of conflict, still acting out in symbolic fashion the impulse that was too much or too little indulged.

The Oral Stage The first year of life constitutes the *oral stage*, in which, as the name indicates, the mouth is the primary focus of libidinal impulses. The infant must suck in order to live, and this sucking is his introduction to sensual pleasure. Soon he is using his mouth not only to satisfy his hunger but also to satisfy his libido. Breast, bottle, thumb, pacifier, blankets, toys—the infant sucks, mouths, and chews whatever he can find in his search for oral stimulation. And the various actions involved in these oral exercises—sucking in, holding on, biting, spitting out, and closing—serve as prototypes for later personality traits such as acquisitiveness, tenacity, destructiveness, contemptuousness, and negativism. Fixation at the oral stage may take a number of forms, of which two of the most common are the "oral-dependent" personality and the "oral-aggressive" personality. In the former, the child experiences repeated anxiety over whether food will be given or withheld—an anxiety which teaches him that he is totally dependent on others. The result is a passive, overly dependent, unenterprising adult personality. In the oral-aggressive personality, on the other hand, the focus of the fixation is a later phase of the oral stage, when the infant's teeth begin to come in and biting becomes a major source of pleasure. Thus the oral-aggressive adult has a biting, sarcastic, scornful personality.

The Anal Stage In the second year of life the child shifts his libidinal attention from the mouth down to the other end of the alimentary canal, the anus. In the *anal stage* the major sources of physical pleasure are the retaining and expelling of feces. In the retention of feces, the pleasurable stimulus is the mild pressure of the fecal material against the walls of the rectum, while in the expulsion of feces, the pleasure is the tension reduction as this pressure is relieved.

Unlike the oral pleasures of the first year, however, the child's anal pleasures are barely established before they are interfered with through the process of toilet training. Freudian theorists tend to regard toilet training as a crucial event, since it is the child's first confrontation with a systematic effort to control his impulses on the part of parents and society. Suddenly his retentive and expulsive pleasures are brought under regulation. He is told when, where, how, and so forth. Caught between these reality-imposed demands and the id's demands for

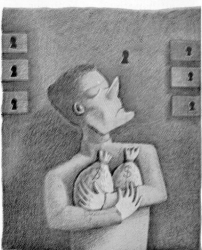

Fig. 2.4 *Possible behavior of a child at each of Freud's first three psychosexual stages, and the adult personality characteristics that might follow if, according to Freud's theory, the behaviors were somehow encouraged and the child became fixated. (Top row) An infant obtains oral gratification by putting just about anything she can find into her mouth. As an adult, this person exhibits a similar lack of discrimination about what she takes into herself. (Middle row) A two-year-old in the anal stage thwarts his mother by refusing to release his feces. As an adult he obtains satisfaction by hoarding. (Bottom row) A four-year-old girl in the phallic stage, observing that she lacks a penis, gives up her hopes of being like a man in any way. As an adult, she adopts a traditionally passive female sex role.*

its own timetable of gratification, the ego may experience considerable conflict and anxiety. And if the anxiety is great enough, it can, as usual, result in fixation. The manifestations of anal fixation depend on whether the fixation takes place in the early "anal-expulsive" phase or in the later "anal-retentive" phase. In the earlier phase, as the name implies, pleasure is derived mainly from the expulsion of feces; hence an anal-expulsive fixation results in pushy, disorderly, messy behavior. On the other hand, fixation at the anal-retentive phase, when the main source of physical pleasure is the retaining of feces, gives rise to a stingy, stubborn, and overly meticulous personality.

The Phallic Stage In the *phallic stage*, which extends from the third to the fifth or sixth year, the focus is shifted to the genitals, and sensual pleasure is derived from masturbation, the stroking and handling of the genitals. During this period, *narcissism*, the erotic preoccupation with one's own body, is assumed to be particularly intense, since for the first time the child is deriving his pleasure not from sensations associated with automatic and life-sustaining body processes such as sucking and excretion, but from a willed manipulation of his organs.

The phallic stage is held to be particularly crucial to psychological development because it is this stage that is the scene of the *Oedipus complex*, the most important determinant of the child's future sexual adjustment. In Greek mythology, King Oedipus has the misfortune to discover that he has killed his father and married his mother. Likewise, according to Freud (1932), all children during the phallic stage long to do away with the parent of the same sex and to take sexual possession of the parent of the opposite sex. In boys, this incestuous desire arouses in the child the feeling of what Freud (1920) called *castration anxiety*—the child's fear that his father will punish him for his forbidden wishes by cutting off the guilty organ, his penis. This fear is supposedly confirmed by the boy's observations of female anatomy. Lacking penises, girls seem castrated to him, and he fears the same fate for himself. At the same time girls, observing that, unlike boys, they have been born unequipped with penises, experience the female counterpart of castration anxiety, *penis envy*.*
While the boy's castration anxiety is what causes him to repress his longing for his mother, the girl's penis envy is what impels her toward her father. In time, however, the girl's Oedipal desires, like the boy's, recede. Rather than war against the parent of the same sex for the unattainable object, both boys and

girls settle for *identification* with the same-sexed parent. Since they can't beat them, they join them, incorporating the parent's values, standards, sexual orientation, mannerisms, and so forth. And it is through the incorporation of the parent's moral values in the process of identification that the child develops his superego.

Latency and the Genital Stage Between the ages of six and twelve, the child goes through the *latency* period, in which, as the term indicates, sexual impulses remain latent. While the libido hibernates, the child's attention is redirected toward the mastery of developmental skills. After this period of presumably asexual behavior, sexual strivings are reawakened as the child enters puberty. Now, however, his sexual functioning undergoes a highly significant change. During the oral, anal, and especially the phallic stages, the child's sexual strivings are, as we have seen, narcissistic. His central erotic love object is his own body, and other people—particularly the mother—are loved in the degree to which they contribute to the child's self-directed physical pleasure. In puberty, on the other hand, the individual begins rechanneling some of this libidinal energy directly toward other people—and not as adjuncts of his body pleasure, but as individuals in their own right. As puberty advances, this altruistic love eventually merges with the more instinctual libidinal energies to produce mature sexual functioning, in which tenderness mingles with the primitive sexual hunger. This final phase of mature sexuality, which to Freud meant heterosexual genital mating, is called the *genital stage* (Blum, 1953).

Normal and Abnormal Behavior

Having outlined the fundamental principles of Freudian theory, let us now draw out from these principles the psychodynamic interpretation of normal and abnormal personality functioning.

Normal Personality Functioning To begin with, Freudian theory views the normal personality as essentially irrational (Blum, 1953). For centuries the most enlightened people had viewed mental disorder

---

*It has only recently been pointed out that concepts such as castration anxiety and penis envy reflect an unjustified assumption that a penis is an exceedingly desirable thing to have and that not to have one is cause for mourning. This assumption, along with such terms as "phallic stage," reflects the degree to which Freud's theories are based on male biology and male psychology—a bias that has made Freud a target of criticism for the women's liberation movement.

as a loss of one's *reason*: the sane person was rational, and the insane person was irrational. In contrast, Freud (1920) saw both the sane and the insane as motivated primarily by the irrational id, with its reckless drives for pleasure and for destruction. While it is true that the ego is eventually developed in order to bend the desires of the id in the direction of reason and practicality, the ego does not originate any desires of its own. It simply acts as administrator to the id.*

The Freudian psyche is not just basically irrational, but basically antisocial as well. Just as the ego is developed to argue the case of reason with the id, so the superego is developed to argue the case of society. But the superego, like the ego, can only deflect the impulses of the id; it cannot substitute any impulses of its own. The motivating power comes from the id, which is as indifferent to society as it is to reason.

Irrational and antisocial, the normal personality is also largely beyond the control of the individual. According to Freud (1932), normal behavior is a symbolic representation of impulses which remain for the most part unconscious, so that whatever conscious strivings a person brings to bear on his behavior are only superficial modifications, affecting the form rather than the content of the behavior. What the content of the behavior will be is determined by two factors: the id impulses with which the person is born and the type of psychic structure that he has developed as the result of his experiences in the oral, anal, and phallic stages extending from birth to age six. Needless to say, the individual has little control over either of these factors.

Finally, the normal personality, according to psychodynamic theory, is characterized by a just balance among the three psychic components of id, ego, and superego (Lindzey et al., 1973). Each is endowed with the proper amount of energy, so the id can obtain sufficient gratification, the ego can keep this gratification within the bounds of reality, and the superego can keep this gratification within the bounds of social morality. This does not mean that the normal personality does not experience conflict. On the contrary, the three psychic components still battle one another for dominance, and thus the normal personality still has its fair share of anxiety. However, such anxiety can be handled and dissipated without any drastic violation of id, ego, or superego. In times of stress, the ego may be

weakened by relying too heavily on defense mechanisms. Under the influence of intense emotion (or of alcohol), the superego may become weak and thus allow the id too much strength, after which the superego will take its revenge by afflicting the psyche with guilt. But these are simply the ups and downs of normal functioning. Once shaken, the balance of power among the three psychic components is again restored, and the person is once again able to keep the id reasonably satisfied and at the same time to meet the requirements both of reality and of morality.

Abnormal Personality Functioning Like normal functioning, abnormal functioning is motivated at bottom by the id. Hence, like normal behavior, abnormal behavior is essentially irrational, antisocial, and determined. What, then, is the difference between the two? The difference lies in the crucial matter of energy balance among id, ego, and superego. In the abnormal personality the distribution of energy among psychic components has either developed in a lopsided fashion or has been knocked askew as a result of some disturbance in pregenital psychosexual development. As we have seen, intense anxiety at any stage of development can result in fixation, which brings further development of ego and superego to a halt. Similarly, anxiety can bring about regression, in which the individual abandons whatever ego or superego maturity he has gained beyond the stage to which he regresses. Improper resolution of the Oedipus complex may leave the individual with a feeble superego. Conversely, an extremely stern and punitive upbringing can shift too much of the id's energy to the superego and cause the ego's power to be depleted through constant repression of id demands.

Once the balance among the three structural components is disrupted, any number of symptoms can occur. If the superego is weakened, aggressive id impulses may gain the upper hand and the individual may take to killing whoever gets in his way. If the superego becomes dominant, then defenses will become exaggerated to the point where they will seriously impair normal functioning. For example, a person who has to rely heavily on projection may end up imagining that everyone is "out to get him"—a condition that would be diagnosed as paranoia. A person having a reaction formation to moral anxiety over masturbation may suddenly lose the sensation in the offending hand, a symptom of hysteria.

---

*It should be noted that later psychodynamically oriented theorists view the ego as having greater autonomy.

While the variety of symptoms is infinite, most of them have one thing in common. No matter what component is strengthened, the ego is usually weakened. And since the individual's contact with reality is only as strong as his ego, any draining of ego strength—whether from the task of repressing an inordinate amount of material or from the task of erecting and maintaining defenses—will result in an impairment of the individual's ability to perceive and adapt to reality. Appointments will be missed; new situations will become terrifying; minor difficulties will become major calamities. As these troubles build, a vicious circle is set up: the troubles create further conflict, which in turn further weakens the ego, which in turn further reduces the individual's ability to adapt to reality. In the extreme case, the ego may end up with all its fingers in the dike, so to speak—thus rendered incapable of doing the work of mediating between the id and reality. When this happens, adaptive functioning simply ceases. Emotions are cut loose from external events. Inner voices are mistaken for outer voices. Speech loses its coherence. Imaginary people appear at the window, and real people are treated as if they did not exist. This condition of total ego collapse, known as psychosis, is the furthest reach of the structural imbalance that Freud (1948) saw as the foundation of abnormal behavior.

THE DESCENDANTS OF FREUD

As we have seen, Freud placed great emphasis on the id. According to his theory, the id is the basic metal from which the personality is hammered out; ego, superego, and reality are merely the hammers. They may pound it into different shapes, but the substance remains the same: primitive, irrational, amoral drives—sexual and aggressive. In general, later contributors to psychodynamic theory tended to shift this emphasis from the id to the ego. That is, they deemphasized sex, instincts, and determinism and instead emphasized goals, creativity, and self-direction. Furthermore, unlike Freud, they began to see the human being as a *social* creature—one whose contacts with reality, and particularly with other people, were major determinants of his behavior.

Jung and Adler

Particularly influential among the followers of Freud were two pupils who broke with him early in their careers, Carl Jung (1875-1961) and Alfred Adler (1870-1937). Jung disagreed vehemently with

Fig. 2.5   Carl Jung, a student of Freud; he rejected Freud's determinism, substituting a goal-oriented psychology.

Fig. 2.6   Alfred Adler, also a student of Freud; he emphasized that human beings should be viewed as social organisms and he stressed the significance of social relationships.

Fig. 2.7 (opposite)   Psychoanalytic theory, as represented by Freud (top), Jung (left), and Adler (right), is perhaps the most systematic and extensive of psychological approaches. It encompasses theories of child development, personality structure and functioning, psychopathology, society, and creativity. Freud stressed the central role of instinctual drives, especially sex and aggression, and of unconscious processes (id, ego, superego) in the development of personality and abnormal behavior (symbols in upper right). Psychoanalytic theorists have generally accepted some Freudian assumptions and have pursued independent directions in areas of disagreement. Jung, for example, proposed that a collective unconscious, in which racial memories were stored, influenced psychic functioning (symbols in lower left). Adler emphasized power relations within the family and the individual's need to overcome a sense of inferiority as major factors in personality development and psychopathology (symbols in lower right).

Fig. 2.8 Neo-Freudians and ego psychologists such as Sullivan, Horney, Erikson, and Fromm have broadened psychoanalytic theory by incorporating interpersonal, societal, and existential views into their theorizing about human behavior. Rather than simply attributing the development of personality to interpsychic conflicts involving biological instincts that occur in childhood, these theorists believe that an individual's personality is greatly determined by a complex of cultural and social factors.

Freud's contention that the basis of human behavior was the combination of early psychosexual history and sexual drives. Against this contention Jung (1933) argued that the unconscious life was not just repressed sexual striving but a combination of many elements, including a stock of *archetypes*, or ancient primordial images common to all mankind which Jung called the *collective unconscious* (Jung, 1972). And whereas Freud stressed the negative character of the unconscious, Jung countered by claiming that the unconscious and the libidinal energy emanating from it gave life its richness and mystery. Furthermore, it was from these sources that the individual acquired the desire and energy to form goals. And in Jung's system, goals were extremely important. Unlike Freud, who saw human beings as determined by their past, Jung saw the individual's behavior as a function of his visions of the future as well as of his experience in the past.

Adler too placed great emphasis on the role of self-generated goals in directing human behavior (Ansbacher and Rowen, 1956). Hypothesizing that all human beings were equipped from infancy with a sense of inferiority (it was Adler who coined the term "inferiority complex"), he saw human behavior

Fig. 2.9 According to the ego psychologists, the kind and quality of human relations that are established between a child and his or her parents are central in determining the outcome of personality development. For example, a young woman's relationship with her parents—the degree of honesty and clearness of communication she can have with them—will definitely affect the type of person she becomes, the type of choices she will therefore make, and the type of parent she, in turn, will be. Thus, the conceptions of personality and of the factors that are said to play major roles in personality development have changed considerably as psychoanalysis has become "modernized."

as a perpetual striving for superiority. However, Adler's most significant contribution to psychodynamic theory was his insistence that the human being be viewed as a social organism. Convinced, like Jung, that Freud had placed an undue emphasis on biological drives, Adler contended that a person's social relationships—the ways in which he was acted upon by others and the ways in which he acted in relationship to others—were much more significant than his biological heritage in shaping his behavior.

Ego Psychology

Set going by Jung and Adler, this movement toward a less deterministic and less biologically oriented psychology has been carried on by a second generation of Freudian theorists, the *ego psychologists*. While still adhering, like Jung and Adler, to the fundamental Freudian notions of the unconscious and the three-part psychic structure, the ego psychologists differ with Freud on the subject of the role of the ego. To Freud, as we have seen, the ego was merely the handmaiden of the id. It took its energy from the id, and its role was simply to find safe and realistic ways of gratifying the id's demands. Against this limited view of the ego's functioning, the ego psychologists have argued that the ego has its own energy and its own autonomous functions, particularly in the areas of perception, motor functioning, and problem-solving. Thus while the id and the superego may underlie an adolescent's willingness to go to school and do his homework, only the ego can account for how he learns to solve an algebra problem, translate a sentence from Latin into English, or throw a ball through a hoop. This new emphasis on the ego has led psychodynamic theorists to extend Jung's and Adler's more positive and optimistic approach to the mind and to concern themselves even more intensely with the creative, individualistic, and interpersonal aspects of personality functioning.

Among the most prominent names associated with ego psychology are those of Karen Horney (1885–1952), Harry Stack Sullivan (1892–1949), Erich Fromm (1900–) and Erik Erikson (1902–). Both Horney (1945) and Sullivan (1953) saw interpersonal relationships as the center of human functioning and disturbed interpersonal relationships as the source of abnormal behavior. Fromm too has given great weight to the social aspect of psychological development and has criticized Freud's dogged adherence to the theory of pregenital psychosexual stages as the final determinants of

the adult psyche. Furthermore, whereas Freud felt that most of mankind's professed ideals were reducible to rationalizations of primitive id strivings, Fromm has placed ideals such as love, generosity, and justice at the center of his psychological system, as true and legitimate goals of the ego.

Of this group of later psychodynamic theorists, perhaps most influential in recent years has been Erikson. Like the others, Erikson (1963) has rejected Freud's limited notion of psychosexual development and has replaced it with his own theory of *psychosocial* development. Furthermore, in answer to Freud's contention that the personality is essentially formed by the end of the fifth year of life, Erikson has charted a series of psychosocial stages of development in which the personality continues to grow and change through a series of challenges extending into old age. Finally, Erikson has considerably expanded Freud's concept of identification, arguing that the ego is not content simply to assimilate the values of a parent or other admired person, but goes on to form an integrated, unique, and autonomous "self," which Erikson calls the *ego identity*.

Post-Freudian Therapies

Both the Freudian technique of psychoanalysis and the therapies that grew out of psychoanalysis will be discussed in Chapter 19. It should be pointed out here, however, that the emphasis on interpersonal relationships in the theories of Freud's followers has given rise to various interpersonal therapeutic techniques. Instead of isolating the patient on the analyst's couch, removed from the stresses and complications of interpersonal interactions, these new therapies attempt to treat the individual's problems within the interpersonal context in which they arose. *Group therapy* operates on the premise that people's problems have to do with other people. Accordingly, in group therapy, participants are given a safe environment in which to reveal their methods of interacting with others and to adjust these methods with the help of the other participants and of the group leader. In *transactional analysis* it is not so much the individuals who are treated but rather the transactions or formulas of communication between them. Thus husbands and wives, brothers and sisters are treated together so that they can rebuild their patterns of dealing with one another. Likewise, in *family therapy*, whole families are seen together, so that their destructive roles and attitudes in relation to one another can be laid bare, reexamined, and modified.

EVALUATING THE PSYCHODYNAMIC PERSPECTIVE

Psychodynamic Theory and Other Models of Abnormal Behavior

There are close ties between the psychodynamic perspective and the medical model. It should be remembered that Freud himself began his career as a neurologist, and though he often argued for a truly psychological, nonorganic approach to abnormal behavior, his medical training did color his interpretation of mental disorder. The Freudian notion of behavioral abnormalities as the surface symptoms of an underlying psychic disturbance is of course very close to the medical model's approach to maladaptive behavior patterns as merely the symptoms of an underlying organic dysfunction. Furthermore, both approaches are deterministic. In the Freudian theory, the individual is a victim of his past. In the medical model, the individual is a victim of his body. In neither case is he himself truly responsible for his behavior. In short, the medical model and the psychodynamic perspective get along well together. And thus it is no surprise that medical schools favor the psychodynamic perspective in their training of psychiatrists and that hospitals for the mentally disturbed tend to be staffed by psychodynamically oriented professionals.

However, notwithstanding this tie with the medical model, the psychodynamic perspective remains the oldest and the most widely used representative of what, in Chapter 1, we have called the psychological model. Indeed, Freud's theory was the first systematic interpretation of the mind to regard abnormal behavior not as a moral, religious, or organic problem, but as a psychological problem—a problem in the history of the individual's emotional life.

Pros and Cons

Freud's theories were no sooner enunciated than they were attacked. And today the psychodynamic perspective is still severely criticized by many psychological theorists (Sarnoff, 1971). A major source of criticism is that psychodynamic formulations lack the support of large-scale scientific studies. Freud's theories were evolved on the basis of his experience with his own patients, and today psychodynamic writers still tend to rely on case studies from private practice as the sole support of their formulations. The problem with such case studies is that their accuracy is always questionable; we can never know to what degree Dr. Jones' ideas and expecta-

Erickson and the Psychosocial Theory of Development

Erik Erikson's psychosocial theory of development differs from Freud's psychosexual theory in at least four major respects. First, whereas Freud saw early childhood as the major arena of psychological development, Erikson views psychological growth as a process that extends from birth to death, leading the individual through a series of "crises," the resolutions of which determine his basic personality traits. Second, while Freud saw the individual psyche in relative isolation except for the influence of parents and siblings, Erikson sees personality development as deeply affected not only by the family but also by the society; teachers, friends, spouses, and the like all do their part in molding the individual. Third, to Freud the psyche was dominated primarily by the instinctual id; in contrast, Erikson stresses the role of the reality-oriented ego in personality development. Finally, Erikson, armed with his faith in the power of the ego, concentrates on the ego's ability to resolve developmental crises, whereas Freud concerned himself primarily with the pathological outcomes of the struggle between the powerful id and the punitive superego. In sum, Erikson's theory is much more hopeful than Freud's: the ego is strong, and there is always a second chance. To Freud, on the other hand, the ego had relatively little influence on the question of how the psyche would develop; furthermore, this question was more or less closed around the age of six.

Erikson's psychosocial stages	Age	Successful resolution of crisis leads to	Freud's psychosexual stages
Basic Trust vs. Mistrust Consistent maternal care vs. negligence, irregular satisfaction of needs	First year	Trust, optimism, warmth	Oral
Autonomy vs. Shame, Doubt Assertiveness and physical self-control vs. dependency on parents and inability to be assertive	Second year	Sense of autonomy, pride of accomplishment	Anal
Initiative vs. Guilt Exploratory behavior and self-initiated activities vs. fearfulness and self-doubt	Third–fifth years	Development of conscience, self-worth, goal definition	Phallic
Industry vs. Inferiority Cooperation and competition vs. fear of failing and feelings of inadequacy	Sixth year to puberty	Competence, mastery of skills, self-confidence	Latency
Identity vs. Role Confusion Integration of identity vs. role diffusion, lack of positive identity	Adolescence	Sense of continuity with one's past, present, and future, healthy sense of identity	Genital
Intimacy vs. Isolation Caring deeply for another person and vulnerability vs. shallow interpersonal relationships and fear of commitment	Early adulthood	Ability to form stable commitments and close relationships	
Generativity vs. Stagnation Need to be needed and desire to contribute vs. self-absorption and early invalidism	Middle adulthood	Productivity, creative concern for the world and future generations	
Integrity vs. Despair Reflection and evaluation vs. regret for past life and strong fear of death	Old age	Acceptance of mortality and of the human life cycle, sense of peace	

Source: Erikson (1964).

THE DESCENDANTS OF FREUD

The descendants of Freud—those who used his concepts of the unconscious and of the three-part structure of the psyche as a basic foundation for their own individual theories of psychological development—have been grouped under various vague headings: the American school, the ego psychologists, the neo-Freudians, and so forth. However, each theorist had his own unique manner of building on, and deviating from, the Freudian system. The following are brief summaries of the theories of psychological disturbance put forth by Freud and his major descendants:

Sigmund Freud: The roots of disordered behavior lie in disturbances (e.g., trauma, over-gratification, undergratification) of psychosexual development during the first six years of life. Psychological disorder develops out of the inevitable conflicts between the infantile pleasure-seeking of the id and the restrictions and censures of the superego and reality. Seeking to avoid the anxiety that arises out of such conflicts, the individual develops a variety of defense mechanisms. Overdependence on these defense mechanisms leads to neurotic behavior (if the person is still in touch with reality) or to psychotic behavior (if he has lost touch with reality).

Carl Jung: Growth involves the integration of the conscious and unconscious forces within the individual. In order to cope with life's stresses, formulate goals, and achieve them, the individual must allow these two forces to balance one another. If he ignores his unconscious forces, he will not achieve the full actualization of his potential. Furthermore, the unconscious forces will have their revenge, manifesting themselves in twisted and distorted fashions, thus creating the rigid behaviors characteristic of neurosis, or in the ex-treme case, the delusions and hallucinations characteristic of psychosis.

Alfred Adler: The individual is born with an innate drive for superiority—the desire to achieve a complete and perfect self. The flip side of this striving for superiority is an inborn feeling of inferiority or incompleteness. Each individual develops a unique "style of life," a set of behaviors through which he attempts to achieve superiority and alleviate his sense of inferiority. Whatever his style of life, it is in the area of social relationships that its value is tested, for human beings are, above all, social creatures. Poor relationships lead to distorted behavior and consequently to increased feelings of inferiority and inappropriate compensatory efforts. The degree of distortion determines whether one suffers a mild neurosis or a full-blown psychosis.

Erich Fromm: The individual develops in an interpersonal context. He is a social being, to be understood in terms of his relationship to others. It is through dynamic interaction with others that the individual realizes his capacity for love and reason and strives toward the ideals of truth, justice, and freedom. However, because the individual is capable of reason and self-awareness, he is conscious of his mixed relationship with nature—his interdependence with nature, and at the same time, his separation from it. This knowledge leads to existential anxiety, which, if properly worked through, may result in a more productive interaction with the world. However, existential anxiety may also lead to a distorted relationship with the world, ranging from self-defeating neurotic interactions to a total psychotic withdrawal.

Karen Horney: Disordered behavior begins with the child's early experiences of negative or actually hostile responses from others. These

tions colored his patients' responses and his reporting of those responses. It is not likely that this scientific deficiency in psychodynamic theory will be easily corrected, for most of the Freudian conceptualizations simply cannot be tested in any scientific manner (Sears, 1943, 1951; Hall, 1956). Though psychosis may in fact stem from a weakened ego, we cannot observe the ego or measure its weakness. Hence to embrace psychodynamic theory requires a certain act of faith and is likely to continue to do so.

A second, related problem with the psychodynamic approach is that it depends so heavily on inference. If a woman decides to become a proctologist, does this mean that she is fixated at the anal stage? If a little boy is afraid of snakes, does this mean that he is anxious about his penis? Does getting drunk really constitute a regression, as Hall claims in the quotation presented earlier? If a person dreams of a little man with a bald head, is this a symbol of the penis? Likewise, if one dreams of a cave, is this a symbol of the vagina? Many psycho-

experiences result in a feeling of basic anxiety, which causes the child, as he grows, to develop rigid and defensive patterns for dealing with others; such patterns almost inevitably lead to failure and rejection, thus causing the individual even more anxiety and making him even more inflexible and defensive—in short, neurotic. When interpersonal relations break down completely and the mind cuts itself loose from its moorings in the social context, then the individual is classifiable as psychotic.

Erik Erikson: Beginning in childhood and continuing throughout his life, the individual is confronted with a series of psychosocial crises which he must resolve in order to become an integrated person. The way in which each crisis is handled depends on the individual's relationships with others. Unsuccessful resolution of early crises results in mistrust, shame, and guilt, which in turn lessen (but do not destroy) the individual's chances of successfully resolving future crises. Anxiety and stress increase with each unresolved crisis. Neurotic behavior may occur as a result of a few unresolved crises; psychotic behavior, as a consequence of many such failures.

Harry Stack Sullivan: In the growing child's interaction with the "significant others" in his life (i.e., parents, siblings, teachers), he invariably experiences some anxiety. Seeking to cope with this anxiety, he gradually develops a self-system made up of attitudes about himself and patterns of dealing with others. If his childhood anxieties have been severe, then his self-system will tend to be limited, rigid, and overdependent on denial. And such a self-system, because it is inadequate for dealing with a variety of experiences and stresses, will eventually give way to extreme anxiety (neurosis) or total breakdown (psychosis).

dynamic theorists would probably answer yes to most of these questions. However, those not already committed to psychodynamic theory tend to regard such leaps of symbolic interpretation with considerable skepticism.

Another point on which psychodynamic theory has been criticized is that it is based on cases drawn from a very limited sample of humankind. Freud's patients were middle-class Viennese neurotics living in a period when all forms of sexual expression were uniformly frowned upon. And even today most psychoanalytic patients are middle-class neurotics. Hence there is serious question as to whether theories based on the treatment of such patients are applicable, as Freud (1926) claimed, to all human beings.

A fourth source of criticism is that psychoanalytic concepts such as ego, superego, and id have become reified—that is, made into entities in themselves. While the ego, for instance, is supposed to stand simply as a metaphor for certain functions of the mind, it is difficult, once the metaphor is accepted, to avoid talking about the ego as if it had a life of its own. Thus in psychoanalytic writings (and in this chapter) the ego is spoken of as "mediating," "protecting," "battling," and so forth, as if it were a little creature efficiently going about its business as president of the psyche. Unfortunately, such thinking may lead to gross oversimplification of psychic processes.

Finally, it has been argued that psychodynamic theory has handed down to the twentieth century an incomparably dismal vision of human life—a vision in which the human being is seen simply as a creature driven by animal instincts beyond his control; in which the individual is virtually helpless to change himself after the die is cast in the first six years of life; in which works of art are merely substitutes for relief of sexual and aggressive impulses; in which acts of great heroism or generosity are neither heroic nor generous but simply the outgrowths of baser motives; in which ideals are nothing more than fancy disguises for self-serving impulses; and in which all that the average individual can know of his own mind is the surface, while all his behavior issues from the murky pool of repressed thoughts that lies beneath that surface. Such a vision did not greatly disturb Freud; he was able to view human life and human achievements in terms of their lowest common denominators and yet still feel that they were not denigrated in the process. As he put it, "One can only characterize as simple-minded the fear which is sometimes expressed that all the highest goods of humanity, as they are called—research, art, love, ethical and social sense—will lose their value or their dignity because psychoanalysis is in a position to demonstrate their origin in elementary and animal instinctual impulses" (1963, p. 50). However, many thinkers, unable to share Freud's double vision, have argued that his reductive interpretation of life is both unsound and destructive.

In answer to such criticisms, it must be acknowledged that psychodynamic theory has made sub-

THE FEMINIST CASE

Over the last decade there has been an increasing clamor that Freudian theory is degrading to women. Nor is it difficult to see why, for Freud's writings are liberally sprinkled with passing references to female inferiority. The basis on which his conceptualization of this inferiority—and indeed of female psychology as a whole—rests is the penis: the fact that boys have one and girls don't. According to Freud, the moment a child notices this basic anatomical difference, that moment he or she begins to become, psychologically as well as biologically, a male or a female. For the little girl, the realization that she lacks this fine piece of equipment gives rise to an ineradicable jealousy, the famous "penis envy." And this is the beginning of her long slide into inferiority. As Freud puts it, "The discovery that she is castrated is a turning point in a girl's growth" (1974, p. 105). He might have said "*the* turning point," for starting with the notion of penis deprivation and penis envy, Freud constructs an elegant chain of reasoning leading directly to female inferiority.

The process may be summarized as follows. Because she lacks a penis, the girl's Oedipal conflict takes a form different from the boy's. Already castrated, she is barred from the healthy process of experiencing and then overcoming castration anxiety. Furthermore, her choice of her father as a love object is a negative rather than a positive choice. Like the boy, she originally preferred her mother, but once she discovers that her mother, like her, is an amputee and is even responsible for bringing her into the world so poorly equipped, she turns to her father out of resentment against her mother. Thus her Oedipal experience lacks both the stable heterosexual orientation and the cathartic resolution of the boy's Oedipal crisis. And as a result, her superego

(the fruit of a successfully resolved Oedipus complex) is stunted in its growth. Throughout her adult life she remains narcissistic, vain, lacking in a fully developed sense of justice, and above all, envious. In short, she is morally inferior because she can never overcome either her bitterness over her castration or the need to compensate for her paltry sexual equipment. Furthermore, she is culturally inferior, since the ability to contribute to the advance of civilization is dependent on the mechanism of sublimation, which in turn depends on a strong, mature superego—the very thing she lacks. According to Freud, there is only one contribution that women have made to civilization, the art of weaving, a practice unconsciously motivated by woman's desire to conceal her "genital deficiency" (1974, p. 111).

Thus, while men, legitimized by their penises, go out to do the work of justice and civilization, women must swallow their disgrace and comfort themselves with substitutes. As a child, a woman can comfort herself sexually with her clitoris, but in order to become psychologically mature, she must abandon this "penis equivalent" (1974, p. 97) in favor of "the truly feminine vagina" (1974, p. 97). (Hence the Freudian notion, recently disputed by Masters and Johnson, that there is a difference between clitoral and vaginal orgasms and that the psychologically mature woman has made the transition to the latter.) The woman's reward for transferring her sexual sensitivity from clitoris to vagina is the ultimate penis substitute, a baby. And if the baby should turn out to be a boy, "who brings the longed-for penis with him" (1974, p. 107), all the better.

To sum up: woman is morally feeble, culturally unproductive, and somehow "other"—a variation on the standard of masculinity, a devia-

AGAINST FREUD

tion from the norm, or, in the words of Simone de Beauvoir, the "second sex" (1961). It should be carefully noted, however, that Freud does not claim that women are born with this inferiority. Though his wording often suggests that he too, like the little girl, sees the penis as an exceedingly desirable thing to have and considers the lack of one to be cause for mourning, what he actually states is that it is the little girl's *perception of herself* as castrated, and her consequent envy, that plunges her into inferiority.

The opposition to this theory was first mounted in 1926 by Karen Horney, who retorted that Freud was in a poor position to know what little girls think. According to Horney (1967), it is not little girls who perceive their condition as degraded. Rather, it is little boys—and the men they eventually become—who see their penisless counterparts as woefully mutilated and deficient and who thus have created the self-fulfilling prophecy that has doomed womankind to inferiority. More recent feminist writers have taken this argument several steps further, claiming that Freud's theory was merely the reflection of an age-old cultural bias against women and that this theory actually constitutes a devious attempt to justify the continuance of male supremacy.

In short, the feminists contend that Freud was simply one more member of the vast male conspiracy aimed, whether consciously or not, at keeping woman in her place. Indeed, not just Freud, but the entire mental health profession appears increasingly suspect to feminist writers. Their basic claim is simply that for thousands of years men have had the privilege of deciding who is crazy and who is not, and that their decisions have been based on sex-role stereotypes. Thus, for example, in reading about the sixteenth and seventeenth centuries, we hear a great deal about witch-burnings but very little about sorcerer-burnings. According to Zilboorg and Henry (1941), the witch-burnings of the late Renaissance actually constituted a pathological outbreak of misogyny and antieroticism. Any woman who stepped out of line was perceived as a diabolical threat: "Never in the history of humanity was woman more systematically degraded. She paid for the fall of Eve sevenfold" (pp. 161-162). And according to Phillis Chesler (1972), woman is still paying. She is born into a society which automatically expects her to be passive, emotional, sexually fearful, and dependent. If she rejects her role assignment, she is either declared mentally disturbed or is made so unhappy by the society that she in fact becomes mentally disturbed. In either case, she is then handed over to the mental health profession, where she is diagnosed and treated by males. And what does her treatment consist of? It consists, Chesler claims, of retraining her to accept her biologically ordained role.

Taken as a whole, Chesler's theory can be argued one way or the other. What cannot be disputed is that the most influential of all psychological theories, that of Freud, was based on the assumption that male biology and male psychology constitute the norm. Nor can it be denied that the vast majority of those who prescribe treatment for the mentally ill are males. Until this latter situation is corrected, whatever women have to say about what it means to be a woman is likely to go on being muffled by whatever men have to say on the subject.

stantial contributions to the modern treatment of abnormal behavior and to modern thought in general. In the first place, it has directed the attention of the twentieth century to the inner life—to dreams, to fantasies, to memory, and to the motives underlying behavior. This intensified subjectivity has extended far beyond the limits of psychology; indeed, it has altered the face of art, literature, history, and education in our century. Furthermore, psychodynamic theory, while deterministic, still holds out the hope that by acquainting ourselves with our inner lives, we can exercise greater control over our destinies. In short, psychodynamic theory has pointed out the adaptive value of self-knowledge.

Second, psychodynamic theory has helped to demythologize mental disorder. By showing that the most bizarre and "crazy" behaviors have their roots in the same impulses and in the same developmental processes as the most adaptive and "sane" behaviors, Freud contributed greatly to the modern effort to treat the mentally disturbed as human beings rather than as freaks. Furthermore, by pointing out what he called the "psychopathology of everyday life"—the ways in which irrational and unconscious impulses come up in dreams, in jokes, in slips of the tongue, in our ways of forgetting what we want to forget—Freud showed that the mentally disturbed had no monopoly on irrationality. This aspect of psychodynamic theory helped to establish the concept of mental health as a continuum ranging from adaptive to maladaptive rather than as a dichotomy of "sick" and "healthy."

Finally, to the treatment of mental problems Freud contributed the new technique of psychoanalysis, in which, through the confrontation and understanding of his unconscious impulses, the patient gains greater mastery over his actions. Psychoanalysis is costly, time-consuming, and limited in its applicability. Yet for some people it clearly works. Furthermore, as we have seen, it has spawned a wide variety of other therapies—family therapy, group therapy, and so on—that have moved out in new and hopeful directions.

While modern thinkers are still arguing with Freud, one cannot argue with his impact on the contemporary conceptualization, assessment, and treatment of abnormal behavior. It is Freudian theory that is responsible for the widespread assumption that abnormal behavior stems from events in the individual's past and that it occurs in response to unconscious and uncontrollable impulses. In terms of psychological assessment, the popular

"projective" tests (e.g., ink-blot tests), in which the person is asked to interpret various pictures and symbols, are based on the Freudian notion that behavior is symbolic and that what a person reads into a picture or an event is actually a reading of his own psyche. As for psychological treatment, it is Freud who truly established what is by now the traditional technique of a one-to-one patient-therapist relationship aimed at increasing the patient's self-knowledge. Though it has been modified in a thousand different ways and though it is used by therapists who disavow any relationship with Freudian theory, this treatment model is essentially a Freudian invention.

The impact of psychodynamic theory has extended far beyond the limited field of professional psychology. Though possibly unfamiliar even with the name of Freud, the man on the street often shows no hesitation in explaining his friends' quirks in terms of their childhood difficulties, in regarding his own children's development as crucial prefigurations of their adult lives, and in using terms such as "inferiority complex," "introvert," "extrovert," "ego," and "narcissistic"—terms coined by Freud and his followers to explain the human psyche (Blum, 1953). In short, psychodynamic theory has colored popular thinking about human behavior. Even more than nineteenth-century man, twentieth-century man tends to regard human behavior both as the function of a deterministic process and as the reflection of a mysterious and irrational inner life. That these two disparate interpretations of life are more firmly entrenched today than ever before is certainly due in part to the fact that it was from two strands of thought, determinism and subjectivism, that Freud wove his famous theory.

SUMMARY

This chapter has presented the basic concepts of psychodynamic theory and has outlined the recent modifications of this theory and the arguments for and against the psychodynamic perspective in general. The basic tenet of Freudian theory is the structural hypothesis, Freud's conceptualization of the human psyche as an interaction of three forces: the id, which is made up of primitive sexual and aggressive drives; the ego, which uses reason to mediate between reality and the demands of the id; and the superego, which represents the moral standards of the society. Freud also divided the mind into three levels of consciousness: the perceptual conscious, the preconscious, and the unconscious, the last of which contains all the individual's repressed thoughts.

The three components of id, ego, and superego exist in a state of perpetual conflict with one another. And this intrapsychic conflict gives rise to three types of anxiety: reality anxiety, moral anxiety, and neurotic anxiety. Though anxiety may be dealt with rationally, a more common response is the use of defense mechanisms (e.g., repression, projection, displacement, denial, reaction formation, intellectualization, fixation, regression, sublimation), which reduce anxiety by concealing its source.

The psychic structure of id, ego, and superego develops gradually as the child progresses through a series of psychosexual stages extending from birth through the sixth year. These include the oral stage, the anal stage, and the phallic stage, in which sensual pleasure is focused on the mouth, anus, and genitals, respectively. Then follows the latency period, when sexual instincts lie dormant, after which the individual emerges into the genital stage, adult sexual functioning.

From these basic theories Freud developed his interpretation of the human personality—both normal and abnormal—as basically irrational, antisocial, and determined. What distinguishes normal from abnormal functioning is the way in which energy is distributed among the three psychic components. In normal functioning the psychic structure is properly balanced, so anxiety can be absorbed without drastically weakening any one of the three psychic components. In abnormal functioning, on the other hand, psychic energy is improperly distributed, with the result that one component becomes disproportionately strong, taking over the personality and forcing it into maladaptive behaviors. This interpretation of normal and abnormal behavior has been modified substantially by such followers of Freud as Jung, Adler, Horney, Sullivan, Fromm, and Erikson. In general, the trend among these later psychodynamic theorists has been to accord a larger role to the ego and to substitute a concern for the individual's goals and his interpersonal relationships in place of Freud's emphasis on sexual drives and psychosexual development.

Related to both the medical and psychological models, the psychodynamic approach has been criticized on a number of points such as its lack of scientific support, its dependence on inference, and its reductive interpretation of human life. But this perspective has also made valuable contributions to modern psychology and has exercised a massive influence on the twentieth century's vision of both normal and abnormal behavior.

The behaviorist approach to abnormal psychology has its roots in the naturalistic philosophy of ancient Greece, particularly in the investigations of Hippocrates and of the philosopher Aristotle in the fifth and fourth centuries B.C. In reaction against current idealistic philosophies, which explained the workings of man and the universe in terms of mystic combinations of numbers or abstract philosophical concepts, Hippocrates and Aristotle devoted themselves to the documentation of actual physical events. To explain the physical universe, Aristotle tirelessly *observed* the physical universe, noting the difference between one flower or one star and the next and classifying them accordingly. Likewise, as we have seen in Chapter 1, Hippocrates attempted to explain disease not by appealing to current superstitions, but by observing the progress of disease in his patients—noting, for instance, the changed facial expression and the rattle of fluid in the chest as death approached. In short, the Greek naturalists sought to explain natural events in terms of other natural events; they looked for causes in observable phenomena, things that they could document through their own five senses.

It is a long leap—twenty-four centuries—from the naturalism of the Greeks to the behaviorism of today, but the basic assumption remains the same. Like the naturalists, the behaviorists hold that the causes of behavior must be sought in empirically observable phenomena.

Thus the behaviorist view presents a striking contrast to the psychodynamic view. As we have seen in the preceding chapter, the psychodynamic approach to mental disorder is based on a theory of psychic structure which, however credible, remains a theory. The movements and conflicts of ego, superego, and id can in no way be weighed, measured, or empirically observed. The behaviorists, on the other hand, attempt to explain abnormal behavior primarily in terms of observable physical circumstances: observable and measurable events in the individual's environment which have molded his behavior into an undesirable form. Furthermore, the behaviorists attempt to treat abnormal behavior by the same empirical route, by subjecting the patient to a new set of environmental stimuli that will remold the behavior into a more desirable form.

The behaviorist approach to specific deviant behaviors will be discussed in the various chapters which deal with them. The purpose of the present chapter is to outline the history of the behaviorist movement, its underlying assumptions, its general interpretation of normal and abnormal psychology,

3
The
Behaviorist
Perspective

and its current impact on the treatment of abnormal behavior.

THE BACKGROUND OF BEHAVIORISM

It was during the first half of the twentieth century, as psychodynamic theory was becoming increasingly popular, that the basic principles of behaviorism were discovered and elaborated. This new movement, which would eventually challenge the psychodynamic school, was based largely on the work of four scientists, whose discoveries we shall discuss in the following section.

Pavlov and the Conditioned Reflex

In conducting research on the salivary responses of dogs, Ivan Pavlov (1849–1936), a Russian physiologist, found that if he consistently sounded a tone at the same time that he gave a dog food, the dog would eventually salivate to the sound of the tone alone. Thus Pavlov discovered what is a basic mechanism of behavioral psychology: the *conditioned*

Fig. 3.1 *Ivan Pavlov, the Russian physiologist and discoverer of the conditioned reflex.*

reflex, whereby if a neutral stimulus (e.g., the tone) is paired with a nonneutral stimulus (e.g., the food), the organism will eventually respond to the neutral stimulus as it does to the nonneutral stimulus.

The implications of Pavlov's discovery were truly revolutionary. Whereas it had always been assumed that human beings' reactions to different things in their environment were the result of complicated subjective processes, Pavlov had raised the possibility that many of our responses, like the dog's, were the result of a simple learning process—that our loves and hates, our tastes and distastes were the consequence of nothing more mysterious than a conditioning process whereby certain things in our environment became associated with automatic responses to food, warmth, pain, and so forth. As we shall see, this astounding notion became the basis of behavioral psychology.

Watson and the Founding of Behaviorism

While Pavlov's discovery gave behaviorism its first basic principle, it is John B. Watson (1878–1958), an American psychologist, who is credited with the founding of the behaviorist movement, since he first outlined and defended the strictly empirical method that has become the hallmark of behaviorism. In doing so, he drew the line that was to separate behaviorism from more subjective psychologies.

In his famous article, "Psychology As the Behaviorist Views It," Watson made his position clear: "Psychology, as the behaviorist views it, is a purely objective, experimental branch of natural science which needs introspection as little as do the sciences of chemistry and physics" (1913, p. 176). Watson

Fig. 3.2 *The apparatus used in early studies of classical conditioning. Saliva dropping from a tube inserted into the dog's cheek strikes a lightly balanced arm, and the resulting motion is transmitted hydraulically to a pen that traces a record on a slowly revolving drum. Pavlov's discovery of conditioned salivation was an accidental by-product of his researches into the activity of the digestive system.*

Fig. 3.3 *The founder of the behaviorist movement, John B. Watson; he argued for an empirical approach to the study of human behavior.*

argued that introspection, the subjective analysis of one's thoughts and emotions was, if anything, the province of theology. In any case, it had no place in psychology. The province of psychology was behavior—that is, observable and measurable responses to specific stimuli. And the goal of psychology was the prediction and control of behavior.

Watson supported his rejection of the introspective method by demonstrating, in a classic experiment, that a supposedly subjective emotion such as fear could, like the salivation response of Pavlov's dogs, result from a simple, objective conditioning process. With the help of one of his students, Rosalie Rayner, Watson conditioned a fear of furry animals in an eleven-month-old boy, Albert B. (Watson and Rayner, 1920). When the experiment began, Albert showed no fear of a white laboratory rat and even tried to reach for it. At this point Watson struck an iron bar with a hammer, causing a very loud noise to occur. Albert jumped, fell forward, cried, and burrowed his head in the mattress on which he was sitting. After seven pairings of these two stimuli, Albert reacted with fright, crying and falling forward in response to the rat alone. Thus a strong conditioned fear reaction had been established. Later tests showed that without further conditioning, Albert exhibited fear of a variety of stimuli similar to the rat: a rabbit, a dog, a fur coat, and a bearded Santa Claus mask. In commenting on these results, Watson argued that many of our "unreasonable" fears are established in the same way that Albert's was—through conditioning.

Thorndike and the Law of Effect

Another psychologist of Watson's time was Edward Lee Thorndike (1874–1949), whose early experiments with animals had a decisive influence on later behaviorism. Unlike Pavlov and Watson, who had studied how the organism responded *after* experiencing certain painful or pleasant stimuli,

Thorndike was interested in how the use of such stimuli as *consequences* of certain responses could affect those responses. In one experiment he placed a hungry cat in a box equipped in such a way that if the cat pulled a cord or pressed a lever, the door of the chamber flew open; when the cat escaped through this door, it got a piece of salmon to eat. Thorndike noted the time it took for the cat to escape on each successive trial. In early trials its behavior was erratic; while the cat often took a long time to escape, on other occasions its escape time was shorter. The pattern was generally irregular. Gradually, however, the time became shorter and shorter, so that finally when the cat was placed in the box, it almost immediately made the desired response, escaped, and received the food. Thorndike concluded that the reason the cat had learned the proper escape response was that this response had become associated with the food, which was the consequence of escaping. Hence Thorndike formulated what he called the *law of effect*, which stated that responses that led to satisfying consequences were strengthened and therefore were likely to be repeated, while responses that led to unsatisfying consequences were weakened and therefore were unlikely to be repeated. Thus another basic principle of behaviorism was established: the importance of reward in the learning process.

Skinner and the Control of Behavior

B. F. Skinner (1904–), the leading behaviorist of today, refined and extended Thorndike's discoveries. Skinner, like Watson, was highly interested in the control of behavior and saw in Thorndike's law, which he renamed the *principle of reinforcement*, the basic mechanism for the control of human behavior. Skinner (1965) pointed out that our social environment is filled with positive and negative reinforcements that mold our behavior as surely as the piece of salmon molded the behavior of the cat in Thorndike's box. Our friends and families control us with their approval or disapproval. Our jobs control us by offering or withdrawing money. Our schools control us by passing us or failing us and thus affecting our access to jobs and therefore to money. In short, in all the areas of our lives our actions are determined by the expectation of pleasant or unpleasant consequences. Thus Skinner finally stated what Pavlov's research had merely suggested: that much of our behavior is based not on internal contingencies but on external contingencies, which, precisely because they *are* external, can be manipulated to control our behavior.

Fig. 3.4   The classic experiment of Watson and Rayner (1920) is re-created in these drawings. The white rat shown in the first drawing elicits no negative reaction from the boy. The loud noise is an unconditioned stimulus (UCS) that elicits an unconditioned response (UCR) of fear. After several occasions during which the rat is present when the boy is frightened by the loud noise, the presence of the rat alone (conditioned stimulus, or CS) elicits a fear response (conditioned response, or CR) that is similar to the UCR. Some theorists claim that many human fears are learned through this process of respondent conditioning, and behavioral methods of treating such fears have been developed on the basis of this theory.

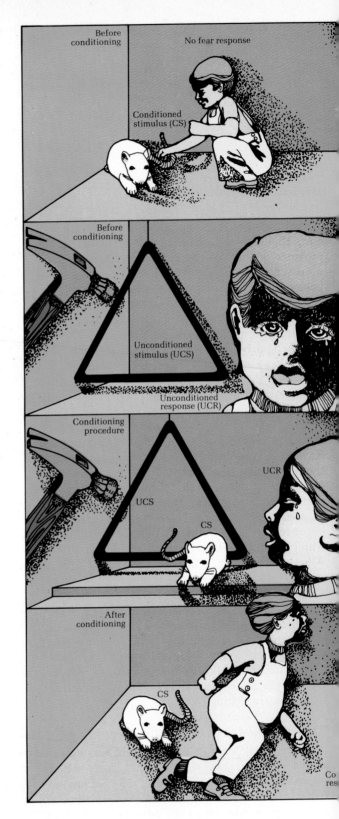

Fig. 3.5   Edward L. Thorndike contributed to behaviorist theory through his formulation of the "law of effect."

Fig. 3.6   B. F. Skinner, the articulate spokesman of modern behaviorism, has done much to refine and extend earlier conceptualizations.

THE MAKERS OF BEHAVIORISM

	Contribution
Ivan Pavlov (1849–1936)	Discovery of conditioned reflex, or respondent conditioning
John B. Watson (1878–1958)	Rejection of introspective psychology; insistence that even the most "subjective" responses are conditioned and therefore objective
Edward Lee Thorndike (1874–1949)	Formulation of the "law of effect," the principle underlying operant conditioning
B. F. Skinner (1904–)	Elaboration of the law of effect into the "principle of reinforcement," stating that almost all behavior is controlled by reinforcements

THE ASSUMPTIONS OF BEHAVIORAL PSYCHOLOGY

Before going on to discuss the mechanisms of learning, it will be useful to review briefly the basic assumptions of behaviorism as it has developed in the hands of the scientists whose work we have just discussed. The first assumption is that the task of psychology is, as Watson claimed, the study of behavior—that is, the study of the responses that an organism makes to the stimuli in its environment. Such stimuli usually come from outside us—people, things, and events in our external environment. However, they may also be internal, such as the stimulus of pressure on the bladder, which will elicit the response of going to the bathroom to urinate. Likewise, responses may be external (e.g., pounding a table in anger) or internal (e.g., the flow of adrenaline in response to whatever makes us angry). And they can range from the simplest reflex, such as a blinking of the eyes in response to bright light, to a highly complex chain of actions such as hitting a baseball or giving a lecture.

A second basic assumption has to do with methodology. According to the behaviorist, both stimuli and responses are objective, empirical events which can be observed and measured, and which *must* be observed and measured in order to qualify as scientific evidence. Hence behavioral studies since the time of Pavlov have always attempted to include careful measurement of responses. Indeed, one of the major innovations of Pavlov's research was that he not only observed the dogs' responses but also quantified them as to *magnitude* (the amount of saliva that occurred in response to the stimulus) and *latency* (the amount of time it took for the salivation response to occur after the presentation of the stim-

ulus). Such measurements—along with *rate*, the frequency with which a response occurs within a given period of time—have become the basic vocabulary of behavioral experimentation.

A third fundamental assumption, again taken from Watson, is that the goal of psychology is the prediction and control of behavior. In declaring this goal, Watson placed behavioral psychology in direct alignment with the natural sciences, whose object is to enunciate general laws. Just as a botanist can predict that a cactus will only grow in warm, dry weather, and can control the development of a sickly cactus by moving it from Massachusetts to Arizona, so the behaviorist attempts to predict how animals, and particularly human beings, will respond under different sets of environmental conditions and to control those responses by controlling the environmental stimuli that affect them. For the behaviorist working in a laboratory, under carefully controlled environmental circumstances and with animals whose conditioning history is known, such prediction and control is a fairly easy matter. But when the behaviorist moves out of the laboratory and into the world at large, where the environmental stimuli are infinitely more varied, complex, and uncontrollable, and attempts to deal with human beings, whose responses are considerably more complicated than those of the average white rat and whose conditioning history is only partially knowable, then the prediction and control of behavior becomes a more difficult task. One might predict, for example, that a hungry child, when called to dinner, might go directly to the dinner table. But if this child has come to associate dinnertime with his parents' fighting, then he might be just as likely to lock himself in his room as to go to the dinner table. Nonetheless, the

Fig. 3.7 (left) Behavioral theories of learning, personality disorder, and psychotherapy derive largely from the work of Pavlov (top center), Watson (upper right), and Skinner (middle left). Each man has had a pioneering and lasting influence on psychology. Pavlov, a Russian physiologist, studied respondent conditioning in animals such as dogs; his work has provided a model by which the acquisition and alteration of certain types of behavior can be studied under controlled conditions. The American psychologist Watson revolutionized psychology by his insistence that observable behavior (such as that recordable on a graph) was the only legitimate focus of study and that human behavior was understandable in terms of the individual's learning history. Skinner, also an American psychologist, has pioneered the study of operant behavior (in experiments with rats pressing a lever or cats discriminating shapes) and has made enormous contributions to psychology in the areas of theory and research design, and in the social and practical applications of operant conditioning (symbolized by the astronaut).

behaviorists hold that human responses to various kinds of environmental stimuli can be stated as general laws and that when a response is interfering with an individual's adjustment, that response can be altered by the careful manipulation of the environmental stimuli.

The final basic assumption of behaviorism is that the major ingredient in behavior is learning. Since Pavlov first discovered his dogs salivating in response to the tone rather than the food, behaviorists have been studying the ways in which behaviors are acquired, maintained, changed, or eliminated. And while they acknowledge the influence of genetics and physiology on human responses, it is primarily in terms of the mechanisms of learning that they attempt to explain both normal and abnormal behavior.

THE MECHANISMS OF LEARNING
Respondent Conditioning

According to behavioral theory, all behavior falls into two classes, respondent and operant. *Respondent behavior*, behavior that is elicited by specific stimuli, consists of *unlearned reflexes* and *conditioned reflexes*. Unlearned reflexes are simple responses such as blinking, coughing, or salivation that occur automatically when elicited by certain stimuli. However, as we have seen, it is possible through the pairing of stimuli to condition an organism so that it will show this same response to a new stimulus, one which would not naturally have elicited the response. The learning of such a conditioned reflex is called *respondent conditioning* (sometimes referred

to as classical conditioning). The classic example is, once again, Pavlov's dogs. Since a dog will naturally salivate when food is placed in its mouth, the food is designated as an *unconditioned stimulus* (UCS) and the natural response of salivation as the *unconditioned response* (UCR). And since the dog's salivation to the tone was the result of conditioning, the tone is called the *conditioned stimulus* (CS) and the salivation to the tone alone, the *conditioned response* (CR).

Generalization and Discrimination

An extremely important aspect of respondent behavior is the process of *generalization*, whereby once an organism has been conditioned to respond in a certain way to a particular stimulus, it will respond in the same way to similar stimuli. As we noted earlier, Watson and Rayner (1920) found that once Albert B. had been conditioned to fear the white rat, he also responded with fear to a rabbit, a dog, a fur coat, and a Santa Claus mask. Likewise, Pavlov discovered that once a dog had been conditioned to salivate upon hearing a tone of a certain sound frequency, tones of similar but different frequencies could also elicit salivation without having been paired with the food. By the same process, a child who grows up under the care of a warm and affectionate German nursemaid may find as an adult that he is immediately attracted to anyone with a German accent.

The effects of generalization can be limited by the process of *discrimination*—that is, the learning to distinguish among similar stimuli and to respond only to the appropriate one. Pavlov, for instance, found that if the food were consistently paired with only one tone, while similar tones were always presented without food, then the effects of generalization would be effaced, and the dog would learn to salivate only at the sound of the tone that had been paired with the food. Likewise, people learn to discriminate between similar stimuli—between a ripe banana and a green banana, between jaywalking on a country road and jaywalking on a major highway—when one of these stimuli is found to be rewarding and the other is not.

Operant Conditioning

While respondent behavior is confined to simple reflexes, *operant behavior*, the second class of behavior, can range in complexity from small, uncomplicated acts such as flicking a light switch to extremely intricate sequences of actions such as writing a novel or building a house. The essential difference

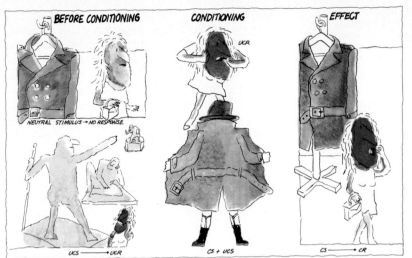

Fig. 3.8   Like salivation, blushing is an involuntary response or reflex controlled by the autonomic nervous system and capable of being classically conditioned. Here a trench coat (neutral stimulus) is paired with male nudity (a UCS for the UCR, blushing). As a result, the trench coat becomes a CS for blushing.

between respondent and operant behavior is implied in the two names: in respondent behavior the organism simply responds to a stimulus, whereas in operant behavior the organism operates upon the environment—in short, *does* something—in order to achieve a desired result. An easy (although, technically speaking, not totally accurate) way of distinguishing between the two is to think of respondent behavior as involuntary and of operant behavior as voluntary (Skinner, 1965). If a person coughs or sneezes (respondent) during a funeral service, we don't blame him because we recognize the behavior as involuntary. But if he reads a magazine (operant) during the service, we do consider this improper, since we see it as a voluntary action.

Unlike respondent behavior, all operant behavior is the result of conditioning. In *operant conditioning* (sometimes referred to as instrumental conditioning), an organism learns to associate certain results with certain actions that it has taken. If the results are desirable, then the organism will repeat those actions, and if they are not desirable, it will avoid repeating them. This is of course Thorndike's law of effect, and the best example is, once again, Thorndike's cat. After a few accidental pressings of the lever, with the result that the door of the box opened and it was allowed to escape and was given a piece of fish, the cat eventually learned to associate these rewards with the pressing of the lever. Consequently, it began pressing the lever as soon as it was put in the box. However, if pressing the lever had resulted in an electric shock, it would have learned, by the same process of operant conditioning, to associate this aversive (that is, painful or

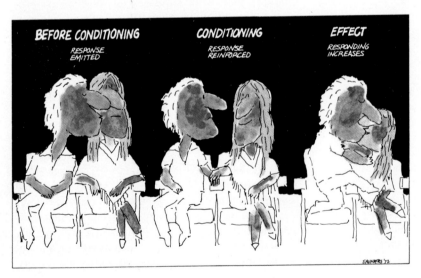

Fig. 3.9   Kissing is a response that is subject to operant conditioning. Here the response is emitted tentatively and if it produced no result would probably be repeated only after a considerable time interval. The kiss is reinforced, however, and immediately the response increases in frequency. Note that the operant behavior increases in vigor, as well as frequency, after reinforcement.

unpleasant) stimulus with the pressing of the lever and thus to avoid pressing it.

In the course of a human life, such operant conditioning goes on every day. The child learns to pick up a cup and put it to his lips because this offers him the reward of a drink of milk. He learns to turn a doorknob because this allows him to enter a room where he wants to go. He learns to speak because speaking brings him the rewards of social interaction, parental approval, and the ability to indicate what he wants. When he grows up he learns to get up in the morning and go to work because working results in money, and money allows him to buy the things he needs and wants.

It is a mistake to assume, however, that most of the actions that we take, complex as they are, are the result of operant conditioning alone. In fact, most behavior is the result of a combination of operant and respondent learning. For example, when the child learns to speak in order to communicate with his parents and gain their approval, this operant conditioning process is based on a prior respondent conditioning process in which the parents, by being paired with food, warmth, and tension reduction (e.g., picking him up and holding him when he is crying), have acquired a positive value. And it is because they have acquired this positive value through respondent conditioning that the reward of their approval can induce the child to learn the operant behavior of speaking. Likewise, it has recently been shown that areas of our behavior such as salivation, heart rate, and blood pressure that were traditionally thought of as solely respondent and beyond the reach of any operant control can in fact be operantly modified (Miller, 1969).

Reinforcement

Were it not for the fish, Thorndike's cat would not have learned to press the lever. Were it not for the food, Pavlov's dogs would not have salivated upon hearing the tone. In all cases, behavior is learned by being reinforced. As Skinner has pointed out, the world is full of reinforcers, positive and negative—food, traffic tickets, money, head colds, people who amuse us, people who annoy us. The simplest type of reinforcer, the *primary reinforcer*, is one to which we respond instinctively, without learning. For example, *primary positive reinforcers* include such basic requirements as food, water, warmth, and sex, while *primary negative reinforcers* include such automatically aversive stimuli as bright lights, extreme heat or cold, and electric shock. However, most of the reinforcers to which we respond are not

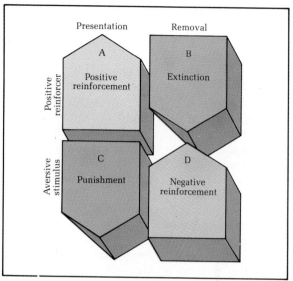

Fig. 3.10   *Reinforcement may be conceptualized in terms of the presentation or removal of a stimulus that is either positive or aversive to an organism. In this book punishment is distinguished from negative reinforcement. Punishment, such as shocking a rat when he presses the bar, is defined as the presentation of an aversive stimulus, and the procedure reduces the frequency of the response (bar pressing). Negative reinforcement, such as terminating the shock when a rat presses the bar, is defined as the removal of an aversive stimulus, and the procedure increases the frequency of the performance. (Adapted from C. B. Ferster and M. L. Perrott,* Behavior Principles. *New York: Appleton-Century-Crofts, 1968, p. 128.)*

the simple primary reinforcers but rather *conditioned reinforcers* (also called *secondary reinforcers*), stimuli to which we have learned to respond by associating them with primary reinforcers. For example, as we have noted above, a newborn baby places no value on his mother's approval. What he does value, however, is being fed and held, and it is by associating his mother with these primary reinforcers that he learns to respond to the mother herself and to her approval as conditioned positive reinforcers, and to respond to her disapproval as a conditioned negative reinforcer.

Modes of Reinforcement   Reinforcement operates on behavior in four basic ways (see Fig. 3.10). In *positive reinforcement* a response is followed by a positive reinforcer, with the result that the response is then more likely to recur. Thus when a child ties his shoes for the first time, his father says, "Good!" (conditioned positive reinforcer) and may even give him a cookie (primary positive reinforcer). A second type of reinforcement that acts to promote behavior is *negative reinforcement*, which involves the removal of an aversive stimulus. (Negative reinforcement should not be confused with punishment, the presentation of an aversive stimulus. This type of reinforcement will be discussed shortly.) If we place a rat in a chamber and turn on an electric shock (primary negative reinforcer) which will continue operating until the rat presses a certain lever in the chamber, the rat will eventually find the lever, and its pressing of the lever will be negatively reinforced by the removal of the shock. As a result, the rat will eventually learn to press the lever as soon as the shock is turned on.

While positive and negative reinforcement have the effect of promoting a response, the two remaining methods of reinforcement, extinction and punishment, act to suppress responses. *Extinction* involves the removal of whatever reinforcement is maintaining a response, with the result that the response gradually dies out. Thus if Thorndike, after teaching the cat to press the lever, had rearranged the box so that pressing the lever no longer resulted in the opening of the door and the offering of the food, then the cat, after a number of attempts with no results, would eventually cease to press the lever. Likewise, in the case of the rat that we have just mentioned, if its action of pressing the lever no longer succeeded in turning off the shock, it would soon give up its lever-pressing. Finally, *punishment*, whereby a response is followed by the presentation of an aversive stimulus, also operates to suppress behavior, as, for instance, when we smack a dog with a newspaper (primary negative reinforcer) for chewing on the furniture or yell, "No! No!" (conditioned negative reinforcer) at a child who is in the process of flushing a towel down the toilet.

Escape and Avoidance   In response to an aversive stimulus, an organism responds through *escape* behavior. For example, you kick off the shoe that is pinching your foot or put up an umbrella to keep yourself dry in the rain. An interesting variant of escape behavior is what is called *avoidance learning*, whereby the organism, once having encountered an aversive stimulus, will arrange its responses in the future so as to prevent any further encounter with the stimulus. Thus if a child has been bitten by a dog, he may in the future simply run the other way whenever he sees a dog. The result of this avoidance behavior is that his fear response will be maintained indefinitely. It can never undergo extinction because extinction would require the child's having contacts with dogs who do not respond to him in the way

he expects. Furthermore, since the avoidance results in a relief of the child's anxiety, this relief acts as a negative reinforcement maintaining the avoidance behavior. As we shall see further along in this chapter, and in later chapters as well, avoidance learning may be closely related to certain kinds of abnormal behavior.

Shaping

Particularly important in learning is a type of operant conditioning called *shaping*, which involves the reinforcement of successive approximations of the desired response in order to "shape out" the response until it finally achieves the desired form. Imagine, for example, that an experimenter wanted to train a pigeon to peck on a disk on the side of its cage. One thing he might do is wait for the pigeon to make the response, at which point he could reinforce it. However, he might find himself waiting by the side of the cage for years, since the chances of this response occurring naturally are minimal. Instead, what he can do is shape the response, first by reinforcing any movement on the side of the cage nearest the disk, then by reinforcing only those movements that the pigeon makes specifically in the direction of the disk, then by reinforcing only pecking-like movements in the direction of the disk. Finally, when the bird at last pecks at the disk, this response will be reinforced, and all other responses will not be reinforced, with the result that they will extinguish.

The process of shaping is extremely important in the development of many of our skills. Let us take the example of a child learning to dive into a swimming pool. First he sits or kneels at the side of the pool, puts his head down, and simply falls into the water. At least he has gone in head first, and

Fig. 3.11 (opposite)   Shaping, a method for producing new responses (such as pressing a bar) by modifying old ones. Shaping is a selective process; the behavior that is closest to the desired response at any point in time is the behavior selected for reinforcement. Here the rat is first rewarded with food for movements in the general vicinity of the bar; then reinforcement is delivered only if it rises on its hind legs; finally reinforcement is withheld until the rat places its forepaws on the bar. When it does this, the shaping process is all but complete. It is highly likely that the rat will soon put enough weight on the bar to activate the automatic circuitry controlling the delivery of food, the reinforcer. (During shaping, before the rat begins to press the bar, the experimenter watches the animal and delivers reinforcement with a manually operated switch.)

accordingly he gets a pat on the back from his swimming teacher. Then the child may start from a standing position and even hazard a little push as he takes off from the edge of the pool. This will be reinforced by further approval from the swimming teacher and by the pleasure of a smoother and deeper descent into the water. Later the child will be ready to move on to the diving board, where he can do higher and fancier jumps and dive even deeper. This final target response will once again be reinforced by the approval of the teacher and by the pleasure of the dive itself. Thus throughout the process there is positive reinforcement of successive approximations of the diving response, while other responses—for example, the child's belly flops—are either extinguished or punished.

Modeling

We have omitted one aspect of the child's diving lesson. It is probable that the swimming teacher would himself dive into the pool to show the child the proper technique and would then reward the child with approval if he could imitate this technique. This type of operant learning, learning via the reinforcement of imitative responses, is known in the vocabulary of behaviorism as *modeling* (Bandura and Walters, 1963). In fact, in actual human development shaping and modeling usually occur in combination: we are rewarded for successive approximations of a model response. A good example of the combination of modeling and shaping is the process by which a child learns to speak his first few words. Babies naturally go through a period of babbling, in which they aimlessly repeat to themselves various vowels, consonants, and combinations of the two—"dada," "gaga," "mmmm," and so on. Let us say that in the presence of his father a baby

begins babbling "dada." The father, delighted at this supposed sign of recognition, says, "Yes! Dada! Dada!" gives the baby a hug, and calls his wife in to observe the great event. In short, he reinforces the random response with attention and affection, thus making it more likely to recur. When it does recur, the father may now try to improve on it, saying, "Yes! Dadee! Daddy!" and pointing to himself. Once this happens a number of times, the baby will eventually model his babbling on the father's speech and say, "Daddy," thus achieving his first actual word, which will again be reinforced with affection. Eventually an entire vocabulary will be built up through the same modeling process, with each new word being reinforced by parental approval and by the pleasure that the child will eventually begin to take in being able to communicate his thoughts and desires.

Schedules of Reinforcement

Up to this point our discussion has implied that each response gets reinforced on every occasion. In fact, such is not the case, either in life or in the laboratory. Behaviors are maintained most effectively when reinforcements are delivered intermittently. We are not always thanked for every favor done, nor are we always praised for each successful accomplishment. Yet we continue in our efforts. Thus we are reinforced on some kind of a schedule, the rewards coming either after a certain lapse of time (interval schedules) or after the performance of a certain number of responses (ratio schedules). The four basic reinforcement schedules are fixed interval (FI), variable interval (VI), fixed ratio (FR), and variable ratio (VR).

In *fixed interval schedules*, the reinforcements are delivered once in every fixed interval of time. For

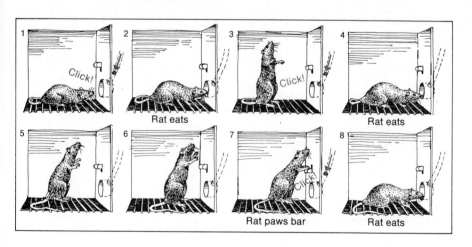

The Mechanisms of Learning

	Definition	*Example*
Respondent conditioning	Pairing a neutral stimulus with a nonneutral stimulus until the organism learns to respond to the neutral stimulus as it would to the nonneutral stimulus	A baby learning to love "mother" because he loves the cuddling and food that she provides
Operant conditioning	Rewarding or punishing a certain response until the organism learns to repeat or avoid that response in anticipation of the positive or negative consequences	A child learning not to lose his homework because he knows from prior experience that his teacher will be angry if he does
Positive reinforcement	"Stamping in" a behavior by rewarding it with a positive reinforcer	Giving special awards to students with high grade-point averages
Negative reinforcement	"Stamping in" a behavior by removing an aversive stimulus in response to that behavior	Allowing a child to forgo his household chores if he cries when asked to do them
Extinction	Suppressing a behavior by removing the reinforcers that are maintaining the behavior	Refusing to loan your lecture notes to a friend who constantly cuts his classes and then inconveniences you by borrowing your notes
Punishment	Suppressing a behavior by subjecting the organism to an aversive stimulus in response to that behavior	Spanking a child for running into the street
Generalization	Transferring a conditioned response from the conditioned stimulus to similar stimuli	A woman, after having been raped, beginning to fear all men
Discrimination	Learning to confine a response only to particular stimuli	A child learning, via aversive encounters with his mother, that finger-painting on the back porch is fine, whereas finger-painting on the living room rug is not fine
Escape behavior	Initiating a response in order to escape an aversive stimulus	Turning on the heater in a cold house
Avoidance learning	Arranging one's responses in order to avoid exposure to an aversive stimulus	Refusing, after a bad experience with marijuana, ever to smoke it again
Shaping	Reinforcing successive approximations of a desired response until that response is gradually achieved	Teaching a child to make his bed by first praising him for pulling up the covers, then for pulling up the covers and smoothing them down, then for pulling up the covers, smoothing them down, and tucking them in
Modeling	Conditioning a response by rewarding imitation of a model	Easing a little girl into her culturally defined sex role by praising her for copying her mother—wearing a dress, combing her hair, setting the table, and so on

example, those of us who get paid by the hour, day, or week (often regardless of how hard we work) are rewarded on a fixed interval schedule. In a *variable interval schedule*, the amount of time elapsing before the payoff comes varies but averages out to a certain stable rate. The frequency with which one is invited to social engagements is an example of such a schedule. Invitations might average out to once a week, but some weeks we may stay home, while other weeks we may have several invitations. The important thing to remember about interval schedules is that the reinforcement is delivered by some outside agency and does not necessarily depend on how many responses we make so long as we respond before the appropriate time interval has elapsed.

In ratio schedules, on the other hand, the number of reinforcements received depends on how many responses we make or how rapidly we make them. Hence it is up to us how many reinforcements we will receive. In *fixed ratio schedules* the reinforcement is given after a certain number of responses. On an FR 5 schedule, for instance, an organism would be reinforced after every fifth response. It can work quickly or slowly, but the reinforcement will not be delivered until the required number of responses has been made. Good examples of a fixed ratio schedule are piecework pay and working on commission. If an insurance salesman working on commission does nothing, he is paid nothing; conversely, if during a particularly energetic week he sells fifty policies, he will earn a lot of money. In *variable ratio schedules* the reinforcements still depend on how many responses we make; here, however, the number of responses that we make in order to receive the reward varies, though averaging out to a certain ratio. A good poker player works on a variable ratio schedule. The more poker games he goes to, the more he is going to win. His winning, however, will be intermittent; when he has a winning streak, the reinforcements will come close together, and in a losing streak they will come only after long stretches. But his winnings will eventually average out to a certain ratio.

THE CONSEQUENCES OF LEARNING: NORMAL AND ABNORMAL DEVELOPMENT

Throughout our discussion of the mechanisms of learning, we have given brief illustrations of how these mechanisms operate in normal human development. To the behaviorist, personality development is simply the result of the interaction of an individual's basic genetic endowment with the types of learning to which he is exposed. Respondent conditioning stamps in many of his most basic responses, including, as we have seen, the value that he places on his parents. Through generalization he learns to value people in general and their approval and affection. Through discrimination he learns that certain stimuli call for certain responses and not for others—that an insult calls for a frown and not a smile, that somersaults are fine on a playground but not in a sickroom. Operant conditioning teaches him his skills—practical, social, and intellectual. Through extinction he learns that whereas crying might have gotten him attention and various other rewards when he was two, it will not work when he is forty-two. Through negative reinforcement he learns to put on a jacket when it gets cold and to apologize when he has offended someone. Through positive reinforcement he learns how to work for rewards and thus prepares himself to earn a living. Through punishment he learns not to touch a hot iron, not to pick up a cat by its tail, and not to be rude. Through shaping and modeling, based on a variety of reinforcers, he learns how to speak, how to write, how to develop an appropriate sexual identity, and how to treat other people. In short, through conditioning the individual learns the so-called normal responses that will allow him to adapt to his environment.

And according to the behaviorist, the so-called abnormal responses that prevent the individual from adapting to his environment are acquired through precisely the same mechanisms of learning. If, for example, there is some disturbance in the respondent conditioning process that teaches an infant to associate food, warmth, and tension reduction with his parents and thus to value his parents and, by extension, people in general, then as a child he may treat people as if they didn't exist, a condition which is likely to result in his being labeled autistic. Respondent conditioning can also account for a sexual deviation such as fetishism, in which sexual interest is focused exclusively on some inanimate object or on some body part not normally considered erotic. If, for example, a boy's earliest masturbation experiences are associated with some article of his mother's clothing, such as a pair of shoes, then he may find as an adult that his sexual interest in women is limited to their shoes. We have already discussed how the operation of generalization and negative reinforcement in avoidance learning can generate a phobia or irrational fear: if a child, after having been bitten by a dog, proceeds to avoid all dogs, then his fear of dogs will persist indefinitely. Similarly, depression has been inter-

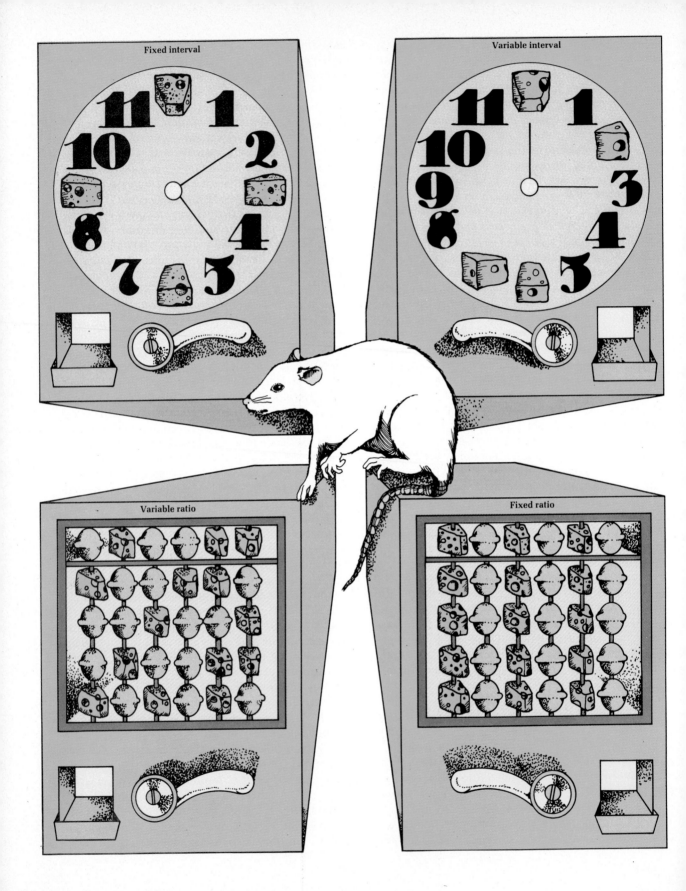

preted by behaviorists as the result of extinction: if significant positive reinforcements are withdrawn from a person, a large proportion of his behaviors will simply extinguish, and he will become weary, withdrawn, and hopeless—in short, according to the diagnostician, depressed. As a final example, modeling may account for a variety of abnormal behaviors. If, for example, a teenage girl models her behavior on that of a street gang and receives reinforcing approval from the gang, then this choice of a model can result in a variety of so-called delinquent behaviors, such as shoplifting and sexual promiscuity.

These are only a very few examples of the behavioral interpretation of abnormal psychology. Others will be detailed more fully in the chapters dealing with specific disorders. However, these few examples are sufficient to illustrate the basic trend of the behaviorist approach, which is that abnormal behavior is the result not of any "illness" or "disorder" but rather of certain variations in the individual's conditioning history—variations that mold his responses into a form different from the social norm.

A corollary to this relativistic view of normal and abnormal behavior is the tendency on the part of the behaviorists to avoid the very use of terms such as "normal" and "abnormal," since these terms imply a clear distinction between something healthy and something sick, or something right and something wrong. Instead, the behaviorists see the range of human responses as a continuum, all the responses being united by the same principle of learning and all of them differing in the kinds of experiences that have shaped them. At one end of the continuum we can indeed identify responses that make it impossible for an individual to interact successfully with his environment—responses that get him in trouble or cause him to give trouble to others. But these responses, according to the behaviorists,

Fig. 3.12 A major breakthrough in the study of behavior was the classic work of Ferster and Skinner concerning schedules of reinforcement. The discovery that an organism's response is markedly influenced by such schedules has provided operant researchers with basic tools by which to better understand behavior. In terms of human behavior, however, the influence of reinforcement schedules is not easily determined because in general there are multiple schedules operating concurrently in an individual's environment. Furthermore, in complex life situations schedules of reinforcement are only one of many important variables that influence a person's behavior.

are best termed "maladaptive" rather than "abnormal," since they are simply less successful outcomes of a single learning principle.

Likewise, the behaviorists tend to avoid labeling people according to diagnostic syndromes, since this labeling process, like the normal-abnormal dichotomy, suggests the operation of an illness and fails to acknowledge that all behaviors, including the most maladaptive, are acquired through the same process. For the behaviorist what is important is not to categorize the behavior as falling within a certain syndrome but rather to specify in what way it is maladaptive, to discover what stimuli gave rise to it, and if possible, to determine how the individual's environmental stimuli can be adjusted in order to alter the behavior (Mischel, 1968; Bandura, 1969).

Types of Maladaptive Behavior

The four categories that the behaviorists do use in describing maladaptive behaviors focus directly on the specific behavior, the stimuli which elicit it, and the reinforcements that maintain it. These four categories are behavior deficit, behavior excess, inappropriate stimulus control, and inadequate reinforcing systems.

Behavior Deficit When a certain behavior occurs at a lower frequency than is expected within the society, with the result that the individual's social, intellectual, or practical skills are impaired, this condition is called a *behavior deficit*. Examples would include a child's unwillingness to go to school (a condition often called "school phobia"), a high school student's unwillingness to answer a question in class, and a man's inability to engage in sexual intercourse with his wife. Some children fail to acquire proper toilet habits, speech, or the ability to engage in cooperative play. Likewise, some adults are totally withdrawn, recoiling from any social interaction whatsoever. All these behaviors would be called behavior deficits. And accordingly, the behaviorist's aim would be to increase the frequency of the behavior.

Behavior Excess A *behavior excess*, as the name indicates, is the opposite of a behavior deficit; here the behavior occurs at a higher frequency than is adaptive according to the standards of the society. The person who constantly talks to himself out loud; the hyperactive child who cannot sit still in class but is constantly in motion and in a state of intense excitement; the college student who washes his hands thirty times a day until they are chapped and raw—these responses would be termed behavior excesses. And the behaviorist's goal would be to decrease their frequency.

Inappropriate Stimulus Control   *Inappropriate stimulus control* is a disruption in the relationship between stimulus and response. Either a response occurs in the absence of any appropriate stimulus, or a stimulus fails to elicit the appropriate response. Examples of the former category would include a person who whenever he sees two people talking infers that they are plotting against him, or a person who hears voices and sees things that are not actually present in the external environment. In both cases, according to the behaviorist, the person is failing to discriminate properly between external and internal stimuli. Likewise, a professor who goes to his classroom at midnight and lectures to an empty room can be said to be lacking appropriate stimulus control. Examples of a stimulus failing to call forth an appropriate response would be the chronic bedwetter, for whom the stimulus of a full bladder does not lead to the appropriate response of getting up and going to the bathroom to urinate, or the so-called anorexic, a person who even when deprived of food for long periods either cannot or will not eat. In the case of a behavior involving inappropriate stimulus control, the behaviorist's major effort would be the establishment of proper discrimination.

Inadequate Reinforcing Systems   Some maladaptive behaviors may be seen as a result of the individual's being controlled by a system of reinforcements different from that of the average person. In short, he hears a different drummer, often to his great inconvenience. In such a situation, the behavior is said to be due to an *inadequate reinforcing system.* A good example is the autistic child's indifference to other people. As we have mentioned earlier, many behaviorists see this indifference as resulting from a failure in the early respondent conditioning process which for the normal child establishes the attention and affection of other people as powerful conditioned reinforcers. Since people are not incorporated into the autistic child's reinforcing system, he simply ignores them. Other examples of an inadequate reinforcing system would be that of a sadist, who is positively reinforced by seeing other people suffer, or that of a masochist, who is positively reinforced by having pain inflicted upon himself. In dealing with a maladaptive behavior that is the result of an inadequate reinforcing system, the behaviorist would attempt to inactivate the old reinforcers and to condition the individual to respond to new, more appropriate reinforcers.

Behavior Modification

The most decisive influence of the behaviorist movement has been in the area of treatment, what the movement calls *behavior modification* or behavior therapy (Bandura, 1969; Kanfer and Phillips, 1970). The various techniques that behaviorists have used to treat specific problems will be brought up in different chapters throughout this book, and the subject of behavior modification as a whole will be discussed in Chapter 19. Here, however, we can introduce the topic by saying that behavior modification attempts to alter specific responses through the same types of learning that engender our responses in the first place—positive reinforcement, negative reinforcement, extinction, punishment, discrimination, generalization, and so forth. One of the earliest attempts at behavior modification was probably a now-famous experiment by Mary Cover Jones (1924), a student of Watson's. What Jones did was essentially the reverse of Watson's respondent conditioning experiment with Albert B. Whereas Watson had used punishment to instill a fear of furry animals in Albert, Jones used extinction to eliminate a fear of furry animals in a boy named Peter. She first got the child busy eating his favorite food and then introduced a rabbit into the room at some distance from where the boy was sitting. On successive occasions the rabbit was brought closer and closer, again while the child was eating, and eventually he was able to touch it without exhibiting any fear. The rabbit was thus paired with the pleasant stimulus of the food, so eventually it took on pleasant associations. At the same time whatever unpleasant consequences the child expected from his encounter with the rabbit did not take place, with the result that the fear, lacking reinforcement, was extinguished.

Another example of respondent conditioning is the use of the so-called Mowrer pad to correct bedwetting. Here a liquid-sensitive pad is placed under the child's bedsheet and is connected by a battery to an alarm. The slightest moisture on the pad sounds the alarm, awakening the child while his bladder is still full. Eventually, after a number of successive pairings of the alarm with the sensations of a full bladder, these latter sensations alone are sufficient to elicit the conditioned response of awakening, and the child is able to get up and go to the bathroom (Baker, 1969).

Operant conditioning has also been widely used in behavior modification. Autistic children have been taught to speak through shaping and modeling (see Chapter 13). Likewise, Rickard and Mundy (1965) have reported a successful treatment of a nine-year-old chronic stutterer through positive reinforcement. At first the experimenters asked the boy to read single words. Each time he did not stutter, he received points, which could later be exchanged for more tangible reinforcements such as candy, gum, or toys. After a few successful sessions, the child was asked to read two words in a row, and again points were used as rewards. Later the child moved on to phrases and finally to sentences. Over a period of twenty-three sessions, the amount of stuttering was reduced to almost zero.

It should be emphasized that such treatment successes do not necessarily support the behaviorists' hypothesis that learning is the source of abnormal behavior. The fact that conditioning can eliminate a response does not prove that the response was originally acquired through conditioning. Aside from the question of what they prove, however, such treatments certainly constitute the most impressive contribution of the behavioral movement. In the first place, because they are carefully documented in terms of specific procedures and specific results, they can be replicated by other scientists. Second, and most importantly, many of these behavioral treatments clearly work. And often they have worked in precisely those areas, such as the psychoses, where more subjective therapies have proved difficult to put into practice and have yielded only questionable results.

CURRENT TRENDS IN BEHAVIORISM

Out of the ideas that form the basis of behavioral theory a number of other ideas have grown. In one direction, behavioral theorists have begun to explore the possibility that if we are controlled by the stimuli in our environment, then perhaps—as individuals, as groups, or as whole societies—we might deliberately manipulate our environmental stimuli in order to make it easier for ourselves to live the kind of lives that we want to live. In another direction, certain investigators have begun to probe the nature of whatever unobservable "mental" constructs mediate between the stimuli that we experience and the responses that we make to them.

Self-Control

If we accept the notion that our behavior is determined by the environmental reinforcements that surround us, then the question naturally arises: Why allow chance or some external agency to arrange these reinforcements? Why not arrange them ourselves so that if our behavior must be controlled, it will at least be self-controlled?

A number of behavioral theorists have explored the possibility of self-control. Goldiamond (1965), for example, has suggested that a person can in fact apply the principles of behavior modification to his own responses. First he must analyze the maladaptive response just as a behavioral psychologist would. Is the response a behavior deficit or a behavior excess? Or is the problem one of inappropriate stimulus control or of an inadequate reinforcing system? Once the person has determined what, in behavioral terms, is wrong, he can then proceed to set it right by manipulating reinforcements in such a way as to steer the behavior in the direction of the target response. For example, a man who overeats would designate this response as a behavior excess. Then he might impose upon himself the rule that every time he gives in and has dessert with lunch, he must, when he gets home from work, spend an hour gardening, a task he despises. Thus he deliberately makes gardening (punishment) a consequence of eating dessert in the hope that he will develop the same aversion to desserts that he has to gardening. Such conditioning can, however, fail if the internal reinforcements maintaining the overeating response are stronger than the aversion to gardening. (If this is the case, the man will remain fat but will have the consolation of a beautifully tended backyard.)

It should be emphasized that according to the behaviorists the possible utility of self-control procedures does not imply that we can of our own free will change our behavior. All we can do is decide, on the basis of our already conditioned ideas and values, which of our responses is displeasing to us and then adjust the environmental stimuli so that these stimuli will alter the unwanted response.

Environmental Planning

The study of the effects of the environment on individuals has suggested the possibility that in some cases environmental influence is so decisive that the nature of the environment is an even better predictor of behavior than is the nature of the individuals operating in that environment. Krasner and Ullmann (1973), for instance, have pointed out that the way in which a room is set up can operate most effectively in setting limits to the range of potential behavior. If, for example, the chairs in a hospital

A Self-Control Experiment Backfires

A prominent behavioral psychologist once described how a carefully arranged self-control procedure could lead to results very different from those intended. This psychologist was very concerned about his smoking. He had tried several times to stop smoking, or at least to cut down, but he had always failed. Then it occurred to him that a possible solution was to use the so-called *Premack principle*, which states that a probable, frequently occurring response can be used to reinforce an improbable, less frequently occurring response (Premack, 1965). For example, in the treatment of obesity, permission to eat a meal (high-probability response) can be an effective reward for doing a set of weight-reducing exercises (low-probability response). The psychologist decided that if he reversed the Premack principle and made smoking (high-probability response) contingent upon the hated task of reading research reports in professional journals (low-probability response), then he could reduce his cigarette consumption. With high hopes he embarked upon his experiment, and his self-control proved equal to the task. Only when he sat down to read a research report would he allow himself to light up a cigarette. The results at first seemed encouraging: his cigarette consumption *did* appear to decline. However, his elation over this progress was soon offset by his growing realization that he was reading more and more research reports. After three weeks of his "therapy," he found, much to his dismay, that his cigarette consumption was the same as before his self-control experiment. The only change in his behavior was that he had become an avid reader of research reports and that he now truly enjoyed this once-loathsome task.

seems to convey a clear message that the teacher is in charge: students are expected to respond to the cues given by the teacher, raising their hands before speaking, speaking only to answer his questions, and generally following where he chooses to lead them. In contrast, a classroom in which all the seats, including the teacher's, are arranged in a circle tends to minimize the teacher's authority, demanding instead that the students speak out, make suggestions, and come up with their own ideas as to the direction in which the class should be going. Not surprisingly, the latter arrangement often causes considerable bewilderment among students accustomed to the more conservative classroom set-up.

Such observations suggest that the immediate environment is a powerful manipulator of whatever behavior is to be enacted in that environment. This lesson is only beginning to be understood and put to use by designers of parks, museums, schools, hospitals, and other environments.

Behavioral Engineering

If behavioral principles can be used to control the responses of an individual in his daily life and the responses of groups in a planned environment, might they not also be used to engineer a whole new society—a society in which carefully structured reinforcements would eliminate the problems that plague our present societies? According to B. F. Skinner, the answer is yes. Skinner believes that it is a waste to confine behaviorism to the laboratory. Instead, if we acknowledge that the frustrations of our daily lives and the evils of our societies are the result not of free choices on our part but simply of the types of stimuli that control us, then we should begin altering those stimuli. The result, according to Skinner, could be an ideal society in which human beings are controlled not by aversive stimuli but by a wealth of positive reinforcements. To describe how such a society could work, Skinner has written a utopian novel, *Walden II* (1948). Walden II is a self-sustaining community, with its own farm, dairy, mills, doctors and dentists, symphony orchestra, and commercial kitchen. Policy is made by appointed "planners," but work and property are shared by all through a system of "labor credits." Each member works the equivalent of four hours a day and then is free to pursue his own creative interests. In the novel one of the planners describes how Walden II, by freeing its inhabitants from aversive stimuli and controlling them through the use of positive reinforcement, has richly compensated them for the lost illusion of free will:

ward are lined up against a wall, this arrangement is likely to cut down considerably on interpersonal communication between patients. Instead of twisting his body toward the person next to him, a patient (or any other person) is likely to follow the lead of the chair and simply stare straight ahead. Likewise, students will have noticed that seating arrangements in a classroom carry strong suggestions as to what is expected of them in the class. The standard arrangement of straight rows facing the teacher

We can achieve a sort of control under which the controlled, though they are following a code more scrupulously than was the case under the old system, nevertheless feel free. They are doing what they want to do and not what they are forced to do. That's the source of the tremendous power of positive reinforcement. There's no restraint and no revolt. By a careful cultural design, we control not the final behavior, but the inclination to behave—the motives, the desires and the wishes (1948, p. 219).

A system similar to that of Walden II has in fact been put into practice in a commune called Twin Oaks in Virginia. But recent reports from Twin Oaks (Kinkade, 1973) indicate that individuals are not as easily controllable as Skinner would seem to believe.

Mediation Theory

Many prominent behaviorists, such as Ullmann and Krasner (1969) and Skinner, hold firmly to Watson's original position that psychology must confine itself strictly to empirical evidence—measurable stimuli and measurable responses. Other behaviorists (Rotter, 1954; Mischel, 1968; Bandura, 1969), however, have begun to explore nonobservable internal variables that may affect our responses to stimuli. These so-called *mediating variables* include our thoughts, assumptions, beliefs, expectations—in short, any mental construct which influences the way we react to our environment and which thus mediates between stimulus and response. The investigators interested in mediation theory argue that in order to learn, an organism has to process and store the information that it gathers from its experiences. Albert B., for instance, had to store in his mind the fact that the rat was connected with a terrible loud noise. This fact then became an expectation, something actually existing though not observable. And this expectation, along with the stimulus of seeing the rat, determined the child's response of fear upon seeing the rat without hearing the noise. Thus what we know of the past and expect from the future becomes a highly significant factor in our responses (Mischel, 1968)—and a factor which, according to mediation theory, cannot be ignored, in spite of the fact that it fits with difficulty into the strictly empirical method of orthodox behaviorism.

EVALUATING BEHAVIORISM

The basic tenets of behaviorism constitute a direct challenge to the medical and psychodynamic models of human behavior. And since these two models are not simply scientific constructs but are outgrowths of some of our most deeply ingrained beliefs—for instance, that our behavior issues from our inner lives and that abnormal behavior is the result of specific "mental" disorders—the challenge from the behaviorists has generated a great deal of controversy.

Behaviorism and the Medical Model

As we have seen in Chapter 1, the medical model interprets abnormal behavior as the result of a sickness—either an actual organic illness or some more intangible "mental" illness. This theory has woven its way in and out of the history of humankind's interpretation of abnormal behavior. It was commonly held in the nineteenth century and remains popular today, as evidenced by the wide use of DSM-II, which is based on the medical model. How this theory of abnormal behavior contrasts with behavioral theory has already been suggested repeatedly throughout this chapter. The most basic assumption of behaviorism—the assumption that most behavior is conditioned behavior and that maladaptive behavior is simply the result of less successful conditioning—constitutes a rejection of the medical model, since it denies that any clear line can be drawn between normal and abnormal. According to the behaviorists, all human beings have different conditioning histories, which mold their responses into different forms. None of these responses can be called either sick or healthy. Some simply work better than others within the context of a society. And those that don't work can be remolded so that they do work.

Such arguments from the behavioral perspective (along with arguments from the humanist and existential perspectives, which will be discussed in Chapter 4) have made some slight headway against the medical model. In contrast to their predecessors, many professionals today tend to be somewhat more suspicious of diagnostic categories, somewhat more hesitant to label people as falling into this or that syndrome, and somewhat more interested in the direct approach of correcting specific *behaviors*. Whatever movement may be seen in this more pragmatic direction is due at least in part to the work of the behaviorists.

Behaviorism and the Psychodynamic Perspective

As we have noted earlier in this chapter, behaviorism in one sense developed as a reaction against the subjective approach of the psychodynamic perspective. When Watson called for an end to the introspective method and for the founding of a new,

TWIN OAKS: Walden II Meets Reality

In 1967 eight people moved to a piece of farmland in Virginia and there founded a community according to the utopian plan outlined by Skinner in *Walden II*. Despite a number of ideological and practical crises, this community, called Twin Oaks, is still in operation today and has expanded to include sixty-five members.

Unlike the fictitious Walden II, Twin Oaks has not yet been able to achieve complete economic self-sufficiency. Part of its livelihood is obtained from farming, keeping cows, and making and selling hammocks; the rest, however, is earned from odd jobs in neighboring towns (where Twin Oaks people also buy the things they don't make or grow). All the work is distributed according to a rather complicated credit system which boils down essentially to the requirement that each member do about forty hours' work a week—somewhat less if the work is tedious, somewhat more if the work is pleasant. Hence members are encouraged to participate both in creative work and in the necessary drudgery. All work is supervised by managers.

To join Twin Oaks, one must agree to participate in this labor system (shirkers are expelled from the community) and to contribute one's earnings and eventually one's property to the community. Furthermore, every member is expected to subscribe to the following code of behavior, borrowed from *Walden II*:

1. We don't use titles [i.e., there is no "Mrs.," "Dr.," or "Mother"].
2. All members are expected to explain their work to any other member who wants to learn it.
3. We do not discuss the personal affairs of other members or speak negatively of other members in the presence of a third party. [Direct feedback given privately is fine, but gossip is taboo.]
4. We don't publicly complain about things we think are wrong in the community. Gripes are best taken up with the appropriate manager. Public bitching is bad for morale.
5. Members who have unconventional views on politics, religion, etc., stay clear of such topics when it is prudent.
6. Seniority is not discussed among us.
7. We try to exercise consideration and tolerance of each other's individual habits.
8. We don't boast of individual accomplishments.
9. We try to clean up after ourselves after any project; we try not to keep articles longer than we need them but return them to their places so that they can be used by other members.
10. Individual rooms are inviolate. No member enters another's room without that other member's permission. ("What Is Twin Oaks Community?" pp. 10–11)

Needless to say, the members of Twin Oaks have given up certain freedoms. For example, gossip, griping, and free expression of unconventional views are all protected by the Constitution of the United States, though not by that of Twin Oaks. In this context, it should be remembered that according to Skinner, freedom is something of an illusion; what matters is positive reinforcement of productive behavior.

However, in exchange for the above privileges, the members of Twin Oaks have gained other freedoms. For example, the confinements of conventional sexual roles are loosened by the official ban on sexism. Furthermore, sexual freedom is condoned, even for those who are married, and sexual jealousy is not reinforced by sympathy. Finally, Twin Oaks members enjoy considerable freedom from the lonely responsibility of parenthood. Children are raised communally. Nevertheless, these freedoms have been accompanied by their fair share of problems. For a few years children had to be excluded from the community because it was felt that the members were not yet capable of providing a properly supportive environment for them. (They are now back and are raised in a communal nursery.) Furthermore, sexual permissiveness at Twin Oaks has in no way eliminated the problem of sexual jealousy, which has resulted in the departures of a few members.

Twin Oaks is still an experiment, and it remains to be seen whether equality, cooperation, and positive reinforcement for adherence to well-defined rules can prove a desirable replacement for the greater freedom and greater inequities of life on the outside.

Source: Kinkade (1973).

objective psychology of behavior, he described what still remains today the major difference between the two perspectives—that is, that while the behaviorists look for the causes of behavior in measurable external events, the psychodynamic theorists look for causes in nonmeasurable internal events.

As has been explained in Chapter 2, Freud and his followers believed that normal behavior could be explained in terms of the workings of a mental apparatus of ego, superego, and id lodged in the so-called unconscious mind. Abnormal behavior could likewise be explained as a disturbance in one or more of these three divisions of the mind—for example, as a failure of ego or superego control, or as a weakening of the ego as a result of its having expended all its energy in keeping repressed urges under control. Similarly, development could be explained by an internal, self-generating progression of psychosexual stages, which if not stalled by psychological trauma followed a natural course into adulthood.

To the behaviorist such explanations are unacceptable because they simply cannot be verified objectively. Instead, as we have seen throughout this chapter, behavioral theory interprets both childhood development and adult behavior as the result of an objective process by which measurable responses are stamped in by measurable stimuli. Like psychodynamic theory, behavioral theory is basically deterministic, interpreting human actions as the inevitable consequence of past experience. But beyond this point, the two interpretations diverge, one into empirical investigation and the other into subjective analysis.

Behaviorism: Pros and Cons

Such disagreements between the behavioral perspective and the other perspectives on human psychology are not simply quarrels over professional details. Though the behaviorists shy away from grand philosophical claims (some, however, are the exceptions that prove the rule; c.f. Breger and Mc-

SYMPTOM SUBSTITUTION

If a problem behavior is merely the "symptom" of an underlying disorder, as the psychodynamic perspective and medical model suggest, then would it not make sense that as soon as one symptom is treated and removed, the underlying disorder, remaining untreated, would simply manifest itself in a new symptom? This notion of "symptom substitution" has for many years been a focus of controversy between the behaviorist and psychodynamic perspectives. Psychodynamic theorists, as we have seen, hold strongly to the view that to treat a problem like bed-wetting without dealing with the psychic conflicts that presumably underlie this behavior is like treating a fever without treating the infection that is causing it. In contrast, the behaviorists hold that a person's problem is whatever problem behaviors he has and that searching for a "deeper" problem is unwarranted.

Recent research tends to fall on the side of the behaviorists. Studies of the treatment of enuresis (Baker, 1969), sexual dysfunction (Masters and Johnson, 1970), obesity (Stuart, 1967; Wollersheim, 1970), phobias (Baudura et al., 1969; Paul, 1969b), and other problems indicate that far from producing new maladaptive behaviors, behavioral treatment for these "symptoms" generally results not only in relief from the "symptom" but in extra behavioral benefits (e.g., renewed self-confidence, improved marital relations, more satisfying sexual relations) as well.

Nevertheless, it is probable that in some cases—despite the therapist's efforts to teach the patient new, adaptive behaviors to replace the old, maladaptive behavior—symptom substitution does take place. The problem, however, is that we can never know whether a symptom that appears after the termination of treatment is actually a replacement or "stand-in" for the symptom at which the treatment was aimed. The new symptom might easily be a response to new environmental pressures; alternatively, this "new" symptom could actually have been there all the while, along with the treated behavior, but might have simply been ignored because it was not as dramatic or as troublesome as the treated behavior (Baudura, 1969). In short, the question of whether or not symptom substitution takes place can never be definitively answered, because we have no precise way of determining whether a new symptom, it it does appear, is in fact a substitution.

Guagh, 1965), the fact remains that their theory of behavior constitutes a drastic revision of Western thought on the subject of human life. And as such, it has been severely criticized.

A primary criticism is that the behaviorists have grossly and unrealistically oversimplified human life—that by excluding man's inner life from consideration, they have chosen to ignore everything that distinguishes a human being from an experimental animal in a cage. As Arthur Koestler (1968) has argued, if mental events are to be banned from psychology, then the only thing left for psychology to study is rats. And indeed, as we have seen, many behavioral principles have been evolved from animal experimentation, a fact which leads critics to ask whether such principles are truly applicable to human beings. Furthermore, the behaviorists' technique of reducing human action to small, measurable units of behavior is viewed both as yet another naïve simplification of human experience and as a methodological and philosophical bias which often distorts the data they are measuring (London, 1969).

The second major focus of criticism is the behaviorists' denial of free will. According to Skinner, this notion of human freedom is simply obsolete and should be abandoned:

> The free inner man who is held responsible for the behavior of the external biological organism is only a prescientific substitute for the kinds of causes which are discovered in the course of a scientific analysis. All these alternative causes lie *outside* the individual. . . . These are the things that make the individual behave as he does. For them he is not responsible, and for them it is useless to praise or blame him. It does not matter that the individual may take it upon himself to control the variables of which his own behavior is a function or, in a broader sense, to engage in the design of his own culture. He does this only because he is the product of a culture which generates self-control of cultural design as a mode of behavior. The environment determines the individual even when he alters the environment (1965, pp. 447–448).

In short, whatever a person does, he is not responsible. If we follow this idea to its conclusion, there is no foundation whatsoever for any kind of legal system, for any religious belief, or for any moral code. Law, religion, and morality are all based on the notion that we are capable of choosing between right and wrong, whereas according to Skinner, whatever we do—whether we care for other people or kill them in their sleep, whether we struggle along in our own aversive environments or go off to create a Walden II—we do these things because our condi-

tioning history has programmed us to do them. Needless to say, such ideas have not been well received by modern thinkers who still cling to the scientifically unverifiable theory that each human being is a unique and free individual. Furthermore, many critics feel that Skinner's social ideas could all too easily be perverted by people seeking to control others for their own selfish ends and that a Walden II could easily become a repressive totalitarian state.

While many of these criticisms seem sound, there is also much that can justly be said in favor of behaviorism. In the first place, the objectivity of behavioral research is not a virtue to be slighted. Indeed, a major problem with all the other psychological perspectives is that their findings are often vague, opinionated, and based more on inference than on fact. In contrast, the behaviorists' findings are expressed much more concisely and as much as possible are based on actual measurable evidence, with the result, as we have noted earlier, that they can easily be retested by other professionals.

Second, while the behaviorists are accused of doing away with individualism, it can be argued that individualism is safer with the behaviorists than with psychologists of other schools of thought. For unlike many other psychologists, the behaviorists recognize a broad range of responses as legitimate and are very sensitive to the adverse effects of labeling behaviors according to supposed syndromes and thus isolating them as "abnormal."

Finally, it bears repeating that the treatment procedures developed by the behaviorists have produced some extremely promising results. Behavior modification takes less time, is less expensive, and in many cases has been found more effective than other forms of treatment. And while whatever treatment success the behaviorists have had in no way constitutes conclusive proof of their learning theories, such success is quite obviously an achievement in itself—and one which no psychological perspective can afford to do without, no matter how convincing its theories.

SUMMARY

The topic of this chapter has been behavioral psychology—its background, its basic principles, and its theories as to normal and abnormal development. The rise of behaviorism is due largely to the work of four scientists: Ivan Pavlov, who discovered the conditioned reflex; John B. Watson, who established behaviorism as an empirical, objective science of behavior; Edward Lee Thorndike, who discovered operant conditioning and enunciated its basic principle in his "law of effect"; and B. F. Skinner, who expanded Thorndike's theory into an interpretation of human life as controlled by the principle of reinforcement. As a result of the work of these men and their followers, modern behaviorism is founded on four basic assumptions: first, that the task of psychology is the study of behavior—that is, stimulus and response; second, that this study of behavior must be confined to empirical evidence; third, that the goal of psychology is the prediction and control of behavior; and fourth, that most behavior is the result of learning.

The fundamental mechanisms of learning are respondent and operant conditioning. Through generalization a conditioned response can be extended to stimuli similar to the conditioned stimulus. However, an organism can also learn discrimination, so that it will respond only to the appropriate stimulus. Common forms of operant conditioning are modeling, in which the response is learned through imitation, and shaping, in which the response is gradually shaped out through the reinforcement of successive approximations.

All operant learning is based on reinforcement. Reinforcers may be either positive or negative, and either primary or conditioned. The types of consequences that can promote a response are positive reinforcement and negative reinforcement. In contrast, the types of consequences that can suppress a response are extinction and punishment. Reinforcement is generally provided not after every response but rather according to one of the following four schedules: fixed interval, variable interval, fixed ratio, and variable ratio.

According to the behaviorists, these mechanisms of learning can account not only for normal development, but for abnormal development as well. In dealing with maladaptive responses, the behaviorists classify the response not as a part of a syndrome but rather as a problem in learning. Such a problem may be a behavior deficit, a behavior excess, inappropriate stimulus control, or an inadequate reinforcing system. Once the behavior has been analyzed according to learning principles, it can then be changed through behavior modification.

Modern behaviorists are now studying the possible use of behavioral principles by individuals in self-control and by designers in creating environments that will promote or suppress certain behaviors. B. F. Skinner has even proposed that an entire new society could be engineered on the basis of behavioral theory. Another recent development in behaviorism is the study of mediating variables—that is, nonobservable mental constructs that mediate between stimulus and response. This last development represents something of a departure from the strictly empirical method that has been the hallmark of classical behaviorism.

In its relativistic approach, behavioral theory constitutes a direct challenge to the medical model, which interprets abnormal behavior as the result of a "sickness" and accordingly classifies it into syndromes. Likewise, the emphatically empirical, nonsubjective method of behaviorism stands in direct contrast to the introspective method of the psychodynamic school. Behaviorism has been widely criticized for its simplistic and deterministic view of man. However, the movement has also been commended for its objectivity and precision, for its caution in labeling behavior as abnormal, and for its treatment successes.

The psychodynamic and behaviorist perspectives, to which our two preceding chapters have been devoted, are in many ways polar opposites. They do, however, agree on one important point: that behavior is essentially *reactive* and *determined*. The organism does not move out on its own toward goals of its own free choice. Rather, behavior occurs in response to some prior circumstance—some memory, stimulus, or impulse. And the form that the behavior will take is determined by the nature of that prior circumstance, just as surely as a knee jerk is determined by the hammer that pounds the knee.

To such an interpretation of human behavior many events of the first few decades of our century seemed to lend support. In particular, the increasing industrialization of Western society, the growing acceptance of Darwin's theory of evolution, and the appalling and senseless loss of life in World War I seemed to convey to the twentieth century the clear message that human beings did not create their own destinies, but that their destinies were created for them by amoral forces beyond their control.

The *humanistic* and *existential* perspectives may be seen as a direct reaction to this deterministic interpretation of life. Against the claims of impulses and learning, the humanists and existentialists have reasserted the claims of the human will, arguing that behavior is both willed and purposive, that human beings choose their lives, that they are accordingly responsible for their lives, and that this responsibility gives life its meaning. The first half of the present chapter, the final chapter of our introductory unit, will be devoted to these two related perspectives: their background, their underlying assumptions, and their interpretations of normal and abnormal behavior. The second half of our chapter will introduce briefly several less comprehensive perspectives on abnormal behavior—the interpersonal, psychosocial, cognitive, physiological, and biological perspectives. Having examined these final perspectives, we will then be in a position to proceed to the central subject matter of this book: the different forms of abnormal behavior that all these perspectives—the psychodynamic, the behaviorist, the humanistic-existential, and the others—have been evolved in order to explain.

THE HUMANISTIC-EXISTENTIAL PERSPECTIVE

While it is convenient for the purpose of clarity to speak of a unified *humanistic-existential perspective*, humanistic and existential psychology can only

4
The Humanistic-Existential Perspective and Other Perspectives

loosely be defined as a single school of thought, or even as two single schools of thought. Rather, what we are dealing with in this section is a group of thinkers who are united by a certain set of basic assumptions but who at the same time remain highly individualistic in their theories. Since they do operate on the basis of shared premises, it is possible to speak, as we shall speak in the following section, of the background, underlying assumptions, impact, and strengths and weaknesses of a single humanistic-existential perspective. However, it should be kept in mind that unlike the psychodynamic and behaviorist theorists, the humanistic and existential thinkers lack any semblance of a unified and comprehensive system of abnormal behavior. Hence, when we refer, in the chapters that follow, to the humanistic-existential perspective on any particular form of abnormal behavior, we are actually referring to the ideas of one or two thinkers who, operating within the framework of humanistic-existential assumptions, have turned their attention to that particular form of disorder.

In order to do justice to the individualism that marks this perspective, we shall place our emphasis in the following section not on a general humanistic-existential interpretation of abnormal behavior but rather on the specific interpretations put forth by three representative thinkers: the humanists Carl Rogers and Abraham Maslow and the existentialist Viktor Frankl.

The Background

The emergence of the humanistic and existential approaches into the field of psychology is a contemporary phenomenon. It was not until the 1950s and '60s, when America first became aware of technology's threat to human values, that humanistic and existential psychology began to receive serious consideration as possibly providing answers to America's spiritual crisis. Nevertheless, both approaches may be traced back to ideas that were already part of Western philosophy in the late nineteenth century.

The humanistic approach is largely an American product. It was the American psychologist and philosopher William James (1842–1910) who laid the cornerstone of humanistic psychology by introducing the notion of a "self-concept," an internal frame of reference within which the individual interpreted the environment. Later, in the 1930s, George Herbert Mead, also an American psychologist, further developed this central humanistic idea by pointing out the role of social interaction in the development of the internal self. According to Mead, the child forged his concept of himself through his perceptions of other people's reactions to him.

While the foundations of humanistic psychology were being laid in America, the European philosophers Sören Kierkegaard, Martin Heidegger, Karl Jaspers, and Jean-Paul Sartre were setting forth the basic tenets of existentialism. Though each of these men made his own distinct contributions to existential philosophy, there are two central themes which may be found in all their works. The first is the conceptualization of human life as a dynamic process, a continual *becoming*. Rejecting the notion that development was ever completed or that it was in any way determined, the existentialists saw the individual as perpetually faced with the decision to grow or not to grow. To grow was to live by one's own principles, to face squarely one's conflicts with existence, and therefore to lead an "authentic" life. Not to grow was to succumb to the principles of others, to evade conflict, and consequently to lead an "inauthentic" life, the equivalent of spiritual death. In either case, it was still the individual who chose—and who chose anew every day of his life.

Hence the second major theme of existential philosophy, the concern with the "here and now." Since the individual's fate was determined not by his past but by the choices that he had to make in the continually evolving present, it was present subjective experience on which the existentialists focused: the "now" in which the individual made his decision as to what he would become.

Underlying Assumptions

Out of the ideas of these philosophers evolved the basic assumptions of the humanistic-existential perspective. Though the humanists and existentialists differ slightly in their emphases, they may be said to agree on at least four basic premises.

The Phenomenological Approach Existentialism has been defined by one proponent as "the endeavor to understand man by cutting below the cleavage between subject and object" (May, 1958b, p. 11)—that is, to understand man by seeing the world through his eyes. The same definition might be offered for humanistic psychology. Both the humanists and the existentialists insist on a *phenomenological* approach to the human being, an approach which sees the individual's world as the product of his own perception. Hence what a person in therapy says about himself and his environment must be accepted as the truths of his own subjective universe. The duty of the therapist is not to go digging below the patient's statements in order to drag up a hidden and supposedly objective "real" truth, but to see the patient's world from the vantage point of the patient's own internal frame of reference and to help him, if necessary, adjust his perceptions.

The Uniqueness of the Individual   Because each person perceives the world in a unique way and creates his "self" from that totally individual perception of the world, each person is therefore unique. According to the humanistic-existential perspective, it is an offense to the dignity of the individual to attempt to reduce him to a set of formulas, be they behavioral or psychodynamic. No human being is an example of anything. Rather, he is a unique, singular, and unreplaceable entity, who is himself the best expert on himself.

Human Potentiality   The humanists, like the existentialists, see the individual as a process rather than a product. For both, human life is a matter of growth through experience. Hence the humanistic-existential perspective places great emphasis on human potentiality—the ability of the individual to become what he wants to be, to fulfill his capabilities, and to lead the life that is best suited to him.

Freedom and Responsibility   The humanistic-existential perspective is unique in its insistence on the freedom of the individual. The life of the human animal, like that of all the other animals, is affected by external events beyond his control. But unlike other animals, human beings are gifted (or cursed) with self-awareness. This self-awareness allows them to transcend their impulses and to *choose* what they will make of the "givens" of their existence. And by doing so, they choose their own destinies.

The corollary of this freedom is that the individual is also responsible for his destiny. What he is, he has himself created. Authentic or inauthentic, fulfilling or nonfulfilling, his existence is the result of his own free choosing. Hence, in the humanistic-existential view, the individual becomes a true adult, damned or saved by his own hand.

Humanistic Psychology

The basis on which humanistic psychology rests is an emphatically antideterministic vision of the human being. Whereas Freud saw the individual as being irrational and antisocial by nature, the humanists hold that if the individual is allowed to develop freely, he will become a rational, socialized

Fig. 4.1   *Carl Rogers has been one of the most prolific and systematic contributors to the humanistic movement.*

being. Furthermore, he will become a *constructive* being, intent on fulfilling not simply his instinctive biological needs, but also some higher vision of his capabilities. Of the humanistic thinkers who have built their psychological theories on this optimistic foundation, the most influential have been Carl Rogers (1902–) and Abraham Maslow (1908–1970).

Rogers and the "Self" Theory   Rogers views the personality as the interaction of two forces: the *organism* and the *self*. The organism is the individual's total perception of his experience, both internal and external. The self is the individual's image of himself. Rogers defines this concept of the self as "the organized, consistent, conceptual gestalt composed of perceptions of the characteristics of the 'I' or 'me' and the perceptions of the relationships of the 'I' or 'me' to others and to various aspects of life, together with values attached to these perceptions" (1959, p. 200). It is the self that tells the individual, "I am industrious, and that is my best point," or, "I am beautiful, which is why people like me." Whether or not the messages that the self sends out are true, they are crucial in that they color the individual's perception of his experience.

These two forces, the self and the organism, become the principal actors in the individual's lifelong striving for *self-actualization*—that is, the fulfillment of all his capabilities. Unlike Freud, who saw behavior as motivated by three opposing forces in the personality, Rogers sees all behavior as a unified whole, motivated by a single overriding force, the actualizing tendency. The actualizing tendency moves the individual to seek out ways to enhance and maintain himself. Thus on one level it includes the drive to reduce tension and satisfy biological demands through drinking, eating, staying warm, and avoiding physical danger—in short, the drive to maintain the organism, to keep it alive. On a higher level, however, the actualizing tendency also includes the individual's drive to seek out fruitful and pleasurable tensions: to expose himself to new experiences, to master new skills, to quit a boring job and find a more exciting one, to travel, to read books, to meet new people, and so on.

In the course of his drive for self-actualization, the individual engages in what Rogers calls the *valuing process*. Experiences that are perceived as contributing to the maintenance and enhancement of the organism are valued as good and are therefore sought after. Likewise, experiences that are perceived as impeding the maintenance and enhancement of the organism are valued as bad and are consequently avoided. Thus, according to Rogers, the individual innately knows what is good for him, since he is equipped from birth with the proper mechanism—the actualizing tendency—for weighing good and bad. As we shall see, this assumption of the innate soundness of the individual's judgment is an important factor in Rogerian therapy.

To return to the concepts of the self and the organism, the degree of self-actualization that a person achieves depends on the degree of congruence between the self and the organism. If the image of the self is broad, flexible, and realistic enough to allow the individual to bring into his consciousness and evaluate all the experiences of the organism, then the individual is in an excellent position to identify and pursue those experiences that are most enhancing to him. In short, the self is the crucial factor in self-actualization. (Hence the name of Rogers' system, the "self" theory.)

How does this all-important self develop? What determines whether it will be broad or narrow, flexible or rigid, realistic or unrealistic? The determining factor is childhood learning experiences. As the child becomes aware of himself, he automatically develops the need for what Rogers calls *positive regard*—that is, affection and approval from the important people in his life, particularly his parents. Invariably, however, this positive regard comes with strings attached—injunctions that the child be mild-mannered, aggressive, boyish, girlish, or what have you in order to be better loved. And these extraneous values, which dictate to the child which of his self-experiences are "good" and which are "bad," are accepted by the child and are incorporated into his self as *conditions of worth*. If these conditions are few and reasonable, then the child can still develop a self that is flexible enough to allow him to entertain a variety of experiences and judge for himself which are enhancing and which are not. If, however, the conditions of worth that the child takes over from his parents are severely limiting, screening out large and significant portions of the experience of the organism, then they will drastically impede self-actualization.

The latter situation is, according to Rogers, the source of abnormal behavior. The problem is essentially one of perception—the self's perception of the experience of the organism. On the one hand, the organism, motivated by its actualizing tendency, perceives the internal and external environment in all its variety. On the other hand, the self, cramped by unrealistic conditions of worth, attempts to filter out whatever organismic experiences do not conform to those conditions. For example, a child who is valued by his mother to the degree that he is gentle and mild may spend the rest of his life denying to himself that he ever experiences anger, since anger does not accord with the self that he has built up with the help of his mother's values. Thus the result of conflict between the self and the organism is the distortion and denial of experience, which in turn blocks self-actualization. Furthermore, if the incongruence between the self and the organism is very great, self-actualization may simply come to a halt. Caught between the organism's experience and the self's rejection of that experience as threatening to its organization, the individual becomes immobilized by anxiety, rechannels all his energy toward the defense of the self, and ceases altogether to engage freely in experience. The result is abnormal behavior.

In order to untie this knot, Rogers has developed a technique which he calls *client-centered therapy* (Chapter 19). Briefly, client-centered therapy aims at providing an environment in which the patient can once again revert to his innately sound valuing process and thus turn himself back in the direction of self-actualization. The role of the therapist is simply to create that environment by mirroring whatever feelings the patient expresses, by attempting to perceive the patient's world as he perceives it, and most of all, by offering the patient unconditional positive regard. In this warm, sympathetic, and accepting atmosphere, the patient is released from the necessity of defending his unrealistic self-image. Hence he can confront feelings and experiences that are inconsistent with the self—a process which will result in the broadening of the self to include the total experience of the organism. In such a way, the self and the organism are brought into congruence, and the patient is free to "*be*, in a more unified fashion, what he organismically *is*" (Rogers, 1955, p. 269).

Maslow and the Hierarchy of Needs Like Rogers, Maslow starts out with the premises that human beings are basically good and that all their behavior issues from a single master motive, the drive toward self-actualization. Maslow's specific contribution to the humanistic program is his concept of the *hierarchy of needs*, a series of needs that must be satisfied one by one in the process of development before the adult can begin pursuing self-actualization.

Maslow proposes five levels of needs. First are the *biological* needs, the need for physical comfort and survival. Second are the *safety* needs, the need for a stable, structured, and predictable environment. The third level of needs is the need for *belongingness and love*, which turn the individual's attention away from the maintenance and protection of his organism and toward the pleasure of affectionate interaction with friends and family. Occupying the fourth level on the hierarchy of needs are the *esteem* needs, which impel the individual to seek the approval and respect of others and eventually to create his own internal fund of self-esteem. Having fulfilled the needs for biological survival, safety, love, and esteem, the individual can then proceed to the fifth level and begin fulfilling the need for *self-actualization*. This final goal Maslow defines "as ongoing actualization of potentials, capacities and talents, as fulfillment of mission, as a fuller knowledge of, and acceptance of, the person's own intrinsic nature, as an increasing trend toward unity, integration or synergy within the person" (cited in *Psychosources*, 1973, p. 140). As is obvious from this definition, self-actualization for Maslow, as for Rogers, is not a process that is ever completed, but rather a continual growing that ends only with death.

In order for the child to progress through the hierarchy of needs, he must have a warm, accepting environment in which those needs can be fulfilled. Given such an environment, he can pass from one level to the next until, having reached adulthood, he has arrived at the point where he can devote himself to self-actualization. If, however, the child's environment is loveless, unstable, or demeaning, then as an adult he will still be concentrating on fulfilling whatever lower need remains unsatisfied and will be incapable of devoting himself to the gratification of higher needs, particularly the need for self-actualization. For example, if a woman has never fulfilled her need for esteem, she may, when offered a job that would be fulfilling to her, turn it down because her father disapproves. Likewise, the unfulfilled need for safety will prevent a person from taking any risk involved in self-actualization.

Fig. 4.2 Abraham Maslow denounced the existing formulations of psychology as pessimistic, negative, and limited because they did not view man as a dynamic, creative, holistic organism.

To Maslow such situations are the essence of what might be called abnormal behavior.

It should be noted, however, that this represents a rather unique outlook on psychopathology. What Maslow is primarily concerned with is not really abnormality as such; rather, it is the individual's failure to progress beyond the prosaic standards of normalcy. According to Maslow, a person may hold down a job, bathe regularly, take care of his children, mow his lawn, keep his clothes on at parties, differentiate between the real and the imaginary, and yet still feel lonely, alienated, and ineffectual—a situation Maslow calls "the psychopathology of the normal." Human beings, Maslow argues, require a great deal more than simple adjustment. Hence human psychology should concern itself not only with the capacity of the personality to break down, but also with its capacity to build up. This theory of Maslow's—along with Rogers' conceptualization of abnormality as blocked self-actualization—has been instrumental in generating humanistic psychology's unique preoccupation with developing the positive and creative capabilities of the individual. And it is this preoccupation which more than anything else sets humanistic psychology apart from other models, most of which are still exclusively concerned with repairing the damage done by the negative and self-defeating capabilities of the individual.

Existential Psychology

As we have seen, existential psychology is an outgrowth of European existential philosophy, with its vision of man as a continual "becoming" and with

its emphasis on the individual's "here and now," his total world of immediate subjective experience—in short, his *existence*. Seeing the individual within this dynamic and subjective context, existential psychology has focused on the individual's effort to discover some meaning to his existence. The existentialists argue that this search for meaning is the major challenge facing twentieth-century man. In the process of seeking his material comforts through the means offered by technology, man has lost his ties to church, region, and family—the very structures which formerly gave life direction and significance. Caught in the midst of a vast and amoral technological society, modern man is left with no values to protect him against the threat of "nonbeing"—that is, depersonalization and ultimately death.

As a means of ministering to the spiritual anguish of modern man—a crisis which the more deterministic psychodynamic and behaviorist models are ill-equipped to handle—existential psychology has gained considerable attention in the last two decades. Though the movement has no single spokesman, its major contributors have been the Swiss psychiatrists Ludwig Binswanger and Medard Boss, the Austrian psychiatrist Viktor Frankl, and the American psychologist Rollo May, the foremost exponent of existential therapy in this country. Our discussion will focus on Frankl's existential psychology, which is both comprehensive and representative.

Frankl and the Search for Meaning A student of Freud's, Frankl (1905–), unlike Freud, was unable to escape from the Nazis and thus spent the years 1942 to 1945 in German concentration camps, including Auschwitz and Dachau. Imprisoned along with him were his parents, his brother, and his wife, all of whom died in the camps. From this harrowing experience Frankl evolved the basic tenets of his psychological theory. In the camps, he observed that those prisoners who were able to survive psychologically, resisting apathy and despair, were those who could find some meaning in their suffering,

Fig. 4.3 Humanistic personality theorists such as Rogers (left) and Maslow (right) have been influenced by existentialism and phenomenology. Their theories stress man's potential for integrative, self-actualizing growth if he is given a wholesome and accepting environment. As long as an individual feels safe and accepted, his integrated self (symbolized by interlocking circles) develops in ways that enhance his being.

Fig. 4.4 Victor Frankl is the foremost proponent of the existential perspective, which emphasizes man's search for personal meaning and value in life.

those who could relate this suffering to their spiritual lives. This observation led Frankl to the conclusion that traditional psychology, in dealing with man only in his biological and psychological dimensions, was omitting an all-important third dimension: the *spiritual life*.

It is this emphasis on the spiritual life that is the central feature of Frankl's existential theory. According to this theory, it is the spirit that gives man his freedom, allowing him to transcend his instincts, his past, and the conditions of his environment. And it is this freedom, in turn, that makes the individual responsible for his life—a responsibility which is the sole source of his dignity as a human being.

Not only is the spirit the foundation of freedom, responsibility, and dignity; it is also, according to Frankl, the source of the prime motivating force of human behavior. This central motive is not the will-to-pleasure or the will-to-power, as psychodynamic theory would have it, but rather the *will-to-meaning*, man's effort to find some reason for this troubled, complicated, and finite existence.

The meaning of life, as Frankl sees it, is not invented by man, but rather "discovered" by him, through the medium of *values*: *creative values*, which are experienced through the achievement of tasks; *experiential values*, which are experienced through appreciating what is good and beautiful in the world, and particularly by loving another human being; and *attitudinal values*, which are experienced by confronting and dealing with one's inevitable suffering.

It should be noted that Frankl views this process of pursuing values as a moral duty. Without the meaning which these values give to life, man evades the role of responsibility offered to him by the spiritual life and thus remains the helpless, puny, driven creature that he appears from the viewpoint of science. Through the discovery of meaning, on the other hand, he accepts his responsibility and thus rises above whatever forces attempt to drive him.

"Ultimately, man should not ask what the meaning of life is, but rather he must recognize that it is *he* who is asked. In a word, each man is questioned by life, and he can only respond by being responsible" (Frankl, 1962, p. 101).

When man cannot discover meaning, he experiences what Frankl calls *existential frustration*, and according to Frankl's theory, this frustration of the will-to-meaning is a major source of abnormal behavior. Thus while still acknowledging the biological and psychological components of psychopathology, Frankl focuses on the spiritual aspects of neurosis and psychosis. He distinguishes two large categories of neurosis, *anxiety neurosis* and *obsessional neurosis*. Anxiety neurosis he interprets as stemming from the neurotic person's guilt over not having sought to realize any values. Obsessional neurosis, on the other hand, is caused by an inability to endure the discrepancy between the real and the ideal. Likewise, the psychoses have been explained by Frankl as disruptions of the individual's quest for meaning.

To deal with the spiritual aspect of psychopathology, Frankl has evolved a technique which he calls *logotherapy* (from the Greek word *logos*, denoting both "meaning" and "spirit"). Psychotherapy, according to Frankl, tends to treat spiritual struggles in a reductive fashion because it is simply unequipped to deal with them. Hence psychotherapy must be supplemented by logotherapy, which addresses spiritual problems in the philosophical terms appropriate to such problems.

The role of the therapist in logotherapy is to confront the patient with his responsibility for his existence and show him his obligation to pursue the values inherent in life. This rather harsh-sounding process is softened, however, by the nature of the patient-therapist relationship. As Frankl views it, this relationship is an existential partnership in which the therapist, by intuiting the patient's subjective world, explores that world with him. The two of them then work together to correct the flaws in the patient's attitude toward life so that he can once again take up the task of discovering meaning through experiencing values.

Comparing Humanism and Existentialism

As we have seen, humanistic and existential psychology are similar enough in their basic assumptions to warrant our use of the term "humanistic-existential perspective." Both approaches emphasize the subjectivity of the individual's world, his individuality and uniqueness, his capacity for growth, his freedom to choose his life, and his responsibility for those choices. Furthermore, both see abnormal behavior as a result of a disturbance in the perception of values, a disturbance that blocks the individual's growth. However, for the humanists the primary motive of human behavior is self-actualization, while for the existentialists this primary motive is the pursuit of meaning. And this difference in interpretation gives rise to a number of other rather subtle differences between the two approaches.

First, the humanists focus solely on the individual—his needs, his perceptions, and his goals—and studiously avoid holding the individual up to any external values. The existentialists, in contrast, see the individual within the context of the human condition and attempt to deal with the larger philosophical question of his relationship to that condition.

Second, the aim of humanistic therapy is to free the patient to satisfy his biological and psychological needs; the individual's responsibility is only to himself, though it is assumed that because he is innately good, he will not harm others in the process of his self-actualization. The aim of existential therapy, on the other hand, is to develop the patient's spiritual life, a process which includes the patient's realizing his responsibility to others and his responsibility to fulfill a rather lofty vision of human life.

Third, humanistic psychology is unremittingly optimistic. All the humanists' emphasis is on freedom, hope, potential, and what they see as the clear possibility of self-fulfillment. The existentialists, in contrast, do not hold out any hopes for total fulfillment. Indeed, many of the existentialists place great emphasis on the sorrows and frustrations that are simply built into life: the anguish of choice, the constant threat of anxiety, and the terror of death. As we have seen, Frankl's whole system is in a way based on the challenge of transcending suffering. To these thinkers, freedom is as much a source of pain as it is a source of satisfaction. For freedom carries with it responsibility: as Frankl says, life expects something from *us* (1955, p. x). The proper fulfillment of this responsibility does not necessarily guarantee self-actualization, though self-actualization may in fact result. Rather, the goal of accepting responsibility is a sort of philosophical peace treaty with the human condition, whereby the individual can rescue his dignity as a human being and transcend spiritually the forces which threaten to dehumanize and annihilate him.

Fig. 4.5 One important aim of existential psychotherapy is to help the person assume responsibility for his own actions, because only through accepting responsibility can the client create meaning in his own life. The goal, as illustrated here, is to help the individual to "control his own chess board" rather than be one of the pawns.

Humanistic and Existential Psychology

Shared Assumptions

Necessity of phenomenological approach
Uniqueness of individual
Human potential
Freedom and responsibility

Different Emphases

Humanism		Existentialism
Self-actualization	*vs.*	Pursuit of spiritual meaning
Satisfaction of needs	*vs.*	Satisfaction of ideals
Individual as a rule unto himself	*vs.*	Individual seen within the context of society and history
Pleasure of freedom	*vs.*	Burden of freedom
Realization of innate goodness and creativity	*vs.*	Transcendence of inevitable suffering, anxiety, and alienation

The Impact of the Humanistic-Existential Perspective

The overall influence of humanistic and existential psychology on traditional psychological theory and practice has been relatively limited. Most psychodynamic therapists still spend a great deal of time analyzing the patient's past history rather than pursuing the humanistic-existential course of focusing on the "here and now." Furthermore, the rather general concepts of self-actualization and will-to-meaning are difficult to incorporate into either psychodynamic or behaviorist theory, since both these approaches insist on a great deal of precision in their concepts. Thus humanistic and existential therapies have not been integrated to any significant degree into psychodynamic or behavioral techniques. Rather, they remain as alternatives to these two approaches.

Nevertheless, a few humanistic and existential concepts have found their way into psychodynamic and behavioral theory, though not always with due credit being given to the originators of these concepts. For example, many therapists now place great emphasis on the necessity of letting the patient know that he is still approved of and accepted even if he behaves in self-destructive ways—an obvious borrowing from Rogers' idea that the therapist must provide unconditional positive regard. Furthermore, the existential technique of confronting the patient with his responsibility for his life has also been quietly appropriated by many psychodynamic and behavioral therapists.

However, the greatest impact of humanistic and existential therapy has been not in the area of the traditional one-to-one patient-therapist relationship, but rather in the rapid proliferation of group therapies, the "group therapy movement," since the 1950s. Group therapy can take any number of forms—Gestalt theory, sensitivity training, psychodrama, encounter groups, marathon groups, and so on. The most common of these therapies will be discussed in Chapter 19. A large part of the group therapy movement, however, is based on humanistic-existential assumptions: that the therapist-patient relationship should be an existential partnership rather than a parent-child-type interaction, involving authority and submission; that interpersonal relations must constitute a central focus of treatment; that therapy should foster growth rather than simply repair maladjustment; and finally, that this growth depends on the achievement of full, uncensored perception of one's internal life. At present, the group therapy movement is riddled by a number of problems, the foremost of which is that groups are not regulated in any way. Thus they invite charlatanry and have seen their fair share of it. But under the direction of competent professionals, many types of group therapy have shown extremely hopeful results (Lieberman et al., 1972).

A smaller sector of the group therapy movement has experimented with some rather radical techniques—hallucinogenic drugs, nude marathons, forty-eight-hour marathons, body massages, and so forth—in order to wear down the participants' rational and moral inhibitions and allow them to get in touch with their "real" selves—that is, the self of impulse and emotion (Shutz, 1967). However, it is questionable whether the state at which participants arrive through such means represents in any way the "real" self. Furthermore, in many cases such methods have been shown to aggravate rather than alleviate psychological problems. Finally, it should be emphasized that this type of therapy may actually be antagonistic to the humanistic-existential approach, which aims not at achieving transient "breakthroughs" to a presocialized or prerational state of mind, but rather at developing the individual's capacity for personal growth within the context of everyday life.

The Humanistic-Existential Perspective and Other Perspectives

The humanistic-existential perspective and the medical model differ radically. The humanists and existentialists allow the person himself to judge whether his behavior stands in need of adjustment. (In this respect they resemble what, in Chapter 1, we called the "personal discomfort" model.) Furthermore, the humanistic-existential theorists believe that the patient must cure himself; the role of the therapist is primarily to provide an environment conducive to such self-cure. The medical model, in contrast, looks to cultural norms—what we could call "typical behavior"—as the measure of whether or not a person's responses are abnormal. And if they are judged to be abnormal, then all efforts are focused on searching out the "bug" within him that is causing the trouble; the patient's will and judgment have virtually no role in the therapy. In sum, both existential and humanistic psychology are "client-centered" in assessment as well as in treatment; medical psychology is society-centered in assessment and body-centered in treatment.

The relationship between the humanistic-existential and psychodynamic perspectives is a complex one, and it should be remembered that many humanistic and existential theorists, like Frankl, began as psychodynamic therapists. The two perspectives are similar in that they both see abnormal behavior as resulting from anxiety when a part of the self is denied. Furthermore, both perspectives envision therapy as a process of rediscovering that lost part

of the self. Thus both approaches are insight-oriented (London, 1964). However, in psychodynamic therapy the insights are provided mainly by the therapist and are presumably interpretations of repressed and unconscious material from the patient's past history. Furthermore, this forbidden material is dredged up not so that the patient can act on it, but so that the ego's energy can be redirected from the task of repression to the task of controlling the basically irrational and instinct-driven self. In humanistic-existential therapy, on the other hand, the insights are supposed to come from the patient himself, as he explores, along with the therapist, his *present* subjective world. These insights are accepted at face value; they are not interpreted as symbols of some darker hidden truth. And the insights are used to fill in the missing pieces in a self which is seen as integrated, rational, and free—a self which, once reinvested with all its parts, can then proceed toward self-actualization.

Like the psychodynamic perspective, the behaviorist perspective in many ways bears a family resemblance to the humanistic-existential perspective. Along with the behaviorists, the humanists see faulty learning as the source of abnormal behavior. And like the behaviorists, the humanists and existentialists focus not on the individual's past, but on his present experience, in the effort to help him find better ways of functioning in the present and future. But whereas the humanistic-existential perspective sees the human being as a free agent, depends on inference in intuiting his subjective world, and concerns itself with human values and with philosophical issues, the behaviorists see humankind as determined by its conditioning and reject as unscientific all inferred material, to say nothing of philosophical inquiries into meaning and values. Furthermore, as we have seen, the humanistic-existential perspective depends on insight as the prime tool of therapy, whereas the behaviorists, in accordance with their stimulus-response thinking, rely on reconditioning—that is, new stimuli aimed at eliciting new responses.

Evaluating the Humanistic-Existential Perspective

Criticisms of the humanistic-existential perspective tend to center on the question of whether the self— that is, the individual's subjective world, as interpreted by himself—can be relied on to the degree that the humanists and existentialists believe. Is the disordered person really capable of deciding whether or not he needs help? Furthermore, is he competent to decide at what point he is "well" again? If a person were to report that his entire subjective network assured him that his self and his organism were in perfect congruence and that he was experiencing values and that his only problem in life was that the world was "out to get" him, could he then be pronounced "healthy"? In short, to what degree can the patient's statements about himself be accepted as truth? And if we assume that each person lives in a uniquely perceived subjective world, how far can the therapist go in crossing the boundary between his phenomenological universe and that of the patient? Moreover, when the humanists and existentialists assert that behavior issues from a person's free will, is it not inviting to ask what circumstances have formed that will (Skinner, 1964)—circumstances that might once again show that the will is not free? Why should the human will be pronounced sacred and thus exempted from scientific study?

The behaviorists have also been quick to point out that humanistic-existential perspective, like the psy-

Three Perspectives on Normal and Abnormal Behavior

	Nature of human psyche	Nature of psychological normalcy	Major cause of abnormal behavior	Preferred treatment methods	Goal of treatment
Psychodynamic perspective	Determined; governed by psychosexual history; basically bent on id gratification	Proper balancing of id, ego, and superego as a result of appropriate levels of gratification in oral, anal, and phallic stages	Anxiety due to unconscious conflicts; consequent imbalance of power among id, ego, and superego	Psychoanalysis; insight-oriented psychotherapy	Uncovering and working through of unconscious conflicts
Behaviorist perspective	Determined; a collection of unlearned reflexes and learned responses to external stimuli	Possession of an adequately large repertoire of adaptive responses	Learning of maladaptive responses and maintenance of these responses through anxiety-motivated avoidance	Behavior therapy and behavior modification	Learning of new, adaptive responses to replace old, maladaptive responses
Humanistic-existential perspective	Free; goal-oriented; unique and individual; basically good	Ability to accept oneself, to actualize one's potentialities, to achieve intimacy with others, and to find meaning in life	Inability to accept and express one's true nature, to take responsibility for one's actions, and to make self-generated choices	Client-centered therapy, logotherapy, Gestalt therapy, encounter groups	Personal growth, including self-acceptance, increased honesty with oneself and others, and clarification of values and goals

chodynamic, places great faith in scientifically un-verifiable inferences. The source of information in Rogerian therapy, for instance, is simply what the therapist thinks about what the patient thinks about his own internal life. The existentialists, of course, are even less scientifically precise, since they deal in spiritual questions and in philosophical issues. Indeed, many hold an almost antiintellectual bias about scientific matters, repudiating formal theory and research and distrusting reason and analysis on the therapeutic plane. As a result, the perspective has been accused of being a religion rather than a science.

The major contributions of this perspective issue from the same sources as the criticisms of the perspective. As we have seen, the humanists' and existentialists' reliance on the value of the individual's subjective vision raises a number of questions. But it also restores to the individual's judgment and perception a measure of dignity and authority that the psychodynamic and behavioral perspectives would deny them. Likewise, by investing the human will with an absolute and autonomous force, humanistic-existential psychology has in a sense rescued the integrity of the will. Such idealism may or may not be justified. But whether justified or not, it can be of great therapeutic value in bolstering the patient's self-esteem and in encouraging him to make constructive changes in his behavior. Furthermore, while the humanistic-existential concern with free will, values, choices, goals, growth, fulfillment, and meaning may be construed as starry-eyed and unscientific, there is no question that such concerns have allowed this perspective to address itself to the major day-to-day concerns of ordinary human beings. Most people do not think of their behavior as being dictated by either environmental stimuli or the warfare between ego, superego, and id. Rather, they think of themselves as free, and thus they worry about the choices that they make. Particularly in the twentieth century, when man is faced with more freedom and fewer firm values than ever before, questions of choice can be extremely anguishing. With this type of struggle the humanistic-existential perspective is better equipped to deal than are other, more strictly scientific perspectives.

Finally, as we have mentioned in connection with Maslow, the humanistic-existential perspective can be credited with calling attention to the "healthy" side of human psychology. While psychodynamic and behavioral theories are typically devoted to "repair" work—that is, the remolding of maladaptive behavior into adaptive behavior—humanistic and

Fig. 4.6 *The counterculture of the 1960s was viewed by many as an expression of anxiety and concern over the depersonalization and dehumanization of contemporary society. The appeal was for a return to closer, more personal contacts among individuals.*

existential psychology has shown that adapting to one's environment is in itself no ideal. Instead, psychology must help people discover or create something for themselves—a sense of meaning or a true feeling of fulfillment—rather than simply ease their adjustment to the world that others have created for them.

OTHER PERSPECTIVES ON ABNORMAL BEHAVIOR

While this text will focus on the psychodynamic, behaviorist, and humanistic-existential perspectives on abnormal behavior, to limit our discussion to these three viewpoints alone would be to ignore some other important psychological and nonpsychological approaches to the question of abnormality. In the remainder of this chapter, we will outline three additional psychological perspectives—the interpersonal, psychosocial, and cognitive approaches—and two nonpsychological perspectives—the physiological and biological views. Our goal is not to present a detailed or comprehensive discussion of these perspectives, but simply to summarize their major features so that when they appear in later chapters their emphases and assumptions will already have been made clear.

Two general points need to be made with regard to these perspectives. The first is that none of them represents a single, consistent, and comprehensive theory of abnormal behavior in general. Rather, each of these views represents simply an *orientation*, a home base—be it family relations, society, genetics, or what have you—from which researchers are attempting to approach certain types of abnormal behavior. Within each orientation, there may be considerable disagreement among researchers and hence many inconsistencies, gaps, and contradictions.

Our second point regarding these perspectives is that by placing them at the end of our final introductory chapter, we do not intend in any way to minimize their importance for the understanding of abnormality. (On the contrary, certain of these perspectives are more important than the psychodynamic, behaviorist, or humanistic-existential approaches in analyzing some of the forms of abnormal psychology that we will deal with in this book.) Rather, our reason for treating them last and more briefly is either that they are less comprehensive than the three major perspectives of this text, as is the case with the interpersonal, psychosocial, and cognitive perspectives, or that they are concerned with organic rather than psychological causes, as is the case with the physiological and biological perspectives. Another, more medically oriented text on abnormal behavior might place greater emphasis on these two latter perspectives. This, however, is a text on abnormal *psychology*, and accordingly our emphasis will be on psychological perspectives.

The Interpersonal Perspective: Sullivan and Berne

The *interpersonal perspective*—along with the psychosocial perspective, which we shall discuss shortly—views the individual's relationships with others as the central breeding ground for psychological disturbance. Hence, according to this view, the disturbed person must not be viewed in isolation, but rather within the context of his contacts with other people.

One of the most important proponents of this view has been Harry Stack Sullivan, whom we have already mentioned briefly in Chapter 2. According to Sullivan, abnormal behavior may be defined as inadequate or inappropriate ways of reacting to interpersonal situations. Such inappropriate behavior arises out of the anxiety one experiences in interpersonal relations.

Logically, Sullivan views disturbed interpersonal relations not only as the manifestation of abnormal behavior, but also as its cause. For Sullivan as for most other interpersonal theorists, the ultimate source of abnormality is family relations. According to Sullivan's theory, social anxiety is learned from

infancy, in either or both of two ways. First, a mother can communicate anxiety to her child through her own anxious behaviors: stiff posture, strained voice quality, rigid routines, and so forth. Second, a child can learn social anxiety simply by being treated cruelly; if he is constantly frightened or abused by his parents, he will eventually become anxious in all interpersonal situations.

Sullivan views anxiety as resulting from a perceived threat to the individual's *self-system* or view of himself—an idea that bears some resemblance to Rogers' interpretation of anxiety. A certain degree of anxiety is normal and accompanies the individual throughout his life. Any time another person places on him a demand that is inconsistent with his view of himself or of his needs and wants, the self-system will be threatened, and anxiety will result. If the individual has been successful in developing an adequate self-system, he will be able to handle these threats with minimal anxiety and thus will be able to negotiate his interpersonal relations successfully. But if the self-system has been repeatedly threatened at its very inception—that is, in childhood—it will not be strong enough to deal with such threats. In consequence, the individual will find himself overwhelmed with anxiety and incapable of maintaining his self-system. Such a situation in turn gives rise to inappropriate behavior, which disrupts interpersonal relationships. In the case of the neurotic, the anxiety does not lead to a total breakdown either in the self-system or in interpersonal relations. It simply impels the neurotic to engage in various self-defeating behaviors in the effort to relieve his psychic discomfort. In the case of the psychotic, on the other hand, the self-system simply crumbles under the weight of anxiety. As a result, interactions with other people become impossible, and the psychotic withdraws into a world of his own, safe from the threats from others.

Another influential interpersonal theorist, Eric Berne, has stressed the effect of the parent-child relationship on the role that the child will assume in his adult years. According to Berne, the transactions between parent and child teach the child what kind of person he is and what attitude he should take toward himself. If these transactions are reality-oriented, warm, and loving, the child will grow up to behave as a mature, rational adult in his interpersonal relations. If, however, the parent-child transactions are repressive, negative, and cold, the child will grow up maintaining his role as a child, never learning to act as an adult in his relationships with others. If such a childlike person encounters enough aversive experiences in his adult years, he may withdraw partially from interpersonal experiences and thus become neurotic. Or he may retreat into a total withdrawal from others, in which case he would be termed psychotic.

Both Sullivan and Berne, therefore, view disruptions in interpersonal relations as both the cause and manifestation of mental disorder. And both theorists point to the family as the all-important interpersonal context in which the child learns his first and most critical lesson in how he is to relate to others. This position is certainly difficult to argue with. And indeed the psychodynamic, behaviorist, and humanistic-existential perspectives all acknowledge the crucial importance of the interpersonal context. The difference is that while these perspectives see the individual's social interactions as one aspect of the self, to interpersonal theorists the self is to a large degree *defined* by its relationships with others.

The Psychosocial Perspective

Like the interpersonal perspective, the *psychosocial perspective* explains abnormal behavior in terms of the social context in which the behavior takes place. However, the psychosocial perspective defines that social context not as the limited range of the individual's personal contacts, but as the entire society or culture. According to this view, it is the society that is the principal determinant of abnormal behavior. Further, it is society that supports or maintains the continued involvement in abnormal behavior.

The central tenet of psychosocial theory is that society crystallizes, maintains, and even aggravates abnormal behavior by defining people as sick. For example, Scheff (1966) argues that while most people frequently deviate from social norms, society singles out certain types of deviations or certain types of people and applies to them the label of "deviant." Once stigmatized with such a label, the individual finds that he is expected to behave in deviant ways and that all his behavior is interpreted within the context of his presumed deviance. Hence he has little choice but to accept the role that society has assigned to him and to become a full-fledged deviant. A similar process may have taken place in the case of the young people who inhabited Haight-Ashbury in San Francisco during the 1960s. Expected to be "freaks," they cheerfully—or perhaps vengefully—fulfilled these expectations.

The relationship among society, mental illness, and the labeling process is strikingly illustrated in the so-called New Haven studies of Hollingshead

and Redlich (1958) and Myers and Bean (1968). These investigators found that people from lower socioeconomic levels, when suffering from behavior disturbances, tended more frequently than middle-class people to be placed in state mental hospitals. The reasons were twofold. First, the lower-class people could not afford private care. Second, they tended to manifest their unhappiness in aggressive and rebellious behaviors. And these behaviors, while acceptable to -members of their own social class as "normal" signs of frustration, appeared unacceptable and, indeed, genuinely bizarre to the mental health professionals who were diagnosing them, since these professionals came from higher socioeconomic brackets and accordingly had different ideas about what constituted normal responses to stress. Hence persons from lower socioeconomic backgrounds were more likely to be labeled as psychotic and to be hospitalized as a result. In contrast, people from higher socioeconomic levels tended not to be hospitalized, not only because they could pay for private outpatient care, but also because the types of deviant behaviors in which they engaged (e.g., withdrawal and self-deprecation) seemed to the doctors, coming from the same social class, less bizarre. Consequently, these people were diagnosed as neurotic—a label which carries much less stigma and which in some segments of society even confers a measure of chic—and with the help of regular therapy were able to return to their daily lives. Unlike the hospitalized and "psychotic" poor, they were not given a "sick" role to fill and thus were more likely to improve. In sum, socioeconomic differences not only determine who is considered truly abnormal, but by doing so, can seriously affect the individual's chances for improvement (Braginsky et al., 1969).

More radical than the labeling theory is the psychosocial view that individual behavioral pathologies are a function of a pathological society. Thus the individual's abnormal behavior is merely a symptom of the sickness of the society. Such is the theme of Alvin Toffler's book *Future Shock* (1970). Toffler claims that our rapidly changing society makes inappropriate demands on its citizens, places them in conflict-producing situations, and as a result brings about the breakdown of normal or adequate functioning. Other theorists have pointed to society's treatment of women and the aged, as well as to the demands which the United States placed on its citizens during the Vietnam War, as further instances of cultural provocation of mental disorder. Such psychosocial views may seem at times to err in plac-

Fig. 4.7 Lucy gets carried away with the labeling game, illustrating Scheff's contention that society gives too much attention to providing a label for every possible disorder.

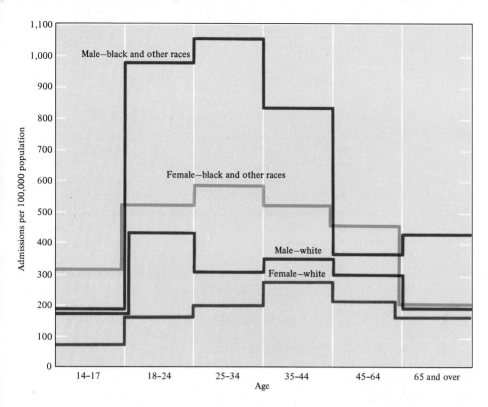

The graph y-axis is labeled "Admissions per 100,000 population" with values from 0 to 1,100. The x-axis is labeled "Age" with categories 14–17, 18–24, 25–34, 35–44, 45–64, and 65 and over. Lines are labeled "Male—black and other races," "Female—black and other races," "Male—white," and "Female—white."

ing the entire responsibility on the society. But the evidence in support of such views is strong enough to indicate that the interaction between individual and society in the development, and particularly in the maintenance, of mental disorder is a factor which we cannot afford to ignore.

The Cognitive Perspective

While the *cognitive perspective* is very clearly a psychological perspective in that it deals with what goes on in the human mind, it differs from the other psychological perspectives in that it views the individual's patterns of thinking as the major determinant of behavior. There are actually two schools of cognitive theory. One holds that abnormal behavior arises from *what* the person thinks, while the other sees the source of the disturbance in *how* the person thinks.

An influential proponent of the former view is Albert Ellis (1958), who argues that when a person behaves inappropriately, he does so because he is operating on the basis of mistaken assumptions— what Ellis calls "irrational beliefs." If, for example, a person believes that he must be loved and approved of by everyone or that it would be catastrophic for him to make a mistake (which, according to Ellis, are two of the most common irrational beliefs), then he will spend inordinate

Fig. 4.8   Breakdown of admission rates to state and county mental hospitals by race, age, and sex, 1970. As we know, many of the poor are black, and very many blacks are poor. Hence this graph, comparing the rate of mental hospital admissions by race, meshes neatly with the findings of the New Haven studies (Hollingshead and Redlich, 1958; Meyers and Bean, 1968) that the lower classes are more likely than any other socioeconomic group to be hospitalized for mental illness. As the graph shows, state and county mental hospitals admit three and a half times as many minority-group males as white males, and three times as many minority group females as white females, in the 18–24 age group. Many reasons have been proposed for this startling racial and socioeconomic differential: that diagnostic guidelines are biased in favor of middle-class behaviors; that the poor and the minorities go to the state and county mental hospitals because they cannot afford private outpatient care; that the mentally disturbed tend to drift into the lower socioeconomic brackets; and finally, that the hardships of ghetto life breed mental disturbance. The answer is yet to be found, though it is likely that all these proposed factors play their part in the over-representation of the poor and the minorities in our publicly funded mental hospitals.

(Source: Executive Office of the President: Office of Management and Budget, *Social Indicators, 1973*. Washington, D.C.: U.S. Government Printing Office, 1973, p. 13.)

amounts of time in trying to please others or in compulsively checking and rechecking his work. As a result, his behavior will appear odd and inappropriate. Furthermore, it will allow no expression of his true preferences and interests—a sacrifice which will eventually give rise to feelings of acute frustration.

In a similar vein, Beck (1967, 1969) proposes that depression is simply the behavioral response to an attitude or cognition of hopelessness. Whereas most theorists hold that the belief that all is hopeless is a symptom or result of the emotional condition called depression, Beck, with classic cognitive reasoning, reverses this causal relationship, making the depressed feelings the result of the cognition of hopelessness. (Beck's theory of depression will be discussed more fully in Chapter 7.)

The second school of cognitive theory, as we have seen, argues that it is how a person thinks that determines whether his behavior will be normal or abnormal. That is, the source of abnormal behavior, according to these theorists, lies in the very mechanics of cognition. Consider, for example, the cognitive mechanics of learning a telephone number. First you look up the number in the telephone directory and read it. This part of cognitive processing is called *input*. Your next step is to try to remember the number. You may do this in a number of ways: by breaking it up into three numbers and then four numbers, by remembering that the number is similar to a friend's telephone number, or in some other way. This part of the cognitive process is known as *storing*. Later on you will try to recall the number so that you can use it to call the person with whom you want to speak, and this final phase of the cognitive process is called *output*.

The second school of cognitive theory holds that abnormal behavior arises from disturbances in this cycle of input, storing, and output. The cause of this disturbance is generally assumed to be biochemical, but it is not with the basic cause, organic or otherwise, that the cognitive theorists are centrally concerned. Rather, their focus is on the precise way in which the cognitive cycle goes awry—whether through a blocking of input, through inappropriate storing, through obstructions to the retrieval of information, or through some other derailment of the cognitive sequence. In any case, the result of this derailment is that the person's ideas are inappropriate. But unlike the unfounded notions that Ellis and Beck propose as the source of abnormal behavior, the ideas that result from impaired cognitive processing are drastically confused and distorted, consisting of bits and pieces of information that have lost their proper connections with one another and hence their connections with objective reality. Thus this theory of abnormal behavior has been advanced to account not for the milder personality disturbances, such as the neuroses with which Ellis deals, but rather for the adult psychoses and for autism, a form of childhood psychosis—disorders in which the individual seems to abandon almost all contact with reality. According to the cognitive theorists, the psychotic withdraws from reality because he simply lacks the cognitive means of negotiating with reality.

The entire cognitive approach is a rather new one and as yet has not exercised a decisive influence on the treatment of abnormal behavior. However, the ideas of Ellis and Beck have been taken to heart by a number of therapists, who are now giving increased attention to the role of inappropriate assumptions in the development of neurotic behavior. As for the cognitive-process view of psychosis, it has so far had little impact on the treatment of psychotics. Nonetheless, it has generated an enormous amount of research and experimentation on the

---

Three Additional Psychological Perspectives

Interpersonal perspective	Abnormal behavior is defined as the inability to establish satisfying relationships and is caused by anxiety-producing parent-child relations.
Psychosocial perspective	Abnormal behavior is produced by social injustice and instability and is maintained by the social process of labeling.
Cognitive perspective	Abnormal behavior is caused either by inaccurate assumptions or by an actual derailment of normal thinking processes.

cognitive processes of adult psychotics and autistic children. And as this research continues, its findings are likely to alter—and perhaps render more hopeful—our therapeutic approach to psychosis.

Nonpsychological Perspectives

Having considered the various psychological perspectives on abnormal behavior, we will now briefly examine two nonpsychological approaches, the physiological and the biological perspectives. The former view focuses on nonhereditary aspects of physical functioning that can contribute to abnormal behavior. The latter is concerned with the relationship between abnormal behavior and hereditary factors, the genetically transmitted biological "givens" with which we are equipped from birth.

Both of these perspectives draw our attention to the important issue of the relationship between the psychic and the somatic aspects of our functioning—the so-called *mind-body problem*, first brought to the attention of modern man by the seventeenth-century French philosopher René Descartes. While the psychological perspectives we have examined so far have viewed the dynamics of the mind in terms of the relationship among the parts of the mind or between the mind and the environment, the physiological and biological perspectives view the mind as inseparable from its *organic* environment, the body. And indeed, as we shall discuss more fully in Chapter 6, physical and mental functioning cannot realistically be considered apart from each other. Each influences the other, and thus to consider one without recognizing its relation to the other is to see only half the picture.

In view of this interrelationship, it is highly possible that psychological and nonpsychological theories of abnormal behavior may be complementary rather than mutually exclusive. At present, the sorry truth is that we know very little about the human mind. Furthermore, as new discoveries are made, the picture often becomes cloudier rather than clearer. (In this book, as the reader will discover, the amount of *theory* presented will far outweigh the amount of *fact*.) With so little certainty to cling to, groups of theorists are tempted to manufacture their own private certainties, sweeping the entire range of abnormal behavior into the bin of their own limited conceptualizations. Thus the biological theorists will claim that all mental disorders are either genetically or biologically based; the behaviorists will argue that all abnormal behavior is the consequence of learning, and so forth. In the case of some truly baffling disorders, such as schizophrenia, many theorists are

willing to acknowledge that a number of different factors—physiological, genetic, and psychological—are probably involved. But in the case of most other disorders, there is hot competition among the various perspectives, with much rigidity on all sides. Nevertheless, it is extremely unlikely that any one perspective will ever be able to account conclusively for all abnormal behaviors in terms of its own special set of principles. Thus in considering the organic dysfunctions proposed by the physiological and biological perspectives as explanations for abnormal behavior, the reader should try to think of these organic factors, like environmental factors, as possible component causes rather than as possible final causes.

The Physiological Perspective Like the psychological perspectives that we have discussed in the latter half of this chapter, the *physiological perspective* is not a comprehensive system of abnormal behavior, but rather a set of theories united by a common orientation—in this case, the physiological orientation. In the chapters that follow, several specific physiological theories will be presented in relation to the forms of abnormal behavior to which they apply. Here we will examine briefly the few more general physiological conceptualizations of abnormal behavior.

One of the more well-known groups of physiological theories are the constitutional theories. These focus on the relationship between personality and bodily features such as height, weight, and build. Some constitutional theorists, such as Ernst Kretschmer (1925) and William Sheldon (1942), argue that both physique and behavior are determined by genetic factors. But others (e.g., Millon, 1969) take the view that one's body build may influence how one responds to the environment. Thus the big, muscular male may respond aggressively, while the "96-pound weakling" may be quite passive. A corollary to this view would be that social stereotypes regarding certain physiques would tend to encourage certain types of behavior. For example, the fat person is expected to be jolly, while the person with a thin, angular body is expected to be high-strung and intense. Constitutional stereotypes can also affect people's self-images, so that the very short male or the very tall female may feel "different" or abnormal. Similarly, an overweight person may feel very negative about himself and may even seek psychological help in dealing with his "problem."

Just as one's physique may be a cause of emo-

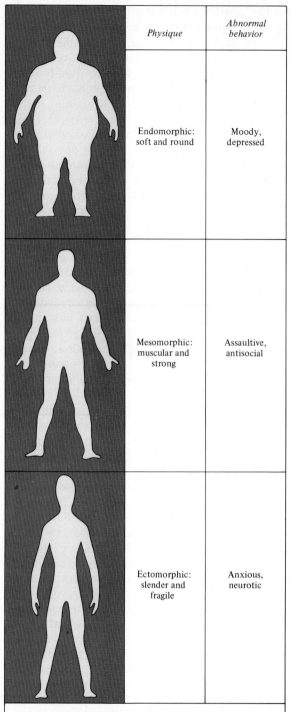

Physique	Abnormal behavior
Endomorphic: soft and round	Moody, depressed
Mesomorphic: muscular and strong	Assaultive, antisocial
Ectomorphic: slender and fragile	Anxious, neurotic

Fig. 4.9   While Sheldon (1940) did not actually argue a causal relationship between physique and abnormal behavior, some small relationship has generally been found, although such a correlation does not prove any cause-and-effect association between body type and behavior.

tional problems, so also can disturbances in growth lead to behavioral abnormalities. Theories that focus on growth disturbances as a basis for pathology emphasize the social implications of deviations in physical development, particularly among children and adolescents. A child who is much smaller than his peers during most of his childhood may find himself excluded from sports and social activities and may suffer considerably as a result. Likewise, a girl who reaches puberty well before her peers may find her early physical development an embarrassment to which it is difficult to adjust. Much more common, however, is the problem of the adolescent who because he is slower than his peers in developing secondary sexual characteristics is filled with shame and self-contempt. While most of these growth disturbances are self-correcting, their damaging influence on the person's self-esteem may continue long after the disturbance has passed and thus breed emotional problems in adulthood.

Even more crucial than variations in physique or in development are physical handicaps resulting either from injury or from disease. Regardless of age, physical impairment creates emotional stress, whether in the child who is born with a cleft palate or in the octogenarian who is suddenly stricken with arthritis. And such stress can result in abnormal behavior (Bernabeu, 1958). The blind and the deaf are typically prone to adjustment problems throughout their lives. And American veterans' hospitals are filled with ex-soldiers still suffering from psychological reactions to wounds received in the Korean and Vietnam wars.

Of all the forms of physiological damage, neurological impairment appears to have the most direct relationship to abnormal behavior (Garmezy, 1968). As we shall see in Chapter 14, any damage to the central nervous system, particularly in the brain, as a result of injuries, tumors or other disease can result in a massive revolution of the personality. Since the 1930s there has been a great deal of research in this area, and we are now able to relate a number of behavioral abnormalities directly to specific kinds of neurological damage. Furthermore, physiological theorists working in this area argue that many other types of abnormal behavior—particularly schizophrenia and depression—may eventually be found to emanate from neurological impairments beyond the scope of our present methods of detection.

In recent years, physiological theorists have also shown increased concern with the effects of drugs and nutritional deficiencies on behavior. Malnutrition has long been known to affect physical development and in severe cases to cause neurological impairment as well, which in turn would affect psychological functioning. Likewise, certain vitamin deficiencies are suspected of having a role in some types of abnormal behavior.

Furthermore, since the 1960s, when marijuana, barbiturates, amphetamines, and heroin suddenly became a part of the American scene, there has been a new interest in the psychological effects of drugs—and not only of these more recent arrivals, but also of such old stand-bys as tobacco, alcohol, and caffeine.

While the above are only a very few of the physiological theories that have been advanced to account for abnormal behavior, they should be sufficient to indicate that the relationship between physiological and psychological functioning cannot be ignored. Indeed, it is because of the unquestionable role of psychological impairment in a number of forms of abnormal behavior (e.g., mental retardation, general paresis, cerebral arteriosclerosis) that the medical model, which we have discussed in Chapter 1, continues to receive so much support. It remains to be proven, however, that this model, which regards psychopathology *solely* as an organic problem, is applicable to all or even to a substantial proportion of behavioral abnormalities.

The Biological Perspective Like the physiological perspective, the *biological perspective* is not a single unified theory of psychopathology, but a group of limited subtheories focusing on specific pathologies and varying widely in the extent of their claims and in their degree of empirical support. Hence our discussion of the biological perspective in this section is in no way intended to cover the subject as a whole, but merely to introduce the reader to the major problems and assumptions of the perspective and thus prepare him for the more specific biological theories that will appear in later chapters.

The role of genetics in abnormal behavior—and for that matter in all aspects of human functioning—is bewilderingly complex. Gregor Mendel, the Austrian monk who "fathered" modern genetics, believed that genes were either dominant or recessive and accordingly either succeeded or failed in translating themselves into the physical traits of the organism. If this theory had survived the test of research, the task of genetic researchers would be a great deal simpler. However, since Mendel's time it has been discovered that the degree to which a gene will be manifested in the organism does not depend simply on dominance or recessiveness but also on that gene's complicated interactions with numerous other genes.

Because of these complexities, it is only in the last two or three decades that researchers have begun to make any genuine progress in relating genetics to behavior disturbances. And to date, only a very few forms of abnormal behavior have been shown to be directly traceable to genetic defects. Two such genetically based abnormalities are mongolism (Down's syndrome) and Turner's syndrome, both of which involve mental retardation. As for direct connections between defective gene combinations and other forms of psychological disorder, there is abundant speculation but little firm evidence.

More popular than the belief in direct genetic causation of abnormal behavior is the *diasthesis-stress* theory, which holds that certain genes or gene combinations give rise to a diasthesis or predisposition toward a disorder and that if this diasthesis is combined with certain kinds of environmental stress, abnormal behavior will result. Studies within the past twenty years seem to indicate that just as a tendency to develop diabetes, heart disease, and certain types of cancer can be genetically transmitted, so can a predisposition toward certain kinds of behavioral disturbances (Kallmann, 1953; Rosenthal, 1971). Research in this area has focused particularly on schizophrenia, and as we shall see in Chapter 12, we now have fairly firm evidence that

---

Nonpsychological Perspectives

Physiological perspective	Abnormal behavior is caused in part by physiological factors such as exaggerated body types, growth disturbances, physical handicaps, and neurological damage.
Biological perspective	Abnormal behavior may be caused either by genetic defects alone or by the combination of genetic predisposition and environmental stress.

genetics does in fact play a role in the development of this form of psychosis.

Genetic research on abnormal behavior is an exceedingly complicated matter, since investigators are constantly faced with the question of whether an abnormal trait is the result of unfriendly genes or an unfriendly environment, or a combination of the two. However, such difficulties seem to have spurred rather than deterred genetic research, and within the past several years such research has been recognized as a whole new field of study, called behavior genetics.

Like physiological findings, the findings of behavior genetics have had the effect of lending support to the medical model, although, as we have seen, these findings are far from conclusive. However, if in the future it is proved, as some genetic theorists argue, that genetic influences are responsible for a substantial number of mental disturbances, then the impact of such a discovery could be very great. The medical model would of course become even more firmly entrenched. Furthermore, people suffering from mental disorders might be encouraged (or required) to refrain from bearing children, and those children who *are* born of such parents might be given special medical and psychological attention in order to compensate for unfavorable genetic influences. Such measures have already been contemplated, but a great deal of further research is necessary before such a decidedly genetic approach to abnormal behavior could be considered justified.

SUMMARY

Arising in reaction to the determinism of psychodynamic and behavioral theory and in response to the spiritual problems of mid-twentieth-century life, humanistic and existential psychology take a uniquely nonmechanical view of human existence. Though differing in certain respects, they are united by their shared emphases on the individual's subjectivity, his uniqueness, his capacity for growth, his freedom to choose his fate, and his responsibility for his fate.

Humanistic psychology, represented in this text by the theories of Carl Rogers and Abraham Maslow, sees the human being as basically good, rational, and socially oriented. The human being's prime motivation is the drive toward self-actualization, the fulfillment of his capabilities. Abnormal behavior results from a blocking of this self-actualization, either because of an incongruence between the individual's experience and his self-image (Rogers' theory) or because of a failure to satisfy basic needs (Maslow's theory).

Existential psychology stresses the individual's state of constant "becoming" and his "here and now"—that is, his present subjective world. Viktor Frankl, a leading existential theorist, has concentrated on the spiritual aspect of behavioral disturbances and argues that many such disturbances are caused by a frustration of the individual's effort to find meaning in his life.

Though similar enough to be united in a single perspective, humanistic and existential psychology differ in that the humanists place greater emphasis on the individual as an isolated unit and on his satisfaction of his biological and psychological needs, while the existentialists focus more on the individual's relationship to the human condition as a whole and on the question of his responsibility.

Differing substantially from the medical, psychodynamic, and behaviorist interpretations of abnormal behavior, the humanistic-existential perspective has had little impact on these more traditional approaches. Its major influence has been on the development of group therapies.

While criticized for its heavy reliance on the concept of the self and for its use of inferred constructs, the humanistic-existential perspective has also been justly credited with treating the individual as a dignified being, with addressing itself directly to the major personal concerns of human beings, and with calling attention to the positive aspects of human psychology.

Other psychological perspectives on abnormal behavior include the interpersonal perspective, which views abnormality as a disturbance in interpersonal relations and focuses particularly on family interactions; the psychosocial perspective, which holds that society contributes substantially to abnormality, particularly by labeling people as "sick"; and the cognitive perspective, which sees the source of abnormal behavior in the individual's assumptions and in his ways of processing information. Finally, there are two major nonpsychological perspectives on abnormal behavior: the physiological perspective, which investigates nongenetic physical determinants of behavioral disturbances, and the biological perspective, which studies genetically transmitted organic causes of abnormality.

II The Emotional Disorders

Of all the forms of psychological distress that we will describe in this book, the neuroses are certainly the most various—and the most common. Many of us have difficulty with certain areas of our own lives: some people, for example, just cannot go to large, crowded parties; others seem to sabotage their own success on examinations or at job interviews; and others feel themselves unsuccessful unless they are constantly in the limelight, the "life of every party." For most of us, these "hang-ups" do not seriously interfere with our lives. For others, however, such quirks become a major source of worry and anxiety—in other words, a major impediment to the person's daily functioning.

For years Ann had been afraid of animals. It began when as a small girl she had been terrified by the huge guard dogs kept by people in the apartment building in which she lived. Since that time, whenever she was around animals—cats, horses, cows, or especially dogs—she felt afraid: her palms became wet; she trembled all over; she had a terrible feeling of apprehension that she was going to get hurt; she even found it hard to "think straight." All that she wanted to do when an animal was present was to get away, to run. She knew this was irrational—particularly in situations in which it was obvious that the animal would not harm her, such as when the dog was on a leash securely held by someone, or when she was in her car with the windows rolled up, or when the animal was on TV—as in a cat-food commercial. Nevertheless, she would feel anxious and afraid. At times, too, it was embarrassing. For example, she might be shopping with friends when they would encounter a Seeing Eye dog; she would have to leave the store. Or if she was visiting someone and a dog or cat wandered into the room, her fear was so great that she would have to get out of her host's home. Most of her friends and family accepted Ann's idiosyncracy and "helped" her avoid confrontation with animals. But the problem of anxiety over animals always plagued Ann, causing her to limit her activities and making her life unpleasant.

The concept of anxiety, which has been introduced and discussed in Chapters 2 through 4, is basic to an understanding of the neuroses. Anxiety may be characterized as a feeling of dread, apprehension, or fear; it can involve such physiological changes as increased heartbeat, breathing, and perspiration; and there may be a sense of confusion or difficulty in thinking. People tend to avoid the situation or situations that lead to these uncomfortable feelings. They develop various ways of doing this. It is when

5 The Neuroses, Personality Disorders, and Transient Situational Disorders

these behaviors themselves become limiting, irrational, and disruptive that the person exhibiting them may be considered neurotic.

Briefly, the *neurotic* may be described as an unadaptable personality. This inability to adapt to the stresses and vicissitudes of life can be reduced to four major components. First, as DSM-II states, "anxiety is the chief characteristic of the neuroses" (1968, p. 39). The neurotic's anxiety may be experienced directly, or he may maneuver it out of awareness through a number of different defensive tactics. However, whether he is fully aware of his anxiety or not, the neurotic feels threatened, fearful, and inadequate in situations that would normally inspire no dismay in others.

Second, in addition to experiencing anxiety directly, the neurotic, because he is so anxious, tends to become a master of some form of avoidance behavior. Rather than confront life squarely—coping with its stresses, savoring its rewards, and enduring its defeats—the neurotic generally develops some means of blocking off a major portion of this unpleasant input. He may narrow his activities down to the constant repetition of some apparently useless and ritualistic behavior. Or he may develop some physical symptom such as blindness or partial paralysis that makes it impossible for him to engage in a normal range of activity. Or in the extreme case, he may simply abandon his identity during stressful periods, either through blacking out his conscious mind or through escaping into another identity. Indeed, it may be said that various types of neurosis are simply descriptions of different types of avoidance behavior—that is, different ways of avoiding anxiety.

Third, the neurotic's interpretations of reality are typically somewhat distorted. Preoccupied with his own fears and inadequacies, he tends to construe everything else in the world in light of his own difficulties. He may brood for days over someone else's random remark that he believes was directed at him. In his mind, work deadlines may assume awesome, Judgment Day proportions. And minor misdeeds can become major sources of guilt. In short, of all the human beings on earth, the neurotic is the most excruciatingly self-conscious, and this intensified consciousness of his own anxious self causes him to interpret all other stimuli in terms of the rigid cognitive formulas created by his anxiety.

Finally, though the neurotic does not know how to correct his behavior—and typically believes that it is beyond any hope of correction—he is at least aware that his mental functioning is disturbed. Despite the fact that most of his perceptions are to some degree distorted, he still knows that things are going badly between him and the world, and it is this limited degree of self-knowledge that constitutes one of the major differences between the neurotic and the psychotic, whose perceptions of himself and of his environment are considerably more distorted. Furthermore, because he has at least this much insight, it is the rare neurotic who is not extremely unhappy.

Considering the unrewarding quality of the neurotic's behavior and the fact that he *knows* it is unrewarding, we are faced with the obvious question of why he persists in such a self-defeating pattern. Mowrer (1948) calls this puzzling situation the *neurotic paradox* and solves the puzzle as follows. While the neurotic response creates a general disturbance in the individual's life, it still satisfies what he experiences as his most pressing single need: the need to reduce his level of anxiety. Furthermore, because the neurotic response allows the individual to avoid confronting the anxiety-producing situation, he never has the opportunity to test his fears against the situation itself, to discover that they are inappropriate, and thus to discard them. Hence through the classic mechanism of avoidance behavior, described in Chapter 3, the neurotic response is "stamped in" by negative reinforcement (i.e., the fact that the response reduces anxiety), and the response can never be extinguished because the feared stimulus is always avoided.

In the present chapter we will examine the major forms of neurosis, along with two related categories of psychological disturbance, personality disorders and transient situational disturbances. We will then discuss how these disorders have been interpreted and treated within the context of the various perspectives outlined in Chapters 2, 3, and 4.

THE NEUROSES

In the following section we will describe six major recognized forms of neurosis—anxiety neurosis,

Fig. 5.1   Types of neurotic disorders and their characteristics. (1) Hypochondriac: chronic preoccupation with bodily functions and fears of developing a disease. (2) Phobic: debilitating fear of an object or situation. (3) Obsessive-compulsive: held by a compelling irrational thought or action. (4) Hysterical: temporary loss or impairment of some function. (5) Neurasthenic: chronic complaints of weakness and exhaustion. (6) Depressive: chronic sadness and apathy. (7) Anxiety: diffuse and generalized fear engulfing the personality.

phobic neurosis, hysterical neurosis, obsessive-compulsive neurosis, neurasthenic neurosis, and hypochondriacal neurosis—each of which may be seen as a different variation on the theme of anxiety and avoidance. (A seventh important category, depressive neurosis, will be treated in Chapter 7, along with the more debilitating forms of depression.) Finally, we shall consider a recently proposed category, existential neurosis.

Anxiety Neurosis

Anxiety neurosis is the most common of the neurotic disorders, accounting for some 30 to 40 percent of the diagnoses of neurosis. Anxiety neurosis is characterized by diffuse and generalized fears impossible to manage through avoidance. Indeed, the whole personality may be engulfed by anxiety.

For the most part, anxiety neurosis manifests itself as a state of *chronic anxiety*, in which the person is jumpy, irritable, and frequently upset. He expresses his apprehensions in a great many verbalized fears and worries. Yet he is unable to specify what it is that is generating his fears—a condition that Freud called *free-floating anxiety*. The anxiety neurotic may have nightmares in which things close in on him or in which he is lost or abandoned. Furthermore, his daily coping is severely impaired. He forgets appointments, has difficulty making decisions, and if placed in a situation of extra stress, may become disorganized.

Various somatic symptoms often accompany chronic anxiety. The person may complain of stiff, aching muscles, the result of sustained muscle tension. His appetite tends to be poor, and he may be troubled by indigestion and by a frequent need to urinate. Sleeping patterns are also disturbed. The individual may have insomnia, or he may begin awakening suddenly in the night. In the morning he feels tired rather than refreshed.

From time to time the person suffering from chronic anxiety may have *anxiety attacks*, episodes in which his already heightened state of tension mounts to an acute and overwhelming level. Usually these attacks last anywhere from fifteen minutes to an hour. The person may report a shivering sensation. His heart begins to pound loudly. He perspires and may gasp for breath. A feeling of inescapable disaster overcomes him. He tries to escape, but there is no place to escape to. When the attack subsides, he feels exhausted, as if he has gone through an extremely traumatic experience, which indeed he has.

One of the most demoralizing aspects of these attacks is their unpredictability. As the following case illustrates, they can occur at any time of the day or night, simply immobilizing the person in whatever situation he happens to find himself:

Ralph was in his last year of law school. For three years he had been extremely tense. Each semester the fear of failing his exams had haunted him, yet each time he had managed to pull himself through. As his last set of final exams approached, however, his thoughts about the embarrassment of failure—and particularly about his family's reactions if he failed— became more intense.

It was then that Ralph began to have a series of anxiety attacks. Since he never knew when they would occur, he began to avoid crowds, fearing he might faint on the spot or even suffocate. If the attacks came while he was in school, he would leave the classroom and pace about in the hall or run out of the building, but these actions accomplished nothing. Sometimes the attacks came at night. Ralph would awaken in a cold sweat, his heart pounding. He would get up, pace the floor, and, when this brought no relief, return to bed, clinging desperately to the mattress until the attack subsided.

Finally, the time for his examinations arrived, and Ralph somehow managed to pass. However, by graduation time, he was worn out and highly irritable, telling people off at the slightest provocation. On the advice of his family, he entered psychotherapy (adapted from Lundin, 1965, pp. 207–208).

Ralph's case is typical in every respect except one: despite chronic and acute anxiety, he managed to struggle through his final ordeal. In most cases, the anxiety is so disruptive the person has to give up certain commitments—perhaps leave school or give up his job—until he is better able to cope with the stresses of everyday life.

In the most extreme form of an anxiety attack, a *panic reaction*, anxiety is so severe and prolonged, possibly lasting even for days, that the person becomes disorganized and disoriented. If a panic reaction occurs, medical attention is necessary.

Phobic Neurosis

A *phobia* is an intense and debilitating fear of some object or situation which, as the phobic person may realize, actually presents no major threat. Most of us can ride in elevators, enter closets, go out in crowds, and meet strangers without feeling anxious. Even in a potentially dangerous situation—on an airplane trip, for example—we manage with varying degrees of success to keep our fears in check. But

Fig. 5.2   The person in this illustration is experiencing an acute anxiety reaction or panic. His subjective experience may be a catastrophic feeling that something terrible but unknown and unexplainable is happening to him. He cannot determine the source of his dread, and he is overwhelmingly anxious and psychologically immobilized. (The Shriek, Edvard Munch; Collection, Museum of Modern Art, New York, Mathew T. Mellon Fund.)

for the phobic person, specific stimuli of this nature can trigger intense anxiety reactions, often involving physical symptoms such as faintness, heart palpitations, nausea, and trembling. Phobias can take many forms, since virtually any stimulus can come to elicit fear. A few of the more common phobias are

1. *acrophobia:* fear of high places.
2. *agoraphobia:* fear of open places.
3. *claustrophobia:* fear of closed places.
4. *gynephobia:* fear of women.
5. *hydrophobia:* fear of water.
6. *mysophobia:* fear of dirt.
7. *ophidiophobia:* fear of nonpoisonous snakes.

Diagnosticians sometimes report other, more idiosyncratic phobias, such as the case of an opera singer whose phobia was specific to singing one specific note, two Cs above middle C, though she could sing higher notes. Once in a public performance her voice had cracked while she was singing this note, and thereafter she avoided any score that included it—a condition which, needless to say, did nothing to further her career and which eventually brought her into treatment.

Although the phobic person may be unable to explain the origin of his phobia or the reasons for its intensity, he is very able to identify the stimulus that arouses his fear and may spend considerable time and energy avoiding that stimulus. For example, a city dweller with claustrophobia would probably spend much time walking up and down

PHOBIAS:
A Brief Catalog

Phobias are named by combining the Greek word for the feared object or situation with the suffix "-phobia," derived from the Greek word "to fear." Since this formula can be applied to any object or situation whatsoever—and since people seem capable of developing phobias for almost any object or situation whatsoever—the naming of phobias has provided considerable diversion for investigators with a fondness for devising diagnostic labels. As a result, phobic neurosis is one of the most extensively subclassified of all psychopathologies. We have already listed seven phobias that are seen with some frequency. Other fairly common phobias and their objects are

algophobia: pain
astrapophobia: lightning
hematophobia: blood
monophobia: being alone
nyctophobia: darkness
zoophobia: animals, or a specific animal
pathophobia: disease
syphilophobia: syphilis
xenophobia: strangers
pyrophobia: fire
ocholophobia: crowds
ailurophobia: cats

Considerably more exotic, but nonetheless duly christened in the literature of phobias, are the following:

melissophobia: bees
entomophobia: insects
homilophobia: sermons
ergasiophobia: work
gephyrophobia: crossing a bridge
erthyrophobia: blushing in public
pnigophobia: choking
haphephobia: being touched
emetophobia: vomiting
taphophobia: being buried alive
parthenophobia: virgins
eosophobia: dawn
gymnophobia: naked bodies
heliophobia: sunlight
gamophobia: marriage
enosiophobia: committing an unpardonable sin

Source: R. M. Goldenson, *The Encyclopedia of Human Behavior: Psychology, Psychiatry, and Mental Health,* Vol. 2. Garden City, N.Y.: Doubleday, 1970.

stairs to avoid elevators. Likewise, a suburban housewife with a phobia for driving will probably have great difficulty. However, it appears that while phobias are fairly common—appearing in 7.7 percent of the population, according to Agras, Sylvester, and Oliveau (1969)—only a very small portion of these are truly debilitating. Particularly if the phobic stimulus is highly specific and is not a usual factor in one's environment, the phobic person is generally able to avoid it with ease and thus can manage quite well. For example, a New Yorker with a phobia for bears need only avoid going to the zoo.

Despite being linked to highly specific stimuli, phobic reactions often show a degree of *generalization* from the object or situation that may have occasioned the original anxiety response. For example, a person who has been pinned in an overturned car for several hours may develop not only a phobia for enclosure in cars but a generalized claustrophobia in which he fears any enclosed place—an elevator, a closet, a subway, and so on.

The mechanics of phobias are still open to a great deal of speculation. One factor, however, is fairly clear, and that is that after the first association of fear with the phobic stimulus, this response undergoes a process called *incubation,* in which the fear intensifies as the person avoids the stimulus. It is to forestall incubation that, for example, a person who has been thrown from a horse is encouraged to take to the saddle again as soon as possible.

Hysterical Neurosis

As we have seen in Chapter 1, the study of hysteria has a long history. First discussed by Hippocrates in the fifth century B.C., this disorder formed the center around which raged the nineteenth century's psychogenic-vs.-somatogenic debate, and it served as the basis for the pioneering work of psychodynamic theory, *Studies in Hysteria,* in which Freud and Breuer described the psychogenic source of hysteria and gave examples of their "cathartic method" of treating the syndrome. Essentially, *hysterical neurosis* involves the involuntary loss or impairment of some normal function, either physical or psychological, with complete denial of anxiety by the person experiencing the loss of function. There are two major categories of hysteria, the conversion type and the dissociative type.

Hysterical Neurosis: Conversion Type In *conversion reactions* the individual develops some motor or sensory dysfunction—typically blindness, deafness, partial or total paralysis, or anesthesia (loss of sensation in some part of the body)—for which there is no organic basis. These symptoms can sometimes appear and disappear with amazing rapidity. Though Charcot felt that hysterics might suffer from neurological weakness, it is he who was responsible for the famous pronouncement that the hysterical symptoms themselves make "neurological nonsense." That is, the symptoms do not conform to those that would be manifested in a true neurological disorder. For example, in *glove anesthesia* the hysterical patient reports that his hand is numb from the tips of the fingers to a clear cutoff point at the wrist, whereas if he were suffering from an actual neurological impairment, the line of demarcation between sensitive and insensitive areas would be much less precise, with some intermediate areas of semisensitivity.

It is important to remember, however, that these reactions, though not organically based, are still developed unconsciously. It is this factor that distinguishes conversion reactions from *malingering*—that is, the conscious faking of symptoms in order to avoid some duty or responsibility. Furthermore, hysterical dysfunctions should not be confused with psychophysiological (also called psychosomatic) disorders (Chapter 6), in which there is an actual neurological conversion of emotional stress into such organic symptoms as ulcers, migraine headaches, and high blood pressure.

One unique characteristic of the conversion reaction is that the individual often seems not at all disturbed by his disability—a response that Charcot's famous pupil, Pierre Janet, called *la belle indifférence*, the "beautiful indifference" of the hysteric. Though the individual can typically describe his symptom for hours in the fullest and most vivid terms, he does not seem particularly anxious to part with it; by repressing his anxiety and converting it into a physical disability, the hysteric experiences considerable relief and thus, at least unconsciously, does not look forward to reversing the conversion process.

The following case is an obvious example of the role of repression in conversion reactions:

At the age of thirteen Kate Fox was admitted to the hospital with partial paralysis of the left leg. She also showed extreme nervousness and a loss of appetite. Kate expressed concern about placing any weight on her left leg while lying down. Prior to this, Kate had been in excellent health and had been progressing well in school.

When first questioned at the hospital concerning her family, Kate spoke of the kindness and care her

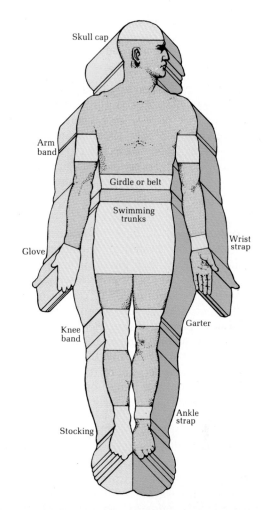

Fig. 5.3   Illustrated above are the areas of the body in which hysterical anesthesia or paralysis typically occurs. Although there is a loss of sensitivity, the pattern of numbness does not correspond to neural pathways and is therefore indicative of psychological rather than neurological disorder. (Adapted from L. J. Karnosh and E. M. Zucker, Handbook of Psychiatry, St. Louis: Mosby, 1945.)

parents had given her but was reluctant to elaborate on these remarks. Only after a sudden emotional outburst did she reveal some of the events that had taken place three years earlier. She told of an affair between her mother and a roomer in their home. One night Kate had overheard them talking about their plans to go off together and to take Kate with them. The couple did in fact leave for a time, without Kate, and divorce seemed imminent. But Mr. Fox, Kate, and her three sisters persuaded Mrs. Fox to return. There ensued a series of violent scenes between the parents, during which Kate and her sisters would cry and pray together. The parents' marital situation did not really begin to improve until one of Kate's sisters threatened to commit suicide (adapted from Carter, 1937, pp. 219–221).

As we have mentioned in Chapter 1, conversion reactions were quite common during the nineteenth century, but they have since become increasingly rare, accounting for only about 5 percent of all treated neuroses. Though they are generally seen in women, they may also occur in men and were in fact an extremely common complaint among combat troops in both world wars.

Hysterical Neurosis: Dissociative Type In *dissociative reactions* the hysterical impairment affects psychological rather than physical functioning. As the name indicates, a dissociative reaction involves the dissociation or splitting off of certain behaviors from the person's normal identity or state of consciousness. DSM-II distinguishes four forms of dissociative reaction: amnesia, somnambulism, fugue, and multiple personality. Like the conversion reactions, these disorders are relatively uncommon; together they constitute only about 5 percent of diagnosed neuroses.

Amnesia As we shall see in Chapter 14, amnesia, the partial or total forgetting of past experiences, often appears in organic brain syndromes. Hysterical amnesia is distinguished from organically based amnesia in several ways. First, it tends to appear and disappear rather suddenly. Second, the hysterical amnesiac is often selective in what he forgets; the "blank" period may include events of a traumatic nature, such as a war experience or perhaps an extramarital affair surrounded by guilt and anxiety. Finally, because the events forgotten by the hysterical amnesiac are simply repressed rather than truly lost altogether (as is the case in organic amnesias), they can often be recovered in hypnosis.

In the typical case of hysterical amnesia, the individual does not know who or where he is. He does not recognize family or friends, nor can he tell you his name, his address, or anything else about himself. However, basic learned abilities generally remain intact: the individual can speak and read, add and subtract, for example. And often he can execute even more specialized tasks. If his profession is carpentry, for example, he may still be able to build a cabinet, although he will not know that he has ever been a carpenter. The amnesic state may last anywhere from a day to several years, and in

some cases it continues for the rest of the person's life. Interestingly, in hysterical amnesia, as in conversion reactions, the individual often seems considerably less perturbed by his condition than those around him. Like *la belle indifférence*, this amnesic calm is often interpreted as an indication of the relief experienced through the repression of anxiety.

Somnambulism Somnambulism, also known as "sleepwalking," is a dissociative disorder in which one part of the personality controls behavior while what is thought to be the usual personality "sleeps" in the sense that it is inoperative. Contrary to popular notions, somnambulism can occur during the day (*diurnal somnambulism*) as well as at night (*nocturnal somnambulism*). Nor does the somnambulist generally walk around with his eyes closed and his hands stretched out in front of him, as is commonly thought.

During a typical diurnal somnambulist episode, the person stops whatever he is doing and wanders about in a daze or acts out an event. He then returns to his previous activity with no recollection of the episode. While in the somnambulist state, he responds only minimally to his environment. For example, he may walk out on a window ledge with no realization of the danger involved. Should he be awakened during the episode, he will act confused and have no memory of how he got to wherever he is. In nocturnal somnambulism, the pattern is the same. The person will get out of bed and begin walking around. He may even dress and leave home, only to return later, undress again, and return to bed. When morning comes he will have no memory of his wanderings.

Sometimes somnambulism may occur as a reaction to some trauma in the patient's history, as in the famous case of Irène, reported by Janet:

Irène was a poor French girl who had nursed her ailing mother through the last stages of tuberculosis. When the mother finally died, Irène desperately tried to blow breath into the dead woman's lungs. After the funeral, Irène began acting strangely. At times she would suddenly stop whatever she was doing and reenact the death of her mother. She would then resume her previous activity. Irène also had episodes in which she seemed to be preparing for her own suicide. She would lie on the floor, arranging her body as though she were lying across a railroad track waiting for a train to run over her. Then, after a startled shriek, she would get up. Sometimes she would repeat this behavior several times before resuming her previous activity (adapted from Janet, 1929, pp. 29–31).

Fugue   A condition related to both amnesia and somnambulism is *fugue*, in which, as the name indicates, the individual actually flees his anxiety-ridden identity and environment. He may leave for work one day and simply not return for days, weeks, or even years. During the period of the fugue, he may just spend the day feeding ducks in the park, or he may travel to another country, assume a different identity, and enter upon a totally new life. During all this time he will appear fairly normal to observers. When at last he "wakes up," he will be completely amnesic for the events which have occurred during the fugue. The last thing he remembers is leaving for work that morning. As for how he got to where he is, he has no idea. In some instances a fugue may begin after a clear precipitating event, as in the following case:

A forty-year-old lawyer who had been married for the last ten years was having an affair with the wife of one of his neighbors. From time to time he would experience intense anxiety over the possibility of being discovered. One evening while driving home from his office, he noticed that the driver behind him was the husband of his mistress, and he assumed he was being followed. Three days later he found himself over two hundred miles from home. The last thing he remembered was getting into his car to go home.

Multiple Personality   An even more extreme form of dissociation is the *multiple personality*, a rare condition which, ever since the publication of Robert Louis Stevenson's story *The Strange Case of Dr. Jekyll and Mr. Hyde*, has held a certain fascination for the layman and which has consequently become a stock in trade of movie and television dramas. Usually a multiple personality consists of two or more complete behavior organizations, each well developed and highly distinct from the other. In what we call the *alternating personality*, there are two identities that alternate one with another, each having amnesia for the thoughts and actions of the other. A second type of multiple personality involves one or more dominant personalities and one or more subordinate ones. While the dominant personality is ostensibly controlling the person's behavior, the subordinate personality, fully aware of the thoughts and actions of the dominant personality, continues to operate subconsciously and to make its presence felt now and again through various covert means. In such cases, the subordinate personality is said to be *coconscious* (Prince, 1905) with the dominant personality. When the coconscious personality finally surfaces, it can discuss in detail the interesting problems of the other personality. Of such a type was the celebrated case described by Thigpen and Cleckley in their book *The Three Faces of Eve* (1957), summarized here:

Eve White was the original dominant personality. She had no knowledge of the existence of her second personality, Eve Black, although Eve Black had been alternating with Eve White for some years. Whenever Eve Black surfaced, all that Eve White could report was that she had "black-outs." Eve Black, on the other hand, was coconscious with Eve White, knew everything that she did, and would talk about her with undisguised flippancy and contempt. Eve White was bland, quiet, and serious—a rather dull personality. Eve Black, on the other hand, was carefree, mischievous, and uninhibited. She would "come out" at the most inappropriate times, leaving Eve White in constant difficulty. During treatment, there emerged a third personality, Jane, who was coconscious with both Eve White and Eve Black, though she had no memory of their activities up to the time of her appearance. More mature than the other two, Jane seemed to have emerged as the result of the therapeutic process. Eventually, a fourth personality, Evelyn Lancaster, developed, and she seemed to be an integration of the other three.

Obsessive-Compulsive Neurosis

In *obsessive-compulsive neurosis* the individual is repeatedly compelled to hold in his mind a thought that he may consider irrational (an *obsession*) or to engage in an action that he may consider irrational (a *compulsion*)—or, most commonly, to do both. In all three cases the person is quite distressed, often by the irrationality of his thought or action, but especially by his inability to control it; it simply forces its way in and takes over.

Mild obsessions strike many of us from time to time. We may dwell repeatedly on some song lyric, or our thoughts may keep running back to a story we read in the paper or to the question of whether we remembered to leave out food for the cat before going to work. But these minor obsessions pass, and we go on about our business. Pathological obsessions, on the other hand, do not pass; they recur day after day. Furthermore, they often have a rather prurient or violent quality, which makes them even more demoralizing to their typically well-behaved victims. An illustrative case is that of Alice James, the sister of philosopher William James and novelist Henry James. As a young adult she became obsessed with the urge to hit her beloved father over the head.

THE TWENTY-ONE FACES OF EVE

Thigpen and Cleckley's case history *The Three Faces of Eve* was a true story as far as it went—that is, until Eve moved away from Augusta, Georgia, where she was being treated by these two doctors. Recently, however, it has come to light that Eve's story by no means ended at that point. In 1975 a woman called Chris Sizemore, an apparently normal and unremarkable middle-aged housewife from Fairfax, Virginia, revealed that she was "Eve" and that Eve Black, Eve White, and Jane were only three of the many personalities with which she has had to struggle throughout her life. Indeed, in her forty-eight years Mrs. Sizemore has manifested twenty-one separate identities, each with its own speech patterns, habits, preferences, and moral code. "I had at one time about every kind of [phonograph] record you could imagine because each personality had its own taste," reported Mrs. Sizemore (p. 26). The personalities invariably came in sets of three, with considerable conflict among them. In one set, there was a personality who collected spoons, while the other two wondered what all those spoons were doing around the house. "If I had learned to sew as one personality and then tried to sew as another, I couldn't do it. Driving a car was the same. Some of my personalities couldn't drive" (p. 4). The same problem had plagued her in school. If one personality went to a lecture or read a book and another personality was in charge when the time came for an exam, this latter personality would have no idea how to answer the exam questions.

When she was younger, a particular personality would dominate for a period of several days. In more recent years, however, her personality would change at least once a day. The transition from one personality to another was usually marked by a sudden and very painful headache. The headache would last for about ten seconds, during which Mrs. Sizemore was conscious of nothing—"there was an instant where there was no personality at all; there was no existence" (p. 26)—and then the pain would disappear, and a new personality would be in control.

Mrs. Sizemore feels that she has now recovered—a fact that she and her present psychiatrist, Dr. Tony Tsitos, ascribe to her realization a year ago that all of her different personalities were truly parts of herself, and not invaders from the outside. Whatever the cause, Mrs. Sizemore has now, for the first time since childhood, clung to one stable personality for over a year. "You don't know how wonderful it is," she said, "to go to bed at night and know that it will be you that wakes up the next day" (p. 4).

Mrs. Sizemore's husband, her second, married Jane, the third face of Thigpen and Cleckley's "Eve." Like all her other personalities, Jane eventually died, and Mr. Sizemore, along with Mrs. Sizemore's children by her first and second marriages, saw her through her various transformations, and witnessed the anguish they caused. Furthermore, the family kept Mrs. Sizemore's secret from everyone until this year.

Thus Chris Sizemore's story is much bigger than *The Three Faces of Eve*. It was not until the summer of 1975 that she finally saw the popular movie that was made from this book. "It was good," she said. "Joanne Woodward did an excellent job of acting. But after all I've lived through, the movie just seemed so unimportant" (p. 26).

Source: Donnell Nunes, "The Anguish Behind the Three Faces of Eve," *New York Post*, September 15, 1975, pp. 4 and 26.

Horrified at this idea, she protected herself from carrying it out by spending most of her adult life in bed and away from her family.

Often, however, obsessions are considerably more lurid. A mother may become obsessed with the idea of drowning her baby in its bath, or a man may become obsessed with the fear that he will sodomize his wife's favorite dog. Predictably, the victims of these more unsavory obsessions are usually swamped with guilt and anxiety. Another common type of obsession occurs in which the individual dwells repeatedly on some problem, often of a rather absurd nature, as in the case (cited by Kolb, 1973) of a well-educated patient whose thoughts were continually dominated by the question of why a chair had four legs rather than one.

Compulsions tend to be more chaste in character, though they may be equally irrational and disruptive to the person's life. Some compulsions have a totally senseless character; for example, a woman may be compelled to open and close all of her desk drawers when she arrives at her office in the morning However, many compulsions are related to a morbid concern for orderliness, cleanliness, or the carrying out of some duty. This category would include the compulsive hand-washer. Also of this type would be the person who has to have everything in his bedroom arranged in a certain highly intricate order before he can go to sleep, or the person who no sooner goes to bed than he is compelled to get up and make sure that he has locked the front door—a process that may be repeated six or seven times before the exhausted and still uncertain individual finally falls asleep. In the latter case, the person is obviously suffering from both an obsession and a compulsion, which is the most common pattern. Hand-washing compulsions, for example, are usually tied to obsessive fears that one's hands are contaminated with germs. Thus the recurrent thought of contamination sends the individual back again and again to the sink to wash his hands, no matter how chapped and raw they are from repeated scrubbing.

Neurasthenic Neurosis

Neurasthenic neurosis, also known as "the fatigue syndrome," is characterized by chronic complaints of weakness and exhaustion. In the sense that it involves somatic symptoms without an organic basis, neurasthenia resembles hysterical conversion reactions. However, according to DSM-II, the neurasthenic differs from the hysteric in that he feels genuine distress about his condition.

Neurasthenic neurosis seems to occur most frequently in the young or middle-aged housewife who feels confined and bored by her domestic duties and who may also harbor considerable resentment of her husband's wider range of activities and of his consequent "neglect" of her. Gradually she begins to complain of chronic tiredness and to restrict her activities. Producing dinner for the family or making a necessary phone call becomes "too much" for her. She begins sleeping more but still awakens feeling listless and weary. She may also begin having more specific complaints, such as headaches, insomnia, and hypersensitivity to light and sound. Typically, she becomes forgetful and finds it difficult to concentrate. A telling point, however, is the selectiveness of her exhausted state; in doing something that she truly wants to do, such as taking a trip or playing a game of golf, she may feel fine. Once she returns home, however, the exhaustion returns. Such a woman is usually extremely demanding in a subtle fashion and is highly dependent on her family, who usually tolerate her condition with a mixture of guilt and resentment.

The term "neurasthenia" (literally, exhaustion of the nerves) was first applied to this syndrome on the theory that it was due to a depletion of nerve energy from overwork. In the early 1900s, S. Weir Mitchell developed a treatment intended to correct the supposed depletion. Complete bed rest was required. The patient was to have no visitors, and the lights and sounds in his room were to be kept to a minimum. Following this treatment, which became known as the "rest cure," patients frequently felt better. However, once they returned to their former duties, the fatigue returned.

The fact of the matter is, of course, that our nerves do not become exhausted. The exhaustion of the neurasthenic is due not to physical stress but to psychological stress: boredom, discouragement, and frustration. Furthermore, in therapy, the neurasthenic often reveals much hostility and anxiety, which by creating increased muscle tension only aggravate the fatigue. And this lack of physical energy may itself contribute to a compounding of the psychological stress.

Hypochondriacal Neurosis

In *hypochondriacal neurosis* the individual converts his anxiety into a chronic preoccupation with his bodily functioning. Unlike the hysteric and the neurasthenic, he never actually translates his neurotic anxieties into a physical disability.* Instead, he simply spends each day waiting for the disability to set in and watching for the first signs of its dreaded onset. Such signs usually do not take long to appear. One day the heart may skip a beat, the bowel movement may not arrive precisely on time, or some suspicious ache or pain may appear. Immediately, the hypochondriac interprets this "symptom" as the first indication of the feared disease that he now assumes is at work throughout his body. Often, when he appears at the doctor's office, he has already diagnosed his condition, for he is usually an avid reader of articles on health in popular magazines. And when the medical examination reveals that he is perfectly healthy, he is typically disappointed and incredulous. Soon he will be back in

---

*It is interesting to consider that, since we live in a society in which physical illness is socially acceptable and anxiety is not, perhaps we are inadvertently fostering hypochondriacal neurosis.

the doctor's office with a further "sure" sign, or he may simply change doctors repeatedly.

It should be emphasized that the hypochondriacal neurotic is not faking either his "symptoms" or his fears. He truly feels whatever twinges, cramps, or bumps he reports, and he is sincerely afraid that he is being eaten up by some sinister malady. However, his misconceptions do not have the bizarre quality of the disease delusions experienced by psychotics, who will report that their feet are about to fall off, that their brains are shrinking, or that their livers are being carried away a piece at a time. Instead, the hypochondriacal neurotic tends to confine his anxieties to more ordinary syndromes, such as heart disease or cancer. His "symptoms," and consequently his diagnosis, may shift regularly, but the fears remain constant. Unable to obtain medical confirmation, he may comfort himself with "miracle" cures, with a vast variety of pills, or with a strenuous health regimen.

Existential Neurosis

We find no mention of *existential neurosis* in DSM-II. Nonetheless, this diagnostic category first named and described by Maddi (1967) is gaining considerable attention. According to Maddi, existential neurosis is characterized primarily by depersonalization (i.e., loss of self-identity) and apathy. It has a cognitive aspect, exemplified by the individual's chronic inability to believe in the truth of anything and by a lack of interest in whatever he is supposed to be doing. On the emotional side, the neurosis involves feelings of boredom that may be accompanied by periods of mild depression; however, the depressions become less frequent as the disorder progresses. In general, the existential neurotic simply feels that life is without meaning and that he himself lacks any personal force or identity.

The increasing appeal of existential neurosis as a legitimate diagnostic category is due in part to the greater attention being paid recently to existential and humanistic psychology. Those who support the new category feel that this disorder results from the stresses of living in a time of rapid social change and in a highly mechanized society which squelches individuality and personal satisfaction in favor of conformity and competition.

PERSONALITY DISORDERS

Like the neuroses, the *personality disorders* involve self-defeating behavior patterns in which, however, the individual remains in fairly good contact with

THE NEUROSES

Type	Symptomatology
Phobic neurosis	Intense fear and consequent avoidance of an object or situation that the individual acknowledges is harmless
Anxiety neurosis	A general sense of anxiety or dread extending over a wide variety of situations and sometimes escalating into periodic anxiety attacks
Hysterical neurosis, conversion type	The impairment of some physiological function (e.g., sight, hearing, sense of touch) without organic cause
Hysterical neurosis, dissociative type	The splitting off of certain behaviors from consciousness, as in amnesia, somnambulism, fugue, or multiple personality
Obsessive-compulsive neurosis	Involuntary rumination on an unwelcome thought and/or involuntary repetition of an unnecessary action
Neurasthenic neurosis	Chronic weakness and fatigue
Hypochondriacal neurosis	Chronic preoccupation with bodily functioning and chronic fear of diseases imagined to be present in the body
Existential neurosis	Apathy, depersonalization, purposelessness, and a sense that life is without meaning

reality. Nevertheless, there are important distinctions between the two categories:

In the psychoneurotic the symptoms are alien to the individual's way of living and are experienced as unwanted intruders. They are also often accompanied by much consciously felt anxiety. In the [individual with a] personality disorder the symptoms, far from being alien to the ordinary mode of existence, are part of the life style which has been adopted. Usually such symptoms, when they cause the patient real concern, may be likened to a dull ache, in contrast to the acute pain suffered by the neurotic. Quite commonly the individual suffering a personality disorder is more of a cause for concern to others than he is to himself (Zax and Stricker, 1963, p. 184).

A personality disorder, in short, is a deeply ingrained maladaptive pattern of behavior. Presumably adopted at an early age in order to cope with specific environmental stresses, the pattern, once adopted, is difficult to abandon. Furthermore, the individual may not be highly motivated to abandon it, since, as Zax and Stricker point out, he does not experience the overwhelming distress of the neurotic. Indeed, on a superficial level, he may think of himself as getting along quite adequately. And, in fact, some of the traits found in certain of the personality disorders may actually have a functional value in helping the individual to succeed financially and in nonintimate social situations. However, such benefits, when they appear, are heavily outweighed by losses in personal satisfaction.

DSM-II outlines ten different types of personality disorders (see box, pp. 24–25). In the present chapter we shall examine three of the more common types: the passive-aggressive personality, the hysterical personality, and the obsessive-compulsive personality. A fourth type, the antisocial personality, will be taken up in Chapter 8.

Passive-Aggressive Personality

As its name implies, the passive-aggressive personality involves both excessive passivity and excessive aggression. The relationship between the two behaviors is often concealed. In the *passive-dependent* form of the disorder, under conditions of mild stress the person acts helpless, anxious, and frankly dependent. He often makes heavy demands on people close to him. Although he goes out of his way to avoid disagreements, his subtle demands are seen as an outlet for the hostility he frequently feels toward those on whom he is so dependent.

In the *passive-aggressive* form of this disorder, the aggressive quality is more overt, but it surfaces in

Fig. 5.4 *The great film comedian W. C. Fields often played the part of characters who could be called passive-aggressive personalities. The type of person that he played was rarely overtly hostile; instead, he was complaining and sarcastic. The character rarely displayed direct aggression or harmed anyone, yet his half-hearted compliance often brought inconvenience, injury, or calamity to others. A good example of the passive-aggressive nature of a typical Fields' character is the contrast between what he said and how he said it. Although his words were sharp and sarcastic, he spoke in a soft, hesitant manner that masked the "bite" of his words.*

a nonthreatening way. The person may be stubborn, sullen, forgetful, or inefficient. He may procrastinate or use some other means of thwarting the demands of others while still seeming to be "doing his very best" to comply. Again, these tactics are interpreted as expressions of the hostility that the individual is afraid to act out directly.

The third form that this disorder can take, identified simply as the *aggressive* type, is marked by a very low threshold for frustration. When thwarted, such a person may have temper tantrums, become extremely abusive verbally, or engage in even more destructive behaviors. This is the person who always seems to have a chip on his shoulder. He may also be very demanding—obviously a common denominator of these three types and one which clearly expresses both their passivity and their aggressiveness.

Hysterical Personality

The name of this diagnostic category, which appeared for the first time in DSM-II (1968), is somewhat misleading, since the *hysterical personality* is quite different from the hysterical neurotic. However, the term appears to have "stuck" and has become something of a catch-all category for women showing personality disorders (Gardner, 1965). The traits of the hysterical personality are emotional instability, egocentricity, vanity, self-dramatization, and overdependence on others. Another significant aspect of this personality is an insatiable desire for attention, which sometimes involves sexual promiscuity along with wildly exaggerated accounts of romantic conquests.

In Edward Albee's play *Who's Afraid of Virginia Woolf?* (1962) the character Martha exemplifies the hysterical personality. Martha's stormy relationship with her husband, George, alternates between violent abuse and tender affection. It is not uncommon in marital relationships to find one partner who is an hysterical personality and the other a passive-aggressive. This was certainly the case with Martha and George. Although he would frequently submit to Martha's abuses in a timid, almost helpless way, at other times he fought back either quietly or aggressively.

Obsessive-Compulsive Personality

Rigid, overconscientious, and excessively concerned with conformity, the *obsessive-compulsive personality* has strong inhibitions against self-expression and self-gratification. Nonetheless, his problems in living are less severe than those of the obsessive-compulsive neurotic, for in the personality disorder the obsessive-compulsive quality is more generalized and involves behavior that is more socially acceptable. Furthermore, since someone with an obsessive-compulsive personality is typically extremely meticulous and hard-working, he may be quite successful if he

PERSONALITY DISORDERS

Passive-aggressive personality	Characterized by stubbornness and by a tendency, expressed either passively or aggressively, to be extremely demanding on others
Hysterical personality	Characterized by insecurity and vain, self-dramatizing, attention-seeking behavior
Obsessive-compulsive personality	Characterized by rigidity, strong inhibitions, highly strained meticulousness, and an inability to relax
Paranoid personality	Characterized by envy, hypersensitivity, self-aggrandizement, and a tendency to blame others and impugn their motives
Cyclothymic personality	Characterized by alternating periods of elation and depression, though not of psychotic proportions
Schizoid personality	Characterized by social withdrawal and absorption in fantasy, though not to the point where reality contact is lost
Explosive personality	Characterized by intense outbursts of rage and aggression inconsistent with the individual's usual behavior
Asthenic personality	Characterized by low energy and lack of enjoyment or enthusiasm
Antisocial personality	Characterized by selfish, callous, impulsive behavior, by a lack of remorse over such behavior, and by an inability to form close personal relationships
Inadequate personality	Characterized by insufficient emotional, intellectual, social, and physical responsiveness

Source: American Psychiatric Association, 1968.

chooses the right profession. For example, an obsessive-compulsive personality might make an excellent research librarian—a field in which extreme fastidiousness is a desirable quality. Thus, in treating the obsessive-compulsive personality, the therapist must take into account the degree to which the patient's behavior is functional. In the following case, the compulsive patterns were functional in only a limited sense:

For twenty-five years Geoffrey V. had been a bookkeeper with a New England industrial concern. He approached both his work and his limited interests—watching baseball and collecting stamps—in a systematic, meticulous way. Although he was a perfectionist and did his work well, he had turned down several opportunities for promotion. Finally, however, he accepted a promotion to a position which put him in charge of several clerical workers. A few weeks after the job change, he took a week's vacation, at the end of which he became extremely anxious at the prospect of returning to work. He did return, but soon his anxiety began to interfere with his work, and it was recommended that he visit a psychiatrist retained by the company. The tranquilizers prescribed by the psychiatrist did not alleviate Geoffrey's condition, and he later requested, and received, a transfer back to his old job (adapted from Zax and Stricker, 1963, pp. 233–235).

TRANSIENT SITUATIONAL DISORDERS

Although this category receives a separate listing in DSM-II, it is relevant to our discussion of neuroses and related disorders. *Transient situational disturbances* are acute reactions to severe stress and are manifested in intense anxiety and other neurotic symptoms. In some cases, the symptoms may actually appear psychotic, involving delusions and exteme disorganization.

The difference between these disturbances and the neuroses and personality disorders is implicit in the words "transient" and "situational." The person suffering from a transient situational disturbance usually has no prior history of psychological difficulties. The symptoms are not expressed until the person is exposed to overwhelming stress with which he is unable to cope. Once the stress passes, so do the symptoms. If the abnormal behavior persists long after the period of stress is over, the diagnosis is changed.

DSM-II classifies these disorders in terms of the patient's developmental stage. In our discussion,

however, we shall simply describe three types of situations that are commonly implicated in transient situational disturbances.

Combat

During both world wars, traumatic reactions to combat were usually referred to as "shell shock." This term was supplanted during the Korean and Vietnam wars by "combat fatigue" and "combat exhaustion." In actuality, none of these terms represent an especially accurate description, since transient situational disturbances due to combat stress often differ markedly from one person to another. Among the symptoms commonly reported are fatigue, hypersensitivity to external stimuli, difficulties in sleeping, chronic anxiety often reaching phobic proportions, depression, and regressive behavior.

The circumstances that prompt such reactions usually involve prolonged exposure to stress, either during field combat or during long periods of combat flying. We know, however, that people differ considerably in their ability to tolerate stress. For some, traumatic reactions can appear during training for flight or ground combat. Others remain calm until the bullets start whizzing past them.

Furthermore, the stress patterns created by actual combat seem to vary with the conditions of combat. For the soldier in the field, stress—in the form of exposure to rifle and machine-gun fire as well as to long-range bombing—is continuous and unrelenting. For the combat pilot and other members of the flight crew, stress may take even more terrifying forms—fighting through antiaircraft fire, and perhaps being shot down over enemy territory—but once the mission is completed, there is a respite, however brief, before the next one. In comparing patterns of stress generated by these two patterns of combat, many observers have suggested that ground troops are more likely to experience chronic fatigue and weariness, whereas aircraft personnel are more likely to experience anxiety.

For some pilots, anxiety becomes so acute that they evince strong phobic symptoms along with such physiological reactions as vomiting, tremors, and "hysterical-like" symptoms, as is illustrated in the following case:

A 23-year-old fighter-bomber pilot on his 38th mission was attacking an important airdrome. In his attempt to destroy it, he pulled out of his dive too low and got caught up in the explosion of his own bomb. He managed to return safely to his base but was tense and fearful. On his 42nd mission, he again escaped death very narrowly. Subsequently he began awakening during the night in cold sweats. When he did sleep, he had nightmares of his plane being shot down. During the day his hands would tremble when he attempted to light a cigarette, and he had difficulty concentrating on anything. After his 65th mission, his efficiency had decreased to the point that he had to be returned to the United States (adapted from Grinker and Spiegel, 1945, p. 18).

Internment as a Prisoner of War

For many of those who fought in World War II or in the Korean or Vietnam wars, it was not combat but the experience of being captured and placed in confinement that occasioned traumatic reactions. The stress to which these prisoners of war (POWs) were subjected took many forms, both physical and psychological: disease, extreme cold, semistarvation, torture or threats of torture, solitary confinement, and anxiety about the prospects of never being released. Frequently these stresses were utilized by captors to bring about changes in the political attitudes of the captives.

One of the best descriptions of this method of attitude change (or "brainwashing") of POWs during the Korean War is given by Farber, Harlow, and West (1956). They call the approach *DDD*, a combination of debility, dependency, and dread.

The *debility* of the POWs grew out of the subtle interaction of the effects of near-starvation, disease, and fatigue. Infections were rampant, and food was scarce and of miserable quality. As the men grew physically weaker, they lowered their activity levels, which in turn aggravated their weakness. This state of debility was also expressed in a general apathy and in an inability to concentrate, which in turn made them more susceptible to pressures from their captors. Leyton (1946) reported similar reactions in German POW camps during World War II.

The *dependency* of the prisoners was often extreme. Placed in solitary confinement, deprived of leadership, and subjected to unpredictable punishment, they soon abandoned any comforting thoughts of their own power and self-sufficiency. Instead, they became passive, helpless, childlike, and easily convertible to new ways of thinking.

Dread—the state of chronic fear which the enemy intentionally instilled in their prisoners—is the final and perhaps the most destructive aspect of the DDD approach. Threats of punishment or even death, warnings that they might never be released or might be permanently deformed—all these contributed to

Fig. 5.5   Continued stress of combat can eventually result in "combat fatigue," a transient situational disturbance. Here a young marine rests on his mortar after an attack in which a fellow soldier was killed at his side.

Fig. 5.6   The face of this American airman in Hanoi reveals the stress produced by the experience of capture and confinement.

the rigors of POWs' lives and further broke down any resistance to new beliefs and viewpoints. With some modifications, the DDD approach could probably be applied to any individual or group of individuals whose lives are under the total control of others.

Civilian Catastrophe

We need not look to war to find shocking and stressful experiences that can induce traumatic reactions. Being in a plane crash, a fire, or a flood; finding oneself suddenly wiped out financially; losing a child; or suddenly realizing that one's spouse has been unfaithful—any experience such as these can trigger a transient situational disturbance.

How a person behaves in response to an event of such gravity varies according to the suddenness of the shock and according to the person's previous psychological adjustments to less severe traumas. However, according to some writers, victims of severe physical trauma show a definite pattern of responses known as the *disaster syndrome*. In the first phase, the *shock stage*, the person is stunned and dazed, frequently to the point of immobility. In extreme cases, there may be disorientation and amnesia as well. During the second stage, the *suggestibility stage*, the person becomes quite passive and is willing to take orders from almost anyone. He may even express concern for other people who were involved in the incident. During the *recovery stage*, he begins to pull himself together to approach his situation in a more rational way. However, he may still show signs of generalized anxiety and may repeatedly keep recounting his experience to others (Raker et al., 1956).

In the more psychologically based catastrophes, we can also see the rough outline of the disaster syndrome. Here, however, shock, suggestibility, and recovery are complicated by feelings of grief and often guilt as well, for the victim, no matter how innocent, often sees himself as being in some way responsible for the catastrophe. This syndrome may be seen in the following case:

Marilyn had spent the first fifteen years of her marriage raising her six children and quietly fulfilling her role as a housewife. The early years of her marriage had been especially hard because the family was of modest financial circumstances. Nonetheless, as far as Marilyn was concerned, her marriage had been a good one.

Suddenly, one day she was told by one of her children that for two years her husband had been having an affair with a young woman in her twenties. Mari-

Fig. 5.7   A tornado struck St. Louis in 1959, causing widespread destruction. Catastrophes such as this can lead to a temporary breakdown in an individual's functioning.

lyn confronted her husband, who reluctantly admitted that it was true. The following day Marilyn began to show a marked apathy and listlessness. She expressed feelings of hopelessness and guilt, wondering what she had done wrong to make her husband look elsewhere. There followed a profound depression, for which she was hospitalized. However, once her husband promised to put a permanent end to his liaison with the young woman, Marilyn began to recover from the depression, and within a year she had resumed her former activities and had regained her good spirits.

After the acute phase of a traumatic reaction, the individual may experience what is called the *post-traumatic syndrome*, which can last for weeks or even months. Here the individual no longer shows glaring signs of grief or depression. Rather, he may simply be anxious and irritable, and he may have difficulty concentrating and phasing back into his daily routines. In this last stage the person may also shy away from social activities and spend many hours in a final sorting out of his responses to the traumatic event.

PERSPECTIVES ON THE NEUROSES AND RELATED DISORDERS

In Chapters 2, 3, and 4 we have presented a general overview of the psychodynamic, behaviorist, and humanistic-existential approaches to abnormal behavior. In the present section we shall see how practitioners utilizing each of these perspectives, along with proponents of the biological and physiological perspectives, would interpret and treat the neuroses and the related disorders that we have described. We have omitted a separate discussion of the personality disorders because when treated, they are treated in the same way as are the neuroses. (Since the various treatment techniques will be discussed in detail in Chapter 19, our coverage of the various treatments for neurosis will be brief.)

Although these approaches are quite different, the three major perspectives do at least agree on one major premise—namely, that anxiety is crucial to the development of neurotic symptoms.

The Psychodynamic Perspective

As we have seen in Chapter 2, the concept of anxiety is absolutely central to the Freudian interpretation of abnormal behavior. And, predictably, psychodynamic theorists view anxiety as the major culprit in the development of neurosis. However, the psychodynamic view of neurosis is difficult to summarize for the simple reason that neurosis has been the major focus of psychodynamic writing. Theories and countertheories have been advanced and readvanced. Even Freud changed his mind repeatedly. As a result, the books and articles offering different psychodynamic interpretations of the various neuroses could, and do, fill whole libraries. It should be understood, therefore, that our discussion of the traditional psychodynamic perspective on neurosis represents only the most general outline.

Cause   Freud, as we have seen, believed that anxiety could take three different forms: reality anxiety, in which the ego is threatened by something in the outside world; moral anxiety, in which the ego is threatened by the superego's punitive response to some forbidden thought or deed; and finally,

neurotic anxiety, in which the ego is threatened by unacceptable and unconscious id impulses that are attempting to overwhelm the constraints imposed on them by the ego. Needless to say, it is this last type of anxiety that psychodynamic theory sees as the major source of neurotic symptoms. The neurotic's problem is that the cold war among his psychic components has turned into open battle. The id pushes in one direction, toward the conscious awareness and enactment of its sexual or aggressive impulse. And the ego, knowing that the id impulse is unacceptable both in terms of reality and in terms of the superego's ideals, pushes in the other direction, toward repression of the impulse back into the unconscious. The result is intense anxiety over the possibility that the id impulses will break out and the individual will "lose control." And the manifestation of this anxiety is neurotic behavior.

As we already know, however, neurosis can take many forms. According to the psychodynamic view, the form that the neurosis takes depends on how the person responds to his anxiety. In a large number of cases the anxiety will be experienced directly, and accordingly anxiety neurosis, the unadulterated experience of neurotic anxiety, is, as we have seen, by far the most common of the neuroses. In the anxiety attack, the state of chronic tension between ego and id is temporarily intensified as the unacceptable id impulse moves closer to the boundaries of the conscious mind. The ego responds with desperate efforts at repression, and consequently a state of maximum conflict ensues. Once the ego regains the upper hand and the impulse is more safely repressed, the anxiety attack passes.

According to psychodynamic theory, however, anxiety neurosis is unique in that the principal defense employed is that of repression. In the other neuroses, the defenses against anxiety are considerably more elaborate, and it is these defenses that appear as the symptoms of neurotic disorder. In phobic neurosis, for example, displacement may be at work. The classic illustration of such displacement in phobia is Freud's famous case study of "Little Hans" (1909). Hans was a five-year-old boy who refused to go out into the street for fear that a horse would bite him. Freud's interpretation of the phobia was that Hans was caught up in an intense Oedipal struggle in which his strong attachment to his mother was accompanied by extreme hostility toward his father, along with the usual fear of the father's retaliation in the form of castration. Thus, because he was afraid to direct such hostile feelings toward his father, he projected his hostility and his fear at horses—an easy substitution, since Hans' father would sometimes play "horsie" with him.

Reaction formation may also be implicated in phobia. For example, a woman with *androphobia* (fear of men)—constantly afraid that some man is following her, hiding under her bed, lurking in her pantry, and so forth—may, according to Freudian theory, unconsciously be harboring an intense desire to be seduced.

In amnesia, and in all the forms of dissociation hysteria in which amnesia plays a part, we see total repression at work. However, psychodynamic theory would suggest that in somnambulism, in fugue, and particularly in cases of multiple personality, the individual acts out in the dissociative state the unconscious impulse, while the ego protects itself from consciousness of the forbidden impulse by maintaining amnesia for the episode.

Obsessive-compulsive neurosis may be interpreted in a number of ways, depending on the nature of the obsession or compulsion. In the case of a man who is obsessed with the fear that he will kill his wife in her sleep, for example, psychodynamic theory would suggest that the unconscious aggressive impulse has in fact made its way into the conscious mind. However, in the wide variety of obsessions and compulsions that have to do with cleanliness, orderliness, and doing one's duty (e.g., presleep orderliness rituals, compulsive hand-washing, obsessive fears of germs), the neurosis would be interpreted as a combination of fixation and reaction formation, the ego defending itself against the anal desire to soil, to play with feces, and to be generally messy and destructive. Likewise, the compulsive eater or drinker might be thought to be fixated at the oral stage, though not employing a reaction formation to his oral impulses.

In hypochondriacal neurosis and neurasthenic neurosis, psychodynamic theory would see a strong element of regression. The hypochondriac and neurasthenic, overwhelmed with the anxiety of adult life, defend themselves by regressing to the state of a sick child, where they hope to receive extra attention, support, and "babying." (These extra satisfactions in the form of comforting that a neurotic receives are called *secondary gains*. The *primary gain* in neurosis is the relief from anxiety through the use of the defense mechanism.)

Finally, the conversion reaction of the hysteric is generally interpreted as a defense against unpermissible impulses, usually of a sexual or aggressive nature. Thus, for example, a person with glove anesthesia may be reacting to an urge to masturbate or to a terrible guilt over past episodes of masturbation. Here we see what Freud considered the *symbolic* meaning of the neurotic's symptoms. Just as the hysteric defends himself against masturbation by anesthetizing his hand, so another person with guilt over masturbation may develop a hand-washing compulsion, or a person who unconsciously wishes to kill some beloved person may develop a phobia about knives.

Treatment We have seen that according to the psychodynamic view the ego has to exert a great deal of its energy in order to maintain repression as well as other defenses. One of the primary aims of psychoanalytic and most psychodynamic therapies is to strengthen the ego by bringing repressed material from the unconscious to the conscious level. In more pragmatic terms, this means guiding the neurotic toward greater self-understanding and freeing the ego to develop new, more flexible ways of responding to conflicts and problems.

There are two essential techniques by which this goal is accomplished. The first technique, *free association*, we have already mentioned briefly in Chapter 2. Here the patient lies back on a couch and simply says whatever comes to his mind, without the censorship of reason, logic, or "decency." Unconscious material will eventually surface and will be interpreted by the therapist. The second is *dream interpretation*, whereby the patient reports his dreams as accurately as possible and the therapist interprets the elements of the dreams as symbols of unconscious wishes and conflicts. Thus through both techniques the person comes to reexperience and understand repressed events from the past and repressed impulses of the present.

For the patient with a transient situational disturbance, treatment may be of the traditional psychoanalytic type just described. Frequently, however, the therapist will use *hypnoanalysis*, a combination of psychoanalysis and hypnosis. Under hypnosis the patient is encouraged to recall the traumatic experiences to which he has been subjected. This unleashing of the traumatic memory relieves some portion of the patient's anxiety. Then the patient and therapist work together to analyze the patient's defenses against this anxiety.

The Behaviorist Perspective

Although many behaviorists agree with the psychodynamic theorists on the central role of anxiety in the development of neurotic disorders,* their conceptualization and treatment methods are, typically, much more straightforward.

Cause According to most learning theorists, anxiety is the result of respondent conditioning. That is, anxiety is a learned negative reaction to a stimulus which was originally neutral but which was then presented simultaneously with a noxious or painful stimulus (Mowrer, 1939). Hence behaviorist theory holds that we learn our anxieties in precisely the same way that Watson's Albert B. (Chapter 3) learned his fear of rats. And like Albert's fear, our specific learned fears generalize into broader anxieties.

Imagine, for example, a family in which every time the father drinks heavily he beats his young daughter. Soon the signs of the father's drinking (CS) will become paired in the child's mind with the pain of the beating (UCS), and she will experience anxiety (CR) at the first sign that the father is intoxicated. Eventually this anxiety may generalize to the father as a whole, drunk or sober, in which case he himself becomes the CS. And if she is able to avoid him—if for example, the parents divorce, and the child lives with her mother, seeing her father only very seldom—then the anxiety will be maintained (since, as we have seen, avoidance prevents extinction from taking place) and may be further generalized to any man who is like her father, any man who drinks, or indeed any man at all.†

A behaviorist would say that when a person exhibits sufficient anxiety to be labeled neurotic, this means that the person's conditioned anxiety and his consequent avoidance behavior have reached the

level where they greatly interfere with his functioning. Likewise, the label "anxiety neurosis" would be applied when a person's conditioned anxiety has become so generalized that he can no longer identify the stimuli that elicit the anxiety. (This may be true even in the case of the anxiety attack.) All he knows is that he experiences a debilitating sense of dread in a wide variety of different situations. And consequent avoidance prevents him from engaging in more constructive and more positively reinforcing behavior.

The difference between phobia and anxiety neurosis from the behaviorist point of view is the degree of generalization. In phobia the degree of generalization is much smaller than in anxiety neurosis, so that the phobic's anxiety remains focused on a discrete stimulus, or on a set of similar stimuli that he can consequently identify. Furthermore, the phobic, unlike the anxiety neurotic, can

---

*Not all behaviorists concur. For example, Ullmann and Krasner (1975) reject the concept of anxiety in favor of specifying the situation to which the individual responds. "At minimum the operations [i.e., context] must be specified each time the concept of 'anxiety' is used. Once having done so, there is little gained from use of the word" (p. 171).

---

†Only if the CS is repeatedly experienced without the reinforcement of the UCS will extinction eventually occur. Say, for example, that the child is forced to spend her summer vacation at the father's house. If the father has by now overcome his drinking problem and the two spend a happy summer together, then the neurotic avoidance mechanism will be undermined: extinction will take place, and the child will cease to respond with anxiety to him. Once the CS (the father) has been experienced repeatedly without the reinforcement of the UCS (the pain from the beating), then the CR (anxiety) will drop out, just as Pavlov's dogs, after repeatedly hearing the bell without the reinforcement of the food, eventually ceased to salivate at the sound of the bell (see Chapter 3).

Fig. 5.8   These illustrations were painted by a fifteen-year-old male named Lonnie during his seven-week period of psychiatric hospitalization. Having attempted suicide several months prior to hospitalization, he was diagnosed as neurotic with tendencies toward paranoia and disorganized thinking. After two weeks of hospitalization, Lonnie began to express anxiety concerning homosexual fantasies and desires, although he denied any real experiences. As a male, he felt quite inadequate; and at the time of release, he still had not resolved his sexual conflict. Through his numerous paintings, which he usually titled and verbally interpreted, Lonnie was able to express his anxieties and desires. The first painting shown at the right, entitled Life and Man, *depicts the blending of a human figure and a tree. The depressed, surrealistic environment surrounding the inhuman male reflects the patient's aggressive fantasies, as well as his fear and rejection of men. Lonnie was in a period of great psychological distress when he painted this picture. Twice he attempted to destroy it but, with encouragement from the art therapist, he finally completed the work. In the painting* What Am I? *(top right), the man-woman figure expresses the patient's uncertainty regarding his sexual identity. As in the previous painting, anxiety and turmoil are evident; the figure is "caught," chained by the wrists, unable to resolve his sexual conflict. The third illustration (bottom right) is entitled* The Failure *and conveys an overwhelming sense of loneliness and depression. Against a stylized background, the small figure is about to enter a tunnel and seems to be borne along, helpless to react. As a self-representation, the figure expresses Lonnie's sense of hopelessness and passivity in the face of life forces.*

actually stave off anxiety altogether if he can manage to avoid those stimuli that arouse his anxiety.

In the case of the less direct neurotic responses to anxiety, the behaviorists once again see avoidance behavior as the central problem. The anxious person, as we know, is in a state of constant tension, and any response which serves to reduce that tension will have strong reinforcing properties. Thus when the anxious individual discovers by chance that some activity, such as washing his hands, leads to a reduction in anxiety, this response will be repeated.

Thus the behaviorist interprets obsessive-compulsive reactions primarily as avoidance responses to situations that arouse anxiety. Whether the individual's compulsion is a simple repetitive act or an elaborate series of ritualistic actions, the fact that it relieves the anxiety acts as negative reinforcement, thus maintaining the compulsive behavior. But the avoidance or reduction of anxiety is only temporary; in order to keep the anxiety at bay, the compulsive act must be repeated again and again, even when the repetition is inconvenient or painful.

Like obsessive-compulsive reactions, hysterical reactions are learned and constitute avoidance behavior. The symptoms of a hysterical paralysis, for example, would enable a person who has just been inducted into the army to avoid the stress of fire under combat. If he cannot walk, he cannot fight. Likewise, the unsuccessful violinist who develops a hysterical cramp in his bowing arm spares himself the fear of bad reviews, poor ticket sales, and difficulties in getting concert engagements. In dissociative reactions like amnesia or fugue, a person avoids a painful situation by failing to remember it.

A behaviorist would also interpret neurasthenia and hypochondria as escape or avoidance reactions. Through "sickness," the person escapes or avoids unpleasant circumstances. The added attention and support he gets from people around him are simply conditioned positive reinforcers, in that they strengthen his maladaptive behaviors.

The transient situational disturbance is viewed by the behaviorist as a response to an extremely aversive situation that cannot be avoided, so that escape from anxiety is impossible. For the POW, for example, there is no way of avoiding the fear of death or punishment that marks his daily existence. And the apathy that POWs often manifest would be interpreted by the behaviorist as the only possible means of escape remaining to them—psychological escape. Similarly, a behaviorist would say that for the person who experiences a civilian catastrophe, such as the death of a spouse or the loss of a job, certain positive reinforcements are suddenly removed and that this extinction results in depressive symptoms.

Treatment We have already mentioned in Chapter 3 the utterly straightforward approach of behavioral treatments. Behavioral therapy is aimed directly at the removal of symptoms. The behaviorist is not interested in tapping the patient's unconscious, nor does he spend a great deal of time determining how the symptoms came about in the first place. His concern is with the patient's current behavioral problems.

In his effort to remove neurotic symptoms, the behaviorist may make use of a number of different behavior-modification techniques. One of the most popular of these is *systematic desensitization* (also called *reciprocal inhibition*). This technique, which was developed by Wolpe (1958), is particularly useful in eliminating anxieties and phobias, although it has also been applied in treating other forms of neurotic behavior. In essence, the patient is trained to relax the muscles of his body while imagining a series of increasingly anxiety-arousing situations. Thus a hierarchy of fears is established for the patient, and by the end of treatment, if it is successful, he is able to imagine the most intensely anxiety-provoking stimulus of his hierarchy and still remain relaxed.

Another behaviorist technique, *reinforcement therapy*, uses positive reinforcement to facilitate shaping, which, as we have seen in Chapter 3, is the gradual development of a desired response through the rewarding of successive approximations of that response. Brady and Lind (1968), for example, report treating a hysterically blind person by reinforcing his approximations to "seeing."

In *extinction therapy*, on the other hand, maladaptive symptoms are extinguished by removing the reinforcements that are maintaining them. For example, the neurasthenic and hypochondriac might be helped if their chronic complaints received neither attention nor sympathy.

The Humanistic-Existential Perspective

As in the case of the other two perspectives, anxiety plays a central role in the humanistic-existential explanation of neurosis. What is unique about this approach, however, is that many humanistic-existential thinkers tend to view both anxiety and neuroses not simply as individual problems, but in a larger sense, as predictable outcomes of conflicts with the inauthenticity of existence in a "sick society." For instance, Rogers (1961) insists that as long as societies thwart man's natural goodness, oppose his innate drive for self-actualization, and frustrate his search for meaning, anxiety and neuroses are inevitable.

Cause On an individual level, humanistically oriented psychologists see the neurotic as a person who has failed to actualize his potential because he has developed a distorted self-concept. The normal person, of course, is in touch not only with the external world but also with what is going on within him. At times he has experiences incompatible with his own self-concept, but he is able to deal with these experiences by simply rejecting them or by modifying his self-concept to accommodate them. The neurotic, on the other hand, is unable to integrate experiences inconsistent with his self-image and therefore holds in his mind two conflicting sets of values and motivational structures. The first set is intrinsic to him; it consists of those realities that maintain, enhance, and actualize his total personality. The second set he derives from others and mistakenly internalizes as his own. For example, if people close to him perceive him as clumsy, inept, or incapable of making sound decisions, he begins to perceive himself in this way, even though this unfavorable self-image conflicts with the other, more self-enhancing image. As a result, a great deal of the energy that the neurotic should be directing toward self-actualization he spends in maintaining and defending this distorted self-concept. Moreover, his failure to express himself authentically impedes his ability to find more appropriate patterns of behavior.

From the humanistic point of view, transient situational disturbances occur when situational stress, whether in military or civilian life, grossly blocks or interferes with the natural drive for self-actualization. The person is suddenly placed in an alien environment—whether it be war, imprisonment, or some domestic disaster—that radically distorts his perceptions of himself and life. Hence he is unable to rely on any of his usual means of self-enhancing behavior. In short, his growth as a person is immobilized.

As might be predicted, humanistic-existential thinkers have given special attention to Maddi's proposed category of existential neurosis, which we described earlier in this chapter. This disorder, if such it be, fits neatly into the humanistic-existential theory of neurosis. For Maddi points out that the deep sense of emptiness experienced by existential neurotics stems from the failure of such persons to develop an adequate sense of themselves as children. Rather, they have been taught only to play a social role, and never to create their own destiny. Thus existential neurotics can manage their affairs by playing their learned social role, but at a deeper level they find none of this satisfying, since they have no sense of their own identity. Furthermore, such individuals have no intrinsic value system and consequently cannot make the important decisions that would enable them to find their own identity.

Treatment Although humanistic-existential therapies are quite individualistic, they all emphasize the individual's responsibility for changing his maladaptive behaviors. The *client-centered therapy* of Carl Rogers (1942) is one of the most popular techniques. In this approach, the therapist makes no value judgments about what the client says and offers no advice about possible courses of action. Instead, he becomes a "mirror of feeling" for the patient. For example, he will respond to the client's remarks by restating their important emotional components, so the client eventually comes to realize that his feelings are understood by someone outside himself. Through such understanding and empathy, the nondirective therapist attempts to create a setting within which the client will be able to restructure his subjective experiences.

The Biological Perspective

As we have seen, the three major psychological perspectives view anxiety as the basic cause of neurosis. However, some researchers have proposed that the development of neurosis may be due to genetic factors as well.

Despite the fact that there is a vast amount of research on the role of heredity in behavior disorders, most of it focuses upon the more severe disorders such as schizophrenia and manic-depressive psychosis—disorders that we shall study in later chapters. And the evidence for a genetic role in these more debilitating disorders is considerably sounder than the evidence for genetic determinants of neurosis. Some studies of neurosis in twins have reported higher concordance rates for monozygotic than for dizygotic twins. For example, in a study of twins in the military, Pollin et al. (1969) reported

THE MECHANICS OF GENETIC STUDIES

Every human being is born with a unique *genotype*—that is, a highly individual combination of genes representing his biological inheritance from his parents. And this genotype combines with the individual's environment to determine his *phenotype*—that is, his equally unique combination of observable characteristics. The entire purpose of genetic research in psychology is to separate these two tangled threads of genotype and environment and thus to discover to what extent different psychological disorders are due to genetic inheritance and to what extent they are due to environmental influence. Needless to say, such information would help considerably in the treatment and prevention of mental illness. Until we know whether a disorder is organic or functional—or, to speak more realistically, to what degree it is organic and to what degree functional—we are in a very poor position to deal with it.

There are two basic categories of genetic studies: family studies and twin studies. Family studies are based on our knowledge that different types of family relationships involve different degrees of genetic similarity. For example, all children receive half their genes from one parent and half from the other. Thus parents and children are 50 percent identical genetically. Likewise, any two siblings have approximately 50 percent of their genes in common. Aunts and uncles, further removed, are approximately 25 percent identical genetically to a given niece or nephew. And first cousins, one step further removed, have approximately 12.5 percent of their genes in common. With these percentages in mind, the genetic researcher puts together a substantial sample of families containing one diagnosed case—referred to as the *index case* or *proband case*—of the disorder in question. Then with each family he studies the other members—grandparents, parents, children, grandchildren, siblings, aunts and uncles, cousins, and perhaps relatives further removed—to determine what percentage of individuals in each of these relationship groups merits the same diagnosis as the index case. When all the families have been examined in this way, the percentages for each relationship group are averaged, so the researcher ends up with an average percentage of aunts and uncles sharing the index case's disorder, an average percentage of siblings bearing the index case's disorder, and so on down the line. And if it should turn out that these percentages roughly parallel the percentages of shared genes—if, for example, siblings prove approximately twice as likely as aunts and uncles to share the index case's disorder—then this evidence would suggest that predisposition to the disorder in question might be passed on genetically.

Such evidence would, however, only suggest, not prove, genetic transmission. For while a person has more genes in common with his siblings than he does with his aunts and uncles, he also has much more of his environment in common with his siblings than with his aunts and uncles. Therefore, if his brothers and sisters are much more likely than his aunts and uncles to join him in his obsessive-compulsive neurosis, this differential could easily be due to shared environment (same parents, same schools, same neighborhood) rather than to shared genes.

The genes-vs.-environment confusion is much less troublesome in twin studies. Here the basic technique is to compare monozygotic and dizygotic twins. *Monozygotic (MZ) twins*, also called *identical twins*, develop from a single fertilized egg and therefore have exactly the same genotype; they are always of the same sex, have the same eye color, share the same blood type, and so on. In contrast, *dizygotic (DZ) twins*, also called *fraternal twins*, develop from two eggs fertilized by two different sperm and therefore, like any pair of siblings, have only approximately 50 percent of their genes in common; thus, like siblings, one may be female and the other male, one blue-eyed and one brown-eyed, and so forth. In sum, monozygotic twins are as likely as dizygotic twins to share the same environment, but they have approximately twice as many genes in common. Therefore, what the genetic researcher does is to assemble one group of index cases, each of whom is one of a pair of MZ twins, and a second group of index cases, each of whom is one of a pair of DZ twins. He then examines all of the *co-twins* (the twins of the index cases) to discover how many of them are *concordant*—that is, share the same disorder—with their index twin. If the researcher should discover that the concordance rate for the MZ twins is considerably greater than that for the DZ twins, then this would be substantial evidence that predisposition to the disorder in question is genetically transmitted.

It should be added, however, that twin studies, like family studies, have their own set of problems. In the first place, there are simply not that many MZ twins in the world. Hence it is no easy task, for example, to assemble a reasonably sized sample of hysterical neurotics all of whom are MZ twins. Second, the question of environmental influence cannot be eliminated completely from twin studies, since it is possible that MZ twins, because they are so similar physically, may be more likely to be raised in a similar way than DZ twins.

Some researchers have attempted to get a firmer hold on the environment-vs.-genes question by assembling very special index groups. For example, restricting an index group to children who are raised, from birth, apart from their parents is one way of separating genetic from environmental influence. If such children proved to share the same psychological disorder with their natural parents, then this would be compelling evidence for genetic transmission of that disorder. (As we shall see in Chapter 12, the present evidence for genetic transmission of the predisposition to schizophrenia is derived from precisely such studies.) Another type of special index group would involve MZ twins who are raised separately. If, with different environments, these twins showed a substantially higher concordance rate for a certain disorder than DZ twins raised together or separately, this would represent the firmest possible support for a genetic hypothesis. However, the difficulty of assembling a sample of people who all have the same disorder, are all MZ twins, and have all been raised separately from their co-twins makes the other problems of genetic studies look small by comparison.

a 1.5 times greater concordance rate for monozygotic twins over that for dizygotic twins. And in a review of genetic studies of neurosis, Rosenthal (1970) reported that for the neuroses in general the concordance rate for monozygotic twins was 53 percent, whereas the concordance rate for dizygotic twins was 40 percent. However, these percentages simply do not show a great enough discrepancy between monozygotic and dizygotic twins to constitute striking evidence. Thus the genetic hypothesis for the etiology of neurosis remains substantially unproven.

The Physiological Perspective

To understand the hypotheses that relate the neuroses to physiological factors we must review very briefly the functions of the central and autonomic nervous systems. The term "autonomic" was first applied in the belief that this system operated separately from the central nervous system. We now know that this is not the case. The *central nervous system*, which comprises the brain and the spinal cord, is connected with the *autonomic nervous system*, which innervates the smooth muscles, the heart muscle, the glands, and the viscera and controls their functions, including physiological responses to emotion.

The autonomic nervous system has two divisions, which operate in opposite directions. During emotional states and times of stress, it is the *sympathetic division* that becomes dominant. At this time blood pressure and heart rate increase, perspiration covers the body, the pupils dilate, and salivation and digestive functions diminish. The action of this division also results in the secretion of adrenalin. In short, the action of the sympathetic division is to heighten the body's arousal in response to stress. In contrast, the *parasympathetic division* of the autonomic nervous system decreases physical arousal and is usually dominant under less emotional conditions. It regulates breathing, heart rate, blood pressure, stomach and intestinal activity, and elimination.

A number of hypotheses have been put forth in the effort to relate the functions of the autonomic nervous system to the neuroses. According to one current hypothesis (e.g., Lacey, 1967), some people inherit a nervous system that is more sensitive to stress. In turn, this autonomic hypersensitivity makes them more easily aroused and consequently might predispose them to anxiety and thus to the formation of neurotic symptoms.

A second hypothesis is that some people *develop* a hypersensitive autonomic nervous system as the result of frequent stress (Seligman, 1971). This means that the sympathetic division is conditioned to go into action at the slightest provocation.

A third hypothesis relating neurosis to the autonomic nervous system involves a portion of this system known as the *reticular formation*. Consisting of a large mass of brain-stem cells connected to other parts of the brain, the reticular formation is particularly important in arousal from sleep and in maintaining alertness in the waking state. In his theory of personality, Eysenck (1967) attempts to relate neurosis to these arousal functions of the reticular formation. It is his belief that the reticular formation controls neurological arousal and that individuals vary inherently in the degree of arousal maintained by their reticular formations. Both Eysenck and Routtenberg (1968) argue that neurotics are characterized by high arousal and that their consequently high emotionality predisposes them to anxieties, obsessions, phobias, and other neurotic reactions. Some of the findings of Eysenck's research (1967) appear to support this hypothesis.

SUMMARY

This chapter has been devoted to an examination of the neuroses, along with a briefer discussion of personality disorders and transient situational disturbances.

In general, neurosis is characterized by anxiety, by avoidance behavior, by impaired perception and impaired insight, and by general unhappiness. Despite its maladaptive quality, the neurotic behavior is maintained because it helps the person to cope with his immediate problem of anxiety and because avoidance prevents the person from testing his fears against the feared situation. The neuroses that we have discussed are anxiety neurosis, phobic neurosis, hysterical neurosis (both conversion and dissociative types), obsessive-compulsive neurosis, neurasthenic neurosis, hypochondriacal neurosis, and finally existential neurosis, a recently proposed category.

Unlike the neuroses, which are marked by acute distress and are seen by their victims as intrusions into their psychic life, the personality disorders are deep-seated lifelong patterns of maladaptive behavior which may cause the individual little intense suffering and may even allow him to function adequately within a limited sphere, although they continue to impair his flexibility and self-fulfillment. We have limited our discussion to three types of personality disorder: the passive-aggressive personality, the hysterical personality, and the obsessive-compulsive personality.

The transient situational disturbances, in contrast to the neuroses and the personality disorders, are temporary episodes of disturbed psychological functioning which occur in response to a specific stress, such as combat, internment as a prisoner of war, automobile accidents, or simply domestic upheavals.

The three major psychological perspectives all see anxiety as the major determinant of neurosis. The psychodynamic perspective interprets neurosis as the result of the ego's struggle with unacceptable id impulses in the unconscious. This struggle gives rise to anxiety, which is then manifested either directly or through a variety of defense mechanisms. Psychodynamic treatment aims at revealing and working through the repressed impulse by means of dream interpretation and free association.

The behaviorist perspective views neurosis as the result of anxiety which is created through respondent conditioning and which is maintained through avoidance behavior. Behavioral therapies aim directly at the suppression of the neurotic response through such methods as systematic desensitization, reinforcement therapy, and extinction therapy.

Humanistic-existential thinkers tend to conceptualize neurosis partly as the product of a dehumanizing society. The neurotic is viewed as a person who because of a distorted self-concept has failed to actualize his potential. A popular therapy within this perspective is Rogers' client-centered therapy.

Finally, genetic and physiological hypotheses have been offered to account for neuroses, but much research remains to be done in this area before we can identify specific organic determinants of neurosis.

Several of the neuroses that we have discussed in Chapter 5 appear to involve physical impairment or discomfort. The neurasthenic, for example, complains of weakness and fatigue, while the conversion hysteric may develop blindness, deafness, paralysis, or any one of a number of other physical dysfunctions. Yet in each of these cases no organic defect can be demonstrated, and it is this fact that distinguishes the somatic complaints of the neurotic from the disorders that are the subject of the present chapter. The *psychophysiological disorders* are physical disorders which, like the neuroses, are thought to be due to emotional factors but which, unlike the neuroses, are also scientifically traceable to a clear organic cause. Typically, the organic dysfunction involves a single organ system (e.g., the digestive system or the respiratory system) under the control of the autonomic nervous system. According to the DSM-II, the organic changes that give rise to the psychophysiological disorder "are those that normally accompany certain emotional states, but in these disorders the changes are more intense and sustained" (1968, p. 46). Indeed, because they involve detectable organic problems and because the individual may be totally unaware of any emotional cause, psychophysiological disorders are often diagnosed and treated without regard to emotional factors. And when such treatments are successful, as they sometimes are, the role of emotional disturbance in creating the disorder is simply ignored.

MIND AND BODY

Until recently almost all textbooks on abnormal psychology stated or at least implied that in the psychophysiological disorders emotional problems were the essential cause of the physical malfunction. The very term "psychophysiological"—along with its commonly used synonym "psychosomatic"—implies that there would be no physiological problem without the accompanying psychological problem. Yet the truth is that we have no justification for assuming such a clear cause-and-effect relationship. Indeed, there has long been, and there remains today, much confusion as to the precise roles "psyche" (mind) and "soma" (body) play in creating the psychophysiological disturbances.

The Mind-Body Problem

Philosophers have been debating the relationship between mind and body since classical times. This longstanding controversy—the mind-body problem—is reflected in current medical and psychiatric practice. Some professionals hold to the *interaction-*

6 Psycho-physiological Disorders

ism theory (Graham, 1967)—that is, that mind and body interact with one another, each influencing the other at various different times. Other professionals assume the *independence* of mind and body. Thus, as Graham notes, a doctor might say to one of his patients, "'There is nothing physically wrong with you, it's all mental'" (Graham, 1967, p. 53). Yet the problem with this approach is that the word "mental" is merely an abstract label for the functions of the brain. And the brain, because it is part of the nervous system, is connected with all the other organ systems in the body. Consequently, whatever is wrong with a person "mentally" is also wrong with him physically.

Misleading as it is, scientists cling to this dichotomy between mind and body simply because it is convenient. Let us consider, for example, the phenomenon of fear from the points of view of a physiologist and a psychologist. "Fear" is a term that a person applies to his own feeling state in relation to something in the environment. For example, most people, upon being shown a large snake, will report that they experience "fear." When the physiologist investigates this state, he is predisposed, because of his specialized training, to study it in terms of changes in physical functioning—changes in heart rate, blood pressure, flow of saliva, and so on. In contrast the psychologist, because of his training, will study the fear response in terms of the environmental events leading up to it. Neither approach is incorrect, but each is limited. So limited, in fact, that a naïve observer, after noting the different vocabularies and different sources of data used by the physiologist and the psychologist, could easily conclude that the two professionals were investigating two different phenomena. However, both these limited approaches to fear are still in use because both have been effective in treatment—the physiological approach through tranquilizers and the psychological approach through systematic desensitization and other psychotherapeutic techniques.

Another reason why the false dichotomy between mind and body still persists is that if a physician cannot account for a patient's apparently physical problem in traditional medical terms, she is likely to invoke a psychosomatic hypothesis. Thus some conditions have been labeled "psychosomatic" only because physicians have been unable to explain them in strictly medical terms. The psychologist is likely to make a comparable error. Because he has scientific evidence that physiological functioning can be drastically altered by manipulating the environment, he is likely to grant emotional factors a larger role than can actually be demonstrated scientifically. For example, investigators of the possible psychological variables involved in mortality rates of cancer patients have quoted a commonly expressed medical opinion that the patient did or did not survive depending upon his "will to live." Similarly, many scientists ascribe *voodoo death*—that is, a death that is directly attributed to a voodoo curse and has no ostensible organic cause—to emotional factors, although reports of such occurrences in primitive societies (Cannon, 1942), to say nothing of their emotional causation, have yet to achieve the status of scientific fact. In short, whatever cannot be accounted for scientifically is quite often marked up to the mysterious emotions and accordingly is dubbed "psychophysiological."

In this chapter we shall take the position that mind and body are a unity. Thus fluctuating emotional states will be accompanied by physiological changes, and physiological changes will be accompanied by alterations in emotional states. There is evidence for this unitary view in the fact that many patients with chronic physiological problems can predict accurately when another attack is imminent, such predictions usually being based on the belief that a certain kind of emotional experience is a sign of another attack. Similarly, patients have shown equal skill in predicting when the attack will end. Furthermore, it has been demonstrated repeatedly that changed anticipations give rise to changed behavior (Ross et al., 1969). Following Graham, then, we propose that "'psychological' and 'physical' (and their synonyms) refer to different ways of talking about the *same* event, and not to different events" (1967, p. 52).

Fig. 6.1 Physical disorders such as migraine headaches, asthma, hypertension, ulcers, and circulatory impairments often occur in the absence of known organic causation. In these cases the disorder is termed psychophysiological or psychosomatic, which indicates that the organic dysfunction or damage is believed to be due to psychological factors, the nature of which have not yet been satisfactorily determined. Environmental stresses, for example, have been associated with psychophysiological disorders. However, the particular chain of events that leads from environmental events to the physiological and emotional response to the stimuli and, in turn, to the physiological dysfunction has not been delineated.

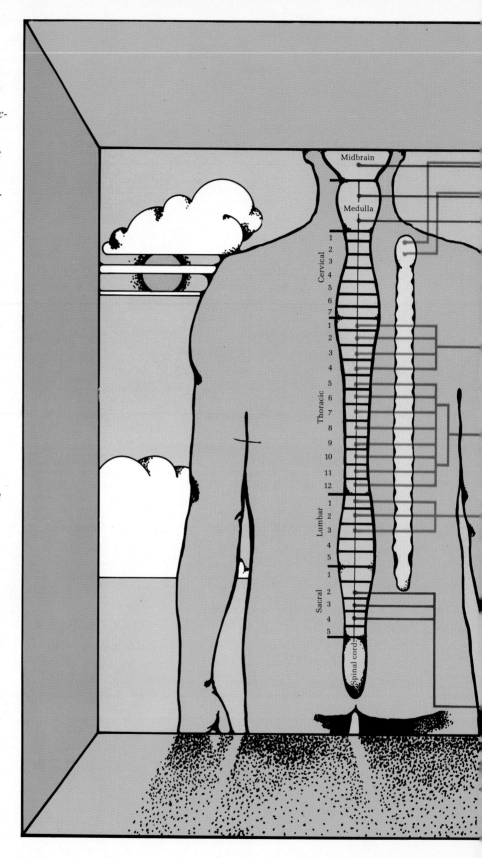

Fig. 6.2 The autonomic nervous system (ANS) includes parasympathetic fibers (green lines), which originate in the brain and sacral vertebrae, and sympathetic fibers (blue lines), which originate in the thoracic and lumbar vertebrae of the spinal cord (far left). Both of these divisions affect each of the internal organs, but in opposite ways. The parasympathetic system controls the organs in all but the most stressful situations, conserves the natural resources of the body, and maintains or returns organ functioning to homeostasis. The sympathetic nervous system prepares the organism for emergency or stressful situations and stimulates the internal organs via the chain ganglia (bottom center) and the celiac ganglia (top center). This division of the ANS signals a decrease in blood flow to and functioning of organs such as the stomach and intestines, increases blood flow from the heart to the brain and muscles of the arms and legs, and stimulates secretion of the adrenal gland, which further prepares the organism for an emergency situation.

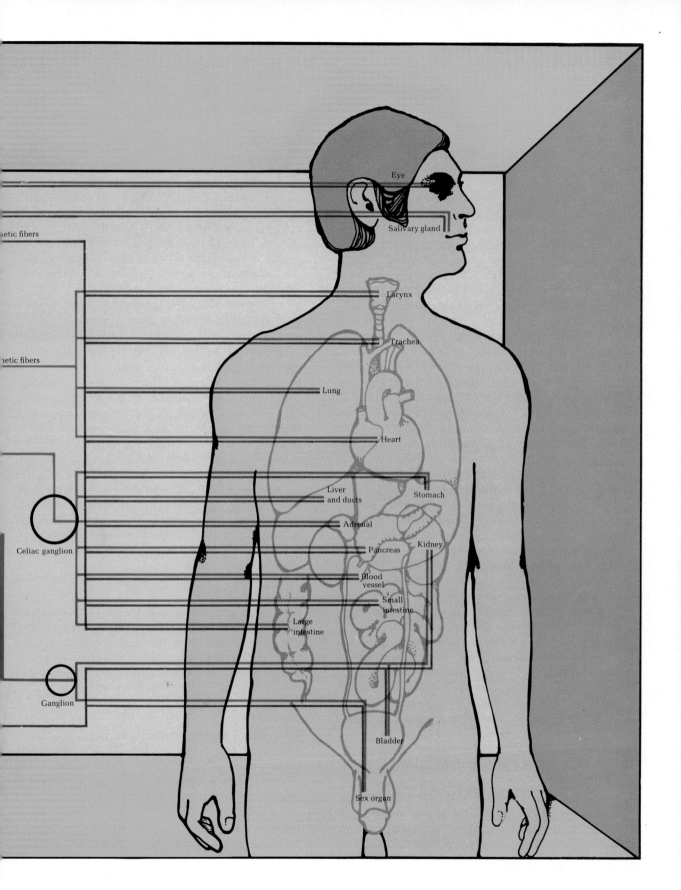

How Psyche and Soma Interact: The Autonomic Nervous System

The autonomic nervous system is, we suspect, the central mechanism of the interaction between what is called psychological functioning and what is called physiological functioning. As we have seen in Chapter 5, the autonomic nervous system, which initiates physiological responses to emotional changes, is made up of two divisions, whose functions we will review briefly. The sympathetic division is responsible for emotional arousal. Among the physiological correlates of sympathetic arousal are dilation of the pupils, increased respiration, diminished digestive functioning, an increased blood-sugar level, and radical changes in blood pressure and blood distribution. The sympathetic division obviously involves all organ systems and thus is a factor in any physical complaints involving emotional arousal.

Normally such arousal will lead to behaviors that change the person's situation usefully, so arousal subsides. However, if a person fails to act on arousal in an effective way, the arousal may simply persist and eventually give rise to a psychophysiological disorder. Suppose that a young man is dissatisfied with his marriage and is constantly angry with his wife. But his fear of jeopardizing their marriage keeps him from discussing what is bothering him. Each time she complains or starts an argument, he changes the subject, but she repeats her complaints. After months or even years of keeping his silence, this person may develop hypertension simply because he has never made an appropriate behavioral response to his state of emotional arousal.

In general, the function of the parasympathetic division is to balance the effect of the sympathetic division by restoring the body to a level state of functioning. Thus, in a sense, it acts in direct opposition to the sympathetic division. However, excessive parasympathetic activity can be just as dangerous as excessive sympathetic activity. For example, an extreme reaction of the parasympathetic division could result in the shutting down of bodily functions altogether—that is, in death. It is thought by some people that this may be what happens in certain kinds of voodoo death.

Classification of Psychophysiological Disorders

Given the fact that there is always a relationship between physiological well-being and emotional response to the environment, we are faced with the question of how a disorder gets included within or excluded from the psychophysiological category. There is no single reasonable answer to this question, since labeling is to a large degree arbitrary. As we have seen, the classification of a syndrome as psychophysiological depends in great part on the success of current treatment methods. If a case responds to medical treatment, the possibility that a psychological factor might be involved tends to be disregarded. But in a case that does not respond to medical treatment, emotional complications are likely to be suspected, although it is of course equally likely that the proper medical treatment has simply not yet been discovered. If the disorder is then treated nonmedically with apparent success, the psychological factor tends to be emphasized, with the result that the disorder is labeled "psychophysiological." Ultimately, the classification tells us little. The fact that Mrs. Jones' migraines improved after psychotherapy is in no way conclusive proof that the etiology of migraine is largely psychological.

In the box on pp. 144–145 we see a list of the disorders that at present are generally considered to be psychophysiological. The box also lists three associated disorders that, as we shall see, can justifiably be considered psychophysiological complaints. Within ten or twenty years these associated complaints will more than likely be elevated to the list of traditional complaints, and some of the latter will perhaps be removed from the list as more effective medical treatments are developed. Thus until we find a totally effective treatment for each of these disorders, the list of psychophysiological complaints is likely to remain unstable from year to year.

THE PSYCHOPHYSIOLOGICAL DISORDERS

Since it is impossible to cover all the complaints listed in the box on pp. 144–145, we will focus our discussion on seven of the most common psychophysiological disorders: ulcer, hypertension, Raynaud's disease, migraine, asthma, eczema, and dysmenorrhea.

Ulcer

Like many psychophysiological disorders, ulcers favor one sex over the other. In the nineteenth century the incidence of ulcers seemed higher among women, but today men are almost twice as likely as women to have ulcers. Approximately 1.6 percent of the general population of the United States suffers from ulcers, but the incidence among middle-aged people is many times greater (U.S. DHEW, 1968).

Voodoo Death and the Autonomic Nervous System

Many anthropologists and physicians working with primitive peoples have reported instances of voodoo death—cases in which perfectly healthy people who have had a spell cast on them or a bone pointed at them or a curse hurled at them, particularly by a medicine man, have simply laid down and died. Cannon (1942), for example, recounts the following story, told to him by a doctor working with natives in northern Australia:

One day a Kanaka came to [Dr. P. S. Clarke's] hospital and told him he would die in a few days because a spell had been put upon him and nothing could be done to counteract it. The man had been known by Dr. Clarke for some time. He was given a very thorough examination, including an examination of the stool and the urine. All was found normal, but as he lay in bed he gradually grew weaker. Dr. Clarke called upon the foreman of the Kanakas to come to the hospital to give the man assurance, but on reaching the foot of the bed, the foreman leaned over, looked at the patient, and then turned to Dr. Clarke, saying, "Yes, doctor, close up him he die" (i.e., he is nearly dead). The next day, at 11 o'clock in the morning, he ceased to live. A postmortem examination revealed nothing that could in any way account for the fatal outcome (p. 171).

While the natives attribute such deaths to evil spirits, European and American scientists tended for many years to mark them up to poisoning or starvation. Cannon, looking for a middle ground between superstition and skepticism, came up with a different physiological explanation. The natives in question, he reasoned, held to their superstitions with iron conviction. Furthermore, their imaginations (particularly their fantasizing of evil spirits) were as potent and vivid as their sense of logic and reason was feeble. Finally, their belief in whatever they imagined would happen to them if they were cursed was firmly supported by their families and fellow tribesmen; once a person was marked for death by the medicine man, all social and physical support was withdrawn from him, and the family began the mourning process as if the person were already dead. These three factors, according to Cannon, would be sufficient to plunge the victim into the most profound terror: the fear of imminent and utterly unavoidable death. And this fear would be sufficient to induce a maximum state of arousal in the sympathetic division of the autonomic nervous system. In turn, this state of arousal would raise the blood pressure to dangerous heights. Studies of human beings and animals have shown that high blood pressure due to shock eventually gives way to dangerously low blood pressure, which in the end can result in death. According to Cannon, this may well be what happens to the victim of a voodoo curse.

However, sudden and mysterious death without apparent organic damage is not confined to the jungle. Seligman (1973) cites the story of a young marine who had survived two years of confinement in a Viet Cong POW camp. Convinced by his captors that they would eventually release him if he cooperated, he became a model prisoner, even to the point of directing the camp's "thought-reform" group. Gradually, however, he realized that he was simply being manipulated and that no matter how "good" a prisoner he was, his captors were not going to release him. Once this hope crumbled, so did he. Whereas previously he had been in relatively good spirits and good health, now he stopped working, took to his bed, rejected whatever food or comfort was offered him, and simply lay there sucking his thumb for hour after hour until he died a few weeks later. According to Seligman, it is possible that such deaths are the result of a feeling of total helplessness which, through the mediation of the parasympathetic division of the autonomic nervous system, causes the heartbeat to slow down to the point where it can no longer sustain life.

Much research remains to be done before it can be scientifically established that either fear or helplessness can actually induce the autonomic nervous system to close down bodily functioning. However, it is possible that sudden death may eventually be added to our list of psychophysiological disorders.

An *ulcer* can be described as an open sore in the wall of the stomach or of the duodenum, the portion of the small intestine lying immediately below the stomach. Ulcers range from the size of a pinhead to roughly the size of a quarter. They are produced by abnormally high levels of gastric activity; in other words, the stomach simply continues to produce the acid necessary for the digestion of food even though food is not present. Some people can tolerate this excess acid without tissue damage. In others, the acid eventually eats into the wall of the stomach, and the result is an ulcer. The first symptom of an ulcer is usually a burning sensation in the stomach, due to the excess acid. Eventually, once the lesion appears, the individual's stomach discomfort turns into actual pain, which may be very intense. If the lesion gets larger, there may be vomiting. Finally, if blood vessels have broken, there will be hemorrhaging in the stomach and vomiting of blood.

There are a number of theories as to why gastric activity should occur in the absence of food. The most popular theory is that this condition is due to psychological stress, a hypothesis that has received substantial support from research on the relationship between stress and gastric activity in both animal and human subjects.

The most well known of the animal studies is Brady's research on monkeys (Brady et al., 1958). Brady and his co-workers found that when a monkey was able to control the occurrence of electric shock both for himself and for a second monkey, the first monkey—Brady called him the "executive monkey"—developed severe gastric ulcers. In fact, if the monkey continued on in the experiment, the ulcers eventually killed him. Initially, Brady found this phenomenon puzzling. His original prediction had been that the second monkey, whose welfare was entirely in the hands of the executive monkey, would be the one to develop the ulcer. As it turned out, it was the monkey who had the pressure and responsibility of deciding when to respond that developed the ulcer. This is reflected in the popular theory that ulcers tend to strike people in responsible, high-level positions. Another of Brady's findings was that monkeys exposed to intermittent stress were more likely to develop ulcers than were those exposed to constant stress. According to this study, then, the degree of stress correlates with ulcer, but the correlation is not absolute; the pattern of stress seems to be equally decisive in determining whether an ulcer will result.

While it is extremely difficult (and ethically questionable) to study humans in similar ways, one

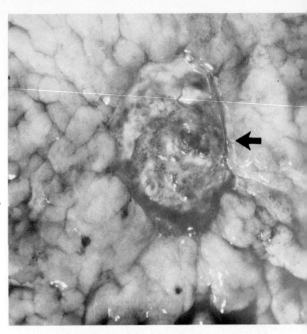

Fig. 6.3 An ulcer is produced by excess acid in the stomach; the one shown here is about the size of a dime.

rather bizarre experiment has in fact supported the correlation between stress and human gastric activity. In 1947 a patient named Tom who had experienced severe gastrointestinal damage was operated upon (Wolf and Wolff, 1947). In the course of that operation a plastic window was installed over Tom's stomach so that his gastric functioning could be observed. Wolf and Wolff found that when the patient was exposed to stress or to any stimulus leading to emotional upset, his flow of gastric juices would increase. This experiment was one of the first clear demonstrations that emotional arousal was indeed directly related to the secretion of gastric juices in human beings.

The following case illustrates the commonly seen relationship between ulcers and disturbed family dynamics:

Although Etta had experienced stomach discomfort for many years, particularly during periods of emotional stress, she did not develop an ulcer until she was forty-two. She had always been very careful about maintaining an adequate diet and having periodic medical examinations. Her life in general could be described as cautious and conventional. She had been raised by devout, hard-working parents who were able to provide for their children adequately though not extravagantly. Etta had married the first man she ever seriously dated and never expressed any regret at having given up her career as a speech therapist after the marriage.

Etta's attachment to her family seemed almost pathological. She consulted her mother about the most trivial of matters. She also talked to each of her four siblings every day if this was at all possible. She particularly deferred to her oldest brother, who was the most financially successful member of the family. Whenever he disapproved of the actions of any of Etta's children—regardless of the reason—she immediately acted upon his disapproval, scolding or spanking the child. In fact, Etta was constantly preoccupied not only with what her brothers and sisters thought of her children but also with what teachers, friends, and neighbors thought. Day after day the children were reproached and disciplined, and their attempted countermeasures precipitated bitter family quarrels. These disagreements intensified as the children grew older and tried to show a degree of independence. Often the quarrels would terminate abruptly as Etta began to experience stomach pains. The children would then slink away, feeling guilty and resentful at the same time.

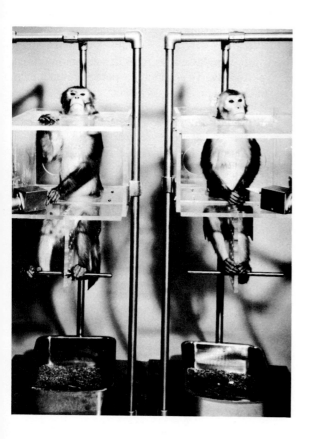

As the children matured and established themselves in the outside world, conflicts within the family diminished. Etta's husband was a reserved person and tried to minimize the number of unpleasant exchanges. By the time Etta was in her late fifties, her ulcers had healed and did not recur.

Hypertension

Like an ulcer, *hypertension* is the result of a physiological function carried to the point of damaging excess. In essence, hypertension can be defined as chronic elevation of the blood pressure with no organic cause. The condition is brought about by the constriction of the arteries, which in turn causes the heart to work harder in pumping blood through these narrowed channels.

In our definition of hypertension, the significant phrase—and one that is sometimes a source of great controversy—is "with no organic cause." Hypertension, like ulcers, appears to be related to continued stress brought about by environmental or psychological conditions. In emotionally arousing situations, any number of people experience, among other reactions, an elevation in blood pressure as a result of temporary constriction of the arteries. However, the prolonged constriction of the arteries that occurs in hypertensive people can be very dangerous, since stress on the heart may cause a heart attack or a stroke. Other damage in the form of kidney and circulatory ailments may also result from this condition. Hypertension is the most common of the serious psychophysiological disorders. Indeed, it represents a severe health problem in this country: the American Heart Association es-

Fig. 6.4   The photograph shows the experimental setup in Brady's "executive monkey" experiments. A shock was delivered to one foot of each monkey at twenty-seconds intervals for a period of six hours. Shock to both monkeys could be avoided or terminated if the monkey on the left (the "executive") pressed a lever; the monkey on the right had no control over the shock. In a series of experiments with pairs of monkeys, the "executive" monkey always developed and died of perforated ulcers, whereas the control monkey showed no ulceration. The constant need to make "decisions" apparently led to increased gastric secretions that resulted in ulceration. Further investigation revealed that the secretion of gastric acids increased in the "executive" following, not during, the six-hour session. Brady's results provide one plausible explanation for the development of ulcers.

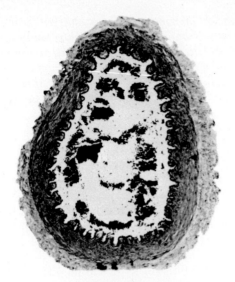

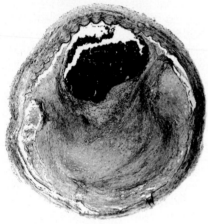

Fig. 6.5 *These photographs show cross-sections of a normal artery (top) and an arteriosclerotic artery (bottom). Normally, the lumen or opening in the artery permits the free flow of blood. In an arteriosclerotic artery, the lumen becomes greatly narrowed or occluded due to fatty deposits, and the blood flow is then reduced or completely blocked. Such arteriosclerosis can result from the prolonged constriction of the arteries that occurs in hypertensive people.*

timates that 23 million Americans—that is, one out of every nine—suffer from this disorder.

The hypertensive person tends to be unaware that there is any correlation between his life style and his hypertensive condition (Davies, 1970). When asked if he is having emotional difficulties, he is likely to give a negative reply. Although psychodynamic theorists usually explain this phenomenon in terms of repression, behavioral theorists explain it as a function of *habituation* or adaptation. The

process of habituation has been demonstrated in laboratory situations: when a constant stimulus is applied, with no change in intensity, to the same sensory receptors, the intensity of the response to the stimulus diminishes over time. Similarly, a person who is under constant tension—a Wall Street stockbroker, for example—comes to experience that persistent tension as a "normal" state. After such habituation occurs, the hypertensive person no longer recognizes that he is tense and therefore sees no reason to modify his life style—by taking a less demanding job, for example—in order to reduce the level of emotional arousal. There is some empirical support for this formulation in the fact that many people are unable to recognize the sensation of relaxation in their own bodies. For example, a person whose arm is supported by an experimenter is told to relax his arm completely and to let the experimenter know when he has complied. When the subject claims that the arm is relaxed, the experimenter withdraws his support and the subject's relaxed arm drops immediately. A hypertensive subject, having followed the same instructions, may report that relaxation has occurred, yet when the experimenter withdraws his support, the "relaxed" arm remains suspended in midair. In other words, a limb the hypertensive subject would describe as "relaxed" the nonhypertensive subject would certainly describe as "somewhat tense."

The following case illustrates this common failing of hypertensive individuals to perceive their own state of arousal.

John W., a high school history teacher, had always been a reserved and meticulous person. He expected a great deal both of his students and of his family. Yet when someone displeased him, he never lost his temper. He felt, as he had often explained, that it was beneath his dignity to let the offending party know just how angry he was. If someone had disappointed him, then they had disappointed him, and that was an end to it.

For the past ten years John's blood pressure had been high enough to be of some concern to his physician. Finally, at the age of forty-five, during the course of an annual checkup, John was told that his blood pressure had reached a dangerously high level. When the doctor asked if anything unusual had happened lately, John said no. The doctor persisted, however, and John finally admitted with great reluctance that the chairman of the history department at his school had recently retired, and that although John had fully expected to be his successor, "some young Turk" from another school had been chosen to fill the position. Furthermore, within a matter of months the new chairman had revamped the entire history program, a curriculum John had developed some fifteen years earlier. Despite these reverses, John vehemently denied being angered by what had taken place. He made a point of lunching now and then with the new chairman, and he had told other members of his department how little he cared for the administrative duties of the chairmanship.

During the year, however, John's blood pressure continued to rise, and his physician finally recommended that he see a psychiatrist.

Raynaud's Disease

Raynaud's disease is a cardiovascular disorder characterized by chronically cold hands and feet but involving no visible impairment of the circulatory system, although the disease is sometimes so severe that gangrene develops. The presumed mechanics of this disorder are that emotional arousal results in constriction of the blood vessels in the extremities without similar constriction of the blood vessels of other parts of the body. Simeons (1961) suggests that the popular idiom whereby someone who is afraid is said to have "cold feet" is a common-sense recognition of the fact that fear produces a physiological readiness to flee, resulting in a reduced flow of blood to the feet and an increased flow to the lungs.

There is experimental evidence to support the concept that emotional arousal can result in a decrease in skin temperature. In one study (Buss, 1966), a group of normal subjects were hypnotized and told that they wanted to take direct, hostile action; a drop in hand temperature ensued. A second group was told, again under hypnosis, that they were about to be subjected to a painful experience and could do nothing to protect themselves; again the result was a decrease in hand temperature.

Raynaud's disease need not involve both the hands and the feet or even an entire hand or foot. Sandy Koufax, a left-handed pitcher considered by many to be one of the greatest talents American baseball had ever seen, was forced to retire at the age of thirty-one because in addition to an arthritic left elbow he had developed Raynaud's disease in the one finger of his left hand that controlled his curve ball. In the case study that follows the disorder was confined to the patient's feet:

Helen L. had grown up in a small Midwestern town and had married her "childhood sweetheart" when she was nineteen. After he completed his military service, Mr. L. decided to take advantage of the GI bill by going to college at a large Eastern university. Helen, who had been looking forward to returning to live in her old hometown, was somewhat dismayed by her husband's decision but complied for the sake of his career. Once he received his bachelor's degree, however, the move was once again deferred as Mr. L. went on to pursue a graduate degree. Meanwhile, Helen began to feel increasingly isolated. Although she enjoyed nothing more than watching television, she found herself surrounded by drama buffs. And although she preferred country music, she dutifully accompanied her husband to chamber-music recitals. These discrepancies between Helen's tastes and those of her husband and his friends increased when he completed his Ph.D. By now the promise of returning to their hometown had been forgotten, and Mr. L. accepted a teaching position at a major university in a large metropolitan area. He was gregarious and adapted easily to his new life. Helen, as usual, joined in without complaining. With the help of some alcohol, however, she was known to mutter about being surrounded by "snobs and phonies."

During her husband's years in graduate school, Helen had begun to complain of cold feet, and much to her distaste, she had to wear woolen socks year-round. By the time her husband took his university job, her condition was complicated by the appearance on her feet of strange-looking sores which resisted medical treatment. She was forced to give up her job as a dental hygienist, which required that she spend a good deal of time on her feet. Thereafter she spent her days at home with few distractions, and soon she became so distressed by her condition that her physician at last referred her to a psychiatrist.

Migraine

Migraine is a condition marked by episodes of severe headache, often unilateral—that is, occurring on one side of the head. The headache may be preceded by an *aura*—a subjective sensation alerting the individual that the headache is about to begin—and it may be accompanied by other somatic symptoms such as dizziness, fainting, nausea, and vomiting. Frequently such episodes occur at night or early in the morning, when the person has rested after a stressful day. Migraine attacks can range from bearable discomfort to complete immobilization and can last anywhere from several hours to several days.

Some clinicians make a distinction between migraine headaches and "tension" headaches, regarding them as two completely different disorders.

Because such a distinction is impossible to verify at present, our discussion will focus on recurrent headaches, whether or not they are preceded by an aura and accompanied by nausea, as is often the case in "classic" migraine.

Like Raynaud's disease, migraine is a cardiovascular disorder in which the difficulty is essentially a disproportionate blood supply. Migraine apparently occurs as a result of the following sequence. First, the blood vessels in the brain constrict as a result of stress. Then once the stress is relieved, the arteries leading to the brain dilate, and more blood is delivered to the area than can be comfortably accommodated. The result of this dramatic change in the flow of blood to the brain is a sharp, painful, throbbing sensation in the head—in short, the migraine. Thus it is not simply stress but rather the period of relief after stress that ushers in the headache.

The incidence of migraine appears to be extremely high. It is estimated that from 10 to 12 million Americans experience migraines either regularly or on occasion as a function of stress. It is also known that the incidence of migraine in women is about twice as high as it is in men. The fact that women usually do not begin experiencing these attacks until adolescence and that the headaches normally subside after menopause has led to a great deal of speculation concerning the possible influence of hormonal factors associated with the appearance and disappearance of the menstrual cycle.

There is no single reliable treatment for migraine. Medical treatments are often complicated by the fact that medication may provide relief for weeks or even months and then lose its effectiveness. Meanwhile, many patients have been helped by nonmedical treatments. We shall examine these psychological treatments for migraine in our discussion of the psychodynamic and behaviorist perspectives.

Asthma

Asthma has been the focus of considerable attention not only because of its high incidence—3 percent of the general American population—but also because it is one of the few psychophysiological complaints common in young children. Approximately one-third of all asthmatics are under the age of sixteen (U.S. DHEW, 1970).

In asthma, stress on the bronchial system results in the narrowing of the air passageways, which in turn causes coughing, wheezing, and general difficulty in breathing. Asthmatic attacks vary in duration, lasting anywhere from a matter of minutes to several hours. They also vary a great deal in their intensity. Some attacks are mild; in others, bronchial spasms cause the air passageways to become so constricted that the asthmatic person has immense difficulty getting air in and out of his lungs. An attack of this severity is a frightening experience; the asthmatic feels that he is suffocating and wheezes and coughs uncontrollably. A series of such attacks can cause a progressive deterioration of the bronchial system, in which mucus accumulates and the muscles lose their elasticity. In such a weakened condition, the bronchial system loses its ability to fight back, and any further attack may prove fatal.

There appear to be at least three factors that can set off an asthmatic attack. First, some asthmas are clearly related to such irritants as pollen, molds, and animal dander and seem to be much like other allergic reactions. Second, there are asthmas that appear to be related to infectious conditions such as whooping cough, tonsillitis, and pneumonia (Rees, 1964). Support for this hypothesis lies in the fact that some asthmatic attacks occur during sleep and thus apparently do not result from interaction with the external environment. Finally, it is a well-established fact that asthmatic attacks can also be triggered by emotional problems. In children, particularly, emotional arousal often leads directly into spasmodic wheezing. Crying spells, for example, are often converted into attacks. And although this fact is not surprising when we consider that sobbing itself greatly modifies respiration, many theorists argue that the attack is symbolic of some underlying conflict. Certainly, only an emotional variable would seem to account for the finding that the condition of an asthmatic child often improves when he is removed from his home. Even when such children have been exposed to dust from their homes—the dust having previously been identified as a triggering agent—their condition remains improved.

In some cases the environmental stimulus that sets off an attack can seem utterly irrelevant or trivial. A most interesting case involved a patient who maintained that if she saw a goldfish she would have an asthmatic attack. The skeptical physician decided to put her claim to the test and brought a goldfish into the room. The patient promptly responded with a genuine attack. His curiosity piqued, the doctor repeated the experiment with a plastic goldfish, and again an attack ensued. Eventually, he found that for this patient the presentation of an empty goldfish bowl was enough to precipitate the attack. In cases such as these, the asthmatic response would seem to be the result of conditioning. Some theorists argue that the apparently neutral stimulus (e.g., a goldfish) is actually symbolic of some anxiety-producing experience the patient underwent earlier in his life, and that consequently, appearances notwithstanding, the attack *is* precipitated by an emotional variable.

Alone or in combination, any of the three variables that we have mentioned—allergic reaction, infection, or psychological stress—can trigger an attack. One study of asthmatic children suggests that multiple causation is usually the rule,

the majority having infective, allergic and psychologic factors in various sequences and combinations. Clinical evidence strongly suggests that these factors often interact with summation of effects. For example, a child who for some years had repeated attacks of bronchitis without wheezing, began having asthma with bronchitis after being frightened by a burglar breaking into her house (Rees, 1964, p. 261).

Eczema

As we can see from the box on pp. 144–145, many kinds of skin disorders—eczema, psoriasis, hives, dermatitis, and even acne—can appear as psychosomatic conditions, and it is often difficult to tell one from the other. Our discussion will focus on *eczema*, probably the most common diagnosis within this category.

Eczema is a fluctuating skin condition that can encompass anything from an itching rash to a cluster of open wounds that may well be the result of uncontrollable scratching. The sensation of itching is extremely difficult to tolerate; indeed, some physicians report that their patients can tolerate pain with more equanimity than they can tolerate itching. Thus the nervousness seen in many people with eczema may be the result rather than—or as well as—the cause of the condition.

The reason for suspecting that emotional factors may be involved in the etiology of eczema derives simply from the observation that many people flush when they are angry and blanch when they are frightened. Thus we know that the circulation of blood immediately beneath the skin can be modified by psychological changes. We also know that the health of the skin depends upon proper blood circulation and that drastic modification of peripheral circulation can be damaging. Hence it would seem to follow that psychological stress, since it can affect peripheral circulation, could cause skin disorders, particularly skin disorders (like eczema) that have shown themselves to be particularly resistant to medical treatment.

However, there are a number of problems with the proposed correlation between eczema and emotional stress. In the first place, the progress of the disorder can seldom be linked directly to events in the patient's life. Second, we have the so-called chicken-and-egg problem. Unlike hypertension or asthma, many cases of eczema are clearly visible and extremely unsightly, so a person with eczema may feel self-conscious and therefore respond in ways that are socially ineffective. Hence emotional distress, like nervousness, may be the result rather than the cause of eczema. If, for example, a depressed and lonely teenaged girl with a raging case of eczema on her hands and face came to a dermatologist, he would have to be extremely biased in favor of the psychosomatic hypothesis in order to conclude that the girl's depression was the cause and the eczema the result rather than vice versa. The process by which eczema is developed and maintained may well be a circular one, in which the emotional stress and the skin condition each aggravate the other. As for which comes first, at present we simply do not know.

Dysmenorrhea

The genitourinary system is primarily under the control of the autonomic nervous system. Thus we would expect elimination, menstruation, and sexual functioning all to be vulnerable to emotional changes. In the case of sexual functioning, this is unquestionably true. However, since sexual inadequacy, probably the most common of the psychophysiological disorders in the genitourinary system, is reserved for a later chapter (Chapter 9), we will confine our discussion to the second most common complaint in this category, *dysmenorrhea*.

Dysmenorrhea is the medical term for irregular or painful menstrual periods. Since so many women accept menstruation as an inherently painful and bothersome process—"the curse," as it is sometimes called—and do not bother to seek medical help for menstrual problems, it is difficult to determine the incidence of this complaint with any degree of accuracy. Estimates of the percentage of American women suffering from dysmenorrhea range from 4 to 62 percent (Santamaria, 1969).

Evidence that psychological difficulties figure in the development of dysmenorrhea comes almost exclusively from clinical practice rather than large-scale studies. Hence what we are left with are a number of plausible but as yet unproved hypotheses. For example, many women report that they have delayed menstrual cycles when they are afraid that

Common Psychophysiological Disorders

DSM-II distinguishes nine major categories of psychophysiological disorders. Listed below are the nine categories, along with a partial listing of the disorders falling under each category. (It is commonly assumed, however, that many of these disorders can also occur strictly as a result of organic causes.)

1. *Psychophysiological skin disorders*

Eczema	Inflammation of the skin
Neurodermatitis	Chronic skin eruptions, ranging from rash to running sores
Psoriasis	Silvery and reddish scaly patches on the skin, especially on the chest, knees, and elbows
Pruritis	Itching skin, especially around the anus or vulva
Hyperhidrosis	Excessive sweating
Acne	Eruption of pustules on the skin
Hives (Urticaria)	An allergic condition characterized by the formation of large, itchy welts or blotches on the skin

2. *Psychophysiological musculoskeletal disorders*

Backache	Pain in the muscles of the upper or lower back, due to chronic tension
Muscle cramps	Spasms in muscles, due to continuous muscle tension
Myalgia	Muscle pain
Tension headaches	Cranial pain due to chronic tension in facial or neck muscles
Arthritis	Inflammation or swollen and painful joints

3. *Psychophysiological respiratory disorders*

Bronchial asthma	Extreme difficulty in breathing, characterized by wheezing, coughing, and difficulty in exhaling air
Hyperventilation	Excessively rapid or deep breathing
Hiccoughs	Chronic spasms of the diaphragm

4. *Psychophysiological cardiovascular disorders*

Hypertension	Chronically elevated blood pressure
Migraine headache	Severe headache, often accompanied by nausea
Raynaud's disease	Chronically cold hands and/or feet
Paroxysmal tachycardia	Spasmodic increases in rate of heartbeat
Vascular spasms	Sudden constriction of blood vessels

5. *Psychophysiological hemic and lymphatic disorders*
Disturbances of the blood and lymphatic systems

6. *Psychophysiological gastrointestinal disorders*

Gastric ulcer	Open sore on the wall of the stomach
Gastritis	Chronic presence of excess gas in the lower digestive tract
Mucous colitis	Inflammation of the colon, often accompanied by disturbances in bowel functions
Constipation	Difficult and infrequent bowel movements
Diarrhea	Chronically loose bowels
Hyperacidity	Discomfort in the upper digestive tract
Pylorospasm	Severe spasm of the sphincter muscle at the far end of the stomach, causing abdominal pain
Heartburn	Burning sensations in the stomach

7. *Psychophysiological genitourinary disorders*

Dysmenorrhea	Irregular or painful menstrual periods
Dyspareunia	Painful coitus
Impotence	Inability, in male, to achieve or maintain erection

8. *Psychophysiological endocrine disorders*

Exophthalmic goiter	Enlargement of thyroid gland
Hyperthyroidism	Overactivity of the thyroid gland
Obesity	Extreme overweight
Diabetes mellitus	Inability to burn up carbohydrates that have been ingested

9. *Psychophysiological disorders of organs of special sense*

Ménière's disease	Disease of the inner ear, often accompanied by ringing in the ears, deafness, dizziness, and nausea
Conjunctivitis	Inflammation of the eyelid membrane

Syndromes Associated with Psychophysiological Disorders

Insomnia	Inability to sleep
Allergies	Hypersensitivity to certain things (such as pollen, types of food, types of drugs, types of animals), resulting in skin rash, breathing difficulty, or other physical symptoms
Anorexia nervosa	Loss of appetite, often resulting in severe malnutrition

they might be pregnant. Such reports have led, of course, to the conclusion that the anticipatory fear may be responsible for the delay. And from this conclusion it is not a long step to the hypothesis that if fear could delay the menstrual cycle, other emotions might also interfere with it. Furthermore, many women have reported that changes in their emotional lives have been followed by changes in the level of menstrual pain. For example, girls who in adolescence have spent three days out of every month in bed with menstrual cramps sometimes find that once they marry, the menstrual pain either decreases considerably or even disappears altogether. Here the correlation might be strictly physical: between the physiological effects of sexual intercourse and the physiological mechanism of menstruation. But it might also be psychological, sexual satisfaction (or perhaps simply release from a disagreeable family environment) giving rise to more normal menstruation. As we have said, these proposals remain merely proposals. And since so many women just accept dysmenorrhea as part of a "woman's burden"—and since dysmenorrhea, unlike hypertension or asthma, is never fatal—research in this area is proceeding more slowly than the study of other psychophysiological disorders.

ASSOCIATED DISORDERS

Of the various disorders associated with psychophysiological complaints we shall discuss only three: insomnia, allergies, and anorexia nervosa.

Insomnia

Insomnia, the chronic inability to sleep, is rarely discussed in textbooks on abnormal psychology except as a symptom of some other more pervasive disorder such as depression. Yet for an extremely large number of people, sleeplessness is the sole complaint, and one which occasions severe physical and psychological distress. Thus there seems ample justification for including it under the psychophysiological disorders.

According to recent surveys, the manufacture and sale of sleeping pills has become big business. In 1973, Americans reportedly spent one and a half billion dollars on sleep-inducing drugs. In England, sleeping pills are said to outsell aspirin (Rechtschaffen and Monroe, 1969). It is estimated that in this country somewhere between 14 and 25 percent of the population have sleeping problems. There is no way of establishing, however, what proportion of these people would report insomnia as their only psychological problem. We do know that women

Is Cancer a Psychophysiological Disorder?

Recently Dr. René Mastrovito conducted a personality study of women suffering from cancer of the reproductive tract. His purpose was to find ways of helping these patients endure the psychological stress of a cancer operation. But in the process he found something else as well: a striking similarity among the personalities of the thirty cancer victims in his study. Indeed, they seemed to represent a type—responsible, idealistic, and emotionally restrained.

Mastrovito claims that his is not the first study to suggest a correlation between cancer and psychological factors. For example, other, more comprehensive psychological tests have also pointed up the emotional restraint of cancer patients. Stoical types apparently have a higher incidence of cancer than those who vent their anger by kicking, swearing, and throwing things.

Another interesting fact is that cancer is much rarer among schizophrenics than in the population at large. Indeed, many years ago a case was reported in which an apparently incurable cancer spontaneously disappeared from a patient's system as he entered a psychotic episode. The psychosis ran its course in about six months, after which the patient enjoyed excellent health until the missing cancer reappeared seven years later.

Should we then, in order to prevent cancer, not only stop smoking but also begin throwing crockery when we are angry? And should we concede that schizophrenia has at least one beneficial side effect? Perhaps. We still know little about the human psyche, less about cancer, and even less about the relationship between emotional and physiological conditions. But it is possible that hormone levels accompanying certain emotional states, even very uncomfortable ones, create an organic climate uncongenial to the growth of cancer and therefore constitute a form of protection.

Source: Harold M. Schmeck, Jr., "Wives' Emotions Linked to Cancer," *The New York Times*, May 11, 1974.

tend to report themselves as having more sleep disturbances than do men. We also know that for both sexes, sleep disturbances tend to increase with age.

Disturbed sleep patterns are of three types. The person may take an extremely long time to fall asleep; he may fall asleep only to awaken repeatedly during the night; or he may wake up much too early each day and be unable to fall asleep again. At some point in our lives each of us has probably experienced some variant of these difficulties. The term "insomnia" is generally applied only if the pattern persists regularly over a period of time.

The disturbance in sleep is almost always a source of concern for the patient, and this concern leads to what is called "anticipatory anxiety" (a problem which, as we shall see, is also a major factor in sexual dysfunction). The minute the person gets into bed, or even while he is putting on his pajamas, he begins to worry: Will I be able to sleep? Will it be like last night? How will I get through work again on three hours' sleep? And since worry of any kind impedes sleep, the worried person probably *will* have another night like last night. Hence insomnia qualifies as a classic example of the vicious circle.

The possibility that sleep patterns can be controlled by past experience is suggested by the following case history:

Edward K. was an attractive career officer who had recently retired. His only complaint was that he usually awakened at about two o'clock in the morning and found it impossible to get back to sleep. He felt himself to be at a total loss. He had tried numerous home remedies of his own and some suggested by friends: reading himself back to sleep, watching old movies on television, listening to soothing music, and so forth. Nothing worked. By about four-thirty every morning he was usually up pacing the floor and wondering anxiously how he would manage to get through the following day with so little sleep.

He readily conceded that he was sometimes lonely. His wife had recently died, and his children were grown up and lived in other communities. However, despite the isolation from his family, Edward was not a man to sit around and brood. He had organized a recreation center for retired people and was busy directing it, as well as planning more programs for the future. Life, he explained to his therapist, was as good as could be expected at his age, and at least he had no financial worries.

After about two months of weekly sessions, the therapist decided to try hypnosis. While Edward was under hypnosis, his therapist gave him the suggestion that he would continue sleeping until six o'clock each morning, his customary rising time in the army. Once the hypnosis was terminated, Edward realized the reason for his apprehension about sleeping past two o'clock: he had once had a nearly fatal heart attack at that time. Another appointment was made for the following week, but Edward called to cancel it, explaining that he was now able to sleep through the night.

Most cures, however, are not so simple. Sleep is still enough of a mystery that guesses about a breakdown in the physiological chain of events leading to sleep and wakening are just that—guesses. Suffice it to say that insomnia is a complex process involving changes in brain activity that may in turn be affected by the internal and external environment.

Since in many cases sleep-inducing drugs are neither safe nor effective and since they are so often implicated in suicides, there have been many efforts to develop other treatments. The Russians have reportedly perfected a machine that will induce sleep electrically (Rosenthal and Wulfsohn, 1970). As for home remedies, about which advice is so freely given, these include everything from the traditional glass of warm milk to vigorous exercise just before retiring.

Allergies

An *allergy* is a hypersensitive reaction to an irritating substance (an *allergen*) in the environment. This reaction, which may develop gradually or after only one or two exposures, is usually manifested either in a skin disorder or in respiratory difficulties. Indeed, some allergic reactions are classified as respiratory or skin disorders. Hives, for example, may be considered a skin disorder, and hay fever can be described as a respiratory problem. Conversely, some forms of asthma, as we have seen, can be described as allergic reactions.

Allergies are extremely various, capricious, and unpredictable. In the first place, it is apparently possible to become allergic to almost anything. A few years ago it was reported in one of the nation's newspapers that a woman and her husband were experiencing a domestic crisis because she had become allergic to him. Other people become allergic to dust, pollen, animal dander, eggs, milk, synthetic fibers, feathers, cotton, bacteria, or fungi. The list is virtually endless.

Furthermore, the intensity of the allergy can vary widely. An allergic reaction can be as mild as a faint reddening of the skin or a slight stuffiness of the nose. In other cases the reaction can be fatal. People allergic to penicillin have been reported to die from a single injection administered by an unknowing physician.

Finally, the course of some allergies seems very odd. For example, a woman who suffers from violent bouts of hay fever may take shots, improve, be free of hay fever for a number of years, then have a single violent attack, and then again become free of the affliction. On the other hand, some allergies are very predictable. A person allergic to cat dander may, upon entering a cat-inhabited house, start sneezing without even knowing that there is a cat on the premises.

Theories about the connections between allergies and other disorders abound. For example, some maintain that allergies are involved in migraine, alcoholism, and even schizophrenia. Likewise, there is much hypothesizing about the relationship between allergies and psychological stress. A review of the literature on allergic disorders reveals that according to several surveys, an emotional factor was present in the attacks of 75 percent of allergic patients (Freeman et al., 1964). And recently it has been reported that some allergies that have resisted medical treatment will in fact yield to psychological therapies. But here, as with other psychophysiological disorders, speculation far outweighs evidence as to the connection between psychic and somatic components.

Anorexia Nervosa

Anorexia nervosa is characterized by a loss of appetite so extreme that it results in a state of severe malnutrition and semistarvation. The loss of weight is of course the most dramatic symptom. Bliss and Branch (1960) cite a case in which the woman's weight dropped from 180 pounds to 60 pounds. As with insomnia, anorexia is often the only presenting complaint, although occasionally anorexic patients become schizophrenic.

Although it is sometimes classified as a neurotic conversion symptom and described as "hysterical loss of appetite," anorexia is associated with psychophysiological complaints because, unlike conversion hysteria, it involves actual damage to the body. Furthermore, while eating is a voluntary action, the autonomic nervous system is involved in the suppression of hunger sensations, and therefore anorexia can reasonably be considered a psychophysiological disorder.

This disorder can take one of two forms: the patient refuses to eat, or she eats and then either

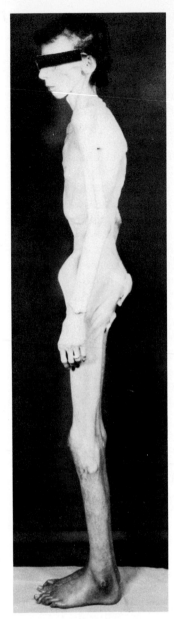

Fig. 6.6 *The dramatic loss of weight characteristic of anorexia nervosa is evident in this emaciated woman, whose weight dropped to 47 pounds.*

induces regurgitation or regurgitates involuntarily. Some patients report that they are so repelled by food that they never experience the normal sensations of hunger. Others show bizarre food preferences or manifest a preoccupation with food in other ways, perhaps by amassing enormous collections of cookbooks. Anorexia is notoriously difficult to treat, and somewhere between 5 and 15 percent of anorexics literally starve themselves to death. One problem with treatment is that once the malnutrition has progressed to a certain point, the anorexic patient may be too weak to eat. But the major problem in treatment is simply that most anorexics refuse, apparently for emotional reasons, to take in any food, often arguing—against overwhelming evidence to the contrary—that they are overweight. (Many anorexics have in fact had histories of obesity [Crisp, 1970].) Finally, even if the anorexia can be reversed, the damage done to the body—and particularly to the liver—by malnutrition is often irreversible (Kessler, 1966).

Anorexia is typically the disease of young women. It occurs in women nine times as frequently as in men, and though it may appear at any age, its onset is typically in adolescence or early adulthood. When anorexia appears in a young woman, it is often thought to represent sexual conflicts, possibly involving fear of impregnation, and to function as a stratagem for avoiding the adult sexual role. Whether or not this theory holds true, anorexia does indeed severely modify the female sexual characteristics: breasts and hips shrink dramatically, and menstrual periods tend to disappear.

The following case of an anorexic teenager is extremely typical:

Karen D. was the shy, plain child of a beautiful and hard-driving mother who had given up a promising career as a magazine editor to raise her daughter. Mrs. D. always hoped, however, that Karen would take over where she had left off and would become a successful career woman.

Karen seemed born to frustrate her mother's ambitions for her. A whiny, anxious child, she had been overweight since infancy. Her mother constantly needled her to lose weight, and once the girl became an adolescent Mrs. D. started offering to buy her a new dress for every 5 pounds she lost. Pictures of gaunt-looking fashion models were pasted on all the kitchen cabinets. All these efforts resulted only in Karen's becoming more withdrawn and obsessive about eating. By age sixteen she weighed 172 pounds. She had few friends and never dated.

Because her relationship with her mother had become intolerable for both of them, it was decided that Karen should continue her education at a boarding school. At the new school, Karen at last seemed able to go on a long-term diet. But she could accomplish this only by eating voraciously and then forcing herself to vomit up what she had eaten. By the end of the school year Karen was down to a normal weight. Despite the improvement in her appearance, she was still too shy to mix with other teenagers.

The dieting did not stop, however, and now Karen's mother was constantly pleading with her to eat. If

forced to eat, the girl gagged or vomited immediately. By the time she returned to school in September she weighed only 90 pounds. By November she was down to 75 pounds and her menstrual periods had stopped. She was then placed in the school infirmary, where she continued to lose weight. Finally she was sent home to her parents. Soon afterward, weighing only 64 pounds, Karen was hospitalized and a program of behavioral therapy was begun.

PERSPECTIVES ON THE PSYCHOPHYSIOLOGICAL DISORDERS

Given the fact that the psychophysiological disorders involve detectable physical symptoms, it is far from surprising that we find theorists from a number of disciplines—including biology, physiology, and medicine—concerned with the nature of these complaints and with how they should be treated.

The Psychodynamic Perspective

Psychodynamic theorists tend to conceptualize the etiology and treatment of the various psychophysiological disorders in essentially the same way that they conceptualize the neuroses. In fact, they call the psychophysiological complaints *organ neuroses.*

Cause In explaining what causes an organ neurosis, psychodynamic theory is still concerned with anxiety, defense mechanisms, trauma at various psychosexual stages, and other concepts already discussed in Chapters 2 and 5. In this view, the same trauma, conflicts, and psychological mechanisms that contribute to the formation of neurotic symptoms contribute to the formation of psychophysiological symptoms. And according to the psychodynamic theorists, the various psychophysiological complaints serve the same functions as do the defense mechanisms: they keep the nature of the underlying conflict from reaching the level of consciousness.

For the psychodynamic theorist, the only difference between explaining a neurosis and explaining a psychophysiological disorder is that in the latter, one must account for the so-called choice of symptom—why, for example, a person develops hypertension rather than asthma. On this subject there is some disagreement. Some psychodynamic theorists would argue that the symptom picture is a form of regression and that the present physiological response reproduces a response elicited at the time of the original conflict. Formulated in these terms, the current complaint would symbolize the time in the patient's life history that was traumatic or at least problematic for him. Thus hypertension might be seen as regression to a time when there was intense anger, coupled with a feeling of helplessness about the situation which provoked that anger. Similarly, since an ulcer patient's disorder relates to his digestive system, a psychodynamic theorist might see his disorder as a lack of gratification during early feeding experiences, resulting in anxiety and dependency needs in adulthood.

Many theorists go a step further. They insist that the symptom picture symbolizes not only the time but the content of early difficulties. They point out, for example, that like crying, an asthmatic attack involves changes both in breathing and vocalization. Thus, according to this interpretation, an asthmatic attack is a symbolic way of crying and represents a repressed need for mothering. For the adult patient a situation that might have resulted in crying when he was a child may now bring on an asthmatic attack. Such theorists are quick to point out that crying can actually precipitate an attack in children, a fact we have already noted.

There are theorists who believe that in addition to the symbolic import of the symptom, its location in the body may also have symbolic value. For example, according to this line of reasoning, the swelling of the fingers in an arthritic hand might represent anxiety about impotence, the shape of the finger suggesting a phallus and the swelling constituting a symbolic erection. Similarly, the appearance of a self-punishing symptom in the hand could represent unconscious guilt associated with masturbation.

In all psychodynamic formulations, self-punishment is a recurring theme. Thus the discomfort and reduction in physical functioning seen in the various psychophysiological disorders are easily interpreted as a form of self-punishment. Here it is important to bear in mind that classical psychodynamic theory often postulates guilt as the result not of actual misdeeds but of unacceptable wishes or fantasies, so evidence of the patient's misbehavior need not be demonstrated.

We should also point out that many psychodynamic theorists, particularly the more orthodox Freudians, employ an extremely broad definition of psychophysiological disorders. For example, in a book devoted to what was then called psychosomatic medicine, Dunbar (1935) had much to say about the unconscious wishes of people who are accident-prone. Freud himself took the position that in the course of human behavior, there was no such thing as an accident. If this premise is granted, a person who has an unusually high number of automobile accidents would certainly qualify as a candidate for psychoanalysis.

Treatment Treatment of psychophysiological disorders does not differ in any significant respect from treatment of the neuroses, according to the psychodynamic school. The therapist makes use of the same techniques; he expects the same course of events to unfold during therapy; and his goals in treating the patient are comparable to those outlined in Chapter 5. These similarities are perhaps best illustrated by describing the treatment of a patient with a psychophysiological complaint.

The patient, a woman of twenty-eight, was an intelligent and highly creative person who suffered from migraine headaches of extreme intensity. These were usually accompanied by an overwhelming feeling of nausea. During such times she was unable to care for her children or to function effectively in any other capacity. She took to her bed and did not get up until the episode had passed—often a matter of many hours. As she mentioned during the first interview, she was well aware that her headaches frequently took place after she had accommodated herself to the wishes of her husband against her better judgment. For example, her husband, a vigorous and often domineering business executive, frequently wanted to invite clients or friends home for elaborate dinner parties. He also pressured his wife into attending various evening discussion sessions and encounter groups. Despite the fact that she preferred to devote her spare time to her own interests in art history and literature, the patient usually gave in to her husband's demands.

During therapy, dream analysis and free association revealed that this young woman had intense guilt feelings because of her many erotic fantasies about her father, and that these guilt feelings had never been resolved. (The guilt was probably intensified by the fact that when the patient was eleven years old, her father had been killed in an automobile accident.) Thus she experienced an intense conflict between her repressed desire to gratify her wishes, and on the other hand, her guilt and fear of punishment by her superego. In therapy the patient came to see that she related to her husband in the same way that she had to her father.

With the help of the therapist, the patient was able to bring those repressed wishes and guilt feelings of early childhood to a conscious level, and her headaches began to diminish in both frequency and intensity. Moreover, she began to speak out more openly when she disagreed with her husband. From a psychodynamic standpoint, this change grew out of the resolution of an unconscious conflict that had its roots in a much earlier period of the patient's life.

The Behaviorist Perspective

As we shall see, behaviorist formulations about the etiology and treatment of the various psychophysiological complaints have undergone significant changes in the last five years.

Cause   For many years the behaviorists could propose little that was original in explaining the origins of psychophysiological disorders. At first it was thought that autonomic responses could be modified only by respondent conditioning. Therefore, a good part of the behavioral position was predicated upon the anxiety-reduction model of psychopathology developed by psychodynamic theorists. Anxiety, as we have seen, was thought to be an involuntary response controlled by the autonomic nervous system, and anything that would reduce that anxiety—even physiological discomfort—would be stamped in through negative reinforcement and would therefore tend to become habitual.

For the behavioral theorists the difficulty of applying such a model to psychophysiological complaints is obvious: How can the lessening of anxiety through the introduction of physical pain or the loss of physical efficiency be reinforcing? Almost the only explanation consistent with behavioral theory was that by being sick, the individual received the positive reinforcement of extra attention—that is, secondary gains. But even this seemed an inadequate explanation in view of the utterly debilitating nature of so many psychophysiological disorders. Faced with this puzzle, behaviorists tended for many years to ignore psychophysiological disorders.

All this was changed in the late 1960s with the development of *biofeedback* techniques, through which subjects, by using various machines, could monitor their own biological processes such as pulse, blood pressure, and brain waves. The interesting finding was that by receiving such feedback, some subjects could actually *control*, within limits, their autonomic processes—slow their heart rate, modify their brain waves, lower their blood pressure, reduce sweat-gland activity, and so forth—though they could not specify how they had attained such control (Shearn, 1962; Hnatiow and Lang, 1965; Lang,

Fig. 6.7 (left)   In the past it was assumed that autonomic responses were related to environmental stimuli primarily through classical conditioning. Recently, numerous studies involving the operant control of involuntary reactions have suggested that these responses may be acquired through operant as well as classical conditioning. This "precocious" rat was trained through operant conditioning methods to regulate his vascular functioning so that one ear flushed while the other paled.

Fig. 6.8 (right)   With the use of biofeedback devices, subjects can monitor their own biological processes. Here, via electrodes attached to the skull, the subject picks up the rhythm of his brain-waves and, in turn, controls them.

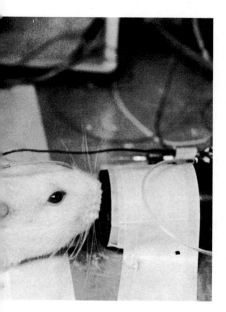

1970). A dramatic example of self-regulation of bodily processes is seen in the case of a precocious animal subject: a rat who learned to produce, upon cue, vascular changes that simultaneously caused flushing in one ear and paling in the other (Miller and DiCara, 1971).

What the results of such biofeedback training meant was that autonomic responses apparently were *not* totally involuntary and that therefore they could be controlled through operant conditioning. In response to these findings, the behaviorists began to invoke principles of reinforcement and degree of feedback as explanatory principles in the development of psychophysiological problems. The basic formulation is a simple one—that the psychophysiological disorders are learned responses. Behaviorists argue that if a change in physiological functioning (impaired respiration, for example) is more or less consistently rewarded (as an asthmatic attack might be in terms of increased attention), the physiological change becomes habituated to the situations that have produced the reinforcement. If habituation, in turn, produces tissue damage or loss of function, behaviorists argue that it is possible to maintain that physical disorders may be a function of operant conditioning.

Treatment The behavioral therapist approaches psychophysiological disorders in precisely the same way that he approaches any other behavior problem. He identifies the maladaptive behavior, specifies a desirable target behavior, and designs a treatment plan that will teach the patient how to move from the maladaptive behavior to the target behavior.

Many behavioral techniques are successful in controlling psychophysiological disorders. Sometimes the complaint is attacked directly. For example, a hypertensive patient may be taught to reduce his blood pressure through relaxation therapy, which is part of Wolpe's systematic desensitization training (Chapter 5). On other occasions, the therapist might make use of strategies designed to prevent an attack or to arrest it in its early stages. Thus the patient may be taught to control his reaction to stress and also to control the situations that lead to that reaction. For example, biofeedback training has been dramatically effective in the treatment of migraine headaches. Thus if a behavioral therapist rather than a psychodynamic therapist were to treat the young migraine sufferer described in the previous section, he might train her to attend to biofeedback so that she knew when she was becoming tense. He might also teach her relaxation techniques to control that

tension so that it would not build up into a full-scale migraine attack. And of course a truly comprehensive treatment plan would include assertive training, to teach her to be more forthright about her own preferences when dealing with her husband. (Assertive training will be discussed in greater detail in Chapter 19.)

The Humanistic-Existential Perspective

Like the psychodynamic theorists, humanists and existentialists equate psychophysiological disorders with neuroses. They depart from a psychodynamic framework, however, in considering these disorders to stem from a conflict between inner demands and those of society. Migraine, ulcers, asthma, and other psychophysiological complaints are seen simply as the physiological expression of the stress felt by a person whose goals or perceptions run counter to those of society and who fears that by conforming to social demands he loses his authentic self.

For example, many humanists and existentialists would view hypertension as an indictment of the society rather than as an abnormal reaction. According to this position, man is constantly victimized by his fear of confronting the Establishment. Such theorists would be surprised only if no psychophysiological or neurotic symptoms appeared in a human being who tends to conform excessively. In their terms, the therapeutic goals in treating any of the psychophysiological complaints would be to check the client's tendency toward social conformity and to help him clarify and act upon his own unique goals.

Personal, Interpersonal, and Cultural Perspectives

In addition to the environmental variables implicated in the psychophysiological disorders from the viewpoints of the preceding perspectives, other perspectives have stressed the etiological role of such factors as learned traits, family disturbances, and cultural stress.

Personality and Attitudes A few decades ago, some theorists, particularly Dunbar (1935), believed that eczema, migraine, ulcer, and other psychophysiological complaints could be linked with specific personality types or trait clusters. The patient with eczema was said to crave affection and to be guilty, self-punitive, unconsciously exhibitionistic, frustrated, and helpless; he was also thought to be the child of conscientious but emotionally distant parents. The migraine patient was described as hard-working and conscientious, something of a perfectionist, and committed to a variety of "good causes." The ulcer patient who achieved worldly success was described as ambitious and self-assertive; the "unsuccessful" ulcer sufferer was passive and dependent.

Although there are so-called classic cases in which the trait constellation once thought to be linked with a given disorder does in fact appear as predicted, recent studies seem to indicate that each of the psychophysiological disorders appears in a variety of personality types. One particularly interesting finding is that ulcers, once thought to be the special province of high-achievers in executive positions, are more likely to develop in chronically discontented blue-collar workers (Kahn, 1969).

Instead of approaching the question in terms of personality traits, Graham (1962) makes use of the concept of attitude. It is his thesis that every psychophysiological disorder is linked with a specific attitude. For example, according to this theory, a person with eczema feels thwarted and unable to take any action; hence he makes himself the target of his own frustration. The hypertensive person feels that he is going to be harmed and that he must therefore be on his guard. A person with Raynaud's disease wants to act in a hostile way—through strangling and hitting, for example. Graham has attempted to test his hypothesis empirically and reports success, but other studies (e.g., Peters and Stern, 1971) contradict his findings.

Attempts to link specific trait clusters to individual psychophysiological disorders are hardly obsolete. In their recent book, *Type A Behavior and Your Heart* (1974), Friedman and Rosenman suggest that a specific type of personality, which they call Type A, is clearly predisposed to hypertension as well as to other cardiovascular disorders. The Type A personality is an aggressive achiever. He moves, walks, and eats rapidly, and feels guilty about relaxing. He cannot bear to be kept waiting. He finishes other people's sentences for them. He fidgets in frustration if he is kept waiting by a traffic light, an elevator, or a line in the bank. The Type A personality prides himself on getting things done in less time than other people, and he measures his own performance by increasingly rigorous standards.

Such a hypertensive "type" may in fact exist, as these investigators insist that it does. However, even if we gather enough clinical evidence to indicate that a certain personality type does carry a predisposition to hypertension or some other psychophysiological complaint, the question remains: Why do certain people with this constellation of traits develop the disorder while others with the same traits remain symptom-free? After all, there are Type As all around us, and many of them go on to the ripe old age of 92 finishing other people's sentences for them.

Stress In our description of the psychophysiological disorders, we already mentioned the role of stress and its capacity to bring about autonomic changes such as increases in gastric activity, heart rate, and blood pressure. As we have seen in our discussion of asthma, stress can be physiological—as with allergens or infective conditions such as pneumonia—or psychological—as in the death of a parent, a financial setback, or family bickering. Moreover, stress is cumulative. Flu is a source of stress; a final exam is a source of stress. And while the organism might be able to tolerate either the flu or the final exam with minimal difficulty, the combination of the two will make him more vulnerable.

The response to stress is the same regardless of whether the stressors are physiological or psychological. Initially the response has a protective function for the organism—as in the release of adrenaline, for example. Under conditions of prolonged stress, however, the protective response may become destructive, upsetting the balance of the bodily systems. Or if the stress is constant, the body's ability to resist stress may become weaker and weaker, and if it is completely exhausted, death can ensue. This latter sequence, demonstrated with laboratory animals, is another mechanism that has been invoked to explain voodoo death. In the more typical case, it is thought that under conditions of constant stress, a person's ability to resist the stress weakens sufficiently to render him more vulnerable to any disorder, psychophysiological or otherwise.

In a provocative volume entitled *Man's Presumptuous Brain* (1961), Simeons suggests that like all animals, man is physiologically programmed to make a "fight-or-flight" response to life stress. That is, under arousal, the organism naturally undergoes changes which help it either respond aggressively or retreat as quickly as possible. Members of species other than man, because they are free of the constraints of an organized society, carry out the natural series of responses and either fight or flee: either activity returns the body to its state of normal balance—provided, of course, that the animal survives. Man, however, is socialized *not* to fight or flee. Instead, we are taught to "reason" with our enemies, turn the other cheek, endure, resist quietly, "stay cool," or try some other civilized remedy. However, these indirect means of handling arousal are much less effective than "fight or flight" in returning the body to a state of balance. And if habitual, they become disruptive enough to produce visible pathology.

Other theorists have speculated about whether the various psychophysiological complaints may each be linked with a particular type of stress. For example, according to Alexander (1950), hypertension results when a person is unable to handle his aggressive impulses and attempts to repress them. Similarly, Alexander has argued that the ulcer sufferer is unable to reconcile his needs for affection and support with social demands that he show more aggressive, independent behavior.

Although current studies do not support such a correlation between specific sources of stress and specific psychophysiological disorders, it has been demonstrated that certain types of stress are connected, in a very broad sense, with certain psychophysiological categories. We know, for example, that under extremely stressful conditions such as those precipitated by an earthquake, a flood, or a social revolution, cardiovascular and gastrointestinal disorders are particularly common (Senay and Redlich, 1968). In general, however, it seems likely that a given stress can lead to any one of a number of complaints (or to no complaint at all) depending on the individual's predisposition and his vulnerability at the time the stress occurs.

Family Variables It is a well-established fact that families tend to share their psychophysiological disorders. Migraine occurs with greater than average frequency in the families of migraine sufferers. Similarly, the incidence of hypertension in the families of hypertensive patients is greater than it is in the general population, and statistics for the families of asthmatics are comparable. But what inferences are to be drawn from such findings? One possibility, which we shall discuss shortly, is that these disorders are passed on genetically. Another possibility is that certain maladaptive ways of responding may be learned and reinforced within the family by many of its members. Yet another, related possibility is that some psychophysiological complaints grow out of disturbed relationships between parents and children—even if the parent himself does not suffer from the particular complaint.

There are several studies that support this third hypothesis, especially with respect to asthma (Wenar et al., 1962; Olds, 1970). One study (Rees, 1963)

Fig. 6.9 *An important biological theory concerning the development of psychophysiological disorders is the stress theory advanced by Hans Selye. According to this approach, the organism's reactions to stress involve a total mobilization of physiological resources. When the stress continues over a long period of time, resources are diminished and "diseases of adaptation" appear. (*Woman II, Willem de Kooning; Collection, Museum of Modern Art, New York.)

suggests that in some cases the cause of asthma may be pathogenic parent-child relationships. Such parents are described as being overprotective and yet, because they are perfectionists, rejecting at the same time. Another study (Purcell et al., 1969) found that the condition of asthmatic children described as having disturbed relationships with their parents improved when they were separated from their parents—a finding which lends further credibility to

Life Change and Physical Ailments

After studying the recent histories of people with medical problems, Holmes and Holmes (1970) have concluded that any number of illnesses, and not just the commonly recognized psychophysiological disorders, can be precipitated by the stress accompanying changes in one's life. To measure the impact of different kinds of changes, Holmes and Rahe (1967) have developed the Social Readjustment Rating Scale, which rates each kind of potentially stressful event in terms of "life change units" (LCUs).

Life event	LCUs
Death of spouse	100
Divorce	73
Marital separation	65
Jail term	63
Death of close family member	63
Personal injury or illness	53
Marriage	50
Fired at work	47
Marital reconciliation	45
Retirement	45
Change in health of family member	44
Pregnancy	40
Sex difficulties	39
Gain of new family member	39
Business readjustment	39
Change in financial state	38
Death of close friend	37
Change to different line of work	36
Change in number of arguments with spouse	35
Mortgage over $10,000	31
Foreclosure of mortgage or loan	30
Change in responsibilities at work	29
Son or daughter leaving home	29
Trouble with in-laws	29
Outstanding personal achievement	28
Wife begins or stops work	26
Begin or end school	26
Change in living conditions	25
Revision of personal habits	24
Trouble with boss	23
Change in work hours or conditions	20
Change in residence	20
Change in schools	20
Change in recreation	19
Change in church activities	19
Change in social activities	18
Mortgage or loan less than $10,000	17
Change in sleeping habits	16
Change in number of family get-togethers	15
Change in eating habits	15
Vacation	13
Christmas	12
Minor violations of the law	11

The more LCUs you compile in a short period of time, the more prone you are to disease. In one sample Holmes found that of those who had absorbed more than 300 LCUs during a one-year period, 86 percent experienced some serious health problem, whereas health changes were found in only 48 percent of those who had scored between 150 and 300 (Colligan, 1975).

Imagine, for example, a woman in her senior year of college. In April, she is notified that the graduate school she wants to attend has not only accepted her, but is offering her a big scholarship (outstanding personal achievement: 28 LCUs). In May her father dies (death of close family member: 63 LCUs), and the trust fund he has established for her begins paying her a generous monthly income (change in financial state: 38 LCUs). In June she graduates (end school: 26 LCUs) and goes to Bermuda for a month in the sun (vacation: 13 LCUs). There she is arrested for marijuana possession, spends two nights in jail (jail term: 63 LCUs), and is deported. Returning home discouraged and depressed, she shies away from drugs, parties, and friends and spends the rest of the summer at home reading and keeping to herself (revision of personal habits: 24 LCUs). In September she leaves for graduate school (change in residence: 20 LCUs) and for the first time in her life takes an apartment of her own (change in living conditions: 25 LCUs). She starts classes (begin school: 26 LCUs), and by October she has fallen in love with a man who, as she soon discovers, is impotent (sex difficulties: 39 LCUs). Leaving her in the middle of her difficulties, we can now stop and total up her score for the last five months: 365 LCUs. According to Holmes, it's time for her to see a doctor, no matter how she feels.

the family hypothesis. Nevertheless, no one has as yet been able to establish with certainty that specific styles of family interaction lead to particular psychophysiological disorders. Furthermore, we should bear in mind that while different family practices will create different degrees of stress, stress has to be defined in individual terms. To an outsider, a highly demanding, achievement-oriented family might seem a source of chronic stress, when in actuality the child is able to meet the parents' demands routinely and unemotionally. Conversely, a more permissive family might appear to be a negligible source of stress, when in fact the very lack of structure makes it difficult for the child to know how to behave and thus constitutes a major source of stress.

Social and Cultural Variables Recently there have been some attempts to view the psychophysiological disorders within the larger social setting in which they occur. Hence a number of questions have been raised as to the incidence of the various disorders and their relationship to such variables as age, sex, race, and social class.

It is of some interest, for example, that there are seven times as many deaths from hypertension among nonwhites as there are among whites (Stamler et al., 1960). And in general, there has been an upsurge of psychophysiological disorders among black people in this country. Moreover, some theorists (Richardson, 1967) believe that there is a strong correlation between illness and social class, the incidence of illness being highest in the lower class.

Evidence from many quarters suggests that the technological advances, increased mobility, and other broad sociocultural changes in this country have made certain groups in our society particularly vulnerable to specific psychophysiological disorders. For example, ulcers were once four times as prevalent among men as among women. This ratio has now been reduced to about two to one. As women become a larger and larger percentage of the work force and begin assuming jobs of greater responsibility, it is possible that the incidence of ulcers among men and women will tend to equalize.

At one time it was thought that psychophysiological complaints were the exclusive property of industrialized cultures. Although cross-cultural studies reveal that these complaints are much less common in primitive societies, such data are difficult to interpret because of the generally high mortality rates in these societies. For example, if a man does not live beyond the age of forty, his chances of developing an ulcer are considerably decreased.

Despite the fact that our data are incomplete and difficult to analyze, however, many theorists insist that unless we see man within the context of his social environment, our understanding of the psychophysiological disorders—and indeed, all forms of illness—will be incomplete. And in view of the fact that the incidence and distribution of psychophysiological illnesses do seem to shift along with social changes, it does seem unrealistic to study these illnesses without reference to the stress of changing cultural demands (Schwab et al., 1970).

The Biological Perspective

Early in this chapter we saw that the tendency to conceptualize mind and body as a dualism has led to some differences in emphasis among those attempting to account for and treat the various psychophysiological complaints. In the biological and physiological perspectives, the emphasis is of course on organic rather than social or interpersonal factors that might predispose a person to psychophysiological problems.

The argument for a genetic factor in psychophysiological disorders rests largely on the evidence, already discussed, that these disorders tend to run in families. It is known, for example, that the incidence of ulcers among the brothers of ulcer sufferers is twice as high as it is in the normal population (Gregory and Rosen, 1965). In itself, this is certainly no basis on which to conclude that ulcers are inherited. Growing up in the same family, two brothers might easily *learn* the same maladaptive way of coping with stress. But it has also been shown that when ulcer patients are anxious, they secrete higher than average amounts of hydrochloric acid. Furthermore, research has established that ulcer sufferers have persistently higher than average levels of uropepsin (an enzyme that aids in digestion of food) in their bloodstream and urine (Mirsky et al., 1958). In fact, using this information, it is possible to predict who in a given population will develop an ulcer. Such data suggest that some people may be biologically predisposed, by higher levels of gastric secretions, to become ulcer sufferers if exposed to a certain degree of stress. But before any broad statements can be made about the influence of genetic variables on the development of ulcers or any other psychophysiological disorder, we will need more extensive research—and research that can carefully control for the many environmental variables involved.

The Physiological Perspective

One of the major current theories as to physiological

factors that might predispose a person to a certain psychophysiological complaint or to any psychophysiological complaint is called the somatic weakness theory.

Somatic Weakness In view of the differences in our genetic endowments and in our physiological histories—diet, illness, accident, and so on—it is unlikely that any two human beings have an equivalent set of organ systems. According to the theory of *somatic weakness*, a psychophysiological complaint is most likely to develop in a person's weakest or most vulnerable organ system. Thus a mildly deficient organ system would not be damaged unless emotional complications were severe, whereas an extremely weak organ system could succumb to a relatively minor stress.

Consider, for example, a person with a superb digestive system, an average vascular system, and a weak respiratory system. Severe stress of any kind would be likely to have a damaging effect on his respiratory system, possibly in the form of asthma. There is some evidence in support of this hypothesis. Rees (1964), for example, has shown that 80 percent of the asthmatic children he studied had previously suffered from respiratory ailments.

The theory of somatic weakness, then, is concerned with a question central to the study of all the psychophysiological disorders: What determines why a person develops one specific psychophysiological complaint rather than another? While this question remains without a definitive answer, the somatic weakness theory represents a plausible hypothesis.

SUMMARY

This chapter has been a consideration of the psychophysiological complaints. In all these disorders we find the presence of detectable physical symptoms that are thought to be related to psychological problems. Usually, each disorder involves a single organ system that is under the control of the autonomic nervous system.

The tendency to conceptualize mind and body as a duality has led to some difficulties as well as to differences in emphasis in explaining the etiology of psychophysiological disorders. Yet the brain, as part of the nervous system, is connected with all the other organ systems in the body, so that the alteration of one system will almost certainly influence the functioning of the others. According to the unitary view, the terms "psychological" and "physical" are simply two different ways of referring to the same event. Moreover, diagnosis and classification of the psychophysiological disorders are to some degree arbitrary, being partly a function of the success or failure of current treatment methods.

The more common psychophysiological disorders include ulcer, hypertension, Raynaud's disease, migraine, asthma, eczema, and dysmenorrhea. Often explained in terms of the patient's high level of gastric acidity, an ulcer is an open sore in the wall of the stomach or duodenum. Research on both animal and human subjects supports the thesis that psychological stress can play an important role in the formation of an ulcer. Another disorder that seems to be related to prolonged stress is hypertension, the chronic elevation of blood pressure with no organic cause. Raynaud's disease is characterized by cold hands and feet, although there is no visible impairment to the circulatory system. In migraine, another cardiovascular disorder, episodes of extremely painful, throbbing headaches may be accompanied by nausea or fainting. Asthma, the most common psychophysiological respiratory ailment, may be triggered by allergic, infective, or psychological variables. Eczema, the most common diagnosis among psychophysiological skin disorders, and dysmenorrhea, painful and irregular menstrual periods, are also discussed, along with three disorders related to psychophysiological illness: insomnia, allergies, and anorexia nervosa.

Theorists may approach the etiology and treatment of psychophysiological disorders from a number of different perspectives. The psychodynamic theorists view such complaints in the same way they view the neuroses. In explaining a psychophysiological disorder, however, they also attempt to account for the "choice" of symptom. With evidence from biofeedback laboratories that the responses of the autonomic nervous system are not necessarily involuntary, the behavioral theorists have intensified their interest in the psychophysiological disorders. As a result, they now invoke the principle of operant conditioning in explaining the development of various psychophysiological complaints. Like the psychodynamic theorists, humanistic and existential theorists equate psychophysiological disorders with neuroses.

Other perspectives emphasize the role of such variables as personality traits and attitudes, stress, family patterns, and social and cultural factors in the development of psychophysiological complaints. Finally, genetic and physiological hypotheses have also been offered, both to account for why psychophysiological disorders develop and to explain why a given person develops one such disorder rather than another.

Emotion—or *affect*, as it is sometimes called by scientists—gives richness and meaning to our world and is an indispensable dimension of human experience. Yet when it ranges too far beyond the limits of reason and reality, emotion can become a source of overwhelming psychological distress. Such is the case in the *affective disorders*, disturbances of mood in which feelings of sadness or elation become so intense and unrealistic as to merit the diagnostic label of *depression* or *mania*, respectively. These disorders have been recognized and written about since the beginning of the history of medicine. Both mania and melancholia (as depression was called in past centuries) were carefully described by Hippocrates in the fourth century B.C. And as early as the first century A.D., the Greek physician Aretaeus observed that manic and depressive behaviors sometimes occurred in the same person and seemed to stem from a single underlying disorder. At the very beginning of the nineteenth century, Pinel (1801) wrote a vivid account of melancholia, using the Roman emperor Tiberius and the French king Louis XI as illustrations. Furthermore, historical figures have given vivid accounts of their own personal experiences of depression. Of his own chronic state of dejection Abraham Lincoln wrote: "If what I feel were equally distributed to the whole human family, there would not be one cheerful face on earth." Winston Churchill also spoke of his struggles with what he referred to as "the mad dogs of depression." More recently, astronaut Edwin Aldrin has written of his bouts of depression following his return from the moon (Aldrin and Warga, 1973).

Yet despite the fact that they have been scrutinized by scientists for many centuries, these debilitating extremes of mood, as we shall see, still remain something of a mystery. The first half of our present chapter will be devoted to a general discussion of mania and depression, to a description of the various syndromes included under the heading of affective disorder, and to an examination of the different perspectives on this form of psychopathology. In the second section of this chapter we shall turn our attention to the phenomenon of suicide, which often occurs as the result of depression.

MANIA AND DEPRESSION: AN OVERVIEW

Some of us respond to stress by trying to sustain a "high"—becoming feverishly active and energetic, surrounding ourselves with friends, going out a great deal, or plowing through unusual amounts of work. In short, many normal people respond to pressure

7
The Affective Disorders

with manic behavior. Pathological mania may be conceptualized as an extreme, prolonged, and uncontrollable form of this "normal" response. The manic person is hyperactive, talkative, and endlessly energetic. He finds great pleasure in things that never pleased him before and becomes intensely involved with a variety of people and activities. His self-image is decidedly positive; he ignores his limits and loves and admires himself. But he also blames others for faults that are clearly his own. Thus he will vehemently deny any suggestion that he may be ill or inadequate in any way. He also makes impulsive, arbitrary decisions that may get him into trouble.

Like the symptoms of mania, the symptoms of depression are distributed across all aspects of the individual's behavior: feeling, thinking, motivation, and physiological functioning are all involved. Most normal people report that they have gone through periods of depression at various times in their lives (Wessman and Ricks, 1966), and their experiences are quite similar in kind to those reported by people who are clinically depressed: sleep disturbances, loss of appetite and/or sexual response, and—most characteristic of all—feelings of guilt, sadness, and even futility. While the symptoms of clinical depression may not differ in kind from the signs of "normal" depression, they do differ drastically in degree. The utter despair reported by depressive patients is foreign to the experience of most people. For the depressive there remains no glimmer of hope, no single source of temporary pleasure. Furthermore, the depressive typically blames himself for his dejection and is filled with self-denunciations. Not uncommonly he simply wishes to die.

While less frequent in occurrence, another factor which distinguishes genuine mania and depression from transient mood swings is that in his extreme states, the true manic or depressive patient may report *delusions* (false beliefs) or *hallucinations* (false sensory perceptions). The delusions of the manic patient typically center on what a wonderful person he is. He is about to solve the world's economic problems or to receive the Congressional Medal of Honor. He is a multimillionaire and is going to give you one of his spare millions. He is going to buy an airplane and fly you and all your friends to Tahiti. In the manic's hallucinations, angels sing to him and disembodied voices congratulate him. Conversely, the depressive patient may with unshakable conviction report that he is the devil, that he has committed unspeakable crimes, that his insides are rotting away, or that he is already dead and is burning in hell for his crimes and failures. If he hears voices, they of course denounce him and warn him of the punishments awaiting him. When this delusional or hallucinatory quality is present, drastically impairing the individual's reality testing, the condition is labeled a psychosis rather than a neurosis—a distinction that we will discuss more fully in Chapter 11.

The Incidence of Affective Disorders

Difficulties of diagnosis and classification make it almost impossible to assess the incidence of the various affective disorders. Nonetheless, there is widespread agreement that in this country, depression constitutes a major health problem. Between 125,000 and 250,000 people are hospitalized each year with depression, and another 4 million have depressive symptoms that are either treated on an outpatient basis or go unrecognized. Often depression accompanies or is disguised by physical symptoms; in such cases, the resulting chronic underachievement, loss of energy, and failure to adapt are the causes of immense suffering. In this country depression is second only to schizophrenia (Chapter 11) in frequency of first and second admissions to mental hospitals, and outside hospitals, depression is five times as common as schizophrenia (Dunlop, 1965).

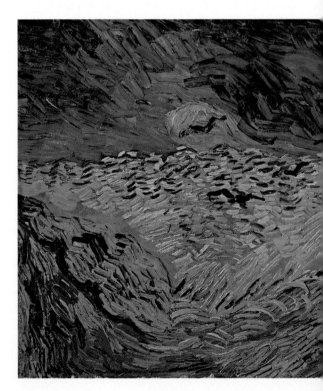

Although the incidence of mania appears to be decreasing (Silverman, 1968), some clinicians believe that the incidence of depression is on the rise, particularly among certain groups. Women are diagnosed as depressives two to three times more often than men (Weissman and Paykel, 1974)—a fact which investigators have sought to account for with theories ranging from hormonal differences between the sexes to the changing social role of women. Furthermore, the risk of depression increases with age, the middle-aged and the elderly being the most common victims. But the incidence of depression among young people has also increased. Some investigators believe that the deviant behavior, drug abuse, and general maladjustment seen in some adolescents are symptomatic of depression (Gallemore and Wilson, 1972). Parallels have also been drawn between the symptoms of depression and the feelings of alienation, powerlessness, and cultural anomie sometimes expressed by the young (Klerman, 1972).

AFFECTIVE DISORDERS: THE INDIVIDUAL SYNDROMES

As we have seen in Chapter 1, our present system of classifying mental disorders, as laid out in DSM-II, is based on the classification system introduced

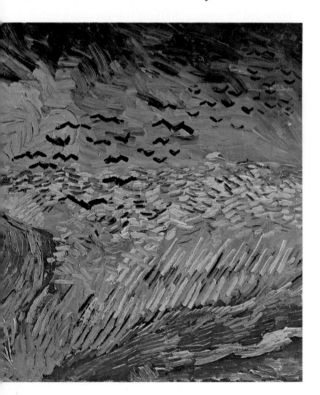

by Kraepelin in the late nineteenth century. To describe the disorders of mood, Kraepelin introduced the term "manic-depressive psychosis." Under this heading, he included patients who had exclusively manic episodes, patients who had exclusively depressed episodes, and the so-called circular types, who had both manic and depressed episodes.

Since its introduction, this grouping has been subdivided somewhat. Today DSM-II lists most of the disorders of mood under the general heading of *major affective disorders*, defined as follows:

This group of psychoses is characterized as a single disorder of mood, either extreme depression or elation, that dominates the mental life of the patient and is responsible for whatever loss of contact he has with the environment. The onset of the mood does not seem to be related directly to a precipitating life experience (1968, pp. 35–36).

Two major categories are included under this heading:

1. involutional melancholia.
2. manic-depressive illness (including the manic type, the depressed type, and the circular type).

Elsewhere DSM-II lists two further disturbances of mood, *psychotic depressive reaction* and *depressive neurosis*, both of which differ from the major affective disorders in that they are precipitated by some identifiable source of stress. In psychotic depressive reaction, a person with no previous history of mood disorder suddenly plunges into depression as a result of some traumatic experience. Similarly, in depressive neurosis the depression is seen as a reaction to some life circumstance, but in this category the individual's contact with reality remains largely intact. He suffers no hallucinations or delusions and manages to function with some adequacy. Hence this disorder is classified as a neurosis, while all the other affective disorders are labeled psychoses. However, no matter what the precise diagnosis, people suffering from depression tend to manifest the same major symptoms. Therefore we will not give separate consideration to these two latter categories.

Fig. 7.1   Vincent Van Gogh's last painting, Wheatfield with Crows *(1890), was completed shortly before he committed suicide. The bleakness, anxiety, and despair that a depressed person feels are conveyed here in the stark colors and intensely bold and rigid brush strokes.*

Involutional Melancholia

Involutional melancholia is a depressive reaction that has its onset in middle age or late middle age—that is, around the time of menopause in women and somewhere between the ages of 50 and 65 in men. According to DSM-II, it is distinguishable from the depressed type of manic-depressive illness not only by the specific age group involved but also by the absence of previous episodes of affective illness.

Involutional melancholia is characterized by agitation, anxiety, insomnia, guilt feelings, and preoccupation with illness. In the typical case, the individual will pace the floor hour after hour, wringing his hands and weeping. He racks his brain as to how he will solve problems that to the observer seem utterly trivial. Both past and future seem to him an endless bleakness. If he has delusions, they tend to be hypochondriacal. He may claim that he has a terrible cancer, that his bowels are stopped up with cement, or that some organ or another is slowly decomposing.

Despite the fact that no precipitating events are thought to have set off these depressive behaviors, some clinicians interpret involutional melancholia as a function of the changes that typically take place in the lives of people during later middle age. For many women, these changes amount to what has been called the "empty nest syndrome"—the depression and dissatisfaction that ensue when grown children leave home and family and household no longer require such an investment of self. For men and women who have invested great energy in their careers, the period between 50 and retirement age may be a time of sobering reassessment, in which they look back over their lives and weigh their present achievements (or failures) against their earlier goals. For both sexes, the signs of physical aging, worries about sexual attractiveness and sexual competence, and the culturally supported notion that with their work, with their children, and with everything else, they have achieved everything that they are going to achieve—all this can arouse feelings of despair. In the following case history of involutional melancholia, we see a painfully critical reassessment of past accomplishments:

At the age of 56, Jim S., a competent and well-respected professor and scholar, began to show an abrupt change in his behavior. At the university where he had been teaching for sixteen years, he suddenly became retiring and withdrawn. He barricaded himself in his office, went less frequently to the research laboratories, and seemed to avoid the faculty club,

where he had lunched fairly regularly for years. As the months wore on, his appearances on campus became less and less frequent. He came only to hold his classes, delivering his lectures in a low monotone and leaving the classroom immediately afterward—apparently in an attempt to avoid any exchanges with his students.

At home, things were also changing for Jim. He withdrew from social activities, was abrasive with his children, and often stormed at his wife. Their sexual relations became less and less frequent and finally ceased altogether. His wife became increasingly concerned when Jim began to stay in bed over the weekend and then finally failed to get up even for classes. At times he would cry or pace anxiously about the house, declaring himself a failure both as a father and as an academician. When not resting in bed or pacing, he would spend long periods of time in his study, rereading the journal articles and books he had written. He began to talk about how he had been a charlatan and a fraud in both his writing and his teaching. He was convinced that he was holding his teaching position under false pretenses. At this point he began composing long retractions of his publications and sending them to the editors of various journals. However, his wife intercepted the letters and at last contacted the family physician, who eventually had Jim hospitalized.

It should be noted that there is some disagreement as to whether involutional melancholia constitutes a different disorder from manic-depressive disturbance. Those who support the distinction claim that involutional melancholia differs from the depressed type of manic-depressive disturbance not only in the particular age of onset and in the absence of previous mood disorders, but also in a more gradual onset, in a longer duration, and in a predominantly agitated rather than a predominantly dejected symptom picture; one further distinguishing factor is a difference in *premorbid* personality (that is, personality before the onset of the disorder): the involutional patient is prone to an even rigidity, whereas the manic-depressive is more inclined to ups and downs of mood. However, there are many investigators who dispute these distinctions (e.g., Hopkinson, 1964; Kendell, 1968), and there are a number who claim that involutional melancholia is simply the name given to manic-depressive disturbance when it occurs in late middle age.

Manic-Depressive Disorder

Manic-depressive disorder is characterized by extreme elation (*manic type*), extreme dejection (*depressed type*), or by some pattern of alternation between the two extremes (*circular type*). Manic-depressive episodes, regardless of type, tend to be of fairly short duration: even if untreated, they rarely last more than a year. However, they also tend to recur, though the chance of recurrence decreases with each episode.

Circular Type While DSM-II uses the label "circular type" for any case of manic-depressive disturbance in which there is a history of at least one manic and one depressed episode, there are actually a number of different patterns, as may be seen in Fig. 7.2. Furthermore, there is also what is called the "mixed type," in which depressive and manic symptoms appear simultaneously. For example, the person may show the typically manic hyperactivity and yet at the same time feel guilty and dejected.

While the circular type is what the layman normally thinks of as manic-depressive disturbance, this type in all its variations is quite rare, accounting for only 15 to 25 percent of the diagnoses of manic-depressive disturbance (Rennie, 1942). The following case illustrates the remarkable swings from one affective extreme to the other:

M.M. was first admitted to a state hospital at the age of 38, although since childhood she had been characterized by swings of mood, some of which had been so extreme that they had been psychotic in degree. At 17 she suffered from a depression that rendered her unable to work for several months, although she was not hospitalized. At 33, shortly before the birth of her first child, the patient was greatly depressed. For a period of four days she appeared in coma. About a month after the birth of the baby she "became excited" and was entered as a patient in an institution for neurotic and mildly psychotic patients. As she began to improve, she was sent to a shore hotel for a brief vacation. The patient remained at the hotel for one night and on the following day signed a year's lease on an apartment, bought furniture, and became heavily involved in debt. Shortly thereafter Mrs.M. became depressed and returned to the hospital in which she had previously been a patient. After several months she recovered and, except for relatively mild fluctuations of mood, remained well for approximately two years.

She then became overactive and exuberant in spirits and visited her friends, to whom she outlined her plans for reestablishing different forms of lucrative business. She purchased many clothes, bought

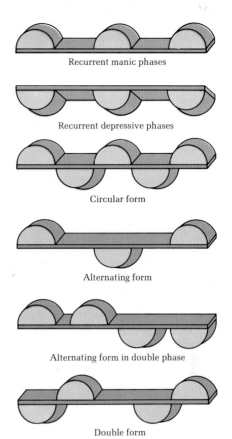

Fig. 7.2 *Six of the many types of manic-depressive reactions distinguished by Kraepelin are represented above. Straight lines indicate normal periods, upward curves signify manic phases, and downward curves represent depressive episodes. The symptoms of both mania and depression vary in intensity from mild to severe, and this variability further increases the possible range of manifestations of affective disorders. (Redrawn from R. W. Lundin,* Principles of Psychopathology, *Columbus, Ohio: Merrill, 1965, p. 421.)*

Recurrent manic phases

Recurrent depressive phases

Circular form

Alternating form

Alternating form in double phase

Double form

furniture, pawned her rings, and wrote checks without funds. She was returned to a hospital. Gradually her manic symptoms subsided, and after four months she was discharged. For a period thereafter she was mildly depressed. In a little less than a year Mrs. M. again became overactive, played her radio until late in the night, smoked excessively, took out insurance on a car that she had not yet bought. Contrary to her usual habits, she swore frequently and loudly, created a disturbance in a club to which she did not belong, and instituted divorce proceedings. On the day prior to her second admission to the hospital, she purchased 57 hats.

During the past 18 years this patient has been admitted and dismissed from the hospital on many occasions. At times, with the onset of a depressed period, she has returned to the hospital seeking admission. At such times she complained that her "brain just won't work." She would say, "I have no energy, am unable to do my housework; I have let my family down; I am living from day to day. There is no one to blame but myself." During one of her manic periods, she sent the following telegram to a physician of whom she had become much enamored: "To: You; Street and No.: Everywhere; Place: the remains at peace! We did our best, but God's will be done! I am so very sorry for all of us. To brave it through thus far. Yes, Darling—from Hello Handsome. Handsome is as Handsome does, thinks, lives and breathes. It takes clear air, Brother of Mine, in a girl's hour of need. All my love to the Best Inspiration one ever had" (Kolb, 1973, pp. 376–377).

Manic Type The manic type of manic-depressive disorder—involving a single episode or recurrent episodes of mania, with no intervening depression—is extremely rare. When it does occur, it tends to do so in women; about 70 percent of hospitalized manic patients are female. And unlike depression, the risk of mania decreases with age (McNeil, 1970).

We have already outlined the basic symptoms of mania: elation, talkativeness, and irritability. In the manic person everything is speeded up. Ideas race through his head, and in order to keep up with them, he talks and moves at a frenetic pace. He has trouble sleeping, but on two hours' sleep he appears to have ten times as much energy as anyone else. In contrast to the depressed person, who cannot bring himself to perform the simplest tasks, the manic is driven to incessant activity and involvement. His need to demonstrate his unique genius is perpetual, and as we have seen, may issue into delusions that he is some great and famous personage. He is uninhibited and sociable, expressing his feelings freely. When frustrated, he may become hostile or violent.

The following case history illustrates the exclusively manic form of manic-depressive psychosis:

Janet S., aged 22, had taken her first job teaching art at one of the local high schools. She first came to the attention of the principal when several angry parents called to complain about the excessive amount of time that their children were spending on various art projects at the school. It was after these complaints that large, vivid murals began to appear in every corner of the school building from the cafeteria to the

locker rooms. These turned out to be the result of a weekend project that Janet had just instituted.

When the principal talked to Janet, he was struck by her excessive energy and stream of verbalizations. Pacing his office, she talked quickly and nonstop about her work at school, her plans for her own art exhibitions, and designs for an outdoor exhibit of student sculpture. When the principal tried to interrupt, she would become irritable and a bit noisier. Otherwise, she seemed cheerful and positive in her outlook. She confidently dismissed the complaints of the parents, assuring the principal that his school would soon be recognized as a model facility for art education.

After she left his office, the principal called Janet's parents to register his concern. When they arrived in the city, they too became alarmed by Janet's excitable and erratic behavior. She was eventually hospitalized for a brief time, following which, with the aid of medication, she returned to her job, still cheerful but much less manic in her general outlook and behavior.

Depressed Type The depressed type of manic-depressive disturbance is characterized by exclusively depressive states. At such times the depressed mood is extreme, and mental and motor activities are inhibited, sometimes to the point of stupor. Because of the high incidence of depression in all its many forms (i.e., depressive neurosis and psychotic depressive reaction in addition to manic-depressive disturbance, circular type and depressed type), we shall not elaborate on the symptoms of the depressed type per se. Rather, we shall discuss the disorder within the broader context of the following section.

Depression

Although some contemporary theorists argue that the distinctions between neurotic and psychotic depressions are quantitative rather than qualitative (Lewis, 1934; Kendell, 1968), others argue that the psychotic form, in which adaptive functioning and reality testing are radically impaired, differs in kind from the milder neurotic form. Those who hold to the latter position tend to regard the neurotic and psychotic categories as *exogenous* and *endogenous* depression, respectively. A depression is called exogenous (literally, "coming from without") when it is clearly linked to an external precipitating event in the person's environment. When depression appears to be physiological, having no connection with an external precipitating event, it is called endogenous (literally, "coming from within"). One patient, for example, described her sudden shift to

The Affective Psychoses

Type	Symptomatology
Manic-depressive illness, manic type	Recurrent episodes of mania—that is, inappropriate elation, boastful talkativeness, hyperactivity, irritability, and impulsive, grandiose behavior
Manic-depressive illness, depressed type	Recurrent episodes of depression—that is, severe dejection, anxiety, agitation, guilt, and insomnia
Manic-depressive illness, circular type	Alternating episodes of mania and depression
Involutional melancholia	Depression occurring in late middle age
Psychotic depressive reaction	A sudden depressive episode, unprecedented in the patient's life and clearly precipitated by a traumatic experience

Depressive neurosis, in which the patient, though chronically dejected, still maintains good reality contact, is the only affective disorder not classified as psychotic.

depression "as if a switch had flipped in my insides"; that describes endogenous depression. However, there is still some question as to whether endogenous depression is truly unrelated to psychological trauma.

As we mentioned earlier, depression appears to be an exaggeration of normal sadness. Psychogenic theorists interpret this similarity as evidence that pathological depression and normal sadness are two extremes on a continuum of mood reactions—a position known as the *continuity hypothesis* (Meyer, 1908). On the other hand, those in the older tradition of Kraepelin hold to the *somatogenic hypothesis*, which regards depression as a discrete disease entity that will ultimately be traced to a biological disorder (Kraines, 1957).

However, most depressions—whether neurotic or psychotic, exogenous or endogenous—tend to look alike. In the symptomatology of depression, the crucial word is "change." The changes that take place in a depressed person are so pervasive that he often seems to resemble other depressed patients more than his former, premorbid personality. The numerous changes that occur during depression involve emotion, motivation, physical and motor functioning, and thinking.

Emotional Changes Almost all severely depressed psychiatric patients report some degree of sadness or unhappiness (Beck, 1967), ranging from a mild melancholy that may be relieved by outside stimuli to total apprehension and hopelessness. This mood of dejection may be expressed in somatic terms or in verbalizations of sadness, loneliness, or boredom. It may also be expressed in the person's feelings about himself, which range from disappointment to total self-loathing.

Many depressed patients characterize the loss of gratification as the predominant aspect of their disturbance. As we have seen, there may be a loss of appetite or a lack of interest in sex. Formerly valued social activities also cease to provide the satisfactions they once did. At first, the reduced gratification from activities involving social responsibilities may be compensated for by an increased enjoyment of such passive recreational activities as lying in bed watching television or reading magazines. This phenomenon has been described as a disturbance in the "give-get" balance (Saul, 1947). In more advanced forms of depression, however, even withdrawal responses become unsatisfying. The loss of emotional involvement with other human beings is also associated with the decline in gratification.

Motivational Changes One of the most striking aspects of depression is the patient's regressive change in motivation, which may range from a simple loss of initiative to a complete "paralysis of the will"—an inability to mobilize oneself to perform even the most elementary of tasks. The latter situation is illustrated in one patient's description of her own bout with depression:

I began not to be able to manage as far as doing the kinds of things that I really had always been able to

Fig. 7.3   The mood state that accompanies depression may involve feelings such as sorrow, fatigability, desolation, and hopelessness. This mood is expressed in de Chirico's Melancholy, *shown above. In the shadows of late afternoon, all is somber and still. A languishing statue, arcades that lead nowhere, and silhouetted figures convey feelings of apathy, indecision, and emptiness. In the background of this static scene is a moving train, symbolizing departure. (*Melancholy, Giorgio de Chirico.*)*

Electroconvulsive Therapy: A Questionable Cure for Depression

For years a popular treatment for depression and involutional melancholia has been electroconvulsive therapy. This procedure (which will be explained more fully in Chapter 19) involves administering to the brain an electric shock of between 70 and 130 volts for a fraction of a second. Therapy for depression usually requires several shock treatments, though the total may be as high as thirty.

When the patient awakens from the sleep which follows the electric shock, he is normally confused and totally amnesic. Then, according to most authorities, his memory for the distant, less distant, and recent past return, in that order (Roueché, 1974). For some patients, however, large memory gaps remain—a fact that has received considerably less attention than the therapeutic usefulness of the technique. Electroconvulsive therapy, it appears, is often extremely effective in lifting depression, but in certain cases the survivor of this therapy may find that he has been relieved not only of his despondency but also of a good part of the knowledge that he has acquired as an adult. For example, the woman quoted below found after eight shock treatments that her appetite, her good spirits, and her self-confidence—all of which she had lost through depression—were restored to her. Most of her memory, however, was gone.

I remember my first morning at home. I thought of breakfast, and my mind was a blank. I turned to Alan [her husband]: "What do I usually have for breakfast?" He looked a little startled, but he told me—an egg and a cookie. Oh, yes. I remembered. I was full of questions. It was like beginning life all over again. I said something one day about the hospital, about the bills, and Alan said Blue Cross was taking care of it. Blue Cross? I didn't know what he was talking about. I'd never heard of it (p. 94).

But the doctors had reassured her that this amnesia was purely temporary. So she stopped worrying about it until the day—three months after her last shock treatment—when she returned to her job as a government economist, a position requiring considerable expertise. At the office she received a chilling surprise:

I started going through my desk—all the current papers and pamphlets and so on. I gathered that I'd been working on the income of securities dealers—relating their earnings to the gross national product. The papers were full of professional terms that seemed familiar. I knew what they were, but I didn't know what they meant. "Over-the-counter," for example. It was a familiar term, but I didn't know—I couldn't remember—exactly what it referred to. "Mutual funds" was another. And "odd-lot dealers." All blanks. . . .

. . .

I came home from the office that first day feeling panicky. I didn't know where to turn. I didn't know what to do. I was terrified. I've never been a crying person, but all my beloved knowledge, everything I had learned in my field during twenty years or more, was gone. I'd lost the body of knowledge that constituted my professional skill. I'd lost everything that professionals take for granted. I'd lost my experience, my knowing. But it was worse than that. I felt that I'd lost my self. I fell on the bed and cried and cried and cried (pp. 95–96).

For two months she tried to relearn her trade. But twenty years of knowledge could not be retrieved in a matter of months. Furthermore, she found that she could no longer retain facts. What she labored to learn during one day would be gone the next. Finally, unwilling to burden her employers any longer, she applied for early retirement. At her request, she remains in the office, without pay, as a "guest employee," doing low-level clerical work. Ten months after the termination of her electroconvulsive therapy, her professional past remains nothing more than a vague shadow in her memory.

do easily, such as cook, wash, take care of the children, play games, that kind of thing. One of the most ... I think one of the most frightening aspects at the beginning was that time went so slowly. It would seem sometimes that at least an hour had gone by and I would look at my watch and it would only have been three minutes. And I began not to be able to concentrate. Another thing that was very frightening to me was that I couldn't read any more. And if awakened early ... earlier than I needed to, I sometimes would lie in bed two hours trying to make myself get up because I just couldn't put my feet on the floor. Then when I did, I just felt that I couldn't get dressed. And then, whatever the next step was, I felt I couldn't do that.*

The depressed person seeks situations in which he is able to be passive and dependent. In his desire to avoid adult responsibilities, he may disavow his professional goals and commitments; he may abandon his friends and even his family. The depressed person seeks rest, yet his inactivity may deepen his depression. This is especially true when he interprets his passivity and dependence as further evidence of his own worthlessness.

A related manifestation is the iron determination with which the depressed person pursues his escape or withdrawal. Despite the inertia with which he encounters most activities, he may mobilize considerable energy in avoiding situations he regards as demanding or in formulating plans for elaborate methods of suicide.

Changes in Physical and Motor Functioning The major physical symptoms of depression are loss of appetite, sometimes reflected in a substantial weight loss; disturbances of sleep, especially the type of insomnia that involves awakening very early in the morning; and the loss of sexual responsiveness. To this list we might add the massive fatigue that accompanies depression, though this symptom seems related to avoidance behavior and loss of motivation rather than to physical changes (Beck, 1967).

Some theorists view the presence of these physical impairments as a signal of "vital depression" and interpret them as evidence that depression is caused by a disturbance in the autonomic nervous system or in the hypothalamus, the portion of the brain stem that controls such processes as hunger, sleep, and sexual functioning (Campbell, 1953; Kraines, 1957).

---

*Source: "Depression: The Shadowed Valley," from the series *The Thin Edge*, © 1975 by the Educational Broadcasting Corporation.

Indicators of Depression

Type	Manifestations
Emotional	Sadness
	Crying spells
	Self-hatred
	Loss of gratification
	Loss of feelings of affection
	Loss of sense of humor
Motivational	Increased dependency
	Loss of motivation
	Avoidance
	Ambivalent wishes
	Suicidal wishes
Physical	Loss of appetite
	Sleep disturbance
	Fatigability
	Loss of sexual interest
Cognitive	Negative self-concept
	Negative expectations
	Exaggerated view of problems
	Attribution of blame to self
Delusions	Worthlessness
	Sinfulness
	Identification with devil
	Expectation of punishment
	Death
	Physical decay
	Physical illness

Source: Adapted from Beck et al. (1961).

However, this theory goes counter to the finding that the physical symptoms of depression have a low correlation with each other and with clinical ratings of depth of depression.

Although some depressives mask their feelings behind a cheerful demeanor—a phenomenon called *masked* or *smiling depression*—most have a stooped posture and a dejected facial expression. And depressive women, in particular, tend to have crying spells.

Depression can often be diagnosed solely on the basis of motor symptoms (Lehmann, 1959). For example, in *retarded depression*, there is little spontaneous activity. Movement is slow and deliberate, gestures are kept to a minimum, and there is little

Fig. 7.4 *Physical manifestations of depression have been characterized for centuries by physicians, novelists, and other observers. Sad facial expressions, stooped posture, physical withdrawal, crying, and vegetative stupor are characteristic of "retarded" depressed persons. An "agitated" depression has also been noted, in which the individual is anxious, restless, and constantly active.*

Fig. 7.5 (right) *Depression is the experience of abject despair and overwhelming loneliness.*

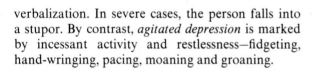

verbalization. In severe cases, the person falls into a stupor. By contrast, *agitated depression* is marked by incessant activity and restlessness—fidgeting, hand-wringing, pacing, moaning and groaning.

Cognitive Changes Typically, the depressed person regards himself as deficient in many attributes that he values—for example, intelligence, physical attractiveness, health, and social skills. His indecisiveness and frequent complaints about loss—whether it be of love, material possessions, social status, or self-esteem—may also reflect his sense of personal inadequacy (Breed, 1967). Compelled to criticize himself and to ruminate over his losses, the depressed person seems to find evidence of his own worthlessness everywhere he looks.

In the depressed person's view of himself, of the outside world, and of his own future, negative expectations predominate. And not surprisingly, these negative expectations have a high correlation with suicidal tendencies (Pichot and Lempérière, 1964; Beck, 1967; Harder, 1967). The deeply depressed person believes that his condition is irreversible, that he will never recover (Sarwer-Foner, 1966). He is sure that he is both unable to help himself and unlikely to be helped by external forces—a way of thinking that has been characterized as the *helplessness-hopelessness syndrome* (Engel, 1968).

At times, cognitive distortions become so rigid and intense that they are properly classified as delusions. Among the most common of the depressive's delusions are those relating to worthlessness, sin and punishment, disease, and poverty.

Since depressive reactions vary so much in their intensity and since we find so many diagnostic classifications of depression, it is virtually impossible to present a "typical" case study of depression. In concluding our clinical description of depression, we shall illustrate a case of manic-depressive disorder, depressed type, in which the delusional and episodic qualities and suicidal intent are illustrated:

E. D., aged 60, was admitted to the hospital because he was depressed, ate insufficiently, and believed that his stomach was "rotting away." The patient was described as a friendly, sociable individual, not quarrel-

Post-Partum Depression

Postpartum depression—that is, depression following childbirth—is normally thought of as a brief period of mild "blues" in which the new mother lapses into crying spells and feels generally dejected for a week or two after the birth of her child. And fortunately, in most cases postpartum depression *is* mild and short-lived. In some instances, however, depression following childbirth reaches psychotic proportions, in which case it may have the same disastrous consequences as any psychotic depression. Occasionally one reads in the news of the murder of an infant by its mother or of the suicide of a new mother. In the absence of other motives, such horrible acts are often thought to be the outcome of severe postpartum depression (Lukianowicz, 1971; Resnich, 1969, 1970). The following is an example of a psychotic postpartum depression:

When Leslie W. was twenty-one, her first child, a boy, was born. She recalls being somewhat depressed when she came home from the hospital, but she realized that many new mothers felt this way. After a few months she no longer had any depressive symptoms. When the boy was two and a half, Leslie gave birth to a second child, this time a girl. On returning from the hospital, some of the old feelings that Leslie had experienced after the first birth returned. Often she found herself listless and unable to get up in the morning. Although her husband was helpful with both children when he was at home, she found it increasingly difficult to care for them while he was working. For the first time, Leslie's house became dirty and unkempt. The children were often unwashed and unattended. Their frequent crying and physical demands became increasingly irritating to her, but instead of dealing with them, she would simply curl up on the living room couch, crying and berating herself for her deficiencies as a mother and housekeeper.

As the months wore on, Leslie became increasingly agitated and often contemplated suicide. She became convinced that world events spelled ultimate misfortune for the children that she had borne. It seemed clear that nothing in her life would ever get better.

One winter morning she bundled the two children into their snowsuits and walked to a bridge spanning a busy freeway. She hurled her son off the bridge and was preparing to jump to the highway below with her baby in her arms when she was stopped by an alert passer-by. Luckily, the boy had fallen on the grassy median of the expressway, and although seriously hurt, he recovered after some weeks in the hospital. After three months of psychiatric treatment, Leslie was able to resume a normal life. She recalls the period of her depression as though it were a dream, not believing that she was capable of attempting to kill her children and herself.

some, jealous, or critical, and with a sense of humor. He was considered even-tempered, slow to anger, tender-hearted, and emotional.

At 51 the patient suffered from a depression and was obliged to resign his position. This depression continued for about nine months, after which he apparently fully recovered. He resumed his work but after two years suffered from a second depression. Again he recovered after several months and returned to a similar position and held it until two months before his admission. At this time he began to worry lest he was not doing his work well, talked much of his lack of fitness for his duties, and finally resigned. He spent Thanksgiving Day at his son's in a neighboring city, but while there he was sure that the water pipes in his own house would freeze during his absence and that he and his family would be "turned out into the street." A few days later he was found standing by a pond, evidently contemplating suicide. He soon began to remain in bed and sometimes wrapped his head in the bedclothing to shut out the external world. He declared that he was "rotting away inside" and that if he ate, the food would kill him. He urged the family not to touch the glasses or towels he used lest they become contaminated.

On arrival at the hospital, he appeared older than his years. He was pale, poorly nourished, and dehydrated, with his lips dry, cracked, and covered with sores. His facial expression and general bearing suggested a feeling of utter hopelessness. He was self-absorbed and manifested no interest in his environment. When urged to answer questions, there was a long delay before he attempted to reply, but he finally spoke briefly, hesitatingly, and in a low tone. He occasionally became agitated and repeatedly said, "Oh, Doctor, why did I ever get into anything like this? Doctor, I am all filled up! I can't get anything through me—what am I going to do? Oh, dear! Oh, dear!" In explaining his presence in the hospital, he said he realized he had been sent by his family because they believed he would be benefited by the treatment, but added, "I don't know how they sent me here when they had not the means. My wife cannot pay for me, and by this time she must have been put out of the house" (Kolb, 1973, pp. 375–376).

PERSPECTIVES ON THE AFFECTIVE DISORDERS

As we have seen, DSM-II defines the major affective disorders as occurring in the absence of any precipitating event in the person's environment—a position that might be supported by the biological and physiological perspectives. But as we shall see in the following section, all the major psychological perspectives predictably view depression as an interaction between psyche and environment and relate depression to some kind of personal loss, whether past or present, real or imagined.

The Psychodynamic Perspective

As with neurosis, the psychodynamic interpretation of the affective disorders is not a single theory but a multitude of theories. Thus, in the interest of brevity rather than completeness, we will concentrate our attention on the early psychoanalytic positions, which have been the most influential. It is important to note that since psychodynamic theory tends to regard mania as a defense or reaction formation against depression, depression is regarded as the primary disorder, and little attention is paid to mania.

Cause   In his classic paper "Mourning and Melancholia" (1917), Freud drew a distinction between grief and depression. While both are reactions to the loss of a loved one, grief is the conscious reaction to the loss, while in depression the true feelings of loss remain unconscious. Hence in depression the perception of loss is distorted, and the ego is weakened in the effort of repressing the true feelings of sorrow and rage. As Freud notes, "in grief the world becomes poor and empty; in melancholia it is the ego itself" that becomes empty. Freud added that this depression need not necessarily be triggered by an actual loss of a love object. It could also stem from some imagined or fantasized loss—even a

symbolic loss, such as not receiving an anticipated raise or promotion.

Much of this Freudian formulation actually constituted an elaboration of an earlier theory put forth by one of Freud's students, Karl Abraham (1911, 1916). Abraham had suggested that depressed persons have ambivalent feelings of love and hate toward the loved object that they perceive as lost—feelings that were previously unconscious. This ambivalence leads to anger toward the love object because the love object has deserted or rejected the individual. And at the same time, the ambivalent feelings give rise to guilt because of the individual's belief that he failed to behave properly toward the now-lost love object. These conflicting emotions combine to create a self-centered sense of loss, suffering, and despair. According to Abraham, it is this self-centered quality that differentiates depression from normal grief. In other words, depression is a narcissistic, inner-oriented state, while grief is a realistic, outer-oriented state.

In keeping with the Freudian theory that psychopathology results from disturbances in psychosexual development, Abraham contended that a person could become predisposed to depression as the result of a withdrawal of love or gratification during the oral stage. One aspect of the consequent oral fixation is an intense dependence on other people for support and emotional gratification. And this dependence, according to Abraham, could contribute to depression, since any minor rejection can lead to a total loss of self-esteem in the highly dependent person.

Another feature of this early psychoanalytic formulation of depression is the concept of *oral incorporation*. According to Abraham and Freud, in the oral stage the primitive child, bent on oral gratification, symbolically "eats up" the loved object, overidentifying with the object and mentally incorporating it into himself in order to avoid losing it. When in later life the individual does in fact lose a loved object, his rage and reproach are turned inward rather than outward and thus become self-reproach and self-loathing. This concept of "anger-in"—the rage directed toward oneself to punish the incorporated love object or the self that was unworthy of the love of the object—is still assumed by many psychodynamic theorists to be a central etiological factor in depression.

However, emphasis in more recent psychoanalytic writings on depression has shifted from disturbances in drives and needs to disturbances in ego organization. Depression is seen as stemming from deficiency in the coping qualities of the ego, due perhaps to a diffuse identity, to ineffective mechanisms of defense, or to inadequate identifications.

Another recent trend in psychodynamic theorizing—and one which has considerably more empirical support than the hypotheses of Abraham and Freud—is the effort to relate depression to actual loss rather than to symbolic loss, loss of self-esteem, or what have you. Bowlby (1960) has minimized the role of suppressed rage, suggesting instead that separation from the parents and its attendant anxiety have a crucial etiological role in depression. One group of investigators found support for Bowlby's thesis in the observation of four young monkeys separated from their mothers for three weeks. Initially the monkeys showed "violent and prolonged protest." Then they lapsed into "despair," abandoning their play activities and becoming withdrawn (Seay et al., 1962). Other studies of depression in rhesus monkeys (e.g., McKinney et al., 1973) also tend to confirm Bowlby's formulation.

Since there have been few psychodynamic theories of depression that have been supported by systematic study of actual groups of depressives, the work of Cohen and his colleagues (1954) is of particular interest. These researchers explored the psychodynamics and family backgrounds of twelve cases of manic-depressive psychosis. They report that manic-depressives show excessive conformity, dependency, and a need for social approval. Moreover, the patients tend to come from families who are eager for advancement and expect their children to further these goals. Evidence suggests that the adult manic-depressive uses expressions of self-reproach as a defense against such demands.

Treatment In general, psychodynamic treatment of the affective disorders has three goals. First, the therapist attempts to bring his patient to a fuller consciousness of the stressful periods of early childhood during which the patient presumably experienced a loss of a love object. Second, the patient is encouraged to explore his evaluation of himself and to remember the conditions that led to his diminished self-esteem. If the patient can recall and work through these early, repressed childhood difficulties, then presumably he may begin to respond to the present situation in a more adequate fashion.

Finally, working on the "anger-in" premise, the therapist will also try to make the patient aware of his own capacity for anger and will encourage him to express his hostile feelings rather than turn them inward. This unleashing of repressed aggression presumably liberates the individual from his depressive self-punishment.

The Behaviorist Perspective

The behavioral school has devoted much less attention to the affective disorders than it has to other syndromes such as compulsions and phobias. Nonetheless, a number of eminent behaviorists have discussed the etiology and treatment of affective illness, particularly depression.

Cause Stated in its simplest terms, the behavioral theory of depression is that it is "a function of inadequate or insufficient reinforcers" (Lazarus, 1968, p. 84). That is, once positive reinforcement is withdrawn and behaviors are no longer rewarded, the person ceases to emit these behaviors. He becomes withdrawn and inactive—in short, depressed.

Ferster (1965) also points to the role of avoidance in depression. He suggests that when certain effective behaviors have been reduced by the withdrawal of reinforcement, the anxiety produced by the "incipient tendency" to engage in these activities suppresses them and encourages avoidance behaviors such as withdrawing from social interaction and spending one's days in bed. The passive quality of the depressed person's behavior is linked to his tendency to respond to the aversive control applied by other people rather than to initiate behaviors on his own. On the other hand, Ferster (1973) explains the agitation—hand-wringing, pacing, compulsive talking, and so on—often found among both depressive and manic patients as a stratagem for avoiding other, more aversive behaviors such as silence or inactivity.

The question of why the withdrawal of positive reinforcement should bring about depression in some people and not in others has been considered by a number of behavioral theorists, who have proposed various factors that might predispose a person to depression. Lewinsohn (1972), for example, suggests that the depressed person's low rate of positive reinforcement may be due not only to events in his life situation but to his own lack of social skills. In support of this hypothesis, Lewinsohn, Shaffer, and Libet (1969) found that in comparison to normal control groups, depressed people elicit and engage in fewer human interactions, convey shorter messages, and time their messages less appropriately.

A different theory is put forth by Ullmann and Krasner (1975), who propose that depression may be to some degree the result of modeling. In opposition to theorists such as Lewinsohn, who claim that depressive behaviors alienate other people, Ullmann and Krasner assert that Americans as a group reinforce depressed behavior with kindness and solicitude, thereby maintaining the depressed role as a potentially desirable one. Thus if a person has seen depressed behavior reinforced, he may, when changes in his own life (such as aging) reduce the level of positive reinforcement, seek new reinforcement by modeling his behavior according to the role of depressed person.

Another variable that may predispose some people to depressive reactions is suggested by Seligman and his colleagues in their theory of *learned helplessness* (Seligman et al., 1971; Seligman, 1974). This theory was based on a series of experimental studies with dogs. After exposing a number of dogs to inescapable electric shocks, these investigators found that when the same dogs were later subjected to escapable shocks, they were either unable to initiate escape responses or were slow or inept at escaping. This conditioned passivity Seligman and his colleagues called "learned helplessness." Noting the similarities between the behavior of the dogs and that of human depressives—that is, fewer and slower responses, a limited range of behaviors, passivity, and helplessness—these investigators hypothesize that the depressive's inability to initiate adaptive responses may, like that of the dogs, be due to a helplessness conditioned by earlier, inescapable trauma.

Treatment In treating the affective disorders, as in treating any other disorder, the behaviorist goes directly to the "symptoms," the depressive behaviors that need to be changed in order to allow the patient to get along more happily and successfully. One basic form of such treatment is the use of direct reinforcement. Lewinsohn (1972), for example, proposes that the patient be rewarded for increasing his activity rate, and particularly his level of social interaction, so that these behaviors can once again assume a reinforcing aspect for the patient. For example, a patient might be asked to perform some simple act that he is otherwise unlikely to perform, such as getting out of bed and dressing himself, or spending fifteen minutes in the day room with the other patients. This behavior is then rewarded by allowing the patient to engage in some activity that he still enjoys, such as reading a magazine or watching television.

In another treatment strategy, proposed by Lazarus (1968), the therapist attempts to evoke responses that are incompatible with depression—a technique similar to systematic desensitization (Chapter 5), in which the therapist attempts to induce a state of relaxation that is incompatible with anxiety. The technique for depression is based on the premise that "anger or the deliberate stimulation of feelings of amusement, affection, sexual excitement or anxiety tends to break the depressive cycle" (p. 88).

Lazarus has also experimented with a technique called *behavioral deprivation*, which involves a period of bed rest without access to external stimuli. An adaptation of the Morita therapy (Kora, 1965) developed in Japan, this method is intended to make the patient more susceptible to incoming stimuli.

In all its aspects, behavior therapy attempts to provide the depressed patient with a new reinforcement schedule, one in which positive reinforcement predominates and thus elicits a normal range and rate of activity.

The Humanistic-Existential Perspective

Predictably, humanistic and existential theorists approach depression from a phenomenological base. That is, no matter how distorted the depressive's perception of himself and of the world may seem, this perception is accepted as his particular "here and now." And it is on the patient's unique subjective experience of his existence that the humanists and existentialists focus in their treatment of affective disorders.

Cause Both the humanists and the existentialists would interpret a person's mood as a good indicator of his total subjective condition: his "being"—that is, his experience of himself—and his "being-in-the-world"—that is, his experience of the environment. In existential terms, the depressive is seized with intolerable angst or existential anxiety, for he knows that he is not living completely in the moment, that he is experiencing "non-being." If a depressive speaks of his guilt feelings, the existentialist, along with the humanist, would say that he *is* guilty because he is failing to make choices, to fulfill his potentialities, and to take responsibility for his own life (May, 1958a). In sum, the depressive is living an inauthentic existence.

Treatment Most humanistic and existential therapists would agree that in treating the affective disorders a central task is to help the patient achieve a fuller and richer sense of his existence, and especially of his being-in-the-world. In essence, the therapist is trying to facilitate the patient's personal experiencing in its entirety: his experience of the natural or external world, his experience of other people, and his experience of himself, his inner world of self-relatedness, self-awareness, and insight.

It is very likely that the depressed patient will feel deeply burdened by environmental demands and unhappy in his interpersonal relationships. Both kinds of perceptions will be reflected in the sad, despairing way in which he experiences himself. But according to the humanistic-existential position, the patient, in order to move beyond despair, must become fully aware of and take full responsibility for his feelings. Only then can he reorient himself toward a more productive and satisfying life. For this reason, the therapist does not allow the patient to dwell on past events except insofar as they give meaning to the present. Instead, the therapist is most concerned with the patient's projections of himself into the future.

The Cognitive Perspective

As we have seen earlier in this chapter, depression involves a number of changes: emotional changes, motivational changes, cognitive changes, and changes in physical and motor functioning. Cognitive theorists hold that the critical variable in depression is the cognitive change, and that it is this factor—the way the person *thinks* about himself—that gives rise to the other factors involved in depression.

Beck, one of the major proponents of this approach, evolved his theory of depression from a clinical study (Beck and Valin, 1953) in which he found that themes of self-punishment occur with great frequency in the hallucinations and delusions of psychotically depressed patients. In a later study of patients in psychotherapy, Beck and Hurvich (1959) found that the dreams of depressed patients contain themes of low self-esteem, loss, deprivation, and frustration in attempting to reach goals. In short, the depressive sees himself in his dreams as a "loser." Beck explains that the content of the depressive's dreams, fantasies, delusions, and meditations are determined not by a desire for suffering or self-punishment but by an idiosyncratic cognitive set or *schema* through which experiences are perceived in a negative light.

Beck (1971) hypothesizes that if a person, because of early childhood experience, develops a cognitive schema involving a negative bias toward himself and

a pessimistic view of the future, that person is then predisposed to depression. For stress can easily activate the negative schema, and the consequent negative perceptions merely serve to strengthen the schema. For example, the sad affect that results from the depressive's persistently negative interpretations of experience is in turn interpreted as further evidence of objective hopelessness. Hence the negative cognitive set becomes progressively more dominant as the depression deepens.

A similar cognitive formulation is that of Lichtenberg (1957), who maintains that depression stems from a person's attributing to himself responsibility for not achieving his goals. Likewise, Ellis (1962) suggests that the way a person thinks about himself may lead him to become self-accusatory and depressed. Ellis believes that many people create for themselves a set of irrational values and unrealistic goals which they then require themselves to live up to. And when they fail, as they almost inevitably must, they become depressed and self-contemptuous, despite the fact that their goals were totally unreasonable.

Another cognitive variable that may be associated with depression is the degree to which a person believes in external as opposed to internal control of reinforcement. Those referred to as "internals" believe that the things that happen to them depend upon their own behavior or personal qualities. "Externals," on the other hand, believe that their success or failure is controlled by other, more powerful human beings or by some arbitrary agency such as "luck" or "fate" (Rotter, 1966). In a review of related research, Strickland (1974) reports strong empirical support for a correlation between depression and the "external" formula.* In other words, those whose cognitive schema tells them that they have little control over their destinies are apparently more prone to depression.

The Biological Perspective

Although most professionals consider the affective disorders to be due to environmental factors, recent genetic studies—along with biochemical and neurophysiological findings which we will examine shortly—suggest that organic dysfunctions may have some role in the etiology of mood disturbances. For example, family studies have shown that first-degree relatives (that is, immediate family members—

---

*Seligman (1975) has drawn a parallel between "learned helplessness" (cf. p.173) and internal-external control. Externals respond as if they had been conditioned like Seligman's dogs.

parents, siblings, and children) of manic-depressives have a much greater chance of developing manic-depressive psychosis than the average person. In contrast to a 1 percent incidence of this disorder in the general population, Stenstedt (1952) found a 15 percent incidence among the first-degree relatives of manic-depressive patients. More recently, Rosenthal (1970) has reported a lower differential, but a substantial one all the same. According to his review of existing family studies, the first-degree relatives of a manic-depressive are ten times as likely as the average person to develop the disorder.

As we know, it is difficult in family studies to separate environmental from genetic influence, and this problem makes family studies the weakest variety of genetic evidence. However, twin studies, where there is much less chance of such confusions, also support the role of genetics in manic-depressive psychosis. In a review of genetic research on manic-depressive psychosis in twins, Price (1972) reported that of the twins studied, 66 out of 97 monozygotic pairs were concordant for the disorder, while only 27 out of 119 dizygotic pairs were concordant. Though not foolproof, this finding constitutes substantial evidence that of the affective disorders, at least manic-depressive psychosis depends to some degree on genetically inherited organic variables.

The Physiological Perspective

If we accept the premise that organic factors may be implicated in the affective disorders, the next logical question is: *What* organic factors? This is the question that physiological researchers are attempting to solve. So far, there are two major lines of inquiry, neurophysiological research and biochemical research.

Neurophysiological Research According to neurophysiological researchers, the basic problem in depression lies with the central nervous system.

One hypothesis, put forth by Whybrow and Mendels (1969), is that in depressives there is an "unstable excitability" of the central nervous system. These investigators suggest that in the nervous system of the depressive the process of electrical transmission of impulses from one nerve cell to the next can be set off by very weak stimuli. Furthermore, they contend that in depressives the nerve cell's recovery period following the discharge is longer than normal. In support of their position, Whybrow and Mendels point to the many studies that have found EEG abnormalities in depressive patients and to the finding that the sleep patterns of depressives differ radically from those of the normal adult (Mendels and Hawkins, 1970). However, it should be noted that EEG and sleep abnormalities could be caused by any number of other factors as well.

Another neurophysiological hypothesis we have already mentioned in passing is that depression may be due to a malfunctioning of the hypothalamus, a portion of the brain known to regulate mood. Kraines (1966) contends that disturbances in appetite, sexual interest, menstruation, and other functions that are regulated by the hypothalamus, point to its role in the genesis of depressive illness. The fact that depressives may also show disturbances in the functioning of the pituitary, adrenal, and thyroid glands, all of which are affected by the hypothalamus, lends some support to this hypothesis. However, as with the "unstable excitability" theory, the evidence is in no way conclusive.

Biochemical Research As we have just seen, there appears to be something wrong with depressives neurologically, but we are not sure exactly what is wrong. Likewise, there is considerable evidence that depressives differ from the rest of us biochemically, but we do not yet know precisely how. At present there are three major theories.

The first is that depression may be due to imbalances in the level of hormones, and particularly of sex hormones. For example, Mendels (1969) argues that the fact that involutional melancholia occurs at a time of change in the sex-hormone levels would seem to indicate a link between affective disorders and these hormones. Reports that oral contraceptives, which contain sex hormones known to have a sedative effect on the central nervous system, have caused depression in some women have been cited in support of this hypothesis.

A second theory is that depression may originate in imbalances in sodium and potassium levels. It appears that the proper transmission of electrical impulses from neuron to neuron within the nervous system depends on a highly delicate balance in the distribution of sodium and potassium inside and outside the nerve cells. If this balance becomes disturbed, so too will the functioning of the nervous system. And in fact a number of studies (e.g., Shaw, 1966; Coppen, 1967) have indicated that psychotic depression is often accompanied by abnormally high sodium levels and that these levels tend to return to their normal state after recovery. Furthermore, Coppen (1967) has shown that lithium salts, which on many occasions have been used successfully in

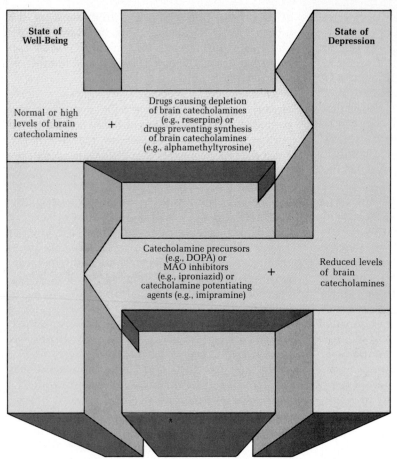

State of
Well-Being

State of
Depression

Normal or high
levels of brain
catecholamines

+

Drugs causing depletion
of brain catecholamines
(e.g., reserpine) or
drugs preventing synthesis
of brain catecholamines
(e.g., alphamethyltyrosine)

Catecholamine precursors
(e.g., DOPA) or
MAO inhibitors
(e.g., iproniazid) or
catecholamine potentiating
agents (e.g., imipramine)

+

Reduced levels
of brain
catecholamines

*Fig. 7.6   One of the current biochemical
theories concerning the etiology of depression is the catecholamine hypothesis.
According to this hypothesis, changes in
the levels of brain catecholamines are related to changes in mental states: low
levels are associated with depression, and
normal or high levels with well-being.
The diagram indicates several types of
drugs that alter catecholamine levels in
the central nervous system.*

the treatment of affective disorders, may achieve their effect by reducing the patient's sodium level.

A final biochemical hypothesis has to do with changing levels of amines, a type of body chemical. It is widely believed that two groups of amines—the catecholamines and the indolamines, both of which facilitate the transmission of impulses between nerve fibers—play a role in the etiology of depressive illness. According to the "catecholamine hypothesis," depression is caused by a deficiency, and mania by an excess, of catecholamines, and particularly of one catecholamine known as norepinephrine (Schildkraut, 1965). More specifically, this theory holds that too much norepinephrine results in over-stimulated nerve fibers and consequently in the overexcitability of mania. Conversely, too little norepinephrine leads to understimulated nerve fibers and hence to the underexcitability of depression. Certain of the indolamines have also been proposed as determinants of affective disorder (Glassman, 1969). In support of such theories, drugs known to increase the amine levels in the brain have been used successfully in the treatment of de-

pression. It should be noted, however, that changes in amine levels may simply be a response to stress and not specific to depression (Bliss, 1966).

In conclusion, it should be emphasized that all these theories—genetic, neurological, and biochemical—may turn out to be equally accurate and to complement one another as parts of a single whole. It is highly possible, for example, that one could be born with a particular genetic makeup that would cause a biochemical malfunctioning resulting in a central nervous system disorder resulting in depression. Certainly, what we know of the interdependence of the various organs of the body renders such a sequence highly plausible. One model, proposed by Aliskal and McKinney (1973), goes even beyond this possibility to argue that affective disorders are a complex interaction of genetic, neurophysiological, biochemical, developmental, and situational variables. These investigators believe that to consider any one cause in isolation would be to ignore the role of the others. And in view of the multitude of current theories—so many of which seem quite logical but remain without conclusive proof—it

Fig. 7.7 Despite their anguish and suffering, most suicidal people have highly ambivalent feelings about taking their lives. Here rescuers try to use that fact to coax a would-be suicide off the superstructure of the Brooklyn Bridge.

seems unwise to ignore any possible variable, whether psychological or organic. Nonetheless, with improved technology and increased numbers of well-trained experimenters, it is likely that our understanding of the precise origins of the affective disorders will increase significantly in the near future.

SUICIDE

In any consideration of the affective disorders we must also include some discussion of suicide, which is often the tragic outcome of mood disturbances. In his book on suicide, *The Savage God* (1971), A. Alvarez claims that "the processes which lead a man to take his own life are at least as complex and difficult as those by which he continues to live" (p. 115). Yet we know that a major factor in this complex process is depression. In a retrospective study of a sample of successful suicides, one group of experimenters found that 94 percent of them had gone through episodes of serious depression (Robins et al., 1959). Another group of researchers found that in their sample of patients who committed suicide, approximately 80 percent had been depressed prior to the fatal attempt (Barraclough et al., 1969).

The Incidence of Suicide

For several reasons statistics about the incidence of suicide are difficult to obtain. Many of those who commit suicide prefer to make their deaths look accidental, whether it be to enable survivors to collect insurance, to spare themselves and their families the shame linked with suicide, or—should the attempt fail—to avoid a criminal charge. (There are eight states that still list suicide as a felony.) For example, Finch, Smith, and Pokorny (1970) estimate that at least 15 percent of all fatal automobile accidents are actually suicides.

However, even with these missing statistics, national estimates of the number of suicides each year range from 25,000 to 60,000, while at least 200,000 more attempt to kill themselves and fail (Epstein, 1974). Two million living Americans have made suicide attempts—that is, almost 1 percent of the population. Among the most common causes of death in the United States, suicide ranks somewhere between tenth and twelfth. Among young people aged 15 to 24, it is considered the second most common cause of death. Furthermore, there are statisticians who argue that if all self-inflicted deaths were recorded, suicide would rank nationally as the fourth or fifth most common cause of death. Whatever the accuracy of the statistics, life-threatening behavior constitutes a serious problem in this country.

Suicidal Types

There is no single suicidal type. Suicide may be undertaken by any variety of personality in any one of a variety of different moods ranging from the most frenzied passion to the most sober and calculating rationalism. Even so formidable a psychological intelligence as Freud's was not immune to suicidal thoughts. At age 29, in the throes of love, he wrote to his fiancée: "I have long since resolved on a decision [i.e., suicide], the thought of which is in no ways painful, in the event of losing you" (Jones, 1963, p. 85).

Though any effort to identify suicidal personalities is apparently futile, Shneidman and Farberow (1970b), in their extensive study of suicides, have attempted a breakdown of the types of reasoning that can lead a person to try to kill himself. The first

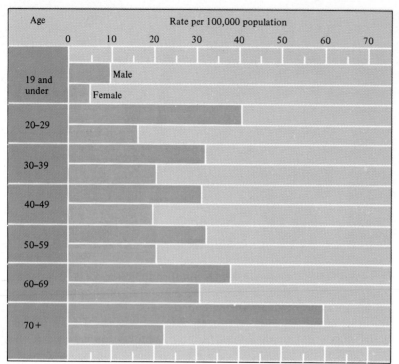

*Rates are for Los Angeles only but are considered to be representative of national statistics.

Fig. 7.8 The chart shows suicide rates by age and sex, 1972–1973. As this chart indicates, suicide rates are considerably higher for men than for women, and the difference becomes more pronounced in old age, with male suicide rates rising dramatically. This increase may be a function of factors such as the male's retirement from work, which reduces his sense of being needed and useful. (Data from J. Green, Suicide Prevention Center, Los Angeles.)

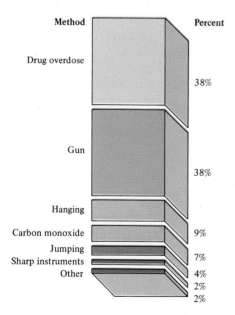

Fig. 7.9 Methods of suicide and the number of persons who used such means are represented by this diagram. These suicide methods range from such passive means as ingesting drugs or inhaling carbon monoxide to active and violent methods that include hanging or gunshot. The more passive methods may be related to the person's ambivalence about living or dying and may also be consistent with his generally passive behavior; active methods may indicate a greater resolve to die. Irrespective of the method, however, the availability of guns, pills, and other means increases the likelihood of impulsive suicidal behavior. (Data from J. Green, Suicide Prevention Center, Los Angeles.)

*The data are for 1972 to 1973 and include Los Angeles only, but they are considered to be representative of national figures.

type, *catalogic* thinking, is essentially despairing and destructive. Here the self as experienced by the self is confused with the self as it is experienced by others. Individuals in this category are often lonely; they feel helpless, fearful, and extremely pessimistic about involving themselves in personal relationships.

At the opposite extreme is the second type of suicidal reasoning, which Shneidman and Farberow call the *logical* type. In this case, the thought processes are rational. The person might be widowed and socially isolated, or he might be in great physical pain because of a long-term illness. To him death offers a release from psychological and physical burdens.

A third type of suicidal reasoning is *contaminated* thinking. Included in this category are people whose beliefs enable them to view suicide as a transition to better life or as a means of saving face. These suicides are most common in societies that hold firmly entrenched religious and cultural beliefs and that surround death with clearly defined meanings and rituals.

The final type of suicidal thinking is *paleologic*. The paleologic thinker is led to his death by delusions or hallucinations. For example, a person might be called upon to end his life by voices accusing him of shameful actions or offering him a glorious transfiguration into a different mode of being.

Myths About Suicide

Common as it is, suicide is still surrounded by an aura of mystery and by a considerable number of popular misconceptions. One of the most unfortunate myths about suicide is that a person who threatens to kill himself will not carry out his threat; only the "silent type" will actually pull it off. This notion is utterly mistaken. The fact is that in approximately 70 percent of all completed suicides, suicidal intent was communicated at some time within the three months before the fatal attempt (Stengel, 1964). Hence, suicidal verbalizations are

Types of Suicidal Thinking

Type	Thinking Process	Example
Catalogic	The person is depressed, despairing, self-destructive, and incapable of thinking rationally	A man who cannot conquer his alcoholism, who has lost his job and destroyed his marriage because of it, and who commits suicide in order to escape his loneliness and self-condemnation
Logical	The person makes a rational decision to rid himself, through death, of an unbearable burden that he cannot rid himself of otherwise	A woman who, after being told that she has terminal cancer, commits suicide in order to save her family the medical expenses and save herself the agony of dying gradually
Contaminated	The person's beliefs in the spiritual ennoblement attached to death lead him to kill himself rather than endure dishonor or some other situation he perceives as intolerable	A Japanese army officer who through his own error has sent a battalion of soldiers to an unnecessary death and commits suicide to save his family and himself the disgrace
Paleologic	The person commits suicide in response to hallucinations and/or delusions	A psychotically depressed woman who is convinced that she has killed her parents and obeys a voice telling her to kill herself so as not to pollute the world with her sins any longer

Source: Shneidman and Farberow (1970).

clear danger signals and should be taken quite seriously.

Another myth is that when a person has attempted suicide and failed, this means that the person was not serious about ending his life. In this view, a mild self-inflicted injury—a superficial cutting of the wrist, for example—suggests that the would-be suicide was making a histrionic gesture, just faking or looking for sympathy. On the contrary, studies show that approximately 12 percent of those who make nonfatal suicide attempts will make a second, successful attempt within two years (Shochet, 1970). In fact, about 75 percent of all completed suicides have made a previous attempt or threat (Cohen et al., 1966). It may be that the initial attempt serves as a trial run, enabling the person to prepare more adequately for a later, more efficient attempt.

As we have mentioned, the issue of suicide is often obscured by a vague cloud of mystery. Our emotional reactions to this phenomenon—fear, horror, curiosity, incomprehension, and perhaps attraction as well—give suicide the status of "unmentionable" in the minds of many people, a taboo which is strengthened by the Judeo-Christian prohibition against suicide. Connected with this cultural response is a third myth about suicide: the myth that in talking to depressed people, suicide is the ultimate unmentionable. According to this popular notion, questioning a depressed person about his suicidal thoughts will either put the idea into his head or, if it is already in his head, will give it greater force. In opposition to this belief, almost all clinicians agree that encouraging a patient to talk about his suicidal wishes often helps him to overcome them and also provides the information necessary for therapeutic intervention.

Suicide Prediction

When a person commits suicide, his family and friends are often astonished. Such comments as "He seemed to be in such good spirits" or "But he had everything to live for" are typical responses. And these responses reveal how frequently people in the immediate social environment of the suicidal person are oblivious to the clues that he leaves. Some suicides, of course, are particularly adept at concealing their intentions. But the majority of suicides do give out signals.

At times clues to suicidal plans may be detected in secretive behavior or in a sudden decision to have a will drawn up. Sometimes a suicidal person makes a very direct verbal statement such as "I don't want to go on living" or "I know I'm a burden to everyone." Once a person has decided to kill himself he may withdraw into an almost contemplative state. He may refrain from conversation or drastically reduce his intake of food. He may sleep more soundly than usual, or he may suffer from insomnia. Often he acts as if he were going on a long trip. In what he presumes will be the last days of his life, the suicidal person frequently gives away his most highly valued possessions. College students tend to give away their skis, watches, and cameras. Wealthier people make outright gifts of money to friends and relatives (Shneidman and Mandelkorn, 1970).

Sometimes the expression of suicidal intent is less direct and can be pieced together only in retrospect. For example, a depressed patient leaving the hospital on a weekend pass might say, "I guess I won't be seeing you again," or, "I want to thank you for trying so hard to help me." It is important to remember that 40 percent of all people about to attempt suicide visit medical or psychiatric services in the week prior to the attempt (Yessler et al., 1961).

Since a period of calm may follow a decision to commit suicide (Keith-Spiegel and Spiegel, 1967), the sudden tranquillity of a previously agitated patient is a danger signal often misinterpreted as a sign of improvement. Since the person seems better, he is watched less carefully. And not uncommonly he will use this new freedom to carry out his suicide. In this connection, it should be pointed out that depressives who commit suicide tend to do so as they are coming out of their depression. It is not clear, however, whether they seem less depressed because they have decided to commit suicide or whether, being less depressed, they at last have the energy to carry out their suicidal wishes.

The psychological variable most frequently associated with serious suicidal intent is the sense of hopelessness (Pichot and Lempérière, 1964; Beck, 1967; Leonard, 1974). Analyses of suicide notes indicate that for many suicides death seems the only way out of an insoluble problem. In a study comparing notes left by successful suicides to simulated notes written by a well-matched control group, Shneidman and Farberow (1970c) found, as we might predict, that the writers of the genuine notes expressed significantly more suffering than the control group. Truly suicidal anguish is evidently hard to feign. Interestingly enough, however, the genuine suicide notes also contained a greater number of neutral statements—instructions, admonitions, lists of things to be done after the suicide has taken place, and so forth. Both the ring of authentic hopelessness and the neutral content are illustrated in the following two notes:

Barbara,
    I'm sorry. I love you bunches. Would you please do a couple of things for me. Don't tell the kids what I did. When Theresa gets a little older, if she wants to cut her hair please let her. Don't make her wear it long just because you like it that way. Ask your Mom what kind and how much clothes the kids need and then buy double what she says. I love you and the kids very much please try and remember that. I'm just not any good for you. I never learned how to tell you no. You will be much better off without me. Just try and find someone who will love Theresa and Donny,

Love Bunches—Charlie

P.S. Donny is down at Linda's
Put Donny in a nursery school

Dear Steve:
    I have been steadily getting worse in spite of everything and did not want to be a burden the rest of my life.

All my love,
Dad

My brown suit is the only one that fits me.

However, by no means do all or even most suicides experience unqualified despair. According to Farberow and Litman (1970), only about 3 to 5 percent of people who attempt suicide are truly determined to die. Another two-thirds of the suicidal population do not really wish to die but instead are trying, through the gesture of a suicide attempt, to communicate the intensity of their suffering to family and friends. Finally, about 30 percent of the suicidal population falls into what Farberow and Litman call the "to be or not to be" group—people who are ambivalent about dying.

In short, the vast majority of suicide attempts are made by people who on one level truly wish to live. In trying to dissuade a would-be suicide, professionals often make use of this fact, pressing the person with the arguments for preserving his life and trying to convince him to postpone irrevocable action until the crisis has passed. If he can be dissuaded, the potential suicide then stands in need of some kind of therapy.

PERSPECTIVES ON SUICIDE

The Psychodynamic Perspective

Freud claimed that psychoanalysis had solved the enigma of suicide by discovering that no one has the psychological capacity to violate the life instinct by killing himself unless in doing so he is also killing an object with whom he has identified himself. In other words, according to Freud, the person who commits suicide is bent not so much on killing himself as on killing another person who has been incorporated within himself. Thus the suicide is directing against himself an unconscious death wish which had been directed against another person. This theory, of course, is simply a logical extension of Abraham's and Freud's theory of depression as "anger-in." In the suicide the anger assumes murderous proportions, but since it is directed inward, the murder is perpetrated against the self.

As we have seen in Chapter 2, Freud believed that such aggressive impulses issued from Thanatos, the death instinct. This theme of the death instinct was picked up by Menninger (1938), who proposed that suicide represented the triumph of man's destructive aspects over his constructive, life-affirming tendencies. According to Menninger, the desire to live depends on the feelings of self-esteem contained in the superego. When this self-esteem is reduced, for whatever reasons, the suicidal person regresses to the state of the hungry, deserted infant who wishes to annihilate the once-incorporated love object. And by committing suicide, he succeeds in annihilating that original object whose incorporation helped to create the superego.

Much of this anger on which Freud and Menninger place so much emphasis has to do with object loss. In psychodynamic theory, object loss, both past and present, plays a significant role in predisposing an individual to suicide. Rejection by significant others early in a person's life may cause him to develop defenses against the pain he unconsciously comes to expect as an adult. If these defenses give way and the person confuses the overwhelming pain of the early loss with a current rejection or separation, he may take his life.

Similarly, psychodynamic theorists maintain that some children who are traumatized by an early devastating loss grow up believing that close interpersonal relationships cannot continue over time. They may even develop some kind of an internal "time clock" by which they gauge how long they can expect such a relationship to endure before the inevitable separation. These are the people who tend to commit *anniversary suicides*, ending their lives on a date that has some special personal meaning, like their birthday or their wedding anniversary or Christmas.

Psychodynamic treatment of the suicidal patient tends to follow the traditional psychoanalytic lines. However, in the case of the potential suicide, the therapist also places great emphasis on providing emotional support. The therapist must carefully avoid any behaviors that might be mistaken for rejection. And in place of, or in addition to, individual therapy, he may recommend family therapy so that the patient will learn how to ask for and accept support from others and so that the family will learn how to provide such support.

The Behaviorist Perspective

According to Ullmann and Krasner (1975), two leading behaviorists, self-destruction is the result of a particular shift in the person's pattern of reinforcements. The basic essential of this new, suicidal pattern is the person's estimate of his current life situation as having no adequate source of reinforcement. Thus suicide results from the real, anticipated, or fantasized loss of highly valued reinforcers—job, health, friends, family, and so on.

At the same time that the person expects no further reinforcements from his life, he may find the thought of his death positively reinforcing, in that it will make the people he leaves behind feel sorry for him and will punish with remorse those he feels have hurt him. In other words, the person may see death as bringing him a number of things that he wants: attention, pity, and revenge.

Thus, from a behaviorist standpoint, suicide appears less of an enigma than it does to the Freudians. Like any other behavior, it involves a movement away from nonreinforcing situations and toward reinforcing situations. In accordance with this interpretation, the behaviorists would treat the suicidal patient, like the depressed patient, by attempting to readjust his pattern of reinforcements.

The Humanistic-Existential Perspective

The humanists and existentialists place great emphasis on the individual's confrontation with death. In fact, May (1958) suggests that death in any of its aspects is the fact that gives life absolute value. He quotes a person in therapy: "I know only two things—one, that I will be dead someday, two, that I am not dead now. The only question is what shall I do between those two points" (p. 90).

Thus, according to humanistic-existential psychology, the possibility of one's own death is something that must be faced and acknowledged by each human being. With this comes the realization that it is entirely within one's power to commit suicide. And the thought of suicide can have positive value, for it makes a person more likely to consider his life with full seriousness.

Humanistic-existential therapy for the suicidal patient would focus on bringing the patient to a full realization of his current existence, in the hope that he would find enough meaning in his life to begin living more authentically. If in spite of this the patient did commit suicide, the therapist might explain that the person was unable to cope with the continuing dread of a meaningless or inauthentic existence. Blocked in his efforts to free himself from overwhelming despair, such a person wills himself to suicide rather than continue in an intolerable situation.

The Psychosocial Perspective

One of the first scholars to study suicide scientifically was the French sociologist Emile Durkheim (1897). Durkheim saw suicide not as the act of an isolated individual, but as the act of an individual within a society. According to his view, whether or not a person commits suicide is determined in large part by the person's adjustment to his society, by the stability or instability of the society, and by the network of values and norms with which the society surrounds the individual.

Working on this premise, Durkheim described three "etiological types" of suicide: anomic, egoistic, and altruistic. *Anomic suicide* takes place when the equilibrium of a society is severely disturbed. For example, in this country the sudden crash of the stock market in 1929 resulted in an immense number of suicides. And in Austria suicide rates took a sharp upturn following World War II, possibly because of the stress created by the loss of the war and the occupation by enemy troops (Havighurst, 1969).

Egoistic suicide, a quite different classification, results from the individual's lack of integration into his society. Loners with no strong ties to community or family, egoistic suicides are people who lacked a supportive social network to see them through periods of stress.

In contrast to egoistic suicide, *altruistic suicide* occurs because the individual is totally immersed in the value system of his culture—a value system that tells him that under certain circumstances it is either necessary or at least honorable to commit suicide. In the modern era, this cultural endorsement of sui-

IS THERE JUSTIFIABLE SUICIDE?

On the night of January 28, 1975, Dr. Henry P. Van Dusen, former president of Union Theological Seminary, and his wife together took deliberate overdoses of sleeping pills before going to sleep. Mrs. Van Dusen died that night. Dr. Van Dusen vomited up his pills and died in a hospital fifteen days later, presumably from heart disease.

Not only because the Van Dusens were well-known people but because they were leaders in American religious life, their suicide pact raises once again an old question—that of justifiable suicide. The Christian religion, to which the Van Dusens had devoted their lives, makes virtually no allowance for suicide, which is considered a sin. Yet many religious thinkers—to say nothing of laymen—feel that in view of modern medical advances, which can prolong life far beyond the individual's capacity to enjoy that life, this traditional Christian attitude is obsolete. Such was the opinion of the Van Dusens, who openly discussed their suicide plans with their friends. Both were in poor health. Mrs. Van Dusen had an arthritic condition that had already rendered her lame and was simply getting worse. Five years earlier Dr. Van Dusen had suffered a severe stroke, which had affected his speech and drastically limited his physical activity. Having been extraordinarily active all their lives, they found these handicaps hard to bear. And, as they stated in their suicide note, they found the prospect of becoming even more disabled impossible to bear. Hence they chose to die—a decision which they felt would be consonant with God's will.

Aside from the religious question, the Van Dusens' suicide raises a number of questions for the mental health profession. Is suicide prevention always justified? Do we have the right to decide for another human being whether or not he can dispose of his own life? Can we justifiably restrain or even hospitalize him against his will? Some people argue that there are cases such as the Van Dusens' in which suicide is a positive and responsible act. Others contend that even if suicide does not violate religious sanctions, a person's life belongs at least in part to those who are close to him. Another pro-prevention argument is that most suicidal persons are too depressed to make a rational decision as to whether they should live or die.

Medical technology has now reached the point where it can prolong almost indefinitely, and at enormous expense, lives that are hardly being lived—lives of patients suffering terrible physical agony and of comatose patients with irreversible brain damage (e.g., Karen Ann Quinlan, the New Jersey girl whose parents petitioned the courts to allow her doctors to detach her respirator). The debate over justifiable suicide and its related issue, euthanasia, is thus particularly relevant now. In the case of suicide, however, it is well to remember that most people who attempt suicide are not suffering from terminal illnesses or debilitating physical handicaps. Rather, they are people with intense personal problems—problems that might be solved. And as we have seen, most suicidal persons, far from having made the type of carefully considered decision that the Van Dusens appear to have arrived at, have intense feelings of ambivalence about ending their lives and at some level would just as soon be rescued.

Sources: Kenneth A. Briggs, "Suicide Pact Preceded Deaths of Dr. Van Dusen and His Wife," *The New York Times,* February 26, 1975, pp. 1 and 43; John Reedy, "The Morality of Self-Destruction," *The New York Times,* March 2, 1975; "Suicide: An Old Debate Is Renewed," *The New York Times,* March 2, 1975.

cide has been much more common in Eastern than in Western cultures. Typical examples would include the practice of hara-kiri or ritual disembowelment in Japan and the suicide missions of the Japanese Kamikaze pilots during World War II. A more recent illustration was provided during the war in Vietnam, when a number of Buddhist monks immolated themselves to protest the fighting.

Following Durkheim's lead, many contemporary investigators continue to explore suicide from a psychosocial perspective. One outcome of their studies is a greater awareness of the relationship between suicide and a number of social variables. We know, for example, that although women attempt suicide considerably more often than men, three times as many men succeed in killing themselves as do women. Statistical studies also show that twice as many single people as married people kill themselves and that in general the likelihood of a person's committing suicide increases as a function of age, especially for males. On the basis of these and other findings, Shneidman and Farberow (1970a) have put together a demographic summary of suicide. According to these investigators, the *modal suicide attempter* (that is, the person who most commonly attempts suicide and survives) is a native-born Caucasian female, a housewife in her twenties or thirties, who attempts to kill herself by swallowing barbiturates and gives as her reason either marital difficulties or depression. In contrast, the *modal suicide committer* (that is, the person who succeeds in killing himself) is a native-born Caucasian male in his forties or older who commits suicide by shooting or hanging himself or by poisoning himself with carbon monoxide for reasons of ill health, depression, or marital difficulties.

We should also point out that although the suicide rate in our own country (11.7 per 100,000) is considered high, several countries have higher rates. For example, Sweden's suicide rate is 22 per 100,000; Czechoslovakia's is 24.5 per 100,000; and Hungary's, the highest in the world, is 33.1 per 100,000.

SUMMARY

This chapter has been an examination of the affective disorders—that is, the disorders of mood—and of suicide. People suffering from affective disorders experience either mania or depression, which are exaggerations of the same kinds of positive and negative feelings experienced by all human beings. The symptoms of both are distributed across all aspects of human behavior: feeling, thinking, motivation, and physiological functioning. Although the incidence of mania appears to be decreasing, the incidence of depression seems to be on the rise. Depression is now a major problem in our society, as is suicide, which often occurs as the outcome of depression.

According to the DSM-II classification, the affective disorders include involutional melancholia, manic-depressive illness, and psychotic depressive reaction—all of which are considered psychoses—and depressive neurosis, a less severe form of depression.

Involutional melancholia is distinguished primarily by age of onset and the absence of previous depressive episodes. Manic-depressive illness is characterized by extreme mood swings, remission, and recurrence. In its circular form, manic and depressive states alternate; in the depressed and manic types, there are simply recurring episodes of depression and mania, respectively. In psychotic depressive reactions there is no previous history of mood disorders; the patient's severe depression is brought on by some direct form of stress. A diagnosis of depressive neurosis is made when the symptoms occur in response to some precipitating event but the person retains adequate reality contact.

The psychodynamic perspective interprets depression as aggression directed toward an incorporated love object. The behaviorist perspective views depression as resulting from the withdrawal of positive reinforcement. From the humanistic-existential perspective, blocked self-actualization and consequent inauthentic living give rise to depression. Another approach, the cognitive perspective, sees depression as the function of a negative cognitive schema. Finally, in addition to these psychological perspectives, biological and physiological research suggests that biochemical or neurophysiological dysfunction may play a part in the etiology of depression.

Suicide, often associated with depression, is surrounded by a number of misconceptions. In answer to these, research has established that people who threaten suicide often do attempt it; that an unsuccessful suicide attempt in no way rules out a later, successful attempt; and that discussing suicidal wishes with depressed patients can be of great therapeutic value, as most suicidal people have highly ambivalent feelings about taking their lives. A sense of hopelessness is the psychological variable most frequently associated with suicidal intent. Other common signs of an impending suicide attempt are secretive behavior, the sudden decision to have a will drawn up, the giving away of material possessions, and a sudden change from agitation to tranquillity, particularly in depressed patients.

Suicide has been interpreted from the psychosocial point of view as well as from the three primary psychological perspectives.

III The Social Disorders

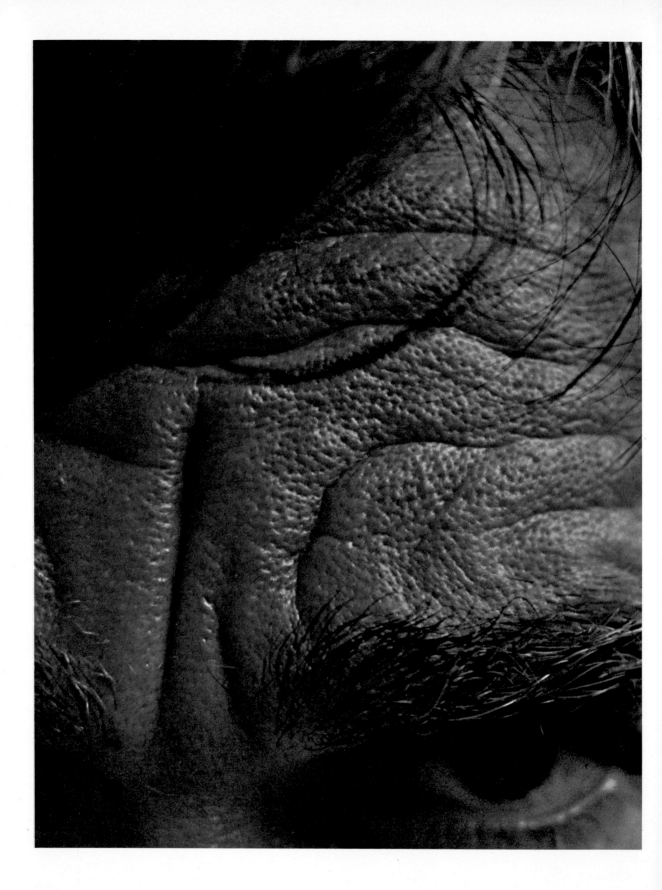

People suffering from the disorders that we have studied so far—the neuroses, the psychophysiological disorders, and the affective disorders—may inconvenience their families and friends considerably, but it is they themselves who bear the major burden of distress. In contrast, *antisocial* and *dyssocial* behavior may bring no mental distress whatsoever to the person engaging in the behavior; it is other people and society at large that suffer. For by definition, antisocial and dyssocial behavior involve disregard for and aggression against others. And such self-serving behavior typically results in the infraction of laws, so that when we speak of antisocial and dyssocial behavior, we are usually speaking of criminal behavior as well.

The question of the relationship between crime and abnormal psychology is extremely complex and forms an interesting chapter in the history of man's conception of mental illness. Immoral and illegal behavior was first officially subsumed into psychiatry by an English psychiatrist, J. C. Prichard, who in 1835 described what he called "moral insanity":

There is a form of mental derangement in which the intellectual functions appear to have sustained little or no injury, while the disorder is manifested principally or alone in the state of feelings, temper or habits. In cases of this nature the moral or active principles of the mind are strangely perverted or depraved; the power of self-government is lost or greatly impaired and the individual is found to be incapable, not of talking or reasoning upon any subject proposed to him but of conducting himself with decency and propriety in the business of life (cited in Preu, 1944, p. 923).

In the late nineteenth century such personalities came to be called *psychopathic personalities*. In keeping with the biogenic thinking of the period, the psychopathic personality was thought to arise from a hereditary constitutional defect—a line of thinking that still seems to capture the popular imagination, as evidenced by the great success of the novel (and play and movie) *The Bad Seed.* This oversimplified bad-seed theory of all disorders involving criminal deviance was widely accepted for many decades, though with the rise of sociology in the twentieth century, investigators began asking whether environmental conditions might not also contribute to the creation of a psychopath. One of the first comprehensive statements of this psychogenic position came from Partridge (1930), who argued that a sizable proportion of "psychopaths" should be relabeled as *sociopaths*, implying that the pathology was not an isolated, genetically determined intrapsychic

8
Sociopathy and Crime

phenomenon, but rather a complicated problem between the individual and the society.

In 1952, the American Psychiatric Association (APA) assimilated Partridge's term into DSM-I, the first edition of its *Diagnostic and Statistical Manual of Mental Disorders.* Under the category of personality disorders (which, as we have seen in Chapter 5, are deep-seated patterns of maladaptive behavior), DSM-I listed the "sociopathic personality," a broad category including not only criminal behavior but sexual deviations, alcoholism, and drug addiction as well—in short, the entire range of social misdeeds that could not be classified under the neuroses or psychoses. However, this classification prompted objections from many professionals, who argued that the average criminal committed his crime not because of a deeply ingrained maladjustment in his personality but for considerably less obscure reasons—to supplement his income, to do away with his girl friend's new lover, to "fix" somebody who has cheated him at cards, or what have you. Consequently, in the second edition of the APA manual, DSM-II (1968), what had been called the "sociopathic personality" was divided up into two separate diagnostic groups. The first label, "antisocial personality," remained in the list of personality disorders as the descriptive name for immoral and illegal behavior of apparently pathological origin. (The terms "psychopath" and "sociopath" are still used interchangeably with this label of antisocial personality.) The second label, "dyssocial behavior," appeared in a new category of "conditions without manifest psychiatric disorder" (1968, p. 51), thus making diagnostic accommodation for the "normal" criminal.

Accordingly, in this chapter we will deal with two broad categories of behavior: the antisocial, which is classified unequivocally as a form of mental disturbance, and the dyssocial, which is not labeled as a form of psychopathology but with which, as we shall see, the psychiatric profession is still very much involved. After describing these two categories, we will examine the various perspectives on antisocial and dyssocial behavior. Finally, we will discuss the complex issue of legal responsibility for crimes that are thought to be pathologically motivated.

THE ANTISOCIAL PERSONALITY

DSM-II defines the antisocial personality as follows:

This term is reserved for individuals who are basically unsocialized and whose behavior pattern brings them repeatedly into conflict with society. They are incapable of significant loyalty to individuals, groups or social values.

Fig. 8.1 *A hostile, sociopathic patient made this doodle of a bloody knife being plunged into a female breast. On a subsequent occasion only the face within the circle was shown to the patient and he identified it as his mother's. (Courtesy of C. Scott Moss)*

They are grossly selfish, callous, irresponsible, impulsive and unable to feel guilt or learn from experience or punishment. Frustration tolerance is low. They tend to blame others or offer plausible rationalizations for their behavior. A mere history of repeated legal or social offenses is not sufficient to justify this diagnosis (1968, p. 43).

Note the caution in the last sentence. This category, as we have seen, does not include everyone who violates laws and social mores but only those who do so in an apparently irrational manner, while remaining relatively free of anxiety (thus excluding the diagnosis of neurosis) and in good contact with reality (thus excluding a diagnosis of psychosis). The syndrome of the antisocial personality has been studied extensively by Cleckley, who lists sixteen interrelated indicators for such a diagnosis (1964, pp. 362–363). These sixteen points may be reduced to five broad aspects of the antisocial personality.

1. *Impulsive and inadequately motivated antisocial behavior.* The destructive actions of the antisocial personality are generally not motivated by any understandable purpose such as financial gain or revenge. Rather, they seem to issue from a sort of aimless perversity and thus sometimes have a rather absurd quality about them. In one of the cases described by Cleckley, for example, the teenaged subject's exploits included "defecation into the stringed intricacies of the school piano, the removal from his

uncle's automobile of a carburetor for which he got 75 cents, and the selling of his father's overcoat to a passing buyer of scrap materials" (1964, p. 86). In keeping with this aimless quality, the antisocial personality is capable of random acts of kindness, but these too seem to lack any firm motivational underpinnings and are therefore likely to tip over into thoughtless disregard of others' feelings at a moment's notice. Thus the antisocial personality may make a great fuss over a sick friend and the next day may steal the friend's car, typically abandoning it a few hours later.

In other words, the behavior of the antisocial personality is impulsive. Carelessly moving from one impulse gratification to the next, he lives for the moment, unable to hold down a job, remain faithful to a spouse, or in any way sacrifice immediate satisfaction for the sake of long-range goals. Hence antisocial personalities tend to make bad criminals. They frequently botch their crimes, as they botch their lives, by acting on the impulse of the moment without benefit of judgment or planning.

2. *Total lack of conscience, of regard for truth, or of any sense of responsibility.* Perhaps the most distinctive quality of the antisocial personality is his utter lack of anxiety or guilt when confronted with

Overcontrolled Hostility

Periodically one reads in the news of a particularly horrible assault committed by an utterly unlikely person—a person described by friends and neighbors as "such a nice quiet boy," who "wouldn't hurt a fly," never got into fights, always helped around the house, and so on. Megargee (1966) cites a number of such cases:

In Phoenix an 11 year old boy who stabbed his brother 34 times with a steak knife was described by all who knew him as being extremely polite and soft spoken with no history of assaultive behavior. In New York, an 18 year old youth who had confessed he had assaulted and strangled a 7 year old girl in a Queens church and later tried to burn her body in a furnace was described in the press as an unemotional person who planned to be a minister. A 21 year old man from Colorado who was accused of the rape and murder of two little girls had never been a discipline problem and, in fact, his step-father reported, "when he was in school the other kids would run all over him and he would never fight back. There is just no violence in him" (p. 2).

In a study of persons who had committed extremely violent crimes, Megargee found that such individuals tended to be one of two personality types. Type X is the perpetual troublemaker: the person who sets fire to his sister's cat at age seven, assaults his teacher at age ten, and from then on builds up a long record of involvement with the police. In short, the Type X criminal is distinguished by an almost total lack of self-control and by a long history of aggressive behavior. Such

individuals, according to Megargee, are likely to be the products of a half-indulgent, half-negligent upbringing.

Type Y—the category into which the examples cited earlier would fall—is almost the exact opposite of Type X. Often the products of a stern and loveless upbringing, these individuals learn too much self-control; they suppress anger, never act on impulse, and never strike out at anyone who offends them. Polite, withdrawn, painfully self-effacing, and generally ignored by those around them, Type Y personalities dam up their aggression until at last the dam breaks and the flood of rage pours forth in a show of grotesquely violent behavior.

Because of the totally irrational, almost convulsive nature of the Type Y's outburst, and because of the intensity of the long-accumulated and festering hostility, Megargee feels that these are the most dangerous of violent criminals. Paradoxically, he also points out that the Type Y personality is the last person who should ever be sent to prison. For once they have released their thunderclap of aggression, they almost invariably revert to their former pattern of passive and overcontrolled behavior, which serves them very poorly in the rough environment of prison life. And though in rare instances they may commit a second offense, no amount of punishment or conventional "rehabilitation"—both of which are aimed at inculcating self-control—will help them refrain from doing so. Indeed, self-control is the lesson they have already learned too well.

his misdeeds, whether they involve petty theft or murder. Typically, he will remain disarmingly calm, will fabricate an extremely plausible lie, and if caught in the lie, will still persist in behaving as if he were quite innocent of any responsibility for the act in question. Zax and Stricker report the case of Thomas, a sixteen-year-old boy who accidentally or otherwise killed a neighborhood child by shooting her in the head. After producing a series of alibis, he was finally forced to admit that it was in fact he who was holding the gun when it went off. Zax and Stricker describe Thomas' initial psychiatric interview as follows:

Thomas was a very attractive and affable boy who was almost defiantly polite. He spoke of the incident which led to his hospitalization in a nonchalant, unfeeling way, and was very suave and unnaturally composed in explaining why he was on the ward. He said, "I was showing her the gun. I didn't know it was loaded. She turned her head and it got her in the temple. I told the police that I was very sorry. You're to find out if there is anything mentally wrong with me. I thought I'd have to go to reform school. . . ." (1963, p. 240)

Even when not covering up for some destructive act, the antisocial personality is often a chronic liar, able to spin out elaborate stories replete with convincing details and to deliver these stories with an air of utter conviction. Like his callous and aggressive actions, the antisocial personality's lies often seem purposeless, though he does appear to take pleasure merely in the ability to deceive people. Of Thomas, mentioned above, his mother said, "Tommy never tells the truth, even when it's easier" (Zax and Stricker, 1963, p. 240). If it is shown to the antisocial personality that he is lying, he may laugh off the incident with no appearance of shame or embarrassment, or he may profess to be contrite and then proceed to tell further lies.

In view of these qualities, it is not hard to understand why antisocial personalities have been called "moral imbeciles." The intellect is intact, but the moral sense is totally absent.

3. *Affective poverty.* Connected to the antisocial personality's moral insensitivity is his lack of any feelings beyond the most superficial. It is difficult to say which is the cause and which the result, but there is no question that the combination of amorality and affectlessness leads to an inability to form close interpersonal relationships. In his dealings with others, the antisocial personality is typically cynical, ungrateful, disloyal, and exploitative. He has no empathy or fellow feeling and therefore cannot comprehend on an emotional level how his actions hurt others. Other people are there to be used. As for giving or receiving love, these are beyond his capabilities. This immunity to emotional ties is well illustrated in the remarks of Dan F., a case reported by McNeil:

I can remember the first time in my life when I began to suspect I was a little different from most people. When I was in high school my best friend got leukemia and died and I went to his funeral. Everybody else was crying and feeling sorry for themselves and as they were praying to get him into heaven I suddenly realized that I wasn't feeling anything at all. He was a nice guy but what the hell. That night I thought about it some more and found out that I wouldn't miss my mother and father if they died and that I wasn't too nuts about my brothers and sisters, for that matter. I figured there wasn't anybody I really cared for but, then, I didn't need any of them anyway so I rolled over and went to sleep (1967, p. 87).

As a consequence of his lack of strong feelings, the sex life of the antisocial personality is typically manipulative and faithless. Likewise, he is unlikely to commit suicide, presumably because despair is beyond his affective range, although he may threaten suicide in an attempt to manipulate and control others.

4. *Lack of insight, and inability to learn from experience.* The antisocial personality does not seem to see the connection between his actions and their consequences. Hence he never learns anything from his experiences. Once punished for some action, the normal person learns either not to repeat the action or to repeat it in such a way that he will not be caught. In contrast, the antisocial personality will repeat the same offense again and again, and in the same manner, no matter how many times he is punished. He lacks any insight into why he does what he does, nor can he understand why he should be punished for so doing. In sum, he behaves as if not only the laws of society but also the law of cause and effect did not apply to him.

5. *Ability to maintain a pleasant and impressive exterior.* As we have seen, the antisocial personality is typically calm, remaining poised and serene even in situations which cause the normal person to perspire from every pore. Furthermore, he is usually of normal or superior intelligence and able to reason quite convincingly. He is, in fact, the ultimate "smooth talker"—charming, affable, good-humored, and convincing. Finally, as noted above, he is an accomplished liar. What all this adds up to is that

the antisocial personality, no matter what objectionable act he has committed or is in the process of committing, is easily able to maintain the appearance of virtue and thus to fool other people into trusting him. McNeil's case of Dan F. again provides a good example. Upon hearing of the suicide of one of his colleagues at the television station where he worked, Dan showed no emotional response whatsoever. McNeil reports:

Later, when I brought it [i.e., the suicide] to his attention, all he could say was that it was "the way the ball bounces." At the station, however, he was the one who collected money for the deceased and presented it personally to the new widow. As Dan observed, she was really built and had possibilities (1967, p. 58).

The Case of Roberta

Though no single human being will conform in every detail to the general pattern outlined above, the following case, taken from Cleckley, is a good illustration of the five qualities that we have listed. Roberta typifies the antisocial personality not only in her aimlessness, shamelessness, affectlessness, lack of insight, and ability to maintain the veneer of virtue, but also in her tendency to pile up minor acts of callousness rather than to commit acts of extreme violence.

"I can't understand the girl, no matter how hard I try," said the father, shaking his head in genuine perplexity. *"It's not that she seems bad or exactly that she means to do wrong. She can lie with the straightest face, and after she's found in the most outlandish lies she still seems perfectly easy in her own mind."*

He had related, in a rambling but impressive account, how Roberta at the age of ten stole her aunt's silver hairbrush, how she repeatedly made off with small articles from the dime store, the drug store, and from her own home. "At first it seemed just the mischievous doings of a little girl," he said, "a sort of play. . . . You know how children sometimes tell a lot of fanciful stories without thinking of it as lying."

Neither the father nor the mother seemed a severe parent. . . . [However,] there was nothing to suggest that this girl had been spoiled. The parents had, so far as could be determined, consistently let her find that lying and stealing and truancy brought censure and punishment.

• • •

As she grew into her teens this girl began to buy dresses, cosmetics, candy, perfume, and other articles, charging them to her father. He had no warning that these bills would come. Roberta acted without saying a word to him, and no matter what he said or did she

went on in the same way. For many of these things she had little or no use; some of them she distributed among her acquaintances. In serious conferences it was explained that the family budget had been badly unbalanced by these bills. As a matter of fact, the father, previously in comfortable circumstances, had at one time been forced to the verge of bankruptcy.

In school Roberta's work was mediocre. She studied little and her truancy was spectacular and persistent. No one regarded her as dull and she seemed to learn easily when she made any effort at all. (Her I.Q. was found to be 135.) She often expressed ambitions and talked of plans for the future. These included the study of medicine, dress designing, becoming an author, and teaching home economics in a nearby college. For short periods she sometimes applied herself and made excellent grades, but would inevitably return to truancy, spending the school hours in cheap movie houses, in the drug store, or wandering through shops stealing a few things for which she seemed to have neither need nor specific desire.

"I wouldn't exactly say she's like a hypocrite," [her father said]. "When she's caught and confronted with her lies and other misbehavior she doesn't seem to appreciate the inconsistency of her position. Her conscience seems still untouched. Even when she says how badly she's acted and promises to do better her feelings just must not be what you take them for."

Having failed in many classes and her truancy becoming intolerable to the school, Roberta, after several more petty thefts from classmates and teachers, was expelled from the local high school. Her family sent her to a boarding school of her choice, from which she wrote enthusiastic letters. Despite this expressed satisfaction, she ran away from school and could not be located for several days.

• • •

Roberta was sent to two other boarding schools from which she had to be expelled. She entered a hospital for training to be a registered nurse but did not last a month. Employed in her father's business as a bookkeeper, she used her skill at figures and a good deal of ingenuity to make off with considerable sums.

• • •

In telling of her initial sexual experience, which had occurred about a year before I first saw her, she seemed frank and by no means embarrassed.

• • •

[This first sexual experience had taken place on yet another of her innumerable episodes of running away.] With no explanation to her parents she suddenly disappeared. To me she explained that she had left with the intention of visiting a boy friend sta-

tioned at a camp in another state. She admitted that she had in mind the possibility of marrying this man but that no definite decision had been made by her, much less by him. She had, it seems, given the matter little serious thought.

She was unable to locate the soldier. Finding herself without funds as night approached, she remembered another friend in the same town. She went to his home and told his parents a story designed to move them to invite her to spend the night. They did, and later that night, when she was alone, Roberta tried to place a long-distance call to the man who was the original reason for the trip.

The call not being completed, she began to fear the operator might ring back. She also was not quite sure her hostess had not overheard her at the telephone. After thinking of this and realizing that her family might trace her in such a nearby place, she slipped off after pretending to go to bed early, leaving no message for these people who had taken her in.

Catching a bus bound in another direction, she rode for a few hours and got off at a strange town where she knew no one. Not having concluded plans for her next step, she sat for a while in a hotel lobby. Soon she was approached by a middle-aged man. He was far from prepossessing, smelt of cheap liquor, and his manners were distinctly distasteful. He soon offered to pay for her overnight accommodations at the hotel. She realized that he meant to share the bed with her but made no objection. As well as one can tell by discussing this experience with Roberta, she was neither excited, frightened, repulsed, nor attracted by a prospect that most carefully brought up virgins would certainly have regarded with anything but indifference.

The man, during their several hours together, handled her in a rough, peremptory fashion, took no trouble to conceal his contempt for her and her role, and made no pretense of friendliness, much less affection. She experienced moderate pain but no sexual response under his ministrations. After giving her $5.00 with unnecessarily contemptuous accentuations of its significance, he left her in the room about midnight.

Next morning she reached her soldier friend by telephone and suggested that he send her sufficient funds to join him. She had not discarded the idea of marrying him, nor had she progressed any further toward a final decision to do so. He discouraged her vigorously against coming, refused to send money, and urged her to return home. She was not, it seems, greatly upset by this turn of events, and, with little serious consideration of the matter, decided to go to

Charlotte, which was approximately 150 miles distant. . . .

Short of funds during her stay in Charlotte, Roberta drifted into random prostitution. She reported that she eventually derived some mild pleasure from sexual intercourse. However, she had never felt any intense sexual temptation or passion, nor had she ever experienced orgasm, as far as she knew. Finally, after three weeks in Charlotte, she was located by her parents, whom she greeted with great affection. Her behavior, however, did not change, and eventually she was hospitalized for psychiatric observation.

During her hospitalization she spoke convincingly of the benefit she was obtaining and discussed her mistakes with every appearance of insight. She spoke like a person who had been lost and bewildered but now had found her way. She did not seem to be making any voluntary effort to deceive her physicians. [Roberta returned home but her old behavior patterns continued.]

· · ·

She returned for psychiatric treatment on several occasions, always saying she had been helped and expressing simple but complete confidence that it was impossible for her to have further trouble. Despite her prompt failures she would, in her letters to us at the hospital, write as if she had been miraculously cured:

"You and Doctor———have given me a new outlook and a new life. This time we have got to the very root of my trouble and I see the whole story in a different light. I don't mean to use such words lightly and, of all things, I want to avoid even the appearance of flattery, but I must tell you how grateful I am, how deeply I admire the wonderful work you are doing. . . . If, in your whole life you had never succeeded with one other patient, what you have done for me should make your practice worthwhile. . . . I wish I could tell you how different I feel. How different I am! . . . " etc. . . .

Though she realized I had been informed of recent episodes quite as bad as those in the past, on several occasions she wrote requesting letters of recommendation for various positions she had applied for or was considering. More than once blank forms appeared in my mail with notices that Roberta had given my name as a reference. It was interesting and not without an element of sad irony to note that these forms made specific queries about "good character," "high moral standards," "reliability," "would you employ the applicant yourself, realizing the position is one of considerable responsibility," etc. Roberta seemed sweetly free of any doubt that such recommendations would be given without qualification and in the highest terms of assurance (1964, pp. 66–74).

DYSSOCIAL BEHAVIOR

As we have seen, DSM-II distinguishes clearly between the antisocial personality and dyssocial behavior, labeling the former as a personality disorder and the latter as a "condition without manifest psychiatric disorder." The DSM-II definition of dyssocial behavior reads as follows:

This category is for individuals who are not classifiable as antisocial personalities, but who are predatory and follow more or less criminal pursuits, such as racketeers, dishonest gamblers, and dope peddlers (1968, p. 52).

The person who engages in dyssocial behavior is, then, presumed to be psychiatrically normal, though capable of preying regularly upon his fellow-man. Cleckley supports this definition, listing four fundamental characteristics which differentiate ordinary criminal behavior—that is, dyssocial behavior —from antisocial behavior (1964, pp. 276–277).

1. *The criminal has a goal and works consistently toward it.* This goal may be directly opposed to the values of society, but it is nevertheless a goal. In contrast, the impulsive antisocial personality cannot stick consistently to anything.

2. *The ends of the criminal are understandable.* These ends may be to make money quickly and easily, or to gain prestige within his peer group, or what have you. The point is that they make sense when viewed by the normal person, although he would not endorse the means that the criminal employs to achieve those ends. The antisocial personality's goals, on the other hand, are for the most part incomprehensible.

3. *The criminal attempts to escape personal harm.* He does not wish to get caught and therefore proceeds with caution in his activities. The antisocial personality, by comparison, shows no such caution. Though he may put together spectacular lies in order to exonerate himself after the fact, in the actual prosecution of his misdeeds he shows little concern for his own well-being.

4. *The criminal is capable of committing major crimes.* A criminal may have the persistence to think through, plan, and carry out, through its successive stages, a major crime such as a full-scale bank robbery, a kidnapping for ransom, or a well-planned murder. Living only for the moment, the antisocial personality is incapable of such intricate undertakings and thus tends to commit more petty offenses.

Occasionally the antisocial personality will commit a brutal murder, but this is rare.

Furthermore, the antisocial personality is traditionally distinguished from the ordinary criminal in that the latter is presumed to have a normal capacity for love, friendship, and loyalty, and hence can establish satisfactory interpersonal relationships. In contrast, the antisocial personality, devoid both of strong feelings and of a sense of duty, can never be consistently loyal or loving to his parents, spouse, children, or friends.

Thus what we are left with is a dichotomy. On the one hand we have the abnormal antisocial personality—shallow, callous, impulsive, and reckless beyond the limits of normalcy; of this syndrome, Roberta's case is a classic example. On the other hand, we have psychiatrically normal dyssocial behavior: the hired killer who, after dispassionately shooting someone down in a dark parking lot, returns home, kisses his wife and children, telephones his mother to find out whether her arthritis is any better, and then sits down with a beer to watch the late show.

Unfortunately, however, most cases are not so clear-cut. What appears as a dichotomy in diagnostic manuals turns out, like so many other distinctions in the field of psychology, to be a continuum when applied to human reality. Consider, for example, the following case:

One day after school two ten-year-old boys, Jim Jones and Bobby Ryan, went shopping for hockey sticks in a large department store. While they were making their purchases in the sports department, they saw two black teenagers bouncing a basketball; a floorwalker appeared, grabbed the basketball, and ordered the two teenagers to leave the store.

Leaving the store with their new hockey sticks, Jim and Bobby were met at the exit by the two teenagers who had been chased from the store. They were Ken Jordan, fifteen years old, and Bill Sherwin, who had just turned fourteen. The two teenagers robbed Jim and Bobby at knifepoint and then ordered them to go back into the store, get refunds for the hockey sticks, and return with the money. Jim and Bobby went back into the store. Though they could easily have sneaked out by another exit or alerted a store guard, they remembered their parents' rule: If you are mugged, give the mugger what he wants. And so they did as they were told, returning to Ken and Bill with the money.

Ken and Bill then took them, by bus, to a construction site. The construction crew had already left for the day. Finding a pay phone, Ken forced Bobby to call his mother and say that he and Jim had been *kidnapped and would be killed unless their parents brought $2,000 to a certain place the following morning.*

Once the call had been made, Ken and Bill took the boys to the sixth floor of the building, out of earshot of the guards. There they proceeded to "have some fun" with them. They defecated on the floor and forced the boys to pick up their feces. They applied lit matches to Jim's body, set fire to his hair, and then tied him to a pulley and immersed him, upside down, in a barrel of water for a minute at a time. They dangled Bobby from a window, pretending that they were going to drop him. Then they took turns beating each of the boys in the face. At one point Bill showed some sign of regret, whispering to Jim as he beat him, "Yell louder and pretend that I'm hitting you harder than I am." Finally exhausted from beating the boys, they made them lie down on the floor and sodomized them.

It was now seven hours since their adventure had begun, and Ken and Bill began to realize that they might be in trouble. Abandoning the kidnapping scheme, they ordered the boys to take off their clothes and "streak" downstairs and into the street. Ken and Bill then escaped. Jim and Bobby, running naked into the street, their faces mangled and bloody, were picked up by a group of black men standing on the corner and were driven to the police station (adapted from Morgan, 1975, pp.9–10).

Was Ken and Bill's behavior antisocial or dyssocial? A case can easily be made for the label of dyssocial. In the first place, they had at least one motive—financial gain—and they pursued it to the point of having the boys go back and get refunds for the hockey sticks. Furthermore, as two disadvantaged black youngsters who were rudely chased from the store while the white boys were being shown hockey sticks by a salesperson, Ken and Bill may have been seeking revenge as well—another understandable motive. (Revenge could also account for their insistence that the hockey sticks be returned.) It should also be noted that at points they showed great caution. The place to which they took the boys was well chosen: they knew the construction crew would be gone at that hour, and they were careful to go up to the sixth floor so that the guards would not hear them. Finally, and rather paradoxically, both the intense cruelty of their abuse of the boys and Bill's one moment of compassion or anxiety are atypical of antisocial criminal behavior.

However, a case can also be made for the label of antisocial behavior. Can revenge against these privileged, hockey-playing white boys constitute

sufficient motive for the utter perversity with which Ken and Bill treated them? And is there not a quality of impulsiveness, almost absurdity, about the ransom scheme? In any case, they showed as much recklessness as caution. When Ken first pulled the knife, he did so in broad daylight on a downtown shopping street crowded with people. Furthermore, dangling Bobby out the window, where he could be spotted from the street, was also extremely imprudent. (But could this recklessness be due to their youth rather than to the typical impulsiveness of the antisocial personality? Possibly. It should be added, however, that at the age of fifteen Ken was a fairly experienced criminal, having been picked up by the police twenty-one times, on charges ranging from petty theft to the robbery and rape of a fifty-six-year-old woman.)

The reader may diagnose Ken and Bill as he chooses. Our point is simply that this case, along with thousands of others, has both its pathological and nonpathological aspects. Furthermore, even when we consider a clear-cut "textbook" case of dyssocial behavior—the hired killer, for example—certain psychological questions are bound to come up. Clear symptoms of pathology are admittedly absent. The man does not commit his crime without motivation, nor does he kill because a "voice from heaven" instructed him to do so. Yet one hesitates to apply the label of "normal" to behavior that so flagrantly violates the most fundamental moral codes, utterly profaning the notion of trust in one's fellow-man. In this vein, one notes a certain hesitation even in DSM-II. Under the general heading of "conditions without manifest psychiatric disorder," dyssocial behavior actually appears as a subcategory of "social maladjustment without manifest psychiatric disorder," a category which DSM-II defines as follows:

This category is for recording the conditions of individuals who are psychiatrically normal but who nevertheless have severe enough problems to warrant examination by a psychiatrist (1968, pp. 51–52).

The question immediately arises: If such people are psychiatrically normal, why do they need to be examined by a psychiatrist? Why, indeed, should they be included in a manual of mental disorders or in a textbook on abnormal psychology? Why should they not be left to the social workers, the police, and the clergy? The answer is that many people obviously still cling to the belief that adherence to basic moral codes is essential to the definition of psychological normalcy and that to sell heroin to a twelve-year-old, for example, requires a certain defect in the personality. Whether or not this belief is justifiable is a question that rests on one's interpretation of human nature. In any case, it is not a question that this book will attempt to resolve. Our purpose is simply to point out that the relationship between psychology and "ordinary" crime remains an open issue. And it is for this reason that in the following section we will briefly consider certain varieties of dyssocial behavior and the psychological questions they provoke.

The Scope of Crime

Pathologically motivated or not, crime is an extremely pressing problem in the United States today. Every 27 minutes someone in this country is murdered; every 10 minutes someone is raped; every 82 seconds someone is robbed; every 76 seconds someone is assaulted; every 34 seconds a car is stolen. Furthermore, the statistics are based only on those crimes that are reported, whereas it is generally agreed that unreported crimes far outnumber reported crimes. The total cost of crime in America is estimated at fifty billion dollars annually. This is to say nothing of the cost of combating crime, which represents an additional twelve billion dollars annually. And even with so great an expenditure on crime control, only one-fifth of all serious crimes result in arrest (FBI, 1975).

Furthermore, the problem is getting worse. In all the major categories of crime, frequency has at least doubled in the last ten years. And rape, for example,

is six times more common than it was ten years ago. Nor is there any indication that next year will not produce even more dismal statistics.

Who is committing these crimes and why? In the following section we will examine very briefly three major categories of crime—*juvenile delinquency*, *organized crime*, and *white-collar crime*—with an emphasis on the psychological questions raised by each of these categories.

Juvenile Delinquency

Juvenile delinquency may be defined as the violation of laws and social mores by people under eighteen years of age. DSM-II includes it not under the heading of dyssocial behavior but rather under "behavior disorders of childhood and adolescence," and accordingly it will be mentioned again in Chapter 16, which deals with childhood developmental disorders. DSM-II distinguishes three different forms of delinquency: (1) the *runaway reaction*, in which, as the term indicates, the juvenile runs away from home and often steals as well; (2) the *unsocialized aggressive reaction*, in which the young person's behavior includes acts of hostility, disobedience, destructiveness, and theft; and (3) the *group delinquent reaction*, in which the juvenile, preferring the mores of his gang to those of society at large, characteristically plays hookey and commits theft, vandalism, and other destructive acts in concert with his fellow gang members.

Whether runaways or unsocialized or socialized into the deviant subculture of a delinquent gang,

Fig. 8.2   Members of the Savage Skulls gang. The deviant subculture of a delinquent gang has its own set of mores for behavior, most of which are viewed as criminal by the larger society.

juveniles commit an alarming number of crimes. Indeed, the most likely age for arrest is sixteen (FBI, 1975), and often the arrested juvenile is actually preadolescent. In such a case in New York City, for example, artist Roger Hane was beaten to death with a tree limb by a gang of six boys to whom he refused to surrender his new bicycle; of the gang, two were sixteen years old, two were fifteen, one was thirteen, and one was twelve.

Such cases raise two rather urgent psychological issues. First, what psychological conditions could possibly "harden" a child to the point that by the age of twelve he would be capable of cooperating in a murder? Second is the issue of psychological intervention. Juvenile delinquency has been shown to be an excellent predictor of adult criminality; the younger the juvenile upon first arrest, and the more serious his first offense, the more likely he is to engage in serious crime as an adult. What psychological remedies could be applied to prevent this "natural" progression from taking place? Current investigators tend to believe that the answers to these questions lie with the family, the slum subculture, and the society at large—matters that we will deal with later in this chapter.

Organized Crime

The term "organized crime" refers to a hierarchically structured organization of criminals variously referred to as the Mafia, the Syndicate, and La Cosa Nostra (literally, "our thing"). Organized crime exists in order to make money, which it does through providing illegal goods and services such as prostitution, narcotics, and especially gambling. And in view of the enormous income of organized crime—annual income from gambling alone is said to be $30 billion (Ogren, 1973)—there is apparently a wide demand for these goods and services. Trafficking in such markets is of course illegal in itself, but protecting these markets involves any number of further criminal acts, including bribery, fraud, extortion, assault, and murder—all for the sake of protecting profits.

What makes organized crime interesting from a psychological viewpoint is the fact that the criminals involved are typically capable of intense loyalties and firm adherence to strict moral codes within their families and subculture, while at the same time exhibiting a total indifference to the harm that they inflict on the society at large—on the young slum dwellers, for example, whom they introduce to hard drugs. Outside the subculture, moral standards no longer apply; all is simply "business." Thus, in

Fig. 8.3   Prostitution. It is estimated that in the United States six million contacts with prostitutes take place each week. (Top) A brothel in Nevada, where such places of business constitute a major industry — neither openly supported by the state nor legally prohibited. (Bottom) A prostitute waits in a doorway where she can be eyed by prospective clients.

psychological terms, members of organized-crime families have a split morality—one half, social responsibility, being totally anesthetized, while the other half, responsibility to the subculture, is highly sensitized.

White-Collar Crime

Though it has been with us for centuries, white-collar crime has only recently gained wide attention. The term was first used in 1949 by Edwin Sutherland, who defined it as "crime committed by a person of respectability and high status in the course of his occupation" (1949, p. 9). It is possible that white-collar crime would have remained of interest only to sociologists had it not been for the recent Watergate affair, in which the citizens of the United States were confronted with the fact that not just persons of "respectability and high status" but in fact the persons who were running the country were engaged in serious crime.

However, politicians have no monopoly on white-collar crime. In a study of seventy large and prestigious business corporations, Sutherland (1949) found that together the executives of these companies—respectable, "law-abiding" upper-middle-class businessmen in impeccable white collars—had been convicted of 980 criminal violations, including false advertising, price-fixing, stock manipulation, restraint of trade, and blatant fraud. The total cost of such white-collar crime is said to be three times that of ordinary property crimes ("White Collar Crime," *Congressional Quarterly*, 1971).

What is the psychologist to make of the white-collar criminal? Here are people who would seem

Fig. 8.5 *(Above) Gambling, one of the major income producers for organized crime. Some states have legalized gambling in order that the larger society instead may benefit from the revenues.*

Fig. 8.4 *(Left) Along with gambling and prostitution, illegal drug trafficking is a major source of business for organized crime.*

to have none of the usual reasons for engaging in criminal behavior; no racial prejudice, no hostile slum environment, no disrupted family structure has stunted their moral development. It is possible that the higher levels of politics and of the business world constitute in themselves a deviant subculture into which the politician and the business executive are socialized, just like the delinquent and the *mafioso*, only at a later age. And since—unlike juvenile delinquency and organized crime, which often involve the direct use of violence against others—white-collar crime typically involves indirect means of cheating people out of their money, the latter variety of crime is probably easier for the middle classes to rationalize.

PERSPECTIVES ON ANTISOCIAL AND DYSSOCIAL BEHAVIOR

Hundreds of theories have been advanced as to the cause and appropriate treatment of antisocial and dyssocial behavior. These theories come not only from the major psychological and nonpsychological perspectives, but also, and especially, from the interpersonal and psychosocial perspectives, since the individual's relations with his family and his society assume a particular importance in the study of crime-related disorders.

However, we may say by way of a discouraging introduction that despite the multitude of theories, the treatment of both dyssocial and antisocial behavior has yielded only minimal results. In the case of dyssocial behavior, the fact that American prisons are failing at the task of rehabilitation is notorious. Of those who are now in penal institutions in the United States, at least 60 percent will return to crime once they are released (Murphy, 1970). Hence it is no surprise that our prisons are generally thought of as part of the problem rather than part of the solution.

The prognosis for antisocial personalities is even poorer. Lacking both insight and the desire to change, they are completely unsuited to the insight-oriented psychotherapies. Furthermore, whatever the form of therapy, the antisocial personality's affectlessness, ingratitude, and lack of motivation place immense demands on the patience of the therapist (Kolb, 1973)—demands which many therapists would sooner avoid. Finally, while there is some evidence that the family and the society may be partially to blame, families are not easy to change, to say nothing of societies. In general, the antisocial personality is likely to end up either in a prison, where he may be introduced to new forms of crime,

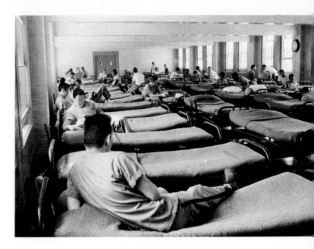

Fig. 8.6   *Rather than retrain the antisocial or dyssocial individual, prisons typically deprive him of opportunities to learn appropriate pro-social behavior and expose him to other antisocial individuals in an antisocial environment.*

or in a mental hospital, where it is likely that he will simply be ignored.

Some of the perspectives outlined below have concentrated primarily on either antisocial or dyssocial behavior, while other theoretical approaches have simply failed to make the distinction. Accordingly, we shall distinguish whenever possible between theories of dyssocial behavior and theories of antisocial behavior. In general, our emphasis will be on the latter.

The Psychodynamic Perspective

According to psychodynamic theory, the development of the antisocial personality may be traced to a failure to develop adequate superego controls due to the child's lack of identification with either parent. As we saw in Chapter 2, the normal development of the superego depends on the boy's identification with his father (or girl's identification with her mother) and his incorporation of his father's values and standards. In a situation in which the child has never developed emotional attachments to either or both parents, the process of identification may never occur, and hence the superego may never develop. This may happen when the parents are particularly cold and rejecting toward the child (Jenkins, 1966).

With this formulation for understanding the development of the antisocial personality, we can see how psychodynamic theorists would conceptualize the criminal as the opposite of the neurotic. Whereas the latter has an overdeveloped superego and hence suffers intense anxiety, the former has an underdeveloped superego and consequently experiences little or no anxiety. Without superego controls, the antisocial personality has little means of resisting the id's amoral demands for gratification. Hence the antisocial personality's impulsiveness and seeming inability even to understand the notion of moral restraint.

This conceptualization may or may not be valid. Unfortunately, it cannot be put to the test of treatment. As we have noted, the very qualities on which psychotherapy most depends—insight and motivation—are two of the qualities that are most strikingly absent in the antisocial personality. Consequently, when psychodynamic treatment is instituted, it is typically unsuccessful (Thorne, 1959).

The Behaviorist Perspective

Cause The behaviorists of course regard antisocial and dyssocial behavior, like most other types of behavior, as learned. Behavioral theorists (e.g., Buss, 1966; Maher, 1966; Ullmann and Krasner, 1975) have described three ways in which a person could be conditioned to engage in such behaviors. The first is *inadequate learning*. That is, the individual simply does not "know any better," either because he has been introduced into the society only recently, as would be the case with new immigrants, or because he has been raised in a culturally deprived environment, with little or no discipline.

The second possible explanation would be *inappropriate learning*, in which behavior is conditioned according to deviant norms, usually those of a deviant subculture. Such an explanation would seem to apply to underground revolutionaries, to delinquent gang members, to people involved in organized crime, and possibly, as we have seen, to white-collar criminals as well. Let us take an example that is probably familiar to most readers. A major turning point in the movie *The Godfather* is the episode in which Don Vito Corleone's son Michael, who has never before committed a crime, shoots down a corrupt police captain and a narcotics racketeer during a meeting with them in a restaurant. According to the mores of the society at large, this action of Michael's, initiating him into a lifetime of crime, is certainly immoral. But according to the mores of the organized-crime subculture, Michael's action is entirely proper, since it serves the dual purpose of protecting the family's financial territory and of taking vengeance for an attempt on his father's life. Indeed, according to the norms of Michael's subcul-

ture, *not* to kill these two men would be entirely improper.

The third behavioral theory of antisocial and dyssocial behavior is that of *"consequenceless" learning*. It has been found that many people who become criminals were raised in homes where, regardless of what they did, they were consistently overindulged or consistently abused. We may take as an example the following words of Albert DeSalvo, who came to be known as the Boston Strangler:

My father—. . . we used to have to stand in front of him, my brother Frank and me, every night and be beaten with his belt. I can still to this very moment tell you the color of the belt and just how long it was—two inches by 36—a belt with a big buckle on it. We used to stand in front of him every night and get beaten with that damn thing—every night, whether we did anything wrong or not. We were only in the fourth or fifth grade. . . . (Frank, 1966, p. 316)

Though DeSalvo's problem was obviously too complicated to be the result merely of consequenceless learning, this type of child-rearing, either arbitrarily accepting or arbitrarily rejecting, may predispose a child toward crime by teaching him that there is no connection between his behavior and the treatment he will receive. Hence he will eventually become desensitized to the social stimuli—laws, conventions, moral norms, and so forth—that indicate to people what the consequences of their behavior will be. He will simply do as he pleases, assuming that the outcome of his behavior will be due not to the nature of that behavior but to arbitrary luck or chance.

Though the inappropriate-learning theory is obviously more applicable to dyssocial than to antisocial behavior, since this type of learning involves loyalty to a group, inadequate and consequenceless learning might apply to both types of deviant behavior. But how do we explain the fact that the dyssocial criminal, no matter what type of deviant conditioning he has been exposed to, eventually learns ways of avoiding punishment, while the antisocial criminal can be punished again and again for the same offense and still never learn how to avoid this aversive consequence? Is it possible that antisocial personalities are exempt from the laws of avoidance learning? The answer might be yes. Recent research suggests that antisocial personalities are inept at avoidance learning by reason of their lack of anxiety. The pioneer in this area of research was Lykken (1957). Lykken subjected a group of college students, a group of nonsociopathic prisoners, and a group of sociopathic (i.e., antisocial) pris-

Charles Manson: *Criminal, Sociopath,*

The case of Charles Manson, who led his "family" of dropouts into the Tate-LaBianca murders, provides an excellent example of the difficulty of distinguishing dyssocial from antisocial or psychotic behavior. Many aspects of Manson's behavior appear typical of the antisocial personality. In his youth, he seemed unable to stay out of trouble or learn any lesson from the endless trouble that he got into. As a result, he spent seventeen of his first thirty-two years in correctional institutions. When paroled, he invariably reverted to crime, graduating from burglary to robbery to car theft to pimping. Furthermore, he had the deceptively charming manner of the sociopath. Psychological reports from the institutions in which he spent his youth show that by the age of seventeen he had learned how to ingratiate himself with others before taking advantage of their trust. Later he used this ability to gather around him what was literally a group of disciples, who feared, obeyed, and loved him. As expressed by one of his followers, "Squeaky" Fromme (later to become well-known on her own), "He gave off a lot of magic" (p. 219).

On the other hand, Manson's control over his "family"—the ways in which he gave off his magic—seems a bit too methodical to fit the mold of the antisocial personality. His careful use of music, drugs, sex, affection, fear, geographical isolation, religious mysticism, and simple cunning to keep the group together and under his complete domination are symptomatic not of the aimless, impulsive sociopath but of an extremely systematic criminal. Likewise, while he had been reckless in his earlier crimes, he did his best to cover the tracks of the "family" after the Tate-LaBianca murders. Upon leaving the LaBianca house, for example, Manson took with him Rosemary La-

Bianca's wallet and deliberately left it in the bathroom of a gas station in the hope that someone would find it, use the credit cards, and thus be held responsible for the murder.

However, there are two major obstacles to labeling Manson either a sociopath or a psychiatrically "normal" criminal. The first is the quality of his interpersonal relationships. Manson had neither the "normal" criminal's capacity for friendship and for give-and-take love relationships nor the sociopath's shallow, callous, and indifferent attitude toward other human beings. Instead, he spent immense energy in arranging his life so that he could dominate others. The women in his "family" cooked, cleaned, and sewed for him. They served him his dinner on top of a high rock and then sat in the dirt at the base of the rock to eat their own meals. They had sex whenever, wherever, and with whomever he told them to. And finally, they killed in accordance with his instructions. The entire existence of his "family" was structured around his authoritarian control.

The second factor which would appear to set Manson apart from the sociopath or "ordinary" criminal is his motive for the murders: his well-publicized "Helter Skelter" plan. Manson felt that certain songs of the Beatles (particularly "Blackbird," "Piggies," "Revolution 1," "Revolution 9," and "Helter Skelter"—all on the White Album) contained a personal message for him. The message was that a full-scale black-white racial war was about to erupt in the United States. In this war, the white population, all of whom Manson identified as the hated "Establishment," would be exterminated. The only whites to survive the slaughter would be the Manson "family," isolated on the remote movie-set ranch where they were living. After the war, the blacks would begin

oners to an ingeniously devised test involving the learning of twenty correct responses in pressing levers on a board. For every correct press, there were three possible incorrect presses, one of which gave the subject a mild electric shock, while the other two simply turned on a red light. Lykken's findings were

that all three groups made approximately the same number of errors, but that the nonsociopathic prisoners managed to avoid the "shock" errors better than the sociopathic prisoners, thus supporting the hypothesis that lack of anxiety renders the sociopath less adept at avoidance learning. Lykken's findings

or Psychotic?

trying to run the country, but would soon discover that they were incompetent to do so. (Manson held a decidedly low opinion of blacks.) And so they would come to Manson and beg him to take over. Manson would then rule the country, the population of which would consist of a pure white master race (the descendants of the "family") and the blacks, who would reassume the role of underlings. This was Manson's dream. And it was to push his dream into reality that he planned the gruesome Tate-LaBianca murders, which he felt would breed such fear among the whites that "Helter Skelter," the racial war, would at last be precipitated. This extravagant notion appears beyond the scope of the more prosaic antisocial and dyssocial mentalities. Indeed, it would seem to indicate a paranoid psychosis, a genuine break with reality. Manson's claims, at various times, that he was Jesus Christ or the devil might also have been the outgrowth of paranoia, though playacting is another possible explanation.

Whatever Manson's problem was, he seems, at least at one point in his life, to have been aware of it. When he was about to be freed from prison in 1967, he begged the authorities to let him stay. Prison, he said, had become his home, and he was afraid that he could not adjust to life on the outside. Manson's request was denied, and he was once again released into the society in which he felt so uncomfortable. Two years later, he and his "family" killed nine people in the space of one month. According to their boasts, the total number of murders committed by the group may be between thirty-five and forty. Manson is now back "home," in prison.

Source: Vincent Bugliosi, with Curt Gentry, *Helter Skelter*. New York: Bantam, 1975.

---

avoid punishment—at least punishment in the form of physical discomfort.

Treatment A common denominator of all behavioral treatments for antisocial and dyssocial behavior—indeed, for behavioral treatments in general—is they are authoritarian. Clear rules of behavior are established, and then one is rewarded for adhering to the rules and punished (generally by not receiving rewards) for violating the rules. The aim of such treatments is of course to socialize the deviant individual. A number of studies have shown that if carried on in a residential setting, such programs can work for juvenile delinquents (Schwitzgebel, 1967) and for antisocial personalities (Burchard, 1967; Crafts et al., 1964). The American Civil Liberties Union has recently raised objections to the use of behavior-modification programs in prisons, on the grounds that such programs violate the civil rights of prisoners. However, though they are hardly democratic, behavioral therapies may in fact represent the most effective means of promoting socialization. Furthermore, the standard prison procedures of offering early parole and special privileges for good behavior, and of using extended incarceration and such measures as solitary confinement as punishments for bad behavior, constitute in themselves behavioral techniques.

The Humanistic-Existential Perspective

Little has been written about the antisocial personality from the humanistic-existential viewpoint. And indeed, antisocial behavior is difficult to deal with from this viewpoint, since the humanists and existentialists tend to give social conformity per se a very low priority—a lesson that the antisocial personality has already learned too well. In dealing with criminals, whether antisocial or dyssocial, existentialists would be likely to focus on the need for the criminal to accept responsibility for his position rather than blame other people or the society, and on his opportunity to make new and more constructive choices rather than simply accepting "being down" as his destiny. The humanists would be likely to interpret the antisocial personality's inability to relate to others and to learn from experience as the functions of a self-concept so distorted that it filters out most of reality. Unfortunately, it is improbable that either of these two approaches could be used in treatment, since humanistic-existential therapy, like psychodynamic therapy, would be undermined from the start by the antisocial personality's lack of insight and of motivation.

---

were later supported by the work of Schacter and Latané (1964), who found that sociopathic prisoners did considerably better on Lykken's test when they had been injected with adrenaline, which promotes anxiety. It would seem, then, that the antisocial personality lacks sufficient anxiety to learn how to

Obedience: *Morality's Loophole*

Psychologists and criminologists have struggled for years with the question of whether a violent criminal can be considered psychologically normal, the assumption being that normal people refrain from doing harm to their fellow-man. However, a recent experiment by Milgram (1974) has shown that when told to do so by an "authority," even quite normal people seem remarkably willing to harm or kill their fellow-man.

Milgram recruited forty male volunteers representing a wide variety of occupations and ranging in age from twenty to fifty for what he claimed was a study of the usefulness of punishment in learning. A so-called experimenter, whose manner was rather stern and professional, interviewed each of the volunteers along with another man who pretended to be a volunteer but who was actually another actor in Milgram's little drama. The volunteers then drew lots with the pseudo-volunteer to see who would play the "teacher" and who would play the "learner" in the supposed learning experiment. But the lots were always rigged so that the actual volunteer became the "teacher" and the pseudo-volunteer the "learner."

The learner was then strapped into a chair, and electrodes were attached to his body. After this was done, the experimenter took the teacher into the next room and showed him a machine labeled "shock generator," with 30 switches labeled according to the voltage and severity (ranging from "slight shock" to "danger: severe shock") of the shock they supposedly generated. The teacher was given a genuine 45-volt shock to convince him that the machine was authentic. (In reality, this was the only shock administered in the experiment.)

The "learning experiment" then began. By prearrangement with Milgram, the learner answered three out of every four questions incorrectly. In response to each of these wrong answers,

the experimenter instructed the teacher to give the learner a shock 15 volts higher than his last shock. When the shock had reached 300 volts, the learner, again by prearrangement, kicked on the wall. At this point the teachers invariably looked to the experimenter for guidance, and they were told to continue the experiment. After the next shock, 315 volts, the learner again kicked on the wall, and the teacher was again advised to ignore this obvious (though feigned) appeal for help. The knocking then ceased, and the experimenter firmly instructed the teacher to continue the shocks up to the maximum voltage.

After the first knocking on the wall, the teachers began to respond in various ways. Five of them walked out. Others, as they continued administering what they assumed were higher and higher shocks to the now-silent learner, began sweating profusely, laughing nervously, shaking, and stuttering. Three eventually had uncontrollable seizures. Most of them repeatedly voiced concern for the learner and said that they wanted to stop the experiment. But the experimenter told them in a firm voice to continue, so they tried to overcome their scruples and go on giving the shocks. To Milgram's astonishment, twenty-six of the forty teachers made it to the end of the experiment, pulling the switch labeled "danger: severe shock" and giving what they thought was a 450-volt shock to the learner.

Many of the Nazi officers who were brought to trial after World War II pleaded that they had simply "followed their orders," and the world looked with righteous loathing at men who could bring themselves to follow such orders. Of the twenty-six apparently normal men from New Haven, Connecticut, who completed Milgram's experiment, not a single one did so without signs of emotional disturbance. But they followed their orders.

The Interpersonal Perspective

The primary agent in a child's socialization process is his family. Hence the most common generalization about antisocial and dyssocial behavior is that it is bred in the home. In what context, after all, would one be prevented from resolving an Oedipal conflict

or be conditioned to ignore the consequences of one's behavior? Within the context of the family.

Investigators have yet to agree on a single family "type" that would bring about antisocial or dyssocial behavior, and it is unlikely that they will ever find such an archetypal pathogenic family pattern. Instead, what we have are a number of theories. And since these family theories are so numerous, we shall confine our discussion to those that deal specifically with the antisocial personality.

One factor that is often pointed to as a major contributor to the development of antisocial behavior is parental deprivation. It has been demonstrated time and again (Greer, 1964; Robins, 1966; Oltman and Friedman, 1967) that the antisocial personality is much more likely than the normal person to have suffered, as a child, the loss of a parent through death, separation, or simple abandonment. The psychological examination of Billy Cook, the so-called hard-luck killer who managed in one month to kidnap nine people and kill six, revealed that Billy's mother had died when he was five years old and that soon afterwards his father had abandoned him in a mine cave, along with his brothers and sisters. Such stories are more common than not in the case histories of antisocial personalities. And many investigators feel that it is the lack of parental affection, either through the loss of the parent (Greer, 1964) or through the parents' rejection of the child (McCord and McCord, 1964), that is the primary cause of antisocial behavior. After all, it is through the love of his parents that the child learns to respect authority, to desire approval, to trade impulse gratification for such approval, to assimilate moral standards, to orient his behavior toward long-term goals, and finally, to care and be cared for, to love and be loved. Hence it is not difficult to understand how a child deprived of such training could become selfish, cynical, unfeeling, irresponsible, and aimless.

Another focus of study from the interpersonal perspective has been the matter of family discipline. Buss (1966) feels that the major factor in the etiology of antisocial behavior is inconsistent discipline, where the parents punish and reward not according to any coherent pattern that the child can understand, but simply according to their whimsy or their mood at the moment. Maher (1966) has also pointed to the damaging effects of allowing a child to worm his way out of punishments through expressions of regret, promises of reform, and other blandishments. The result, according to Maher, is that the child learns to avoid punishment by becoming a good talker rather than by correcting his behavior.

In evaluating such theories, one should remember that broken homes, parental rejection, and faulty discipline have also been implicated in the etiology of neurosis, schizophrenia, autism, alcoholism, and any number of other disturbances. Thus these family

Fig. 8.7 *Billy Cook, the hard-luck kid from Joplin, Missouri, was executed in the gas chamber at San Quentin. His motto "hard luck" (tattooed on his knuckles) typified his life: he was abandoned as a child, grew up in foster homes, was rejected and unwanted by most, liked by few. He went to prison for the last time after kidnapping nine people and killing six.*

problems, while they may well contribute to the development of the antisocial personality, can also produce a very different kind of adult, including one who has managed to overcome the handicap of an aversive childhood and to turn out exquisitely normal. (Conversely, there are many antisocial personalities, such as Roberta, who seem to have suffered no parental deprivation whatsoever and to have been carefully and consistently disciplined.) In dealing with this question, Robins (1966) suggests that it is not family disruptions that cause antisocial behavior; rather, it is emotional instability on the part of the parents that causes both family disruptions and antisocial behavior in the child. According to Robins, the best predictor of antisocial development is the personality of the father. If the father is antisocial or impulsive, the child has a good chance of becoming antisocial as well.

The Psychosocial Perspective

Most professionals would agree that the injustices built into our society contribute their fair share to the development of dyssocial behavior. To what degree might the society also act as a pathogenic factor in antisocial behavior? According to Gough (1948), the society does its part:

There are very definite aspects of our cultural pattern which give [antisocial personalities] encouragement. In America we put great value on the acquisition of material gain, prestige, power, personal ascendance, and the competitive massing of goods. . . .

We have very short memories about the origins of some of our great national fortunes, toward the holders of which we hold so much respect. At the other end, of course, our machine civilization tends to level, and strangle individuality, leaving large groups within our culture fearful, anxious, resentful and even occasionally openly hostile. In such an atmosphere psychopathy rises, grows and fattens. . . . (pp. 359–366)

There are three major current theories as to the psychosocial component in dyssocial behavior (McKee and Robertson, 1975). The first is the *labeling theory*. We have already mentioned in Chapter 1 the adverse effects of applying to a person the label of "sick" or "crazy." The same holds true for the label of "criminal" or "deviant." Labeling theorists (e.g., Becker, 1963) argue that while most people commit crimes of one sort or another, certain types of people and certain types of crime are much more likely than others to be labeled "criminal." This label tends to result in harsher punishment. Furthermore, like the "sick" label, it acts as a self-fulfilling prophecy, affecting the person's self-image and encouraging him to become wholeheartedly what the society has already told him he is.

A good illustration of differential labeling is the case of white-collar crime. Because of his social status, the white-collar criminal tends to escape the labeling process. Consequently, not only does he tend to escape severe punishment as well, but his reputation and self-image remain relatively unblemished.

For example, most Americans would probably not define former Vice President Spiro Agnew as a "criminal." It seems that the judicial system also had difficulty in labeling him as such, since he was allowed to avoid a prison sentence by pleading "no contest" to a minor tax evasion charge; nothing was said of the fact that the income on which he had failed to pay those taxes was apparently in the form of bribes. Meanwhile, thousands of other people—less wealthy, less white, less "reputable"—had been labeled as criminals and were accordingly serving prison sentences for stealing considerably smaller amounts of money than those that were allegedly delivered in brown paper bags to Agnew's suite in the Executive Office Building (McKee and Robertson, 1975).

A second major psychosocial approach to crime is the *differential-association theory*, similar to the behavioral theory of inappropriate learning. According to differential-association theorists (e.g., Sutherland and Cressey, 1970), a person becomes a criminal by associating with people who embrace deviant norms. And in a society rife with injustices, deviant subcultures are bound to develop and to pass along their dyssocial norms to whoever joins the subculture.

Finally, there is the theory of *anomie* as an explanation for crime (Merton, 1957). Anomie may be defined as a state of normlessness. Such a state certainly prevails in many of our urban ghettos, where filth, poverty, family disorganization, violence, despair, and the lack of any opportunity to escape from these conditions discourage many young people from embracing any norms whatsoever, to say nothing of the norms of a society that would permit such conditions to exist.

As we have seen, these three theories have been evolved, largely by sociologists, as explanations of dyssocial behavior. However, they might also apply, as secondary if not primary causes, to antisocial behavior. Anomie in particular would seem to be an extremely likely factor in the development of the antisocial personality's cynicism, impulsiveness, lack of goals, and general incomprehension of moral values.

The Biological Perspective

As we mentioned at the beginning of this chapter, the most popular approach to antisocial and dyssocial behavior in the late nineteenth century was the biogenic view. Particularly active in this area of speculation was the Italian school of criminology led by Cesare Lombroso, who held that criminality was genetically transmitted just like blue eyes and red hair. According to Lombroso, this hereditary taint could be recognized by certain physical features such as a low forehead and protruding ears. While Lombroso's theory of the physically stigmatized "born" criminal was discredited decades ago, researchers are still attempting to discover whether genetic factors might not figure, in a more subtle fashion, in the etiology of antisocial and dyssocial behavior. As with other forms of abnormal behavior, twin studies have been conducted on criminals (Lange, 1929; Kranz, 1936). However, not only have the findings been very inconclusive, but moreover these early studies failed to distinguish between antisocial and dyssocial behavior patterns, with the result that whatever findings we have are too vague to constitute substantial evidence for genetic influence.

More spectacular, though perhaps no more conclusive, was the recent discovery that a certain percentage of violent criminals showed the XYY chromosomal abnormality. Every cell in the human body is equipped with twenty-three chromosome pairs, one of which determines the sex of the individual. In the female, this sex-related pair is made up of two female (X) chromosomes; thus the female is an XX type. The male, in contrast, carries one female and one male (Y) chromosome and is therefore an XY type. In the last decade, however, it was found that a number of more dangerous male criminals were XYY types—that is, they carried an extra male chromosome (Jacobs et al., 1965). This discovery, which received a great deal of publicity, set off a flurry of genetic research on violent criminals. Such efforts were given further impetus when it was reported that Richard Speck, who murdered eight student nurses in Chicago one night in 1966, was an XYY type (Montague, 1968). However, so far these genetic studies have failed to prove the hypothesis that the XYY type has a double dose of "male aggressiveness" and is thus genetically predisposed toward crimes of a brutal nature. The XYY type *has* been found to be four times more common among male criminals than among males in general. Nevertheless, the fact that the incidence in both cases is so low (.4 percent in the general male population; 1.5 percent in the criminal male population) and that most XYY types are not criminals but perfectly normal, peace-loving types makes it impossible to conclude that there is any significant relationship between this genetic aberration and violent crime (U.S. PHS, 1970).

The Physiological Perspective

Somewhat more fruitful than genetic research has been physiological research on brain-wave activity in antisocial personalities. It has been shown that somewhere between 31 and 58 percent of all antisocial personalities show some form of *electroencephalogram** (EEG) abnormality (Ellington, 1954). One type of aberration is the appearance of *positive spikes*—that is, brief and sudden bursts of brain-wave activity—which in some studies showed up on 40

---

*An electroencephalogram is a record of brain waves obtained by connecting sensitive electrodes to the skull where they pick up and record the minute electrical impulses generated by the brain.

percent of the EEGs of antisocial personalities with histories of sudden, impulsive acts of aggression (Hughes, 1965; Kurland et al., 1963). However, by far the most common abnormality in the EEG of the antisocial personality is slow-wave activity, which is typical of the infant and the young child but not of the normal adult. This finding has led some investigators—notably Eysenck (1960a) and Hare (1968)—to hypothesize that brain-wave "immaturity" in the antisocial personality prevents him from developing normal fear responses, and that this absence of anxiety in turn results in the antisocial personality's presumed immunity to avoidance learning, a matter that we have discussed earlier.

In evaluating this proposed relationship between brain-wave abnormalities and antisocial behavior, we are still confronted with the fact that a goodly number of antisocial personalities have perfectly normal EEGs, and conversely, that many apparently normal people have abnormal EEGs. However, the percentage of antisocial personalities with brain-wave abnormalities (unlike the percentage with the XYY abnormality) *is* strikingly large. Furthermore, the hypothesis of brain-wave immaturity dovetails neatly with the finding that antisocial personalities tend to settle down after the age of forty. Hence it is possible that their fear responses simply do not reach maturity until middle age. (However, it is also possible that antisocial behavior eventually diminishes because biological drives eventually become weaker, or because the antisocial personality, after forty years of trouble, is simply worn out.)

Another interesting recent physiological finding is that the autonomic nervous system of the antisocial personality seems to operate at a lower level of arousal than that of the normal person. This finding is consistent with the discoveries of Lykken and of Schacter and Latané discussed above: that under normal conditions antisocial personalities do poorly at avoidance learning, but that their performance can be improved by injections of adrenaline, a chemical which the body naturally produces in a state of high autonomic arousal. According to Hare (1970), autonomic underarousal could explain a number of the antisocial personality's behavioral oddities. In the first place, as we have indicated earlier, the antisocial personality is generally characterized by an unshakable serenity, even in situations that would prove unnerving to anyone else (e.g., being caught in a lie, being interrogated by the police). This composure could easily be due to the fact that the antisocial personality's autonomic nervous system is simply unable to achieve the degree of arousal necessary to produce fear. If so, this factor would in turn account for the antisocial personality's difficulties with avoidance learning. Furthermore, Quay (1965) has proposed that the impulsive behavior of the antisocial personality is not so much passive as active; according to Quay, it is a form of "thrill-seeking." If this is the case, the antisocial personality's quest for stimulation could be a function of the body's need to compensate for autonomic underarousal. Research in this area is still going on. Should the data prove conclusive, it is possible that the antisocial personality could be helped through the use of medications that would adjust his level of arousal.

ANTISOCIAL BEHAVIOR AND LEGAL RESPONSIBILITY

In studying antisocial behavior as a form of psychological disturbance, we are confronted with an interesting question: To what degree should a person be held legally responsible—and therefore legally punishable—for a crime which is either pathologically motivated or which he would presumably not have committed if some psychological disturbance had not prevented him from exercising proper behavioral controls? This is a question that has haunted the courts of law for many years and has resulted in three landmark legal decisions. The first is an 1834 ruling, in an Ohio case, that a person can be acquitted by reason of insanity if he has committed his crime under the influence of an "irresistible impulse." The second decision is the so-called McNaughten rule, emanating from the trial of Daniel McNaughten, who after being instructed by "the voice of God" to kill the English Prime Minister, Sir Robert Peel, proceeded to kill Peel's secretary by mistake. In acquitting McNaughten, the English court ruled that a person could be judged legally insane if at the time of committing the crime he either did not know what he was doing or did not know that what he was doing was wrong. Hence the commonly used criterion of "Did the defendant know right from wrong?" Finally, a third decision, rendered in 1954 in the case of *Durham* v. *United States*, stated that a person could not be held legally responsible for a crime that was "the product of mental disease or mental defect."

Thus we have four criteria for an insanity plea: (1) irresistible impulse; (2) unawareness of what one was doing; (3) unawareness that what one was doing was wrong; and (4) mental disease or mental defect. However, these criteria raise a number of problems, of which we will mention only a few. In the first place, how is one to decide whether a person was laboring under any one of these psychological handicaps at the time of committing his crime? Having him examined by a psychiatrist or clinical psychologist does not solve the problem. Diagnostic disagreement among psychiatrists and clinical psychologists often reaches absurd proportions, and the difficulty of making a *retrospective* diagnosis only makes it that much more unlikely that a diagnostic consensus can be reached. For example, in the pre-trial hearing convened to determine whether Albert DeSalvo, quoted above, was psychologically competent to stand trial, three different psychiatrists managed to apply to DeSalvo the following diagnostic descriptions: "chronic undifferentiated schizophrenia," "sociopath with dangerous tendencies," "sexual deviation," "acute anxiety hysteric," "obsessive and compulsive," "wild overt psychosis," and "homosexual panic, or sexual panic of some sort" (Frank, 1966, pp. 358–359).

A second problem is that a liberal interpretation of the above-listed criteria could result in the acquittal of many criminals whom society has traditionally considered responsible for their crimes. It has been shown, for example, that the majority of murderers are apparently normal, benign individuals who on one occasion, in extreme passion, attack and kill a friend or relative. They are extremely remorseful afterwards and are very unlikely to repeat the crime. If such murderers are not driven by irresistible impulse, who is? Yet if this rule were applied to all such murders, most murderers would be acquitted.

The last question that we will raise is by far the most difficult: If a person is judged to be not legally responsible for his crime, what then is to be done with him? Typically, in such a case, the person is committed for an indeterminate period of time to a federal or state mental hospital, where he will be labeled as "sick," be deprived of his civil rights, and, according to one estimate (Graham, 1968), be seen by a psychiatrist for fifteen minutes per month. Here he will remain—under conditions possibly worse than those that he would have encountered in prison—until the psychiatrists with whom he has had so little contact determine that he is at last "cured." Worse yet, if he has been committed without a trial (on the grounds that he is psychologically incompetent to participate in his own defense), he may then have to undergo both a trial and a prison sentence. Such a state of affairs has prompted a number of people to call for the abolition of the insanity plea. For example, Thomas Szasz (1963), whose criticism of the medical model we have discussed in Chapter 1, argues that deviant behavior is almost invariably of a purposive character, and that by calling it insane, we are simply refusing to acknowledge what the necessary and inevitable tensions between individuals and their society are. Szasz further contends that almost anyone is better off in a prison, where he is subject to laws and where he serves a specific amount of time, than in a mental hospital, where his treatment and the length of his stay is subject entirely to the whim and subjectivity of psychiatric professionals. Szasz's argument must be granted a certain legitimacy. However, considering the brutal conditions prevailing in most prisons, one still hesitates to agree that people suffering from psychological problems should be exposed to such stresses, even for a determinate sentence. The matter can be argued either way and will continue to be arguable until either our prisons or our mental hospitals can show that they are truly equipped to rehabilitate their inmates.

SUMMARY

The subject of our chapter has been antisocial and dyssocial behavior, which differ from other forms of deviant behavior in that they are characterized primarily by disregard for and/or aggression against others. The antisocial personality, which historically has also been called the psychopath and the sociopath, is typically marked by five major characteristics: (1) impulsive and inadequately motivated antisocial behavior; (2) total lack of conscience, of regard for truth, or of any sense of responsibility; (3) affective poverty; (4) lack of insight, and inability to learn from experience; and (5) ability to maintain a pleasant and impressive exterior. This syndrome is considered clearly pathological.

By contrast, the label of dyssocial behavior is reserved for persons who engage in predatory behavior but who appear psychiatrically normal. The criminal engaging in dyssocial behavior differs from the antisocial personality in that the former has a goal and works consistently toward it, pursues an *understandable* goal, attempts to escape personal harm, may commit major crimes, and may have normal interpersonal relationships. Nevertheless, despite these differences and despite the official distinction between antisocial and dyssocial behavior, it is often hard to draw the diagnostic line in dealing with actual cases. Furthermore, there are those who would question the presumed psychiatric normalcy of the criminal engaging in dyssocial behavior.

Whether antisocial or dyssocial, criminal behavior is an immensely serious social problem in our country. Three major categories of crime are juvenile delinquency, organized crime, and white-collar crime.

The prognosis for the antisocial personality is dismally poor, and treatment methods aimed at modifying either antisocial and dyssocial behavior have shown only isolated successes, whether in hospital or prison settings. Our study of the perspectives on criminal behavior has emphasized theories of antisocial rather than dyssocial behavior. Psychodynamic theory traces the growth of the antisocial personality to a child's lack of identification with his parents and a consequent failure to develop an adequate superego. Humanistic-existential therapy would tend instead to implicate a distorted self-concept and a failure to assume responsibility. Unfortunately, neither of these theoretical perspectives can be adequately tested in treatment, since both psychodynamic and humanistic-existential treatment require insight and motivation, both of which, by definition, are lacking in the antisocial personality. Behavioral theories of antisocial and dyssocial behavior tend to emphasize inadequate, inappropriate, or "consequenceless" learning. The behaviorists have also proposed that antisocial behavior may be due to an inability to engage in avoidance learning. Behavioral treatments, which predictably involve the rewarding of good behavior and the punishing of bad behavior, have had some success in residential settings. The interpersonal perspective has pointed up various patterns of family interaction—including parental deprivation and inconsistent discipline—that could generate antisocial behavior, while the psychosocial perspective has pointed to the role of differential labeling, differential association, and anomie in contributing to crime. Finally, somatogenic theories of antisocial behavior range from chromosomal abnormality to brain-wave immaturity to abnormally low levels of autonomic arousal.

The judgment of whether a specific criminal is psychiatrically normal or abnormal of course has great bearing on his legal standing, and for this reason the courts of law, in addition to the psychologists, biologists, and sociologists, have had their say about the "normalcy" of criminal acts. Criteria for a plea of "not guilty by reason of insanity" have been developed over the years, but they continue to prove less than helpful when applied to actual cases. Furthermore, a successful plea of insanity often results in indeterminate incarceration in a mental hospital, which may in the end leave the individual more helpless than would a determinate prison sentence. Neither alternative—prison or hospitalization—is likely to prove therapeutically helpful. Hence the treatment of criminals in our society remains an open and extremely pressing question.

Unlike antisocial and dyssocial behavior, the most common forms of abnormal sexual behavior involve no direct harm to one's fellow-man. Yet like antisocial and dyssocial behavior, sexual abnormalities are often construed as a crime against the society. If a person becomes depressed and spends his days in bed complaining that all is lost, the society is likely to label him as sick. But if a person manifests a sexual aberration, he is likely to be labeled repulsive and perverted. In short, we place an immense *moral* value on our sexual norms. The vast majority of states have laws prohibiting not only homosexual acts but also such equally heterosexual practices as oral-genital contact and anal intercourse. And many people would sooner admit to beating their children every night than confess that they regularly masturbate while fondling and smelling a pair of old shoes—a practice which, when viewed objectively, would seem considerably less offensive. Thus of all the varieties of abnormal behavior, sexual abnormalities are perhaps the most intimately connected with social norms. And consequently, a discussion of these norms—and of the extent to which they correspond to our actual sexual makeup and sexual habits—is a necessary prerequisite to discussing sexual abnormality.

DEFINING SEXUAL ABNORMALITY

DSM-II classifies sexual deviation among "personality disorders and certain other nonpsychotic mental disorders" and defines it as follows:

This category is for individuals whose sexual interests are directed primarily toward objects other than people of the opposite sex, toward sexual acts not usually associated with coitus, or toward coitus performed under bizarre circumstances as in necrophilia [sexual contacts with dead bodies], pedophilia [sexual contacts with children], sexual sadism [sexual gratification through inflicting pain], and fetishism [exclusive reliance on a single body part or on an inanimate object for sexual gratification]. Even though many find their practices distasteful, they remain unable to substitute normal sexual behavior for them (1968, p. 44).

What is meant in the second sentence by "normal sexual behavior" can be inferred at least vaguely from the first sentence. What the American Psychiatric Association accepts as normal is sexual behavior that is focused primarily on *coitus* (i.e., penile-vaginal intercourse) with a consenting member of the *opposite sex*. This of course rules out anyone whose sexual interests are predominantly homosexual, as well as heterosexuals who generally prefer other forms of sexual gratification to coitus.

9
Sexual Disorders and Sexual Variance

However, when we come to the requirement that coitus, in order to be normal, should take place under nonbizarre circumstances, we are on much shakier ground. Few people would deny that sexual intercourse with corpses or with children is bizarre. However, there is a wide range of other circumstances that might or might not be judged bizarre, depending on who is doing the judging. Kinsey (1948), for example, found that many people regard having coitus while fully unclothed as bizarre, while others consider keeping the lights on during intercourse as equally odd. Likewise, there is no question that while many people regard oral-genital stimulation as a normal part of sexual foreplay, other people find this practice weird and repulsive in the extreme.

Despite this area of vagueness, however, the DSM-II definition clearly implies that a person who is normal sexually is a person whose sexual goals are generally confined to coitus with a member of the opposite sex. And this standard is backed up by centuries of moral and religious teaching. While the ancient Greeks not only tolerated but actually glorified homosexuality, the Judeo-Christian tradition that supplanted classical thought has been consistently adamant in its condemnation of homosexuality. God's attitude toward homosexuals was presumed by the Jews to have been clearly manifested in his raining fire and brimstone on the cities of Sodom and Gomorrah (Genesis 19), where homosexuality was practiced. Further along in the Bible, Leviticus 20:13 specifically spells out the prohibition: "If a man also lies with mankind, as he lieth with a woman, both of them have committed an abomination; they shall surely be put to death; their blood shall be upon them." As for masturbation, God's striking down of Onan, who in Genesis 38:9 "spilled [his seed] on the ground" rather than in the proper place, was taken as a precedent for centuries of religious teaching that masturbation (also called *onanism*) was both abhorrent and dangerous to mind and body.* Indeed, Roman Catholic doctrine still holds that the begetting of children within wedlock is the sole legitimate objective of sexual activity; hence any source of sexual gratification other than coitus with one's spouse is by definition sinful, a stand reaffirmed as recently as 1976 (*New York Times*, 1976).†

This rather narrow definition of normal sexual behavior has served for many centuries to help guarantee the continuation of the human species and the survival of the family structure. However, there is very little to indicate that human beings are in any way programmed biologically to confine their

Fig. 9.1 Despite a greater tolerance today toward sexual behaviors, some acts, such as this man's kissing his doll, are still considered abnormal by most people.

sexual gratification to coitus. On the contrary, while there is no question that the sex drive itself is inborn, the direction that it will take is, according to anthropological evidence, a result of socialization. For example, while Western culture considers the female breast an erotic object, many societies consider it utterly neutral sexually. Likewise, while homosexuality is frowned on in our society, in other societies it is not only accepted but actually institutionalized as the proper sexual outlet for adolescent boys (Ford and Beach, 1951). In short, while our norms are rather rigid, our impulses are in fact highly flexible. Furthermore, what studies we have on sexual behavior in our society indicate that not only our impulses but also our actions tend to range far afield from our declared standards of sexual normalcy. For example, Kinsey (1948) found that of the white American males sampled in his study, over 90 percent had, by the age of eighteen, committed at least

---

*Actually Onan was not masturbating, but practicing a form of birth control called coitus interruptus (i.e., withdrawal immediately before ejaculating); he was struck down because by this act he avoided impregnating the wife of his dead brother, for whom religious regulation decreed that he provide a child.

†It should be noted, however, that most Catholic priests under the age of 40 tend to interpret such rulings quite liberally in counseling parishioners (Gallup and Davies, 1971).

one sexual act for which they could be imprisoned according to state law.

This incongruence between our norms and laws on the one hand and our impulses and actions on the other hand has led in recent years to a widespread questioning of traditional sexual morality and to a gradual loosening of the prohibitions on such practices as masturbation and premarital sex. Nonetheless, the list of psychiatrically recognized sexual abnormalities remains a long one, and those sexual activities that continue to be judged deviant are the subject of our chapter. We shall deal with three aspects of sexual abnormality: sexual inadequacy, the inability to achieve sexual gratification; sexual deviations, individual patterns of unconventional sexual activity; and finally, homosexuality, which is common enough and controversial enough to be dealt with as a separate case.

SEXUAL INADEQUACY

As we have just mentioned, the last decade has been a crucial period of questioning and change in the area of sexual morality. Many Americans have begun to doubt the "abnormality" of a number of traditionally decried sexual practices; we have also come to place a heavy emphasis on sexual technique and sexual gratification. The enormous success of such recent best sellers as *Everything You Always Wanted to Know About Sex . . . But Were Afraid to Ask* (Reuben, 1969), *The Sensuous Woman* ("J," 1970), and *The Joy of Sex: A Cordon Bleu Guide to Lovemaking* (Comfort, 1972) attests to our current preoccupation with plumbing the depths of our sexual capabilities. Whereas twenty years ago people wondered whether what they were doing was right, now they simply ask themselves whether they are doing it right. And while this concern with sexual gratification has had the undoubtedly beneficial effects of easing the flow of information on sex and of increasing sexual communication between partners, it is not without its own burdens of anxiety and guilt. As Rollo May has noted:

The challenge a woman used to face from men was simple and direct—would she or would she not go to bed?—a direct issue of how she stood vis-à-vis cultural mores. But the question men ask now is no longer, "Will she or won't she?" but "Can she or can't she?" The challenge is shifted to the woman's personal adequacy, namely, her own capacity to have the vaunted orgasm—which should resemble a *grand mal* seizure (1969, p. 40).

Where the so-called "sexual revolution" will take us as a society remains to be seen. However, its impact on the field of psychology is already evident in the increasing attention being given to problems of *sexual inadequacy*, the inability to achieve gratification in normal sexual activity.

The Forms of Sexual Inadequacy

The two most widely recognized experts in this field of psychopathology, William Masters and Virginia Johnson, have listed eight types of sexual inadequacy (1970). Four of these are specifically male problems. In *primary impotence*, apparently the most difficult to cure of all the forms of inadequacy, the male has never been able to sustain an erection sufficient for the successful completion of intercourse. In *secondary impotence*, the male has had at least one episode, and usually many episodes, of successful intercourse but eventually becomes impotent in at least 25 percent of his attempts at intercourse. In *premature ejaculation*, the erection is easily achieved, but the man is unable to postpone his ejaculation long enough to satisfy the female; ejaculation takes place immediately before, immediately upon, or very shortly after insertion, with the result that successful intercourse cannot take place. Somewhat the opposite problem is *ejaculatory incompetence*, a rare condition in which the male is able to achieve erection and insertion but is incapable of ejaculating in the woman's vagina.

Formerly, any failure to gain sexual gratification on the part of the female came under the all-inclusive and somewhat misleading heading of "frigidity." Masters and Johnson, however, have distinguished three separate forms of female sexual inadequacy. In *primary orgasmic dysfunction*, the woman has never achieved orgasm through coitus, masturbation, or any other means. In *situational orgasmic dysfunction*, the woman is orgasmic only in certain situations and not in others. For example, she may experience orgasm only by means of manual stimulation, or only when coitus takes place outdoors. In *vaginismus* the outer third of the vagina spasmodically contracts when insertion is attempted, rendering intercourse either impossible or very painful. A final problem—which may afflict both men and women, though it is more commonly a female complaint—is *dyspareunia*, pain during intercourse.

These problems, all of which would be classified in DSM-II as psychophysiological disorders, apparently occur with astounding frequency. Masters and Johnson estimate that fully half the marriages in the United States suffer from some form of sexual inadequacy. And the vast majority of cases, particu-

What Is Normal Sexual Response in a Woman?

Should a woman consider herself somehow deficient if she does not always reach orgasm during intercourse or if she is orgasmic only when direct clitoral stimulation is present? The definition of a normally functioning woman, whether explicitly stated or not, includes the expectation that she be able to reach orgasm through intercourse; when this proves difficult, her reaction is often a feeling of failure, of somehow "just not being able to make it." In fact, one of the major changes in our attitude toward sexuality since Masters and Johnson began publishing the results of their pioneering work is that more women, and their partners, expect and demand this of themselves.

Of all the varieties of sexual inadequacy treated by Masters, Johnson, and their fellow therapists at the Reproductive Biology Research Foundation, only primary impotence, with a failure rate of 40.6 percent (1970, p. 211), has proven more resistant to treatment than random orgasmic inadequacy, with a failure rate of 37.5 percent (1974, p. 314). In fact, Masters and Johnson have stated that "infrequent or rare orgasmic return with both masturbatory and coital experience has defied the Foundation's current therapeutic approaches" (1970, p. 315).

Dr. Helen Singer Kaplan, director of the Sex Therapy and Education Program at New York Hospital, has suggested that the definition of a normally sexually responsive woman be expanded to include women who do require direct clitoral stimulation (1974, p. 379). Research has shown that it is the clitoris that triggers orgasm in women, and as Kaplan notes, "paradoxically, coitus provides only relatively mild clitoral stimulation which is often insufficiently intense . . ." (p. 378).

In addition, after noting the importance to women of the emotional component in lovemaking, Kaplan points out that orgasmic response in women seems to form a continuum, with points from one end to the other as follows: women who are orgasmic from erotic fantasizing, from brief foreplay, from coitus, from coitus plus additional manual clitoral stimulation, from intense stimulation such as that provided by a vibrator, and those women, approximately 10 percent of the female population, who cannot have an orgasm at all. Women who require clitoral stimulation of one sort or another seem to make up a large part of the population; Kaplan feels that these women are "merely exhibiting a normal variation of female sexuality and should be reassured to that effect" (p. 383).

More research is needed before the question of what is normal sexual response in women can be answered. Until then the range of responses considered normal is reassuringly wider for the present college generation than it was for their mothers' and grandmothers' generations. And the growing body of information being made available to more and more women makes sexual responsiveness increasingly less mysterious and hence easier to attain.

---

larly those involving female sexual inadequacy, go untreated.

The disorders that we have listed are manifested over a period of time and should in no way be confused with the random episodes of inadequacy that an adult can easily experience when tired, sick, unhappy, desensitized by alcohol, or simply distracted. Nor should the label of inadequacy be applied to the common occurrence of premature ejaculation, impotence, or orgasmic failure in young people who have not yet established a regular pattern of sexual activity and whose satisfaction is often inhibited by overconcentration on either "doing it right" or get-

ting to do it at all. Indeed, a very great misfortune often revealed in the course of sexual counseling is that one episode of failure may lead to another and another simply because the first episode generates enough anxiety to impair sexual receptivity on the next occasion. This second failure in turn aggravates the anxiety, which in turn further undermines sexual performance, and so on until a regular pattern of inadequacy is established. Furthermore, such anxiety is communicable, with the result that sexual inadequacy is often found in both members of a couple. For example, vaginismus and primary impotence often go hand in hand. Likewise, orgasmic dysfunction and either secondary impotence or premature ejaculation are often seen together in the same marriage.

PERSPECTIVES ON SEXUAL INADEQUACY

In some cases sexual inadequacy may be due to biological or physiological problems. Internal lacerations left over from childbirth can easily cause dyspareunia in women. Likewise, diabetes can in some instances give rise to secondary impotence, as can overuse of alcohol or tranquilizing drugs. However, in the majority of cases the causes of sexual inadequacy are apparently psychological.

The Psychodynamic Perspective

Psychodynamic theorists tend to regard the cause of sexual inadequacy as a failure to resolve the Oedipal conflict and thus to achieve mature genital sexuality. This line of thinking may be seen in the interpretation of impotence offered by Otto Fenichel, a leading psychoanalytic theorist:

> Impotence is based on a persistence of an unconscious sensual attachment to the mother. Superficially no sexual attachment is completely attractive because the partner is never the mother; in a deeper layer, every sexual attachment has to be inhibited, because every partner represents the mother (1945, p. 170).

Similarly, psychoanalytic formulations of orgasmic

Types of Sexual Inadequacy

	Form of dysfunction	Overall treatment success rate reported by Masters and Johnson after five-year follow-up
Primary impotence	Male has never maintained an erection long enough to complete intercourse successfully	59.4%
Secondary impotence	Male, after at least one episode of normal intercourse, lapses into impotence in at least one-fourth of his attempts at intercourse	69.1%
Premature ejaculation	Male cannot postpone ejaculation long enough to satisfy the female sexually	97.3%
Ejaculatory incompetence	Male cannot ejaculate inside the woman's vagina	82.4%
Primary orgasmic dysfunction	Female has never experienced orgasm through any means of sexual stimulation	82.4%
Situational orgasmic dysfunction	Female is unable to achieve orgasm except in certain specific circumstances	75.2%
Vaginismus	The outer third of the female's vagina spasmodically contracts, so that insertion of the penis is either impossible or very painful	100%*
Dyspareunia	Either the male or the female experiences pain during intercourse	‡

*Since the women who were relieved of vaginismus were reclassified, during the treatment program and the five-year follow-up, under the headings of primary or situational orgasmic dysfunction, this percentage for vaginismus represents only the initial success rate.

‡Unreported. Many cases are physiological and are treated medically or surgically.

Source: Masters and Johnson, 1970.

dysfunction tend to stress the role of continued penis envy, and vaginismus too has been interpreted as the expression of an unconscious desire to reject or injure the male's envied penis (Fenichel, 1945). However, beyond selected anecdotal evidence from clinical practice, there is little empirical support for these theories. And psychoanalytic treatment of sexual inadequacy, aimed at the revelation and working through of an unconscious Oedipal conflict, has had considerably less success than the behavioral therapies we shall discuss next.

The Behaviorist Perspective

Behavioral theories of sexual inadequacy have focused consistently on the role of early respondent conditioning in which sexual feelings are paired with shame, disgust, fear of discovery, and especially anxiety over possible failure, all of which then proceed to block sexual responsiveness (Cooper, 1969; Wolpe, 1969; Kaplan, 1974). In keeping with this etiological theory, behavioral treatment has relied primarily on systematic desensitization and on the creating of situations in which sexual arousal can take place in the absence of its conditioned accompaniment, anxiety. By far the most comprehensive theory and the most influential treatment approach within this behavioral context are those offered by Masters and Johnson in their book *Human Sexual Inadequacy* (1970).

Masters and Johnson: The Etiology of Sexual Inadequacy
In their extensive study and treatment of sexual dysfunctions at the Reproductive Biology Research Foundation in St. Louis, Masters and Johnson have evolved the theory that the major source of sexual inadequacy is the fear of sexual inadequacy. For any one of a number of reasons, the individual becomes anxious that he or she will be unable to perform adequately—will not achieve erection, will "come" too soon, will not produce the required orgasm, or whatever. As a result of this anxiety, the worried partner assumes what Masters and Johnson call the "spectator role"—that is, instead of simply relaxing and enjoying himself or herself, the individual is constantly watching and judging his or her performance. And, with cruel irony, the performance is almost inevitably a failure, because the individual's tense and critical attitude blunts his responsiveness to sexual stimuli.

As for the original factors which trigger performance anxiety and consequently lead to the adoption of the spectator role, Masters and Johnson point to a number of contributing causes. One important

Fig. 9.2   Drs. Masters and Johnson, whose teamwork in treating couples with sexual problems has been highly successful.

etiological factor can be a background of strict religious orthodoxy, in which the individual is taught that sex is sinful and repulsive. One woman seen by Masters and Johnson was told by her mother on her wedding day that

It would be her duty as a wife to allow her husband "privileges." The privileges were never spelled out. She also was assured that she would be hurt by her husband, but that "it" would go away in time. Finally and most important, she was told that "good women" never expressed interest in the "thing." Her reward for serving her husband would be, hopefully, in having children.

She remembers her wedding night as a long struggle devoted to divergent purposes. Her husband frantically sought to find the proper place to insert his penis, while she fought an equally determined battle with nightclothes and bedclothes to provide as completely a modest covering as possible for the awful experience. The pain her mother had forecast developed as her husband valiantly strove for intromission.

Although initially there were almost nightly attempts to consummate the marriage, there was total lack of success. [The marriage remained unconsummated for nine years.] . . . When seen in therapy, Mrs. A. had no concept of what the word masturbation meant. . . . As would be expected, at physical examination Mrs. A. demonstrated a severe degree of *vaginismus in addition to the intact hymen. . . . When vaginismus was described and then directly demonstrated to both husband and wife, it was the first time Mr. A. had ever seen his wife unclothed and also the first time she had submitted to a medical examination* (1970, pp. 232–233).*

The denigration of sexual feelings need not be communicated within the context of religion, however. Sometimes general sociocultural attitudes alone suffice. This is true particularly in the case of female inadequacy, which is often perversely supported by the sociocultural message that women are required to suppress, adapt, and bend their sexual feelings and sexual preferences for the sake of modesty and decency, and in deference to their mates.

Not surprisingly, another factor often implicated in the development of sexual dysfunction is early psychosexual trauma, which can range from gang rape to the more typical variety of sexual humiliation illustrated in the following case:

During [Mr. D.'s first sexual] episode the prostitute took the unsuspecting virginal male to a vacant field and suggested they have intercourse while she leaned against a stone fence. Since he had no concept of female anatomy, of where to insert the penis, he failed miserably in this sexually demanding opportunity. His graphic memory of the incident is of running away from a laughing woman.

The second prostitute provided a condom and demanded its use. He had no concept of how to use the condom. While the prostitute was demonstrating the technique, he ejaculated. He dressed and again fled the scene in confusion (1970, p. 177).

Other psychological causes that have turned up regularly in the cases treated by Masters and Johnson are homosexual inclinations, which predictably dull heterosexual response; disturbances, in "partner orientation," whereby one partner devalues the femininity or masculinity of his or her partner; maternal or paternal dominance, in which one partner cannot separate his sexual responses from continuing resentment of or competition with a parent; and overuse of alcohol, which can give rise to secondary impotence through the vicious circle described

above, one alcohol-caused erective failure leading to anxiety and further drinking, which in turn cause further episodes of impotence.

Finally, Masters and Johnson have pointed to the occasional role of ill-informed counseling from physicians, psychologists, psychoanalysts, marriage counselors, and religious advisers in creating and maintaining sexual dysfunction. Couples seen by Masters and Johnson had been given such advice as "once a grown man has a homosexual experience, he always ends up impotent," and "any man masturbating after he reaches the age of thirty can expect to become impotent" (p. 189). Another couple "was assured that the symptoms of impotence would disappear if there were regularity in church attendance for at least one year. Two years later, despite fanatical attendance at all church functions, the symptoms of impotence continued unabated" (p. 189). Careless and mistaken advice can actually initiate sexual inadequacy, as may be seen in the following case:

The husband and wife in a three-year marriage had been having intercourse approximately once a day. They were somewhat concerned about the frequency of coital exposure, since they had been assured by friends that this was a higher frequency than usual. Personally delighted with the pleasures involved in this frequency of exposure, yet faced with the theoretical concerns raised by their friends, they did consult a professional. They were told that an ejaculatory frequency at the rate described would certainly wear out the male in very short order. The professional further stated that he was quite surprised that the husband hadn't already experienced difficulty with maintaining an erection. He suggested that they had better reduce their coital exposures to, at the most, twice a week in order to protect the husband against developing such a distress. Finally, the psychologist expressed the hope that the marital unit had sought consultation while there still was time for his suggested protective measures to work.

The husband worried for 48 hours about this authoritative disclosure. When intercourse was attempted two nights after consultation, he did accomplish an erection, but erective attainment was quite slowed as compared to any previous sexual response pattern. One night later there was even further difficulty in achieving an erection, and three days later the man was totally impotent to his wife's sexual demands with the exception of six to eight times a year when coitus was accomplished with a partial erection. He continued impotent for seven years before seeking further consultation (1970, p. 191).

---

*It should be noted that the demonstration of vaginismus is the only case in which a couple's sexual problem is physically observed, rather than simply discussed, by the therapists and the couple together. All other sexual activity takes place in the privacy of the couple's bedroom. In the case of vaginismus, however, a specialist is needed to demonstrate to the couple the automatic and purely physiological nature of the response.

Masters and Johnson: The Treatment of Sexual Inadequacy The treatment methods developed by Masters and Johnson deserve special attention simply in view of their apparently excellent success rate. A five-year follow-up study of 790 marital units treated revealed an overall success rate of 80 percent, with success rates for the individual disorders ranging from 97 percent for premature ejaculation to 59 percent for primary impotence. As Masters and Johnson themselves point out, these cases were in no way a random sampling of sexually dysfunctional Americans. They were better educated and better off financially than the average American; furthermore, they were generally married couples who were highly motivated to solve the sexual problems that were threatening their marriages. However, even with an unrepresentative sampling, the success rates noted above are certainly impressive.

Masters and Johnson's treatment of married couples rests on two basic assumptions. The first is that sexual inadequacy is not an individual problem—"her" problem or "his" problem—but a problem of the marital unit in which sexual communication has broken down. The second assumption is that in order to reactivate the individual's natural ability to respond to sexual stimuli, the couple must be relieved of all performance pressures; essentially, they must return to a goalless, nondemand "petting" stage in order to rediscover their ability to be "pleasured" by touching and caressing.

In accordance with the former principle, the first three days of Masters and Johnson's two-week therapy program are devoted to extensive interviewing—the wife by the female therapist and the husband by the male therapist, and then vice versa—leading up finally to a round-table meeting of the couple and the therapists. In this meeting, the couple's sexual problem, their communication difficulties, and the information culled from the interviews are discussed openly and frankly. Resentments, fears, and secret premarital histories are laid bare so that impediments to communication can be removed. The next stage of therapy is devoted to "sensuous exercises." In this stage (as during the first three days), the couple observes a ban on sexual intercourse. Instead, they are given specific instructions on how simply to "pleasure" each other in private through gentle stroking and caressing in the nude so that they can rediscover their natural sexual responses without feeling any pressure to manipulate these responses into a sexual performance. Very gradually the allowance of sexual play is increased, always without any performance goals and always

with the couple returning to the therapists the following day to discuss their responses, their mistakes, their misgivings, and so forth. Then after a few days the therapists provide the couple with more detailed "pleasuring" instructions aimed at dealing with the couple's specific problem. And eventually, through these gradated, nondemand exercises, the couple proceeds to complete intercourse when they are fully ready and fully anxiety-free.

In the sense that this program relies on the development of insight and on the communication of feelings, it bears some resemblance to psychotherapy. However, in their willingness to focus primarily on the couple's *sexual* problem (which psychodynamic theorists would consider merely the symptom of the underlying true disorder) and in their extensive use of stimulus-response exercises to increase arousal and decrease anxiety, Masters and Johnson can properly be said to be using traditional behavior-modification techniques. This combination of "insight" therapy with behavioral treatment has since become increasingly popular. Programs similar to that of Masters and Johnson are now operating in many different cities throughout the country, while at the same time other individual therapists are experimenting with combinations of psychodynamic interpretation and behavioral exercises in imitation of Masters and Johnson's successful "mixed" formula.

SEXUAL DEVIATIONS

Earlier in this chapter we have already quoted DSM-II's definition of sexual deviance. Under this heading we shall discuss the following disorders:

1. *Fetishism:* sexual gratification via inanimate objects or via some body part to the exclusion of the person as a whole.
2. *Transvestism:* sexual gratification through dressing in the clothes of the opposite sex.
3. *Transsexualism:* gender identification with the opposite sex.
4. *Exhibitionism:* sexual gratification through displaying one's genitals to an involuntary observer.
5. *Voyeurism:* sexual gratification through clandestine observation of other people's sexual activities or sexual anatomy.
6. *Pedophilia:* child molesting—that is, gratification, on the part of the adult, through sexual contacts with children.
7. *Incest:* sexual relations between members of the same immediate family.
8. *Rape:* the achievement of sexual relations with another person through the use or threat of force.

9. *Sadism:* sexual gratification through inflicting pain on others.
10. *Masochism:* sexual gratification through having pain inflicted on oneself.

The first thing that we should note about these various behaviors is that they all occur in mild, playful, or sublimated forms in what we would call normal everyday life. The wife who regularly chooses to take her bath while her husband is shaving and the husband who regularly chooses to shave while his wife is taking her bath are engaging in what would be called socially allowable exhibitionism and voyeurism. It is only when peeping and exhibiting—or for that matter, the use of aggression or of inanimate objects—become the central focus and *sine qua non* of the person's arousal and gratification that they are generally deemed abnormal by the society and by diagnosticians. Similarly, rape fantasies, intrafamilial flirtations, and arousal by children are not uncommon in normal individuals. It is only when these impulses are acted upon that they are labeled pathological.

Fetishism

The case of fetishism is a fine example of the fact that sexual disorders, like so many other psychological disorders, exist on a continuum ranging from the normal to the abnormal, with many variations in between. Thus the diagnostic decision as to where the line is to be drawn and the case deemed pathological is by necessity a subjective judgment. It is of course not unusual for people to concentrate sexual interest on some particular attribute of the opposite sex. Certain women consider the size of a man's penis to be particularly important, while many men are utterly fascinated by large breasts or by a well-formed bottom. Other men prefer as sexual partners women who are stylishly dressed, and the sight of a pair of underpants held together with a safety pin can leave them considerably discouraged sexually. In general, however, such people, despite their marked preferences, do not totally disregard the rest of the person and can in fact respond to conventional sexual stimuli.

Further along the continuum we can place the following case, originally reported by Krafft-Ebing in 1886:

A lady told Dr. Gemy that in the bridal night and in the night following her husband contented himself with kissing her, and running his fingers through the wealth of her tresses. He then fell asleep. In the third night Mr. X produced an immense wig, with enor-

mously long hair, and begged his wife to put it on. As soon as she had done so, he richly compensated her for his neglected marital duties. In the morning he showed again extreme tenderness, whilst he caressed the wig. When Mrs. X removed the wig she lost at once all charm for her husband. Mrs. X recognized this as a hobby, and readily yielded to the wishes of her husband, whom she loved dearly, and whose libido *depended on the wearing of the wig. It was remarkable, however, that a wig had the desired effect only for a fortnight or three weeks at a time. It had to be made of thick, long hair, no matter of what colour. The result of this marriage was, after five years, two children, and a collection of seventy-two wigs (1965, pp. 157–158).*

Here the question of whether Mr. X's "hobby" deserves the label of pathological is somewhat more difficult to answer. The wigs were admittedly an utterly necessary prerequisite for sexual arousal; yet with the help of the wigs, the couple enjoyed an otherwise conventional and very satisfactory sexual relationship.

However, most of the cases of fetishism that come to the attention of diagnosticians are those in which the person's sexual fascination with a single body part or, more commonly, with some type of object has totally crowded out any interest in normal sexual interplay with another human being. Much of the person's life will be occupied with collecting new examples of his favored object. (Every year a number of people convicted of breaking and entering turn out to be fetishists in search of a new supply of whatever it is that arouses them. Some fetishists have reported that the risk of being caught in the theft adds considerably to their sexual arousal.) Typically, the fetishist's sexual activity will consist of fondling, kissing, and smelling the fetish, and often masturbating in the process. Common fetishistic objects are fur, women's stockings, women's shoes, women's gloves, and especially women's underpants, but more exotic fetishes have also been reported. Bergler (1947), for example, has cited the case of a man whose major source of sexual gratification was the sight of well-formed automobile exhaust pipes.

It is interesting to note that virtually all the reported cases of fetishism involve males. In fact, most of the deviations treated in this section are exclusively male aberrations. This fact is often interpreted as suggesting that female sexuality is so repressed in the process of socialization that women have little opportunity to develop either truly normal or truly abnormal forms of sexual expression.

Transvestism

Similar to the fetishists in that they are sexually excited by inanimate objects, transvestites go one step further and actually put on their fetish, which is the clothing of the opposite sex. Once cross-dressed, the transvestite typically masturbates privately, though he may also enjoy appearing publicly in his costume. A relatively rare aberration, transvestism should not be confused with homosexuality. Some homosexuals are in fact transvestites, in which case they are referred to in the homosexual vernacular as "drag queens." But according to one

Fig. 9.3   A transvestite parade-marcher, protesting social discrimination against transvestism and other forms of sexual variance.

study of 262 transvestites (Buckner, 1970), the vast majority of transvestites think of themselves as heterosexuals.

Transvestites usually do not come into conflict with the law, and recent social attitudes toward transvestism seem to range from indifference to curiosity. Indeed, nightclubs featuring transvestite performers have become increasingly popular in the last decade. Partly as a result of this social tolerance, there has been little psychological investigation of transvestism. However, some insight into the psychology of the transvestite has been provided by the studies of Bentler and Prince (1969, 1970) and of Bentler, Shearman, and Prince (1970), who, with the help of a national transvestite organization, administered standardized personality tests to a large sample of male transvestites. These tests revealed what a number of clinicians had already suspected: that as a group, transvestites appear to be no more neurotic or psychotic than the population at large. However, the tests did show transvestites to be more indifferent to other people and to social approval than the average person.

Transsexualism

Unlike transvestites, transsexuals—almost all of whom, again, are males—believe that they truly *do* belong to the opposite sex and that their physiological gender is simply an ugly mistake. Typically cross-dressing on a regular basis, they do not feel the sexual arousal that the transvestite feels in women's clothes; rather, they feel relaxed, "at home" (Green, 1971). In short, transsexuals have a reversed *gender identity*, a condition which may date from very early childhood. In a thorough study of fourteen male transsexuals, Money and Primrose (1968) found that without exception all of these men had been branded as "sissies" in childhood and had presented a feminine rather than a masculine appearance.

In increasing numbers, transsexuals are attempting to solve their gender problems through sex-reassignment surgery. While the first of these operations was performed in the thirties, sex reassignment did not receive much attention until the highly publicized case of Christine Jorgensen, whose successful surgery was reported by Hamburger in 1953. In the case of the male, such surgery involves the removal of the penis and testicles and their replacement by an artificially constructed vagina, which in some cases apparently works well enough to allow the individual to experience orgasm in intercourse. This surgery is then supplemented by regular injections

Fig. 9.4 *Most sex changes by transsexuals are from male to female, but Annie M., at age sixteen (left), underwent surgery for sex reassignment as a man (right, six years after surgery).*

of sex hormones to inhibit beard growth and stimulate breast development. Surgical reassignment of female transsexuals involves the removal of the breasts and internal reproductive organs and the attachment of a penis constructed of tissue and cartilage taken from other parts of the body. However, the penis does not function normally, and in general, this operation has been less successful than male-to-female reassignment. While follow-up studies of surgically reassigned transsexuals has revealed an extremely high rate of satisfaction (Benjamin, 1966; Pauly, 1968), such operations, because they are irreversible, remain exceedingly controversial, and surgery is usually undertaken only after prolonged and careful screening.

Exhibitionism

Exhibitionism and voyeurism are the two sex offenses most often reported to the police. And while it may be said in both cases that there is a victim involved, exhibitionists and voyeurs are very rarely dangerous. Again, virtually all reported exhibitionists are men. This fact may be due in part to a reversed "double standard." Should a woman choose to undress regularly in front of a window, male observers are unlikely to be disgusted or to report the incident to the police. Furthermore, modern dress codes give women ample opportunity for mild exhibitionism—an advantage not shared by men.

In the typical case the exhibitionist is a young male, probably caught in an unsatisfactory and sexually inhibited marriage (Mohr et al., 1964). Experiencing an irresistible impulse to exhibit himself,

he will usually go to a public place such as a park, a movie house, or a department store, or will perhaps simply stroll down a city sidewalk, and upon sighting the appropriate "victim"—usually a young woman, though sometimes a young girl—will show her his penis. The penis is usually, but not always, erect. The exhibitionist's gratification is derived from the woman's response, which is generally horror, fear, and revulsion. Observing the reaction, the exhibitionist experiences intense arousal and either ejaculates immediately, masturbates to ejaculation, or in some cases simply experiences psychic relief. He then flees. It is very uncommon for an exhibitionist to attack his victim or to attempt any physical contact whatsoever with her.

In some cases, exhibitionism occurs as a symptom of a more pervasive disturbance such as schizophrenia, epilepsy, senile brain deterioration, or mental retardation (Chapters 11, 14, and 15). But exhibitionists generally turn out to be simply shy, submissive, immature men who remain attached to their possessive mothers and who have uncommonly puritanical attitudes about sex (Witzig, 1968), and particularly about masturbation. Furthermore, they often experience feelings of social and sexual inferiority and serious doubts about their masculinity. Thus, it has been suggested, they display their genitals for shock value in a desperate effort to convince themselves of their masculine prowess (Blane and Roth, 1967; Christoffel, 1956), all the while arranging the circumstances so that the woman is utterly unlikely to respond positively and thus place any sexual demands on them. In this connection, it is worth noting that in the rare instance where the woman evinces indifference or scorn rather than the expected shock and dismay, the exhibitionist will generally be cheated of his sexual gratification.

Voyeurism

As is the case with exhibitionism, there is usually an element of voyeurism in normal sexual activity. Most people would regard going through a sex act blindfolded as a serious deprivation. What distinguishes the true voyeur (or "peeping Tom," as he is sometimes called) from the average sexual participant is that the pleasures of looking replace, rather than supplement, normal sexual interplay with another person. Furthermore, the voyeur, again typically male, is not aroused by observing his wife or his girl friend disrobe for his pleasure. Rather, he is almost invariably interested in watching only strangers—usually women who are undressing or couples engaged in sex play. And the element of risk

INTERVIEWER: . . . *In other words, you feel you were born a female with male organs?*

DEBBIE: *Exactly. That's the way I view the situation. Essentially, what a transsexual is is an individual who has, for some reason—usually many reasons—decided to change sex and is being supported by physicians in this decision. I've always felt that I was a female, period, and just the way I view myself in essence is simply this: I am a female with a physical problem—that is, I look like a male, and this had to be changed if I was going to be happy at all.*

I maybe had other reasons—I was first raised as a female. I did not know I wasn't until age seven.

I was born in Brooklyn and was raised near the Brooklyn waterfront—a very poor area—under-developed, as they call it these days. As I said, I was raised as a female until just prior to my entrance into elementary school—which made this whole situation come as quite a shock to me [She laughs]. *. . .*

I was with a group of girls and we were playing in the street, and a group of nice, uh, nasty boys came along and decided to rape the whole group and we were taken off to an abandoned house and after they finished raping the first three or four girls, they got to me. And found out that things weren't quite the same [She laughs]. *So they decided to rape me anyway—it didn't seem to make any difference to them* [More laughter]. *And that's really when I sort of got frantic, because up until that time I hadn't known any difference, I didn't suspect anything. I assumed I was just the same as all other girls and that they were all the same as me. And that was the first time, really, that the actual difference between the sexes was pointed out to me in a physical way.*

I was hysterical for quite some time, and I didn't want to accept it at all. I thought I was being terribly misled by somebody—I didn't know who at the time. When I went to my mother, she explained the whole thing away in that it was just a temporary problem that I had, that it would be solved. That I really was a girl in essence, and that the situation would have to be straightened out, and that she would help me do it. But in the meantime we had to fool everybody and continue the big masquerade. If they thought I was a male, we'd just have to pretend that until such time as it could be straightened out.

. . .

I continued in school. By age thirteen I was living in the streets on my own. My family left New York City and told me that if I wanted to finish school I could finish it on my own, which also meant that I would have to survive on my own, which I did. For a year and a half I lived in the streets, stealing food and clothes and all sorts of things, until I met up with some nice guy from my high school who very nicely took care of me for the rest of my high-school career. And I did a lot of traveling with him in Europe. In fact, I was even married to him in Maryland.

He never made any unnecessary demands on me, but I guess he might have been homosexual. . . . He treated me well right up until the time he died, which was just after my high-school graduation.

We had a big argument concerning sexual activity and he vacated the premises and was so angry that he, uh, smashed a car into a telephone pole. . . .

I was attending school as a male, because that's the way I was registered, but outside of school I was living as a female. I went to Syracuse University and at the time was put in a boys' dorm. That situation didn't last long before I suffered a breakdown—I couldn't take the environment. A single girl in a boys' dorm, particularly when the boys don't want to recognize what your sex is, is a difficult situation to handle. After about six months of it I had a breakdown and spent the entire second semester in the hospital.

. . .

Of course, I went to several psychiatrists. . . . They refused to discuss the problem itself, they refused to face what the situation was. They always tried to avoid the issue by saying the problem was something else and this was only symptomatic of something much more severe. A resentment for authority, for instance, or something along those lines, or not having any faith in my elders [She laughs]. *These were basically the problems that all this first series of psychiatrists seized upon as the outlet for avoiding what the problem really was.*

. . .

A TRANSSEXUAL

When I was at Syracuse University I had a really good friend from another college. And she was quite understanding at the time. We were always together and everything, and most people always viewed my situation as one of a male, whether I tried to convince them one way or another—they wouldn't accept my interpretation of what I was.

But this particular friend of mine and I really became very good companions and eventually we got married—as a male and female. As to who was who was hard to say [She laughs]. But as I say, Toni and I became very good friends, we seemed to understand each other. She knew about the situation. We didn't know at the time what could and could not be done. She was also a social worker and felt that she might be able to help the situation, and she sort of got involved and so did I, in the sense that we thought very highly of each other—but as friends—and there was nothing ever sexually involved, there couldn't be—I had no interest in a sexual way. From a male point of view, I couldn't possibly ever consider having relations with women—it's something totally beyond my comprehension. It's just not the way I am at all.

After the marriage I tried, maybe if I did my attitude might change. I was willing to try almost anything to see if it would help. And it didn't help, I'll tell you, it certainly didn't help [She laughs]. It certainly made things more complicated, because the harder I would try, the more involved Toni would get—the more she would assume I could do or change things by just deciding I would change things. And then it really got kind of involved, and after three years we separated, and finally last month the annulment was decreed.

. . .

I feel that my circumstance is something that would have happened regardless of what my mother did. In many ways I can thank my mother for doing what she did, because it at least helped me over many of the socialization processes that I would normally have to go through. It helped instill the feeling in me of really being a girl at a very early age. That adjustment is very easy for me to make now.

It's simply a matter of a freak of nature, a physical freak of nature. Siamese twins are born, something has to be done, and I happen to be de-formed in this way. Now some people consider it quite acceptable, the way I looked as a male, but I personally didn't and this is, I think, the big difference: it was my personally not accepting it for what it was and wanting to modify a situation that I consider was a gross mistake, a freak of nature.

. . .

When I was in high school most of my friends were girls, with the exception of a few guys I dated. When I was in college, at Syracuse especially, I had very few friends at all. In most cases, I never had to explain. Most of my relationships were so transitional that it wasn't even practical to explain. Those who knew me as a male assumed I was a male, and those who knew me as a female never thought of me any other way. A year ago, when people found out what I was about to do [i.e., that she was beginning hormone treatments preparatory to sex-change surgery], it cost me all the friends I had. Without exception, all of them.

. . .

After surgery, I expect that I'll do the same thing with my life that every other girl wants to, and that is eventually get married. . . .

But really, I just want to be as happy as . . . I feel that I'm just approaching, right now, the best part of my life, and once the surgery is complete I will have a lot more to offer someone. Because I think that once you're happy as an individual, you can make someone else happy, and not before then. And I feel that up until that time I won't quite be as happy with myself as I should be. Once the surgery is achieved I will have a lot more to offer and I can start leading what I consider the normal life that I have been deprived of up until this time.

. . . I've gotten over everything, I adjust to everything very well. I may joke around about the tragedy, but it's only because, like many other things, you laugh instead of crying, you know? You laugh in many places where if your true feelings were known you'd rather cry. . . . But, um, I don't cry about many things anymore—not in public, anyway [Soft laughter]. . . .

Source: Steve Post, *Playing in the FM Band: A Personal Account of Free Radio*. New York: Viking, 1974, pp. 112–118, 125. Copyright© 1974 Steve Post.

necessarily involved in watching strangers seems to be a desirable adjunct to his pleasure. The thought of being discovered in his perch on the tree branch, fire escape, balcony, or whatever adds to the sexual thrill of the peeping, which normally leads to masturbation.

Like exhibitionism, voyeurism seems to provide a substitute gratification and a reassurance of power for otherwise sexually anxious and inhibited males. Voyeurs are typically withdrawn both socially and sexually, with little in their developmental histories to support the learning of more appropriate interpersonal skills.

As sadism interacts with masochism, so voyeurism sometimes interacts with exhibitionism, as is illustrated in the following rare case of voyeurism on the part of a woman:

A forty-year-old single woman complained that a middle-aged man who lived in the opposite house was creating a public nuisance by exposing his erect penis while lying on his bed. The man admitted his exposure but denied that he was creating a public nuisance, because the woman had to stand on a piece of furniture in order to see him. Furthermore, she had been observing him for many years and because she had never complained, he had thought that he was doing her a favor. In the course of the legal investigation, it was learned that the woman not only stood on a piece of furniture but also used binoculars. The man was acquitted. However, the mystery remained as to why the woman, after so many years, complained about the man's behavior (Hirschfeld, 1944, pp. 505–506).

Sadism and Masochism

There appears to be an element of aggression in even the most "natural" sexual activity. As we have mentioned, aggressive sexual fantasies—of raping or of being raped—are not uncommon. And indeed, most sexual acts involve some degree of force. For example, human beings, like most other mammals, exhibit some biting and scratching during intercourse—behavior that would be considered cruel and aggressive in almost any other context. Conversely, there is often a sexual element underlying aggression. Both men and women have reported becoming sexually excited at boxing matches and football games or while watching fires or executions—observations which have led some theorists to propose that our society's preoccupation with violence may be sexually motivated.

In sadism and masochism, however, the element

Fig. 9.5 As these two photographs illustrate, the circumstances under which one takes off one's clothes determine how one will be regarded—as degenerate or star.

of physical cruelty—giving and receiving, respectively—assumes a central role in sexual functioning. Both disorders are named for literary figures who publicized the sexual pleasures of cruelty. The term "sadism" is taken from the name of the Marquis de Sade (1740–1814), whose novels included numerous erotic scenes featuring the delights of whipping a woman. "Masochism" is named for an Austrian novelist, Leopold von Sacher-Masoch (1836–1895), whose male characters tended to swoon with ecstasy when physically abused by women—a source of excitement which apparently played a central part in Sacher-Masoch's personal fantasy life as well.

Individual patterns of sadism turn up, as usual, primarily in men. The degree of cruelty indulged in may range from sticking a woman with a pin to horrifying acts of murder and mutilation, numerous hair-raising examples of which may be found in Krafft-Ebing's *Psychopathia Sexualis* ([1886] 1965). Between these two extremes are sadists who bind, whip, bite, and cut their victims. For some, the mere sight of blood or the victim's cries of pain are sufficient to trigger ejaculation; for others, the act of cruelty merely intensifies arousal, which eventually leads to rape. Similarly, the masochist may need to suffer only a mild degree of pain, such as spanking or verbal abuse, or he may choose to be chained and whipped. And like the sadist, he may reach orgasm through the experience of pain alone, or the abuse stage may serve simply as "foreplay," leading eventually into intercourse. While individual sadists may prey on strange women or prostitutes, individual masochists usually have to resort to prostitutes, some of whom specialize in catering to masochistic tastes.

Fig. 9.6 *Some of the paraphernalia used by sadists and masochists in their sexual activities.*

Podolsky and Wade (1961) present an interesting case of a female sadist:

Margie is a 30-year-old, raven-haired, oval-faced young lady, an attractive figure, intelligent. She is a secretary to a large steamship corporation president, well respected and admired by everyone. Yet, she is still single. She wants to get married but is convinced that it is impossible to find a man who will submit to being punished . . . as part of the sexual act. Margie is a female sexual sadist.

Margie was one of seven children. As far back as she can remember, her mother was scrubbing, ironing, washing, cooking, taking care of her children and the factory-working husband. Her mother always said to her, "Margie, never let any man take advantage of you. All men want to do is hurt women, getting them pregnant all the time. A man will use you, punish you, if you let him." Margie recalls the misshapen and ugly appearance of her mother's body whenever she became pregnant. And because the walls of their shack-like home were thin, she vividly remembers the cries and screams of pain her mother made when her father would gratify his own . . . urges. Later, whenever boys tried to get fresh with her, she would push them away, hating them, hating all males for what they did to women—hating them because she transferred that hatred to her father who had been abusive to her mother.

Margie escaped into a world of illusion. She would daydream about punishing men. She envisioned herself as a mythical queen in a legendary land, standing naked on a throne while dozens of helpless males writhed and twisted at her feet while she flogged them, the steel-tipped burred whip just ripping and tearing at their naked flesh. Margie pretended in this illusionary world that she was Master of all males . . . that she had power over them all—and that all desired her sexually. Only when she would completely flog them, torture them, was she able to feel her own sexual powers welling up. . . .

Margie recalls having had too much to drink one night at an office party, and being taken to a motel by a man whom she had befriended at the bar. While she was still heady from the liquor, she had most of her senses. The man made some attempts at love, slowly stripping Margie. But she failed to respond. Meanwhile, the strange man became prepared for the consummation but he did something else. He forced Margie to her knees and roughly demanded that she participate in a distasteful act [presumably fellatio, oral stimulation of the penis]. "He wanted pleasure only for himself," recalls Margie with bitterness. "He wanted me to do . . . what he asked . . . but it meant nothing to me. Through the haze of alcohol came the words of my mother, telling me never to give in to men, to look at her and see where it had gotten her . . . at the door of poverty—being reduced to a sexual rag by a greedy man. It made me angry. There was a sudden surge of power. I got to my feet, suddenly seized the man and hurled him to the floor.

"Then, right there in the motel, I seized the belt from his trousers which had been placed on a chair and began to whip him. He tried to scream, but I placed my high heel upon the small of his back, crushing him to the floor, and soundly whipped him. The sound of the whispering belt as it whistled through the air, his struggles to get free from my capture, his rippling muscles as they were lashed with the belt . . . it so excited me that I could no longer control myself. Fortunately, he sensed my aroused emotions and we had a violent but satisfying sexual session" (pp. 107–112).

However, the vast majority of cases of sadism and masochism are not individual patterns, but dual patterns in which a sadist and a masochist pair up in a relationship to satisfy their mutually complementary tastes. Such *sadomasochistic* sexual relationships are sometimes found within otherwise conventional marriages. Other sadists and masochists prefer homosexual relationships, and in fact there is a substantial so-called S-and-M segment within the homosexual subculture. In many large American cities, there are now "sex shops" which specialize in selling sadomasochistic equipment: whips, chains, handcuffs, and belts with metal studs, as well as the leather costumes often favored by homosexual sadomasochists. Such shops also carry numerous pictures, books, and magazines graphically illustrating sadomasochistic acts for the benefit of those who prefer to experience such gratifications vicariously.

Pedophilia

Of the sexual deviations that we have discussed so far, it can be said that with the striking exception of individual sadistic patterns, these aberrations are largely "victimless." The exhibitionist certainly imposes on his audience, and the voyeur unquestionably invades the privacy of those whom he observes. But the major sufferers, if any, are those who engage in these behaviors. In contrast, pedophilia—

along with the two disorders that we will discuss next, incest and rape—involves a flagrant violation of the rights of another person, who may suffer serious psychological damage as a result. The social sanctions on these three forms of deviance are accordingly very high. And in the case of pedophilia, where the victim is by definition a child, social response is perhaps the most punitive.

Pedophilia (from the Greek, meaning "love of children") can take a number of different forms, ranging, in order of increasing rarity, from covertly or overtly masturbating while talking to the child and perhaps stroking her hair, to manipulation of the child's sex organs, to masturbation between the child's thighs, to having the child masturbate or fellate him, or to actual intromission.

Though cases of female pedophilia occasionally turn up, most pedophiles are adult males, ranging in age from adolescence to their seventies, but generally in their thirties or forties. They are usually either married or divorced and have children of their own. And like exhibitionists, they usually hold rather puritanical attitudes toward sex. In the vast majority of cases the victim is a girl, and one who is well-known to the pedophile; indeed, he is typically a neighbor, a relative, or a friend of the family (Gebhard et al., 1965). And it is not unlikely that a child's innocently uninhibited show of affection for Uncle Joe or for Mr. Jones down the block may initiate the first episode, if Uncle Joe's or Mr. Jones' behavioral controls have been lowered by alcohol, loneliness, or marital unhappiness (MacNamara, 1968). Once the first episode has taken place, the pedophilic relationship may continue for months or even years until it is discovered or until the child at last tells her parents.

The pedophile has been described in much the same terms as the voyeur and the exhibitionist—that is, as a man who has failed socially, sexually, and occupationally in the adult world and thus goes in search of a less threatening sexual outlet, in this case a relationship with a nondemanding and innocent child. However, according to Mohr, Turner, and Jerry (1964), motivation seems to vary considerably with age of the offender. Adolescent pedophiles tend to be sexually inhibited and inexperienced boys. Young adult pedophiles show a more serious degree of social maladjustment and mental disturbance, often accompanied by alcoholism, the alcohol serving as the disinhibiting factor. Older pedophiles, those in their middle or late fifties, tend to be more normal psychologically but suffering from loneliness, which the relationship with the child relieves.

Fig. 9.7 Sado-masochism is given widely differing explanations by psychodynamic theorists and behaviorists. As with its other explanations, the psychodynamic approach focuses on unconscious conflicts. The behaviorists emphasize the conditioned arousal properties of previously neutral stimuli; that is, that inflicting and/or receiving pain in either fantasy or reality may be repeatedly associated with orgasm, and thus the individual eventually becomes aroused only through sado-masochistic interactions. This painting, Autumnal Cannibalism, *by Salvador Dali, may be interpreted as depicting both sadism and masochism.*

Incest

Almost all human societies have—and have had throughout their known histories—a taboo on incest. (One exception would be ancient Egypt, where Pharaohs married their sisters on the assumption that the royal blood should be kept pure. Cleopatra, for example, was married successively to two of her younger brothers.) Explanations of this universal taboo range from the argument that it encouraged families to establish wider social contacts to the contention, supported by scientific studies, that inbreeding fosters genetic defects in offspring (Adams and Neel, 1967; Lindzey, 1967).

However, despite this very strong taboo, incest is more common than would usually be assumed. Kinsey and co-workers (1948) reported that .5 percent of the males interviewed in their study admitted to acts of incest, and in view of the fact that incest tends to remain an extremely well-kept family secret,

incidence is assumed to be considerably higher. By far the most common pattern is brother-sister incest. Father-daughter incest is about one-fifth as common (Kinsey, 1948; Gebhard et al., 1965), and mother-son incest is apparently quite rare.

Brother-sister incest is difficult to label as pathological, since it often seems to occur almost accidentally in lower-class families where brothers and sisters share the same beds (Bagley, 1969). (This is not to deny that guilt over such a relationship may seriously interfere with psychological functioning in adulthood.) In father-daughter incest the pathological element seems clearer. Whereas one might suspect the incestuous father of simply being promiscuous and of fastening upon his daughter as simply one of his many unselective sexual contacts, studies show that this is decidedly not the case. Cavallin (1966) reports that the typical incestuous father tends to confine his extramarital sexual contacts to his daughter alone, and sometimes to several daughters, starting with the oldest and going down the line as the years pass. Furthermore, far from being indiscriminately amoral, fathers who seduce their sexually mature daughters are likely to be highly moralistic and devoutly attached to fundamentalistic religious doctrines (Gebhard et al., 1965). Father-daughter incest often occurs in connection with disturbed marital relationships and may even be tacitly encouraged by the mother as a means of escaping her husband's sexual advances.

Rape

Legally, there are two categories of rape: *statutory rape*, sexual intercourse with a minor, which usually occurs in the absence of force; and *forcible rape*, sexual gratification under coercion with a person over eighteen. Our discussion will be limited to the latter type, usually committed by married men in their twenties or even younger.

It is difficult to estimate the incidence of rape, since many jurisdictions disagree on what actually constitutes rape. In some states any attempt on the part of a man to force his sexual attentions on a woman, even if he fails to achieve intercourse, may be interpreted as rape. In other jurisdictions the criteria for a rape conviction are considerably more stringent. Indeed, until recently, New York State required that rape could not be established without a witness to the crime, whereas, needless to say, most rapists tend to steer clear of witnesses. The most precise statistics available (FBI, 1975) indicate that in 1974 there were more than 55,000 cases of forcible rape in the United States. However, rape is the least commonly reported of violent crimes, since many women, knowing that it is notoriously difficult to get a rape conviction, prefer not to add the trauma of a rape trial to the trauma of the rape. Hence, the statistics quoted above are estimated to represent approximately one-third of the actual cases of rape in our society (President's Commission, 1967).

In dealing with rape, we are faced with the serious question of why the rapist, who, as has been mentioned, typically has a wife at home, should go out and force his sexual attentions on another adult woman. In some cases the rapist is clearly a sociopath—a person who simply follows his impulses in seizing whatever he wants—and thus would properly be classified as an antisocial personality rather than as a sexual deviant. In many other cases, however, it appears that for the rapist sexual gratification is inextricably bound up with the release of aggression—a condition which obviously bears some relationship to sadism. In other instances we find the same syndrome that has been described in the case of the voyeur and the exhibitionist: a timid, submissive male who has grave doubts about his masculinity and who is so fearful of rejection that he is unable to seek sexual gratification through more acceptable channels (Cohen and Seghorn, 1969).

In the case of rape, as in the case of pedophilia and incest, psychology must concern itself not only with the perpetrator but also with the victim. Rape victims often suffer substantial physical and psychological damage, with the result that after the rape they may have great difficulty responding sexually even to the most loving and beloved male. Furthermore, as the women's liberation movement has pointed out, social and judicial attitudes are often anything but helpful to the rape victim, commonly serving to aggravate rather than relieve her sense of shame. Fortunately, recent attention to this type of injustice has resulted in the establishment of centers for the counseling of rape victims, in the inclusion of policewomen in vice squads responsible for investigating rape reports, in the repeal of many laws which seemed designed to protect the rapist from conviction, and finally, in a less self-deprecating attitude on the part of rape victims.

PERSPECTIVES ON SEXUAL DISORDERS

Both the psychodynamic and the behaviorist perspectives tend to interpret a number of different sexual deviations as resulting from the same mechanisms. Hence we will not attempt a complete rundown of etiological theories of all the disorders from each of these perspectives, but instead will summarize what each perspective views as the major causative factors and the most hopeful therapeutic approaches for sexual disorders in general.

The Psychodynamic Perspective

Cause   According to Freud (1905), sexual disorders represent a continuation into adulthood of the diffuse sexual preoccupations of the child. Children normally enjoy "showing off" their sexual equipment and peeping at that of others. Furthermore, according to Freudian theory, they are capable of resorting to any number of defensive maneuvers in attempting to deal with the castration anxiety and penis envy supposedly endemic to the Oedipal period. In accordance with this line of thinking, psychodynamic theorists generally conceptualize sexual disorders as the result of fixation at a pregenital stage, and in general, with sexual disorders as with sexual dysfunctions, it is the Oedipal stage, with its attendant castration anxiety, that is considered the major source of mischief. Incest is of course easily interpretable as simply an acting out of Oedipal attractions. As for fetishism, Freud (1928) theorized that it was intimately related to castration anxiety and that the fetish, particularly if it is a shoe, is a symbol of the mother's lost penis. Likewise, transvestism is seen as a denial of the mother's presumed castration. Dressed in the clothes of a woman, but still equipped with a penis underneath, the transvestite can momentarily convince himself that his mother did not suffer castration after all and that therefore he need not fear the same fate for himself (Nielson, 1960). Similarly, Fenichel (1945) interprets sadism as an attempt, through cruelty and aggression, to take the part of the castrator rather than that of the castrated and thus to relieve anxiety. Indeed, castration anxiety is often seen as paramount in any sexual deviation involving the avoidance of coitus. For the male who fears losing his own penis, the thought of coming into contact with the supposedly truncated genitals of the woman and of watching his penis "disappear" inside her involves intolerable levels of anxiety. Hence he defends himself by redirecting his sexual impulses toward a safer outlet, such as a fetish, a child, or vicarious participation in the sexual activities of his neighbors across the way.

Other psychodynamic interpretations of sexual disorders have stressed the individual's inability to disentangle and control his basic id impulses. Thus sadism has been explained as a continuation of the child's confusion of sexual and aggressive impulses. And though masochism is sometimes seen as a manifestation of the death instinct, it is more often conceptualized as a redirection onto the self of aggressive impulses originally aimed at a powerful, threatening figure.

Treatment In individual psychotherapy or psychoanalysis, the procedure with the sexual deviant would follow the traditional lines: the therapist would interpret symbolic remarks, behaviors, and dreams in the attempt to bring to the conscious level the unconscious sexual conflict so that it can be confronted and "worked through." A variation on this technique has been the use of group therapy, which has recently been employed as a substitute for imprisonment in the cases of some rapists, pedophiles,* and other criminal offenders. The group technique has the obvious advantage of placing the troubled and often deeply remorseful individual in

a situation where he can take comfort from the knowledge that he is not "the only one"—a reassurance which can hasten his confrontation of his problem. Cohen and Seghorn (1969) have reported successful results with certain types of rapists in group therapy.

The Behaviorist Perspective

Cause The most common behavioral interpretation of sexual deviations is that the deviation results from a respondent conditioning process in which early sexual experiences, particularly masturbation, are paired with some unconventional stimulus which then becomes the discriminative stimulus for arousal. Thus according to this interpretation, Alexander Portnoy, the hero of Philip Roth's novel *Portnoy's Complaint*, might have been expected to develop a fetish for women's underpants, since much of his youth was spent in the family bathroom masturbating into his sister's underpants, retrieved from the laundry basket. This formulation, at least with regard to fetishism, has been given some support by an experiment (Rachman, 1966) in which male subjects were repeatedly shown slides of women's boots in alternation with slides of nude women in explicit erotic poses. Eventually the subjects began to register sexual response at the signal of the boots alone. (The fetishist attraction was, however, weak and easily dissipated.)

In the case of sadism and masochism, behavioral theorists have noted that sex, aggression, and the experience of pain all involve strong emotional and physiological arousal; hence it has been proposed that the sadist and the masochist are simply persons who never learned to make the discrimination among the various types of arousal. Another learning theory of masochism is that as a child the masochist may have been cuddled and loved by his parents only after being punished, with the result that love and punishment become paired. Likewise, classical conditioning may have some role in the development of transvestism and transsexualism. In the case histories of these people, it often turns out that they were reinforced by being given attention and being told that they were "cute" when they dressed up in their mother's or sister's clothes.

---

*One of the major problems in treating convicted pedophiles is their denial of the crime. This is particularly true in prison, where sex offenders are considered to be at the bottom of the hierarchy and hence are looked down upon by the other inmates. Denial in this case serves as an attempt to preserve self-respect in such a hostile society.

Treatment The behavioral theories reviewed above, like the psychodynamic theories, have as yet very little firm empirical support, and the truth is that we still know very little about how most sexual disorders develop. In the case of behavioral treatments, however, we are on somewhat more solid ground, for the simple reason that behavior-modification techniques do seem to work in a large number of cases of sexual deviation. The technique utilized in many such cases is aversive conditioning. In this treatment, the person will be shown slides or will listen to tapes which present to him the discriminative stimulus that triggers his arousal, whether it be a blond little girl, a patent-leather shoe, or a woman undressing in front of a window. Once the subject is aroused, he is then given a mild electric shock, which he can turn off by verbalizing a more appropriate sexual behavior or by flipping a switch which changes the slide to one representing a socially acceptable object of sexual interest, typically a seductively posed woman. Emetics—that is, nausea-producing drugs—have also been used in place of shock. This rather simple technique has proved successful in a number of cases of fetishism (Meyer et al., 1968; Bandura, 1969; Marks and Gelder, 1967), masochism (Abel et al., 1970), transvestism (Lavin et al., 1961), and exhibitionism (Evans. 1967), and in some cases of pedophilia and sadism. Of central importance is that the aversive conditioning is combined with a program to develop new, more acceptable sexual behaviors. One such approach is to use systematic densensitization, to desensitize the individual to anxieties that may be contributing to the abnormal response and particularly to fears of normal sexual activity. Finally, the therapist may also use assertive training to develop the patient's confidence in normal social and sexual interactions.

HOMOSEXUALITY

Technically, the term *homosexuality* (from the Greek word *homo*, meaning "same as") designates sexual activity directed toward one's own sex, whether that be male or female, and we will use the term in this sense in our discussion. However, in popular usage *homosexuality* means male homosexuality, while female homosexuality, which has received much less attention than its male counterpart, is called *lesbianism*. (The term is taken from the name of the Greek island of Lesbos, home of the presumably lesbian poet Sappho [c. 620–c. 565 B.C.].) Of all the forms of deviance from the supposed norm of heterosexual coitus, homosexuality and lesbianism together constitute the most common and the most controversial variation. As we noted earlier in this chapter, homosexuality is an ancient practice, but in most societies, including our own, it has been severely stigmatized and equally severely punished. Today most American homosexuals are still faced with the difficult choice of remaining "in the closet"—that is, maintaining the pretense that they are heterosexual, while engaging in clandestine homosexual activity—or "coming out"—that is, making no secret of their preferences and facing the adverse consequences involved, including possible loss of housing, loss of employment, arrest, and imprisonment, to say nothing of social ostracism, scorn, and mockery.

For Elaine Noble, 31, the first avowed lesbian to be elected to state office [to the Massachusetts legislature in 1974], coming out . . . cost her her job as an advertising executive, her female lover, who was afraid to be seen with her, "and at least for a time, a certain portion of my sanity." There were obscene phone calls, dirty words written on her car, slashed tires. People looked on her as "a freak, a tattooed lady." "I wonder, if we knew the cost," she says, "would we still have done it" (*Time*, 1975, p. 33).

Yet the mere fact that an avowed lesbian could be elected to state office is an indication of the increasing liberalization of our attitudes toward homosexuality. In England and in a few American states such as Illinois and Connecticut, antihomosexual legislation has recently been repealed. And several large cities, including Seattle and San Francisco, have passed bills protecting homosexuals from discrimination in housing and employment. This trend has also been reflected in official psychiatric nomenclature. Though not without cries of protest from within their own ranks, the Board of Trustees of the American Psychiatric Association voted in 1973 to remove homosexuality per se from the list of sexual disorders and to replace it with the label of "sexual orientation disturbance," to be applied only to people "who are disturbed by, in conflict with, or wish to change" (p. 44) their homosexual orientation. However, this revision, while welcomed by many liberals, still begs the question of whether the homosexual who is in conflict with his sexual leanings might not be experiencing this conflict simply as a result of social disapproval rather than as a result of a natural drive toward the presumably normal state of heterosexuality.

The Incidence of Homosexuality

Virtually nothing was known about the incidence of homosexuality in the United States until 1948, when

Fig. 9.8 Perhaps the increasing openness about homosexuality in American society will result in a more accepting attitude toward marriages between members of the same sex.

Alfred C. Kinsey and his associates shocked a substantial number of Americans by presenting evidence that homosexual and heterosexual orientation in males was not a dichotomy of "them *versus* "us" but rather a continuum, with a large percentage of "us" falling somewhere between the two extremes of exclusive heterosexuality and exclusive homosexuality. On the basis of interviews with 5,300 American males, Kinsey reported that 37 percent of his male sample had had at least one homosexual experience to orgasm since the onset of adolescence, while 18 percent revealed as much homosexual as heterosexual experience. Another 13 percent experienced, but did not act upon, homosexual impulses. Of those men who remained unmarried to the age of 35, 50 percent had engaged in homosexual activity to orgasm since the beginning of adolescence. In all, only 63 percent of Kinsey's sample had had exclusively heterosexual experience, and only 4 percent had exclusively homosexual histories (Kinsey et al., 1948). And while Kinsey's data on women indicated a much lower incidence of homosexual experience—only 13 percent (Kinsey et al., 1953)—even this percentage was considered startling when first published.

Kinsey's report has been criticized on a number of points. In the first place, the sample may be considered unrepresentative in the sense that only white males and females were interviewed. Second, any sexual data based on self-report tend to be viewed with some skepticism, since many people are hesitant to share the intimate details of their sex lives even with the most objective interviewer. However, other surveys of sexual behavior have tended to confirm Kinsey's findings (Gebhard, 1972). And these findings—revealing, as they do, that homosexual experience is by no means uncommon in the general population—have certainly played a role in the current questioning of the "abnormality" of homosexuality.

Homosexual Myths and Realities

The issue of homosexuality is surrounded by a good deal of misinformation. One prevailing myth is that homosexuals generally suffer from the type of gender confusion that we have described as typical of the transsexual. Consequently, many people believe that male homosexuals are invariably swishy, limp-wristed effeminate types and that lesbians are generally tough-looking "dykes." The evidence indicates, however, that while some homosexuals do adopt the mannerisms of the opposite sex, these are a small minority; most homosexuals are indistinguishable from heterosexuals in their superficial appearance. Another popular misconception is that there is a distinctly homosexual personality type. On the contrary, it appears that homosexuals differ as much from one another in personality makeup as do heterosexuals (Hooker, 1957). Finally, it is widely assumed that homosexuals, whether male or female, tend to assume either an "active" or a "passive" role in their sexual relations, whereas surveys (Saghir and Robins, 1969; Saghir et al., 1969) show that both female and male homosexuals commonly alternate between active and passive roles.

What homosexuals *do* do in their sexual interplay can be stated without great mystery, since most homosexual activities are also regularly practiced by many heterosexuals. As with heterosexuals, homosexual foreplay involves kissing, fondling, and tactile stimulation of genitals. For male homosexuals, orgasm is achieved through mutual masturbation, fellatio, or anal intercourse, the latter being the least common method. Lesbians generally reach orgasm through mutual masturbation, or less commonly through *cunnilingus* (oral stimulation of the female genitals). However, some lesbian couples imitate heterosexual intercourse by using an artificial penis called a *dildo*.

A Letter from Freud on Homosexuality

Four years before his death, Freud, now world-famous, received a letter from an American woman desperately asking for advice regarding her son's "problems." Freud's kindly reply—written, as it was, thirteen years before the publication of the Kinsey report—seems extremely modern in its approach to homosexuality. Predictably, he ascribes this condition to arrested psychosexual development. Note, however, that he adamantly rejects the notion that homosexuality can be classified as either a vice or an illness, suggests that it need not be accompanied by neurosis, is skeptical about the advisability or success of any treatment, and appears to consider the happiness of the woman's son of greater importance than his sexual orientation. Forty years of research later, the most avant-garde psychologists have had little to add to this position.

April 9, 1935

Dear Mrs.——

I gather from your letter that your son is a homosexual. I am most impressed by the fact that you do not mention this term yourself in your information about him. May I question you, why you avoid it? Homosexuality is assuredly no advantage, but it is nothing to be ashamed of, no vice, no degradation, it cannot be classified as an illness; we consider it to be a variation of the sexual function produced by a certain arrest of sexual development. Many highly respectable individuals of ancient and modern times have been homosexuals, several of the greatest among them (Plato, Michel-

angelo, Leonardo da Vinci, etc.). It is a great injustice to persecute homosexuality as a crime, and cruelty too. If you do not believe me, read the books of Havelock Ellis. [Ellis, a contemporary of Freud, was famous for his seven-volume Studies in the Psychology of Sex.]

By asking me if I can help, you mean, I suppose, if I can abolish homosexuality and make normal heterosexuality take its place. The answer is, in a general way, we cannot promise to achieve it. In a certain number of cases we succeed in developing the blighted germs of heterosexual tendencies which are present in every homosexual; in the majority of cases it is no more possible. It is a question of the quality and the age of the individual. The result of treatment cannot be predicted.

What analysis can do for your son runs in a different line. If he is unhappy, neurotic, torn by conflicts, inhibited in his social life, analysis may bring him harmony, peace of mind, full efficiency, whether he remains a homosexual or gets changed. If you make up your mind, he should have analysis with me!! I don't expect you will!! He has to come over to Vienna. I have no intention of leaving here. However, don't neglect to give me your answer.

Sincerely yours with kind wishes,
Freud

P.S. I did not find it difficult to read your handwriting. Hope you will not find my writing and my English a harder task [cited in Jones, 1963, p. 490].

Lesbianism vs. Male Homosexuality

Since the publication of Kinsey's findings, a number of studies have been conducted in the effort to dissipate the haze of mystery surrounding homosexuality. One very interesting finding reported by Saghir and his co-workers (Saghir and Robins, 1969; Saghir et al., 1969) is that there is apparently a substantial difference between lesbian relationships and male homosexual relationships. Perhaps not surprisingly, these investigators found that "when it comes to sexual behavior, homosexual men are more like heterosexual men (or the stereotype) and homosexual women are more like heterosexual women (or

the stereotype)" (Saghir et al., 1969, p. 228). In the first place, male homosexuals are much more promiscuous than lesbians. Indeed, in the Kinsey survey (1953), only 29 percent of those claiming to be exclusively lesbian had had sexual contacts with more than two partners, whereas the number of different partners reported by the typical male homosexual was considerably higher. And whereas a large proportion of male homosexuals tend to engage in short-term relationships—often "one-night stands" resulting from a pickup in a gay (i.e., homosexual) bar—lesbians tend to establish longer-lasting unions. Finally, as could be predicted from the above, male homosexuals find it easier to separate sex from emotional involvement. In contrast, lesbians are more "romantic" (Simon and Gagnon, 1970) and tend to look for relationships in which caring, love, and emotional support are more important than sexual gratification.

PERSPECTIVES ON HOMOSEXUALITY

The Psychodynamic Perspective

Cause   The classical psychodynamic view of male homosexuality, like that of the sexual disorders described earlier, centers on the problem of unresolved Oedipal conflicts. According to this theory, the male homosexual is unable to overcome his attachment to his mother, to identify with his father, and thus to proceed to the mature stage of genital sexuality. Hence he continues to suffer from acute castration anxiety, and consequently he strenuously avoids contact with female genitals for fear of injury to or loss of his penis.

This family-centered theory received some support from a famous study in which Bieber and his associates (1962) asked a number of their psychiatric colleagues to fill out detailed questionnaires on the family histories of their homosexual patients. What these investigators found, in comparing the information they received, was a frequent occurrence of what might be called the "smother mother" syndrome. Briefly, the pattern involves a disturbed relationship between the parents, with the result that the mother transfers her love to her son and becomes overprotective of him. Meanwhile the father, like a rejected suitor, becomes withdrawn, resentful, and very negative in his interactions with his rival, the son. The mother is either explicitly or subtly seductive with the son but at the same time discourages erotic displays on his part and communicates to him her contempt for the male role in general. Needless to say, such a pattern would be hardly conducive to any successful resolution of the Oedipal complex. Thus Bieber's findings have been hailed as definitive evidence for the psychodynamic formulation. And while perhaps not definitive, such a family theory does seem to merit serious consideration. At the same time it should be noted that the Bieber pattern turns up in the histories of heterosexuals as well, and conversely, that many homosexuals fail to manifest such a pattern.

Treatment   The psychodynamic treatment of homosexuality follows the traditional route of free association, dream analysis, and "talking out," with

Fig. 9.9   In contrast to male homosexuals, female homosexuals or lesbians tend to have more stable, romantic, and lasting relationships.

special attention, of course, to the confrontation of the Oedipal conflicts. Such treatment procedures, particularly with highly motivated patients who are not exclusively homosexual, have shown some success. Currently, however, they are receiving less attention than behavioral treatment, while at the same time all attempts to modify homosexual orientation have come under attack from critics who claim that the only fair treatment for a homosexual is to help him accept and pursue successfully his sexual preferences. It should be noted that most homosexuals do not seek treatment for their sexual orientation on their own volition. Rather, they are often pressured to change by people who are upset by their behavior.

The Behaviorist Perspective

Cause   Predictably, most psychologists who follow a learning theory regard homosexuality simply as a learned sexual preference. If we regard most human beings as potentially responsive to stimulation from both males and females, then the development of the individual's sexual orientation will depend upon his personal experiences in sexual arousal and satisfaction. Males who have had punishing experiences with females, including their mothers, will tend to avoid females, and if such avoidance is coupled with sexual satisfaction from males, then the situation is clearly conducive to the development of homosexual orientation.

It can be noted that many elements of this behavioral analysis are very much in keeping with the psychodynamic theory of the conflict-ridden mother-son relationship. The similarity between these two points of view is nicely illustrated in a study by Evans (1969) of 43 male homosexuals, all members of a West Coast Gay Liberation group. In contrast to a matched group of heterosexuals, the homosexuals recalled themselves during their childhood as frail, clumsy, and less athletic. Most were afraid of physical injury, tended to play with girls rather than boys, and thought of themselves as loners who seldom entered into competitive games. The mothers of the homosexuals were more likely to be seen as cold and puritanical, demanding of the son's attention, preferring the son to the father in an open and demanding sort of way, interfering with the development of relations with girls during adolescence, and generally encouraging feminine attitudes while discouraging masculine attitudes. The homosexuals spent less time with their fathers, reported more negative feelings toward their fathers, and were in general more afraid that their fathers might harm or injure them. While certain of these findings are clearly supportive of the psychodynamic position—indeed, they have been taken as further evidence for Bieber's family theory—the results of Evans' study are also in keeping with the view of homosexuality as learned predisposition or preference.

Treatment In treating homosexuals who are clearly desirous of initiating heterosexual contacts, behavior therapists have had some success with systematic desensitization, assertive training, and modeling procedures (Stevenson and Wolpe, 1960; Ellis, 1965), all aimed not at homosexual behaviors, but rather at training the patient in effective heterosexual behaviors. Other treatment successes have been reported through the use of such aversive conditioning techniques as administering mild electric shocks to the penis while showing homosexual pictures or while eliciting homosexual fantasies (Wilson and Davison, 1974; Barlow, 1974). Some behavioral treatments have also experimented with a technique called *behavioral contracting*, in which the patient commits himself, perhaps even through a written contract, to making a certain number of behavioral changes within a certain period of time (Freeman and Meyer, 1975).

The Humanistic-Existential Perspective

Humanistic-existential theory may see homosexuality, male or female, as a lack of authentic choice, but only where homosexuality is part of a total pattern of disturbed functioning. Humanists have been at the forefront of the movement to recognize homosexuality as a potentially valid form of sexual expression. Humanists emphasize the risks of a commitment to homosexuality in a society that is so heavily geared to heterosexuality, but they would validate such a choice if it was made with full awareness. In such a case, the humanistic or existential therapist, instead of attempting to reorient the patient to a more socially acceptable pattern, would concentrate on the patient's accepting responsibility for his choice and on his development of honest, authentic, and fulfilling relationships. And in view of the finding, by the Task Force on Homosexuality of the National Institutes of Mental Health, that only about one-fourth of the people who are exclusively homosexual can effect any change in this pattern through current therapies, the humanistic-existential approach may represent the most pragmatic as well as the most humane treatment of the exclusively homosexual patients.

The Biological Perspective

The oldest theory of homosexuality, and one that is still widely accepted by the general public, is that it is due to genetic or hormonal defects. The scientific support for this formulation is extremely flimsy. In the case of genetic etiology, Kallman (1952) originally reported 100 percent concordance rates for homosexuality in monozygotic twins, as compared to a concordance rate of less than 15 percent for dizygotic twins. However, later research (Pritchard, 1962; Parker, 1964) has failed to confirm this evidence, and at the moment the genetic theory of homosexuality remains one of the least convincing.

The hormonal theory centers on the role of testosterone, the hormone that is largely responsible for the development of such male secondary sexual characteristics as beard growth, deepening of the voice, and sperm production. According to the hormonal hypothesis, abnormally low levels of testosterone might be responsible for the development of homosexuality. And, in fact, testosterone abnormalities have been found in studies of homosexuals. Loraine and co-workers (1971) found less urinary testosterone in homosexual men than in heterosexual men, and more testosterone in lesbians than in heterosexual women. Similarly, Kolodny and his colleagues (1971) found lower plasma tes-

Fig. 9.10 *Psychologists and psychiatrists have applied conditioning methods to homosexual behavior. This photograph illustrates the procedure of visual desensitization, in which a subject who experiences anxiety in response to female stimuli is given relaxation training. When the subject is in a relaxed state, an image of a woman is projected onto a screen, and the subject is told to indicate the point at which he begins to feel anxious. After a time, the subject remains in a relaxed state for progressively longer periods, until he feels no anxiety in the presence of female stimuli.*

tosterone as well as poorer-quality sperm in male homosexuals than in heterosexuals. However, Brodie et al., (1974) found higher plasma testosterone in a group of homosexuals than in a carefully matched group of heterosexuals. In sum, the "born homosexual" theory still lacks any substantial support.

SUMMARY

This chapter has been devoted to sexual abnormalities, the social sanctions on which are very stringent. While the human sexual impulse is capable of gratification through a wide range of outlets, society and the psychiatric profession tend to regard heterosexual coitus as the only normal outlet. Our discussion has been devoted to three forms of abnormality: sexual inadequacy, sexual deviations, and homosexuality.

Sexual inadequacy—which may take the form of primary impotence, secondary impotence, premature ejaculation, ejaculatory incompetence, primary orgasmic dysfunction, situational orgasmic dysfunc-

tion, vaginismus, or dyspareunia—has been studied intensively in recent years by Masters and Johnson, who see performance anxiety and the spectator role as primary etiological factors. These investigators have had considerable treatment success through what are basically behavior-modification techniques.

The sexual disorders that we have discussed include fetishism, transvestism, transsexualism, exhibitionism, voyeurism, pedophilia, incest, rape, sadism, and masochism. These behaviors occur primarily in males, and many of them are thought to result from feelings of sexual inadequacy that prevent the male from pursuing more acceptable forms of gratification. While psychodynamic theorists stress the etiological role of continuing castration anxiety, behavior theorists see sexual disorders primarily as the result of early respondent conditioning.

In both schools of thought, essentially the same mechanisms are invoked as explanations of homosexuality. However, homosexuality differs from the other disorders in that it is a much more common behavior and is currently being reconsidered by both psychological professionals and the society as a possibly legitimate sexual preference. At the same time, a number of misconceptions about homosexuality are being disproven, and investigators are exploring the various coping styles of different types of homosexuals, as well as the difference between male homosexual and lesbian relationships. While genetic and hormonal theories of homosexuality lack scientific evidence, both the psychodynamic and the behavioral interpretations have received some measure of scientific support, and both schools have had some treatment successes. However, homosexuality remains extremely difficult to treat, and some thinkers, including humanistic-existential theorists, have argued that the best treatment for the homosexual without other adjustment problems may be to help him to accept his orientation and to establish fulfilling homosexual relationships.

234

The very word "drug" sends shivers down the spines of many Americans. Yet by far the majority of Americans indulge either occasionally or regularly in some form of *psychoactive drug*—that is, a drug that alters one's psychological state. While certain people go to the trouble of seeking out illegal drugs, most Americans confine their "kicks" to such legal drugs as alcohol, nicotine, and caffeine, which, precisely because they *are* legal, tend not to be looked upon as drugs. Yet the fact is that the legal drugs may be equally as harmful, if not more harmful, than many of the illegal drugs. However, in the case of almost all these drugs, legal or illegal, occasional dabbling in minor doses rarely results in any great harm. The point at which psychological and physiological damage begin to set in is when the indulgence becomes habitual, and when the body seems to crave the drug. This is the condition that we call drug abuse, a psychological problem considerably more pervasive than most of the other disorders discussed in this book.

Discussion of drug abuse is difficult because neither the society nor the mental health professions have as yet agreed on a clear and consistent terminology. Nevertheless, there is a fairly general consensus that when the individual begins to orient his existence around the drug experience, there is cause for serious concern. Whether conscious or unconscious, it is this focusing of life on the drug and the drug experience that seems to separate the pathological use of a drug from simple recreational use.

The term *addiction* may be defined in either a broad or a narrow sense. The broad definition may be seen in the description of addiction offered by the World Health Organization (WHO):

Drug addiction is a state of periodic or chronic intoxication detrimental to the individual and to society, produced by the repeated consumption of a drug (natural or synthetic). Its characteristics include: 1) an overpowering desire or need (compulsion) to continue taking the drug and to obtain it by any means, 2) a tendency to increase the dosage, and 3) a psychic (psychological) and sometimes physical dependence on the effects of the drug (1965, p. 722).

However, many professionals confine the term "addiction" to the state of *physiological* need. According to this definition, addiction is the condition whereby the body's chemical functioning has altered in such a way that its "normal" state is the drugged state. To maintain homeostasis—that is, relatively normal functioning—the drug must be present in the body. Furthermore, once the body has become ha-

10
The Addictive Disorders

bituated to the drug, the usual dosage may no longer provide the desired "high"—a phenomenon known as *tolerance*. Some alcoholics, for example, can drink a quart of whiskey a day without seeming intoxicated (Mello and Mendelson, 1970). And as tolerance develops, the individual will begin taking larger and larger amounts of the drug. Whatever the amount, the addicted person, if deprived of the drug, will undergo *withdrawal symptoms*, temporary psychological and physiological disturbances resulting from the body's attempt to readjust to the absence of the drug. It is important to note, however, that not all drugs result in physiological addiction. Hence the term *drug dependence* has been introduced to describe the condition of *psychological* need for a drug that is not physiologically addictive. Such psychological dependence can be every bit as potent and destructive as physiological addiction.

In terms of their effects on behavior, there is very little difference between addiction and dependence. In both cases, the person's existence, as we have mentioned, becomes centered around obtaining and using the drug. All other considerations—personal appearance, family, job, studies—become secondary. Thoughts of safety and morality also go down the drain. Needing money to support his habit, the addict may resort to mugging or prostitution. Furthermore, the simple lowering of behavioral controls under the influence of drug intoxication often leads to assault or to automobile accidents. In short, there is ample justification for the current rise in social concern over drug abuse. This concern is evidenced in the recent establishment of the National Institute of Drug Abuse and the National Institute of Alcohol Abuse and Alcoholism as equal to the much older National Institute of Mental Health. In the last few years there has also been a rapid proliferation of alcohol- and drug-treatment centers and of educational programs aimed at the prevention of alcohol and drug abuse—ideas whose time has most definitely come.

In this chapter we will discuss five classes of drugs: alcohol, depressants, stimulants, hallucinogens, and marijuana. Alcohol is actually a depressant, but because it is one of the most heavily abused drugs in our society, it will be treated separately and will be given greater emphasis than the other drugs. In the case of alcohol and the other drugs, we will review the current theories as to the etiology and treatment of abuse.

One fact that bears mentioning before we go on to discuss the individual drugs is that in many cases they are not used individually. Some drug users like

to combine effects, the usual combination being marijuana and alcohol. Other drug users switch repeatedly from one drug to another. Apparently, once they enter the illegal-drug abuse subculture, they use whatever is available on the street, and in some cases they will use just about anything. (People have been known to inject peanut butter.) As a result, the current trend in drug-treatment centers is to deal with the patient as a person who seeks *a* drug experience—any alteration in his state of consciousness—rather than to worry over whether he is an alcoholic, a heroin addict, or an acid head. Yet despite this trend, information on multiple drug use is still very scarce. Current researchers have difficulty enough in studying the effects of single drugs, to say nothing of various combinations. Hence we will have to confine our discussion to what we know something about: the individual effects of the most common drugs.

ALCOHOLISM

For thousands of years alcohol has been the traditional "high" of Western culture. And of all the drugs that we will discuss in this chapter, it is the only one that is legally purchasable in most parts of the United States. For both these reasons, alcohol is the most widely used of all the psychoactive drugs. In 1974 about two-thirds of the population of the United States over fifteen years of age drank alcoholic beverages on some occasion, and 58 percent reported that they drank once a month or more. Ten percent of the over-fifteen population drank more than 1.0 ounce of absolute alcohol each day. That 1.0 ounce of absolute alcohol can be obtained in either 2.5 ounces of distilled spirits (about 2 mixed drinks), *or* 7 ounces (about 2 glasses) of wine, *or* 22 ounces (about 2 cans) of beer. The average yearly consumption of those who drink more than once a month is about 4.4 gallons of distilled spirits, *and* 3.7 gallons of wine, *and* 45.2 gallons of beer. Substantial as this ration may seem, many people consume alcohol at a much higher rate: an estimated 9 million Americans are alcoholics (U.S. DHEW, 1974).

Estimates of the incidence of alcoholism of course vary in relation to one's definition of the disorder. A commonly accepted definition of *alcoholism* is that provided by DSM-II:

This category is for patients whose alcohol intake is great enough to damage their physical health, or their personal or social functioning, or when it has become a prerequisite for normal functioning (1968, p. 45).

Fig. 10.1   An individual's use or abuse of drugs is determined by a combination of psychological, sociological, and physiological factors that vary from person to person.

A crucial phrase in this definition is the last one. Contrary to popular belief, in order to be a drunk, one needn't look drunk. Indeed, according to the rather arbitrary guideline set up by DSM-II, one can be an alcoholic and still not show intoxication—that is, slurring of speech, stumbling, and so forth—more than four times a year. But while he may not become intoxicated, the alcoholic must constantly maintain a certain level of alcohol in his blood in order to function "normally." Without alcohol in his system, he feels tense, "out of sorts," and physically sick.

The Social Cost of Alcoholism

It is impossible to measure the suffering endured by the society at large as a result of alcohol abuse. Easier to measure is the amount of money it costs. It is estimated that alcohol-related problems cost American society $25 billion in 1971. Most of this

Smoking: *The Most Common Form of Drug Dependence*

Discussions of psychoactive drugs often give little if any attention to the most common form of drug dependence in the United States: tobacco-smoking. The reason smoking tends to be ignored in discussions of drug abuse is that of all the psychoactive drugs, nicotine is the least destructive psychologically. Indeed, it appears to do no psychological damage whatsoever. Thus the heavy smoker can go through three packs a day, year after year, well into his eighties or nineties without ever worrying that the nicotine will cloud his memory, distort his perceptions, or warp his mental functioning in any way. However, the chances of his reaching his eighties or nineties are poor. For tobacco is almost as dangerous physiologically as it is benign psychologically.

In 1964, years of suspicions and research regarding the hazards of tobacco finally culminated in the famous "Surgeon General's Report" (U.S. Public Health Service, 1964), which presented compelling evidence that smoking was a major contributor to lung cancer, heart disease, emphysema, and other fatal illnesses. Since 1964 further studies have merely confirmed this claim. Those who smoke less than a pack of cigarettes a day have a death rate four times higher than the nonsmoker; those who smoke more than a pack a day have a death rate seven times higher than the nonsmoker. For certain specific ailments, the risks shoot even higher. For example, any man who smokes is ten times as likely as a nonsmoker to die of lung cancer (U.S. Department of Health, Education, and Welfare, 1974).

These findings have resulted in legislation banning tobacco advertisements from radio and television and requiring that each pack of cigarettes sold in this country carry an advertisement of its own potentially lethal effects: "Warning: The Surgeon General Has Determined That Cigarette Smoking Is Dangerous to Your Health." But strangely enough, these dismal warnings appear to have had no effect on smoking patterns in the United States. In 1964, the year of the Surgeon General's Report, cigarette consumption did decline by approximately 2 percent (Skinner, 1970, p. 27). But the following year Americans were once again smoking just as much as they had

in 1963. And since then, annual consumption has remained at approximately the same level—that is, about 210 packs per person over the age of 18 ("Tobacco: Basic Analysis," 1975).

Thus it is clear that smoking is one of the most potent of all drug habits, but why this should be so is not at all clear. Some investigators (e.g., Brecher, 1972) argue that the cause is simply physiological addiction to nicotine, which is a central nervous system stimulant. Others (e.g., Bernstein, 1969) contend that the dependence is psychological, though the psychological reward most often reported—a mild sense of relaxation—would appear slight compared to the enormity of the hazards involved. In either case, whether physiological or psychological, the tobacco habit is one that many people seem utterly unable to break. A pathetic example is that of Sigmund Freud's addiction. Knowing full well that his practice of smoking as many as twenty cigars a day was weakening his heart and engendering cancerous growths in his mouth and jaw, Freud, after numerous futile attempts to end the habit, decided that without his cigars he simply could not maintain the psychological strength to continue his work. And so, even after his entire jaw had to be replaced by a clumsy artificial jaw, he continued smoking as long as his mouth could hold a cigar. Finally, in 1939, after cancer had eaten through his cheek as well, Freud died. It cannot be said that he died young—he lived to be eighty-three—but his death came only after years and years of harrowing physical pain.

Freud's helplessness in the face of his deadly habit is in no way unique. Treatment programs for smokers tend to report the same results that Freud showed repeatedly: successful abstention followed by relapse. Mark Twain summed it up neatly. He could stop smoking, he said, with the greatest of ease; indeed, he had done so hundreds of times. Some people do break the habit for good, but they are the exceptions. In the face of alarming medical evidence, increasing social disapproval, much nagging by nonsmokers, and rising cigarette prices, it appears that as many Americans are smoking as ever before.

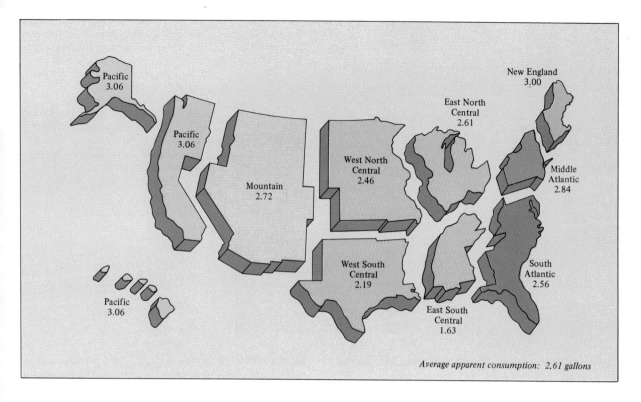

Pacific
3.06

New England
3.00

Pacific
3.06

East North
Central
2.61

Mountain
2.72

West North
Central
2.46

Middle
Atlantic
2.84

Pacific
3.06

West South
Central
2.19

South
Atlantic
2.56

East South
Central
1.63

Average apparent consumption: 2.61 gallons

economic loss was concentrated in three areas: motor vehicle accidents, decreased work productivity, and health problems.

The largest portion of this loss is due to decreased work productivity. Alcohol and work do not mix. The worker with a drinking problem is slower and less efficient, loses time on the job (e.g., coming in late because of a hangover, leaving early after having too many drinks at lunch), makes hasty decisions, causes accidents, and lowers the morale of his co-workers. Furthermore, he is more likely to become prematurely disabled and to die young. What all of this adds up to is an estimated loss of $9 billion in decreased productivity. And this estimate is conservative, since it covers only male workers and does not take into account the loss of productivity of institutionalized or skid-row alcoholics.

As for the health services required to minister to America's drinking problems, the annual cost is over $8 billion. Astoundingly, $5.3 billion—that is, *20 percent of the country's total annual expenditure for the hospital care of adults for any reason*—was spent for the hospital care of alcoholics.

Finally, $6.4 billion is lost annually in alcohol-related motor vehicle accidents. Before commenting on the relationship between drinking and driving, it is necessary to clarify the matter of blood alcohol

Fig. 10.2   This map shows the apparent alcohol consumption, in gallons per person (age fifteen and over), by region of the United States in 1970. The Pacific and New England regions consume the greatest amount, the South Central regions the least.

levels. The effects of alcohol on the nervous system—and consequently, on the drinker's behavior—are directly proportionate to the amount of alcohol in the bloodstream. This latter factor is called the *blood alcohol level*, which is expressed in terms of the amount of alcohol in relation to a specific volume of blood. Table 10.1 indicates the approximate relationship between alcohol intake and blood alcohol levels. Note well that there is a sex difference. Women have less body fluid (but more fat) per pound of body weight. Therefore, if a 150-pound woman and a 150-pound man go out and have five drinks apiece, she will have a higher blood alcohol level, and consequently will be more intoxicated, than he.

In most states a person with a blood alcohol level of 0.10 percent is labeled as intoxicated. In all states a level of 0.15 percent is clear legal evidence of intoxication. And well it should be. As Table 10.2 indicates, a person with a blood alcohol level of 0.15 percent is in no position to be trusted with his own

Body Weight (lbs.)	Number of Drinks*											
	1	2	3	4	5	6	7	8	9	10	11	12
100	.038	.075	.113	.150	.188	.225	.263	.300	.338	.375	.418	.450
120	.031	.063	.094	.125	.156	.188	.219	.250	.281	.313	.344	.375
140	.027	.054	.080	.107	.134	.161	.188	.214	.241	.268	.285	.321
160	.023	.047	.070	.094	.117	.141	.164	.188	.211	.234	.258	.281
180	.021	.042	.063	.083	.104	.125	.146	.167	.188	.208	.229	.250
200	.019	.038	.056	.075	.094	.113	.131	.150	.169	.188	.206	.225
220	.017	.034	.051	.068	.085	.102	.119	.136	.153	.170	.188	.205
240	.016	.031	.047	.063	.078	.094	.109	.125	.141	.156	.172	.188

Under .05 Driving not seriously impaired	.05 to .10 Driving increasingly dangerous (.08 legally drunk in Utah)	.10 to .15 Driving dangerous (legally drunk in many states)	Over .15 Driving VERY dangerous (legally drunk in any state)

*One drink equals 1 ounce of 100 proof liquor or 12 ounces of beer.

Fig. 10.3 As this chart shows, increased consumption of alcohol results in higher blood levels of alcohol and greater danger in driving an automobile. Excessive alcohol consumption has a variety of consequences, including psychological, social, and organic dysfunctions. Although psychological effects are incalculable, statistics on the traffic fatalities involving intoxicated drivers are indeed staggering. (Data from the New Jersey Department of Law and Public Safety, Division of Motor Vehicles, Trenton, New Jersey.)

or anyone else's safety. Some European countries, more cautious than we are, put the intoxication level at 0.05 percent.

The relationship between blood alcohol level and motor vehicle accidents is unequivocal enough to make one want to give up driving permanently. About 40 percent of motor vehicle deaths are attributable to drivers with a blood alcohol level above 0.05 percent. Much could be discussed here, but three points must suffice. First is the obvious fact that blood alcohol level is directly proportionate to the probability of an accident, a serious injury, and/or a fatality while driving. The more you have drunk—and unfortunately, the more the driver coming toward you has drunk—the more likely you are to have an accident. Thus the motto "If you drive, don't drink, if you drink, don't drive" is no empty homily.

The second point is that most motor vehicle fatalities involve drivers with blood alcohol levels above 0.10 percent. These are not social drinkers. To reach a blood level this high, a 180-pound man would have to consume 5 drinks within an hour on an empty stomach—hardly the thing that a moderate drinker would do. For the most part, motor vehicle fatalities are caused by alcoholics, not by drunk social drinkers.

Finally, while plenty of sober drivers have automobile accidents, accidents involving alcohol are much more likely to result in death. Two out of three single-car fatalities involve a driver with a blood

alcohol level of about 0.10 percent. In one out of three fatal adult pedestrian accidents, the *pedestrian* has a blood alcohol level of above 0.10 percent. Hence the New Year's Eve roadblock is not just to let you know that the police are working. Crossing the street or behind the wheel, the drunk stands a good chance of ending his days without having to wait for cirrhosis of the liver.

There is another area in which the social damage associated with alcohol is very visible but less frequently studied. This is the contribution of alcohol use to physical assault and sexual offenses. In one careful study of young offenders (Tinklenberg and Woodrow, 1974), alcohol use was involved in 30 percent of all the corroborated assaults in which tissue damage occurred and in 30 percent of the deaths. In fact, alcohol use was involved in about half of those physical assaults in which the assailant was under the influence of some drug. In the area of sexual offenses—pedophilia and forcible rape—alcohol was involved in 32 percent of the cases. These alcohol-related sexual offenses accounted for 90 percent of the drug-related sexual offenses. In commenting on this evidence, Tinklenberg and Woodrow conclude that violence in the adolescent under the influence of alcohol tends to be "a process of enhanced irritability and indiscriminate assaultive tendencies directed toward anyone who might happen to be present" (p. 223). In short, the drunk can cause serious social damage long before he is old enough to get a driver's license.

Table 10.1 Relationships Among Sex, Weight, Oral Alcohol Consumption, and Blood Alcohol Level

Absolute alcohol (ounces)	Beverage intake*	Blood alcohol levels (mg/100ml)					
		Female (100 lbs.)	Male (100 lbs.)	Female (150 lbs.)	Male (150 lbs.)	Female (200 lbs.)	Male (200 lbs.)
½	1 oz. spirits[+] 1 glass wine 1 can beer	0.045	0.037	0.03	0.025	0.022	0.019
1	2 oz. spirits 2 glasses wine 2 cans beer	0.09	0.075	0.06	0.05	0.045	0.037
2	4 oz. spirits 4 glasses wine 4 cans beer	0.18	0.15	0.12	0.10	0.09	0.07
3	6 oz. spirits 6 glasses wine 6 cans beer	0.27	0.22	0.18	0.15	0.13	0.11
4	8 oz. spirits 8 glasses wine 8 cans beer	0.36	0.30	0.24	0.20	0.18	0.15
5	10 oz. spirits 10 glasses wine 10 cans beer	0.45	0.37	0.30	0.25	0.22	0.18

*In 1 hour.
[+] 100 proof spirits.

Source: O. S. Ray. *Drugs, Society and Human Behavior*, St. Louis, Mo.: Mosby Company, update 1974.

Table 10.2 Blood Alcohol Level: Physiological and Psychological Results

Blood alcohol level	Effect	Blood alcohol level	Behavior
0.05%	Lowered alertness; usually good feeling	0.03%	Dull and dignified
0.10%	Slowed reaction times; less caution	0.05%	Dashing and debonair
0.15%	Large, consistent increases in reaction time	0.10%	May become dangerous and devilish
0.20%	Marked depression in sensory and motor capability, decidedly intoxicated	0.20%	Likely to be dizzy and disturbing
0.25%	Severe motor disturbance, staggering; sensory perceptions greatly impaired	0.25%	May be disgusting and disheveled
0.30%	Semistupor	0.30%	Delirious and disoriented and surely drunk
0.35%	Surgical anesthesia; minimal lethal dose	0.35%	Dead drunk
0.40%	Probable lethal dose	0.60%	Chances are that he is dead

Source: O. S. Ray. *Drugs, Society and Human Behavior*, St. Louis, Mo.: Mosby Company, update 1974.

The Personal Cost of Alcoholism

The Immediate Effects of Alcohol Pharmacologically, alcohol is a depressant. It slows down and interferes with the transmission of electrical impulses in the higher brain centers, areas that control, organize, and inhibit some of our more complex mental processes. And it is precisely because of this disinhibiting effect that we use alcohol to ease our way in social situations. It helps us to relax, stop worrying about what other people think of us, and just have a good time.

By the time the blood alcohol level reaches 0.03 to 0.06 percent, two types of effect occur. First, the behaviors and thoughts that were being controlled and inhibited begin to appear and get expressed. Since what was inhibited will vary from individual to individual, the behaviors released by the alcohol will also vary. Some of us become amorous, some boisterous, some belligerent. The second effect is that judgment and the ability to make discrim-inations are impaired. Amorous types will begin making wanton remarks to the boss's wife, belligerent types will start fights with people twice their size, and so forth.

As the blood alcohol level continues to rise, the depressant effect of alcohol becomes more obvious. We slow down, stumble over nothing, and slur our words. Judgment is further impaired, and we begin engaging in some even riskier behaviors. Whatever anxieties we would normally feel gradually dissolve. Remorse over past misdeeds and fear of future failures recede. Likewise, we cease to feel guilty over whatever ugly or foolish behaviors we are engaged in at the moment, whether it be running through a stop sign or kicking our dog or giving a detailed account of our first sexual experience to our great-aunts over Thanksgiving dinner. It is probably this level—the release from anxiety over past, present, and future sins, real or imaginary—that the alcoholic seeks to maintain. And because he builds up a toler-

ance for alcohol, he has to drink more and more in order to maintain it.

The Long-Term Effects of Alcohol Abuse The process of intoxication that we have just described is something that most of us experience at some time in our lives, usually to no great harm. However, the habitual overuse of alcohol can result in severe psychological and physiological deterioration.

Alcohol abuse is usually resorted to as a way of coping with, or at least enduring, life's problems. The sadly ironic result is that the alcoholic ends up with many more problems than he had before and with fewer resources for dealing with them. Hence he drinks more. Hence he has more problems. In short, a classic vicious circle. In the process, his mental acuteness is lost; memory, judgment, and the power to concentrate are all diminished. Because of his unruly behavior, he loses both respect and self-respect. He neglects and alienates his friends, and his family life becomes a bitter stew of remorse and abuse. Often unable to work, the alcoholic typically feels guilty toward his family, but at the same time he takes out his problems on them. Child-beating, for example, is very often connected with alcohol abuse. In the end, the alcoholic may find himself deserted by his employer, his friends, his family, and his former talents. In short, the psychological damage can be devastating.

Equally serious are the physiological consequences of alcoholism. Habitual overuse of alcohol can cause stomach ulcers, hypertension, or heart failure. Furthermore, the alcoholic is subject to grave physical malfunctions simply as a result of malnutrition. Alcohol is high in calories and therefore provides energy, but it is totally devoid of any known nutrient. Deriving his energy from alcohol, the alcoholic typically eats very little and very unselectively, with the result that his protein and vitamin intake are dangerously insufficient. In one out of every ten alcoholics, the protein deficiency leads to cirrhosis of the liver, a circulatory problem that often leads directly to death. In addition, older alcoholics may develop Korsakoff's psychosis (Chapter 14), a severe memory loss thought to be caused by vitamin B deficiency.

Should the chronic alcoholic's blood alcohol level drop suddenly, he may enter *delirium tremens*, literally translated as "trembling delirium" and better known as the DTs. This psychotic reaction, which is actually a withdrawal symptom, is perhaps the most dramatic demonstration of the profound physical change that the chronic alcoholic undergoes. Deprived of his needed dosage, the patient with DTs trembles furiously, perspires in streams, becomes disoriented, and suffers delusions that he is being stalked and attacked by all manner of disgusting and terrifying creatures—snakes in this corner, rats in that corner, cockroaches and spiders under his clothes. This condition usually lasts for three to six days, after which the typical patient vows he will never take another drink in his life, demands to be discharged from the hospital, and heads for the nearest bar.

The Making of an Alcoholic

As we shall see further along in this chapter, there is considerable confusion as to what type of person is likely to become an alcoholic. Nevertheless, it does appear that alcoholics, however much they may differ from one another, tend to go through the same general sequence of behaviors in their progression toward total dependence on alcohol. On the basis of a study of two thousand alcoholics, Jellinek (1946) has outlined the sequence as follows:

1. *Periodic excessive drinking.* Ninety percent of alcoholics begin drinking excessively in social situations; only 10 percent begin with solitary drinking. In both cases, however, the alcoholic-to-be discovers that drinking provides a welcome release from tension.
2. *Blackouts.* Eventually the drinker begins to experience "blackouts"—periods of time in which, under the influence of alcohol, he remains conscious and may carry on in a fairly normal fashion, but of which he has no memory the following day. About 30 percent of moderate drinkers also experience blackouts at some time in their lives. But since the incidence of this reaction is three times as great among people who become alcoholics, the blackout can be regarded as an ill omen.
3. *Sneaking drinks.* Around the time of the blackouts, the future alcoholic is likely to begin "sneaking drinks"—that is, finding a chance to have a few more drinks than the rest of the company without their knowing it. For example, at a dinner party in a restaurant, he may excuse himself to go to the bathroom and then hurry off to the bar to gulp down a quick one.
4. *Loss of control over drinking.* Around two years after the beginning of the blackouts, the drinker finds that he is almost always drinking more than he means to. He is not yet compelled, when sober, to take a drink. But once he starts drinking, he seems unable to stop.

Fig. 10.4 Factors that affect an individual's use or abuse of alcohol include family background, prior experience, social customs, and personal expectations.

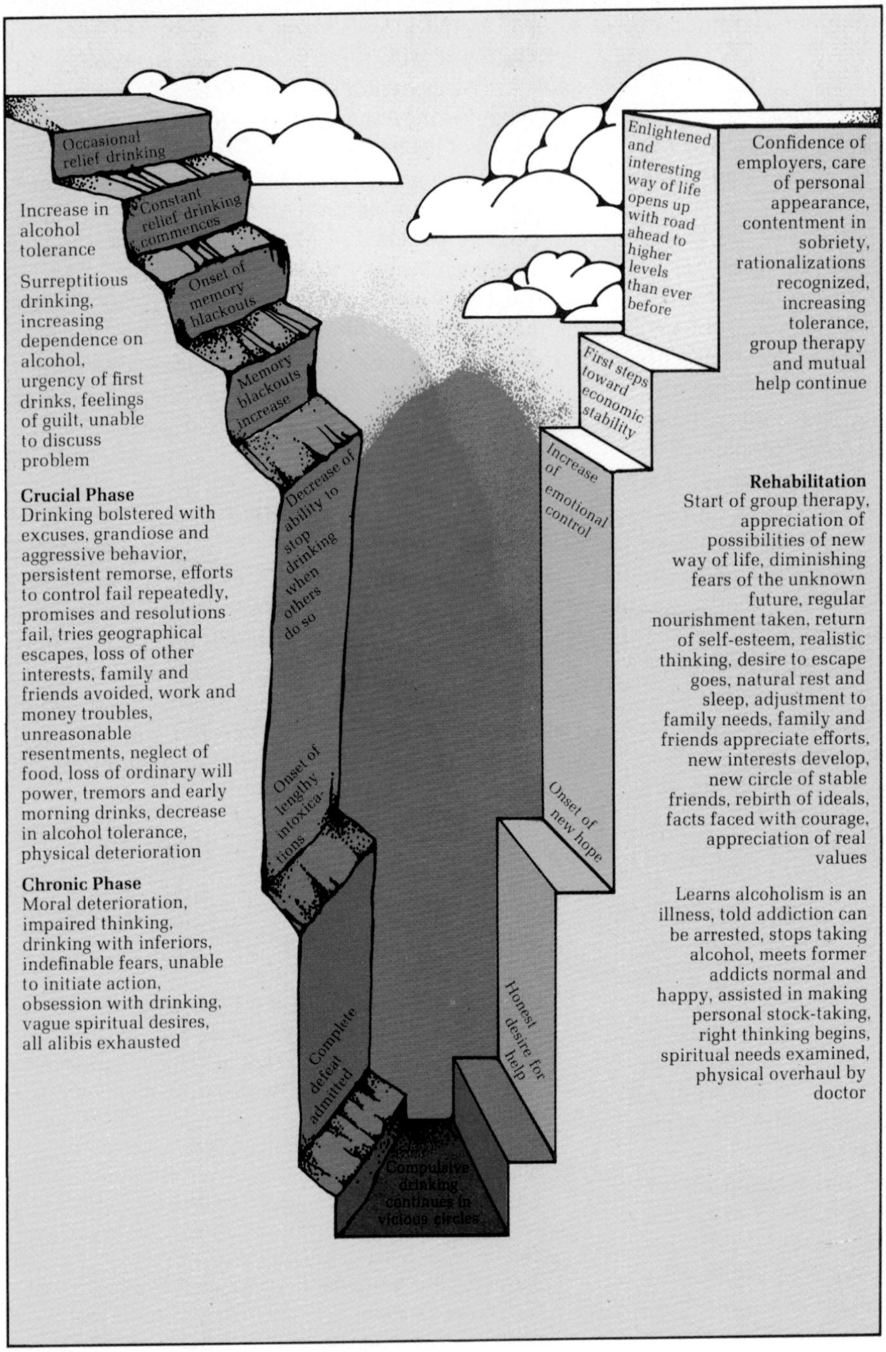

Fig. 10.5 Stages of alcoholism and steps toward recovery are depicted in this diagram. (Adapted from H. M. Glatt, "Group Therapy in Alcoholism," British Journal of Addiction, 54, 1957.)

According to Jellinek, this response marks the beginning of the crucial phase of alcoholism.

5. *Remorse and rationalization.* As the crucial phase progresses, the drinker begins to be seriously worried about his drinking and increasingly remorseful about his drunken behavior. At this point he begins rationalizing his drinking, convincing himself that he got drunk not because he lost control but because he had a "good reason"—trying job, nagging wife, good-for-nothing kids, whatever—to drink too much.

6. *Changing pattern of drinking.* In a last-ditch attempt to regain control over his alcohol consumption, the drinker may, in the crucial phase, decide that his problem is what he drinks or the way he drinks rather than the fact that he drinks too much. Hence he will alter his pattern of drinking—swear off alcohol before a certain hour, switch from whiskey to wine, or make some other change that he presumes will solve his problem.

7. *Morning drinking.* About one year after the beginning of the rationalizations, the drinker, regardless of what his changed pattern is, will usually begin taking a drink in the morning in order to "get himself going."

8. *Benders.* One to three years after the onset of morning drinking, the drinker begins going on "benders"—that is, alcoholic binges lasting several days, during which he totally disregards work and family. Jellinek claims that the onset of benders marks the beginning of the compulsive phase of alcoholism.

9. *Defeat.* Within a few years after the beginning of the benders, the alcoholic's life becomes centered on drinking. Now he begins to suffer alcohol-related physical ailments, possibly including the DTs, and may have to be hospitalized periodically. At this point also the rationalization system breaks down, and whether or not he does anything to save himself, the alcoholic knows that he is "licked."

Jellinek found that this entire sequence, from the beginning of excessive drinking to the utter surrender to alcohol, took between twelve and eighteen years. However, for some the road to alcoholism may be much shorter. Others may never have blackouts. Others may never change their drinking pattern beyond increasing their intake. In short, the sequence outlined by Jellinek must be seen as simply a general outline. Furthermore, it must be seen as an outline of the typical *male* progression, since Jellinek's study was confined to men. There is still a great scarcity of information on alcoholism in women.

The following case history may put some flesh on the bones of Jellinek's analysis:

This 45-year-old white male, who works as a construction foreman during his sober periods, completed eight years of education and served two years in the army during the Korean War. He started drinking at the age of eighteen, and although he reports that his drinking has been a problem only for the last ten years, he also admitted that he had been court-martialed three times in the army and had spent six months in the stockade for alcohol-related offenses.

He described himself as a "spree" drinker, but his heavy-drinking episodes now last three to four weeks and occur about six times a year. During these drinking periods, according to his statement, he consumes at least a quart of whiskey, a gallon of wine, and one to three six-packs of beer per day. He has had loss of memory and times of extreme shakes and hallucinations on a "few" occasions. He has had so many

arrests for public drunkenness that he cannot even estimate their number. He has also had one arrest for drunk driving. He reports that both of his brothers are also alcoholics. His father drank heavily for years but was dry for the year before his death.

On his first known admission five years ago, the patient denied that he had been drinking heavily and said he had only a few beers a day. He was brought to the hospital by his wife because he was talking to the television, hearing strange music, and seeing bugs and snakes. He was detoxified [that is, withdrawn from alcohol through a medical procedure that we will discuss later in this chapter]. On his next admission, two years ago, he said that he had not been working more than a day or two at a time and that his wife supported him by working as a manager at a local department store. His mother lives in the same apartment complex and contributes some money whenever possible.

During his second admission he said that he was ready to go into a treatment program, but he managed to miss all of his scheduled appointments and evaluations. He requested a long pass to "look for work," and when he was told that he wasn't ready to leave the hospital, he returned to his room, dressed, and left.

A year later his wife brought him to the hospital because she had returned from work to find him unconscious on the floor. His heart was pounding furiously, and he was blood-red in color and gasping for breath. After sobering up in the hospital, he said that he had "too many troubles" to handle and that these troubles depressed him. He drank to feel better, but sometimes he just thought he would be better off dead. He said he didn't feel that way now that he was sober and in the hospital. And he swore that he was "willing to do anything to get better."

Everyone was convinced, and eight days later he was given a one-day pass to visit his wife before entering the alcohol treatment program. He returned sober from the pass, but he must have brought a bottle with him, since the next morning he was intoxicated and unable to begin the treatment program. He left the hospital two days later against the advice of the staff.

The staff's last contact with this patient took place six months ago, when he was brought to the hospital by ambulance after passing out in a downtown alley. A companion reported that the patient had drunk a case of beer in one hour (which is not possible). He left the hospital three days later and has not yet returned.

PERSPECTIVES ON ALCOHOLISM

What causes alcoholism? Why is it that some people are able to drink heavily and regularly for long periods of time without becoming addicted or centering their life on alcohol, while others seem to become dependent on alcohol the first time they smell it? What is the basis for this difference in sensitivity? The answer is yet to be found. As we shall see in the following section, there is a vast grab bag of theories regarding the origins of alcoholism, but even with the most popular and convincing theories, there is often as much evidence to dispute them as to support them. As far as we know at this point, there are as many different kinds of alcoholics as there are different kinds of people. The alcoholic may be the solitary drinker at the end of the bar who talks to no one. He may be the noisy one at the pinball machine. He may be the Junior Chamber of Commerce Man of the Year. He may be your congressman, your father, your roommate, or even you. The only trait that we know for certain is shared by all alcoholics is the need for alcohol.

This is not to say, however, that there are no predisposing factors—only that there is no single etiological agent that can be traced in all or even most cases. Furthermore, as with most other types of abnormal behaviors, there are probably multiple factors underlying each case of alcoholism. It is also likely that the importance of different factors will vary from individual to individual.

The Psychodynamic Perspective

Cause The psychodynamic theorists of course hold that alcoholism is merely the symptom of an unconscious emotional problem. As for what that problem might be, there are at present two major theories. The first is that alcoholism is a reflection of unsatisfied dependency needs. This dependence, in turn, is thought to stem from oral fixation. There is some evidence that alcoholics may in fact have more intense oral needs than other people. For example, alcoholics are much more likely than nonalcoholics to be heavy cigarette smokers (Maletzky and Klotter, 1974). Other research has shown that boys with high oral needs are more likely than others to become alcoholics. As for the dependency of the alcoholic, this theory is supported by a wealth of research data (McCord et al., 1960) and is likely to receive the hearty assent of anyone who has lived with an alcoholic. It is no secret that alcoholics are not self-sufficient types, willing to take responsibility for their actions. On the contrary, they tend to seek out anyone and anything—including, of course,

Fig. 10.6 *The social and personal consequences of alcoholism are enormous. While relatively few alcoholics end up on skid row, most nevertheless cause irreparable damage—in the physical harm they do themselves and in the havoc they wreck in their homes and jobs.*

the drinking—on which to pin the blame for their troubles. It wasn't *they* who caused the accident or the divorce; it was the alcohol! However, most of the evidence for this dependency theory is retrospective evidence, and thus it is possible that the dependency of alcoholics develops out of their drinking problem rather than vice versa, or at least that the two problems feed one another in the form of a vicious circle.

Somewhat the opposite of the dependency theory, the second major theory to develop out of current research is that alcoholics are power-seekers who take to drink in order to foster within themselves the comforting illusion that they are in control. McClelland and his co-workers (1972) have built an entire treatment program around this theory, though whether the theory will prove truly applicable to alcoholics in general remains to be seen.

Treatment Psychodynamic treatment of the alcoholic of course aims not so much at the "symptom"—that is, the drinking—as at the underlying psychic cause, since according to psychodynamic theory there will be no symptom relief until there is relief of the unconscious conflict. But as we have seen, there is no clear consensus as to what the unconscious conflict is. Perhaps for this reason, psychodynamic therapy has a relatively low success rate with alcoholism and is not a common form of treatment for this disorder.* Indeed, if it were the preferred treatment, we would be in great trouble, since there are nowhere near enough therapists around to handle in individual therapy the multitude of alcoholics produced by our society.

The Behaviorist Perspective

Cause   In the case of alcoholism, behavioral theory is, as usual, disarmingly simple. According to this view, the development of alcoholism is an operant-conditioning procedure based on negative reinforcement. Specifically, the dynamics are as follows. All of us have our share of troubles—anxiety, self-doubt, depression, guilt, annoyance, and so forth. In the process of emitting different behaviors in an attempt to reduce our psychological discomfort, some of us will take a drink. And alcohol, as we have seen, can definitely do the job; acting as a depressant, it dulls or deadens entirely whatever psychological distress we are experiencing. Thus alcohol use becomes associated with the alleviation of psychological pain. And because of this negative reinforcement, the drinking behavior is likely to be repeated.

Actually, learning theory views the development of alcoholism as a two-stage process. At first the individual may drink excessively only at times of psychological stress, just as Skinner's rat jumped for the lever only when the electric shock was turned on (Chapter 3). However, in our society, regular heavy drinking is frowned upon. Hence the person may begin to feel guilty about his episodes of heavy drinking and about the behaviors that go with it. In short, the "solution" to stress (alcohol) becomes itself a source of stress. And what does he do to relieve this increasing stress? He of course resorts to the behavior that he has learned is effective in reducing psychological stress: drinking. Hence he drinks to reduce the feelings of guilt and anxiety that have developed because he drinks too much. This is, of course, the vicious circle that we have described earlier in this chapter.

It bears mentioning that modeling is another behavioral principle that may apply to the development of alcoholism. A number of studies (e.g., Wood and Duffy, 1966; MacKay, 1961) have shown that people who become alcoholics are much more likely than others to have had an alcoholic parent. Thus it is possible that the young person, when confronted

with problems—and since he has been raised in a home with an alcoholic parent, his problems are likely to be substantial—resorts to the same coping method that he saw his parent resort to: drinking.

Treatment   In order for the alcoholic to "unlearn" the drinking response, this response must either be extinguished—that is, no longer be reinforced by anxiety reduction—or be made aversive through some kind of punishment. And since it is difficult to arrange things so that alcohol intake is not followed by a reduction in anxiety, most behavioral treatments of alcoholism rely on the use of aversive techniques.

One such aversive method involves the use of a drug called Antabuse. Antabuse (disulfiram) is a chemical that interferes with the normal metabolic processing of alcohol for about two days after it is taken. When the Antabuse taker drinks alcohol, a

Fig. 10.7   In some cases aversive conditioning techniques can effectively reduce alcohol consumption by pairing an unpleasant sensation, such as electric shock (below), with the act of drinking.

*An additional reason for poor success is that the inevitable anxieties raised by psychodynamic therapy can often drive the alcoholic to his favorite anxiety-reducing device—having a drink.

toxic agent accumulates in the bloodstream, causing an extremely unpleasant reaction. The individual flushes, his heart rate increases, he experiences intense nausea, and generally he feels as though he is about to die. The pairing of this reaction with alcohol is of course a classic case of aversive conditioning. Furthermore, Antabuse treatment is also based on the assumption (yet to be established as fact) that it will help the alcoholic avoid impulsive drinking (Baekeland et al., 1971), since if he wants to take a drink without becoming violently ill, he has to stop taking the Antabuse at least two days in advance. However, a problem with Antabuse is that many patients, after taking the drug in the hospital, simply discontinue it once they are discharged. Consequently, treatment rarely relies on Antabuse alone. Instead, the drug is used as part of a more general rehabilitation program.

There are also more direct forms of aversive conditioning. In one method, the individual is "allowed to drink," but every time he reaches for a glass he receives an electric shock. Another approach is once again to allow the individual to drink but to administer apomorphine, an emetic, at the same time so that alcohol becomes associated with nausea and vomiting. Because this approach is so Pavlovian, it is *the* preferred mode of treatment for alcoholism in Russia. Each Russian outpatient dispensary that treats alcoholics has its vomitorium. This is a room with four to six cots and an equal number of sinks. The patients are allowed to drink as long as they take the emetic as well. Then they vomit into the sink, collapse onto the cot, and when they are ready, repeat the sequence. Whether this incredibly simple treatment actually serves as a long-term deterrent remains to be proven.

The Humanistic-Existential Perspective

Cause The humanistic-existential perspective views the alcoholic as someone who has rejected, or indeed never located, his real identity. Instead of giving expression to his true self and accepting the risks involved in such a choice, the alcoholic attempts to cope with the problems of existence by playing a role which is unacceptable to himself and which is not favored by but is understandable to society. In doing so, he gives up his freedom to choose self-actualizing behaviors, behaviors more congruent with his true self. And the longer he continues in this self-defeating process, the more isolated he becomes from his true self and from other human beings.

Treatment Humanistic treatment for alcoholism, as for other disorders, emphasizes the necessity of the individual's looking inside himself and working hard to identify the real self—the self that he would truly choose to become. Equally important is the confrontation with the nonchosen self, the role that he has been playing. Through his therapeutic dialogues, the individual is helped to realize that he alone must make the choice between the two different behavior patterns. This philosophy is actually quite close to the basic tenet of Alcoholics Anonymous, a group that we will discuss shortly. AA's position is simply that every day the individual must decide anew whether he will escape from the self into alcohol or whether he will deal directly with the difficulties and anxieties each of us must confront sooner or later.

The Psychosocial Perspective

Do certain social groups produce more than their fair share of alcoholics? And if so, can we assume that cultural pressures have a role in the development of alcoholism? According to the widely noted study of McCord, McCord, and Gudeman (1960), the answer is yes. In a follow-up study of a number of young men who had been interviewed carefully as adolescents, these investigators found that the major factors dividing those who became alcoholics from those who did not were ethnic background and social class. For example, the boys of American Indian and Irish extraction were more prone to become alcoholics, while those of Italian and other Latin backgrounds were the least likely. Likewise, the higher the educational and socioeconomic level, the higher the incidence of alcoholism.

Another cultural correlate of alcoholism is religious affiliation. The one religious group that seems particularly resistant to alcohol problems is, predictably, the conservative Protestants, who have a notably high percentage of alcohol abstainers and a notably low percentage of heavy drinkers. Catholic, Jewish, and liberal Protestant groups all contain a fairly high proportion of alcohol users, with the Catholics leading the other groups in the percentage of heavy drinkers. In all religious groups it appears that the rate of church attendance correlates highly with abstinence.

Furthermore, it has been found that rural residents and small-town dwellers are less likely to drink and less likely to be heavy drinkers than their urban cousins (Cisin and Calahan, 1970). This finding may be related to a longstanding hypothesis that as environmental stress and cultural confusion increase—and they *do* tend to increase as one moves from country to city—so does the incidence of alcoholism. However, regardless of where a person lives, his culture's ingrained attitudes toward alcohol use will to some degree determine the likelihood of his becoming alcoholic. Likewise, among adolescents, peer-group sanctions appear to be a major determinant of alcohol consumption. If a young college student lives in a fraternity where weekends are given over to beer, he is likely, no matter what his background, to join in the festivities.

Finally, it should be mentioned that cultural expectations may have something to do with the fact that at present men are much more likely than women to be heavy drinkers and to be alcoholics. Perhaps the pressures on men have been greater. Or perhaps the recourse to alcohol as a pressure valve has been more culturally acceptable in men than in women. If so, the fact that women are now moving into the man's world may account for the finding that the incidence of alcoholism in women is rising. Alcoholism, it seems, may be one of the less attractive adjuncts of liberation.

The Biological Perspective

A number of researchers and clinicians believe that the critical predisposing factors in alcoholism are genetically based and have to do with physiological and biochemical abnormalities. The evidence here is as mixed and varied as it is for the other possible predisposing factors that we have discussed. One type of genetic evidence comes from cross-cultural studies. It has been reported, for example, that Japanese, Koreans, and Taiwanese respond with obvious facial flushing and clear signs of intoxication after drinking amounts of alcohol that have no detectable effect on Caucasoids ("Ethnic Differences in Alcohol Sensitivity," 1972). Such ethnic differences have led some investigators to conclude that sensitivity to alcohol is related to genetic factors, possibly affecting the autonomic nervous system.

Goodwin and his co-workers (1973) have conducted an even more revealing study, having to do with a group of male adoptees. Each of the men in the index group under study had been separated in infancy from his biological parents, one of whom had been hospitalized at least once for alcoholism. These children were then adopted by other families. Compared to a matched control group of adoptees, many more of the index children grew up to have drinking problems and to seek psychiatric treatment. They also had a higher divorce rate than the control group. The adoptive parents of both groups were of comparable socioeconomic standing and had similar proportions of alcoholism and other psychiatric disorders. Hence, contrary to the family studies cited above, this study would seem to suggest that the critical variable is not environmental (i.e., growing up with an alcoholic parent) but genetic (i.e., having the genes of an alcoholic parent).

Since the possible biochemical, endocrine, or physiological factors have not been explored, we cannot elaborate further on the subject of genetic influence. It should be noted, however, that if genetic characteristics do turn out to be of primary importance, treatment methods are likely to change radically.

Multimodal Treatments

Any treatment of alcoholism generally begins with a medical treatment called *detoxification*—that is, getting the alcohol out of the alcoholic's system and seeing the alcoholic through his withdrawal symptoms. The patient is hospitalized, and a tranquilizer such as Valium or Librium is substituted for the alcohol. Withdrawal to this substitute drug is generally completed in about five to seven days. High levels of vitamins, especially the B complex, are administered daily to counter the nutritional deficiencies. Since dehydration is also common in withdrawal, a high liquid intake is maintained. Finally, depending on the severity of the alcoholism, an anticonvulsant such as Dilantin may be administered to eliminate the possibility of seizures.

Once detoxification is completed, the difficult part of treatment begins—the effort to change the alcoholic from a drinking social dropout, with disrupted interpersonal, family, and job relationships, to an integrated, self-sustaining, coping member of the society. This is no easy task. Since rehabilitation has to do with so many aspects of the alcoholic's life, the better-designed alcohol rehabilitation programs are multimodal in nature. Within a supportive and nonthreatening environment, the alcoholic is provided with occupational therapy, to help him learn or relearn a hobby; relaxation therapy, to teach him how to reduce tension without alcohol; group and individual therapy, to help him learn something about himself and to show him how to relate to others without a drink in his hand; family and marital therapy, to resolve some of the problems at home that may have contributed to and/or resulted from the patient's drinking; and industrial or job-seeking therapy, to get the patient back to work, thus keeping him busy, boosting his self-esteem, and relieving his financial worries. These different forms of treatment are given concurrently, and most, if not all, patients will participate in them daily.

Why so many kinds of treatment? One reason is that no one knows what specific treatment is most important, other than trying to give the alcoholic some way other than drinking to solve his problems. Hence all approaches are tried, in the hope that one or a combination may work. Second, a full and varied schedule keeps the alcoholic busy and distracts him from thinking about or wanting alcohol.

One part of most successful rehabilitation programs is a follow-up component. Usually the ex-patients meet one or more times a week for three to six months or perhaps for the rest of their lives. This continued contact provides support for the individual, reminding him once again that he is not the only alcoholic in the world and that people are there to help him. Furthermore, the follow-up meetings give the alcoholic the opportunity to continue working on his problems and to learn additional interpersonal coping skills.

The most successful of these regular meeting programs for alcoholics is Alcoholics Anonymous, better known as AA. The AA program started in the mid-thirties, soon after the end of Prohibition, and has since spread around the world. There are now over 10,000 groups in the United States alone. AA is not a panacea. Not all alcoholics benefit from—or can even tolerate—the group's approach. But it is an option to which every alcoholic should be exposed.

The success of AA seems to be based on two of its basic tenets: (1) once an alcoholic, always an alcoholic, and (2) no one can stop drinking without help. AA sees alcoholism as a lifelong problem from which the individual never recovers. Consequently, he must abstain completely from alcohol and must rely on AA for comradeship and support in doing so. Such support is provided not only through the meetings, but also through AA's famous "buddy system." When a member feels that he can't keep from taking a drink, he calls AA. One or two members will then come to him, wherever he is, as soon as possible and help him get over the urge. In the process, it is believed, they will be helping themselves.

After this lengthy discourse on the causes and treatment of alcoholism, it is discouraging to have to report that there is no basis for optimism about rehabilitation. From the few follow-up studies that we have, it appears that in the more successful programs about 40 percent of the members actually stop drinking permanently. This is probably not much higher than the percentage that would even-tually stop without treatment. On the more positive side, it may be said that better treatment programs may arise from refinement of our current programs. Furthermore, even if complete rehabilitation does not occur, the programs now in operation do appear to help in keeping alcoholics functioning in the community for longer periods of time and at higher levels of efficiency.

ILLEGAL DRUGS

For the person in search of a potent psychoactive drug other than alcohol, there is a wide variety of illegal drugs—depressants, stimulants, hallucinogens—that can be equally destructive if used habitually. Most of these drugs are nothing new. Opium, for example, has been easing man's pain for almost nine thousand years. And indeed, until recently, most of these drugs were sold legally over the counter in the United States. During the nineteenth century countless numbers of self-respecting ladies thought nothing of taking laudanum, a form of opium, to help them sleep. In the Civil War morphine was commonly administered as a cure for dysentery and other ailments, with the result that many soldiers returned from the war as morphine addicts. At the beginning of this century, the major ingredient in the best-selling cough syrups was a recently discovered miracle drug called heroin. Freud himself took cocaine to relieve depression and publicized its miraculous effects. These miraculous effects were soon available to Americans in the form of a new drink called Coca-Cola, first introduced in 1896 and not purified of its cocaine ingredient until 1906. By 1914, however, the nonmedical use of most of the drugs that we will discuss in this section was made illegal in the United States. And though widely used, illegal they remain.

Depressants

As we have seen in the case of alcohol, a *depressant* is a drug that acts on the central nervous system to reduce pain, tension, and anxiety, to relax and disinhibit, and to slow down intellectual and motor reactivity. Along with alcohol, the narcotics and the barbiturates probably account for over 95 percent of all depressant drug use, both legal and illegal. All three types have a number of important effects in common: physiological addiction occurs; tolerance develops; high dosages depress the functioning of vital systems such as respiration and thus may result in death.

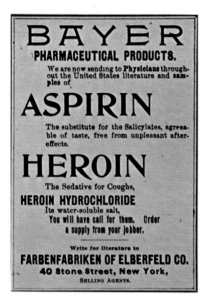

Fig. 10.8 This advertisement for the sale of certain patent medicines appeared during a period when massive advertising campaigns assailed the public with thousands of remedies.

Fig. 10.9 (below) A photograph of a nineteenth-century opium den depicts the bleak surroundings in which individuals smoked themselves into an oblivion of beautiful sensory hallucinations, free from pain and anxiety but often leading to addiction.

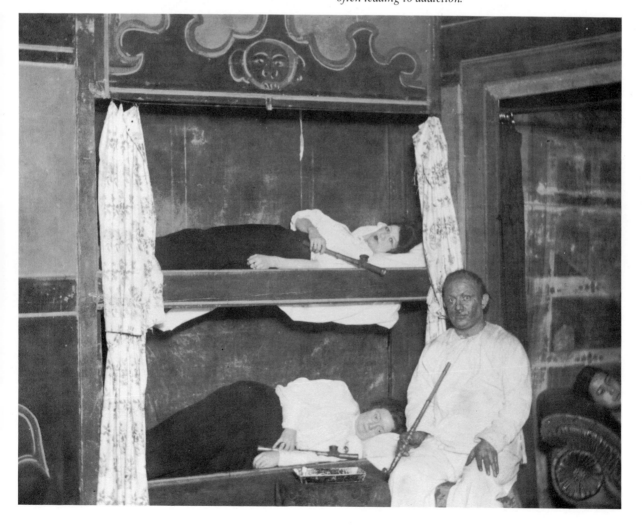

Narcotics The *narcotics* are a class of drugs which induce relaxation and reverie and provide relief from anxiety and physical pain. The narcotics include opium, the derivatives of opium, and chemically synthesized drugs which imitate certain effects of opium. The grandfather of the narcotics is of course *opium*, a chemically active substance derived from the opium poppy. Early in the nineteenth century, scientists succeeded in isolating one of the most powerful ingredients in opium. This new narcotic, which they called *morphine* (after the Greek god of dreams, Morpheus), was soon widely used as a pain reliever. As the years passed, however, it became clear that morphine was dangerously addictive, and so scientists went back to work, this time attempting to find a narcotic that would relieve pain without causing addiction. In 1875 this research culminated in the discovery, by Heinrich Dreser (who also discovered aspirin), that a minor chemical change could transform morphine into a new miracle drug, *heroin*, much stronger than morphine and presumably nonaddictive. This presumption was, of course, cruelly mistaken. Finally, the problems of narcotics addiction have led in recent years to the discovery of the final entry in our list of narcotics, *methadone*, a synthetic chemical which satisfies the craving for narcotics but does not produce narcotic euphoria. Our discussion will focus on the most popular of the narcotics, heroin.

It is impossible to give an accurate picture of the extent of illegal narcotics use. Up through the early 1970s heroin use increased each year, and in 1972–1973 a reasonable estimate was that there were about 600,000 narcotic addicts in the United States. In 1974 it was widely believed that the "epidemic" was over. However, reports indicate that the number of new users has rapidly increased through 1974 and 1975.

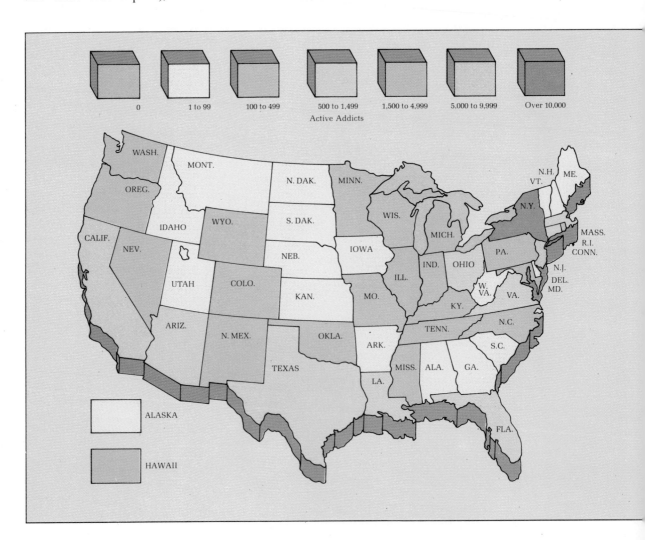

| 0 | 1 to 99 | 100 to 499 | 500 to 1,499 | 1,500 to 4,999 | 5,000 to 9,999 | Over 10,000 |

Active Addicts

Heroin is normally taken by injection, either directly beneath the skin ("skin-popping") or into a vein ("mainlining"). The immediate positive effects of mainlining heroin are twofold. First is the "rush," which is best described as a whole-body orgasm lasting five to fifteen minutes. As one addict described it, "Imagine that every cell in your body has a tongue and they are all licking honey." The second effect is a simple state of satisfaction, euphoria, and well-being, in which all positive drives seem to be gratified and all negative feelings—guilt, tension, anxiety—disappear completely. Unfortunately, from the addict's point of view, this artificial paradise lasts for only three to five hours, after which he needs a further injection.

Such are the positive effects. The negative effects are even more impressive. In the first place, not all people have the honey-licking experience. All users respond initially with nausea, and for some, this response outweighs the euphoric effects.

Second, if heroin use becomes regular, both addiction and tolerance develop. Thus in order to avoid withdrawal symptoms, the heroin addict has to begin injecting larger and larger doses.

Third, should withdrawal take place, it is an extremely disagreeable experience. Withdrawal symptoms begin about four to six hours after the injection and vary in intensity according to the dosage regularly used. The first sign of withdrawal is anxiety. Then the addict enters a period of three to five days during which he feels utterly wretched throughout his body. Specifically, withdrawal symptoms generally include watering eyes, a runny nose, yawning, hot and cold flashes, tingling sensations in the body, increased respiration and heart rate, profuse sweating, diarrhea and vomiting, headache, stomach cramps, aches and pains in other parts of the body, and possibly delirium and hallucinations as well—all

this combined with a state of intense craving for the drug. Though this experience is probably more uncomfortable than any physical reaction most of us have ever endured, it is not as devastating as addicts—and novels and movies—depict it to be, particularly since in a hospital setting drugs are commonly used to relieve the symptoms. Furthermore, unlike withdrawal from alcohol or barbiturates, heroin withdrawal very rarely results in death.

Much worse are the long-term effects of heroin addiction. Reduced to devoting his existence to acquiring the drug, the addict soon abandons his employment, his family, his interests, and his self-respect. In the end, nothing matters except the drug. Equally as serious as this personality deterioration is the physical deterioration involved. Heroin addicts generally have very poor and scanty diets, and thus they tend to suffer from malnutrition and lowered resistance to disease. Sexual interest declines, and respiratory ailments may develop. Furthermore, addicts are often careless about injection techniques and about the sterility of needles, with the result that they are prone to tetanus, blood poisoning, and hepatitis. Finally, if the addict injects too large a dose or if he combines a substantial dose of heroin with a substantial dose of another drug, he may lapse into a coma and die.

Barbiturates The *barbiturates* are a group of powerful sedative (i.e., calming) drugs, whose major effects are to alleviate tension and bring about relaxation and sleep. The most commonly used barbiturates are Nembutal (pentobarbital), Seconal (secobarbital), and Butiserpine (butabarbital). Legally, these drugs are prescribed by many physicians as sleeping pills. Illegally, they are sold on the street as "downers," providing an alcohol-like experience without the alcohol taste, breath, or expense. Sidney Cohen, one of the giants in the field of drug-abuse research, told a U.S. Senate investigating committee:

For the youngster, barbiturates are a more reliable "high" and less detectable than "pot." They are less strenuous than LSD, less "freaky" than amphetamines, and less expensive than heroin. A school boy can "drop a red" [i.e., a Seconal capsule] and spend the day in a dreamy, floating state of awayness untroubled by reality. It is drunkenness without the odor of alcohol. It is escape for the price of one's lunch money (1971, p. 2).

In the panic over heroin, LSD, and marijuana, the public has largely ignored the dangers of barbiturates. Yet they pose a clear psychosocial threat. In

Fig. 10.10 This map shows the number of active narcotics users in the United States, by state, in 1970. It should be noted that these statistics are based on reports submitted by state and local authorities on a "strictly voluntary basis" and therefore represent only reported cases of narcotics use. Among the many factors associated with drug use are the psychological, social, and economic conditions of a given area. Research has indicated that drug use is highest in areas where economic depression, deprivation, and related conditions are prevalent. One implication of this finding is that improvement of social and economic conditions, for example, in ghetto areas, may lead to a decrease in the use of narcotics. (Data from the Bureau of Narcotics and Dangerous Drugs, 1971.)

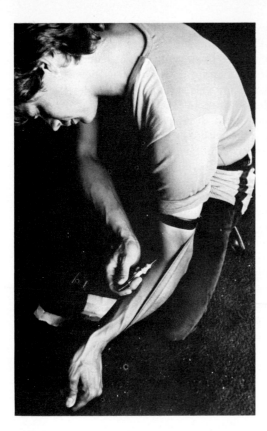

Fig. 10.11   Heroin users with some of their paraphernalia.

the first place, they are far too readily and cheaply available. Adolescents can often gather a supply of barbiturates simply by discreet and regular lootings of the family medicine cabinet. Adult addicts can insure their supply with relative ease merely by going from doctor to doctor with complaints of insomnia and thus obtaining multiple prescriptions.

Second, as we have seen in Chapter 7, the barbiturates are the drug of choice for suicide attempts. With an overdose, the depressant effect first induces sleep and then stops respiration. Furthermore, the overdose need not be made up solely of barbiturates. The barbiturates are additive in their effects with alcohol. Thus the person who combines the two drugs runs the risk, intentionally or unintentionally, of becoming a suicide-overdose statistic. The deaths of Judy Garland and Marilyn Monroe from barbiturate overdoses received a good deal of publicity. However, accidentally or otherwise, approximately three thousand people die in precisely the same way every year (Bayh, 1971), with no publicity.

Generally, the use of barbiturates by the young is recreational and sporadic, reflecting the multiple-drug-use pattern mentioned earlier. The true addicts, on the other hand, are usually middle-aged

housewives and marginally employed males who don't see themselves as addicts until hospitalization becomes necessary. Typically, such adult addicts begin using barbiturates for the standard reason—to relieve insomnia. However, since tolerance eventually develops, they will gradually increase the dose until it finally reaches the level—about two to three times the standard sleep-inducing dose—necessary for addiction. From that point on, barbiturate intoxication becomes a way of life.

In their effects, which generally last from three to six hours, the barbiturates are extremely similar to alcohol. Like alcohol, they disinhibit, induce relaxation and mild euphoria, and impair judgment, speech, and motor coordination. Like the alcoholic, the barbiturate addict will stagger, slur his speech, slow down intellectually, and become confused. Again like alcohol, the barbiturates, though they are technically depressants, may have a stimulating effect, especially if they are taken with the expectation of "having some fun" rather than of getting to sleep (Wesson and Smith, 1971). Indeed, one of the major concerns of those studying barbiturates is the relationship between aggression and Seconal, a favored barbiturate of the young. We have already mentioned the study conducted by Tinklenberg and Woodrow (1974) on the relationship between drugs and aggression in young men arrested for assault. These young offenders reported that they expected to be more aggressive when they used "reds"—and they were. They took Seconal when they "wanted to have a party." To counteract the sedative-depressant effects of the drug, they literally "fought to stay awake"—that is, they used aggression as a form of stimulation to keep themselves from slowing down. These offenders also reported that after taking Seconal they had less control over their behavior than usual and that they would persist in an assault even when their opponent was already devastated.

A final area of similarity between barbiturates and alcohol is the matter of withdrawal. Withdrawal from barbiturate addiction is very similar to withdrawal from alcohol addiction and is equally harrowing and dangerous. Without medical supervision, it can easily result in death.

Stimulants

The *stimulants* are a class of drugs whose major effect, as the name indicates, is to provide energy, alertness, and feelings of confidence. Aside from caffeine, which is available legally and which most of us consume daily in the form of coffee, tea, or cola drinks, there are two classes of illegally sold stimulants, the amphetamines and cocaine.

The *amphetamines* are a group of synthetic stimulants, the most common of which are Benzedrine (amphetamine), Dexedrine (dextroamphetamine), and Methedrine (methamphetamine). When taken, they dispel any feelings of boredom or weariness. Suddenly the individual finds himself alert, confident, full of energy, and generally ready to take on the world. The amphetamines depress appetite—hence their use by people with weight problems. They improve motor coordination—hence their use by professional athletes. And they inhibit sleepiness—hence their use by college students preparing for exams. Contrary to campus rumors, however, they do not improve complex intellectual functioning (Tinklenberg, 1971a).

As long as they are taken irregularly and in low or moderate doses, amphetamines do not appear to pose any behavioral or psychological problem. As with most other psychoactive drugs, the problems arise from high doses and habitual use. And once use becomes habitual, tolerance develops, and accordingly higher doses become necessary.

The problems of amphetamine abuse are epitomized in the "speed freak," the person who injects liquid amphetamine into his veins for periods of three to four days during which he neither eats nor sleeps but remains euphorically and intensely active. This heightened activity level can easily lead to paranoid and violent behavior—a fact which did not endear speed freaks to the more peaceable drug users during the late sixties. Although the speed freaks were mostly an East and West Coast phenomenon, they struck fear everywhere into the communes and pads of the hallucinogen users and other flower children. The rule was: when the speeders move in, you move out. The anathema against speed freaks was formally proclaimed by Allen Ginsberg:

Let's issue a general declaration to all the underground community *contra speedamos ex cathedra.* Speed is antisocial, paranoid making, it's a drag, bad for your body, bad for your mind, generally speaking, in the long run uncreative and it's a plague in the whole dope industry. All the nice gentle dope fiends are getting screwed up by the real horror monster Frankenstein speed-freaks who are going around stealing and bad-mouthing everybody (cited in Pittel and Hofer, 1972, p. 105).

Of special importance to the student of abnormal psychology is the clear resemblance between the effects of amphetamine abuse and the symptoms of paranoid schizophrenia (Chapter 11). Under the influence of heavy doses of amphetamines, the individual commonly expresses the same delusions of persecution and the same emotional condition that we see in the paranoid schizophrenic (Bell, 1973). This amphetamine psychosis appears to be unrelated to any personality predispositions and is thus assumed to be the direct result of the drug. As a result of this finding, considerable research is now in progress with both animals and human beings to determine whether paranoid schizophrenia might not be caused by the same chemical changes that amphetamines induce in the brain. It should be noted that this amphetamine psychosis is the only drug-induced psychosis that is virtually identical to a clinically observed "functional" psychosis.

Unlike the synthetic amphetamines, *cocaine* is a natural stimulant. It is the active ingredient in the coca plant, and as has been mentioned, was also the most active ingredient in Coca-Cola for a number of years. (Now caffeine is the only psychoactive drug remaining in Coca-Cola.) Producing feelings of euphoria and omnipotence unsurpassed by any other drug, cocaine is now the "in" stimulant and is probably used by three to four times as many people as heroin. Since it is expensive, most of its users are middle- and upper-class white-collar and executive types. The drug is taken now primarily by "snorting"—that is, by inhaling the drug into the nostrils, where it is absorbed into the bloodstream through the mucous membranes. Repeated use, however, will irreversibly damage these membranes.

A Twin Death from Barbiturate Abuse

On July 17, 1975, a pair of 45-year-old identical twins, Stewart and Cyril Marcus—both eminent and well-to-do gynecologists, both known for their correct, conventional, and highly meticulous behavior—were found dead and partially decomposed in the apartment that they shared in New York City. Cyril, dressed only in his socks, was lying on the floor. Stewart, with only his shorts on, was sprawled on his bed. Both showed signs that advanced malnutrition had preceded their death. The floors of the apartment were strewn with layer upon layer of litter and garbage, a foot and a half deep: fast-food packages, old newspapers, chicken bones, paper bags, feces, and, notably, over a hundred empty barbiturate bottles.

The immediate conclusion of the police was that the brothers had killed themselves with barbiturate overdoses, in fulfillment of a suicide pact. But the Medical Examiner's office later revealed that Stewart had died several days before Cyril and furthermore that there was no trace of barbiturates in their systems. Thus the hypothesis was revised: the Marcuses had died not from barbiturate overdoses but rather from the severe withdrawal symptoms associated with the drug. But soon this theory too came into question, as later evidence from the Medical Examiner's office revealed that one of the brothers (it was not specified which) did in fact have substantial amounts of barbiturates in his brain—further support for the suicidal-overdose hypothesis.

A survey of the Marcuses' past history does little to help solve the mystery. What it does reveal is that the brothers were so similar and led such similar lives that somehow, in spite of the law of probabilities, it seems natural that they should have died together. Indeed, they did almost everything together: went to the same college (both graduating Phi Beta Kappa), attended the same medical school, and undertook the same medical specialty. Both then entered the army, each attaining the rank of captain and becoming chief of obstetrics and gynecology at a different

army hospital. After leaving the army, both joined the staff at Lenox Hill Hospital in New York and later switched over to New York Hospital, where they became assistant professors. Both were experts on fertility problems. When they wrote, they wrote together; they coauthored several scientific papers as well as a leading gynecology textbook, which contributed substantially to their eminence. And when they relaxed, they did so together at their jointly owned summer home. Finally, they shared the same office and, in the last months of their lives, the same apartment. The only deviation in their otherwise parallel lives was that Cyril had been married and divorced, while Stewart remained a bachelor.

And in the end, they went downhill together, with Cyril apparently leading the way. Whereas previously both had been known for their fastidious habits—Cyril, according to a former nurse of the Marcuses, could not bear the sight of a used Kleenex in a wastebasket—now their office became filthy; urine specimens, never analyzed, filled the refrigerator. The brothers began missing appointments, stopped sending out bills and filling out insurance forms, and admitted fewer and fewer patients to the hospital. When they did appear at the hospital, their behavior was increasingly bizarre. Once during surgery one of the brothers ripped the anesthesia mask from the patient's face and put it over his own face. Excused from the operating room, he was replaced by his brother, who appeared equally "out of it." Finally, after more than a year of such behavior, the Marcuses were dismissed from the New York Hospital. Then, apparently, they virtually barricaded themselves in their apartment until a month later a strange smell in the hallway of the apartment building alerted the building handyman that something was amiss. The door of the apartment was broken down by the police. By that time the Marcuses' struggle had been over for about a week.

This strange story received a great deal of

attention from the press, not simply because it was strange but also because it raises two serious questions. First is the question of how well the medical profession is policing itself. This issue, at which consumer protection advocates have been hammering for years, was brought squarely before the eyes of the public as they read the Marcuses' story. Many of their colleagues knew that the Marcuses were unfit to practice, yet month after month nothing was done.

The second issue is that of the role of twinship in the addiction and death of the two brothers. Stewart and Cyril Marcus, like all monozygotic twins, had the same genetic makeup. Could it be that their common genotype predisposed them both to barbiturate addiction, or to drug addiction in general, or perhaps to some personality disorder that caused them to seek refuge in drugs? Or was it simply the natural sympathy between twins that led them down the same dark alley? Cyril reportedly became addicted approximately two years before his death, while Stewart's addiction was only a few months old. Could Stewart have chosen, out of a sense of symbiotic oneness with his twin, to share his destructive habit?

The Marcuses were buried side by side on July 20, 1975. But the questions surrounding their death have not yet been laid to rest. Their story, particularly because it involves two such eminent physicians working at such an eminent hospital, places the entire medical profession in a dubious light. At the same time it lends an aura of eeriness to the psychology of twinship.

Sources: Boyce Rensberger, "Death of Two Doctors Poses a Fitness Issue," *The New York Times*, August 15, 1975, pp. 1, 32; Anna Quindlen, "Death of Marcus Twins Still a Puzzle," *New York Post*, November 17, 1975, pp. 4, 38; Anna Quindlen, "Experts Disagree on Autopsy Data," *New York Post*, November 17, 1975, p. 38; Anna Quindlen, "The Marcus Brothers—Who Was Who?" *New York Post*, November 18, 1975, pp. 5–7; Linda Wolfe, "The Strange Death of the Twin Gynecologists," *New York*, September 8, 1975, pp. 43–47; Ron Rosenbaum and Susan Edmiston, "Dead Ringers," *Esquire*, March 1976, pp. 98–103, 135–136, 138, 140, and 142.

One of the more horrifying effects that may result from the intense stimulation of the nervous system by high doses of either amphetamines or cocaine is a condition called *formication*, in which the individual feels that there are bugs crawling under his skin. This hallucination, which probably results from the drug-induced hyperactivity of the nerves in the skin, is sometimes so intense and terrifying that the individual will try to "cut the bugs out" with a knife.

As with amphetamines, tolerance develops with regular use of cocaine. In the case of both drugs, there is still debate about whether they involve physiological addiction and withdrawal symptoms. When extended high-level use of either of these stimulants is suddenly terminated, the individual shows both physical and psychological symptoms of depression. However, it has not yet been resolved whether this depression is an inevitable and organically based result of cessation of use and therefore truly classifiable as a withdrawal symptom.

Hallucinogens

The *hallucinogens* are a class of drug that acts on the central nervous system in such a way as to cause distortions in sensory perception; hence their name, derived from the word "hallucination." Unlike the stimulants or depressants, they achieve their effect without substantial changes in the level of arousal. Tolerance develops rapidly to most hallucinogens, but there is no evidence that they are physiologically addictive. If they were, our society might have a problem on its hands, since according to a 1973 report by the federal government, one out of every twenty Americans over the age of twelve has tried one of the major hallucinogens at some time in their life. (This seems high, but there is no hard evidence to the contrary.)

There are many hallucinogens, including mescaline, psilocybin, THC, DMT, and, best-known of all, LSD, referred to by pharmacologists as lysergic acid diethylamide and by users as "acid." Despite this variety, rarely can any hallucinogen other than LSD or PCP, an animal tranquilizer, be bought on the street. These two drugs are usually combined with nonactive material, or with amphetamine or strychnine, which in large doses is fatal, and are sold as THC or mescaline. Several studies have shown that no matter what you think you are buying, you are probably getting LSD or PCP (Student Association for the Study of Hallucinogens, 1973).

LSD was originally synthesized by a Swiss chemist, Albert Hoffman, in 1938. Five years later, Dr. Hoffman reported an interesting experience that he

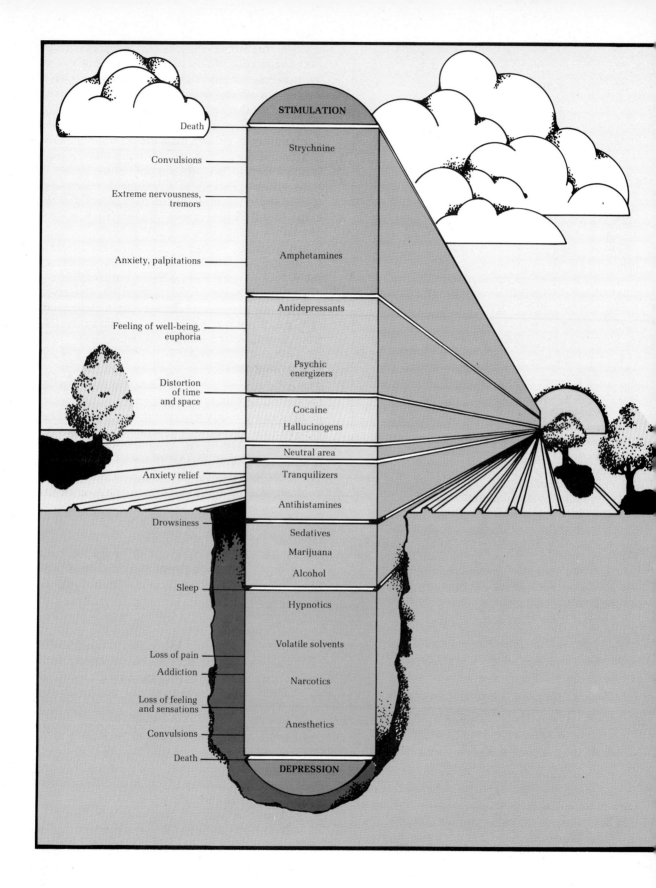

STIMULATION

Death

Strychnine

Convulsions

Extreme nervousness, tremors

Amphetamines

Anxiety, palpitations

Antidepressants

Feeling of well-being, euphoria

Psychic energizers

Distortion of time and space

Cocaine

Hallucinogens

Neutral area

Anxiety relief

Tranquilizers

Antihistamines

Drowsiness

Sedatives

Marijuana

Alcohol

Sleep

Hypnotics

Volatile solvents

Loss of pain

Addiction

Narcotics

Loss of feeling and sensations

Convulsions

Anesthetics

Death

DEPRESSION

had had after a morning's work in his laboratory:

Last Friday, . . . I was forced to stop my work in the laboratory . . . and to go home, as I was seized by a peculiar restlessness associated with the sensation of mild dizziness. On arriving home, I lay down and sank into a kind of drunkenness which was not unpleasant and which was characterized by extreme activity of imagination. As I lay in a dazed condition with my eyes closed (I experienced daylight as disagreeably bright) there surged upon me an uninterrupted stream of fantastic images of extraordinary plasticity and vividness and accompanied by an intense, kaleidoscope-like play of colours. This condition gradually passed off after about two hours (1971, p. 23).

Hoffman guessed that this experience might have been due to his having ingested some of the new chemical on which he was working. So he purposely swallowed a small amount of LSD and found that he had indeed guessed correctly.

LSD soon came to be called a "psychotomimetic" drug, on the assumption that it mimicked the effects of psychosis. And it was this assumption—along with the hope that LSD would provide some key to the cause of psychosis—that led to the extensive research with the drug in the fifties and sixties. This research did not prove fruitful, and no one any longer believes that an LSD "trip" is similar to a psychotic episode. So far the only use for which LSD has proved effective is the achieving of experiences like the one reported by Dr. Hoffman. In retrospect, the hallucinogens will probably be best remembered because they reopened the study of states of awareness (Holden, 1973; Grant, 1972)—an area of psychology that had lain fallow since about 1900, when William James wrote about these matters.

More than any other psychoactive drug, LSD and the other hallucinogens interfere with the processing of information in the nervous system. That is both their danger and their attraction. They do produce a kaleidoscope of colors and images. They do give the user a new way of seeing things. And they may open up new states of awareness, allowing the user to find out things about himself that he never imagined before. These are attractive benefits. And for the stable, mature individual who uses hallucinogens under controlled, nonthreatening conditions, there is little chance of a negative outcome from the experience (Cohen and Ditman, 1963).

The problem arises with people who are unable to process or accept the new kinds of perceptions induced by hallucinogens. Perhaps for some of us there are things about ourselves that we are better off not knowing. In any case, if a person's grasp on reality is not firm, if he derives great support from the stability of the world around him, or if he is somewhat immature or somewhat neurotic, then he may suffer negative effects, possibly for years, from using any of the hallucinogens.

In terms of negative effects, the trouble generally begins with a "bad trip" in which the user becomes terrified and disorganized in response to his changed perceptions. Such an experience is extremely unsettling and slowly forgotten. For some people the drug-induced disruption of their relationship with reality is so severe that they require some kind of long-term therapeutic assistance (Frosch et al., 1965). Furthermore, some users are haunted by LSD "flashbacks"—that is, spontaneous repetitions of terrifying hallucinatory perceptions experienced during a bad trip—which may disrupt their functioning considerably. Short-term psychotherapy is generally effective in relieving flashbacks.

Marijuana and Hashish

Though *marijuana* and *hashish* are often classified as minor hallucinogens, they deserve separate treatment. In the first place, their use is considerably

Fig. 10.12 This diagram illustrates the continuum of drug effects on mood and related symptoms. Although stimulants and depressants cause radically different reactions, overuse of certain drugs of either type may lead to convulsions and death. Through extensive and controlled research, more detailed knowledge will become available regarding the specific effects of these drugs and the effects of psychological factors such as expectation and prior experience. (Adapted from R. W. Earle, Ph.D., Department of Medical Pharmacology and Therapeutics, University of California, Irvine, California College of Medicine.)

Fig. 10.13 (succeeding pages) Accurate information is a prerequisite to meaningful communications about drugs, to research, and to treatment and prevention of their misuse. This chart provides a compendium of information about many commonly used pharmacological agents, and the accompanying photographs illustrate the various substances. (Adapted from J. Fort, M.D., The Pleasure Seekers, *Indianapolis: Bobbs-Merrill, 1969, pp. 236–243.)*

*Crucial to an evaluation of these drugs is the amount consumed, purity, frequency, time interval since ingestion, food in the stomach, combinations with other drugs and, most important, the personality of the individual taking it and the context in which it is taken. The determinations made in this chart are based on evidence with human use of these drugs rather than on isolated experimental situations or animal research.

†Only scattered, inadequate health, education, or rehabilitation programs (usually prison hospitals) exist for narcotic addicts and alcoholics (usually outpatient clinics), with nothing for the others except, sometimes, prison.

Name	Slang Name	Typical Single Adult Dose	Duration of Action (hours)	How Taken	Legitimate Medical Uses (present and projected)	Psychological Dependence Potential	Toler Poten
Alcohol Whisky, gin, beer, wine	Booze Hooch	1½ oz. gin or whisky, 12 oz. beer	2–4	Swallowed	Rare; sometimes used as a sedative	High	Yes
Caffeine Coffee, tea, Coca-Cola, No-Doz, APC	Java	1–2 cups 1 bottle 5 mg.	2–4	Swallowed	Mild stimulant; treatment of some forms of coma	Moderate	Yes
Nicotine (and coal tar) Cigarettes, cigars	Fag	1–2 cigarettes	1–2	Smoked	None	High	Yes
Barbiturates Nembutal Seconal Veronal Doriden Chloral hydrate	Yellow jackets Red devils Phennies Goofers	50–100 mg. 500 mg. 500 mg.	4	Swallowed	Treatment of insomnia and tension; induction of anesthesia	High	Yes

Stimulants
Amphetamines
  Benzedrine
  Methedrine
  Dexedrine
Cocaine
	Bennies
	Crystal, speed
	Dexies
	Coke, snow
		2.5–5.0 mg.
		
		Variable
			4	Swallowed or injected
				
				Sniffed or injected
					Treatment of obesity, narcolepsy, fatigue, depression
					Anesthesia of the eye and throat
						High	Yes

Tranquilizers Valium Miltown Librium Thorazine Stelazine		5-10 mg. 5-10 mg. 5-10 mg. 10-25 mg. 2 mg.	4–6	Swallowed	Treatment of anxiety, tension, alcoholism, neurosis, psychosis, psychosomatic disorders, and vomiting	Minimal	No

Sedatives and Barbiturates

Tuinal

Nembutal

Phenobarbital

Amytal

Seconal

Doriden

Meprobamate

Chloral hydrate

Stimulants and Amphetamin

D

Methamphetamin

Obetrol

	Overall Abuse Potential	Reasons for Use	Typical Short-term Effects*	Typical Long-term Effects	Form of Legal Regulation† and Control
	High	To relax; to escape from tensions, problems, and inhibitions; to get "high"	CNS depressant; relaxation; sometimes euphoria; drowsiness; impaired judgment, reaction time, coordination, and emotional control; frequent aggressive behavior and driving accidents	Possible obesity with chronic excessive use; irreversible damage to brain and liver, addiction with severe withdrawal illness (DTs); habituation	Available and advertised without limitation in many forms, with only minimal regulation by age (21 or 18), hours of sale, location, taxation, ban on bootlegging, and driving laws; some "black market" for those under age and those evading taxes; minimal penalties
	None	For a "pickup" or stimulation	CNS stimulant; increased alertness	Sometimes insomnia or restlessness; habituation	Available and advertised without limit, with no regulation for children or adults
	Moderate	For a "pickup" or stimulation	CNS stimulant; relaxation (or distraction) from the process of smoking	Lung (and other) cancer, heart, and blood vessel disease, cough, etc.; habituation	Available and advertised without limit, with only minimal regulation by age, taxation, and labeling of packages
	High	To relax or sleep; to get "high"	CNS depressants; sleep induction; sometimes euphoria; drowsiness; impaired judgment, reaction time, coordination, and emotional control; relief of anxiety-tension	Irritability, weight loss, addiction with severe withdrawal illness (like DTs); habituation, addiction	Available in large amounts by ordinary medical prescription, which can be repeatedly refilled or can be obtained from more than one physician; widely advertised and "detailed" to M.D.s and pharmacists; other manufacture, sale, or possession prohibited under federal drug abuse and similar state (dangerous) drug laws; moderate penalties; widespread illicit traffic
	High	For stimulation and relief of fatigue; to get "high"	CNS stimulants; increased alertness, loss of appetite, insomnia, often euphoria	Restlessness; irritability, weight loss, toxic psychosis (mainly paranoid); habituation; extreme irritability, toxic psychosis	Amphetamines, same as sedatives above; cocaine, same as narcotics below
	Minimal	Medical (including psychiatric) treatment of anxiety or tension states, alcoholism, psychoses, and other disorders	Selective CNS depressants; relief of anxiety-tension; suppression of hallucinations or delusions, improved functioning	Sometimes drowsiness, dryness of mouth, blurring of vision, skin rash, tremor; occasionally jaundice, agranulocytosis	Same as sedatives above, except not usually included under the special federal or state drug laws; negligible illicit traffic

Cocaine

Tranquilizers

Librium

Valium

Thorazine

Compazine

Stelazine

Name	Slang Name	Typical Single Adult Dose	Duration of Action (hours)	How Taken	Legitimate Medical Uses (present and projected)	Psychological Dependence Potential	Tol... Pot...
Cannabis Marijuana Hashish	Pot, grass, tea, weed, stuff	Variable— 1 cigarette or 1 drink or cake (India)	4	Smoked Swallowed	Treatment of depression, tension, loss of appetite, sexual maladjustment, and narcotic addiction	Moderate	No
Narcotics Opium Heroin	Op Horse, H	10–12 "pipes" (Asia) Variable—bag or paper with 5–10 percent heroin	4	Smoked Injected	Treatment of severe pain, diarrhea, and cough	High	Yes
Methadone Morphine Codeine Percodan Demerol Cough syrups		15 mg. 30 mg. 1 tablet 50–100 mg. 2–4 oz. (for euphoria)		Swallowed			
Hallucinogens LSD Psilocybin Mescaline (peyote) DMT (dimethyl-tryptamine) THC (tetra-hydrocannabinol)	Acid, sugar Cactus	150 micrograms 25 mg. 350 mg. 25 mg.	12 6 12	Swallowed Chewed Injected	Experimental study of mind and brain function; enhancement of creativity and problem solving; treatment of alcoholism, mental illness, and the dying person	Minimal	Yes (rar...
Antidepressants Elavil Tricyclics (Tofranil, Sinequan) MAO inhibitors (Nardil, Parnate)		10 mg. 25 mg., 10 mg. 15 mg., 10 mg.	4–6	Swallowed	Treatment of moderate to severe depression	Minimal	No
Miscellaneous Glue Gasoline Amyl nitrite Antihistamines Nutmeg Nonprescription "sedatives"		Variable 1–2 ampules 25–50 mg. Variable	2	Inhaled Swallowed	None except for antihistamines used for allergy and amyl nitrite for some episodes of fainting	Minimal to moderate	?

Marijuana

Narcotics

Raw opium

Heroin

nce	Overall Abuse Potential	Reasons for Use	Typical Short-term Effects*	Typical Long-term Effects	Form of Legal Regulation† and Control
	Moderate	To get "high"; as an escape; to relax	Relaxation, euphoria, increased appetite, some alteration of time perception, possible impairment of judgment and coordination; (probable CNS depressant)	Usually none	Unavailable (although permissible) for ordinary medical prescription; possession, sale, and cultivation prohibited by state and federal narcotic or marijuana laws (laws are changing); moderate to severe penalties; widespread illicit traffic
	High	To get "high"; as an escape; to avoid withdrawal symptoms	CNS depressants; sedation, euphoria, relief of pain, impaired intellectual functioning and coordination	Constipation, loss of appetite and weight, temporary impotence or sterility; habituation, addiction with unpleasant and painful withdrawal illness	Available (except heroin) by special (narcotics) medical prescriptions; some available by ordinary prescription or over-the-counter; other manufacture, sale, or possession prohibited under state and federal narcotics laws; severe penalties; extensive illicit traffic
	Moderate	Curiosity created by recent widespread publicity; seeking for meaning and consciousness expansion	Production of visual imagery, increased sensory awareness, anxiety, nausea, impaired coordination; sometimes consciousness expansion	Usually none; sometimes precipitates or intensifies an already existing psychosis; more commonly can produce a panic reaction when person is improperly prepared	Available only to a few medical researchers (or to members of the Native American Church); other manufacture, sale, or possession prohibited by state dangerous drug or federal drug abuse laws; moderate penalties; extensive illicit traffic
	Minimal	Medical (including psychiatric) treatment of depression	Relief of depression; stimulation	Basically the same as tranquilizers above	Same as tranquilizers above
	Moderate	Curiosity; to get "high"	When used for mind alteration, generally produces a "high" (euphoria) with impaired coordination and judgment	Variable—some substances can seriously damage liver or kidney	Generally easily available; some require prescriptions; in several states glue banned for those under 21

cinogens

Various forms of LSD

Mescaline (peyote)

Antidepressants

Elavil

Ritalin

Nardil

Tofranil

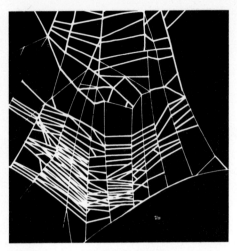

Fig. 10.14 *The left photograph shows a beautifully precise web spun by a spider under the influence of LSD. In contrast, the distorted, erratically executed web in the right photograph was constructed by the same spider, at another time, after being given a dose of mescaline. A great deal of knowledge about the effects of drugs is gained through research with animals; operant conditioning research involving rats and pigeons also contributes to knowledge about the effects of drugs on learning and performance. With human subjects it is difficult to ascertain the "specific" effects of agents such as LSD because of variables introduced by nonspecific factors such as the subject's expectations, prior experiences, and situational characteristics.*

more widespread. As frequently as the major hallucinogens are used, the use of marijuana and hashish is at least three times more common. According to government figures, approximately one out of every seven Americans over the age of fifteen uses marijuana in any given week. In the second place, the effects of marijuana and hashish are considerably milder than those of the major hallucinogens.

Marijuana and hashish are both derived from cannabis, a hemp plant that grows, cultivated and wild, in many countries, including the United States. Marijuana consists of the dried and crushed leaves of cannabis. Though it is usually rolled into a cigarette or "joint," and smoked, it can also be eaten. Hashish, derived from the resin rather than the leaves of cannabis, is about five to six times stronger than marijuana. Like marijuana, it can be eaten, but it is usually smoked in a specially designed pipe.

In both forms of the drug, the active ingredient is the same: THC (delta 9, tetrahydrocannabinol), which is not physiologically addictive. THC is unique among the psychoactive agents in that it is quite fat-soluble. As a result it accumulates in the body, and this accumulation may be the basis for the "reverse tolerance" reported by many marijuana users. Apparently, with repeated use, the body becomes sensitized to the drug, and consequently the individual eventually requires *less* of the drug in order to achieve a "high."

There are only two consistent physiological effects worthy of mention. The first is an accelerated heart rate. As the dose increases, so does the heart rate, which may go up to 140–150 beats per minute. The second change is a reddening of the whites of the eyes—reason enough to wear sunglasses. Both effects disappear as the drug wears off.

The behavioral effects of marijuana have been studied in a variety of situations. The effects of a mild marijuana high on simple behaviors is either nil or minimal. The person can easily turn on the record player, dial a phone number, make an acceptable pot of coffee, and so forth. However, as the complexity of the task increases, as speed of response becomes more important, and as a more accurate sense of time and distance are required, the impairment of ability from a single-joint marijuana high becomes more apparent. In this connection, it has been clearly established that no one should drive under the influence of marijuana (Klonoff, 1974).

Having discussed the physiological and behavioral effects, we now come to the major reason for using marijuana and hashish—the psychological effects. These have been summarized by Tinklenberg (in press):

Initial effects of cannabis at low doses usually include euphoria, heightening of subjective sensory experiences, alterations in time sense, and the induction of a relaxed, laissez-faire passivity. With moderate doses, these effects are intensified with impaired immediate memory function, disturbed thought patterns, lapses of attention, and a subjective feeling of unfamiliarity.

It should be noted that the latter group of reactions are generally not at all disturbing. The individual simply feels somewhat "spaced out"—a not unpleasant experience for most people under relaxed conditions.

As for the possibility of a bad trip with marijuana or hashish, the issue is probably as settled now as it will ever be: rarely does a significantly bad experience occur from smoking a single joint of marijuana or a small amount of hashish. However, as the amount of THC consumed increases, there is a corresponding increase in the possibility of a bad drug experience. At high levels of THC intake, the effects and the dangers are similar to those involved in the use of LSD. Some people experience sensory distortions, depersonalization, and changes in body image—all of which can result in a panic reaction and a fear of going crazy. At this point, intervention by a professional or a trained layperson becomes necessary, and short-term psychotherapy may eventually be required. However, it must be emphasized that these severe reactions to the use of THC are the exception, not the rule, and that they occur at the higher dose levels.

Much less clear than the short-term effects of THC use are the long-term effects. Can regular use of marijuana or hashish cause psychological or physiological damage? This question has polarized scientists as well as generations (Maugh, 1974). While many laymen feel that smoking a single joint can be the first step on the road to complete personality deterioration, for scientists there are essentially three areas of specific concern.

The first has to do with the effect of prolonged heavy marijuana use on the blood levels of the male sex hormone, testosterone. There seems to be general agreement that almost daily marijuana use (about nine joints a week) for six or more months will result in a reduction of the testosterone level in the blood (Miller, 1975). The degree of testosterone reduction is directly related to the amount of marijuana smoked. However, even the 40 percent reduction in testosterone reported in the original study of this problem (Kolodny et al., 1974) does not seem to be enough to impair significantly the sexual activity of males *with established patterns of sexual activity.* However, it is a well-established fact that variations in sex-hormone level have a greater impact on the sexual activity of individuals who have not yet stabilized their patterns of sexual behavior. Therefore it is possible, though it has not yet been proven, that heavy chronic marijuana use by males who have not yet established a regular pattern of sexual activity could result in impaired sexual functioning.

The second current question is with whether marijuana use suppresses immune reactions—that is, the body's mechanisms for fighting off the invasion of foreign substances such as germs. The evidence is fairly solid that chronic marijuana smoking does in fact impair the functioning of one part of the immune system (Miller, 1975). However, this impairment has yet to show any recognizable clinical effect. Therefore, as with the testosterone problem, there is no clear basis on which to make a decision about the significance of the immune response effect.

A third problem centers on the psychological effects of chronic marijuana use. Some professionals feel quite strongly that prolonged use of marijuana eventually results in impaired judgment, apathy, and—as with the more potent drugs—a focusing of one's existence on the drug experience. Related to this line of thinking is the argument that those who begin by smoking marijuana will go on to more dangerous drugs such as heroin. However, a simple comparison of the figures on frequency of marijuana use and narcotics use will show that very few marijuana smokers make the transition to narcotics. As for the more general hypothesis that regular marijuana use results in a blunting of intellect, drive, and emotion, there are simply no acceptable long-term studies to prove or disprove this argument.

In sum, the problems and issues are clear, but the answers aren't. Testosterone levels go down, but maybe sexual activity doesn't. One immune response is suppressed, but there is no observable effect. The personality may be affected, and then again it may not. The only thing that we know for sure about long-term marijuana use is that it increases the likelihood of respiratory ailments. Much more data is needed before the marijuana issue can ever be reasonably settled. Indeed, it may never be *reasonably* settled. The chances are good that as marijuana use increases and as young marijuana users grow up and begin assuming positions of power, the issue will be settled—at least in the sense of legalization—long before science has been able to accumulate conclusive evidence as to the actual long-term effects of this drug.

PERSPECTIVES ON ILLEGAL-DRUG ABUSE

As we have mentioned earlier, the current trend in the study and rehabilitation of drug abusers is to consider these individuals as a group rather than to attempt fine distinctions among the alcoholic, the narcotics addict, the barbiturate addict, the speed freak, and so on. Hence the theoretical perspectives that we have discussed in relation to alcoholism tend to apply as well in the case of illegal-drug abuse. The psychodynamic theorists would still tend to implicate dependency; the behaviorists, negative reinforcement; the humanists and existentialists, refusal to choose the true self over the false self. In the following section we will examine briefly the possible correlation between illegal-drug use and personality type, the social issues pertaining to illegal drugs, and the various current approaches to rehabilitation.

Illegal Drugs and Personality Factors

We must introduce this discussion by stating that attempts to relate personality types to specific types of drug abuse and to drug abuse in general have been largely fruitless. Suggestions are offered, but they are vague. Furthermore, in the case of some illegal drugs, use is so widespread that generalizations as to the type of user are, by necessity, hopelessly broad. It has been said of hallucinogen users, for example, that they are primarily white and middle or upper class, and are generally better educated than the average American (Braucht et al., 1973). Likewise, in a 1971 study that is probably outdated by now, the federal government reported that marijuana users tended to be young, single, male, and middle or upper class; most did not participate in any formal religion. Other personality studies on users of specific drugs offer conclusions that seem applicable to any form of drug addiction. Braucht and his co-workers (1973) reported that narcotics users were generally immature, insecure, irresponsible, and egocentric. But it is highly improbable that such a constellation of characteristics is the unique property of narcotics users. The very same description could easily apply, for example, to barbiturate addicts and alcoholics. In sum, little progress has been made in identifying predisposing personality factors.

According to our best evidence, the strongest predisposing factor in the case of adolescents is drug use by peers (Rohr and Densen-Gerber, 1971). The adolescent will tend to smoke pot if his friends are smoking pot. Drug use by parents also exerts an influence, though not as great as drug use by peers (Kandel, 1973).

In the case of the physiologically addicting drugs, socioeconomic status may play a role. For example, the two factors most commonly related to narcotics use are membership in an ethnic minority and, of course, the availability of narcotics.

Finally, for adolescents and young adults, drug use may be related to a period of confusion and transition in their lives. A recent study (Salzman and Lieff, 1974) of a group of young people who had discontinued heavy use of hallucinogens supports this notion. The subjects reported that they began using hallucinogens at a point when they were facing major life decisions—choosing a career, deciding whether to go on to graduate school, and so forth. Likewise, they discontinued their hallucinogen use when the transitions were finally made. "Drug use ceased as problems resolved. Relationships and goal directions were often clarified, sometimes solidified. Commitments to people and tasks were often established, and the drug experience lost prominence" (p. 332).

Drugs and Society

Like alcoholism, addiction to illegal drugs is damaging to the society. Here, as with alcoholism, work productivity is decreased, medical resources are wasted, and lives are lost in drug-related accidents. Furthermore, the money spent on illegal drugs generally goes into the coffers of organized crime—a cause which, as we have seen in Chapter 8, society has little reason to support. Finally, there appears to be a clear correlation between the use of addictive drugs and the incidence of crime. For the most part, this is not violent crime, but rather shoplifting, burglary, and theft. The narcotics addict, for example, has to come up with a substantial amount of money every day in order to support his habit. He is generally unemployable, and therefore, unless he is independently wealthy, he has to steal. One study (Hekimian and Gershon, 1968) estimates that in New York City alone, crimes committed by heroin addicts in order to finance their habits cost 10 million dollars *per day*. (It should be noted that although marijuana was first made illegal in 1937 because it was thought to encourage crime, there is little evidence of any clear relationship between marijuana and crime, though it is thought by some that the tranquilizing effect of marijuana may actually discourage crime, particularly violent crime [Tinklenberg, 1971b].)

ADOLESCENT ADDICTS

How do adolescents drift into drug addiction? Flender (1972) has assembled thirteen case histories of young ex-addicts, most of whom were heavily into drugs by the age of fifteen. As for why, each had his own reasons. But in the accounts of their entry into the drug subculture, two themes do tend to recur. The first is peer pressure—the desire to be part of a group:

I got into drugs when I was twelve or thirteen years old by trying to be like the older dudes in the neighborhood. I would look up to those fellows of sixteen or seventeen who had the slickest clothes and all the girls. If they used drugs, then I wanted to use drugs. They used drugs (p. 50).

Trying to get in with a crowd in order to have friends was [one] reason for drugs, probably the most important reason. I began to go steady with this boy I met in high school. He was into shooting speed. At first I was afraid to fool around with it, even by popping pills. But then when I got in with my boyfriend's crowd of people, I felt I had to do what they were doing. . . .

It wasn't long before I realized that I really dug amphetamines. At first, two would get me off for the whole day. But the trouble with amphetamines is that you gradually build up a resistance to them, and it wasn't long before I was taking twenty to thirty amphetamines a day (p. 15).

I got into drugs, I guess . . . because of things that happened to me like, you know, the way I felt about myself. I was a very, very skinny, ugly little kid.

And it made me feel even worse that the only kids I could hang out with, that would accept me, were the kids who did crazy wild things—like taking drugs. So you can say I started fooling around with drugs . . . when I was about ten. I started by sniffing glue (p. 78).

I took drugs because of the great need I had to be accepted. And dope fiends very easily accept anyone who's on drugs, no matter what drugs

they're on, whether it's heroin or speed or anything (p. 136).

The second major theme in these young people's accounts of how they began using hard drugs is problem-"solving." Like forty-year-olds, fourteen-year-olds take drugs in order to forget their troubles:

What got me started on heroin was being so disgusted with life. I had left this really bad neighborhood in Denver, where nobody would give you a chance, and come all the way to California. And nobody would give me a chance there either. I just couldn't get a job. They always said they wanted somebody with some experience. Well, how could I get some experience if nobody would hire me for my first job?

So I said, "I don't care, I'm just going to forget about everybody else." And as long as I was on heroin I forgot about everybody else. It really worked, you know? (p. 33)

It was after I'd gotten out of the unwed mothers' home and given my second baby for adoption that I went from using acid to heroin. I just didn't see any future for myself. First I started sniffing, and then I started shooting it in my arms (pp. 59–60).

I guess one of the reasons I felt this big need for drugs was because I had a big hang-up about chicks. I was so skinny and ugly, no girl would go for me. Even if we were in a group where there was an extra girl, she wouldn't go for me. She'd go over to somebody else even if he already had a girl, and hang around with the two of them rather than be alone with me (p. 81).

These two factors, peer influence and the need to forget one's troubles, combined with the startling availability of most illegal drugs—on the streets, in the high schools, in the detention centers—make drug abuse appear an easy "solution" for teenagers with a greater-than-average share of adolescent woes.

There is, of course, one solution to the problem of addiction-related crime, and that is to legalize the drugs and dispense them to addicts, under medical supervision, at a nominal cost. Such a system has been in effect in Great Britain now for almost ten years. Opponents of this approach claim that it will simply encourage addiction, and the fact that the number of British addicts does appear to have increased in the last decade would seem to support this argument. However, defenders of the British system claim that it is the only reasonable way to prevent addicts from doing as much harm to society as they do to themselves.

The other great legalization question has to do, of course, with marijuana. While legal penalties for the possession of marijuana are very severe in many states, this strict prohibition, as we have seen, has only the flimsiest scientific support. As far as we know, the supporters of legalization of marijuana may be quite correct in their contention that marijuana is safer than alcohol, since it is nonaddictive and appears to do very little physical damage. Marijuana possession was in fact decriminalized in Oregon in the fall of 1973, and one year later there was no evidence of a substantial increase in use or abuse (Drug Abuse Council, 1974). As we have suggested earlier, it seems likely that marijuana will be legalized in many more states within the next few decades, though it may be many more decades before scientists are able to discover whether the drug is truly harmful or harmless.

Drug Rehabilitation

Therapy recommendations for abuse of specific illegal drugs are generally as vague as our knowledge of the effects of these drugs. The following, for example, is a suggestion for the treatment of barbiturate addicts:

Supporting a Drug Habit

I supported my habit by becoming a "cattle rustler." That's our name for somebody who steals meat from supermarkets and sells it at half-price. Me and three other guys, we had this kind of team.

I'd take the meat from the racks and put it right down my pants. When I'd get undressed at night my underwear . . . would be saturated with blood.

I never got caught. Veal cutlets, however, were dangerous to steal. They would bleed like a son of a gun and you'd be walking through the store and the blood would be running out your pants all over the place.

. . . I had to go out and start turning tricks. I looked so terrible that I could only get as tricks the lowest of the low, I mean creeps who would only pay two dollars. I was five feet five inches tall, but I only weighed ninety pounds. I was sick all the time, plus I had my son and I was dragging him all over the city. It was awful. I'd go into an apartment with a bunch of creepy guys and walk out with about ten dollars. . . . That's the way it was for quite a long time.

To support my habit, I robbed and stole. Wherever the money was, that's where I was. Stores, dudes, *anything and anyone. I used a gun. It's very easy to get a gun in Washington. . . .*

I got caught robbing stores a number of times. But since I was only fourteen or fifteen, it was easy for me to get released in my father's custody. I had about thirteen charges of armed robbery against me. But I'd never spend more than a few days or a couple of weeks in jail for each charge. But then I got picked up on a charge of attempted murder, and that was more serious.

One of the things that I did was when I was fifteen years old. I met this retarded girl on the train who was coming back from a special school in Manhattan and talked to her for a while and weaseled my way into getting her to take me home. Once I got in the house, I started fooling around and she really didn't know what was going on. She was very much out of it, in her own little world.

I cleaned out the whole house. I took a gold charm bracelet with four gold coins. I don't know whether it was hers or her mother's. I took a brass microscope, a twenty-one-carat gold watch and another watch, a couple of bottles of champagne, and about a hundred dollars in cash.

Source: Flender (1972), pp. 92, 60, 50-51, 82.

Psychotherapeutic management of the patient, designed to help him find better ways of adapting to stress, coping with guilt feelings and communicating affects is begun in the hospital. Since learning to use human sources to help rather than seeking pharmacological refuge may be difficult for this patient, a long-term relationship with his physician, a psychiatrist or a mental health center is desirable.... The family's enlightened cooperation is essential and it may be useful to engage the patient and the spouse in conjoint psychotherapy (Bakewell and Ewing, 1969, p. 143).

The very same recommendations could apply to any type of drug abuse.

However, three specific current types of therapy merit our attention. One is aversive conditioning, which follows essentially the same lines as the behavioral treatment of alcoholism. Here, however, the painful stimulus, usually electric shock, is paired not with the drug itself but with oral descriptions, in the patient's own language, of the need for the drug and the taking of it. Several investigations (e.g., O'Brien et al., 1972) have reported successful treatment of heroin addicts by combining this type of aversive conditioning with techniques such as relaxation training (Chapter 19) and systematic desensitization, which are designed to reduce the anxiety that may trigger the drug-taking.

A second type of treatment is the therapeutic residential community, of which the best-known is Synanon, a community for narcotics addicts. Founded in the late fifties by an AA member, Synanon, like AA, has a reputation for successful rehabilitation, but hard data are almost nonexistent. Synanon and its imitators base their treatment on two principles: (1) once an addict, always an addict (note the resemblance to AA doctrine), and (2) the first step in learning new, nondrug ways of coping with stress is to learn about oneself. In accordance with the second principle, an integral part of Synanon's rehabilitation program is regular attendance at encounter-group sessions. Since Synanon members believe that all the addict's defenses must be peeled away and his core problem revealed in all its nakedness before he can go straight, these group therapy sessions are often anything but gentle. For some, however, such an approach appears to work.

A third rehabilitation method, again specific to narcotics addiction, is the methadone maintenance approach. As we have seen earlier in this chapter, methadone is a synthetic narcotic, which, like the other narcotics, is highly addictive. It produces no high, but it does satisfy the craving for heroin and prevents heroin withdrawal. In short, what metha-done maintenance programs do is to switch the individual from heroin addiction to methadone addiction, thus relieving him of his "doped" behavioral symptoms and of the necessity of stealing to finance his drug-craving. When this technique is combined with job training, group therapy, and employment assistance, it seems to be an effective way of reducing illegal narcotic use.

Despite successes with these programs, however, there are still thousands of addicts whom we truly do not know how to help. Drug use appears to be increasing, and historical evidence suggests that increased use will lead to increased abuse (Ray, 1974). If this is the case, it is likely that the pace of research will also increase and will eventually open therapeutic doors that at present are only dimly perceived.

SUMMARY

The subject of our chapter has been the abuse of psychoactive drugs, in which most Americans indulge at least occasionally. When a person's indulgence reaches the point where he *must* have the drug in order to satisfy a physiological craving, he may be said to be addicted. Generally, the addict develops tolerance for the drug, and if deprived of it, will experience withdrawal symptoms. Psychological need for a nonaddictive drug is termed "drug dependence." Both forms of drug abuse are severely damaging to the individual and to the society.

Alcohol, sanctioned in our society by both law and tradition, is one of the most heavily abused drugs. Its social cost is enormous, particularly in the area of automobile accidents. And its personal cost, in terms of psychological and physical deterioration, is equally ruinous.

No one knows what causes alcoholism or what "type" of person becomes an alcoholic. The most popular psychodynamic theory is that the alcoholism is due to dependency resulting from oral fixation. The humanistic-existential perspective, equally introspective, views the alcoholic as a person who has denied his true self. In contrast, the behaviorists argue that alcoholism is the result of operant conditioning, based on negative reinforcement (i.e., the relief of anxiety)—a process which behavioral therapies attempt to reverse through aversive conditioning. The psychosocial and biological perspectives have pointed up possible cultural and genetic causes. The most successful treatments of alcoholism are generally multimodal treatments, dealing with the entire spectrum of the alcoholic's problems—job, spouse, family, self, and so on. Generally, such programs include follow-up meetings of the type offered by Alcoholics Anonymous.

There is a wide variety of illegal drugs, with a wide variety of effects. The depressants include not only alcohol but the narcotics (e.g., opium, morphine, heroin) and the barbiturates (e.g., Nembutal, Seconal). The narcotics, normally taken by injection, provide euphoria and relief from anxiety. They are rapidly addictive; tolerance develops; and withdrawal is extremely uncomfortable.

The barbiturates, legally prescribed as sleeping pills, are sold illegally for their alcohol-like effects: disinhibition, relaxation, and mild euphoria. In some users, however, they may prompt aggression. Physiologically, barbiturates can be extremely dangerous. Barbiturate overdoses are often implicated in suicides. Likewise, barbiturate withdrawal can be lethal.

The stimulants, including the amphetamines (e.g., Benzedrine, Dexedrine, Methedrine) and cocaine, induce alertness, energy, and feelings of confidence. Amphetamine addicts—colloquially known as "speed freaks"—can become quite violent; indeed the symptoms of amphetamine abuse are strikingly similar to those of paranoid schizophrenia. Cocaine,

which is inhaled, produces an extravagant and short-lived euphoria.

The hallucinogens (e.g., mescaline, psilocybin, THC, DMT, and especially LSD), originally thought to mime the effects of psychosis, are now used only for their ability to expand and distort perception.

Finally, marijuana and hashish, both derived from cannabis, induce euphoria, passivity, and intensified sensory perception. Neither is physiologically addictive, and irregular use appears, from the evidence, to have no harmful effects. However, the increasing popularity of marijuana and increasing demands for its legalization have led to investigation of the possible long-term ill effects of regular marijuana use on sexual potency, immune reactions, and psychological acuteness. The evidence remains quite inconclusive.

Personality type, socioeconomic status, and peer-group habits may all play a role in predisposing a person to illegal drug abuse. Like alcoholism, abuse of illegal drugs exacts a high toll from the society, particularly in the area of crime—a fact which has led many to argue that these drugs should be legalized. Drug rehabilitation, still in its infancy, may be attempted through aversive conditioning. Other methods used with narcotics addicts are the therapeutic residential community and methadone maintenance.

IV The Psychotic Disorders

Madness, though a terrible and at present a very frequent calamity, is perhaps as little understood as any that ever afflicted mankind. The names alone usually given to this disorder and its several species, *viz. Lunacy, Spleen, Melancholy, Hurry of the Spirits, etc.* may convince any one of the truth of this assertion. . . (Battie [1758], 1969, pp. 1–2).

Over two hundred years have passed since England's first teacher of psychiatry, William Battie, began his *Treatise on Madness* with these somber words. During this period some progress has been made in the study of psychosis, the severest form of what Battie calls "madness," but that progress has been slow and often discouraging. Indeed, in the spectrum of calamities which befall mankind, the psychoses are still "perhaps as little understood as any."

According to DSM-II there are two major categories of psychoses: the *biogenic psychoses*—those associated with organic brain syndromes (to be covered in Chapter 14)—and the *functional psychoses*, those not attributed to known physical conditions. The functional psychoses are further divided into three major categories:

1. the schizophrenias, which are characterized primarily by disorders of *thought*.
2. the major affective disorders, in which disturbances of *mood* predominate.
3. the paranoid states, in which the essential, and possibly the only, abnormality is a circumscribed system of *delusions*.

The affective psychoses have already been described in Chapter 7. The present chapter will focus on the two remaining types of functional psychosis, schizophrenia and paranoid states, with particular emphasis on schizophrenia, as it is by far the more common of the two types. We will begin, however, by considering the general features of psychosis and the history of our modern conception of psychosis and of schizophrenia.

PSYCHOSIS

As we have seen in our opening chapter, the history of severe mental disorder is as long as the history of the human species. However, it is only within the last hundred years, with the birth of modern science, that specialists have attempted to develop a comprehensive and systematic theory of mental illness: to distinguish between the milder and more common forms, the neuroses, and the more severe and less common forms, the psychoses, and to identify and label the different types of psychosis.

11
Schizophrenia and Paranoia

Psychosis vs. Neurosis

At some point in a series of lectures on abnormal psychology, a seasoned professor will generally point out that cases involving actual human beings are seldom as clear-cut as textbook cases. When it comes to the question of differentiating between the psychoses and the neuroses, however, even the textbooks can't be clear-cut. For every attempt to draw a "definitive" distinction between the two, there are at least a thousand exceptions from well-documented research or case studies to invalidate that distinction. Nevertheless, there are enough *apparent* differences between neurosis and psychosis that the habit of distinguishing between them has survived a century of professional dispute.

For the layman, the distinction between psychosis and neurosis might best be characterized in terms of the difference between behavior which is continuous with his own experience and that which is discontinuous. That is, to most of us, psychotic behavior would appear totally foreign to anything we have experienced or can imagine experiencing. Neurotic behavior, on the other hand, is something we can usually empathize with, because it appears to be only an exaggeration of some of our own bothersome fears, habits, and quirks.

From a more formal standpoint, the distinction between the two has traditionally focused on the matter of reality contact—that is, the ability to perceive and interact with one's environment in a reasonably efficient manner. Such, for example, is the emphasis of the definition of psychosis provided by DSM-II:

Patients are described as psychotic when their mental functioning is sufficiently impaired to interfere grossly with their capacity to meet the ordinary demands of life. The impairment may result from a serious distortion in their capacity to recognize reality (p. 23).

Neurotics, as we have mentioned in Chapter 5, may be seriously incapacitated, but they can seldom be characterized as out of contact with reality. In the psychoses, on the other hand, mental functioning has become impaired to the point where the psychotic can no longer deal effectively with the stimuli that he receives from the world around him. The consequent distortion of reality, often involving hallucinations and delusions, presents major barriers to even the most marginal adaptive functioning. It is for this reason that psychotics, unlike neurotics, are usually institutionalized.

Table 11.1 summarizes McNeil's system of comparative dimensions between psychosis and

Fig. 11.1   Social withdrawal, bizarre behavior, and distorted, disorganized thinking, the marks of "madness" throughout history, are now recognized as symptoms of schizophrenia. It remains, however, a little understood, much misunderstood breakdown of human functioning (The Madwoman, *Chaim Soutine*).

Table 11.1 Psychosis and Neurosis: A Comparison

	Psychosis	Neurosis
Emotional distortion	Severe	Mild
Cognitive distortion	Severe	Mild
Hallucination	Present	Absent
Delusion	Present	Absent
Reality contact	Distorted	Not distorted
Decompensation	Severe	Mild
Disturbed social relations	Severe	Mild

Source: E. B. McNeil, *The Psychoses* (Englewood Cliffs, N.J.: Prentice-Hall, 1970), p. 12.

Fig. 11.2 Emil Kraepelin, the German psychiatrist who established separate diagnostic categories; his use of the Latin term "dementia praecox" was the first attempt to isolate the "dementing" syndromes we now call schizophrenia.

Fig. 11.3 Eugen Bleuler, the Swiss psychiatrist who introduced the term "schizophrenia" (meaning "split mind") to describe the cognitive disorganization characteristic of those suffering from the disorder.

neurosis. You will note that on a number of these dimensions the symptoms of the neurotic and the psychotic differ in terms of "mild" vs. "severe," suggesting that neurosis is nothing more than a "little" psychosis. Although some writers do hold this position—that neurosis and psychosis differ quantitatively rather than qualitatively—the majority of professionals in the field of abnormal psychology, including even some noted behaviorists (e.g., Eysenck, 1960b), believe there is a difference in kind between the two types of disorders. In general, writers who emphasize qualitative differences between the two do so on etiological grounds, stressing that the psychoses have at least a predisposing biological basis, whereas the neuroses are attributable more to environmental stresses. These theories will be discussed more fully in Chapter 12, which will take up the various conceptualizations and treatments of schizophrenia.

Kraepelin and Bleuler: The History of Our Terminology

Until the end of the nineteenth century the different forms of what we now call psychosis were generally considered to be the result of a single disease. The first major break with this unitary theory came in 1896, when Emil Kraepelin proposed the idea that there were three separate psychoses, representing three separate disease entities: dementia praecox, paranoia, and manic-depressive psychosis.

It was to what other authors had called the primary "dementing" syndromes—those syndromes which involved delusions, hallucinations, attention deficits, and bizarre motor behavior—that Kraepelin applied the Latin term "dementia praecox," meaning "premature mental deterioration." Implied in the term were his beliefs that the illness normally

began in adolescence (hence "premature") and that it involved an irreversible mental deterioration.

That Kraepelin was wrong on both counts was pointed out less than ten years later by Eugen Bleuler, a highly influential Swiss psychiatrist. Not only was the term "dementia praecox" grossly inaccurate, Bleuler argued, but furthermore this inaccuracy was hindering professional recognition of the disease entity that the term was intended to describe.

There is hardly a single psychiatrist who has not heard the argument that the whole concept of demetia praecox must be false because there are many catatonics and other types who, symptomatologically, should be included in Kraepelin's dementia praecox, and who do not go on to complete deterioration. Similarly, the entire question seems to be disposed of with the demonstration that in a particular case deterioration has not set in precociously but only in later life (1950, p. 8).

To do away with these problems, Bleuler proposed the adoption of a new, more accurate term.

We are left with no alternative but to give the disease a new name, less apt to be misunderstood. I am well aware of the disadvantages of the proposed name but I know of no better one. I call the dementia praecox "schizophrenia" [from the Greek words *schizein*, meaning "to split," and *phren*, meaning "mind"] because the "splitting" of the different psychic functions is one of its most important characteristics. For the sake of convenience, I use the word in the singular although it is apparent that the group includes several diseases (1950, p. 8).

Hence the term "schizophrenic," which in the past half century has become the commonly accepted label. Because of its association with "splitting," laymen are apt to misunderstand the term as designating the multiple or "split" personality, which is actually a form of hysterical neurosis (see Chapter 5). What Bleuler was referring to was not a splitting of the personality into two or more personalities, but rather a split or disconsonance within or between different psychic functions in a single personality. In the mind of the schizophrenic, emotions, ideas, and perceptions cease to operate as an integral whole. One set of ideas may dominate the personality, while other thoughts or drives are split off and become impotent. Furthermore, emotions may be split off from perception and thus seem very inappropriate to a given situation. In short, to use Bleuler's words, "the personality loses its unity" (1950, p. 9).

Thus Bleuler's term "stuck" simply because it was so much more accurate than Kraepelin's. To Kraepelin, however, goes the credit (or the blame, according to some professionals) for having established separate diagnostic categories for the different psychoses, and indeed, for most of the mental disorders recognized by modern psychology. As we have seen in Chapter 1, the American Psychiatric Association's diagnostic manual, DSM-II, to which we have repeatedly referred in this book, is merely a revised version of Kraepelin's pioneering classification scheme.

Fig. 11.4   A significant behavioral manifestation of schizophrenia is the withdrawal from meaningful relationships. The top illlustration, painted by a young schizophrenic during the early stage of his disturbance, depicts a partially faceless woman alone in a desertlike setting and reflects the sense of anonymity and isolation experienced in emotional withdrawal. The middle painting depicts a globe being struck by lightning and splitting apart—a schizophrenic's symbolic expression of his own intense conflict and personality disintegration. In the bottom illustration the ghostlike figure conveys another patient's marked feelings of depersonalization, a state in which a person experiences the loss of a sense of identity, frequently with the feeling of being someone or something else. Also note the large and sinister eyes, which often occur in the art of schizophrenic persons.

SCHIZOPHRENIA

In diagnostic terms, *schizophrenia* is the label given to a group of psychoses marked by severe distortion and disorganization of thought, perception, and affect, by bizarre behavior, and by social withdrawal. Schizophrenia constitutes a major mental health problem in our society; at present almost half of the total resident populations in mental hospitals in the United States are schizophrenics (Taube and Redick, 1973). It is encouraging to note that there has been a progressive decline in the number of schizophrenic patients in mental hospitals since 1966, but we should not allow such statistics to lull us into believing that schizophrenia itself is on the decline or even that it is being dealt with more effectively. Rather, the decline is probably a reflection of recent efforts to treat schizophrenics outside mental hospitals—in short-term psychiatric wards of general hospitals, in nursing homes, and in outpatient facilities such as community mental health centers.

Fig. 11.6 shows the rate of schizophrenic patient care episodes—that is, new admissions plus those already under care—in all types of mental health facilities in the United States for the year 1971. As the chart shows, the rate is low for those under 18. Then it almost quadruples in the postteenage years, ages 18 to 24. In early adulthood, ages 25 to 44, it increases further, doubling for the men and quadrupling for the women. Then after 44 the rate begins to decline, reaching a low level in the 65-and-over age group.

The Symptoms of Schizophrenia

Buss (1966) has pointed out that though there is general agreement on the major symptoms of schizophrenia, no two authorities seem to agree as to which are the fundamental symptoms. DSM-II names the thought disorders as the predominant symptom, but as we have noted, the schizophrenic almost invariably displays other abnormalities as well, including disorders of language, perception, affect, and motor behavior. Although there is some overlap among these categories, they are listed separately below for descriptive convenience. It should be noted that while all schizophrenics do display some of these symptoms some of the time, none display all of the symptoms all of the time. Indeed, some people labeled schizophrenic behave quite normally most of the time.

Disorders of Thought
I try to think and all of a sudden I can't say anything because it's like I turn off in my mind . . . emptiness.

I can't remember that I was going to say. See, my memory leaves like that and I can't remember . . . it can happen any time.

Fig. 11.5 These drawings, entitled "My Life in the Hospital," depict a psychotic woman's self-perceptions during hospitalization. In the first series (top two rows), she shows herself as she had entered the hospital, bent over and depressed. Then, as she became involved in such activities as cooking and art therapy, she regained a measure of self-confidence, which is reflected in the erect posture and outstretched arms. Unfortunately she experienced a relapse of the depression in her attempts to deal with questions and fears. The second series of drawings (bottom two rows) shows the patient's interaction with the hospital chaplain, who seems to have answered some of her questions. After the chaplain had been transferred to another post, the woman expressed her sense of loss at his departure. She is again bent over; the rest of the world—her bed and her home—has been crossed out, lost; and the last drawing is as the first.

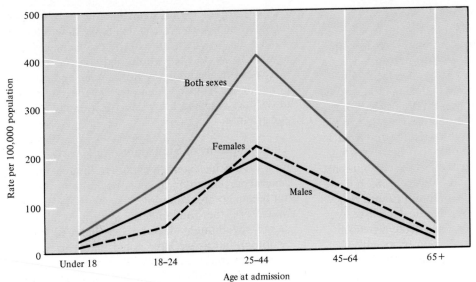

Fig. 11.6 The rate by age and sex of schizophrenic admissions to all types of mental health facilities in the United States in 1971. (Adapted by C. A. Taube, "Utilization of Mental Health Facilities, 1971." National Institute of Mental Health, 1973. DHEW Publication No. NIH-74-657.)

Dispersal is the word that I keep thinking of . . . dispersal meaning from the center out in all directions. . . . There is a circle and arrows all heading outward and meeting many different objects. So your attention is just whew—360 degrees.

My mind was so confused I couldn't focus on one thing, I had an idea and I was wondering whether I should press charges and then all of a sudden my mind went to something pleasant, and then it went back to my work, and I couldn't keep it orderly (Freedman and Chapman, 1973, pp. 46–54).

The above are firsthand reports from four different patients of the disturbed thinking so typical of schizophrenics. Disorders of thought may take a number of forms, including blocked or inappropriate associations, overinclusion, inability to conceptualize, and delusions.

Association We pointed out earlier that in looking for a term to replace "dementia praecox," Bleuler chose "schizophrenia" because it described the central symptom of a lack of association (a "split") either among ideas or between ideas and emotions in the patients whom he had observed. Bleuler summed up the schizophrenic association disturbance as follows:

In the normal thinking process, the numerous actual and latent images combine to determine each association. In schizophrenia, however, single images or whole combinations may be rendered ineffective, in an apparently haphazard fashion. Instead, thinking operates with ideas and concepts which have no, or a completely insufficient, connection with the main idea and should therefore be excluded from the thought-process. The result is that thinking becomes confused, bizarre, incorrect, abrupt. Sometimes, all the associative threads fail and the thought chain is totally interrupted; after such "blocking," ideas may emerge which have no recognizable connection with preceding ones (1950, p. 22).

The breakup of coherence in the mind of the schizophrenic may result in the association of words not on the basis of any logic whatsoever, but only, for example, because they rhyme. Such a series of rhyming or similar-sounding words is called a *clang association*. The following is a transcript of a conversation between a doctor and a schizophrenic patient who could be considered an expert at clang associations. (About half of all his daily speech was rhymed.)

Dr.: How are things going today, Ernest?
Pt.: Okay for a flump.
Dr.: What is a flump?
Pt.: A flump is a gump.
Dr.: That doesn't make any sense.
Pt.: Well, when you go to the next planet from the planet beyond the planet that landed on the danded and planded on the slanded.

Dr.: *Wait a minute. I didn't follow any of that.*
Pt.: *Well, when we was first bit on the slip on the rit and the man on the ran or the pan on the ban and the sand on the man and the pan on the ban on the can on the man on the fan on the pan.* [*All spoken very rhythmically, beginning slowly and building up to such a rapid pace that the words could no longer be understood.*]
Dr.: *What's all that hitting your head for . . . and waving your arms?*
Pt.: *That's to keep the boogers from eatin' the woogers. Well, it was a jigger and a figger and a figger and a bigger and me and I'll swap you for a got you and a fair-haired far for a bar and a jar for a tar and a rang dang, ting tang with a bee shag, he shag.*

Cohen, Nachmani and Rosenberg (1974) have pointed out that schizophrenic speech is ordinarily quite competent syntactically—that is, subject, predicate, modifiers, and so forth are usually present, and in their proper order as well. It is not the sentence structure but the meaning of the words themselves that is so frustratingly elusive. Hence, the listener's response is often "He seems to be speaking ordinary English, but I can't tell what in the world he's driving at." According to Cohen and his co-workers, schizophrenics can make very common primary associations to a given stimulus about as easily as normal people. It is the more subtle secondary associations that a schizophrenic cannot make without becoming confused and incoherent.

This phenomenon is illustrated in an experiment conducted by Cohen and his colleagues. A group of normal subjects and a group of schizophrenics were shown two colors and were asked to describe one of the colors in such a way that a listener who also had those two colors before him could pick out the one being described. When the colors were quite dissimilar, the schizophrenics did about as well as the normals—that is, the schizophrenics could deliver the obvious response almost as readily as the normal subjects. For example, when one color was red and the other a purple-blue and subjects were asked to describe the latter, responses were as follows:

Normal Speaker 1: Purple.
Normal Speaker 2: Purple.
Normal Speaker 3: This is purple blue.
Schizophrenic Speaker 1: Blue.
Schizophrenic Speaker 2: Purple.
Schizophrenic Speaker 3: The bluer.

Thus when dealing with a clear difference between red and blue, the schizophrenics, like the normal subjects, could make the simple association between the visual stimulus of the purple-blue card and the word used to describe that color. In the next stage of the experiment, however, the two colors were quite similar, requiring that the speaker make subtle associations in order to describe the slight difference between the two. Faced with this task, the normal speakers managed to combine and refine their associations in such a way as to indicate which color they

Fig. 11.7 In this painting by a chronic undifferentiated schizophrenic, the disjointed bodies and the random, mixed phrases illustrate the schizophrenic's tendency to form incoherent, inappropriate associations, characteristic of his disordered thinking.

meant. The schizophrenics, on the other hand, began reeling off associations which, while quite vivid, failed to convey the appropriate information:

Normal Speaker 1: Both are salmon colored. This one, however, has more pink.

Normal Speaker 2: My God, this is hard. They are both about the same, except that this one might be a little redder.

Normal Speaker 3: They both are either the color of canned salmon or clay. This one here is the pinker one.

Schizophrenic Speaker 1: A fish swims. You call it a salmon. You cook it. You put it in a can. You open the can. You look at it in this color. Salmon fish.

Schizophrenic Speaker 2: This is a stupid color of a shit ass bowl of salmon. Mix it with mayonnaise. Then it gets tasty. Leave it alone and puke all over the fuckin' place. Puke fish.

Schizophrenic Speaker 3: Make-up. Pancake make-up. You put it on your face and they think guys run after you. Wait a second! I don't put it on my face and guys don't run after me. Girls put it on them.

Common to all three of the schizophrenic responses is the characteristic schizophrenic "split"—in this case, the splitting off of the associations from the task at hand, that of distinguishing between the two colors. Furthermore, the ways in which the schizophrenics lose track of the point illustrate two typical patterns of schizophrenic thinking. First, in the response of Schizophrenic Speaker 1, we see the tendency to *perseverate* (dwell repeatedly) on the primary association to a given stimulus; the speaker makes the connection between the colors in front of him and the color of salmon, and then he simply pursues that association rather than refining it with any further association. A second characteristically schizophrenic quality, evident in the responses of Schizophrenic Speakers 2 and 3, is the seemingly spontaneous generation of each sentence from some mental stimulus in the sentence immediately preceding, with the result that the mind wanders further and further away from the point at which it began. This aspect of schizophrenic thinking, called *"overinclusion"* or looseness of association, is the subject of the following section.

Overinclusion   Cromwell and Dokecki (1968) have suggested that the schizophrenic has difficulty "disattending to" a stimulus after having attended to it. The hypothesis is similar to that presented many years ago by Cameron (1938), who saw schizophrenic thought as an overinclusion of stimuli. Like a normal person, a schizophrenic forms many tangential associations to stimuli, including the stimulus of his own speech, but unlike a normal person, the schizophrenic cannot filter out the irrelevant associations. Therefore, his thinking and his speech may zigzag rapidly from one topic to the next without any coherence other than the irresistible linkage of associations. This quality of schizophrenic thought may be seen in the following excerpt from a letter by a schizophrenic patient:

Dear Mother,

I am writing on paper. The pen which I am using is from a factory called "Perry & Co." This factory is in England. I assume this. Behind the name of Perry Co. the city of London is inscribed; but not the city. The city of London is in England. I know this from my school days. Then, I always liked geography. My last teacher in that subject was Professor August A. He was a man with black eyes. I also like black eyes. There are also blue and gray eyes and other sorts, too. I have heard it said that snakes have green eyes. All people have eyes. There are some, too, who are blind. These blind people are led about by a boy. It must be very terrible not to be able to see. There are people who can't see and, in addition can't hear. I know some who hear too much. One can hear too much (Bleuler, 1950, p. 17).

Bleuler, who first published this letter, points out that the only common denominator of the ideas expressed in it is that they are all present in the patient's awareness. London—geography lesson—geography teacher—his black eyes—gray eyes—green snake eyes—human eyes—blind people—deaf people, and so on. The terrible irony is that while all the ideas expressed are perfectly correct, the letter itself, because of its lack of any unifying logic, is meaningless.

Conceptualization

Dr.: I'd like you to continue this series: dog, cat, horse, lion, tiger, leopard, cow, donkey, elephant, fox . . .

Pt.: Spider, sparrow, bluefish (adapted from Arieti, 1974a, p. 297).

Most of us, listening to the doctor's series, could have abstracted the category "mammals." The schizophrenic's inability to go beyond the fact that all the items in the series were animals shows a weakness in the area of thinking known as *conceptualization,* the ability to think in terms of general concepts. Conceptualization encompasses a broad array of mental skills: imagining what "might be," grasping the essential of a given whole, isolating that which is common to a number of parts, and thinking in terms of symbols. The breakdown of these skills in the mind of the schizophrenic results in a drastic impairment of the ability to conceptualize. In studying this aspect of schizophrenic thought disorder, Goldstein (1944) stressed the schizophrenic's inability to move from the abstract to the concrete and vice versa. A normal person, when presented with a general rule, can think of a concrete example to illustrate it; conversely, when presented with a concrete object or event, he can relate it to a general principle. However, according to Goldstein, the schizophrenic, like the brain-damaged person, can experience objects only in their discrete, concrete form and is incapable of relating them to any general concept which transcends that single particular instance. While Goldstein's conclusions have been supported by a number of studies involving proverb interpretation tests (e.g., Gorham, 1956; Elmore and Gorham, 1957; Johnson, 1966), others (e.g., Brown, 1958) argue that not all schizophrenics have difficulty conceptualizing. Table 11.2 provides illustrations of the schizophrenic's inability to grasp the abstract larger meaning of a proverb.

Delusions

"Well, I know your psychology," Clyde said, "and you are a knick-knacker, and in your Catholic church in North Bradley and in your education, and I know all of it—the whole thing. I know exactly what this fellow does. In my credit like I do from up above, that's the way it works."

"As I was stating before I was interrupted," Leon went on, "it so happens that I was the first human spirit to be created with a glorified body before time existed."

"Ah, well, he is just simply a creature, that's all," Joseph put in. "Man created by me when I created the world—nothing else" (Rokeach, 1964, pp. 10–11).

On a midsummer day in 1959, three men, each of whom claimed to be Jesus Christ, were transferred to the same ward of a hospital in Ypsilanti, Michigan. The excerpt above is from one of their first encounters. Milton Rokeach had "the three Christs" assigned to adjacent beds, a shared table in the dining hall, and similar jobs in the laundry room. He then observed them for two years in order "to explore the processes by which their delusional systems of belief and their behavior might change if they were confronted with the ultimate contradiction conceivable for human beings: more than one person claiming the same identity" (Rokeach,

---

Table 11.2 Schizophrenic Interpretations of Proverbs

Proverb	Interpretation
A stitch in time saves nine.	If you had a tear in your clothing and sewed it up right away, you'd be saving time.
	If I would take one stitch ahead of time, I would know nine times better how to do another stitch.
	I could do something and it would help everyone.
A rolling stone gathers no moss.	It won't grow any grass.
	A person could answer that better if they were a stone.
	The stone keeps rolling endlessly.
People in glass houses shouldn't throw stones.	Because they'd break the glass.
	You shouldn't throw stones at people.
	You shouldn't throw stones through windows—that's what I've been trying to avoid doing.
A golden hammer breaks an iron door.	If we'd love the Russians, they'd probably love us back.
Barking dogs seldom bite.	It depends on what they're barking for. When they are loose it is all right, but when they are tied up they get mean and will bite.

Source: Adapted from I. Gregory, *Fundamentals of Psychiatry* (Philadelphia: Saunders, 1968), pp. 430–431.

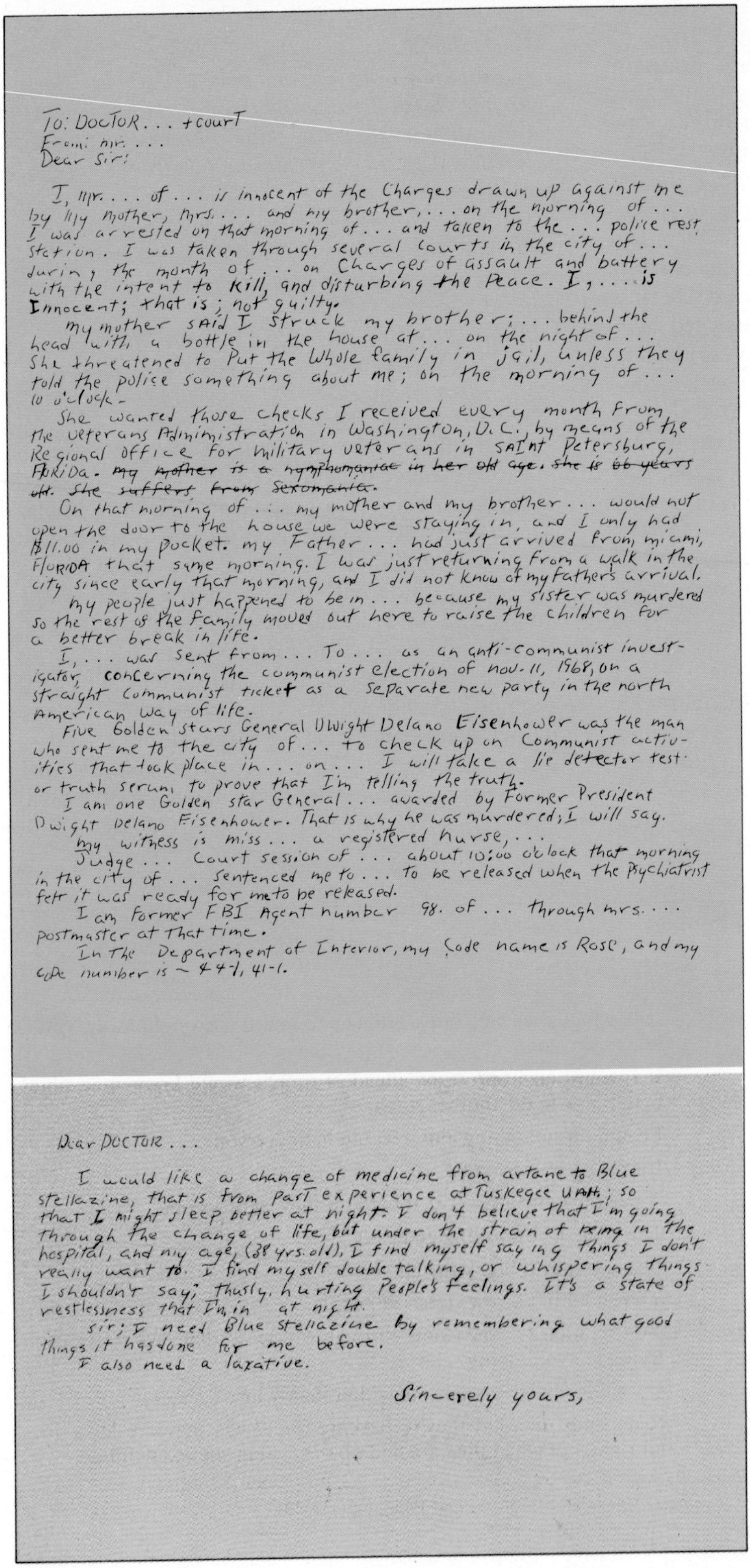

To: Doctor... + court
From: Mr...
Dear Sir:

I, Mr.... of... is innocent of the charges drawn up against me by my mother, Mrs.... and my brother,... on the morning of... I was arrested on that morning of... and taken to the... police rest station. I was taken through several courts in the city of... during the month of... on charges of assault and battery with the intent to kill, and disturbing the peace. I,...is innocent; that is; not guilty.

My mother said I struck my brother;... behind the head with a bottle in the house at... on the night of... She threatened to put the whole family in jail, unless they told the police something about me; on the morning of... 10 o'clock.

She wanted those checks I received every month from the Veterans Administration in Washington, D.C., by means of the Regional office for Military veterans in Saint Petersburg, Florida. My brother is a nymphomaniac in her old age. She is 66 years old. She suffers from sexomania.

On that morning of... my mother and my brother... would not open the door to the house we were staying in, and I only had $11.00 in my pocket. My Father... had just arrived from Miami, Florida that same morning. I was just returning from a walk in the city since early that morning, and I did not know of my father's arrival.

My people just happened to be in... because my sister was murdered so the rest of the family moved out here to raise the children for a better break in life.

I,... was sent from... to... as an anti-communist investigator, concerning the communist election of Nov. 11, 1968, on a straight communist ticket as a separate new party in the north American way of life.

Five Golden stars General Dwight Delano Eisenhower was the man who sent me to the city of... to check up on Communist activities that took place in... on... I will take a lie detector test or truth serum, to prove that I'm telling the truth.

I am one Golden star General... awarded by Former President Dwight Delano Eisenhower. That is why he was murdered; I will say.

My witness is Miss... a registered nurse,...

Judge... Court session of... about 10:00 o'clock that morning in the city of... sentenced me to... To be released when the Psychiatrist felt it was ready for me to be released.

I am former FBI Agent number 98. of... through Mrs.... postmaster at that time.

In the Department of Interior, my code name is Rose, and my code number is ~ 447, 41-1.

Dear Doctor...

I would like a change of medicine from artane to Blue stellazine, that is from past experience at Tuskegee VAH; so that I might sleep better at night. I don't believe that I'm going through the change of life, but under the strain of being in the hospital, and my age, (38 yrs. old), I find myself saying things I don't really want to. I find myself double talking, or whispering things I shouldn't say; thusly, hurting people's feelings. It's a state of restlessness that I'm in at night.

Sir; I need Blue stellazine by remembering what good things it has done for me before.

I also need a laxative.

Sincerely yours,

Fig. 11.8 These letters were written by a psychiatric patient who was diagnosed as paranoid schizophrenic. The first letter, reflecting fragmentation of thought and delusions of persecution and grandeur, was written before a plan was set up which required that the patient earn his discharge from the hospital by being rational for increasing periods of time each day. In the second letter, written after the plan was in effect, the patient attempts to control his delusions and blames the occurrence of "double talking, or whispering things I shouldn't say" on lack of sleep. (Letters courtesy of Dr. Robert Liberman, Camarillo State Hospital.)

The View from the Eden Express

In 1971, on a commune in British Columbia, Mark Vonnegut, son of novelist Kurt Vonnegut, Jr., began behaving very strangely. He gave up wearing clothes altogether; he made so much noise that the neighbors constantly threatened to call the police; he threw a huge rock through the picture window of someone's living room. Eventually he gave up eating as well. Though his friends on the commune clung to the Laingian belief that schizophrenia is a sane response to an insane society, they still felt unable to handle Vonnegut's particular response, sane or insane. And so he was committed to a mental hospital. For the next few years he struggled with recurrent schizophrenic episodes and underwent recurrent hospitalizations—a story which he has since recounted in his book, *The Eden Express* (1975). The following excerpts, all taken from Vonnegut's descriptions of his experiences in the mental hospital, illustrate the tangle of confusion and delusion typical of schizophrenic thinking:

I have a fuzzy recollection of walking up to some doctor-looking person and being totally absorbed by his gold tie clip. I suspected it was the button to end the world so I didn't touch it. I'm pretty sure it was Dr. Dale. I didn't know who else could be so tasteless as to walk around a mental hospital wearing a button to end the world.

· · ·

"The first time you were in here you were the Father. Now you're the Son. Next time you'll be the Holy Ghost and you won't need me and my keys any more." It was said affectionately. It was an orderly bringing me some food.

"Oh boy," I said slowly, just shaking my head. "Oh boy, I've f—— up again." Shrug.

"Oh boy," he said, agreeing, nodding as he left.

"Oh boy, oh boy, oh boy." I ate slowly. I didn't have the faintest idea how I had gotten there but I knew where I was.

And then I wouldn't know where I was or wouldn't care or the place was some elaborate hoax or sinister plot, and back and forth several times a day for about a week.

Dr. Dale came into my little windowless seclusion room one day and asked if I'd like to see my mother. I figured he was just asking to torment me. Of course I wanted to see my mother, but even if I wasn't dead and in hell or being kidnapped by Martians, even if I was a real patient in a real mental hospital, my mother was in Jamaica. And then alakazam he materialized my mother and she was hugging me and we were both sobbing and sobbing under Dale's tight satanic grin. "That guy really is the devil."

Our first few visits were fairly disjointed. I tried to explain what I thought was being done to me. They were draining my blood and replacing it with something else and changing the lines on my palms.

· · ·

McNice [one of the doctors] came in one day with three of the meanest orderlies. I had been utterly alone for days.

"I think I'm dead, I'm dead, aren't I?" pleading and grasping for his arm.

"Yes, I know you feel like that." He left quickly. The orderlies held me down and jabbed another needle in my ass (pp. 130, 185,189).

1964, p. 3). After two years of continuous daily contact, each of the three men remained quite unmoved in his belief that he alone was the son of God.

A *delusion* is an irrational belief which an individual will defend with great vigor despite overwhelming evidence that the belief has no basis in reality. Delusions are among the most common of the schizophrenic thought disorders. In a sample of 405 schizophrenics, Lucas and his colleagues (1962) found 71 percent to be delusional. The delusions themselves may take many forms. In Rokeach's study cited above, all three of the schizophrenics had *delusions of grandeur,* in which an individual believes that he is some famous person such as Napoleon or, as in the case above, Christ himself. Other types of delusions are also common. *Delusions of persecution* involve the belief that one is being plotted against, spied upon, threatened, interfered with, or otherwise mistreated. In *delusions of control* (also called *delusions of influence*), the individual is convinced that other people or even extraterrestrial beings are controlling his thoughts or actions, often by means of electronic devices which send signals directly to his brain. *Hypochondriacal delusions*, also common, differ from the hypochondriacal beliefs seen in some neurotic patients in that the delusions generally are marked by a bizarre quality; a schizophrenic patient, for example, may believe that his insides are rotting or that his brain is full of mold. *Delusions of sin and guilt* involve the unfounded belief that one has committed "the unpardonable sin" or has brought great harm to others.

It should be pointed out that occasionally it is very difficult for the psychiatrist or psychologist to distinguish between what is delusional and what is real. And, no doubt, diagnostic mistakes do occur. For example, Kraft and Babigian (1972) report the case of a woman, Mrs. M., who appeared one day in the hospital emergency room complaining that she had needles in both her arms. Upon questioning, the woman revealed that she had spent a total of nine years in psychiatric hospitals. Each of her eight hospitalizations had been precipitated by an episode of self-mutilation in which Mrs. M., obeying voices that told her that she was bad and that she should kill herself, had slashed her wrists, thighs, or abdomen. She also reported seven years of alcohol abuse. This history, along with the physical examination, which revealed no needle marks on her arms nor any foreign bodies inside the arms, convinced the examining physicians that Mrs. M. was delusional. However, they were thorough enough to order an x-ray and were very much surprised when the x-ray showed that the woman did indeed have a number of needles in both arms. Apparently, in a suicide attempt the year before, she had inserted several sewing needles in each arm, and the needles had remained undetected during three subsequent hospitalizations. It is not improbable that during these hospitalizations Mrs. M. reported the presence of the needles and that her reports were simply assumed to be delusional.

Disorders of Language   In describing schizophrenic symptomatology most specialists make little distinction between disorders of thought and disorders of language, reasoning that the confused speech of the schizophrenic is simply the result of confused thinking. Thus, for example, we have considered clang associations under the heading of thought disorders, since this bizarre rhyming speech seems closely related to the schizophrenic's inability to make appropriate mental associations. However, it has been suggested by some writers (e.g., Kleist, 1960; Fish, 1957) that schizophrenic language disturbances may result not from disordered thought processes but rather from a disorganization and inaccessibility of verbal symbols. Hence the schizophrenic might know what word he wants but simply be unable to find it. Two typical schizophrenic language disorders that might possibly be explained by this hypothesis are neologisms and word salad, but they might also be interpreted as merely the reflection of disordered thinking.

Neologisms   Schizophrenic speech often includes words and phrases not found even in the most comprehensive dictionary. These usages, called *neologisms* (literally, "new words"), are often formed by combining parts of two or more regular words. Or the neologism may simply involve the using of common words in a unique fashion. In either case, what is interesting about neologisms is that while sometimes they are totally unintelligible, at other times they manage to communicate ideas quite clearly and vividly, as may be seen in the following transcript. (Possible intended meanings are indicated within brackets.)

Dr.: Sally, you're not eating supper tonight. What's the problem?

Pt.: No, I had belly bad luck and brutal and outrageous. [I have stomach problems, and I don't feel good.] I gave all the work money. [I paid tokens for my meal.] Here, I work. Well, the difference is I work five days and when the word was [when I am told to work] but I had escapingly [I got out of some work]. I done it for Jones. He planned it and had me work and helped me work and all and had all the money. He's a tie-father. [He's a relative.] Besides generation ties and generation hangages [relationships between family generations—the way generations hang together] . . . he gave love a lot. I fit in them generations since old-fashion time [since long ago]. I was raised in packs [with other people] . . . certain times I was, since I was in littlehood [since I was a little girl] . . . she said she concerned a Sally-twin [my twin sister]. She blamed a few people with minor words [she scolded people], but she done goodship [good things]. I've had to suffer so much. I done it United States long.

Dr.: Sally, is there anything else you want to tell me before you go?

Pt.: Well, I expect there's a lot of things, but I would know what they were, especially the unkind crimery [the bad things].

Word Salad Schizophrenic speech aberrations range from only slight peculiarity to total disorganization. The latter extreme may be seen in the following statement made by the same patient whose clang associations were quoted earlier in this chapter.

The lion will have to change from dogs into cats until I can meet my father and mother and we dispart some rats. I live on the front part of Whitton's head. You have to work hard if you don't get into bed. She did. She said, "Hallelujah, happy landings." It's all over for a squab true tray and there ain't no squabs, there ain't no men, there ain't no music, there ain't no nothing besides my mother and my father who stand alone upon the Island of Capri where there is no ice, there is no nothing but changers, changers, changers. That comes like in first and last names, so that thing does. Well, it's my suitcase, sir. I've got to travel all the time to keep my energy alive.

Appropriately, this type of speech, in which words and phrases are combined in what appears to be a completely disorganized fashion, is referred to as *word salad*. Unlike neologisms, word salad seems to have no communicative value whatever. Nor does it appear to reflect thoughts which generalize on the basis of tangential associations, as did the letter quoted earlier, in which the writer's associations progressed from a geography teacher to his black eyes, to other color eyes, to green snake eyes, and so on. Seemingly devoid not only of logic and meaning, but even of associational links, word salad is defined by its total inaccessibility to the listener.

Disorders of Perception There is considerable evidence that schizophrenics perceive the world differently from normal people. In the first place, schizophrenics consistently *report* perceptual dysfunction. In a comparative study of newly admitted schizophrenic and nonschizophrenic patients, Freedman and Chapman (1973) found that the schizophrenics reported a significantly greater number of changes in their perceptual functioning, including visual illusions, disturbingly acute auditory perception, inability to focus attention, difficulty in identifying people, and difficulty in understanding the speech of others. Schizophrenics have also reported olfactory changes, complaining that their own body odor is more pronounced and more unpleasant, that other people smell stronger, and that objects smell funny (Hoffer and Osmond, 1962).

Second, these reports are confirmed by standard laboratory perceptual tests, which indicate that schizophrenics do poorly on such perceptual tasks as size estimation (Strauss, Foureman, and Parwatikar, 1974), time estimation (Johnson and Petzel, 1971; Petzel and Johnson, 1972), and *proprioceptive discrimination* (Ritzler and Rosenbaum, 1974)—that is, discrimination of the orientation of their bodies in space: where their hands and feet are, for example. Other tests have shown schizophrenics to be generally deficient in sensory sensitivity (Broen and Nakamura, 1972).

To the normal observer, the most dramatic type of schizophrenic perceptual disorder is the *hallucination*, a sensory perception which occurs in the absence of any appropriate external stimulus. Most of us are able, with varying degrees of vividness, to hear imagined voices, to form pictures "in the mind's eye," and even to re-create experiences of taste, touch, and smell in the absence of primary stimulation. But when this occurs, we are aware that these sensory experiences are products of the imagination rather than responses to external stimuli. Furthermore, we feel that we control such experiences. Hallucinations differ from such "normal" imaginings in two respects. First, they are not conjured up or created at will; they occur spontaneously. Second, while many schizophrenics do recognize that the voices they hear are "only in my head," many others are unsure as to whether their hallucinations are real or imagined, and a fair percentage—presumably the more severely psychotic (Buss, 1966)—are in fact convinced that their hallucinations are perceptions of objectively real events.

The common clinical observation is that auditory hallucinations are the most frequent, followed by visual hallucinations, followed by hallucinations involving the other senses. These frequencies have been confirmed by Malitz, Wilkens, and Esecover (1962), who found that out of a random sample of one hundred schizophrenics, 50 percent reported auditory hallucinations, while 9 percent reported visual hallucinations. Buss (1966), observing that this frequency pattern for hallucinations in the various senses parallels the frequency with which the different senses are used in interpersonal contact, has proposed a correlation between the two factors: "The more the sense modality is used in dealing with others, the more likely it is that a hallucination will occur in its sphere" (p. 194). Thus since the most common type of interpersonal communication is listening to one another, the most common type of hallucination is auditory; since the second most common type of interpersonal sensory contact is looking at one another, the second most common

Fig. 11.9 (above)   Visual hallucinations are rarely reproduced in drawings, especially while the hallucination is in progress. However, this drawing in black chalk was made by a girl during an acute hebephrenic outburst. She reportedly saw herself "threatened on all sides by hideously grimacing heads of monsters, large birds and the like who wanted to tear her to bits." (Source: J. H. Plokker, Artistic Self-Expression in Mental Disease: The Shattered Image of Schizophrenics. *I. Finlay, tr., The Netherlands: Mouton & Co., 1964, p. 170).*

type of hallucination is visual; and since the remaining sense modalities—smell, taste, and touch—are less commonly used in interpersonal exchanges, likewise hallucinations in these modalities are less common.

Mintz and Alpert (1972) have offered an alternative interpretation of the varying hallucination frequencies in the different senses. These writers point out that research has shown that 10 percent of the normal population is able to experience vivid visual imagery, while 48 percent is able to experience vivid auditory imagery; these figures are very close to the percentages of schizophrenics who report visual and auditory hallucinations—according to the study cited above, 9 percent and 50 percent respectively (Malitz et al., 1962). Hence the distribution of vivid imagery among the sensory modalities is the same for schizophrenics as for normal people. Accordingly, Mintz and Alpert have proposed that schizophrenics differ from normal people not in the fact that they have imagined sensory experiences, nor in the frequency or modality of these experiences, but simply in the

Fig. 11.10 (right, above)   A professional artist made this pen drawing of a visual hallucination which had made him very frightened and depressed. As described by Plokker, "the work . . . shows a large, cavernous and bare room in a prison where a cruel looking soldier is on guard with a bayonet on his rifle. The artist himself is balancing, with a rope around his neck which ends in a rope around the neck of another man, on a narrow beam above the large room. If one of them falls, then both will be strangled. Clusters of corpses of men who have been subjected to the same test of equilibrium and who tripped illustrate in no uncertain way the danger of death which he is experiencing. His wife and child (in the lower right-hand corner) do not dare to look at the horrible scene. A 'bird of death' is looking at the scene and waiting for him. Although he accomplished the feat of balancing above the abyss without falling down, the return to his old and familiar surroundings remains barred to him." (Source: J. H. Plokker, Artistic Self-Expression in Mental Disease: The Shattered Image of Schizophrenics. *I. Finlay, tr., The Netherlands: Mouton & Co., 1964, p. 171).*

ability to *distinguish* between those sensory experiences that are responses to actual external stimuli and those that are not. In short, the schizophrenics have impaired reality testing. And thus we call their sensory imagery, which they mistake for objective reality, by a different name: "hallucinations."

A challenge to the accuracy of the frequencies reported above comes from a former patient, Louise Pfeifer, who has written about her own hallucinatory experiences during a schizophrenic episode. Pfeifer believes tactile hallucinations to be much more prevalent among schizophrenics than reported, primarily because these hallucinations are so difficult to describe that the patient is prone to pass them off as "pain." This former patient, however, has not only made a drawing of her hallucinations, showing the areas of sensation and their associated strengths (see Fig. 11.11), but she has also, apparently for the first time in the literature of schizophrenia, written a vivid firsthand report of what it is like to suffer from tactile hallucinations:

These hallucinations consist of the subjectively real feeling that patches of flesh are painfully stretching in an elastic manner past the boundaries of the head—sometimes as far as twelve inches past the boundary of the head. These hallucinations contract into the head as well as expand past the head. They are concentrated in the area of the head, though they do extend briefly to other parts of the body. They are chronic and constantly active but they are variable in their intensity and in the scope and speed of their activity. Sometimes the "stretch" to these hallucinations becomes so taut that it results in a sharp cutting pain. There is also a quality of numbness to these hallucinations. It suffices to say that the essential nature of these hallucinations is utterly frustrating and incapacitating, and thus vastly frightening, as is manifested in the devastating effect they have on the personality, thinking and behavior of the patient.

A curious thing about these hallucinations is that even though they are painful and unbearable, once one falls asleep one remains asleep, indicating that they are not active during sleep. This, however, does not hold true in the acute stage of the illness—sometimes one can feel the sensations even while one is dreaming. Sleep at this stage is very sporadic and disturbed.

Running the tongue across the teeth will increase the activity of these hallucinations as will rubbing the head with the hand. These hallucinations tend to follow the movement of the tongue and hand (1970, pp. 57–58).

Disorders of Affect   As we have noted, the affective psychoses are characterized primarily by disturbances in mood or affect, while schizophrenia is characterized primarily by disturbances in thought. But, in fact, schizophrenia often involves disturbances in affect as well. The schizophrenic affective abnormalities differ from those that mark the affective psychoses in two important respects. First, as we have seen, the affective psychoses involve either deep depression or manic elation, or a combination of the two; in schizophrenia, on the other hand, what we see is either a lack of affect or affect which is inappropriate to the immediate context. Second—again, as we have seen—the affective psychoses may involve sudden and extreme reversals in mood; the manic-depressive psychotic is capable of progressing rapidly from a state of expansive euphoria to a state of bleak despair. In contrast, the schizophrenic is unlikely to undergo such extreme mood shifts.

DSM-II identifies three types of affective abnormality commonly found in schizophrenics. The first

Fig. 11.11   *A representation of typical tactile hallucinations. (Adapted from I. Pfeifer, "A Subjective Report of Tactile Hallucinations in Schizophrenia."* Journal of Clinical Psychology, *1970, 26 (1), 57–60.)*

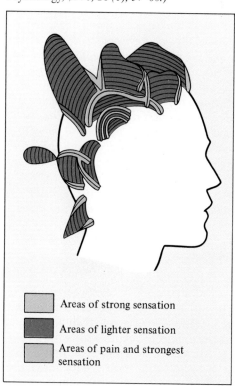

Areas of strong sensation

Areas of lighter sensation

Areas of pain and strongest sensation

is *ambivalent affect*—that is, the schizophrenic may manifest both a strong positive reaction and a strong negative reaction toward another person at the same time. Second, the schizophrenic may show a "constricted" emotional responsiveness, often described as *flat affect*. In this case, nothing can elicit from him any emotional response whatsoever; regardless of what is going on around him, he remains totally apathetic. Finally, many schizophrenics display *inappropriate affect*, meaning that their emotional responses seem totally unsuitable to the immediate context. For example, a patient may giggle upon hearing of his wife's death, or he may become very angry when given a present.

Disorders of Motor Behavior

The variety of unusual behaviors, including the absence of normal behavior, manifested by schizophrenics seems to be limited only by the boundaries of behavior itself. The following portrait of a schizophrenic ward shows a typical mix of behaviors that might be observed daily in hundreds of schizophrenic wards throughout the country.

In the day room Lou stands hour after hour, day after day, never saying a word, just rubbing the palm of his hand around and around on the top of his head. Jerry, more active, spends hours not only rubbing his hand against his stomach but also running around a post at the same time. Helen paces back and forth, her head down, mumbling about enemies who are coming to get her, while Vic grimaces and giggles over in the corner. Virginia stands in the center of the day room vigorously slapping her hand against the fullness of her dress, making a rhythmical smacking sound which, because of its tireless repetition, goes unnoticed. Nick tears up magazines, puts bits of paper in his mouth, and then spits them out, while Bill sits immobile for hours, staring at the floor. Some behaviors are not bizarre, but merely inappropriate to the setting: Betty sits quietly masturbating on the couch, while Paul follows one of the young nurse's aides on her room check, hoping to get a chance to see up her dress as she leans over to smooth a bed. Other behaviors appear perfectly normal: Geraldine is reading her Bible; Lillian is watching television; and Frank is hard at work scrubbing the floor.

Whether or not a person would feel comfortable working on or visiting such a ward would depend largely on the extent of his experience with schizophrenics. There is little doubt, however, that a first-time visitor would feel uneasy. This uneasiness appears to be related to a common equation of odd

behavior with potential danger. To be sure, people are sent to mental hospitals specifically because they are considered a danger to themselves or to others. However, the majority of mental hospital patients who exhibit bizarre behaviors are no more dangerous to be around than the average individual outside the hospital. In fact, most people would be far safer spending an afternoon in a local mental hospital ward than they would be taking a walk in many parts of their own cities. With certain types of mental patients the possibility of danger does exist, but the general fear of danger from present and former mental patients is considerably greater than available evidence would warrant (Giovannoni and Gurel, 1967).

In spite of the wide range of behaviors both usual and unusual taking place on the ward described above, there is one behavior that is strikingly absent: interpersonal interaction. Rarely do the patients engage in small talk. Rarely do they address one another except to ask for a cigarette or a light. Indeed, one of the most salient characteristics of severely disturbed patients is withdrawal from interpersonal relationships. This is particularly true of the chronic long-term schizophrenic, the type of patient in the ward described above. Is this social withdrawal a response to living year after year amid the unchanging drabness of the ward? Or is it due specifically to an avoidance of interpersonal involvement on the part of schizophrenics? Several investigators believe the latter to be the case and have provided data to support their positions.

Duke and Mullins (1973), for example, found that chronic schizophrenics preferred greater interpersonal distances (that is, the actual amount of space between oneself and the person standing or sitting closest to one) than either nonschizophrenic psychiatric patients or a group of normal people. Although hospitalization did have some effect upon interpersonal distance, hospitalization alone did not account for the magnitude of interpersonal distance preferred by the schizophrenics (Duke and Mullins, 1973). Furthermore, it has been found that schizophrenics tend to look at other people less than do normal people and that they tend to avoid the gaze of anyone looking directly at them (Harris, 1968). To test whether this gaze avoidance was a function of stimulus aversion in general—perhaps because the schizophrenic finds stimulation overarousing—or whether it was specifically other *people* that the schizophrenic avoided looking at, Williams (1974) compared the amount of time three different groups of subjects—schizophrenics, psychiatric patients not

The Symptoms of Schizophrenia

Disorders of thought

Blocked or inappropriate associations
  (e.g., clang associations, perseveration)
Overinclusion
Difficulty in conceptualization
Delusions (especially of grandeur and
  persecution)

Disorders of language

Neologisms
Word salad

Disorders of perception

Intensification or dulling of sensory perception
  (e.g., hypersensitivity to sound)
Hallucinations (especially auditory and visual)

Disorders of affect

Ambivalent affect
Flat affect
Inappropriate affect

Disorders of motor behavior

Bizarre behavior
Lack of interpersonal interaction
Catatonic stupor

diagnosed as schizophrenic, and normal people—spent looking at either a television program or at a person who was trying to engage them in conversation and was looking directly at them. No differences were found between the normal people and the nonschizophrenic patients; in comparison to the two other groups, however, the schizophrenics spent considerably less time looking at the person and considerably more time looking at the television program. Williams interprets these results to mean that gaze avoidance shown by schizophrenics is in fact "person avoidance" not just "stimulus avoidance."

Gaze avoidance, however, falls only in the middle range of withdrawal behaviors seen in schizophrenics. In the most extreme form of withdrawal, called *catatonic stupor* (to be discussed later in this chapter), the schizophrenic, retreating into a completely immobile state, shows a total lack of responsiveness not only to all interpersonal stimuli but to most other forms of stimulation as well.

The Dimensions of Schizophrenia

Early research in schizophrenia simply compared groups of undifferentiated schizophrenics with groups of normal individuals. But these studies found that the heterogeneity or variety of behavior represented by the schizophrenic groups was much too great for the purposes of certain kinds of research. Hence investigators began searching for dimensions along which subgroups of schizophrenics could be formed, so as to reduce the extreme heterogeneity. Among the dimensions of schizophrenia that have since been proposed, the two that have received the most attention and that have proved most useful are the process-reactive dimension and the paranoid-nonparanoid dimension.

The Process-Reactive Dimension In the *process-reactive dimension* the schizophrenic is classified according to whether the onset of symptoms is gradual (process) or whether it is abrupt (reactive) and apparently precipitated by some traumatic event. Garmezy (1970) reminds us that the process-reactive dimension of schizophrenia has a long history, finding its roots in the writings of Kraepelin and Bleuler. In terms of etiology, these two investigators divided the psychoses into two basic groups: those which are biogenic in origin—that is, the result of an abnormal physiological *process*—and those which are psychogenic in origin—that is, *reactions* to life experiences. Although this dichotomous construct, based on etiology, is still held by many investigators today, most current workers in the field view the process-reactive dimension more in terms of a continuum (Ullmann and Krasner, 1975). This change reflects an increasing emphasis on those aspects of the dimension which have to do with the schizophrenic's *premorbid adjustment*—that is, his level of social and sexual adjustment before hospitalization. Needless to say, weighing the normality or abnormality of a patient's entire life prior to hospitalization involves a great many more gray areas than does the simple black-or-white distinction between biogenic or psychogenic etiology.

Thus investigators differ somewhat in their interpretation of the process-reactive dimension, but there is a fairly general agreement on the basic behavioral elements which define the poles of the dimension. Kantor, Wallner and Winder (1953) have provided an excellent summary of case-history criteria for differentiating between process and reactive schizophrenics (see Table 11.3). In general, the process case involves a long history of inadequate social, sexual, and occupational adjustment. Apathy, isolation, and lack of emotional responsibility to others have usually been evident for many years prior to hospitalization. The history of the process schizophrenic typically shows that he did not belong to a group of friends in school, did not date regularly during adolescence, did not continue his education after high school, never held a job for longer than two years, and never married (Ullmann and Krasner, 1975). Furthermore, there appears to have

Table 11.3   Case-History Criteria for Differentiating Process and Reactive Schizophrenia

Process Schizophrenia	*Reactive Schizophrenia*
Birth to the Fifth Year	
a. Early psychological trauma.	a. Good psychological history.
b. Physical illness, severe or long.	b. Good physical health.
c. Odd member of family.	c. Normal member of family.
Fifth Year to Adolescence	
a. Difficulties at school.	a. Well adjusted at school.
b. Family troubles paralleled with sudden changes in patient's behavior.	b. Domestic troubles unaccompanied by behavior disruptions. Patient had "what it took."
c. Introverted behavior trends and interests.	c. Extroverted behavior trends and interests.
d. History of breakdown of social, physical, mental functioning.	d. History of adequate social, physical, mental functioning.
e. Pathological siblings.	e. Normal siblings.
f. Overprotective or rejecting mother. "Momism."	f. Normal protective, accepting mother.
g. Rejecting father.	g. Accepting father.
Adolescence to Adulthood	
a. Lack of heterosexuality.	a. Heterosexual behavior.
b. Insidious, gradual onset of psychosis without pertinent stress.	b. Sudden onset of psychosis; stress present and pertinent; later onset.
c. Physical aggression.	c. Verbal aggression.
d. Poor response to treatment.	d. Good response to treatment.
e. Lengthy stay in hospital.	e. Short course in hospital.
Adulthood	
a. Massive paranoia.	a. Minor paranoid trends.
b. Little capacity for alcohol.	b. Much capacity for alcohol.
c. No manic-depressive component.	c. Presence of manic-depressive component.
d. Failure under adversity.	d. Success despite adversity.
e. Discrepancy between ability and achievement.	e. Harmony between ability and achievement.
f. Awareness of change in self.	f. No sensation of change.
g. Somatic delusions.	g. Absence of somatic delusions.
h. Clash between culture and environment.	h. Harmony between culture and environment.
i. Loss of decency (nudity, public masturbation, etc.).	i. Retention of decency.

Source: R. E. Kantor, J. M. Wallner, and C. L. Winder, "Process and Reactive Schizophrenia," *Journal of Consulting Psychology,* 17 (1953), pp. 157–162.

been no precipitating event—no sudden change such as a divorce, the loss of a job, or the death of someone close—immediately preceding hospitalization. Rather, what the history usually reveals is a gradual eclipse of thoughts, interests, emotions, and activities until at last the person becomes so withdrawn that he is hospitalized.

In contrast, the reactive schizophrenic's premorbid adjustment turns up smooth and normal. The patient fit in nicely at home and at school, had friends, dated, and simply got along well in general. The onset of the schizophrenic symptoms after a clear precipitating event is sudden and spectacular, often involving hallucinations and delusions as well as considerable panic on the part of the sufferer, who suddenly discovers that he no longer has control over his thought and emotions.

The process-reactive distinction has been particularly useful in predicting which patients will recover and which will not (Garmezy, 1970). Process schizophrenics are more likely to have longer hospitalizations and are less likely to be discharged than reactives. It is largely this factor that allows the terms *chronic* and *acute* to be used, for all practical purposes, interchangeably with "process" and "reactive," or "poor premorbid" and "good premorbid." As the terms are generally defined for research purposes, "chronic" refers to patients who have been hospitalized for more than about two years, while "acute" refers to those who have had shorter hospitalizations.

The Paranoid-Nonparanoid Dimension

Like the process-reactive dimension, the *paranoid-nonparanoid dimension* has been used by investigators to reduce the wide variety of schizophrenic symptomatologies by classifying them into manageable subgroups. The criterion by which schizophrenics are grouped on this dimension is the presence (paranoid) or absence (nonparanoid) of delusions of persecution and/or grandeur. Although some studies have found the paranoid-nonparanoid dimension to be independent of the process-reactive dimension (e.g., Johannsen et al., 1963; Zigler and Levine, 1973), other studies have presented substantial evidence of a correlation between the two dimensions. Buss, for instance, points out that in general paranoid schizophrenics, like reactive schizophrenics, "are more intact intellectually, perform better in a variety of tasks, and have a higher level of maturity" (1966, p. 230). Not surprisingly in view of these findings, the length of hospitalization is briefer and the number of rehospitalizations fewer for paranoid schizophrenics. Thus the paranoid-nonparanoid dimension, like the process-reactive dimension, has had some prognostic value, indicating whether a patient is likely to be chronic or acute. Paranoid schizophrenia will be discussed more fully in the following section.

The Subtypes of Schizophrenia

DSM-II lists the following ten types of schizophrenia: simple, hebephrenic, catatonic, paranoid, acute, latent, residual, schizo-affective, childhood, and chronic undifferentiated. Then, just in case the diagnostician cannot quite fit the patient into one of these categories, an eleventh is listed: "other (and unspecified) types." It might be said that attempts to derive conceptual order out of such descriptive and semantic chaos are the province as well as the despair of specialists in behavior pathology. Rarely does the active, treatment-oriented clinician have the time, patience, or motivation to quibble about such

Dimensions of Schizophrenia

Process-reactive	Gradual onset with no precipitating event vs. sudden onset with precipitating event
Good-poor premorbid	Normal social and sexual adjustment prior to schizophrenic breakdown vs. inadequate social and sexual adjustment prior to breakdown
Chronic-acute	Hospitalized for more than about two years vs. hospitalized for less than about two years
Paranoid-nonparanoid	Presence vs. absence of delusions of persecution or grandeur

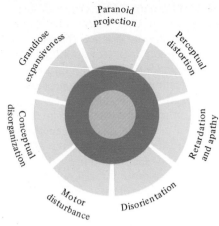

Paranoid
projection

Grandiose
expansiveness

Perceptual
distortion

Conceptual
disorganization

Retardation
and apathy

Motor
disturbance

Disorientation

Fig. 11.12   Schizophrenic subtypes: an alternative system. In response to diagnosticians' complaints regarding the imprecision of the DSM-II schizophrenic subtypes, Lorr et al. (1963) have proposed an alternative method of classification: the so-called schizophrenic circle, pictured here. Through factor analysis (Chapter 16) — that is, computerized comparison — of the symptoms revealed in interviews with over 500 psychotic patients, Lorr and his colleagues broke these symptoms down into large symptom-clusters or syndromes, seven of which appeared characteristic of schizophrenia. These seven syndromes were then assembled into a circle, indicating the degree to which each syndrome appeared related to another. According to this system, the closer together two syndromes are on the schizophrenic circle, the greater the likelihood of their occurring together in the same patient. Conversely, the greater the distance between two syndromes on the circle, the more unlikely it is that any one patient will manifest symptoms associated with both syndromes. Thus, for example, the paranoid patient is most likely to suffer from perceptual distortion and grandiose expansiveness, while he is least likely to manifest motor disturbances and disorientation. Lorr and his colleagues have developed a similar circle, made up of eight syndromes, for the classification of psychotics in general. But Lorr's circles have yet to supplant the DSM-II classification system. Consequently, while it seems likely that this alternative method would increase diagnostic agreement, we do not know whether it would prove a better tool for prescribing treatment. (Adapted from M. Lorr, C. J. Klett, and D. M. McNair, Syndromes of Psychosis. New York: Macmillan, 1963.)

fine nuances of diagnostic distinction, especially since in the case of schizophrenia the subcategory is totally unrelated to treatment. Some of these subcategories, however, are more easily distinguished than others, and for descriptive purposes, we will consider four of the more clear-cut types: simple, hebephrenic, catatonic, and paranoid. Fig. 11.12 shows a typical breakdown of the frequencies with which the various schizophrenic subtypes are seen in hospitals. The paranoid type is by far the most frequent, accounting for 45 percent of the cases, while the catatonic, hebephrenic, and simple types are less common, accounting for 8 percent, 5 percent, and 2 percent, respectively.

Simple Schizophrenia   As we have just seen, diagnostic breakdowns of hospitalized schizophrenics show *simple schizophrenia* as being a comparatively rare subtype. But this statistical rarity may be due in large part to the ability of simple schizophrenics to avoid hospitalization by making a marginal adjustment in the outside world. The simple schizophrenic is generally in better contact with his environment and shows fewer overtly bizarre behaviors than do other types. As a consequence, many simple schizophrenics are cared for by their families, particularly during adolescence and early adulthood. And often they either support themselves or contribute to their support by working at low-level, unskilled jobs, showing minimal motivation and seldom advancing. Such an individual may be accepted by his family simply as "weird Uncle George, who at forty-five still lives with Grandma and Grandpa and never seems interested in much of anything." Because George has been this way for many years and has never really disturbed anyone or shown any severe psychotic symptoms, friends of the family shrug and dismiss his pattern of behavior with "Oh, that's just George." Many other simple schizophrenics become hobos, prostitutes, or hermits, some preferring the anonymity afforded by the rundown sections of large cities, and others isolating themselves in rural areas.

Similar in many ways to the description we have given above of process schizophrenia, simple schizophrenia usually involves a slow onset beginning in adolescence or early adulthood. Gradually the individual withdraws from interpersonal contacts, abandons whatever ambitions he had, and becomes sloppy in personal habits. Hallucinations and delusions may occur, but they are rare. Rather, the typical simple schizophrenic shows a highly undramatic symptomatology, in which the most striking features

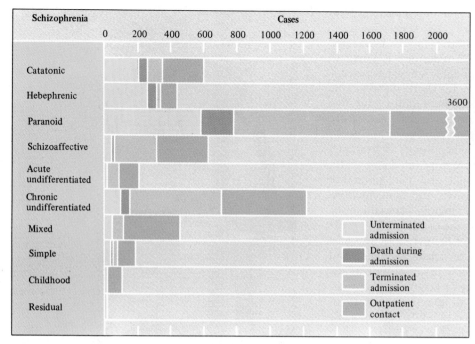

Fig. 11.13 shows how a sample of 8,094 cases, all diagnosed schizophrenic, were distributed among ten of the eleven categories listed in DSM-II. (Adapted from F. G. Guggenheim and H. M. Babigian, "Catatonic Schizophrenia: Epidemiology and Clinical Course." Journal of Nervous and Mental Disease, 1974, 158(4), 291–305.)

are apathy, dullness, scattered attention, and constant daydreaming. Not surprisingly, simple schizophrenics are generally quiet and placid, though they may become irritable if pressure is put on them to change their behavior or to show any initiative.

Since the diagnosis of simple schizophrenia is largely established negatively, by the absence of more bizarre schizophrenic symptoms, diagnostic confusion is probably widespread. Because of their apathy, poor attention, and slowness of thinking, many simple schizophrenics are mistakenly thought to be mentally retarded. Furthermore, there is often some question as to whether the simple schizophrenic might not as easily be diagnosed as suffering from a personality disorder such as schizoid personality or inadequate personality (see Chapter 5). The following case illustrates the major characteristics of this subtype:

Lester's record contained very little information except that he had been at the state hospital for seventeen years. Although the ward treatment program was highly active, involving daily trips to the gym, classes in academic subjects and in self-care, social activities, and jobs caring for the ward and serving the meals, Lester was generally to be found lying on his bed looking out the window or occasionally reading. His beard seemed never to be clean-shaven, but, on the other hand, neither did his scraggly stubble ever seem to grow—at least not as fast as the long brown splotch on his T-shirt, where the tobacco juice col-

lected as it dribbled from his chin. Occasionally, if he were pressed into relating some tale from the early part of his life when he rode the rails, his eyes might show a glint of light. But in general those who ventured into his world were greeted with nothing more than a dull scowl and a few grudging words.

Lester's behavior was never bizarre, and in fact it rarely drew any notice at all except at activity time. On his ward, patients were organized in groups, and all members of a group were expected to be present before an activity could begin—a requirement that Lester invariably resisted with obstinacy and annoyance. He was the last member of his group to arrive, and then only after a great deal of haranguing by his group members. The only times he had ever shown anger or appeared to be physically menacing were those few occasions on which his group members had voted to turn his bed over if he didn't get up and join them.

Hebephrenic Schizophrenia The term *hebephrenic* is adapted from the Greek words meaning "youthful mind," an apt description of some of the behaviors typically observed in patients so diagnosed. Giggling wildly, making funny faces, and assuming absurd postures, the hebephrenic often resembles nothing so much as a normally silly seven-year-old boy trying to get a rise out of his parents. Even neologisms, so often a part of the hebephrenic's speech, are also typical of a young child's attempts to express himself.

In addition to "immature" motor behaviors, however, the hebephrenic's repertoire is likely to include disturbances of thought, language, perception, and affect as well. In short, hebephrenic schizophrenia seems to run the gamut of the five categories of disorder that we have described earlier as characteristic of schizophrenia in general. Speech is often distorted: it is the hebephrenic, for example, who is most likely to produce word salad and neologisms. Disorders of thought and perception are prominent, including delusions and hallucinations which often focus on sex, religion, persecution, or bodily harm but which lack the continuity and organization of the imaginings of the paranoid. It is also the hebephrenic who with his constant giggling and silliness is most likely to show inappropriate affect. Armed with this wide array of bizarre mannerisms, the hebephrenic, out of all the types of schizophrenia, is the one who best fulfills the layman's stereotype of a crazy person.

Despite their apparent retreat from reality, many hebephrenics have a certain knowing quality about them and tend to perform their antics only for carefully chosen audiences. For example, the word salad and clang associations quoted earlier in this chapter were produced by a hebephrenic who would perform these verbal antics only if an attentive staff member was nearby. Furthermore, it was obvious to anyone listening to him that the patient took real pride in the speed and facility with which he could pour forth his gibberish. There are also other indications that the hebephrenic is often keenly aware of what is going on around him. White and Watt (1973) report that when a young psychiatrist decided to live for two weeks as a patient in a schizophrenic ward, his playacting was quickly detected by a hebephrenic, who at the end of the doctor's second day on the ward "came over to the doctor, put his hand protectively on his shoulder and confided with mock earnestness, 'You know, Doc, I think you're much better already.'"

The onset of this increasingly rare form of schizophrenia is usually gradual and tends to occur at an earlier age than simple schizophrenia. The major distinguishing mark of the onset—the withdrawal into a realm of bizarre and childlike fantasies—is illustrated in the following case:

Doris, Sam's wife, reported that she was bothered by his behavior at times but she attributed it to the pressure of business and the series of disasters that befell

Fig. 11.14   Disturbance of affect is illustrated by this young man who laughs and giggles. Such inappropriate affect is characteristic of individuals diagnosed as hebephrenic schizophrenics.

him. As Doris said, "What hurt me most was the feeling I began to get more and more of the time that I was losing contact with him. It was as if he were drifting away from me and I didn't know what to do about it. I would talk to him for a while, but when I looked at him, I would realize he wasn't listening. He was off somewhere lost in thought and never heard a word I said. Then he began to do scary and creepy things. I would wake up in the middle of the night and he would be gone. Once I found him sitting on the grass in the middle of the backyard at 4:00 A.M. and he didn't seem to know where he was or what was going on. He was confused, but he was all right the next day and never mentioned what had happened the night before. . . ."

About three weeks later, Sam was arrested at 3:00 A.M. in a small town about 40 miles from where he lived. The police report said that he was driving through town at nearly 85 miles an hour when he was stopped and that he told the arresting officers that he was trying to "get up escape velocity for a trip to Mars."

• • •

Some of the ideas Sam spoke about freely to doctors and fellow patients were extremely bizarre. At one time he was convinced he was Robin Hood, for example. He had not notified anyone of this sudden shift in his identity and it was discovered only [after] he leaped from a perch atop a door and landed on the back of an unsuspecting attendant who had just entered the room (McNeil, 1970, p. 98).

The hebephrenic's fantasy life, however, is not all playful fun. Along with Robin Hood and Bopeep, a number of grisly horrors people his private world. Enemies stalk him through the night, and voices accuse him of unspeakable sexual taints. McNeil, who reported the case of Sam, has commented on this darker aspect of the hebephrenic's imaginings:

There is no exact replica of a hebephrenic experience in normal existence. Probably the closest match is the occasional bizarre, frightening, nonsensical nightmare that sometimes awakens us in a cold sweat in the dark of night. In a nightmare we are entangled in delusions, hallucinations, and distorted logic. But we wake up to a rational, ordered life. The hebephrenic is caught in a nightmare from which he may never awaken (1970, p. 99).

Catatonic Schizophrenia

There was no family history of mental illness in the case of F.C. He had been an average scholar but introspective and solitary at school, with no liking for games and no hobbies. He became a mill-worker at the age of 15 and was "more a boy for home, never keen on girls." He served in the Army during the Second World War and had some sort of transient mental breakdown, of which no records are available. After demobilization he was idle for six months: he appeared depressed and mixed up, seemed to take no interest in things around him and did not even respond to questioning. Then he had a job for six months, but was dismissed and again hung around the house, making no attempt to seek further employment. Thereafter he became even more dull and apathetic, looked vacant and faraway, refused to get out of bed or take food. He declared that . . . some unknown individual was "making him think about things," and that he himself was a "riddle of bones." In the year following his demobilization from the Army he was admitted to a mental hospital, aged 23 years.

In hospital at first he lay in bed with an occasional vacant smile, and refused food. . . . He complained of hearing buzzing noises, sounds like someone squealing, and voices which he could sometimes understand but whose messages he could not remember, and he described flashes of light and shadows in the middle of the room. He expressed the belief that the doctors and nurses could manipulate their shadows, and that there was another person in his bed. Later he complained of tasting soap in his mouth and of receiving poison from the post beside his bed. Often he could not be engaged in conversation, sat vacantly by the hour and had both to be taken to his meals and pressed to eat. At times he was incontinent, chewed the end of his tie and hoarded rubbish. For weeks on end he would be in a state of stupor or near to it. . . . Then a period of excitement would intervene, when for days or weeks on end he would be hyperactive and talk a great deal in a disjointed and usually incoherent way. At these times he would strike out impulsively at the nursing staff. On occasion he clowned in a crude way and would walk on his hands (Henderson and Gillespie, 1969, pp. 278–279).

This patient was diagnosed as *catatonic* primarily on the basis of what might be called his "nonbehavior"—the slowing down of motion and eventual cessation of all adaptive behavior. The onset of catatonic symptoms often seems rather sudden, but as in the case above, the patient's history will usually reveal earlier tendencies toward withdrawal.

To the visitor first entering a ward for severely disturbed mental patients, the catatonic is likely to be the most easily identifiable type of schizophrenic. He may be huddled in a painfully awkward position in a corner, or he may simply be standing rigid and immobile, eyes staring blankly ahead. It is in this stuporous state that catatonics occasionally show *waxy flexibility*, a condition in which the patient may report that his limbs have a plastic feel and he may leave them for long periods of time in positions imposed by some other person, as if he were a flexible rubber doll. McNeil points out, however, that the catatonic's immobility is by no means a sign of passivity. On the contrary, it appears to be an active and strenuously controlled resistance to some kind of subjectively perceived threat, "as if the catatonic fears making a voluntary or willful mistake that would further jeopardize his already anxiety-ridden and dangerous situation" (1970, p. 100). It is obvious that an extraordinary amount of physical energy must be expended to hold, sometimes for hours, the bizarre postures that are assumed.

Furthermore, while the catatonic's mute and frozen immobility would seem to indicate that he

is out of contact with reality and oblivious to his environment, this too appears to be deceptive. As with the hebephrenic, there are clear indications that the catatonic is acutely aware of what is going on around him. For example, many catatonic patients will not only refuse to do what is requested of them, but will continually do just the opposite, indicating that they understand very well the nature of the requests. Moreover, while stuporous catatonics can remain seemingly unmoved in response to a wide range of painful stimuli, certain stimuli have been known to rouse them into taking a quick detour back into reality. An incident reported by O'Kelly and Muckler amply illustrates this point:

A class of student nurses were gaining experience on the psychiatric section as part of their regular training course. One girl, possibly from reasons of insecurity, was given to making rather free and frank comments out loud about the patients as she moved around the ward. One patient, a catatonic, had for several days sat immobile on the side of his bed. The nurse, as she was making the adjacent bed, remarked to a fellow worker concerning the "stupidity" of the catatonic. Her back was to the patient and she was bent over adjusting a sheet. Suddenly, in the midst of her comments about the patient, he let out a loud cry and placed a well-aimed foot on the nurse's posterior. When she recovered, straightened up, and looked around, the catatonic had resumed his "wooden Indian" expression and his former posture (1955, p. 285).

Even though this category is seldom used, DSM-II distinguishes two subtypes of catatonic schizophrenia, one of which is marked by stupor, mutism, negativism, and/or waxy flexibility, and another marked by highly excited and sometimes violent motor activity. Like F.C., many catatonics fluctuate between these two extremes. Regardless of which state they are in, however, reports from patients who have recovered indicate that delusions and hallucinations predominate a good deal of the time.

Fig. 11.15   In the stuporous state of catatonic reaction, the patient may assume a strained posture, such as sitting folded in a chair or crouching on the floor, and maintain it for long periods of time. The body is generally quite malleable and if, for example, an arm is extended by the patient himself or by another person, the limb remains in that position for any period of time—a condition known as waxy flexibility. Although he appears mute and uncomprehending, the catatonic may do the opposite of what is asked, indicating that he does understand the request.

Fig. 11.16 *This illustration was done by a male patient diagnosed as schizophrenic with paranoid tendencies. There is strong emphasis on eyes, with a figure watching over the shoulder. The torso of the central figure is surrounded by hands, and the figure in the background is reaching out. Religiosity as well as delusions of persecution and grandeur may be seen in the cross and the Christlike figure bestowing a wreath.*

Fig. 11.17 *"Nijinsky has faults, but Nijinsky must be listened to because he speaks the words of God . . . I am God, Nijinsky is God. 'He is a good man and not evil. People have not understood him and will not understand him if they think. If people listened to me for several weeks there would be great results. I hope that my teachings will be understood.' All that I write is necessary to mankind"* *(cited in Kaplan, 1964, pp. 424–428). These words are taken from the diary of Vaslaw Nijinsky, one of the most celebrated dancers the world has ever known. The diary is signed "God and Nijinsky, . . . February 27, 1919." In that year, at the age of twenty-nine and at the height of his fame, Nijinsky was diagnosed as schizophrenic by the doctor who invented the term, Eugen Bleuler. And though he lived thirty years longer, Nijinsky never recovered, nor did he ever dance again.*

Paranoid Schizophrenia Though many writers have taken Kraepelin to task for the elaborate diagnostic system that he authored, no one has ever accused him of having been a poor observer of behavior. The following description of *paranoid schizophrenic* behaviors, penned by Kraepelin three-quarters of a century ago, captures in dramatic fashion the most prominent features of the disorder.

The patients . . . divulge a *host of delusions*, almost entirely of persecution; people are watching them, intriguing against them, they are not wanted at home, former friends are talking about them and trying to injure their reputation. These delusions are changeable and soon become *fantastic*. The patients claim that some extreme punishment has been inflicted upon them, they have been shot down into the earth, have been transformed into spirits, and must undergo all sorts of torture. Their intestines have been removed by enemies and are being replaced a little at a time; their own heads have been removed, their throats occluded, and the blood no longer circulates. They are transformed into stones, their countenances are completely altered. . . .

Hallucinations, especially of hearing, are very prominent during this stage; fellow-men jeer at them, call them bastards, threaten them, accuse them of horrible crimes, . . . Occasionally faces and forms are seen at night, or a crowd of men throwing stones at the window. . . .

The *emotional attitude* soon changes and becomes more and more exalted. At the same time the delusions become less depressive and more expansive and fantastic. The patient, in spite of persecution, is happy and contented, extravagant, and talkative, and boasts that he has been transformed into the Christ; others will ascend to heaven, have lived many lives, and traversed the universe. They have the talent of poets, have been nominated for President, and have represented the government at foreign courts. The delusions may become most florid, foolish, and ridiculous. A patient may say that he is a star, that all light and darkness emanate from him; that he is the greatest inventor ever born, can create mountains, is endowed with all the attributes of God, can prophesy for coming ages, can talk to the people in Mars; indeed, is unlike anything that has ever existed (1902, pp. 257–258).

Paranoia is a term borrowed from the ancient Greek, in which it means "beside or outside of reason," a fitting description of the delusions of persecution that constitute the most prominent symptom of paranoid schizophrenia. In terms of continuity, the delusions of the paranoid schizophrenic can range from a jumble of vague and contradictory suspicions to an exquisitely worked out system of imagined conspiracies. As Kraepelin points out, the delusions are commonly accompanied by a wide range of hallucinations—faces at the window, voices in the dark—supporting the . delusional belief. Furthermore, they often involve a grandiose expansiveness of personal worth and position; in order to have so many and such relentless enemies, one must, after all, be someone very important. Thus the patient may suddenly become Napoleon, Beethoven, George Washington, or, as we have seen, Christ.

As we have seen, this subtype of schizophrenia is the most prevalent, accounting for almost half the schizophrenic population of mental hospitals. Although the full-blown disorder usually does not appear until after age 25, the onset has generally been preceded by years of fear and suspicions leading to tense, uneasy, and fragile interpersonal relationships. The onset and development of a paranoid schizophrenic episode is illustrated in the following case, reported by Arieti:

Laura was a 40-year-old married woman. A few weeks prior to her first examination, her husband had noted restlessness and agitation, which he interpreted as being due to some physical disorder. A physician who was consulted prescribed a tonic. Later Laura started to complain about the neighbors. A woman who lived on the floor beneath them was knocking on the wall to irritate her. According to the husband, this woman had really knocked on the wall a few times; he had heard the noises. However, Laura became more and more concerned about it. She would wake up in the middle of the night under the impression that she was hearing noises from the apartment downstairs. She would become upset and angry at the neighbors. Once she was awake, she could not sleep for the rest of the night. The husband would vainly try to calm her. Later she became more disturbed. She started to feel that the neighbors were now recording everything she said; maybe they had hidden wires in the apartment. She started to feel "funny" sensations. There were many strange things happening, which she did not know how to explain; people were looking at her in a funny way in the street; in the butcher shop, the butcher had purposely served her last, although she was in the middle of the line. During the next few days she felt that people were planning to harm either her or her husband. In the neighborhood she saw a German woman whom she had not seen for several years. Now the woman had suddenly reappeared, probably to testify that the patient and her husband were involved in some sort of crime.

Laura was distressed and agitated. She felt unjustly accused, because she had committed no crime. Maybe these people were really not after her, but after her husband. In the evening when she looked at television, it became obvious to her that the programs referred to her life. Often the people on the programs were just repeating what she had thought. They were stealing her ideas. She wanted to go to the police and report them. At this point the husband felt that the patient could not be left alone, and after a brief telephone conversation with the family doctor, a consultation with me was arranged.

When I saw Laura, she repeated all her allegations to me. She was confused, agitated, and afraid. Everything seemed to have a hidden meaning, but she did not know how to put all these meanings together. She was very distressed and unwilling to explain. If the husband or someone else doubted the validity of

DSM-II Listing of Schizophrenic Subtypes

Simple type	Characterized by gradual impoverishment of thought, affect, and social relations, with apathy the outstanding feature
Hebephrenic type	Characterized by silly, childlike behavior, inappropriate giggling, and disorganized thinking
Catatonic type	Characterized either by excessive and sometimes violent motor activity or by drastic reduction of motor activity, along with mutism and general withdrawal
Paranoid type	Characterized by delusions of persecution and/or grandeur, often accompanied by hallucinations, and by bizarre and sometimes hostile behavior consistent with these delusions and hallucinations
Acute type	Characterized by sudden, terrifying onset of schizophrenic disorganization, often manifested in extreme confusion, emotional agitation, fragmented thinking, fear, excitement, or depression
Latent type	Characterized by schizophrenic symptoms in a patient with no history of a clear-cut schizophrenic episode
Residual type	Characterized by mild symptoms of schizophrenia in a patient recovering from a schizophrenic episode
Schizo-affective type	Characterized by a combination of schizophrenic symptomatology with either extreme elation or extreme depression
Childhood type	Characterized by the appearance, before puberty, of extreme withdrawal, bizarre behavior, and loss of developmental progress
Chronic undifferentiated type	Characterized by a mixed schizophrenic symptomatology that does not lend itself to classification under one of the other types

Adapted from DSM-II (1968).

her beliefs, she would become infuriated (1974, pp. 165–166).

It should be evident from this description of Laura that she manifests all of the "classic" symptoms of paranoid schizophrenia—a host of delusions, hallucinations, heightened emotional attitudes, and general interpersonal disorientation and disorganization. We shall see how this differs from the paranoid states described below.

PARANOID STATES

Of the third major category of functional psychosis, *paranoid states*, DSM-II gives the following definition:

These are psychotic disorders in which a delusion, generally persecutory or grandiose, is the essential abnormality. Disturbances in mood, behavior and thinking (including hallucinations) are derived from this delusion. This distinguishes paranoid states from the affective psychoses and schizophrenias, in which mood and thought disorders, respectively, are the central abnormalities (1968, p. 37).

Paranoid schizophrenia, as we have seen in the preceding section, is distinguished from the other schizophrenic subtypes by the *prominence* of delusions of persecution. In the paranoid schizophrenic, however, this delusional quality is only one item— the outstanding item—in a cluster of abnormalities, all of which may function independently of one another. In paranoid states, on the other hand, the delusional system is, as DSM-II states, the *essential* abnormality. In many cases, in fact, it may be the only abnormality; outside the circumscribed delusional system, the patient will appear to have normal reality contact. In other cases disturbances of affect, thinking, and motor behavior may be manifested, but in such a way as to indicate that they are caused by, and therefore dependent upon, the delusional complex. Thus, it is assumed, if there were no delusions, there would be no apparent abnormality.

It should be noted, however, that authorities have been arguing for over a hundred years as to just how many types of paranoia deserve to be listed as separate categories. And there are many specialists who believe that the conditions now labeled as paranoid states are simply variants of schizophrenia (Buss, 1966).

As defined by the rigorous criteria outlined above, paranoid states are extremely rare. Estimates of incidence vary from 1 percent of the mental hospital population (McNeil, 1970) to only one case in several thousand patients (Sullivan, 1956), depending on the purity of symptomatology demanded by the diagnostician. It is possible, of course, that many more exist. In the course of our daily lives we have all probably encountered a few likely candidates for this diagnostic label: jealous husbands, ignored geniuses, self-styled prophets, people who phone up radio talk shows to describe in detail some fantastic scheme to solve the world's problems—a scheme which the world has so far perversely refused to adopt. Because such people tend, apart from their isolated delusional systems, to have relatively good contact with reality, many of them remain within the community. In the case described below, for instance, the woman's symptoms were limited to her intricate set of delusions regarding sexual involvements on her husband's part. In all other respects she appeared perfectly normal, and it was only because her false beliefs had begun to endanger her marriage that she was forced to consult a psychiatrist:

Rose's idea at the time of her psychiatric examination . . . involved her husband, her brother-in-law, the secretary [in her husband's office], a bachelor friend of her brother-in-law, and several unspecified other women. She thought that this group was meeting in the bachelor's apartment for cocktail parties and immoral activities. The bachelor originally aroused her suspicion by putting a rug in his apartment which she thought did not match the decor, and which she felt was being used solely to muffle footsteps. When he put a muffling device on his telephone, she felt certain that this was done to prevent anyone from knowing when he was receiving phone calls. Rose felt that the secretary wore clothing which was at the same time too expensive for her salary and too informal for her job. She also felt that in doing such things as asking Tom [Rose's husband] for change for bus fare, the secretary was being unproperly familiar.

On occasions when Tom went to his office at night in order to work, Rose insisted on going with him, suspecting that he otherwise would go to the bachelor's apartment. Recently she had been spending a great deal of time in Tom's office in order to watch him, and the remainder of her time was spent sitting by the window, watching for the arrival and departure of the bachelor's car. She insisted on accompanying Tom wherever he went, and if he left to visit his family at night she would rouse their sleeping child in order to accompany him. During this period her housework was neglected, so that her time could be spent observing her husband. . . . She believed that Tom and the secretary were disturbed by her presence in the office, and that they developed a system of signals to get around this. When Tom opened a certain desk drawer, Rose felt, he was signaling to the secretary to come to him so that he could tell her something. Rose also felt that when the secretary saw Rose coming she made a noise, such as a shuffling of her feet, to warn Tom. . . .

. . . Rose appeared to be a generally relaxed woman, neat in her dress and manner, and reasonably content with life, except for her frequent battles at home. She denied being openly suspicious of anything apart from her husband and his relationships.

Under Tom's insistence, Rose sought psychiatric help (Zax and Stricker, 1963, pp. 113–114).

SUMMARY

The distinction between psychosis and neurosis centers on the matter of reality contact. In the psychoses, unlike the neuroses, mental functioning is so severely impaired that the individual can no longer effectively process the stimuli in the environment There are two major categories of psychosis: the biogenic psychoses—associated with organic brain syndromes—and the functional psychoses, which are not attributed to known physical causes. The functional psychoses are further divided into: (1) the schizophrenias, characterized primarily by disorders of thought; (2) the major affective disorders, characterized primarily by disorders of mood; and (3) the paranoid states, in which the essential abnormality is a circumscribed delusional system. The purpose of our chapter is to describe the symptomatology of the two latter disorders.

Although DSM-II names thought disorders as the predominant symptom of schizophrenia, the schizophrenic usually displays disorders of language, perception, affect, and motor behavior as well. The most striking symptom, however, is the disruption of thought processes, as manifested in blocked or inappropriate associations, overinclusion, and difficulties in conceptualization. Furthermore, the schizophrenic's thinking is usually clouded by delusions, particularly delusions of grandeur and of persecution.

Closely related to—and perhaps simply a function of—schizophrenic disorders of thought are schizophrenic disorders of language. Two language aberrations typical of schizophrenics are neologisms, coined usages whose meaning can often be divined, and word salad, a jumble of words whose meaning is totally obscure.

The schizophrenic's perceptual abilities may be impaired in various subtle ways. Not subtle at all, however, is the most common schizophrenic perceptual disorder, the hallucination, or imaginary perception. Auditory hallucinations are by far the most frequently reported, followed by visual hallucinations.

Unlike the monolithic depression and elation seen in the affective psychosis, schizophrenic disorders of affect rarely involve sustained extremes of mood. Rather, the schizophrenic's affective responses tend to be either inappropriate, markedly ambivalent, or simply flat, that is, apathetic.

The final category of schizophrenic symptomatology, disorders of motor behavior, includes an almost unlimited range of behaviors. The only common denominator is the absence of interpersonal interaction.

Schizophrenics are normally classified according to certain dimensions or scales. The most useful of these are the process-reactive dimension, which takes into account the patient's premorbid adjustment, and the paranoid-nonparanoid dimension. Patients are also grouped according to certain traditionally accepted, though not necessarily useful, subtypes, including the simple, hebephrenic, catatonic, and paranoid subtypes. Paranoid schizophrenia is by far the most common classification.

The third category of functional psychosis, the paranoid state, resembles paranoid schizophrenia in that its most prominent symptom is delusion. In the paranoid state, however, the delusional system is thought to be the essential abnormality, from which any other abnormalities emanate, rather than simply the most striking among a cluster of symptoms. Indeed, in this extremely rare form of psychosis, the delusional system may be the only apparent abnormality.

In the last chapter, we discussed the behavior patterns typical of schizophrenia and paranoia, but we have not yet raised the question of "why." What causes people to act in such bizarre and seemingly self-defeating ways? It is with this question—the question of etiology—that the bulk of scientific writing on the psychoses is concerned. And it is this question that is the subject of our present chapter. Theories as to the causes of the affective psychoses have already been reviewed in Chapter 7. And since, of the two remaining categories of functional psychosis, schizophrenia has been much more thoroughly researched than paranoia, our discussion will focus primarily on theories of schizophrenia.

PROBLEMS IN THE STUDY OF SCHIZOPHRENIA

If schizophrenia is really as widespread and as debilitating as the last chapter claimed, why don't we appropriate the necessary funds, hire a team of researchers, and simply go to work until we have found both cause and cure? The answer to this question is that what we need in order to solve the enigma of schizophrenia is not simply money, brains, and the will to do the research. Unfortunately, the research itself is hampered by problems so abundant and so serious that of all the many researchers who apply themselves to the study of schizophrenia, only the most dedicated end up making any contributions of worth. And generally even they have to make compromises that affect the level of their research product. A brief look at some of these problems will help us understand why research on schizophrenia has progressed so slowly; it may also help us appreciate the magnitude of the progress that has been made.

What Is Being Studied?

Recently I was invited to present a technical paper on schizophrenia at a New England medical school. Having arrived unexpectedly early, I met with a group of residents on an informal basis before the lecture. One young resident asked innocently, "What is schizophrenia?" Before evading his question I could not help thinking, "God only knows" (Cancro, 1974, p. 1).

This candid admission, by a nationally known expert in schizophrenia, points up one of the major difficulties in the research into schizophrenia, a difficulty so basic that many people overlook it entirely: the fact that there is no general agreement as to what schizophrenia actually is. What in fact do we mean when we use the term? Is schizophrenia a disease, caused perhaps by a microorganism or

12
Schizophrenia: Perspectives

Is Psychosis Universal?

Insanity belongs almost exclusively to civilized races of men: it scarcely exists among savages, and is rare in barbarous countries.

J. C. Prichard
A Treatise on Insanity, 1835

This opinion expressed by the English psychiatrist Prichard would have been endorsed by most professionals in the nineteenth century. Even as late as the 1920s, it was widely assumed (e.g., Van Loon, 1928; Seligman, 1929) that psychosis was the bitter fruit of civilization, while "backward" peoples continued to enjoy a pristine sanity reminiscent of Adam and Eve before their expulsion from Eden. However, within the last fifty years a large number of cross-cultural studies reporting instances of psychosis in the tribal societies of Samoa, New Guinea, Brazil, India, Indonesia, and other countries have led to the widespread adoption of the opposite view: that psychosis is a universal affliction unrelated to the pressures of industrialization, and that it is as likely to strike the "noble savage" as the harassed commuter. But this revised opinion has not gone unchallenged either. Some researchers (e.g., Torrey, 1973) still argue that in non-Western cultures the prevalence of psychosis is in fact directly proportionate to the degree that these cultures have undergone "Westernization."

Unfortunately, the question can never really be answered definitively, because any answer depends on cross-cultural studies, and cross-cultural studies depend on a number of rather slippery variables. In the first place, the studies, and consequently the "diagnoses," are usually done by anthropologists whose training in psychology is of necessity limited. A second and more serious problem is that of cultural differences between the researcher and the people he is studying. If we define schizophrenia by the presence of hallucinations, then schizophrenia may in fact be universal. But if we define it as behavior that is maladaptive in the extreme or as loss of reality contact, then we have to consider what the individual's society requires him to adapt to and what it considers reality to be. Some cultures, for example, are quite tolerant of eccentric behavior. And other cultures consider the world of good and evil spirits to be as much a part of reality as the workaday world of eating, sleeping, and waking up in the morning. Indeed, in many of the American Indian and Eskimo tribes, a person who communed with spirits or engaged in public combat with invisible devils was given the prestigious role of shaman or medicine man. In short, what would be grounds for hospitalization in our culture may be grounds for sanctification in another. Consequently, even the most accurate cross-cultural research can only tell us how many people in tribe X or tribe Y would be considered psychotic in the researcher's culture.

What, then, can we say about the universality or nonuniversality of psychosis? We can say that all human populations appear to have their share of members who manifest unconventional thinking patterns, hear supernatural voices, and engage in other so-called psychotic behavior. But not all human populations designate these behaviors as abhorrent or even abnormal. And this difference in cultural attitudes renders all comprehensive cross-cultural studies relative in the extreme, no matter what their conclusions.

some inherited biological malfunction? Or is "schizophrenic" merely a label that we assign to a person who acts in certain ways, just as we assign the label "postman" to the person who delivers our mail? Researchers differ widely in their views on this subject. Some insist that schizophrenia is a disease entity, like diabetes or cancer. Others believe that the term describes a recognizable set of behaviors caused by biological and/or social factors. Still others reject the term altogether, claiming that it is simply too vague to be of any use. In sum, there is no consensus whatsoever as to what it is that we are studying, or whether it even exists. Consequently, our research is built on a rather shaky foundation.

Problems with Diagnosis

However much researchers may disagree on a theoretical level as to the validity of the concept of schizophrenia, they are required, when conducting

Fig. 12.1 *Any researcher who attempts to compare psychiatric patients in an institution with "normal" people on the outside must consider the circumstances of hospitalization such as overcrowding.*

experiments, to establish an *operational definition* of the term—that is, a definition specifying precisely what observable phenomena the term designates. However, every researcher's operational definition of the term *schizophrenic* is simply a matter of his own way of diagnosing patients. And diagnostic agreement among professionals is nowhere near perfect.

Fig. 12.2 *Scenes of lethargy, despondency, and apathy are not uncommon in many mental institutions.*

Consider, for example, the interesting finding, published in a recent cross-national study, that schizophrenia is more common in New York than in London, while the affective disorders are more common in London than in New York. A group of investigators (Cooper et al., 1972), guessing that this disparity might have more to do with national diagnostic favorites than with an actual difference in the psychic life of Londoners and New Yorkers, decided to test their hypothesis by showing groups of psychiatrists in New York and in London identical videotapes of doctor-patient interviews. The results confirmed the investigators' skepticism. In cases involving disturbances of both thought and mood, the American psychiatrists tended to give more weight to the thought disturbance and consequently were more likely to diagnose the patient as schizophrenic. The British psychiatrists, on the other hand, tended to see the mood disturbance as the primary symptom and therefore to diagnose the patient as either manic or depressive. Hence the cross-national difference.

Not only do such inconsistencies exist from one country to another, but a given patient, having received one diagnosis by one professional, might very well be given a different diagnosis by another professional in the next state, the next hospital, or even the next office. In recent studies (e.g., Beck et al., 1962; Sandifer et al., 1964), the percentage of agreement among professionals on a general diagnosis of schizophrenia has ranged from only 53 percent to 74 percent. Worse yet, when attempts have been made to specify the subcategory of schizophrenia, rate of agreement has generally dropped to between 35 and 50 percent. What this means is that if Dr. Green in one hospital and Dr. Brown in another hospital are each doing research on paranoid schizophrenia, there is only a 35 to 50 percent chance that they are talking about the same thing. Consequently, any attempt to make meaningful comparisons between their research findings is practically useless. Needless to say, this bodes very poorly for our ability to learn from one another in the effort to discover the causes of psychosis.

Problems in Experimentation

The most common scientific procedure for finding out the effect of a given set of conditions is the *randomized groups design*. In its simplest form, this method involves the random assignment of subjects to two different groups: the *experimental group*, which is then exposed to whatever conditions are being studied, and the *control group*, which is not exposed to the conditions. The two groups are then compared to determine the effects, if any, of the conditions.

For obvious reasons, however, this method cannot be used for etiological research in schizophrenia. Consider, for example, the well-established fact that the lower socioeconomic strata have a disproportionately high incidence of schizophrenia. This finding suggests that the stresses of poverty may contribute significantly to the development of schizophrenia. But how do we test this hypothesis? Do we send a group of normal subjects to live in a ghetto and wait to see if they begin showing schizophrenic symptoms? Obviously not. Even if willing subjects could be found, one still could not for the sake of an experiment expose people to conditions that might produce psychological damage.

The only alternative is to gather our evidence ex post facto—that is, to compare groups of people who are already schizophrenic to groups of normal people on whatever variable we are interested in, whether it be socioeconomic background, academic success, or what have you. However, in this method there are two major problems that make it almost impossible to identify clear cause-and-effect relationships.

The Chicken-and-Egg Problem   Whenever existing

groups of people are found to differ on two characteristics, we can speculate about one characteristic causing the other, but we can never firmly establish which is the cause and which is the result. Consider once again the correlation between socioeconomic status and schizophrenia. We have suggested above that the hardships of life in the lower socioeconomic strata may contribute to the development of schizophrenia. But it is equally plausible that because schizophrenics adapt poorly to life, they may be unable to get decent jobs and thus may gravitate into the lower socioeconomic strata. In other words, having established the existence of a correlation between two variables, we still have no clue as to the *directionality* of a causal relationship between the two.

The Third-Variable Problem   In the discussion so far, we have assumed that a causal relationship might exist between two correlated variables, one being the cause and the other the result. But it is equally possible that both factors are the results of an unidentified cause, a *third variable*. Thus, it is possible that both socioeconomic disadvantage and schizophrenia may be the result of an unknown genetic factor. Likewise, the well-established correlation between heterosexual maladjustment and schizophrenia may have no causal significance whatsoever, since both factors might easily be due either to psychosocial stresses or to a biological defect.

Fig. 12.3   This typical scene of a ward "day room" effectively portrays the general inactivity and inattention of the patients, due in large part to the heavy tranquilizing medications and the sterility of the surroundings.

In comparing hospitalized schizophrenics with normal subjects there are hundreds of third variables that may be lurking behind whatever cause-and-effect conclusions the researchers attempt to draw. Some of this uncertainty can be removed by matching the patients with the normal subjects on certain critical variables such as age, intelligence, or socioeconomic status. However, even after scrupulous matching efforts, the researcher is still usually faced with two third variables that are notoriously difficult to control: hospitalization and drugs, both of which clearly influence behavior.

Since most studies comparing schizophrenics to normal subjects use hospitalized schizophrenics and nonhospitalized normal subjects, any oddities of behavior that show up in the comparison may be symptoms not of schizophrenia but of hospitalization. Overcrowding, inadequate diet, difficult sleeping conditions, lack of exercise, lack of privacy, loss of freedom—each of these all-too-ordinary circumstances of hospitalization can bring about physical and psychological changes that are easily mistaken for "pure" schizophrenic symptomatology.

Likewise, tranquilizing drugs, which are taken regularly by the vast majority of hospitalized schizophrenics, can cause a wide variety of changes in cognitive, perceptual, and motor functioning, thus preventing researchers from making any truly precise comparison between actual schizophrenic behavior and normal behavior. Of course, it is always possible either to take the schizophrenic subjects off drugs for several weeks before research is begun (to allow the body to "clear" itself of the drug) or to use new admissions before they are put on drugs. But neither of these methods is foolproof, and both raise the ethical question of whether a "treatment" should be withheld or withdrawn for research purposes.

The Problem of Expectations

The well-known fact that the expectations of researchers and their staffs can affect the results of their research (Rosenthal, 1967) is one that haunts all seasoned investigators. Expectation effects are particularly difficult to control in studies assessing the outcome of different treatments, since this type of research necessarily involves a great deal of personal contact between staff and subjects.

In such studies, the staff usually have fairly strong ideas about which treatment should be the most effective (or which treatment they would like to see demonstrated to be the most effective), and these biases or expectations can lead to many subtle differences in effort and enthusiasm—differences which may have a powerful effect on the subjects' responses to the various treatments. Hence the common saying among clinicians with regard to new treatments: "Hurry up and use it while it still works," the implication being that the most powerful ingredient in a new treatment is the element of expectation which both therapist and client share. The good researcher takes great pain to reduce the effects of

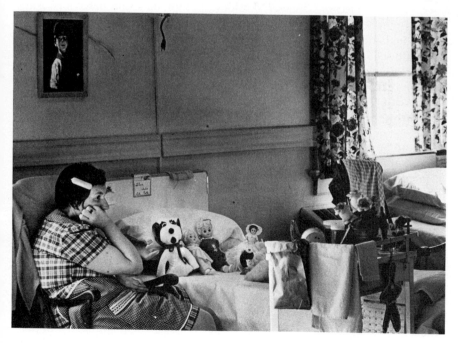

Fig. 12.4 Some of the more "progressive" mental institutions allow patients to have personal belongings, but this does not necessarily alleviate a patient's apathy and boredom.

differential expectations, but it is probably impossible to eliminate them altogether.

PERSPECTIVES ON SCHIZOPHRENIA

We have already devoted a number of pages to reviewing the many problems that surround any effort to solve the riddle of schizophrenia. However, we have not yet discussed what is really the basic problem—that is, that the riddle seems to have no single answer. Quite unlike most medical problems, which can be traced to a single microorganism or a single organ dysfunction, schizophrenia appears to be the result of a highly complex interaction of psychological, interpersonal, and biological factors, each of which has claimed the attention of a number of different theoretical perspectives. In the following section we will examine the various etiological and treatment theories put forth by each of these perspectives.

The Psychodynamic Perspective

Cause   There is no single psychodynamic formulation of the psychoses; instead, there is a variety of positions, all of which are offshoots of the theories of Freud (Freeman et al., 1966). Although Freud devoted his attention primarily to the neuroses, he did offer an interpretation of psychosis as well, and especially of paranoia. In his earliest psychoanalytic study of psychosis (1911), Freud viewed the development of the disorder as a two-stage process. The first stage involves a complete or partial withdrawal of *cathexes* (emotional investment) from the *object world*, the world of people and things. In the second phase, the restitution phase, the individual attempts to regain the lost object world by substituting imaginary events and relationships for the real ones that he has abandoned. Thus hallucinations can be accounted for as remembered sensory events that the psychotic uses to take the place of his lost object relations.

The psychotic's disturbed thinking can be seen as the result of a similar two-stage process. First, there is a withdrawal of cathexes from internal forms of object representation—that is, the mental pictures that the individual has of the object world. Then, in the restitution phase, the cathexes are redirected toward words which remain in the memory but which are no longer tied to appropriate objects. As a result, the words come out but they are no longer coherent, since they have lost their value as symbols of real things (Freud, 1915).

After Freud's elaboration in 1923 of the structural concepts of ego and superego, the psychoanalytic interpretation of psychosis shifted from object decathexis to ego insufficiency or disintegration. According to this later view, the psychotic is a person who because he is unable to cope with unacceptable id impulses regresses to an early phase of the oral stage. In this phase of infancy there is as yet no separate ego to exercise the basic cognitive functions of perception, memory, judgment, and so forth. Hence the psychotic's loss of contact with reality, since the phase to which he has regressed provides no equipment for reality testing.

Whereas regression is the mechanism which has received theoretical emphasis in psychoanalytic accounts of schizophrenia, projection has been seen as the basic mechanism of paranoia. In all his cases involving paranoia, Freud inferred a connection with repressed homosexuality (Jones, 1955). Presumably, when the ego is threatened by these unacceptable id impulses, the projection mechanism enables the individual to externalize them. That is, the source of the threat is no longer seen as coming from within oneself, but rather from someone else: "It is not my own desires that are threatening me; it's that guy over there who is threatening me." Hence the development of delusions of persecution.

The neo-Freudians view schizophrenia as a developmental disorder (White and Watt, 1973): the child, having experienced relations with other people as painful and hostile, withdraws into a world of fantasy, a withdrawal which he expresses in his behavior. Having withdrawn from others, the child never develops appropriate social behaviors, which results in further unpleasantness and consequently in further withdrawal. Such continually negative social experience severely damages the child's self-esteem. While young, the child may manage to cope with his world of unhappiness. However, at some point later in life he may experience such sufficiently strong negative social encounters that the resulting anxiety, pain, and withdrawal cause a general breakdown in functioning—a schizophrenic breakdown.

Treatment   Strict classical psychoanalytic treatment is not generally applicable to the psychoses, since it requires a degree of psychological coherence that the psychotic patient usually does not have (McNeil, 1970). Hence the psychoanalytically oriented therapist often has to combine the principles of psychoanalysis with principles that generally receive greater support from other schools of thought, such as the behaviorists' emphasis on reinforcement and the humanists' concern for personal autonomy. In treating the schizophrenic, psychodynamically oriented therapists proceed in many respects as they would with a neurotic. However, a major difference is that with the schizophrenic, much more attention is given to creating a warm, nurturant therapeutic relationship (Arieti, 1974b). Through this relationship and through analysis of the transference (that is, the feelings of anger, love, and the like that the patient originally felt toward his parents and now transfers to the therapist—see Chapter 19), the therapist aims at healing the psychic wounds left over from childhood and at reorienting the schizophrenic toward interpersonal relations. In short, the therapist becomes a sort of second parent, providing the sympathy, support, and esteem that that patient needs in order to rediscover the sources of value and pleasure in himself and in others.

The Behaviorist Perspective

Cause   The most recent comprehensive interpretation of schizophrenia within the behaviorist tradition is that of Ullmann and Krasner (1975). According to these investigators, the schizophrenic is subject to the same principles of learning and behavior as so-called normal people; however, because of a failure of reinforcement, the schizophrenic has ceased to attend to the social stimuli to which most of us respond. Instead, he attends to his own idiosyncratic cues, and as a result, his behavior seems odd or bizarre to the "normal" observer. To clarify their interpretation, Ullmann and Krasner offer the following analogy:

A question [is] asked of a college student whose mind has been on more enjoyable things than the lecture. The response made under these circumstances is likely to seem "illogical," "childish," and "concrete" rather than the abstract, insightful verbalization expected of him. The listener who knows and expects the right answer may not understand the student's answer. In short, the person who was not paying attention may display poor social judgment (not respond to the cues emitted by others which indicate the nature of the situation) and may display disorganization of thinking (concrete, irrelevant, bizarre associations which the listener cannot follow) (1975, p. 357).

As Ullmann and Krasner point out, attention responses require effort: "When they do not pay off, they decrease in emission" (1975, p. 357). And this is what has happened with the schizophrenic. Furthermore, the following vicious cycle may be instituted: when an individual ceases responding to certain accepted social cues, he may become the target of disciplinary action and social rejection, leading to additional feelings of alienation and to the belief that others are out to "get" him. Hence his behavior becomes even more bizarre. In addition, other sources may begin providing reinforcement for his deviant behavior, in the form either of social attention or of any of the other advantages one gains by being viewed as "sick." Once reinforced, these behaviors will of course increase in frequency.

In support of their argument that schizophrenia is a learned behavior, Ullmann and Krasner point to two basic lines of evidence. First, there is good reason to believe that schizophrenics know what they are doing. For instance, their bizarre behaviors are not equally distributed across situations; rather, like other learned behaviors, they are often responses to specific stimuli, as was the case with the hebephrenic described in Chapter 11 who would produce his word salad and clang associations only if a staff member was within earshot. Schizophrenics have also been found to engage in impression management—that is, they can "look good" or "look bad" depending on the advantages or disadvantages of each. Moreover, schizophrenics appear to be much more socially sensitive than one would expect; studies have shown, for example, that psychotic patients have been able to predict the posthospital adjustment of other patients as well as staff could.

Ullmann and Krasner's second line of evidence has to do with the demonstrated ability of schizophrenics to unlearn their maladaptive behaviors. It has been shown, as we shall see below, that when the advantages of acting out the schizophrenic role are withdrawn and socially valued behaviors are instead reinforced, schizophrenics can abandon many of their bizarre behavior patterns with impressive speed.

As Ullmann and Krasner have themselves acknowledged, none of this evidence proves conclusively that schizophrenia is actually a learned role. The fact remains, however, that the behaviorist formulation has encouraged us to look much more closely at the reinforcing contingencies which exist in the milieu of the schizophrenic, and it has prompted the development of a number of very promising new treatments.

Treatment   As we have seen in Chapter 3, the behaviorist does not attempt to root out the causes of psychopathology and then "cure" it. Instead, he analyzes the individual's actions, identifies which behaviors are maladaptive, and then attempts, through the manipulation of reinforcement, to correct these behaviors.

Basic to the behaviorist treatment of schizophrenia is the idea, discussed above, that the schizophrenic engages in his bizarre behaviors because these behaviors are reinforced. An impressive array of recent data (Braginsky et al., 1966, 1969; Braginsky and Braginsky, 1967) actually indicates that many patients enter a mental hospital "in order to pursue an hedonic life in a comfortable, nondemanding milieu" (Braginsky et al., 1969, p. 180). These patients do not actually seek treatment, nor do they perceive themselves as ill or as particularly different from others, though they will sometimes act "crazily" in order to maintain their hospitalized status.

Such findings suggest that our custodial-care hospitals are fostering deviant behavior by providing a refuge for those who are either unwilling or unable to cope with the demands of everyday life. If this is the case, it would then seem reasonable to restructure hospital settings in such a way that "craziness" is no longer rewarded and that adaptive, socially acceptable behaviors are. Such a goal is the very essence of the behavioral treatment strategies that have been developed during the past two decades. Derived from the principles of both operant and respondent conditioning, these treatments range

---

THE MENTAL HOSPITAL AS RESORT

As we have seen in this chapter, studies by Braginsky and his colleagues (Braginsky and Braginsky, 1967; Braginsky et al., 1966, 1969) indicate that many people act "crazily" in order to gain admission to mental hospitals and thus shield themselves from the harassments of daily life. Such evidence can be—and in this chapter has been—invoked as support for the behaviorist approach to schizophrenia, whereby "crazy" behaviors are punished or extinguished and socially acceptable behaviors—cleaning one's room, feeding oneself, and generally pulling oneself up by the bootstraps—are rewarded. This, however, is not what Braginsky and his colleagues propose. Instead, they suggest that if people need periodic refuge from the difficulties of life on the outside, they should have it. And they should have it without having to act crazy as the cost of admission.

The paradigm we put forth suggests that, short of a transformation of society, the best solution would be to provide opportunities [other than mental hospitals] for withdrawal and renewal; opportunities that would eliminate the otherwise unavoidable hypocrisy of mental hospitals that require people to assume the degrading status of patienthood in order to obtain some relief from societal pressures.

Any member of a community, when he desires, may go to the cooperative retreat and stay as long as he wants, at no cost to him . . . residents may pursue their own preferred life styles—it would be Everyman's resort. Persons who wish to remain permanent residents may participate . . . in the running of the establishment. Persons, however, who do not want to work will not be required to do so (Braginsky et al., 1969, pp. 182–185).

One is immediately tempted to ask whether "Everyman's resort" wouldn't be overrun in a day. Why would anyone remain on the outside—working, coping, studying for exams, emptying the garbage—when he could be peacefully renewing himself, free of charge? And if no one remained on the outside, who would pay the taxes to support Everyman's resort? To Braginsky and his colleagues these questions are not pertinent, since their proposal is based on a humanistic interpretation of human nature. If human beings are essentially hedonistic and opportunistic, as many behaviorist and psychodynamic thinkers would agree, then of course everyone would rush off to register for a lifetime of cost-free renewal. However, if, as Braginsky and other humanists believe, human beings are inherently motivated toward productivity, creativity, and the full realization of their potential, then such retreats would constitute excellent way stations for those who are temporarily blocked in their self-actualization. Unfortunately, Braginsky's proposal has never been implemented, so we still don't know whether it would provide a useful retreat for the well-meaning or simply a free lunch for the lazy.

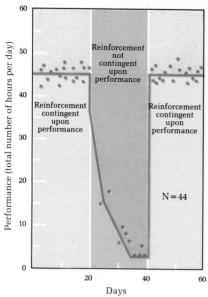

Fig. 12.5 *The above graph shows the critical effect of reinforcement on the work behavior of a group of hospitalized chronic psychotic patients. Reinforcement with tokens contingent upon performance resulted in high, stable levels of work; withdrawal of reinforcement immediately resulted in drastically decreased performance. Upon reinstatement of the token system, the patients' work behavior resumed at its previous level. One implication of this finding is that successful post-hospital adjustment of long-term psychotic patients requires that they be frequently reinforced for appropriate performance in their environment outside the hospital. Failure to provide such reinforcement may result in behavioral deficits that lead to rehospitalization. (Adapted from T. Ayllon and N. H. Azrin, "The Measurement and Reinforcement of Behavior of Psychotics." Journal of Experimental Analysis of Behavior, 8, 1965, 357–383.)*

from the most simple and commonsensical to the highly sophisticated and intricate. We shall look at only a few of the many applications currently in use.

Direct Reinforcement

Mr. C.'s most obnoxious behaviors were: urinating and defecating on the floor, shouting, swearing, name-calling, begging cigarettes, demanding other things, striking at other patients. It . . . seemed evident that Mr. C.'s inappropriate conduct usually was followed by some kind of staff attention. Two procedures for eliminating Mr. C.'s disruptive behavior were [implemented]. 1. Social attention should no longer be given following inappropriate behavior. 2. Social attention and cigarettes . . . would be the consequence of socially acceptable behavior (Sushinsky, 1970, p. 24).

The result was that in two weeks' time not only had all of Mr. C.'s "obnoxious" behaviors disappeared, but furthermore he was now striking up conversations, participating in rehabilitation therapy, and even insisting on buying his own cigarettes.

This example illustrates what is certainly one of the most practical and powerful contributions of behavior modification as applied to hospitalized patients: the discovery that the direct manipulation of attention can be extremely effective in producing more acceptable behavior. For years, the prevailing view that psychotic behaviors were caused by some underlying "disease" kept hospital staff from even considering that their own attention to such behaviors might be maintaining them. Now we know that the systematic use of social reinforcement in the form of attention can effect dramatic changes. Rickard, Dignam, and Horner (1960), for example, reported that the behavior of a patient who constantly engaged in delusional and irrational speech improved significantly after the staff began looking away when such delusional talk occurred and attending only when the patient spoke rationally. To cite another example, Agras (1967) suspected that attention was maintaining the refusal to eat on the part of a male schizophrenic who weighed only 85 pounds; once the staff began systematically ignoring the patient for not eating, he established satisfactory eating habits within five days.

Procedures which involve the giving or withholding of more tangible reinforcers, such as the cigarettes in the case of Mr. C., are surrounded by a number of ethical and legal questions that are as yet unresolved. There is no question, however, about the power of such procedures to effect behavior change. In one of the earliest operant-conditioning studies, Ayllon and Haughton (1962) reported increases in attending meals on time and in the performance of both simple and complex tasks when food was contingently given or withheld. Other researchers have succeeded in instituting or increasing speech in mute and near-mute patients through the use of such direct reinforcements as fruit, chocolate, milk, cigarettes, and magazines (Baker, 1970, 1971; Thomson et al., 1974; Kassorla, 1974).

The direct application of aversive stimuli has been used only minimally because of associated ethical problems. However, such techniques clearly work and occasionally seem quite appropriate. Ayllon and Michael (1959), for example, used an avoidance procedure with two female patients who refused to feed themselves—a behavior that was not only detrimental to rehabilitation but which also wasted many

Shaping Speech After Thirty Years of Silence

In 1967 a team of behavioral therapists decided to try shaping a normal behavior in the most severely regressed schizophrenic they could find. The patient they finally settled on was Mr. B., a catatonic whose hospital record had read the same for thirty years: "mute, negativistic, sits motionless for much of the day, needs full nursing care" (Kassorla, 1974, p. 300). The target behavior the researchers decided upon was speech.

Mr. B.'s verbal repertoire was limited to two sounds: "ugh" and something that sounded like "crack 'em." "Crack 'em" was chosen as the first object of reinforcement. The therapy then began.

Stage 1. The experimenter would say "crack 'em" to Mr. B., and he would be rewarded with food for any attempt at responding, even for simply moving his lips. After five days, Mr. B. was repeating the experimenter's "crack 'em" about 10 percent of the time.

Stage 2. Again the experimenter repeatedly said "crack 'em" to Mr. B., but now he was rewarded with food only for saying "crack 'em" in return. Less articulate sounds (e.g., grunts) were reinforced with praise, but not with food. After fourteen days, Mr. B. was repeating "crack 'em" about 92 percent of the time.

Stage 3. A new word was added: "dog." The experimenter would hold up a picture of a dog and say the word. If Mr. B. responded by saying "dog," he was given food. "Crack 'em" responses were merely praised. Grunts were ignored. After nine days, Mr. B. was responding with "dog" 90 percent of the time.

Stage 4. A hitch developed. Moving toward a higher level of communication, the experimenter held up the same dog picture as in stage 3 and asked, "What's this?" Instead of replying "dog," as expected, Mr. B. said, "I don't know." Although the experimenters were delighted to hear him utter a three-word sentence, their delight dissipated rapidly as Mr. B. continued for seven days to reply, "I don't know," when asked to identify the dog picture.

Stage 5. To extinguish the negativistic "I don't know" replies, the experimenters had Mr. B. taken out of the room and returned to his ward every time he produced this response. After four days he stopped saying, "I don't know," and identified the picture by saying "dog" almost 100 percent of the time.

Stage 6. The experimenters began pointing to things in the room, identifying them, and then saying, "What's that?" If Mr. B. said, "I don't know," he was again shown out of the room. Correct responses, on the other hand, were reinforced with food, as usual. After thirty-one days Mr. B. could name 150 objects correctly.

Stage 7. Mr. B.'s horizons were broadened. He was shown pictures in magazines, was taken around the hospital grounds, and was even guided through a supermarket, all the while identifying objects and being rewarded with food. His vocabulary began to increase spontaneously.

Stage 8. In order to wean Mr. B. from the continual reinforcement of food to more natural reinforcers, the experimenters began rewarding him intermittently rather than regularly. At the same time they trained him to make requests (e.g., "I want candy," "I want tea") so that he could solicit his own reinforcers. The requests eventually generalized to objects not demonstrated, so that he could spontaneously say, for example, "I want a cigarette."

Stage 9. The experimenters taught Mr. B. one final behavior that was likely to be reinforced naturally: the ability to ask questions. He was encouraged to talk to the other patients, and they to him.

Mr. B.'s training took 138 days. When it was terminated, his speech still lacked much in the way of spontaneity, but it was speech all the same. And as such, it was reinforced by responses to his requests, by conversation with the other patients, and by training from the hospital's occupational therapy department, which had previously given him up as hopeless. Furthermore, this type of interaction kept him moving; he was no longer catatonic. Indeed, his occupational therapist reported, "He'll run to you across the room if you give him the slightest nod." According to his last follow-up report, made one year after the end of his training, Mr. B. is still on the move and still talking.

hours of valuable staff time. The nurses who customarily fed the patients were instructed to spill food on the patients' clothes during the feeding process. Since both patients were extremely fastidious about their appearance, they learned very quickly to feed themselves and thus avoid any mealtime contact with the sloppy nurses.

The Token Economy Efforts to extend operant-conditioning methods to entire wards have generally involved the *token economy*, a system whereby patients are given tokens or points or some other kind of generalized conditioned reinforcer in exchange for performing certain target behaviors, such as personal grooming, cleaning their rooms, or doing academic or vocational-training tests. The patients can then exchange the tokens for any number of backup reinforcers, such as cigarettes, snacks, coffee, new clothes, or special privileges. The procedure is really very much like that which operates outside the hospital: we earn money by performing certain tasks and then exchange this money for the privileges and goods that we want. Indeed, one of the major advantages of the token economy may be its value in preparing the patient for reentry into the community.

The Humanistic-Existential Perspective

Cause Most humanistic and existential writers have directed their attention primarily to the neuroses, but a few systematic attempts have been made to apply the humanistic-existential model of man to the problem of psychosis. The writer who has contributed by far the most in the area is R. D. Laing, a British existential psychiatrist. Laing's interpretation may be reduced to two central arguments. The first is that madness is all a matter of perspective:

The concept of schizophrenia as a form of madness implies a concept of sanity as the norm against which madness is judged. . . . The psychiatrist seems to us in varying degrees sane, and the patients in varying degrees mad. This is because the psychiatrist's behavior is assumed axiomatically to be the yardstick against which the abnormality of the patient is scaled (1964, pp. 185 and 189).

This relativistic argument leads directly into Laing's second point, which is that schizophrenia is simply "a special sort of strategy that a person invents in order to live in an unlivable situation" (1964, p. 187). In his earlier work, Laing did support the notion that the schizophrenic was in some way "ill" as a result of pressures both from the society and from the

family; he held the view that the schizophrenic individual had as a child never developed a secure sense of personal identity. As a consequence of this failure, he is in constant fear of being overwhelmed, forgotten, or destroyed by others; other people represent a constant threat or danger to him. In the face of this, the individual seeks ways to protect himself. But this desire for security, which drives the individual to withdraw from others, is in conflict with an equally powerful desire to be loved, acknowledged, and understood by others. Thus the schizophrenic is torn, is divided, between love and fear ([1960] 1969). In his more recent writings (1967), however, Laing takes a much more radical stand: he argues that the schizophrenic may well be more sane than the society that labels him mad. According to this theory, schizophrenia is not "insanity," but rather "hypersanity," a voyage from our own mad reality into another reality in the existential search for autonomy and meaning. Psychiatrists, Laing argues, have no right to interfere with this quest: "Can we not see that this voyage is not what we need to be cured of, but that it is itself a natural way of healing our own appalling state of alienation called normality?" (1967, p. 116)

The Antipsychiatric Movement In his defense of the schizophrenic experience against the presumptions of conventional psychiatry, Laing is supported by a group of writers whose major contention is that the state called "insanity" is simply a label fabricated by society in order to justify the exploitation of persons so labeled. This group, which includes Thomas Szasz and a number of other eminent writers along with Laing, sees the schizophrenic virtually as a victim of an Establishment plot; they would like to do away with conventional psychiatry and to redefine psychosis as a disruption of social or interpersonal relations.

Mosher (1974) lists four major criticisms raised by this group concerning the traditional views and treatment of people labeled schizophrenic. First, they argue that by classifying so-called schizophrenics "mentally ill" or "diseased," society justifies detention in distant, dehumanizing, impersonal institutions and sanctions "treatment" methods which do no more than persuade deviant individuals to conform more closely to society's norms. Second, these critics point out the adverse social consequences of the labeling process; for example, a person who has at any time been labeled "schizophrenic" will probably have difficulty for the rest of his life both in establishing social relationships

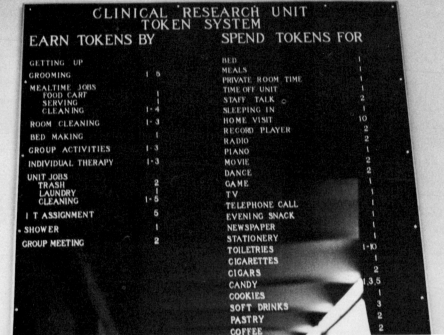

CLINICAL RESEARCH UNIT
TOKEN SYSTEM

EARN TOKENS BY		SPEND TOKENS FOR	
GETTING UP		BED	1
GROOMING	1-5	MEALS	1
MEALTIME JOBS		PRIVATE ROOM TIME	1
FOOD CART	1	TIME OFF UNIT	1
SERVING		STAFF TALK	2
CLEANING	1-4	SLEEPING IN	1
ROOM CLEANING	1-3	HOME VISIT	10
BED MAKING	1	RECORD PLAYER	2
GROUP ACTIVITIES	1-3	RADIO	2
INDIVIDUAL THERAPY	1-3	PIANO	1
		MOVIE	2
UNIT JOBS		DANCE	2
TRASH	2	GAME	1
LAUNDRY	1	TV	1
CLEANING	1-5	TELEPHONE CALL	1
I T ASSIGNMENT	5	EVENING SNACK	1
SHOWER	1	NEWSPAPER	1
GROUP MEETING	2	STATIONERY	1
		TOILETRIES	1-10
		CIGARETTES	1
		CIGARS	2
		CANDY	1,3,5
		COOKIES	1
		SOFT DRINKS	3
		PASTRY	2
		COFFEE	2

Fig. 12.6 Aspects of a token economy program at Camarillo State Hospital in Camarillo, California, are shown in these photographs. (Top) The "rent" for a private room is five tokens; (middle) a chart posted on a wall indicates the ways in which tokens can be earned and spent; and (bottom) a patient exchanges tokens for a candy bar. In a token economy, required behaviors and achievable privileges are clearly specified. The aim of such a program is to produce behaviors that the patient needs for successful post-hospital adjustment. For a token economy to be effective, cooperation of the staff at all levels is necessary; a program can be rendered ineffective by inequitable token distribution, inconsistent requirements for behavior, and other sources of error.

and in getting a job. Scheff (1970), in particular, believes the labeling process to be the single most important cause of continuing deviance. A third source of criticism is psychiatry's preoccupation with finding out what kind of "disease" the person has, to the neglect of the person himself. And fourth, these writers object to the traditional doctor-patient relationship, which as they see it allows the physician unlimited power to manipulate—often for the satisfaction of his own needs—the submissive, dependent patient. By its very nature, this relationship destroys any possibility of the patient's achieving the independence he is supposed to achieve.

Treatment In summary, the humanistic-existential and antipsychiatric schools construe psychosis as either fabricated, caused, or aggravated by a social environment that blocks off the quest for personal autonomy and growth. Hence the treatment strategies proposed by these writers invariably emphasize the establishment of an open, warm, nurturant environment "where the patient is able freely to dispose of his innermost existential resources" (Binswanger, 1970, p. 351). Therapy does not involve training or education, as in the behavioral treatments; rather, it is a process of healing and growing. As Laing says: "The schizophrenic is one who is broken-hearted. But even broken hearts can mend, if we have the heart to let them" (1964, p. 193).

From a humanistic standpoint, the ultimate treatment for all mental disorders would be a drastic restructuring of society so that impossible demands, debilitating pressures, and dehumanizing conditions would be eliminated. But since this ideal, even if it were possible, is unlikely to be brought about, humanistic therapists have concentrated on designing "mini-communities" aimed at fostering the personal growth of immediate members. Depending on the degree to which their designers view psychosis as an actual "disturbance" requiring "cure," these communities range from mild to radical departures from the traditional mental hospital.

Among the less radical treatments are various forms of *milieu therapy*, some of which have produced promising results (Artiss, 1962; Cumming and Cumming, 1962). Like the traditional mental hospital, milieu therapy involves a residential community which is still run by mental health professionals with fairly conventional notions of what constitutes normal and abnormal behavior. Unlike most mental hospitals, however, milieu therapy programs place as few restraints as possible on the freedom of the patient and actively encourage him to take part in

a wide variety of activities. Patients are expected to take responsibility for their own behavior, to participate in their own rehabilitation and that of others, and to help in the making of decisions which affect the entire community.

Considerably less traditional is the type of residential community first founded by Laing in London in 1965, under the name of Kingsley Hall, and since imitated by another community, Soteria House in San Jose, California. These communities differ from milieu therapy and from any other type of mental health facility in two very basic respects. First, there is very little dichotomy between patients and staff. For instance, Soteria House staff members are selected not on the basis of their knowledge or experience in working with schizophrenics, but rather on the basis of their ability to "tune into the patients' altered state of consciousness" (Mosher, 1972, p. 233). In fact, those with preconceived notions are rejected. Basically, the residence is a commune of people who are regarded simply as people, those who are "up" helping those who are "down." The second major difference is in the attitude toward psychotic behavior. In keeping with Laing's theories (1967), a schizophrenic reaction is viewed not as a breakdown, but as a potential "breakthrough"—as an experience which the individual has a valid reason for going through and which has meaning for him. The job of the staff in relation to the schizophrenic is to perform "a role similar to that of the LSD-trip guide" (Mosher, 1972, p. 233), supporting him and working *with* him as he goes through his process of growth.

Adequate evaluation of such programs is yet to be made (Mosher, 1974; Cooper, 1967). Nevertheless, the humanistic-existential perspective and the antipsychiatric movement have no doubt already

Fig. 12.7 R. D. Laing, the British existential psychiatrist, feels that madness is a matter of perspective and schizophrenia is strategy for living in an unlivable situation.

A VOYAGE THROUGH PSYCHOSIS AT KINGSLEY HALL

If, as R. D. Laing argues, what we call a psychotic breakdown is actually a quest—and a quest that psychiatry has no right to interfere with—what does this mean in terms of day-to-day treatment of the psychotic? According to Laing, the psychotic's bizarre behaviors are part of a natural healing process; the patient must be allowed to "go down" if he is ever truly to "come up." But what if "going down" means kicking, biting, refusing food, smearing feces, and yelling from the rooftops? If these behaviors cannot be "interfered with" through such means as drug therapy, electroshock, or operant conditioning of more socially acceptable behaviors, what is the therapist to do with the patient?

One answer to this question is given in *Two Accounts of a Journey Through Madness* (1973), in which Mary Barnes and her therapist, Joseph Berke, describe Barnes' five-year stay at Kingsley Hall, the residence established by Laing for people who needed a noncoercive environment in which to "go down." Within a month after her arrival at Kingsley Hall, Barnes had indeed gone down. Regressing to a womblike state, she refused to take any nourishment other than warm milk mixed with honey, which she sucked from a baby bottle. And this she would normally take only from Berke. There were other prerequisites as well. Berke reports:

All I had to do was turn my head, or look inattentive, or blink an eye while feeding her, and Mary began to pinch her skin, twist her hair, contort her face, and moan and groan. Worse shrieks followed if I had to leave the room and get involved in another matter at about the time she was due for a feed (p. 235).

After months of severe regression, Barnes began slowly to "come up." And now her behavior changed from total withdrawal to what outsiders would consider total obnoxiousness. Venting jealousy and rage that she had contained since childhood, she used her own feces to paint pictures on the walls of Kingsley Hall, much to the disgust of the other residents. She hung on Berke and followed him around like a puppy; if he had to speak to someone else privately or worse yet, leave Kingsley Hall, she tore at his clothes and howled with grief; if he succeeded in leaving, she sat huddled in front of the door to his room, whining until he returned. When Berke's wife-to-be moved in with him at Kingsley Hall, Barnes' jealous possessiveness simply escalated:

Mary wouldn't leave us alone. If we were sitting together she would come between us. If we were asleep in our room, she would walk in and lie down between us. If we locked the door she would stand outside and howl. If we forgot to lock the door and went out, she would steal into our room and pee on the bed. Several times we had to drag her screaming out of the room. She wouldn't leave of her own accord (p. 267).

When he could not tune in with her mood on a given day, she would often respond by simply "bashing him one" (p. 231).

To all of these behaviors, Berke responded with heroic patience. Nor was this simply a function of kindness on his part. His tolerance of Barnes' behaviors was grounded on the belief, which he shared with Laing, that "psychosis is a potentially enriching experience if it is allowed to proceed full cycle, through disintegration and reintegration, or death and rebirth" (p. 231). Thus at every point, he tried to meet her on her own terms, allowing her to go where her voyage was taking her. "The resultant transactions often took place at a psychotic level, and if that was the way of the day, fine" (p. 233).

When Barnes regressed to the womb, he bottle-fed her. Later, when she had moved along to the level of a young child, he bought her toys, took her out for ice cream cones, played catch with her, and worked to discern the meaning in her speech, which was often limited to a small repertoire of different grunts. When she needed to exorcise her rage, he took her up to the roof and let her scream. He also encouraged her to kick and bite him when she was angry: "I used my superior size and weight to absorb her squeezes and bites and blows. Deft footwork kept me from being kicked in more vital places" (p. 268).

Most important of all, when Barnes started painting on the wall with her feces, he praised her pictures. (His praise was sincere; he writes: "Mary smeared shit with the skill of a Zen calligrapher" [p. 249].) Then he brought her cans of real paint. This was a major turning point in her "voyage." She began painting furiously, pouring onto vast canvases the images of her desires and her rages. Gradually her paintings began to interest people outside Kingsley Hall. They were exhibited, written up, and praised. This creative outlet and the attention it brought were important factors in her regeneration. Today she is a recognized artist, lives in an apartment of her own, and makes her living from painting and writing.

But the central factor in Barnes' regeneration, according to her own account, was Berke's respect for the process she was going through, his belief in its value and necessity, and his willingness to meet her at whatever level she was operating on at the moment.

Not all existential therapists, no matter how thoroughly convinced by Laing's theory, could see such a treatment through on a day-to-day basis as Berke did. Indeed, many of the confirmed Laingians inhabiting Kingsley Hall at the same time as Barnes were utterly disgusted with her behavior and wanted her expelled from the Hall. This is to say nothing of the neighbors, who viewed the goings-on at Kingsley Hall with increasingly sour disapproval. In short, Mary Barnes' "journey through madness" was a noisy, violent, messy, time-consuming, and utterly inconvenient business, the likes of which would never be tolerated in the average mental hospital. But in Kingsley Hall it was allowed to run its course. Whether such therapy would work for other patients is a serious question. An even more serious question is whether the society could ever provide enough Kingsley Halls and enough Joe Berkes to try out this therapy on a sizable number of patients. But for Mary Barnes it *did* work. She was allowed to take her journey, and she arrived at her destination: an independent and fulfilling life.

performed a service to mental health by insisting on the integrity and validity of the individual's experience, be it schizophrenic or otherwise, and by calling for critical reappraisals of such matters as the ethics of labeling and commitment, the effectiveness of traditional treatments, and the overall social significance of the disease model of mental illness.

The Interpersonal Perspective

All three of the perspectives that we have covered so far give some attention to the schizophrenic's interactions with others; however, the primary emphasis of these perspectives is on the psychological processes of the individual (e.g., regression, operant conditioning, or the blocking of growth processes) as he responds to these interactions. The interpersonal perspective, on the other hand, focuses primarily on the interactions themselves in an effort to determine what kind of interpersonal relations could possibly bring about schizophrenia.

The Family

Will J., a nineteen-year-old youth, fluctuated between states of catatonic stupor and wild excitements that, in those preshock and pretranquilizer days, were difficult to manage. With the help of a special nurse, Will began to improve, but clearly became worse after each of his mother's semi-weekly visits. Despite Will's desperate condition, his mother would spend her time with him seeking to have him pray with her and in admonishing him to remember to move his bowels regularly, to take his vitamins, to do deep breathing exercises, and so forth. When Mr. J., a dignified industrialist, was asked to persuade his wife to return to their home in another state and leave their son's care to the hospital staff, he said that it would not be possible: he had given up trying to get his wife to permit Will to have some independence and grow up, and now that Will was so desperately ill, she would never leave him. When the hospital decided to ban her visits temporarily, she sent imploring notes to her son daily, and when these were returned to her, she sent him a box of chocolates. The brand had been selected carefully, for instead of the customary brown paper "trays," these contained white ones, on each of which Mrs. J. had carefully printed a message such as "eat your prunes at breakfast," "breathe deeply five times each hour," "say your prayers morning and night" (Lidz, 1973, p. 8).

It is generally agreed that the family has a greater impact on the individual's psychosocial development

Schizophrenia as an Aid to Evolution

If schizophrenia is such a debilitating mental illness and if its cause is partly genetic, why has it not been eliminated from our gene pools through the process of natural selection? Why, on the contrary, does it continue to appear in all the populations in the world? Edward F. Foulks, an anthropologist and a physician, has advanced the rather novel view that schizophrenia has survived because, like bipedalism in the earliest ancestors of man and like long necks in giraffes, it is adaptive. Foulks claims that schizophrenia tends to flourish in times of social disorganization due to rapid change. In such periods most people are completely at a loss because their thinking is traditional; they cannot part with their old habits—habits tied to conditions that no longer obtain. This is where the schizophrenic comes in. Because his thinking is not traditional, but rather visionary and unorthodox, he can teach his people new and more adaptive patterns of behavior.

As an example, Foulks cites Joan of Arc, whose visions commanded her to mobilize her people and rid France of English rule. Foulks also points to the case of an American Indian named Handsome Lake. When Handsome Lake's people, the Seneca Indians, were confined to reservations in the eighteenth century and could no longer hunt, this change caused severe psychological stress. The Senecas drank, quarreled, and became idle and superstitious. At this point Handsome Lake began to hear voices telling him that the people should organize themselves in families rather than clans, and that they should farm rather than hunt. As might be expected in a small traditional society, Handsome Lake's visions were valued as prophecies rather than ignored as the ravings of a madman. The Senecas followed his instructions and consequently adapted to their new circumstances.

Foulks' theory bears some relation to Laing's conception of the schizophrenic as a mental voyager in search of a state beyond our own cramped and distorted notions of sanity. Against this rather elated vision of schizophrenia, it must be said that most of the grand schemes put forth by schizophrenics are not as practical as converting to farming or liberating one's country from foreign dominion. Rather, they tend to focus on such matters as the necessity of building a bridge from Earth to Mars or fortifying the hospital against enemy invasions. A second objection to Foulks' theory is that of necessity it depends on retrospective diagnosis, and retrospective diagnosis is always risky. Who knows but that Handsome Lake, in order to convince his people, merely converted what he thought were good ideas into messages sent from heaven? Joan of Arc is equally problematic. Scientific age or no scientific age, there are many people who would object to labeling her as schizophrenic.

Source: *The New York Times*, December 9, 1975, p. 11.

than any other element of society. Hence it is no surprise that several generations of investigators have looked to the family for the causes of schizophrenia, particularly in cases such as the above.

Arieti (1974) sees the schizophrenic's family milieu as one in which the child is deprived of all security and is surrounded by anxiety and hostility in all family interactions. In setting the tone of such interactions, the relationship between the parents is of course particularly decisive. Lidz (1973) claims that a great number of schizophrenic children come from families that fall into either one of two categories: the "schismatic family," in which parental discord has divided the family into opposing factions, and the "skewed" family, which remains reasonably calm, but only because one spouse is totally dominated by the pathology of the other. In both situations the child is denied the emotional support necessary for a sense of security and self-worth. Furthermore, role-modeling may become extremely problematic, particularly in the "schismatic" family, where identification with one parent might antagonize the other and thus cause even greater hostility.

Such family-based theories of schizophrenia do, however, give rise to a further question: If the total family setting is of major importance in the etiology of schizophrenia, why does one child in the family grow up schizophrenic while another develops normally? Bowen (1960) hypothesizes that one child may be selected as the focal point toward which both parents direct their emotional immaturity, thus achieving an uneasy stabilization of their own rela-

Fig. 12.8 Institutionalized patients often exhibit withdrawal and inactivity. There is a great deal of evidence indicating that this passivity and stupor are not symptoms of a "schizophrenic process" but are aspects of the social breakdown syndrome. Overcrowding, understaffing, and prevailing treatment approaches result in the reinforcement of docility and the punishment of assertiveness; residents in an institution quickly learn the patient role. In contrast, milieu therapies and token economy programs reward patients for constructive, assertive behavior. Token economies, which are more systematic than milieu programs, seem to be successful in preventing and overcoming patients' withdrawal. Therapies involving vocational or creative activities also ameliorate passivity and involve the patient in constructive activities such as painting, cooking, sewing, and woodworking.

tionship. In addition, Mosher, Pollin, and Stabenau (1971) suggest that such a focal child may be selected from among the others because he is weaker or less intelligent or otherwise constitutionally inferior to his siblings. It is of course also possible that one child may inherit a genetic predisposition toward schizophrenia, while another child in the same family may be genetically "free and clear" and thus better equipped to withstand the emotional stresses imposed by the family.

Double-Bind Communication

A young man who had fairly well recovered from an acute schizophrenic episode was visited in the hospital by his mother. He was glad to see her and impulsively put his arm around her shoulders, whereupon she stiffened. He withdrew his arm and she asked, "Don't you love me any more?" He then blushed, and she said, "Dear, you must not be so easily embarrassed and afraid of your feelings." The patient was able to stay with her only a few minutes more and following her departure he assaulted an aide (Bateson et al., 1956, p. 251).

Bateson and his co-workers offer this case as an example of what they call *double-bind communication*, which they feel may be a strong causative agent in schizophrenia. In the double-bind situation the mother gives the child mutually contradictory messages (for example, both rejection and affection in the above example), meanwhile implicitly forbidding the child to point out the contradiction. The

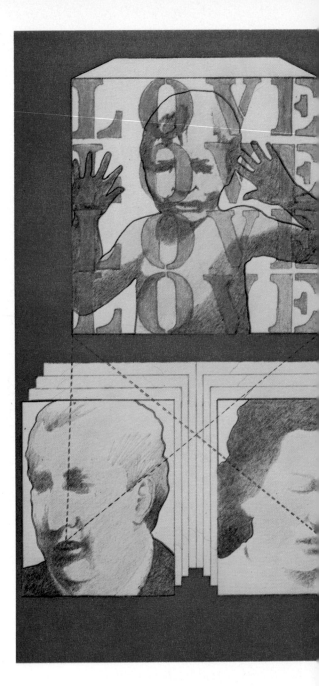

Fig. 12.9 *Double-bind situations have been hypothesized as a primary factor in the development of childhood psychosis. One particularly destructive form of double-bind situation is when the child is verbally told that he is loved and nonverbally told that he is unloved and rejected. One or both parents, for example, may say, "Of course, we love you," and then recoil at the child's attempts to embrace them. Other types of double-bind conditions involve one parent contradicting the other's message, with neither acknowledging the contradiction. In such situations the child is without effective communication, for if he responds to either message he incurs disapproval, and if he verbalizes a double bind he is ignored or rejected.*

child is thus caught in the middle; no matter which alternative he chooses, he is the loser. In short, he is in a double bind. Bateson and his colleagues propose that the type of mother most likely to engage in double-bind communication is one who finds closeness with her child intolerable but who also finds it intolerable to admit this to herself. Thus she pushes the child away, but when the child withdraws, she accuses him of not loving her.

This emphasis on the mother as the principal culprit in producing schizophrenia was not new when Bateson and his colleagues wrote their now-famous article. In 1948, Frieda Fromm-Reichmann coined the term *schizophrenogenic mother* to describe the type of mother who was capable of inducing schizophrenia in her children. Such mothers were typically characterized as cold, domineering, rejecting, and yet overprotective. The father, meanwhile, was faulted mainly for his passivity in not interfering in the pernicious mother-child relationship. More recent investigations (e.g., Caputo, 1968), however, have suggested that the fathers are as responsible as the mothers for the hostile, aggressive atmosphere which seems to permeate many homes of schizophrenic children. In fact, the trend of recent studies has been to focus attention on the communication patterns among *all* members of the family (Mishler and Waxler, 1968).

It should be noted, however, that while many writers accept the correlation between schizophrenia and disordered family relationships, drawing etiological conclusions from studies of the families of schizophrenic children is always hazardous. In the first place, there is the chicken-and-egg problem: it is not clear whether the family disruptions are causing the child's disorder or whether the presence of an abnormal child produces abnormal relationships among other family members (Gunderson et al., 1974). Furthermore, there is the third-variable problem: it is certainly possible that both the child's

disturbance and the abnormal family interactions are the result of yet another factor, such as a shared genetic defect (Reiss, 1974). Studies of the families of schizophrenics are extremely difficult to conduct, both because of the multitude of uncontrollable variables and because of ethical problems (e.g., the invasion of the family's privacy, the implication that the parents are to blame for the deviance of the child). Nevertheless, developments in family-study methodology—particularly the high-risk family studies, which we shall discuss shortly—are making it increasingly possible for investigators to address the critical questions in this area.

The Biological Perspective

There is . . . reason to fear that . . . this disorder is haereditary. For, altho' even in such case it may now and then be excited by some external and known cause, yet the striking oddities that characterise whole families derived from lunatic ancestors, and the frequent breaking forth of real Madness in the offspring of such ill-concerted alliances, and that from little or no provocation, strongly intimate that the nerves or instruments of sensation in such persons are not originally formed perfect and like the nerves of other men (Battie, [1758] 1969, pp. 59–60).

William Battie, the eighteenth-century physician whom we have already encountered in Chapter 11, was not alone in holding to a genetic theory of psychosis. The idea that "madness" was an inherited trait became particularly popular in the latter half of the nineteenth century, and as we have seen in Chapter 11, was shared by Kraepelin and Bleuler. It is only within the past decade, however, that we have been able to produce studies sophisticated enough to provide what seems to be conclusive evidence in support of the genetic hypothesis. In the words of Rosenthal, one of the world's foremost authorities on the genetics of abnormal behavior, "the issue must now be considered closed. Genetic factors do contribute appreciably and beyond any

reasonable doubt to the development of schizophrenic illness" (1970, pp. 131–132).

If there is in fact a genetic component in the etiology of schizophrenia, it must of course manifest itself in some biochemical or physiological abnormality—perhaps, as Battie put it, in imperfect "nerves or instruments of sensation" or perhaps in some other imperfection. Hence genetic, biochemical, and physiological studies of schizophrenia are very closely linked. And accordingly, we will consider the perspectives from these three areas within a common section in this chapter. The reader should keep in mind that these views are in no way mutually exclusive; rather, they are interdependent, each focusing on some particular aspect of organic etiology.

The Genetic Approach

The Evidence: Family, Twin, and Adoptive Studies Family studies of the genetics of schizophrenia show clearly that the more closely one is related to a schizophrenic, the more likely one is to develop schizophrenia. Fig. 12.10 shows the data from a representative study, that of Kallmann (1953). As may be seen from this graph, the child of one schizophrenic parent has a 16.4 percent chance, and the child of two schizophrenic parents a 68 percent chance, of becoming schizophrenic, as compared to an incidence of less than 1 percent in the general population. However, because families tend to share the same environment as well as the same genes, it

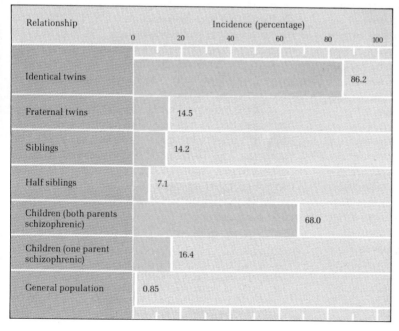

Fig. 12.10 Kallmann's pioneering research, summarized in the accompanying chart, indicates that an individual's chances of becoming schizophrenic are a function of the closeness of his blood relationship to a person already having schizophrenia. Kallmann's data have been criticized because of methodological flaws in his research design, the principal flaw being that Kallmann himself conducted the examinations to determine diagnosis, thus making his findings particularly vulnerable to the interference of expectation and bias. Nevertheless, numerous studies have produced data which are roughly comparable to Kallmann's. (Adapted from F. J. Kallmann, Heredity in Health and Mental Disorder. New York: Norton, 1953.)

is nearly impossible in family studies to determine whether correlations are the function of genetic or environmental influences. Hence family studies are the weakest class of genetic evidence.

A great deal more precision on the question of genetics *vs.* environment can be achieved in twin studies. As we have seen in Chapter 5, these studies are based on the difference between monozygotic (MZ) and dizygotic (DZ) twins in the degree of genetic similarity. Any pair of twins tends to share a highly similar environment. However, MZ twins, having developed from the same sperm and the same ovum, have exactly the same genetic constitution, whereas DZ twins are no more alike genetically than any pair of siblings. Hence a wide disparity in concordance rates between MZ and DZ twins would seem to be a function of genetic factors alone.

In the case of schizophrenia, such a disparity in concordance rates does indeed exist. In twin studies conducted over the past fifty years, the mean concordance rates for schizophrenia in MZ twins comes to 43.9 percent, approximately five times as great as the mean concordance rate of 8.8 percent for DZ twins (Rosenthal, 1970; Ban, 1973). As more recent studies have improved in research methodology, the concordance rates have tended to diminish for both MZ and DZ twins (Mosher and Gunderson, 1973; Allen et al., 1972). Nevertheless, the MZ-DZ concordance ratios found in these studies generally lie between 3:1 and 6:1.

Such data must be considered to be very strongly in favor of a genetic theory of schizophrenia. However, it is possible to muster arguments to the effect that MZ twins share not only a more similar genotype but also a more similar environment, in that they are always the same sex, tend to be dressed alike, are often confused with one another by friends, and so forth. Hence even the twin studies cannot be considered altogether conclusive.

It is only within the past ten years that researchers have developed studies in which environmental influences can be distinguished from genetic influence with truly scientific precision. These are the adoptive studies—studies of children who were adopted away from their biological families at birth and who thus have the genetic endowment of one family and the environmental history of another. If such a study could show that children who were born to schizophrenic mothers* but who were adopted away at birth—thus having no experience of the adverse environmental influences that might be present in their biological families—still developed schizophrenia at the same rate as those children who were born of one schizophrenic parent and were not adopted away, then this would indeed be highly conclusive evidence for the genetic hypothesis.

Such a study has been done, and such, in fact, were the findings. By going through psychiatric hospital and foundling home records, Heston (1966) was able to identify 58 adoptees who had been born to hospitalized schizophrenic mothers. He also selected a control group of individuals adopted through the same foundling homes and matched for age, sex, type of placement, and length of time in child-care institutions. From a large variety of sources, mostly firsthand interviews, information was gathered on all these subjects. A dossier was then compiled on each subject, all identifying information was removed, and diagnoses were made by several independent psychiatrists. The results were that schizophrenia was found only in the children of schizophrenic mothers. Furthermore, the age-corrected† rate for schizophrenia among this group was 16.6 percent, almost exactly the same as Kallmann's figure of 16.4 percent for children who were not adopted away from their biological families. Heston also found that about half of the children born of the schizophrenic mothers exhibited signs of major psychosocial disability, such as mental deficiency, sociopathic personality, or neurosis.

A study similar to Heston's but covering a much larger sample was recently conducted in Denmark by Rosenthal and his colleagues (1971). The scope of the project is truly astounding. Through various central registries which have been maintained by the Danish government for some fifty years, these investigators identified 5,500 adoptees and 10,000 of their 11,000 biological parents. Then they identified all of those biological parents who had at some time been admitted to a psychiatric hospital with a diagnosis of either schizophrenia or manic-depressive psychosis. The 76 adopted-away children of these parents (index children) were then matched with a control group of adopted children whose biological parents had no history of psychiatric hospitalization. (The most significant difference between the design of this study and that of Heston's study is that the

---

*Studies of children of schizophrenic parents sometimes limit their subjects to children of schizophrenic mothers, since paternity can never be established with absolute certainty.

†An *age-corrected* figure is a figure adjusted to take into account the age of the subjects being studied. A subject who is only twenty years old at the time when the study is done may develop schizophrenia at a later time. Thus the figures are adjusted slightly to make allowance for this possibility.

majority of the Danish index parents were not hos-pitalized until some time after the births of their children, thus eliminating the possibility of a mother's abnormal mental condition affecting her child's gestation or birth.) According to the results published so far, only 1 of the 76 index children has been hospitalized for schizophrenia (as compared to none of the control children); however, a sizable proportion of the risk period still remains for most subjects, and the rate of hospitalization may in-crease. Perhaps of greater interest is the finding, derived from extensive interviews and psychological testing, that approximately twice as many index children as control children were listed as having schizophrenic characteristics.

Using the same Danish records, Kety, Rosenthal, Wender, and Schulsinger (1971) did another study from a slightly different perspective. From the same group of 5,500 adoptees, 33 were identified as having psychiatric histories that warranted a diagnosis of schizophrenia. A matched control group of adoptees was selected from the same records. Then 463 biological and adoptive parents, siblings, and half-siblings were identified for both the index and con-trol groups. A search through a variety of state and agency records revealed that 21 of these biological and adoptive relatives could be labeled schizo-phrenic. However, while the incidence of schizo-phrenia among the adoptive relatives, those who shared only a common environment with the adop-tees, was the same for both the index and control groups, the incidence among the biological relatives, those who shared only a common genetic endow-ment with the adoptees, was significantly higher for the index group than for the control group. This study, like the other two adoptive studies, meets the highest standards of scrutiny for scientific method-ology, and along with the other two, it constitutes very strong evidence for the operation of a genetic component in the etiology of schizophrenia.

Modes of Genetic Transmission: Monogenetic-Biochemical vs. Diathesis-Stress While most genet-ic investigators consider data such as the above conclusive (Reiss, 1974), there remains a great deal of disagreement over the particular mode of genetic transmission. Early researchers tended to hold to the *monogenetic-biochemical* theory: that a single gene—dominant, recessive, or intermediate—was re-sponsible for a specific metabolic dysfunction which in turn produced the behavioral manifestations of schizophrenia. Within the past few years, however, there has been a stronger movement toward a *dia-*

thesis-stress position; according to this theory, what is inherited is a diathesis or predisposition toward schizophrenia, and the schizophrenia itself will develop only if certain stresses are encountered.

The most widely known diathesis-stress model is that proposed by Paul Meehl (1962). Meehl pos-tulates that the phenotypic consequence of the ge-netic abnormality is a neural defect which he labels *schizotaxia.* The normal stresses and strains of any social learning environment produce in schizotaxic individuals a somewhat peculiar personality organi-zation which Meehl calls *schizotypy.* If the schizotype has the good fortune to be raised in a favorable social milieu, he will remain fairly normal, though perhaps slightly eccentric. But if he is raised in a highly stressful milieu—if, for example, he has a mother who engages in double-bind communi-cation—then he will develop clinical schizophrenia.

Research Extensions from Genetic Findings: High-Risk Studies A vast number of studies have been conducted with children who have been born to schizophrenic parents and who have shown at least some symptoms of schizophrenia. These studies have revealed a wealth of information, but they are almost always contaminated by serious method-ological problems. If, for example, you wanted to identify significant events in the background of a child who is now showing schizophrenic symptoma-tology, your theoretical notions might well bias your attention toward certain details of the child's history. Furthermore, if you interview people who have known the child—parents, grandparents, and so forth—their recollection will usually be influenced by what they know of the child's present condition. In short, retrospective information is often highly questionable. In addition, some of your subjects would probably already have experienced hospitali-zations and drug therapies, factors which could de-cidedly affect their responses to present testing.

The solution, of course, would be to conduct a *longitudinal study*—that is, a study involving testing and interviews at regular intervals over a period of time—of a large random sample of children. Then when certain of these children became schizo-phrenic, you would already have on file a reliable record of their physiological, psychological, and social histories and could begin searching for corre-lations. Unfortunately, there is one major problem with such a project. As we have seen, less than 1 percent of the general population becomes schizo-phrenic. Hence in order to end up with a reliable sample of schizophrenics, you would have to do longitudinal studies of thousands of children—a prohibitively expensive and time-consuming project.

In the early 1960s, Mednick and Schulsinger effected a clear breakthrough in schizophrenic research by devising a longitudinal project that would largely resolve all of the problems outlined above (Mednick, 1970). Recognizing the impossibility of studying a random sample of normal children, Mednick and Schulsinger selected instead a group of children who had a "high risk" for schizophrenia—that is, children who were born of schizophrenic mothers. A number of previous studies had demonstrated that about 50 percent of the children of schizophrenic mothers could be expected eventually to show deviant life styles and that about 15 percent would become schizophrenic. Thus by choosing 200 normally functioning children of schizophrenic mothers, the investigators were able to predict that a large enough number would become schizophrenic so that meaningful comparisons could be made with appropriate control children (see Fig. 12.11).

Mednick lists the following advantages of this project over previous studies:

1. The children have not yet experienced the confounding effects of the schizophrenic life, such as hospitalization and drugs.
2. No one—teacher, relative, child or researcher—knows who will become schizophrenic, which eliminated much bias from testing and diagnosis.
3. Our information is current; we do not have to depend on anyone's recollection.
4. We have two built-in groups of controls for the children who become ill: the high-risk subjects who stay well and the low-risk subjects (1971, p. 80).

Considering its longitudinal nature, the project is still in its infancy; nevertheless, some fascinating preliminary data have already been published. As of 1971, 27 of the high-risk children had been identified as mentally ill. Five critical differences appear to separate these children from those high-risk children who were still normal and from the control subjects:

1. The mothers of the deviant children were more severely schizophrenic, and they were hospitalized while their children were at an earlier age.
2. School reports showed that the deviant children were more domineering, aggressive, and unmanageable in class.
3. On a word-association test, deviant children quickly drifted away from the stimulus. The word "table," for example, might elicit a sequence of associations such as "chair, top, leg, girl, pretty, sky."
4. Upon the presentation of a very loud, irritating noise, the galvanic skin responses (GSRs) of the deviant group were quite different from those of the other two groups. Whereas the GSRs of the two nondeviant groups showed characteristic increases in *latency*—that is, they eventually habituated or got used to the noise and thus began responding to it only at longer

Fig. 12.11 *In this research design for the study of "high-risk" vs. "low-risk" children, Mednick (1970) gathered comparative data at three levels. At the first level, the distinguishing characteristics of children with and without schizophrenic mothers were studied. At the second level, the high-risk children who became deviant were compared with those who did not. At the third level, the characteristics of high-risk children who became schizophrenic were compared with those who were deviant but not schizophrenic, with those who did not become deviant, and with "low-risk" control children. (Adapted from S. Mednick, "Breakdown in Individuals at High Risk for Schizophrenia: Possible Predispositional Perinatal Factors." Mental Hygiene, 1970, 54, 50–63.)*

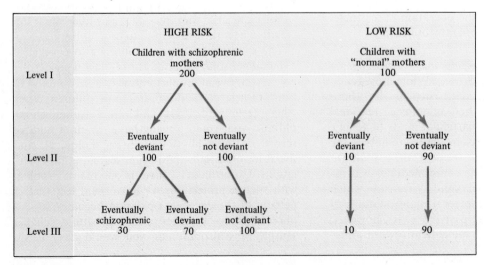

intervals—the GSRs of the deviant group showed no *habituation* and actually decreased in latency. Furthermore, once the stimulus was removed, the GSRs of the deviant group showed a much more rapid recovery to normal state than those of the two nondeviant groups. (It should be noted that these findings give some support to an earlier theory of Mednick's [1958] that schizophrenia is a thought disorder learned as an avoidance response to overarousal of the autonomic nervous system.)

5. Mednick (1971) points out that the most striking finding of all is that complications during pregnancy or birth had occurred for 70 percent of the deviant children as compared with 15 percent of the nondeviant high-risk group and 33 percent of the controls. These pregnancy and birth complications included oxygen deprivation, prematurity, prolonged labor, difficulty with the placenta or the umbilical cord, multiple birth, breech birth, and maternal illness during pregnancy.

The Mednick-Schulsinger program is just beginning to produce results, and already more than twenty similar projects are under way (Garmezy, 1974). It will be years, of course, before all these high-risk studies are completed, but it is hoped that their findings will aid substantially in the development of preventive intervention programs.

The Biochemical Approach If there is a genetic factor in schizophrenia, what is the phenotypic mechanism that translates the genetic abnormality into behavioral abnormality? Many investigators today believe that this mechanism has to do with body chemicals, but for the reasons mentioned earlier in this chapter—particularly interference by third variables such as hospitalization, drugs, diet, and exercise—the progress in biochemical research has been torturously slow and has suffered many embarrassing setbacks. We will review only a few of the theories that have been offered during the past several decades.

Protein Abnormalities In the late 1950s, Robert Heath isolated a factor in the blood serum of schizophrenics that he believed disturbed neural functioning in the brain, thus causing schizophrenia. This factor, a simple protein, Heath (1960) called *taraxein*, from the Greek word meaning "to disturb." When Heath injected taraxein into monkeys, marked changes in behavior and in EEGs were observed. In addition, when the substance was injected into prison volunteers, subjects showed a number of characteristically schizophrenic symptoms, such as severely disorganized thought processes, withdrawal,

and feelings of depersonalization. These startling findings received a great deal of attention at the time of their publication, but because other investigators have had difficulty replicating Heath's work (Siegal et al., 1959), further investigation is necessary before any firm conclusions can be drawn.

Transmethylation Theories The biochemical theories most popularly held today are all based on the hypothesis that schizophrenia is caused by substances known as methylated amines which are produced by the body and which act as hallucinogens (like LSD or mescaline), causing hallucinations and disorganized thinking. In one line of research, a group of neurotransmitters known as the indolamines, principally serotonin and tryptamine, are believed to be chemically altered (methylated) in an abnormal way to form hallucinogenic compounds. For example, Mandell and his colleagues (1972) have reported that under certain conditions an enzyme in the brain known as indolamine-N-methyltransferase can convert serotonin and tryptamine into an hallucinogeniclike compound.

Another group of neurotransmitters which has gained attention are the catecholamines, principally epinephrine, norepinephrine, and dopamine. It has been proposed that in the schizophrenic these catecholamines are abnormally methylated into a mescalinelike compound. For example, Friedhoff (cited in Mosher and Gunderson, 1973) has demonstrated that the human organism is able to synthesize, from dopamine, compounds which are similar to the dimethoxy hallucinogens, of which mescaline is one.

Somewhat conversely to these positions, it has been suggested by other researchers that schizophrenia is caused not by the production of abnormal methylated amines, but rather by an inability to *demethylate* hallucinogenic amines which are normally found in everyone and thus to prevent their accumulation. Evidence for this position and for the others outlined above is still subject to a great deal of speculation. As yet, none of these hypotheses are supported by anything resembling conclusive proof.

The Physiological Approach Studies in physiological aspects of schizophrenia do not compete with genetic or biochemical views. Rather, by concentrating on the functions and processes of the body rather than on qualitative biological differences between individuals, they tend to complement the other views, adding another facet to what may be a many-faceted organic-based condition. It should be kept in mind, however, that a physiological abnormality, like a biochemical abnormality, may well be the result rather than the cause of schizophrenia. Or, as usual, both the abnormality and the schizophrenia may be the results of a third variable. We will consider two recent physiological hypotheses: neurophysiological dysfunction and low stress tolerance.

Neurophysiological Dysfunction A number of studies (e.g., Mednick and Schulsinger's findings with regard to the GSRs of the high-risk children) have shown that autonomic arousal patterns among schizophrenics are different from those observed in normal people (Fenz and Velner, 1970). What researchers have discovered is that in resting states, the arousal level of schizophrenics is higher than normal, but in situations that call for a reaction to some stimulus, the arousal level of schizophrenics is lower than normal. In short, the schizophrenic is "overactive" and "under-reactive" (Buss, 1966). To account for this apparent contradiction, it has been suggested that faulty metabolism of neurotransmitters produces the autonomic overactivity of schizophrenics, and that the low level of reactivity is simply a normal reaction of the nervous system to high resting levels. For example, in normal subjects it has been shown that at extremely high resting levels of autonomic arousal a stimulus will generally not elicit further arousal; rather, a paradoxical decrease in arousal may be effected (Lacey, 1956). Thus the lower reactivity of schizophrenics may be not a primary characteristic but rather a secondary one, reflecting the "normal" functioning of a hyperactive nervous system (Buss, 1966).

Low Stress Tolerance Investigators have also suggested that the schizophrenic does not have a store of adaptive energy that may be mobilized in order to cope with stress. Such a deficiency might be genetic. On the other hand, some researchers have suggested that it might be a physiological consequence of the strains imposed on the body by a prolonged schizophrenic condition (Beckett et al., 1963; Luby et al., 1962). One study has shown, for example, that during acute schizophrenic episodes certain steroid hormones are excreted at abnormally high levels (Sachar et al., 1970). It is possible that a series of such episodes might in the end simply exhaust the adrenal glands, which would then cease to excrete the hormones necessary for dealing with stress.

Chemotherapy In conclusion, a word must be said about the various antipsychotic drugs that are cur-

rently being used with schizophrenics to modify the effects of the supposed biological abnormalities that we have discussed in this section. Lehmann (1974) lists three principal uses which are made of these drugs: to bring the patient out of an acute schizophrenic breakdown; to make management and control of patients easier; and to prevent the recurrence of schizophrenic symptoms in patients in remission. That chemotherapy does in fact attain these goals in a large number of cases is beyond dispute. The question that remains is whether such effects are due to the chemicals themselves or whether they are the result of the expectations of the patients and the staff.

Consider, for example, one pharmacological treatment known as megavitamin therapy. This treatment, which involves administering large doses of nicotinic acid, has been quite popular for twenty years, and schizophrenic patients provide fervent testimonials as to its effectiveness (Mosher, 1973). However, carefully controlled studies comparing megavitamin therapy to placebo treatment (that is, "medicine" with no chemical effect) have repeatedly found no significant difference between the effects of the two (Mosher and Gunderson, 1973). Other studies have found antipsychotic drugs to be quite effective, but in very few of these studies has it been shown that both the clinical staff administering the drugs and the observers collecting data were truly unaware of the nature of the study and of the identity of the experimental and control groups. Hence expectations may well have affected the findings.

While the late 1950s and early 1960s saw a rapid proliferation of new antipsychotic agents, relatively few psychopharmacological advances have been made during the past several years (Mosher and Gunderson, 1973). Instead, researchers have been concentrating on expanding their knowledge of the drugs currently in use, on assessing more carefully the advantages, disadvantages, and limitations of these treatments, and on refining the treatments to eliminate the possibility of side effects and complications.

SUMMARY

The purpose of this chapter has been to review the current theoretical perspectives on schizophrenia. No single one of these perspectives has any greater authority than another, since the cause of schizophrenia remains largely an unsolved mystery.

One reason why so little progress has been made

is that research into schizophrenia is bedeviled by a number of serious problems. First, there is little agreement as to what schizophrenia actually is. Second, there is little consistency among professionals in the diagnosis of schizophrenia. Third, while studies of schizophrenics often uncover interesting correlations between variables, such correlations seldom reveal causality. Finally, the expectations of the researcher are likely to affect findings.

Current theoretical approaches to schizophrenia include the psychodynamic, behaviorist, humanistic-existential, interpersonal, and biological perspectives. Psychodynamic theories, derived from the writings of Freud, view schizophrenia as the result either of a de-cathexis of the object world or of regression. Psychodynamic treatment tends to combine the techniques of classical psychoanalysis with methods borrowed from other perspectives in order to accommodate the psychotic's cognitive weaknesses.

The behaviorist perspective interprets schizophrenia as a learned inattention to socially accepted cues. Behaviorist treatment uses various kinds of direct reinforcement, as well as the more comprehensive token economy, to alter the schizophrenic's social learning environment in such a way that adaptive behaviors are rewarded and maladaptive behaviors are not.

The humanistic-existential perspective tends to emphasize the social aspects of psychosis and to see schizophrenia as a label that society applies to a person who has abandoned modern civilization's distorted realities in search of a more meaningful reality. Likewise, the antipsychiatric movement has called attention to the injustice and hypocrisy of the current psychiatric treatment of schizophrenics. Both schools of thought support treatments which protect the schizophrenic's individualism, develop his sense of responsibility, and provide a warm, supportive environment conducive to personal growth.

While the humanistic-existential perspective stresses the individual's interaction with society at large, the interpersonal perspective tends to focus on smaller units of interaction, particularly within the family; this perspective has called attention to hostile and anxiety-ridden family relations and to double-bind communications as possible sources of schizophrenia.

In contrast to these four psychological perspectives, the biological perspective looks to organic factors for the cause of schizophrenia. Through family studies, twin studies, and especially adoptive studies, this perspective has amassed convincing evidence of the role of genetic inheritance in the etiology of schizophrenia, though the mode by which this genetic abnormality is transmitted remains unknown. In the effort to pinpoint the essential biological deficiency that results in schizophrenic behavior, biochemical studies have suggested the possible involvement either of protein abnormalities or of abnormally methylated neurotransmitters, acting as hallucinogens. Physiological research has proposed both low stress tolerance and disturbed patterns of autonomic arousal as possible fundamental causes of schizophrenic symptomatology. Presumably to correct or at least to control such organic abnormalities, antipsychotic drugs are widely administered to schizophrenics. However, researchers as yet know very little about how these drugs actually work, nor is it certain that their effects are in fact due to chemical action rather than to the patients' expectations.

In Chapters 11 and 12 we have discussed psychosis as it is seen in adults. However, profound psychological disturbance is in no way limited to those who have reached adulthood. It is estimated that 31 out of every 10,000 children in the United States are psychotic (Kolb, 1973). And because research on childhood psychosis is surrounded by the same problems that impede the investigation of adult schizophrenia, the prognosis for many of these children remains discouragingly poor.

Moreover, as with adult schizophrenia, there is little agreement as to what we are actually studying. Some investigators see childhood psychosis merely as a subcategory of adult schizophrenia. Thus in DSM-II childhood psychosis is not given a separate listing but instead appears simply as one of the eleven subtypes ("schizophrenia, childhood type") of adult schizophrenia. Other investigators see childhood psychosis as a syndrome similar to, but separate from, adult psychoses. Furthermore, while many professionals view childhood psychosis as divisible into two separate syndromes, *childhood schizophrenia* and *early infantile autism*, others argue that there is no justification for such a division and that what we are dealing with is a single disorder.

In the following chapter we will consider the common features of childhood psychosis, the question of classification into separate syndromes, the primary features of early infantile autism and of childhood schizophrenia, and finally, the various current theories as to cause and treatment.

CHILDHOOD PSYCHOSIS

Many professionals lump all psychotic children into one category based on the appearance of "schizophrenic symptoms" before puberty (twelve to fourteen years.) According to this view, what some have called autism is simply the appearance in children under six of what is called childhood schizophrenia in children over six. Working according to this unitary theory, a group of British researchers (Creak, 1963) have proposed a list of nine basic symptoms leading to a diagnosis of "schizophrenic syndrome of childhood," by which they mean childhood psychosis in general:

1. Serious and sustained impairment of personal relationships.
2. Apparent unawareness of personal identity, as manifested in grotesque posturing and in self-mutilation.
3. Pathological preoccupation with certain inanimate objects or with certain characteristics of these objects, without any regard for their function.

13
Childhood Psychosis

4. Sustained resistance to any change in the environment, and compulsive rituals aimed at maintaining sameness.
5. Abnormal perceptual experiences, which may lead to exaggerated, diminished, or unpredictable responses to sensory stimuli.
6. Acute, excessive, and seemingly illogical anxiety, which may manifest itself as terror of common objects.
7. A loss of, or failure ever to acquire, speech.
8. Distortion of motor behavior, which may take the form of catatonia, of contortions, of hyperactivity, or—most commonly—of endlessly repeated ritualistic mannerisms.
9. Retardation in general skills, with a pattern of near-normal, normal, or exceptional intellectual functioning in specific areas.

This list is comprehensive enough to cover all psychotic children, but it should be kept in mind that only rarely will a single psychotic child manifest all these symptoms. Nevertheless, any child diagnosed as either autistic or schizophrenic will usually show serious impairment in speech and social relationships, as well as bizarre motor behavior.

Sometimes identified as the cardinal trait of childhood psychosis, the disturbance in social relationships may take the form of total withdrawal, at the other extreme, of obsessive attachment, either to the mother or in some cases to an inanimate object such as a vacuum cleaner, a garden hose, or something equally unlikely. In short, the psychotic child either fails to respond to his social environment or responds in an excessive and inappropriate manner.

No doubt closely linked to the impaired social skills of the psychotic child is his equally severe impairment of speech. Many psychotic children are actually mute, in which case they merely babble, whine, and howl like a three- to six-month-old infant. When speech is present, it is marked by a number of peculiarities and may be used either in a totally noncommunicative fashion or for the communication of bizarre or incoherent ideas.

To the observer, however, the most striking oddity of the psychotic child is his bizarre motor behavior. These behaviors can vary considerably, ranging from a total lack of movement (catatonia) to wild tantrums, self-induced vomiting, and feces-smearing. Most typical, however, is the psychotic child with a limited repertoire of movements that he repeats endlessly, in stereotypic fashion, with no observable goal. These self-stimulatory responses may involve fine or gross motor movements of the hands, face, arms, and/or trunk, in combination or in isolation. Examples include twirling, toe-walking (a sort of prolonged tiptoeing), hand-flapping, rocking, and tensing of various parts of the body. If left to themselves, psychotic children, especially those in institutions, are likely to spend up to 90 percent of their waking hours engaged in these apparently nonfunctional behaviors (Lovaas et al., 1971a).

Even more striking are those cases in which these repetitive movements result in actual physical harm. Self-mutilating behaviors such as head-banging, eye-gouging, and hand-biting are not uncommon. Psychotic children have been known to pull out their teeth, bite off the ends of their fingers, and chew their shoulders down to the bone. Oddly enough, in many cases these behaviors are disturbing not only to the horrified observer, but apparently to the child as well, who will often cry out from the pain all the while that he goes on inflicting it.

Classification: Early Infantile Autism and Childhood Schizophrenia

As we have just seen, it is possible to describe a single large syndrome for childhood psychosis, and

Fig. 13.1 This series of drawings was done by Joey, a young autistic boy who was treated at Bruno Bettelheim's Orthogenic Training School at the University of Chicago. Joey was called "the mechanical boy" because he perceived himself as a machine and regulated all of his behavior and interactions with others through a series of machines. For example, he thought that he was powered by electricity from his machines, and he built a machinelike apparatus to "live him" while he slept; also, he held onto vacuum tubes while he eliminated, both to "power" his elimination and to prevent his body from being drawn into the toilet. The extent to which he perceived himself and his world through machinery is illustrated by his expression of hurt when he was rebuffed by another little boy: Joey said, "He broke my feelings." These drawings illustrate Joey's problems as well as his progress. His self-portrait (1) is that of a machine. Bettelheim interprets pictures 2 and 3 as indicative of Joey's increasing self-esteem. Initially, he saw himself as an "electric papoose," completely controlled by wireless signals. In picture 2 his figure is larger, although he is still being controlled. The third drawing reflects Joey's ability to picture the machine that controls him and, more important, he now has hands with which to manipulate his surroundings. The next drawings also indicate Joey's progress. Drawings 4–6, which show the imaginary "Carr" (car) family, reflect his increasing sense of control. He initially draws an empty car, then proceeds to show a car with a passive passenger, and finally draws a figure driving the car, with a pet as a passenger. The last illustration is a landscape that Joey painted at age twelve, after his recovery. The painting reflects the human emotions that he had regained. Having learned to realize and express his emotions, Joey was no longer a machine.

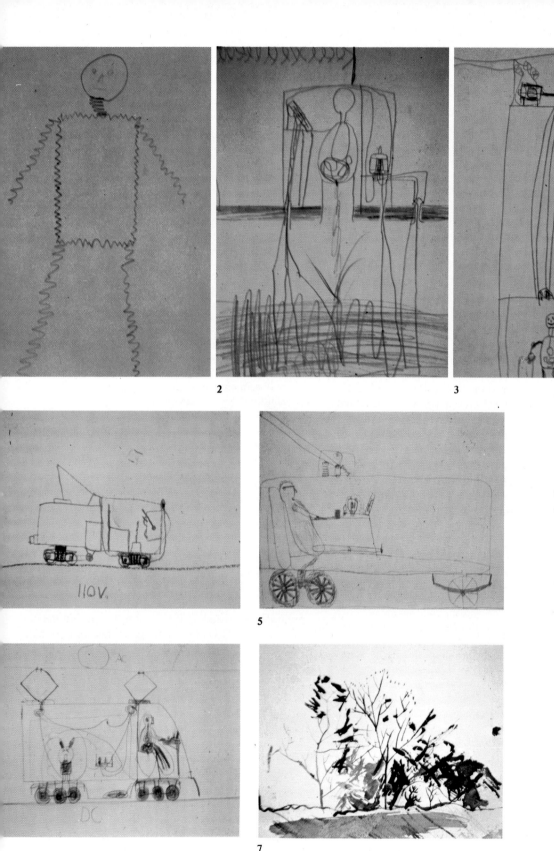

2

3

5

7

for many years it was generally believed that childhood psychosis was in fact a single disorder. Then in 1943 Leo Kanner described eleven cases in which an inability to relate to others, an obsession with sameness, and impaired speech were shown to appear in early childhood. Kanner proposed that these children suffered from an inborn disorder that could be differentiated from other psychotic disturbances of childhood. Since the primary symptom seemed to be an inability apparent from infancy to relate to anything beyond the self, Kanner named the new syndrome *early infantile autism*, from the Greek word *autos*, meaning "self."

Since Kanner's proposal, a number of attempts have been made to develop a classification scheme which would take into account autism and other proposed subcategories of childhood psychosis. In general, such classification schemes, including those proposed by the World Health Organization (Rutter et al., 1969) and by the Group for the Advancement of Psychiatry (GAP, 1966), divide childhood psychosis into two large subcategories, on the basis of age at onset: the psychoses of infancy and early childhood (onset at five years or younger), of which autism is the major syndrome, and the psychoses of later childhood (onset between six and twelve), of which childhood schizophrenia is the major syndrome. Those who support such a two-part classification argue that autism and schizophrenia can be distinguished from one another on the following dimensions (Rimland, 1964; Rutter, 1968; Wing, 1972):

1. *Onset and course:* The autistic child appears to be disordered from birth, while the schizophrenic child experiences a period of normal or near-normal development, after which he regresses.
2. *Health and appearance:* Autistic children are not only in very good physical health, but are also identified as being "beautiful" children, whereas schizophrenic children may have health problems and are no more or less beautiful than the rest of us.
3. *Physical responsiveness:* In contrast to the stiff withdrawal of the autistic child, schizophrenic children are physically responsive to social contact.
4. *Autistic aloneness:* While autistic children are severely withdrawn, schizophrenic children do respond to their social environment.
5. *Preservation of sameness:* Schizophrenic children do not share the autistic child's obsession with maintaining his physical environment intact.
6. *Personal orientation:* While the schizophrenic child is disoriented, the autistic child is unoriented. That is, while the schizophrenic child may have a distorted perception of his environment, the autistic child generally gives no indication of perceiving his environment, beyond the need to preserve sameness.
7. *Hallucinations:* While hallucinations are not common in childhood psychosis, they have been reported in schizophrenic children, but not in autistic children.
8. *Motor performance:* In contrast to the schizophrenic child, who generally has a number of motor problems, the autistic child is well coordinated and able to perform complex motor tasks.
9. *Language:* Autistic children who can speak use their speech in noncommunicative ways, whereas schizophrenic children use speech to communicate bizarre thoughts.
10. *Intellectual abilities:* Though autistic children are more likely than schizophrenic children to have IQs indicating severe retardation, they have a better intellectual potential.
11. *Idiot savant performances:* Idiot savant performances— that is, displays of remarkable ability in isolated areas—may be seen in autistic children, but not in schizophrenic children.
12. *Family background:* Parents of autistic children are of higher intellectual ability and come from higher socioeconomic strata than parents of schizophrenic children.
13. *Family history of mental disorder:* The incidence of mental illness in parents and grandparents is lower than average in the case of the autistic child and higher than average in the case of the schizophrenic child.
14. *Sex ratio:* While the incidence of autism in males is anywhere from three to eight times higher than in females, there is no such sex differential in the case of childhood schizophrenia.

Thus it does appear that there is some justification for classifying autistic children separately from schizophrenic children. It may turn out, in fact, that the primary defect in the autistic child, as in the mentally retarded child, is simply an intellectual impairment. However, here again researchers have pointed out a number of differences between the two syndromes. Bettelheim (1967) and Rimland (1964) claim that the autistic child, unlike the retarded child, has a good cognitive or intellectual potential. Rutter (1968, 1971) has also shown that the pattern of intellectual abilities in the two syndromes differs in that the retarded child is slow in all areas, whereas the autistic child may be severely retarded in the verbal areas while performing quite well on rote memory and visual motor tasks. Additionally, a good 25 to 30 percent of autistic children have IQs in the dull-normal range or above, indicating that retardation is not in fact the primary defect. Further evidence for a differentiation between the autistic child and the mentally retarded child has been provided by the parents themselves. In a comparison of questionnaires filled out by the parents of autistic and mentally retarded children, Douglas and Sanders (1969) found that autistic children were much more frequently described by their parents as being unresponsive to social stimuli, noncuddly, attractive, distant or aloof, and interested in the preservation of sameness than were the retarded children.

In view of all this evidence, it does seem that autism deserves the status of a diagnostic category separate from schizophrenia and mental retardation. However, the diagnosis of autism remains a serious problem. In the first place, as we have seen, there is still abundant confusion and disagreement among diagnosticians, some denying the existence of autism altogether, others differing on critera for diagnosis. Furthermore, compared to other forms of childhood psychosis, the incidence of autism is quite low. Hence we simply don't have a large enough sample of autistic children against which to measure the usefulness of any set of diagnostic criteria.

EARLY INFANTILE AUTISM

While, as we have just seen, the incidence of autism still remains relatively low, the number of children diagnosed as austistic has grown by leaps and bounds since Kanner's first report in 1943. The incidence of autism is now estimated at 4 to 5 per 10,000 in the general population (DeMyer et al., 1973; Lotter, 1974), though many professionals, including Kanner himself, believe that only a few of the children currently being labeled autistic actually belong in that category.

It remains an open question to what degree this increase in the diagnosis of autism is a result or a cause of the recent growth of interest in the disorder. But there is no question that there has been such a recent growth of interest, as evidenced by the establishment of the National Society for Autistic Children, by the calling of conventions and the founding of journals for the study of autism, and by the allocation of federal funds for research into autism. Some states—California for example—are now requiring that local school districts provide special-education programs for autistic children. Much of this recent stir may be due to the hope that autism, unlike childhood schizophrenia, will eventually be traced to a single, clear-cut, and curable organic impairment. Furthermore, since the parents of autistic children tend to come from the middle and upper-middle classes, they have the money and influence to draw attention to the problem. Finally,

there may be a subjective factor involved: it is not unlikely that the physical attractiveness ascribed to autistic children makes people believe that they can be cured, and possibly makes the autistic child preferable to the schizophrenic child as an object of public concern.

Symptoms

As we have seen, the autistic child is said to differ from other psychotic children on a number of different dimensions. However, several of these distinguishing features are based on nothing more than guesswork, while others have failed to receive confirmation from subsequent research. For example, there is no empirical support for the belief that autistic children have better intellectual potential than other psychotic children. In fact, subsequent research reports just the opposite (e.g., Hingtgen and Churchill, 1971). Likewise, there is no firm evidence that parents of autistic children are above average in intelligence (Florsheim and Peterfreund, 1974). And reports of idiot savant performances, while very appealing to the lay press, are also open to serious question. However, there does remain a distinct cluster of correlated symptoms of psychotic children. And it is this set of basic symptoms that we call autism.

Social Isolation   The social withdrawal of the autistic child—what has been called "extreme autistic aloneness"—is usually evident in the first or second year of the child's life. Parents often recall that their autistic children were "good babies." That is, they didn't pester adults for attention; in fact, they seemed happier when left alone. Furthermore, they were very difficult to hold and cuddle, because unlike normal babies, who instinctively mold to the body of an adult who is holding them, they arched their backs and stiffened when picked up. As the autistic infant grows into a child, this recoil from personal contact becomes even more marked. The child avoids looking anyone in the eye and treats people as if they simply didn't exist. If he forms any attachments at all, it is to inanimate objects.

Speech Deficits   The autistic child's social isolation is increased by his failure to use language to communicate. Many autistic children are mute. In others, speech is limited to *echolalia*, in which the child merely repeats, either immediately or at some later time, words or phrases that he has heard. These snatches of speech are echoed not in any apparent attempt to communicate, but simply aimlessly,

THE SEPARATE UNIVERSE OF THE AUTISTIC CHILD

Literally, autism means "self-ism." For those who accept the distinction between childhood schizophrenia and autism, a prime distinguishing feature of the autistic child is his total absorption in himself. While the schizophrenic child is unable to respond appropriately to reality, the autistic child seldom gives any indication that what we call reality has ever even entered his field of awareness. Instead, he seems to inhabit a totally different world, a world closed to everyone but himself. And across the frontiers dividing his world from ours, no communication is possible. This striking feature of autism—along with the autistic child's typically good motor coordination and his love of manipulating objects—is well illustrated in the following quotation, a father's description of his autistic child's play activity:

His little hands hold the plate delicately, his eyes surveying its smooth perimeter, and his mouth curls in delight. He is setting his stage. This is the beginning of his entry into the solitude that has become his world. Slowly, with a masterful hand, he places the edge of the plate on the floor, sets his body in a comfortable and balanced position, and snaps his wrist. The plate spins with dazzling perfection. It revolves on itself as if set in motion by some exacting machine . . . as indeed it was.

This is not an isolated act, a mere aspect of some childhood fantasy . . . it is a great and skilled activity performed by a very little boy for a very great and expectant audience . . . himself.

As the plate moves swiftly and spins hypnotically on its edge, he bends over it and stares squarely into its motion.

For a moment, his body betrays a just-perceptible motion similar to the plate's. His eyes sparkle. He swoons in the playland that is himself . . . Raun Kahlil, our very "special" child. Seldom does he cry or utter tones of discomfort. His contentment and solitude seem to suggest a profound and inner peace. He is seventeen months old and seems to be contemplating another dimension (Kaufman, 1975, p. 43).

without any concern for the meaning of the words. If any actually communicative speech does develop in the autistic child, it is accompanied by problems of pronoun reversal (i.e., the child refers to himself not as "I" but as "you" or "he," or by his proper name), extreme literalness, and repetitiveness. Where an autistic child falls on this scale of speech deficits seems to be an excellent prognostic indicator: it has been shown that the child most likely to benefit from almost any attempt at treatment is the one who has developed some meaningful speech by age five (Lotter, 1974; Rimland, 1964; Rutter, 1971).

Preservation of Sameness Another distinguishing characteristic of the autistic child is his anxiously obsessive desire to maintain sameness in his environment. Toys must always be placed in the same position on the same shelves. At breakfast the egg must be eaten first, then the vitamin pill, then the toast. In the bath, the face must be washed first, then the arms, and so on. If any item in this intricate order is disturbed, a tantrum may ensue. Interestingly enough, this concern for sameness is also commonly observed in the normally developing child of two and a half, thus raising the possibility that the autistic child's development is stalled at this point.

Other Behavior Problems The autistic child frequently has a number of other problems as well. As we have noted, tantrums and self-mutilation are common. Even more common is the total absorption in some endlessly repetitive movement such as spinning or rocking, or in the manipulation of some mechanical object. Such activities often take preference to food; hence eating may be sporadic. One study, for example, found that when engaged in ritualistic movements, a group of autistic children who had not eaten for twenty-four hours either would not respond or would delay their responses to an auditory signal indicating that food was available. The remarkable finding was that these same children would immediately respond to the same signal when they were not engaged in such movements. Thus they knew very well what the signal

Fig. 13.2   Among the behaviors typically displayed by autistic children are repetitive movements, echolalia, self-destructive acts, and withdrawal. Persons who attempt to interact with a severely autistic child often feel that the child acts at best as though they were objects to be investigated or moved aside or at worst as though they were not there at all.

meant but were simply more interested in their repetitive motor activities than in eating (Lovaas et al., 1971a).

This total self-absorption, along with the other basic symptoms of autism, may be seen in the story of Peter, as reported by his mother:

Peter nursed eagerly, sat and walked at the expected ages. Yet some of his behaviour made us vaguely uneasy. He never put anything in his mouth. Not his fingers nor his toys—nothing.

. . .

More troubling was the fact that Peter didn't look at us, or smile, and wouldn't play the games that seemed as much a part of babyhood as diapers. While he didn't cry, he rarely laughed, and when he did, it was at things that didn't seem funny to us. He didn't cuddle, but sat upright in my lap, even when I rocked him. But children differ and we were content to let Peter be himself. We thought it hilarious when my brother, visiting us when Peter was 8 months old, observed that "that kid has no social instincts,

whatsoever." Although Peter was a first child, he was not isolated. I frequently put him in his playpen in front of the house, where the school children stopped to play with him as they passed. He ignored them too.

. . .

Peter's babbling had not turned into speech by the time he was three. His play was solitary and repetitious. He tore paper into long thin strips, bushelbaskets of it every day. He spun the lids from my canning jars and became upset if we tried to divert him. Only rarely could I catch his eye, and then saw his focus change from me to the reflection in my glasses. It was like trying to pick up mercury with chopsticks.

His adventures into our suburban neighborhood had been unhappy. He had disregarded the universal rule that sand is to be kept in sand-boxes, and the children themselves had punished him. He walked around a sad and solitary figure, always carrying a toy aeroplane, a toy he never played with. At that time, I had not heard the word that was to dominate

our lives, to hover over every conversation, to sit through every meal beside us. That word was autism.

Peter's mother took him to various doctors and therapists and finally he was sent to a special school, where he spent nine years (see pp., 340–341).

I'm not qualified to discuss the programme at the [school]. It apparently gave Peter the help he needed.... Peter has made a marginal adjustment, but a "near-miracle" nevertheless, according to his psychiatrist.

Peter chose his own vocation. He tunes pianos, giving them the same devotion that many teenage boys give to their cars. At present he needs help with transportation and arrangements. He does his own book-keeping. He is happy in his work and happy to be home again. We have found a programme for him, where young adults with a history of emotional difficulties meet for recreation and group therapy. I'm sure this is a factor in his continuing improvement (Eberhardy, 1967).

CHILDHOOD SCHIZOPHRENIA

Of all the diagnostic terms associated with childhood psychosis, "childhood schizophrenia" is undoubtedly the most confusing. In the first place, for years the term was used—and by some professionals (e.g., Creak, 1963) it is still used—to designate all psychotic children, including those whom many professionals would now call austistic. Second, the term implies that childhood schizophrenia is simply an earlier version of adult schizophrenia. This may in fact be the case, since the two syndromes have several fundamental symptoms in common. However, there are a number of very important differences as well. For example, while schizophrenic children may experience hallucinations and delusions, these seem to be rare, as is not the case with adult schizophrenics. Likewise, while schizophrenic adults generally seem indifferent to other people, the schizophrenic child may be obsessively attached to his mother. These differences, along with a number of very obvious cognitive differences, may simply be a function of the difference in age at onset. However, they may also be a function of a difference in etiology. Since we do not know the answers to these questions, the Group for the Advancement of Psychiatry (1966) has proposed that the term "childhood schizophrenia" be replaced by a new term, "schizophreniform," in order to avoid confusion with adult schizophrenia. The term, however, has not stuck.

Symptoms

In general, a child is diagnosed as schizophrenic if after six years or more of normal or near-normal development, his reality contact and social adjustment begin to show a severe decline. Specific symptoms include social withdrawal, disorientation, distorted sensory perception, speech disintegration, and intellectual retardation. Motor peculiarities are usually present, including agitated hyperactivity and catatonic nonactivity as well as the ritualistic movements that we have discussed in relation to the autistic child.

The specific areas in which childhood schizophrenia differs from autism have been listed earlier in this chapter. In general, it may be said that childhood schizophrenia manifests itself in symptoms that are somehow more familiar, albeit no more curable, than those of autism. Though the schizophrenic child may also spend hours contorting his body and engaging in repetitive and nonfunctional motor behaviors, he is much less likely than the autistic child to mutilate himself. Though his behavior is bizarre, it is less obsessive than autistic behavior. And finally, though often withdrawn, the schizophrenic child lacks the mysterious and seemingly impenetrable aloofness of the autistic child.

Several common signs of childhood schizophrenia—catatonia, sudden speech disturbance, and especially the general history of normal development followed by decline—are illustrated in the following poignant case:

Ann D. was nine years old when her parents took her to the state hospital. She acted extremely frightened and insisted on being held while her parents went through the process of admitting her.

Ann was the third of six children born to a hard-working bus driver and mechanic and a distraught mother, whose marriage had been necessitated by the first pregnancy. Mrs. D. was a single child from a broken home, and both parents refused to have anything to do with her when she became pregnant before getting married. After her marriage, she remained ignorant of appropriate birth control measures, and six children were born in rapid succession. She found raising the children extremely difficult. Her husband had to maintain two jobs to support the family; he expected her to be totally responsible for the children.

Ann's birth and early development had been quite normal. Toilet training was accomplished at about three years with no problems. She was an active, curious child and did well in her first years in school, becoming very interested in science. She had very few friends, but she was friendly with most of the people in the neighborhood. She liked to help her mother at home, especially with the cooking.

As Ann grew older, her mother's emotional state became steadily worse. Always feeling the burden of caring for six children, Mrs. D. was often severely upset and anxious. At such times she would often ignore her family altogether, refusing to care for the children or the home. Her treatment of Ann was very inconsistent. At times she would coddle her and at other times for no apparent reason would ignore her.

Finally, after one month in which Mrs. D. did nothing in the way of caring for herself or her family, she was taken to the nearby state mental hospital by Mr. D. Six months later, Mrs. D. was able to return home. But at the advice of the hospital psychiatrist, several of the children were sent to live with relatives. Ann and her youngest brother stayed at home. She was expected to help her mother with the housework and to care for the little boy.

It wasn't until a month later that Ann's parents learned from the school psychologist that Ann had become quite withdrawn and had not spoken to any of the children for the past several weeks. Ann's teacher had noted her unusual behavior and had asked the school psychologist to observe her. On seeing Ann, the psychologist became very concerned by the withdrawn, frightened way in which Ann was acting.

Ann's father became very angry at Ann and scolded her for her behavior. Ann's mother got very upset and appeared to be on the verge of a relapse. Her parents' responses upset Ann, who became more withdrawn and frightened. Over the next several days Ann ceased to help her mother. She acted frightened if someone spoke to her, and insisted that the bedroom light be on at night. She often talked about her parents leaving her and not loving her, and she kept saying she was going to be fed to the wild animals in the woods. After about a week of this behavior, Ann's parents took her to the hospital.

During her stay at the hospital, Ann gradually began to communicate with the other patients and the staff. In describing her parents, she stated that she felt she was to blame for her mother's "nervous breakdown"; she felt that she had somehow let her parents down and that they were going to leave her. Ann remained at the hospital for about three months. Through conjoint therapy with her parents, Ann was successfully reunited with her parents and returned to school.

PERSPECTIVES ON CHILDHOOD PSYCHOSIS

Since many professionals view childhood psychosis as a single disorder, much of the theory and research in the area has failed to distinguish between autism and schizophrenia. Thus in this section the two syndromes will be discussed separately only when appropriate.

The Psychodynamic Perspective

Cause This perspective views childhood psychosis as a failure in ego development. Psychodynamic theorists are fairly unanimous in holding the parent-child relationship responsible for this ego block, and though Mahler (1965) sees the origin of psychosis as a symbiotic relationship between mother and child, most psychodynamic theorists take the opposite view: that is, that a child becomes autistic as the result of being raised by parents who are "emotional refrigerators" (Kanner and Eisenberg, 1955)—cold and detached.

While this idea has been explored by a number of researchers (Kanner and Eisenberg, 1955; Eisenberg and Kanner, 1956; Singer and Wynne, 1963; Rimland, 1964), its foremost publicist has been Bruno Bettelheim, whose conceptualization of autism is presented in his book *The Empty Fortress* (1967). According to Bettelheim, autism is a child's response to an extreme situation in which his parents reject him and fail to respond to his slightest attempts to influence his environment. Particularly crucial is the parents' failure to provide stimulation during the early phases when object relationships develop (birth to six months) and when language and locomotion begin to emerge (six to nine months). As a result of this lack of stimulation, the child has no basis on which to form emotional attachments or to develop proper speech and motor skills. Most important of all, because of his parents' unresponsiveness, he feels unable to control the external world in any way. Hence he withdraws into a private fantasy world, while attempting to impose some order and constancy through the insistence on sameness.

This emphasis on parental unresponsiveness as a major etiological factor in autism has been questioned by many investigators, particularly in view of the fact that the siblings of autistic children are likely to turn out quite normal. Furthermore, if it

A Case of Bettelheim's

When Marcia entered the University of Chicago's Sonia Shankman Orthogenic School, directed by Bruno Bettelheim, she had shown autistic behavior for nine of her eleven years. Nearly mute and completely antisocial, she tolerated no stimulation from the external environment; her total activities included rocking her body, staring at lights and shiny objects, ritualistically twiddling the fingers of one hand, and thwarting all attempts at interaction by closing her eyes and stuffing her fingers in her nostrils and ears. She refused to eat unless alone and never defecated without the administration of enemas and laxatives. Tests had ruled out brain damage and retardation, but there was no means of testing her intelligence.

Marcia's history was typical of that which Bettelheim reports finding in most of his patients. Her parents, both melancholy and anxious types, did not welcome her birth. She received from them only the most perfunctory attention. Feeding and bathing were handled as hurriedly as possible, without pleasure on the part of the parents or the child, and aside from these activities the child was largely ignored. Nonetheless, she did not begin to behave abnormally until the age of two, when both her parents suffered serious depressions and

their previous ambivalence toward the child turned to deep resentment. In response to her mother's toilet-training attempts, Marcia began to withhold her feces. This led to weekly enemas, painful experiences during which both parents had to fight the child to hold her still. Bettelheim notes that "if the close bodily contact the small child normally loves and reaches out for turns out to be painful, then he concludes he must shun what he seeks, and disbelieves that anything good can come from his body or seeking" (1967, p. 160). Marcia now stopped speaking, expressed no emotions, and rejected human interaction altogether. She spent the next nine years in and out of psychiatric and custodial institutions. Her condition remained unchanged.

The therapy program at the Orthogenic School aims at correcting the three major problems Bettelheim finds in autistic children: first, the child's profound sense of rejection; second, his distrust of the human and physical environment; and third, his inability to perceive himself as an autonomous, worthwhile individual. In the end, it is the child himself who must remove these barriers. But in order to do so, he requires the warm attentiveness that is the basis of the school's therapeutic program, for "only as a human being persistently seeks the autistic child with his positive emotions does the child become interested in the external world" (p. 230).

The initial phase of Marcia's therapy involved total, loving acceptance by the school staff of everything she did. At first she preferred to be left

Fig. 13.3 Bruno Bettelheim, the controversial spokesman of the psychodynamic approach to autism, sees the child's behavior as a response to a pathological parental relationship.

alone, seemingly content with the staff's assurances that there would be no more forced feedings or enemas. After three months, she had a bowel movement, her first assertive act in nine years. Slowly she began to notice the environment the staff had prepared for her—a strip of material left on a table for her to find and twiddle in her hand, a sandbox to sit in, a baby bottle left near her sink. She gradually incorporated these and a few other objects into her world, and began on her own initiative to use the water, the bottle, and a baby doll to reenact her earlier unhappy feedings and enemas, playing the roles of both mother and child. Frustration, anger, and some destructive behavior emerged at length, as did some fragmented speech.

It was apparent to the staff from these behaviors that a prime causal factor in Marcia's autism was her feeling of having been robbed of her basic functions—eating and defecating—and so of her *self*. To her mind, everything beyond her threatened to overwhelm and destroy her. This feeling had led to her withdrawal, and only after many months of acting out and thus mastering the initial source of her fears could she begin to get a sense of safeness in the external world and of her own individuality.

Her interest in other people increased slowly until, after three years in the school, she would allow staff members to hold her and would play briefly with other children. Now that she no longer had to keep others away from her, she was able to show positive as well as negative feelings.

She grew very attached to one female counselor, Karen, and for many months spoke of "you-Marcia" and "you-Karen" interchangeably, unwilling to differentiate herself from this special other person. With Karen's help, Marcia's recognition of and concern for other individuals eventually led to recognition of her own self. At the end of four years she began to use "I" and "me" to refer to herself. Indeed, her entire range of verbal self-expression expanded greatly. At the same time her emotional reactions were tempered to an appropriate level.

At fifteen and a half, Marcia left the school to return to her parents, who had undergone therapy in the meantime and who now had another child, a normal three-year-old. Marcia was now a cheerful and uninhibited adolescent, able to express a complete range of emotions and to interact socially. Her intellectual level, however, was that of a slow fourth-grader. "While it seems possible," Bettelheim writes, "to restore the mute autistic child to full emotional life ... the same is not true for his grip on reality, for his ego. ... If the requisite emotional experiences [of trust and autonomy] are not available to the child before puberty sets in—that is, at the time when it is necessary for the unfolding of his full intellectual (or ego) development, then the ego remains stunted, even though he may catch up in emotional development ..." (p. 231). But in the sheltered environment of her home Marcia takes care of herself, enjoys doing simple chores, and lives a relatively full, normal life.

is indeed the case that autistic children have cold, detached parents, we are once again faced with a chicken-and-egg question: while it is possible that unresponsive mothers give rise to autistic children, it is equally possible that children who from birth are unresponsive to mothering may give rise to "autistic" mothers (Harlow, 1969).

Treatment Psychodynamic treatment generally requires that the child be removed from the home situation and placed in a residential treatment facility. Here he is provided with a counselor who is constantly available and sympathetic—a steady, reliable image which the child can internalize and around which he can unify his own personality (Freud, 1954). The basis of this treatment is constant responsiveness to the child's needs on the part of the counselor and the staff. Thus in an example cited by Sanders (1974), when a new child was being shown around the school and said, "Mashed potatoes," during a visit to the kitchen, the kitchen staff responded by giving him a special serving of mashed potatoes at every meal.

In this way the child learns what, according to psychodynamic theory, he could not learn at home: that by communicating his needs through speech and movement, he can influence his environment. Once this foundation is laid, the child can begin to develop emotional attachments and to build a stable personality.

A major problem in evaluating psychodynamic treatments is the general lack of concrete suggestions for actual therapy (Wieland, 1971). Ruttenberg (1971) has recently made an attempt to dispel this vagueness by offering a highly specific outline of treatment procedures. Ruttenberg sees the autistic

The story of Peter, presented on pp. 335–336, has another side to it, and that is the story of Peter's mother, Frances Eberhardy—her attitude toward her autistic child, her experiences with the professionals to whom she brought Peter, and her dismay at the current theories of autism, particularly Bettelheim's theory:

A magazine [Newsweek, March 27, 1967] *article on Dr. Bettelheim's (1967) latest book* [The Empty Fortress] *was shown to me, since my son was once an "empty fortress." The reporter's first paragraph was as biting as a Wisconsin blizzard. "For the withdrawn and psychotic child, the yellow door (of the Orthogenic School) is their first experience with warmth and brightness" (1967, pp. 70–71).*

Dr. Bettelheim's own words proved to be no more comforting. "The precipitating factor in infantile autism is the parent's wish that his child should not exist" (p. 125). (1967, p. 257)

Eberhardy claims that in her seven years' association with a group of parents of emotionally disturbed children, she has yet to meet a parent who was markedly aloof or indifferent to his child. As for her own autistic child, he was welcomed into the world with joy:

To us, Peter, our first born, was an unfolding miracle. He was our chance to see the world through a fresh pair of eyes, a reality to the oneness of our marriage, our vote of confidence in the future. But most of all he was himself, a new personality to be cherished.

He was a golden child, so handsome he might have been a girl. So agile—he scared his grandmothers green when he jumped from chair to couch to coffee table. And smart! We delighted in telling how he had outwitted us when he was so young that he could do little more than scoot around on his fat bottom (p. 257).

Once Peter was diagnosed as severely disturbed, however, his parents' early delight in him became inadmissible evidence. The prevailing belief, then

as now, was that serious psychological disturbance in a child was the result of parental neglect or abuse. Whatever was wrong with the child was due to whatever was wrong with the parents:

I told my psychiatric social worker about Peter but her questions were directed to me.

How did I get along with my parents, siblings, the people at work? As well as most people, I thought.

Had I wanted the baby? Yes, I had gone through sterility studies to get pregnant.

Why had I wanted a baby? Why? I had never reasoned it out. They are a part of life, just like food, sunshine, friends and marriage.

How did I get along with my husband? Very well. She snapped to attention. "Why?" she asked, "Are you afraid to quarrel with him?" Well—we were both in our thirties. We had no serious problems and could laugh at our small differences. Years of separation by the war had made us treasure the ordinary joys of life.

How could I expect Peter to be warm when I was so cold to him? How could I be anything but cold after years of trying to warm up this icy child of mine? Even with your own son, friendship is a two-way street. We hadn't rejected Peter, he had rejected us. Even rejection was too strong a word. Peter accepted us as he did the furniture, as tools to get what he wanted. He simply didn't recognize us as people. Proving this was as difficult as proving which came first, the chicken or the egg.

I asked the psychiatric social worker for suggestions, but she had none to offer. What I did was not so important as how I felt about it. What could I read that would help me understand Peter? She could suggest no reading nor would she advise it. I sounded like a school teacher already. My use of the Tracy course [a series of parent-child exercises designed to help deaf children] was held up as an example of my intellectual approach to motherhood (pp. 259–260).

With professional after professional, Eberhardy met with the same accusatory line of ques-

AGAINST BETTELHEIM

tioning. The result of such counseling was predictable. Eberhardy's confidence, already eroded by her helplessness in the face of Peter's condition, was further undermined:

I alternated between being overwhelmed with guilt, and feeling resentful at being treated like a child who couldn't face an unpleasant truth. If I could have felt that it was true, that we had been cold and dominating, or cold and indifferent parents, I think I could have faced that fact. At least I would have had something concrete to work with. Anything would have been better than that nameless, formless, faceless fear. My self-confidence was fast disappearing. I was less and less able to cope with the problems each day brought (p. 260).

When at last Peter was placed in a special school, the family's sacrifices and sufferings were still not over:

Each year when we brought him home, we were filled with plans, high resolve, and optimism. And each fall we sent him back with a sense of failure, sadness and relief. For the job was too big for us. We underwrote psychotherapy, field trips, music lessons and orthodontia. We did not miss the luxuries we might otherwise have had, but we were saddened to see our bubbling extrovert daughter turn into a quiet, withdrawn child in the shadow of Peter's illness, and the changes it made in our lives.

For Peter too, life has been very hard. As a small boy, he had expressed his unhappiness by saying dejectedly, "out-of-tune" or "all mixed up." My mother used to say of us on our off days that we had gotten out of the wrong side of the bed. Peter got out of the wrong side of bed every day and life was heart-breakingly difficult for him. When he was about 12 years old, he asked me, "What is wrong with me? I feel like a freak."

What could I say? If I said he was like everyone else, wouldn't that put the burden of his difficulties on him? If I told him that we all differ, that would be an evasion and he would know it.

How does the parent of any handicapped child explain that he has an extra burden to carry through life? It takes most of us adults a lifetime to develop a philosophy or religious outlook that enables us to live with the inequalities and suffering we see around us. And when the suffering is in your own child, you never really do accept it (p. 261).

Thus despite the fact that Peter grew up to make a much better adjustment than most autistic children, his mother's story is a painful one. And it raises serious questions regarding our current approach to autism. The psychodynamic, behaviorist, and interpersonal perspectives all side with Eberhardy's social worker: look to the parent for what is troubling the child. The best-known proponent of this interpretation has been Bettelheim, whose eloquent accounts of his successes with autistic children such as Marcia (see case on pp. 338–339) have been widely read and widely applauded. Yet even if we accept Bettelheim's reported success rates, must we necessarily accept his etiological hypothesis? If an autistic child can be helped by constant attention to his needs, does this mean that his autism is the result of parental indifference to his needs? Because Bettelheim's school has a bright yellow door, does this mean that there has been no other brightness in his patients' lives?

As Eberhardy's story illustrates, Bettelheim's theory places a heavy burden on the parents. In general, parents who bring a disturbed child in for treatment already feel guilty, whether justifiably or not. The question is whether, on the basis of a theory that has yet to be proven scientifically, professionals have a right to make them feel more guilty. Future research may in fact confirm the theory that cold, indifferent parenting is a major contributor to autism. But as long as this theory remains only a theory and not a fact, the type of counseling that Peter's mother received—and it is not atypical—seems a good example of the arrogance of which Szasz (1970) has accused the psychiatric profession as a whole.

child as being fixated at a preoral period, with the result that the child is totally absorbed in autoerotic and autoaggressive behaviors at a very primitive sensorimotor level. Treatment is therefore aimed at activating the stalled developmental processes by furnishing optimal gratification through a consistent, positive, and accepting "mother." The "mother" (i.e., the therapist) must meet the needs of the child at his primitive level of sensorimotor functioning. Treatment consists of holding, cuddling, rocking, singing, feeding, and so forth in an attempt to provide the child with necessary tactile-kinesthetic, visual, and aural contact. Once an object relationship has been established with the mothering figure, social, motor, perceptual, and cognitive skills can be developed through (1) imitation of the child's behaviors and vocalizations, (2) verbalization of affect, (3) naming and conceptual verbalizations of activities, functions, body parts, and objects that the child encounters, and (4) gradual introduction of expectations for self-care, impulse control, and problem-solving. The result of this gradual treatment is a progression through a sequence of lesser psychotic states—that is, the child becomes symbiotic, then oral omnipotent, then anal sadomasochistic, and so on until he finally arrives at his appropriate stage of psychosexual development.

Psychodynamic therapy, however, is long-term and expensive, and as yet there is no truly firm evidence of its effectiveness. In evaluating the progress of some forty children who had received treatment at the school he founded in Chicago, Bettelheim (1967) claimed that 42 percent had made a "good" adjustment. This figure compares quite favorably with the usual follow-up reports of good adjustment for only 5 to 15 percent of autistic children (DeMyer et al., 1973). However, the children on whom Bettelheim reported were evaluated by Bettelheim himself, thus raising the possibility that his expectations and hopes may have colored his judgments. Furthermore, over 65 percent of Bettelheim's forty cases had evidenced functional speech by the age of five—a factor which, as we have noted, indicates a good prognosis. Hence these children were much more likely to benefit from treatment than the average autistic child.

The Behaviorist Perspective

Cause Ferster (1961) has probably presented the most thorough conceptualization of childhood psychosis from the behavioral perspective. In defining the psychotic child, Ferster makes no distinction between autism and schizophrenia. Instead, each child is described functionally—that is, problems are defined in terms of behavior deficits and excesses. In the case of the psychotic child, the deficits include an impoverished repertoire of social, verbal, and cognitive responses, while the excesses include violent and inappropriate behaviors such as tantrums and self-mutilation.

While as usual the behaviorist perspective differs from the psychodynamic in shifting the emphasis from internal subjective processes to observable external behaviors, in the case of childhood psychosis the two perspectives agree on at least one matter: the parents are responsible. According to Ferster, the reason the child fails to develop appropriate language skills, social responses, and cognitive abilities is that when he directs appropriate responses at his parents, they either ignore him or deliver feedback only intermittently. Hence these responses are weakened and eventually drop out. The child may then resort to some kind of violent and inappropriate behavior, such as head-banging or a tantrum, and find that unlike the appropriate behavior, this *does* get attention. For example, a child may ask his mother for a cookie and get no response. If he then throws himself on the floor, yelling and kicking and banging his head, the mother is likely to give him the cookie simply in order to stop the tantrum. The tantrum behavior is then likely to recur, since it has been reinforced by the attention and the cookie, both of which the child was unable to obtain by more civilized means.

It is difficult to imagine any normal adult consistently dealing with his child in this way, but as Ferster points out, such a response pattern might easily result either from a severe disruption in the parental response repertoire (e.g., depression) or from a preoccupation with work. It is also possible that a child who frequently engages in tantrums or who constantly diverts the parent's attention from matters that he finds more reinforcing (e.g., professional concerns) might acquire conditioned aversive properties for the parent, who would then avoid the child.

Treatment While there is no direct evidence to support the behaviorist interpretation of childhood psychosis, its utility has been demonstrated by numerous empirical reports of successful treatment. Behavior modification techniques used to eliminate undesirable behaviors include direct reinforcement (e.g., giving the child a cookie if he refrains from engaging in the undesirable behavior or if he does engage in a desirable behavior), extinction (e.g., withdrawing attention in response to a tantrum), and punishment (e.g., administering a spanking or a mild electric shock in response to unacceptable behavior). Thus, whereas the child's upbringing has reinforced unacceptable behaviors and allowed acceptable behaviors to extinguish, the behavioral therapist simply reverses this pattern.

Reports indicate that all of these techniques are effective but that their effectiveness depends greatly on what behavior is being eliminated. For example, self-mutilative responses such as head-banging will eventually extinguish if social attention is withdrawn when the child hits himself. In one case, however, it took nearly eight days and 1,800 head bangs before the response dropped out (Simmons and Lovaas, 1969). Another problem with extinction procedures is that some behaviors seem to be maintained by internal rather than external rewards, in which case withdrawing social attention or food will have little, if any, effect. For example, psychotic children's ritualistic motor behaviors—which, as we have seen, they will prefer over food even when they are hungry—are highly resistant to extinction through the withdrawal of food or attention (Reuter et al., 1974), apparently because they satisfy an internal need for stimulation (Litrownik, 1969).

Punishment procedures that involve the application of negative stimuli appear to be highly successful in immediately suppressing undesirable behaviors. But even though this immediate effect may be desired in some cases—as, for example, in the case of self-mutilation—moral, ethical, and legal concerns frequently limit the use of aversive procedures. Many people believe that punishing a psychotic child for undesirable behaviors only compounds the problem. For example, Bettelheim (1967), whose goal is to provide a warm, nurturant relationship, argues that the autistic child cannot be helped by treating him like an object. On the other hand, Lovaas, whose goal is to shape appropriate responses to adults (Chance, 1974), contends that a psychotic child is more likely to respond to therapy if he is treated like a person—that is, rewarded, punished, and generally held responsible for his behavior —rather than like a patient.

Another major problem in eliminating inappropriate behaviors is that the behavior, once eliminated, may later reappear, or the child may engage in other inappropriate behavior. Once a child's rocking behavior is eliminated, for example, he may suddenly begin hyperventilating (Reuter et al., 1974). What this seems to mean is that once we have eliminated a behavior in which a child has been engaging frequently and at long stretches, we can't expect the child simply to sit quietly and wait for someone to teach him a new, appropriate behavior with which to fill the void. Hence the most effective therapy is one which not only eliminates inappropriate behaviors but at the same time teaches the child appropriate behaviors that he can substitute for the inappropriate ones (e.g., Simmons and Lovaas, 1969; Wolf et al., 1964).

Procedures aimed at developing appropriate responses in psychotic children have first and foremost focused on establishing people as secondary reinforcers—that is, the child must first see people as being important and valuable. This can be accomplished through respondent conditioning, by pairing praise by the therapist (social reinforcement) with primary positive reinforcers such as food or with primary negative reinforcers such as pain relief (Lovaas et al., 1965). Next, through shaping and modeling, with the use of social reinforcement as well as direct reinforcers such as food, the child is taught new motor and verbal responses (Lovaas et al., 1966; Wolf et al., 1964). Once he has learned basic skills for playing and communicating, food rewards can be withdrawn, though social reinforcement is continued, and the child can be placed in a group learning situation (Koegel and Rincover, 1974), which will allow him to learn from observing others and which, it is hoped, will prepare him to enter a public school special-education program.

As in eliminating inappropriate behaviors, so in developing appropriate behaviors, there are problems in maintaining the change. Follow-up reports frequently indicate relapse, especially in children who after behavior therapy are returned to institutions. There is no question that institutions foster such relapsing, since in the usual institutional setting patients are expected to act in an inappropriate fashion and no rewards are given for acting otherwise. For example, one therapist who was visiting an institution decided to stop in and see a child with whom he had worked with considerable success. He found her crouched in a corner, flapping her hand and making bizarre sounds. But as soon as she saw the therapist, she got up, walked over, and said, "Hi, how are you?" She continued to talk and act appropriately while the therapist was there. After he left, she presumably returned to her corner.

Recent efforts to get around this problem have involved keeping the child at home and directing treatment efforts at the parents as well as at the child. In this method the parents are actually trained to act as behavioral therapists. Recent reports indicate that such home therapy can be very successful (Lovaas et al., 1973). Once the parents see the child improving as a result of their efforts, they are likely to try even harder, with the result that the child will not only maintain his improvements but will make further gains.

While the evidence appears to indicate that this and other behavioral methods are effective, some people argue that children treated by behavioral therapy are no better than performing robots (Bettelheim, 1967). In some instances this seems to be the case. For example, one psychotic child, when asked, "What did you have for breakfast?" would tell you that she had had "eggs, toast, jelly, juice, and milk" even on days when she hadn't had any breakfast at all. In short, she had no understanding of the concept; she was simply responding with a programmed answer to a specific question. However, there are many other cases in which behavioral treatment has resulted in the development of responses that are spontaneous as well as appropriate.

The Humanistic-Existential Perspective

Cause While the humanists have devoted most of their attention to the adult neuroses and psychoses rather than to childhood disorders, a general humanistic conceptualization of childhood psychosis is that it results from interplay between, on the one hand, the child's drive to adapt to his psychosocial environment, and on the other, the demands made by that environment. While the child attempts to organize his environment in a positive manner, this adaptive drive is frustrated by the environment itself.

Though Niko and Lies Tinbergen are not usually thought of as either humanistic or existential psychologists, their explanation of childhood psychosis is a good example of a humanistic-existential approach to the problem. According to the Tinbergens (Hall, 1974), autism, which they define very broadly as failed socialization, is on the rise because environmental changes are occurring too fast for genetic evolution. These rapid changes place on the organism a constant pressure to adapt and readapt. Normal children manage to withstand such stress. They explore their environment and interact with it, becoming more confident and competent with each additional experience. In short, they become socialized. In the child who becomes autistic, however, this environmental stress gives rise to an intense motivational conflict. The child naturally desires to interact with and adapt to his world, but the very instability of that world makes him appre-

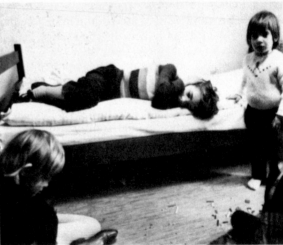

Fig. 13.4 *An autistic boy at a residential facility for disturbed children. Whether alone or with others, he covers his ears to cut off interaction with his environment; in humanistic-existential terms he is an example of failed socialization.*

hensive. While the child is starved for social contact, his fears prevent him from responding to others. Likewise, language fails to develop not because the child can't talk, but because he is too afraid to engage in the kind of social interactions that would lead to speech. The result is a general failure to respond to the environment—in other words, failed socialization.

Treatment Treatment of this societal casualty involves the type of therapy so often favored by the humanists, milieu therapy. The child is placed in a residential facility where his development is encouraged by an empathetic, warm staff who provide the reassurance and structure necessary to alleviate the child's apprehension. In this way the child is freed to establish social relationships and to explore his world. Throughout the day, events such as eating, sleeping, dressing, and studying provide opportunities for human interaction and evoke behaviors to which the adults can respond on an individual basis, helping the child to increase his confidence and self-awareness (Goldfarb, 1965).

Such treatment in many ways resembles that recommended by psychodynamic theorists such as Bettelheim. And as with the psychodynamic therapy, one problem with the humanistic therapy is that actual day-to-day treatment procedures are not specified. Hence, if such therapies are reported to be successful, it is difficult for others to initiate similar programs in an effort to replicate those results.

The Interpersonal Perspective

As we have seen earlier in Chapter 4, the interpersonal perspective differs from other psychological perspectives mainly in that its central focus, both in theory and in treatment, is on the individual's in-

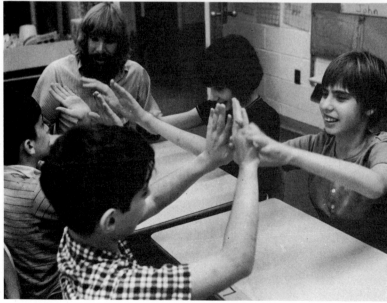

Fig. 13.5   Milieu therapy involves a total environment that maximizes the psychotic child's opportunities for interaction, self-care, and rehabilitation. Within such a realistic social environment, the child is given the chance to perform a variety of functions that may enhance his self-esteem and thus improve his social interactions with adults and other children.

teractions with others. There are actually very few professionals who would argue with the basic contention that interpersonal factors, despite the presence or absence of organic factors, contribute to the development of childhood psychosis. The problem, as Rosenthal (1968) points out, is in trying to identify in the family, the society, or the culture the specific type of pathogenic interaction that is responsible.

The effort to locate the kind of family interaction that could contribute to psychosis in a child has prompted a number of studies, one of the most influential of which is the study of double-bind communication (Bateson et al., 1956) cited in Chapter 12. In a more recent study (Goldfarb et al., 1973), the verbal communications of mothers of schizophrenic children and mothers of normal children were observed, on the assumption that this sample might reflect the general communication patterns in the families. The investigators found that in general, when the mother of a schizophrenic child was asked to describe to her child an object he was to pick up from among a number of objects, she conveyed less information, was more ambiguous, and was less supportive than the mother of a normal child.

Once again, however, one must be very cautious about drawing etiological conclusions from such evidence. It is highly possible, for instance, that the inefficient verbal communication of the mothers of the schizophrenic children in this study was the result of simple weariness and pessimism after years of having their verbal communications ignored. But one thing we can be sure of is that once disturbed family interactions appear, they hinder attempts at treatment. Hence, if the child is to remain at home, the most hopeful therapy is one which involves the parents, as in the behavioral home therapy (Lovaas et al., 1973) mentioned earlier in this chapter.

The Cognitive Perspective

All the perspectives on childhood psychosis that we have discussed so far have two things in common. First, they all view the primary defect as a disturbance in the child's relationship with other people, usually with his parents. Second, there is very little empirical evidence to support any one of these perspectives, and it is only because of reports of some success in treatments based on these perspectives that we continue to rely on them. In contrast, the cognitive perspective—along with the perspective we shall take up next, the biological perspective—sees the primary defect in the autistic child not as social withdrawal, but as an organic problem. In the case

of the cognitive perspective, this organic problem is viewed as an impairment in the child's equipment for perceiving and interpreting the environment.

Rutter (1968, 1971) claims that in autism the basic defect is an impaired comprehension of sounds. Thus autism is seen as comparable to other developmental disorders of language (e.g., *aphasia*, the loss or impairment of speech as a result of brain lesions), differing from these only in that the autistic child's defective comprehension of sounds is accompanied by other perceptual deficits as well. In support of this view, Rutter points out that retarded speech has an early onset in the autistic child and is one of the most important defining symptoms. In addition, autistic children show a number of signs of improper sound comprehension: they are often suspected of being deaf; they either don't respond to sounds or ignore a loud sound and then respond to a soft sound; they aren't easily distracted; and they tend to echo words and reverse pronouns. The pattern of cognitive abilities observed in autistic children—the fact that they are as good in visual motor and rote memory tasks as they are poor in verbal and conceptual tasks—also suggests a language deficit. Finally, one of the strongest arguments in support of Rutter's thesis is the fact, which we have noted before, that it is language ability that is the best predictor of the autistic child's chances of benefiting from treatment.

Another cognitive hypothesis, put forth by Lovaas and his colleagues (e.g., Koegel and Wilhelm, 1973; Lovaas et al., 1971b; Schreibman and Lovaas, 1973), is that the basic impairment of the autistic child is that he is overselective in his attention—that because of a perceptual defect he can only process, and thus respond to, one kind of sensory input at a time, be it tactile or visual or whatever. Such an impairment, which has also been proposed as the basis of adult schizophrenia, could easily account for the social and intellectual retardation of the autistic child. Much of a child's intellectual and emotional development is based on the association of paired stimuli through the process of respondent conditioning. Thus as a child's mother comes to be paired in his mind with food and with holding, she comes to be loved. If, however, when a child is being fed or held, his perceptual faculties can only process the stimulus of the food or of the holding and not of his mother's presence as well, the mother fails to take on any positive meaning. Furthermore, it is highly possible that with limited processing abilities, the child will select irrelevant aspects of his environment on which to base his responses. One autistic child, for example, appeared to base his identification of his father on the father's eyeglasses. When the father was wearing his glasses, the child was extremely responsive to him. But when the father did not have his glasses on, the child ignored him completely.

In contrast to the theories of Rutter and Lovaas, Wing (1969) argues that autism is the result not of a single basic perceptual defect, but of a cluster of defects. Wing had parents rate the behaviors of their autistic, aphasic, partially blind/partially deaf, mongoloid, and normal children when they were between the ages of two and five. His findings were that autistic children had basic problems in several areas, including speech and auditory perception, execution of skilled movement, visual perception, and social behavior. The partially blind and deaf children resembled the autistic children, while the aphasic and mongoloid children evidenced difficulties in more specific and limited areas. From these comparisons Wing (1969, 1972) concludes that autism is a condition of multiple handicaps, including problems in the comprehension and use of speech, in pronunciation and voice control, and in right-left, up-down, back-front orientation.

As a result of such findings, there has been much recent experimentation with behavioral treatment approaches designed to circumvent the child's supposed cognitive defects. For example, in an attempt to avoid the use of auditory input channels, researchers have taught autistic children sign language, which utilizes the tactile and kinesthetic stimuli to which they are most likely to respond (Webster et al., 1973). In an effort to develop reinforcers more effective than auditory stimuli such as the therapist's saying "Good!" other scientists have found that certain sensory stimuli, such as lights that flash when the child gives the correct response, are even more rewarding than food (Newsom et al., 1974). The treatments that are emerging from such experimentation, treatments based on cognitive and behavioral theory, appear to be very promising, at least for autistic children. No such encouraging results have as yet emerged from the use of such therapy with schizophrenic children.

The Biological Perspective

Evidence supporting the belief that organic factors are responsible, at least in part, for childhood psychosis is rapidly accumulating. Much of the recent work, stimulated by the cognitive perspective, supports the cognitive theory that the psychotic child does not perceive his world in the same way as the normal child. But while the cognitive theorists con-

Fig. 13.6 An autistic child in a behavioral treatment center is rewarded with pieces of food for making speech sounds. Autistic children speak little, if at all, and are emotionally unresponsive to other people. The therapist must be adept at recognizing sounds that approximate the words she is trying to teach the child so that she can immediately reinforce the child's attempt to speak. She must also be capable of great patience, warmth, and sensitivity to the child. The goal of this program is to bring the child to a level at which natural social reinforcers such as hugs and smiles will maintain talking and other outward-directed behaviors.

centrate on determining in what way the psychotic child's perception is impaired, the biological researchers have directed their efforts toward determining whether that perceptual defect is organic, and if so, what specific organic defect is responsible.

Genetic Research As we have seen in Chapter 12, there has been a great deal of highly sophisticated and highly productive research on the genetics of adult schizophrenia. As yet, however, there have been very few genetic studies dealing specifically with the psychotic child. Kallmann and Roth (1956) did report that concordance rates in twins for childhood schizophrenia followed the same pattern found in adults. In their study, eight of thirty-five dizygotic pairs were both diagnosed as schizophrenic before age fifteen, while fifteen of seventeen monozygotic pairs were concordant—in short, a strong indication that genetic factors are at work. It should be noted, however, that in this study most of the concordant co-twins were not diagnosed as schizophrenic until early adolescence, and consequently they were more similar to adult schizophrenics in their functioning than to their proband twin.

In the case of autism, Rimland (1964) has reported that of the eleven cases known to him of autism in a monozygotic twin, all the co-twins were concordant. As we have noted earlier, however, families of autistic children appear to be relatively free of psychosis in general. And though a sibling of an autistic child is more likely himself to be autistic—the incidence in siblings is 2 percent, as opposed to a .05 percent incidence in the general population—this finding in no way proves that autism is genetically determined (Rutter, 1968).

Thus there is some evidence, though weak, that genetic factors figure in the development of childhood schizophrenia. In the case of autism, on the other hand, the role of genetic inheritance is still quite obscure. And in view of the difficulties involved in finding psychotic children who have twins and getting reliable diagnoses, it seems unlikely that these questions will be resolved in the near future.

Monogenetic-Biochemical and Diathesis-Stress Theories
Monogenetic-biochemical conceptualizations of psychosis have suggested that autism may be due to abnormalities either in the level of serotonin, the indolamine that has also been investigated in relation to depression (Chapter 7) and schizophrenia (Chapter 12), or in blood platelets, substances in the blood that aid in coagulation (Campbell et al., 1974; Rimland, 1973). It has also been pointed out that certain allergies give rise to symptoms similar to those of autism—for instance, screaming, head-banging, and cessation of speech (Rimland and Meyer, 1967). Consequently, efforts have been made to treat autism, as these allergies are treated, through orthomolecular therapy—that is, through special diets, especially low-carbohydrate diets, and through megavitamin therapy. However, there is still no firm evidence to support any of these monogenetic-biochemical theories.

Many genetic theorists (e.g., Gottesman and Shields, 1972; Rosenthal, 1968) feel whatever the organic factor is that predisposes a person to psychosis, this factor must interact with environmental stresses in order for the psychosis to develop. An example of such a diathesis-stress conceptualization of autism is that of Zaslow and Breger (1969). These investigators feel that the primary defect in autism is an early disturbance in affective and social attachment and that this failure in attachment results from the interaction between a particular type of child and a particular mode of parental handling.

Normal attachment develops through the pairing of stress reduction with sensorimotor stimulation from the parents. That is, the child develops an attachment for the parents through repeatedly having his stress relieved by the tactile-kinesthetic stimulation which they provide in the form of holding, cuddling, patting, rocking, and so forth. However, if a child is constitutionally active, noncuddly, and disease-prone, and if at the same time his parents tend to be distant and withdrawn, then it is likely that the child will never be held long enough for his stress to dissipate. As a result, the parent-child attachment will not develop. According to Zaslow and Breger, this is what happens in the case of the autistic child.

Because of the attachment failure, the child and the parent become locked into an increasingly negativistic relationship, which prevents the child from developing cognitively or socially. Instead, attachments are attempted with objects, while cognitive activity is arrested at the earlier stages of sensorimotor development. The child relies on "negative motor resistance"—tantrums, stiffening, gaze aversion, and other such tactics—to maintain his independence and to avoid any further attempt at tactile-kinesthetic stimulation.

To break this vicious circle, Zaslow and Breger have developed a treatment based on the pairing of stress reduction with parental holding. But their theory, like the monogenetic-biochemical theories, has yet to be confirmed by any conclusive evidence.

Neurological Studies
Within the last decade researchers have accumulated a good deal of evidence suggesting that psychotic children suffer from neurological impairments. It has been hypothesized that such impairments might result from damage to the central nervous system during pregnancy or birth, and some reports have in fact indicated that the incidence of prenatal and perinatal complications is higher in schizophrenic and autistic children

than in the general population (Gittelman and Birch, 1967; Rimland, 1964). Other researchers, however, have found no such differences, and thus the source of the supposed neurological defect of the psychotic child remains an open question.

The evidence that psychotic children do in fact have such defects is somewhat clearer, though still not wholly definitive. One problem in gathering neurological evidence is that the tests involved, such as readings of EEGs and CEVs (*cerebral evoked voltages*, the electrical measurement of neurological responses to specific stimuli), often require a degree of cooperation on the part of the patient, and psychotic children are not always willing to cooperate (Walter et al., 1971). However, with the recent technological refinement of testing methods, researchers have been reporting increasingly strong evidence of neurological abnormalities in psychotic children. For example, DeMyer et al. (1973) recently reported that 73.4 percent of the psychotic children they had observed showed signs of neurological dysfunction and that 69 percent had grossly abnormal EEG patterns. Furthermore, recent studies of the CEVs of psychotic children tend to support the cognitive theory that these children do not receive input, attend to it, or process it in the same way as normal children. Small (1971), for instance, reported that CEVs to auditory and visual stimuli in autistic children appear to be of lower amplitude, to show shorter latencies to the peak response, and to be more unstable than those of normal children. What this indicates is that in the auditory and visual modalities, psychotic children have weaker responses, reach their maximum response more quickly, and show less consistent responses than do normal children. A direct cause-effect relationship remains to be demonstrated, however. Schopler and Reichler (1971) have proposed that this attention deficit is in fact limited to the audiovisual modalities—a fact which would explain the preference that psychotic children show for tactile-kinesthetic stimuli (Hermalin and O'Connor, 1970).

The question of what specific biological defect causes the psychotic child's neurological abnormalities has prompted a number of hypotheses. Rimland (1964) has proposed that the reticular formation in the brain stem of the autistic child is failing to provide the proper degree of arousal. DeMyer et al. (1973) have suggested that a brain lesion may be responsible for both verbal and perceptual dysfunctions. Other researchers (Ornitz and Ritvo, 1968; Des Lauriers and Carlson, 1969) have pointed to other possible biological sources. However, none of these theories has been confirmed.

In sum, as research continues, the biological hypothesis is becoming increasingly convincing. At this moment it does seem probable that psychotic children are the victims of some organic defect which causes them to fail socially and intellectually. But we are still very far from identifying this organic defect. As a result, no useful drugs have been developed for psychotic children, and all the treatments now in use remain entirely experimental.

SUMMARY

Childhood psychosis may be conceptualized as a single syndrome, of which the most common and striking symptoms are disturbed social relationships, impairment of speech, and bizarre motor behavior, which may involve self-mutilation. However, many professionals see childhood psychosis as divisible into the two separate syndromes: early infantile autism, which has its onset before the age of six, and childhood schizophrenia, which has its onset between ages six and twelve. Aside from the difference in age of onset, many other distinctions have been drawn between the two syndromes, particularly in the areas of language skill, obsessiveness, and degree of social isolation. While some of these distinctions lack empirical support, others appear to be genuine and would seem to justify the classification of autism and childhood schizophrenia as two different syndromes. In general, the autistic child is characterized primarily by his total social withdrawal, by his failure ever to acquire speech at all or to use what speech he has for meaningful communication, and by his obsessive resistance to any change in the environment—all of which symptoms may be evident from very early childhood. The schizophrenic child, on the other hand, experiences a period of normal development, after which he begins to show severe disturbances in social adjustment and in reality contact.

The psychodynamic perspective interprets childhood psychosis as a failure in ego development, resulting from the parents' unwillingness to respond to the child or to provide him with sufficient stimulation. Accordingly, psychodynamic treatment aims at promoting ego development by providing stimulation through warm, accepting, and responsive "mothering."

The behaviorist perspective, like the psychodynamic, views childhood psychosis as the result of parental unresponsiveness, which, according to the behaviorists, results in the extinction of appropriate behaviors and the reinforcement of inappropriate behaviors. Treatment aims at reversing this pattern, through direct reinforcement, extinction, and sometimes punishment as well.

The humanistic-existential perspective tends to indict the society rather than the parents for the fostering of childhood psychosis. A recent humanistic interpretation is that the psychotic child is caught in a conflict between his natural adaptive drive and his apprehension in the face of an unstable social environment. Humanistic theory favors a milieu therapy in which the child's fears are alleviated and he is encouraged to explore and interact with his environment.

The interpersonal perspective, like the others, focuses primarily on the psychotic child's social disturbance and attempts to identify specific patterns of interpersonal communication, particularly in the family, which could give rise to the development of childhood psychosis.

Unlike the preceding perspectives, the cognitive perspective views the essential defect in childhood psychosis not as a disturbance in social relations but as a perceptual impairment in one or more sensory modalities. This conceptualization, which has received a good deal of empirical support, has given rise to the development of behavioral therapies which attempt to circumvent the child's supposed cognitive handicaps.

The biological perspective has produced some evidence, though inconclusive, of a genetic component in childhood psychosis, and these findings have given rise to various monogenetic-biochemical and diathesis-stress theories. As yet, however, the most substantial contribution of the biological perspective is the rapidly accumulating evidence of neurological dysfunction in psychotic children, evidence which tends to support the cognitive theory that the child suffers from a perceptual deficit. However, the organic defect responsible for such a condition has not yet been identified.

V The Organic Disorders

In the last nine chapters we have devoted our discussion to psychological disorders that are generally thought to be primarily psychogenic. As we have seen in the case of schizophrenia, autism, depression, and other syndromes, organic causation can by no means be ruled out. But the primary emphasis in the study of these disorders has been on psychological etiology—the relation of an individual to his experience and environment. In contrast, the *organic brain disorders*, as the name indicates, are by definition biogenic; they are clusters of behavioral problems that are directly traceable to the destruction of brain tissue or to biochemical imbalances in the brain. And though we have given considerably more attention to the functional disorders, the organic brain syndromes constitute a major mental health problem. At present they account for one-fourth of all first admissions to mental hospitals in the United States.

In our chapter we will first examine the difficulties involved in the diagnosis of organic brain disorder. Second, we will discuss the symptoms and—where they are known—the causes of the major organic brain disorders.

PROBLEMS IN DIAGNOSIS

There are two major problems in the diagnosis of organic brain disorder: deciding whether the disorder is in fact organic, and if so, what type of organic impairment is involved. As we shall see, neither decision is a simple matter.

Biogenic vs. Psychogenic

According to DSM-II (1968), there are essentially five major symptoms that accompany most organic brain disorders:*

1. *Impairment of orientation.* The person will be confused as to who he is, where he is, what the date is, and so forth.
2. *Impairment of memory.* The person may forget events of the distant past or, more typically, of the very recent past and may invent stories to fill in these memory gaps.
3. *Impairment of other intellectual functions, such as comprehension, calculation, knowledge, and learning.* The person will be unable to define simple words, do ordinary addition and subtraction, name the President of the United States, and the like.

---

*Although one or more of these symptoms may accompany most brain disorders, it is unlikely that all five would appear simultaneously. Further, with the exception of certain deficits in judgment and orientation, these symptoms are most often correlated with specific areas of damage and not with general destruction of brain tissue.

14
Organic Brain Disorders

4. *Impairment of judgment.* The person ceases to be able to make appropriate decisions—cannot decide what to have for lunch, when to keep his clothes on and when to take them off, and so forth.

5. *Lability or shallowness of affect.* The person passes quickly and inappropriately from apathy to hostility or from laughing to weeping.

These symptoms should by now sound familiar. Impaired judgment, as we know, is common in manic patients, while disorientation, impaired intellectual functioning, and inappropriate affect are well-recognized symptoms of schizophrenia. Thus behavioral signs serve as very vague guidelines to the diagnostician attempting to differentiate between a functional and an organic condition. Consider, for example, the following case:

M., aged 41, a roofing salesman, was transferred to a state hospital from the jail to which he had been sentenced for violation of the motor vehicle laws. The prodromal [i.e., early warning] symptoms of the patient's oncoming disease were apparently slight. The informant, his sister, who has seen him but infrequently, stated that she had not noticed any change in him except that for a year he had seemed somewhat "worried." While driving his car, he disregarded the collector at a toll bridge and drove across the structure at high speed. When overtaken by a police officer, the patient was found to have no license to drive an automobile, the permit having been revoked several years previously. Three days later, while awaiting trial for this offense, he was again arrested for driving an automobile without a license. He was given a short sentence in jail, where a physician soon recognized the patient's disorder and had him committed to the hospital.

On arrival at the admission office of the hospital, he told the office attendant that he was going to give her a million dollars because she was "a nice lady." As he was being questioned for the usual admission data, he began to boast of his wealth, claiming that he had three automobiles, thousands of dollars in the bank, and a "diamond watch," and much other valuable jewelry. His son, he said, was lieutenant governor of the state, was soon to be governor, and later would be president of the United States. After having expressed various absurdly grandiose plans, he added, "I have another plan, too. I'm going to the wardens of the prisons in this state and all the other states and I'm going to buy the prisoners. I'll have an agreement with the warden to take their prisoners and put them to work on farms, and I'll charge each prisoner $300 for doing it and for getting him out of jail. I made $105,000 with prisoners just last week, and when I get

going, I'm going to make plenty of money" (Kolb, 1973, p. 229).

What was the disorder that the physician in the jail so quickly recognized? On the basis of a number of the man's symptoms—a year in which he had seemed "worried," followed by a bout of expansive, grandiose, and imprudent behaviors—one might guess that the problem was manic-depressive illness. In fact, the man was suffering from an advanced case of syphilis, which had infected his brain. (We shall discuss this condition shortly.)

Thus there is considerable overlap between the symptoms of organic and functional disorders. Furthermore, the symptoms of an organic disorder may be complicated by emotional disturbances developing *in response to* the organic impairment. For example, if a person who is unknowingly suffering from an organic brain disorder suddenly finds that his cognitive skills are deteriorating—that he is continually making mistakes on the job or repeatedly taking the wrong bus to get home—he is likely to become anxious, depressed, or defensive. Thus by the time he is seen by a diagnostician, his primary symptoms, the symptoms of the organic impairment, may well be obscured by an overlay of secondary functional disturbances.

In sum, differential diagnosis between functional and organic disturbances is an extremely complicated matter. Furthermore, it is an extremely crucial matter. If a particular syndrome has an organic basis, then the primary treatment should be medical—that is, drugs and/or surgery. And if such treatment is not provided, the patient's condition will not only fail to improve but may worsen and end in death. It is not unknown for an autopsy to reveal that a patient whose symptoms have been curiously resistant to several years of psychotherapy was actually suffering from a brain tumor (Waggoner and Bagchi, 1954; Patton and Sheppard, 1956). George Gershwin, for example, in the midst of conducting a concert of his works momentarily lost consciousness. In the months that followed he began to act peculiarly; he was irritable, restless, and suffered from painful headaches. At the urging of his family he entered a hospital for a complete physical examination; he was released, the physicians insisting that he was "a perfect specimen of health" (Ewen, 1956, p. 298). He began daily treatment with a psychoanalyst who decided that Gershwin needed rest and seclusion; this seemed to help. But less than a month later, Gershwin collapsed and went into a coma. He was rushed to a hospital where exploratory surgery located an inoperable brain tumor. Gershwin never regained consciousness and died that day at the age of thirty-eight. And it is precisely such cases that make the accurate diagnostic distinction between functional and organic disorders so very important.

How, then, does the diagnostician make this distinction in any particular case? He draws on all the sources available to him: direct observation of the patient, a detailed history of the onset and progress of the symptoms, interviews with the patient's family and physician. In addition, he will usually put the patient through a variety of tests: neurological tests to assess his reflexes, which may prove faulty if there is damage to the nervous system; EEGs, brain x-rays, and chemical analyses of cerebrospinal fluids; and finally, various psychological tests specifically designed to detect organic impairment (Chapter 18).

Specifying the Impairment

If a patient appears in an emergency room with a revolver in his hand and bullet holes on either side of his head, the physician on duty will have little difficulty determining the source—to say nothing of the existence—of organic brain damage. However, in most cases, specifying the source of the organic impairment—that is, what area of the brain has been damaged and what has damaged it—is even more difficult than making the primary distinction between psychogenic and biogenic pathology. And like the psychogenic-biogenic distinction, the accurate specification of the source of a biogenic disorder is utterly essential, as it is on this decision that treatment is based. Needless to say, one does not wish to treat for a brain tumor only to discover that the patient is suffering from lead poisoning.

THE ANATOMY OF THE BRAIN

Knowledge of the anatomy of the brain—its various components and their functions—can aid in understanding why damage to certain areas of the brain produces certain types of behavioral problems.

The *cerebral cortex*—the intricately convoluted "gray matter"—is the outer covering of the brain. The external surface of the cerebral cortex has many *sulci* (fissures) and *gyri* (ridges between sulci), which are "landmarks" in studying the brain. A major sulcus called the *longitudinal fissure* divides the brain along the midline into two symmetrical, mirror-image cerebral hemispheres, connected by the *corpus callosum*, a band of nerve fibers. Each hemisphere is further divided into four lobes: the *central sulcus* (or *fissure of Rolando*) divides the cortex into the *frontal lobe* and the receptive cortex, made up of the *parietal, temporal*, and *occipital lobes*. Another major fissure, the *lateral sulcus* (or *fissure of Sylvius*), runs along the side of each hemisphere, separating the temporal lobe from the frontal and parietal lobes.

The functions of these different lobes of the brain have been the subject of much debate and research. The frontal lobes are a particular enigma, but at present it appears that they are related essentially to language ability, to the regulation of fine voluntary movements, and to the ordering of stimuli and sorting out of information. The temporal lobes control auditory perception and some part of visual perception; furthermore,

damage to the temporal lobes generally involves memory loss. The parietal lobes are the center of intersensory integration (e.g., the ability to recall the visual counterpart of an auditory stimulus) and of motor and sensory-somatic functions; damage to the parietal lobes frequently results in spatial disorientation and in loss of control over gross motor behavior (e.g., walking). Finally, the occipital lobes appear to control visual discrimination and visual memory.

A cross section of the brain reveals further important structural features: the *hypothalamus*, which controls body temperature and metabolism and helps regulate emotions; the *thalamus*, which relays sensory messages to the appropriate parts of the brain; the *cerebellum*, involved in posture, physical balance, and fine motor coordination; the *pons*, a major relay station connecting the cerebellum with other areas of the brain and with the spinal cord; and the *medulla*, which regulates such vital functions as heartbeat, breathing, and blood pressure. The *brain stem* includes the pons, the medulla, and the *reticular formation*, which regulates arousal and alertness.

This is a bare outline of what we know about the brain. And, in truth, what we know is not a great deal. There are somewhere between 10 and 12 billion neurons in the brain, and we are far from solving the mystery of how each interacts with the others to make up the entire complex of human behavior.

In making this important diagnostic decision, there are a number of possible sources of confusion. In the first place, the symptoms of the various organic brain disorders, like symptoms of biogenic vs. psychogenic disorders, show considerable overlap. For example, if it is determined that a patient's amnesia is biogenic, this condition could still be due to a number of possible brain pathologies, each requiring a different treatment approach. Second, just as different organic brain disorders may result in the same symptoms, so too the same disorder may result in widely different symptomatologies. A brain tumor may cause violent outbursts of rage in one patient and double vision in another. Indeed, the source of the brain pathology and the exact location and extent of the damage are only a very few of the many factors determining the patient's behavioral responses to his disease. His age, his general physical condition, his premorbid personality, his emotional reaction to his new disability, the extent of his outside supports, including family, friends, and finances—all these factors will affect the patient's symptoms. A patient who feels that he is alone in the world or one who is basically rigid and pessimistic or one to whom a serious medical problem may spell financial ruin may respond to his unwelcome symptoms with considerable panic or total dejection. Conversely, a patient who is happily married, well insured, and blessed with a resilient disposition may show a surprisingly moderate response to what is actually a severe impairment. From this bewildering array of variables, the diagnostician must ferret out the single primary variable: the source of the brain pathology.

There is one final problem in the diagnosis of organic brain syndromes. As with so many of the functional disorders, there are many organic brain disorders about which we simply know very little. Unfortunately it often happens that the better-understood syndromes—those in which we can chart with substantial accuracy the cause, the symptoms, the course, and the prognosis—are those which occur least frequently, while many of the most common organic disorders remain somewhat baffling. For example, brain poisoning due to the ingestion of toxic mushrooms is both very well understood and very rare, while the senile psychoses, which may be witnessed in almost every mental-hospital ward in the country, remain something of a mystery.*

In diagnosing an organic brain syndrome, the clinician classifies the syndrome according to its etiology—trauma, infection, poisoning, or what have you. And accordingly it is by etiology that these

Fig. 14.1 *These three drawings show the major areas and structures of the human brain. (Top) side view, (bottom left) top view, and (bottom right) cross-section of the right cerebral hemisphere.*

brain syndromes will be discussed in our chapter. (The one exception to this classification system is epilepsy, which, because its etiology is unknown, is classified by its symptomatology.)

In addition to specifying the source of the brain syndrome—and if possible, the location and extent of the damage—the diagnostician makes three further distinctions. First, he must determine whether the pathology is exogenous or endogenous. An *exogenous* pathology is one that originates from outside the patient, as would be the case with a mushroom toxin or a bullet through the head. By contrast, an *endogenous* pathology, such as a brain tumor or a hardening of the brain arteries, is one that originates from within the organism.

Second, the diagnostician will determine whether the patient's condition is psychotic or nonpsychotic. As we have seen in Chapter 11, the decision as to whether or not a patient is psychotic hinges on his degree of reality contact. Interestingly, what may seem a mild impairment from a medical point of view may cause a severe psychotic reaction, including vivid hallucinations and delusions, whereas more pervasive organic damage may result in only mild behavioral changes.

Finally, the patient's disorder will be classified as either acute or chronic. These terms (which, again, we have covered in Chapter 11) are sometimes used to differentiate, respectively, between conditions that are considered reversible and those that are thought to be permanent (DSM-II, p. 22). And, as with schizophrenia, an organic brain syndrome which is classified as acute but which does not clear up after a certain period of time will be reclassified as chronic.

---

*The distinction between brain damage due to a localized lesion (whether from trauma, stroke, tumor, infection, etc.) and damage due to the more diffuse types of brain disease (some toxic effects, presenile dementia, and other degenerative disorders) has important implications for diagnosis and treatment. In the field of human neurospsychology today there is considerable understanding of specific intellectual impairment and behavioral syndromes resulting from highly localized brain lesions. Little, however, is understood of the mechanism of general intellectual disruption caused by diffuse degenerative changes and atrophy.

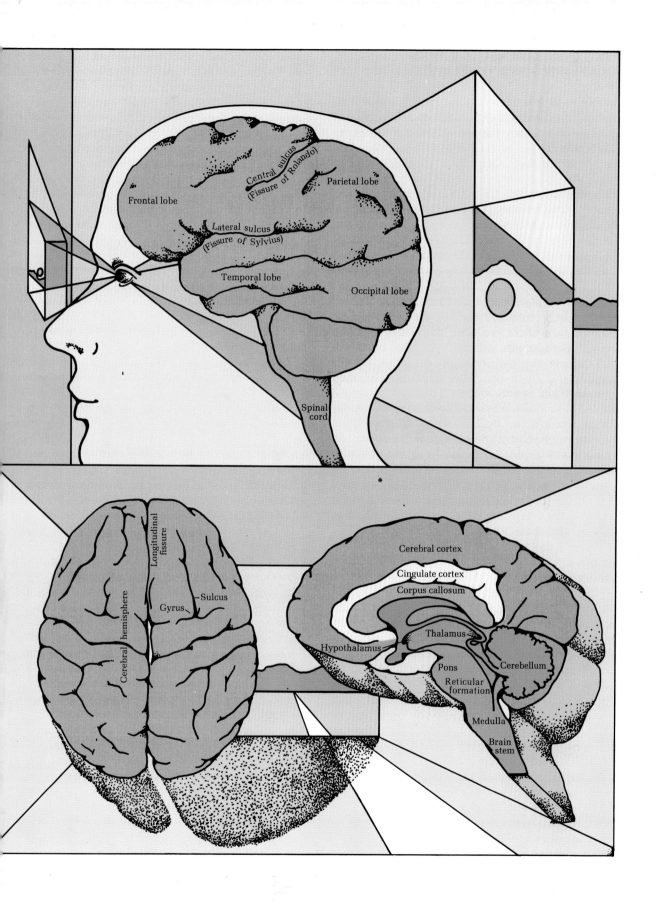

ORGANIC BRAIN DISORDERS CLASSIFIED BY ETIOLOGY

Cerebral Infection

Behavior disorders may result from infections that damage and destroy the neural tissue of the brain. There are two major categories of brain infection: encephalitis and neurosyphilis.

Encephalitis In the United States, encephalitis, a generic term meaning any inflammation of the brain, was a more serious problem earlier in this century than it is today. One form, *epidemic encephalitis* (also called *von Economo's disease*, after the Viennese physician who first identified it), was particularly widespread following World War I. Because its most striking symptoms were profound lethargy and prolonged periods of sleep, often for days or even weeks at a time, the disease came to be called "sleeping sickness." In his periods of wakefulness, the patient might paradoxically become extremely hyperactive, irritable, and then breathless and unable to sleep. Other symptoms included convulsive seizures, disorientation, and delirium marked by hallucinations. Furthermore, striking psychological aftereffects could be observed in victims of the disease, especially in children, who are more susceptible to it than are adults. After an episode of sleeping sickness, a premorbidly cheerful and affable child might demonstrate a marked moral deterioration, including such offensive behaviors as lying, cheating, cruelty, and sexual aggression. In short, such children came to resemble young sociopaths—a condition which often persisted into adulthood.

The virus responsible for epidemic encephalitis, while still active in certain areas of Asia and Africa, is now virtually unknown in the Western world. However, there remain scores of other viruses that can cause different types of encephalitis, most of which are grouped under the general heading of *unspecified encephalitis*. Typically transmitted by such animals as mosquitoes, ticks, and horses, these viruses induce many of the same symptoms that we have described as typical of epidemic encephalitis: lethargy, irritability, convulsions, and the like.

A final variety of encephalitis is *meningitis*, an acute inflammation of the *meninges*, the membranous covering of the brain or spinal cord. Meningitis may be caused by bacteria, viruses, protozoa, or fungi transmitted to the brain either by an infection elsewhere in the body or by an exogenous agent such as a bullet. Among the psychological symptoms usually observed in the various forms of meningitis are drowsiness, confusion, irritability, inability to concentrate, memory defects, and sensory impairments. In milder cases the primary infection may be effectively eradicated, but residual effects such as motor and sensory impairments and, in infants, mental retardation are not uncommon. In more severe cases, meningitis progresses rapidly from drowsiness to coma to death. Autopsies on such cases generally reveal that the brain is swollen and covered with pus and that the pressure from the swelling has caused the gyri (i.e., the convolutions in the surface of the brain) to be flattened against the skull.

Neurosyphilis More common than any of the forms of encephalitis is *neurosyphilis*, the deterioration of brain tissue as a result of syphilis. As we have seen in Chapter 1, it was not until the late nineteenth century that the degenerative disorder called general paresis was finally linked with syphilis. Throughout the previous centuries syphilis had raged unchecked through Europe, taking a fantastic toll in infant mortality, blindness, madness, and death. Among its more famous victims were Henry VIII, along with most of his many wives, and probably Columbus. Indeed, it is thought that the disease was first introduced into Europe by Columbus' crew, who were apparently infected by the natives of the West Indies (Kemble, 1936). Nearer our own times, Lord Randolph Churchill, father of Winston Churchill, and Al Capone both suffered gruesome deaths from neurosyphilis.

Syphilis begins when the spirochete known as *Treponema pallidum* invades the victim's body through tiny skin lesions or, more commonly, through the mucous membranes in the mouth or genital areas. The transmission almost invariably occurs during sexual intercourse (genital or anal) or oral-genital contact with a syphilitic sexual partner. Once contracted, the disease runs its course through four well-defined stages. In the first stage a *chancre* or sore appears at the site of the infection—be it the mouth, the genitals, or the anus—about ten to twenty days after the disease has been contracted. Unfortunately, the chancre is often painless and disappears without treatment, the result being that many people either do not recognize this early warning sign or conclude that they are cured once the chancre disappears. The second stage, occurring about three to six weeks after the appearance of the chancre, is marked by a copper-colored rash which covers the body and may be accompanied by fever, headaches,

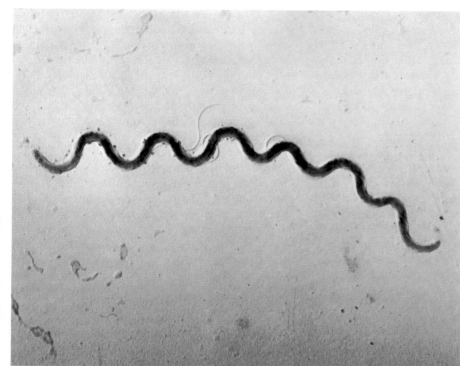

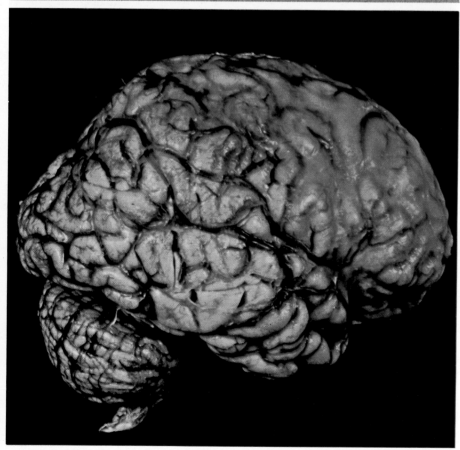

Fig. 14.2 (Top) A photomicrograph shows the spirochete Treponema Pallidum, *the causative organism of syphilis. (Bottom) A photograph of a syphilitic brain illustrates the tissue deterioration in general paresis, the most advanced state of neurosyphilis. Typically, there is a thickening of the meninges of the brain and atrophy of the convolutions of the cortex, particularly in the frontal and temporal lobes.*

and other indispositions. However, this symptom also passes quickly, after which either the spirochetes may be eliminated by the body's immune system, or in less fortunate individuals, the spirochetes simply multiply, carrying the individual into the decisive third and fourth stages of the disease. In the third stage, the latent stage, which may last anywhere from ten to thirty years, the spirochetes slowly and insidiously invade the vital organs of the body. Finally, in the fourth stage, whatever damage has been done during the latent period now becomes apparent, in any one of a wide variety of organ failures, including heart attack, blindness, or—if the spirochetes have infiltrated the brain—general paresis, which develops in approximately 3 percent of untreated syphilitics. The onset of general paresis is usually marked by a vague but pervasive slovenliness of behavior. The person begins to show up late for work, ignores the feelings of others, dispenses casual insults, loses interest in his appearance, evades responsibilities, and so forth.

As the disease becomes more advanced, a number of better-defined symptoms make their appearance, including tremors, slurring of speech, deterioration of handwriting, a shuffling gait (called *locomotor ataxia*), and, almost invariably, disturbances of vision. One very common indication is the so-called Argyll Robertson symptom, in which the pupil of the eye makes an accommodation to distance but not to light.

This physical deterioration is accompanied by an equally grave deterioration of the personality, in which the individual becomes increasingly sloppy, indifferent, and callous. Memory losses begin to appear. At the same time the individual may become severely depressed or, as in the case cited at the beginning of this chapter, expansive, delusional, and euphoric. When the disease has progressed to this stage, the only possible treatment is custodial. In the final stage preceding death, both body and mind are virtually nonfunctional. The individual is paralyzed, inarticulate, utterly cut off from reality, and subject to frequent convulsive seizures.

In *congenital syphilis* the spirochetes are transmitted by a syphilitic mother to her unborn child, causing *juvenile paresis* in the child. While the child may appear normal at birth, the same symptoms of intellectual and physical deterioration seen in general paresis generally appear sometime between the ages of five and twenty. As in the case of general paresis, juvenile paresis is irreversible, usually resulting in death approximately five years after the onset of symptoms.

With the development of such early-detection procedures as the Wassermann test and with the advent of penicillin, the incidence of syphilis decreased dramatically in the 1940s and 1950s. The reward of this conquest is that at present general paresis accounts for only 1 percent of all first admissions to United States mental hospitals. However, the conquest may have been short-lived. With the increasing sexual permissiveness of the 1960s and early 1970s, particularly among the young, there was a parallel increase—reportedly at the rate of 200 percent each year—in the incidence of primary and secondary syphilis. Thus within the next decade or so, we can expect a corresponding rise in mental-hospital admissions for general paresis.

Major Forms of Cerebral Infection

	Major symptomatology
Encephalitis (inflammation of the brain)	
Epidemic encephalitis ("sleeping sickness")	Lethargy, irritability, convulsions, moral deterioration after recovery
Unspecified encephalitis	Lethargy, irritability, convulsions
Meningitis	Drowsiness, memory defects, sensory impairments, inability to concentrate
Neurosyphilis (infection of the brain by syphilis)	
General paresis	Slovenliness, moral deterioration, impairment of speech, memory, and motor control
Juvenile paresis	Gradual physical, intellectual, and moral deterioration in youth

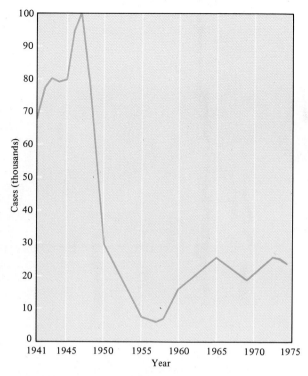

Fig. 14.3   Incidence of syphilis reported by state health departments, 1941–1975. The high incidence of only the reported cases of syphilis in the United States over the last fifteen years, as shown in this graph, lends validity to the grim prediction that many individuals with organic psychoses due to undetected and untreated syphilis will be admitted to hospitals in the next several decades. (Source: "VD Fact Sheet," USDHEW Publication No. COC 75–8195.)

Brain Trauma

Behavior disorders ranging from the mild to the debilitating can result from *trauma*, in which brain tissue is jarred, bruised, or cut by some exogenous source. Although automobile accidents are the most frequent cause of brain trauma, alcoholics and epileptics are particularly prone to head injuries due to falls. However, any extreme physical force suddenly applied to the head, whether from an automobile windshield, a policeman's baton, or an ill-aimed baseball bat, may result in brain damage. Head injuries may be grouped into three categories: concussions, contusions, and lacerations.

Concussions   In the case of a *concussion*, the blow to the head simply jars the brain, momentarily disrupting its functioning. The result is a temporary loss of consciousness, often lasting for only a few minutes, after which the individual is typically unable to remember the events immediately preceding the injury. A familiar example of a concussion is a knockout in a boxing match. The fighter loses consciousness, falls to the floor of the ring (probably hitting his head a second time), and may then show some reflexive twitching of the arms or legs. Soon he is up again and ready to reciprocate.

Nonetheless, concussions may involve posttraumatic symptoms lasting for as long as several weeks, particularly if there has been a prolonged period of unconsciousness. In addition to headaches and dizziness, the person may display apathy, general memory difficulties, inability to concentrate, insomnia, irritability, fatigue, and a decreased tolerance for noise, light, heat, alcohol, and exertion. However, these symptoms also pass, leaving no residual damage.

Contusions   In a *contusion* the trauma is severe enough so that the brain is not simply jarred; it is actually shifted out of its normal position and pressed against one side of the skull, thus bruising the sensitive neural tissue. The results of a contusion are correspondingly more severe than those of a concussion. The person typically lapses into a coma lasting for several hours or even days, and afterwards he may suffer convulsions and/or a temporary speech loss. Furthermore, upon awakening from the coma, the person may fall into a state of disorientation called *traumatic delirium*, in which, for example, he may imagine that the hospital staff are enemies holding him captive. Other patients may simply wander away if they are not carefully watched. Another interesting form of traumatic delirium is *occupational delirium*, in which the patient carries on his conversation as if he were at his job rather than in the hospital. These symptoms generally disappear within a week or so, but a very severe contusion or repeated contusions (such as are often suffered by boxers) can result in permanent emotional instability and intellectual impairment.

Lacerations   *Lacerations*, in which a foreign object, such as a bullet or a piece of metal, enters the skull and directly ruptures and destroys brain tissue, are the most serious of the brain injuries. The effects of a brain laceration depend greatly upon the exact site of the damage. Lacerations in certain areas of the brain result in death or in extremely debilitating impairments of intellectual, sensory, or motor functioning; damage to other sites may lead to only relatively minor consequences. Periodically the newspapers will report a case in which a person, after

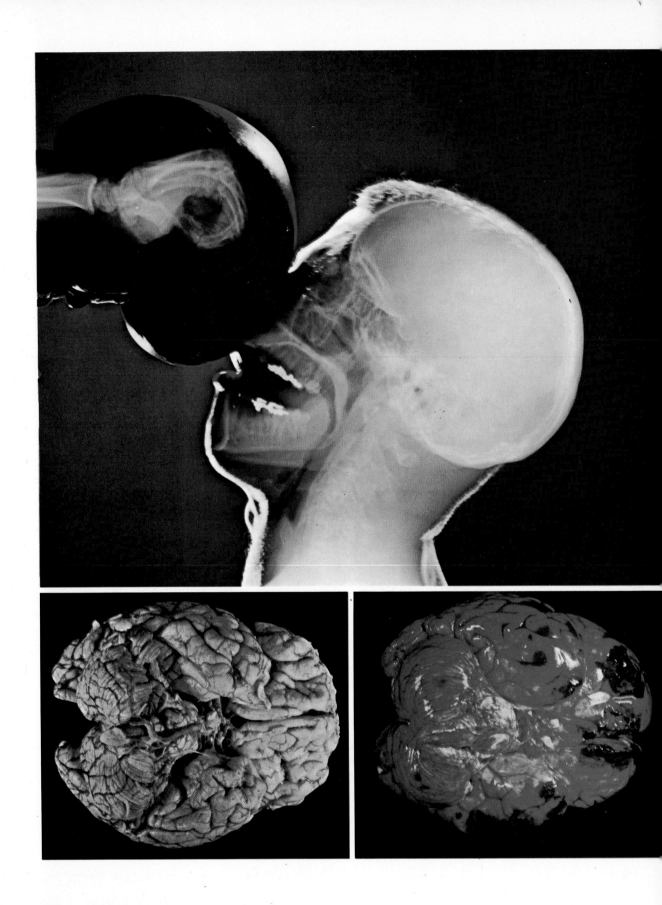

Forms of Brain Trauma

	Form of damage	Major symptomatology
Concussion	Brain jarred	Temporary loss of consciousness
Contusion	Brain shifted out of normal position and bruised against side of skull	Coma followed by convulsions and delirium
Laceration	Brain tissue cut by foreign object entering skull	Variable symptoms ranging from minor discomfort to major intellectual, sensory, and motor impairments or death

being shot in the head, simply resumes normal functioning after his external wounds have healed and goes about his daily business with a bullet or two lodged in his brain. Such cases, however, are exceedingly rare. Normally, a cerebral laceration results in some form of physical impairment or personality change, whether major or minor. The following classic case, reported in 1868, illustrates the subtle, variable, and unpredictable nature of the effects of cerebral laceration:

Phineas P. Gage, age 25 and strong and healthy, was the popular foreman of a railroad excavation crew. While working at a site, a premature explosion drove a tamping iron into the left side of his face and up through his skull. Gage, thrown onto his back by the force of the blast and by the entry of the rod, convulsed. However, he quickly regained speech and was placed in a cart, in which he rode in a sitting position for three-quarters of a mile to his hotel. He got out of the cart by himself and was able to walk up a long flight of stairs to his room. Although bleeding profusely, he remained fully conscious during the doctor's ministrations. And soon afterwards he appeared completely recovered physically. However, his personality had undergone a radical change. The equilibrium between his intellectual faculties and his instincts seemed to have been destroyed. He was now inconsiderate, impatient, and obstinate, and yet at the same time capricious and vacillating in decision-making. He also began indulging in the grossest profanity. The change in temperament was so extreme that his employers had to replace him as foreman. To his friends he was simply "no longer Gage" (adapted from Harlow, 1868, pp. 330–332, 339–340).

Vascular Accidents

A third category of organic brain disorders includes those due to endogenous *vascular accidents*, in which blockage or breaking of cranial blood vessels results in injury to the brain tissue. Such vascular accidents to the left cerebral hemisphere, particularly those due to cerebral thrombosis (which we shall discuss in a moment), often result in language impairments, which are called *aphasias*. Aphasias are subdivided into *sensory aphasias* (also called *receptive aphasias*), which involve difficulty in understanding, and *speech aphasias* (also called *expressive aphasias*), which involve difficulty in articulation. The speech aphasias occur somewhat more frequently than the sensory. Common sensory aphasias include

1. *Auditory aphasia*: inability to understand spoken language.
2. *Visual aphasia* (or *alexia*): inability to understand the written word.

Fig. 14.4   Head punches sustained by a boxer produce a series of brain traumas, usually involving concussions and contusions. (Top) An x-ray of a boxer's head as a punch is landed shows that the force of the blow causes the brain to be momentarily displaced toward the back of the skull. (Bottom right) This photograph, in comparison to that of a normal brain (bottom left), illustrates the effects of an acute massive cerebral contusion and subsequent hemorrhaging.

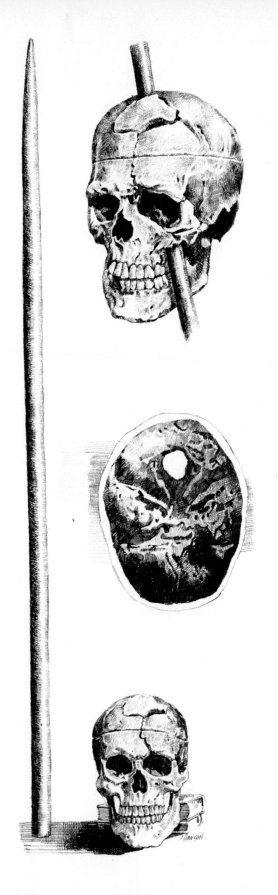

Characteristic speech aphasias include

1. *Nominal aphasia* (or *anomia*): inability, in speaking, to recall the names of common objects.
2. *Paraphasia*: inability to order speech grammatically or syntactically, so that the syllables of words, for example, are transposed.

These defects, though circumscribed, rarely appear in isolation. Typically, a patient will manifest several forms of aphasia. In addition, aphasias are almost invariably accompanied by psychological disturbances, partly organic and partly a functional response to the new impairment. One extremely typical reaction is emotional lability; the patient may pass from laughing to weeping in an instant. Another response that is sometimes seen is a *catastrophic reaction* (Goldstein, 1948), in which the patient, utterly bewildered by his inability to perform elementary tasks that he has long since taken for granted—walking across a room, forming a sentence, reading a magazine—reacts, understandably, with disorganization and sometimes violent fury.

Cerebral Thrombosis As we have mentioned, the culprit normally lurking behind aphasia is *cerebral thrombosis*, in which a blood clot forms in one of the blood vessels feeding the brain and thus cuts off the circulation in that vessel. The result is that the portion of the brain served by that blood vessel can no longer take in nourishment or dispose of chemical wastes. An occurrence of cerebral thrombosis is technically labeled a *cerebrovascular accident* (CVA), though it is known in the popular vocabulary simply as a "stroke." The most common organic brain disorders, CVAs are found in 25 percent of routine autopsies, even though death may have resulted from a totally unrelated cause. Often CVAs are fatal. If they are not, the patient may suffer a variety of aftereffects, the most common of which are paralysis

Fig. 14.5 The cerebral laceration suffered by Phineas Gage is illustrated in these drawings, which are adapted from original sketches done by Dr. Harlow, the physician who attended Gage. The drawings at the bottom and left show the relative sizes of the skull and the tamping iron that passed through it. The top drawing illustrates the position in which the iron lodged and a large section of the skull that was torn away and later replaced. The middle sketch, an upward view of the inside of the skull, shows the hole made by the iron and a new bone deposit that partially filled the hole. Gage's survival of the accident is considered remarkable; however, profound personality changes, discussed in the text, were noted following the traumatic event.

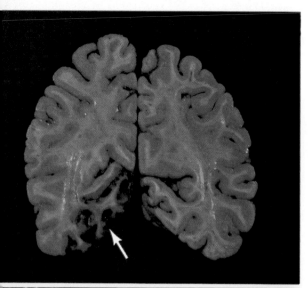

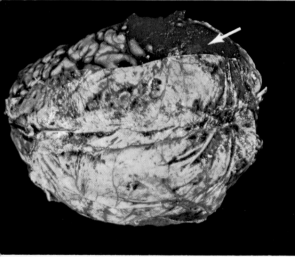

Fig. 14.6   If not fatal, the effects of a CVA often last throughout the life of the individual. (Top) A photograph of a brain section shows the atrophy of tissue (arrow) that results from a cerebral hemorrhage which, in this case, involves gray matter in the left cerebral hemisphere. (Bottom) A photograph of a hemorrhaged brain shows the position of the blood clot (arrow) between the dura (membrane covering of the brain) and the cortex.

ruptures as a result of the pressure exerted by the bloodstream. Blood then spills directly onto brain tissue, damaging or destroying it. Other common causes of vessel rupture are trauma, hypertension, tumors, drug usage, and bacterial infection (Yarnell and Stears, 1974). As with other brain disorders, the specific effects depend on the location and extent of the damage. Usually the patient lapses into a coma, sometimes accompanied by convulsions. Victims of extensive hemorrhaging usually die within two to fourteen days, but if the patient survives, he will probably suffer paralysis, speech difficulties, and severe psychological impairment, such as confusion or loss of memory. The experience of a brain hemorrhage, with subsequent speech and memory disturbances, is described in the following personal account. Undoubtedly, the account itself suffers from distortions and memory gaps of which the patient, a neuroanatomist, was probably not aware.

I found that I was extremely tired. I did not feel quite well, and I was conscious of a tingling and numbness in my right arm. . . . I found the lucid formulation of my train of reasoning impossible. I felt almost desperate; I searched for the dictionary for expressions which at other times were familiar and while so doing I forgot what I wanted to say. . . . My condition now seemed to me critical. . . . It was obvious to those about me that I had difficulty in finding certain words. . . . I became suspicious, and I began to think I had had a slight stroke. . . .

. . . [My] impediment of speech recurred, and was more apparent. I fumbled for phrases, my speech became uncertain and indistinct. . . . I was very tired and even rather dizzy.

Next morning, after a good sleep, I got up and went, half-dressed, to the[toilet]. . . . I turned giddy, and fell down. I did not lose consciousness, but I felt very vague. . . . [Supporting myself] and swaying on my feet, I crept away. . . . However, I could still walk, dress myself, and even take my breakfast. My secretary told me later that I had looked very absent-minded, and had spread the butter on my sugar instead of my bread (Forel, 1937, pp. 288–290).

of one half of the body (*hemiplegia*) or of one limb and disturbances of speech, sensory receptivity, and motor coordination. Some of these impairments may disappear spontaneously, while others can be remedied through rehabilitation therapy. In some cases, CVA patients recover completely, but more often they continue to labor under some form of impairment for the rest of their lives.

Cerebral Hemorrhage   Unlike cerebral thrombosis, in which the affected part of the vascular system remains intact, although useless because of blockage, *cerebral hemorrhage* involves an actual rupture of the vessel wall. Vessel breakage most commonly occurs when a weak part of the vessel wall balloons out into what is called an *aneurysm* and eventually

Brain Tumors

Although the actual cause of tumors, both *benign* (noncancerous) and *malignant* (cancerous), has not yet been determined, the clinical course of a *brain tumor* is clear. For some reason, a few cells begin to grow at an abnormally rapid rate, destroying the surrounding healthy brain tissue and resulting in a wide variety of psychological symptoms. Because of the inexplicable cellular growth, brain tumors are referred to technically as *intracranial neoplasms*—that is, new growths within the brain.

The first sign of a temporal or frontal lobe tumor is often a sudden, terrifying, and incomprehensible outburst of emotion or behavior, completely incompatible with the person's premorbid personality and unrelated to any particular provocation. It sometimes happens, for example, that a "solid citizen" will go suddenly berserk and wantonly shoot at passers-by or commit some other wild crime, to the universal bafflement of family and friends. In such cases, it is not uncommon for an autopsy to reveal a brain tumor. Splitting headaches and visual problems are often other common initial symptoms. With the progressive destruction of brain tissue, the patient eventually experiences abnormal reflexes, blunting of affect, poor memory and concentration, double vision, and jerky motor coordination. The actual kind and severity of symptoms is directly related to the location of the tumor in the brain; the functions controlled by that section will probably be impaired earlier and more severely than other functions. Malignant tumors are much more likely to bring on any of these symptoms than benign tumors. However, if any tumor continues to grow undetected and untreated, the patient will eventually suffer headaches, nausea, vomiting, seizures, and personality changes that can reach psychotic proportions. Prior to death, the patient becomes overtly psychotic and finally lapses into a coma. Surgical removal of the growth is the standard therapy and is sometimes quite successful, especially with benign tumors. However, the surgical intervention itself usually results in some form of permanent brain damage.

Degenerative Disorders

Degenerative disorders are those organic brain syndromes in which intellectual, emotional, and motor functioning appears to deteriorate as a function of advancing age. However, since degenerative disorders can strike long before old age, this diagnostic category has been subdivided into two groups: the presenile psychoses, affecting the 40-to-60 age group, and the senile psychoses, affecting those over 60.

Presenile Psychosis The *presenile psychoses*, involving deterioration of the brain and central nervous system, are both rare and poorly understood. We shall study four syndromes: Huntington's chorea, Parkinson's disease, Pick's disease, and Alzheimer's disease, each named for the physician who first described it.

Huntington's Chorea *Huntington's chorea* is one of the very few psychological disorders that is known to be transmitted genetically. Passed on by a dominant gene from either parent to both male and female children, Huntington's cannot be detected at birth. Indeed, whether or not a person has been unlucky enough to inherit Huntington's cannot be determined until after the age of thirty, when the symptoms typically appear. At present, there are 7,000 to 10,000 Americans showing overt symptoms of Huntington's chorea (Boll et al., 1974).

The first indications of Huntington's are vague behavioral and emotional changes. The patient may become slovenly and indifferent to everyday social amenities. Furthermore, his moods may become unpredictable and inconsistent, running the gamut from obstinacy, passivity, and depression to inexpli-

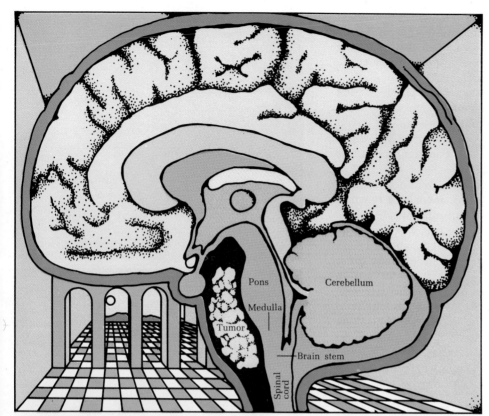

Fig. 14.7 (Top) This illustration shows the position of a tumor located beneath the brain stem. The major symptom of such a tumor is spontaneous outbursts of inappropriate laughing or crying, which may last for thirty to ninety seconds. (Bottom) A photograph of a brain section shows a tumor in the central portion of the left hemisphere (arrow). (Top illustration adapted from R. C. Cantu, "Importance of Pathological Laughing and/or Crying as a Sign of Occurrence or Recurrence of a Tumor Lying Beneath the Brainstem," Journal of Nervous and Mental Disease, 143, 1966, 509.)

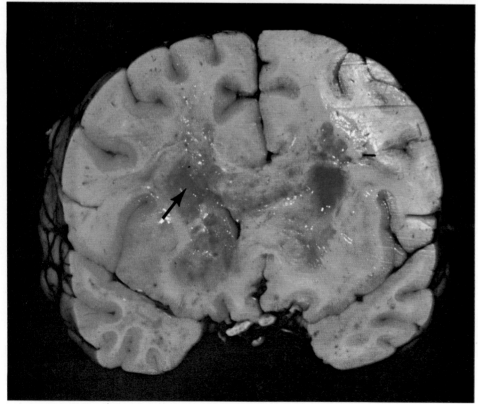

cable euphoria. Intellectual functions, particularly memory and judgment, are also disrupted. As the disease progresses, delusions, hallucinations, and suicidal tendencies commonly appear (Boll et al., 1974).

In addition to the psychological problems that have surfaced, the patient may begin to show the characteristic *choreiform* movements—that is, involuntary spasmodic jerking of the limbs—from which the term "chorea" is derived. This sign appears to signal irreversible brain damage (James et al., 1969). The victim's behavior becomes increasingly bizarre; he smacks his tongue and lips involuntarily, spits, barks out words (often obscenities) explosively, and walks with a jerky or shuffling gait. Eventually he loses complete control of his bodily functions. Death is the inevitable result, but some people may suffer the overt symptoms of Huntington's for ten to twenty years before dying. Such was the case with folksinger Woody Guthrie. And at present Arlo Guthrie must live with the knowledge that along with his father's talent, he has a 50-50 chance of also having inherited his father's disease, though it is still several years before he will know whether he carries the fateful gene.

Parkinson's Disease *Parkinson's disease*, first described in 1817 by James Parkinson (who also suffered from it), involves degenerative lesions of midbrain nerve tracts responsible for relaying motor impulses. The cause of this condition is unknown, although it has been attributed to a variety of sources, including encephalitis, heredity, viruses, toxins, and deficient brain metabolism. The illness occurs most frequently between the ages of fifty and seventy.

The primary symptom of this disorder is tremor, occurring at a rate of about four to eight movements per second. The tremors are usually present during rest periods, but tend to diminish or cease when the patient is sleeping. Interestingly, the patient can often abruptly stop the tremors, at least temporarily, if someone orders him to do so, and for a short time he may even be able to perform motor activities requiring very fine muscular coordination. However, such remissions are always quite temporary, and the patient once again lapses into the typical rhythmic jerking of his arms, hands, jaws, and /or head.

Another highly characteristic physical sign of Parkinson's is an expressionless, masklike countenance, probably due to a degeneration of cortical tissue. Examples of this facial rigidity may be seen in late photographs of the American playwright Eugene

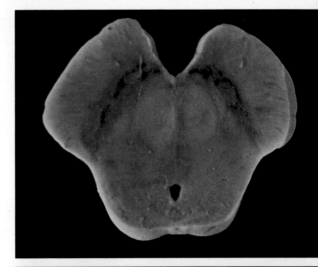

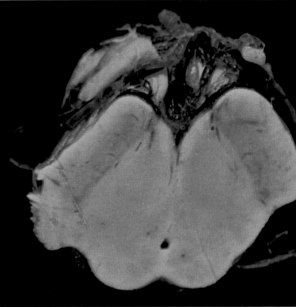

Fig. 14.8 *At the top is a photograph of a section of the midbrain from a normal brain. In comparison, note the tissue degeneration in the bottom photograph of a midbrain section from a Parkinsonian brain. The degeneration occurs on both macroscopic and microscopic levels, and the etiology is unknown. (Bottom photograph courtesy of R. Rowen, M.D., San Diego.)*

O'Neill, who died of Parkinson's in 1953. Parkinson's patients also tend to walk, when they *can* walk, with a distinctive slow, stiff gait, usually accompanied by a slight crouch.

Psychological disturbances associated with Parkinson's disease are a withdrawal from social contact, difficulty in concentration, and apathy. In more severe cases there may be highly systematized delusions and severe depression, including suicidal tendencies. However, it is difficult to determine whether these symptoms are due directly to the brain pathology or simply to the patient's distress over his physical helplessness.

Parkinson's is rare among the presenile psychoses in that it can be treated with some success. With the help of a new drug called L-dopa, some patients have shown substantial improvement.

Pick's Disease *Pick's disease* is an extremely rare disorder in which the frontal and temporal lobes of the brain gradually atrophy. The disorder usually appears between the ages of forty-five and sixty and results in death four to seven years later.

Initial symptoms vary from difficulty with simple reasoning and memory tasks to confusion, indifference, and occasionally, suspiciousness. Interestingly, victims of Pick's disease may exhibit either marked underactivity or marked hyperactivity in their cognitive, emotional, and motor functions. Extremely hyperactive patients may also show explosively violent and destructive behavior.

As the disease advances, intellectual abilities slowly deteriorate, resulting in distractibility, concrete thinking (Chapter 11), and aphasias. Eventually the person is reduced to an utterly vegetative state, which may last for several years before death.

Alzheimer's Disease Like Pick's disease, *Alzheimer's disease* results from an atrophy of the brain, though in the case of Alzheimer's the damage is more diffuse, involving the entire cerebral cortex and the basal ganglia, clusters of nerve cell bodies deep within the cerebral hemispheres. The characteristic early signs are irritability and difficulties in concentration and memory (Miller, 1973). As the disease progresses, a wide array of further deteriorative symptoms appear, including facial paralysis, involuntary movements and convulsions, physical aggression, hallucinations and delusions, and a strikingly rapid intellectual decline, involving multiple aphasias. The course of the fatal disease averages approximately four years.

A differential diagnosis between Pick's disease and Alzheimer's disease is sometimes difficult because the two syndromes strike the same age group, those in their forties and fifties, and share many of the same clinical signs. A general difference is that the deterioration of functioning is more widespread and occurs more rapidly in the more common Alzheimer's disease. A rule of thumb sometimes used is that Pick's disease patients are typically indifferent, whereas Alzheimer's disease patients generally appear quite anxious. Furthermore, clinicians suggest that patients suffering from Pick's disease are more likely to show motor underactivity. However, there are numerous exceptions to these rules, and in practice the decision as to whether a patient is suffering from Pick's or Alzheimer's usually depends on biopsy, on vascular radiographic techniques (a type of x-ray), or finally on autopsy.

Senile Degenerative Disorders Almost all old people experience some psychological changes as a result of a general slowing down of the central nervous system. And while certain old people may respond to these changes—and the other physical and social changes implicit in aging—with confusion, depression, and anxiety, these are functional disorders, which we shall discuss in Chapter 17. By contrast, the two major *senile degenerative disorders*, senile psychosis and cerebral arteriosclerosis, are the direct result of serious organic deterioration of the brain. Both syndromes are extremely common and will become even more so as life expectancies increase.

The differential diagnosis of these two syndromes is often extremely complicated. In the first place, they have many of the same clinical signs. Second, both syndromes involve many of the same symptoms as general paresis, with the result that blood tests are often necessary in order to rule out the possibility of neurosyphilis. Then to make matters even more complicated, it is not uncommon for any two of these three syndromes—senile psychosis, cerebral arteriosclerosis, and general paresis—to appear together in the same patient. A final source of diagnostic confusion is one that we have mentioned earlier: the symptoms in any individual case of organic brain disorder have everything to do with the patient's premorbid personality, his psychosocial history, the availability of outside supports, and any number of other rather intangible factors. Of all the organic brain disorders, this is perhaps most true of the senile degenerative disorders. Thus it is not rare for a proper diagnosis to be arrived at only after postmortem examination.

Senile Psychosis Autopsies of victims of *senile psychosis* commonly reveal extensive atrophy of brain tissue. Precisely why this condition leads to the bizarre habits and intellectual incapacities typical of senile psychosis has not been fully explained. When the link is discovered, some kind of rehabilitation may enable many old people to live out their lives with greater emotional and intellectual fulfillment.

In terms of symptoms, the senile psychotic shows a gradual increase in general behavioral problems. He may neglect personal hygiene and go for days without bathing or changing his clothes. Oblivious to himself and those around him, he may explode in bursts of impulsive behavior, such as ordering a houseful of new furniture when he can barely afford his monthly rent, or he may take a sudden interest in unusual activities (such as, for example, sexual deviations) atypical of his premorbid personality.

The senile psychotic may also begin saving items that others regard as worthless, such as old papers and magazines or bits of string. In such cases, the old person will typically spend a great deal of time arranging and cataloging his collection and may become quite distraught if anyone comments on it or attempts to remove it to the trash pile.

As the disease progresses, cognitive defects—particularly loss of memory for recent events—become increasingly severe, further isolating the person from reality. Thus the senile psychotic may be able to give you the line-up of his favorite baseball team sixty years ago, complete with batting averages and runs batted in, but will not remember what he ate for lunch. (On the other hand, some patients exhibit permanent memory loss for distant events.) Some patients mutter in unusual verbal patterns, stringing together the same jumbled phrases over and over again—a condition called *logorrhea*. They may also develop a taste for vivid obscenities. Other symptoms include emotional lability and *misoneism*, a pronounced hatred of anything new.

Cerebral Arteriosclerosis　We shall now deal with a misnamed disorder. *Arteriosclerosis* is a hardening of the walls of the blood vessels in the brain, a condition which in many cases has no psychotic effects. The condition under consideration is actually one of *artherosclerosis*, in which there is a narrowing, and sometimes an obstruction, of the opening of the vessels, thereby cutting off the blood supply to the brain and resulting in psychotic behavior. In spite of this difference, the majority of clinicians continue to describe the latter disorder as "arteriosclerosis," and this minor inconsistency will be perpetuated in our discussion in order to conform to the most widely accepted terminology.

There are certain physiological signs—periods of blackouts, indications of cardiac insufficiency, symptoms of kidney failure, hypertension, and retinal sclerosis (a hardening of the retina of the eye)—that suggest to the physician that cerebral arteriosclerosis is the proper diagnosis. The prominent psychological symptoms are similar to those of senile

DEGENERATIVE DISORDERS

Major symptomatology

Presenile psychoses	Deterioration of intellectual, emotional, and motor functioning prior to age sixty
Huntington's chorea	Emotional extremes, bizarre behavior, and intellectual impairment, accompanied by spasmodic jerking of the body
Parkinson's disease	Emotional withdrawal, facial rigidity, stiff gait, and continual tremor
Pick's disease	Confusion, indifference, underactivity or hyperactivity of cognitive, emotional, and motor functioning
Alzheimer's disease	Symptomatology similar to Pick's disease, though indifference and underactivity less common in Alzheimer's
Senile degenerative disorders	Deterioration of intellectual, emotional, and motor functioning after age sixty
Senile psychosis	Bizarre, impulsive, and slovenly behavior; loosening of moral controls; cognitive impairment, especially loss of short-term memory
Cerebral arteriosclerosis	Symptomatology similar to that of senile psychosis, though cognitive defects tend to fluctuate rather than remain constant, as in senile psychosis

Organic Brain Disorders Due to Nutritional Deficiency

	Nutritional deficiency	Major symptomatology
Korsakoff's psychosis	Lack of B complex vitamins as a result of alcoholism	Anterograde amnesia and confabulation
Pellagra	Lack of niacin	Depression, anxiety, and delirium
Beriberi	Lack of vitamin B_1	Lassitude, lack of appetite, insomnia, cognitive defects, irritability

psychosis: confusion, memory defects, emotional lability, a declining interest in hygiene. However, according to Rothschild (1956), if the psychological manifestations are complex and are marked by alternating periods of lucidity and confusion, the patient is more likely to be suffering from arteriosclerosis than from senile psychosis. Another specific indication of cerebral arteriosclerosis is a fluctuation in the ability to recall distant events, which may be remembered in exquisite detail on one day and totally forgotten the next day. By contrast, the senile psychotic's memory deficits are constant and permanent.

Nutritional Deficiency

Avitaminosis, the lack of one or more essential vitamins from a person's diet, can result in neurological damage and consequently in psychological disturbances. The most common syndromes in this category are Korsakoff's psychosis, pellagra, and beriberi.

Korsakoff's Psychosis *Korsakoff's psychosis*, considered irreversible, is invariably associated with alcoholism, and there is still debate as to whether the primary cause of this syndrome is alcohol poisoning, as DSM-II claims, or whether it is due to a shortage of B-complex vitamins in the typically deficient diet of the alcoholic (Redlich and Freedman, 1966; Brion, 1969).

There are two classic behavioral signs of Korsakoff's psychosis, anterograde amnesia and confabulation. *Anterograde amnesia* is the loss of memory for immediately preceding events, and *confabulation* is the tendency to fill in these memory gaps with invented stories. For example, in response to questioning, the patient may placidly offer an utterly outrageous account of why he is in the hospital, if indeed he even admits that the place is a hospital. Such patients usually seem calm and affable, while at the same time their total unawareness of the fantastic quality of their stories reveals a psychotic impairment of judgment. This impairment gradually spreads to other aspects of psychological functioning and may include disorientation.

Pellagra *Pellagra*, caused by a severe deficiency of the B vitamin niacin, is most common in geographical areas where corn is a major part of the diet of the population. In the early 1900s, pellagra accounted for about 10 percent of all admissions to state mental hospitals in some areas of the United States, particularly the South (Millon, 1969), but since that time improvements in the average American's diet have virtually eliminated this syndrome in our society. The major psychological symptoms of pellagra are depression, anxiety, and eventually delirium and hallucinations prior to death. Massive vitamin therapy, if instituted in time, can halt the progress of the disease.

Beriberi *Beriberi*, caused by a deficiency of vitamin B_1, often appears in association with other disorders, such as chronic alcoholism, pellagra, pernicious anemia, or diabetes. The most prominent clinical signs of beriberi include lack of appetite, insomnia, disturbances in memory and concentration, irritability, and above all, extreme lassitude. This disorder has been a particular problem in areas such as the Far East, where polished rice constitutes a major portion of the diet.

Endocrine Disorders

The *endocrine glands* are responsible for the production of hormones which, when released into the bloodstream, affect various bodily mechanisms, such as sexual functions, physical growth and development, and the availability of energy. Disturbances in the endocrine system, and particularly in the thyroid and adrenal glands, can give rise to a variety of psychological disorders.

Thyroid Syndromes Overactivity of the thyroid gland—a condition called *hyperthyroidism*, or *Graves' disease*—involves an excessive secretion of the hormone thyroxin, which in turn gives rise to a series of physical and psychological difficulties. Psychological symptoms accompanying the disorder may include severe apprehension and agitation, hallucinations, excessive motor activity, sweating, and other anxietylike symptoms.

Opposite in both cause and effect is *hypothyroidism*, sometimes referred to as *myxedema*, in which underactivity of the thyroid gland results in deficient production of thyroxin. Hypothyroidism may be due to an inadequate iodine consumption, a problem that has become much less common in the United States since the advent of iodized table salt. Individuals suffering from hypothyroidism are frequently sluggish, have difficulties with memory and concentration, and appear to be lethargic and depressed. However, here, as with hyperthyroidism, symptomatology depends greatly on premorbid personality.

Another condition resulting from thyroid deficiency is *cretinism*, in which the thyroid has not developed, has been injured, or has undergone degeneration. When the deficiency occurs during the prenatal or perinatal periods, the unwelcome result is mental retardation (Chapter 15). Cretinism has become relatively rare as a result of public health measures involving prevention, early detection, and treatment. With early treatment, normal intellectual and personality functioning can usually be restored.

Adrenal Syndromes The *adrenal glands* are a pair of ductless glands located above the kidneys and consisting of an outer layer called the *cortex* and an internal portion called the *medulla*. Chronic un-

Fig. 14.9 The endocrine system, including the glands as well as their functions and dysfunctions, is illustrated in this diagram. Psychological disorders accompanying thyroid and adrenal dysfunctions are discussed in the text.

deractivity of the adrenal cortex gives rise to *Addison's disease*, which involves both physical and psychological changes. Again, the psychological symptoms vary considerably according to the individual's premorbid psychosocial adjustment. Some patients may simply appear moderately depressed and withdrawn; a more violent reaction may involve debilitating extremes of depression, anxiety, irritability, and invalidism. Appropriate medical therapy can alleviate the symptoms of even a severe case of Addison's disease. With such therapy the individual can resume normal functioning, as was the case with President John F. Kennedy, who suffered from Addison's (Lasky, 1966).

When the adrenal cortex is excessively active, several disorders may arise, one of which is *Cushing's syndrome*. This relatively rare disorder usually affects young women. As with the other endocrine disorders, Cushing's syndrome involves both physical symptoms (e.g., obesity and muscle weakness) and psychological difficulties, especially extreme emotional lability, with fluctuations in mood ranging from total indifference to violent hostility.

Toxic Disorders

Various plants, gases, drugs, and metals, when ingested or absorbed through the skin, can have a toxic or poisonous effect on the brain. The resulting symptoms range from temporary distress to permanent brain damage.

Organic Brain Disorders Due to Endocrine Dysfunction

	Major symptomatology
Thyroid syndromes	
Hyperthyroidism (Graves' disease)	Hyperactivity, anxiety, agitation
Hypothyroidism (myxedema)	Lethargy, depression, defects in memory and concentration
Cretinism	Mental retardation
Adrenal syndromes	
Addison's disease	Mild or severe depression, anxiety, irritability
Cushing's syndrome	Extreme fluctuations in mood

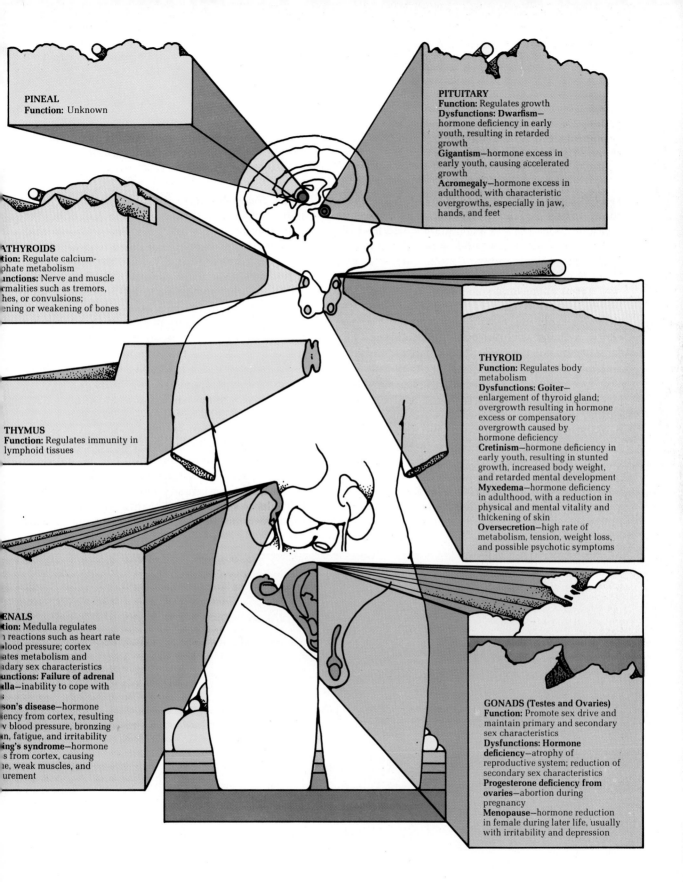

Mushroom Toxins The ingestion of certain species of mushrooms can cause extreme physical illness as well as a number of psychological symptoms. For example, most mushrooms of the genus *Amanita* cause disorientation, hallucinations, delirium, and periods of extreme excitement alternating with periods of sleep. Such symptoms are typically transitory. Eating certain members of this genus, however, can be fatal.

Lead Poisoning Much more common than mushroom toxins is lead poisoning. The excessive ingestion of lead causes a condition called lead *encephalopathy*, in which fluid accumulates in the brain, causing extraordinary intracranial pressure. Early symptoms include abdominal pains, constipation, facial pallor, and sometimes convulsions and bizarre behaviors such as hair-pulling. In severe cases, the symptoms may be similar to those of psychosis, including delirium and hallucinations. The most common victims of lead poisoning are children, who may become mentally retarded as a result.

In recent years, consumer advocacy groups have identified a number of sources of lead contamination, including old lead-lined water pipes, lead-based paint on children's toys and furniture, old plaster walls, candles with lead-core wicks, certain electric tea kettles which release lead from soft solder joints when heated, pottery glazes from which acetic foods (e.g., grape juice) can leach lead, exhaust from automobiles burning leaded gasoline, and industrial pollution. As may be seen from this list, the issue of metal poisoning often involves a conflict between the needs of industry and the needs of the individual. An illustrative case is the community of Kellogg, Idaho, whose primary industry is a lead-smelting plant which, at the same time that it provides the economic support for most of the people of Kellogg, is probably damaging the brains of many of these people's children with the lead dust that it releases daily into the air.

Other Heavy-Metal Toxins The "industry vs. the individual" conflict also crops up in two of the more common varieties of heavy-metal poisoning, mercury and manganese poisoning. Victims of these toxic disorders are usually those whose jobs bring them into close daily contact with these metals. However, other victims are simply unwitting citizens whose food or air has been contaminated by industrial wastes containing metallic toxins. One notorious source of such poisoning is fish taken from waters polluted by mercury wastes from nearby factories. In Japan, for example, thousands of people have been permanently paralyzed and brain-damaged as a result of eating mercury-contaminated fish (Kurland et al., 1960).

Early signs of damage due to mercury poisoning are memory loss, irritability, and difficulty in concentration. As the disease develops, the individual typically develops tunnel vision (that is, loss of peripheral vision), faulty motor coordination, and difficulty in speaking and hearing. In extreme cases, these symptoms lead to paralysis, coma, and death.

TOXIC DISORDERS

Source of brain poisoning	Major symptomatology
Toxic mushrooms	Disorientation, hallucinations, alternation between hyperactivity and sleepiness
Lead	Convulsions, bizarre behavior, delirium, hallucinations, and, if untreated, mental retardation
Heavy metals (e.g., mercury and manganese)	Mercury: irritability, defects in memory and concentration, impairment of speech, hearing, and motor coordination Manganese: emotional instability, agitation, motor and speech impairments
Drugs (e.g., bromide)	Bromide: intoxication, hallucinations, withdrawal, paranoid suspiciousness
Carbon monoxide	Apathy, confusion, memory impairment

Manganese poisoning is manifested in motor and speech impairments, restlessness, and emotional instability. In the case of both types of poisoning, some clinicians believe that personality changes are often simply pathological exaggerations of the individual's premorbid personality traits.

Drugs As we have seen in Chapter 10, abuse of psychoactive drugs such as alcohol, narcotics, and amphetamines can cause severe psychological disturbances. Other drugs have also been implicated in organic brain damage. In recent years, for example, the inhalation of aerosol gases and fumes of certain glues have become popular means of getting "high" among adolescents. Unfortunately, the toxins in these gases and fumes tend to accumulate in the vital organs and may cause permanent damage not only to the liver and kidney but also to the brain, which in turn may result in severe psychological deterioration, and in extreme cases, death.

Another example of drug-induced brain disorder is *bromide psychosis.* Many popular nonprescription sleeping pills consist of compounds containing bromides, even though bromides are not particularly useful in producing sleep. The chronic insomniac may take so many of these pills that he inadvertently ingests a toxic dose of bromides, which may result in permanent brain damage if appropriate medical treatment is not instituted quickly. Depending on the dose ingested, the symptoms of bromide overdose range from simple intoxication to what is called "bromide schizophrenia," involving hallucinations, withdrawal, and extreme suspiciousness (Levin, 1948).

Carbon Monoxide Carbon monoxide, an odorless, tasteless, and invisible gas usually inhaled from automobile exhaust fumes, combines with the hemoglobin in the blood in such a way as to prevent the blood from absorbing oxygen. The usual result of this process is a swift and rather painless death, a fact which makes carbon monoxide inhalation a favored means of suicide. If, however, the patient lives, he will suffer a number of psychological consequences, typically including apathy, confusion, and memory defects. While these symptoms usually clear up within two years, some patients suffer permanent mental impairment (Kolb, 1973).

THE EPILEPSIES

It is estimated that about .5 percent of the American population suffers from the enigmatic disease called epilepsy. *Epilepsy* is actually a generic term covering a variety of organic disorders characterized by irregularly occurring disturbances in consciousness in the form of seizures or convulsions. These seizures appear to be due to a disruption in the electrical and physiochemical activity of the discharging cells of the brain. And accordingly, about 85 percent of epileptics manifest brain-wave abnormalities in EEG recordings. However, the remaining 15 percent of epileptics have normal EEGs—a fact that suggests that the abnormal discharges may occur too infrequently for detection by this instrument or that the disturbance arises from deeper within the brain and consequently is not detectable by surface electrodes.

In most cases, epilepsy, regardless of its type, can be controlled with medication. However, there are some very severe cases in which surgery may be considered in order to remove the portion of the brain responsible for the seizures. In such cases, the affected area can often be localized by EEG studies (Rasmussen and Branch, 1962).

Etiology

As we have seen in our foregoing discussion, convulsions occur in a number of brain syndromes—for example, neurosyphilis, acute alcohol or other drug intoxication, tumors, encephalitis, trauma, and cerebral arteriosclerosis. Though such seizures are labeled *symptomatic* or *acquired epilepsy* because they are a function of the brain damage caused by these other pathologies, the appropriate diagnosis is not epilepsy but rather the primary organic condition. However, in about 77 percent of all cases of epilepsy, there is no known cause for the convulsive disorder (Kolb, 1973); such cases are called *idiopathic epilepsy.* Idiopathic epilepsy usually has its onset between the ages of ten and twenty, though it may also appear in early childhood.

Personality and Intellectual Characteristics

For many years the clinical lore attributed a certain type of personality to all epileptics. It is now generally accepted that there is no single, stereotypic epileptic personality (Tizard, 1962). In fact, some individuals with epilepsy show no psychological abnormalities whatsoever. And in those epileptics who do show mild personality disturbances, such disturbance is likely to be, at least in part, a response to the social stigma attached to epilepsy and to the embarrassment and inconvenience of having such seizures.

As for the intellectual characteristics of epileptics, as a group their functioning is in the low-normal range. Some have IQ scores that are lower than average, others have scores above average (Kolb, 1973). It should be noted that a great many epileptics—including, for example, Julius Caesar, Feodor Dostoevsky, and Vincent van Gogh—had very little trouble intellectually, no matter what other problems, such as those caused by war, poverty, or psychosis, were present.

Precipitation of Seizures

Factors that may precipitate an epileptic attack include blows to the head, high fevers, deep breathing (*hyperventilation*), low blood sugar level (*hypoglycemia*), alcohol, fatigue, highly charged emotional situations, and sleep deprivation. In some cases, what seems to be a very mild or innocuous stimulus can provoke an epileptic seizure; for example, certain musical notes or lights flickering at certain frequencies have been known to set off seizures in susceptible individuals. Other examples of known precipitative factors are prolonged reading and, in women, hormonal changes during the menstrual period.

Once the attack has been precipitated, many epileptics experience a warning sign known as the *aura*. The aura may take many different forms. Some patients always note a strong aroma or small involuntary movements before the onset of convulsions; others simply become aware of a diffuse fear or "funny feeling" (*epigastric aura*), a sensation of dizziness, or sudden cramps. Despite its frightening aspects, the aura does permit the patient to prepare for the attack and thereby reduce the chance of his being injured.

Types of Epilepsy

Historically, epilepsy has been classified according to four main types: petit mal, Jacksonian, psychomotor, and grand mal.

Petit Mal In *petit mal* (literally, "small illness") the seizure generally lasts for only a few seconds and involves only a brief, and not necessarily total, loss of consciousness. During the attack the individual remains immobile, becomes completely unaware of his surroundings, and simply stares straight ahead. A loss of muscle tone may or may not accompany the seizure. After the attack the individual, unaware that anything has happened, simply resumes whatever he was doing prior to the attack. Such attacks can occur as often as a hundred times a day, but usually their occurrence is much less frequent, in which case the individual may not even require treatment.

Jacksonian Epilepsy *Jacksonian epilepsy*, first described by the neurologist Hughlings Jackson, begins with a muscular twitching or a tingling in the hands and feet, which then spreads to the rest of the body. The part of the brain from which the seizure originates is thought to be quite localized, and treatment sometimes involves removing that portion of the brain, which typically contains a structural lesion or tumor. The Jacksonian seizure is often a prelude to a full-scale grand mal seizure, a type that we will examine shortly.

Psychomotor Epilepsy In *psychomotor epilepsy*, the attack, preceded by an aura, usually involves nothing more dramatic than a loss of contact with reality lasting anywhere from a few seconds to several minutes. During this time the person may appear quite normal and may engage in some rather mechanical activity. After the attack has passed, he will resume his former business and will be amnesic for the episode.

Psychomotor attacks are unique among the epilepsies in two respects. First, between attacks, psychomotor epileptics may show bizarre, schizophreniclike behavior, such as public disrobing and urination, hallucinations and paranoid delusions, and possibly violent aggression as well (Standage, 1973). Second, in very rare instances a person will commit a crime or an act of violence during a psychomotor seizure. Turner and Merlis (1962), for example, reported that 5 out of the 337 epileptics included in their study had engaged in illegal activities during a seizure. Part of the defense of Jack Ruby, who killed Lee Harvey Oswald, the alleged assassin of President Kennedy, was that Ruby had carried out Oswald's murder during a psychomotor seizure.

Grand Mal What most people think of when they think of epilepsy is grand mal. *Grand mal* (literally, "great illness"), the most common and the most dramatic of the epilepsies, involves a generalized seizure throughout the brain. There are thought to be four stages of grand mal, the first of which is the *aura phase*, which may or may not occur. The second stage is the *tonic phase*, in which the person's body becomes very rigid—with arms flexed, legs outstretched, and fists clenched—and undergoes strong muscular contractions. During this phase, which may last for as long as a minute, breathing ceases. In the third stage, or *clonic phase*, breathing resumes and the muscles begin to contract and relax in a rhythmic way, though the body continues to jerk

THE EPILEPSIES

Nature of seizures

Petit mal	Loss of consciousness for only a few seconds, during which the epileptic remains immobile
Jacksonian epilepsy	Twitching or tingling progressing from hands and feet to rest of body; often a prelude to grand mal seizure
Psychomotor epilepsy	Aura followed by a brief loss of reality contact, during which epileptic may remain active and appear normal
Grand mal	Aura followed by body rigidity and intense muscular contractions and then by coma

in violent and rapid generalized spasms. In this stage there is some danger that the patient may bite or swallow his tongue or otherwise injure himself because of the violent jerking movements. The clonic phase also lasts about a minute, after which the convulsions dissipate. In the last stage, the *coma*, the muscles slowly relax while the patient remains unconscious. When the patient regains consciousness, he typically is somewhat confused, has a headache, and feels quite exhausted and sleepy. In severe cases, such attacks may occur as often as several times a day.

SUMMARY

This chapter has been devoted to the organic brain disorders, which differ from most of the syndromes discussed in this book in that they are definitely biogenic. There are five major symptoms of organic brain disorder: impairment of orientation, of memory, of general intellectual functioning, of judgment, and of control over affect. However, since these symptoms overlap considerably with those of functional disorders, differential diagnosis is often extremely complicated. And since many different organic syndromes share similar symptom pictures, specifying the precise type of impairment—along with location, source, severity, and prognosis—involves a host of diagnostic difficulties.

Most of the organic brain syndromes are classified by etiological categories. These include the following: cerebral infection, whether from encephalitis or from neurosyphilis, the latter leading to general paresis; brain trauma, including, in order of severity, concussions, contusions, and lacerations; vascular accidents, including cerebral thrombosis ("strokes") and cerebral hemorrhage, both of which commonly result in multiple aphasias; brain tumors; presenile degenerative disorders, including Huntington's chorea, Parkinson's disease, Pick's disease, and Alzheimer's disease, all of them rare and all but Parkinson's being virtually untreatable; the much more common senile degenerative disorders, including senile psychosis and cerebral arteriosclerosis; nutritional deficiencies (especially of B-complex vitamins), including Korsakoff's psychosis, pellagra, and beriberi; endocrine disorders, including disturbances in thyroid and adrenal functioning; and toxic disorders, in which the brain is essentially poisoned, whether by mushrooms, lead, heavy-metal toxins (e.g., mercury and manganese), drugs, or carbon monoxide. A final category of organic brain syndromes, epilepsy, is classified by symptomatology rather than etiology, as the etiology is unknown. The four types of epilepsy, all of which are usually treatable, are petit mal, Jacksonian epilepsy, psychomotor epilepsy, and grand mal.

Although mental retardation has been recognized and written about for over 2,500 years, no universally accepted definition has been developed. The standards of a given society form the primary basis upon which the judgment of retardation, regardless of its cause or form, is made. There has long been controversy over the nature of intelligence, its organization, its predictability, and its susceptibility to change. Thus consensus on just what mental retardation *is* has been impossible to achieve.

Because there is no one definition of retardation, there are also no absolute statistics on its incidence. However, the President's Panel on Mental Retardation estimated that in 1962 there were nearly 6 million retarded persons in the United States, or approximately 3 percent of the population; this figure has changed little, if at all (Robinson and Robinson, 1970). This is more than twice the combined number of people afflicted with polio, blindness, rheumatic heart disease, and cerebral palsy. Only four seriously disabling conditions are more prevalent than retardation: mental illness, cardiac disease, arthritis, and cancer (Scheerenberger, 1964). And the retarded account for almost 70 percent of the permanently disabled population (Robinson and Robinson, 1970). These figures define the enormity and indicate the seriousness of the problem for society.

APPROACHES TO DEFINITION

The most widely accepted current definition of mental retardation is that presented in the *Manual on Terminology and Classification in Mental Retardation*, published by the American Association on Mental Deficiency (1973):

Mental retardation refers to significantly sub-average general intellectual functioning existing concurrently with deficits in adaptive behavior, and manifested during the developmental period (p. 11).

The most important aspects of this definition are the determination of retardation in terms of levels of functioning and the requirement that deficits occur in *both* intellectual and adaptive behavior. That is, an individual of below-average intelligence who nevertheless demonstrates successful adaptive behavior would not be judged retarded. The same would be true of an individual whose behavior is maladaptive but who is of normal intelligence. (See Fig. 15.1.)

This represents a change in the concept of retardation. Many previous attempts to arrive at a definition were founded largely upon the concept of a

15 Mental Retardation

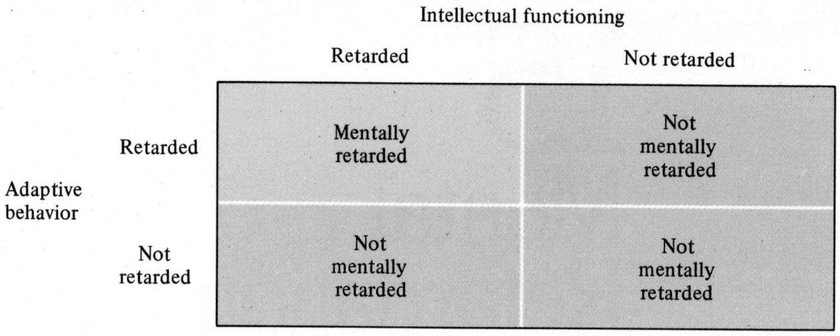

Fig. 15.1 *This chart illustrates the possible combinations of intellectual and adaptive behavior deficits. Only those individuals who displayed both retarded intellectual functioning and retarded adaptive behavior would be classified as mentally retarded. (Adapted from the AAMD Manual on Terminology and Classification in Mental Retardation, 1973.)*

unitary or singular mental ability that was impervious to change. These definitions focused largely upon the retarded *adult's* intellectual deficiencies and inability to achieve social competence. Retardation was believed to be constitutional (physical) in origin and essentially incurable.

Seen from this perspective, the AAMD's succinct definition has significant implications. The diagnosis of mental retardation is limited to the description of present behavior rather than to estimates of untapped potential or predictions of future capability. Objective, individually administered tests of general intelligence are relied upon *in conjunction with* other sources of information. There is a developmental emphasis, in that diagnosis is tied to behavioral descriptions related to the norms of the individual's age group. Unlike earlier definitions, the AAMD definition does not insist upon a physical cause or upon incurability. Thus, on the basis of this definition, a child who is experiencing great academic difficulty, who scores low on an IQ test, and who is having difficulty adjusting to the school environment might be labeled retarded, even though there is no evidence of organic or constitutional impairment and no presumption of continued disability once he leaves the more stringent intellectual demands of the school setting.

Interestingly enough, the incidence of retardation seems to be directly related to age. The lowest incidence seems to occur among the very young and the very old, whereas the highest incidence occurs between the ages of five and nineteen (Scheerenberger, 1964). It would seem that the demands of preschool life are within the capabilities of nearly all children. Hence the mildly retarded are not easily identifiable at an early age. Similarly, the less verbal and less academically oriented demands of adult life are again within the capabilities of most individuals. Thus the mildly retarded adult is also not so readily identifiable. The incidence among adults is further reduced by the relatively high preadult mortality

rate among the more severely retarded. Apparently it is during the school years, when heavy emphasis is placed upon learning abstract academic skills and mastering complex verbal concepts, that even mild retardation becomes apparent.

Levels of Retardation

The AAMD manual describes four levels of retardation, each representing one standard deviation* (about 16 points) on the normal curve of the distribution of intelligence. The highest level to be judged retarded is two standard deviations below the mean (100 points). The approximate percentage of the retarded population and the estimated number of individuals who fall within each of the four levels are presented in Table 15.1. (A fifth level, called "borderline mental retardation" and representing those who fell between one and two standard deviations below the mean, was included in the AAMD's 1961 manual but was deleted from the 1973 edition. This indicates a significant change in the estimate of the potential for social adaptability on the part of persons of low intelligence.) The following description of the characteristics of each of the four levels of retardation is based on the work of Robinson and Robinson (1970).

Mild Mental Retardation (Binet IQ 52 to 67) Individuals in this category constitute nearly 90 percent of all people labeled retarded. Mildly retarded children are usually eligible for placement in special classes for the "educable" mentally retarded, yet only one in three is so placed. Their rate of progress is slower and their levels of achievement lower than a child of average intelligence, but with the help of a special curriculum, they are usually capable of

---

*A standard deviation is a statistical measure or distribution. Hence one standard deviation above or below the mean (average) includes 34 percent of the people, two standard deviations above or below average includes 48 percent of the people, or a normal (bell-shaped) curve—see Table 15.1.

Table 15.1 Incidence and Percent of Mental Retardation, by Levels (United States)

Level	IQ Obtained Stanford-Binet	Wechsler Scales	Percentage of Mentally Retarded	Estimated Number
Mild	67–52	69–55	89.0	5,340,000
Moderate	51–36	54–40	6.0	360,000
Severe	35–20	39–25*	3.5	200,000
Profound	19 and below	24 and below*	1.5	90,000

*Estimated scores.
Source: Adapted from the AAMD *Manual on Terminology and Classification in Mental Retardation* (1973) and based on percentages presented by the President's Committee on Mental Retardation, 1967.

learning basic academic skills. Mildly retarded adults are generally able to maintain themselves in the community through employment in relatively unskilled jobs, but they may need assistance in coping with social situations and in handling their financial affairs. Only about 1 percent of this group is institutionalized, usually because of behavior problems.

Moderate Mental Retardation (Binet IQ 36 to 51) Children who are classified as moderately retarded are eligible for placement in special classes for the "trainable" mentally retarded. These classes focus on the development of self-help and day-to-day living skills. Until recently, a sizable proportion of this group was institutionalized. But today, mod-

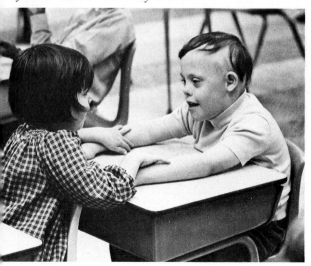

Fig. 15.2 Learning to get along with other people, to function socially, is an important part of the school years for the "educable" mentally retarded.

erately retarded adults are usually found living dependently within the family. Those who are employable generally work in family businesses or in *sheltered workshops*, places where simple work is done under supervision. Their social contacts tend to be limited. Most adults in this category have few friends, and marriage is rare.

Severe Mental Retardation (Binet IQ 20 to 35) Both children and adults in this category usually require constant supervision. These individuals exhibit very little independent behavior. Lethargy and apathy are common. (This may, however, be largely a result of an unstimulating environment.) Communication usually remains at the momentary and concrete level; such individuals talk very little and very simply. Those who are in the upper portion of this category may be able to benefit from placement in classes for the trainable mentally retarded, but most severely retarded individuals will not be helped by these special classes. Special programs are required for the teaching of language and self-help skills, and such instruction is a prolonged undertaking. Although often institutionalized, with self-help skills training an increasing number of the higher-level severely retarded are now able to remain at home with their families.

Profound Mental Retardation (Binet IQ below 20) These individuals usually cannot protect or care for themselves and require total supervision. Through the use of behavior-modification techniques, most profoundly retarded persons can be toilet-trained and taught to feed themselves. However, in some cases, physical or neurological damage will make this impossible. Although these people are by no means impervious to things around them, they seem unable to learn very much. Some

Fig. 15.3 Artwork of mentally retarded children reflects a level of intellectual development comparable to that of normal children who are chronologically several years younger. This drawing of a man on a horse was done by a twelve-year-old retarded boy with an IQ of 33. It indicates a developmental level comparable to that of a normal child in the age range of four to six years. As with other developmental stages and learning tasks, the retarded child goes through the same artistic stages and learns according to the same principles, but his pace is slower, his attention span is shorter, and his ultimate intellectual capacity is much more limited.

may learn to walk and to vocalize a greeting, but little other communication is apparent. Due to the increased incidence of organic impairment and increased susceptibility to disease, the preadult mortality rate is very high.

Systems of Classification

Throughout history, the mentally retarded were variously viewed as immoral, lazy, possessed, or unfortunates needing to be cared for. But in the 1850s, a more scientific approach to retardation began to develop. Along with new ideas about treatment came the need for a means of identifying and classifying types of retardation. From the outset, attempts to establish an effective classification system have led to confusion and controversy. Much of the confusion arose from the practice of dealing with causation and levels of function at the same

time. Today, however, the trend is to deal with these issues separately.

The AAMD manual, which is now the major influence on procedures and guidelines for the diagnosis of retardation, uses a dual system of classification. The two systems are complementary. The biomedical system focuses on physical disorders and is based on current medical findings and the individual's medical history; the functional system focuses on behavior and is based on assessments of current intellectual and adaptive functioning in comparison with age-appropriate norms for the general population.

Biomedical Classification System This system, which regards mental retardation as a manifestation of an underlying disease process or physical condition, is designed to distinguish groups according to demonstrated or presumed etiology. However, be-

LEVELS OF MENTAL RETARDATION

Degree of intellectual and adaptive deficiency

Mild	Can learn basic academic skills and, as adults, can usually be employed in simple jobs; very rarely institutionalized
Moderate	Can learn self-help skills and, as adults, can work under close guidance and supervision; social skills remain very limited
Severe	With prolonged training, can learn some language and self-help skills; generally apathetic, noncommunicative, and in need of constant supervision
Profound	May be taught, through behavior modification, to feed and toilet themselves; otherwise require total care; most never learn to walk or communicate verbally

cause this classification is based entirely on organic factors (i.e., excluding functional consideration), not all individuals in a particular group will be functioning at the same level. (Nor will all necessarily be retarded.) The biomedical classification system is divided into ten major groupings: (1) infections and intoxications, (2) trauma and physical agents, (3) metabolism and nutrition, (4) gross brain damage (postnatal), (5) unknown prenatal influence, (6) chromosomal abnormalities, (7) gestational disorders, (8) psychiatric disorders, (9) environmental influences, and (10) other conditions (AAMD, 1973). Within each group, there are a number of subgroups and specific syndromes. For example, phenylketonuria is a specific syndrome in the subgroup of amino acid disorders, which falls within the major grouping of metabolism and nutrition.

The biomedical system suffers from certain limitations. Although it is medically and statistically useful, it is of limited use in devising remedial instruction or in predicting who will benefit from which type of instruction.

Functional Classification System   This system is designed to distinguish between the four levels of functioning (mild, moderate, severe, and profound). It encompasses the two criteria for determining retardation: "sub-average general intellectual functioning" and "deficits in adaptive behavior."

Intellectual functioning is evaluated on the basis of performance on recognized tests of general intelligence.* These individually administered tests, based on well-established norms, are considered reasonably objective, reliable, and valid tools for estimating intellectual functioning.

Adaptive behavior includes performance in a wide range of areas: intellectual, affective, motivational, social, and motor. Because expectations of adaptive behavior vary with age, the nature and extent of deficits also vary with age. Therefore, different aspects of behavior are assessed at different ages. During infancy and early childhood, sensorimotor, language, self-help, and social skills are considered particularly significant. During the school years, skills essential to academic functioning and social interaction are emphasized. During adulthood, overall social adjustment as reflected in the individual's ability to support himself and conform to the standards of the community are of greatest interest. However, the instruments for measuring adaptive behavior are less precise and based on less well established behavioral norms than the measures of intellectual functioning, and therefore the estimates obtained are cruder.†

The functional system of classification also has its shortcomings. Although it is used to develop remedial programs, it is essentially a system of description and thus says little about cause. Other criticisms have been made: errors in measurement and in the administration of the tests may produce IQ score differences of up to 10 points. The most frequently used tests are thought to be biased in favor of middle-class children, a matter to which we shall return in Chapter 18. The functional system is particularly open to criticism in the area of measuring adaptive behavior. Because the instruments measuring adaptive behavior are not entirely satisfactory, classification often involves too great a reliance upon estimates of intellectual deficits—an imbalance which has been referred to as the "tyranny of the IQ."

Relationship of the Two Systems   The great majority of mildly retarded individuals exhibit no demonstrable evidence of brain injury or other organic anomalies. Thus a child functioning at this level might be culturally disadvantaged and educationally retarded. The incidence of brain damage, mongolism—which we shall discuss—and other pathological medical conditions is frequent among the moderately retarded. Either genetic disorders (e.g., phenylketonuria) or environmental trauma resulting in neurological damage (e.g., brain damage due to lead poisoning) are found in almost all severely retarded individuals. Among the profoundly retarded, the severity of neurological damage and physical deformity (e.g., blindness, deafness, and gross physical deformities caused by congenital infections) often result in confinement to a wheelchair or bed. Thus the lower the level of functioning, the higher the probability of demonstrable organic impairment.

ORGANIC FACTORS

In some cases, a particular biological factor can be identified as contributing to mental retardation. But the actual mechanism through which it operates to

---

*Tests of general intelligence include the Stanford-Binet, the Wechsler Scales (WPPSI, WISC, and WAIS), the Cattell Scale, the Kuhlmann-Binet, and the Bayley Infant Scale. See Chapter 18.

†However, rating scales such as the Vineland Social Maturity Scale and the AAMD Adaptive Behavior Scale have begun to lend some order and standardization to the measurement of adaptive behavior.

IDIOT SAVANTS

There have been reports over the years of the occurrence of very special abilities in individuals who are otherwise seriously retarded in their intellectual functioning. Some of the amazing feats performed include the ability to tell the day of the week of any date of any year, without looking at a calendar or using pencil and paper; the ability to repeat page after page of a phone book after a single reading; and demonstrations of remarkable musical talent. The presence of these abilities in the behavior of otherwise retarded individuals has been explained by the fact that the performance of these tasks requires no abstract reasoning ability.

David Viscott, a psychiatrist, has reported (1970) the history of a musical idiot savant, Harriet G., a forty-year-old woman who had been considered mentally retarded all her life. Harriet G. lived with and cared for her very demanding, invalid mother and worked in the kitchen of a large hospital, where she did her tasks faithfully, dependably, and unvaryingly. She came to Viscott's attention when, after an accident in which she broke her ankle, her carefully structured world fell apart; she subsequently became deluded and confused, and was thought to be suicidal. The story of her life and remarkable abilities unfolded during the course of her therapy.

While pregnant with Harriet, her mother, a music teacher, had observed a terrible accident. She thought her child would be defective as a result. After Harriet's birth, to protect her, she kept the infant with her during the music lessons she gave; the crib was placed next to the piano. When Harriet was seven months old, her father heard her humming an operatic aria, with perfect pitch, tempo, and phrasing. At three she played the piano. At seven she could read music and play the violin, trumpet, clarinet, and French horn. She did not speak at all, however, until she was almost seven, when a younger sister taught her.

Harriet showed other signs of what is known as idiot savantism. She memorized the telephone numbers of all the family's friends and her mother's students. Before she was seven she knew three hundred numbers and never made a mistake reciting them. She could give the date and weather report of any day of the past five years, and could repeat poems she hadn't heard since she was two. When Viscott met her she remembered the entire history of music in Boston for the past quarter of a century. Until her accident she had lived her quiet life of service in the hospital kitchen and at home; the only recreation she had known was playing the piano for a church choir and regular attendance at concerts and other musical occasions. After four years of psychotherapy, Viscott was able to help her to gain self-confidence and to return to her job and to musical activity.

It should be noted that although idiot savants have traditionally been considered mentally retarded, there is considerable evidence that points to their actually being autistic children. Harriet showed many of the signs of autism: aside from her lateness in talking, she banged her head repeatedly and spent much time rocking herself. Rimland, whose theories of autism were discussed in Chapter 13, considers idiot savantism a sign of autism.

produce the retardation is seldom understood. For example, most individuals with Down's syndrome (mongolism) have an extra chromosome, but the pathological action of that chromosome has not yet been clearly demonstrated. Furthermore, individuals may have the same medical diagnosis and yet very different levels of retardation. Mental retardation is not a single disease, syndrome, or symptom; its causes may be many and diverse. Finally, there is the problem of differential diagnosis. In the individual case, it is not always clear whether a diagnosis of retardation, autism, emotional disturbance, or learning disability is appropriate. All four may result in generally impaired or deficient behavior and development.

The AAMD manual, for example, lists more than a hundred distinct organic or genetic anomalies that are associated with retardation. Obviously, it is beyond the scope of this chapter to describe in detail all, or even most of, these diseases. Therefore, we will discuss only some of the more common and better-known syndromes in each of the five etiological categories: chromosomal anomalies, metabolic disturbances, congenital infections, toxins, and physical trauma.

Chromosomal Anomalies

Perhaps the best-known and the most common syndrome in the category of chromosomal anomalies is *mongolism*, or *Down's syndrome*. Its incidence is approximately 1 in every 700 births, and there are an estimated 65,000 Down's syndrome individuals in the United States today (Koch et al., 1971b). It was first described in 1886 by John Down, a British physician. He used the term "mongolism" to refer to the characteristic slanting eyes and flat nose of most individuals with this condition. Other common characteristics are a small, round head; an extra fold of skin on the upper eyelids; a small mouth with drooping corners; a thickened, protruding tongue; short, stubby fingers; poor muscle tone; and almost always mental retardation. (Most Down's syndrome individuals have IQs of 50 or less.) Of course, not all mongoloid individuals have all these characteristics. Furthermore, there appears to be no direct relationship between the number of physical characteristics and the level of retardation.

It was not until 1959, however, that the genetic basis of Down's syndrome was identified. The normal human cell has 23 pairs of chromosomes. But the French geneticist Jérôme Lejeune and his colleagues (1963) found that individuals with Down's syndrome have an extra chromosome in pair 21, or *trisomy 21* (see Fig. 15.4). In the normal production of sperm and ova, through a type of cell division called *meiosis*, each reproductive cell receives one chromosome from each of the 23 pairs. In trisomy 21, however, something goes wrong during the meiotic division of the ovum, and pair 21 does not divide (*nondisjunction*). If this ovum is fertilized, the fetus will have 47 chromosomes. The likelihood of nondisjunction seems to be directly related to the mother's age. That is, the older a woman is, the greater the chances that she will conceive a mongoloid child. For women age 29 or under, the chances are about 1 in every 3,000 births; but for women between the ages of 45 and 49, the chances are about 1 in 40 (Koch et al., 1971b).

Although children with Down's syndrome generally have a somewhat limited life span because they have a tendency to develop serious cardiac and respiratory disorders, modern medical care has increased the survival rate considerably. Today, if the mongoloid child survives his first few months, he has a good chance of living into adulthood.

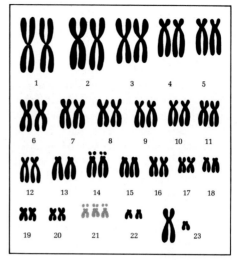

Fig. 15.4 *Mongolism is one of the few specifiable syndromes for which there is a known etiology. The chromosomes of a male mongoloid child are shown in the illustration above. In most cases the presence of an extra chromosome in the twenty-first pair is the causative factor of this abnormality. Sometimes the trisomy occurs in the twenty-second pair. The twenty-third pair is the normal male sex chromosomes. Mongoloid children characteristically have small skulls, slanting eyes with an extra fold of skin on the upper eyelids, small ears, and a flat nose and face. Many mongoloid children show an affectionate and passive disposition. Their intellectual development generally reaches an IQ level of 30 to 50, which is considered moderate retardation. Their tendency to develop physical disorders, including cardiac problems, makes their life span limited.*

Nondisjunction of the sex chromosomes (pair 23) results in a condition known as *Kleinfelter's syndrome*, which affects only males. Whereas the normal male has one X and one Y chromosome in pair 23, a male with Kleinfelter's syndrome has an extra X chromosome. An individual with this condition will have underdeveloped testes and is sterile. Although not all such persons are retarded, those who are, are usually mildly retarded.

Metabolic Disturbances

Another form of genetic defect results in metabolic disturbances. One of the best known is *phenylketonuria* (PKU), which occurs with a frequency of about 1 in every 10,000 to 15,000 live births (Melnyk and Koch, 1971). It is believed to be caused by a recessive defective gene. PKU children are unable to metabolize the amino acid phenylalanine because they are deficient in the liver enzyme phenylalanine 4-hydroxylase. This results in an accumulation of phenylalanine and its derivatives in the body, which in turn damages the developing central nervous system. The result is usually severe retardation, hyperactivity, and erratic and unpredictable behavior. Seizure disorders and severe eczema are also common. Fortunately, this disorder can be detected soon after birth. Many states now require the testing of newborn infants for PKU. A special low-phenylalanine diet during infancy and childhood (until about the age of six) appears promising in minimizing its deleterious effects (Koch et al., 1971a).

Another metabolic disorder is *Tay-Sachs disease*. This disorder, transmitted by a recessive gene, is a defect of the lipid metabolism marked by the absence of the enzyme hexosominidase A in the cerebral tissues. It is usually detected between the ages of four and eight months and is largely confined to children of northeastern European Jewish ancestry. It is characterized by progressive deterioration to the point of complete immobility, but with isolated episodes of convulsions. Under intensive hospital care, only 17 percent of afflicted infants survive beyond four years, and death is virtually certain before the age of six (Aronson and Volk, 1965).

Congenital Infections

Congenital infections are communicated to the fetus by the mother during pregnancy. Thus they are not inborn disorders; rather, they are contracted from the uterine environment. Two of the best-known diseases in this group are rubella and syphilis.

In the case of *rubella* (German measles), the frequency, type, and severity of abnormality are related to the stage of pregnancy during which the mother contracts the disease. The likelihood of recognized congenital anomalies is 50 percent if rubella is contracted during the first month of pregnancy, 22 percent during the second month, and 6 percent during the third month. However, if the infection occurs during the second or third trimester, the risk is considerably lower (Wright, 1971). Children affected by congenital rubella may be born with eye lesions, deafness, brain lesions, cardiac defects, jaundice, and bone lesions. Wright has speculated that retardation occurs when the rubella virus affects the development of brain cells, with the result that brain function is impaired.

Congenital syphilis produces a variety of abnormalities, including prematurity, rashes, pseudoparalysis of the limbs, and enlargement of the liver and spleen. The syphilis spirochete attacks the central nervous system, resulting in retardation; this may be accompanied by convulsions and hydrocephalus. Fortunately, because of compulsory premarital and prenatal blood tests and the availability of penicillin therapy, this form of retardation is uncommon today.

Toxins

Toxic substances either taken by the mother and communicated to the fetus during pregnancy or ingested by the child during infancy or childhood can cause organic damage associated with retardation. Lead poisoning resulting from ingestion of lead-based paints is one of the most common forms of poisoning associated with retardation. If ingestion is chronic, lead deposits accumulate in various tissues and interfere with brain-cell metabolism, resulting in permanent damage. Retardation is usually severe (Koch, 1971a).

Drugs taken by the mother during pregnancy may also result in malformation of the fetus. A recent example was the drug thalidomide, which produced retardation and/or severe limb malformation. Koch (1971a) points out that antidiabetic drugs may be dangerous and that quinine, taken to induce abortion when other means are not available, may, in unsuccessful attempts, produce deafness in the child.

Physical Trauma

Physical trauma of various sorts can result in brain damage. Two sources of such damage are anoxia (insufficient oxygen content of the blood) and head injuries. Anoxia may occur during childbirth as a result of inappropriately administered anesthesia, hypertension in the mother, prolonged labor, or rupture of the umbilical cord. Head injuries may occur when labor is too rapid because the infant's head compresses quickly and then reexpands too rapidly, rupturing capillaries and causing intercranial hemorrhaging. If a woman becomes exhausted by prolonged labor, forceps may be employed to facilitate delivery. Although low-forceps delivery (i.e., use of forceps low in the birth canal) may actually minimize the chances of birth injury, high- or mid-forceps delivery is a very delicate procedure that increases the chances of such injuries.

Brain damage may also be produced by a condition known as *hydrocephalus*, which is characterized by an overabundance of cerebrospinal fluid in the ventricles of the brain. This overabundance may result from obstruction of its normal flow or from inadequate absorption into the bloodstream. In either case, the ventricles become enlarged, causing pressure atrophy of the cortex—that is to say, the brain is actually slowly crushed between the expanding ventricles and the skull.

Other Anomalies

Several well-known medical anomalies associated with retardation do not fit well into any of these categories. One is the problem of Rh incompatibility. Approximately 85 percent of the population has Rh positive blood, which means that the Rh (Rhesus) factor is present. Problems may occur when an Rh negative (Rh factor absent) woman is carrying an Rh positive fetus. When some of the fetal blood enters the mother's bloodstream (through the placental membrane), the mother's system begins to produce antibodies. When small amounts of the antibodies are communicated to the fetus (again through the placental membrane), an antigen-antibody (or tissue rejection) reaction occurs. This can result in the destruction of red blood cells in the fetus. Brain damage may result from anoxia and the toxic effects of red blood cell destruction on nerve tissue. Fortunately, this condition can be identified by testing the mother's blood for antibodies, and the newborn child can be given a complete transfusion immediately (Koch and Dobson, 1971). And an even simpler way to prevent the problem has recently been discovered, in which the mother is treated with an injection of Rh antibodies (Glasser, 1976). There need no longer be children born mentally retarded because of Rh incompatibility.

Premature births are also associated with 15 to 20 percent of all cases of retardation (Koch, 1971b). Immaturity of certain organs (such as liver, kidneys, and lungs) increases the risks of brain damage in premature infants.

A congenital hormonal imbalance, specifically a thyroxine deficiency, causes *cretinism*, a condition marked by serious mental retardation and physical disabilities. If a pregnant woman's diet lacks iodine, or in the case of injury to the thyroid during birth, the thyroid gland of the fetus will be damaged. It may be partially or totally absent or present but defective. However, the extensive use of iodized salt has contributed to a very significant reduction in the incidence of cretinism, and when it does occur, if it is detected early (in the first year) and treated with thyroid extract, the child can be restored to normality.

Some Known Organic Causes of Mental Retardation

Chromosomal anomalies

Mongolism (Down's syndrome)
Kleinfelter's syndrome

Metabolic disturbances

Phenylketonuria (PKU)
Tay-Sachs disease

Congenital infections

Rubella (German measles)
Congenital syphilis

Toxins

Lead poisoning
Poisoning of fetus by drugs (e.g., thalidomide) taken by mother during pregnancy

Physical trauma

Anoxia or head injury during childbirth
Hydrocephalus

Other anomalies

Rh incompatibility
Cretinism (thyroxine deficiency)

ENVIRONMENTAL FACTORS

Among the mildly retarded (who constitute the majority of the retarded population), the contribution of organic factors is least clear, and it is here that environmental factors are believed to have their greatest impact.

The issue of cause and effect is crucial and as yet unresolved. Certainly, environmental variables can prevent the full development of intellectual abilities that may already have been limited by organic factors. But the degree to which environmental factors may be primarily responsible for intellectual deficits labeled retardation is less well understood. The available data on humans are almost totally correlational: that is, the factors were observed to occur together, but none were manipulated to determine what the effect of changing one would be on the other. Considerably more experimental data have been provided by animal studies, but these studies present the problem of generalizing findings from animals to human beings.

Attempts have been made to examine specific variables in order to gain a more accurate understanding of their relationship to retardation. But this area is so broad that statements about the effects of environmental factors must be considered only suggestive.

Cultural Deprivation

There has been much investigation and controversy surrounding the multifaceted factor called *cultural deprivation*. It consists of socioeconomic, political, cultural, and other variables that may affect intellectual and adaptive functioning. Poverty has been cited as a major factor affecting mental retardation (Robinson and Robinson, 1970), for the incidence of retardation increases rapidly at the lower end of the socioeconomic scale. Poor diet and malnutrition, particularly inadequate protein and vitamin intake, are common among the poor and have been linked to lowered intellectual functioning (Eichenwald and Fry, 1969). Inadequate medical care is associated with an increased incidence of prematurity, illnesses, and other medical problems related to retardation. Lead-based paint is common in the poor and older housing in poor neighborhoods, and lead poisoning caused by ingestion of chips of such paint can cause brain damage. The lack of adequate training and instruction frequently found in schools in poverty areas certainly aggravates the problem of deficient intellectual functioning.

Attitudes and social outlooks associated with socioeconomic status may well have an effect on intellectual development. Children from poverty families tend to show lower self-esteem, a greater degree of behavioral disturbances, and more difficulty in accepting personal responsibility than their middle-class contemporaries (Ausubel and Ausubel, 1963; Battle and Rotter, 1963). This would certainly interfere with the child's adjustment to school and thus could hinder intellectual growth. Positive attitudes toward school and the desire for and expectation of academic success are much more prevalent among middle-class than among lower-class children (Hieronymus, 1957).

These attitudinal differences are also found among adults and are reflected in child-rearing practices. Adults from poverty circumstances tend to have low expectations of success and a feeling that they are unable to have any impact on the world around them. This feeling of hopelessness extends to their children, whom the parents feel will not greatly be affected by anything they can do. Teachers, too, tend to expect less of these children; neither the child nor the teacher is motivated to try, so low achievement becomes a self-fulfilling prophecy (Rosenthal and Jacobson, 1966).

Language differences related to social class may also be a factor in the retardation of intellectual development, at least as it is reflected in IQ scores. Numerous studies have indicated that the language of children from lower socioeconomic backgrounds is less abstract than that of middle-class children (Deutsch, 1965). Jensen (1963) and John (1963) both found a much more limited use of language as a cognitive tool among lower-class children. Ausubel (1963) has suggested that a delay in the acquisition of certain language forms results in difficulty in making the transition from concrete to abstract thinking that is necessary for academic achievement.

Family Factors

The effects of family and child-rearing factors are of great interest. Severe abuse and neglect are clearly disruptive to development. For example, in the case of abuse, physical injury resulting in brain damage may well cause mental retardation. And in the case of neglect, malnutrition can have a detrimental effect on the development of the central nervous system (Eichenwald and Fry, 1969); the effect of emotional disturbances associated with child abuse and neglect is more indirect.

Other aspects of parenting have more subtle effects. The slower intellectual development noted in children of lower socioeconomic status is associated with parenting practices that considerably limit the amount and quality of verbal interaction between parents and child. One study showed that the parents of these children felt that talking to their infants was inappropriate or foolish (Tulkin and Kagan, 1972). There also is some evidence to indicate that parent training can improve the situation. Gordon (1969), for example, found that one- and two-year-old children whose parents participated in a training program outstripped control children in cognitive development. However, if the parents did not remain in the training program, the beneficial effects were lost, apparently because the parents ceased to apply what they had learned in the program.

Environmental Deprivation

The institutionalization or hospitalism phenomenon has been studied as a type of stimulation deprivation. It is of particular interest in its relationship to parenting patterns. The pioneering work in this area was done by René Spitz (1945). He found that whereas infants cared for by their mothers in the normal fashion developed at an average rate, children cared for in an institutional setting by professional nurses showed an average loss in developmental quotient from 124 to 72 within a year. In work done even earlier, Skeels and Dye (1938) found that the IQs of thirteen mentally retarded children increased an average of 27.5 points over two years after they had been moved from an overcrowded orphanage to living conditions where they were the center of attention. They also found that twelve average to dull-normal children left at the orphanage decreased in IQ by an average of 26.2 points during the same two years. Although there has been considerable debate over the meaning and methodology of both studies, more recent research has confirmed the possible negative impact of institutional living.

Much research has been done to determine what the effects of various types of deprivation might be. Studies on rats have shown that deprivation or lowering of general levels of stimulation results in adverse effects ranging from decreased problem-solving ability to fear of exploration to reduction in the size of the cortex of the brain (Hebb, 1947; DeNelsky and Dennenberg, 1967; Rosenzweig, 1966). In one study, animals with experimentally inflicted brain injuries were studied along with normal animals. Some animals were raised in an environment rich in stimulation, while others were raised in an environment lacking stimulation. Although the normal rats did better than the brain-injured animals within each group, the brain-injured raised in the "rich" environment did better than the normal animals raised in the "poor" environment (Schwartz, 1964). This shows the interaction of organic and environmental factors, at least in the rat.

Other studies have attempted to look at more specific types of deprivation. Using monkeys as subjects, Harlow (1964) and his co-workers studied social deprivation. They found that the most extreme form of social isolation (no contact whatever) led to

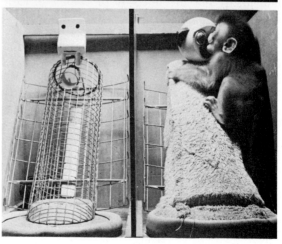

Fig. 15.5 Infant monkeys in the Harlow experiments on social deprivation. When a large and frightening toy bear was placed near a baby monkey (top), it ran to the cloth-covered surrogate mother for comfort (middle), then later (not shown) ventured out to explore the bear. The monkey remained fearful of the bear if it had only a wire mother (bottom left) rather than a cloth mother (bottom right) to cling to.

severe disruption in social behavior. If the isolation was maintained through the first twelve months of life, the animals showed severe lack of social and sexual behavior, and the deficits could not be completely remedied by later experience. Animals that remained isolated until the twenty-fourth month were totally deficient in social skills and were even unable to defend themselves. The longer the animals experienced social isolation, the greater the incidence of stereotyped, bizarre, and self-destructive behavior. Surprisingly, the socially deprived animals did not show a deficit when tested on a cognitive problem-solving task. However, they were much more difficult to test and showed comparable cognitive ability to the control group only under special optimal conditions. In general it seems that adequate stimulation in many areas is good for development and that deprivation can be harmful. But just what "adequate" means or what constitutes deprivation is far from clear.

ISSUES FOR THE FAMILY AND SOCIETY

In recent years, greater attention has been focused on the problem of mental retardation and on understanding and meeting the needs of the retarded and their families. More than ever before, the retarded individual is recognized as having the same needs and rights as any other member of society. It is becoming accepted that the retarded individual deserves to develop his or her innate potential to the fullest degree possible.

Impact on the Family and the Community

Parental Reactions Parents' reactions to the diagnosis that their child is mentally retarded are highly individual, and the intensity of responses varies widely, depending on such factors as individual personality, stability of the marriage, and socioeconomic status. Some reactions, however, are more prevalent than others: these include denial, intense disappointment, anger, and guilt. This is not the looked-forward-to child, the heir, the embodiment of hopes and dreams for the future. Parents may become ambivalent toward the child. They have the normal impulses to love and nurture this child, but at the same time they have feelings of anger, shame, and hopelessness (Schild, 1971). Frequently parents view the birth of a retarded child as a punishment for some action on their part (Kramm, 1963). Solnet and Stark (1961) have likened the emotions to the grief felt over the death of a child. However, as

Olshansky (1962) has observed, the parents of a retarded child suffer from chronic sorrow—a natural, normal response to a tragic fact. They must live with the daily burden of their child's prolonged and exhausting dependency.

Some parents find it difficult to accept the initial diagnosis and go from professional to professional, seeking additional opinions. This so-called shopping behavior is considered maladaptive because it costs them time, energy, and money. Inevitably, it disrupts the entire family and takes the parents' attention away from constructive efforts to work with their child (Anderson, 1971). Often, however, the professionals themselves contribute to shopping behavior. When parents have been given conflicting diagnoses, they will continue to shop for a definitive opinion (Anderson, 1971). The diagnostician may even intentionally withhold the truth from parents in the mistaken belief that this will spare them grief. Furthermore, as the retarded child grows and develops, he will have different needs and problems. Thus parents may not be shopping at all; they may be attempting to find services that will meet their child's new and changing needs.

One of the first problems parents must face is telling friends, neighbors, and relatives that the child is retarded. Negative and stigmatic attitudes about mental retardation are still prevalent. Mental abnormalities are looked upon with superstition and fear, and ignorance about them continues to be widespread, in spite of the fact that the problem of mental retardation affects a broad cross section of society. Thus clinicians give considerable attention to helping parents to communicate their situation to family and friends. They are advised to approach the problem honestly and calmly and to describe the child's handicap in the simplest terms possible (Murray, 1973; Champaign County Association for the Mentally Retarded, undated).

Special Child-Rearing Problems Current approaches favor an effort to care for the retarded (even the profoundly retarded) within the community. The family is encouraged to manage and rear the child at home. Parents who assume the responsibility for the day-to-day care of a retarded child inevitably have many questions about child-rearing techniques. Furthermore, the presence of a retarded child in the home puts new and different strains upon the family. If parents are to raise their retarded child at home, they must have supportive training and counseling. Therefore, professionals in the field of mental retardation are concentrating on teaching

Fig. 15.6 These photographs show scenes from the family life of Annie, a twelve-year-old mongoloid girl. During the day, Annie attends a school that specializes in the education of retarded children. At home, she handles chores and responsibilities suited to her capabilities. Annie has remained an integral part of the family structure and partakes in a full range of activities with her parents, siblings, and pets. As a result, she is an active, happy child. This type of integration with family and peers is necessary in order to alleviate the serious effects of unnecessary institutionalization and to counteract the misconceptions about retarded children.

parents the skills they will require to handle their child's needs and problems.

All too often the only professional advice parents receive is to "go home and treat him like a normal child." To some extent this is appropriate, because the retarded child has many of the same needs as a normal child: to be fed and kept warm and clean and dry; to be loved and cuddled and played with; to be given structure, discipline, and training in keeping with his abilities. Like the normal child, the retarded youngster must have social interaction with other children and with adults in order to develop interpersonal skills. He needs to be encouraged to be as independent as possible. But parents and professionals must realize that the retarded child does have special needs and problems. The child may suffer from physical handicaps. Learning will be slower, and achievement more limited. He may experience social rejection and be subjected to ridicule.

The retarded adolescent presents additional concerns to his family and his community. Parents must deal with some very sensitive issues and must walk a narrow line between the child's need for independence and his lack of normal adolescent maturity. They must help their child to deal with the physical changes he is undergoing, with sexual feelings, with threats to his self-esteem (an especially difficult task if he is aware of being "different"), and with interaction with members of the opposite sex and with a peer group that is increasingly outgrowing him. The extent to which these problems become an issue depends, of course, upon the young person's level of retardation. They are of greatest concern for parents of mildly and moderately retarded individuals.

Problems of the Retarded Adult   As the adolescent nears adulthood, his family and community must consider carefully the extent to which he will be able to live independently. Although parents may be confident of their ability to provide for their retarded child when he is small, they become uneasy when thinking about the stresses and demands placed upon the retarded adult. One of the most complex issues is that of sex and/or marriage.

Historically, attitudes toward the mentally retarded person's sexual development have favored complete desexualization, physically, intellectually, and emotionally (Perske, 1973). It was incorrectly believed that the mentally retarded had abnormal sex drives and feelings (were likely to be child molesters, oversexed, and the like). Any relationships between retarded men and women were discouraged, and involuntary sterilization was common. Today, a more humane approach is being taken. The trend is toward the belief that each retarded individual has the right to his own sexual development and that he can be taught sexual behavior appropriate to his level of functioning. Furthermore, state laws prohibiting marriage for the retarded and permitting sterilization without consent are being challenged (Krischef, 1972).

Many of the more severely retarded adults are not capable of a long-term relationship with a person of the opposite sex. But with proper guidance and supervision, many other retarded adults can have emotional and/or sexual relationships without

Fig. 15.7   *In contrast to the varied and more normal life of Annie, many of the mentally retarded are abandoned to a monotonous, depressing existence in an institution.*

destructive consequences such as promiscuity or unwanted pregnancies (Perske, 1973). Those who are able to maintain such a relationship should demonstrate a certain amount of self-sufficiency before contemplating marriage. Studies show that with some support and assistance from families or social agencies, many mildly retarded people are able to marry and maintain themselves as functioning units in society (Andron and Strum, 1973).

Another major concern is arranging for a living situation outside the home. At some point, it is likely that parents will no longer be able to care for their retarded child. A variety of solutions are available. The less retarded can be taught to live independently (Perske and Marquiss, 1973). Other alternatives being explored are group homes (Shapiro, 1973), foster homes (Justice et al., 1971), and sheltered workshops, many of which have residential facilities.

Society and the Mentally Retarded

Educational Programs The formation of parents' organizations has produced a strong surge of interest in providing the specialized services needed to maintain retarded people within the community. This movement was led by the National Association for Retarded Children (NARC), which was founded in 1950. By 1965, NARC had over 100,000 members and more than 1,000 local units in all fifty states. Many local units sponsored parent-run day-school programs for their children. As a result of the actions of parent groups and interested individuals, the public education systems have begun to take responsibility for these programs. Most states now provide classes for the mildly and moderately retarded (Koch and Dobson, 1971). A small but growing number of states have passed legislation requiring the public schools to provide educational services for all children, regardless of the extent of their mental handicap; in other states, class-action suits are being brought demanding such programs for all school-age children (Friedman, 1971).

Employment Most retarded adults enter the labor force. Although some need the closely supervised work and/or training programs of a sheltered workshop, many can be trained to join the regular work force. Employers are realizing that there are advantages to hiring properly trained and qualified retarded workers (President's Committee on Employment of the Handicapped, 1964). With on-the-job supervision, the retarded can function successfully, particularly in jobs calling for simple skills, repetitive tasks, few decisions, and established routines. Furthermore, in the past decade, there has been a noticeable increase in the numbers and types of occupations that are available to the qualified mentally retarded. They can work with the public or behind the scenes on farms and in shops, factories, offices, and restaurants as clerks, messengers, mechanics, stock clerks, painters, and so forth (President's Committee on Mental Retardation, 1969). In some factories, retarded workers are being taught to put together complicated electrical equipment.

It has long been assumed that, in spite of their

Fig. 15.8 Sheltered workshops are centers designed to teach a variety of vocational skills and tasks to mentally retarded persons. Some activities, such as the sorting task shown here, enable a person to learn an intellectual skill such as visual discrimination. A sheltered workshop setting helps many retarded persons to acquire a degree of self-sufficiency, from which they derive a sense of usefulness and a feeling of pride in a constructive accomplishment.

contributions in individual situations, mentally retarded people belong to America's socioeconomic surplus population, and that retarded workers are among the first to lose their jobs in times of general unemployment. More recent information suggests that things are changing. Studies show that properly placed retarded people make good workers and are consequently not necessarily the first to be fired when jobs become scarce (Halpern, 1973). And aside from the personal satisfaction that the retarded adult derives from a job, there are advantages to society as a whole in employing them. Instead of becoming a financial burden to society, the retarded adult will actually lessen the burden because some of his earnings will be paid to the community in the form of state and local taxes (President's Committee on Employment of the Handicapped, 1964).

Civil Rights Many personal freedoms and civil rights that "normal" Americans take for granted have been and to some extent still are denied to mentally retarded individuals. In the past, the retarded were often denied the right to education, the freedom to marry and have children, and the right to vote. They were committed to institutions without due process, and when institutionalized, were denied treatment and forced to work without pay. Today, the trend is toward the view that the mentally handicapped are entitled to the same rights as other members of society. Each individual is regarded as entitled to the greatest extent of his civil rights that his own particular limitations will allow.

Since the early 1970s, there has been a great deal of litigation focused primarily on three areas: the right to treatment, the right to education, and the freedom from involuntary servitude (Department of Social and Health Services, State of Washington, 1972). Lawyers are demanding the right of the mentally retarded criminal offender to due process rather than to an indeterminate sentence in an institution for the retarded. In addition, there is new emphasis on citizenship training that will enable retarded individuals to exercise their civil rights, such as the right to vote, knowledgeably (Olley and Fremouw, 1974; Gozali and Gonwa, 1973). Many individuals and groups are working together to see to it that the retarded will not continue to be treated as second-class citizens (Boggs, 1972).

TREATMENT AND PROGRAMING

Throughout history, a wide variety of approaches to treatment of the retarded have been tried, ranging from allowing the handicapped individual to die to

accepting him and supporting him in society. Early in the nineteenth century, experimental psychologists began to take a closer look at environmental effects on learning. Attempts at training retarded children were undertaken, and this stimulated the development of the first residential schools for the retarded.

Institutionalization

The movement for institutional care of the mentally retarded began in a spirit of great hope and optimism. Its founders did not envision great warehouses of human suffering and neglect. Rather, they believed that the retarded could be trained and returned to their homes and communities as more successful, contributing citizens. Edouard Seguin, the driving force behind the establishment of state and private training schools, saw these facilities as a link in the chain of common schools (1866). Optimism dwindled somewhat when it became apparent that not all students could return to the community. Around 1890, longer-term custodial care of the retarded became the major function of the state institutions (Fernald, 1893). Still, the emphasis was on training, on developing new ways of preparing the retarded for a more self-sufficient life, and on establishing new programs such as boarding out and special industries operated by the retarded—all of which, it was hoped, would lead to the return of greater numbers of the mentally handicapped to the community.

By the second decade of the twentieth century, the increased financial burden of a greatly enlarged institutional population, along with a devastatingly naïve notion of genetics, brought this hopeful era to a sad end. In 1912, Goddard published his study of the Kallikak family (see box, p. 395), in which he popularized the notion put forth earlier by Tregold and the British Royal Commission that at least 90 percent of all mental retardation was familial in origin. Consequently, it was believed that retardation was a problem of genetics and should be dealt with through segregation and sterilization. This in turn led to inadequate funding for facilities and programs. The resulting period of dismal custodial care is only now being ended in many parts of the country. In the 1960s, public awareness of the deplorable conditions in many institutions and the realization that the simplistic program of segregation was both inadequate and inhumane led to support for change in the area of institutional care. The widespread attention gained by the photo story *Christmas in Purgatory* (Blatt and Kaplor, 1966),

THE KALLIKAK FAMILY

Today it is recognized that the vast majority of the mentally retarded can learn enough skills to enable them to make an acceptable adjustment to society. However, this recognition is a fairly recent phenomenon. At the beginning of this century, in this country, Dr. Henry H. Goddard, the director of a school for what were then called "feeble-minded and backward children," published an account (1912) of his study of mental retardation, or "feeble-mindedness." Goddard's book remains on library shelves today, a reminder that in the not very distant past a respected member of the scientific community could publish and be acclaimed for a study which states that retardation is due entirely to "bad stock" and that the solution to the problem lies in "segregation through colonization" and, to prevent the birth of more "defectives," enforced sterilization of those already so labeled. In other words, round them up, sterilize them, and send them away.

Goddard's investigations were just getting started when an eight-year-old girl arrived at his school for "training"; she and her family provided most of his source material. He observed the progress of this little girl, whom he calls Deborah Kallikak, interviewed members of her family and people who knew them or had heard of them, studied old documents, and went over the Kallikak family tree back to colonial times. He stated his conclusions as follows:

How do we account for this kind of individual? The answer is in a word "Heredity,"—bad stock. We must recognize that the human family shows varying stocks or strains that are as marked and that breed as true as anything in plant or animal life. Formerly such a statement would have been a guess, an hypothesis. We submit . . . what seems to be conclusive evidence of its truth (p. 12).

Goddard defined the feeble-minded as those who are "wayward" and "get into all sorts of trouble and difficulties, sexually and otherwise" (p. 11). He pointed out a group of girls who "could not be made to stay in the homes that were found for them, nor to do reasonable and sensible things in these homes, which fact, of itself, pointed toward feeble-mindedness" (pp. 57–58). Alcoholism was another sure sign; in fact, Goddard felt that it "was the result of feeble-mindedness and that one way to reduce drunkenness is to first determine the mentally defective people" and then to remove them from the temptation to drink (p. 68).

Using these distinguishing characteristics as his diagnostic criteria, Goddard set out to present his "conclusive evidence." This was his version of the history of the Kallikak family, six generations of the descendants of Martin Kallikak, Sr., a soldier in the Revolutionary War who fathered two children, one by his "normal" legal wife and one by a nameless "feeble-minded girl." Among these many descendants Goddard identified a large group of mental defectives, all of whom fell on one side of the family tree, that which derived from Martin Kallikak's liaison with the nameless feeble-minded girl. Herein, according to Goddard, lay the proof that mental retardation was an inherited trait: "The striking fact of the enormous population of feeble-minded individuals in the descendants of [the feeble-minded girl] and the total absence of such in the descendants of [the legal wife] is conclusive on this point" (p. 53).

While Goddard pored over old records and interviewed neighbors in his quest for the cause of the Kallikaks' "feeble-mindedness," there was one rather striking aspect of their lives that he did not consider, except as further proof of their defectiveness: most of the descendants of the feeble-minded girl lived in abject poverty. Over the years a few children had escaped this grim existence; somehow their families were able to place them in better homes, with people who could feed, clothe, and educate them. The normalcy of these individuals Goddard ascribed to their being either "high-grade morons, who, to the untrained person, would seem . . . nearly normal" or illegitimate (p. 52). Actually it is the existence of these people throughout the family tree that disproves Goddard's thesis once and for all. These were children of hope and expectation; brought up with care and attention, their lives fulfilled a different prophecy.

which depicted the dehumanizing conditions in some institutions and contrasted them with what can be done in a modern treatment and rehabilitation center, is an example of the change in public attitude. More recently, Willowbrook, a New York state institution, was the subject of similar attention (see box, pp. 396–397).

There are about 200,000 residents in over 150 public institutions for the retarded; in addition, an estimated 10 percent of the residents of mental hospitals are mentally retarded (Butterfield, 1969). The care and programs provided in these facilities ranges from desperately inadequate to innovative and creative. Smaller training centers in or near the communities they serve are gaining favor over large, isolated institutions. Furthermore, the institution is seen as only a part of a broader range of services for the retarded. The residential program has its place in providing care and training, especially when it is not possible for the retarded individual to be cared for by his family or in a foster family. However, these programs must be viewed as they were by their originators: as places for training and enrichment through the use of methods leading to growth and development.

Education

One reason that the early training schools encountered difficulty in attempting to return retarded students to the community was the lack of community programs and services available for them. But in recent years, the expansion of programs has been extraordinary.

This expansion began with the extension of the principle of universal public education to the mild and moderately retarded. Children termed *educable* have been provided with special classrooms and programs at both the elementary and the secondary levels. Classes are smaller, and there is increased teacher-student contact to facilitate learning. Acquisition of the skills and information necessary for independent or semi-independent living is stressed, and there is less concentration on some of the more formal academic subjects. Many feel that these programs have provided new opportunities for children who would otherwise have been lost in the shuffle; others are concerned over evidence that similar children who remain in regular classrooms make greater academic gains. However, the special-education students appear to achieve better social and personal adjustment than the children who remain in regular classes (Blackman and Sparks, 1965).

WILLOWBROOK:

What happens to a mentally retarded child in a state institution? Little good and much harm, according to recent reports. In 1972 Geraldo Rivera of ABC-TV did a series of newscasts on Willowbrook State School for the Mentally Retarded in New York. The following was what he found.

In 1972 Willowbrook, the largest institution for the mentally retarded in the world, housed 5,300 patients. According to Dr. Mike Wilkins, a former employee at Willowbrook, the sanitary conditions on the wards were so bad that 100 percent of the patients contracted hepatitis within their first six months in the institution. Furthermore, because there were not enough attendants to feed the patients properly, many of them got food lodged in their lungs, which resulted in pneumonia, the major cause of death at Willowbrook. The mortality rate was either three to four children per week (according to Dr. Wilkins), or three to four children per month (according to the school's administration).

Only 20 percent of the children at Willowbrook took part in any rehabilitative training. The rest tended to simply lie about—often naked, often smeared with their own excrement—moaning ceaselessly. Many of these children were given major tranquilizers daily. As it was explained to Rivera, a ward filled with sixty or seventy undrugged children would be too much for the attendants. No wonder, since at the time of Rivera's report, the patient-attendant ratio at Willowbrook was 30 or 40 to 1. For working in these wards, attendants were paid an average of $115.38 per week. Their turnover rate was 50 per month.

Rivera describes his first glimpse of Willowbrook:

Public school programs for the more severely retarded are a more recent development. There are an increasing number of programs for children termed *trainable*. These programs teach self-care and practical living skills to children who are moderately or severely retarded. These skills will help them to live in a supervised community-living situation (Lance, 1968). As they get older, the youngsters are taught prevocational skills that prepare them for work in sheltered workshops.

Day-care centers for the severely and profoundly

A Case Study in Institutional Neglect

When Dr. Wilkins slid back the heavy metal door of B Ward, building No. 6, the horrible smell of the place staggered me. It was so wretched that my first thought was that the air was poisonous and would kill me. I looked down to steady myself and I saw a freak: a grotesque caricature of a person, lying under a sink on an incredibly filthy tile floor in an incredibly filthy bathroom. It was wearing trousers, but they were pulled down around the ankles. It was skinny. It was twisted. It was lying in its own feces. And it wasn't alone. Sitting next to this thing was another freak. In a parody of human emotion, they were holding hands. They were making a noise. It was a wailing sound that I still hear and that I will never forget. I said out loud, but to nobody in particular, "My God, they're children" (1972, p. 3).

Why, then, would parents place their children in an institution such as Willowbrook? To begin with, 80 percent of the children at Willowbrook in 1972 came from poor families, families unable to afford more humane private institutions. As for keeping the retarded child at home, it is the rare family that can manage this. The time, the emotional investment, and the physical strain of caring for a retarded child (or adult) on a 24-hour-per-day basis add up to a staggering burden. Thus without the help of community programs, families with retarded children are faced with an all-or-nothing choice. Either they shoulder, alone, the immense responsibility of caring for the child, or, as is usually the case, they send him away to an institution such as Willowbrook.

Some states have begun to solve this problem by providing the needed community services—day-care centers, special nonresidential schools, work programs—where the retarded child can spend the day learning whatever skills he is capable of learning and then return home at night. At the same time the family receives counseling, comfort, and some relief from the total care of the child. Through such a program of community services, California was able in five years to cut in half the number of institutionalized retarded persons. At the present time in California, only the utterly untrainable child is institutionalized. Other states are slowly following California's example, on the theory that even the most average quality parental care is preferable to the treatment of the retarded in many of the state institutions.

And in fact New York, after Rivera's shocking television reports and the court intervention that followed, is also coming around. Despite its current fiscal crisis, the state is now offering a monthly allowance of $291 to any parent of a Willowbrook patient who will remove his child from the facility and care for him at home. In addition to the allowance, which is designed to cover the special needs (babysitters, medicine, etc.) of the retarded child, free day-care treatment or special schooling has been provided for any patient who returns to his community. Thus it is possible that many of the children who have been languishing for years in the dismal wards of Willowbrook may finally go home.

Sources: Geraldo Rivera, *Willowbrook: A Report on How It Is and Why It Doesn't Have to Be That Way.* New York: Vintage, 1972. "Stipend Offered to Parents of Willowbrook Children," *The New York Times,* January 17, 1976, p. 29.

retarded are the most recent development in services for the mentally handicapped, and they are still not available in all areas of the country. (These facilities are separate from the public school systems, although they are sometimes partially funded by the public schools.) Basic training in self-help skills such as toileting and feeding is provided to children previously thought untrainable. Additional services are available for those with other handicaps. These programs have demonstrated that even the most profoundly retarded children respond to the stimu-lation and care provided by a supportive environment. And they have made it possible for a larger percentage of the severely retarded to remain in their homes and communities (Murphy and Scheerenberger, 1967).

The basic service program for the more severely retarded adults has been the sheltered workshop. These workshops teach work habits and job skills. In many instances, there are also programs to increase the development of social and interpersonal skills. As a result of workshop training, some indi-

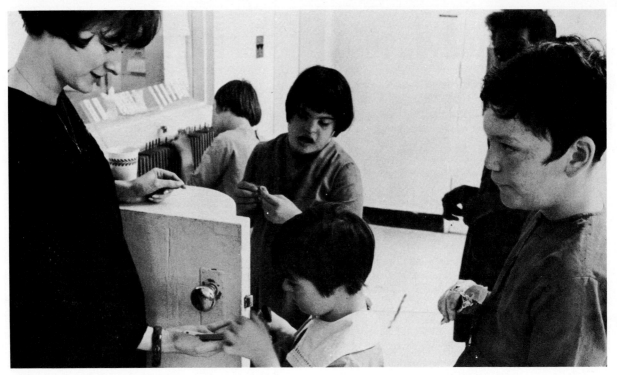

Fig. 15.9 In Mimosa Cottage at Parsons State Hospital and Training Center, Parsons, Kansas, mentally retarded girls are educated and trained in a setting that is based on a token economy. The girls are in the IQ range of 25 to 55 and are between the ages of eight and twenty-one. Here girls are exchanging tokens they have earned for candy. The Mimosa Cottage program includes personal grooming, occupational skills, academic subjects, and improvement of social interaction. The ultimate aim is to train a girl until she can live and work outside an institution or, if that is impossible, to make her as self-sufficient and independent as possible within the institution. Occupational training is closely geared to the kind of job a girl will have; and training in social interaction includes sex education and instruction in dancing and conversation with boys. Such programs attempt to help a person develop his or her life as fully as possible; the "retarded" label is not interpreted as preventing certain aspects of life, but simply means that different methods are required to bring about personal development.

viduals are able to become part of the regular labor force. For those who cannot, the workshop offers a permanent job placement where they may feel the dignity of work and the satisfaction of contributing to their support and care (Cohen, 1966). Programs for very severely and profoundly retarded adults are just beginning to be developed. *Adult activities centers*, as they are often called, take over where the day-care centers leave off and continue training in the areas of self-care and socialization (Conover,

1967). Those who make sufficient progress move into a sheltered workshop. Also new are the community-living centers: smaller residential programs located in or near the community that the retarded adult comes from. In a homelike atmosphere, these facilities provide care and supervision as well as training in self-help, socialization, and daily-living skills.

Learning Theory

New and diversified programs and services for the retarded have created a need for new techniques and procedures in training and behavior management. Since the early 1960s, various researchers have demonstrated the usefulness of learning theory in filling this need. The technology of behavior modification, which utilizes such established principles as reinforcement, extinction, and modeling, has generated great enthusiasm in the field (Altman and Talkington, 1973). These techniques are being used extensively in the home, in schools and workshops, and in institutional settings. They have been used successfully in improving both general and specific behavior.

In recent years, methods for teaching behavior-modification techniques to parents of retarded children have developed rapidly. Parents are trained

Fig. 15.10 Aspects of a farm training school for mentally retarded children in Santa Cruz County, California, are depicted in these photographs. Learning plant care (top left) and how to operate a tractor (bottom left) are features of the program. An unscheduled event was the birth of a lamb (right), for which classes were interrupted. The school is operated by the Santa Cruz public school system and teaches academic subjects and personal grooming in addition to farming skills. As with the Mimosa Cottage project, pictured on the facing page, the aim is to enable retarded children to become self-sufficient and feel a sense of accomplishment in their efforts.

to teach their child a wide range of skills such as dressing, feeding, toileting, and speaking (Lance and Koch, 1973). Furthermore, studies have shown that when retarded children are given intensive preschool training, they are able to reach much higher levels of functional development. Therefore, parents are taught to devise and implement preschool educational programs in which their children learn to sit quietly in a chair, play appropriately with toys for short periods of time, imitate sounds and movements, and follow simple instructions (Freeman and Thompson, 1973). In addition, parents can learn to teach their children appropriate social behavior, such as cooperative play and interaction with persons of the opposite sex, and independent living skills, such as the use of money and the comprehension of street signs (Ray, 1974). Parents can also employ behavior-management techniques to decrease inappropriate behavior, such as temper tantrums, aggressiveness, and hyperactivity (Ray, 1974).

In the past, teachers had few practical methods for helping retarded children increase their social and academic skills (Neisworth and Smith, 1973). But today, behavior-management techniques give teachers concrete methods for improving both the personal and social behavior and the academic skills of their pupils. For example, token economies are used to teach appropriate social skills such as cooperative play, sitting and listening to the teacher, and waiting in lines. Token economies have also helped children learn to complete assignments, participate in class discussions, and so forth.

The technique is effective with retarded individuals in all age groups. It has been used successfully to control the disruptive or negative behavior of retarded children in nursery schools (Baker et al., 1972) and of retarded adolescents in high school special-education programs (Gardner, 1971). Token economies are also used extensively in vocational training programs for retarded adults. In sheltered workshops, they have been effective in improving job performance rates (Logan et al., 1971); in teaching work habits such as arriving on time, punching in and out, and taking breaks and lunch periods at appropriate times; and in improving social interaction.

For more severely retarded individuals, especially those confined to institutions, behavior-modification techniques are considered one of the few appropriate therapeutic approaches. They have been effective in teaching self-help skills (Colwell et al., 1973) and in decreasing hyperactivity (Whitman et al., 1971) and self-destructive behavior (Ausman et al., 1974). Token economies are frequently used on wards in institutions to improve the general level of functioning of the entire group (Bath and Smith, 1974).

As with most serious human problems, the problems involved in retardation outstrip the knowledge and resources currently available to provide solutions. Nevertheless, retardation is at present one of the most hopeful areas of abnormal psychology. The trend toward community- and family-based programs, along with the general upgrading of institutional care, is gradually bringing us toward the desired goal: the acceptance and treatment of the mentally retarded as fully *human* beings who simply think more slowly than the rest of us.

SUMMARY

Mental retardation—defined as deficient intellectual performance and adaptive behavior occurring in the developmental period—is a handicap borne by a vast number of Americans: 3 percent of the population. Of these retarded individuals 90 percent are classified as mildly retarded. The three remaining levels of retardation, in order of increasing severity and rarity, are moderate, severe, and profound retardation.

These groupings are designed to describe the functional status of the retardate: his intellectual, affective, social, and motor behavior. In addition to this functional classification, the retarded are also classified on a biomedical scale indicating demonstrable organic impairments. The two classification systems are related in that the lower the level of functioning, the higher the probability of clear organic dysfunction.

Organic factors commonly implicated in retardation are chromosomal anomalies (e.g., mongolism), metabolic disturbances (e.g., PKU), congenital infections (e.g., rubella), toxins (e.g., lead poisoning), and physical trauma (e.g., anoxia). Environmental factors—including cultural deprivation, neglect, and lack of environmental stimulation, all of which are more likely to affect the poor than the middle classes—are thought to contribute to retardation. But it is not yet known whether these factors are actually primary causes or whether they simply elicit and aggravate an organically caused condition.

Retardation causes problems not only for the individual afflicted with it, but also for his parents, who must deal with the disappointment of having produced a mentally handicapped child and with the difficulties of arranging for him an appropriate academic and social life. Likewise, the society is faced with the problems of providing adequate education and employment for the retarded and of seeing that they are protected from all-too-easy infringements of their civil rights.

Almost every retarded person can be taught self-help skills, and the majority can learn basic academic skills as well. At present, treatment is aimed at tapping this potential rather than allowing it to atrophy under custodial care. Accompanying this emphasis on education is a trend away from institutionalization. Family care and community-based programs—including special-education classes, day-care centers, and sheltered workshops—are now the favored approaches. And with the help of behavior-modification techniques, they are producing encouraging results.

VI The Developmental Disorders

Unlike a troubled adult, a child with psychological problems cannot seek help for himself. Often he cannot be helped at all without the consent and full cooperation of his family. If the child is autistic or schizophrenic, the chances of his being brought for treatment are good, if only because his behavior is so disturbing that the rest of his family finds it difficult to function without guidance. But a child with a developmental disorder—a milder, less dramatic disorder than a psychosis—is more easily ignored. For this reason, the vast majority of children suffering from developmental disorders tend to go untreated.

Before we examine the developmental disorders of childhood, the term "developmental" requires some explanation. To most people, the word "development" is linked with childhood. Properly speaking, however, the term refers to the entire process of growth and change through which we all progress from birth to death. Thus a developmental problem is not necessarily a problem of childhood, but rather any problem that is specific to a certain stage of life. Middle-aged people have developmental problems. So do the aged, as we shall see in Chapter 17.

Our present chapter will deal with the developmental disorders of childhood, which of all the kinds of developmental disorders have received the most intense study. There are two reasons for this special attention. First, the childhood developmental disorders are probably the most common of developmental disorders. The period from birth to the beginning of adolescence is a period of extremely rapid change. In this short span of approximately twelve years, the child learns to stand up, to walk, to speak, to manipulate objects in his environment, to feed himself, to establish toilet habits, to develop his cognitive skills (remembering, judging, planning, etc.), to control his aggressive drives, to deal in a civilized manner with other people, and so on—an endless list of developmental hurdles. Indeed, if a comparable set of demands were placed on adults, it would probably be the end of most of us. Because he is subject to these changes and stresses, however, the normal child can easily experience normal hitches in his development.

A second reason for the careful attention given to the developmental disorders of childhood is the belief that if these minor problems go untreated in childhood, they are likely to become major problems in later life. Although this notion has been disputed, it is still widely accepted and provides a central justification for the special emphasis placed on psychological disorders in children.

16 The Developmental Disorders of Childhood

In the present chapter we will first discuss the general issues surrounding the childhood developmental disorders: incidence, the definition of normal and abnormal, methods of classification, and the long-term consequences of childhood disorders. We will then describe the more common disorders, and finally, will examine the interpretations and treatments offered by the various perspectives.

CHILDHOOD DEVELOPMENTAL DISORDERS: GENERAL ISSUES

Incidence

A recent report by the President's Joint Commission on the Mental Health of Children (1970) confirms the widespread belief that the incidence of serious emotional difficulties among children in this country is alarmingly high. The report estimates that 8 to 10 percent of all children have difficulties serious enough to be diagnosed as neurotic; that an additional 2 to 3 percent are severely disturbed; and that over one-half of 1 percent are clearly psychotic.

When do the troubles begin? And are there any particularly problematic ages? A summary of information on children terminating treatment in mental health clinics in 1961 provides some answers to these questions. Admission rates begin to increase gradually at about age six or seven—a phenomenon that most professionals interpret as indicating that early problems may not be detected until the child begins to attend school and that the added stress of school itself may intensify other problems. Thereafter, there are two age periods when clinic admission peaks. The first is nine to ten years of age; the second, in which clinic admission is even higher, is fourteen to fifteen years of age (Rosen et al., 1964). (Although this pattern holds true for children of both sexes, in every age group the clinic admission rates for boys are higher—sometimes two or three times higher—than for girls.) The reasons for the early peak at nine to ten years of age are obscure. Perhaps, as some theorists suggest, developmental stresses and environmental demands, particularly in school, are especially burdensome at this age. The even higher peak at ages fourteen and fifteen probably has to do with the fact that at this age normal developmental problems are coupled with the incipient difficulties of adolescence. The child is now no longer quite a child; physically, he is able to act on his sexual and aggressive drives. If he does act on them, he may get into trouble with authorities, who now hold him more responsible for his behavior. (Boys are generally more likely to act on these impulses and are therefore more likely to be referred for treatment as "behavior problems.") If the child does not act on these impulses, he may still experience a great deal of conflict, which will show up in other problem behaviors.

Fig. 16.1 *The development of a child's personality is greatly influenced by his family environment—the presence or absence of such factors as love, support, security, discipline. There are so many things that a child must learn during the years between birth and adolescence that even a normal child will probably experience periods of stress; sometimes the family will be able to provide the extra support needed. Sometimes, however, the child will show some of what are called "developmental disorders."* (Family Group, *Henry Moore; Collection, Museum of Modern Art, New York; A. Conger Goodyear Fund.*)

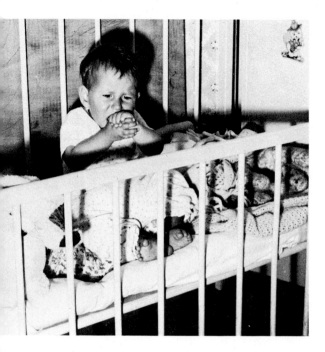

Fig. 16.2 For some infants, the absence of a parent or the disruption of a secure relationship can lead to strong feelings of loss, which can have a deep and lasting negative effect on emotional development.

Normal and Abnormal

Whatever figures we choose to consult on the incidence of childhood developmental disorders, these figures must be regarded with some skepticism, as it is impossible to define clearly the difference between normal and abnormal difficulties in childhood. At some point during their development, many children bite their nails, develop tics, or have nightmares, often in reaction to normal developmental stress. Whether their behavior is regarded as normal or abnormal usually has a great deal more to do with the attitude of parents, teachers, and physicians than with the problematic behavior itself. Moreover, what is considered normal or abnormal is in part influenced by cultural norms, which change over time. For example, masturbation, once widely considered a dangerous sign of moral degeneration, is now more generally accepted as a normal childhood behavior. Likewise, nail-biting, which most people now think of as a minor response to transient stress, has at various times been considered a "stigma of degeneration," an "exquisite psychopathic symptom," and "a sign of an unresolved Oedipus complex" (Kanner, 1960).

Then, too, behavior considered normal or of only limited importance at one age may be considered deviant at another. For example, irrational fears are quite common among children under six, but if a twelve-year-old is still afraid of the boogeyman and insists on sleeping with the light on, then this might have diagnostic significance. Likewise, the failure of a child to achieve normal developmental goals (speech, walking, etc.) at appropriate ages may in itself be considered abnormal. But where we place the outside limit for walking, developing speech, forgetting about the boogeyman, and other developmental achievements is once again to some degree a subjective diagnostic decision.

For all these reasons, normality and abnormality in childhood cannot be thought of as two clear-cut, mutually exclusive categories of behavior, but rather as two extremes, with most children falling somewhere in between. On such a continuum, where one draws the line between normal and abnormal is to some extent arbitrary.

Systems of Classification

There is substantial disagreement as to how childhood disorders should be classified, and accordingly, there are quite a few different classification systems. First, there are what we might call "theoretical" systems, diagnostic groupings based on a theory of childhood development. A good example of this type is the "developmental profile" proposed in 1965 by Anna Freud, Sigmund Freud's daughter and one of the foremost experts in the psychodynamic theory of childhood disorders. In the "developmental profile," the child is rated on a number of items described in terms of psychoanalytic theory: the status of his ego defenses and their adequacy for his age; the manner in which he handles sexual and aggressive drives; the psychosexual stage he has reached; and so on.

A second type of classification, which we might call the "descriptive" type, may be seen in the DSM-II grouping of childhood disorders or in a similar system devised by the Group for the Advancement of Psychiatry (GAP, 1966). Here problem behaviors that, according to clinicians, tend to occur together are grouped together as syndromes, and then each syndrome is given a name, such as "overanxious reaction of childhood." Such systems have the advantage of being the combined work of many clinicians. But since each category has to be acceptable to all these clinicians, innovative approaches to classification tend to be tabled in favor of more traditional approaches, which are more likely to satisfy everyone simply because they *are* traditional. It should be noted, however, that whereas DSM-I tended to ignore children altogether, DSM-II now includes a category entitled "Behavior Disorders of Childhood and Adolescence."

A newer and more sophisticated variation on the descriptive technique is the use of *factor analysis*, a computerized statistical method designed to isolate the common elements or factors that contribute to a complex behavior pattern. The hope on which factor analysis is based is that if the basic factors underlying various behavioral complexes could be identified, then we would be in a better position not only to classify childhood disorders but also—most important—to treat them.

The most promising application of factor analysis to the problem of describing childhood disorders is that of Achenbach (1966). Achenbach began by rating six hundred children, all of whom were receiving psychiatric treatment, on the presence or absence of a number of specific symptoms. These figures, once analyzed, produced a two-part grouping. In other words, the symptoms fell into two clusters, each of which correlated negatively with the other; a child who scored high on one cluster of symptoms scored low on the other.

Achenbach labeled one cluster "internalizing" and the other "externalizing." Children who scored high on the internalizing scale had symptoms indicative of internal conflict: phobias, frequent nausea, withdrawal tendencies, and so on. By contrast, children who scored high on the externalizing scale had symptoms indicative of conflict with the external world: stealing, lying, fighting, and so on. Achenbach's work suggests that there may be two mutually exclusive ways in which psychological problems are structured, one involving conflict with oneself and a second involving conflict with others.

All of these classification systems have their virtues and vices. Theoretical systems such as Anna Freud's rest, like all psychodynamic constructs, on untestable hypotheses. Descriptive systems such as DSM-II's often tell us very little and tend to be modeled far too closely on adult disorders. Factor-analysis systems such as Achenbach's look suspiciously simple. Yet there is little chance of our coming up with a foolproof classification system. The diagnosis of childhood disorders will probably always remain problematic, not only because diagnosticians are as likely to disagree about childhood disorders as they are about adult disorders, but also because children change so rapidly. Today's bed-

Fig. 16.3   Childhood fears are common, although children differ in the particular objects that they fear. Shown here are drawings by children of what they fear: (1) being chased by the mother and running to the father's car; (2) being chased by a police car; (3) someone "peeking" through the bedroom window; (4) a monster; (5) a snake; and (6) a dinosaur. Some fears (for example, being chased by mother) reflect a developmental stress or problem that the child is experiencing. Others may result from guilt concerning an act performed or fantasized. Certain fears occur with greater frequency than others.

wetter may be tomorrow's model child—or tomorrow's stutterer. Hence even the most solid diagnosis is likely to be undermined by the simple process of natural growth (Kessler, 1971).

The Long-Term Consequences of Childhood Disorders

As we have mentioned earlier, one of the reasons why childhood developmental disorders have received such wide attention is that most theorists believe that early problems are predictive of later problems. This notion has received support from numerous studies (e.g., Stennett, 1966; O'Neal and Robins, 1958). Thomas and his co-workers (1963) have even argued that children prone to psychological disturbances can be identified in infancy. The obvious conclusion of such studies is that every attention should be given to problem children so that their difficulties can be "nipped in the bud," thus avoiding more serious problems in adolescence and adulthood.

It should be noted, however, that these assumptions about the long-term consequences of childhood psychological problems have not gone unchallenged. Leavitt (1971), for example, has summarized several studies comparing children who had psychological problems but received no treatment with comparable children who did receive treatment. In 60 to 70 percent of the cases, the problem seemed to disappear regardless of whether or not it was treated.

However, there are a number of problems with this study. In the first place, as Leavitt himself points out, while a child may eventually stop his bed-wetting, he may engage in other related or unrelated problem behaviors later on—a fact that we have already noted. For example, it has long been accepted that the syndrome known as hyperkinesis (to be discussed later in this chapter) disappears in adolescence and thus may be said to be "cured." However, the learning problems associated with hyperkinesis generally continue to haunt the child throughout his later development. Thus when a specific problem disappears, there is still no reason to assume that the child is or will remain problem-free.

Furthermore, the disorders manifested by the children in the Leavitt study tended to be precisely those disorders—such as bed-wetting, nail-biting, fears, and temper tantrums—that *do* seem to run their course and then disappear, particularly if undue parental concern is not exhibited. And this fact may well account for the high improvement rates cited by Leavitt. Had he studied children with

Fig. 16.4   Life styles that depart from traditional nuclear family arrangements offer child-rearing conditions that are likely to have differing effects on personality development. Although there is little controlled data on child development in communal environments, such as American communes and Israeli kibbutzim, one possible outcome may be that the many parental figures available in such situations provide multiple sources of nurturance, guidance, identification, and affection.

problems such as encopresis (soiling), anxiety, and extreme aggressiveness—problems that tend either to persist or to be exchanged for more serious disturbances—his spontaneous improvement rates might well have been less impressive. In short, some childhood disturbances do seem to take care of themselves. Others do not, and therefore they merit professional attention.

SPECIFIC DEVELOPMENTAL DISORDERS

Having walked around our topic, we shall now examine the major childhood developmental disorders themselves, some of which extend into adolescence. We shall cover three types of disorder: habit disturbances, neurotic disturbances, and conduct disturbances.

Habit Disturbances

Among the most common developmental disorders are the *habit disturbances*—that is, disruptions of the child's most natural functions, such as eating, sleeping, and toileting.

Feeding Disturbances Since the time of Freud, feeding has been regarded as one of the most crucial aspects of development. Because the young child must depend on others for his food, his experiences during feeding will be a major influence on his future interpersonal relationships. For some, the taking in of food can come to symbolize being loved and cared for and thus can provide a foundation for loving and caring relationships. For others, the feeding situation may be fraught with anxiety and dissatisfaction, carried over from the parent-child relationship and carrying over in turn to other relationships.

Bulimia In *bulimia*, excessive overeating results in extreme obesity. Bulimia is a difficult diagnosis to apply, for what is "fat" to some is simply "substantial" to others. However, many investigators consider a child obese if his weight is 25 percent above the normal weight for children of the same sex, age, and height.

There is some dispute as to the relative importance of hereditary and physiological variables in cases of extreme obesity. Although constitutional predisposition may play some role, most professionals emphasize psychological and social factors as the primary determinants.

Bruch (1957), who is one of the leading theorists on obesity, distinguishes three different, though not mutually exclusive, categories of obesity. First, a child may become obese not because of any emotional problem, but because overeating is the "normal" thing to do in his family and in his ethnic group. Second, obesity may occur in response to some acute emotional stress (e.g., the death of a parent or the birth of a sibling), and in this case may function as a form of consolation and reassurance. Third, obesity may occur as a function of family problems, and especially of marital problems between the parents. When parents are in conflict with each other, they often attempt to satisfy their own needs through their children. The response of the mother, in particular, may be to overprotect and overfeed the child. As a result, the child becomes obese and maintains his obesity by overeating whenever he is subject to stress and frustration.

Regardless of its causes, this disorder, like so many of the other disorders that we will discuss in this chapter, has a snowball effect. A child who is obese (or who wets his pants in school or who stutters) is a child who is made fun of. Guilt, rejection, self-contempt, and exclusion from peer-group activities then become sources of further stress, causing the child to overeat (or wet his pants or stutter) even more than before.

Anorexia Nervosa Anorexia nervosa is a disorder involving the inability or refusal to eat, a situation that often leads to severe malnutrition and sometimes to death. As we have already discussed anorexia in Chapter 6, we will elaborate only by saying that while adolescent girls and young women seem most prone to anorexia, the disorder also appears in children, both male and female. (Even among children, however, female anorexics vastly outnumber males.) In the child as well as in the adolescent, the disorder often seems to function as the child's weapon in a power struggle with the parents, and particularly with the mother, who is forced to plead with the child to eat. And precisely because it so often appears to be a manifestation of family warfare, one of the popular current treatments for anorexia is family therapy, which we will discuss later in this chapter.

Pica A third feeding disturbance is pica, which takes its name from the Latin word "magpie," a bird reputed to have indiscriminate eating habits. *Pica* refers to a child's persistent and intentional ingestion of inedible substances past the age (one to two years) at which children usually can discriminate between edible and inedible substances. The child with pica tends to favor plaster, paint chips, clay, and charcoal, though he may also swallow paper clips, buttons, earrings, gravel—indeed, anything that he can get down his trachea.

The reason why pica is cause for serious concern is, of course, that grave physical harm may result from the ingested substances. This is especially true when a child eats paint chips, painted plaster, or any other substance coated with lead-based paint. Such habits can result in lead poisoning, which in turn can cause permanent and severe brain damage, and if the dose is sufficiently large, even death.

A number of studies (e.g., Cooper, 1957) have reported that black children and poor children seem particularly prone to pica. The reasons offered for these findings are many. Some investigators have proposed that poor nutrition and family disorganization, both of which are problems among the poor, contribute to the development of pica. Another possible factor is the simple matter of supervision. After all, children learn not to swallow inedible things mainly because they are told again and again not to. However, if a child receives inadequate supervision—as would be more likely in poor families, where mothers who are forced to work often lack decent child-care facilities—then he might never learn to take seriously the difference between edible and inedible substances.

Disturbances of Toilet Training   Like feeding, toilet training may be the arena of intense conflict. This is the first time that the child is forced to comply with demands that run counter to his natural impulses. And sometimes these demands can be extreme, for our society places a great deal of emphasis on the achieving of eliminative control at an early age.

Enuresis   The term *enuresis* is usually defined as a lack of bladder control past the age when such control is usually achieved. In this country the average child usually attains daytime control between the ages of two and three; nocturnal control is generally established about a year later. There are, however, great individual differences in the age at which control is achieved. When a child falls behind in his bladder control, the problem is usually nocturnal wetting—that is, bed-wetting. The inability to control daytime wetting is much less common and is usually considered more serious from a psychological point of view.

The incidence of enuresis is difficult to estimate, for at least two reasons. First, professionals have yet to agree on the age that separates late but essentially normal development of bladder control from an enuretic condition in need of treatment. Kanner (1957) suggests age three as the dividing line. Other theorists set it higher, although no one places it higher than age eight (Kessler, 1966). (It should be noted that whatever the cutoff age, enuresis is much more common in boys than in girls.)

A second difficulty in establishing the criteria for a diagnosis of enuresis concerns the frequency of wetting. If a six-year-old child wets his bed every two weeks or so, is he enuretic? Some would say yes; others would say no. However, the fact remains that many otherwise normal children wet their beds now and then. One study, for example, reports that 8 percent of all normal school-age children wet their beds more frequently than once a month (Lapouse and Monk, 1959). In view of such evidence, many professionals use a criterion of once a week or more in diagnosing the condition.

Enuresis can appear as either a chronic or a regressive condition. In *chronic enuresis*, bladder control has never been achieved. The child simply wets his pants whenever he has to, day or night. Typically, chronic enuresis lasts until middle childhood, but occasionally it extends into adolescence or even beyond. Some authorities (e.g., Bakwin and Bakwin, 1972) have suggested a hereditary basis for this condition.

In *regressive enuresis* bladder control has been achieved and is then abandoned. The loss of control is almost invariably precipitated by the onset of some stress in the child's life. The birth of a sibling, with the feelings of jealousy and insecurity that this often engenders, is probably the most common cause. Whether treated or not, such enuresis is usually transient. In this respect and in others, the following case is quite typical:

At the age of five, Jimmy, who had been successfully toilet-trained at age two and a half, began wetting his bed every night. At first his parents attempted to deal with the problem by alternately cajoling and punishing him, but their procedures only led to exasperation on their part and increased embarrassment on Jimmy's part. Finally they brought him to a guidance clinic.

Jimmy's mother could give no reason for the enuresis. Indeed, she described him as having been a "beautifully behaved" infant. Yet in exploring the history of Jimmy's sudden return to wetting, the therapist discovered that its onset roughly coincided with the birth of Jimmy's baby sister. Additional questioning revealed that Jimmy did not interact with his sister. In fact, he did his best to pretend that she did not exist. As the baby sister grew older, she slept less and became more active, thus making it more difficult for Jimmy to ignore her presence. Now, in addition to wetting his bed, Jimmy had adopted a number of other infantile behaviors. He sucked his thumb and refused to eat unless his mother fed him. Each night at bedtime he insisted on an elaborate ritual involving the tucking in of his covers; not surprisingly, they had to be tucked in just as his baby sister's were. He also appeared to demand more attention from his mother than he had previously, and he was often petulant.

Because all these behaviors seemed to reflect Jimmy's resentment of his sister and because they also gained for him a great deal of parental attention, the parents were advised to treat the enuresis in a matter-of-fact way and to give Jimmy more attention when the baby sister was out of the way. Within a few weeks, the enuresis diminished in frequency, and finally it disappeared altogether.

Whether enuresis actually constitutes a serious problem is a question that remains unresolved. Some (e.g., Tapia et al., 1960) argue that because enuresis is common and often occurs as an isolated behavior pattern, it is not necessarily indicative of a psychological problem. On the other hand, others (e.g., Kanner, 1957) report that seriously enuretic children often have other maladaptive behavior patterns and are generally immature. However, regardless of whether enuresis per se constitutes a serious problem, this disorder, like obesity, can *cause* serious problems. The child who wets his pants in school is likely to have a hard time of it with his schoolmates. He will be teased and rejected, and his self-esteem and social adjustment will suffer accordingly.

Encopresis Earlier we used "soiling"—that is, defecating in one's pants instead of in the toilet—as a synonym for "encopresis," but this is actually an oversimplification. In *encopresis* episodes of soiling generally alternate with periods during which feces are retained for an abnormally long time. Although we have little precise data on the incidence of encopresis, we do know that it is a much rarer condition than enuresis and, again, is much more common among males than females. Unlike wetting, soiling usually does not occur during sleep.

Like enuresis, some cases of encopresis may be due to neurological or anatomical abnormalities. However, most cases are thought to be psychogenic, and psychogenic encopresis is generally considered a much more serious problem than psychogenic en-

uresis. In the first place, from the psychological standpoint, encopresis is usually regarded as a definitely antisocial action and thus as indicative of serious psychological problems, while enuresis can be considered, and is often called, an "accident." Second, encopresis, whatever its cause, is a matter of substantial concern from a medical standpoint, since continual retention of feces can lead to impaction, whereby the stool becomes so dried out, hard, and large that defecation becomes extremely difficult. Hemorrhoids may result. Furthermore, when the stool is passed, it may stretch the anus sufficiently to produce skin lesions (Bakwin and Bakwin, 1972). In severe cases, surgical procedures may be necessary before the child can evacuate normally.

Sleep Disorders The sleep disorders occurring in children include somnambulism (Chapter 5), restless sleep, nightmares, night terrors, and other complaints associated with bedtime. With the exception of night terrors, adults are also prone to all these problems.

A *night terror*, which should not be confused with a nightmare, is a particularly harrowing variety of bad dream. When it occurs, generally during the early part of the night, the child shows marked physical changes (e.g., rapid breathing, escalated heartbeat, thrashing, and often somnambulism), usually talks in his sleep, and often screams as well. When awakened, he is confused, disoriented, and difficult to calm. He cannot seem to pull himself out of the dream and may, for example, go on yelling at the bear (or whatever) that is attacking him. What he remembers of his dream is usually confined to a single, overwhelmingly violent feeling or memory. Eventually, however, he goes back to sleep, and in the morning he has no memory of the episode. In contrast, a *nightmare* is the garden-variety "bad dream" (also called "anxiety dream" by professionals). Nightmares occur at any time during the night and involve much less dramatic physical responses and fewer and more subdued verbalizations. When awakened, the child soon becomes calm and lucid and often can relate a substantial narrative of his dream (Keith, 1975). He will recall not only the bear, but what color the bear was and what his cave looked like and how he (the brave child) fought back with a ray gun and so on.

All young children probably go through occasional periods of sleep disturbance. Moreover, bad dreams seem to be quite common at certain ages. Although some three-year-olds are troubled by bad dreams, as a rule they are easily reassured. By age four and a half or five, however, dreams are often a great source of anxiety for children. Children of this age often have nightmares about wild animals, monsters, robbers, and other strange figures who chase them or appear at the bedroom window. After age six, nightmares seem to decrease in frequency, though they often increase again at age nine.

It often is difficult to draw the line between pathological and normal sleep disturbances. In most children, sleep disturbances appear to represent normal and transient responses to stress. However, the child who is constantly plagued by sleep disturbances may have a serious problem. One study, for example, reports that children who consistently experienced nightmares, night terrors, or sleepwalking were more tense, fearful, and suggestible than a control group of children who did not (Anthony, 1959). Here one must wonder whether the tenseness of these children might not be the result rather than the cause of their sleep disturbances. But in any case, a child who suffers continually from sleep disturbances over a substantial period of time may be harboring fears that should be relieved through some form of therapy.

Tics and Motor Habits   Tics and motor habits are far from uncommon: they occur in about 15 percent of all children. *Tics* are involuntary, periodic movements of muscle groups, such as shoulder-shrugging, head-twisting, and grimacing. A distinction is normally made between transient tics and nontransient tics. A *transient tic* usually appears as the reaction of a high-strung child to a situational pressure; it tends to disappear quickly after the stressful period. In contrast, the *nontransient tic*, often interpreted as an indication of anxiety or other neurotic symptom, may persist for years; about 6 percent of nontransient tics seen in children actually continue into adulthood. However, such tics usually disappear or diminish considerably during adolescence (Bakwin and Bakwin, 1972).

Closely related to tics are *motor habits*, repetitive and nonfunctional patterns of motor behavior that seem to occur in response to stress. Among the most common are thumb-sucking and nail-biting.

Although *thumb-sucking* is extremely common in young children, it usually disappears completely by age five, while the majority of children abandon it much earlier. For a number of years parents went to great lengths to stop their children from thumbsucking. Taping mittens on the child's hands or applying a repulsive-tasting substance to his thumb

Fig. 16.5   *Nightmares are common sleep disturbances among children. The child can usually be comforted when he awakens from a frightening dream, but more frequent and extreme nightmares may lead the parents to seek treatment for the child.*

were two common stratagems. Today a much more relaxed attitude toward thumb-sucking prevails. The behavior is no longer considered harmful; rather, it is viewed as a source of gratification for the child in times of stress. Some theorists believe, however, that thumb-sucking in an older child reflects immaturity and that when it is engaged in to an extreme degree, it constitutes a neurotic symptom. For example, Kessler (1966) cites the case of an eleven-year-old girl whose finger-sucking was so extreme that it produced calluses on her fingers and wore down the enamel on her teeth. Apparently, this child felt that she had not been given enough affection by her mother. Thus the finger-sucking not only provided a substitute gratification but also represented an aggressive act against the mother by provoking parental guilt and concern.

Unlike thumb-sucking, *nail-biting* often continues into adolescence and even into adulthood. In fact, nail-biting actually increases with age. In children it is apparently most common between the ages of twelve and fourteen (MacFarlane et al., 1954). Like thumb-sucking, nail-biting provides the child with a means of reducing tension in situations involving stress. We know that the arousal produced by stress tends to generate physical activity. This phenomenon is apparently an evolutionary throwback to the time when "fight or flight" would have been the response most appropriate to the stress (Chapter 6). Since under most circumstances fighting or fleeing is no longer adaptive, motor activities provide a substitute way of reducing tension. Hence, in general, nail-biting is not thought to have serious psychological significance.

Disturbances of Speech   Despite the fact that there are many different types of speech disturbances, psychological disturbances appear to be implicated in only two of these conditions, delayed speech and stuttering.

Delayed Speech   Although the child to some extent comprehends speech before he can reproduce it, the average child says his first words within a few months after his first birthday. And between eighteen and twenty-four months, he usually begins to formulate two- or three-word sentences.

There are wide individual differences in this schedule, and a few months' delay in developing normal speech is rarely thought to have any diagnostic significance. Some normal children put off speaking for considerably longer than a few months;

Albert Einstein, for example, did not utter his first words until he was fully three years old. In most cases, however, a prolonged delay in speaking is taken very seriously as a possible indication of an organic or functional disorder. Organic problems that may interfere with the acquisition of normal speech include aphasia, deafness, mental retardation, and autism. As for functional causes of delayed speech, these may include a lack of encouragement or verbal stimulation from the parents, a trauma such as hospitalization or other long separation from the mother, or a discouragement of the child's independence on the part of the mother.

Stuttering   *Stuttering* refers to the interruption of speech fluency through blocked, prolonged, or repeated words, syllables, or sounds. Many people stutter on occasion, and speech hesitation in young children is a very common phenomenon, especially at the ages of two and a half, three and a half, and six. Thus, with the exception of extreme cases, it is sometimes difficult to draw the line between pathological and nonpathological stuttering. Estimates of the incidence of serious stuttering in children range from 1 to 3 percent (Kessler, 1966). This is yet another area in which boys far outnumber girls. Furthermore, in some cases stuttering appears to run in families.

Some theorists (e.g., Johnson, 1955) argue that parents who become extremely concerned about their child's speech hesitation and apply the label "stuttering" to this behavior may in fact cause him to become a stutterer. According to this theory, the parent's concern makes the child self-conscious and anxious about his speech; this anxiety in turn disrupts his speech performance; the disrupted speech in turn increases the anxiety; and this cycle continues until the stuttering becomes chronic.

Many children outgrow stuttering as their motor skills and confidence increase. Even those who do not outgrow it completely tend, as they develop, to stutter less or simply to confine their stuttering to stressful situations. It is estimated that as many as 80 percent of all children who stutter achieve fluent speech by late adolescence, while 40 percent overcome the problem before they start school (Sheehan and Martyn, 1970).

Although at one time organic theories of stuttering were quite popular, in recent years professionals have tended to regard the problem as psychologically based. Almost all theorists agree that anxiety plays a major role in generating, maintaining, and aggravating stuttering.

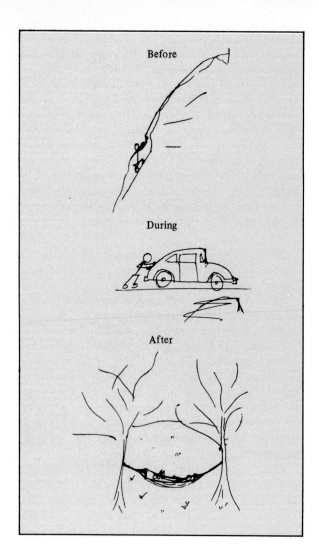

Before

During

After

Fig. 16.6 Speech disturbances can be incapacitating to the individual because of the prominent role that vocal communication plays in social development and interaction. Stuttering, for example, may involve chronic difficulty in speaking, and social conversation then becomes associated with anxiety and anticipation of failure. These drawings illustrate the ways in which a stutterer viewed her own speech disturbance. Attempting to speak is likened to climbing a mountain or pushing a car; completing the effort may bring a sense of relief and accomplishment. Anxiety is considered by most theorists to play a major role in stuttering problems.

Withdrawing Reaction and Overanxious Reaction While, as we have seen in Chapter 13, DSM-II classifies childhood schizophrenia under the same heading with the adult schizophrenias, the withdrawing reaction of childhood and the overanxious reaction of childhood are placed under "Behavior Disorders of Childhood and Adolescence" rather than under the general grouping of neuroses. The implication seems to be that these childhood problems are not as stable or as resistant to treatment as the term "neurosis" would suggest. However, these two reactions may be considered neurotic in two very fundamental respects. First, as we mentioned, they are produced by anxiety. And second, they in turn produce avoidance behavior. It is the way in which the child handles his anxiety that constitutes the major difference between the two syndromes.

In the child who is said to have an *overanxious reaction*, anxiety is overt and unmistakable. Such a child is overdependent, timid, shy, and extremely fearful in almost all new situations. Because he lacks self-confidence, he tends to conform and to seek constant approval and reassurance from others. Typically he is haunted by many groundless fears, along with nightmares and insomnia.

In school and in social situations, where he cannot receive the degree of support and individualized attention that he may get at home, the overanxious child becomes a victim of the familiar vicious cycle. Because he is anxious, he tends to give up in the face of even the smallest difficulties. This results in failure, which results in further anxiety, and so on.

Like the child with the overanxious reaction, the child with the *withdrawing reaction* is terribly anxious and excruciatingly shy. But instead of expressing his anxiety overtly and clinging to others for approval and comfort, the withdrawing child, as the term indicates, withdraws. He hides his anxiety and avoids close contact with others. And apparently

Neurotic Disturbances

Our discussion so far has been confined to the habit disturbances, circumscribed areas of troubled functioning which may result from anxiety or from any number of other causes. In contrast, the *neurotic disturbances* of childhood seem invariably to stem from anxiety and may in some cases engulf almost the entire repertoire of the child's behavior. (It should be noted that habit disturbances—enuresis, tics, night terrors, and so forth—may appear as part of a neurotic disturbance.) As we have seen in Chapter 5, neurotic anxiety in adults can involve specific unrealistic fears—that is, phobias—or a more vague and pervasive feeling of dread, with no specific focus. In children, as we shall see, the picture is largely the same.

Habit Disturbances of Childhood

Feeding disturbances	
Bulimia	Chronic overeating resulting in obesity
Anorexia nervosa	Inability or refusal to eat
Pica	Chronic ingestion of inedible substances
Toileting disturbances	
Enuresis	Failure to achieve bladder control (chronic enuresis) or loss of previously mastered bladder control (regressive enuresis)
Encopresis	Inappropriate bowel control, manifested in alternating periods of soiling and of prolonged retention of feces
Sleep disturbances	
Somnambulism	Sleepwalking
Night terrors	Particularly bad dreams occurring during the earliest stage of sleep; child talks and often screams, shows marked physical signs of anxiety, and remains terrified and disoriented upon awakening
Tics and motor habits	
Tics	Periodic involuntary movements of muscle groups
Thumb-sucking	
Nail-biting	
Speech disturbances	
Delayed speech	Prolonged failure to acquire speech
Stuttering	Interruption of speech fluency by blocked, prolonged, or repeated sounds

in an effort to block off the sources of his anxiety, he seems to shun the world as well, losing himself in a private world of fantasy and daydreams which he may eventually have trouble distinguishing from reality. Not surprisingly, in view of this detachment, he often does very poorly in school, though he may be quite intelligent. Most of all, however, the withdrawing child is noticeable as a social isolate. To his teacher and classmates, he is the "odd kid" in the back of the room.

Neither the withdrawing reaction nor the overanxious reaction appears to be uncommon. Though there are no definitive data on incidence, Jenkins (1969) reports that almost 20 percent of children referred for treatment are diagnosed as having either overanxious or withdrawing reactions.

Childhood Fears and Phobias Phobias—that is, morbid and unrealistic fears—have already been discussed in detail in Chapter 5. However, in distin-

guishing between adult and childhood phobias, we have to keep clearly in mind the word "unrealistic." When a six-foot-tall man runs in the other direction every time he sees an Irish setter, this may be said to be an unrealistic fear or a phobia. But when a three-foot-tall child manifests the same reaction to the Irish setter, this must be called a fear. After all, the dog is taller than the child; his bark is loud; his teeth are big. Children—all children—fear such things, and their response is in no way pathological.

The fears of the very young child tend to involve objects of this concrete type; dogs, loud noises, subway trains. However, as the child becomes older, sees more television, reads more comic books, and becomes more adept at imagining hypothetical situations, his fears tend to take on a more fantastic quality. An early survey of fears in children between the ages of five and twelve revealed that while concrete fears such as accidents and injury were still common, the two most frequently reported sources of fear in this age group were supernatural agents (e.g., ghosts, witches, boogeymen) and "spooky" situations (e.g., being alone in a dark, strange place) (Jersild et al., 1960).

When is a child's fear called a phobia? Generally, when the child becomes morbidly preoccupied with the source of the fear and begins arranging his activities so as to avoid it (Kessler, 1966). A good example, already cited in Chapter 5, is Freud's case of Little Hans, who would not leave the house for fear that he would encounter a horse. Such phobias are quite common in young children—so common, in fact, as to merit the term "normal neuroses" of early childhood. However, phobias that persist into later childhood merit professional attention.

One phobia that is particularly common and particularly troublesome is *school phobia,* one of the few childhood developmental disorders (along with anorexia nervosa) that is more common in girls than in boys. School phobia is taken seriously for the obvious reason: if the child misses too many days of school, he will fall behind academically. Typically, the school-phobic child expresses fear of some aspect of school (e.g., "the teacher is mean," or "the children don't like me") and bolsters his argument with a complaint of illness. Parents are often inconsistent in responding to this problem; at different times they may punish the child, plead with him, or bribe him to attend school. Interestingly, school phobia is very seldom related to achievement difficulties. In the following case, for example, there was no prior history of school difficulties:

When Vicky was eight, she started becoming nauseated each morning when it was time to go to school. After she had missed class for a week and seemed to be getting no better, the child was taken to her pediatrician. He found no physical basis for her complaints and referred her to a child guidance clinic.

At first Vicky would not speak about school. Finally, however, she admitted that she was afraid that if she left home for any length of time, her mother might abandon her. This fear of abandonment was quite intense. Indeed, during the initial interview, Vicky had to run out to the clinic waiting room twice to make sure that her mother was still there.

After several interviews with Vicky and her parents, it became clear that the child's conflict with school was being played out against the backdrop of a bitter marital conflict. The father had tried to involve Vicky in the marital problem by complaining to her about her mother and thus making the child his confidante. As a result of listening to these confidences, Vicky felt

Fig. 16.7   School phobias involve strong fears and dread about attending school. As in all phobias, approaching the situation creates anxiety that is reduced by avoidance; "staying away" is thus reinforced. The illustrations shown here were done by school-phobic children. The top picture was drawn by a young boy who had run away from elementary school and who was regarded by his teacher as a "manipulator." In discussing what he had drawn, the boy said that he did not like being separated from his classmates and working by himself. He also indicated that his teacher made him stay inside during recess and that she yelled at him. The bottom illustration was done by a fourth-grade girl who said that she was afraid to meet other children and that she felt alone. In her picture, she drew a girl with a smile (left), then said that she "wasn't like that," and made the smiling face a sad one.

Neurotic Disturbances of Childhood

Overanxious reaction	Overtly expressed anxiety, timidity, and overdependence; need for constant reassurance
Withdrawing reaction	Withdrawal from others and retreat into daydreams as an escape from anxiety
Phobia	Morbid preoccupation with a feared stimulus and curtailment of normal activities in order to avoid the stimulus

not only that the breakup of the family was imminent, but also that because she had listened to her father's complaints, she had betrayed her mother and would be punished by maternal desertion. Consequently, she had no intention of letting her mother out of her sight for any period of time—school or no school.

The therapist referred the parents to a marriage counselor but decided that the resolution of Vicky's school difficulties could not be postponed until after the complex marital problems were settled. Therefore, he insisted that after full reassurance that her mother would be there when she got home, Vicky should return to school as quickly as possible so that the absence from school would not generate new problems.

We should note here that not all therapists believe that a school-phobic child should return to school as soon as possible. Some advise that the child be allowed to stay home until there has been some resolution of the parent-child difficulties.

Conduct Disturbances

In a sense we can say that neurotic disturbances are analogous to Achenbach's internalizing symptoms, whereas conduct disturbances are analogous to externalizing ones. In contrast to the neurotic disturbances, which, as we have seen, typically involve anxiety and avoidance, *conduct disturbances* generally manifest themselves in disruptive, aggressive, and antisocial behaviors—that is, in the acting out of impulses that are normally suppressed. It is the child with the conduct disturbance who gets sent to the principal's office.

In DSM-II there are three classifications that would fall under the heading conduct disturbance: hyperkinetic reaction, unsocialized aggressive reaction, and group delinquency reaction.

Hyperkinetic Reaction The major symptoms of *hyperkinesis* (also called *hyperactivity*) are constant activity, restlessness, short attention span, distracti-bility, and fidgeting. Werry (1968a, b) has defined hyperkinesis as a chronic sustained level of motor activity that is a cause of complaint both at home and at school. The likelihood of such complaint is very good; even the most patient parent or teacher is eventually worn thin by a child who simply never sits still. Unable to tolerate even the smallest degree of frustration, the hyperkinetic child tends to engage in temper tantrums and other inappropriate displays of anger. He is also emotionally overresponsive and socially immature. As a result, his interpersonal relations are generally very fragile. In the area of schoolwork, matters become even worse. Indeed, it is usually in the classroom setting, with its demands for concentration and for restrained physical behavior, that the hyperkinetic child first becomes a source of concern. Aside from the simple facts that his attention span is minimal and that he can't sit still long enough to complete a task, his academic progress is impeded by multiple learning difficulties. His perceptual motor skills are typically poor; he may suffer from left-right confusion; and he usually has problems interpreting verbal and written language. The following is a typical case:

Robby first came to the attention of the school psychologist when he was eight. At that time he was in the third grade. His teacher, who was thoroughly exasperated with the child, complained, among other things, of his constant fidgeting, his messy handwriting, and his inability to complete his classwork. Despite his obvious intelligence, Robby had had difficulties since his first day at school. He was not able to work independently, or for that matter, in a group. At eight, he still had serious reading problems, and when writing or printing he often reversed letters in words.

At home Robby was highly irritable, aggressive, and explosive. If he asked his mother for something, he had to have it immediately; the slightest delay threw him into a rage. Robby's mother was frequently

Hyperactivity and Amphetamines

One of the major problems in our schools is the presence of children who constantly disrupt their classes and annoy their teachers and fellow students. At home these children wear out their parents and seem generally unable or unwilling to contain their actions or curtail their speech for any length of time. When worried parents bring these children to the attention of a doctor, more often than not the diagnosis will be some term such as "hyperactivity," "hyperkinesis," a "learning disability," or minimal brain dysfunction (MBD). And for from 500,000 to 1 million of these children, the treatment is drug therapy—specifically, the use of amphetamines. For those children who actually do suffer from MBD, the amphetamines are demonstrably helpful. Though the cause is still unknown, these drugs have a paradoxical effect: instead of stimulating these children, amphetamines suppress their hyperactivity, enabling them to function more normally.

In many instances, however, the hyperactive child may not be hyperactive at all—at least not neurologically or organically. Many people believe that this label and the subsequent drug therapy have become substitutes for parental control and teacher guidance. A child is no longer spanked or punished for misbehaving, no longer tutored or counseled for lack of concentration, but is labeled as hyperactive, learning-disabled, pre-delinquent, or any of many other such names. This places the blame for a child's lack of self-control on some obscure neurological condition for which no one can really be held responsible. In their book *The Myth of the Hyperactive Child* (1975), Schrag and Divoky give an example of this:

Shawn, a four-year-old, is brought to a suburban general practitioner by his mother, who has heard from several of her friends that the doctor is a strong advocate of Ritalin [a stimulating drug]. Her complaint is that Shawn is overactive and mean, and can't get along with his playmates. Even Shawn's brother and sister think he's mean, she explained tearfully. In addition, the boy wants everything right away and can't seem to wait for rewards. She said she found it almost impossible to love this child.

Medical records showed a history of a normal delivery, and a physical examination of the child revealed nothing unusual from a neurological or organic standpoint. The doctor then prescribed 10 milligrams of Ritalin twice daily. The mother reported back that the child was easier to get along with, but now he wanted to "talk, talk, talk." The doctor then cut the dosage to 5 milligrams three times daily, and this "decreased some of his loquaciousness." The mother told the doctor she "was delighted. . . . I can love this child again" (p. 70).

Though the side effects of the dosages of drugs given for hyperactivity seem to be minimal, there is no way of knowing just what will be the effect of the sustained use of drugs during a child's physical and emotional growing years.

But even if there is no long-term physical effect, there is one more unanswered question: How much does the use of these drugs help to solve the problem? Schrag and Divoky suggest that they are a temporary remedy:

In theory it is a temporary remedy, something to help "manage" a child and permit him to sit still and concentrate until the normal processes of maturation or the obvious rewards of good behavior enable him to develop other forms of control; such management, according to the rationale, prevents or mitigates academic failure, social ostracism and the resulting cycle of emotional problems. Increasingly, however, there are indications that chemotherapy may become indefinite, that it masks the problems, and that it simply defers, perhaps forever, the more permanent remedies. What is certain is that for roughly one of every ten children labeled "hyperactive" or "learning disabled," chemotherapy is the first line of "treatment," that their ranks have been growing at a phenomenal rate, and that for an increasing number, the temptation to extend medication indefinitely may be producing a new way of life (p. 71).

upset and angry because of his overactivity and his failure to meet her high standards. And her responses, in turn, led to more tense and overactive behavior on his part. Because he had always been aggressive socially, even as a very young child, he had few friends and rarely remained in a group for very long. In fact, Robby seemed able to play with other children only if he could make the rules.

The school psychologist found Robby's performance on the intelligence tests she had given him to be quite high. Robby was then referred to a psychiatrist, who prescribed daily medication as well as remedial help with certain visual-perceptual skills. Robby's parents were also counseled as to how they should respond to his hyperactive behavior. Soon afterwards Robby's performance began to change considerably. There was a great improvement in his ability to concentrate, and he began to advance rapidly in his schoolwork, particularly his reading, although he continued to have difficulties in writing (adapted from Davids, 1974, pp. 110–121).

Estimates of the incidence of hyperkinesis in the general population of children vary between 4 and 10 percent. As we stated earlier, hyperkinesis itself—that is, the virtually ceaseless motor activity—tends to disappear in adolescence, but the problems associated with this disturbance do not.

Unsocialized Aggressive Reaction and Group Delinquent Reaction The diagnostic approach to aggression tends to depend on the age of the child. For several reasons, the aggression of a young child is not taken as seriously in diagnostic terms as that of the older child. First is the simple matter of the consequences of aggression. A young child may have a furious temper tantrum—yelling, kicking, throwing things, and so on—yet the chances are that he will still do very little harm. In contrast, the aggression of a twelve-year-old, who is stronger and more ingenious, can have ruinous consequences; a twelve-year-old can commit murder. Second is the matter of socialization. The very young child has better

excuses for his aggression: his socialization is still in its early stages, and thus he has had fewer opportunities to learn alternative ways of dealing with his destructive impulses. In contrast, when an older child is consistently destructive, we can assume that his socialization has gone awry. In sum, the older the child, the more severe the psychiatric (and legal) response to his aggression. Accordingly, the syndromes described below would tend to be applied to preadolescents and adolescents rather than to younger children.

The characteristics ascribed to a child diagnosed as having an *unsocialized aggressive reaction* include destructiveness, hostile disobedience, cruelty, vindictiveness, displays of temper, and bullying. He may steal, lie, set fires, or be sexually aggressive. Such a child tends to come from an unstable family in which the parents are inconsistent in their dealings with each other and in their discipline of the children. One study reports that almost a third of clinic-referred children—most of them male—are diagnosed as having an unsocialized aggressive reaction (Jenkins, 1969).

A related conduct disturbance, again more common in males than in females, is *group delinquent reaction*—the label used to describe the child who belongs to a delinquent gang, who embraces the deviant value system and behavioral norms of the gang, and who tries to master the skills that its members hold in esteem. In the company of the gang, he may cut school, set fires, commit vandalism, steal, and engage in various acts of violence. Such a child is likely to come from a poor family. His delinquency is often a function of family negligence as well as exposure to delinquent influences outside the home.

Predictably, the child diagnosed as having an unsocialized aggressive reaction is more likely to have serious problems throughout his life than is the member of a delinquent gang. The distinction between the two is something akin to the distinction we drew in Chapter 8 between antisocial and dys-

Conduct Disturbances of Childhood

Hyperkinetic reaction	Distractibility, restlessness, and constant motor activity
Unsocialized aggressive reaction	Destructiveness, hostile disobedience, and cruelty
Group delinquent reaction	Destructive and other socially disapproved behavior carried on in concert with a gang and in conformity with the gang's deviant norms

social behavior. Whereas the group delinquent reaction is partly a function of loyalty and the desire to belong, the unsocialized aggressive reaction is not a response to social pressure. Rather, it resembles and seems to prefigure the random perversity of the adult sociopath, and it is likely to become a lifelong pattern. However, both types of reaction are cause for serious social concern. Whether in gangs or on their own, these children commit many crimes—a large percentage of them serious. Police records show that in 1973, in New York City alone, there were 94 arrests for murder, 181 for rape, and 4,449 for robbery in the under-16 age group (Morgan, 1975).

In general, regardless of the specific diagnosis, the prognosis for these children is poor. Serious aggressive and antisocial behavior in later childhood tends to increase rather than diminish (O'Neal and Robins, 1958), partly because of the aversive life circumstances that support such behavior and partly because of the inability of our legal and mental health institutions to deal effectively with the young offender.

PERSPECTIVES ON THE DEVELOPMENTAL DISORDERS OF CHILDHOOD

The Psychodynamic Perspective

Because of its emphasis on the childhood determinants of adult behavior, the psychodynamic perspective probably interests itself more than any other perspective in the developmental problems of childhood.

Cause   It may be said as a general rule that psychodynamic theorists interpret childhood developmental disorders as stemming from a conflict between, on the one hand, the child's sexual and aggressive impulses and, on the other hand, the prohibitions imposed by his parents and his own developing superego. For example, nightmares and night terrors may result when forbidden wishes, repressed during the waking hours, surface in the child's dreams. And this process can then give rise to insomnia, as the child refuses to go to sleep for fear that the unacceptable desire will once again be reenacted in his dreams.

Toileting problems may be interpreted according to the same formula. Encopresis, for example, is often seen as a disguised expression of hostility. If toilet training has been coercive, leading to a power struggle between the child and his parents, then instead of expressing his aggression directly—a response that would arouse too much anxiety—the child revenges himself upon his parents by withholding his feces (thus causing them worry) and then finally releasing his feces at inappropriate times and in inappropriate places (thus causing them annoyance, mess, and bother).

Enuresis, on the other hand, tends to be viewed as a sign of regression. For example, in Jimmy's case, cited above, the therapist would be very likely to assume that out of envy of the attention being lavished on the new baby, Jimmy simply regressed to the baby's level. By wetting, he was letting his parents know that he too required attention—as much attention as the unwelcome newcomer.

We have already mentioned in Chapter 6 the sexual connotations that psychodynamic theory attaches to anorexia nervosa in the young woman. According to some theorists, the same rule may apply to young girls. Here again, unacceptable wishes, particularly Oedipal wishes, may be at work. Desiring to possess her father and to become pregnant by him—and deathly afraid of this desire—the little girl may refuse to eat because the act of sending food down to her stomach is associated in her mind with the fear of oral impregnation. (For lack of better information, many children do believe that one becomes pregnant through the mouth. This misconception is associated with the fact that adults, in discussing pregnancy with a child, often say that Mrs. So-and-so has a "baby in her tummy"—that is, in the very same place where, as the child knows, the food goes.)

Forbidden wishes may also play a role in the development of childhood phobias. Once again, the most obvious example is Freud's case of Little Hans (Chapter 5), who because of his Oedipal desires for his mother feared castration by his father. But since this fear of his father was intolerable to him, he displaced it to horses and consequently developed a horse phobia.

While all these interpretations sound very much of a piece, we should keep in mind that psychodynamic theory is not monolithic. Different cases of a single disorder can be explained differently. Moreover, psychodynamic theorists may disagree among themselves about the etiology of a given case. Finally, they are not totally unreceptive to non-psychodynamic explanations. For example, they acknowledge that a phobia is sometimes generated by a single traumatic experience, uncomplicated by conflict, repression, displacement, and so on.

Treatment As we have seen, the preferred mode of psychodynamic treatment for adults is psychoanalysis or its less specialized form, psychotherapy. Through this therapy the patient relives and gains insight into his unconscious conflicts. In treating children, however, the therapist has to modify his analytic procedures in several ways.

The technique of Anna Freud (1965), who is the best-known exponent of child psychoanalysis, is probably closest to traditional adult psychoanalysis. Like adults, children are seen four or five times a week and engage in a verbal dialogue with the therapist. And as with adults, the therapist provides interpretations. For example, if a child commented, "You must see a lot of kids in this office," the therapist might respond, "Would you like to have me all to yourself?" On the other hand, the therapist is more active in helping the child to clarify his feelings and is more cautious in the use of interpretation. Furthermore, the child is given more warmth, support, and encouragement than an adult would receive. Finally, the therapist is likely to request sessions with the parents as well, to clarify his understanding of family interactions and to give advice on how the parents should respond to the child.

Other psychodynamic theorists, in treating children, go much further afield from traditional psychoanalysis. In informal sessions, often once or twice a week, the child is encouraged to solve his problems through symbolic fantasy. Rather than using interpretation to promote insight into past conflicts, such therapists instead emphasize the venting of the child's *immediate* conflicts. A very popular technique for this purpose is *play therapy*. Here symbolic play expressive of internal conflict takes the place of verbal expression, which is often more difficult for the child. Typically, the therapist's office looks something like a small-scale nursery schoolroom, with blocks, paints, clay, sand, and sinks with running water. Other essentials are toys for expressing aggression—toy guns, rubber darts, toy soldiers—and dolls and puppets for playacting family conflicts. (While such therapy is usually done individually, group play therapy has also been used with success [Slavson, 1952].) However, as the child reaches the age of ten or eleven, the therapist may shift to a more verbal form of therapy.

While such techniques are characteristic of the general psychodynamic treatment of children, we do not always find a one-to-one relationship between theoretical orientation and treatment method. To a large degree, the type of treatment depends on the type of problem. Freud herself (1968) notes that child analysis is suitable only for children with neuroses.

The Behaviorist Perspective

In treating children, as in treating adults, the behaviorist focuses directly on the problem behavior. Hence his major concerns are: (1) What environmental variables have conditioned this behavior? and (2) How can these variables be changed so that the behavior will change accordingly?

Cause Behaviorists believe that developmental disorders in children stem from either inadequate learning or inappropriate learning, concepts that have already been discussed in Chapter 3.

For example, inadequate learning—that is, a failure to learn relevant cues for performing desired behaviors—may play a role in chronic enuresis. According to behavioral theory, the child has simply failed to learn what cues are relevant to urination. And missing his cues, he of course botches the performance. Ross (1974) suggests that inadequate learning may also figure in regressive enuresis if the toileting is newly learned and has not yet been completely mastered. Since positive reinforcement such as praise from his mother may have helped the child to master the sequence, early removal of such positive reinforcement can lead swiftly to the extinction of the behavior. To counteract this process, external reinforcement (i.e., praise) should be resumed until internal reinforcers—pride in accomplishment, for example—are strong enough to maintain the newly developed sequence of responses.

Similarly, encopresis may be the result of inadequate learning. We have seen that bowel control involves both holding and releasing responses. Ross (1974) suggests that if parents use punishment in toilet training a child, he may overlearn the holding response in order to avoid punishment. Eventually, of course, he becomes constipated, and when he can no longer maintain control, he defecates involuntarily. In short, he becomes encopretic.

A number of other childhood problems are also interpreted as being the result of inadequate learning. Behaviorists believe, for example, that a child's failure to develop social skills may stem from the fact that he has never been reinforced for appropriate interaction with other children.

As for the development of problems through inappropriate learning—that is, the reinforcement of undesirable behavior—the behaviorist's prime example would be aggressive behavior. Ross (1974) suggests that aggression may be reinforced through positive or negative reinforcers. In the latter situation, the aggressive response has the effect of reducing the tension produced by anger and is therefore stamped in through negative reinforcement. If this process is supplemented by positive reinforcement (e.g., parental attention or peer-group approval) of aggression, then the aggressive response is even more likely to recur.

Modeling may provide another form of inappropriate learning. A classic study by Bandura and Walters (1963) found that parents who used physical punishment when their children behaved aggressively actually increased the frequency of aggressive behavior in their children. Apparently, the punishing parent provides the child with a model for aggression, so the child learns to behave aggressively himself when the parent is absent. Movies, television, comic books, and advertising may provide children with further models for aggressive behavior.

In Chapters 3 and 5 we have already discussed the importance of avoidance learning—combining negative reinforcement with the absence of any opportunity for extinction—in the development of phobias. According to behavioral theory, this sequence is as applicable to school phobia as to any other phobia. Furthermore, in the case of school phobia, the extra parental attention and special privileges associated with staying home may simply cement the aversion to school. And according to the behaviorists, this phobia-producing sequence of avoidance, negative reinforcement, lack of extinction, and secondary gains may become generalized enough to produce what are called the overanxious and withdrawing reactions of childhood.

Treatment In altering the child's reinforcement pattern to replace maladaptive with adaptive behaviors, the behaviorists use the entire behavior-modification repertoire: positive reinforcement, negative reinforcement, extinction, punishment (usually in the form of the withdrawal of rewards), shaping, modeling, and so on. To begin with the simplest technique, respondent conditioning, an excellent example of the use of this mechanism in curing developmental disorders is the Mowrer pad, which, as we have seen in Chapter 3, has been used with substantial success in the treatment of enuresis.

In treating anxiety-mediated disorders such as phobias and overanxious reactions, behaviorists have used systematic desensitization (Wolpe, 1958), in which, just as with adults, the child is taught relaxation or another response incompatible with anxiety all the while that he is being gradually ex-

posed to the situations that he fears, usually by imagining them at the therapist's request. A predecessor of this technique was Mary Cover Jones' famous desensitization of the boy Peter to his fear of furry animals by bringing a rabbit successively closer and closer to him while he was eating (Chapter 3).

Another technique that has proved successful with phobic children is *emotive imagery*, in which the child is asked to imagine a story involving his favorite heroes; then the therapist gradually incorporates the objects or situations that the child fears into the story (Lazarus and Abramovitz, 1962). Imagine, for example, that Stephen has a phobia for dogs. With the encouragement of the therapist, he begins making up his story. He, Stephen, has taken the place of Robin as Batman's sidekick. He and Batman ride around continually in the Batmobile, bringing culprits to justice. "But let's imagine that Batman has a dog, Growler," says the therapist. "Batman loves Growler very much and always brings him along in the Batmobile. Would you stay home if Growler came along?" Stephen reluctantly concedes that he would not. The adventures of Batman, Stephen, and now Growler continue. Then the therapist suggests that Growler might like to sit in the front seat of the Batmobile. Again Stephen concedes, to please Batman. "And would you pet Growler? Batman does," suggests the wily therapist. Stephen concedes that he might pet Growler. And so it goes. At times this procedure has proved more successful than systematic desensitization.

Modeling has also proved very valuable in the treatment of phobias. The child, for example, is given the opportunity to watch the therapist or another person play with a dog, handle a snake, or deal in a carefree manner with whatever it is that the child fears so intensely (Bandura et al., 1969).

Multifaceted operant conditioning programs are popular in the treatment of conduct disturbances. Patterson (1965) reports the successful use of operant techniques in a classroom setting to eliminate hyperactive behavior. His technique involves extinguishing problem behaviors, such as the distracting of one's schoolmates, while reinforcing more positive behaviors, such as remaining seated at one's desk long enough to finish a task.

Finally, one of the most effective therapeutic applications of operant principles is the token economy, a technique that we have already mentioned in earlier chapters. With children it is used just as with adults. Desirable behavior is rewarded with stars or points or some other token that the child can save and later exchange for candy, a turn with

Fig. 16.8 These drawings illustrate a behavioral method of treatment known as "emotive imagery," which was devised and reported by Lazarus and Abramovitz (1962). A young child, having been taught by his grandmother to fear the dangerous persons who inhabit the darkness, is afraid of being alone in the dark, especially in the bathroom. The therapist helps the child to be comfortable in the dark by teaching him to imagine himself on a secret mission with his heroes, Superman and Captain Silver. Because the child's absorption in the fantasy is incompatible with anxiety, therapy proves successful. This treatment technique is based on the assumption that anxiety is reduced if the individual makes a response to the feared stimulus, such as relaxation or assertion, that is incompatible with anxiety.

a special toy, a trip to the zoo, or some other coveted privilege or object. Tokens seem particularly suitable in working with children, since they provide almost immediate gratification.

Token systems have proved successful in institutions for delinquent children. Furthermore, O'Leary and his co-workers (1969) report that token systems can also work well in schoolroom settings. When used with children, the token system is usually supplemented with aversive techniques for extinguishing undesirable behavior. These include *time-out*, which involves the temporary removal of the child to an area lacking in reinforcing stimuli, and *response cost*, whereby the child has to give back tokens that he has earned.

The Humanistic-Existential Perspective

Although humanistic and existential clinicians have written relatively little on the specific psychological problems of the child, most of them, like the psychodynamic theorists, believe that the genesis of psychopathology lies in the experiences of childhood.

Cause   In explaining the evolution of psychological disorders, humanists and existentialists typically emphasize the loss of self-integrity in childhood. According to Rogers (1951), the child, in order to win social approval, denies or distorts aspects of his experience that are inconsistent with the perceptions of his parents and other people whose approval he values.

Moustakas (1959) appears to express a similar concept when he argues that a child's psychological difficulties are caused by the denial of his unique self. Both Rogers and Moustakas seem to agree that although the child's problems begin with the judgments of others, he comes to internalize these judgments and gradually restricts his own experience in order to live up to them. As Moustakas phrases it, the rejection of the child by others becomes the rejection of the child by himself.

Another concept that seems to have some bearing on this process is Laing's notion of mystification (1965). By *mystification*, Laing means a habitual mode of interaction between parent and child that causes the child to doubt the adequacy or legitimacy of his own thoughts, feelings, and perceptions. As described by Laing, these doubts appear much more profound and radical, in degree if not in kind, than those discussed by Rogers and Moustakas. This difference is perhaps due to the fact that Laing's primary concern is with the development of

schizophrenia, whereas Rogers and Moustakas concentrate on less serious disorders.

Treatment   According to the humanistic-existential perspective, the preferred mode of treatment for troubled children is play therapy. The major exponents of such treatment are Axline (1969) and Moustakas (1959).

At first glance, humanistically oriented play therapy resembles other forms of play therapy. However, there are subtle but important differences. Unlike the psychodynamic therapist, for whom play is the symbolic expression of unconscious fantasies, humanistic therapists such as Axline see the play itself as the therapy; the child uses his play to express his feelings and deal with his conflicts. Adapting Rogers' client-centered therapy to children, Axline argues that since the child has an innate drive for self-actualization, the therapist's role is simply to clarify feelings and to provide a positive relationship and conditions under which the child will be able to resolve his own problems. Unlike psychoanalytic play therapy, there is little interpretation of behavior. And beyond observing rudimentary safety limits, the child is free to do as he wishes.

Although Moustakas' approach is similar to Axline's, he emphasizes the relationship between patient and therapist even more than she does. One of his central contentions is that in the process of developing a relationship with his therapist, the child will clarify his problems and begin to tap his own creativity. This notion of the liberating value of the patient-therapist relationship is of course a very basic humanistic-existential idea.

The Interpersonal Perspective

In the view of Haley (1963), Satir (1967), and several other theorists, the family is a miniature social system in which each member plays a major role. Childhood developmental disorders, when seen within this frame of reference, take on an entirely different meaning. When a child develops a problem, the problem is interpreted as symptomatic of difficulties within the family as a unit. Indeed, it may be the child who has the symptoms, but it is the family that has the problem.

Consider the case of one highly intelligent boy of fourteen who was referred for treatment because he was doing very poorly in school. When the family was seen together, problems between the boy's mother and father soon became apparent. The mother repeatedly undercut the father, making invidious comparisons between him and his son. For

Humanistic Play Therapy

The following dialogue between Virginia Axline (1969) and a nine-year-old patient illustrates the two major goals of Axline's Rogerian brand of play therapy: to allow the child, through play, to externalize his conflicts and to mirror and clarify his feelings as they emerge. Richard, the patient in the following dialogue, lives in an institution. His parents are divorced, and his father has remarried. He is about to go on a home leave for his birthday, but instead of staying with his mother, whom he loves very much, he has been told that he will spend the two weeks of his leave at his aunt's house. As the dialogue begins, Richard and the therapist have been playing checkers:

Richard: (Suddenly he stops this game. He arranges the checkers as though for an ordinary game, then places a red king over in the left corner of the king row on the therapist's side of the board.) This is the little boy, see? He is lost. In fact his mother sent him away. She couldn't help it, see? There was no place for him and she had to work. *(Richard is very nervous. He moves his fingers quickly over the board and touches the checkers lightly.)*

Therapist: The little boy has been sent away from his mother.

Richard: This is the boy's father. This is his grandfather. This one here is the other mother that the father married. And this is his aunt. And this one *(the checker in the opposite corner from all the other checkers)* is the boy's mother. Now these people— *(He moves them out in between the boy and the mother.)* None of these people are going to let him get to his mother and this other mother won't let the father get to the boy and the boy cries, "Help! Help!" These soldiers hear him. They hurry out. They fight the father. The mother sneaks around this way. The father sneaks around that way. The other mother watches. Then— *(Richard sweeps the father clear off the board. He goes rolling across the floor.)* Oh, no, you don't! *(Richard is yelling now, very excited.)* The mother is getting closer. This other mother goes at her. They fight. *(He messes the checkers up. Then he sweeps all the checkers off the board. They roll in all directions.)* Mother! Mother! *(Richard is crying. He stands up and wipes his eyes.)*

Therapist: You want to be with your mother. The father and mother both want to help the boy, but the other mother won't let them get close enough.

Richard (nodding his head in agreement): Yes. That's it (pp. 122–123).

---

his part, the father was quite gruff with his wife. And despite his apparent concern about his son's academic difficulties, he continually made snide remarks about the uselessness of "book learning" and the effeminate qualities of "sissies with high marks."

Looked at from an interpersonal perspective, the boy's problems in school soon become understandable. The boy was caught in a struggle between his parents. He wanted to do well in order to please his mother. Yet by succeeding academically, he would become a sissy in his father's eyes and—worse yet— he would give his mother one more reason to prefer the boy to his father, thus further endangering the father-son relationship. Thus for the family therapist, the boy's underachievement is truly comprehensible (and treatable) only when viewed as a symptom of a family psychopathology. (This is not to suggest family therapists do not use psychodynamic and behavioral concepts. Likewise, psychodynamic and behavioral therapists in no way ignore family dynamics. On the contrary. However, rather than consider the present family interaction in its totality, the psychodynamic therapist would tend to concentrate on past experiences, including possible Oedipal conflicts, while the behavioral therapist would emphasize the reinforcement patterns of the one-to-one relationships between father and child and between mother and child rather than explore the complexity of the triangular interaction among the three family members.)

A developmental disorder that has been treated with some success through family therapy, and with less success through other therapies, is anorexia nervosa. Minuchin (1974) describes a typical family therapy interaction with a hospitalized anorexic teenaged girl. First the therapist allows both parents to try to get their daughter to eat. Inevitably they fail, and the therapist points out to them why, in terms of intrafamily struggles, the child is responding in this way. Then the therapist, who interprets the girl's refusal to eat as a fight for independence within the family, tells the patient she has triumphed over the parents and can savor that triumph, but that in order to stay alive she must eat. After a time this strategy begins to work; the patient begins eating surreptitiously. Once the patient is released from the hospital, the parents are instructed to use behavior-modification techniques at home. The girl must eat enough to gain a certain amount of weight each week. If she falls short of the goal, she must remain in bed.

At present, it is still unclear whether all childhood developmental disorders can be regarded as family disorders or whether some do in fact represent essentially individual problems. However, the family perspective does appear to be a promising one for conceptualizing and treating at least some disorders in childhood, especially those that seem clearly to originate in, or at least to be aggravated by, pathogenic family problems.

The Physiological Perspective

As we have mentioned earlier, it is thought that some childhood developmental disorders, such as chronic enuresis and encopresis, are physiological in origin. In fact, there are a number of hot disputes between somatogenic and psychogenic theorists in the area of childhood disorders. One of the most controversial of these etiological questions concerns the relationship between hyperkinesis and minimal brain damage (MBD). Wender (1971), along with a number of other theorists, points out that the behavior of hyperkinetic children resembles that of children suffering from neurological defects. He suggests that because drugs have so often been successful in suppressing hyperactivity, the problem is probably organic in origin.

On the other hand, critics of the MBD hypothesis charge that it is unjustifiable to infer brain damage solely on the basis of behavior. Furthermore, they point out that many children who are not hyperkinetic and who have no apparent brain damage manifest the same kinds of minor behavioral disturbances from which brain damage is inferred in hyperkinetic children.

We should mention that competing psychogenic theories of hyperkinesis have not gone uncriticized. For example, such theories do not seem able to account for the fact that although the psychological environments of some hyperkinetic children appear to be conducive to behavioral disturbance, many other hyperkinetic children (like many autistic and schizophrenic children) seem to come from fairly stable and loving families (Werry, 1968b).

The etiology of hyperkinesis remains an open question. Because of the increasing popularity of hyperkinesis as a diagnosis and because the syndrome is so often treated with drugs, the issue is likely to receive even more attention in future research.

SUMMARY

In this chapter we have examined the developmental disorders of childhood—that is, disorders related to processes of growth and change occurring during the years from birth to puberty and sometimes extending into adolescence as well. Childhood is important from a mental health standpoint not only because later problems may have their origin during the early years, but also because the rapid change that characterizes childhood itself seems to produce a number of transient disturbances. In fact, most children at one time or another develop minor problems. Thus in childhood the distinction between normal and abnormal behavior is even less clear-cut that it is in adulthood.

Developmental change also creates difficulties in formulating adequate classification systems for childhood disorders. Since symptoms may change with development while the problems that produced them may not, systems based on symptom description are particularly open to criticism. The DSM-II classification system, as well as those of Achenbach and Anna Freud, were briefly discussed.

Although there is still some question as to the long-term consequences of childhood disorders, the best available evidence suggests that serious problems in childhood tend to persist into later life, whereas minor disturbances seem to pass without further repercussions.

Developmental disorders of childhood can be grouped under three categories: habit disturbances, neurotic disturbances, and conduct disturbances.

Habit disturbances are those which involve disruption of some restricted area of the child's normal daily functioning. These include disturbances of feeding (bulimia, anorexia nervosa, and pica), of toilet training (enuresis and encopresis), and of speech (delayed speech and stuttering), as well as sleep disorders, tics, and motor habits such as thumb-sucking and nail-biting.

The neurotic disturbances of childhood, like those of adulthood, are more pervasive disorders, involving a high degree of anxiety that may manifest itself in very specific fears and phobias or in more generalized conditions such as withdrawing and overanxious reactions.

In the conduct disturbances, behaviors that are usually held in check are acted out in disruptive and/or aggressive behavior. Included in this category are hyperkinesis, unsocialized aggressive reaction, and group delinquent reaction.

Interpretations of childhood developmental disorders from the various perspectives range from unconscious conflict (the psychodynamic view) to inadequate or inappropriate learning (the behaviorist view) to the denial or distortion of the child's experience (the humanistic-existential view). In addition, the interpersonal perspective emphasizes the role of pathogenic family interactions, while the physiological perspective would implicate organic defects in a number of developmental disorders, particularly hyperkinesis, which, it is argued, may involve brain damage.

As we have pointed out in the preceding chapter, developmental disorders are in no way the special province of children. They may occur at any stage in a person's life, as a function of the stresses of that stage. However, there are two stages in which the pressures of changing life circumstances seem particularly numerous and intense, increasing the likelihood of developmental disorder. One of these two stages is childhood, which we have already discussed. The other is old age. When a child who has spent three years at home with his mother is suddenly dropped off at nursery school to play with strange toys and strange children in a strange room under the direction of a strange woman, this is a developmental stress. And as we have seen, the child may respond by becoming enuretic, stuttering, or manifesting some other developmental disorder. Likewise, when a seventy-five-year-old widow finds that she can no longer handle the upkeep of the house in which she has been living for the last fifty years and consequently is forced to move to a small apartment in a strange neighborhood, this too is a developmental stress. And the woman, like the child, may respond by showing signs of developmental disorder. Once settled in her new "efficiency" apartment, suddenly she doesn't hear as well as she did before; she can't seem to sleep through the night; she seems depressed. Her children might say that she is simply "growing old"—that is, undergoing a *natural* process—but there is no denying that *how* one grows old has everything to do with the stresses of aging. The greater the stresses, the greater the developmental problems.

Such problems merit considerably more attention than they have been given, particularly in view of the size of the population involved. Because of lower birth rates and higher life expectancies, America is graying at a rapid pace. In 1900, only one out of every twenty-five Americans was over 65. Today one out of every ten Americans falls into this age group. And if present trends continue, the over-65 population will simply become a larger and larger segment of the total citizenry. Thus whether we choose to acknowledge them or not, our society is faced with a whole new set of very serious social, medical, and psychological problems. In the Middle Ages, when the average life expectancy was around forty years, there was little reason to worry about the problems of the aged. But in today's America, when the average life expectancy is 71.3 years, there is little justification for ignoring the stresses faced by old people.

17
The Disorders of Aging

THE PHYSIOLOGICAL STRESSES OF AGING
Physical Appearance
Psychomotor Skills
Sensation and Perception
Intelligence
Organ Function and Illness

THE SOCIAL STRESSES OF AGING
Lack of Function
Poverty
Where to Live
Loneliness
Social Attitudes Toward the Aging

THE PSYCHOPATHOLOGY OF AGING
Anxiety
Depression
Case Histories

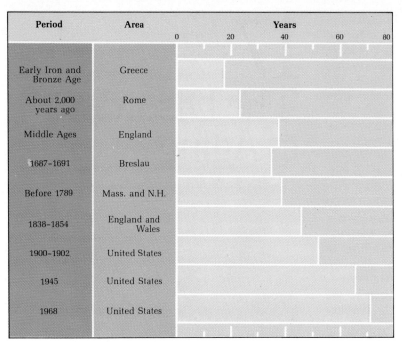

Period	Area	Years

Fig. 17.1 Man's average life span at different periods in history is illustrated in this chart. Only in the twentieth century have substantial numbers of persons in technologically advanced societies lived into their sixth decade. The presence of such persons and the conditions in which they find themselves thus create the issues that necessitate a consideration of aging and death in the study of psychopathology. (Data courtesy of Metropolitan Life Insurance Company.)

Just as most children make their way over the developmental hurdles of childhood without showing any serious symptoms, so thousands of old people manage the difficulties of aging with relative serenity and truly enjoy their later years. However, there are thousands of other old people who fall prey to what may be called the two major developmental disorders of the aging: depression and anxiety. And since our subject is abnormal psychology, it is with this latter group that our chapter will be concerned.

Our discussion is divided into three parts. The first two will cover the physiology and the social aspects of aging, the two major sources of developmental stress. In our final section we will examine the psychological disorders of the aging. (Our discussion will be limited to the functional disorders of the aged; the organic brain disorders associated with old age have been covered in Chapter 14.)

THE PHYSIOLOGICAL STRESSES OF AGING

In considering the physical problems of the aged, we must keep in mind the unity of mind and body—a matter already discussed in Chapter 6. When a depressed old man begins walking more slowly, is this because he is old or because he is depressed? In the case of many of the physiological changes that we will discuss in this section, there is no question that they are due in some part to the natural and inevitable process of physiological aging. Others of these changes are clearly due to psychological stress. In most cases, however, there appears to be a complex interaction of physiological and psychological causes.

In any case, numerous physiological changes—some severe, some mild—accompany the process of aging. We will briefly outline these changes and then indicate what they mean in terms of the individual's ability to cope.

Physical Appearance

Among the obvious physiological changes affecting the aged are modifications in external appearance. These changes are familiar to all of us; they are what allow us to identify a person as being old. In the first place, the old person's skin becomes less elastic. As a result, his facial expression tends to take on a different appearance; lines deepen and features sharpen as the skin and the tissue supporting it begin to sag. This process is not confined to the face. Indeed, the connective tissue covering the entire body loses its firmness and elasticity, and muscles tend to shrink while fatty tissue increases. Men may lose their hair; in women, height may be reduced as a function of lowered estrogen levels. Both men and women may begin losing teeth.

What all this means to the scientist is that a seventy-year-old looks different from a forty-year-old, who in turn looks different from a ten-year-old. What it means to the individual seventy-year-old, however, may be total catastrophe. This is particularly true in the case of women, as our society tends to equate a woman's value with her youthful physical appearance. However, men are not impervious to balding, as hairpiece manufacturers will gleefully testify. In general, more and more older people are dying their hair, buying toupees, getting face lifts. There is nothing wrong with these compensatory techniques in themselves, but their increasing popularity would seem to indicate a general panic on the part of the American people in the face of growing old. The message sent out by our cosmetics industries is that while it is fine for a ten-year-old to look ten, and for a forty-year-old to look forty, it is rather horrible for a seventy-year-old to look seventy. And this message constitutes a serious source of stress for those who take it to heart, as apparently thousands of Americans do. The individual may respond by doing nothing and simply feeling unhappy every time he looks in the mirror. Or he may, as the years pass, spend more and more of his time, energy, and money disguising his age—combing solutions into his hair and having his face lifted higher and higher, all in the effort to make it seem that his physiological development came to a halt at age forty-five. Whichever way he responds, chances are that his self-esteem will suffer.

Psychomotor Skills

Of all the physiological changes that affect the aging, perhaps the most characteristic is the tendency to slow down (Botwinick, 1967). Some investigators have argued that this slowness is mainly a *reactive* slowness due to reduced sensory input—that, for example, the reason the older driver hits the brakes more slowly is that he sees the stop sign later and more dimly than does the younger person. However, it appears that old people are equally slow in self-initiated behaviors. Indeed, it seems that all behavior mediated by the central nervous system slows down in the aging organism (Birren, 1974). This change is thought to be due to a process called *primary neural aging*, in which the transmission of electrical impulses in the nervous system becomes slower and less efficient because of loss of cells and because of physiological changes in nerve cells and nerve fibers. The central nervous system processes information more slowly, and consequently the organism reacts more slowly.

What does this mean in terms of the life of the old person? One thing it means is that he is more likely to have an automobile accident. (Indeed, while much furor has been raised over the frequency of accidents in the 16-to-17-year age group, the over-70 driver is more likely to have an accident.) It also means that when he goes on a hike with the family, he will always be bringing up the end, even if the rest of the group has slowed down to accommodate him. And how can the older person respond to these new conditions? One alternative—probably the one most often chosen—is simply to stop driving, to stay home when the family goes on an outing, and generally to curtail all demanding activities. But this of course increases the isolation of the aged person and decreases his sources of pleasure—in short, another potential source of stress.

Sensation and Perception

We have already mentioned the matter of reduced sensory input in the aged. The fact is that in old age, sensory receptivity may decline rapidly. This change is a function not only of primary neural aging but also of changes in the specialized anatomical structures on which sense perception depends. One such special structure, for example, is the lens of the eye, which often in the elderly loses transparency because cataracts develop.

Reduced sense perception can affect all five senses. However, by far the most common and the most crucial sensory impairments are those of sight and hearing. Visual acuity, the measure of the smallest object that can be discriminated by the observer, diminishes rapidly in many people after the age of fifty (Chapanis, 1950). Furthermore, the older person has greater difficulty in focusing his eyes and in adapting to darkness. As for hearing, the older person often begins to have difficulty hearing at many different sound frequency levels. Most importantly, there is reduction in hearing ability in the frequency range of 500 to 2,000 cycles per second, the frequency range of speech.

The ramifications are obvious. If the older person has trouble seeing, then a lifelong pleasure in reading may have to be abandoned. Worse yet are the stresses associated with hearing problems. Many of us have probably responded with mild amusement or annoyance in dealing with a slightly deaf older person. We ask our great-aunt a question and then have to repeat it three times. Finally we may get an answer that has no bearing whatsoever on our question. But how many of us have considered this problem from the point of view of the great-aunt, who is likely to be embarrassed and worn out by such an interchange and who finally, in desperation, hazards an interpretation that she is fully aware may be completely off the mark? Of all the physical changes involved in aging, hearing difficulties are probably the major cause of the social isolation from which so many old people suffer. When you have to ask a person to repeat again and again what he has said, and when at the same time you are aware that the other person may be nearly shouting in order to help you out, then these conditions tend to make conversation a strain rather than a pleasure. As a result, you converse less, keeping your thoughts, problems, and complaints to yourself. Others, responding to your silence, address fewer remarks to you. You are not asked your opinion of the new drapes or of the energy shortage. Fewer people share *their* problems with you. In short, hearing problems can lead directly to loneliness.

Intelligence

Perhaps the most common stereotype of the aged is that they are doddering and dull-witted. Many people simply assume that senility is as inevitable after sixty-five as tomorrow after today. Baltes and Schaie (1975) have remarked on this stereotype:

News reporters never tire of pointing out that Golda Meir works 20-hour days, yet is in her mid-70s, and a grandmother. *Time*, in a recent story on William O. Douglas, noted that the blue eyes of the 75-year-old Justice "are as keen and alert as ever. So, too, is [his] intellect." This sort of well-intended but patronizing compliment betrays a widespread assumption that intelligence normally declines in advanced adulthood and old age, and that people like Meir and Douglas stand out as exceptions (p. 93).

Likewise, the public was given to marveling at Pablo Casals, Pablo Picasso, Grandma Moses, Eleanor Roosevelt, and other creative people whose intellects still managed to burn brightly in what were supposed to be their "twilight years."

For many years the notion of the inevitable dimming of intellect in the aged went unchallenged. Indeed, it was supported by various intelligence tests. However, there was much that these tests did not take into account, including the fact that generations unexposed in their youth to IQ tests, SATs, and GREs are likely to consider a number of test questions stupid and irrelevant. More recent research seems to indicate that a general decline in intellectual ability in old age is largely a myth (Baltes and Schaie, 1975). Advanced age *is* accompanied by changes in intellectual functioning, but these changes need not represent serious impediments to intellectual functioning.

The most important change is a shift of power between two categories of intelligence: crystallized intelligence and fluid intelligence (Cattell, 1963). *Crystallized intelligence* is the storehouse of information that one has accumulated over a lifetime—vocabulary, numerical skills, and reasoning patterns that are organized, relatively durable over time, and available for association and retrieval. Not surprisingly, as a person grows older and experiences more, his crystallized intelligence increases. By contrast, *fluid intelligence* is the more dynamic component of intelligence, involving attention, inhibition of irrelevant associations, perception of environmental changes, and the ability to select the most appropriate response from a repertoire of learned behaviors. In short, fluid intelligence allows us to make efficient mental connections between past and present and to act on them swiftly and appropriately. As crystallized intelligence increases with age, fluid intelligence may decline. Thus, compared to the younger person, the older person has more knowledge available to him but cannot sort out, connect, and manipulate as many pieces of information per unit of time. Hence some older people may have difficulty in problem-solving and in decision-making.

It is important to point out, however, that these conclusions as to the intellectual idiosyncrasies of the aged are based on laboratory tests, and laboratory conditions are often very different from life conditions. Pacing, for example, can make a great difference in intellectual performance (Canestrari, 1963). Whereas in the laboratory a person has only so many seconds in which to solve a problem, in his daily life he may simply give himself more time and thus compensate for the slowdown in fluid intelligence. Another way of compensating is practice (Taub and Long, 1972), from which older people benefit just as much as do younger.

This matter of practice leads us to what appears to be the most critical variable in the intellectual development of the aged—that is, the degree to which their intellects are exercised. If an older person is isolated from others, assumed and expected to be slightly dotty, and left with little more to do than watch television, then his intellectual performance may in fact decline. If, however, he has people to talk to and interesting things to do—if, in short, he is allowed to *use* his mind—then there is no reason for any blunting of his intellectual powers. Indeed, there is no reason why they should not become sharper. In sum, expectations and opportunities have everything to do with the intellectual performance of the aged.

Coming of Age in Abkhasia

For years doctors and anthropologists have been making a long trek to Abkhasia, a small agricultural region between the Black Sea and the Caucasus Mountains in the Soviet Union. The reason for this scientific pilgrimage is to discover the secret of the longevity of the Abkhasian people. For the Abkhasians routinely live past the age of 100. Reporting on her visit to Abkhasia, Sula Benet, an American anthropologist, recounts the following faux pas:

In the village of Tarnish . . . I raised my glass of wine to toast a man who looked no more than 70. "May you live as long as Moses [that is, 120 years]," I said. He was not pleased. He was 119 (1971, p. 3).

While some early investigators considered the Abkhasians' claims of being 100, 110, and 120 to be part of the local folklore, it now appears that these people, like the rest of us, lie about their age only to reduce it. For example, one man who claimed that he was only 95 turned out to be 108. The reason for the lie soon came out: the man was engaged to be married. As another Abkhasian explained, "A man is a man until he is 100, you know what I mean. After that, well, he's getting old" (Benet, 1971, p. 29).

Why *do* the Abkhasians live so long? Natural selection is one possible answer. Abkhasia, dominated in turn by the Turks, the Greeks, and the Russians, has had a long history of hand-to-hand combat, which may have removed from the Abkhasians' gene pool the predisposition toward deafness, blindness, obesity, and other physical handicaps. Another possible explanation is the Abkhasians' diet, which is low in saturated fats and consists mainly of fruits, vegetables, corn meal, and buttermilk. Furthermore, overeating is very rare, and fat people are considered ill. Other peoples, however, have fought for centuries, eat little saturated fat, and still consider themselves lucky to live into their 80s.

Benet suggests that the central reasons for the Abkhasians' longevity are cultural stability and cultural expectations. Social norms in Abkhasia have been the same for centuries. The people live in large extended families, sometimes numbering fifty or more, where roles are clearly defined, where manners and mores are clear and strictly enforced, and where the people eat the same foods, do the same work, play the same games, propose the same toasts, and value the same things (e.g., thinness, good horsemanship, sex when it is strictly private) that they did a hundred years ago. Hence the elderly suffer no "culture shock." On the contrary, their world remains stable, familiar, and predictable from birth to death.

Even more important, perhaps, is the Abkhasians' conception of old age. According to their vocabulary, they have no "old" people. Those who live past 100 are called "long-living" people. All the rest are simply people. And even the "long-living" people have clearly defined roles and functions. While the Abkhasians concede that after 100, sexual potency may decline, they fully expect to enjoy themselves until it does. As for physical condition, they expect to remain healthy until the day they die, and to a large degree they do exactly that. The rate of visual impairment, hearing deficiencies, memory deterioration, mental illness, cancer, and cerebral arteriosclerosis in Abkhasians over 90 is astoundingly low. Finally, there is no such thing as a retired Abkhasian. They expect, and are expected, to work throughout their lives. After the age of 80, they tend to reduce their work loads and to rest between tasks. Furthermore, they may stop herding the sheep and stay closer to the farm, feeding the chickens and weeding the vegetable garden. But they consider their work essential, and though their productivity may decrease, their status within the family and the society increases with age. In sum, the older Abkhasians are not relegated to the rocking chair. While in their 80s and 90s, and even when past 100, they still have everything to live for. And live they do.

Organ Function and Illness

It should come as no surprise to anyone that older people suffer from more physical complaints than younger people. Many of us, in telephoning our grandfathers, hesitate to ask the usual "How are you?" for fear of hearing a long litany of complaints—his dinner didn't agree with him, his joints are swollen, his bowels don't move, he doesn't sleep well, and so on. The fact is that, according to the statistics, 86 percent of people over sixty-five suffer from some type of chronic illness (Butler and Lewis, 1973). Compared to younger groups, they are admitted to hospitals twice as often and stay there twice as long. Highest on the list of the complaints of the aged is heart disease. Almost equally common is arthritis. Going down the list of other frequent complaints, hernias affect 21 percent of the over-65 population; cataracts, 15 percent; varicose veins, 15 percent; hemorrhoids, 14 percent; hypertension without heart disease, 14 percent; and prostate disease, 14 percent (Commission on Chronic Illness, 1957). Other common somatic complaints include sleep disturbances—particularly early-morning waking—and indigestion.

These statistics raise a number of questions, of which we will discuss three. First, how "inevitable" are these problems? Or, to put the problem differently, how many of them are caused by the sorrows and worries that so often accompany old age in our society? There is fairly general agreement among clinicians that the vast majority of sleeping and digestive problems of the aged are due to depression and anxiety. How many other complaints fall into this category?

Second, to what extent do boredom and loneliness *aggravate* these problems? A fifty-year-old woman who has a job as well as a hemorrhoid condition is likely, at least between the hours of nine and five, to have enough on her mind so that she has little attention to spare for her hemorrhoids. By contrast, an eighty-year-old woman with little to do has plenty of time to worry about her hemorrhoids—whether they will get better or worse, whether they will bleed or not, how they will interfere with her next bowel movement, and so on. In short, the elderly, because they are so often left idle, have ample opportunity to develop anxiety about whatever somatic com-

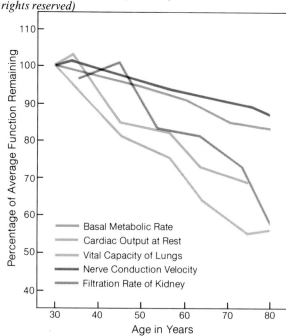

Fig. 17.2   This graph shows the percentage of change with age in cardiac output and certain other physiological functions, using 100 percent at age thirty as the standard. (Adapted from Nathan W. Shock, The Physiology of Aging, copyright © 1962 by Scientific American, Inc. All rights reserved)

plaints they have. And this anxiety may in turn aggravate the complaints considerably.

Finally, there is the rather delicate question of the quality of medical attention given to the physical problems of the elderly. When confronted with a seventy-five-year-old man complaining of varicose veins, which to him may be very distressing, the physician is not unlikely to tell him that at seventy-five he is lucky if all he has is varicose veins. There appears to be an unspoken agreement among some doctors that since so many of the old are sick, it is natural for the old to be sick. And what is "natural" will of course fall very low on the list of things requiring the busy doctor's attention. (We shall return later to this notion that the problems of the aged are natural.)

In sum, old people have numerous physical problems, have enough anxieties to generate even more physical problems, have too much empty time in which to worry about these problems, and are less likely than young people to have their physical complaints taken seriously by doctors. Such a situation is, needless to say, an added source of stress on the elderly.

THE SOCIAL STRESSES OF AGING

In this section we will actually say nothing that we haven't already suggested. The physiological and social problems of the aging are so deeply interconnected that it is impossible to speak of one without

implying the other. Consider, for instance, our example of the eighty-year-old woman with the hemorrhoids. The hemorrhoids are a physiological problem, but the fact that she had nothing to do but brood on them is a social problem. Thus the woman's "condition" is both physiological and social. Likewise, there are social problems lurking behind all the physiological problems of the aged. These social problems include lack of function, lack of money, lack of a proper place to live, lack of interpersonal communication, and lack of respect and understanding from the society. In short, thousands of the aged live without many of the material and psychological supports which the rest take for granted and on which we heavily depend.

Lack of Function

In traditional societies, where the extended family was the rule, as long as a person could still move, he never lacked a function. Women bore many more children over longer periods of time. Thus once your own children no longer needed looking after, your grandchildren did. There was no such thing as retirement. Instead, there were big jobs and little jobs, field jobs and home jobs. If an older man could no longer fell a tree, he could feed the chickens—and not just to give him something to do, for the chickens *had* to be fed. Thus older men and women not only had work to do, but they also had the pride of knowing that far from just being "kept busy," they were doing essential work, work that had to be done in order for the family group to survive. In short, they had a true function.

By now the statement that the change from the extended family of traditional cultures to the nuclear family of modern technological culture had massive ramifications has become a textbook cliché. However, like most clichés, it holds true. And one of these massive ramifications is that the older person has been left without function and without pride of function. Once his own children are grown, there are no more children around to play with and clean up after. And once he reaches his mandatory retirement age, the job to which he has devoted most of the waking hours of his adulthood is gone in a day.

Some older people respond very cheerfully both to retirement and to what has been called post-

Fig. 17.3 Aging and disease tend to go together. Older people have more chronic illnesses, are ill longer, and visit the doctor more often than do younger adults.

Fig. 17.4   To many older people, the retirement years mean a lack of social function and an idle, joyless existence.

parental life. They relax, let their hair down a bit, go to the movies more often, spend more time in the garden and truly *enjoy* spending more time in the garden. The following are one woman's remarks on having the children gone:

There's not as much physical labor. There's not as much cooking and there's not as much mending and, well, I remarked not long ago that for the first time since I can remember, my evenings are free. And we had to be very economical to get the three children

through college. We're over the hurdle now; we've completed it. Last fall was the first time in 27 years that I haven't gotten a child ready to go to school. That was very relaxing (cited in Deutscher, 1975, p. 307).

For thousands of older people, however, relaxing is not enough. And for these people involuntary retirement and the termination of the parental role may constitute psychological disasters. Our society has for many years considered it entirely proper and normal for a woman to invest twenty or thirty years of hope and energy in her children's development, to the exclusion of her own potential interests outside the home. However, once the children finally depart, women who have followed this socially approved course may find themselves utterly devastated by the "empty nest" syndrome. The thing they lived to take care of is gone; it now chooses to take care of itself. What is there left to live for?

Reactions to involuntary retirement can be even more extreme. For while the growing up and moving on of children may be seen as a natural process, in no way denigrating the parent's competence, the message of compulsory retirement—"You are too old to be of any further use to us"—may be taken as a direct blow to the person's self-esteem (Buhler, 1969). Not only does the retiree have nothing left

The "Empty Nest" Syndrome

The following is a sample of the "empty nest" syndrome: the depression and sense of futility that haunt many mothers once their children—the object against which they have defined themselves as "mothers"—leave home:

Yes, here I am fifty-five—fifty-five, but I don't feel old. I feel disgusted but not old. I would lay down and die if I wasn't a coward. I was kinda depressed when my first girl married. I thought that was the end. I just died. I don't even care very much how I look. Look, I'm thirty pounds overweight. My daughters were both nineteen when they married. I didn't want them not to marry, but I missed them so much. I felt alone. I couldn't play golf. I couldn't even play bridge. I don't have a profession, and I couldn't take just any job. . . . I wanted my girls to wait until they were 30 before they got married (cited in Deutscher, 1975, p. 309).

Fig. 17.5 *Reactions to advancing age, as to other life periods, are markedly influenced by the individual's surroundings. The reduced stimulation found in many convalescent homes, for example, contributes to the psychological decline of the residents. If an older person is given opportunities to be active and useful, the outcome is likely to be a greater sense of vitality and satisfaction. The occupational and familial practices of American society often orient a person to the grim expectation that he will be discarded or unappreciated as he grows older. This situation creates stresses that can be avoided by changing the opportunities afforded older persons.*

to do, but it is *because* he is old and thus "incompetent" that he can no longer be trusted with a job. Of men stricken with this involuntary retirement syndrome, anthropologist Margaret Mead had the following to say: "One day they have life, the next day nothing. One reason women live longer than men is that they can continue to do something they are used to doing [such as marketing and cooking] whereas men are abruptly cut off—whether they are admirals or shopkeepers" (cited in *Time*, June 2, 1975, pp. 47–48).

"Cut off" is the essential phrase here. Just as American society has encouraged women to give their entire selves to their children, so men have been encouraged to give even more of themselves to their careers. Yet all the while the society has made no allowance for the fact that when these people reach their sixties, their children and their careers will disappear, depriving the aging person not only of his function but also of his pride—that "self" that was invested and is now gone. This freezing out of the functionless aged is well described in one man's comments on his retirement: "I am over 60 and most distressed, not only by failing vision, missing teeth, barnacles on the spine, aching joints, gray hair and wrinkles, but because every effort is being made to separate and isolate me from a portion of my life and the rest of the living" (Perera, 1975, p. 359). Indeed, to many older people it seems that without their work and the self-respect that came with it, they are dropped into a limbo between the living and the dead, with a decade or so to wait before death puts a final end to their idle and joyless existences.

How should they cope? Some begin second careers; Palmore (1967) reports that in 1962, 40 percent of men between the ages of 65 and 72 were working to some extent. But these figures are now somewhat dated. In a depressed economy, we may assume that those older people who are working are vastly outnumbered by those who wish they were working. This is to say nothing of those whose self-esteem has suffered so badly as a result of their functionlessness that they no longer feel qualified to do any useful work. Finally, we should not forget those for whom the lack of a productive role has led to physical and emotional problems which, in a fine example of self-fulfilling prophecy, have rendered them truly unable to fulfill a productive role.

Poverty

Aside from reducing a person's sense of self-worth, retirement has another serious consequence. It reduces his income. In view of the gravity of this problem, the poverty of the American aged has been astoundingly underpublicized. A fine example of this lack of understanding of the actual problems of old people is shown in a study done by Kogan and Shelton (1962), in which groups of young people and old people were asked to complete the statement "One of the greatest fears of many old people is . . . ." The young people, many without the slightest hesitation, chose death as the greatest fear of the aged. But the number one choice of the older interviewees was financial insecurity. And with good reason. One out of every four Americans over sixty-five has an annual income below the 1970 poverty index of $1,852 (Butler and Lewis, 1973). And among those living on their own, almost half fall below the poverty line (Kahn, 1974).

Their ways of coping are well known to the doctors in public clinics. They subsist on peanut-butter sandwiches. They live in clammy rooming houses. They stay on, long after most members of the middle class have departed, in depressed neighborhoods where they can't take a walk after dark for fear of being mugged. Small pleasures and minor conveniences are of necessity eliminated: no concerts, no ball games, no long-distance calls. When the television breaks down, they have to wait for their next Social Security check in order to call the repairman. Even then they may not be able to afford it. Such deprivations constitute a tremendous source of stress and are likely to contribute heavily to the isolation, anxiety, and depression of the elderly person.

Where to Live

Where do the old people live? Or, in view of what we have just discussed, perhaps the question should be: Where can they afford to live? This problem is particularly pertinent to those older people, by far the majority of the over-65 group, who are widowed or otherwise spouseless. Some of them—20 percent of the over-65 group (Sheldon, 1958)—live with relatives other than their spouses. These are the widows and widowers who go to live with their children and grandchildren—the last remnants of the extended family. And these old people should probably count themselves among the lucky few. As we have seen, the modern nuclear family—efficient, mobile, and usually without extra bedrooms—cannot easily accommodate the older generation. And even if there is room for a widowed parent, many women today either work or are otherwise active outside the home and are thus unable or unwilling to stay around the house looking after an older person. Consequently, many older people find themselves

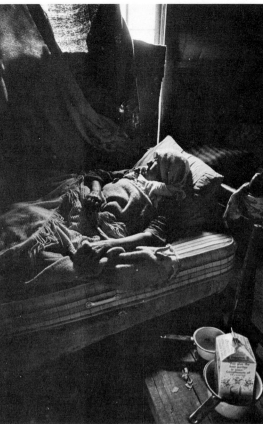

Fig. 17.6 Poverty is a major source of stress for the aged; the privations and hardships exacerbate the feelings of isolation, anxiety, and depression.

The Nursing Home Scandal

The following are a few vignettes from a recent report by Jacoby (1974) on the nation's nursing homes:

A thin, graying woman wanders up and down the corridor of a Michigan nursing home in search of a nurse's aide. "Could you help my husband out of bed?" she asks. "He didn't feel well earlier in the day but he'd like to get up now."

It is 11 in the morning, but the aide says it is the wrong time of day for patients to be getting out of bed. "Oh, I didn't mean this minute," the woman replies timidly. "We know you're very busy." The aide stalks off down the hall and yells to a colleague, "I don't know who the hell her husband is, do you?"

"How should I know?" snaps back the other aide. "I can't remember people's names."

The home is located on a quiet residential street in Lansing, Mich., and is owned by National Health Enterprises, Inc., the largest nursing-home chain in the United States (p. 13).

• • •

According to Federal law, Medicaid patients are supposed to receive a $30-a-month allowance for personal use. However, many patients do not receive the allowance. . . . One man in a New York home told me he had been a patient for three years before he learned about the personal allowance from a niece. "She wondered why I was always begging her for cigarettes when she came to visit, and I told her I had no money to buy them. She went to the administrator and threatened to get a lawyer, and then they started giving me the money." The man asked that his name be withheld because he was afraid of retaliation from the nursing home staff (p. 76).

• • •

In a Michigan nursing home, an emaciated woman was sitting in a wheel chair. The blanket covering her legs had fallen to the floor. "You'd better pull that blanket back up, honey," said an aide. "No one around here wants to look at your skinny old legs" (p. 82).

Source: Susan Jacoby, "Waiting for the End: On Nursing Homes," *The New York Times Magazine*, March 31, 1974, pp. 13–93.

living alone—often, as mentioned earlier, in sub-standard housing and in the rougher parts of the city. And when their health fails, they are removed to nursing homes, which at this point house 5 percent of the nation's elderly. The conditions in these institutions have lately become a national scandal. While some are quite faultless, thousands of others are raking in prodigious profits from Medicaid while maintaining their patients in filthy surroundings, with brutal or indifferent attendants and wretched food. One nursing-home owner prided himself on "feeding his patients for 54¢ a day, less than the county jail spent on its prisoners" (*Time*, June 2, 1975, p. 47).

Combined with the stresses inherent in whatever quarters they move to, the moving itself may constitute a psychological trauma for the aged person. The children have grown; the spouse is dead; the old person can no longer keep up the house. But to leave the house, the place where he had some standing—where he was known by the neighbors, the grocer, the owner of the dry cleaner; where he raised his children, earned his money, established his place in the world, made his own rules—is to him a potent symbol of his loss of status. Whether he moves in with his children, finds himself a small apartment, or is placed in an institution, he is no longer in any way the person who makes the rules. Hence it is no surprise that this transition can be a severe blow to the self-esteem of the older person. For many, the move from the "old house" marks the beginning of psychological withdrawal.

Loneliness

We have already commented several times on the isolation that can plague the elderly. One of the inevitable pains of growing old is watching others die. In the over-65 age group, 20 percent of men and 50 percent of women are widowed. A third no longer have any living children. And of course, one by one their friends die. Thus whether his life is fulfilling or not, the older person tends to live among the ghosts of the dead—his spouse, his old friends, even his children. Some older people energetically compensate for these losses. Many of the over-65 group remarry, and according to McKain (1972), the chances of such marriages being successful are very good. Others can afford to live in retirement communities where they may, if they wish, find plenty of older people equally in need of companionship. Others, undaunted by their personal losses, simply go about finding new ways to involve themselves with other people. But again, these are the

Fig. 17.7   Nursing homes vary widely in their atmosphere and accommodations; some residents can enjoy a more "home style" environment, while others suffer the isolation of an institutional setting.

fortunate ones. For many other older people, the deaths of loved ones and companions, and the loneliness that follows, are a major source of personal distress.

These personal losses have a number of ramifications. First, there is the obvious matter of bereavement, which can lead to serious emotional problems (Williams, 1973); Paul (1966) argues that the majority of older persons seeking help in community clinics are suffering from unvented grief. And as several studies have shown, the psychological stress of bereavement can often hasten the bereaved person toward his own death. In a study comparing the relatives of 371 deceased persons with a matched control group of the relatives of 371 living persons, it was found that after one year of bereavement, 12.2

percent of the index group died, in comparison to 1.2 percent of the control group (Kraus and Lilienfeld, 1959).

Second, the older person who confronts the death of a loved one also confronts his own death, which now seems to him that much more real, inevitable, and imminent. Thus his grieving for the dead person may include a sizable portion of grief for himself.

Third and most important of all is the simple fact that the other person is gone, along with whatever he contributed to the happiness of the elderly survivor. Even if an older mother manages fairly well in getting over the loss of her adult child, the card on Mother's Day still doesn't come. And even if Sam seems relatively unshaken by the death of his pinochle partner, George, there is still no one to play pinochle with next Tuesday. In sum, the older person inevitably suffers from the attrition of interpersonal supports. He has fewer people to talk to him, call him up, or care about him. If he wants to go to a ball game, the chances are good that he will have to go alone. And the chances are even better that under these circumstances, he won't go at all. In some older persons it appears that this social isolation may contribute to the development of depression and other forms of mental disorder (Blau, 1961; Connally, 1962; Gruenberg, 1954; Lowenthal and Haven, 1968). For others, the loss of friends and family simply means that the basic human need for intimacy, as strong in the elderly as in the young (Angyal, 1965; Bowlby, 1958; Erikson, 1959), remains unfulfilled. In short, they are just lonely.

Social Attitudes Toward the Aging

However many difficulties the aging may have simply because they are aging, our society's attitude toward old people does little to alleviate, and much to aggravate, these problems. We live in a youth-oriented culture. One has only to view a series of television commercials (an activity that occupies a good deal of the older person's time) to appreciate how much value we place on youthfulness. Even the paper towels and scouring powders—to say nothing of the cars and perfumes—have their virtues demonstrated by younger actors and actresses, as if to suggest to the viewer that if he uses the product, he too will become imbued with that infinitely desirable quality, youth. Only in advertisements for hospitalization insurance, savings accounts, denture adhesives, and laxatives do old people typically appear. The message is clearly that the role of old people in our society is simply to worry about their health, their savings, their dentures, and their bowels.

The old people hear this message loud and clear. It has been shown that not only the young but also the old hold negative stereotypes of the aged (Bennett and Eckman, 1973). Typically, old people are thought to be lonely, rigid, mentally slow, unhealthy, and uninterested in sex. (Small wonder that so many of the aged feel bad about themselves!) Indeed, it may be said that our entire society has a positive horror of old age. As Simone de Beauvoir puts it, "Society looks upon old age as a kind of shameful secret that it is unseemly to mention" (1972, p. 38). And in fact we do our best not to mention it, at least by name. The old are not old; they are "senior citizens" living out their "Golden Years." The very word "aging," which we have used so many times in this chapter, is an inaccurate euphemism. We are all aging. A person over sixty-five, however, is aged; he is old.

The negative stereotype that we camouflage in these pretty words has two extremely damaging effects. The first is, of course, that it acts as a self-fulfilling prophecy. As we have seen, a person who is put in a mental hospital and told that he is "crazy" is likely to act crazy. By the same token, an old person who is told that old people are sick, muddle-headed, and useless is likely to feel and act sick, muddle-headed, and useless.

A second effect, more subtle and more sinister, of this negative stereotype is to convince everyone, young and old, that the problems of the aged are "natural." Bright and active older people, the Picassos and Eleanor Roosevelts of the world, are, as we have seen, considered the exception. The rule is that loneliness, depression, inactivity, anxiety, ill health, and all the other pains and sorrows that we have listed in this chapter are the *inevitable* companions of the aged. And when something is inevitable, no efforts need be expended to change it. If Grandma is worried and complains all the time, that's because all old people worry and complain all the time. And thus Grandma's complaints—that she has nothing to do, that her money might run out, that she doesn't know what will happen to her when she can no longer take care of herself—do not incite anyone, either individuals or the society as a whole, to go in search of a remedy.

As we have seen, this "naturalness" fallacy regarding the problems of the aged has had its effect on the medical profession. And it appears to have affected the mental health professions as well. In mental hospitals older people are less likely than young people to receive psychotherapy—a fact that may have a great deal to do with diagnostic habits, since it appears that no matter what the symptoms of the elderly patient, he is often almost automatically diagnosed as having an untreatable organic brain syndrome (Gurland, 1973). Lawton and Gottesman (1974) also claim that clinical psychologists tend to ignore the complaints of the elderly—a phenomenon that these investigators call the "brownout of the aged." Finally, as Lawton and Gottesman (1974) further point out, there is a depressing scarcity of research and professional writing on the treatment of elderly. In recent years, a number of researchers (Eisdorfer and Lawton, 1973; Gaitz, 1972; Neugarten, 1968; Palmore, 1970, 1974) have given close attention to the developmental aspects of aging—that is, the changes that take place with age. But as for *treatment*, the therapeutic reversal of the ill effects of these changes, very few professionals seem interested.

Sex Among the Aging   One area in which social attitudes toward the aging appear to have had a particularly ruinous effect is the area of sexual activity. As we have noted above, many older people remarry in their later years. What we didn't note was that, in general, society disapproves of such marriages (McKain, 1972). Marriage is apparently for the young, and so is that essential component of marriage, sex.

As a result of hormonal changes, the sexual functioning of the aged is not precisely identical to that of the young. Certain changes do take place, and these may be listed quite succinctly. In older women, vaginal lubrication decreases. In older men, the erection may take two or three times longer to achieve, the orgasm may be less intense, and restimulation after orgasm may take a longer time. However, these changes need not interfere with

BEER AND CRACKERS:
A Cure for the Psychoses of the Aged

Many thousands of beds in our mental hospitals are occupied by the aging. How many of these people are suffering from treatable functional disorders that have been mistaken—or simply written off—as untreatable organic brain disorders? Worse yet, how many of these old people are simply suffering from a case of lowered expectations—the society's expectation that they will have nothing to offer anyone and their own internalization and fulfillment of this expectation?

Working with a hospitalized group of elderly men, Volpe and Kastenbaum (1967) decided to put his question to the test. The patients involved were serious cases. They could not dress themselves, feed themselves, or go to the toilet. Furthermore, they were generally agitated and confused, had a record of exposing themselves, and limited their personal interactions to randomly hitting one another without provocation. The "treatment" instituted by Volpe and Kastenbaum consisted of the following unspectacular innovations: the men's rumpled pajamas were taken away and replaced by trousers, white shirts, and ties; every day at two o'clock they were served a snack of beer, crackers, and cheese; and their ward was supplied with a record player, a few games, some decks of cards, and a bulletin board with pictures on it. Within a month after these

few amenities were introduced on the ward, the men's behavior had changed substantially. They began going to the toilet or asking to be taken there. They managed to consume their beer and crackers without help. Furthermore, they became less agitated; accordingly, their dosages of tranquilizers were reduced, and they became more alert. Finally, they participated in hospital parties and dances and began requesting more of the same.

Volpe and Kastenbaum concluded that the men's increasingly adaptive behavior and much of their prior maladaptive behavior were the results of self-fulfilling prophecies. The difference was in the prophecy. Implicit in their earlier hospital environment (and probably their pre-hospitalization environment as well) was the expectation that they would be sick and incompetent people—patients who needed *care*. Likewise, the beer and crackers, the record player, the cards, and the street clothes carried the implication that, hospital or no hospital, they were dignified and sociable adults—people who get dressed during the day and enjoyed listening to music, playing cards with one another, and having a beer at two o'clock. Once the expectations changed, so did the men.

Fig. 17.8 *There is no reason why an older couple should not continue sexual activity for as long as they desire.*

sexual functioning. If the older couple is in reasonably good health, if they can get themselves to the drugstore to buy a lubricant, and if they can adjust their thinking so that they don't expect the male's erection to appear with the same speed as it did when he was forty, then there is no reason why they should not continue sexual functioning well into their eighties and possibly into their nineties as well. And according to a large-scale longitudinal study of sexual activity in the elderly (Pfeiffer et al., 1968; Pfeiffer and Davis, 1972), many people do just that. However, this same study indicates that many more old people are interested in sex than are actually engaging in sexual activity.

There appear to be two major reasons for this biologically unwarranted continence. The first is the lack of an available partner—a problem particularly for women, who, as we have seen, are much more likely to be widowed than men. The second reason is the commonly held notion that decent older people can't, shouldn't, and don't engage in sexual activity. It is widely believed that a right-minded woman loses interest in sex after menopause. Likewise, an older man who still shows an interest in sex runs a heavy risk of being labeled a "dirty old man." But however strong the belief that older people *shouldn't* have sexual activity, it is not as strong as the belief that normally they *can't* have sexual activity because, presumably, old men are impotent. As we have indicated above and as Masters and Johnson (1970) have forcibly pointed out, old men are not impotent. However, this common misconception, combined with the changes in the aging male's speed of erection, often leads directly to a cessation of sexual activity. Once the erection begins to arrive more slowly, both partners say to themselves, "Oh, here it is," "it" being the beginning of the end. Embarrassed by what is a perfectly natural slowing down—not a disappearance—of the erective response, fearful of the effects of "failure" on the male's self-esteem, and assured by their society that termination of sexual activity is natural—indeed, proper—in the elderly, each member of the couple gradually ceases making sexual demands on the other until at last their sex life comes to an end. Thus it is not biological destiny, but rather a combination of misinformation, timidity, and social pressure that is the most common cause of sexual abstinence in older couples. And the consequences of this absti-

SEXUAL CHANGES IN THE AGED

Women	Decrease in vaginal lubrication upon stimulation
	Decrease in elasticity of vagina
Men	Increase in time necessary to achieve erection
	Decrease in intensity of orgasm
	Increase in time before restimulation to erection is possible
	Decreased need to ejaculate as climax to coitus

Otherwise, sexual functioning in the aged is much like sexual functioning in the young or middle-aged. It is in the psychology of sex, not in the physiology of sex, that the aged differ drastically from the young. And for this difference social attitudes are responsible.

Sex Among the Aging

One of the major misconceptions attached to the aging process is the belief that people over the age of sixty no longer have the ability, desire, or need for sexual intimacy. Sexual dysfunction among the old is not a natural process, and although the act itself may alter slightly, there is no biological reason for termination of sexual contact at any age.

The following composite case study from Masters and Johnson (1970) illustrates a typical problem:

Mr. and Mrs. A were 66 and 62 years of age when referred to the Foundation for sexual inadequacy. They had been married 39 years....

They had maintained reasonably effective sexual interchange during their marriage. Mr. A had no difficulty with erection, reasonable ejaculatory control, and ... had been fully committed to the marriage. Mrs. A, occasionally orgasmic during intercourse and regularly orgasmic during her occasional masturbatory experiences, had continued regularity of coital exposure with her husband until five years prior to referral for therapy....

At age 61, ... Mr. A noted for the first time slowed erective attainment. Regardless of his level of sexual interest or the depth of his wife's commitment to the specific sexual experience, it took him progressively longer to attain full erection. With each sexual exposure his concern for the delay in erective security increased until finally ... he failed for the first time to achieve an erection quality sufficient for vaginal penetration.

When coital opportunity [next] developed ... erection was attained, but again it was quite slow in development. The next two opportunities were only partially successful from an erective point of view, and thereafter he was secondarily impotent.

After several months they consulted their physician and were assured that this loss of erective power comes to all men as they age and that there was nothing to be done. Loath to accept the verdict, they tried on several occasions to force an erection with no success. Mr. A was seriously depressed for several months but recovered without apparent incident....

The marital unit ... accepted their "fate." The impotence was acknowledged to be a natural result of the aging process. This resigned attitude lasted approximately four years.

Although initially the marital unit and their physician had fallen into the sociocultural trap of accepting the concept of sexual inadequacy as an aging phenomenon, the more Mr. and Mrs. A considered their dysfunction the less willing they were to accept the blanket concept that lack of erective security was purely the result of the aging process. They reasoned that they were in good health, had no basic concerns as a marital unit, and took good care of themselves physically.... Each partner underwent a thorough medical checkup and sought several authoritative opinions (none of them encouraging), refusing to accept the concept of the irreversibility of their sexual distress. Finally, approximately five years after the onset of a full degree of secondary impotence, they were referred for treatment [to Masters and Johnson] (pp. 326–328).

Within a week after the beginning of therapy, full sexual functioning between the couple was restored. The realization that physiological changes—the longer time required for an older male to attain erection, the reduction in seminal fluid, and the decrease in female lubrication—are natural but uninhibiting responses was all that was needed to rebuild confidence and destroy the psychological barriers that had brought about the original dysfunction.

nence are simply that one more source of pleasure and self-esteem is removed from the grasp of the older person. The meaning of this loss is detailed by Kastenbaum:

What does an older person lose if and when he no longer has a loving sexual partner? (It might be more accurate to turn convention aside and employ the female pronoun, considering the greater likelihood of women outliving their men.) Is it possible that the loss of intimate sharing may prove more critical than the orgasm deprivation? Where else is the old man or woman to receive immediate proof that his body can be a source of pleasure both to himself and others? In what other context than the boudoir will he have the opportunity for the whisperings, the nonverbal communications, the private world of people very close to each other? Strangers and young people may tend to stereotype him as Another Old Man. They see him with all his clothes on, more or less playing the public role. They do not fathom that he has been lover and beloved. When the identity-enhancing intimacy of loving sex has terminated, where is the elder to turn for a convincing reminder that there is more to him than his new and skimpy public role? (1973, p. 705)

THE PSYCHOPATHOLOGY OF AGING

The aged form a massive sector of the mental-hospital population. In 1968, state and county mental hospitals housed 629.7 patients per 100,000 in the over-65 population, as compared to 157.8 patients, 226.4 patients, and 312.2 patients per 100,000 in the 25–34, 35–44, and 45–54 age brackets, respectively. Many of these old people who occupy so many beds in our mental hospitals are suffering from organic brain syndromes. The others are there because they have functional disorders. In both cases, the old people, unlike the young, tend to stay in the hospital until they die.

As we have noted earlier, the organic brain syndromes that strike the elderly are not the province of this chapter. Our concern is with the functional disorders of the aged. Of what are they a function? There are essentially two major predisposing factors. The first is personality. As a person grows old, he becomes more like himself than ever before. If when young he was a curious, flexible, resourceful person, he is likely to remain curious, flexible, resourceful in old age, and this will work in his favor. Likewise, if he was a rather rigid or dependent type when young, he will become even more rigid or dependent as he ages, and this will work against him.

The second predisposing factor is stress, the very factor that has been the subject of most of this chapter so far. As we have seen, the stresses with which the elderly have to cope can be enormous: a vast vicious circle of physiological changes which induce psychological distress, which in turn produces further physiological changes, and so on. And as we have further seen, the old person caught in this circle has also to cope with the social expectation that he will "naturally" be morose, sedentary, mentally befuddled, depressed, unhealthy, and sexless.

Many old people are extremely successful in defying such expectations. While they themselves may harbor negative stereotypes of the elderly, they exempt themselves from the rule. Throughout our society there are older people who are leading happy, active, and fruitful lives—a fact which by necessity has received little attention in this chapter.

In contrast, there are many old people who fulfill society's expectations to the hilt. Why do they succumb while others manage to resist? As we have seen, happiness and unhappiness in old age have everything to do with personality and stress. If the personality is enterprising and adaptable, quick to find substitutes for satisfactions that have been lost, then this personality is supremely adapted for growing old (Schwartz, 1974). Likewise, if stresses are few and minor—in short, if not too many satisfactions have been lost—then the person's chances are even better. But if the old person is basically rather an inflexible type—one who, having lost old friends, finds it hard to make new friends, or one who simply cannot shift his enjoyment from reading to music if his vision begins to dim—then his chances are that much poorer. And if the stresses with which he has to cope are very great, making heavy demands on his flexibility, this too will diminish his chances. Should the last two factors be combined in a single person—low adaptability and high stress—then this person may easily succumb to one of the two major functional disorders of old age, anxiety and depression.

Anxiety

Free-floating anxiety, described in Chapter 5, is quite common in the older population. What causes this anxiety? First and most important is the old person's concern over his last years. Will I be incapacitated by illness? If so, where will I go? Who will take care of me? Will my money run out? Will I be alone? These questions can run incessantly through the minds of the aging, creating a vast and threatening "unknown"—an ideal climate for the cultivation of anxiety.

A second important source of anxiety is the process of making decisions and adapting to change. As his life circumstances change, the older person is often faced with many decisions, and the shift, noted above, between fluid and crystallized intelligence does not help him in this area. Because his crystallized intelligence is greater, he can think of many more alternatives and many more possible consequences for each of these alternatives. Thus whereas a younger person making a decision juggles maybe three balls in his hands, the older person juggles nine. And confronted with this vast range of possibilities, the older person's reduced fluid intelligence makes it more difficult for him to sort them out, choosing the most promising alternative. Hence for the aging, decision-making can be an extremely anxiety-laden experience, fraught with danger and risk.

Furthermore, whether or not it is the result of his own decision, the older person is faced with change—change in his body, change in his relationship to his environment—and coping with change means learning new skills. This relearning process can generate extreme anxiety in the aged, particularly since their limited options make the consequences of failure seem particularly serious. If they cannot learn to adapt to living with Cousin Josie, who else is there for them to live with?

Finally, whereas younger people may approach change, uncertainty, and new challenges with a sense of their own fitness to the task at hand, old people are likely to approach these risky matters with a keen sense of vulnerability. They are weaker, have fewer ways out, are closer to death. Their time is running out, and there is nothing they can do about it. This sense of powerlessness alone can make an old person extremely anxious in the face of each new day.

The anxiety of the elderly is manifested in a number of ways. One common sign is extreme self-preoccupation. Besieged with worries about themselves, they have little concern for or patience with the problems of others. Instead, all their energies are directed toward what they see as a last-ditch attempt to control their own destinies and satisfy their own needs (Neugarten, 1968). Likewise, they may appear extremely rigid, intent as they are on defending themselves against the threats that they perceive all around them (Butler and Lewis, 1973). Furthermore, the extreme suspiciousness and paranoid thinking sometimes seen in the elderly and often considered a sign of senility is likely instead to be a sign of anxiety. The more powerless they feel, the more it seems to them that the grocer is cheating them or that things that they gave away years ago were actually stolen out from under their eyes by greedy relatives. Finally, a common sign of anxiety in the aged, and particularly in older women, is hypochondria. In a study of 250 normal people ranging in age from sixty to ninety-three, Busse (1970) found that 33 percent showed hypochondriacal tendencies. And in fact hypochondria may constitute a fairly useful outlet for the anxieties of the aged. We must not forget that whereas we live in a time where young people are often encouraged to express any and every feeling and need, many old people were raised in an environment where it was considered commendable to be strong, to not talk about your troubles, and to "stand on your own two feet." As a result, the direct expression of deeply personal feelings may be difficult for many of the aged. However, by transferring their doubts and disap-

pointments from the emotional to the physical realm—in short, by becoming hypochondriacal—they can find it acceptable in themselves to solicit attention from a doctor, a relative, or a friend, and to give vent to some of their fears, albeit disguised as somatic complaints.

Depression

Erik Erikson describes old age as the point at which the individual chooses between ego integrity—that is, acceptance of his life, past and future, and of his death as part of the grand cycle of human experience—and despair. But for many old people the stress of change may be so intense and their capacity for coping with it so enfeebled that ego integrity is not among their range of available choices. And for these people, despair can be very bitter, leading to a clinical diagnosis of depression.

As we have seen in Chapter 7, there are a number of competing theories of depression, including genetic theories. However, family studies indicate that hereditary factors play a lesser role in depression among the aged. Post (1965), for example, found in his sample of depressives that a family history of depression showed up in only 44 percent of those who experienced their first attack of depression after the age of sixty-five, whereas 80 percent of those whose first attack occurred before the age of fifty had such a family history. In reviewing his evidence, Post concludes that in the elderly most depressions are reactive—that is, they occur in response to some loss or the threat of some loss. This sounds very close indeed to the behavioral theory of depression (Chapter 7), the theory that depression is the result of a removal of positive reinforcers. As we have seen above, there is virtually no end to the list of reinforcers that can swiftly and inexorably be removed from the aging: job, children, spouse, friends, familiar territory, good health, youthful looks, sex, money, and so on. Hence it is no surprise that many of the elderly manifest the extreme sadness and withdrawal that we call depression.

There is yet another loss that can contribute to the depression of the older person, and that is the impending loss of his own life. The elderly are keenly aware of the closeness of death. And though their anxieties may center on the circumstances of their death (whether it will be long, costly, painful, lonely and so forth), their depression centers on the more existential aspect of death—the special poignancy and meaning that death gives to the way one has spent one's life. A young person can always take comfort in the thought that there is still time

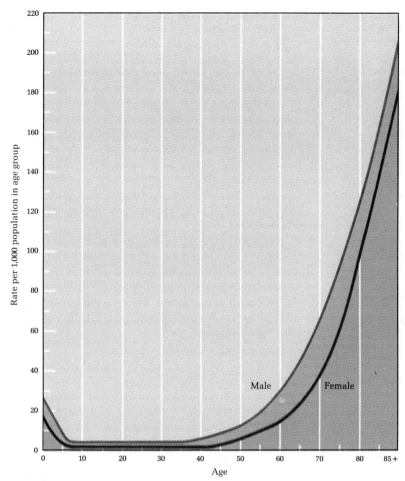

Fig. 17.9 Death rates by age and sex in the United States in 1968 are represented by the graph above. In addition to indicating the obvious fact that the likelihood of dying increases with age, the curves show that life expectancy is greater for females than for males. (Data from U.S. Department of Health, Education, and Welfare, Facts of Life and Death, Washington, D.C.: Government Printing Office, 1970, p. 11.)

for change, that if his destiny seems headed in the wrong direction, he can always turn it around. The aged do not have this comfort. They know that however they have spent their years, those years are nearly all spent. Hence missed opportunities, unwise choices, or perhaps the simple fact that they do not have some great thing that they can point to and say, "This is my achievement"—such broodings on the past can lead older people to the conclusion that their lives were wasted and that they themselves are nothing. In short, such thoughts can lead to depression.

Furthermore, the matter of existential anxiety aside, there is no question that most people do not wish to die. And the fact that the elderly are closer to death does not make them any more comfortable with the idea. Hence, if the older person lacks reinforcers to keep his attention focused on life, the specter of death may haunt his mind continually and provide the entry into depression.

Depression, as we know from Chapter 7, can lead to suicide. And according to the statistics, this lethal sequence is more common among the old than among the young. Though suicide rates for elderly women are increasing, the white elderly male still has the highest suicide rate of any American age/sex/race group. Together, elderly men and women account for 5,000 to 8,000 suicides annually in this country (Resnik and Cantor, 1970). Some of these old people commit suicide upon finding out that they have what they know to be a terminal illness, the agony of which they have no desire to prolong for themselves or their families. However, the majority of elderly suicides, like the majority of younger suicides, are people who are simply miserable. And as we have seen, old age in our society is met with ample opportunities, and very few cures, for misery.

Case Histories

As the life of any old person, happy or unhappy, is bound to include many of the changes and stresses catalogued in this chapter, we have saved our case histories for the end. In the first, we see an average degree of stress but also considerable adaptability and hence, predictably, a not unhappy ending. In the second case, we see greater stress, less adaptability, and, not surprisingly, an unhappy ending.

Miss Greene

The oldest daughter in a large German-Jewish family, Miss Greene never married. She took a job as an assistant in a large dressmaking concern in Germany, and as the years passed she became an excellent seamstress. When the Nazis started their climb to power, Miss Greene, then in her forties, came to America. She settled in New York, and due to her skill at sewing, earned a more-than-comfortable living. When she retired, she had many friends and quite a bit of money saved. For the next twenty years she lived in a small apartment right next door to her closest friend, a slightly younger widow. They cooked for each other, took trips together, went to concerts, and so forth. As the years went by, Miss Greene became frail, but she managed the three-flight climb to her apartment, slept from eight at night to eight in the morning, and, even though her eyesight was failing, continued to make very beautiful little dresses and shirts for the many great-nieces and great-nephews and great-great-nieces and great-great-nephews whose births she awaited with much excitement.

Then her friend became ill and was hospitalized. Miss Greene made her way to the hospital every day. When, after surgery, the friend returned to her apartment, Miss Greene, who was by this time eighty-seven years old, took total charge of her, changing the bed, cooking the meals, and spending hours reading aloud and talking to her friend. However, as each day passed, the sick woman became weaker. Finally, caring for her became too much for Miss Greene. The friend returned to the hospital, and soon afterwards she died there.

This event precipitated a great change in Miss Greene's life. She stopped going to the market, stopped going outside at all. A cousin, a year older than Miss Greene, began bringing cooked meals for her, but often Miss Greene ate nothing but cake, her favorite food, for days. Though she continued to dress with care, she began to pace the hallway at all hours; occasionally she was found sitting on the steps. She remained perfectly lucid, but her conversation, which until this time had been about whatever she had found interesting that day—a new book, the world situation, her plants' growth—became more and more restricted

to how she was feeling. She slept little, ate less, and suffered from a series of illnesses.

One day almost a year after her friend's death, Miss Greene finally left the building. She had written to several homes for the aged, and after receiving their brochures and selecting a few homes that sounded acceptable, she began a series of visits to them. After a few weeks of inspections, she packed some clothes, some old photographs, a carton of books, and several plants and went to "visit" the institution she had chosen. After a month there, she returned to her old apartment, packed a few more things, called the Salvation Army to take away the rest, took her name off the mailbox, and moved into the home for good.

She has been in this institution now for over two years. She says that her greatest pleasure comes from being able to do some real gardening (the home has a sizable garden), but she admits to being happy to be with other people again. The only thing that worries her is the possibility that her savings will run out before she dies.

Joe

Born in Eastern Europe, Joe came to America at the age of fourteen. For years he took whatever work he could get—and as much as he could get—delivering ice, loading cargos in the shipyards, cleaning up after hours in factories. Finally, in his early twenties, shortly after his marriage, he was given a regular job as a janitor in a large company, and he stayed with this company for the next forty years, receiving one promotion, to door attendant. He was loyal to the company and did his work faithfully, but he valued his job merely as a source of steady income. The only work he ever really enjoyed was carpentry. His one ambition had been to buy a house in a better section of town than the bleak neighborhood occupied by his fellow Slavic immigrants. This ambition he realized, after strenuous economizing, at the age of thirty-two. The big new house was soon equipped with a neatly planted vegetable garden and a workshop. On weekends Joe spent most of his time in the workshop, constructing with utterly precise workmanship an endless train of bookshelves, tables, little benches, and big benches. After he had furnished his own house, he still went on carefully making these things, which he then gave away to friends and relatives.

In the big house Joe went through two wives and raised nine children. Having a rather gruff and compulsive personality, he was never an affectionate husband or father. But everyone in the family understood his or her duties, and everyone put up with everyone else. Eventually the children grew up, married, and went off to have their own children. But they usually came for Sunday dinner and thus provided Joe with his greatest pleasure (next to carpentry): sitting at the head of the head table in his big kitchen with all his descendants in view. He loved being boss, the man in charge.

But by the time he was seventy-five, Joe no longer knew what to do with the big house or with himself. He had been forced to retire ten years earlier; his second wife had been dead for three years. He tried taking in roomers, but their habits annoyed him, and he staged quarrels in order to get rid of them. He could still play at carpentry, and every Thursday afternoon he had a regular card game with three old friends who still managed to put up with his imperious temperament. But he had too little money, too much time on his hands, and too big a house to maintain. His solution was to sell the house, divide the money among his children, and move in with his son's family in the suburbs. However, their habits annoyed him too. They were very kind to him and were genuinely happy to have him. Nevertheless, he was painfully aware that it was their house, not his, and that things were no longer arranged around his well-defined tastes and preferences. So he moved in with another son and his family in another suburb. Again he was welcomed, but again he was unhappy. They didn't clean the tops of the kitchen cabinets often enough to please him; they let their teenaged daughter, his granddaughter, "run wild" (i.e., stay out past ten on Saturday night); they invariably bought the wrong kind of crackers. To add to his unhappiness, he developed arthritis and began having difficulty doing his carpentry.

In a fit of pique, he returned to the city, moved into an apartment in a low-income housing project, took a mistress, a widow in her early seventies, and rejoined his Thursday-afternoon card party. Though disgusted with the habits of the other people in the housing project, he seemed relatively content for a while. He was once again boss, at least of his own little apartment and of the mistress, whom he treated as gruffly as he had treated his two wives. But within a few years, his card-playing friends had died and he himself was confined to a wheelchair with arthritis. Finally he fell and broke his hip, and had to spend a month in the hospital. There he became truly depressed and told his favorite grandson that he was dying, "little bit by little bit." The grandson assured him that he had years to live and tried to cheer him up by telling him gossip about the crooked city poli-

ticians, stories that Joe had once loved to hear. But he was hard to cheer up.

When Joe returned from the hospital it became clear to him that the mistress, though still in residence and still cooking for him, had "taken up" with the man down the hall, a man younger and healthier than Joe. Joe's depression deepened. He would call his children at all hours of the night, complaining that he was dying. He lost interest in television. Some days he did not even bother to get out of bed.

One day, about three months after his return from the hospital, the mistress returned from church to find Joe hanging from a rope attached to a pipe running across the ceiling. His children, overwhelmed with guilt, shock, and grief, were convinced that he had been murdered; somehow someone had managed to hang him. This belief was dispelled when they took a closer look at the rope. It was carefully anchored to the radiator and then wound around the pipe tightly and neatly for many more inches than was necessary; it was knotted after every fifth turn; the noose was tied with utter precision. It was unmistakably Joe's work.

SUMMARY

Our subject has been the stresses of aging and the developmental disorders that can result from these stresses. There are two major sources of such stress: physiological changes and social changes.

The physiological changes that accompany aging include changes in physical appearance, to which many older people respond with dismay; a slowing down of psychomotor activity; possible impairments of sensory perception, particularly sight and hearing; a decrease in fluid intelligence and an increase in crystallized intelligence; and a greater vulnerability to disease. All of these changes can cause psychological suffering, which in turn can aggravate whatever impairment the older person has or thinks he has.

Intimately related to these psychological changes are the social changes that accompany aging—changes in the way the older person relates to his environment. However, unlike the physiological changes, which may or may not cause the person psychological distress, depending on how he responds to them, the social changes are often very difficult to adapt to, no matter what the older person's attitude. These social changes include lack of function—that is, the absence of any useful role after retirement and the departure of the children; poverty, another common painful consequence of retirement; unavailability of suitable living quarters; loneliness due to social isolation and the death of friends and family; and finally, negative social stereotypes, which can act as self-fulfilling prophecies and at the same time discourage people from trying to solve the problems of the aging, since, according to the stereotype, these problems are "natural." It is also natural, according to the social stereotype, for older people to terminate sexual activity—a misconception that often discourages continued sexual functioning in the aged and thus deprives them of an important source of pleasure and intimacy at a time in their lives when sources of pleasure and intimacy are few and precious.

Some older people cope with these stresses very efficiently, either because they have adaptable personalities or because they are faced with fewer and milder stresses. Others who are less adaptable and who have to cope with extremely heavy stress may succumb to either anxiety or depression, the two major functional disorders of the aged.

The anxiety of the aged stems primarily from concern over their last years, from the stress of making decisions and of learning new ways of coping with new circumstances, and from their sense of vulnerability in the face of these questions and challenges. Such anxiety tends to be manifested in self-preoccupation, rigidity, suspiciousness, and—very commonly—hypochondria.

Depression in the elderly appears to be largely reactive, occurring in response to the many losses which they must endure. The confrontation with death may add considerably to this depression, both because the closeness of death reminds the older person that whatever he has not achieved in his life will remain unachieved and because the older person is often no more willing to die than is the younger person. When serious depression occurs in the elderly, it can easily lead to suicide.

VII Dealing with Disorder

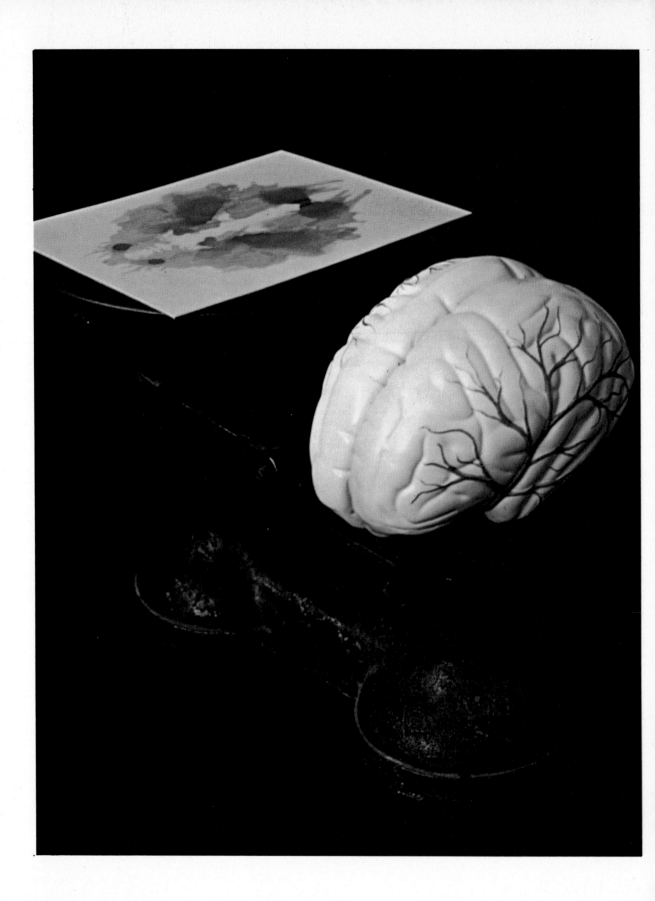

Our last thirteen chapters have been devoted to a study of the most common categories of abnormal behavior. And as categories, such disorders are relatively easy to study: we chart the symptoms, give illustrative case histories, weigh the possible causes, and review the suggested treatments. However, it is only in our professional vocabulary that these abnormal behaviors exist as categories. In reality, they are the complex and ambiguous things that people do and say. And the first job of the mental health professional is to look hard at what the person says and does and to make some sense out of his behaviors. This process is called *psychological assessment*, which Sundberg and Tyler define as "the systematic collection, organization and interpretation of information about a person and his situation" (1962, p. 81). In the following chapter we will examine the issues surrounding psychological assessment, the various types of assessment techniques, and the relationship between these assessment techniques and the major psychological perspectives.

ASSESSMENT: THE ISSUES

Why must a person be assessed? Does this assessment involve diagnostic labeling? If so, how useful is that label? How can we tell a good assessment technique from a bad one? And what are the outside factors that can influence assessment? All of these are very tricky questions, to which only imperfect answers can be given. The very practice of psychological assessment—to say nothing of the various assessment methods—is extremely controversial. Assessment was originally developed as a scientific tool, which, like all scientific tools, was aimed at describing, predicting, and controlling phenomena (Kaplan, 1964)—in this case, the phenomenon of human behavior. But just as there is some question as to whether psychology is a science, there is a great deal of question as to whether our present methods of psychological assessment can meet even the loosest standards of scientific precision. Thus, like psychological treatment, which we will examine in our next chapter, psychological assessment, though it is carried on every day of the week, is still in a thoroughly experimental stage.

Why Assessment?

There are basically two reasons for psychological assessment. The first is the need to measure the individual's psychological condition in order to make decisions about his future. Outside the clinical context, people are given psychological tests in order to determine who goes to which college, who should

18
Approaches to Assessment

be promoted within a company, who can withstand the pressures of a particularly trying government assignment, and so on. Those chosen to be astronauts or undercover agents, for example, are the survivors of extensive batteries of tests designed to measure their resistance to psychological stress. Within the clinical context—that is, the context of abnormal behavior—people are subjected to psychological assessment in order to determine what kind of behaviors they might be likely to display and what kind of treatment they require. Should this child be put in a special education program? Should his parents be called in for family therapy? Would that patient benefit from drugs? Would he do well in insight therapy? Should he be hospitalized—even against his will? It is these questions that assessment aims to resolve. And, needless to say, they are very critical questions indeed, the answers to which may determine the direction of the individual's entire future.

The second reason for psychological assessment has less to do with the needs of the individual than with the needs of the various institutions that surround his life. The fact is that these institutions require labels, and psychological assessment provides those labels. In order to get funding for its special-education program, a school system has to say how many mentally retarded children or how many autistic children it is handling. Hospitals and clinics, in applying for their funds, have to list the number of schizophrenics, neurotics, alcoholics, and so on that they are treating. Insurance companies require a diagnosis before they will begin paying the bills. The law courts, as we have seen, have to know whether or not a person is psychologically competent to stand trial. The mental health profession needs a diagnostic vocabulary for the purpose of research and even for the purpose of discussion. And finally, the society itself needs to know what its major mental problems are—which disorders are rare, which are on the rise. In short, institutions need statistics. And in order to fit the individual into the statistics, psychological assessment, in addition to weighing the problem and recommending treatment, must *name* the problem.

Assessment and Classification: DSM-II

Where does the assessor find a name for the problem? Generally he finds it in DSM-II, the diagnostic manual to which we have referred so frequently in this book. As we have seen in Chapter 1, DSM-II is based on the classification system developed by Kraepelin in the late nineteenth century. Closely tied

to the medical model, which in Kraepelin's time was the most popular approach to abnormal behavior, the manual, after various revisions, remains a prime target of criticism. These criticisms boil down to three basic arguments. The first argument is the humanistic contention that once the diagnostic label is applied, the human being in all his uniqueness and complexity is ignored; he is stamped as Brand X or Brand Y of deviant, and that label becomes his identity. Szasz (1965) has further pointed out that diagnostic labeling often results not only in a loss of individuality but also in a loss of social status and civil rights—a fact which leads Szasz to conclude that current diagnostic practices represent an illegitimate exercise of power on the part of mental health professionals.

The second argument—which, unlike the first, can be and has been empirically documented—is that diagnostic labels tell us very little about the people to whom they are applied. The basic assumption of DSM-II—and the rationale for its use—is that patients who receive the same classification will manifest essentially the same symptoms for essentially the same reasons and thus require essentially the same treatment. In other words, the diagnostic nomenclature is supposed to *help* in the job of describing, predicting, and controlling behavior. However, as numerous studies have pointed out, the diagnosis may have more to do with the socioeconomic status of the individual or with the comments of the diagnostician's more prestigious colleagues (Tremerlin, 1968; Langer and Abelson, 1974) than with the actual symptom picture. As a result of such interferences and the built-in inadequacies of the classification system, individuals receiving the same diagnosis may in fact behave quite differently. And conversely, individuals receiving different diagnoses may share a number of the same behavioral oddities. In short, there is little homogeneity within diagnostic categories. This fact was made clear in a famous study by Zigler and Phillips (1961) of the relationship between symptoms and diagnoses in 793 patients who had already been diagnosed by hospital psychiatric staffs. Rating the patients on a number of symptoms, these investigators found, for example, that the manic-depressives and the neurotics were equally likely to be self-deprecating and almost equally likely to be depressed; that somatic complaints were almost equally common in the manic-depressives, the neurotics, and the schizophrenics; that the occurrence of hallucinations was approximately the same in the manic-depressives and in those diagnosed as having character disorders; and that there were numerous other disturbing similarities among differently labeled patients. In view of such evidence, it is no surprise that the relationship between diagnosis and treatment is, at best, extremely loose (Stuart, 1970). In sum, knowing how a person has been diagnosed, we still know very little about what he does and what should be done with him.

A third focus of criticism with regard to DSM-II is a matter that we have already mentioned in previous chapters, particularly in Chapter 12—that is, the truly embarrassing lack of agreement among diagnosticians. This problem is particularly acute in the making of finer diagnostic distinctions (Schmidt and Fonda, 1956). Blashfield (1973), for example, asked a number of psychologists and psychiatrists to evaluate a series of simulated patient profiles and assign each "patient" to a schizophrenic subcategory; the resulting rate of agreement among any two judges assigned to the same profile was a dismally low 25 percent. The rate of agreement in assigning patients to broader categories is higher (Beck et al., 1962) but is in no way reassuring. Furthermore, the broader the category, the less, by definition, it tells us about the patient.

In view of these shortcomings,* we are faced with the question of why DSM-II is still used. The answer is that the mental health profession still requires a vocabulary and the institutions that surround the profession still require diagnoses, for the reasons stated above. Thus DSM-II continues to be widely used simply because it is the only comprehensive classification system we have.

Assessing the Assessment: Reliability and Validity

The shortcomings of DSM-II provide an excellent introduction, albeit a negative one, to the two major criteria used in judging assessment procedures: reliability and validity.

Reliability The *reliability* of any measurement device is the degree to which its findings can stand the test of repeated measurements. Thus, in its simplest sense, reliability is a measure of the consistency of such a device under varying conditions. In the

case of psychological assessment techniques, there are three tests of reliability:

1. *Internal consistency.* Do different parts of the test yield the same results?
2. *Test-retest reliability.* Does the test yield the same results when administered to the same person at different points in time?
3. *Inter-judge reliability.* Does the test yield the same results when scored or interpreted by different judges? (As we have just seen, DSM-II fares very poorly with regard to inter-judge reliability.)

As an example of the three measures of reliability, let us imagine that you are reading this book as part of a course in abnormal psychology. Midway through the semester, your instructor gives you a fifty-item multiple-choice examination in order to assess (i.e., grade) how much information you have absorbed from your reading. If the exam has a high degree of internal consistency, then we would expect that if the class material were randomly arranged within the exam and the whole arbitrarily split into two equal parts, you would do approximately as well on one part as you do on the other.

Now let us imagine that your class is given exactly the same exam once again two weeks later. If the test-retest reliability of the exam is high, then we would expect each student to score approximately the same, in relation to the other students, as he did two weeks earlier. If on the first round Maria and Nick scored fifteen points higher than Jenny and Sam, then this differential should be approximately the same on the second round. But—given that we ignore the possibility that the students have either forgotten the material or studied again—if the second round shows Jenny and Sam performing considerably better than Maria and Nick, then the test-retest reliability of the exam is suspect.

Finally, let us imagine that you and your classmates are at the end of the semester and have taken a final exam consisting of six essay questions. All the exams are graded both by the instructor and by a teaching assistant. If these two judges consistently agree on the grade to be given an exam, then the inter-judge reliability of the test is high; in other words, there are objective grading criteria. Conversely, if the assistant is repeatedly giving Bs where the professor has given Ds, then the inter-judge reliability of the exam is poor, and you have cause to question its adequacy as a measurement of your knowledge.

If an exam fails to measure up on these three scores of reliability, then it may cause considerable grumbling in the classroom. However, if a psycho-

---

*There are other criticisms, including the fact that DSM-II is based on a particular theoretical model of abnormal psychology—the medical model—and is therefore subject to the criticisms made of that model. And although DSM-II makes no claim to give the possible causes of the disorders it lists, the fact that it does not makes it less than an optimal classification system.

logical test proves unreliable, the consequences are somewhat more serious. If the test lacks internal consistency, then it will yield conflicting results: one item will show the patient to be a serene type while another item shows him to be racked with anxiety. If the test lacks test-retest reliability—so that, for example, a group that tested out as generally cheerful on one round tests out as generally depressed two weeks later—then the test is obviously a poor sample

of the individual's stable psychological characteristics. Finally, if the test fails to show inter-judge reliability, then it is obviously too vague to allow the making of clear interpretations. In any one of these three cases, the test will bring no one any nearer an answer as to what the individual's problem is.

Validity Whereas reliability is the measure of how consistently a test performs under various condi-

"On Being Sane in Insane Places"

Can the sane be distinguished from the insane with current diagnostic methods? In an attempt to answer this question, D.L. Rosenhan (1973) set up an experiment whereby eight psychologically stable people with no history of mental disorder would try to get themselves admitted to mental hospitals. The eight "pseudopatients"—three psychologists, a psychiatrist (Rosenhan himself), a graduate student in psychology, a pediatrician, a painter, and a housewife—presented themselves at separate hospitals in five different states. They all went under assumed names, and those involved in mental health lied about their professions. Otherwise they gave completely accurate histories, adding only one false detail: each of them claimed that he had been hearing voices that seemed to say something like "hollow," "empty," or "thud."

The pseudopatients' greatest fear in embarking on their experiment was that they would be unmasked as frauds and thrown out of the hospital, much to their embarrassment. It turned out that they had no reason to fear. With only one exception, they were diagnosed as schizophrenic, and without exception they were all admitted as mental patients.

Once they were admitted, the pseudopatients made no future reference to the voices. They behaved completely normally, except that they made special efforts to be courteous and cooperative. Yet not a single one of them was ever exposed as a fraud. Apparently, the staff simply assumed that because these people were in a mental hospital, they were disturbed. This assumption persisted despite the fact that all the pseudopatients spent a good part of the day taking copious notes on what went on in the ward. Far from being judged as a sign of normalcy, the note-taking was either ignored or interpreted as an indication of pathology. On one pseudopatient's hospital record, the

nurse recorded, day after day, this same suspicious symptom: "Patient engages in writing behavior" (p. 253). The genuine mental patients, however, were not so easily fooled. They regularly accused the pseudopatients of being completely sane and speculated out loud that they were either journalists or professionals sent in to check up on the hospital.

Without ever having had their "insanity" questioned, each of the patients was eventually discharged. Their stays ranged from seven to fifty-two days, with an average of nineteen days. Upon discharge, they were classified not as being "cured" or as showing no behavior to support the original diagnosis, but rather as having psychosis "in remission." In other words, their "insanity" was still in them and might rear its head at any moment—an assumption that would deeply influence any future employer's judgment of them (to say nothing of their judgment of themselves), had they been true patients.

From the evidence of this study, Rosenhan concludes that while there may in fact be a genuine difference between sanity and insanity, those whose business it is to distinguish between them are unable to do so with any accuracy whatsoever. Often on the basis of a single behavior, diagnosticians assign a label (such as "schizophrenic") that means nothing other than that the person in question manifests at least one behavior in common with other people who have been given that label. And thereafter the label—along with the fact that it has landed the person in a mental hospital—suffices as proof that the person is insane. Rosenhan suggests that it is time for diagnosticians to discard this circular process and to ask themselves again the question that appears to have been forgotten long ago: "If sanity and insanity exist, how shall we know them?" (p. 250)

tions—in other words, how consistent the test is with itself—*validity* is the measure of how consistent a test is with other sources of information about the same subject. For example, if a psychological test shows a child to be mentally retarded but his grades in school are good, his mother reports that he reads *The New York Times* every morning, and he appears normal during a psychiatric interview, then we have reason to suspect the validity of the test. In this case the test appears to lack *concurrent validity*—that is, consistency with other *current* findings on the same subject. Another type of validity is *predictive validity*, the degree to which a test's findings are consistent with the subject's *future* performance. Imagine, for example, that an intelligence test shows that a child is extremely gifted intellectually. The child is then put in special classes for gifted children, where he consistently falls behind the rest of the class, has no idea what the teacher is talking about, and feels very badly about himself as a result. In this case the predictive validity of the intelligence test would be called into question.

Essentially, validity and reliability are two different ways of measuring the same thing—that is, whether a test is equipped to tell us something *true* about a person. Hence it is not surprising that the two measures correlate well with one another. In the case of DSM-II, for example, inter-judge reliability, as we have noted, is notoriously poor; what is schizophrenic to one diagnostician may easily be manic-depressive to another. Consequently, it is almost inevitable that diagnoses based on DSM-II criteria should in many cases give us very little truly substantial information as to the patient's behavior (concurrent validity), and that many of these diagnoses should prove to be of little use in determining how the patient will respond to a particular treatment (predictive validity).

Assessment Interferences

When the findings of a test prove faulty, then what is showing up in the findings is something other than what is being tested. In other words, some outside factor is interfering with the accurate and objective assessment of whatever the test claims to be assessing. A test can be subject to a discouraging multitude of possible interferences. Furthermore, the objectivity of the test can be knocked askew at any one of the stages from the making up of the questions to the recording of an individual test result. If the test itself is fair and objective, the testing conditions may still influence the subject's performance considerably. And even if the making up

and administering of a test are miraculously free of interference, that same test is still vulnerable to the biases of whoever does the scoring or interpreting of results. Finally, to come full circle, a test may be administered and interpreted with exemplary objectivity yet still reflect the prejudices of whoever made up the test.

Cultural attitudes based on race and socioeconomic status represent one very serious source of interference, particularly in the creation of an assessment technique. For example, as we have noted in Chapter 2, the widely cited New Haven study (Hollingshead and Redlich, 1958) reported that lower-class people have a better chance of being diagnosed as psychotic, while the middle classes have a better chance of being diagnosed as neurotic. Hence it is highly possible that our diagnostic criteria for distinguishing between neurosis and psychosis are based on middle-class assumptions as to what is an appropriate response to stress, with the result that lower-class styles of responding to stress are designated as "crazier." It has also been charged repeatedly (e.g., Mischel, 1968; Williams, 1970) that intelligence tests, because they are generally made up by white middle-class psychologists, are measures not of intelligence but rather of the kind of knowledge typical of white middle-class culture. If a white middle-class six-year-old cannot identify a giraffe, then this might seem unusual. But if a black lower-class six-year-old who has limited access to books, has never been taken to a zoo, and has not gone to nursery school cannot identify the giraffe, is this to be interpreted as a sign of deficient intelligence?

Another major source of interference is the testing situation, where any number of variables can affect the subject's performance. One of the most notable of these situational variables is the examiner himself (Masling, 1960; Mischel, 1968; Barber and Silver, 1968). Examinations may be standardized, but not examiners. If the examiner is typically cold and aloof in assessment situations, the subject—particularly a child or a troubled adult—may respond in a highly guarded and apprehensive manner. And if the examiner then writes down that the subject seems withdrawn and suspicious or that his intellectual responses are slow, how is the next person reading this report supposed to know what influences determined these interesting behaviors? Even personal attributes that the examiner cannot control, such as physical appearance, race, and sex, may affect test performance.

Not unpredictably, a second major situational variable known to affect test performance is the way

IS IQ INHERITED?

For years civil-rights-minded critics have been protesting against the cultural bias of the standard IQ tests. However, it was not until 1969 that this debate reached a fever pitch. In that year Arthur Jensen, an educational psychologist, published a long article entitled "How Much Can We Boost IQ and Scholastic Achievement?" Attempting to account for the failure of the Head Start program to effect any lasting change in IQ, Jensen suggested, on the basis of his own research and that of others, that the 11- to 15-point differential between the average IQ scores of blacks and whites was largely due to genetic rather than environmental factors. In support of his antienvironmental argument, Jensen claimed that even within the same socioeconomic brackets, the average scores of blacks were lower than those of whites; that while American Indians generally suffered greater environmental deprivation than blacks, their average IQ was higher than that of blacks; that lower IQ scores among blacks did not correlate with the absent-father syndrome from which many lower-class black families suffer; and finally, that the race of the examiner did not have any substantial effect on the IQ scores of black children.

No sooner was this paper published than Jensen's argument and Jensen himself were virulently attacked. From the storm of racial bias and racial hatred that was unleashed on both sides, however, a few cogent rebuttals of Jensen's thesis emerged:

1. Jensen took no account of environmentally based *organic* factors, such as intellectual impairment due to lead poisoning, which is particularly common among black children.

2. To rule out environmental influence by comparing scores of "middle-class" blacks with "middle-class" whites is to ignore the fact that there are still differences between the life styles of black and white children who are supposedly of the same class. For example, not only the parents but also the grandparents of a middle-class white child may have been educated professionals; in contrast, the middle-class black family is likely to be a new arrival and thus to retain certain ties to lower-class culture.

3. When faced with a test, black children are handicapped by having greater anxiety, less confidence and motivation, and less-developed test-taking skills than white children. These factors, while nonintellectual, can profoundly affect IQ test performance.

4. Jensen's conclusions were based in large part on studies of heritability of intelligence among whites, whereas there has been little research on heritability of intelligence among blacks.

5. Finally, there is the matter of cultural bias built into the tests. The tests assume familiarity with the objects, vocabulary, and skills typical of middle-class life. Critics continue to insist that it is this middle-class know-how, and not intellectual acumen, that the IQ tests measure, and that it is this fact that accounts for the lower average scores of black children.

It should be pointed out that most scientists acknowledge that heredity plays some part in determining intelligence. The question under debate is whether its influence can so enormously outweigh that of environment—and whether the gene pool of an entire race of people can be said to contain less "intelligence" than that of another race. These questions, raised by Jensen, remain unanswered. The controversy, while no longer raging, is still quite active, and it has led to renewed efforts to develop bias-free intelligence tests. In the meantime, however, the dominant culture in the United States remains a white middle-class culture, and consequently the ability to maneuver in that culture remains a central component of school and career success. If it is this ability that the standard IQ tests measure, it is difficult to say what predictive value a culturally neutral IQ test would serve. If there is such a thing as raw "intelligence," where will we find a society in which this intelligence alone—and not culturally transmitted values, customs, and skills—determines success?

Fig. 18.1 The young woman's test responses are influenced by her reactions to the examiner, whom she perceives as a cold, threatening, sharklike person. The extent of his effect on her responses is difficult to measure, although it may be considerable. "Experimenter effects" present formidable difficulties in psychological assessment. Clinical observations and extensive research have shown that personality factors such as warmth or aloofness, sex, and racial or ethnic characteristics of the examiner can alter an individual's responses to intelligence or personality test items. Furthermore, the scoring and interpretation of test responses may vary according to the examiner's own personality variables and expectations. Such immeasurable effects contribute to the unreliability of psychological tests and can reduce the plausibility of test interpretations and experimental conclusions.

The Dove Counterbalance Intelligence Test
by Adrian Dove

A "Gas Head" is a person who has a
(a) Fast moving car (b) Stable of "lace" (c) Process (d) Habit of stealing cars (e) Long jail record for arson

If a man is called a "Blood," then he is a
(a) Fighter (b) Mexican-American (c) Negro (d) Hungry Hemophile
(e) Redman or Indian

In "C. C. Rider," what does "C. C." stand for?
(a) Civil Service (b) Church Council (c) County Circuit, preacher of an old-time rambler (d) Country Club (e) "Cheating Charley" (the "Boxcar Gunsel")

Cheap "chitlings" (not the kind you purchase at the frozen-food counter) will taste rubbery unless they are cooked long enough. How soon can you quit cooking them to eat and enjoy them?
(a) 15 minutes (b) 2 hours (c) 24 hours (d) 1 week (on a low flame)
(e) 1 hour

If a judge finds you guilty of "holding weed" (in California), what's the most he can give you?
(a) Indeterminate (life) (b) A nickel (c) A dime (d) A year in county
(e) $100.00

A "Handkerchief Head" is
(a) A cool cat (b) A porter (c) An "Uncle Tom" (d) A hoddi (e) A "preacher"

"Tell it like it
(a) Thinks I am" (b) Baby" (c) Try" (d) Is" (e) Y'all"

"You've got to get up early in the morning if you want to
(a) Catch the worms" (b) Be healthy, wealthy, and wise" (c) Try to fool me" (d) Fare well" (e) Be the first one on the street"

"Walk together, children,
(a) Don't you get weary—there's a great camp meeting" (b) For we shall overcome" (c) For the family that walks together talks together" (d) By your patience you will win your souls" (Luke 21:19) (e) Find the things that are above, not the things that are on Earth" (Col. 3:3)

Which word is most out of place here?
(a) Splib (b) Blood (c) Gray (d) Spook (e) Black

If a Pimp is up tight with a woman who gets California State aid, what does he mean when he talks about "Mother's Day"?
(a) Second Sunday in May (b) Third Sunday in June (c) First of every month (d) None of these (e) First and fifteenth of every month

Fig. 18.2 It has often been noted that members of minority groups do not perform as well on intelligence tests as white middle- or upper-class individuals do. Recently, charges have been leveled against intelligence tests on the grounds that they are prepared by white middle-class psychologists for the testing of white middle-class values and knowledge. To emphasize these inequities and to point out the different values and knowledge inherent in minority group environments, Adrian Dove, a black social worker, developed the Dove Counterbalance Intelligence Test, examples from which are shown here.

the subject happens to be feeling that day. If his girl friend has just broken up with him, if he has just been turned down for a coveted job, or even if he is simply tired or has a cold, this can influence his responses to test questions.

So far we have limited our discussion to variables affecting the makeup of tests, the testing situation, and the subject's performance. However, perhaps the most likely and the most controversial area of possible interference is the evaluation and interpretation of test performance—in short, the biases of the examiner. This is not to imply that examiners consciously distort truth; rather they, like everyone else, have certain cognitive sets that color their perceptions. Furthermore, any interchange between one human being and another is bound to carry some positive or negative charge. However, there is serious question as to how strenuously examiners try to *control* for these cognitive sets and positive and negative charges.

There are many possible types of examiner bias. One is simply personal bias. Masling (1959) points out that even when scoring is standardized and comparatively objective, as on most intelligence tests, the responses of more attractive people may be scored more generously. Political or cultural bias can also interfere with evaluation. Facing an examiner whose cultural assumptions include the notion that minorities should, by way of compensation, be given the benefit of the doubt, a black person will have an advantage over a white person.

Likewise, an examiner's theoretical orientation, if

given the chance, almost inevitably affects evaluation. An apathetic young college student, if evaluated by a humanistic psychiatrist, might be said to have denied his true identity and to be suffering from existential neurosis. The same student, if assessed by a Freudian psychoanalyst, will appear to have serious conflicts left over from his psychosexual development, particularly conflicts having to do with aggressive impulses, to which his present apathy is a reaction formation. In this case, the diagnosis might be depressive neurosis. Finally, if the student were evaluated by a behaviorist, the report might include no label at all but rather a detailed discussion of the recent changes in the student's pattern of reinforcements. In sum, the examiner—like the lawyer, the politician, and so on—tends to find what he is looking for, particularly in the less objective testing situations. And what he is looking for is determined by his own theoretical loyalties.

Finally, a major criticism of traditional psychological assessment is that examiners and the tests they use are biased in favor of pathology. The diagnostician often has neither the tools nor the training to assess areas of strength, whereas he is rigorously trained to spot signs of weakness or deviance. Consequently, it is weakness and deviance that he tends to find. For example, in a study of court-appointed psychiatric examiners conducting interviews to determine sanity, Scheff (1966) found that the examiners tended to presume mental illness or incompetence on the part of interviewees. In fact, even though the behaviors of many of the interviewees were judged by independent outside observers to be quite unexceptional, the psychiatrists recommended treatment for mental disturbance in every one of the 116 cases studied. These decisions were often reached with lightning speed. Twenty-six of the interviews took only five to seventeen minutes, with an average length of ten minutes.

For many modern mental health workers, such biases—along with the traditional assumption that whatever the examiner finds is a sign of a stable psychological trait rather than a situational variable—are clear signs of the type of inbred arrogance with which Szasz (1965) charges the entire psychiatric profession. And the recognition of the role of bias and presumption in psychological assessment has led to a widespread suspicion of assessment procedures as a whole. This professional disenchantment has been supported by the recent public reaction against psychological tests and particularly intelligence tests, which are said to constitute an invasion of privacy and to invite misuse. As a result, many professionals now deemphasize assessment in

---

Test Interferences

Creating the test

Cultural bias in the makeup and wording of test problems

Administering the test

Subject's personal response to examiner, to examination room, and to being examined

Subject's mood in response to variables extraneous to test

Scoring the test

Examiner's personal, political, cultural, and theoretical biases

Examiner's bias toward pathology

---

favor of direct treatment, prevention, and the analysis of the situational and ecological stresses that can generate abnormal behavior. However, these recent trends have in no way put an end to psychological assessment. On the contrary, psychological testing and evaluation go on every day in thousands of rooms across the country, often for very good reasons. Our next section will review the various assessment methods most commonly used today.

METHODS OF ASSESSMENT

Current assessment techniques fall into four general categories: the interview, psychological tests, situational observation, and physiological tests.

The Interview

Of all the methods of assessment, the *interview*, the face-to-face conversation between subject and examiner, is the oldest, the most commonly used, and the most pliable. It may be highly structured, with the subject answering a prearranged sequence of questions, or it may be highly unstructured, giving the subject the chance to describe his problem and his thoughts about it in his own way and at his own speed. The degree to which the interview is structured and the type of questions asked will of course depend on the interviewer's purpose. If his aim is simply to put the client at ease, in the effort to promote confidence and candor, then the structure will be loose. However, usually the interviewer has a fairly clear idea of the type of information he requires in order to recommend or proceed with treatment. Consequently, most interviews have some definable structure guiding the subject as to what kind of information the interviewer wants—whether it be about his childhood and development or about the stresses and rewards of his current life situation.

The possible pitfalls of assessment by interview are not hard to imagine. Both the interviewer's personality and the subject's transient mood can have a great impact on the quality of the subject's responses. Likewise, the interview, because it is structured and interpreted solely by the interviewer, can give uncontrolled free play to the interviewer's subjectivity and biases. For this reason, a fairly structured interview is often recommended, even though it does restrict the subject's responses.

Psychological Tests

More structured than the normal interview, the *psychological test* presents the subject with a unified series of stimuli to which he is asked to respond. This procedure, like the highly structured interview, gives the subject little freedom in responding, but because of its restrictive quality, the psychological test can be scored more easily and more objectively. Most psychological tests follow what is called the *psychometric approach*. This historically dominant method of measuring human behavior aims at locating stable underlying characteristics or *traits* (e.g., anxiety, passivity, aggression, intelligence) which are assumed to exist in differing degrees in the entire testing population. Because it assumes the existence of stable traits and aims to measure these traits, the psychometric method considers response variability due to situational influences to be simply a source of error and makes every effort to screen out such influences.

There are many different kinds of psychological tests. We shall examine only the most important categories: intelligence tests, projective personality tests, self-report personality inventories, and tests for organic impairment.

Intelligence Tests *Intelligence tests* were the first widely used psychological assessment technique. Modern intelligence tests are based on the work of Alfred Binet, the French psychologist who in 1916 introduced the first intelligence test, to be used in the French school system in order to decide which children should go on to higher education. Since revised by Lewis Terman of Stanford University and now known as the Stanford-Binet Intelligence Scale, the test measures a child's ability to recognize objects in a picture, to remember a series of digits, to define simple words, to complete sentences in a logical fashion, and so forth. The final score is rendered as an *intelligence quotient* (IQ) which is computed by dividing the subject's "mental age"—that is, the age level on which he is presumably operating intellectually—by his chronological age and then multiplying by 100.

In recent years the Stanford-Binet has taken second place to the Wechsler Intelligence Scales. Developed by the American psychologist David Wechsler, these tests, unlike the Stanford-Binet test, are adapted to adults as well as children and yield not only general IQ, but also a Verbal IQ, measuring knowledge and comprehension, and a Performance IQ, measuring the ability to solve problems. For example, to measure Verbal IQ, an adult might be asked how many days there are in a year or how many state capitals there are in the United States. To measure Performance IQ, he might be asked to decode a simple message or to reproduce a block design with differently shaped blocks. There are three Wechsler tests: the Wechsler Adult Intelligence Scale (WAIS), the Wechsler Intelligence Scale for Children (WISC), and the Wechsler Preschool and Primary Scale of Intelligence (WPPSI), each geared to the age group specified.

In evaluating intelligence tests, which have been under heavy attack in recent years, it must be remembered, as Wechsler (1958) himself has pointed out, that intelligence is not an existing *thing*, such as heart rate or blood pressure, that can be objectively quantified. Rather, it is a mental construct; it is whatever the people who make up the test construe intelligence to be. And basically the notion of intelligence reflected in intelligence tests is equivalent to the ability to handle the types of tasks meted out by our current educational system. In short, what these tests predict—and predict fairly accurately—is success in school. As for whether they measure intelligence as well, this depends on one's definition of intelligence.

Projective Personality Tests *Projective personality tests* are based on the psychodynamic assumption

Fig. 18.3 These test items are similar to those included in the various Wechsler intelligence scales. (Top left) A sampling of questions from five of the verbal subtests; (top right) a problem in block design, one of the performance subtests in which the subject is asked to arrange the blocks to match a pattern on a card that he is shown for a brief period of time; and (bottom) another example of a performance subtest in which the subject is required to put together puzzle pieces to form an object such as a duck. (Reproduced by permission of The Psychological Corporation, New York.)

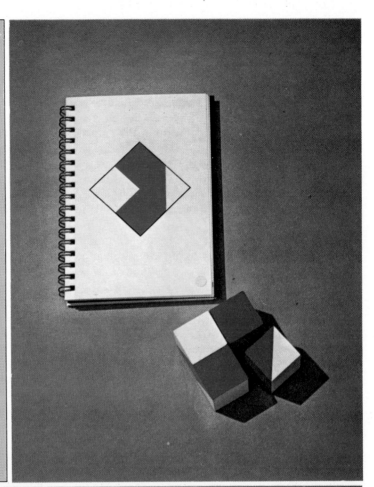

Paraphrased Wechslerlike Questions

General Information
1. How many wings does a bird have?
2. How many nickels make a dime?
3. What is steam made of?
4. Who wrote "Paradise Lost"?
5. What is pepper?

General Comprehension
1. What should you do if you see someone forget his book when he leaves his seat in a restaurant?
2. What is the advantage of keeping money in a bank?
3. Why is copper often used in electrical wires?

Arithmetic
1. Sam had three pieces of candy and Joe gave him four more. How many pieces of candy did Sam have altogether?
2. Three men divided eighteen golf balls equally among themselves. How many golf balls did each man receive?
3. If two apples cost 15¢, what will be the cost of a dozen apples?

Similarities
1. In what way are a lion and a tiger alike?
2. In what way are a saw and a hammer alike?
3. In what way are an hour and a week alike?
4. In what way are a circle and a triangle alike?

Vocabulary
This test consists simply of asking, "What is a _____?" or "What does _____ mean?" The words cover a wide range of difficulty or familiarity.

that an individual's true conflicts and motives, because they are largely unconscious, must be drawn out indirectly by presenting the individual with ambiguous stimuli and allowing him to project his private self into his responses. Thus projective tests expose the subject to vague stimuli into which he himself must read meaning; there is no right or wrong answer. And whatever meaning the subject gives to the stimulus, this response is thought to contain clues, which the interviewer must interpret, as to the subject's unconscious thoughts. Murstein (1961) has further pointed out that the projective tests assume (1) that no response is accidental, so every response is interpretable, (2) that the subject is unaware of what he is revealing about himself, and (3) that verbal responses to the test parallel the subject's behavior in his social environment.

Perhaps the most famous of the projective tests is the Rorschach Psychodiagnostic Inkblot Test (Rorschach, 1942), in which the subject is asked to respond to ten cards, each showing a symmetrical ink-blot design. The designs vary in complexity and shading, becoming increasingly colorful as one looks through the sequence. Administration of the test involves three phases. In the first phase, the *free association* phase, the testee is asked to describe as specifically as possible what each card reminds him of. The examiner records all of the subject's comments, as well as the time that he takes to respond and any pertinent nonverbal behavior (e.g., nail-biting, shifting about in the seat) that accompanies the response. The second phase, called the *inquiry* phase, involves questioning the testee as to which characteristics of each ink blot contributed to forming his impression of that ink blot. If, for example, the subject said that a card reminded him of two little girls fighting over a toy, then the examiner might ask the subject to state exactly what in the ink blot made him conclude that the figures were girls rather than boys. The final phase, called *testing the limits*, consists of telling the subject what other people usually report when exposed to a particular card and asking him to point out which characteristics of each ink blot would justify the typical response. Using such information, some diagnosticians claim to be able to rate the subject on such matters as anxiety, hostility, possible homosexual involvement, neurosis, psychosis, and organic brain damage.

A second projective technique which enjoys wide popularity is the Thematic Apperception Test—the TAT (Morgan and Murray, 1935). In this test the subject is presented with up to thirty pictures in black, white, and shades of gray. Unlike the utterly ambiguous ink blots, the TAT pictures show a person, or possibly two or three people, doing something, but the scenes are still vague enough to allow for a variety of interpretations. With each card, the subject is asked to describe what has happened prior to the scene presented in the picture, what is going on in the picture itself and what the characters are thinking and feeling, and what the final outcome will be. Some researchers (e.g., Rapaport et al., 1968) have argued that certain cards are particularly useful in eliciting certain types of information, such as the presence of underlying depression, suicidal ideation, or strong aggressive impulses. Like the Rorschach, the TAT includes an inquiry phase to clarify ambiguous responses. Then, through a complex scoring system, the subject's responses are converted into an interpretation of his unconscious conflicts and motivations. A children's version of this test, the Children Apperception Test or CAT (Bellak, 1954), follows the same principles as the TAT except that animals are substituted for human figures, on the assumption that children can tell stories about animals more readily than they can stories about people. The animals are clearly presented in feeding, toileting, and rivalry situations, and thus responses readily lend themselves to psychodynamic interpretation.

Another subclass of projective devices requires the subject to draw pictures of common objects. One popular test in this category is the Draw-A-Person Test, or DAP (Machover, 1949). The assumption underlying this test is that whenever a person draws a human figure, he is drawing a self-portrait. Many characteristics of the drawing—including placement of the figures, shading, size, and erasures—are studied to provide information regarding the anxieties, impulses, and defenses of the testee. For example, Machover, who developed the test, suggested that a prominent mouth is indicative of sexual difficulties, while oversized eyes and ears are signs of suspiciousness or paranoia.

Sentence-completion tests and word-association tests may also be considered projective techniques, although the assumptions underlying these methods are not as tightly bound to traditional psychoanalytic theory as are the assumptions behind the Rorschach, TAT, or DAP. A widely used sentence-completion test is the Rotter Incomplete Sentences Blank (Rotter and Rafferty, 1950), a printed form which contains sentence stems such as "I feel foolish . . ." or "Women . . ." which the subject is asked to complete. This test is very often used in clinical settings

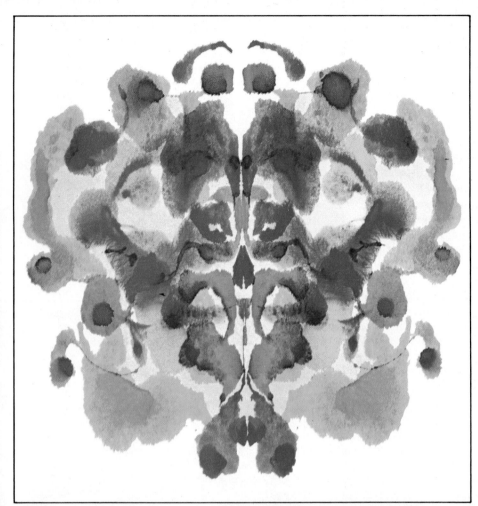

Fig. 18.4 *Shown at the left is an ink blot card similar to those found in the Rorschach Inkblot Test, and below are pictures comparable to those used in the Thematic Apperception Test (TAT). Both the Rorschach and the TAT have been widely used in clinical situations as projective techniques. The subject is assumed to project aspects of his personality in his responses to the ambiguous test stimuli.*

to provide the diagnostician with insights about specific areas of personality functioning. Word-association tests require the subject to give connotative associations to a stimulus word. For example, if the examiner says "table," the subject may say, "chair, floor, linoleum, glue," and so on. After the train of associations is completed, the stimulus word may be read again and the subject asked to reproduce the original associations. Thus, the word-association tests provide information about cognitive processes and memory as well as the usual presumed clues to the subject's unconscious.

Of all the varieties of psychological testing, the projective techniques incontestably allow the subject the greatest freedom in expressing himself. However, they also allow the interviewer the greatest freedom in interpreting the subject's responses, and herein lies the major problem with this type of testing. Opponents of the projective tests claim that the chain of inference leading from the subject's response to the interviewer's report is simply too long, too complex, and too subjective, with the result that the report may tell more about the interviewer than about the subject (Ullmann and Krasner, 1975). This argument has been supported by numerous studies (e.g., Datel and Gengerelli, 1955; Little and Shneidman, 1959; Howard, 1962) revealing the poor inter-judge reliability of the projective tests. And as may be expected with a method that can lend itself to many different clinical interpretations, the validity of the projective tests has been found by many researchers to be disturbingly low (Nunnally, 1967; Mischel, 1968; Peterson, 1968, Chapman and Chapman, 1969). In response to such evidence, supporters of the projective techniques claim that these tests are still the only assessment methods that are open and flexible enough to tap the unconscious.

Self-Report Personality Inventories *Self-report personality inventories*, unlike the projective tests, ask the subject direct questions about his personality and his feelings. Such a test may ask the subject to rate a long list of descriptive statements—e.g., "I am afraid of the dark" or "I prefer to be alone most of the time"—according to their applicability to him-

Fig. 18.5   Three of the stimulus cards from the Children Apperception Test (CAT) are shown here. Test assumptions and directions are similar to those of the TAT. The use of animals in humanlike interactions is believed to facilitate the child's identification with the stimulus materials. The responses to these cards give the examiner material for interpreting the child's personality dynamics and for formulating a diagnosis, prognosis, and probable treatment.

Fig. 18.6   Among the projective tests used in conjunction with interviews and therapy techniques are the Draw-A-Person, House-Tree-Person, and Draw-A-Family, all of which yield relatively inert figure drawings. Burns and Kaufman (1970) have developed an approach to assessment known as "kinetic family drawings," in which the subject is instructed to produce a drawing that shows figures doing something. The authors maintain that the kinetic family drawings produce dynamic material with which to attempt an understanding of disorder in a family environment. The drawings shown here and the interpretations that follow are adapted from a case study presented by Burns and Kaufman (1970) in Kinetic Family Drawings (K-F-D). (1) This picture was done by a thirteen-year-old girl named Chris when she was asked to draw a person. It reflects a degree of compulsivity in the exactness of the drawing and in the off-center design of the blouse. In addition, the pants-skirt and flat bosom suggest sexual ambivalence. Chris' drawing of a family (2) depicts a somewhat rigid group of people. Several notable features include the pock marks on the father's face and his relatively apathetic expression. Although the mother and older sister have pockets in the breast areas, which reveal their sexuality, the drawing of the "self" features a pattern of crosshatching, which suggests obsessive thoughts as well as a denial, or crossing out, of her sexuality. The only significant aspects of the house-tree-person drawing done by Chris (3) are the compulsive balancing of the features of the house and the fact that the person in the drawing is again wearing pants, although female sexual traits are beginning to appear. In the kinetic family drawing (4), there is a reversal of roles, with the father working at the stove in the kitchen and the mother smoking a cigarette in the living room. Unlike the other members of the family, the father is turned away. Interpretations of projective test responses are particularly risky if the diagnostician does not have accurate information about the subject and his life situation. In this case study, the diagnostician could not blindly interpret the parents' role-reversal without information about their respective participation in family life. Because of the father's emotional problems, all of the children had been removed from the family. The mother reported that Chris' father had sexually molested all of the children and had been institutionalized. Through the dynamics illustrated in Chris' drawings, especially the kinetic family drawing, the authors were better able to understand Chris and therefore to help her.

I have never indulged in any unusual sex practices.

Someone has been trying to poison me.

I am afraid of losing my head.

I feel anxiety about something or someone almost all the time.

Fig. 18.7   Four of the test items used in the Minnesota Multiphasic Personality Inventory are reproduced above. The MMPI profile sheet is the usual basis for interpretation of this test; MMPI "manuals" and computer-based analyses have been developed to help the psychologist with the formulation of objective personality descriptions based on MMPI statistical profiles. In addition, the clinical psychologist draws upon his own experiences with the MMPI profiles of patients in order to formulate personality descriptions and make predictions and decisions. Several new MMPI scales have recently been devised and are being subjected to extensive research in order to establish their reliability and validity. (Reproduced by permission. Copyright 1943, renewed 1970 by the University of Minnesota. Published by The Psychological Corporation, New York. All rights reserved.)

self. Or the test may consist of a list of things or situations which the subject is asked to rate according to how much they appeal to him or frighten him. In any case, in the self-report inventory, as the name indicates, the subject assesses himself. This self-assessment may not be taken at face value by the psychologists interpreting the test, but it is given some weight.

Thus the self-report inventory differs considerably from the projective test. Whereas the latter involves ambiguous stimuli, ambiguous responses, and a highly subtle and complex process of interpretation aimed at seeing through distortions and defense mechanisms, the former assesses direct answers to direct personal questions. In short, the projective test takes the subject's responses as suggestive *signs* of his underlying personality dynamics, while the self-report inventories take the subject's responses as actual *samples* of his behavior. For example, a person who shows up as paranoid on a self-report inventory would do so primarily because he has answered yes to such statements as "Someone is out to get me" or "People often talk about me behind my back." Conversely, when a person is diagnosed as paranoid on the basis of a Rorschach test, this diagnosis is generally founded on a rather sinuous

interpretation of such factors as the presence of eyes in the subject's ink-blot interpretations or the suggestion of hostility in his responses.

The most widely used of the self-report personality inventories is the Minnesota Multiphasic Personality Inventory or MMPI (Hathaway and McKinley, 1943). This test was developed to simplify the process of differential diagnosis of psychiatric patients by comparing their statements about themselves to those provided by already diagnosed groups of schizophrenics, paranoids, depressives, and so on. Thus it is important to note that a subject's self-description is not actually taken at face value. If he answers yes to such statements as "Voices speak to me in the night" or "Someone is pouring filthy thoughts into my head," he is not automatically diagnosed as schizophrenic. Rather, the diagnosis depends on whether his responses to these statements conform to those of "known" schizophrenics.

The test items range from statements of rather workaday vocational and recreational preferences to descriptions of truly bizarre behaviors. We have already given a few examples of the latter. Other items similar to those on the MMPI checklist would be

"I go to a party every week."
"I am afraid of picking up germs when I shake hands."
"I forgive people easily."
"I sometimes enjoy breaking the law."

The test items were originally put together from a list of statements that a number of clinicians felt would be typical of certain diagnostic groups. Then these items were tried out on groups of already diagnosed hysterics, schizophrenics, and so forth, and only those statements on which a group showed substantial agreement were retained. Then the items were tried out on groups of normal individuals, and only those items on which the normal groups substantially disagreed with the pathological groups were retained. In the end, the test was made up of 550 statements, yielding a rating of the subject on ten clinical scales: hypochondriasis, depression, hysteria, psychopathic deviation, masculinity-femininity (i.e., the degree to which the subject shows presumably masculine or feminine traits), paranoia, psychasthenia (i.e., rigidity and anxiety), schizophrenia, hypomania (i.e., manic behavior), and social introversion (i.e., shy, self-effacing behavior). In addition to the clinical scales, the MMPI rates the subject on three control scales designed to measure the validity of the subject's responses. The L (Lie) scale indicates the degree to which the subject appears to be falsifying his responses to show himself in a more favorable light. For example, if a subject has answered yes to some extremely improbable statement, such as "I can't remember ever having lied to anyone," then this would boost his score on the L scale. The F scale is a measure of the subject's carelessness or confusion in responding; if many of his answers seem improbable, though not necessarily faked in order to look good, he will score high on the F scale. The K scale indicates to what degree the subject has responded with unusual defensiveness or unusual candor.

While the control scales do allow the clinician to make some correction in a person's MMPI scores, there is a fair amount of distortion that can slip past these controls. A good deal of attention has been given recently to the matter of *response sets*—that is, test-taking attitudes that lead the subject to distort his responses, often unconsciously. One such response set is the *social desirability* set, leading the person to ascribe to himself qualities that will make him look good; this problem can be controlled to some degree by the L scale but cannot be entirely eliminated in a test such as the MMPI (Edwards, 1953). Another response set that can distort an MMPI profile considerably is the *acquiescence* set, in which the subject tends to agree with a statement regardless of its applicability to him.

The interference of response sets, which can lead to highly inaccurate profiles, constitutes the major drawback to self-report inventories such as the MMPI. Critics of this assessment method have also pointed out that the test has no way of controlling for external variables affecting the test-taking situation. Finally, it has been argued that little accuracy can be hoped for from an assessment method that compares subjects to patients diagnosed according to DSM-II, which, as we have seen, has a poor record for validity and reliability. In response to this last criticism, it should be noted that the pathological groups on whose responses the test was standardized included only patients whose diagnosis was agreed upon by a number of psychiatrists. However, the major argument in support of the MMPI is that it is an extremely convenient and time-saving method of screening patients; indeed, the computers which now analyze the answer sheets and make up the profiles can do so in less than one and a half seconds. Furthermore, while, as we have seen, MMPI is not immune to error, it has been found to agree substantially with personality descriptions derived from elaborate case histories (Little and Shneidman, 1954).

The MMPI has had a number of descendants, self-report inventories designed to assess specific traits rather than the total personality. One such test is the California F Scale, designed to assess the subject's degree of authoritarianism by analyzing his responses to statements such as "In order to succeed, you have to learn how to control people." Another widely used self-report measure is the Fear Survey Schedule II (Geer, 1965) or FSS-II. This test lists a number of stimuli (e.g., seeing a fight, being with a member of the opposite sex, looking down from the top of a tall building) which the subject rates according to how much fear each of the stimuli elicits from him. The FSS-II is used not only to reveal areas of anxiety that require treatment but also to assess the progress of such treatment. Somewhat the opposite of the FSS-II, the Reinforcement Survey Schedule (Cautela and Kastenbaum, 1967) or RSS is a self-report measure aimed at discovering what the subject most enjoys. This test lists 54 stimuli, such as playing cards, being praised, or going to a movie, and asks the subject to rate these items according to how pleasurable he finds them. The RSS also asks for the individual's positive or negative reactions to six specific situations and asks him to list thoughts and activities in which he engages five, ten, fifteen, and twenty times a day. In the hands of the astute clinician, this scale can suggest areas of conflict and avoidance as well as fulfilling its primary goal of pinpointing the types of reinforcement to which the subject is likely to respond.

Unlike the MMPI, the FSS-II and the RSS tend to be taken largely at face value. Two other self-report tests go a step further than this, basing their value on their ability to measure not the "objective" truth about a person but rather his special and perhaps distortive way of perceiving. The Role Construct Repertory Test (Kelly, 1955) or "Rep" test attempts to identify the subject's "personal constructs"—that is, the sets of values and assumptions through which he perceives his world. Better-known than the Rep test is the Q-sort (Butler and Haigh, 1954), which aims at measuring a person's self-concept. In this test, the subject is given a pile of cards, each of which describes a certain personal quality (e.g., "Is well-liked," "Evades responsibility," "Works diligently"). He is then asked to sort the cards into nine piles, ranging from those which he feels are most descriptive of himself to those which he feels are least descriptive of himself. Often this procedure is followed by a second step, in which the subject re-sorts the cards in order to describe his "ideal self," the kind of person he would *like* to be. Repeated Q-sorts have been used to measure changes in self-concept as a result of therapy. Humanistic therapists have shown, for example, that discrepancies between real and ideal Q-sorts often decrease as psychotherapy progresses—a fact which makes the Q-sort useful in determining whether a therapeutic procedure is having any success (Rogers and Dymond, 1954; Rogers, 1959).

Tests for Organic Impairment As we have seen in Chapters 14 and 15, psychological problems may be organic rather than, or as well as, functional. The diagnosis of "organicity"—that is, neurological damage—may be arrived at through medical procedures such as surgery or biopsy, which allow direct observation of brain tissue. Less direct but also less dangerous are procedures such as the x-ray, which can detect the presence of tumors, and the EEG, which can reveal disturbances in the electrical functioning of the brain. However, with the increasing sophistication of psychological assessment techniques, certain types of pencil-and-paper tests have been developed that may actually be superior to these medical procedures in providing accurate and specific information as to neurological damage.

One device that is widely used in screening patients for organicity is the Bender Visual-Motor Gestalt Test (Bender, 1938). In this test the subject is shown nine simple designs, each printed on a different card, and is asked to reproduce these designs on a piece of paper. If certain errors such as rotation of the figures or rounding of the corners consistently appear in the subject's drawings, the examiner is likely to suspect neurological impairment. In some cases the test involves a second phase, in which the examiner asks the subject to reproduce the designs from memory. Failure to reproduce more than two designs is generally viewed as further evidence of impairment.

Skilled clinicians have also used projective techniques, primarily the Rorschach and various figure-drawing tests, to diagnose organicity. When the subject consistently provides primitive and poorly formed responses, this may be taken as a sign of organic damage. However, while projective devices can provide reliable general information about organicity, they cannot determine the specific location or magnitude of the suspected tissue damage.

Much more helpful in providing such specific information is a series of tests called the Halstead-Reitan Neuropsychological Battery. This battery involves a number of performance measures, including the Wechsler Adult Intelligence Scale. It also includes tests of perception of speech and rhythm as well as a test measuring the subject's ability to place various wooden forms into properly shaped receptacles while blindfolded. These latter tests allow the diagnostician to determine whether it is the left or the right sensory modality that is impaired and thus help him in pinpointing which hemisphere of the brain contains the lesion.

Filskov and Goldstein (1974) compared the predictive accuracy of the Halstead-Reitan Battery to that of six medical diagnostic techniques and concluded that the Halstead-Reitan surpassed all of the medical measures as a screening device. Since neuropsychological assessment done by means of tests such as the Halstead-Reitan poses no danger of injury to the subject, this type of testing for organic damage will undoubtedly enjoy increasing popularity in the future.

Situational Observation

As we have noted earlier, the psychometric approach to psychological assessment aims at the measurement of what are presumed to be the individual's stable characteristics. Accordingly, any variability due to situational influences is considered simply a form of troublesome interference, which the test-makers and examiners make every effort to eliminate. This approach has lately been challenged by a number of psychologists, who argue that most behavior—including those very characteristics or "traits" (e.g., depression, anxiety, introversion) that psychometric tests assume to be the bedrock of individual psychology, underlying situational influence—is actually situation-specific. According to this essentially behaviorist argument, the individual's thoughts and actions are based not on stable "traits" but rather on the changeable stimuli that surround him. Hence a person's behavior cannot be properly assessed outside the context of his everyday environment.

As a result of this recent shift in attitude toward assessment, researchers and clinicians are giving much more attention to the assessment of individuals through situational observation—that is, by unobtrusively assessing their behavior within a specific environmental context, particularly the context of their daily lives. In hospital settings, where patients are accustomed to having hospital personnel milling around, this type of observation is rather easy and has been used effectively in evaluating both individual patients and specific hospital environments. For example, Veit (1973) developed a complex recording system for evaluating the interactions

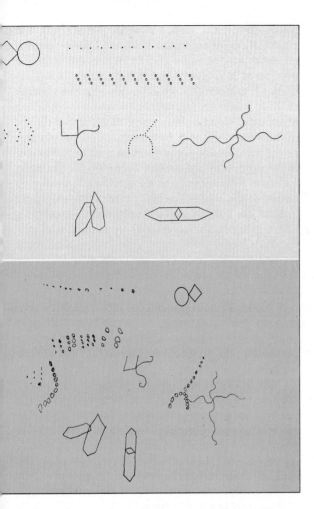

Fig. 18.8   The nine figures of the Bender Visual-Motor Gestalt test are shown. (Bottom) The reproductions of the Bender drawings done by a ten-year-old boy with an average IQ show evidence of his diagnosed brain damage. Characteristics of the boy's drawings, such as the reversal of the square and the circle in the first figure and the rotation of the last figure, strongly suggest organic impairment. Neurological tests are generally recommended for children whose test records reveal characteristics such as the ones cited in this case.

classroom to analyze precisely what environmental conditions provoke his outbursts—for example, ostracism by peers, punitive treatment by the teacher, academic tasks that are either frustratingly difficult or tediously simple. Once this information is collected, the examiner is in a better position to determine what the child's problem actually is and how his classroom environment can be altered to discourage his disruptive behavior. Likewise, observers can go into the home to assess problems that appear to be specific to the family environment.

This type of assessment by direct observation cuts down considerably on assessment errors due to the subject's response to the examiner or to the examiner's interpretive flights of fancy. Whereas a projective test may show that a child's problem is unresolved castration anxiety, situational observation may reveal that his "problem" is entirely specific to certain types of interaction with his mother—a variable that is much more easily dealt with than the presumed castration anxiety. However, situational observation is not without its own problems. In the first place, this technique requires an immense amount of time not only in the observation itself but also in the training of observers so that criteria are thoroughly understood and so that ratings of behavior are reliable and unbiased.* Second, observers often have to go to great lengths to disguise their function in the school and particularly in the home setting. A third problem is that while covert situational observation of a child may be authorized by his parents, there is no question that surreptitious observation of adults without their permission constitutes an invasion of privacy, no matter how useful therapeutically.

Physiological Testing

A final category of psychological assessment technique is the use of physiological testing. As we have seen, certain physiological techniques such as the

between attendants and retarded children in a large state training school. He found that 91 percent of all interactions were initiated by attendants, but that these interactions were positive in nature only about half as often as the interactions initiated by the children. A subsequent study by Dailey, Allen, Chinsky, and Veit (1974) found that when the attendants did initiate positive interactions, it was generally with children whom they perceived as physically attractive and likable. These studies were then used as a basis for recommending improved procedures for the training school.

In the case of these two studies, what was being assessed was essentially the impact of the environment and the responses of the individual to it. Other researchers and clinicians have sent trained observers into classrooms and homes to assess the relationship between individuals being assessed and the settings in which they operate. For example, if a child is consistently having behavior problems in school, then an observer may be sent into the

---

*Such training, however, is probably less extensive and expensive than training "expert" projective testers.

Common Assessment Techniques

INTERVIEW

PSYCHOLOGICAL TESTS

INTELLIGENCE TESTS

Stanford-Binet Intelligence Scale

Wechsler Adult Intelligence Scale (WAIS)

Wechsler Intelligence Scale for Children (WISC)

Wechsler Preschool and Primary Scale of Intelligence (WPPSI)

PROJECTIVE PERSONALITY TESTS

Rorschach Psychodiagnostic Inkblot Test

Thematic Apperception Test (TAT)

Children Apperception Test (CAT)

Draw-a-Person Test (DAP)

Rotter Incomplete Sentences Blank

SELF-REPORT PERSONALITY INVENTORIES

Minnesota Multiphasic Personality Inventory (MMPI)

California F Scale

Fear Survey Schedule II (FSS-II)

Reinforcement Survey Schedule (RSS)

Role Construct Repertory Test

Q-Sort

TESTS FOR ORGANIC IMPAIRMENT

Bender Visual-Motor Gestalt Test

Halstead-Reitan Neuropsychological Battery

SITUATIONAL OBSERVATION

BEHAVIORAL AVOIDANCE TEST (BAT)

PHYSIOLOGICAL TESTING

POLYGRAPH

EEG can aid in the diagnosis of organically based disorders. Such techniques can also be used to identify functional disorders. We have already examined in Chapter 6 the relationship between emotion and physiological changes, a relationship mediated by the autonomic nervous system. When a person's hostility level rises, so may his blood pressure. When his anxiety level rises, so may the level of activation in his sweat glands. Such changes can be monitored by physiological recording devices such as the *polygraph*, a machine equipped with a number of sensors, which when attached to the body can pick up subtle physiological changes. These fluctuations, in the form of electrical impulses, are amplified within the polygraph and activate pens which then record the changes on a continuously moving roll of paper. When sensors are attached to the scalp, the result is an EEG, a reading of the person's brain waves. When the sensor measures changes in the electrical resistance of the skin, then the result is a galvanic skin response (GSR). When the sensor is used to pick up subtle changes in the electrical activity of muscles, the result is an *electromyograph* (EMG). Likewise, the polygraph may also measure heart rate, blood volume, and blood pressure. All of these measures may be used as indicators of emotional responses to certain stimuli and thus may aid in the process of assessment. Consider, for example, a person who appears to be suffering from a pervasive anxiety, with no clear cause. If the examiner hooked the subject up to a polygraph, read him a list of possible anxiety-producing stimuli, and saw the EMG and GSR pens jump when the words "mother" and "homosexual" were read, then he might at least have some preliminary clues as to the source of the person's anxiety state.

A more situation-oriented means of gathering data on the relationship of physiological changes and various stimuli is to have the subject wear a portable blood-pressure recorder so that he can take his own blood pressure at regular intervals during the day, at the same time recording in a notebook what he is doing at the time of each reading. When the two records are compared and elevations in blood pressure correlate consistently with some specific environmental stimulus, such as the patient's interactions with his children, then once again the clinician is in a better position to design some kind of therapeutic treatment for the patient's problem, be it anxiety or hypertension.

ASSESSMENT AND THEORETICAL ORIENTATION

In our discussion of assessment interferences, we have already mentioned the relationship between an examiner's theoretical orientation and his assessment conclusions—the fact that psychodynamic clinicians tend to discover unconscious conflicts, that behaviorists tend to discover disadvantageous reinforcement patterns, and that humanists and existentialists tend to discover problems in self-concept and in responsibility taking. This is not to say that examiners wear blinders, but only that most psychologists and psychiatrists have a certain loyalty to one or another of the three major psychological perspectives discussed in this book. And basically what each of these perspectives constitutes is a notion of why human beings have problems. Hence it should come as no surprise that an examiner trained in a certain perspective tends to stress the same etiological principle in assessing the problems of a number of different patients. Likewise, it is predictable that examiners from the three different perspectives should favor three different varieties of assessment techniques, techniques which in each case are useful in detecting what the examiner expects to find—conflict in the unconscious, faulty reinforcement, or a distorted self-concept.

The Psychodynamic Approach to Assessment

As we have seen in Chapter 2, two basic assumptions of psychodynamic theory, as derived from Freud, are (1) that the individual's behavior is primarily determined not by his will or by his current environment, but by his inborn drives and his psychosexual history, and (2) that these latter factors operate unconsciously in motivating his behavior. Proceeding on these two assumptions, psychodynamic assessment procedures attempt to filter out all situational influences and to provide the subject with the freest and loosest atmosphere so that the "core" personality of unconscious memories, drives, and conflicts will reveal itself in its purity.

Basically this assessment strategy involves two techniques. The first is the *depth interview*, in which the subject is encouraged to talk about his past, and particularly his childhood history, as freely and as candidly as possible. Of special interest to the examiner is the subject's handling of sexual and aggressive impulses during the pregenital psychosexual stages, along with any possible traumas that occurred during these presumably crucial states. Hence the examiner may prompt the subject to talk about these matters.

The second major psychodynamic assessment tool is the projective test. This technique, as we have seen, gives the subject some stimulus to respond to, but at the same time keeps the stimulus vague enough so that rather than restrict the subject's verbalizations to a specific context and consequently allow his defenses to remain intact, the ambiguous stimulus will force him to fall back on his own imagination and thus to project, in symbolic fashion, whatever is lurking in his unconscious.

These psychodynamic assessment techniques may be said to have the same virtues and vices as psychodynamic theory itself. On the one hand, they represent one method of tapping the inner reaches of the personality, levels that lie below the individual's surface behaviors. On the other hand, they tend to accord the status of fact to assumptions that cannot be empirically validated—assumptions regarding the primacy of sexual and aggressive drives, the ineradicable influence of psychosexual development, the importance of Oedipal conflicts, and so forth. Furthermore, psychodynamic theory assumes,

as we have seen, that any verbalization is interpretable in terms of unconscious motivation. But if a person who is asked to use his imagination in interpreting an ink blot sees in that ink blot two staring eyes, does this really mean that he is paranoid? Is this not something like saying that because Shakespeare wrote a play about the melancholic Hamlet, he himself must have been depressed?

Essentially, what all these criticisms come down to is a serious concern regarding the faith that psychodynamic assessment places in the clinician's subjective judgment. Numerous studies have been conducted on the predictive validity of clinical interpretations (Meehl, 1954; Goldberg, 1959; Holtzman and Sells, 1954), on the reliability of such interpretations when aided by projective tests and self-report inventories (Little and Shneidman, 1959), and on the validity of interpretations made by trained clinicians as opposed to those made by laymen (Goldman, 1959; Soskin, 1959). Reviewing this vast literature on the accuracy of clinical judgment, Mischel makes the following rather discouraging summation:

In sum, studies of clinical inference generally have led to negative conclusions about its predictive validity. . . . Experienced clinicians tend to be no more accurate than inexperienced nonprofessionals like secretaries. . . . The accuracy of trait inferences is not improved by clinical training; when the judge departs from common stereotypes he may become less accurate. . . . Moreover, these conclusions generally obtain regardless of the test data on which judges base their interpretations. . . . Thus while clinical judgments are often better than random guesses, they usually provide poorer predictions than those available from cheaper and simpler sources like biographical and social case history information, or from the combination of facts by statistical rules . . . (1976, pp. 187–188).

The problem of clinical judgment is one that plagues mental health workers of all persuasions. But in view of the unparalleled freedom of interpretation exercised by psychodynamic clinicians, this difficulty is particularly pertinent to psychodynamic approaches to assessment.

The Behaviorist Approach to Assessment

Unlike psychodynamic theorists, who see behavior as controlled from within, the behaviorists, as we have seen in Chapter 3, regard behavior as controlled primarily by external stimuli. Thus when a person reports that his actions or feelings are distressing to him, the behaviorist, in assessing the problem, will focus his attention on determining with the greatest possible accuracy what stimulus patterns are reinforcing the maladaptive response (Kanfer and Phillips, 1970).

Because they see behavior as variable in relation to the environment, the behaviorists place little faith in such stable-trait-oriented assessment methods as the projective tests and the MMPI. Instead, they derive their information primarily from interviews, self-report check lists and journals, and situational observation.

An interview conducted by a behaviorist bears little relation to the depth interview favored by psychodynamic clinicians. Generally, a behaviorist assessment interview takes the form of what is called a *functional analysis*. What this involves is a systematic dissection of the person's complaint: what precisely the problem behavior is, how it developed, what the person has done to try to combat it, and—most important of all—what specific situations (i.e., reinforcing and punishing stimuli, which maintain, increase, or decrease behavior) tend to provoke the maladaptive response. Furthermore, the interviewer will also try to get some picture of the person's strengths and his preferences, since these are important in formulating a treatment program. It should be noted that in such an interview, unlike the psychoanalytic depth interview, the subject's remarks are assumed to be fairly frank statements of the problem rather than veiled clues to underlying dynamics.

In gathering his information, the behavioral examiner will often make use of behavioral check lists such as the FSS-II and the RSS in order to determine with greater accuracy the various stimuli that the patient tends to avoid and those which he finds most reinforcing. Furthermore, the examiner may ask the subject to keep a journal of his problem behaviors. For example, a patient who is afflicted with vague anxieties would be asked to keep a record of the times when his anxiety occurs and the circumstances surrounding these episodes. If the journal should reveal that one situation in which his anxiety regularly occurs is when he is taking the bus home from work, then this correlation will provide a starting point for determining the stimuli that are maintaining his anxiety.

Finally, a widely used behavioral assessment method is situational observation. As described earlier, the subject may be observed in his school, work, or home environment in order to identify the discriminative stimuli that trigger his maladaptive responses. Or the behavior sampling may take place in the clinical situation itself. For example, a person reporting a dog phobia may be asked to participate in a Behavioral Avoidance Test (BAT). Here the subject would be asked to enter a room in which there is a caged dog, to approach the dog, and, if possible, to play with the animal. In the meantime, his responses—not only his behavior toward the dog but also his extraneous signs of nervousness—would be viewed by observers seated behind a one-way mirror. This technique is helpful not only in determining the severity of the phobia (Bandura et al., 1967), but also in assessing the progress of treatment.

In evaluating the behavioral approach to assessment, it should be noted first of all that in general this approach fulfills very well its stated objective—that is, the detailed and concrete analysis of the problem behavior and the environmental conditions which support the behavior. On the negative side, behavioral assessment is subject to the same criticisms that have been leveled at behavioral theory in general: that it regards human beings as being on a par with experimental pigeons and white rats; that it attends only to the symptoms and ignores what are presumed to be the underlying causes, rooted in the total personality structure; that it tends to overlook organic factors; and finally, that its methods (e.g., covert situational observation) are not designed to take into account the individual's right to privacy and self-determination and thus at times bear a discomforting resemblance to authoritarianism. In answer to these charges, the behaviorists point out that a technique which works for human beings should not be discarded because it also works for white rats; that if problems can be solved by dealing with environmental contingencies, then there is no need for speculations as to unverifiable "underlying" causes; and that the behaviorists' excellent record of publicizing their research and therapeutic techniques in specific and quantifiable terms should protect them from the charge of authoritarianism.

The Humanistic-Existential Approach to Assessment

As we have mentioned in Chapter 3, behaviorist assessment procedures tend to avoid diagnostic labeling because the behaviorists feel that such labels obscure the actual problem. The humanists and existentialists also avoid labeling in the assessment process, mainly because they consider diagnostic labels an affront to the patient's individuality. The central focus of humanistic-existential psychology, as we have seen in Chapter 4, is precisely this matter of individuality—the uniqueness of each human being and the validity of his unique perceptions. And the central aim of humanistic-existential therapy is to restore to the patient his power as an individual—the power to be true to his own "self," to choose his own goals, and to take responsibility for his actions. In accordance with this orientation, humanistic-existential assessment procedures are aimed at helping both the therapist and the patient become more fully aware of precisely what the patient's unique self really is. In addition to the loosely structured interview, there are two assessment procedures that are particularly helpful in defining the individual's particular manner of perceiving himself and the world. The first is the Q-sort, described above, which Carl Rogers and other humanists have used extensively in measuring patient's self-concepts. Second is the Rep test, also described above, which was developed by a leading humanist, George Kelly. By revealing the mental constructs through which the individual perceives himself and his environment, the Rep test can be of considerable help to the examiner in viewing the subject's problem phenomenologically—that is, through the subject's own eyes—and thus assessing his difficulties in pursuing the dictates of his own true personality.

Such assessment techniques have two unique advantages. First, they focus on systematically obtaining a clear picture of the individual in all his idiosyncratic reality rather than on reducing and distorting his problems to fit theoretical formulas. Second, of all the assessment procedures that we have discussed, these techniques are probably the least contaminated by the pathological bias that we discussed earlier in this chapter. The major weakness of this phenomenological approach to assessment is that it must assume that what the individual says in his interviews or in a Q-sort or Rep test are true, at least for himself. Hence no account is taken of the possibility of intentional or semi-intentional distortion, which could seriously interfere with the therapist's effort to participate phenomenologically in the patient's internal world.

SUMMARY

Psychological assessment involves the systematic analysis of a person and of his life circumstances. In the case of clinical assessment, such analysis also involves defining the person's psychological problem. Assessment is carried out for two reasons: to help in making decisions regarding the person's future, particularly if he requires some form of therapy, and to assign a diagnostic label for the sake of the various institutions that surround the mental health profession. Such a diagnostic label is almost invariably based on the classification system provided by DSM-II. This system is of questionable accuracy in describing behavior and of questionable utility in determining treatment procedures. But at present it is our only comprehensive classification system, and it does function to provide mental health professionals with a diagnostic vocabulary, albeit an imperfect one.

There are two major criteria used in judging an assessment technique. The first is reliability, the degree to which an assessment device can produce the same findings under a variety of circumstances. The second is validity, the degree to which the assessment device produces findings that conform to findings from other sources. The weaknesses of DSM-II are essentially weaknesses in reliability and validity.

When an assessment technique proves to be wanting in either validity or reliability, this generally means that its findings have been distorted by some kind of extraneous interference. Particularly troublesome sources of interference are cultural biases embedded in the test itself, environmental variables (such as the subject's mood or the examiner's manner) affecting the subject's performance, and finally, personal, theoretical, and pathological biases on the part of the examiner interpreting the subject's responses.

There are four common methods of assessment. First is the interview, which may be structured and conducted in a variety of ways. A second technique is the administering of psychological tests, of which there is a wide variety: intelligence tests (e.g., the Stanford-Binet and Wechsler scales), projective personality tests (e.g., Rorschach, TAT, DAP), self-report personality inventories (e.g., MMPI, FSS-II, RSS, Q-sort), and tests for organic impairment (e.g., Halstead-Reitan Battery). A third and increasingly popular assessment method is situational observation, aimed at assessing the environmental determinants of the subject's behavior. Finally, physiological testing of such autonomic responses as blood pressure, brain waves, and galvanic skin response can provide clues as to the subject's emotional reactions to various stimuli.

An examiner's choice of assessment techniques is very often tied to his theoretical orientation. Psychodynamic clinicians tend to favor the depth interview and projective techniques, both of which require a great deal of interpretation on the part of the examiner. Behaviorist assessment, in contrast, eschews subjective interpretation and focuses instead on functional-analytic interviews, behavioral check lists, and situational observation. Finally, humanistic-existential assessment generally relies on a loosely structured form of interview and on assessment techniques (e.g., the Q-sort and the Rep test) which reveal the subject's individual manner of perceiving himself and others.

Centuries ago, when a woman could not get along with her husband or manage her child, or when she thought all her neighbors despised her, or when she simply found her life utterly dismal, she might go to her great-aunt or perhaps her priest and receive condolence and a dose of conventional wisdom: to try to understand her husband better, to spank her child more often or less often, to ignore her neighbors or woo them, and so on. Today the advice may be much the same, but the adviser has changed. Gone or weakened are the therapeutic institutions of the church and the extended family. And their place has been taken by the institution of psychotherapy.

Psychotherapy may be defined as a systematic and more or less structured series of interactions between a therapist—that is, a person trained and authorized by the society to minister to psychological problems—and a client who is troubled, or is troubling others, because of such a problem. The goal of psychotherapy is to produce in the client certain emotional, cognitive, or behavioral changes in order to alleviate the problem. Thus the new therapy differs from the old in that it is a sort of formal contract and, furthermore, a business contract. (The therapist is, after all, paid.) In addition, psychotherapy in many cases aspires to the level of science—that is, the level of constant and empirically verifiable laws of behavior—a goal undreamed of by the great-aunts and clerics of former centuries.

In the following chapter we shall examine first the recent changes in psychotherapy as an institution. Second, we will review the three major psychological approaches to therapy—the psychodynamic, behaviorist, and humanistic-existential—along with the recent trends in group therapy. Finally, we shall discuss the biological approach to treatment.

PSYCHOTHERAPY AS AN INSTITUTION

As we have seen in Chapter 1, men such as Philippe Pinel and William Tuke were already practicing, in the late eighteenth and early nineteenth century, a type of therapy not radically different from our own. But such therapy was reserved for the deeply disturbed and was merely the exception to the far more brutal rule of dealing with the mentally ill. Only in the first half of the twentieth century, after the widespread publication of Freud's theories of the human psyche, did psychotherapy truly come into its own. And no sooner did it become established and respectable than it began to undergo a number of changes, particularly after World War II.

19
Approaches to Treatment

In the first place, the rise of psychotherapy has been accompanied by increasingly vociferous challenges to the medical model. Rather than see psychological disturbance as the mere symptom of an underlying organic pathology, more and more therapists have come to see human problems, including even the severest psychosis, as the result of a conflict between the individual and his environment. This new line of thinking has led to two recent trends. First, the disturbed person's environment, and particularly the people closest to him, are being much more carefully scrutinized. For example, when a child is brought into treatment as a "behavior problem," the therapist may go into the home to try to correct the child's *interaction* with his family. Likewise, as we have seen in Chapter 9, a number of therapists are now treating sexual problems such as impotence and orgasmic dysfunction as a disturbance in the couple's communications rather than in the individual's psyche or genitals. In short, the focus of therapy has shifted somewhat from the individual to his personal relations and his daily world.

The second consequence of the recent emphasis on environment as a major pathogenic factor is a new questioning of the role of the therapist. If the client's problem is not that he has a "screw loose" but rather that his habits and preferences conflict with the demands of the environment, whose side should the therapist take? In the case of homosexuality, for example, should the psychiatric profession devote its energies to finding new ways to turn homosexuals into heterosexuals because the society prefers heterosexuality, or should the profession help homosexuals and the society to accept this minority sexual orientation? A number of writers, including Szasz, Scheff, and Laing, whose theories we have discussed earlier, charge that psychiatrists are little more than policemen bent on enforcing conformity to questionable social norms. Such arguments have led to some liberalization both of treatment practices and of diagnostic habits. As we have seen, DSM-II now no longer regards the contented homosexual as mentally disturbed.

A second major change in psychotherapy within the last three decades is simply that it has become vastly more popular. As both cause and result of this new popularity, less of a stigma is attached to therapy. Not only psychotics and neurotics but also people who simply find existence less fulfilling than they think it should be are seeking out psychological counseling and often show no hesitation in discussing their therapy in the classroom, at the office, or

wherever. Psychotherapy, indeed, has become a social institution—vast, various, and open to the public. With its growth, it has lost a good deal of its unity. Freudian psychology, which once dominated the field, now has formidable challengers in behaviorism and in humanistic-existential psychology. And each of these larger groups has spawned its own rebellious subgroups. Along with this loss of unity, psychotherapy has lost a good deal of its mystique. As each group challenges the other, the actual techniques of each type of therapy have been brought more explicitly before the eyes of the public. And accordingly, therapists are faced with a much stricter demand to justify their techniques both to their colleagues and to the public. Thus the assessment of therapy—does it work? And if so, how?—is currently receiving unprecedented emphasis.

All these current developments must be regarded as welcome. It should be understood that our treatment methods in no way constitute the last word. We occupy only a tiny point in time between the past and the future, and frankly, the therapies now in use are simply what we happen to have at the moment. Indeed, it is extremely likely that our current approaches to such problems as schizophrenia may seem to our grandchildren as incredibly primitive as trephining now seems to us. And in order to hasten the process of sorting out useful techniques from useless techniques, and thereby to eliminate much suffering, we can profit greatly from a climate of questioning—professionals questioning other professionals and the society questioning the profession as a whole.

In our earlier chapters we have discussed a number of specific treatments. In the remainder of this chapter, we shall try to draw together these loose ends and present a unified summary of each of the current approaches to treatment. It has often been said that the number of types of psychotherapy is equal to the number of practicing therapists. There is some truth to this adage, for each therapist has his own style, and many good therapists are truly eclectic, willing to use whatever techniques appear to work rather than adhering strictly to any school of thought. However, because of their training, most therapists do approach therapy with certain assumptions, assumptions which generally correspond to one or another of the theoretical perspectives that we have outlined in our preceding chapters. In addition to its repertoire of techniques, each perspective has its own notion of who should be treated (e.g., the individual alone or the family), what the focus of treatment should be (e.g., the client's past, his present subjective perceptions, his environmental reinforcements), what the client's role should be (e.g., sitting back and taking a pill or engineering his own self-actualization), and finally, what the therapist's role should be (e.g., creating an atmosphere of unconditional acceptance, telling the client that his ideas are hogwash, climbing out on balconies or fire escapes with him in order to overcome a fear of heights). In the case of each of these approaches, impressive arguments can be marshaled for and against. Thus what we have said of psychological assessment is equally true of psychological treatment: it remains in an entirely experimental stage.

THE PSYCHODYNAMIC APPROACH TO TREATMENT

Psychodynamic therapy can be, and is, varied in any number of ways. However, all psychodynamic therapy is based to some degree on the famous technique developed by Freud, *psychoanalysis.* Hence we shall give first consideration to traditional psychoanalysis and then discuss some of the major variations introduced by later psychodynamic theorists.

Freudian Psychoanalysis

As we have seen in Chapter 2, Freud's experience in treating neurotics led him to the conclusion that the source of neurosis was the anxiety experienced by the ego when unacceptable unconscious drives threatened to break through into the conscious mind. In order to deal with this threat, the ego had recourse to a number of defense mechanisms, the most important of which was repression, the simple pushing back of the threatening impulse into the unconscious. But while the impulse could be gotten out of sight, the effort involved weakened the ego considerably. Furthermore, the anxiety remained, forcing the individual into various self-defeating postures and generally making him miserable. Thus, according to Freud, the proper treatment for neurosis was to get the patient to allow the unconscious impulse to emerge into the full light of consciousness and to help him confront and accept the forbidden material. Once faced and "worked through," this material—be it castration anxiety, hatred of one's mother, or what have you—would lose its power to terrorize the ego. Self-defeating defense mechanisms could accordingly be abandoned, and the ego would then be free to devote itself to more constructive pursuits.

It is on this theory that the techniques of psychoanalysis are founded. In the first place, because the

trouble is thought to be with the individual's past history, which the analyst is helping him explore, psychoanalysis is strictly a one-to-one client-analyst relationship. The client lies on a couch, the better to relax him and thus loosen the restraints on the unconscious. And the analyst typically sits outside the client's field of vision. What the client then does is talk, usually for one hour a day, four to six days a week, over a period of several years. And generally what he talks about is, of course, the past. The analyst remains silent much of the time, in order not to detour the client from his journey into his unconscious. When the analyst does speak, it is generally to *interpret* the client's remarks—that is, to point out their possible connection with unconscious material. This dialogue between client and therapist revolves around four basic techniques: free association, dream interpretation, analysis of resistance, and analysis of transference.

Free Association As we pointed out in Chapter 2, Freud early in his career became dissatisfied with hypnosis and felt that the purpose of dislodging repressed material from the unconscious could be better achieved by a technique called *free association,* whereby the patient, while lying on the couch, is asked to verbalize whatever thoughts come to his mind in whatever order they come. The primary directive to the client is that he must in no way structure or censor his remarks in order to make them appear logical, coherent, mature, morally sound, or otherwise admirable. The rationale behind this technique is that the unconscious has its own logic and that if the client reports his thoughts in a totally unstructured and undirected situation, the connective threads between verbalizations and unconscious impulses will be revealed. (This is essentially the same rationale as that underlying the Rorschach ink-blot tests [Chapter 18].) When such connections do become clear to the analyst, he interprets them to the client, thus cutting through defenses and furthering the client's access to knowledge of his unconscious motivations.

Dream Interpretation A second important source of clues to the unconscious is dreams. Freud believed that when a person is asleep, his defenses are lowered; thus unconscious material can make its way into the individual's dreams. But defenses are never completely lowered, even in sleep, and therefore the repressed impulses reveal themselves in dreams only in symbolic fashion. A long, dark tunnel, for example, might represent a vagina, or a threatening figure

such as a bear might represent the client's father as perceived through the eyes of childhood. Thus a dream has both its *manifest content*—that is, its content as seen and reported by the individual—and its *latent content*—that is, the unconscious material that is being expressed in disguised fashion through the symbols contained in the dream. For example, one patient, a new mother who (like most new mothers) was up at all hours of the night tending to her baby, reported to her analyst a dream in which she had given birth to identical twin boys, one of whom had died. The analyst felt that underlying this manifest content was the latent content of the dream: the woman, while she loved her newborn son, also wished him dead for destroying her peace of mind; but her defenses, still in partial operation in the dream, had managed to multiply the baby into two babies and to kill off only one (Ildiko Mohacsy, personal communication, 1975).

Analysis of Resistance As the client is guided toward the unwelcome knowledge of his unconscious motivations, he may begin to manifest *resistance*, whereby his well-practiced defenses cause him to avoid confronting certain memories or impulses. Resistance can be manifested in a number of ways. The client may break up a fruitful train of thought by changing the subject; he may suddenly fail to remember the upshot of an episode from his childhood; he may disrupt the session by making jokes

Fig. 19.1 Psychoanalytic methods, such as free association, encourage the person to focus on and report his fantasies. The analyst then interprets the content of these fantasies as symbolic expressions of disturbing childhood situations, which are usually thought to involve sex and aggression. Sometimes the content is interpreted as resistance, that is, the person's defensive refusal to experience his unconscious conflicts. Free association and interpretation therefore focus on what the analyst considers to be the individual's "problems." Other therapeutic methods also use the person's ability to fantasize, but the focus differs from that of psychoanalysis. Jungian analysis, for example, emphasizes the interpretation of dreams and fantasies in terms of the universal symbols and strivings of human beings. Gestalt therapy and related experiential methods use fantasies and dreams to help the individual to become aware of his ongoing experiences in the present situation. The Gestalt therapist assumes that each aspect of dream content represents some part of the dreamer, and he therefore instructs the client to play the role of each part of his dream and to become aware of the experiences, or meanings, that emerge with the different roles. (The Dream, Henri Rousseau; Collection, Museum of Modern Art, New York; Gift of Nelson A. Rockefeller.)

A PSYCHOANALYTIC DREAM ANALYSIS

In the following psychoanalytic dialogue the patient reports the manifest content of a dream, and then the therapist guides her toward discovery of the latent content.

"Well," she said, "this is what I dreamed. . . . I was in what appeared to be a ballroom or a dance hall, but I knew it was really a hospital. A man came up to me and told me to undress, take all my clothes off. He was going to give me a gynecological examination. I did as I was told but I was very frightened. While I was undressing, I noticed that he was doing something to a woman at the other end of the room. She was sitting or lying in a funny kind of contraption with all kinds of levers and gears and pulleys attached to it. I knew that I was supposed to be next, that I would have to sit in that thing while he examined me. Suddenly he called my name and I found myself running to him. The chair or table—whatever it was—was now empty, and he told me to get on it. I refused and began to cry. It started to rain—great big drops of rain. He pushed me to the floor and spread my legs for the examination. I turned over on my stomach and began to scream. I woke myself up screaming."

Following the recital Laura lay quietly on the couch, her eyes closed, her arms crossed over her bosom.

"Well," she said after a brief, expectant silence, "what does it mean?"

"Laura," I admonished, "you know better than that. Associate, and we'll find out."

"The first thing I think of is Ben," she began. "He's an interne at University, you know. I guess that's the doctor in the dream—or maybe it was you. Anyhow, whoever it was, I wouldn't let him examine me."

"Why not?"

"I've always been afraid of doctors . . . afraid they might hurt me."

"How will they hurt you?"

"I don't know. By jabbing me with a needle, I guess. That's funny. I never thought of it before. When I go to the dentist I don't mind getting a needle; but with a doctor it's different. . . ." Here I noticed how the fingers of both hands clutched her arms at the elbows while her thumbs nervously smoothed the inner surfaces of the joints. "I shudder when I think of having my veins punctured. I'm always afraid that's what a doctor will do to me."

• • •

"What about gynecological examinations?"

"I've never had one. I can't even bear to think of someone poking around inside me." Again silence; then, "Oh," she said, "I see it now. It's sex I'm afraid of. The doctor in the dream is Ben. He wants me to have intercourse, but it scares me and I turn away from him. That's true. . . .

• • •

"But why, Laura?"

"I don't know," she cried, "I don't know. Tell me."

"I think the dream tells you," I said.

"The dream I just told you?"

"Yes. . . . There's a part of it you haven't considered. What comes to your mind when you think of the other woman in the dream, the woman the doctor was examining before you?"

"The contraption she was sitting in," Laura exclaimed. "It was like a—like a wheel chair—my mother's wheel chair! Is that right?"

"Very likely," I said.

"But why would he be examining her? What would that mean?"

"Well, think of what that kind of examination signifies for you."

"Sex," she said. "Intercourse—that's what it means. So that's what it is—that's what it means! Intercourse put my mother in the wheel chair. It paralyzed her. And I'm afraid that's what it will do to me. So I avoid it—because I'm scared it will do the same thing to me. . . (pp. 93–95).

In fact, the mother's paralysis was totally unrelated to sex. However, the patient had unconsciously connected her mother's condition with the muffled cries and moans which, as a child, she had heard through the walls during her parents' love-making.

Source: Robert Lindner (1955).

Mechanics of Freudian Psychoanalysis

Free association	Patient freely verbalizes whatever thoughts pass through his mind, without regard to logic or propriety
Interpretation	Analyst points up the connection between a patient's remark or action and the presumed contents of his unconscious
Dream interpretation	Patient reports his dreams (manifest content) and analyst interprets them as symbolic representations of unconscious material (latent content)
Analysis of resistance	Analyst interprets to patient his various defenses against confronting his unconscious memories and motivations
Analysis of transference	Analyst interprets the ways in which the patient's responses to him are reflections and reenactments of the patient's childhood responses to important persons, particularly his parents

or by trying to pick a quarrel with the analyst; or he may even begin missing appointments. Once again, the analyst's duty is to interpret—in this case, to point out to the client that he is unconsciously avoiding confronting certain conflicts from his past and to suggest to the client what that threatening material might be.

Analysis of Transference As the psychoanalysis progresses, with the client revealing to the analyst truths that he has never revealed to anyone else, the relationship between the two partners becomes understandably complex. In his own practice Freud noted that while he sat impassively in his chair, many of his patients began responding to him with very strong and often very mixed feelings—sometimes with a childlike love and dependency, and other times with snarling hostility and rebellion. Freud interpreted this phenomenon as a *transference* on to him of the client's childhood relationships with important people in his life, most particularly with his parents. It has since become a basic assumption of traditional psychoanalysis that in order for the therapeutic process to be successful, the client must go through this stage, called *transference neurosis*, of reenacting with the analyst his childhood conflicts with his parents, including, typically, unsatisfied dependency needs along with feelings of anger and hatred—emotions which he has repressed out of shame and which may currently be subverting his adult relationships. The belief is that once these central emotions are brought out, the client has reached the core of his neurotic conflict. With the analyst's help, the client at last faces up to his leftover childhood emotional conflicts and evaluates them realistically, thus depriving them of

their power, as shadowy and fearful presences, to manipulate his behavior into self-defeating patterns. This is the essence of what psychodynamic therapists mean when they speak of "working through" a conflict.*

Post-Freudian Variations in Psychodynamic Therapy

At present Freud's techniques are rigorously followed only by a small percentage of psychodynamic therapists. The others, while they may retain the Freudian vocabulary, practice a considerably modified form of psychoanalysis, often based not simply on Freud's theory but also on the theories of his followers. As we have seen in Chapter 1, Alfred Adler departed from Freud in emphasizing man's social relationships and his striving for superiority. Likewise, Carl Jung virogously rebelled against Freud's deterministic vision of man as driven by his instincts and his past, and postulated instead an interpretation of human life as striving, goal-forming, and future-oriented. These theories, along with those of other post-Freudians, have contributed to making psychodynamic therapy what it is today.

What psychodynamic therapy is can be stated only in broad generalizations, as techniques vary considerably from therapist to therapist. However, in general, such therapy differs from Freudian

---

*Transference is not the exclusive province of the client. The analyst, though he makes every effort to remain objective, is subject to the problems of *countertransference*, whereby he projects on to the client emotions originating in his own personal history. One of the reasons psychoanalysts are required to undergo analysis themselves before attempting to practice it is so that they can identify their areas of emotional vulnerability and thus better control for countertransference.

psychoanalysis first in that the therapist takes a more active part, usually approaching the client face-to-face (the couch is typically disposed with) and speaking, interpreting, directing, and advising much more extensively than Freud would have considered permissible. Second, while the client's past history is certainly not ignored, modern psychotherapy places considerable emphasis on the client's present life, and especially on his personal relationships. Here the directive therapist may suggest new methods of dealing with other people and in general may try to help the client formulate a set of goals to be achieved in his day-to-day life. Finally, modern psychodynamic therapy is briefer and less intensive than orthodox psychoanalysis. Therapist and client typically meet once or twice a week for anywhere from a few months to a few years. This broad category of therapy is probably the most commonly practiced of all forms of psychological treatment (Parloff, 1976).

We shall examine very briefly two specific forms of this post-Freudian psychotherapy, ego analysis and Sullivanian therapy.

Ego Analysis We have already pointed out in Chapter 2 that a major revision of Freudian theory was that of the ego psychologists, a loosely formed group including, among others, Karen Horney, Harry Stack Sullivan, Erich Fromm, and Erik Erikson. The basic contention of ego psychology is that human beings are at least as much ego as they are id. As we have seen, Freud's conceptualization of the psyche was one in which the ego, borrowing its energy from the id, merely served as a sort of reality-oriented administrator of the id's sexual and aggressive demands. In contrast, the ego psychologists argue that the ego has substantial energy of its own and thus allows man to control his behavior—through such important ego functions as memory, judgment, perception, and planning—rather than simply being controlled by the id.

Ego analysis as a form of therapy places great emphasis on social interactions and on strengthening the ego so that it can allow the client to control his environment and his personal relations for his maximum satisfaction and fulfillment.

Sullivan and Human Interactions Because of its central emphasis on social relationships, Sullivan's form of ego psychology bears separate mention. As we have seen in Chapter 1, Sullivan proposed that psychological disturbance was essentially an interpersonal disturbance, a disruption in the individual's

way of relating to others. Such a disruption was usually due to what Sullivan called *paratoxic distortions*—that is, self-protective styles of relating to others which the individual develops in childhood and then carries through into his adult life, much to the detriment of his interpersonal relations. (Note that this notion bears some resemblance to the Freudian theory of transference.) Accordingly, Sullivanian therapy is devoted first to an exploration of the client's past to discover how his paratoxic distortions developed, and second to an examination of how these distortive patterns have affected his past and present interactions with other people, including his interaction with the therapist.

Psychodynamic Therapy: Pros and Cons

There is perhaps no hotter issue in the field of psychology than psychodynamic theory and treatment. On the one hand, the psychiatric literature abounds with vivid testimonials, such as Robert Lindner's popular book *The Fifty-Minute Hour* (1955), to the profound insights and equally profound behavior changes achieved through psychoanalysis. On the other hand, there are a number of problems surrounding this kind of therapy. In the first place, it is based on a series of assumptions (e.g., the existence of the unconscious; the triad of ego, superego, and id; the symbolic nature of behavior) that must simply be accepted or rejected, since they cannot be empirically validated.

Second, the argument that psychodynamic therapy actually *works*—that exploration leads to insight, and insight to change—is equally lacking in empirical support. The vivid testimonials of which we have just spoken are almost invariably written by the therapists themselves, who can hardly be considered disinterested evaluators. As for large-scale, scientifically controlled studies of the outcomes of psychodynamic therapy, there have been very few, and the one most widely cited, that of Eysenck (1952, 1961), concludes that the improvement rate for patients undergoing such therapy is approximately the same as that for patients who receive no formal treatment but simply sit tight and perhaps talk over their problems now and then with a clergyman or with the family doctor. In short, there is no substantial scientific documentation of the effectiveness of psychodynamic treatment (Luborsky and Spence, 1971).

Finally, there is much question as to the general utility of psychodynamic treatment methods. In the first place, any psychodynamic therapy requires a substantial expenditure of time and money on the part of the patient. And in the case of traditional psychoanalysis, the cost is so great as to exclude a major portion of the middle classes, to say nothing of the lower classes. Second, because it is such a highly verbal enterprise and because it requires a certain subtlety of perception on the part of the patient, psychodynamic therapy is likely to be successful only for those who are highly verbal, highly articulate, above average in intelligence, and neurotic rather than psychotic (Luborsky and Spence, 1971). Finally, psychodynamic techniques appear to be relatively useless beyond the four walls of the therapist's office. It has been shown, for example, that the techniques employed by other perspectives, such as behaviorism, can be used by parents of disturbed children (Patterson, 1971) and by aides and paraprofessionals in mental hospitals (Allyon and Azrin, 1968). In contrast, the practice of psychodynamic therapy is generally confined to highly trained professionals working with patients on an individual basis. Hence, aside from any questions of effectiveness, the value of this type of therapy is limited by the fact that it simply cannot reach very many people.

In sum, Freud's pioneering treatment method, along with all its descendants, is subject to numerous limitations and even more numerous challenges, most of them unanswerable in scientific terms. Those who reject the approach consider it, in no uncertain terms, an expensive waste of time. Those who espouse it view it not only as an effective but also as an heroic journey into the inner reaches of the self.

THE BEHAVIORIST APPROACH TO TREATMENT

Like the techniques of psychodynamic therapy, the methods of behavior modification have already been examined to some degree in the introductory section of this book and in the chapters dealing with the various forms of abnormal behavior. Likewise, in Chapter 3, we have discussed in full the principles on which behavioral therapy is based. The most fundamental of these principles is the theory that most behavior, both normal and abnormal, is learned through reinforcement and consequently can be unlearned through reinforcement. Thus the focus of behavior modification is not on the total personality, as is the case with the "insight" therapies of the psychodynamic and humanistic-existential perspectives, but rather on specific, measurable behaviors and the specific, measurable stimuli that serve to reinforce those behaviors. What this means

is that the behaviorists, in contrast to other theorists, place considerably less emphasis on the individual's past and on his inner life, since neither of these can be evaluated scientifically. This is not to say, however, that the behaviorists ignore the troubled individual's past altogether; typically they will give it careful consideration. However, the behaviorists believe that the reinforcements that are currently maintaining a maladaptive response may be very different from those earlier reinforcements that engendered the response. Hence they have little faith in the curative powers of "insight" into the historical origins of the behavior. Likewise, most of the less radical behaviorists acknowledge the existence and the power of the unobservable and unmeasurable inner life of the mind—the mediating constructs (Chapter 3), in the form of thoughts, beliefs, and assumptions, that stand between stimulus and response. But most forms of behavioral therapy concentrate on modifying tangible behaviors, usually with the assumption that intangible mental constructs will change along with the behavior.

In contrast to the grander goals of personality restructuring or self-actualization that characterize the insight therapies, the goals of behavior modification appear rather modest. The behavioral therapist's objectives are simply to identify the maladaptive behavior through functional analysis (Chapter 18), determining whether it is a behavior excess or a behavior deficit (Kanfer and Saslow, 1969); to specify a target behavior to replace the troublesome behavior; and then, by dint of exposing the individual to a new set of reinforcements, to transform the maladaptive behavior into the adaptive target behavior. In sum, behaviorist therapy is no way grandiose or philosophical; it is simple, concrete, and extremely pragmatic.

Similarly, the behavioral therapist's approach to his client differs somewhat from the role of the therapist in insight therapy. The Greek philosopher Socrates once described himself as a "midwife"—that is, his function, as he saw it, was not to reveal truth but rather to help other people give birth to their own revelations of truth. Such, in many ways, is the role of the therapist in insight therapy. By contrast, the behavior therapist is much more directive and does not hesitate in the least to give specific instructions and to model appropriate behavior. He is not there, after all, to help the client "find himself," but rather to teach him how not to run in the other direction when he sees a dog or a woman or what have you.

The techniques that behavior modification

Fig. 19.2   The individuals shown here are undergoing a behavioral treatment for their fear of dogs. Called "systematic desensitization," the treatment consists of first relaxing the patients and then presenting a series of progressively frightening pictures of dogs to them. If the patients are able to remain relaxed while viewing the pictures, they should be able to generalize this response to the real world and soon be able to observe and touch real animals without fear.

systematic desensitization (also called *reciprocal inhibition*) is essentially an extinction technique, in which, by inducing a state of relaxation in the patient and then presenting the anxiety-arousing stimulus, the therapist prevents the anxiety response and negatively reinforcing avoidance behavior from taking place and consequently allows the anxiety to extinguish. First named and developed as a formal treatment procedure by Wolpe (1958), systematic desensitization involves three steps. In the first step the therapist trains the patient in muscle relaxation, usually through a technique involving the progressive contracting and relaxing of the different muscle groups in the body (Jacobson, 1938). In the second step the therapist and the patient construct a *hierarchy of fears*—that is, a list of anxiety-producing situations in order of their increasing horror to the patient. The following, for example, is the hierarchy of fears established for a basketball player who suffered from extreme anxiety and vomiting before games:

(1) He meets an assistant coach in the gym and the coach doesn't say "hello," (2) he is in the gym changing for practice and he notices his hands beginning to sweat, (3) he is trying to study and he can't get the day's practice out of his thoughts, (4) he finishes practice and some observers speak to the other players but ignore him, (5) he is on the court and he gets a tired, draggy, no-good feeling, (6) he is on the court and notices that the coaches are keeping a record of each player's performance, (7) he is visiting at home and his mother makes a remark about another player, (8) he is eating dinner with his mother when she asks him something about how his game is going, (9) it is time for the late afternoon pre-game dinner and he is on the way to the cafeteria, (10) he is in the cafeteria line and the sight of food makes him feel sick, (11) he is in the gym changing for a game and he is sick to his stomach (Katahn, 1967, pp. 310–311).

Once both the relaxation training and the hierarchy of fears have been established, then the two can be combined in the third step, the actual desensitiza-

employs in order to impart such practical skills to the client are based on the two fundamental learning principles outlined in Chapter 3—respondent conditioning and operant conditioning—along with the principle of social learning, which combines operant and respondent techniques with the persuasive powers of social influence.

Respondent Conditioning and Extinction

As we have seen in Chapter 3, the behaviorists hold that a primary learning mechanism is respondent conditioning, whereby the individual's positive or negative response to a certain stimulus is transferred to another stimulus through the pairing of the two stimuli. The behavior-modification techniques that we shall discuss in this section work on precisely this same principle. Their effort is to *recondition* the individual, either by removing the stimuli that reinforce his maladaptive response (extinction) or by pairing the maladaptive response with incompatible positive or negative stimuli. Among the many different techniques that fall into this broad category, we shall discuss five popular methods: systematic desensitization, emotive imagery, assertive training, implosive therapy, and aversion therapy.

Systematic Desensitization   Perhaps the earliest known example of systematic desensitization was the famous experiment in which Mary Cover Jones cured the furry-animal phobia of the little boy named Peter by giving him his favorite food to eat, consequently relaxing him, and then bringing a rabbit closer and closer to him (Chapter 3). Thus

tion. Here the patient is asked to relax himself and then to imagine himself experiencing, one by one, the anxiety-producing stimuli listed in his hierarchy, starting with the lowest item and moving upward on the anxiety scale. The process continues until the patient reports that his relaxation has given way to anxiety. Then relaxation is reestablished and the process is continued until the patient can vividly imagine the scene at the top of his hierarchy of fears and still remain relaxed. The entire process may require one or more sessions of therapy.

The success of this technique depends, of course, on the carrying over of the relaxed response from the imagined situation to the actual situation. And in most cases it appears that this transfer does in fact take place. Bandura (1969) has documented the successful use of systematic desensitization in the treatment of an extremely wide variety of phobias. It has also been effective in relieving incapacitating obsessions and compulsions; recurrent nightmares; insomnia; chronic alcoholism; and complex interpersonal problems involving fears of social and sexual intimacy, of aggressive behavior, of social disapproval, of rejection, and of authority figures (Wolpe, 1958; Walton and Mather, 1964; Haslam, 1965; Geer and Katkin, 1966; Hain et al., 1966; Wolpe and Lazarus, 1966; Geer and Silverman, 1967; Kraft and Al-Issa, 1967b; Madsen and Ullmann, 1967; Kanfer and Phillips, 1970).

Though systematic desensitization is preferred, a technique called *induced anger* is sometimes successful when an alternative method is necessary, or when systematic desensitization fails. Here, the patient is taught to respond to imagined anxiety-producing situations not with relaxation but with anger, another response that is incompatible with anxiety (Goldstein et al., 1970).

Emotive Imagery *Emotive imagery* is essentially the Mary Cover Jones technique transferred from reality to the imagination. Here the therapist asks the client to imagine an extremely positive situation. Then, as this fantasy is being pursued, the anxiety-producing stimulus is gradually introduced into the scene. For example, Lazarus and Abramowitz (1962) had a dog-phobic child imagine that he was driving a fancy sports car along a road. As he sped along in this splendid vehicle, he passed a number of extremely pleasurable scenes, as related to him by the therapist. Then images of dogs were very gradually introduced into these otherwise glorious scenes until the dogs eventually became paired with the child's fantasied pleasures. Thus in emotive imagery the

principle is essentially the same as that of systematic desensitization: the anxiety-inducing stimulus is paired with an emotional response incompatible with anxiety—in this case, pleasure and self-confidence.

Assertive Training One problem in treating anxiety solely with the type of extinction techniques described above is that the client's anxiety may in fact be due to real external dangers (Bernstein and Paul, 1971). For example, if a client is immobilized by anxiety at the thought of social encounters, this fear may be due not simply to conditioning but also to the fact that the client actually does lack the interpersonal skills necessary for navigating social situations. Hence in addition to extinction techniques, behavior modification often employs procedures designed to *create* adaptive responses which can then take the place of extinguished maladaptive responses.

One such procedure is *assertive training*, whereby the client is taught how to assert himself properly with other people and thus avoid being either passive or overaggressive. Often conducted in groups, assertive training, as outlined by Alberti and Emmons (1974), involves reenacting as vividly as possible in the consulting room the interpersonal situations to which the client tends to respond inappropriately, either by letting himself be stepped on or by stepping on others. First the client plays himself and the therapist plays the "other guy"—for example, the nosy friend, the bossy mother, the rude salesperson, or what have you. After the skit is over, the therapist will point out to the client the flaws in his responses and then switch roles with him, modeling a properly assertive (but not overly aggressive) response. Then the roles are again switched, with the client attempting to imitate the assertive response. These rehearsals continue until the client can transfer the appropriate response to real-life situations. It should be noted that this procedure, while it involves modeling and positive reinforcement (i.e., the therapist's praise for assertive responses), is also an extinction therapy, in that it teaches the client that the sky will not fall (as he often expects it will) if he insists on his rights as a human being.

Implosive Therapy *Implosive therapy* might be described as a cold-turkey extinction therapy. Unlike the gradual extinction paired with relaxation that constitutes systematic desensitization, here the aim is to maximize the client's anxiety through imagined

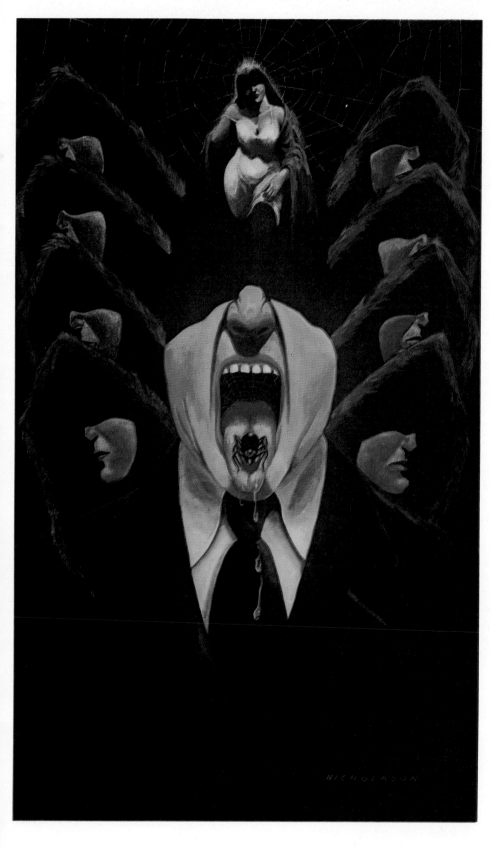

Fig. 19.3 *Implosive therapy contrasts markedly with systematic desensitization. Both methods attempt to help people overcome their anxiety in and avoidance of certain situations. Both methods also involve the construction of graded hierarchies of anxiety-producing stimuli. At this point, the two therapies diverge. The implosive therapist quickly exposes his client to intense and exaggerated accounts of high anxiety-inducing situations in the attempt to arouse and thereby extinguish great anxiety. Conversely, the therapist who uses systematic desensitization teaches his client how to relax and then exposes him to the least anxiety-provoking stimulus, only gradually working through the hierarchy to the highest-anxiety situations as his client masters each step with relaxation. Thus, although both methods have the same end, their theoretical justifications and their methods are quite different.*

fear-producing situations and to hold the anxiety at this pitch until the client realizes that these imaginings do not result in any aversive consequences. As a result, the anxiety extinguishes (Stampfl, 1961; Stampfl and Levis, 1968). As with systematic desensitization, the therapist must first find out exactly what situations the client most fears. Then he has the client sit back and imagine highly vivid anxiety-provoking scenes, often embellished with painful details taken from the patient's past history, with stimulus cues based on psychodynamic theory and with whatever gruesome additions the therapist's imagination can provide. Hogan (1968) has provided the following example of a scene used in implosive-therapy research with snake-phobics:

[*Imagine that the snakes are*] *touching you, biting you, try to get that helpless feeling like you can't win, and just give up and let them crawl all over you. Don't even fight them anymore. Let them crawl as much as they want. And now there is a big giant snake, it is as big as a man and it is staring at you and it is looking at you; it's ugly and it's black and it has got horrible eyes and long fangs, and it is coming towards you. It is standing on its tail and it is looking down at you, looking down on you. I want you to get that feeling, like you are a helpless little rabbit, and it's coming toward you, closer and closer; feel it coming towards you. Horrible, evil, ugly, slimy, and it's looking down on you, ready to strike at you. Feel it in your stomach, feel it coming, oooh, it is getting closer and closer and it snaps out at you. Feel it biting at your head now, it is biting at your head; it opens its giant mouth and it has your whole head inside of its mouth. And it is biting your head right off. Feel it; feel it biting, the fangs going right through your neck. Feel it, and now it is starting to swallow you whole. It is pulling you right inside its body, feel yourself being pulled and dragged into its body. Feel yourself inside, helpless, lost, and now you are starting to turn into a snake. Feel yourself turning into a slimy snake. And you are crawling out of its mouth. All the other snakes see you. And they start to attack you. Feel them; they are coming to bite and rip you apart. Do you know how animals attack each other? Look at the snakes attacking you, feel them biting you, ripping you to shreds (p. 429).*

Aversion Therapy As we have seen in preceding chapters, *aversion therapy*, whereby a maladaptive response is paired with an aversive stimulus such as electric shock or a nausea-producing drug, has been used extensively in the treatment of homosexuality, sexual deviations, and alcoholism. Though such therapy, particularly when it involves electric shock, may seem extremely harsh to most laymen and to many clinicians as well, a number of clients consider it far preferable to whatever behavior it is that they are trying to eradicate. Furthermore, the mere fact that it seems to work in cases where other therapies fail is a strong argument for its use. For example, Ivar Lovaas has made extensive use of electric shock in halting self-mutilation and in eliciting attention in autistic children, with some very encouraging results (Simmons and Lovaas, 1969).

In *convert sensitization*, a tamer version of aversion therapy, the patient is asked simply to imagine the aversive stimuli along with a visualization of the maladaptive behavior (Cautela, 1966, 1967). For example, Davison (1968), in treating a young man who was disturbed by sadistic sexual fantasies, asked his client to conjure up his typical sadistic fantasy and at the same time to imagine himself drinking "a large bowl of 'soup' composed of steaming urine with reeking fecal [matter] bobbing around on top" (p. 86). Likewise, a therapist treating a problem drinker might ask his client to imagine having a pleasurable first and second drink at a party, then becoming progressively more drunk, then telling off his boss, then vomiting all over his hostess's expensive couch, then urinating on the rug in front of the assembled company, and so forth. Such therapy, like other forms of aversion therapy and like the extinction therapies, is most successful when combined with techniques aimed at teaching the client adaptive responses to take the place of his maladaptive responses. For example, if a client is being voluntarily deprived of a sexual fetish, he will require some training in how to initiate a sexual encounter with a woman rather than with a glove or a shoe.

Operant Conditioning

As we have seen in Chapter 3, the second major principle of learning, according to the behaviorists, is operant conditioning, whereby the positive or negative consequences of a certain behavior condition the individual either to repeat or avoid that behavior, respectively. And like respondent conditioning, operant conditioning has served as the basis for a wide repertoire of behavior modification techniques. While respondent techniques are often used in the clinician's office, operant techniques are most effective when they are made part of a complete environment—whether a prison, a mental hospital, an institution for delinquents or mental retardates, a classroom, or a home—since the success of such techniques depends on the client's being reinforced or deprived of reinforcements, hour after hour and day after day, according to an inexorably consistent pattern. Only in this way can the individual eventually internalize the pattern, thus learning to reinforce himself with self-approval for adaptive responses.

The Token Economy A technique that we have already touched upon in previous chapters, the *token economy* is an operant-conditioning system built in to the individual's total environment. According to Ullmann and Krasner (1975), there are three essential components to a token economy. First, the rules of the game must be utterly clear; the clients must know precisely which behaviors are considered desirable and which undesirable. Second, desirable behavior must be reinforced by generalized conditioned reinforcers or tokens, which may take the form of poker chips, play money, gold stars pasted on a board, or whatever. Third, these tokens must be exchangeable for a range of backup reinforcers—gum, candy, movies, a private room, a weekend pass, and so forth—which the patient himself chooses.

Originally tried out on hospitalized psychotics (Atthowe and Krasner, 1968; Allyon and Azrin, 1968), this system has proved useful with numerous other kinds of groups, including retardates, juvenile delinquents, and even ordinary children in their schoolrooms (O'Leary and Drabman, 1971). In institutional token economies, there is typically a board listing the various desirable behaviors and their token rewards (e.g., combing hair—1 token; making bed—2 tokens; scrubbing day-room floor—5 tokens) and then a commissary where the patients can exchange their tokens for backup reinforcers. Some institutions even have department store catalogs from which the patients can order their rewards.

The advantages of the token system are many. First, tokens, unlike reinforcers such as cookies, are

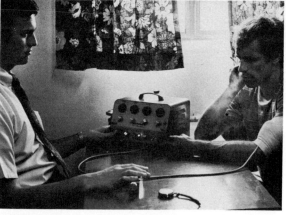

Fig. 19.4 *The top photograph shows a hospitalized patient with a severe body tic. The behavior modification approach to treatment involved the use of aversive stimulation (shock) immediately following performance of the tic (bottom). The patient readily agreed to this treatment because of the great discomfort and embarrassment that the tic caused him. Progress was slow, however, because he rarely emitted the tic during the initial therapy sessions, although it was clearly evident when he was on the ward. In order for aversive methods to be successful, the behavior under treatment must be exhibited relatively frequently during the therapy sessions.*

Before
conditioning

Behavior whose
frequency is to be
increased: playing
well with other
children

Conditioning
procedure

Reward

After
conditioning

Fig. 19.5   These draw-
ings illustrate the way in
which operant behavior,
such as a child's socializ-
ing with peers, can be influenced by positive reinforcement. Although the
child initially plays
alone, he may, for a variety of reasons, attempt to
be included in the group
play. He and the other
children are then re-
warded with ice cream.
This reward, or positive
reinforcement, increases
the child's tendency to
play with the children
and encourages the chil-
dren to accept a new
member into the group.
It is likely that the
child's play activities
eventually will be main-
tained by the generalized
reinforcers, such as at-
tention, approval, and
success, that occur in the
play situation itself.

not subject to satiation, since they can be exchanged for different kinds of rewards; a patient who is tired of candy can simply switch to comic books or movies. Second, the token system allows the patient a certain freedom both in choosing whether or not to earn the tokens and in choosing how he will spend them. Finally, the token system provides a sort of bridge to life on the outside, where we are rewarded with money, approval, and so forth for tidiness, hygiene, work, and other socially valued behaviors. However, since the rate of reinforcement in the outside world is much less consistent than that in the token economy, an attempt is usually made to wean patients from tokens to more realistic reinforcers such as social approval and self-approval before they reenter the community.

Reinforcement Deprivation: Response Cost Contingencies and Time-Out In addition to offering reinforcement for desirable behaviors, operant therapies often include techniques for withdrawing reinforcements in response to undesirable behaviors. *Response cost contingencies* (Sherman and Baer, 1969) constitute one such technique. Here an undesirable response is "punished" by the withdrawal of a reinforcement, just as a child who has been acting up may be deprived of his television time for one evening. Another technique for weakening maladaptive responses is called *time-out from reinforcement*, whereby the subject, upon engaging in some undesirable behavior, is temporarily removed from the situation and placed in some neutral environment (e.g., an empty room) where he can receive no reinforcement. (Hence this technique is a cousin of the time-honored system of sending a naughty child to his room and also, at the extreme other end of the spectrum, of solitary confinement as it is used in prisons.) Time-out, which is usually practiced with children and can be utilized by the parents at home (Patterson and Gullion, 1968), has been successful in discouraging self-mutilation and tantrums (Wolf et al., 1964) and in insuring that children sit still and pay attention during various kinds of therapy, such as speech therapy (Risley and Wolf, 1967).

Shaping As a learning technique, *shaping*, whereby the subject is reinforced for successive approximations of the target behavior, has already been examined in Chapter 3. And as we have seen in the foregoing chapters on the various forms of abnormal behavior, it has also proved useful as a therapeutic technique, particularly in treating children. For example, in teaching a retarded child to feed

Fig. 19.6 *Time-out procedures, which involve removing the person from a given situation and placing him in another situation in which reinforcement is unavailable, are usually applied to the treatment of specific problem behaviors. In a classroom situation, for example, the child is removed to a barren room (photo above) when he performs the undesirable behavior and is returned to the classroom after a previously specified period of time. In prisons, solitary confinement is essentially a vindictive time-out procedure. Parents often use a form of the time-out procedure by ordering a child to "Go to your room." Used in this way, however, the procedure is not very effective because the situation to which the child is banished, that is, his bedroom, does contain reinforcing stimuli such as toys and books.*

himself, the child would first be reinforced for picking up the spoon, then for messing around in the food with the spoon rather than with his hands, then for getting some food on the spoon and raising it from the plate, then for aiming the spoon toward his face, and then, at last, for delivering the food to its proper destination, his mouth. While shaping requires a good deal of patience on the part of the therapist, it has proved helpful in speech therapy (Chapter 16) and in teaching certain self-sufficient behaviors—not only self-feeding but dressing and toileting as well—to retarded, mildly disturbed, and psychotic children (Wolf et al., 1964).

Contingency Contracting *Contingency contracting* is essentially a highly specific give-and-get system, in which a contract is drawn up indicating that for desirable behavior X, the subject will be given reward X; for desirable behavior Y, reward Y; and so on. Along with other behavior-modification techniques, this procedure has the great advantage of being usable in the home; it has proved successful, for example, in establishing truces between "hard-core" delinquent children and their parents (Stuart, 1971). Contingency contracting has also been used in marital therapy (Azrin et al., 1973). In one type of marital contract, for example, communicativeness on the part of the husband is exchanged for sexual favors on the part of the wife—a technique devised by Stuart (1969) and since dubbed "prostitution therapy."

Social Learning

Social learning is another area in which cognitive processes, so suspect to the more orthodox behaviorists, have insinuated their way into behavior modification. Here the intangible is essentially the influence that people have over one another—one person's desire to please another person by doing what that other person does or tells him to do. Under this category of techniques come two highly successful treatment procedures, modeling and cognitive restructuring.

Modeling *Modeling*, whereby the subject learns a new behavior by imitating another person performing that behavior, depends of course on the subject's wanting in some way to be like the model and to win his approval. Thus, for example, little boys learn to urinate while standing up by watching their fathers or older brothers, and schoolchildren learn to speak French by hearing their teachers do so. The same monkey-see-monkey-do principle applies to behavior modification. If the therapist can capture the subject's attention and regard, then he can teach the subject a new adaptive response simply by performing it himself and then encouraging and helping the subject to imitate him. This procedure has proved particularly useful in defusing phobias. Bandura (1969), for example, has reported a 90 percent success rate in curing snake phobias through modeling. Likewise, Bandura, Grusec, and Menlove (1967) were able to eliminate dog phobias in children by

allowing them, in a number of successive sessions, to watch another child (dubbed "Fearless Peer") approach a dog, touch it, pet it, and eventually engage in active play with it. Modeling can also be used to relieve more diffuse fears. For instance, O'Connor (1969) successfully modified extreme social withdrawal in a group of children by showing them films of other socially withdrawn children who were gradually drawn into play with a group and visibly enjoyed the interaction.

It has already been pointed out that modeling is an important component of assertive training. Indeed, it might be said that modeling plays some part in almost all nonmedical therapies. Whatever the treatment approach, be it psychoanalysis, response shaping, humanistic group therapy, or whatever, the therapist's example—the fact that *he* is not alcoholic or obese or afraid of heights or sexually excited by whipping (or at least that he appears to be free of these afflictions)—will play some part in any successful outcome.

Cognitive Restructuring Only by extension can *cognitive restructuring* be considered a form of behavior modification, since its central focus is on an intangible, the client's ways of perceiving. The assumption of this technique is that the client behaves in self-defeating ways because he is laboring under a set of false assumptions. Consequently, therapy aims at identifying these assumptions and then demolishing them with the tools of reason. As we have mentioned in Chapter 4, a major proponent of cognitive restructuring is Albert Ellis (1962). Ellis argues that thousands of people manage to make their lives miserable by unthinkingly embracing certain irrational beliefs, such as "I must be loved and approved of by everyone whose love and approval I seek" or "I must be utterly competent in everything that I do." Through a "talking cure" that he calls *rational-emotive therapy*, Ellis helps his patients to trace their emotional problems back to these "musts," to realize that their distress over failing to meet such standards is quite unrealistic, and finally to establish a more pragmatic cognitive framework.

Behavior Modification: Pros and Cons

The most frequently voiced criticisms of behavior modification are that it denies individual freedom and that it is a "mechanistic, manipulative, and impersonal approach which deliberately sets out to control behavior" (O'Leary and Wilson, 1975, p. 28). In fact all therapy is directed toward controlling behavior, whether through "insight," "self-actuali-

PRIVILEGES	RESPONSIBILITIES
General	
In exchange for the privilege of remaining together and preserving some semblance of family integrity	Mr. and Mrs. Bremer and Candy all agree to concentrate on positively reinforcing each other's behavior while diminishing the present overemphasis upon the faults of the others.
Specific	
In exchange for the privilege of riding the bus directly from school into town after school on school days	Candy agrees to phone her father by 4 p.m. to tell him that she is all right and to return home by 5:15 p.m.
In exchange for the privilege of going out at 7 p.m. on one weekend evening without having to account for her whereabouts	Candy must maintain a weekly average of B in the academic ratings of all of her classes and must return home by 11:30 p.m.
In exchange for the privilege of going out a second weekend night	Candy must tell her parents by 6 p.m. of her destination and her companion and must return home by 11:30 p.m.
In exchange for the privilege of going out between 11 a.m. and 5:15 p.m. Saturdays, Sundays, and holidays	Candy agrees to have completed all household chores before leaving and to telephone her parents once during the time she is out to tell them that she is all right.
In exchange for the privilege of having Candy complete household chores and maintain her curfew	Mr. and Mrs. Bremer agree to pay Candy $1.50 on the morning following days on which the money is earned.
Bonuses and Sanctions	
If Candy is 1–10 minutes late	she must come in the same amount of time earlier the following day, but she does not forfeit her money for the day.
If Candy is 11–30 minutes late	she must come in 22–60 minutes earlier the following day and does forfeit her money for the day.
If Candy is 31–60 minutes late	she loses the privilege of going out the following day and does forfeit her money for the day.
For each half hour of tardiness over one hour	Candy loses her privilege of going out and her money for one additional day.
Candy may go out on Sunday evenings from 7 to 9:30 p.m. and either Monday or Thursday evening	if she abides by all the terms of this contract from Sunday through Saturday with a total tardiness not exceeding 30 minutes, which must have been made up as above.
Candy may add a total of two hours divided among one to three curfews	if she abides by all the terms of this contract for two weeks with a total tardiness not exceeding 30 minutes, which must have been made up as above, and if she requests permission to use this additional time by 9 p.m.
Monitoring	
Mr. and Mrs. Bremer agree to keep written records of the hours of Candy's leaving and coming home and of the completion of her chores. Candy agrees to furnish her parents with a school monitoring card each Friday at dinner.	

Fig. 19.7   Contingency contracts specify the behaviors that each party agrees to perform and to reinforce. Such contracting procedures are useful in problem family situations, such as marital conflicts and delinquent children, and in institutional situations, such as classrooms. In situations in which there is great dissatisfaction and the people involved have grown indifferent to one another or repeatedly use aversive stimulation with each other, contracting procedures offer a chance to develop interactional behaviors that are mutually gratifying and to still obtain personally important goals (reinforcements). The contingency contract presented here was formulated by a therapist for a juvenile delinquent girl and her family. (Adapted from R. B. Stuart, "Behavioral Contracting Within the Families of Delinquents," Journal of Behavior Therapy and Experimental Psychiatry, *2, 1971, 9.)*

Fig. 19.8 These photographs illustrate the desensitization of a snake phobia through live modeling and guided participation. (Top) The therapist calmly handles the snake in front of a frightened girl. In a series of anxiety-reducing steps, the subject is encouraged to slowly approach the snake: at first while it is safely in its cage (middle) and later while the therapist is holding it. The last step of the desensitization procedure involves the girl's actual handling of the snake (bottom), a behavior that formerly would have aroused great anxiety. Modeling and imitation have been shown to be important factors in a number of behavior modification methods. Their incorporation into behavior therapy is an example of the contributions of experimental social psychology to behavioral methods. Modeling and imitation were widely studied in the 1960s, with the general aim of understanding the processes that influenced the acquisition and modification of social behavior.

Techniques of Behavior Modification

Systematic desensitization	Extinction of anxiety through pairing of anxiety-arousing stimulus with induced state of relaxation
Induced anger	Extinction of anxiety through teaching patient to respond with anger to anxiety-producing stimulus
Emotive imagery	Extinction of anxiety through the creation of fantasies in which the anxiety-producing stimulus is gradually paired with strong reinforcers
Assertive training	The conditioning of self-assertive responses through role-playing of social situations by patient and therapist
Implosive therapy	Extinction of anxiety by verbally bombarding the patient with anxiety-provoking imagery, which, when it produces no harmful consequences, loses its power to induce fear
Aversion therapy	The suppression of a maladaptive response through pairing that response with an aversive stimulus (e.g., electric shock)
Covert sensitization	Eradication of a maladaptive response through fantasied pairing of that response with vividly imagined noxious stimuli
Token economy	The operant conditioning of a range of adaptive responses by rewarding them with tokens that can be exchanged for backup reinforcers
Response cost contingency	The suppression of a maladaptive response by punishing the subject through the withdrawal of a reinforcer
Time-out	The suppression of a maladaptive response by removing the subject to a neutral environment, void of reinforcements, when he manifests the response
Shaping	Gradual conditioning of an adaptive response through positive reinforcement of successive approximations of that response
Contingency contracting	The conditioning of adaptive responses and suppression of maladaptive responses through drawing up a contract indicating the rewards and punishments contingent on the responses in question
Self-control	The replacement of maladaptive responses with adaptive responses through rearranging one's own environment and habits in such a way that these responses are appropriately rewarded or punished
Modeling	The establishment of an adaptive response through rewarding the subject's initiation of that response as modeled by another person
Cognitive restructuring	The eradication of a maladaptive response through demonstrating the irrationality of the assumptions on which the response is based

zation," or "conditioning." In the psychodynamic and humanistic-existential therapies, the values of the therapist are implicit, while in behavior therapy the goals of treatment are carefully and explicitly worked out between the therapist and client. There is no assumption that the therapist "knows best." Getting control of one's own life is a major goal of all behavior modification.

Behavior modification has been further criticized for its insistent emphasis on the individual's present environment—an emphasis that may lead the thera-

pist to ignore important etiological factors from the patient's past history or even from his biological makeup. Furthermore, because behavioral treatment does not aim at leading the individual through a "growth experience"—a process that many psychodynamic and humanistic-existential therapists consider essential—it has been widely accused of superficiality. However, given these possible limitations, behavior modification still deserves very serious attention in that it does tend to work in solving certain specific problems. Systematic desensitization, for example, has an excellent record in eliminating many different types of conditional anxiety (Paul, 1969a, 1969b); modeling has proved very helpful in relieving phobias; and aversive conditioning has been shown to be effective in establishing impulse control. (On the other hand, no behavioral technique has so far shown any great success in eliminating alcoholism, extreme depression, or schizophrenia.) Moreover, such success as behavior therapy has had can be measured and reported scientifically, as is not the case with psychodynamic therapy. Further advantages of the behaviorist approach to treatment are that it tends to be faster and cheaper than other therapies; that its techniques can be taught to nonprofessionals and paraprofessionals, so therapy can be extended beyond the consulting office and into the hospital ward, the classroom, and the home; and finally, that it is utterly precise in its goals and techniques, so it can be discussed, reported, and evaluated with equal precision.

THE HUMANISTIC-EXISTENTIAL APPROACH TO TREATMENT

We have just mentioned the concept of psychological treatment as a growth experience. Of no treatment approach is this goal of personal growth more characteristic than of the humanistic and existential therapies. While humanistic and existential therapists tend to be highly individualistic in their specific techniques, they share the common objective of helping the patient to become more truly "himself"—to find out what it is that he wants out of life and then to make deliberate choices in order to fulfill his desires. In keeping with this therapeutic goal, the humanistic-existential approach to treatment differs from the psychodynamic and behaviorist approaches in that it maximizes the client's sense of freedom, discourages deterministic thinking (e.g., "passing the buck" to a stern father, a cruel wife, a dreary job), turns him face-front toward the future, and asks him to "become"—to choose his own destiny. This approach further differs from the other treatment philosophies that we have discussed in that it encourages a greater intimacy in the client-therapist relationship, with the therapist attempting to enter the client's phenomenological world and the client drawing strength from the warmth and honesty of the therapeutic relationship.

Client-Centered Therapy

The best-known and most popular humanistic therapy is the *client-centered therapy* of Carl Rogers

(1951). The fundamental principle of this treatment approach, which we have already outlined in Chapter 4, is that human beings are innately good and innately motivated to actualize their potential. However, if the individual adopts a value system that conflicts with his true self, then he will be forced to block out portions of his experience that violate this adopted value system. As a result, the unfolding of the self will be impeded, and the individual will become poorly adjusted and generally unhappy.

According to Rogers, the only way to solve this problem is to bring the self back into harmony with its experience—hence client-centered therapy. As the name indicates, this treatment is focused directly on the client himself, on *his* unique personality, and not on any system of theories or laws regarding human behavior in general. In the effort to reconcile the client to his true self, the therapist offers him unconditional positive regard (that is, total acceptance) and attempts to see the world through the client's eyes so that finally *his* experience of the world can be seen as a thing of value. Unlike psychodynamic and behavioral therapists, the Rogerian therapist does not interpret or instruct. Rather, he listens to the client's remarks and then mirrors back to him the feelings that seem to emerge from these remarks. In the process, the client clarifies his true feelings and learns to regard them as acceptable. What this means is that the client gradually begins to recement the disrupted unity of his self and his experience, to approve of himself as a totality, and to allow that total and integrated personality to emerge in the form of constructive choices.

Thus Rogers' technique is definitely an insight therapy. And accordingly it is subject to all the criticisms that have been leveled at insight therapies: that they can benefit only a small percentage of the population (i.e., those who are verbal, intelligent, highly motivated, and not severely disturbed); that insight in no way guarantees change (Loevinger and Ossorio, 1959); that such therapies are long and costly; and that their effectiveness cannot be scientifically validated. Furthermore, Truax (1966), himself a Rogerian, has shown that Rogers' interactions with his patients are not as nondirective as has been claimed. However, Rogers himself has been extremely active in advocating and originating scientific methods such as the Q-sort (Chapter 18) for testing the effectiveness of insight therapies and for studying what in fact goes on in such therapies. Because of this show of good faith, and because of his timely insistence on individuality and self-determination, Rogers' approach to treatment has been ex-

Fig. 19.9 The client-centered therapist attempts to understand what his client is experiencing and then to communicate this understanding to him. Because the therapist often restates what he considers to be the emotional content of the client's communication, he functions as a "mirror of feeling." In this way, he provides understanding and positive regard, without making value judgments. Feeling safe in such an environment, the client learns to relax the defenses that he has used to deny or distort his experiences and, in turn, to develop a more realistic self-concept and a more accurate perception of events. In addition to "reflecting," the client-centered therapist tries to be "transparent" or "congruent"; that is, he is open and spontaneous in relating to the client. Thus, the client-centered therapist acts as an elicitor, a model, and a reinforcer of openness and honesty in a relationship.

tremely influential. Indeed, the fact that many behaviorists are now willing to acknowledge the role of subjective constructs in shaping behavior (Mahoney, 1974) is due in part to the influence of Rogers' phenomenological approach.

Existential Therapy

We have pointed out in Chapter 4 that existential psychology differs somewhat from humanistic psychology in the approach to the question of freedom. While the humanists tend to assume, optimistically, that an integrated personality will automatically use its freedom by bringing into full and beautiful flower all of its potentialities, the existentialists less optimistically stress the arduous responsibility of making "authentic" choices. In short, where the humanists speak of acceptance and self-actualization, the existentialists speak of values and self-confrontation.

As popularized by such figures as Ludwig Binswanger, Medard Boss, Viktor Frankl, and Rollo May (Chapter 4), the major efforts of existential therapy are to encourage the patient to take responsibility for his symptoms as something that he himself has chosen and to show him that he is free—and, indeed, almost morally bound—to choose better ways of coping, ways that will give meaning to his life. Hence whatever the patient's complaint, the existential therapist will consistently turn the patient's attention to the "here and now," emphasize the active rather than the passive aspects of his mode of "becoming," and encourage him to formulate for himself a system of values that will give his life an ultimate meaning. For the existentialists, this sense of meaning is tightly bound to interpersonal relationships, which, if they are honest and open, can give to existence that sense of worth and direction that the existentialists seek.

Because existential therapists tend to be so individualistic in their techniques, it is difficult to spell out exactly what transpires between therapist and client. However, two techniques originated by Viktor Frankl, dereflection and paradoxical intention, will serve to illustrate the application of the abstract principles of freedom and responsibility to specific behavior problems. *Dereflection* involves turning the

---

A Logotherapy Dialogue

The following dialogue, between Viktor Frankl and an 80-year-old woman dying of cancer, illustrates some of the major themes of existential therapy: the search for sources of value in the patient's life, the effort to find meaning in suffering and thereby to transcend suffering, and the forthright confrontation with the idea of death. As the excerpt begins, the patient has just been talking of the pleasures of her youth:

DR. FRANKL: *You are speaking of some wonderful experiences; but all this will have an end now, won't it?*

PATIENT (thoughtfully): *In fact, now everything ends. . . .*

DR. FRANKL: *Well, do you think now that all of the wonderful things of your life might be annihilated and invalidated when your end approaches? (And she knew that it did!)*

PATIENT (still more thoughtfully): *All those wonderful things. . . .*

DR. FRANKL: *But tell me: Do you think that anyone can undo the happiness, for example, that you have experienced? Can anyone blot it out?*

PATIENT (now facing me): *You are right, Doctor; nobody can blot it out!*

DR. FRANKL: *Or can anyone blot out the goodness you have met in your life?*

PATIENT (becoming increasingly emotionally involved): *Nobody can blot it out!*

DR. FRANKL: *What you have achieved and accomplished—*

PATIENT: *Nobody can blot it out!*

DR. FRANKL: *Or what you have bravely and honestly suffered: Can anyone remove it from the world—remove it from the past wherein you have stored it, as it were?*

PATIENT (now moved to tears): *No one can remove it!* (Pause) *It is true, I had so much to suffer; but I also tried to be courageous and steadfast in taking life's blows. You see, Doctor, I regarded my suffering as a punishment. . . .*

DR. FRANKL: *But cannot suffering sometimes also be a challenge? . . . What counts and matters in life is . . . to achieve and accomplish something. And this is precisely what you have done. You have made the best of your suffering. You have become an example for our patients by the way and manner in which you take your suffering upon yourself. I congratulate you on behalf of this achievement and accomplishment. . . .*

Source: Frankl (1967), pp. 92–94.

---

patient's attention away from his symptom, be it anxiety or depression or whatever, and pointing out to him what he *could* be doing, or "becoming," if he were not so self-preoccupied; in short, the therapist offers the patient his freedom. Somewhat different in technique but not in aim, *paradoxical intention* involves asking the patient to go ahead and indulge his symptom, even to exaggerate it. If he has been washing his hands fifty times a day, he should now aim for a hundred. The purpose is to show the patient that he controls his symptom and that it can therefore be approached with nonchalance and even humor rather than with terror and loathing.

Like humanistic therapy, existential therapy has all the shortcomings (if such they be) of any insight therapy. Furthermore, the actual dynamics of existential therapy, unlike those of humanistic therapy, have not been subjected to any systematic efforts at scientific evaluation. This, it might be said, is in the nature of the beast. Existential psychology is deeply philosophical, almost religious, and its proponents would answer their critics by saying that a unique human being's search for meaning in life is not something that can be weighed and measured with the tools of science.

Gestalt Therapy

The founder of *Gestalt therapy,* Frederick (Fritz) Perls (1951, 1970) was trained in Europe as an orthodox Freudian psychoanalyst; then as his career progressed, he repudiated large portions of Freudian theory. Thus Gestalt therapy is both an outgrowth and a rejection of psychoanalysis. On the Freudian side, Perls adhered to the theory that disordered behavior is the result of unresolved conflicts left over from the past—conflicts that must be located and "worked through." Furthermore, Perls, like Freud, believed in the symbolic content of dreams and made extensive use of dream interpretation. On the other hand, Perls' handling of childhood conflicts, repressed feelings, dreams, and all the other Freudian materials is decidedly un-Freudian in that all these matters are brought to bear solely on the present, the *now*, in which the client chooses what he will become and whether or not he will allow his past to control his future. In short, Perls detached a number of Freudian concepts from Freud's deterministic view of human behavior and redirected these concepts toward humanistic ends: freedom, responsibility, openness, the active control of one's "becoming."

In Gestalt therapy, the client is asked to root out his past conflicts and reenact them in the consulting

A Gestalt Therapy Dialogue

The following brief patient-therapist exchange exemplifies one of the fundamental goals of Gestalt therapy: getting the patient to take frank and open responsibility for his emotions rather than allowing him to hide behind devious and often manipulative quasi-expressions of emotion. The dialogue also illustrates a major Gestalt technique for reaching this goal—namely, encouraging the patient literally to act out his emotions and their sources in his personal history:

> PATIENT: *I would like to understand . . .*
> THERAPIST: *I hear a wailing in your voice. Can you hear it?*
> PATIENT: *Yes . . . There is a trembling . . .*
> THERAPIST: *Be your voice now.*
> PATIENT: *I am a weak, complaining voice, the voice of a child that doesn't dare to demand. He is afraid . . .*
> THERAPIST: I *am . . .*
> PATIENT: *I am a little boy and I am afraid to ask for anything, can only ask for what I want by showing my sadness, so that mommy will have pity and take care of me . . .*
> THERAPIST: *Could you be your mother, now?*

Source: Naranjo (1975), p. 39.

room. If the client is still smarting, at the age of forty, over the way his father treated him when he was ten, then Perls would assume the role of the father and have the client act out the conflict—reopen the quarrel and perhaps this time close it as well. The patient is encouraged to "act out" as violently and as vividly as he needs to: he should swear, kick the chair, yell, weep, and so on. In this way, Perls argued, the patient would confront his feeling, take responsibility for it, and learn to control it rather than letting it control him. And by doing so, he would learn to unify his feelings and his actions into a new whole (the word *Gestalt* means "whole") and begin living a more spontaneous, open, and honest life—a life of decisive feeling and decisive action.

Gestalt therapy has been quite influential, particularly in the group therapy movement, where it has helped a number of people to get in touch with their feelings and to deal with others more openly. However, like the other insight therapies, Gestalt therapy has offered no sound empirical support for its effectiveness. Furthermore, Perls' techniques have been criticized for giving an authoritarian control to the therapist, for devaluing reason in favor of emotion, and for training patients to develop a type of extreme candor that is inappropriate outside the consulting room.

GROUP TREATMENT

There is no question that the most significant change in psychological treatment in recent years is the group therapy movement. Treatment in groups has the obvious advantage of saving time and money. The therapist can handle more clients in a single hour, and therefore the clients pay less for the therapist's time. However, economy alone cannot account for the spectacular rise of group therapy. Rather, the popularity of this type of treatment is due primarily to the current belief that many psychological difficulties are basically interpersonal difficulties—problems in dealing with other people—and that consequently these difficulties must be worked out in an interpersonal context—that is, with other people. These other people may be one's "significant others"; thus a married couple or an entire family may be treated together. Or the members of a group may have nothing more in common than the fact that they are all human beings with problems.

The number of different kinds of groups is staggering. There are behavioral groups, psychodynamic groups, and many, many varieties of humanistic groups. There are groups for married couples, for unmarried couples, for homosexuals, for delinquents, for parents of problem children, for alcoholics, for spouses of alcoholics, and so on. And most of all, there are groups for anyone who cares to come. Since we can in no way cover this entire range,

we shall discuss below only a few representative types of group therapy.

Family Therapy, Marital Therapy, and Transactional Analysis

In *marital therapy* and *family therapy* the therapeutic focus is shifted from the individual to the interaction between the couple or to the relations between the members of a family. Every couple and every family builds up patterns of relating to one another, sets up roles for each person to fill, and unconsciously enforces these expectations on one another. For example, married couples often have a designated "weak" member and a designated "strong" member—roles that may cramp each member's potentialities considerably. Likewise, families will

Fig. 19.10 Through the technique of psychodrama, group members have the opportunity to act out their fears, anxieties, and obsessions.

often create equally constricting roles for their members: the scapegoat, the disciplinarian, the one who needs looking after, the one who is expected to take care of everyone else, and so on. The assumption of marital or family therapy is that while one member of the couple or family may "break down" because he is somehow more vulnerable, it is the interpersonal unit, and not the symptomatic member, that is disturbed (Martin Stein, personal communication, 1975). Hence therapy aims at pinpointing the role expectations and patterns of communication within the unit, encouraging members to examine their roles and the roles they impose on the others, and opening up the lines of communication so that the relationships within the unit can become less restrictive, more sympathetic, and more mutually reinforcing (Satir, 1967).

An interesting recent variant of marital therapy is *transactional analysis*, a technique originated by Eric Berne and often used in groups of married couples. Berne's basic tenet, as set forth in his popular book *Games People Play* (1964), is that people, and particularly husbands and wives, "play games" with one another—that is, that they go on for years interacting with one another according to a set of rules that may fulfill neurotic needs but at the same time undermine mutual respect and comfort. For example, in the game that Berne calls "Now I've Got You, You Son of a Bitch (NIGYYSOB)," one member invites the other one to take advantage of him and then turns around, with much righteous indignation, and accuses the other one of exploiting him, a charge that the exploiter is hard put to deny. Such games, according to Berne, can be extremely destructive to a marriage. The purpose of transactional analysis is to uncover these games or transactions and change the rules that need changing.

Psychodrama

Originated in the 1930s by J. L. Moreno, a Viennese psychiatrist, *psychodrama* is a psychoanalytically oriented form of group therapy in which members get up on an actual stage and together with other members act out their emotional conflicts. For example, if a male member of the group is basically terrified of women, he will be put on the stage with a female member of the group playing his mother, and will be asked to act out a childhood scene with her. If necessary, other members may enter the play as his father, his brothers, or his sisters. The aim is not simply to encourage the client to confront and act out his feelings, as in Gestalt therapy, but also to allow him to reveal the unconscious roots of these feelings, which are then examined according to Freudian theory.

Milieu Therapy

Milieu therapy (also called the *therapeutic community*), which we have already discussed in Chapter 12, is basically an institutional group therapy in which severely disturbed patients live together in an atmosphere designed to maximize their independence, their activity level, and their sense of dignity. Everyone in the community is valued as a therapeutic agent: the patients for one another, the staff for the patients, and the patients for the staff. Hence the atmosphere is warm, open, democratic, and, above all, busy, involving the patients in occupational therapy, recreational activities, self-governmental meetings, and other projects.

Milieu therapy grew up in the 1940s as a reaction against the type of custodial care typically offered to the chronic patient: care which tended to reinforce withdrawal (and hence chronic institutionalization), as withdrawn behaviors posed fewer problems for the staff. As an antidote, milieu therapy has shown some success. The discharge rates in milieu programs are much higher than those in custodial programs (Paul, 1969c). But readmission rates are also high, indicating that the warm and permissive atmosphere typical of milieu programs may not be an appropriate preparation for reentry into the community.

Encounter Groups and T-Groups

One of the central pillars of the "human potential movement" as it has emerged in the sixties and seventies is humanistically oriented group therapy. The two originals of this form of therapy were the *encounter group*, originating in such human-potential centers as California's Esalen Institute, and the *sensitivity-training group* or *T-group*, first introduced in the late forties in order to help business executives improve their relations with their co-workers and hence increase their efficiency. Originally the encounter group was the more radical of the two, encouraging touching exercises, yelling, weeping, and the type of no-holds-barred emotional expressiveness typical of Gestalt therapy. In contrast, the T-groups limited themselves to somewhat more sober verbal interchanges. However, as the group therapy movement has grown, the distinctions between the two types have blurred considerably.

The central goals of humanistically oriented group therapy are, predictably, personal growth—that is, understanding of and experimentation with one's own behavior—and increased openness and honesty

Fig. 19.11 Group psychotherapy, whether highly structured (as in group psychoanalysis) or relatively unstructured (as in encounter group psychotherapy), has certain features that sometimes make it preferable to individual treatment. A cohesive group can offer support and a source of identification to persons whose problems include a sense of isolation or alienation. Also, the group as a miniature society helps members to understand how they respond to persons of different personality styles; an individual may become better able to relate to persons in authority, for example, by exploring his reactions to the leader and to assertive members of the group. He may also come to understand people better through hearing the group members disclose their own problems. In addition, he may learn how others respond to him through the feedback he receives from many different members. Such feedback may provide consensual validation of his behavior or may help him to understand how he responds defensively to critical input. Another valuable feature of groups is that they can function as "social learning laboratories" in which a person can experiment with new behaviors in a safe atmosphere and thereby learn more adequate social and coping skills.

in personal relations. Note that the emphasis is positive rather than negative, as is typical of humanistic psychology. The members are there not to become less sick, but rather to become more well. Indeed, hundreds of people join groups not because they feel they are psychologically disturbed but simply because they find their lives somewhat lacking in excitement, intensity, or intimacy.

During sessions, group members may talk about the problems they encounter in their outside lives, but the emphasis usually shifts to the members' reactions to one another, which they are encouraged to express with complete candor. Love, anger, warmth, suspiciousness—whatever a member feels toward another member he is free to express. And the other member is free to respond in kind, so that both will gain practice in venting their emotions honestly, achieve some insight into how they affect other people, and eventually learn how to work out interpersonal conflicts with patience, tolerance, and sympathy. During such interchanges, the group leader (sometimes called the "facilitator") straddles a fence between directing and participating. On the one hand, he is fair game for the other participants; he is not to play boss or fount of wisdom, as in other therapies. On the other hand, he must also make sure that each person is allowed his fair say and that no member is scapegoated by the group (Aranson, 1972).

Such are the basic themes of the humanistic group, and they are subject to hundreds of different variations. In the effort to break down defenses, some groups are conducted as marathons, others in the nude. Many groups use touching, staring, and other exercises in order to loosen inhibitions (Schutz, 1967).

Group Therapy: Pros and Cons

Any form of group therapy, no matter what its orientation, has the advantage of giving its members a unique insight into the nature of human relationships. The members can learn vicariously from one another; can practice new interpersonal skills on one another, receiving frank and immediate feedback; and can come to understand that their worries,

Fig. 19.12 Humanistically-oriented groups sometimes focus on techniques involving sensory awareness and bodily experience. Various exercises, such as those shown in the photographs, are used to emphasize physical awareness and physical expression among group members. Such activities are usually enjoyable and often result in intensely positive experiences.

Common Varieties of Group Therapy

Marital therapy and family therapy	Married couples or entire families meet together to examine and adjust their roles and patterns of communication.
Transactional analysis	Husbands and wives examine the destructive "games" that they play with each other and devise better ways of meeting their own and each other's needs.
Psychodrama	Groups act out, in skits, the conflicts of their members, and these conflicts are analyzed in psychodynamic terms.
Milieu therapy	Groups of disturbed persons live together with staff on a democratic basis and in a supportive atmosphere aimed at promoting individualism, autonomy, and self-respect.
Encounter groups and T-groups	Groups of people meet to interact with one another, and to express their reactions to one another, candidly and spontaneously, in the effort to promote honesty, emotional receptivity, and personal growth in their daily lives.

problems, faults, and deep, dark secrets are not a cross they bear alone but rather are the burden of most human beings. A number of highly respected professionals, including Rogers (1970), have testified to the effectiveness of this process in bringing about constructive changes in behavior outside the group.

However, this latter point—the ability of members to transfer their new skills to their daily lives—has been disputed by some critics (Houts and Serber, 1972). And there is also question as to whether the skills learned in humanistically oriented groups—for example, utter bluntness in expressing positive and negative reactions to others—are in any way appropriate beyond the confines of the group; indeed, they may get the newly "liberated" individual into deep trouble. Finally, another criticism that has been directed specifically at humanistically oriented groups is that for particularly vulnerable members intense "encountering" may be quite the opposite of constructive, serving as an entry into psychotic episodes or suicides (Bednar and Lawlis, 1971; Yalom and Lieberman, 1971).

THE BIOLOGICAL APPROACH TO TREATMENT

The treatment methods that we have discussed so far in this chapter are all psychological treatments, aimed at giving the client new insights into his personality or teaching him new psychological responses. In contrast, biological therapies bypass the psyche and go directly to the neural pathways that mediate between the environment and the individual's behavioral response to it. We shall examine three major biological treatments: drugs, psychosurgery, and electroconvulsive therapy.

Drugs

There are three major categories of drugs used in treating abnormal behavior: antianxiety drugs, antipsychotic drugs, and antidepressant drugs.

Antianxiety Drugs The *antianxiety drugs* (or *minor tranquilizers*) are very widely used to reduce tension and anxiety. Indeed, it might be said that at least half the medicine cabinets in the United States have at one time or another housed either Miltown (meprobamate), Librium (chlordiazepoxide hydrochloride), or Valium (diazepam), which are the three most common antianxiety drugs. While they are most commonly used by normal people going through difficult periods in their lives, antianxiety drugs are also prescribed for neurotics, people with psychosomatic symptoms, and people withdrawing from alcohol and other drugs. In such cases they may serve as a helpful aid to psychological treatment. However, they often have inconvenient side effects, such as drowsiness, and prolonged use may lead to addiction. Furthermore, heavy doses of minor tranquilizers taken along with alcohol can result in death.

Solving Problems with Valium

At present Valium is the most widely prescribed drug in the world. And along with its predecessor, Librium, it has made Hoffmann-La Roche, the manufacturer of these two tranquilizers, one of the most profitable corporations in the world. The company has spent millions of dollars promoting the two drugs, and doctors, particularly general practitioners, have responded willingly. Valium alone is now taken by approximately 15 percent of the population of the United States.

But Valium is not without its problems. The most common side effects are fatigue, drowsiness, and staggering—reason enough for the Valium taker to avoid driving. Furthermore, Valium, like all central nervous system depressants (e.g., alcohol) may have a disinhibiting effect, in which case whatever the person's anxiety was covering—irritability, hostility, or any other type of antisocial behavior—may surface once Valium releases the hold. Another unwelcome effect of Valium, especially when taken in large doses, is that once the drug treatment is terminated, the symptom that it was originally prescribed to eliminate may return with redoubled strength. This is particularly true of insomnia and nightmares, for which Valium is often prescribed. Finally, Valium can be very dangerous and even fatal when taken in combination with other central nervous system depressants.

However, many people report no adverse side effects and are simply grateful to have something that will help them get through the minor crises of daily existence. Even so, the vast popularity of Valium still leaves us with two serious questions. First, is the suppression of anxiety the best way of solving problems? Is it not possible that a person who suffers regularly from anxiety *needs* to experience that anxiety in order to force him to get to the bottom of his difficulties? The second question has to do with our social environment. If 15 out of every 100 Americans are experiencing so much stress that they have to rely on Valium—and this is to say nothing of those who depend on other tranquilizers, on alcohol, or on barbiturates—then we must ask ourselves whether our society is not moving and changing too quickly and too haphazardly to make it fit for comfortable habitation by the average nervous system. Perhaps we need a prescription for the society rather than for the individual.

Source: Deborah Larned, "Do You Take Valium?" *Ms.*, November 1975, pp. 26–30.

Antipsychotic Drugs The *antipsychotic drugs* (or *major tranquilizers*) are used to relieve symptoms such as extreme agitation, hyperactivity, and hallucinations and delusions in psychotic patients (Cole, 1964; Davis, 1965; Goldberg et al., 1965). The most popular of these drugs are the phenothiazines, including Thorazine (chloropromazine) and Stelazine (trifluoperazine hydrochloride), which appear to be effective in calming down even chronic schizophrenics. However, there is still no substantial information on exactly how they work. (Like most drug treatments, they were discovered by accident.) And like the antianxiety drugs, they are not without side effects, including fatigue and fainting.

Antidepressant Drugs *Antidepressant drugs*, as the name indicates, are used to elevate mood in depressives. The first of these drugs, iproniazid, was originally introduced as a treatment for tuberculosis, and it was found, quite by accident, that its major effect was simply that it made the tubercular patients sud-denly cheerful and optimistic. This discovery led to the development of further mood-elevating drugs. Today the major antidepressants are (1) the monoamine oxidase inhibitors, or MAO inhibitors, including Nardil (phenelzine sulfate) and Parnate (tranylcypromine sulfate) and (2) the tricyclics, including Tofranil (imipramine hydrochloride) and Sinequan (doxepin hydrochloride). The use of MAO inhibitors has declined recently because of their toxic side effects. The tricyclics, on the other hand, are widely used and appear to be effective, particularly for endogenous depressions (Chapter 7) (Lapolla and Jones, 1970).

Psychosurgery

In prehistoric times, as we saw in Chapter 1, abnormal behavior was treated with a type of surgery known as trephining. Surgery did not again appear as a common treatment for psychological problems until 1935, when Egas Moniz and Almeida Lima developed the *prefrontal lobotomy*, a surgical proce-

THORAZINE: The Tedium of Tranquillity

While Thorazine definitely has a calming effect on psychotic patients, some patients complain that in addition to its inconvenient physiological side effects, it is *too* calming psychologically—that it induces a bland indifference, making all of reality seem uniformly colorless. In *The Eden Express* (1975) Mark Vonnegut describes his response to Thorazine during his recovery from schizophrenia:

Thorazine has lots of unpleasant side effects. It makes you groggy, lowers your blood pressure, making you dizzy and faint when you stand up too quickly. If you go out in the sun your skin gets red and hurts like hell. It makes muscles rigid and twitchy.

The side effects were bad enough, but I liked what the drug was supposed to do even less. It's supposed to keep you calm, dull, uninterested and uninteresting. No doctor or nurse ever came out and said so in so many words, but what it was was an antihero drug. Dale [Vonnegut's doctor] kept saying to me, "You mustn't try to be a hero." Thorazine made heroics impossible.

What the drug is supposed to do is keep away hallucinations. What I think it does is just fog up your mind so badly you don't notice the hallucinations or much else.

• • •

On Thorazine everything's a bore. Not a bore, exactly. Boredom implies impatience. You can read comic books and Reader's Digest *forever. You can tolerate talking to jerks forever. Babble, babble, babble. The weather is dull, the flowers are dull, nothing's very impressive. Muzak, Bach, Beatles, Lolly and the Yum-Yums, Rolling Stones. It doesn't make any difference.*

When I did manage to get excited about some things, impatient with some things, interested in some things, it still didn't have the old zing to it. I knew that Dostoyevsky was more interesting than comic books, or, more accurately, I remembered that he had been. I cared about what happened at the farm [the commune where he had been living before his breakdown], but it was more remembering caring than really caring (pp. 196–197).

---

dure in which a cut is made between the frontal lobes (the thought center) and the thalamus (the emotional center) of the brain. The lobotomy was expected to aid very disturbed patients by cutting down the communication between these sections, thereby reducing disturbing stimuli. Other methods of psychosurgery were rapidly developed (see Fig. 19.13), and over the next twenty years many thousands of these operations were performed.

It cannot be denied that there were many patients who were helped by psychosurgery, people who were able to leave the hospitals in which they had been expected to spend the rest of their lives. There were, however, enormous problems. Patients and their families were horrified at the prospect of this type of surgery, and many people, both inside and out of the medical profession, decried it as unethical. The side effects were, in many cases, extreme: some patients emerged from surgery in a vegetative state, in which they remained; others were hostile, childlike, lethargic, or generally devoid of affect; some suffered recurring convulsions; some died (Redlich and Freedman, 1966).

The side effects of psychosurgery were almost always irreversible. It was, therefore, with considerable relief that professionals welcomed the introduction of the phenothiazines in the 1950s as a safer method of calming the severely disturbed. Psychosurgery is now resorted to only very rarely and only in the most extreme cases.

Electroconvulsive Therapy

Electroconvulsive therapy (ECT) involves administering to the patient an electric shock of approximately between 70 and 130 volts, thus inducing a convulsion similar to a grand mal epileptic seizure. Typically therapy will involve about twenty such treatments, spaced over a period of several weeks,

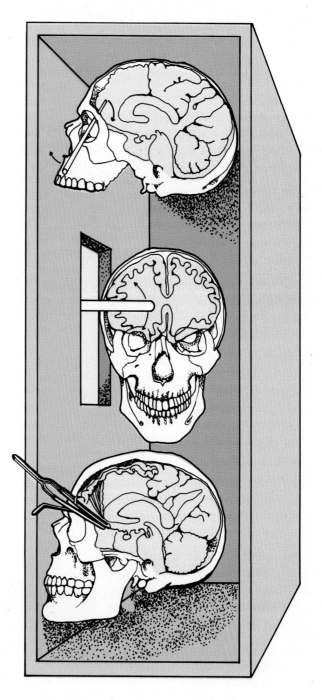

Fig. 19.13   Various techniques were developed to make the procedure of psychosurgery more effective and efficient and to reduce side effects. (Top) One method, known as transorbital lobotomy, involved the insertion of a needle through the optic cavity, thereby eliminating the necessity of drilling through the skull. (Middle) The "closed" standard lobotomy technique involved the drilling of a hole in the side of the skull, through which an instrument was inserted to cut a selected area of brain tissue. A later modification of this technique substituted electrical cauterization of brain tissue for cutting. (Bottom) Another major technique, orbital undercutting, involved the insertion of instruments through a hole or holes drilled in the frontal area of the skull and the selective removal of brain tissue. Very few lobotomies of any kind are performed today; the few that are offer a chance of improvement to those patients who have been unsuccessfully treated in all other available ways.

though the total may be much lower or higher. This technique, first discovered in the late thirties (Bini, 1938), has been found to be quite effective in the treatment of depression (Greenblatt et al., 1964), but as with the drug treatments discussed above, no one as yet knows exactly how it works. One current theory is that the shock in some way "clears out" the nervous system, allowing it to return to normal functioning. A more skeptical opinion is that the therapy is so aversive to the client that he improves simply to avoid its repetition.

ECT, like other medical treatments, has its complications. A typical aftereffect is loss of memory, and though this problem usually clears up within a month, some patients continue to be troubled with amnesia for several years. A second problem is simply that many patients are deathly afraid of the treatment, in spite of the evidence documenting its effectiveness.

Biological Therapy: Pros and Cons

As we have just seen, some biological treatments do in fact relieve certain distressing symptoms. But for how long? And at what cost in terms of side effects? Let us take drugs as an example. Critics of drug therapy argue that medications, because they focus on symptom reduction rather than resolution of psychological problems, cannot be considered an actual cure. This argument is supported by hospital statistics. Though the introduction of antipsychotic drugs has allowed many patients to be released from mental hospitals on maintenance doses of these drugs, the patients generally make only a minimal adjustment to life on the outside and often have to be rehospitalized (Rickles, 1968; Gurel, 1970). Thus antipsychotic drugs have allowed us to progress from long-term institutionalization to "revolving-door" institutionalization. This can hardly be considered substantial progress. Furthermore, many critics charge that a state of tension or anxiety may be a thoroughly appropriate response to certain life situations or internal conflicts and that by relieving the patient's agitation, professionals also relieve themselves of the responsibility—and relieve the patient of his motivation—for solving his continuing problem.

On the other hand, there is no question that the use of drugs to control extreme emotional and motor responses in psychotic patients is preferable to the use of strait jackets and has introduced a calmer atmosphere into modern mental hospitals. This latter improvement should not be minimized, since it makes patient-staff interactions, organized ward activities, and formal therapy easier to institute. Unfortunately, however, in many institutions drugs are themselves the major form of treatment rather than serving as aids to more constructive treatments. In short, the society may be comforted that its mental institutions are no longer the "bedlams" of former years, and for this, drugs are largely responsible. What is less comforting but more easily ignored is that for many severely disturbed patients, drugs are the only relief available.

MAJOR BIOLOGICAL THERAPIES

DRUGS

Antianxiety drugs
Miltown
Librium
Valium

Antipsychotic drugs
Thorazine
Stelazine

Antidepressant drugs
MAO inhibitors
   Nardil
   Parnate

Tricyclics
   Tofranil
   Sinequan

PSYCHOSURGERY
Lobotomy

ELECTROCONVULSIVE THERAPY

SUMMARY

The purpose of this chapter has been to summarize the goals and techniques of the various treatments for abnormal behavior, professional therapies which together constitute something of an institution in modern society. The major approaches to treatment are psychodynamic therapy, behavior modification, humanistic-existential therapy, group therapy, and biological therapy.

Psychodynamic therapy may take the form of orthodox Freudian psychoanalysis, which relies heavily on the techniques of free association, dream interpretation, and analysis of resistance and transference. However, most current psychodynamic therapies use Freudian techniques only in modified form, and many incorporate the emphasis on ego strength and on interpersonal relations typical of ego analysis and Sullivanian therapy, respectively.

Behavior modification is much more precise in its goals and techniques than any of the insight therapies. It aims simply at altering the client's specific maladaptive behavior through such procedures as respondent conditioning (e.g., systematic desensitization, aversion therapy), operant conditioning (e.g., token economies, contingency contracting, shaping), and social learning (e.g., modeling, cognitive restructuring).

Humanistic-existential therapy differs from both psychodynamic and behaviorist treatments in that it stresses personal growth and freedom and rejects deterministic interpretations of human behavior. Humanistic client-centered therapy depends on an atmosphere of acceptance and on a nondirective approach to promote personality integration, and consequently, self-actualization. Existential therapy also aims at self-determination but places greater stress on the responsibilities attached to freedom. Gestalt therapy, again growth-oriented, encourages the client to reenact his past conflicts and to accept and express freely his feelings.

Group therapies, which have become extremely popular in the last two decades, come in many varieties: family and marital therapy, psychodrama, milieu therapy, and humanistically oriented encounter groups and T-groups. Most group therapies are based on the belief that individual psychological problems are the result of disturbed or inadequate interpersonal relations—relations that can be improved by the kind of practice in candid interaction that the group approach offers.

Biological therapies include drugs (antianxiety, antipsychotic, and antidepressant), psychosurgery, and electroconvulsive therapy. These techniques have been shown to relieve symptoms in many cases, but they are often criticized for ignoring the problems underlying these symptoms.

We began this text by asking three questions: How is deviance defined? How is it explained? How is it handled? And our text so far has been essentially an attempt to answer these questions in light of our present knowledge. Let us recapitulate briefly. Deviant behavior is culturally defined (Benedict, 1934)—that is, what we call abnormal is whatever seriously conflicts with the current norms of the society in which we live. In measuring behavior against these norms, the behaviorists tend to take a relativistic approach, whereas the psychodynamic and humanistic-existential perspectives still cling to some ideal or absolutist standard of normality, be it self-actualization or a successful balancing of ego, id, and superego. As for the explanation and handling of deviant behavior, here the disagreements among different orientations begin to multiply. Few people believe any longer that the emotionally disturbed are inhabited by devils and are thus in need of exorcism, flogging, or burning. Yet this medieval position is no more distant from our present outlook than many of the various current theories are from one another. In the meantime, some of the most interesting research—for example, the studies of high-risk children of schizophrenic mothers (Chapter 12) and the studies of the role of lithium carbonate in the affective disorders (Chapter 7)—comes from the much-criticized medical model. Should these studies prove productive, it would not be rash to predict that future professionals will abandon the functional-vs.-organic dispute regarding the so-called functional psychoses and adopt instead an interactive theory, in which both environment and biology would be seen as equally potent etiological factors.

This, then, is where we are now—in a state of competing theories, competing treatments, and competing research, with most of the serious questions (e.g., what causes schizophrenia?) unanswered. And the aim of the last nineteen chapters has been to spell out in some detail the unanswered questions and the conflicting approaches to these questions. The purpose of this final chapter is to discuss briefly where we are going from here. Our subjects will be, first, the recent movement toward community mental health services, toward the use of paraprofessionals, and toward prevention programs, and second, the larger unresolved issues surrounding the mental health profession as a whole.

20
Abnormality: Today and Tomorrow

CHANGING SERVICES: THE RETURN TO THE COMMUNITY

The State Institution

As we have seen, one of the fruits of the eighteenth-century Enlightenment was the widespread development of large hospitals for the mentally disturbed.* Most of these hospitals, both in the United States and elsewhere, were built in relatively isolated rural or suburban areas. There were a number of reasons for these locations. First, it was thought that patients would recover sooner if they were removed from the stresses of community life and allowed to repose in the fresh country air (and, as we have seen in Chapter 1, this did result in a higher rate of cures than was achieved by most other treatments). A second reason was economy. The land necessary for the construction of these large hospitals was much less expensive far out in the countryside than it would have been in the cities. Furthermore, until fairly recently, most of these state mental hospitals had large farms attached to them, where the patients, as part of their "therapy," worked to produce their own food, thus further saving the taxpayers money. A third and equally important reason for removing these patients to remote locations was that no one wanted to see them. Though the mentally ill were no longer tortured and hanged, they were still considered rather unsightly and dangerous to have around—an attitude that is still widely held today.

Whatever the reasons, the isolation of the large state mental hospitals did not contribute to their efficiency. Very few competent professionals were willing to join the patients in their retreat and thereby remove themselves from centers of research and opportunities for advancement. As a result, staffing became a serious problem. (It was not uncommon to find hospitals with over a thousand patients and only one licensed psychiatrist on the staff.) The consequence, of course, was that care was custodial rather than remedial. Furthermore, the very fact that patients were removed from their communities proved counterproductive. Families and friends were far away and therefore could not be mobilized to aid in the treatment process. Worse yet, the patients simply forgot how to assume their social roles—how to be a father, a mother, a son, a daughter, an employee, a friend. Hence returning to the community was made doubly difficult. Finally, the remoteness of the hospitals made it impossible for the patients to engage in any kind of *partial* treatment through halfway houses, work-release programs, outpatient follow-up services, and so on. It was all or nothing. Once removed from the community and hidden away in a remote hospital, the mentally disturbed person's identity was confined to his role as a *patient*—that is, a failure, an "other." Erving Goffman has summed up the crushing loss of status involved in this transition:

> In the mental hospital, the setting and the house rules press home to the patient that he is, after all, a mental case who has suffered some kind of social collapse on the outside, having failed in some overall way, and that here he is of little social weight, being hardly capable of acting like a full-fledged person at all (1961, pp. 151–152).

The Community Mental Health Center

Some efforts have been made to improve the state mental hospitals, bringing them closer to the therapeutic-community model (Jones, 1953), where patients are given more respect, more actual treatment, and more autonomy. However, the sad truth is that most of the state institutions remain ill-staffed, dreary, and boring places—warehouses where forgotten people are encouraged simply to keep quiet. And at present the major efforts at improvement in mental health services are aimed not at the large state hospitals but rather at a totally new kind of service, the *community mental health center*.

These centers, organized and funded by the Community Mental Health Centers Act of 1963 as part of President Kennedy's drive for a "bold new approach" to mental illness, were a direct response to the problems involved in isolating the mentally disturbed from their communities. The law provided for the establishment of one mental health center for every 50,000 population. In these centers, anyone, rich or poor, from the center's *catchment area* (i.e., its area of geographical coverage) would receive the psychological services he required and still retain whatever he could handle of his normal role in the community. Furthermore, the centers were to implement programs for the prevention of mental disturbance; to educate other community workers, such as teachers, clergymen, and policemen, in the principles of preventive mental health; to train professionals and nonprofessionals to work in the centers; and finally, to carry out research. We shall have more to say later in this chapter about training and prevention. For the moment we will concentrate on the types of services that the commu-

---

*Many of these very buildings, now in greatly deteriorated physical condition, are still in use; this contributes further to the problems of staffing and treatment.

Fig. 20.1   A patient and therapist greet each other in a mental hospital; the importance to successful treatment of greater human contact and more personalized relationships between staff and patients is beginning to be recognized.

nity mental health centers provide directly to the troubled people who walk through their doors and to other workers in the community. It should be noted that many of these services are at present of limited availability; a country-wide system of community mental health care is still in the future.

Outpatient Services   The outpatient service, the first place to which the disturbed person or his family turns for help, is the primary and most heavily used service of the community mental health center. Here the individual can receive therapy once or twice a week without leaving his family (indeed, his family can be brought into the therapy) and without abandoning his schooling, his work, his friends, his turf—all the things that make him feel like a person. Furthermore, the services are convenient and available, only a short trip away. And many community mental health centers have additional satellite operations—storefront offices and traveling teams—that attempt to bring help even closer to all the members of the community. Thus a person with problems can receive therapy quickly and conveniently and still be home in time for dinner—a fact which encourages him to see his problems as natural and solvable rather than hideous and extreme.

Another important aspect of the community mental health center's outpatient services is the provision of *aftercare*—for example, weekly therapy or perhaps just monthly checkups—for patients who have been hospitalized. Here the patient can often be treated by the same people who treated him in the hospital, thus providing continuity and promoting the patient's feeling that he is looked upon as a human being rather than simply as another manila folder in the files of some vast institutional bureaucracy.

Inpatient Services   While effective outpatient services can reduce the need for hospitalization, there are still patients who require hospitalization, either because they are intensely disturbed and pose a threat to themselves and others or because they lack family or other resources to support them in their difficulties. In such cases, the community mental health center provides hospitalization, usually in a general hospital in the community. Because these facilities are readily and quickly available, because family and friends can easily visit, and because coordinated aftercare can be provided, it is hoped that this system of hospitalization can speed up the patient's release. Furthermore, in many centers patients can receive partial hospitalization through the innovative systems of the day hospital and the night hospital. In the *day hospital*, the patient is hospitalized only on a nine-to-five basis. He takes part in the hospital's therapeutic activities during the day, and then at night he returns home to his family, his friends, his poker game, and so on. Conversely, in the *night hospital*, the patient goes to his job from nine to five and then returns to the hospital. In both cases, the emphasis is once again on preserving whatever can be preserved of the person's sources of gratification, self-respect, and social interaction so that he will not fall into the role of the chronic patient.

For some people, however, partial or short-term hospitalization simply does not work, in which case the patient will usually be transferred to a state mental hospital for longer-term care. Nevertheless, the innovative inpatient services of the community mental health centers do allow the hospitalized patient to retain his ties to the community.

Emergency Services   Before the advent of the community mental health center, emergency psychological services were virtually nonexistent. The mental hospitals, as we have seen, were miles away from major population centers, and even communities that were rich in mental health services generally provided such services only during ordinary work hours, and almost never on weekends or holidays. Hence, people who did not time their personal crises, acute anxiety attacks, acute depressions, suicidal impulses, bad drug experiences, and other psychological emergencies to fit this schedule usually either spent the night in jail (supposedly for their protection), sat for hours on the low-priority bench in the emergency room of the local general hospital, or in most cases simply weathered their crises alone. To solve this problem, the community mental health centers have established various kinds of emergency services. In some cases a satellite storefront clinic will remain open for emergencies at night; here the troubled person can come for an informal talk (and possibly a tranquilizer) and make an appointment to go to the regular outpatient clinic in the morning. Other community centers provide teams of mental health workers to serve in the emergency rooms of the community's general hospitals so that acute psychological problems can be given the same swift attention as acute physical problems. In addition to filling the obvious need for emergency psychological services, the presence of these mental health professionals in hospital emergency rooms has had the beneficial side effect of sensitizing the rest of the emergency room staff to the psychological responses of people involved in automobile accidents, fires, and other catastrophes. In this way the psychological trauma can be dealt with at the same time as the physical trauma, thus obviating or at least minimizing transient situational disturbances.

Consultation A chronic problem in the delivery of psychological services is that there are simply not enough professionals to go around. One solution to this problem is consultation, whereby trained mental health professionals, instead of working with specific cases themselves, advise other types of professionals—teachers, police, clergymen, and the like—on how to deal with the psychologically troubled people that they encounter in the course of their work. For example, if a teacher is having great difficulty with a particular child, one way of handling the problem would be simply to refer the child's family to the local community mental health center. On the other hand, using the consultation approach, the school could ask a psychiatrist or psychologist from the community mental health center to come in and observe the child in question during a class hour and then to advise the teacher, and perhaps other teachers at the same time, on how to deal with the kind of behavior problem in question. This type of consulting service is being given increasing attention by community mental health centers, not only because it saves professional manpower but also because it allows behavior problems to be dealt with at the moment and in the context in which they occur.

A fine example of the usefulness of the consultation approach was a recent program in which a group of New York City policemen were trained by mental health professionals in how to intervene in family quarrels (Bard, 1970). It is a little-known fact that such quarrels are a major source of assaults and homicides—crimes which the public tend to assume occur in the streets. Domestic quarrels are dangerous not only for the family members involved but also for the policemen who are called in to handle them—hence New York City's innovative consultation program. In one precinct, eighteen policemen received 160 hours of training, including lectures, demonstrations, role-playing exercises, and so on, in how to intervene more sensitively in family crises. These trained policemen then worked as family-crisis intervention teams in that precinct. In contrast to policemen in a neighboring district, who witnessed and suffered the same amount of violence normally involved in such calls, the trained team members were able to decrease the number of assaults on family members, did not themselves suffer a single assault, and did not witness a single family homicide in 1,388 family crisis calls. The spectacular success of this program has led to the adoption of similar programs by police departments all over the United States and provides strong support for the effectiveness of providing consultation services to other human service agencies.

Since they are still so new, it is difficult to measure the effectiveness of the community mental health centers. There is little question that they have made psychological services more widely and quickly available to the population at large. On the other hand, many of the services that they offer—psychotherapy, drug therapy, short-term hospitalization, and the like—are rather traditional in nature, while the more innovative services such as consultation, day hospitals, and night hospitals are less widely available. Indeed, the major criticism leveled at this program is that while the idea of local centers is new and promising, the centers themselves are staffed by old-line therapists who are more interested in Oedipal conflicts and sibling rivalry than in the unique and more pressing problems (e.g., drugs, racism, the pressures on migrant-worker families) of the population groups they are supposed to serve (Holden, 1972). In sum, while they have the incontestable virtue of serving the troubled individual on his home ground, the community mental health centers still have a number of shortcomings. And with recent cutbacks in federal and state funds, these shortcomings will not be easily eradicated.

Halfway Houses

Another type of community service that has proliferated in recent years is the halfway house, a service closely related to the partial hospitalization programs offered by many of the community mental health centers. A *halfway house* is a residence for people (e.g., ex-drug addicts or newly released mental patients) who no longer require institutionalization but who still need some support system in the trying process of readjusting to community life. In the halfway house these people with similar problems live together, talk out their difficulties with one another, and relearn appropriate social skills. Many such houses even set up stores, handyman services, and other money-making concerns that both support the members and at the same time train them to support themselves on their own once they leave the house. For many people, these residences appear far preferable to a cold-turkey return to the community, and early reports (e.g., Fairweather et al., 1969) indicate that halfway-house graduates are less likely to require rehospitalization than ex-patients who have not had the benefit of this transitional support.

Crisis Intervention: The Hot Line

As we have seen, the community mental health centers have devoted considerable energy to providing emergency psychological services. But face-to-face emergency counseling is simply one part of a whole new trend toward crisis intervention, the handling of severe emotional stress on the spot. An-

other important innovation in this area is the development of telephone *hot lines*—that is, round-the-clock telephone services where people who are in trouble can call and receive immediate comfort and advice, usually from trained but nonprofessional volunteers. The best-known example of this type of service is the suicide-prevention hot line, the most famous of which is the Los Angeles Suicide Prevention Center, established by Shneidman and Farberow in 1958. But there are other types of hot lines as well—numbers for people with drinking, gambling, or drug problems, and even so-called Dial-a-Shoulder numbers, where volunteers take calls from people who simply need a kindly ear to listen to their troubles. Aside from providing sympathy, a major function of hot-line volunteers is to try to induce the caller to take advantage of whatever community services are available to help him. The following case illustrates the combination of sympathy, intuition, and solid information that a good hot-line volunteer can offer:

The caller began timidly to inquire about how venereal disease was acquired, indicating that he was writing a paper on the subject for his high school class. His frightened manner and the indirect manner in which he phrased his questions (e.g., "How many times is it necessary for a person to have sex in order to get VD?" and "How can someone be sure if he gets VD?" and "If a high school student gets VD, do his parents have to know?") suggested to the staff person that the caller's concerns were more personal than he was willing to admit.

"Perhaps there's some reason for you to be personally concerned that you or someone you know might have been exposed to VD," suggested the staff person after some twenty minutes of more indirect discussion. "Perhaps" was the reply. "Did you know that the city health department runs free VD clinics and that there is no requirement that parents know that someone has come into the clinic?" "No," replied the caller, with interest. Discussion of the high school research paper was now dropped. Very tactfully, the interviewer managed to find out which neighborhood clinic was the most convenient to the caller and then told him the clinic's hours and exactly how to get there. After receiving this information the caller was audibly relieved, thanked the interviewer, and hung up.

Not all hot-line conversations are such obvious successes. Indeed, volunteers on suicide hot lines often have no idea, once they have hung up the phone, whether the person they have just talked to will keep the clinic appointment they have just made for him or whether he will jump out the nearest window. Thus manning a hot line is often frustrating and depressing. At the same time, these services can be of immense help to many callers who need immediate assistance and have no one else to turn to.

CHANGING STAFF: THE RISE OF THE PARAPROFESSIONAL

As we have mentioned in our discussion of consulting services, a problem that has plagued the mental health field is that there are simply not enough trained professionals to minister to all the people with problems that need attention. Thus thousands of people have problems that have simply not been dealt with. Or when the problem was serious enough, the person was often placed in a mental hospital where most of his daily contact was with ill-trained and ill-paid hospital aides whose major duty, as they saw it, was simply to keep the patients from acting up.

In attempting to deal with this manpower shortage, the mental health profession has begun during the last few decades to expand its concept of who is equipped to handle psychological problems. Traditionally there were only three types of professionals who were considered competent to deal with mental disturbance: first (in order of status, pay, and years of schooling), the psychiatrist, a medical doctor with an additional three years' training (a *residency*) in psychiatry; second, the clinical psychologist, with a Ph.D. in psychology and a one-year internship in psychotherapy; third, the psychiatric social worker, with a two-year postgraduate training focused particularly on psychological problems related to family and social difficulties. These professionals were, and still are, in short supply. Furthermore, they are largely white, middle-class, well-educated people to whom nonwhite, non-middle-class, and uneducated people are often reluctant to unburden their special problems.

How to handle these two serious limitations? A partial answer to this question was provided in a now classic study in which Margaret Rioch (1967) showed that housewives who had had no prior experience in psychology but who were carefully selected and then given two years of intensive supervised training made excellent "mental health counselors"—that is, psychotherapists. Rioch's paper suggested that simply by choosing well-balanced and sympathetic people and giving them a relatively short but intensive training, the mental health profession could add to its numbers a whole new group of professionals,

including professionals who shared a common background with the poor and the minorities. And this is precisely what the community health centers have done, particularly those that deal mainly with the lower socioeconomic classes. Such centers routinely select, train, and employ local residents to provide a wide variety of mental health services—interviewing, testing, counseling, home visits, and so on—that just a few years ago would have been impossible to provide on a wide basis with the limited staff of psychiatrists, psychologists, and social workers. In recent years these new mental health professionals, called *paraprofessionals*, are also being trained in colleges, particularly community colleges. At present there are in the United States 174 such programs, usually leading to an Associate of Arts degree (True and Young, 1974). However, most psychological paraprofessionals are recruited, trained, and put to work in the communities in which they live, with the result that they usually have intimate knowledge of the types of problems of that particular community.

How well do these paraprofessionals do their jobs? Research (e.g., Rioch, 1967; Carkhuff, 1968; Brown, 1974) indicates that they are as skillful in their work as "professionals." Because their training is more narrow, they can generally assume only a few specific tasks, such as interviewing or home visits. But in performing these tasks they have an advantage over the professionals in that they are more readily accepted by the community residents. Furthermore, community mental health centers tend to be quite selective about the personal qualifications of the people that they admit to their paraprofessional training programs. Hence it might be argued that simply in terms of personality traits the paraprofessionals may be better suited to deal with the mentally disturbed than the professionals, who are not generally screened for sympathy, objectivity, or emotional stability. There is still considerable objection to the use of paraprofessionals, mainly by professionals suspicious of workers with more limited training. However, since the present data tend to confirm the effectiveness of the paraprofessionals and since they are so sorely needed, it is likely that they will become an increasingly large and important sector of the mental health profession.

CHANGING APPROACHES: PREVENTION

So far in this chapter we have examined a number of new services and new programs. Though different

Fig. 20.2 Through the use of paraprofessionals, more personal attention can be given to patient needs and problems. Here a paraprofessional helps patients examine men's fashion ads in order to make them become more aware of their appearance.

in kind, all of these recent developments have a common aim: the effort to bring psychological care to the doorsteps of ordinary people—to make help available immediately, cheaply, locally, and somehow *naturally*, so that if a person is seriously troubled, he does not have to wait until he suffers a total breakdown before he can get some psychological attention. In short, all of these newly developed services, whatever their specific aims, share the goal of preventing small problems from developing into large problems.

This common emphasis on prevention is no coincidence. In recent decades many professionals, aware of the adverse effects of hospitalization, have argued that mental health workers, following the lead of public health medicine, should direct their energies primarily toward preventing rather than curing mental disturbance. Preventive mental health, now an extremely important trend, is normally divided into three categories: primary, secondary, and tertiary prevention.

Primary Prevention

Primary prevention is the prevention of the *development* of psychological disturbance. Just as polio vaccines prevent polio from occurring, primary preventive mental health would attempt to prevent schizophrenia, depression, sociopathy, and other psychopathologies from occurring. However, polio is a specific and an organic problem, whereas mental disturbance, as we have seen, is an infinitely vast and vague problem—indeed, a collection of vast and

vague problems, partly organic and partly environmental, or psychological. How are we to "vaccinate" our population against all these problems? Caplan (1964) argues that primary prevention involves seeing that every individual, throughout his life, has free access to physical supplies (adequate food, shelter, and protection from bodily harm), psychosocial supplies (adequate intellectual, affective, and social stimulation), and sociocultural supplies (useful roles and equal opportunities). In other words, primary prevention involves a total restructuring of our society. This, of course, is an unlikely eventuality. And were it to be undertaken, there is little reason to assume that the society would turn the job over to the mental health profession.

Even if we tailor our primary-prevention goals down to the wiping out of a specific pathology such as schizophrenia, how are we to proceed when, as we have seen, we still have little insight into what causes schizophrenia? In short, before we can truly devote our efforts to primary prevention, we still have to complete our research in etiology—a long, costly, and tedious process. In the meantime, certain programs such as family planning, Medicaid, Medicare, and other social reforms do their part in reducing environmental stress, while genetic counseling can help in preventing genetic disorders. But large-scale primary prevention still remains a distant ideal.

Secondary Prevention

Secondary prevention, the preventing of manageable disorders from becoming unmanageable, chronic

Types of Schizophrenic Process		
Feature	**Observational Factors**	**Sociocultural Factors***
Simple	*Least* frequently reported by those requiring delusions and hallucinations as criteria of diagnosis, and *most* frequently by those working only *inside* mental hospitals	*Most* frequent in Asians; *least* frequent in Euro-Americans
Hebephrenic	*Most* frequently noted by those who exclude confusional cases from schizophrenia group and by those working only *outside* mental hospitals	*Most* frequent in Japanese and Okinawans
Catatonic	*Least* frequently noted by psychiatrists requiring chronicity as criterion of schizophrenia	*Least* frequent in Euro-Americans
Paranoid	Nil	*Most* frequent in urban middle classes; *least* frequent in rural groups
Disturbances of Reality Contact		
Visual hallucinations	Nil	*Least* frequent in urban Euro-Americans; *most* frequent in peoples of Africa and Near East
Tactile hallucinations	Nil	*Most* frequent in peoples of Africa and Near East
Delusions of grandeur	Nil	*Most* frequent in rural groups
Delusions of destruction	Nil	*Most* frequent in Christian samples
Religious delusions	Nil	*Most* frequent in Christian samples; *least* frequent in Buddhist, Hindu, and Shintoist samples
Delusions involving jealousy	Nil	*Most* frequent in Asian groups
Depersonalization	Nil	*Least* frequent in rural groups
Disturbances of Affect		
Social and emotional withdrawal	*Least* frequently noted by psychiatrists working only *inside* mental hospitals	*Most* uniformly frequent in Japanese and Okinawans
Flatness of affect	*Most* frequently reported by those working only *outside* mental hospitals	*Most* frequent in Japanese and Okinawans and, after them, in peoples of South America
Types of Catatonic Disturbance		
Catatonic mannerisms	*Most* frequently noted by those requiring chronicity as criterion of schizophrenia	*Most* frequent in rural groups
Catatonic negativism	*Most* frequently noted by those requiring chronicity as criterion of schizophrenia	*Most* frequent in peoples of India and South America
Catatonic excitement	*More* frequently reported by those working only *outside* and *less* frequently by those working only *inside* mental hospitals	*Most* frequent in peoples of Africa and South America; *least* frequent in peoples of Anglo-Saxon origin
Catatonic stupor	*Least* frequently reported by those insisting on delusions and hallucinations as criteria for diagnosis	*Most* frequent in rural groups
Stereotypy	*Least* frequently noted by those excluding confusional cases from schizophrenic category	*Most* frequent in East Indians; *least* frequent in Euro-Americans
Catatonic rigidity	Nil	*Most* frequent in East Indians
Other Behavioral Disturbances		
Bowel and bladder incontinence	*Least infrequently* noted by psychiatrists insisting on chronicity as criterion for schizophrenia	Nil
Temper outbursts	*Most* frequently noted by those working only *outside* and *least* frequently by those working only *inside* mental hospitals	*Most* frequently reported in Christian groups
Sexual assault	Nil	*Least* frequently reported in Euro-Americans
Suicide	Nil	*Most* frequently reported in Japanese

Fig. 20.3 In an attempt to compare the symptomatology of schizophrenia among various cultures, Murphy and his colleagues found certain factors that seem to affect the world-wide distribution of reported schizophrenic symptoms. On the basis of their data, they concluded that this distribution appears to vary according to cultural and observational factors. That is, culture may affect the schizophrenic process or, at least, the individual's reaction to the process. (Adapted from H. B. M. Murphy, E. D. Wittkower, J. Fried, and H. Ellenberger, "A Cross-Cultural Survey of Schizophrenic Symptomatology," International Journal of Social Psychiatry, 9, 1963, 240–241.)

Significance of sociocultural factors was recalculated after allowing for influence of observational factors.

disorders, is basically what we have been talking about throughout most of this chapter. Secondary prevention requires prompt detection and equally prompt treatment of psychological problems *as they occur*—a goal which consulting programs, outpatient clinics, emergency services, hot lines, and other recently developed programs are aiming to achieve. However, secondary prevention, though not so difficult as primary prevention, is still not easy. Assessment procedures for detecting latent disturbances are, as we have seen in Chapter 18, of limited usefulness. And consulting programs, which would allow people such as teachers to spot early signs of emotional difficulty, are still not widely available. Furthermore, the community mental health centers have enough difficulty dealing with the numbers of

Fig. 20.4   Individual counseling and problem solving are major factors in the secondary prevention of psychological disturbance.

troubled patients that they already have, without sending workers out to locate people whose troubles are still in their earliest stages. Hence we are not yet equipped truly to nip psychological problems in the bud. However, once the individual experiences enough distress to cause him to look for help, the new services that we have discussed in this chapter can make some efforts so that his distress will not develop into chronic mental disturbance.

Tertiary Prevention

Tertiary prevention aims at reducing the consequences of an already fully developed psychological disturbance. Since it does focus on people with serious mental problems, there is some question as to whether tertiary prevention is in fact a form of prevention. The time for prevention would seem to have passed. However, when we consider, for example, the unwelcome effects of custodial hospitalization, it is not hard to see that even in the case of seriously disturbed people, there is still much to prevent. Good illustrations of tertiary prevention are the partial hospitalization programs that we have already discussed, the day hospitals and night hospitals. In a day hospital, for example, a person who is seriously depressed can take advantage of whatever programs the hospital has to offer him during the day, and then at night can return to the potential sources of pleasure and stimulation available to him at home rather than simply languishing in his hospital bed and forgetting that there *is* an outside world. Other examples of tertiary prevention are halfway houses and in-hospital group therapy and occupational therapy—indeed, any program that goes beyond custodial care and aims at rehabilitating the mental patient, preparing him for release from the hospital, and preventing rehospitalization.

THE UNRESOLVED QUESTIONS

In a sense, our entire book has been a series of unresolved questions. The minute we describe a particular syndrome, a host of riddles present themselves. Is there really a difference between schizophrenia and paranoia or between depression and involutional melancholia? Are autistic children suffering from parental hostility or simply from neurological impairments? Can criminal behavior be regarded as psychiatrically normal? Why do only a small percentage of syphilitics develop neurosyphilis? In twenty or thirty years some of these questions may have been answered. However, abnormal psychology is also beset by a number of larger questions. These questions, because they have to do with values and attitudes, can never be answered in the laboratory. Nor do we have any reason to expect an answer within the next few decades.

Who Needs Changing?

The normal assumption of the mental health professional in dealing with an abnormal behavior is that it is the person displaying this behavior who needs changing. However, as we have seen, what is abnormal is defined against what we consider normal, and what we consider normal is defined by our norms. These norms are not absolute; they were not handed down from heaven on stone tablets. They have changed in the past and will change again in the future. Yet in psychological treatment these norms do tend to be regarded as absolutes. As Hallek (1971) has pointed out, psychotherapy is essentially an enforcer of the status quo. In opposition to this approach, a number of eminent professionals have asked whether it is not the status quo that needs changing, rather than the individuals who have to deal with it (Sager, 1968; Hallowitz, 1970). Existential writers such as Laing (1967) have questioned whether anyone can be truly sound psychologically amid the brutalities and injustices of our society. Others have asked, more specifically, whether middle-class mental health professionals have any right to impose their notions of what is normal on people without similar backgrounds. If a ghetto teenager sees himself and his family as being "ripped off" by the larger society, should he be considered abnormal if he shows a total lack of remorse about ripping off the society in return? In general, it must be said, each person tends to deal with such questions according to how many comforts he or she has been able to extract from the present social system. And until the access to such comforts is equalized, until we truly have equal opportunities, our answers to the question of what needs changing—the social norms or the person who deviates from them—will differ as greatly as, and in proportion to, our levels of gratification within the society.

Psychology vs. Individual Rights

In July 1975 the United States Supreme Court rendered a decision which has enormous potential implications for the field of mental health. A man named Kenneth Donaldson had sued the State of Florida for damages, claiming that he had been involuntarily imprisoned in the state's mental hospitals for fourteen years and that during his first ten years of confinement he had seen a psychiatrist for a total of only three hours, or approximately eighteen minutes a year. Judge John Minor Wisdom of the Federal Court of Appeals ruled in Donaldson's favor, stating: "We hold that where a nondangerous patient is involuntarily civilly committed to a state mental hospital, the only constitutionally permissible purpose of confinement is to provide treatment, and that such a patient has a constitutional right to such treatment as will help him be cured or improve his mental condition" *(Donaldson v. O'Connor*, 493 F, 2nd 507 [5th Circ. 1974]). Upon appeal, the Supreme Court upheld Judge Wisdom's decision. What this means, in essence, is that custodial care is now for the most part illegal.

Shortly after the Donaldson decision, the Federal Court of Appeals ruled, in the case of *Wyatt* v. *Stickey,* that mental patients in Alabama are constitutionally entitled to privacy, nutritionally sound and complete meals, access to recreational facilities (including television and interaction with persons of the opposite sex), visitors, minimum pay for institutional work (even if the work is regarded as primarily therapeutic in nature), and, when medically possible, ground privileges and an open ward (i.e., a ward in which people are free to come and go as they wish). What this means is that the token economy, which

---

PREVENTION IN MENTAL HEALTH

Primary prevention	Preventing the development of psychological disturbance. Examples: genetic counseling, public welfare programs such as family planning.
Secondary prevention	Preventing psychological disorders from developing into disabling conditions. Examples: hot lines, consulting programs.
Tertiary prevention	Preventing serious psychological disorders from becoming worse. Examples: day hospitals and night hospitals.

Fig. 20.5 Standards of beauty and adornment vary among cultures. For example, scarification in Africa, face-lifting surgery in the United States, and tattooing in both Africa and the United States are acceptable, and sometimes expected, in the respective societies; each practice enhances the attractiveness of the person to other members of the culture. In a different society, however, the same practice is regarded as bizarre, and the individual is considered abnormal. Dimensions such as beauty and normality are therefore culturally relative, and behavior must be understood in the context of what a culture expects, tolerates, and rewards.

grants these privileges not as constitutional rights but as rewards for good behavior, may soon be illegal throughout the country.

Another matter with which the courts have concerned themselves in the past few years is the so-called indeterminate sentence conferred on mentally disturbed criminals (Chapter 8). In one recent case (Trotter, 1975), a young man convicted of assault with intent to rape and assault of a police officer was sent to Patuxent Institution, a Maryland mental health facility for "defective delinquents." Because he protested his innocence and was appealing his original conviction, the prisoner refused to cooperate in a psychological evaluation. As a consequence, he served nearly six years in the institution, whereas in an ordinary prison he would have been eligible for parole after fifteen months. His prison record cited him for his refusal to cooperate with the mental

health professionals who operate the institution, and he apparently would still be incarcerated there if the United States Supreme Court had not ordered his immediate release in June of 1971.

These are only three of the many recent cases in which the courts have clashed head-on with the mental health profession. As we have pointed out in Chapter 19, as psychological treatment has become increasingly popular, it has also become, paradoxically, increasingly suspect. Psychiatry has lost much of its mystique, and thousands of people, along with the law courts, are beginning to question whether the mentally disturbed are not better off within the community, with the legal protections that it affords, than in the hands of mental health professionals, who for many years have practiced their skills virtually unchecked by any external agency. This is not to imply that psychiatrists and psychol-

HARD TIMES

A former alcoholic, a woman in her mid-thirties who had straightened herself out and obtained a job as a substitute teacher, is now drinking again.

A couple, married for seventeen years, are suddenly forced to spend day after day together, and decide to divorce.

The twelve-year-old son of a married couple who have had an unusually close relationship, both at home and in the store they run together, has become such a problem in school that he faces expulsion.

What these people have in common is that all their troubles are a result of the economic depression in this country. A cutback in school funds resulted in the former alcoholic not being called to substitute teach; she lost the self-confidence she needed. The husband in the seventeen-year-old marriage was laid off, causing him to be around the house all day. The forced togetherness led to enormous amounts of tension. And the loss of income from the store run by the parents of the twelve-year-old boy, and the resultant problems, caused them to be extremely hard on their son. These people, and hundreds more with related problems, have been flooding the agencies that offer secondary prevention of mental disturbance.

Community mental health clinics and counseling agencies throughout the country have been inundated as the recession has resulted in family discord and psychological difficulties that people are not able to handle by themselves. And as Louis E. Kopolow and Frank M. Ochberg, psychiatrists associated with the National Institute of Mental Health, point out, the great need for the type of assistance these agencies provide comes at a time when the funds for them are reduced.

A more encouraging point has been made by other experts in the field: since we now know that economic change and stress cause psychological problems, instead of merely reacting to them, as our secondary prevention agencies have been attempting to do, we are in a position to change our approach to a primary prevention one. By using economic statistics, we can determine the communities in which economic change is anticipated; by setting up preventive programs in schools, factories, and unions, we can greatly lessen the distressing rise in psychological problems.

Source: Ann Crittendon, "The Recession Takes Its Toll: Family Discord, Mental Illness," *The New York Times*, April 19, 1976, p. 32.

ogists are unconcerned for the welfare of their patients. Nor do we wish to take a stand against indeterminate sentences or token economies, the virtues of which can be very convincingly argued. Rather, what we are up against is a serious dilemma.

On the one hand, what can we reasonably expect from the mental health profession? The community offers virtually no resources for dealing with the deeply disturbed. Their families cannot handle them. And so they are sent off to overcrowded and underfunded mental hospitals, where they either go untreated, because there are neither staff members nor facilities for treating them, or are treated through programs aimed at maximum efficiency and practicality rather than maximum protection of individuality and civil rights. Who, then, is to blame—the mental health profession, the families, or the entire society?

On the other hand, it can be argued that many mental health professionals, though they may be compassionate and hard-working in their attempts to help the disturbed, often forget that these people are indeed people, deserving of the same rights that the mental health professionals themselves take for granted. Once a person appears to have lost his "reason," he also tends to lose, in the eyes of those who treat him, his status as a human being. At best, he is a "case," a riddle to be solved. At worst, he is simply a nuisance, uncooperative and unsightly.

Yet abnormal behavior is a common and universal problem, and therefore, while it may be distressing, it is fully as human as normal behavior. This fact is too often ignored. Indeed, the very word "abnormal"—technically meaning only that which deviates from our norms—conjures up all the images that our book has tried to dispel: images of freakishness, "weirdness," that which is alien to the rest of us. People with psychological problems—the withdrawn child, the hallucinating schizophrenic—are in fact not so very different from the rest of us. Like all of us, they have difficulties and are trying to cope. Their difficulties are simply much greater than ours; their particular amalgam of genes, past history, and present circumstance is less likely to see them successfully through an average day in our society. Their coping methods therefore take the form of rather desperate maneuvers. But they are by no means alien to the human condition, nor can we help them by regarding them as such. Paracelsus, for all that he believed that mental disturbances were caused by planetary movements, was aware of this truth, which is still—more than four centuries and many scientific discoveries later—so elusive to many of us. His words, already quoted in Chapter 1, bear repeating: "The insane and the sick are our brothers. Let us give them treatment to cure them, for nobody knows whom among our friends or relatives [or, we might add, among ourselves] this misfortune may strike."

SUMMARY

The purpose of this chapter has been to indicate the directions in which we appear to be moving in the treatment of abnormal behavior and to review the unsettled issues surrounding the mental health profession. In recent years there have been three major innovations in the general treatment of mental disturbance. First, the focus of treatment has shifted from the large state institutions to local community services. Foremost among these services are the new community mental health centers, which provide inexpensive outpatient therapy, inpatient services (including short-term hospitalization, day hospital programs, and night hospital programs), emergency psychological care, and consultation with other community workers such as teachers and police. Additional local programs include halfway houses and telephone hot lines. The central aim of all these services is to make psychological assistance widely and immediately available, within the community, to those who need it.

A second development in the effort to increase the availability of psychological care is the training of paraprofessionals to serve as mental health workers in their communities. These paraprofessionals have not only added considerably to the manpower of the profession; they also have the advantage of being more familiar with community problems and, in lower-class communities, of appearing more approachable to local residents than do middle-class professionals.

Related to the development of widely available community services and to the training of paraprofessionals to man these services is the third major innovation in modern mental health, the new emphasis on prevention. This effort includes the prevention of the occurrence of mental disturbance (primary prevention), the prevention of minor mental disturbances from becoming major mental disturbances (secondary prevention), and the prevention of major mental disturbances from becoming chronic, lifelong conditions (tertiary prevention).

While such progressive measures are being discussed or undertaken, the mental health profession continues to be plagued by two larger issues. First is the question of whether the society might not need changing more than the individuals who deviate from the norms of the society. Second is the conflict between the needs and limitations of psychological treatment on the one hand and the needs and rights of disturbed individuals on the other hand. While the riddle of schizophrenia or of autism or of depression may be solved within the next few decades, these larger questions will remain to haunt us as long as science, the society, and the individual continue to pose different sets of demands.

Contributors

George J. Allen, who holds his Ph.D. from the University of Illinois, is associate professor of psychology at the University of Connecticut. In 1972 he won an award for distinguished research from the American Personnel and Guidance Association, and in 1974 he received the Phillip A. Goodwin Consulting Psychology Research Award. He is a member of the editorial board of *Behavior Therapy.* He has published extensively in the areas of behavioral treatment of test anxiety among students and behavior modification in educational and community settings. He is especially interested in the assessment of psychotherapeutic processes and outcomes and in the behavioral measurement of "real-life" interaction patterns. Dr. Allen is responsible for the chapter on approaches to assessment.

James E. Birren, who received his Ph.D. from Northwestern University, became interested in gerontology during his commission at the Naval Medical Research Institute, Bethesda, Maryland. He is currently director of the Gerontology Center, Dean School of Gerontology, and professor of psychology at the University of Southern California. Dr. Birren contributed to the chapter on the disorders of aging.

James F. Calhoun received his Ph.D. in clinical psychology from the University of Illinois. He is associate professor of psychology at the State University of New York at Stony Brook and has been director of the Psychological Center there since 1971. He is also a fellow of the Academic Administration Internship Program of the American Council of Education. He is especially interested in social learning approaches to therapy and in environmental design, and his articles have appeared in a number of journals. Dr. Calhoun served on this book as coordinating author.

James P. Curran received his Ph.D. in psychology from the University of Illinois. He is associate professor of psychology at Purdue University, where his areas of special interest are clinical psychology and personality development. Dr. Curran is responsible for the chapter on approaches to treatment.

Karen K. Evans is a partner at the Institute for Behavioral Services, Hinsdale, Illinois. She received her master's degree in social work from the University of Illinois at Champaign. She has been program director of the day school for behavioral problemed children at the Scalabrinian Education Center, Stone Park, Illinois, and is actively involved in the Community Intervention Program for Retarded Children and Adults at the Illinois State Pediatric Institute. She contributed to the chapter on mental retardation.

Michael B. Evans received his Ph.D. in psychology from the University of Illinois at Urbana, where he specialized in behavior therapy. He is currently director of the Behavior Therapy Program at the Institute for Juvenile Research, Illinois Department of Mental Health. He is also assistant professor of psychology at the Abraham Lincoln School of Medicine. He has published widely on the use of behavior modification in the classroom and on biofeedback techniques. Dr. Evans contributed to the chapter on mental retardation.

Louis R. Franzini received his Ph.D. in clinical psychology from the University of Pittsburgh and completed a postdoctoral fellowship in behavior modification at the State University of New York at Stony Brook before joining the faculty at San Diego State University. His research and clinical interests include behavior modification theory and techniques, behavior therapy, applied training programs, and self-regulatory processes in the trainable mentally retarded. Dr. Franzini is responsible for the chapter on organic brain disorders.

Leonard D. Goodstein, professor and chairman of the Department of Psychology at Arizona State University, received his Ph.D. from Columbia University. He was a fellow in psychology at the City College of New York and held faculty positions at Hofstra University, the University of Iowa, and the University of Cincinnati. He is editor of the *Journal of Applied Behavioral Science,* consulting editor of the *Journal of Abnormal Psychology,* and has published many articles in various areas of psychology. Dr. Goodstein served as the adviser on this book and is also responsible for the first and last chapters dealing with past and present treatment of abnormality.

Richard L. Hagen, associate professor of psychology at Florida State University, received his Ph.D. in clinical psychology from the University of Illinois at Urbana. His special research interest is in obesity. His publications have been primarily on theoretical and applied problems related to behavior therapy. He has contributed to various workshops and symposia and has served as editorial consultant for the *Journal of Abnormal Psychology,* the *Journal of Applied Behavioral Analysis,* and the *Journal of Clinical and Consulting Psychology.* Dr. Hagen is responsible for the two chapters on schizophrenic disorders.

Ella Lasky, assistant professor of psychology at Manhattan Community College, the City University of New York, received her Ph.D. from Columbia University. She specializes in clinical and social psychology and has been a frequent lecturer on women's therapy and the role of the feminist psychotherapist. She is also active in New York City community affairs as co-director of Women's Psychotherapy Referral Service and as co-coordinator of the psychology and psychotherapy committee, National Organization for Women. Her articles have appeared in a number of professional journals, and she is the author of *Humanness: An Exploration into the Mythologies About Women and Men* and a forthcoming book, *Physical Attractiveness, Self-Esteem and Interpersonal Behavior.* Dr. Lasky is responsible for the chapter on the humanistic-existential perspective.

Alan J. Litrownik, who received his Ph.D. from the University of Illinois (Champaign-Urbana), is associate professor of psychology at San Diego State University. His area of special interest is the analysis and remediation of handicapped children. He has been consultant to numerous programs dealing with the autistic and the retarded, and his articles have appeared in many professional journals. Dr. Litrownik is responsible for the chapter on childhood psychosis.

Robert W. Lundin, professor of psychology and chairman of the department at the University of the South, holds his Ph.D. from Indiana University. He is an associate editor of *The Psychological Record* and author of *An Objective Psychology of Music*; *Personality: An Experimental Approach*; *Principles of Psychopathology*; *Personality: A Behavioral Analysis*; and *Theories and Systems of Psychology*. Dr. Lundin is responsible for the chapter on the behaviorist perspective and the chapter on the neuroses.

Willard A. Mainord, professor and director of clinical training in the Department of Psychology at the University of Louisville, received his Ph.D. from the University of Washington, Seattle. He is involved in weekend institutes for agencies concerned with group problem solving, and he has published several articles in professional journals concerning therapy from social and behavioral points of view.

Robert G. Meyer, associate professor of psychology at the University of Louisville, received his Ph.D. from Michigan State University. He is a senior consultant partner with Riddick, Flynn and Associates in Louisville, Kentucky, and consultant both to the Kentucky Department of Human Resources and to the Southern Indiana Mental Health Center. His interests are primarily in issues on the interface of law and clinical psychology and in hypnosis and psychotherapy. He is board certified in clinical psychology by the American Board of Professional Psychology and has published in the areas

of sexual disorders, forensic psychology, and hypnosis in such journals as *Behavior Therapy*, the *Journal of Clinical and Consulting Psychology*, and the *International Journal of Clinical and Experimental Hypnosis*. Dr. Meyer is responsible for the chapter on sexual disorders and sexual variance.

C. Scott Moss is coordinator of mental health for the Federal Correctional Institution at Lompoc, California. Since receiving his Ph.D. from the University of Illinois, he has held professorships at the universities of Washington (St. Louis), Missouri, Kansas, and Illinois and was for seven years a consultant for the National Institute of Mental Health. He has published extensively in the areas of clinical, community, and criminal psychology and hypnosis. His most recent books are *Black Rover, Come Over: The Hypnosymbolic Treatment of a Phobia*; *Recovery with Aphasia*; and, with Ray Hosford, *The Crumbling Walls: Treatment and Counseling of Prisoners*. Dr. Moss is responsible for the chapter on the psychodynamic perspective and the chapter on sociopathy and crime.

Robert C. Neubeck is co-director of the Institute for Behavioral Services, Hinsdale, Illinois. He received his Ph.D. in clinical psychology from Southern Illinois University at Carbondale. Dr. Neubeck is co-founder of the Scalabrinian Education Center, Stone Park, Illinois, and is a consultant at Mercy Hospital and Medical Center and the John Madden Mental Health Center. His area of special interest is behavior modification approaches to learning disabilities and mental retardation. He is also assistant professor of psychology at Lewis College, Lockport, Illinois. Dr. Neubeck is responsible for the chapter on mental retardation.

Oakley S. Ray received his Ph.D. in clinical psychology from the University of Pittsburgh, after which he began research in the area of drug effects on animal behavior. He is currently professor in the Department of Psychology and associate professor in the Department of Pharmacology at Vanderbilt University,

as well as chief of the Mental Health Unit at the Veterans Administration Hospital in Nashville, Tennessee. He has published extensively in the area of drug-behavior and brain-behavior relationships and is the author of *Drugs, Society, and Human Behavior*. Dr. Ray is responsible for the chapter on the addictive disorders.

Robert L. Solnick is a faculty member of the Andrus Gerontology Center, Summer Institute for Study of Gerontology, at the University of Southern California, where he is also a candidate for his Ph.D. in psychology. His area of specialization is clinical psychology, with particular emphasis on the problems of the middle-aged and older adults. He is currently completing his internship at Long Beach Veterans Administration Hospital. He is responsible for the chapter on the disorders of aging.

Bonnie R. Strickland, professor of psychology at the University of Massachusetts at Amherst, received her Ph.D. in clinical psychology from Ohio State University. She previously taught at Emory University and in 1970 was awarded a diploma in clinical psychology by the American Board of Professional Psychology. She is a fellow of the American Psychological Association and advisory editor of the *Journal of Consulting and Clinical Psychology*. She has published widely in the areas of her special research: the internal-external locus of control in children, the function of sex role and personality characteristics in children's aspirations, and the learned helplessness syndrome in depression. Dr. Strickland is responsible for the chapter on the affective disorders.

Fredric Weizmann, associate professor of psychology at York University, Toronto, received his Ph.D. from Ohio State University in clinical psychology. He has held faculty positions at the University of Illinois and Purdue University. In 1975 he was a visiting scientist at the Tavistock Institute of Human Relations in London. His forthcoming book, co-edited with Ina Uzgiris, is entitled *The Structuring of Experience*. Dr. Weizmann is responsible for the chapter on childhood developmental disorders.

Illustration Credits and Acknowledgments

CHAPTER 1. ABNORMALITY: YESTERDAY AND TODAY

2 Karl Nicholason; 5 The American Museum of Natural History; 9–11 The Bettmann Archive; 14 The Granger Collection; 15 (top) San Diego Fine Arts Gallery; 15 (bottom) The Bettmann Archive; 16 Rapho/Photo Researchers, Inc.; 17–20 The Bettmann Archive; 21 Edmund Engleman; 22 Douglas Armstrong

CHAPTER 2. THE PSYCHODYNAMIC PERSPECTIVE

30 John Oldenkamp/IBOL; 34 Terry Lamb; 37, 39 Gary Van der Steur; 42 (top) Courtesy, The New York Academy of Music; 42 (bottom) Photo by Emery I. Gondor, courtesy, The New York Public Library Picture Collection; 43 Philip Kirkland; 44 Karl Nicholason

CHAPTER 3. THE BEHAVIORIST PERSPECTIVE

54 Robert Van Doren; 56 (top) Culver Pictures, Inc.; 56 (bottom) John Dawson; 57 Culver Pictures, Inc.; 58 (top left) Courtesy, New York Academy of Medicine; 58 (bottom left) photograph ©1976, Jill Krementz; 58 (right) Joyce Kitchell; 60 Masami Teraoka; 62 (top and bottom) Howard Saunders; 65 John Dawson; 68 Joyce Kitchell

CHAPTER 4. THE HUMANISTIC-EXISTENTIAL PERSPECTIVE AND OTHER PERSPECTIVES

78 Tom Suzuki; 81 John Oldenkamp/IBOL; 83 Ted Polumbaum; 84 Terry Lamb; 85 Raimondo Borea; 87 Karl Nicholason; 91 Bob Fitch/Black Star; 94 United Feature Syndicate, Inc.

CHAPTER 5. THE NEUROSES, PERSONALITY DISORDERS, AND TRANSIENT SITUATIONAL DISORDERS

102 Robert Van Doren; 105 Ignacio Gomez; 115 Courtesy, Universal Pictures; 118 (top and bottom) Wide World Photo; 119 Courtesy, The American Red Cross; 123 Courtesy, Margaret Howard, from Jakab and Howard, "The Artistic Talent of an Adolescent with Borderline Psychoneurotic Life Adjustment," in Jakab (ed.), *Psychiatry and Art* (S. Karger, 1971) vol. 3, pp. 32–51

CHAPTER 6. PSYCHOPHYSIOLOGICAL DISORDERS

130 Robert Van Doren; 133 Richard Jones; 134–135 Joyce Kitchell; 139 Joseph V. Brady; 140 Louisiana State University Medical Center; 148 Courtesy, Behavioral Sciences Department, Navy Medical Research Institute; 151 (left) Bernard Gotfryd/*Newsweek* magazine; 151 Frank Owen/Stock, Boston

CHAPTER 7. THE AFFECTIVE DISORDERS

158 Robert Van Doren; 160 National Museum, Vincent Van Gogh, Amsterdam; 163 Douglas Armstrong; 166 Scala Fine Arts Publishers, Inc.; 169 (left) Gene Brownell; 169 (right) Jack Spratt/Black Star; 176 Douglas Armstrong; 177 T. Cowell/Black Star

CHAPTER 8. SOCIOPATHY AND CRIME

186 Robert Van Doren; 188 Courtesy of C. Scott Moss; 195 Michael Abramson/Black Star; 196 (top) Woodfin Camp & Associates; 196 (bottom) Peter Southwick/Stock, Boston; 197 (left) Dan McCoy/Black Star; 197 (right) Peter Southwick/Stock, Boston; 198 Werner Wolff/Black Star; 203 Allan Grant/Time-Life Picture Agency, ©Time, Inc.

CHAPTER 9. SEXUAL DISORDERS AND SEXUAL VARIANCE

208 Rowland Scherman; 210 Alan Mercer; 214 Bob Levin/Black Star; 218 Jean-Claude Lejeune/Black Star; 219 Associated Press Photo; 222 (top) Alan Mercer; 222 (bottom) Bruce Davidson/Magnum; 223 Sepp Seitz/Magnum; 225 Courtesy, The Edward James Foundation, England; 229 Alan Mercer; 231 Michael Abramson/Black Star; 233 Bernie Cleff

CHAPTER 10. THE ADDICTIVE DISORDERS

234 Robert Van Doren; 237 Karl Nicholason; 240 Douglas Armstrong; 242 Karl Nicholason; 244 Joyce Kitchell; 246 Richard Lawrence/Black Star; 247 Curt Gunther/Camera 5, Schick Center, courtesy of Arnold Carr Public Relations; 251 (top and bottom) Culver Pictures, Inc.; 252 Douglas Armstrong; 254 (left) Dan McCoy/Black Star; 254 (right) Steve Schapiro; 258 Joyce Kitchell; 260–263 (top) Douglas Armstrong, (bottom) Werner Kolber, PPS; 264 Courtesy, Schering Corporation

CHAPTER 11. SCHIZOPHRENIA AND PARANOIA

272 Robert Van Doren; 274 National Museum of Western Art; 275 National Library of Medicine; 276 Otto Billig; 277 Irene Salab; 279–282 Courtesy, Al Vercoutere, Camarillo State Hospital; 294 Benyas Kaufman/Black Star; 296 Bill Bridges; 297 (left) Courtesy, Al Vercoutere, Camarillo State Hospital; 297 (right) The Bettmann Archive

CHAPTER 12. SCHIZOPHRENIA: PERSPECTIVES

302 Robert Van Doren; 305 (top) Bill Stanton/Magnum; 305 (bottom) Jack Spratt/Black Star; 306–307 Roy Zalesky/Black Star; 314 (top) John Oldenkamp/IBOL; 314 (center and bottom) Hugh Wilkenson; 319 (top) Bill Bridges/Globe Photographs, Inc.; 319 (bottom) Photograph ©1976, Jill Krementz; 320 Gillian Theobald; 321 Douglas Armstrong

CHAPTER 13. CHILDHOOD PSYCHOSIS

328 Robert Van Doren; 331 Dr. Bruno Bettelheim from *Scientific American*, March 1959; 335 Costa Manos/Magnum; 338 Photograph ©1976, Jill Krementz; 344 Krämer/Black Star; 345 Costa Manos/Magnum; 347 Steve McCarroll

CHAPTER 14. ORGANIC BRAIN DISORDERS

352 Robert Van Doren; 357 Joyce Kitchell; 359 (top) Venereal Disease Research Lab, Center for Disease Control, H.E.W.; 359 (bottom) California Medical Publications, all rights reserved; 362 (top) Howard Sochurek; 362 (bottom right) Courtesy, Robert Keefe, M.D.; 362 (bottom right) California Medical Publications, all rights reserved; 364 John Dawson; 365 California Medical Publications, all rights reserved; 367 (top) Joyce Kitchell; 367 (bottom) and 368 (top) California Medical Publications, all rights reserved; 368 (bottom) Courtesy, R. Rowen, M.D.; 373 Joyce Kitchell; 376 Douglas Armstrong

CHAPTER 15. MENTAL RETARDATION

378 John Oldenkamp; 380 Taken from the *AAMD Manual on Terminology and Classification in Mental Retardation*, 1973; 381 Bruce Roberts/Rapho/Photo Researchers, Inc.; 382 John Oldenkamp/IBOL; 385 Douglas Armstrong; 389 H. F. Harlow, Oregon Regional Primate Research Center; 391 John Oldenkamp/IBOL; 392 Jeff Albertson/Stock, Boston; 393, 398 John Oldenkamp/IBOL; 399 Neil Heilpern/Globe Photos, Inc.

CHAPTER 16. THE DEVELOPMENTAL DISORDERS OF CHILDHOOD

402 Robert Van Doren; 405 Tom Blau/Camera Press, Ltd.; 407 (top) Rhonda Hughes; 407 (bottom left) David Wilkerson, courtesy, Early Achievement Center; 407 (bottom right) Jon Schmidt; 408 (top) Hugh Wilkerson; 408 (bottom left) Moshe Lapidot; 408 (bottom right) Hugh Wilkerson; 412 Joyce Fitzgerald; 414 Courtesy, Irene Jakab, from Bar and Jakab "Graphic Identification of the Stuttering Episode as Experienced by Stutterers," in Jakab (ed.), *Psychiatry and Art* (S. Karger, 1969), vol. 2, pp. 2–15, Fig. 5; 416 Courtesy, Martha Karson; 423 Howard Saunders

CHAPTER 17. THE DISORDERS OF AGING

429 Robert Van Doren; 430 Douglas Armstrong, data courtesy Metropolitan Life Insurance Company; 434 Douglas Armstrong; 435 Department of Housing and Urban Development; 436 (top) Harry Crosby; 436 (bottom) Eve Arnold/Magnum; 437 (top left) Joe Molnar; 437 (top right) Elliott Erwitt/Magnum; 437 (bottom left) Mitchell Payne/Jeroboam, Inc.; 437 (bottom right) Eileen Christelon/Jeroboam, Inc.; 439 (left) Mark Jury/Rapho/Photo Researchers, Inc.; 439 (right) Don Getsug/Rapho/Photo Researchers, Inc.; 440 (top) Peeter Vilms/Jeroboam, Inc.; 440 (bottom) David Powers/Jeroboam, Inc.; 443 Kirk Breedlove/Photophile; 447 Douglas Armstrong

CHAPTER 18. APPROACHES TO ASSESSMENT

452 Robert Van Doren; 459 John De Marco; 460 Courtesy, Adrian Dove; 463 Douglas Armstrong; 465 (top) Tom Gould; 465 (bottom) Karl Nicholason; 466 C.P.S., Inc., P.O. Box 83, Larchmont, N.Y.; 467 Courtesy, Robert R. Burns, from Burns and Kaufman, *Kinetic Families' Drawings; An Introduction to Understanding Children Through Kinetic Drawings* (Brunner/Mazel, Inc., 1970); 471 Courtesy, Dr. Lauretta Bender and the American Orthopsychiatric Association, Inc., reproduced with permission

CHAPTER 19. APPROACHES TO TREATMENT

476 Robert Van Doren; 485 The New York Times; 487 Karl Nicholason; 489 Hugh Wilkerson; 490 Joyce Kitchell; 491 John Oldenkamp/IBOL; 493 Douglas Armstrong; 494 Steven McCarroll/IBOL; 497 Cliff McReynolds; 500, 502, 503 (top left) Arthur Schatz; 503 (bottom left) J. M. Vincent/Camera 5; 503 (right) Arthur Schatz; 507 Joyce Kitchell after William Scoville, M.D.

CHAPTER 20. ABNORMALITY: TODAY AND TOMORROW

510 Bill Call; 513 Anders/Black Star; 517 Paul Fusco/Magnum; 518 Douglas Armstrong; 519 David Powers/Jeroboam, Inc.; 521 (left) Robert Isaacs; 521 (right) George Rodgers/Magnum

Glossary

acquiescence set. A test-taking attitude in which the subject tends to agree with a statement regardless of its applicability to him.

acrophobia. The fear of high places.

addiction. A physiological dependence on a drug developed through continual use in increasing dosage.

Addison's disease. A disease caused by chronic underactivity of the adrenal cortex, which results in both physical and psychological changes.

adequacy model. A conceptual approach to the study of abnormal behavior in which normalcy is judged on the basis of a person's ability to interact successfully with his environment.

adrenal glands. A pair of ductless endocrine glands located above the kidneys.

affect. A term sometimes used by scientists meaning emotion.

affective disorders. Disturbances of mood in which feelings of sadness or elation become intense and unrealistic.

aggressive personality. A type of personality disorder characterized by a very low threshold for frustration, which can result in temper tantrums, verbal abuse, or even more destructive behaviors.

agitated depression. A form of depression characterized by incessant activity and restlessness.

agoraphobia. The fear of open places.

alcoholism. As defined by DSM-II, the disorder in which an individual's alcohol intake is great enough to damage his physical health or his personal or social functioning, or when it has become a prerequisite for normal functioning.

allergen. An irritating substance which produces a hypersensitive reaction.

allergy. A hypersensitive reaction to an irritating substance; usually manifested in either a skin disorder or in respiratory difficulties.

altruistic suicide. Durkheim's classification of a suicide that occurs because the individual is totally immersed in his culture's value system—a value system that tells him that under certain circumstances it is either necessary or at least honorable to commit suicide. A type of suicide more prevalent in Eastern cultures.

alternating personality. A type of multiple personality disorder in which two identities alternate with each other, each one unaware of the thoughts and actions of the other.

Alzheimer's disease. A fatal presenile psychosis that results from atrophy of the cerebral cortex and the basal ganglia. Symptoms include impairment of memory and concentration, facial paralysis, involuntary movements and convulsions, physical aggression, hallucinations, and rapid intellectual decline.

ambivalent affect. A subjective feeling or tone in which the individual experiences both a strong negative feeling and a strong positive feeling toward another person.

amnesia. The partial or total forgetting of past experiences, which can be associated with organic brain syndromes or hysteria.

amphetamines. A group of synthetic stimulants, the most common of which are Benzedrine, Dexedrine, and Methedrine.

anal stage. In psychodynamic theory, the second stage of psychosocial development in which the focus of the child is on the pleasurable feelings of retaining and expelling the feces; occurs in the second year of life.

aneurysm. A vessel breakage in the brain in which a weak part of the vessel wall balloons out and ruptures.

angst. In existential theory, a state of extreme anxiety.

anniversary suicides. The ending of one's life on a date that has some special, personal meaning, such as a birthday, a wedding anniversary, or Christmas.

anomic suicide. Durkheim's classification of a suicide that takes place when the equilibrium of a society is severely disturbed, as, for example, in war or economic collapse.

anomie. A stage of social normlessness, which could cause an individual to develop antisocial or dyssocial behavior patterns.

anorexia nervosa. A psychophysiological disorder characterized by an extreme loss of appetite that results in severe malnutrition, semistarvation, and sometimes death.

anterograde amnesia. The loss of memory for immediately preceding events.

antianxiety drugs (minor tranquilizers). Drugs used to reduce tension and anxiety. They are used by normal people during times of stress, by neurotics, by people with psychosomatic symptoms, and by people withdrawing from alcohol and other drugs.

antidepressant drugs. Drugs used to elevate mood in depressives.

antipsychotic drugs (major tranquilizers). Drugs used to relieve symptoms such as extreme agitation, hyperactivity, and hallucinations and delusions in psychotic patients.

antisocial personality. An individual who is in repeated conflict with society, does not feel guilt, and does not learn from experience or punishment. The term is used interchangeably with psychopath and sociopath.

anxiety. A state of increased physiological arousal and generalized feelings of fear and apprehension.

anxiety attacks. Episodes in which the chronically anxious person's already heightened state of tension mounts to an acute and overwhelming level.

anxiety neurosis. The most common neurotic disorder, characterized by diffuse and generalized fears which may engulf the whole personality.

aphasia. A language impairment resulting from vascular accidents.

archetypes. According to Jung, the ancient primordial images common to all mankind.

artherosclerosis. A narrowing and sometimes obstruction of the opening of the blood vessels; the blood supply to the brain is cut off and psychotic behavior results. (See also *cerebral arteriosclerosis.*)

assertive training. A behavior modification technique whereby the client is taught how to assert himself properly with other people and thus avoid being either passive or overaggressive.

asthma. A psychophysiological disorder of the bronchial system caused by a narrowing of the air passageways which, in turn, causes coughing, wheezing, and general difficulty in breathing.

auditory aphasia. A language impairment characterized by inability to understand spoken language.

aura. A warning sign experienced before the onset of an epileptic attack, such as an aroma, involuntary movements, or diffuse fear.

aura phase. Often the first stage of grand mal seizure.

autism. See *early infantile autism.*

autonomic nervous system. That part of the nervous system which governs the smooth muscles, the heart muscle, the glands, and the viscera, and controls their functions, including physiological responses to emotion.

aversion therapy. A behavior modification technique in which the patient's maladaptive response is paired with an aversive stimulus such as an electric shock or a nausea-producing drug; used extensively in the behavioral treatment of homosexuality, sexual deviations, and alcoholism.

avitaminosis. A condition that results from the lack of one or more essential vitamins in a person's diet; may cause neurological damage and hence psychological disturbances.

avoidance learning. A variant of escape behavior whereby an organism, having encountered an aversive stimulus, will arrange its responses in the future so as to prevent any further encounter with the stimulus.

barbiturates. A group of powerful sedative drugs whose major effects are to alleviate tension and bring about relaxation and sleep.

behavior deficit. A condition that results when a certain behavior occurs at a lower frequency than is appropriate to the situation, with resulting impairment of an individual's social, intellectual, or practical skills.

behavior excess. A condition that results when certain behavior occurs at a higher frequency than is adaptive, according to what is appropriate to the situation.

behavior modification. A behaviorist method of psychotherapy which uses such learning principles as reinforcement, extinction, and modeling to improve behavior.

behavioral contracting. A behaviorist treatment procedure in which the patient commits himself to making a certain number of behavioral changes within a certain period of time.

behavioral deprivation. A behaviorist technique developed by Lazarus for the treatment of depression which involves a period of bed rest without access to external stimuli in order to make the patient subsequently more susceptible to incoming stimuli.

bender. An alcoholic binge lasting several days.

beriberi. A disease caused by deficiency of vitamin B_1 and marked by lack of appetite, insomnia, irritability, and extreme lassitude.

biofeedback. A technique by which subjects, with the help of various machines, can monitor their own biological processes such as pulse, blood pressure, and brain waves.

biogenic psychosis. A severe mental disorder associated with organic brain syndromes.

biogenic theory. The view that mental disturbance is due to organic disorders.

biological perspective. An approach that focuses on the genetically transmitted organic causes of abnormal behavior.

blackout. A period of time in which a drinker, under the influence of alcohol, remains conscious but has no memory of it after.

blood alcohol level. The amount of alcohol in the bloodstream, expressed in terms of the number of milligrams of alcohol per 100 milliliters of blood.

bromide psychosis. A drug-induced brain disorder, usually caused by excessive ingestion of sleeping pills containing bromides.

bulimia. A childhood developmental disorder characterized by excessive overeating resulting in extreme obesity.

castration anxiety. In psychodynamic theory, the male child's fear that his penis will be cut off as punishment for his sexual desire of his mother.

catastrophic reaction. A condition in which the victim of aphasia, bewildered by his inability to perform elementary tasks, responds with disorganization and sometimes violent fury.

catatonic schizophrenic. A psychotic patient whose behavior is characterized by the slowing down of motion and eventual cessation of all adaptive behavior.

catatonic stupor. An extreme form of withdrawal in which the individual retreats into a completely immobile state, showing a total lack of responsiveness to stimulation.

cathexes. The emotional energy invested in people and objects. In psychodynamic theory, the first stage of psychosis involves the total or partial withdrawal of cathexes.

central nervous system. That part of the nervous system comprised of the brain and spinal cord.

cerebral arteriosclerosis. A hardening of the walls of the blood vessels in the brain.

cerebral hemorrhage. A rupture of a vessel wall in the brain; blood then spills directly onto brain tissue, damaging or destroying it.

cerebral thrombosis (cerebrovascular thrombosis, "stroke"). The formation of a blood clot in one of the blood vessels feeding the brain which cuts off circulation in the vessel.

cerebrovascular accident (CVA). See *cerebral thrombosis.*

childhood psychosis. A childhood disorder characterized by disturbed social relationships, impairment of speech, and bizarre motor behavior.

childhood schizophrenia. A childhood disorder which manifests itself after a period of normal development, when the child begins to show severe disturbances in social adjustment and in reality contact.

choreiform. Involuntary spasmodic jerking of the limbs, often a symptom of Huntington's chorea.

chronic anxiety. A manifestation of anxiety neurosis in which the individual appears to be jumpy, irritable, and frequently upset and cannot specify the cause of his fears.

chronic enuresis. A condition in which bladder control has never been achieved.

circular type. A pattern in manic-depressive disorders characterized by an alternation between extreme elation and extreme dejection.

clang association. A characteristic speech pattern of schizophrenics in which a series of words are used together because they rhyme or sound similar, without regard to logic.

claustrophobia. The fear of closed places.

client-centered therapy. A therapeutic procedure developed by Rogers in which the therapist provides a safe environment for the patient by mirroring the patient's own perceptions and offering unconditional positive regard, thus releasing the patient from the necessity of defending his unrealistic self-image.

clonic phase. The third stage of grand mal seizure in which muscles contract and relax rhythmically while the body jerks in violent spasms.

cocaine. A natural stimulant made from the coca plant which produces feelings of euphoria and omnipotence.

coconscious. A type of multiple personality disorder in which the subordinate personality is fully aware of the dominant personality's thoughts and actions.

cognitive perspective. An approach to abnormal behavior which regards the individual's patterns of thinking as the major determinants of his behavior; some theorists argue that *what* the person thinks is the source of abnormal behavior, others that it is *how* the person thinks.

cognitive restructuring. A behavioral therapy procedure which attempts to alter the client's ways of perceiving his life in order to change his behavior.

coitus. Penile-vaginal intercourse.

collective unconscious. According to Jung, the unconscious life of all mankind, which is composed of many common elements and not just sexual strivings as Freud contended.

coma. In a grand mal seizure, the final stage in which the muscles slowly relax while the patient remains unconscious.

compulsion. An action which an individual may consider irrational but feels compelled to do.

conceptualization. The ability to think in terms of general ideas or concepts; in schizophrenic thought disorders, the patient has difficulty with conceptualization.

concordant. A genetic term which means sharing the same disorder.

concussion. A head injury caused by a blow to the head that jars the brain and momentarily disrupts functioning.

conditioned reinforcer (secondary reinforcer). A stimulus or need that one learns to respond to by associating it with a primary reinforcer.

conditioned response. A simple response to a neutral stimulus that is the result of repeatedly pairing the neutral stimulus with another non-neutral stimulus that would have naturally elicited the response.

conditioned stimulus. The neutral stimulus which elicits a particular response as a result of repeated pairings with a non-neutral or unconditioned stimulus that naturally elicits that response.

conditions of worth. According to Rogers, the values incorporated by the child that dictate which of his self-experiences are "good" and which are "bad."

conduct disturbances. The acting out of impulses that are normally suppressed; the behavior is disruptive, aggressive, and antisocial.

confabulation. A tendency to fill in memory gaps with invented stories.

congenital syphilis. Syphilis transmitted by a syphilitic mother to the unborn child, which causes mental retardation and severe physical deformities.

"consequenceless" learning. In behaviorist theory, the inappropriate learning that results when a child is either consistently overindulged or consistently abused.

contingency contracting. A technique of behaviorist therapy in which a contract is drawn up indicating that for desirable behavior X, the subject will receive reward X, and so on.

continuity hypothesis. A theory which sees pathological depression and normal sadness as two points on a continuum of mood reactions.

control group. Those subjects in an experiment who are not exposed to whatever conditions are being studied; see *randomized groups design*.

contusion. A head injury in which the brain is shifted out of its normal position and pressed against one side of the skull, thus bruising the neural tissue.

conversion reaction. A type of hysterical neurosis in which the individual develops some motor or sensory dysfunction for which there is no organic basis.

cortex. Outer layer of the adrenal glands.

co-twin. A term used by genetic researchers to refer to the twin of the index case.

countertransference. In a psychoanalytic relationship, the analyst's projection on to the client of emotions which originated in his own personal history. (Cf. *transference*.)

covert sensitization. An aversion therapy technique in which the patient is asked to imagine an aversive stimulus at the same time that he visualizes his maladaptive behavior.

cretinism. A congenital hormonal imbalance caused by a thyroxine deficiency and marked by mental retardation and physical disabilities.

crystallized intelligence. The storehouse of information that one has accumulated over a lifetime—vocabulary, numerical skills, and reasoning patterns. (Cf. *fluid intelligence*.)

cultural deprivation. The situation in which socio-economic, political, cultural, and other factors adversely affect intellectual and adaptive functioning.

cultural model. A conceptual approach to the study of abnormal behavior in which the standard of normalcy is a person's ability to conform to the norms of his culture.

cunnilingus. Oral stimulation of female genitals.

current validity. The degree to which a test's findings are consistent with other current findings on the same subject.

Cushing's syndrome. A disease caused by an excessively active adrenal cortex; it usually affects young women and involves both physical and psychological difficulties.

day hospital. A partial hospitalization service in which the patient is treated on a nine-to-five basis and then returns home for the night.

DDD (debility, dependency, and dread). The syndrome of attitudinal change experienced by prisoners of war.

defense mechanisms. Psychic stratagems that reduce anxiety by concealing the source of anxiety from the self and the world.

degenerative disorder. An organic brain syndrome in which intellectual, emotional, and motor functioning appear to deteriorate as a function of advancing age.

delirium tremens (DTs). A withdrawal symptom experienced by the chronic alcoholic when his blood alcohol level drops suddenly; characterized by trembling, sweating, and hallucinations.

delusion. An irrational belief which an individual will defend with great vigor despite overwhelming evidence that the belief has no basis in reality. Delusions are among the most common schizophrenic thought disorders.

delusions of control (delusions of influence). The belief that other people or even extraterrestrial beings are controlling one's thoughts or actions.

delusions of grandeur. The belief that one is a famous person.

delusions of persecution. The belief that one is being plotted against, spied upon, threatened, or otherwise mistreated.

delusions of sin and guilt. The unfounded belief that one has committed "the unpardonable sin" or has brought great harm to others.

dementia praecox. The Latin term used by Kraepelin meaning "mental deterioration"; replaced by Bleuler's more accurate term, "schizophrenia."

denial. The refusal to acknowledge the source of distress.

depressants. Drugs which act on the central nervous system to reduce pain, tension, and anxiety, to relax and disinhibit, and to slow down intellectual and motor reactivity.

depressed type. A type of manic-depressive disorder characterized by extreme dejection.

depression. An emotional state characterized by intense and unrealistic sadness.

depressive neurosis. A mood disturbance in which the individual experiences sudden, deep depression as a reaction to some life circumstance, although his contact with reality remains largely intact.

depth interview. A psychodynamic assessment method in which the subject is encouraged to talk about his past, particularly about sexual and aggressive impulses during his childhood.

dereflection. A technique of existential therapy originated by Frankl, which involves turning the patient's attention away from his symptom and pointing out to him what he could be doing if he were not so self-preoccupied.

detoxification. A medical treatment in which the alcohol is gotten out of the alcoholic's system and his withdrawal symptoms supervised.

diasthesis-stress theory. The belief that certain genes or gene combinations give rise to a diasthesis or predisposition toward a disorder and that if the diasthesis is combined with environmental stress, abnormal behavior will result.

differential association theory. The view that a person becomes a criminal by associating with people who embrace deviant norms.

dildo. Artificial penis, sometimes used by lesbian couples to imitate heterosexual intercourse.

directionality problem. When two variables are found to be correlated, the difficulty of determining which variable causes the other.

disaster syndrome. A pattern of response to severe physical trauma involving three stages—shock, suggestibility, and recovery.

discrimination. The process of learning to distinguish among similar stimuli and to respond only to the appropriate one.

displacement. A defense mechanism which involves the transfer of emotion from an unacceptable object to a safer one.

dissociative reaction. A type of hysterical neurosis which affects psychological functioning and involves the dissociation or splitting off of certain behaviors from the person's normal identity or state of consciousness. (Cf. *conversion reaction*, which affects physical functioning.)

dizygotic twins (DZ twins, fraternal twins). Twins who develop from two eggs fertilized by two different sperm and who have only approximately 50 percent of their genes in common.

Down's Syndrome. See *mongolism*.

dream interpretation. A psychoanalytic technique in which the patient reports his dream as accurately as possible and the therapist interprets the elements of the dream as symbols of unconscious wishes and conflicts.

drug dependence. Psychological dependence on a drug that is not physiologically addictive.

DSM-II (Diagnostic and Statistical Manual of Mental Disorders, second edition). The medically based diagnostic classification system of the American Psychiatric Association.

dysmenorrhea. Irregular or painful menstrual periods.

dyspareunia. Pain during intercourse; it may afflict both men and women, though it is more commonly a female complaint.

dyssocial behavior. A type of behavior in which the individual follows criminal pursuits but is presumed to be psychiatrically normal.

early infantile autism. A disorder in children in which the primary symptom, apparent from infancy, seems to be the inability to relate to anything beyond the self.

eczema. A psychophysiological skin disorder that encompasses conditions ranging from an itching rash to a cluster of open wounds.

ego. In Freudian theory, the psychic component of the mind which mediates between the id and reality.

ego identity. Erikson's belief that the ego does more than just assimilate values of a parent, that it goes on to form an integrated, unique, and autonomous "self."

ego psychologists. The second generation of Freudian theorists who believe in less deterministic and less biologically oriented psychology and who argue that the ego has its own energy and autonomous functions apart from the id.

egoistic suicide. Durkheim's classification of a suicide that results from the individual's lack of a supportive social network (community or family).

ejaculatory incompetence. The inability of the male to ejaculate in the female's vagina after erection and insertion.

electroconvulsive therapy (ECT). The administering of an electric shock to the patient, which induces a convulsion; used in the treatment of depression.

electroencephalogram. A record of brain wave activity obtained by connecting sensitive electrodes to the skull which pick up and record the minute electrical impulses generated by the brain.

electromyograph. The measurement of changes in the electrical activity of muscles.

emetics. Nausea-producing drugs, sometimes used in behavioral therapy.

emotive imagery. A behaviorist respondent conditioning technique in which the anxiety-inducing stimulus is paired with an emotional response incompatible with anxiety, such as pleasure or self-confidence.

encephalitis. An inflammation of the brain caused by infection.

encopresis. A childhood developmental disorder in which episodes of defecating alternate with longer periods of fecal retention.

encounter group. A humanistic form of group therapy which emphasizes personal growth and increased openness and honesty in personal relations by means of free and candid expression within the group.

endocrine glands. Glands responsible for the production of hormones that, when released into the bloodstream, affect various bodily mechanisms such as physical growth and development.

endogenous. That which originates from an internal cause. (Cf. *exogenous.*)

endogenous depression. A type of depression in which the cause appears to be physiological.

enuresis. A lack of bladder control past the age when such control is normally achieved.

epidemic encephalitis (von Economo's disease). A brain infection characterized by profound lethargy and prolonged periods of sleep; often called "sleeping sickness."

epigastric aura. A "funny feeling" often experienced by epileptics before an attack.

epilepsy. An organic disorder characterized by irregularly occurring disturbances in consciousness in the form of seizures or convulsions. The seizures are due to a disruption in the electrical and physiochemical activity of the discharging cells of the brain.

Eros. According to Freud, the constructive life instinct of the id, which deals with survival, self-propagation, and creativity.

escape behavior. Behavior directed toward removing a present and persistent aversive stimulus.

exhibitionism. Sexual gratification through displaying one's genitals to an involuntary observer.

existential neurosis. A disorder characterized primarily by depersonalization and apathy.

exogenous. That which originates from an external cause. (Cf. *endogenous.*)

exogenous depression. A type of depression in which the cause is clearly linked to an external precipitating event in a person's environment.

exorcism. The ritualistic casting out of "devils" and "evil spirits" believed to have invaded possessed persons.

experimental group. Those subjects in an experiment who are exposed to whatever conditions are being studied. See *randomized groups design.*

extinction therapy. A behavior-modification technique for eliminating a maladaptive response by removing the reinforcement that maintains it.

factor analysis. A computerized statistical method designed to isolate the common elements that contribute to a complex behavior pattern.

family therapy. The therapeutic technique in which an entire family is seen together so that destructive roles and attitudes can be exposed and treated.

fellatio. Oral stimulation of the penis.

fetishism. Sexual gratification via inanimate objects or via some part of the body to the exclusion of the person as a whole.

fixation. A defense mechanism in which an individual experiences anxiety at a certain stage of development and refuses to progress beyond that stage.

fixed interval schedule. In operant conditioning, a reinforcement schedule structured so that the reward is delivered once in every fixed interval of time.

fixed ratio schedule. In operant conditioning, a reinforcement schedule structured so that the reward is given after a certain number of responses.

flagellants. People who roamed Europe in the Middle Ages whipping themselves to atone for their sins.

flashbacks. Spontaneous repetitions of terrifying hallucinatory perceptions experienced under drugs.

flat affect. A subjective feeling or tone in which there is a lack of any emotional response to one's surroundings or to other people.

fluid intelligence. The dynamic component of intelligence, involving attention, inhibition of irrelevant associations, perception of environmental changes, and the ability to select the most appropriate response from the range of learned behaviors. (Cf. *crystallized intelligence.*)

formication. A condition resulting from intense stimulation of the nervous system by high doses of amphetamines or cocaine, in which the individual feels that there are bugs crawling under his skin.

free association. A psychoanalytic technique whereby the patient verbalizes whatever thoughts come to his mind, without structuring or censoring his remarks.

free-floating anxiety. A condition associated with anxiety neurosis in which the individual is continually anxious but unable to specify what is generating his many fears and worries.

fugue. A dissociative episode in which an individual flees his anxiety-ridden identity and environment, not returning for days, weeks, or even years. Upon "waking up," nothing about the particular fugue period is remembered.

functional analysis. A behaviorist assessment which involves a systematic dissection of the person's complaint. In an interview situation, the subject's remarks are assumed to be straightforward statements of the problem rather than oblique clues to underlying dynamics.

functional psychosis. A severe mental disorder which cannot be attributed to known physical causes.

gender identity. The individual's sense of being a man or a woman.

general paresis. A mental syndrome associated with syphilis, involving the gradual and irreversible breakdown of physical and mental functioning.

generalization. The process by which an organism, conditioned to respond in a certain way to a particular stimulus, will also respond to similar stimuli in the same way.

genital stage. According to Freud, the final phase of mature sexuality, by which he meant heterosexual genital mating.

genotype. That unique combination of genes which represents one's biological inheritance from one's parents.

Gestalt therapy. An existential-humanistic form of therapy in which the patient acts out past conflicts with the therapist in order to confront his feelings and learn to take responsibility for them.

glove anesthesia. A form of hysterical neurosis in which the individual reports a numbness in his hand from the tips of the fingers to a clear cut-off point at the wrist.

grand mal. The most common and most dramatic of the epilepsies, involving a generalized seizure throughout the brain, with violent convulsions and loss of consciousness.

group delinquent reaction. A form of juvenile delinquency in which the child joins a gang, embraces the deviant value system and behavioral norms of the gang, and tries to master the skills that its members hold in esteem.

group therapy. A therapeutic technique, based on the assumption that people's problems have to do with other people, in which the individual is given an opportunity to interact with others in a safe environment under a trained leader.

gynephobia. The fear of women.

habit disturbances. Childhood disorders consisting of disruptions of one's most natural functions, such as eating, sleeping, and toileting. (Cf. *neurotic disturbances.*)

habituation. The process whereby an individual's response to the same stimulus decreases with successive presentations.

halfway house. A residence for people who no longer require institutionalization but who still need some support system in readjusting to community life.

hallucination. A sensory perception that occurs in the absence of any appropriate external stimulus.

hallucinogens. A class of drugs that acts on the central nervous system in such a way as to cause distortions in sensory perception.

hashish. A nonaddictive hallucinogen derived from the resin of the cannabis and about five to six times stronger than marijuana.

hebephrenic. A form of schizophrenia characterized by childlike behavior, such as giggling wildly, making faces, and assuming absurd postures.

helplessness-hopelessness syndrome. The depressed person's conviction that he is both unable to help himself and unlikely to be helped by external forces.

hemiplegia. Paralysis of one half of the body; a common aftereffect of cerebrovascular accidents.

heroin. An addictive narcotic drug derived from morphine.

hierarchy of needs. Maslow's concept of a series of needs that must be satisfied one by one in the process of development before the adult can begin pursuing self-actualization.

homosexuality. Sexual activity directed toward one's own sex.

hot line. Round-the-clock telephone service where people in trouble can call and receive immediate comfort and advice from trained volunteers.

humanistic-existential perspective. A diverse approach to abnormal psychology whose proponents generally agree that behavior is both willed and purposive and that human beings choose their lives and therefore are responsible for their lives.

humors. According to Hippocrates, the four vital fluids in the body; an imbalance between them was thought to cause personality disorders.

Huntington's chorea. A fatal presenile psychosis which is transmitted genetically. The symptoms include spasmodic jerking of the limbs, bizarre behavior, and mental deterioration.

hydrocephalus. A brain disorder caused by an overabundance of cerebrospinal fluids in the ventricles of the brain. The ventricles become enlarged, crushing the brain against the skull.

hydrophobia. The fear of water.

hyperkinesis (hyperactivity). A chronic sustained level of motor activity by the child.

hypertension (high blood pressure). Chronic elevation of the blood pressure due to constriction of the arteries; a psychophysiological disorder.

hyperthyroidism (Grave's disease). Overactivity of the thyroid gland which causes excessive secretion of the hormone thyroxin. The disorder is accompanied by anxiety-like symptoms.

hyperventilation. Rapid and deep breathing.

hypnosis. An artificially induced sleeplike state in which the subject is highly susceptible to suggestion.

hypoanalysis. A technique combining psychoanalysis and hypnosis; frequently used with patients suffering from transient situational disturbances.

hypochondriacal delusions. The belief in some bizarre physical ailment, such as that one's brain is full of mold.

hypochondriacal neurosis. A disorder in which an individual converts his anxiety into a chronic preoccupation with his bodily functioning.

hypoglycemia. Low blood sugar level.

hypothyroidism (myxedema). Underactivity of the thyroid gland which results in deficient production of thyroxin, due possibly to inadequate iodine consumption. Symptoms include lethargy and depression.

hysteria. A physical disability for which no organic cause can be found.

hysterical neurosis. A condition which involves the involuntary loss or impairment of some normal function, either physical or psychological, with complete denial of anxiety by the person experiencing the loss of function.

hysterical personality. A type of personality disorder characterized by emotional instability, egocentricity, self-dramatization, overdependence on others, and an insatiable desire for attention.

id. According to Freud, the mass of biological drives with which the individual is born.

identification. In psychodynamic theory, the incorporation of the same-sexed parent's values, standards, sexual orientation, and mannerisms, as part of the development of the superego.

idiopathic epilepsy. A convulsive disorder for which there is no known cause; the disorder usually has its onset between the ages of ten and twenty.

implosive therapy. A behavior modification technique to extinguish anxiety by maximizing the client's anxiety through imagined fear-producing situations and holding the anxiety at this pitch until the client realizes that these imaginings do not result in any aversive consequences.

inadequate learning. In behaviorist theory, one of the ways in which a person is conditioned to engage in antisocial or dyssocial behavior; the individual simply does not know better, because either he is new to the society (as in the case of an immigrant) or he has been raised in a culturally deprived environment with little or no discipline.

inadequate reinforcing system. A pattern of maladaptive behaviors which results from an individual's being controlled by a system of rewards different from that of the average person.

inappropriate affect. A subjective feeling or tone in which emotional responses are totally unsuited to the immediate context.

inappropriate learning. In behaviorist theory, one of the ways in which a person is conditioned to engage in antisocial or dyssocial behavior; the individual is conditioned according to deviant norms, usually those of a deviant subculture.

inappropriate stimulus controls. A disruption in the relationship between stimulus and response, either because a response occurs in the absence of any appropriate stimulus or because a stimulus fails to elicit the appropriate response.

incest. Sexual relations between members of the same immediate family.

incubation. A period of time in which a phobic reaction intensifies as the person avoids the original stimulus.

index case (proband case). In genetic family studies, the individual in the family who has the diagnosed case of the disorder being studied.

induced anger. A behaviorist extinction technique in which the patient is taught to respond to imagined anxiety-producing situations not with relaxation but with anger, since anger is a response incompatible with anxiety.

insomnia. The chronic inability to sleep.

intellectualization. The avoidance of unacceptable feelings by repressing these feelings and replacing them with an abstract intellectual analysis of the problem.

intelligence quotient (IQ). The score on an intelligence test which is computed by dividing the subject's mental age by his chronological age and then multiplying by 100.

intelligence test. A psychological assessment technique effective in predicting success in school.

interactionism. The theory that the mind and body interact with one another, each influencing the other at various times.

intercranial neoplasm. A new growth within the brain; the technical term for brain tumor.

inter-judge reliability. The degree to which a measurement device yields the same results when scored or interpreted by different judges.

internal consistency. The degree to which different parts of a measurement device yield the same results.

interpersonal perspective. The view that the individual's relationships with others are the central breeding ground for psychological disturbance and that the disturbed person must not be viewed in isolation but within the context of his contacts with others.

involutional melancholia. A depressive reaction that has its onset in middle age or late middle age and is characterized by anxiety, agitation, insomnia, guilt feelings, and preoccupation with illness. Often there is no previous episode of affective disorder in the individual.

Jacksonian epilepsy. A form of epilepsy in which the origin of the seizure is localized in one part of the brain.

juvenile delinquency. The violation of laws and social mores by people under eighteen years of age.

juvenile paresis. Irreversible syphilis that the child contracts in the womb from his syphilitic mother.

Kleinfelter's syndrome. A condition that affects only men in which the nondisjunction of the sex chromosomes results in an extra X chromosome, causing underdeveloped testes, sterility, and sometimes mild mental retardation.

Korsakoff's psychosis. An irreversible nutritional deficiency due either to alcohol poisoning or to vitamin B deficiency associated with alcoholism; characterized by anterograde amnesia and confabulation.

labeling theory. The view that applying a label of "sick," "crazy," "criminal," or "deviant" has an adverse effect on the individual; the label acts as a self-fulfilling prophecy, affecting the person's self image and encouraging him to become what he has been labeled.

la belle indifférence. A characteristic of the conversion reaction in which the individual does not seem at all disturbed by his disability.

laceration. A serious kind of brain damage, in which a bullet or piece of metal enters the skull and directly ruptures and destroys brain tissue.

latency. The dormancy of a particular behavior or response.

latent content. In psychoanalytic theory, the unconscious material of a dream that is being expressed in disguised fashion through the symbols contained in the dream.

law of effect. Thorndike's formulation of the importance of reward in the learning process which states that responses that lead to satisfying consequences are strengthened and therefore are likely to be repeated, while responses with unsatisfying consequences are weakened and therefore unlikely to be repeated.

lead encephalopathy. A toxic disorder due to excessive ingestion of lead, which causes fluid to accumulate in the brain and results in extraordinary intracranial pressure.

learned helplessness. In behaviorist theory, the depressive's inability to initiate adaptive responses, possibly due to a helplessness conditioned by earlier, inescapable trauma.

lesbianism. Female homosexuality.

libido. In psychoanalytic theory, the energy of the life instinct, which Freud saw as the driving force of personality.

locomotor ataxia. A shuffling gait; a symptom characteristic of advanced syphilis.

logorrhea. A condition in which the patient repeats unusual verbal patterns over and over; a symptom of senile psychosis.

logotherapy. Frankl's technique for dealing with the spiritual aspect of psychopathology, in which the therapist confronts the patient with his responsibility for his existence and his obligation to pursue the values inherent in life.

longitudinal study. A type of experimental study which involves testing and interviewing a random sample population at regular intervals over a period of time.

lycanthropy. A delusion in which a person believes he is a wolf and acts accordingly.

major affective disorders. As defined by DSM-II, a group of psychoses characterized by a single disorder of mood, either extreme depression or elation, that dominates the patient's mental life and is reponsible for his loss of

reality contact. The mood does not seem to be caused by a precipitating life experience.

mania. An emotional state characterized by intense and unrealistic feelings of elation.

manic-depressive disorder. Affective disorder characterized by extreme elation, extreme dejection, or some pattern of alternation between the two. Manic-depressive episodes are usually of fairly short duration but tend to recur.

manic type. A type of manic-depressive disorder characterized by extreme elation.

manifest content. In psychoanalytic theory, the content of a dream as seen and reported by the individual. (Cf. *latent content.*)

marijuana. A nonaddictive hallucinogen derived from the dried and crushed leaves of the cannabis plant.

marital therapy. A therapeutic procedure which aims at pinpointing the role expectations and patterns of communication between the couple, encouraging each member to examine his or her role and the role he or she imposes on the other.

masked or smiling depression. A type of depression in which the individual hides his feelings behind a cheerful demeanor.

masochism. Sexual gratification through having pain inflicted on oneself.

mediating variable. In behaviorist theory, any mental construct which influences the way individuals react to the environment and thus mediates between stimulus and response.

medical model. The conceptualization of psychological abnormality as a group of diseases analogous to physical diseases.

medulla. The internal portion of the adrenal glands.

meiosis. A type of cell division in which each reproductive cell receives one chromosome from each of twenty-three pairs.

meninges. The membranous covering of the brain or spinal cord.

meningitis. A brain infection involving an acute inflammation of the meninges, characterized by drowsiness, confusion, irritability, and sensory impairments.

methadone. A synthetic narcotic which satisfies the craving for narcotics but does not produce narcotic euphoria.

migraine. A psychophysiological disorder characterized by episodes of severe headache.

milieu therapy (therapeutic community). An institutional group therapy in which severely disturbed patients live together in an atmosphere designed to maximize their independence, their activity level, and their sense of dignity.

mind-body problem. The issue of the relationship between the psychic and somatic aspects of human functioning.

misoneism. A pronounced hatred of anything new; a symptom of senile psychosis.

modeling. In behavioral theory, the learning of a new behavior by imitating another person performing that behavior.

mongolism (Down's syndrome). A form of mental retardation caused by an extra chromosome. Individuals with this condition usually have IQs of 50 or less and distinctive physical characteristics, such as slanting eyes and flat nose.

monogenetic-biochemical theory. The theory that a single gene—dominant, recessive, or intermediate—is responsible for a specific metabolic dysfunction which, in turn, produces the behavioral manifestations of schizophrenia.

monozygotic twins (MZ twins, identical twins). Twins who develop from a single fertilized egg and have exactly the same genotype; they are always of the same sex, have the same eye color and blood type, and so on.

moral anxiety. In psychoanalytic theory, a state in which the source of danger is the superego, which threatens to overwhelm a person with guilt or shame.

moral therapy. A treatment procedure developed in the early nineteenth century based on providing a pleasant and relaxed atmosphere for the mentally ill.

morphine. An addictive narcotic derived from opium.

motor habits. Repetitive and nonfunctional patterns of motor behavior that seem to occur in response to stress, such as thumbsucking and nail-biting.

multiple personality. An extreme form of dissociative reaction in which two or more complete behavior organizations, each well-developed and highly distinct, are found in one individual.

mysophobia. The fear of dirt.

mystification. As used by R. D. Laing, a habitual mode of interaction between parent and child that causes the child to doubt the adequacy or legitimacy of his own thoughts, feelings, and perceptions.

narcissism. The erotic preoccupation with one's own body.

narcotics. A class of drugs which induces relaxation and reverie and provides relief from anxiety and physical pain.

necrophilia. Sexual contacts with dead bodies.

negative reinforcement. A conditioning procedure in which a response is followed by the removal of an aversive event or stimulus, which has the effect of promoting the response.

neologisms. A schizophrenic speech pattern in which new words are formed by combining parts of two or more regular words or in which common words are used in a unique fashion.

neurasthenic neurosis. A disorder characterized by chronic complaints of weakness and exhaustion.

neurosyphilis. Deterioration of brain tissues as a result of infection by the spirochete *Treponema pallidum*.

neurotic anxiety. In Freudian theory, a state in which danger comes from id impulses that threaten to burst through ego controls.

neurotic disturbances. Those disturbances which sometimes occur in childhood and which stem from anxiety and may influence all aspects of behavior. (Cf. *habit disturbances*.)

neurotic paradox. The situation in which an individual persists in unrewarding behavior patterns even while realizing that these patterns are self-defeating.

night hospital. A partial hospitalization service in which the patient goes to his job from nine to five and then returns to the hospital for the night.

night terror. A particularly harrowing variety of bad dream experienced by a child, which generally occurs during the early part of the night.

nightmare. A bad dream which is less frightening and dramatic than a night terror.

nominal aphasia (anomia). Language impairment characterized by the inability, in speaking, to recall the names of common objects.

nondisjunction. In the meiotic division of the ovum, the failure of a pair of chromosomes to divide.

object world. The environment of people and things.

obsession. A thought which an individual may consider irrational but which recurs repeatedly, compelling him to dwell on it.

obsessive-compulsive. A type of personality disorder characterized by rigidity, overconscientiousness, and strong inhibitions against self-expression and self-gratification.

obsessive-compulsive neurosis. A disorder in which the individual is repeatedly compelled to hold a thought in his mind that he may consider irrational (obsession) or to engage in an action he may consider irrational (compulsion).

occupational delirium. A form of traumatic delirium in which the patient carries on his conversation as if he were at his job rather than in the hospital.

Oedipus complex. According to Freud, the desire that all male children have during the phallic stage to do away with the parent of the same sex in order to take sexual possession of the parent of the opposite sex, a crucial stage of development which determines the child's future sexual adjustment.

operant behavior. In behaviorist theory, a class of complex behavior in which an organism acts upon the environment in order to achieve a desired result; all operant behavior is the result of conditioning. (Cf. *respondent behavior*.)

operant conditioning (instrumental conditioning). The process by which an organism learns to associate certain results with certain actions it has taken.

operational definition. The working definition of a term which specifies precisely what observable phenomena the term designates; essential in psychological experiments.

ophidiophobia. The fear of nonpoisonous snakes.

opium. A chemically active substance derived from the opium poppy; one of the narcotics.

oral incorporation. In psychoanalytic theory, the child's overidentification in the oral stage with a loved object.

oral stage. In psychoanalytic theory, the first stage of psychosocial development in which the mouth is the primary focus of libidinal impulses and pleasure; occurs in the first year of life.

organ neuroses. The psychodynamic term for the various psychophysiological disorders.

organic brain disorders. Behavioral problems that are

directly traceable to the destruction of brain tissue or to biochemical imbalance in the brain.

organic theory. The concept that attributes abnormal behavior to physical disorders; first developed by Hippocrates.

overanxious reaction. A condition in which the child's anxiety is overt and unmistakable, causing him to be overdependent, timid, shy, and lacking in self-confidence. (Cf. *withdrawing reaction*.)

overinclusion. An aspect of schizophrenic thinking in which topics are linked in irrelevant associations, without coherence or logic.

panic reaction. An extreme form of anxiety attack in which the anxiety is severe and prolonged, possibly lasting for days.

paradoxical intention. A technique of existential therapy originated by Frankl, in which the patient is asked to indulge or exaggerate his symptom in order to prove to the patient that he controls his symptom and that it can be approached with nonchalance and humor rather than terror and loathing.

paranoia. A psychotic state characterized by delusions of persecution.

paranoid-nonparanoid dimension. The classification of schizophrenics according to the presence (paranoid) or absence (nonparanoid) of delusions of persecution and/or grandeur.

paranoid schizophrenic. A type of psychotic behavior often characterized by delusions, hallucinations, and extreme emotional changes.

paranoid state. A major category of functional psychoses in which the delusion, either of persecution or grandeur, is the essential abnormality, or in many cases the only one.

paraphasia. Language impairment characterized by the inability to order speech grammatically or syntactically.

paraprofessional. A mental health worker who lacks a Ph.D. or M.D. but who is trained to provide certain mental health services, often in the community in which he lives.

parasympathetic division. That division of the autonomic nervous system which decreases physical arousal and is usually dominant under less emotional conditions. It regulates breathing, heart rate, blood pressure, stomach and intestinal activity, and elimination. (Cf. *sympathetic division*.)

paratoxic distortions. According to Sullivan, the self-protecting styles of relating to others which the individual develops in childhood and then carries through into his adult life, to the detriment of his interpersonal relations.

Parkinson's disease. A presenile psychosis involving degenerative lesions of midbrain nerve tracts responsible for relaying motor impulses. Symptoms include tremors, a masklike countenance, stiff gait, and withdrawal.

passive-aggressive personality. A type of personality disorder characterized by excessive passivity and excessive aggression; the aggression is more overt than in the passive-dependent type.

passive-dependent personality. A type of personality disorder characterized by excessive helplessness, anxiety, and dependency.

pedophilia. Child molesting—that is, gratification, on the part of the adult, through sexual contacts with children.

pellagra. A disease caused by severe deficiency of the B vitamin niacin. It occurs most often in areas where corn is a major part of the diet of the population. Symptoms include depression, anxiety, delirium, and hallucinations.

penis envy. In psychoanalytic theory, the female child's feeling that she has been born unequipped with a penis because of her sexual desire toward her father; female counterpart of castration anxiety.

perceptual conscious. In Freudian theory, the first level of the mind's consciousness which contains whatever requires no act of recall.

perseverate. A characteristic schizophrenic thought pattern in which the individual dwells repeatedly on the primary association to a given stimulus and applies it to different stimuli.

personal discomfort model. A conceptual approach to the study of abnormal behavior which, in judging disorder, gives primary importance to the individual's own perception of his mental functioning.

personality disorder. A deeply ingrained, maladaptive pattern of behavior, presumably adopted at an early age. The individual, however, remains in fairly good contact with reality.

petit mal. An epileptic seizure lasting only a few seconds and involving a brief loss of consciousness.

phallic stage. In psychoanalytic theory, the third stage of psychosocial development in which pleasure is derived from masturbation, the stroking and handling of the genitals; occurs from the third to the fifth or sixth year of life.

phenomenological approach. A therapeutic procedure in which the therapist attempts to see the patient's world from the vantage point of the patient's own internal frame of reference.

phenotype. The unique combination of observable characteristics that results from the combination of a person's genotype with his environment.

phenylketonuria (PKU). A genetic defect caused by a deficiency in a liver enzyme, phenylalanine hydroxylase, which results in severe retardation, hyperactivity, and erratic behavior.

phobia. An intense and debilitating fear of some object or situation which actually presents no real threat.

physiological perspective. The approach to the study of abnormal behavior which investigates nongenetic physical determinants of behavior disturbances.

pica. A development disorder in which the child willfully ingests inedible substances after the age of two years.

Pick's disease. A rare but fatal presenile psychosis in which the frontal and temporal lobes of the brain gradually atrophy, causing impairment of memory and cognitive, emotional, and motor functions.

play therapy. A psychodynamic technique which encourages the child to vent his conflicts through symbolic play rather than verbal expression.

pleasure principle. In Freudian theory, the tendency of

the id to devote itself exclusively to the immediate reduction of tension.

polygraph. A physiological recording device equipped with sensors which, when attached to the body, can pick up subtle physiological changes in the form of electrical impulses. These changes are recorded on a moving roll of paper.

positive regard. As defined by Rogers, the individual's need for affection and approval from those most important to him, particularly his parents.

positive reinforcement. A situation in which a response is followed by a positive event or stimulus which increases the probability that the response will be repeated.

positive spikes. Brief and sudden bursts of brain-wave activity, which some studies have found in the EEGs of some antisocial personalities with histories of sudden, impulsive acts of aggression.

posttraumatic syndrome. In the disaster syndrome, the period following an acute phase of traumatic reaction in which the individual shows no outward signs of grief or depression but may be anxious and irritable and have difficulty getting back into daily routines.

preconscious. In Freudian theory the second level of the mind's consciousness which consists of whatever the person can remember without great difficulty.

predictive validity. The degree to which a test's findings are consistent with the subject's future performance.

prefrontal lobotomy. A surgical procedure in which a cut is made between the frontal lobes (the thought center) and the thalamus (the emotional center) of the brain in order to cut down the communication between these sections, thereby reducing disturbing stimuli.

premature ejaculation. Inability of the male to postpone ejaculation long enough to satisfy the female.

premorbid adjustment. The level of social and sexual adjustment before the onset of a disorder.

premorbid personality. The personality before the onset of a disorder.

presenile psychosis. The deterioration of the brain and central nervous system that affects the 40-to-60 age group.

primary gain. In neurosis, the relief from anxiety through the use of a defense mechanism.

primary impotence. The inability of the male to ever sustain an erection sufficient for the successful completion of intercourse.

primary neural aging. A physiological change believed to be caused by the slowing of electrical impulse transmission in the central nervous system because of loss of cells and because of physiological changes in nerve cells and nerve fibers.

primary orgasmic dysfunction. The inability of the woman to ever achieve orgasm through coitus, masturbation, or any other means.

primary prevention. The prevention of the development of psychological disturbances.

primary process thinking. In Freudian theory, one of the id's methods of self-gratification which involves conjuring up a mental image of the source of satisfaction.

primary reinforcer. A stimulus or need that one responds to instinctively, without learning.

principle of reinforcement. According to Skinner, the basic mechanism for the control of human behavior in which actions are determined by pleasant or unpleasant consequences.

process-reactive dimension. The classification of schizophrenics according to whether the onset of symptoms is gradual (process) or abrupt and precipitated by some traumatic event (reactive).

projection. A defense mechanism whereby internal threats are transformed into external threats.

projective personality test. An assessment technique used to draw out, indirectly, an individual's true conflicts and motives by presenting him with ambiguous stimuli and allowing him to project his private self into his responses.

proprioceptive discrimination. A perceptive disorder in which schizophrenic individuals have difficulty determining where their bodies are in space (for example, where their hands and feet are).

psychoactive drug. A drug that alters one's psychological state.

psychoanalysis. The psychodynamic therapy method which relies heavily on the techniques of free association, dream interpretation, and analysis of resistance and transference: the aim is to give the patient insight into his unconscious conflicts, impulses, and motives.

psychodrama. A psychoanalytically oriented form of group therapy in which members get on a stage and together act out their emotional conflicts. The purpose is for the client to confront his feelings and also to get at the unconscious roots of these feelings, which are then examined according to Freudian theory.

psychogenic theory. The view that mental disturbance is due primarily to emotional stress.

psychological assessment. The systematic analysis of a person and his life situation.

psychological model. A conceptual approach to the study of abnormal behavior which emphasizes psychosocial factors and learning in the development and maintenance of all behaviors and which views behaviors on a continuum ranging from "normal" to "abnormal."

psychometric approach. A method of psychological testing which aims at locating and measuring stable underlying traits.

psychomotor epilepsy. A form of epilepsy in which the individual loses contact with reality but appears normal and performs some mechanical activity. He will be amnesic for the episode after the attack has passed.

psychopath. See *antisocial personality*.

psychophysiological disorders. Physical disorders which are thought to be due to emotional factors and which are also scientifically traceable to a clear organic cause.

psychosocial perspective. The view that regards society as the principal determinant of abnormal behavior and which explains abnormal behavior in terms of the social context within which it takes place.

psychotherapy. A systematic and rather structured series of interactions between a therapist and a client. The goal is to produce in the client emotional, cognitive, or behavioral changes.

psychotic depressive reaction. A disturbance of mood in which an individual with no previous history of mood disorder suddenly plunges into depression as a result of some traumatic experience.

punishment. In behavioral theory, the process for suppressing behavior whereby a response is followed by an aversive stimulus.

randomized groups design. A scientific procedure for finding out the effect of a given set of conditions. The method involves assigning subjects at random to two groups: one group is exposed to the conditions being studied (experimental group), the other not (control group), and the two groups are then compared to determine the effects, if any, of the conditions.

rape. The achievement of sexual relations with another person through the use or threat of force.

rational-emotive therapy. The "talking cure" method of Albert Ellis in which the patient is helped to establish more pragmatic goals for the unrealistic ones he has set.

Raynaud's disease. A cardiovascular disorder characterized by chronically cold hands and feet but involving no visible impairment of the circulatory system.

reaction formation. A state in which a person represses feelings that are arousing anxiety and then vehemently professes the exact opposite of these feelings.

reality anxiety. A state in which a person is threatened by something actual in the outside world. (Cf. *moral anxiety*, *neurotic anxiety*.)

reality principle. In Freudian theory, the concern of the ego with finding safe and realistic means to satisfy the id.

reciprocal inhibition. See *systematic desensitization*.

reflex action. Instinctive and automatic behavior that immediately reduces the biological tension involved.

regression. A defense mechanism which involves the return to an earlier, less threatening developmental stage that one has already passed through.

regressive enuresis. A condition in which bladder control has been achieved but then abandoned.

reinforcement therapy. A behavior modification technique utilizing positive reinforcement for the gradual development of a desired response through the rewarding of successive approximations of that response (shaping).

reliability. The degree to which a measurement device yields consistent results under varying conditions.

repression. A defense mechanism in which unacceptable id impulses are pushed down into the unconscious.

resistance. In psychoanalytic theory, a defense mechanism on the part of the patient to avoid confronting certain memories and impulses.

respondent behavior. In behaviorist theory, that behavior which is elicited by specific stimuli, both unlearned and conditioned.

respondent conditioning (classical conditioning). The process of learning a conditioned response.

response cost contingencies. In behavioral therapy, an operant conditioning technique in which undesirable behavior is "punished" by the withdrawal of a reinforcement.

response set. A test-taking attitude that leads the subject to distort his responses, often unconsciously.

retarded depression. A type of depression in which there is little spontaneous motor activity; movement is slow and deliberate, with a minimum number of gestures and little verbalization.

reticular formation. A portion of the autonomic nervous system which consists of a large mass of brain cells connected to other parts of the brain; it is particularly important in arousal from sleep and in maintaining alertness while awake.

Rorschach test. A projective test in which the subject is shown a series of ink blot designs and asked to describe them.

rubella (German measles). A congenital infection that, if contracted by the mother during the first three months of pregnancy, has a high risk of causing mental retardation and physical deformity in the child.

runaway reaction. A form of juvenile delinquency characterized by running away from home and often by stealing as well.

sadism. Sexual gratification through inflicting pain on others.

sadomasochism. The pairing up of a sadist and a masochist to satisfy their mutually complementary sexual tastes.

schizophrenia. A group of psychoses marked by severe distortion and disorganization of thought, perception, and affect, by bizarre behavior, and by social withdrawal.

secondary gains. In neurosis, the extra attention and "babying" that an adult receives when responding inappropriately to anxiety.

secondary impotence. A type of sexual inadequacy in which the male is impotent in at least 25 percent of his attempts at intercourse.

secondary prevention. The preventing of manageable psychological disorders from becoming unmanageable, chronic disorders.

secondary process thinking. In Freudian theory, the remembering, reasoning, and evaluating done by the ego in mediating between the id and reality.

self-actualization. According to Rogers, the fulfillment of all an individual's capabilities.

self-report personality inventory. An assessment technique in which the subject is asked direct questions about his personality and feelings; in other words, the subject assesses himself.

self-system. According to Sullivan, the individual's view of himself, his needs, and his wants; when demands are placed on the individual inconsistent with his self-system, anxiety will result.

senile degenerative disorders. Organic deterioration of the brain in persons over the age of sixty.

senile psychosis. A senile degenerative disorder brought on by extensive atrophy of brain tissue and marked by a gradual increase in behavioral problems.

sensory aphasia (receptive aphasia). A language impairment caused by a vascular accident in which the individual has difficulty in understanding.

sex-reassignment surgery. An operation to remove the genitalia of an individual and to provide an artificial substitute for the genitals of the opposite sex.

sexual deviation. As defined by DSM-II, "sexual interest directed primarily toward objects other than people of the opposite sex, toward sexual acts not usually associated with coitus, or toward coitus performed under bizarre circumstances."

sexual inadequacy. The inability to achieve gratification in normal sexual activity.

shaping. A type of operant conditioning used often with children, whereby the subject is reinforced for successive approximations of target behavior.

sheltered workshops. Places where moderately retarded adults are employed to do simple work under supervision.

simple schizophrenia. A comparatively rare subtype of schizophrenia in which the individual may exhibit very few overtly bizarre behaviors and be in better contact with his environment than other types of schizophrenics; often the individual is not hospitalized.

situational orgasmic dysfunction. The ability of the female to achieve orgasm only in certain situations and not in others.

social desirability set. A test-taking attitude in which the subject distorts his responses in order to ascribe to himself qualities that will make him look good.

social learning. That branch of behavioral theory which is based on the influence that people have on one another.

sociopath. See *antisocial personality*.

somatic weakness. The vulnerability of an organ system to psychological stress.

somatogenic hypothesis. The theory that pathological depression is a discrete disease entity that will ultimately be traced to a biological disorder.

somnambulism (sleepwalking). A dissociative disorder in which one part of the personality controls behavior while what is considered to be the usual personality is inoperative; it can occur during the day (diurnal somnambulism) as well as the night (nocturnal somnambulism).

speech aphasia (expressive aphasia). A language impairment caused by a vascular accident in which the individual has difficulty in articulation.

statistical model. A conceptual approach to the study of abnormal behavior which defines abnormality as any substantial deviation from a statistically calculated average.

statutory rape. Sexual intercourse with a minor, which usually occurs in the absence of force.

stimulants. A class of drugs whose major effect is to provide energy, alertness, and feelings of confidence.

stroke. See *cerebral thrombosis*.

structural hypothesis. Freud's conceptualization of the human psyche as an interaction of three forces—the id, the ego, and the superego.

stuttering. The interruption of speech fluency through blocked, prolonged, or repeated words, syllables, or sounds.

sublimation. A defense mechanism by which impulses are channeled away from forbidden outlets and toward socially acceptable ones.

superego. In Freudian theory, that part of the mind in which the individual has incorporated the moral standards of the society.

sympathetic division. That division of the autonomic nervous system which becomes dominant in times of stress and which heightens the body's arousal, causing blood pressure, heart rate, perspiration and adrenalin to increase, pupils to dilate, and salivation and digestive functions to diminish. (Cf. *parasympathetic division*.)

symptomatic epilepsy (acquired epilepsy). Convulsions which are a function of brain damage caused by other pathologies, such as neurosyphilis, alcohol or drug intoxication, tumors, encephalitis, or trauma.

syndrome. The distinct cluster of symptoms which tends to occur in a particular disease.

systematic desensitization (reciprocal inhibition). A behaviorist extinction technique in which the patient, in a relaxed state, is presented with the anxiety-rousing stimulus while the therapist prevents the anxiety response and the negatively reinforcing behavior from taking place, which consequently allows the anxiety to be extinguished.

tarantism. A hysterical dancing frenzy of epidemic proportions during the Middle Ages; then believed to be caused by the sting of a tarantula.

Tay-Sachs disease. A genetic disorder of lipid metabolism marked by the absence of the enzyme hexosominia A in cerebral tissues; causes mental retardation, muscular deterioration, convulsions, and death before the age of six.

tertiary prevention. The reducing of the consequences of an already fully developed psychological disturbance.

test-retest reliability. The degree to which a measurement device yields the same results when administered to the same person at different points in time.

testosterone. The hormone largely responsible for the development of such male secondary sexual characteristics as beard growth, deepening of the voice, and sperm production.

T-group (sensitivity training group). See *encounter group*.

Thanatos. In Freudian theory, the death instinct of the id.

third variable. An unidentified factor which may have a causal effect on the relationship between two correlated variables.

tic. An involuntary, periodic movement of muscle groups. A *transient tic* usually appears as a reaction to a situational pressure and tends to disappear quickly after the stressful period. A *nontransient tic* may persist for years.

time-out (from reinforcement). An operant conditioning technique whereby the subject is "punished" for undesirable behavior by being temporarily removed from the situation and placed in a neutral environment where he can receive no reinforcement.

token economy. A behavior modification procedure, based on operant conditioning principles, in which patients are given artificial rewards for socially desirable behavior; the rewards or tokens can then be exchanged for a range of further established rewards which the patients choose.

tolerance. The physiological condition in which the usual dosage of a drug no longer provides the desired "high."

tonic phase. The second stage of a grand mal seizure in which the person's body becomes very rigid and undergoes strong muscular contractions, and breathing is suspended.

topographical approach. Freud's original conceptualization of the mind in terms of levels of consciousness.

transactional analysis. A therapy technique originated by Eric Berne, in which the games married couples play with each other are uncovered and the rules are changed in order to foster more healthy, satisfying relationships.

transference. In psychoanalytic theory, the process by which the patient identifies the therapist with important people in his life, usually with his parents, and projects on to the therapist his relationship with those people.

transference neurosis. A stage in psychoanalytic therapy in which the patient reenacts with the analyst his childhood conflicts with his parents.

transient situational disturbances. Acute reactions to temporary severe stress, which are manifested in intense anxiety and other neurotic symptoms.

transsexualism. Gender identification with the opposite sex.

transvestism. Sexual gratification through dressing in the clothes of the opposite sex.

trauma. A severe physical injury to the body from an external source; or a severe psychological shock.

traumatic delirium. The state of disorientation that a patient suffering from contusion may experience upon awakening from the coma.

trephining. An ancient and crude surgical technique which involved cutting a hole in the skull of a possessed person in order to allow the evil spirits to escape.

trisomy 21. A condition in which there are three rather than the usual pair of chromosomes in the human cell.

ulcer. An open sore in the wall of the stomach or in a portion of the small intestine produced by abnormally high levels of gastric activity; a psychophysiological disorder.

unconditioned response. A natural, unlearned response to a stimulus.

unconditioned stimulus. A stimulus which elicits a natural or unconditioned response.

unconscious. In Freudian theory, the largest level of the mind's consciousness which contains all memories not readily available to the perceptual conscious, either because they have been forgotten or repressed.

unlearned reflexes. Simple responses, such as blinking or coughing, that are elicited automatically by certain stimuli.

unsocialized aggressive reaction. A type of juvenile delinquency characterized by hostility, disobedience, destructiveness, and theft.

unspecified encephalitis. A brain infection typically transmitted by mosquitoes, ticks, and horses. The disorder is characterized by lethargy, irritability, convulsions, and the like.

vaginismus. The spasmodic contractions of the outer third of the vagina, which render intercourse either impossible or very painful.

validity. The measure of how consistent a test is with other sources of information about the same subject.

valuing process. The assigning of positive or negative values to experiences according to whether they enhance or impede the maintenance of the individual.

variable interval schedule. In operant conditioning, a reinforcement schedule so structured that the amount of time elapsing before the reward varies but averages out to a certain stable rate.

variable ratio schedule. In operant conditioning, a reinforcement schedule so structured that the number of responses made in order to receive the reward varies but averages out to a certain ratio.

vascular accident. An organic brain disorder in which blockage or breaking of cranial blood vessels results in injury to the brain tissue.

visual aphasia (alexia). A language impairment characterized by inability to understand the written word.

voodoo death. A death which has no ostensible organic cause and is directly attributed to emotional factors.

voyeurism. Sexual gratification through clandestine observation of other people's sexual activities or sexual anatomy.

waxy flexibility. A stuporous state that catatonic schizophrenics occasionally exhibit in which the patient may report that his limbs have a plastic feel and may leave them for long periods of time in positions arranged by another person.

will-to-meaning. In existential philosophy, man's effort to find some reason for existence.

withdrawal symptoms. Temporary psychological and physiological disturbances resulting from the body's attempt to readjust to the absence of a drug.

withdrawing reaction. A condition in which the child is anxious, shy, and withdrawn, living in his own fantasy world. (Cf. *overanxious reaction.*)

word salad. A schizophrenic speech pattern in which words and phrases are combined in a disorganized fashion, seemingly devoid of logic and meaning and even associational links.

References

ABEL, G. G., D. J. LEVIS, and J. CLANCY. Aversion therapy applied to taped sequences of deviant behavior in exhibitionism and other sexual deviations: A preliminary report. *Journal of Behavior Research and Experimental Psychiatry* 1970, *1*(1), 59–66.

ABRAHAM, K. Notes on psychoanalytic investigation and treatment of manic-depressive insanity and allied conditions (1911). In *Selected papers of Karl Abraham, M.D.*, D. Bryan and A. Strachey, trs. London: The Hogarth Press, 1948.

ABRAHAM, K. The first pregenital stage of the libido (1916). In *Selected papers of Karl Abraham, M.D.*, D. Bryan and A. Strachey, trs. London: The Hogarth Press, 1948.

ACHENBACH, T. M. The classification of children's psychiatric symptoms: A factor analytic study. *Psychological Monographs*, 1966, *80* (Whole No. 615).

ACHENBACH, T. M. *Developmental psychopathology*. New York: The Ronald Press, 1974.

ADAMS, M. S., and J. V. NEEL. Children of incest. *Pediatrics*, 1967, *40*, 55–62.

AGRAS, W. S. Behavior therapy in the management of chronic schizophrenia. *American Journal of Psychiatry*, 1967, *124*(2), 240–243.

AGRAS, S., D. SYLVESTER, and D. OLIVEAU. The epidemiology of common fears and phobias. Unpublished manuscript, 1969.

ALBEE, E. *Who's afraid of Virginia Woolf?* New York: Atheneum, 1962.

ALBERTI, R., and M. L. EMMONS. *Your perfect right: A guide to assertive behavior*, rev. ed. San Luis Obispo, Calif.: Impact, 1974.

ALDRIN, E., and W. WARGA. *Return to earth*. New York: Random House, 1973.

ALEXANDER, F. *Psychosomatic medicine*. New York: Norton, 1950.

ALISKAL, H. S., and W. T. McKINNEY. Depressive disorders: Toward a unified hypothesis. *Science*, 1973, *182*, 20–29.

ALLEN, M., S. COHEN, and W. POLLIN. Schizophrenia in veteran twins: A diagnostic review. *American Journal of Psychiatry*, 1972, *128*(8), 939–945.

ALTMAN, R., and L. W. TALKINGTON. Modeling: An alternative behavior modification approach for retardates. *Mental Retardation*, 1973, *9*, 20–23.

ALVAREZ, A. *The savage god: A study of suicide.* London: Weidenfeld and Nicolson, 1971.

AMERICAN PSYCHIATRIC ASSOCIATION. *Diagnostic and statistical manual of mental disorders* (DSM-II), 2nd ed. Washington, D.C.: American Psychiatric Association, 1968.

ANDERSON, K. A. The "shopping" behavior of parents of mentally retarded children: The professional person's role. *Mental Retardation*, 1971, *9*, 3–5.

ANDRON, L., and M. STRUM. Is "I do" in the repertoire of the retarded? *Mental Retardation*, 1973, *11*, 31–34.

ANGYAL, A. *Neurosis and treatment: A holistic theory*. New York: Wiley, 1965.

ANSBACHER, H. L., and R. ROWENA, eds. *The individual psychology of Alfred Adler*. New York: Basic Books, 1956.

ANTHONY, E. J. An experimental approach to the psychopathology of childhood: Sleep disturbances. *British Journal of Medical Psychology*, 1959, *32*, 18–37.

ARIETI, S. *Interpretation of schizophrenia*. New York: Basic Books, 1974a.

ARIETI, S. An overview of schizophrenia from a predominantly psychological approach. *American Journal of Psychiatry*, 1974b, *131*(3), 241–249.

ARONSON, E. *The social animal.* San Francisco, Calif.: Freeman, 1972.

ARONSON, S. M., and B. W. VOLK. The nervous system sphingolipodoses. In C. H. Carter, ed., *Medical aspects of mental retardation.* Springfield, Ill.: Charles C Thomas, 1965.

ARTISS, K. L. *Milieu therapy in schizophrenia.* New York: Grune & Stratton, 1962.

ATTHOWE, J. M., and L. KRASNER. A preliminary report on the application of contingent reinforcement procedures (token economy) on a "chronic" psychiatric ward. *Journal of Abnormal Psychology*, 1968, *73*, 37–43.

AUSMAN, J., T. S. BALL, and D. ALEXANDER. Behavior therapy of pica. *Mental Retardation*, 1974, *12*, 16–18.

AUSUBEL, D. P., and P. AUSUBEL. Ego development among segregated Negro children. In A. H. Passow, ed., *Education in depressed areas.* New York: Bureau of Publications, Teachers College, Columbia University, 1963.

AXLINE, V. M. *Play therapy*, rev. ed. New York: Ballantine, 1969.

AYLLON, T., and N. H. AZRIN. *The token economy: A motivational system for therapy and rehabilitation.* New York: Appleton-Century-Crofts, 1968.

AYLLON, T., and E. HAUGHTON. Control of the behavior of schizophrenic patients by food. *Journal of the Experimental Analysis of Behavior*, 1962, *5*, 343–352.

AYLLON, T., and J. MICHAEL. The psychiatric nurse as a behavioral engineer. *Journal of the Experimental Analysis of Behavior*, 1959, *2*, 323–334.

AZRIN, N. H., B. J. NASTER, and R. JONES. Reciprocity counseling: A rapid learning based procedure for marital counseling. *Behavior Research and Therapy*, 1973, *11*, 365–382.

BAEKELAND, F., L. LUNDWALL, B. KISSIN, and T. SHANAHAN. Correlates of outcome in disulfiram treatment of alcoholism. *The Journal of Nervous and Mental Disease*, 1971, *153*(1), 1–9.

BAGLEY, C. Incest behavior and incest taboo. *Social Problems*, 1969, *16*(4), 505–519.

BAKER, B. L. Symptom treatment and symptom substitution in enuresis. *Journal of Abnormal Psychology*, 1969, *74*, 42–49.

BAKER, R. The use of operant conditioning to reinstate the speech of mute schizophrenics: A progress report. In L. Burns and J. L. Wors-

543

ley, eds., *Behavior therapy in the 1970's*. Bristol, Eng.: John Wright, 1970.

BAKER, R. The use of operant conditioning to reinstate speech in mute schizophrenics. *Behavior Research and Therapy*, 1971, *9*, 329–336.

BAKER, R., J. GARRY, B. STANISH, and B. FRASER. Comparative effects of a token economy in nursery school. *Mental Retardation*, 1972, *10*, 16–19.

BAKEWELL, W. E., JR., and J. A. EWING. Therapy of non-narcotic psychoactive drug dependence. *Current Psychiatric Therapies*, 1969, *9*, 136–143.

BAKWIN, H., and R. M. BAKWIN. *Behavior disorders in children.* Philadelphia, Pa.: W. B. Saunders, 1972.

BALTES, P. B., and K. W. SCHAIE. The myth of the twilight years. In F. Rebelsky, ed., *Life, the continuous process: Readings in human development.* New York: Knopf, 1975.

BAN, T. *Recent advances in the biology of schizophrenia.* Springfield, Ill.: Charles C Thomas, 1973.

BANDURA, A. *Principles of behavior modification.* New York: Holt, Rinehart and Winston, 1969.

BANDURA, A., E. B. BLANCHARD, and B. RITTER. Relative efficacy of desensitization and modeling approaches for inducing behavioral, affective, and attitudinal changes. *Journal of Personality and Social Psychology*, 1969, *13*, 173–199.

BANDURA, A., J. E. GRUSEC, and F. L. MENLOVE. Vicarious extinction of avoidance behavior. *Journal of Personality and Social Psychology*, 1967, *5*, 16–23.

BANDURA, A. and R. WALTERS. *Social learning and personality development.* New York: Holt, Rinehart and Winston, 1963.

BARBER, T. X., and M. J. SILVER. Fact, fiction, and the experimenter bias effect. *Psychological Bulletin Monograph*, 1968, *70*, 1–29.

BARD, M. *Training police as specialists in family crisis intervention.* Washington, D.C.: U.S. Government Printing Office, 1970.

BARLOW, D. H. The treatment of sexual deviation: Toward a comprehensive behavior approach. In K. Calhoune, H. Adams, and K. Mitchell, eds., *Innovative treatment methods in psychopathology.* New York: Wiley, 1974.

BARNES, M., and J. BERKE. *Two accounts of a journey through madness.* New York: Ballantine, 1973.

BARRACLOUGH, B. M., B. NELSON, J. BUNCH, and P. SAINSBURY. The diagnostic classification and psychiatric treatment of 100 suicides. Proceedings of the Fifth International Conference for Suicide Prevention, London, 1969.

BATESON, G., D. JACKSON, J. HALEY, and J. WEAKLAND. Toward a theory of schizophrenia. *Behavioral Science*, 1956, *1*, 251–264.

BATH, K. E., and S. SMITH. An effective token economy system. *Mental Retardation*, 1974, *12*, 41–43.

BATTIE, WILLIAM. *A treatise on madness* (1758). New York: Brunner/Mazel, 1969.

BATTLE, E. S., and J. B. ROTTER. Children's feelings of personal control as related to social class and ethnic group. *Journal of Personality*, 1963, *31*, 482–490.

BAYH, B. (Senator). Opening statement on hearings on the abuse of barbiturates. December 15, 1971.

DE BEAUVOIR, S. *The second sex*, H. M. Parshley, tr. and ed. New York: Bantam, 1961.

DE BEAUVOIR, S. Frank talk on a forbidden subject. *The New York Times Magazine*, March 26, 1972, pp. 38ff.

BECK, A. T. *Depression: Clinical, experimental, and theoretical aspects.* New York: Harper & Row, 1967.

BECK, A. T. The meaning of depression. *Science News*, 1969, *96*(24), 554.

BECK, A. T. Cognition, affect, and psychopathology. *Archives of General Psychiatry*, 1971, *24*, 495–500.

BECK, A. T., and M. S. HURVICH. Psychological correlates of depression: I. Frequency of "masochistic" dream content in a private practice sample. *Psychosomatic Medicine*, 1959, *21*, 50–55.

BECK, A. T., and S. VALIN. Psychotic depressive reaction in soldiers who accidentally killed their buddies. *American Journal of Psychiatry*, 1953, *110*, 347–353.

BECK, A. T., C. H. WARD, M. MENDELSON, J. MOCK, and J. ERBAUGH. An inventory for measuring depression. *Archives of General Psychiatry*, 1961, *4*, 561–571.

BECK, A. T., C. H. WARD, M. MENDELSON, J. MOCK, and J. ERBAUGH. Reliability of psychiatric diagnoses 2: A study of consistency of clinical judgments and ratings. *American Journal of Psychiatry*, 1962, *119*, 351–357.

BECKER, H. S. *Outsiders: Studies in the sociology of deviance.* New York: Free Press, 1963.

BECKETT, P. G., R. SENF, C. E. FROHMAN, and J. S. GOTTLIEB. Energy production and premorbid history in schizophrenia. *Archives of General Psychiatry*, 1963, *8*, 155–162.

BEDNAR, R. L., and G. F. LAWLIS. Empirical research in group psychotherapy. In O. E. Bergin and S. L. Garfield, eds., *Handbook of psychotherapy and behavior change: An empirical analysis.* New York: Wiley, 1971.

BEERS, C. W. *A mind that found itself* (1908), rev. ed. New York: Doubleday, 1970.

BELL, D. S. The experimental reproduction of amphetamine psychosis. *Archives of General Psychiatry*, 1973, *29*(1), 35–40.

BELLAK, L. *The Thematic Apperception Test and the Children's Thematic Apperception Test in clinical use.* New York: Grune & Stratton, 1954.

BENDER, L. A visual motor gestalt test and its clinical use. *Research Monograph of the American Orthopsychiatric Association*, 1938, *3*, xi and 176.

BENEDICT, R. Anthropology and the abnormal. *Journal of General Psychology*, 1934, *10*, 59–82.

BENET, SULA. "Why They Live to Be 100 or Even Older in Abkhasia," *The New York Times Magazine*, December 26, 1971, pp. 3, 28–29, 31–34.

BENJAMIN, H. *The transsexual phenomenon.* New York: Julian Press, 1966.

BENNETT, R., and J. ECKMAN. Attitudes toward aging: A critical examination of recent literature and implications for future research. In C. Eisdorfer and M. P. Lawton, eds., *The psychology of adult development and aging.*

Washington, D.C.: American Psychological Association, 1973.

BENTLER, P. M., and C. PRINCE. Personality characteristics of male transvestites, III. *Journal of Abnormal Psychology*, 1969, *74*(2), 140–143.

BENTLER, P. M., and C. PRINCE. Psychiatric symptomology in transvestites. *Journal of Clinical Psychology*, 1970, *26*(4), 434–455.

BENTLER, P. M., R. W. SHEARMAN, and C. PRINCE. Personality characteristics of male transvestites. *Journal of Clinical Psychology*, 1970, *26*, 287–291.

BERGLER, E. Analysis of an unusual case of fetishism. *Bulletin of the Menninger Clinic*, 1947, *2*, 67–75.

BERNABEU, E. P. The effects of severe crippling on the development of a group of children. *Psychiatry*, 1958, *21*, 169–194.

BERNE, E. *Games people play*. New York: Grove Press, 1964.

BERNSTEIN, D. A. The modification of smoking behavior: A review. *Psychological Bulletin*, 1969, *71*, 418–440.

BERNSTEIN, D. A., and G. L. PAUL. Some comments on therapy analogue research with small animal "phobias." *Journal of Behavior Therapy and Experimental Psychiatry*, 1971, *2*, 225–237.

BETTELHEIM, B. *The empty fortress*. New York: Free Press, 1967.

BIEBER, I., H. DAIN, P. DINCE, M. DRELLECH, H. GRAND, R. GRUNDLACH, M. KREMER, A. RITKIN, C. WILBUR, and T. BIEBER. *Homosexuality: A psychoanalytic study of male homosexuals*. New York: Basic Books, 1962.

BINI, L. Experimental researches on epileptic attacks induced by the electric current. *American Journal of Psychiatry*, 1938. Supplement 94, 172–183.

BINSWANGER, L. Existential analysis of schizophrenia. In W. S. Sahakian, ed., *Psychopathology today*. Ithaca, Ill.: Peacock Publishers, Inc., 1970.

BIRREN, J. E. Translations in gerontology—From lab to life: Psychophysiology and speed of response. *American Psychologist*, 1974, *29*, 808–815.

BLACKMAN, L. S., and H. L. SPARKS. What is special about special

education revisited: The mentally retarded. *Exceptional Children*, 1965, *31*, 242.

BLANE, L., and R. H. ROTH. Voyeurism and exhibitionism. *Perceptual and Motor Skills*, 1967, *24*, 391–400.

BLASHFIELD, R. An evaluation of the DSM-II classification of schizophrenia as a nomenclature. *Journal of Abnormal Psychology*, 1973, *82*, 382–389.

BLATT, B., and F. KAPLAN. *Christmas in purgatory*. Boston: Allyn and Bacon, 1966.

BLAU, Z. S. Structural constraints on friendship in old age. *American Sociological Review*, 1961, *26*, 429–439.

BLEULER, E. *Dementia praecox or the group of schizophrenias* (1911). J. Zinkin, tr. New York: International Universities Press, 1950.

BLISS, E. L., V. B. WILSON, and J. ZWANZIGER. Changes in brain norepinephrine in self-stimulating and "aversive" animals. *Journal of Psychiatric Research*, 1966, *4*, 59–63.

BLISS, E. W., and C. H. BRANCH. *Anorexia nervosa: Its history, psychology, and biology*. New York: Hoeber Medical Book, 1960.

BLUM, G. S. *Psychoanalytic theories of personality*. New York: McGraw-Hill, 1953.

BOCKOVEN, J. S. *Moral treatment in American psychiatry*. New York: Springer, 1963.

BOGGS, E. M. Rights of the retarded—Who's listening. *Journal of Clinical Child Psychology*, 1972. *2*(1), 13–15.

BOLL, T. J., R. HEATON, and R. M. REITAN. Neuropsychological and emotional correlates of Huntington's chorea. *Journal of Nervous and Mental Disease*, 1974, *158*, 61–69.

BOTWINICK, J. *Cognitive processes in maturity and old age*. New York: Springer, 1967.

BOWEN, M. A. A family concept of schizophrenia. In D. D. Jackson, ed., *The etiology of schizophrenia*. New York: Basic Books, 1960.

BOWLBY, J. The nature of the child's tie to his mother. *International Journal of Psychoanalysis*, 1958, *39*, 350–373.

BOWLBY, J. Grief and mourning in

infancy and early childhood. *Psychoanalytic Study of the Child*, 1960, *15*, 9–52.

BRADY, J. P., and D. L. LIND. Experimental analysis of hysterical blindness. In L. P. Ullmann and L. Krasner, eds., *Case studies in behavior modification*. New York: Holt, Rinehart and Winston, 1968.

BRADY, J. V., R. W. PORTER, D. G. CONRAD, and J. W. MASON. Avoidance behavior and the development of gastroduodenal ulcers. *Journal of Experimental Analysis of Behavior*, 1958, *1*, 69–73.

BRAGINSKY, B., and D. BRAGINSKY. Schizophrenic patients in the psychiatric interview: An experimental study of their effectiveness at manipulation. *Journal of Consulting Psychology*, 1967, *21*, 543–547.

BRAGINSKY, B. M., D. D. BRAGINSKY, and K. RING. *Methods of madness: The mental hospital as a last resort*. New York: Holt, Rinehart and Winston, 1969.

BRAGINSKY, B. M., M. GROSSE, and K. RING. Controlling outcomes through impression management: An experimental study of manipulative tactics of mental patients. *Journal of Consulting Psychology*, 1966, *30*, 295–300.

BRAUCHT, G. N., D. BARKARSH, D. FOLLINGSTAD, and K. L. BERRY. Deviant drug use in adolescence: A review of psychosocial correlates. *Psychology Bulletin*, 1973, *79*(2), 92–106.

BRECHER, E. M., and the Editors of *Consumer Reports*. *Licit and illicit drugs*. Mount Vernon, N.Y.: Consumers Union, 1972.

BREED, W. Suicide and loss in social interaction. In E. S. Shneidman, ed., *Essays in self-destruction*. New York: Science House, 1967.

BREGER, L., and J. L. McGUAGH. Critique and reformulation of "learning theory" approaches to psychotherapy and neurosis. *Psychological Bulletin*, 1965, *63*, 338–358.

BRION, S. Korsakoff's syndrome: Clinico-anatomical and physiopathological considerations. In G. A. Talland and N. C. Waugh, eds., *The pathology of memory*. New York: Academic Press, 1969.

BRODIE, H. K. H., N. GARTRELL, G.

DOERING, and T. RHUE. Plasma testosterone levels in heterosexual and homosexual men. *American Journal of Psychiatry*, 1974, *131*(1), 82–83.

BROEN, W. E., JR., and C. Y. NAKAMURA. Reduced range of sensory sensitivity in chronic nonparanoid schizophrenics. *Journal of Abnormal Psychology*, 1972, *79*(1), 106–111.

BROWN, R. W. *Words and things.* New York: Free Press, 1958.

BROWN, W. F. Effectiveness of paraprofessionals: The evidence. *Personnel and Guidance Journal*, 1974, *53*, 257–263.

BRUCH, H. *The importance of overweight.* New York: Norton, 1957.

BUCKNER, H. T. The transvestic career path. *Psychiatry*, 1970, *33*(3), 381–389.

BUHLER, C. Loneliness in maturity. *Journal of Humanistic Psychology*, 1969, *9*, 167–181.

BURCHARD, J. Systematic socialization: A programmed environment for the habilitation of antisocial retardates. *Psychological Record*, 1967, *17*, 461–476.

BUSS, A. H. *Psychopathology.* New York: Wiley, 1966.

BUSSE, E. W. Psychoneurotic reactions and defense mechanisms in the aged. In E. Palmore, ed., *Normal aging.* Durham, N.C.: Duke University Press, 1970.

BUTLER, J. M., and G. V. HAIGH. Changes in the relation between self-concepts and ideal concepts consequent upon client-centered counseling. In C. R. Rogers and R. F. Dymond, eds., *Psychotherapy and personality change.* Chicago: University of Chicago Press, 1954.

BUTLER, R. N., and M. I. LEWIS. *Aging and mental health.* St. Louis, Mo.: C. V. Mosby, 1973.

BUTTERFIELD, E. C. Basic facts about public residential facilities for the mentally retarded. In R. B. Kugel and W. Wolfensberger, eds., *Changing patterns in residential services for the mentally retarded.* Washington, D.C.: President's Committee on Mental Retardation Monograph, 1969.

CAMERON, N. Reasoning, regression and communication in schizophrenia. *Psychological Mono-*

graphs, 1938, *50*, Whole No. 221.

CAMPBELL, J. D. *Manic-depressive disease: Clinical and psychiatric significance.* Philadelphia, Pa.: Lippincott, 1953.

CAMPBELL, M., E. FRIEDMAN, E. DeVITO, L. GREENSPAN, and P. J. COLLINS. Blood serotonin in psychotic and brain damaged children. *Journal of Autism and Childhood Schizophrenia*, 1974, *4*, 33–41.

CANCRO, R. An overview of the schizophrenic syndrome. In R. Cancro, N. Fox, and L. Shapiro, eds., *Strategic intervention in schizophrenia: Current developments in treatment.* New York: Behavioral Publications, 1974.

CANESTRARI, R. E. Paced and self-paced learning in young and elderly adults. *Journal of Gerontology*, 1963, *18*, 165–168.

CANNON, W. B. "Voodoo" death. *American Anthropologist*, 1942, *44*(2), 169–181.

CAPLAN, G. *Principles of preventative psychiatry.* New York: Basic Books, 1964.

CAPUTO, D. V. The parents of the schizophrenic. In E. G. Mishler and N. E. Waxler, eds., *Family processes and schizophrenia.* New York: Science House, 1968.

CARKHUFF, R. R. Differential functioning of lay and professional counselors. *Journal of Counseling Psychology*, 1968, *15*, 117–126.

CARTER, J. W. A case of reactional dissociation. *American Journal of Orthopsychiatry*, 1937, *7*, 219–224.

CATTELL, R. B. The theory of fluid and crystallized intelligence: A critical experiment. *Journal of Educational Psychology*, 1963, *54*, 1–22.

CAUTELA, J. R. Treatment of compulsive behavior by covert sensitization. *Psychological Record*, 1966, *16*, 33–41.

CAUTELA, J. R. Covert sensitization. *Psychological Reports*, 1967, *20*, 459–468.

CAUTELA, J. R., and R. KASTENBAUM. A reinforcement survey schedule for use in therapy, training, and research. *Psychological Reports*, 1967, *20*, 1115–1130.

CAVALLIN, H. Incestuous fathers: A clinical report. *American Journal of Psychiatry*, 1966, *122*(10), 1132–1138.

CHANCE, P. A conversation with Ivar Lovaas. *Psychology Today*, January 1974, *7*, 76–84.

CHAPANIS, A. Relationships between age, visual acuity, and color vision. *Human Biology*, 1950, *22*, 1–31.

CHAPMAN, L. J., and J. P. CHAPMAN. Illusory correlation as an obstacle to the use of valid psychodiagnostic signs. *Journal of Abnormal Psychology*, 1969, *74*, 271–287.

CHESLER, P. *Women and madness.* New York: Doubleday, 1972.

CHRISTOFFEL, H. Male genital exhibitionism. In S. Lorand and M. Bolint, eds., *Perversions: Psychodynamics and therapy.* New York: Random House, 1956.

CISIN, I., and D. CALAHAN. The big drinkers. *Newsweek*, July 6, 1970, p. 57.

CLECKLEY, H. *The mask of sanity*, 4th ed. St. Louis, Mo.: C. V. Mosby, 1964.

COHEN, B. D., G. NACHMANI, and S. ROSENBERG. Referent communication disturbances in acute schizophrenia. *Journal of Abnormal Psychology*, 1974, *83*(1), 1–13.

COHEN, E., J. A. MOTTO, and R. H. SEIDEN. An instrument for evaluating suicide potential: A preliminary study. *American Journal of Psychiatry*, 1966, *122*, 886–891.

COHEN, J. S. Vocational rehabilitation of the mentally retarded: The sheltered workshop. *Mental Retardation Abstracts*, 1966, *3*, 163–169.

COHEN, M., G. BAKER, R. A. COHEN, F. FROMM-REICHMAN, and E. V. WEIGART. An intensive study of twelve cases of manic-depressive psychosis. *Psychiatry*, 1954, *17*, 103–137.

COHEN, M., and T. SEGHORN. Sociometric study of the sex offender. *Journal of Abnormal Psychology*, 1969, *74*, 249–255.

COHEN, S. Statement to the Subcommittee to Investigate Juvenile Delinquency of the Committee on the Judiciary, U.S. Senate, on control of drug abuse. December 15, 1971.

COHEN, S., and K. S. DITMAN. Prolonged adverse reactions to lysergic acid diethylamide. *Archives of General Psychiatry*, 1963, *8*, 479.

COLE, J. O. Phenothiazine treatment in acute schizophrenia: Effectiveness. *Archives of General Psychia-*

try, 1964, *10*, 246–261.

COLLIGAN, D. That helpless feeling: The dangers of stress. *New York*, July 14, 1975, pp. 28–32.

COLWELL, C. N., E. RICHARDS, R. B. MCCARVER, and N. R. ELLIS. Evaluation of self-help habit training. *Mental Retardation*, 1973, *11*, 14–18.

COMFORT, ALEX. *The joy of sex*. New York: Crown, 1972.

COMMISSION ON CHRONIC ILLNESS. *Chronic Illness in a large city*, Vol. IV. Cambridge: Harvard University Press, 1957.

CONNALLY, J. The social and medical circumstances of old people admitted to a psychiatric hospital. *The Medical Officer*, August 1962, 95–100.

CONOVER, J. V. Community day-care programs for severely and profoundly retarded children. *The New Jersey Welfare Reporter*, 1967, *18*, 19–25.

COOPER, A. J. A clinical study of "coital anxiety" in male potency disorders. *Journal of Psychosomatic Research*, 1969, *13*, 143–147.

COOPER, D. *Psychiatry and anti-psychiatry*. London: Tavistock Publications, 1967.

COOPER, J. E., R. E. KENDELL, B. J. GURLAND, L. SHARP, J. R. M. COPELAND, and R. SIMON. *Psychiatric diagnosis in New York and London: A comparative study of mental hospital admissions*. New York: Oxford University Press, 1972.

COOPER, M. *Pica*. Springfield, Ill.: Charles C Thomas, 1957.

COPPEN, A. The biochemistry of affective disorders. *British Journal of Psychiatry*, 1967, *113*, 1237–1264.

CRAFTS, M., G. STEPHENSON, and C. GRANGER. A controlled trial of authoritarian and self-governing regimes on adolescent psychopaths. *American Journal of Orthopsychiatry*, 1964, *34*, 543–554.

CREAK, E. M. Childhood psychosis: A review of 100 cases. *British Journal of Psychiatry*, 1963, *109*, 84–89.

CRISP, A. H. Premorbid factors in adult disorders of weight, with particular reference to primary anorexia nervosa (weight phobia). *Journal of Psychosomatic Medicine*, 1970, *14*(1), 1–22.

CROMWELL, R. L., and P. R.

DOKECKI. Schizophrenic language: A disattention interpretation. In S. Rosenberg and J. H. Koplin, eds., *Developments in applied psycholinguistics research*. New York: Macmillan, 1968.

CUMMING, J., and E. CUMMING. *Ego and milieu*. New York: Atherton, 1962.

DAILEY, W. F., G. J. ALLEN, J. M. CHINSKY, and S. W. VEIT. Attendant behavior and attitudes toward institutionalized retarded children. *American Journal of Mental Deficiency*, 1974, *78*, 586–591.

DAIN, N. *Concepts of sanity in the United States, 1789–1895*. New Brunswick, N.J.: Rutgers University Press, 1964.

DATEL, W. E., and J. A. GENGERELLI. Reliability of Rorschach interpretations. *Journal of Projective Techniques*, 1955, *19*, 372–381.

DAVIDS, A. *Children in conflict: A casebook*. New York: Wiley, 1974.

DAVIES, M. Blood pressure and personality. *Journal of Psychosomatic Research*, 1970, *14*, 89–104.

DAVIS, J. M. Efficacy of tranquilizing and anti-depressant drugs. *Archives of General Psychiatry*, 1965, *13*, 552–572.

DAVISON, G. C. Elimination of a sadistic fantasy by a client-controlled counterconditioning technique: A case study. *Journal of Abnormal Psychology*, 1968, *73*, 84–90.

DEMYER, M. K., S. BARTON, W. E. DEMYER, J. A. NORTON, J. ALLEN, and R. STEELE. Prognosis in autism: A follow-up study. *Journal of Autism and Childhood Schizophrenia*, 1973, *3*, 199–246.

DENELSKY, G. Y., and V. H. DENENBERG. Infantile stimulation and adult exploratory behavior: Effects of handling upon tactual variation seeking. *Journal of Comparative and Physiological Psychology*, 1967, *63*, 309–312.

DES LAURIERS, A. M., and C. F. CARLSON. *Your child is asleep: Early infantile autism, etiology, treatment, parental influences*. Homewood, Ill.: Dorsey, 1969.

DEUTSCH, A. *The mentally ill in America*, 2nd ed. New York and London: Columbia University Press, 1949.

DEUTSCH, M. The role of social class in language development and cognition. *American Journal of Orthopsychiatry*, 1965, *35*, 78–88.

DEUTSCHER, I. The quality of post-parental life. In F. Rebelsky, ed., *Life, the continuous process: Readings in human development*. New York: Knopf, 1975.

DOUGLAS, V. I., and F. A. SANDERS. A pilot study of Rimland's Diagnostic Checklist with autistic and mentally retarded children. *Journal of Child Psychology and Psychiatry*, 1969, *10*, 105–109.

DRUG ABUSE COUNCIL. *Marijuana survey—State of Oregon*. December 15, 1974.

DRUG USE IN AMERICA: Problem in perspective. U.S. Government Printing Office, Washington, D.C., #5266-00003, March 1973.

DUKE, M. P., and M. C. MULLINS. Preferred interpersonal distance as a function of locus of control orientation in chronic schizophrenics, nonschizophrenic patients, and normals. *Journal of Consulting and Clinical Psychology*, 1973, *41*(2), 230–234.

DUNBAR, H. F. *Emotions and bodily changes*. New York: Columbia University Press, 1935.

DUNLOP, E. Use of antidepressants and stimulants. *Modern Treatment*, 1965, *2*, 543–568.

DURKHEIM, E. *Le suicide*. Paris: Librarie Felix Alcan (1897). J. A. Spaulding and G. Simpson, trs. Glencoe, Ill.: Free Press, 1951.

EATON, J., and R. J. WEIL. The mental health of the Hutterites. *Scientific American*, 1953, *189*, 31–37.

EBERHARDY, F. The view from "the couch." *Journal of Child Psychology and Psychiatry*, 1967, *8*, 257–263.

EDDY, N. B., H. HALBACH, H. ISBELL, and M. H. SEEVERS. Drug dependence: Its significance and characteristics. WHO Bulletin, 1965, *32*, 721–733.

EDWARDS, A. L. The relationship between the judged desirability of a trait and the probability that the trait will be endorsed. *Journal of Applied Psychology*, 1953, *37*, 90–93.

EICHENWALD, H. F., and P. C. FRY. Nutrition and learning. *Science*, 1969, *163*, 644–648.

EISDORFER, C., and M. P. LAWTON, eds. *The psychology of adult development and aging.* Washington, D.C.; American Psychological Association, 1973.

EISENBERG, L., and L. KANNER. Early infantile autism. *American Journal of Orthopsychiatry*, 1956, *26*, 556–566.

ELLINGSON, R. J. Incidence of EEG abnormality among patients with mental disorders of apparently nonorganic origin: A criminal review. *American Journal of Psychiatry*, 1954, *111*, 263–275.

ELLIS, A. Rational psychotherapy. *Journal of General Psychology*, 1958, *59*, 35–49.

ELLIS, A. *Reason and emotion in psychotherapy.* New York: Lyle Stuart, 1962.

ELLIS, A. *The case for sexual liberty.* Tucson, Ariz.: Seymour Press, 1965.

ELMORE, C. M., and GORHAM, D. R. Measuring the impairment of the abstracting function with the proverbs test. *Journal of Clinical Psychology*, 1957, *13*, 263–266.

ENGEL, G. A life setting conducive to illness: The giving-up-given-up complex. *Bulletin of the Menninger Clinic*, 1968, *32*, 355–365.

EPSTEIN, H. A sin or a right? *The New York Times Magazine*, September 8, 1974, pp. 91–94.

ERIKSON, E. H. Identity and the life cycle. In *Psychological Issues*, Vol. 1. New York: International Universities Press, 1959.

ERIKSON, E. H. *Childhood and society,* rev. ed. New York: Norton, 1963.

ETHNIC DIFFERENCES IN ALCOHOL SENSITIVITY. *Science*, 1972, *175*, 449–450 (Abstract).

EVANS, D. R. An exploratory study into the treatment of exhibitionism by means of emotive imagery and aversive conditioning. *Canadian Psychologist*, 1967, *8*, 162.

EVANS, R. B. Childhood parental relationships of homosexual man. *Journal of Consulting and Clinical Psychology*, 1969, *33*, 129–135.

EWEN, D. *Journey to greatness: The life and music of George Gershwin.* New York: Holt, Rinehart and Winston, 1956.

EYSENCK, H. J. The effects of psychotherapy: An evaluation. *Journal of Consulting Psychology*, 1952, *16*, 319–324.

EYSENCK, H. J. *Behavior therapy and the neuroses.* London: Pergamon, 1960a.

EYSENCK, H. J. Classification and the problem of diagnosis. In H. J. Eysenck, ed., *Handbook of abnormal psychology.* London: Pitman, 1960b.

EYSENCK, H. J. The effects of psychotherapy. In H. J. Eysenck, ed., *Handbook of abnormal psychology.* New York: Basic Books, 1961.

EYSENCK, H. J. *The biological basis of personality.* Springfield, Ill.: Charles C Thomas, 1967.

FAIRWEATHER, G. W., D. H. SANDERS, H. MAYNARD, and D. L. CRESSLER. *Community life for the mentally ill: An alternative to institutional care.* Chicago: Aldine, 1969.

FARBER, I. E., H. F. HARLOW, and L. J. WEST. Brainwashing conditions and DDD (debility, dependency and dread). *Sociometry*, 1957, *20*, 271–285.

FABEROW, N. L., and R. E. LITMAN. A comprehensive suicide prevention program. Suicide Prevention Center of Los Angeles, 1958–1969. Unpublished final report DHEW NIMH Grants No. MH 14946 and MH 00128. Los Angeles, 1970.

FEDERAL BUREAU OF INVESTIGATION. *Uniform Crime Reports.* Washington, D.C.: U.S. Government Printing Office, 1975.

FENICHEL, O. *The psychoanalytic theory of neurosis.* New York: Norton, 1945.

FENZ, W. D., and J. VELNER. Physiological concomitants of behavior indexes in schizophrenia. *Journal of Abnormal Psychology*, 1970, *76*(1), 27–35.

FERNALD, W. E. The history of the treatment of the feeble-minded. *Proceedings of the National Conference on Charities and Correction*, 1893, *20*, 203–221.

FERSTER, C. B. Positive reinforcement and behavioral deficits of autistic children. *Child Development*, 1961, *32*, 437–456.

FERSTER, C. B. Classification of behavioral pathology. In L. Krasner and L. P. Ullmann, eds., *Research in behavioral modification.* New York: Holt, Rinehart and Winston, 1965.

FERSTER, C. B. A functional analysis of depression. *American Psychologist*, 1973, *28*, 857–870.

FILSKOV, S. B., and S. G. GOLDSTEIN. Diagnostic validity of the Halstead-Reitan neuropsychological battery. *Journal of Consulting and Clinical Psychology*, 1974, *42*, 382–388.

FINCH, J. R., J. P. SMITH, and A. D. POKORNY. Vehicular studies. Paper presented at meetings of the American Psychiatric Association, May 1970.

FISH, J. F. The classification of schizophrenia. *Journal of Mental Science*, 1957, *103*, 443–465.

FLENDER, H., ed. *We were hooked.* New York: Random House, 1972.

FLORSHEIM, J., and O. PETERFREUND. The intelligence of parents of psychotic children. *Journal of Autism and Childhood Schizophrenia*, 1974, *4*, 61–70.

FORD, C. S., and F. A. BEACH. *Patterns of sexual behavior.* New York: Ace Books, 1951.

FOREL, A. *Out of my life and work.* B. Miall, tr. London: Allen and Unwin, 1937.

FOUCAULT, M. *Madness and civilization.* Richard Howard, tr. New York: Random House, 1965.

FRANK, G. *The Boston strangler.* New York: New American Library, 1966.

FRANKL, V. E. *The doctor and the soul.* New York: Knopf, 1955.

FRANKL, V. E. *Man's search for meaning.* Boston: Beacon Press, 1962.

FRANKL, V. E. *Psychotherapy and existentialism.* New York: Washington Square Press, 1967.

FREEDMAN, B., and L. J. CHAPMAN. Early subjective experience in schizophrenic episodes. *Journal of Abnormal Psychology*, 1973, *82*(1), 46–54.

FREEMAN, E. H., B. F. FEINGOLD, K. SCHLESINGER, and F. J. GORMAN. Psychological variables in allergic disorders: A review. *Psychosomatic Medicine*, 1964, *26*, 543–575.

FREEMAN, S. W., and C. L. THOMP-

SON. Parent-child training. *Mental Retardation*, 1973, *11*, 8–10.

FREEMAN, T., J. L. CAMERON, and A. McGHIE. *Studies on psychosis.* New York: International Universities Press, 1966.

FREEMAN, W., and R. G. MEYER. A behavioral alteration of sexual preferences in the human male. *Behavior Therapy*, 1975, *6*, 206–212.

FREUD, A. The widening scope of indications for psychoanalysis. *Journal of the American Psychoanalytic Association*, 1954, *2*, 607–620.

FREUD, A. *Normality and pathology: Assessment of development.* New York: International Universities Press, 1965.

FREUD, A. Indications and contraindications for child analysis. *Psychoanalytic Study of the Child*, 1968, *23*, 37–46.

FREUD, S. Three essays on sexuality (1905). In J. Strachey, ed., *The standard edition of the complete psychological works of Sigmund Freud*, Vol. III. London: The Hogarth Press, 1953.

FREUD, S. Analysis of a phobia in a five-year-old child (1909). In *Collected papers*, Vol. III. London: The Hogarth Press, 1953.

FREUD, S. Psycho-analytic notes upon an autobiographical account of a case of paranoia (Dementia Paranoides) (1911). In *Collected papers*, Vol. III. London: The Hogarth Press, 1925.

FREUD, S. Mourning and melancholia (1917). In *Collected papers*, Vol. IV, J. Riviere, tr. London: The Hogarth Press, 1924.

FREUD, S. Beyond the pleasure principle (1920). In J. Strachey, ed., *The standard edition of the complete psychological works of Sigmund Freud*, Vol. XVIII. London: The Hogarth Press, 1953.

FREUD, S. *The ego and the id* (1923). London: The Hogarth Press, 1947.

FREUD, S. *The questioning of lay analysis* (1926). In J. Strachey, ed., *The standard edition of the complete psychological works of Sigmund Freud*, Vol. XX. London. The Hogarth Press, 1953.

FREUD, S. *The interpretation of dreams.* New York: Macmillan, 1932.

FREUD, S. Analysis terminable and interminable (1937). In *Collected papers*, Vol. V. London: The Hogarth Press, 1950.

FREUD, S. *An autobiographical study.* J. Strachey, tr. London: The Hogarth Press and the Institute of Psychoanalysis, 1948.

FREUD, S. Femininity. In Jean Strouse, ed., *Women and analysis: Dialogues on psychoanalytic views of femininity.* New York: Dell, 1974.

FRIEDMAN, M., and R. H. ROSENMAN. *Type A behavior and your heart.* New York: Knopf, 1974.

FRIEDMAN, P. R. Mental retardation and the law: A report on the status of current cases. *Journal of Clinical Child Psychology*, 1971, *2*(1), 37–39.

FROMM-REICHMANN, F. *Psychoanalysis and psychotherapy: Selected papers.* D. M. Bullard, ed. Chicago: University of Chicago Press, 1974.

FROSCH, W. A., E. S. ROBBINS, and M. STERN. Untoward reactions to lysergic acid diethylamide (LSD) resulting in hospitalization. *The New England Journal of Medicine*, 1965, *273*(23), 1236.

GAITZ, C. M. *Aging and the brain.* New York: Plenum Press, 1972.

GALLEMORE, J., and W. WILSON. Adolescent maladjustment or affective disorder? *American Journal of Psychiatry*, 1972, *129*, 608–619.

GALLUP, GEORGE, JR., and JOHN O. DAVIES III. *Religion in America: 1971*, The Gallup Opinion Index, April 1971, Report No. 70.

GARDNER, E. A. The role of the classification system in outpatient psychiatry. In M. N. Katz, J. O. Cole, and W. E. Barton, eds., *The role and methodology of classification in psychiatry and psychopathology.* Washington, D.C.: Public Health Service Publication No. 1584, 1965.

GARDNER, W. I. *Behavior modification in mental retardation.* Chicago: Aldine Atherton, 1971.

GARMEZY, N. Process and reactive schizophrenia: Some conceptions and issues. *Schizophrenia Bulletin*, 1970, *2*, 30–67.

GARMEZY, N. Vulnerability research and the issue of primary prevention. *American Journal of Orthopsychiatry*, 1971, *41*, 101–116.

GARMEZY, N. Children at risk: The search for the antecedents of schizophrenia. Part I. Conceptual models and research methods. *Schizophrenia Bulletin*, 1974, No. 8, 14–90.

GEBHARD, P. H. Incidence of overt homosexuality in the United States and Western Europe. In J. M. Livingood, ed., National Institute of Mental Health Task Force on Homosexuality: Final Report and Background Papers. Rockville, Md.: National Institute of Mental Health, 1972.

GEBHARD, P. H., J. H. GAGNON, W. B. POMEROY, and C. V. CHRISTENSON. *Sex offenders.* New York: Harper & Row, 1965.

GEER, J. H. The development of a scale to measure fear. *Behavior Research and Therapy*, 1965, *3*, 45–53.

GEER, J. H., and E. S. KATKIN. Treatment of insomnia using a variant of systematic desensitization. *Journal of Abnormal Psychology*, 1966, *71*, 161–164.

GEER, J. H. and P. SILVERMAN. Treatment of a recurrent nightmare by behavior modification procedures: A case study. *Journal of Abnormal Psychology*, 1967, *72*, 188–190.

GIOVANNONI, J. M., and L. GUREL. Socially disruptive behavior of ex-mental patients. *Archives of General Psychiatry*, 1967, *17*, 146–153.

GITTLEMAN, M., and H. G. BIRCH. Childhood schizophrenia: Intellect, neurologic status, perinatal risk, prognosis, and family pathology. *Archives of General Psychiatry*, 1967, *17*, 16–25.

GLASSER, R. J. *The body is the hero.* New York: Random House, 1976.

GLASSMAN, A. H. Indoleamines and affective disorders. *Psychosomatic Medicine*, 1969, *2*, 107–114.

GODDARD, H. H. *The Kallikak family.* New York: Macmillan, 1912.

GOFFMAN, E. *Asylums: Essays on the social situation of mental patients and other inmates.* New York: Doubleday, 1961.

GOLDBERG, L. R. The effectiveness of clinicians' judgments: The diagnosis of organic brain damage from the Bender-Gestalt Test. *Journal of Consulting Psychology*, 1959, *23*, 25–28.

GOLDBERG, S. C., G. L. KLERMAN, and J. O. COLE. Changes in schizophrenic psychopathology and ward behavior as a function of phenothiazine treatment. *British Journal of Psychiatry*, 1965, *111*, 120–132.

GOLDFARB, W. Corrective socialization: A rationale for the treatment of schizophrenic children. *Canadian Psychiatric Association Journal*, 1965, *10*, 481–496.

GOLDFARB, W., E. YUDKOVITZ, and N. GOLDFARB. Verbal symbols to designate objects: An experimental study of communication in mothers of schizophrenic children. *Journal of Autism and Childhood Schizophrenia*, 1973, *3*, 281–298.

GOLDIAMOND, I. Self-control procedures in personal behavior problems. *Psychological Reports*, 1965, *17*, 851–858.

GOLDSTEIN, A. J., M. SERBER, and G. PIAGET. Induced anger as a reciprocal inhibitor of fear. *Journal of Behavior Therapy and Experimental Psychiatry*, 1970, *1*, 67–70.

GOLDSTEIN, K. Methodological approach to the study of schizophrenic thought disorder. In J. S. Kasanin, ed., *Language and thought in schizophrenia*. Berkeley: University of California Press, 1944.

GOLDSTEIN, K. *Aftereffects of brain injuries in war: Their evaluation and treatment*. New York: Grune & Stratton, 1948.

GOODWIN, D. W., F. SCHUISINGER, L. HERMANSEN, S. B. GUZE, and G. WINOKUR. Alcohol problems in adoptees raised apart from alcoholic biological parents. *Archives of General Psychiatry*, 1973, *28*, 238–243.

GORHAM, D. R. A proverbs test for clinical and experimental use. *Psychological Reports*, 1956, *2*, 1–12 (Monograph Supplement No. 1).

GOSHEN, C. E. *Documentary history of psychiatry*. London: Vision, 1967.

GOTTESMAN, I., and J. SHIELDS. *Schizophrenia and genetics*. New York: Academic Press, 1972.

GOUGH, H. C. A sociological theory of psychopathy. *American Journal of Sociology*, 1948, *53*, 359–366.

GOZALI, J., and J. GONEVA. Citizenship training. *Mental Retardation*, 1973, *11*, 49–50.

GRAHAM, D. T. Some research on psychophysiologic specificity and its relation to psychosomatic disease. In R. Roessler and W. S. Greenfield, eds., *Physiological correlates of psychological disease*. Madison: University of Wisconsin Press, 1962.

GRAHAM, D. T. Health, disease, and the mind-body problem: Linguistic parallelism. *Psychosomatic Medicine*, 1967, *39*, 52–71.

GRAHAM, F. P. Curbs on psychiatrist in court. *New York Times*, October, 27, 1968, Section 4, p. 13.

GRANT, C. T. States of consciousness and state-specific sciences. *Science*, 1972, *176*, 1203–1210.

GREEN, R. Guidelines to the management of the transsexual patient. *Roche Reports*, 1971, *11*(8), 3, 6.

GREENBLATT, M., G. H. GROSSER, and H. WECHSLER. Differential responses of hospitalized depressed patients to somatic therapy. *American Journal of Psychiatry*, 1964, *120*, 935–943.

GREER, S. Study of parental loss in neurotics and sociopaths. *Archives of General Psychiatry*, 1964, *11*, 177–180.

GREGORY, I., and E. ROSEN. *Abnormal psychology*. Philadelphia, Pa.: W. B. Saunders, 1965.

GRINKER, R. R., and J. P. SPIEGEL. *Man under stress*. New York: Blakiston, 1945.

GROSSMAN, H. J., ed. *Manual on terminology and classification in mental retardation*. Washington, D.C.: American Association on Mental Deficiency, 1973.

GROUP FOR THE ADVANCEMENT OF PSYCHIATRY, COMMITTEE ON CHILD PSYCHIATRY. *Psychopathological disorders in childhood: Theoretical considerations and a proposed classification*. GAP Report No. 62, New York, June 1966.

GRUENBERG, E. M. Community conditions and psychoses of the elderly. *The American Journal of Psychiatry*, 1954, *110*, 888–896.

GUNDERSON, J. G., J. H. AUTRY, and L. R. MOSHER. Special report: Schizophrenia, 1973. *Schizophrenia Bulletin*, 1974, No. 9, 15–54.

GUREL, L. A ten-year perspective on outcome in functional psychosis. Highlights of the 15th Annual Conference, Veterans Administration Cooperative Studies in Psychiatry, Houston, Texas, 1970, 92–102.

GURLAND, B. J. A broad clinical assessment of psychopathology in the aged. In C. Eisdorfer and M. P. Lawton, eds., *The psychology of adult development and aging*. Washington, D.C.: American Psychological Association, 1973.

HAIN, J. D., R. H. BUTCHER, and I. STEVENSON. Systematic desensitization therapy: An analysis of results in twenty-seven patients. *British Journal of Psychiatry*, 1966, *112*, 295–307.

HALEY, J. *Strategies of psychotherapy*. New York: Grune & Stratton, 1963.

HALL, C. S. Current trends in research of dreams. In D. Bower and L. E. Abt, eds., *Progress in clinical psychology*, Vol. 2. New York: Grune & Stratton, 1956.

HALL, E. A conversation with Nobel Prize winner Niko Tinbergen. *Psychology Today*, March 1974, *7*, 65–80.

HALLEK, S. Therapy is the handmaiden of the status quo. *Psychology Today*, 1971, *4*(11), 30–32, 98–100.

HALLOWITZ, E. The challenge to the group therapist created by a society in flux. *International Journal of Group Psychotherapy*, 1970, *20*, 423–434.

HALPERN, A. General unemployment and vocational opportunities for EMR individuals. *American Journal of Mental Deficiency*, 1973, *78*, 123–127.

HARDER, T. The psychopathology of infanticide. *Acta Psychiatrica Scandinavia*, 1967, *43*, 196–245.

HARE, R. D. Psychopathology, autonomic functioning and the orienting response. *Journal of Abnormal Psychology*, 1968, *73* (Monograph Supplement 3, part 2), 1–24.

HARE, R. D. *Psychopathy: Theory and research*. New York: Wiley, 1970.

HARLOW, H. A brief look at autistic children. *Psychiatry and Social Science Review*, 1969, *3*(1), 27–29.

HARLOW, H. F. Early social deprivation and later behavior in the monkey. In H. H. Garner and J. E. P. Toman, eds., *Unfinished tasks in the behavioral sciences*.

Baltimore, Md.: Williams and Wilkins, 1964.

HARLOW, J. Recovery from the passage of an iron bar through the head. *Publication of the Massachusetts Medical Society*, 1868, *2*, 327–340.

HARRIS, S. E. Schizophrenics' mutual glance patterns. *Dissertation Abstracts*, 1968, *29B*, 2202.

HASLAM, M. T. The treatment of an obsessional patient by reciprocal inhibition. *Behavior Research and Therapy*, 1965, *2*, 213–216.

HATHAWAY, S. R., and J. C. McKINLEY. *Minnesota Multiphasic Personality Inventory: Manual*. New York: The Psychological Corporation, 1943.

HAVIGHURST, R. J. Suicide and education. In E. S. Shneidman, ed., *On the nature of suicide*. San Francisco, Calif.: Jossey-Bass, 1969.

HEATH, R. G. A biochemical hypothesis on the etiology of schizophrenia. In D. D. Jackson, ed., *The etiology of schizophrenia*. New York: Basic Books, 1960.

HEBB, D. O. The effects of early experience on problem solving at maturity. *American Psychologist*, 1947, *2*, 306–307.

HEKIMIAN, L. J., and S. GERSHON. Characteristics of drug abusers admitted to a psychiatric hospital. *Journal of the American Medical Association*, 1968, *205*(3), 125–130.

HENDERSON, D., and R. D. GILLESPIE. *Textbook of psychiatry for students and practitioners*, Ivor R. C. Batchelor, ed. London and New York: Oxford University Press, 1969.

HERMALIN, B., and N. O'CONNOR. *Psychological experiments with autistic children*. London: Pergamon Press, 1970.

HESTON, L. L. Psychiatric disorders in foster home reared children of schizophrenic mothers. *British Journal of Psychiatry*, 1966, *112*, 819–825.

HIERONYMUS, A. N. A study of social class motivation: Relationships between anxiety for education and certain socio-economic and intellectual variables. *Journal of Educational Psychology*, 1951, *42*, 193–205.

HINGTGEN, J. N., and D. W. CHURCHILL. Differential effects of behavior modification in four mute autistic boys. In D. W. Churchill, G. D. Alpern, and M. K. DeMyer, eds., *Infantile autism*. Springfield, Ill.: Charles C Thomas, 1971.

HIRSCHFELD, M. *Sexual anomalies and perversions*. New York: Emerson Books, 1944.

HNATIOW, M., and P. J. LANG. Learned stabilization of cardiac rate. *Psychophysiology*, 1965, *1*, 330–336.

HOFFMAN, A. LSD discoverer disputes "chance" factor in finding. *Psychiatric News*, 1971, *6*(8), 23–26.

HOGAN, R. A. The implosive technique. *Behavior Research and Therapy*, 1968, *6*, 423–431.

HOLDEN, C. Nader on mental health centers: A movement that got bogged down. *Science*, 1972, *177*, 413–415.

HOLDEN, C. Altered states of consciousness: Mind researchers meet to discuss exploration and mapping of "inner space." *Science*, 1973, *179*, 982–983.

HOLLINGSHEAD, A. B., and F. C. REDLICH. *Social class and mental illness*. New York: Wiley, 1958.

HOLMES, T. H., and R. H. RAHE. The social readjustment rating scale. *Journal of Psychosomatic Research*, 1967, *11*, 213–218.

HOLMES, T. S., and T. H. HOLMES. Short-term intrusions into the life style routine. *Journal of Psychosomatic Research*, 1970, *14*, 121–132.

HOLTZMAN, W. H. and S. B. SELLS. Prediction of flying success by clinical analysis of test protocols. *Journal of Abnormal and Social Psychology*, 1954, *49*, 485–490.

HONIGMAN, J. J. *Personality in culture*. New York: Harper & Row, 1967.

HOOKER, E. The adjustment of the male overt homosexual. *Journal of Projective Techniques*, 1957, *21*(1), 18–31.

HOPKINSON, G. A genetic study of affective illness in patients over 50. *British Journal of Psychiatry*, 1964, *110*, 244–254.

HORNEY, K. *Our inner conflicts*. New York: Norton, 1945.

HORNEY, K. *Feminine psychology*. Harold Kelman, ed. New York: Norton, 1967.

HOUTS, P. S., and M. SERBER, eds. *After the turn-on what? Learning perspectives on humanistic groups*. Champaign, Ill.: Research Press, 1972.

HOWARD, K. I. The convergent and discriminant validation of ipsative ratings from three projective instruments. *Journal of Clinical Psychology*, 1962, *18*, 183–188.

HUGHES, J. R. A review of the positive spike phenomenon. In W. Wilson, ed., *Applications of electroencephalography in psychiatry*. Durham, N.C.: Duke University Press, 1965.

"J." *The sensuous woman*. New York: Lyle Stuart, 1970.

JACOBS, P. A., M. BRUNTON, and M. M. MELVILLE. Aggressive behavior, mental subnormality, and the XYY male. *Nature*, 1965, *208*, 1351–1352.

JACOBSON, E. *Progressive relaxation*. Chicago: University of Chicago Press, 1938.

JAMES, W. E., R. B. MEFFORD, and I. KIMBELL. Early signs of Huntington's chorea. *Diseases of the Nervous System*, 1969, *30*, 556–559.

JANET, P. *The major symptoms of hysteria*, 2nd ed. New York: Macmillan, 1929.

JELLINEK, E. M. *Phases in the drinking history of alcoholics*. New Haven, Conn.: Hillhouse Press, 1946.

JENKINS, R. L. Psychiatric syndromes in children and their relation to family background. *American Journal of Orthopsychiatry*, 1966, *36*, 450–457.

JENKINS, R. L. Classification of behavior problems of children. *American Journal of Psychiatry*, 1969, *125*(8), 68–75.

JENSEN, A. R. Learning ability in retarded, average and gifted children. *Merrill-Palmer Quarterly*, 1963, *9*, 123–140.

JENSEN, A. R. How can we boost IQ and scholastic achievement? *Harvard Educational Review*, 1969, *39*, 1–123.

JERSILD, A. T., F. V. MARKEY, and C. L. JERSILD. Children's fears, dreams, wishes, daydreams, likes, dislikes, pleasant and unpleasant memories. In A. T. Jersild, ed., *Child psychology*. Englewood Cliffs, N. J.: Prentice-Hall, 1960.

JOHANNSEN, W. J., S. H. FRIEDMAN, T. H. LEITSCHUK, and H. AMMONS. A study of certain schizophrenic dimensions and their relationship to double alternation learning. *Journal of Consulting Psychology*, 1963, *27*, 375–382.

JOHN, V. P. The intellectual development of slum children: Some preliminary findings. *American Journal of Orthopsychiatry*, 1963, *33*, 813–822.

JOHNSON, J. E., and T. P. PETZEL. Temporal orientation and time estimation in chronic schizophrenics. *Journal of Clinical Psychology*, 1971, *27*(2), 194–196.

JOHNSON, M. H. Verbal abstracting ability and schizophrenia. *Journal of Consulting Psychology*, 1966, *30*, 275–277.

JOHNSON, W. *Stuttering in children and adults*. Minneapolis: University of Minnesota Press, 1955.

JOINT COMMISSION ON MENTAL HEALTH OF CHILDREN. *Crisis in child mental health*: *Challenge for the 1970's*. New York: Harper & Row, 1970.

JONES, E. *The life and works of Sigmund Freud*, 3 vols. Vol. 1. *The formative years and the great discoveries, 1856–1900*. 1953. Vol. 2. *Years of maturity, 1901–1919*. 1955. Vol. 3. *The last phase, 1919–1939*. 1957. New York: Basic Books.

JONES, E. *The life and work of Sigmund Freud*. L. Trilling and S. Marcus, eds. New York: Doubleday Anchor, 1963.

JONES, M. *The therapeutic community*: *A new treatment method in psychiatry*. New York: Basic Books, 1953.

JONES, M. C. A laboratory study of fear: The case of Peter. *Pedagogical Seminary*, 1924, *31*, 308–315.

JUNG, C. G. *Modern man in search of a soul*. New York: Harcourt, 1933.

JUNG, C. G. *Mandala symbolism*. R. F. C. Hull, tr. Princeton, N.J.: Princeton University Press, Bollingen Series, 1972.

JUSTICE, R. S., J. BRADLEY, and G. O'CONNOR. Foster family care for the retarded: Management concerns of the caretaker. *Mental Retardation*, 1971, *9*, 12–15.

KAHN, E. J., JR. The American people. New York: Weybright and Talley, 1974.

KAHN, R. L. Stress: From 9 to 5. *Psychology Today*, 1969, *3*(4), 34–38.

KALLMANN, F. J. Twin and sibship study of overt male homosexuality. *American Journal of Human Genetics*, 1952, *4*, 136–146.

KALLMANN, F. J. *Heredity in health and mental disorder*. New York: Norton, 1953.

KALLMANN, F. J., and B. ROTH. Genetic aspects of preadolescent schizophrenia. *American Journal of Psychiatry*, 1956, *112*, 599–606.

KANDEL, D. Adolescent marihuana use: Role of parents and peers. *Science*, 1973, *181*, 1067–1069.

KANFER, F. H., and J. S. PHILLIPS. *Learning foundations of behavior therapy*. New York: Wiley, 1970.

KANFER, F. H., and G. SASLOW. Behavioral diagnosis. In C. M. Franks, ed., *Behavioral therapy*: *Appraisal and status*. New York: McGraw-Hill, 1969.

KANNER, L. *Child psychiatry*, 3rd ed. Springfield, Ill.: Charles C Thomas, 1957.

KANNER, L. Do behavior symptoms always indicate psychopathology? *Journal of Child Psychology and Psychiatry*, 1960, *1*, 17–25.

KANNER, L., and L. EISENBERG. Notes on the follow-up studies of autistic children. In P. Hoch and J. Zubin, eds., *Psychopathology of childhood*. New York: Grune & Stratton, 1955.

KANTOR, R. E., J. M. WALLNER, and C. L. WINDER. Process and reactive schizophrenia. *Journal of Consulting Psychology*, 1953, *17*, 157–162.

KAPLAN, B., ed. *The inner world of mental illness*. New York: Harper & Row, 1964.

KAPLAN, H. S. *The new sex therapy*: *Active treatment of sexual dysfunctions*. New York. A Brunner/Mazel Publication published in cooperation with Quadrangle/The New York Times Book Co., 1974.

KASSORLA, I. For catatonia: Smiles, praise, and a food basket. In *Readings in Psychology Today*, 3rd ed. Del Mar, Calif.: CRM Books, 1972.

KASTENBAUM, R. J. Epilogue: Loving, dying and other gerontologic addenda. In C. Eisdorfer and M. P. Lawton, eds., *The psychology of adult development and aging*. Washington, D.C.: American Psychological Association, 1973.

KATAHN, M. Systematic desensitization and counseling for anxiety in a college basketball player. *Journal of Special Education*, 1967, *1*, 309–314.

KAUFMAN, B. Reaching the "unreachable" child. *New York*, February 3, 1975, pp. 43–49.

KEITH, P. R. Night terrors: A review of the psychology, neurology and therapy. *Journal of the American Academy of Child Psychiatry*, 1975, *14*(3), 477–489.

KEITH-SPIEGEL, P., and D. SPIEGEL. Affective states of patients immediately preceding suicide. *Journal of Psychiatric Research*, 1967, *5*, 89–93.

KELLY, G. A. *The psychology of personal constructs*. New York: Norton, 1955.

KEMBLE, J. *Idols and invalids*. New York: Doubleday, 1936.

KENDELL, R. E. *The classification of depressive illnesses*. New York: Oxford University Press, 1968.

KESSLER, J. W. *Psychopathology of childhood*. Englewood Cliffs, N.J.: Prentice-Hall, 1966.

KESSLER, J. W. Nosology in child psychopathology. In H. E. Rie, ed., *Perspectives in child psychopathology*. Chicago: Aldine Atherton, 1971.

KETY, S. S., D. ROSENTHAL, P. H. WENDER, and F. SCHULSINGER. Mental illness in the biological and adoptive families of adopted schizophrenics. *American Journal of Psychiatry*, 1971, *128*, 302–306.

KINKADE, K. *A Walden II experiment*: *The first five years of Twin Oaks Community*. New York: William Morrow, 1973.

KINSEY, A. C., W. B. POMEROY, and C. E. MARTIN. *Sexual behavior in the human male*. Philadelphia, Pa.: W. B. Saunders, 1948.

KINSEY, A. C., W. B. POMEROY, C. E. MARTIN, and P. H. GEBHARD. *Sexual behavior in the human female*. Philadelphia, Pa.: W. B. Saunders, 1953.

KLEIST, K. Schizophrenic symptoms and cerebral pathology. *Journal of Mental Science*, 1960, *106*, 246–253.

KLERMAN, G. L. Depression among youths. Paper presented at a symposium on man and his moods at

Taylor Manor Hospital, Ellicott City, Maryland, 1972.

KLONOFF, H. Marijuana and driving in real-life situations. *Science*, 1974, *186*, 317-323.

KOCH, R. Postnatal factors in causation. In R. Koch and J. C. Dobson, eds., *The mentally retarded child and his family*. New York: Brunner/Mazel, 1971a.

KOCH, R. Prenatal factors in causation (general). In R. Koch and J. C. Dobson, eds., *The mentally retarded child and his family*. New York: Brunner/Mazel, 1971b.

KOCH, R., P. B. ACOSTA, and J. C. DOBSON. Two metabolic factors in causation. In R. Koch and J. C. Dobson, eds., *The mentally retarded child and his family*. New York: Brunner/Mazel, 1971a.

KOCH, R., and J. C. DOBSON. Intrapartum and neonatal factors in causation. In R. Koch and J. C. Dobson, eds., *The mentally retarded child and his family*. New York: Brunner/Mazel, 1971.

KOCH, R., K. FISHLER, and H. M. MELNYK. Chromosomal anomalies in causation: Down's syndrome. In R. Koch and J. C. Dobson, eds., *The mentally retarded child and his family*. New York: Brunner/Mazel, 1971b.

KOEGEL, R. L., and A. RINCOVER. Treatment of psychotic children in a classroom environment: I. Learning in a large group. *Journal of Applied Behavior Analysis*, 1974, *7*, 45-59.

KOEGEL, R. L., and H. WILHELM. Selective responding to the components of multiple visual cues. *Journal of Experimental Child Psychology*, 1973, *15*, 442-453.

KOESTLER, A. *The ghost in the machine*. New York: Macmillan, 1968.

KOGAN, N., and F. C. SHELTON. Beliefs about old people: A comparative study of older and younger samples. *Journal of Genetic Psychology*, 1962, *100*, 93-111.

KOLB, L. C. *Modern clinical psychiatry*, 8th ed. Philadelphia, Pa.: W. B. Saunders, 1973.

KOLODNY, R. C., W. H. MASTERS, J. HENDRYX, and G TORO. Plasma testosterone and the semen analysis in male homosexuals. *New England Journal of Medicine*, 1971, *285*, 1170-1174.

KOLODNY, R. C., W. H. MASTERS, R. M. KOLODNER, and T. GELSON. Depression of plasma testosterone levels after chronic intensive marihuana use. *The New England Journal of Medicine*, 1974, *290*(16), 872-874.

KORA, TAKEHISA. Morita therapy. *International Journal of Psychiatry*, 1965, *1*, 611-645.

KRAEPELIN, E. *Clinical psychiatry: A textbook for physicians*. A. Diffendorf, tr. New York: Macmillan, 1902.

VON KRAFFT-EBING, R. *Psychopathia sexualis* (1886), F. S. Klaf, tr. New York: Bell, 1965.

KRAFT, D. P., and H. BABIGIAN. Somatic delusion or self-mutilation in a schizophrenic woman: A psychiatric emergency room case report. *American Journal of Psychiatry*, 1972, *128*(7), 127-129.

KRAFT, T., and I. AL-ISSA. Alcoholism treated by desensitization: A case report. *Behavior Research and Therapy*, 1967, *5*, 69-70.

KRAINES, S. H. *Mental depressions and their treatment*. New York: Macmillan, 1957.

KRAINES, S. H. Manic-depressive syndrome: A physiologic disease. *Diseases of the Nervous System*, 1966, *27*, 573-582.

KRAMM, E. R. *Families of mongoloid children*. Washington, D.C.: U.S. Government Printing Office, 1963.

KRANZ, H. *Lebenschicksale krimineller Zwillinge*. Berlin: Springer-Verlag, 1936.

KRASNER, L., and L. P. ULLMAN. *Behavior influence and personality: The social matrix of human action*. New York: Holt, Rinehart and Winston, 1973.

KRAUS, A. A., and A. M. LILIENFELD. Some epidemiologic aspects of the high mortality rate in the young widowed group. *Journal of Chronic Diseases*, 1959, *10*, 207-217.

KRETSCHMER, E. *Physique and character*. New York: Harcourt, 1925.

KRISCHEF, C. H. State laws on marriage and sterilization. *Mental Retardation*, 1972, *10*, 29-38.

KURLAND, H. D., C. T. YEAGER, and R. J. ARTHUR. Psychophysiologic aspects of severe behavior disorders. *Archives of General Psychiatry*, 1963, *8*, 599-604.

KURLAND, L. T., S. N. FARO, and H. SIEDLER. Minamata disease. The outbreak of neurologic disorder in Minamata, Japan, and its relationship to the ingestion of seafood contaminated by mercuric compounds. *World Neurology*, 1960, *1*, 370-395.

LACEY, J. I. The evaluation of autonomic responses: Toward a general solution. *Annals of the New York Academy of Science*, 1956, *67*, 123-164.

LACEY, J. I. Somatic response patterning and stress: Some revisions of activation theory. In M. H. Appley and R. Trumbull, eds., *Psychological stress*. New York: McGraw-Hill, 1967.

LAING, R. D. Is schizophrenia a disease? *International Journal of Social Psychiatry*, 1964, *10*, 184-193.

LAING, R. D. Mystification, confusion and conflict. In I. Boszormenyi-Nagy and J. L. Framo, eds., *Intensive family therapy*. New York: Hoeber Medical Division, Harper & Row, 1965.

LAING, R. D. *The politics of experience*. New York: Pantheon, 1967.

LAING, R. D. *The divided self*. New York: Pantheon, 1969.

LANCE, W. D. School programs for the trainable mentally retarded. *Education and Training of the Mentally Retarded*, 1968, *3*, 3-9.

LANCE, W. D., and A. C. KOCH. Parents as teachers. *Mental Retardation*, 1973, *11*, 3-4.

LANG, P. J. Autonomic controls or learning to play the internal organs. *Psychology Today*, 1970, *4*(5), 37-41.

LANGE, J. *Verbrechen als Schicksal*. Leipzig: Georg Thieme Verlag, 1929.

LANGER, E. J., and R. P. ABELSON. A patient by any other name...: Clinician group difference in labeling bias. *Journal of Consulting and Clinical Psychology*, 1974, *42*, 4-9.

LANVIN, N. I., J. G. THORPE, J. C. BARKER, C. B. BLAKEMORE, and C. G. CONWAY. Behavior therapy in a case of transvestism. *Journal of Nervous and Mental Disease*, 1961, *133*, 346-353.

LAPOLLA, A., and H. JONES. Placebo-control evaluation of desipromine in depression. *American*

Journal of Psychiatry, 1970, *127*, 335–338.

LAPOUSE, R., and M. MONK. Fears and worries in a representative sample of children. *American Journal of Orthopsychiatry*, 1959, *29*, 803–818.

LASKY, V. *J.F.K.: The man and the myth*. New Rochelle, N.Y.: Arlington House, 1966.

LAWTON, M. P., and L. E. GOTTESMAN. Psychological services to the elderly. *American Psychologist*, 1974, *29*, 689–693.

LAZARUS, A. A. Learning theory and the treatment of depression. *Behavior Research and Therapy*, 1968, *6*, 83–89.

LAZARUS, A. A., and A. ABRAMOVITZ. The use of "emotive imagery" in the treatment of children's phobias. *Journal of Mental Science*, 1962, *108*, 191–195.

LEAVITT, E. E. Research in psychotherapy with children. In R. E. Bergin and S. C. Garfield, eds., *Handbook of psychotherapy and behavior change: An empirical analysis*. New York: Wiley, 1971.

LEHMANN, H. E. Psychiatric concepts of depression: Nomenclature and classification. *Canadian Psychiatric Association Journal*, 1959, Supplement 4, 1–12.

LEONARD, C. V. Depression and suicidality. *Journal of Consulting and Clinical Psychology*, 1974, *42*, 98–104.

LEVIN, M. Bromide psychoses: Four varieties. *American Journal of Psychiatry*, 1948, *104*, 798–800.

LEWINSOHN, P. M. Clinical and theoretical aspects of depression. In H. E. Adams and W. K. Boardman, eds., *Advances in experimental psychology*. New York: Pergamon Press, 1972.

LEWINSOHN, P., M. SHAFFER, and J. LIBET. A behavioral approach to depression. Paper presented at meetings of the American Psychological Association, 1969.

LEWIS, A. Melancholia: A clinical survey of depressive states. *Journal of Mental Science*, 1934, *80*, 277–378.

LEYTON, G. B. The effects of slow starvation. *Lancet*, 1946, *251*, 73–79.

LICHTENBERG, P. A definition and analysis of depression. *Archives of Neurology and Psychiatry*, 1957, *77*, 519–527.

LIDZ, T. *The origin and treatment of schizophrenic disorders*. New York: Basic Books, 1973.

LIEBERMAN, M. A., I. D. YALOM, and M. B. MILES. Impact on participants. In L. Solomon and B. Berzon, eds., *New perspectives on encounter groups*. San Francisco, Calif.: Jossey-Bass, 1972.

LINDNER, R. *The fifty minute hour*. New York: Holt, Rinehart and Winston, 1955.

LINDZEY, G. Some remarks concerning incest, the incest taboo, and psychoanalytic theory. *American Psychologist*, 1967, *22*, 1051–1059.

LINDZEY, G., C. S. HALL, and M. MANOSEVITZ. *Theories of personality: Primary sources and research*, 2nd ed. New York: Wiley, 1973.

LITROWNIK, A. J. The relationship of self-stimulatory behavior in autistic children to the intensity and complexity of environmental stimulation. Unpublished master's thesis, University of Illinois, Champaign-Urbana, 1969.

LITTLE, K. B., and E. S. SHNEIDMAN. The validity of MMPI interpretations. *Journal of Consulting Psychology*, 1954, *18*, 425–428.

LITTLE, K. B., and E. S. SHNEIDMAN. Congruencies among interpretations of psychological test and anamnestic data. *Psychological Monographs*, 1959, *73*, No. 6 (Whole No. 476).

LOEVINGER, J., and A. OSSORIO. Evaluation of therapy by self report: A paradox. *Journal of Abnormal and Social Psychology*, 1959, *58*, 392–394.

LOGAN, D. L., J. KINSINGER, G. SHELTON, and J. M. BROWN. The use of multiple reinforcers in a rehabilitation setting. *Mental Retardation*, 1971, *9*, 3–6.

LONDON, P. *The modes and morals of psychotherapy*. New York: Holt, Rinehart and Winston, 1964.

LONDON, P. *Behavior control*. New York: Harper & Row, 1969.

LORAINE, J. A., D. A. ADAMOPOULOS, E. E. KIRKHAM, A. A. ISMAIL, and G. A. DOVE. Patterns of hormone excretion in male and female homosexuals. *Nature*, 1971, *234*, 552–555.

LOTTER, V. Social adjustment and placement of autistic children in Middlesex: A follow-up study. *Journal of Autism and Childhood Schizophrenia*, 1974, *4*, 11–32.

LOVAAS, O. I., J. P. BERBERICH, B. F. PERLOFF, and B. SCHAEFFER. Acquisition of imitative speech in schizophrenic children, *Science*, 1966, *151*, 705–707.

LOVAAS, O. I., A. LITROWNIK, and R. MANN. Response latencies to auditory stimuli in autistic children engaged in self-stimulatory behavior. *Behavior Research and Therapy*, 1971a, *2*, 39–49.

LOVAAS, O. I., B. SCHAEFFER, and J. Q. SIMMONS. Building social behavior in autistic children by use of electric shock. *Journal of Experimental Research in Personality*, 1965, *1*, 99–109.

LOVAAS, O. I., L. SCHREIBMAN, R. KOEGEL, and R. REHM. Selective responding by autistic children to multiple sensory input. *Journal of Abnormal Psychology*, 1971b, *77*, 211–222.

LOWENTHAL, M. F., and C. HAVEN. Interaction and adaptation: Intimacy as a critical variable. *American Sociological Review*, 1968, *33*, 20–30.

LUBORSKY, L., and D. P. SPENCE. Quantitative research on psychoanalytic therapy. In A. E. Bergin and S. L. Garfield, eds., *Handbook of psychotherapy and behavior change: An empirical analysis*. New York: Wiley, 1971.

LUBY, E. D., J. L. GRISELL, C. E. FROHMAN, H. LEES, B. D. COHEN, and J. S. GOTTLIEB. Biochemical, psychological, and behavioral responses to sleep deprivation. *Annals of the New York Academy of Science*, 1962, 96, 71–78.

LUCAS, C., P. SANSBURY, and J. G. COLLINS. A social and clinical study of delusions in schizophrenia. *Journal of Mental Health*, 1962, *108*, 747–758.

LUKIANOWICZ, N. Infanticide. *Psychiatria Clinica*, 1971, *4*, 145–158.

LUNDIN, R. W. *Principles of psychopathology*. Columbus, Ohio: Charles E. Merrill, 1965.

LYKKEN, D. T. A study of anxiety in the sociopathic personality. *Journal of Abnormal and Social Psychology*, 1957, *55*(1), 6–10.

McCLELLAND, D. C., W. N. DAVIS, R. KALIN, and E. WANNER. *The drinking man.* New York: Free Press, 1972.

McCORD, W., and J. McCORD. *The psychopath: An essay on the criminal mind.* New York: Van Nostrand, 1964.

McCORD, W., J. McCORD, and J. GUDEMAN. *Origins of alcoholism.* Stanford, Calif.: Stanford University Press, 1960.

MacFARLANE, J. W., J. ALLEN, and M. P. HONZIK. *A developmental study of the behavior problems of normal children over fourteen years.* Berkeley, Calif.: University of California Press, 1954.

MacKAY, J. R. Clinical observations on adolescent problem drinkers. *Quarterly Journal of Studies in Alcoholism*, 1961, *22*, 124–134.

McKAIN, W. C. A new look at older marriages. *The Family Coordinator*, 1972, *21*, 61–69.

McKEE, M., and I. ROBERTSON. *Social problems.* New York: Random House, 1975.

McKINNEY, W. T., S. J. SUOMI, and H. F. HARLOW. New models of separation and depression in rhesus monkeys. In J. P. Scott and E. C. Senay, eds., *Separation and depression: Clinical and research aspects.* Washington, D.C.: Publication No. 94 of the American Association for the Advancement of Science, 1973.

MacNAMARA, D. E. J. Sex offenses and sex offenders. *Annals of the American Academy of Political and Social Science*, 1968, *376*, 148–155.

McNEIL, E. B. *The quiet furies.* Englewood Cliffs, N.J.: Prentice-Hall, 1967.

McNEIL, E. B. *The psychoses.* Englewood Cliffs, N.J.: Prentice-Hall, 1970.

MACHOVER, K. *Personality projection in the drawing of the human figure.* Springfield, Ill.: Charles C Thomas, 1949.

MADDI, S. The existential neurosis. *Journal of Abnormal Psychology*, 1967, *72*, 311–325.

MADSEN, C. H., JR., and L. P. ULLMANN. Innovations in the desensitization of frigidity. *Behavior Research and Therapy.* 1967, *5*, 67–68.

MAHER, B. A. *Principles of psychopathology.* New York: McGraw-Hill, 1966.

MAHLER, M. On early infantile psychosis: The symbiotic and autistic syndromes. *Journal of the American Academy of Child Psychiatry*, 1965, *4*, 554–568.

MAHONEY, M. J. *Cognition and behavior modification.* Cambridge, Mass.: Ballinger, 1974.

MALETZKY, B. M., and J. KLOTTER. Smoking and alcoholism. *American Journal of Psychiatry*, 1974, *131*(4), 445–447.

MALITZ, S., B. WILKENS, and H. ESECOVER. A comparison of drug-induced hallucinations with those seen in spontaneously occurring psychoses. In L. J. West, ed., *Hallucinations.* New York: Grune & Stratton, 1962.

MANDELL, A. J., D. S. SEGAL, R. T. KUCZENSKI, and S. KNAPP. The search for the schizococcus. *Psychology Today*, 1972, *6*(5), 68–72.

MARKS, I. M., and M. G. GELDER. Transvestism and fetishism: Clinical and psychological changes during faradic aversion. *British Journal of Psychiatry*, 1967, *113*, 711–729.

MASLING, J. M. The effects of warm and cold interaction on the administration and scoring of an intelligence test. *Journal of Consulting Psychology*, 1959, *23*, 336–341.

MASLING, J. M. The influence of situational and interpersonal variables in projective testing. *Psychological Bulletin*, 1960, *57*, 65–85.

MASTERS, W. H., and V. E. JOHNSON. *Human sexual response.* Boston: Little, Brown, 1966.

MASTERS, W. H., and V. E. JOHNSON. *Human sexual inadequacy.* Boston: Little, Brown, 1970.

MAUGH, T. H. II. Marihuana (II): Does it damage the brain? *Science*, 1974, *185*, 775–776.

MAY, R. Contributions of existential psychotherapy. In R. May, E. Angel, and H. F. Ellenberger, eds., *Existence: A new dimension in psychiatry and psychology.* New York: Basic Books, 1958a.

MAY, R. The origins and significance of the existential movement in psychology. In R. May, E. Angel, and H. F. Ellenberger, eds., *Existence: A new dimension in psychiatry and psychology.* New York: Basic Books, 1958b.

MAY, R. *Love and will.* New York: Norton, 1969.

MEDNICK, S. A. A learning theory approach to research in schizophrenia. *Psychological Bulletin*, 1958, *55*, 316–327.

MEDNICK, S. A. Breakdown in individuals at high risk for schizophrenia: Possible predispositional perinatal factors. *Mental Hygiene*, 1970, *54*, 50–63.

MEDNICK, S. A. Birth defects and schizophrenia. *Psychology Today*, 1971, *4*(11), 49–50, 80–81.

MEEHL, P. E. *Clinical versus statistical prediction.* Minneapolis: University of Minnesota Press, 1954.

MEEHL, P. E. Schizotaxia, schizotypy, schizophrenia. *American Psychologist*, 1962, *17*, 827–838.

MEGARGEE, E. I. Undercontrolled and overcontrolled personality types in extreme antisocial aggression. *Psychological Monographs*, 1966, *80*, 3 (Whole No. 611).

MELLO, N. K., and J. H. MENDELSON. Experimentally induced intoxication in alcoholics: A comparison between programmed and spontaneous drinking. *Journal of Pharmacology and Experimental Therapy*, 1970, *173*, 101.

MELNYK, J. M., and R. KOCH. Genetic factors in causation. In R. Koch and J. C. Dobson, eds., *The mentally retarded child and his family.* New York: Brunner/Mazel, 1971.

MENDELS, J. Urinary 17-ketosteroid fractionation in depression: A preliminary report. *British Journal of Psychiatry*, 1969, *115*, 581–585.

MENDELS, J., and D. R. HAWKINS. Sleep studies in depression. In *Proceedings of the symposium on recent advances in the psychobiology of affective disorders.* Bethesda, Md.: National Institute of Mental Health, 1970.

MENNINGER, K. *Man against himself.* New York: Harcourt, 1938.

MERTON, R. K. *Social theory and social structure*, 2nd ed. Glencoe, Ill.: Free Press, 1957.

MEYER, A. The problems of mental reaction types, mental causes and diseases (1908). In E. E. Winters, ed., *Collected papers of Adolf Meyer*, Vol. II. Baltimore, Md.: Johns Hopkins Press, 1951.

MEYER, R., R. DUKE, and C. MOORE. Aversion treatment for voyeurism.

Unpublished paper, Chapel Hill, North Carolina, 1968.

MILGRAM, S. *Obedience to authority*: *An experimental view*. New York: Harper & Row, 1974.

MILLER, E. Short- and long-term memory in patients with presenile dementia (Alzheimer's disease). *Psychological Medicine*, 1973, *3*, 221–224.

MILLER, L. L., ed. *Marihuana: Current research*. New York: Academic Press, 1975.

MILLER, N. E. Learning of visceral and glandular responses. *Science*, 1969, *163*, 434–445.

MILLER, N. E., and L. DiCARA. Instrumental learning of heart-rate changes in curarized rats: Shaping and specificity to discrimination stimulus. *Journal of Comparative and Psychological Psychiatry*, 1967, *63*, 12–19.

MILLON, T. *Modern psychopathology*. Philadelphia, Pa.: W. B. Saunders, 1969.

MINTZ, S., and M. ALPERT. Imagery vividness, reality testing and schizophrenic hallucinations. *Journal of Abnormal Psychology*, 1972, *79*(3), 310–316.

MINUCHIN, S. *Families and family therapy*. Cambridge, Mass.: Harvard University Press, 1974.

MIRSKY, I. A., P. FUTTERMAN, and S. KAPLAN. Physiologic, psychologic, and social determinants in the ecology of duodenal ulcer. *American Journal of Digestive Diseases*, 1958, *3*, 285–314.

MISCHEL, W. *Personality and assessment*. New York: Wiley, 1968.

MISCHEL, W. *Introduction to personality*, 2nd ed. New York: Holt, Rinehart and Winston, 1976.

MISHLER, E. G., and N. E. WAXLER. Family interaction processes and schizophrenia: A review of current theories. In E. G. Mishler and N. E. Waxler, eds., *Family processes and schizophrenia*. New York: Science House, 1968.

MOHR, J. W., R. E. TURNER, and M. B. JERRY. *Pedophilia and exhibitionism*. Toronto: University of Toronto Press, 1964.

MONEY, J., and C. PRIMROSE. Sexual dimorphism and dissociation in the psychology of male transsexuals. *Journal of Nervous and Mental Disease*, 1968, *147*, 472–486.

MONTAGUE, A. Chromosomes and crime. *Psychology Today*, *2*(5), 43–49.

MORGAN, C. D., and H. A. MURRAY. A method for investigating fantasies: The Thematic Apperception Test. *Archives of Neurology and Psychiatry*, 1935, *34*, 289–306.

MORGAN, T. They think, "I can kill because I'm 14." *The New York Times Magazine*, January 19, 1975.

MOSHER, L. R. A research design for evaluating a psychosocial treatment of schizophrenia. *Hospital and Community Psychiatry*, 1972, *23*, 229–234.

MOSHER, L. R., ed. Megavitamin therapy—some personal accounts. *Schizophrenia Bulletin*, 1973, No. 7, 7–9.

MOSHER, L. R. Psychiatric heretics and extra-medical treatment of schizophrenia. In R. Cancro, N. Fox, and L. Shapiro, eds., *Strategic intervention in schizophrenia: Current developments in treatment*. New York: Behavioral Publications, 1974.

MOSHER, L. R. and J. G. GUNDERSON. Special report: Schizophrenia, 1972. *Schizophrenia Bulletin*, 1973, *7*, 12–52.

MOSHER, L. R., W. POLLIN, and J. R. STABENAU. Identical twins discordant for schizophrenia: Neurologic findings. *Archives of General Psychiatry*, 1971, *24*, 422–430.

MOUSTAKAS, C. E. *Psychotherapy with children*. New York: Harper & Row, 1959.

MOWRER, O. H. A stimulus-response analysis of anxiety and its role as a reinforcing agent. *Psychological Review*, 1939, *46*, 553–565.

MOWRER, O. H. Learning theory and the neurotic paradox. *American Journal of Orthopsychiatry*, 1948, *18*, 571–610.

MURPHY, P. V. Crime and its causes—A need for social change. *Los Angeles Times*, December 13, 1970.

MURPHY, W. K., and R. C. SCHEERENBERGER. Day centers for the mentally retarded. In *Establishing day centers for the mentally retarded*. Springfield, Ill.: Illinois Department of Mental Health, 1967.

MURRAY, MRS. MAX A. *Needs of parents of mentally retarded chil-*dren. Arlington, Texas: National Association for Retarded Children, 1973.

MURSTEIN, B. I. Assumptions, adaptation level and projective techniques. *Perceptual and Motor Skills*, 1961, *12*, 107–125.

MYERS, J. K., and L. L. BEAN. *A decade later: A follow-up of social class and mental illness*. New York: Wiley, 1968.

NARANJO, C. I and thou, here and now. In F. D. Stephenson, ed. *Gestalt therapy primer*. Springfield, Ill.: Charles C Thomas, 1975.

NEISWORTH, J. T., and R. SMITH. *Modifying retarded behavior*. Boston: Houghton-Mifflin, 1973.

NEUGARTEN, B. L., ed. *Middle age and aging*. Chicago: University of Chicago Press, 1968.

New outlook for the aged. *Time*, June 2, 1975.

NEWSOME, C. D., E. A. CARR, and A. RINCOVER. Identifying and using sensory reinforcers. Paper presented at Western Psychological Association, San Francisco, April 1974.

NIELSON. P. E. A study in transsexualism. *Psychiatric Quarterly*, 1960, *34*, 203–235.

NUNNALLY, J. C. *Psychometric theory*. New York: McGraw-Hill, 1967.

O'BRIEN, J. S., A. E. RAYNES, and V. D. PATCH. Treatment of heroin addiction with aversion therapy, relaxation training, and systematic desensitization. *Behavioral Research and Therapy*, 1972, *10*, 77–80.

O'CONNOR, R. D. Modification of social withdrawal through symbolic modeling. *Journal of Applied Behavioral Analysis*, 1969, *2*, 15–22.

OGREN, R. W. The ineffectiveness of the criminal sanction in France and corruption cases: Losing the battle against white-collar crime. *American Criminal Law Review*, 1973, *11*(4), 959–988.

O'KELLY, L. I., and F. A. MUCKLER, *Introduction to psychopathology*. Englewood Cliffs, N.J.: Prentice-Hall, 1955.

OLDS, S. Say it with a stomach ache. *Today's Health*, 1970, *48*(11), 41–43, 88.

O'LEARY, K. D., W. C. BECKER, M. B. EVANS, and R. A. SAUNDER-GAS. A token reinforcement program in a public school: A replication and systematic analysis. *Journal of Applied Behavior Analysis*, 1969, *7*, 377–380.

O'LEARY, K. D., and R. DRABMAN. Token reinforcement programs in the classroom: A review. *Psychological Bulletin*, 1971, *75*, 379–398.

OLLEY, G., and W. J. FREMOUW. The voting rights of the M.R. *Mental Retardation*, 1974, *12*, 14–16.

OLSHANSKY, S. Chronic sorrow: A response to having a mentally defective child. *Social Casework*, 1962, *43*, 191–194.

OLTMAN, J., and S. FRIEDMAN. Parental deprivation in psychiatric conditions. *Disturbances of the Nervous System*, 1967, *28*, 298–303.

O'NEAL, P., and L. N. ROBINS. The relation of childhood behavior problems to adult psychiatric status: A thirty-year follow-up study of 150 subjects. *American Journal of Psychiatry*, 1958, *114*, 961–969.

ORNITZ, E. M., and E. R. RITVO. Perceptual inconsistency in early infantile autism. *Archives of General Psychiatry*, 1968, *18*, 76–98.

PALMORE, E. Employment and retirement. In L. A. Epstein and J. H. Murray, eds., *The aged population of the United States*. Washington, D.C.: U.S. Government Printing Office, 1967.

PALMORE, E., ed. *Normal aging: Reports from the Duke Longitudinal Study, 1955–1969*. Durham, N.C.: Duke University Press, 1970.

PALMORE, E., ed. *Normal aging 2: Reports from the Duke Longitudinal Study, 1970–1973*. Durham, N.C.: Duke University Press, 1974.

PARKER, N. Twins: A psychiatric study of a neurotic group. *Medical Journal of Australia*, 1964, *2*, 735–741.

PARLOFF, M. B. Shopping for the right therapy. *Saturday Review*, February 21, 1976, pp. 14–20.

PARTRIDGE, G. E. Current conceptions of psychopathic personality. *American Journal of Psychiatry*, 1930, *87*, 53–99.

PATTERSON, G. R. Behavioral intervention procedures in the classroom and in the home. In A. E. Bergin and S. L. Garfield, eds., *Handbook of psychotherapy and behavior change: An empirical analysis*. New York: Wiley, 1971.

PATTERSON, G. R., and M. E. GULLION. *Living with children*. Champaign, Ill.: Research Press, 1968.

PATTERSON, G. R., R. JUNES, J. WHITTIER, and M. S. WRIGHT. A behavior modification technique for the hyperactive child. *Behavior Research and Therapy*, 1965, *2*, 217–226.

PATTON, R. B., and J. A. SHEPPARD. Intercranial tumors found at autopsy in mental patients. *American Journal of Psychiatry*, 1957, *113*, 319–324.

PAUL, G. L. Outcome of systematic desensitization I: Background procedures and uncontrolled reports of individual treatment. In C. M. Franks, ed., *Behavior therapy: Appraisal and status*. New York: McGraw-Hill, 1969a.

PAUL, G. L. Outcome of systematic desensitization II: Controlled investigation of individual treatment technique variations and current status. In C. M. Franks, ed., *Behavior therapy: Appraisal and status*. New York: McGraw-Hill, 1969b.

PAUL, G. L. Chronic mental patient: Current status—future directions. *Psychological Bulletin*, 1969c, *71*, 81–94.

PAUL, L. Crisis intervention. *Mental Hygiene*, 1966, *50*, 141–145.

PAULY, I. B. The current status of the change of sex operation. *Journal of Nervous and Mental Disease*, 1968, *147*, 460–471.

PAVLOV, I. P. *Conditioned reflexes*. C. V. Anrep, tr. London: Oxford University Press, 1927.

PERLS, F. S. Four lectures. In J. Fagan and I. L. Shepherd, eds., *Gestalt therapy now: Therapy, techniques, applications*. Palo Alto, Calif.: Science and Behavior Books, 1970.

PERLS, F. S., R. F. HEFFERLINE, and P. GOODMAN. *Gestalt therapy: Excitement and growth in the human personality*. New York: Julian Press, 1951.

PERSKE, R. About sexual development. Mental Retardation, 1973, *11*, 6–8.

PERSKE, R., and J. MARQUISS. Learning to live in an apartment. *Mental Retardation*, 1973, *11*, 18–19.

PETERS, J. E., and R. M. STERN. Specificity of attitude hypothesis in psychosomatic medicine: A reexamination. *Journal of Psychosomatic Research*, 1971, *15*, 129–135.

PETERSON, D. R. *The clinical study of social behavior*. New York: Appleton-Century-Crofts, 1968.

PETZEL, T. P., and J. E. JOHNSON. Time estimation by process and reactive schizophrenics under crowded and uncrowded conditions. *Journal of Clinical Psychology*, 1972, *28*(3), 345–347.

PFEIFER, L. A subjective report of tactile hallucination in schizophrenia. *Journal of Clinical Psychology*, 1970, *26*(1), 57–60.

PFEIFFER, E., and G. C. DAVIS. Determinants of sexual behavior in middle and old age. *Journal of the American Geriatrics Society*, 1972, *20*, 151–158.

PFEIFFER, E., A. VERWOERDT, and H. WANG. Sexual behavior in aged men and women. *Archives of General Psychiatry*, 1968, *19*, 753–758.

PICHOT, P., and T. LEMPÉRIÈRE. Analyse factorielle d'un questionnaire d'auto-evaluation des symptômes depressifs. *Revue de Psychologie Appliques*, 1964, *14*, 15–29.

PINEL, P. *A treatise on insanity* (1801). D. D. Davis, tr. New York: Hafner, 1962.

PITTEL, S. M., and R. HOFER. The transition to amphetamine abuse. *Journal of Psychedelic Drugs*, 1972, *5*(2), 105–111.

PODOLSKY, E., and C. WADE. *Sexual sadism: The sexual urge of love and pain*. New York: Epic, 1961.

POLLIN, W., G. ALLEN, A. HOFFER, J. R. STABENAU, and Z. HRUBEC. Psychopathology in 15,909 pairs of veteran twins. *American Journal of Psychiatry*, 1969, *126*, 597–609.

POST, F. *The clinical psychiatry of later life*. New York: Pergamon Press, 1965.

PREMACK, D. Reinforcement therapy. In D. Levine, ed., Nebraska Symposium on Motivation. Lincoln: University of Nebraska Press, 1965.

PRESIDENT'S COMMISSION ON LAW

ENFORCEMENT AND ADMINISTRATION OF JUSTICE. The challenge of crime in a free society. Washington, D.C.: U.S. Government Printing Office, 1967.

PRESIDENT'S COMMITTEE ON EMPLOYMENT OF THE HANDICAPPED. *Guide to job placement of the mentally retarded.* Washington, D.C.: U.S. Government Printing Office, 1964.

PRESIDENT'S COMMITTEE ON MENTAL RETARDATION. *M.R. 67: A first report to the President on the nation's progress and remaining great needs in the campaign to combat mental retardation.* Washington, D.C.: U.S. Government Printing Office, 1967.

PRESIDENT'S COMMITTEE ON MENTAL RETARDATION. *These, too, must be equal.* Washington, D.C.: U.S. Government Printing Office, 1969.

PRESIDENT'S PANEL ON MENTAL RETARDATION. *A proposed program for national action to combat mental retardation.* Washington, D.C.: U.S. Government Printing Office, 1962.

PREU, P. W. The concept of the psychopathic personality. In J. McV. Hunt, ed., *Personality and the behavior disorders*, Vol. 2. New York: The Ronald Press, 1944.

PRICE, R. H. *Abnormal behavior: Perspectives in conflict.* New York: Holt, Rinehart and Winston, 1972.

PRINCE, M. *The dissociation of a personality.* New York: Longmans, Green, 1905.

PRITCHARD, M. Homosexuality and genetic sex. *Journal of Mental Sciences*, 1962, *108*, 616–623.

PsychoSources: A psychology resource catalog. New York: Bantam, 1973.

PURCELL, K., K. BRADY, H. CHAI, J. MUSER, L. MOLK, N. GORDON, and J. MEANS. The effect of asthma in children of experimental separation from the family. *Psychosomatic Medicine*, 1969, *31*, 144–164.

QUAY, H. C. Psychopathic personality as pathological stimulus seeking. *American Journal of Psychiatry*, 1965, *122*, 180–183.

RACHMAN, S. Sexual fetishism: An experimental analogue. *Psychological Record*, 1966, *16*, 293–296.

RAKER, J. W., A. F. WALLACE, and

J. F. RAYMER. *Emergency medical care in disasters.* Disaster Study No. 6, National Academy of Sciences, Washington, D.C.: National Resources Council Publication No. 457, 1956.

RAPAPORT, D., M. GILL, and R. SCHAEFER. *Diagnostic psychological testing.* New York: International Universities Press, 1968.

RASMUSSEN, T., and C. H. H. BRANCH. Temporal lobe epilepsy: Indications for and results of surgical therapy. *Postgraduate Medicine*, 1962, *31*, 9–14.

RAY, J. S. The family training center. *Mental Retardation*, 1974, *12*, 12–13.

RAY, O. S. *Drugs, society, and human behavior.* St. Louis, Mo.: C. V. Mosby, updated 1974.

RECHTSCHAFFEN, A., and L. MONROE. Laboratory studies of insomnia. In A. Kales, ed., *Sleep: Physiology and pathology.* Philadelphia, Pa.: Lippincott, 1969.

REDLICH, F. C., and D. X. Freedman. *The theory and practice of psychiatry.* New York: Basic Books, 1966.

REES, L. The significance of parental attitudes in childhood asthma. *Journal of Psychosomatic Research*, 1963, *7*, 181–190.

REES, L. The importance of psychological, allergic, and infective factors in childhood asthma. *Journal of Psychosomatic Research*, 1964, *7*, 253–262.

REISS, D. Competing hypotheses and warring factions: Applying knowledge of schizophrenia. *Schizophrenia Bulletin*, 1974, No. 8, 7–11.

RENNIE, T. A. C. Prognosis in manic-depressive psychosis. *American Journal of Psychiatry*, 1942, *98*, 801–814.

RESNICH, P. J. Child murder by parents: A psychiatric review of filicide. *American Journal of Psychiatry*, 1969, *126*, 325–334.

RESNICH, P. J. Murder of the newborn: A psychiatric review of neonaticide. *American Journal of Psychiatry*, 1970, *126*, 1414–1420.

RESNICK, H. L., and J. M. CANTOR. Suicide and aging. *Journal of the American Geriatrics Society*, 1970, *18*, 152–158.

REUBEN, D. *Everything you always wanted to know about sex ... but were afraid to ask.* New York:

David McKay, 1969.

REUTER, K. E., A. D. WALSH, J. A. BUCK, and A. J. LITROWNIK. Comparison of instructions, time-out, and punishment for controlling self-stimulatory behavior in autistic-like preschoolers. Paper presented at Western Psychological Association meeting, San Francisco, April 1974.

RICHARDSON, W. C. Dimensions of economic dependency. Health administration perspectives, No. A4, 1967.

RICKARD, H. C., P. J. DIGNAM, and R. F. HORNER. Verbal manipulation in a psychotherapeutic relationship. *Journal of Clinical Psychology*, 1960, *16*, 364–367.

RICKARD, H. C., and M. C. MUNDY. Direct manipulation of stuttering behavior: An experimental-clinical approach. In L. P. Ullmann and L. Krasner, eds., *Case studies in behavior modification.* New York: Holt, Rinehart and Winston, 1965.

RICKLES, K. Nonspecific factors in ·drug therapy of neurotic patients. In K. Rickles, ed., *Nonspecific factors in drug therapy.* Springfield, Ill.: Charles C Thomas, 1968.

RIMLAND, B. *Infantile autism.* New York: Appleton-Century-Crofts, 1964.

RIMLAND, B. High-dosage levels of certain vitamins in the treatment of children with severe mental disorders. In D. Hawkins and L. Pauling, eds., *Orthomolecular psychiatry.* San Francisco, Calif.: W. H. Freeman, 1973.

RIMLAND, B., and D. I. MEYER. Malabsorption and the celiac syndrome as possible causes of childhood psychosis: A brief discussion of evidence and need for research. Unpublished manuscript, Institute for Child Behavior Research, San Diego, 1967.

RIOCH, M. J. Pilot projects in training mental health counselors. In E. L. Cowen, E. A. Gardner, and M. Zax, eds., *Emerging approaches to mental health problems.* New York: Appleton-Century-Crofts, 1967.

RISLEY, T., and M. M. WOLF. Establishing functional speech in echolalic children. *Behavior Research and Therapy*, 1967, *5*, 73–88.

RITZLER, B., and G. ROSENBAUM. Proprioception in schizophrenics and normals: Effects of stimulus intensity and interstimulus interval. *Journal of Abnormal Psychology*, 1974, *83*(2), 106–111.

ROBINS, E., J. GASSNER, J. KAYES, R. WILKINSON, and G. E. MURPHY. The communication of suicidal intent: A study of 134 successful (completed) suicides. *American Journal of Psychiatry*, 1959, *115*, 724–733.

ROBINS, N. L. *Deviant children grow up.* Baltimore, Md.: Williams and Wilkins, 1966.

ROBINSON, H. B., and N. M. ROBINSON. Mental retardation. In P. H. Mussen, ed., *Carmichael's manual of child psychology*, 3rd ed. New York: Wiley, 1970.

ROGERS, C. R. *Counseling and psychotherapy.* Boston: Houghton Mifflin, 1942.

ROGERS, C. R. *Client-centered therapy: Its current practice, implications and theory.* Boston: Houghton Mifflin, 1951.

ROGERS, C. R. Persons or science? A philosophical question. *American Psychologist*, 1955, *10*, 267–278.

ROGERS, C. R. A theory of therapy, personality, and interpersonal relationships, as developed in the client-centered framework. In S. Koch, ed., *Psychology: A study of a science*, Vol. 3. New York: Basic Books, 1959.

ROGERS, C. R. *On becoming a person.* Boston: Houghton Mifflin, 1961.

ROGERS, C. R. *Carl Rogers on encounter groups.* New York: Harper & Row, 1970.

ROGERS, C. R. and R. F. DYMOND, eds. *Psychotherapy and personality change: Coordinated studies in the client-centered approach.* Chicago: University of Chicago Press, 1954.

ROHR, C. C., and J. DENSEN-GERBER. Adolescent drug abuse: An evaluation of 800 inpatients in the Odyssey House program. Paper presented at American Psychiatric Association annual meeting, Washington, D.C., May 3–7, 1971.

ROKEACH, M. *The three Christs of Ypsilanti.* New York: Random House, 1964.

RORSCHACH, H. *Psychodiagnostics: A diagnostic test based on perception.* New York: Grune & Stratton, 1942.

ROSEN, B. M., S. K. BAHN, and M.

KRAMER. Demographic and diagnostic characteristics of psychiatric outpatients in the U.S.A., 1961. *American Journal of Orthopsychiatry*, 1964, *24*, 455–467.

ROSENHAN, D. L. On being sane in insane places. *Science*, 1973, *179*, 250–258.

ROSENTHAL, D. The heredity-environment issue in schizophrenia: Summary of the conference and present status of our knowledge. In D. Rosenthal and S. S. Kety, eds., *The transmission of schizophrenia.* London: Pergamon Press, 1968.

ROSENTHAL, D. *Genetic theory and abnormal behavior.* New York: McGraw-Hill, 1970.

ROSENTHAL, D. *Genetics of psychopathology.* New York: McGraw-Hill, 1971.

ROSENTHAL, D., P. WENDER, S. S. KETY, J. WELNER, and F. SCHULSINGER. The adopted-away offspring of schizophrenics. *American Journal of Psychiatry*, 1971, *128*(3), 307–311.

ROSENTHAL, R. Covert communication in the psychological experiment. *Psychological Bulletin*, 1967, *5*, 356–367.

ROSENTHAL, R., and L. JACOBSON. Teachers' expectancies: Determinants of pupils' I.Q. gains. *Psychological Reports*, 1966, *19*, 115–118.

ROSENTHAL, S. H., and N. L. WULFSOHN. Electrosleep—A clinical trial. *American Journal of Psychiatry*, 1970, *127*(4), 175–176.

ROSENZWEIG, M. R. Environmental complexity, cerebral change, and behavior. *American Psychologist*, 1966, *21*, 321–332.

ROSS, A. O. *Psychological disorders of children.* New York: McGraw-Hill, 1974.

ROSS, L., J. RODIN, and P. G. ZIMBARDO. Toward an attribution therapy: The reduction of fear through induced cognitive emotional misattribution. *Journal of Personality and Social Psychology*, 1969, *12*, 279–288.

ROTHSCHILD, D. Senile psychoses and psychoses with cerebral arteriosclerosis. In O. J. Kaplan, ed., *Mental disorders in later life*, 2nd ed. Stanford, Calif.: Stanford University Press, 1956.

ROTTER, J. B. *Social learning and clinical psychology.* Englewood Cliffs, N.J.. Prentice-Hall, 1954.

ROTTER, J. B. Generalized expectancies for internal versus external control of reinforcement. *Psychological Monographs*, 1966, *80*, 1–28.

ROTTER, J. B., and J. E. RAFFERTY. *Manual for the Rotter Incomplete Sentences Blank. College form.* New York: The Psychological Corporation, 1950.

ROUECHÉ, B. Annals of medicine: As empty as Eve. *The New Yorker*, September 9, 1974, pp. 84–100.

ROUTTENBERG, A. The two-arousal hypothesis: reticular formation and limbic system. *Psychological Review*, 1968, *75*, 51–80.

RUTTENBERG, B. A. A psychoanalytic understanding of infantile autism and its treatment. In D. W. Churchill, G. D. Alpern, and M. K. DeMyer, eds., *Infantile autism.* Springfield, Ill.: Charles C Thomas, 1971.

RUTTER, M. Concepts of autism: A review of research. *Journal of Child Psychology and Psychiatry*, 1968, *9*, 1–25.

RUTTER, M. The description and classification of infantile autism. In D. W. Churchill, G. D. Alpern, and M. K. DeMyer, eds., *Infantile autism.* Springfield, Ill.: Charles C Thomas, 1971.

RUTTER, M., S. LEBOVIC, L. EISENBERG, A. V. SNEZNEVSKIJ, R. SADOUN, E. BROOKE, and T. LIN. A tri-axial classification of mental disorder in childhood. *Journal of Child Psychology and Psychiatry*, 1969, *10*, 41–61.

SACHAR, E. J., S. KANTER, D. BUIE, R. ENGLE, and R MEHLMAN. Psycho-endocrinology of ego disintegration. *American Journal of Psychiatry*, 1970, *126*(8), 1067–1078.

SAGER, C. J. The group psychotherapist: Bulwark against alienation. *American Journal of Group Psychotherapy*, 1968, *18*, 419–431.

SAGHIR, M. T., and E. ROBINS. Homosexuality: I. Sexual behavior of the female homosexual. *Archives of General Psychiatry*, 1969, *20*, 192–201.

SAGHIR, M. T., E. ROBINS, and B. WALBRAN. Homosexuality: II

Sexual behavior of the male homosexual. *Archives of General Psychiatry*, 1969, *21*, 219–229.

SALZMAN, C., and J. LIEFF. Interviews with hallucinogenic drug discontinuers. *Journal of Psychedelic Drugs*, 1974, *6*(3), 329–332.

SANDERS, J. An autistic child in residential treatment. Paper presented at American Psychological Association meeting, New Orleans, September 1974.

SANDIFER, M. G., JR., C. PETTUS, and D. QUADE. A study of psychiatric diagnosis. *Journal of Nervous and Mental Disease*, 1964, *139*, 350–356.

SANTAMARIA, B. A. G. Dysmenorrhea. *Clinical Obstetrics and Gynecology*, 1969, *12*(3), 708–723.

SARNOFF, I. *Testing Freudian concepts: An experimental social approach*. New York: Springer, 1971.

SARWER-FONER, G. J. A psychoanalytic note on a specific delusion of time in psychotic depression. *Canadian Psychiatric Association Journal*, 1966, Supplement 2, 221–228.

SATIR, V. *Conjoint family therapy*, rev. ed. Palo Alto, Calif.: Science and Behavior Books, 1967.

SAUL, L. J. *Emotional maturity: The development and dynamics of personality*, 2nd ed. Philadelphia, Pa.: Lippincott, 1947.

SCHACHTER, S., and B. LATANÉ. Crime, cognition, and the autonomic nervous system. In D. Levine, ed., *Nebraska Symposium on Motivation*, Vol. 12. Lincoln: University of Nebraska Press, 1964.

SCHEERENBERGER, R. C. Mental retardation: Definition, classification, and prevalence. In J. H. Rothstein, ed., *Mental retardation readings and resources*. New York: Holt, Rinehart and Winston, 1971.

SCHEFF, T. J. *Being mentally ill: A sociological theory*. Chicago: Aldine, 1966.

SCHEFF, T. J. Schizophrenia as ideology. *Schizophrenia Bulletin*, 1970, No. 2, 15–19.

SCHILD, S. The family of the retarded child. In R. Koch and J. C. Dobson, eds., *The mentally retarded child and his family*. New York: Brunner/Mazel, 1971.

SCHILDKRAUT, J. The catecholamine hypothesis of affective disorders: A review of supporting evidence.

American Journal of Psychiatry, 1965, *122*, 509–522.

SCHMIDT, H. O., and C. P. FONDA. The reliability of psychiatric diagnosis: A new look. *Journal of Abnormal and Social Psychology*, 1956, *52*, 262–267.

SCHOPLER, E., and R. J. REICHLER. Psychobiological referents for the treatment of autism. In D. W. Churchill, G. D. Alpern, and M. K. DeMyer, eds., *Infantile autism*. Springfield, Ill.: Charles C Thomas, 1971.

SCHRAG, P., and D. DIVOKY. *The myth of the hyperactive child*. New York: Pantheon, 1975.

SCHREIBMAN, L., and O. I. LOVAAS. Overselective response to social stimuli by autistic children. *Journal of Abnormal Child Psychology*, 1973, *2*, 152–168.

SCHUTZ, W. C. *Joy: Expanding human awareness*. New York: Grove Press, 1967.

SCHWAB, J. J. Comprehensive medicine and the concurrence of physical and mental illness. *Psychosomatics*, 1970 *11*(6), 591–595.

SCHWAB, J. J., N. H. McGINNIS, L. B. NORRIS, and R. B. SCHWAB. Psychosomatic medicine and the contemporary social scene. *American Journal of Psychiatry*, 1970, *126*, 108–118.

SCHWARTZ, A. N. A transactional view of the aging process. In A. N. Schwartz and I. Mensh, eds., *Professional obligations and approaches to the aged*. Springfield, Ill.: Charles C Thomas, 1974.

SCHWARTZ, S. Effect of neonatal cortical lesions and early environmental factors on adult rat behavior. *Journal of Comparative and Physiological Psychology*, 1964, *57*, 72–77.

SCHWITZGEBEL, R. Short-term operant conditioning of adolescent offenders on socially relevant variables. *Journal of Abnormal Psychology*, 1967, *72*, 134–142.

SEARS, R. R. *Survey of objective studies of psychoanalytic concepts*. New York: Social Science Research Council, 1943.

SEARS, R. R. *Survey of objective studies of psychoanalytic concepts*. New York: Social Science Research Council, 1951.

SEAY, B., E. HANSEN, and H. F.

HARLOW. Mother-infant separation in monkeys. *Journal of Child Psychology and Psychiatry*, 1962, *3*, 123–132.

SEGUIN, E. *Idiocy: And its treatment by the physiological method*. New York: Wood, 1866.

SELIGMAN, C. G. Temperament, conflict and psychosis in a stone age population. *British Journal of Psychology*, 1929, *9*, 187–202.

SELIGMAN, M. E. P. Phobias and preparedness. *Behavior Therapy*, 1971, *2*, 307–320.

SELIGMAN, M. E. P. Fall into hopelessness. *Psychology Today*, 1973, *7*(1), 43–48.

SELIGMAN, M. E. P. Depression and learned helplessness. In R. J. Friedman and M. M. Katz, eds., *The psychology of depression: Contemporary theory and research*. New York: Halsted Press, 1974.

SELIGMAN, M. E. P., S. F. MAIER, and R. L. SOLOMON. Unpredictable and uncontrollable aversive events. In F. R. Brush, ed., *Aversive conditioning and helplessness*. New York: Academic Press, 1971.

SELLING, L. S. *Men against madness*. New York: Greenberg, 1940.

SENAY, E. C., and F. C. REDLICH. Cultural and social factors in neuroses and psychosomatic illnesses. *Social Psychiatry*, 1968, *3*(3), 89–97.

SHAPIRO, H. Circle of homes. *Mental Retardation*. 1973, *11*, 19–21.

SHAW, D. M. Mineral metabolism, mania, and melancholia. *British Medical Journal*, 1966, *2*, 262–267.

SHEARN, D. Operant conditioning of heart rate. *Science*, 1962, *137*, 530–531.

SHEEHAN, J. G., and M. MARTYN. Stuttering and its disappearance. *Journal of Speech and Hearing Research*, 1970, *13*, 279–289.

SHELDON, H. D. *The older people of the United States*. New York: Wiley, 1958.

SHELDON, W. H. (with the collaboration of S. S. Stevens). *The varieties of temperament: A psychology of constitutional differences*. New York: Harper & Row, 1942.

SHERMAN, J. A., and D. M. BAER. Appraisal of operant therapy techniques with children and adults. In C. M. Franks, ed., *Behavior therapy: Appraisal and status*. New

York: McGraw-Hill, 1969.

SHNEIDMAN, E. S., and N. L. FARBEROW. Attempted and completed suicide. In E. S. Shneidman, N. L. Farberow, and R. E. Litman, eds., *The psychology of suicide*. New York: Science House, 1970a.

SHNEIDMAN, E. S., and N. L. FARBEROW. The logic of suicide. In E. S. Shneidman, N. L. Farberow, and R. E. Litman, eds., *The psychology of suicide*. New York: Science House, 1970b.

SHNEIDMAN, E. S., and N. L. FARBEROW. A psychological approach to the study of suicide notes. In E. S. Shneidman, N. L. Farberow, and R. E. Litman, eds., *The psychology of suicide*. New York: Science House, 1970c.

SHNEIDMAN, E. S., and P. MANDELKORN. How to prevent suicide. In E. S. Shneidman, N. L. Farberow, and R. E. Litman, eds., *The psychology of suicide*. New York: Science House, 1970.

SHOCHET, B. R. Recognizing the suicidal patient. *Modern Medicine*, 1970, *38*, 114–117, 123.

SIEGEL, M., G. D. NISWANDER, E. SACHS, and D. STRAVROS. Taraxein: fact or artifact? *American Journal of Psychiatry*, 1959, *115*, 819–820.

SILVERMAN, C. The epidemiology of depression: A review. *American Journal of Psychiatry*, 1968, *124*, 883–891.

SIMEONS, A. T. W. *Man's presumptuous brain: An evolutionary interpretation of psychosomatic disease*. New York: Dutton, 1961.

SIMMONS, J. Q., and O. I. LOVAAS. Use of pain and punishment as treatment techniques with childhood schizophrenia. *American Journal of Psychotherapy*, 1969, *23*, 23–36.

SIMON, W., and J. H. GAGNON. Psychosexual development. In J. H. Gagnon and W. Simon, eds., *The sexual scene*. Chicago: Aldine, 1970.

SINGER, M., and L. C. WYNNE. Differentiating characteristics of the parents of childhood schizophrenics, childhood neurotics, and young adult schizophrenics. *American Journal of Psychiatry*, 1963, *120*, 234–243.

SKEELS, H. M., and H. B. DYE. A study of the effects of differential stimulation on mentally retarded children. AAMD *Proceedings*, 1938–39, *44*, 114–136.

SKINNER, B. F. *Walden II*. New York: Macmillan, 1948.

SKINNER, B. F. Behaviorism at fifty. In T. W. Wann, ed., *Behaviorism and phenomenology*. Chicago, Ill.: University of Chicago Press, 1964.

SKINNER, B. F. *Science and human behavior*. New York: Free Press, 1965.

SKINNER, B. F. *Beyond freedom and dignity*. New York: Knopf, 1971.

SKINNER, W. I. *Tobacco and health: The other side of the coin*. New York: Vantage Press, 1970.

SLAVSON, S. R. *Child psychotherapy*. New York: Columbia University Press, 1952.

SOLNET, A. J., and M. H. STARK. *Mourning and the birth of a defective child*. New Haven, Conn.: Yale University School of Medicine, Department of Pediatrics and Child Study Center, 1961.

SOSKIN, W. F. Influence of four types of data on diagnostic conceptualization in psychological testing. *Journal of Abnormal and Social Psychology*, 1959, *58*, 69–78.

SPITZ, R. A. Hospitalism: An inquiry into the genesis of psychiatric conditions in early childhood. *Psychoanalytic Study of the Child*, 1945, *1*, 53–74.

SROLE, L., T. S. LANGNER, S. T. MICHAEL, M. K. OPLER, and T. A. C. RENNIE. *The Midtown Manhattan Study: Mental health in the metropolis*, Vol. 1. New York: McGraw-Hill, 1962.

STAMLER, J., M. KJELSBERG, and Y. HALL. Epidemiologic studies on cardiovascular-renal disease: I. Analysis of mortality by age-race-sex-occupation. *Journal of Chronic Diseases*, 1960, *12*, 440–542.

STAMPFL, T. G. Implosive therapy: A learning-theory derived psychodynamic therapeutic technique. Paper presented at a colloquium of the University of Illinois, 1961.

STAMPFL, T. G., and D. J. LEVIS. Implosive therapy—A behavioral therapy? *Behavior Research and Therapy*, 1968, *6*, 31–36.

STANDAGE, K. F. Schizophreniform psychosis among epileptics in a mental hospital. *British Journal of Psychiatry*, 1973, *123*, 231–232.

STENGEL, E. *Suicide and attempted suicide*. Baltimore, Md.: Penguin, 1964.

STENNETT, R. G. Emotional handicap in the elementary years: Phase or disease. *American Journal of Orthopsychiatry*, 1966, *36*, 444–449.

STENSTEDT, A. A study of manic-depressive psychosis: Clinical, social, and genetic investigations. *Acta Scandinavica Supplementum*, 1952, *79*.

STEVENSON, I., and J. WOLPE. Recovery from sexual deviations through overcoming non-sexual neurotic responses. *American Journal of Psychiatry*, 1960, *116*, 737–742.

STRAUSS, M. E., W. C. FOUREMAN, and S. D. PARWATIKAR. Schizophrenics' size estimations of thematic stimuli. *Journal of Abnormal Psychology*, 1974, *83*(2), 117–123.

STRICKLAND, B. R. Locus control and health-related behaviors. Paper presented at XV IntraAmerican Congress, Bogotá, Colombia, 1974.

STUART, R. B. Behavioral control of overeating. *Behavior Research and Therapy*, 1967, *5*, 357–365.

STUART, R. B. Operant-interpersonal treatment for marital discord. *Journal of Consulting and Clinical Psychology*, 1969, *33*, 675–682.

STUART, R. B. *Trick or treatment*. Champaign, Ill.: Research Press, 1970.

STUART, R. B. Behavioral contracting within the families of delinquents. *Journal of Behavior Therapy and Experimental Psychiatry*, 1971, *2*, 1–11.

STUDENT ASSOCIATION FOR THE STUDY OF HALLUCINOGENS, INC., PHENCYCLIDINE (PCP). *Stash Capsules*, 1973, *5*(2), 1–4.

SULLIVAN, H. S. *The interpersonal theory of psychiatry*. H. S. Perry and M. L. Gawel, eds. New York: Norton, 1953.

SULLIVAN, H. S. *Clinical studies in psychiatry*. New York: Norton, 1956.

SUSHINSKY, L. An illustration of a behavioral therapy intervention with nursing staff in a therapeutic role. *Journal of Psychiatric Nursing and Mental Health Services*, 1970, *8*(5), 24–26.

SUTHERLAND, E. H. *White collar crime*. New York: Dryden, 1949.

SUTHERLAND, E. H., and D. R.

CRESSEY. *Criminology*, 8th ed. Philadelphia, Pa.: Lippincott, 1970.

SZASZ, T. S. *The myth of mental illness*. New York: Harper & Row, 1961.

SZASZ, T. S. *Law, liberty, and psychiatry*. New York: Macmillan, 1963.

SZASZ, T. S. *The manufacture of madness*. New York: Harper & Row, 1970.

TAPIA, F., J. JEKEL, and H. DOMKE. Eneuresis: An emotional symptom? *Journal of Nervous and Mental Disease*, 1960, *130*, 61–66.

TARTER, R. E. Intellectual and adaptive functioning in epilepsy. *Diseases of the Nervous System*, 1972, *33*, 763–770.

TAUB, H. A., and M. K. LONG. The effects of practice on short-term memory of young and old subjects. *Journal of Gerontology*, 1972, *27*, 494–499.

TAUBE, C. A., and R. REDICK. *Utilization of mental health resources by persons diagnosed with schizophrenia*. DHEW Publication No. (HSM) 73-9110. Rockville, Md.: National Institute of Mental Health, 1973.

THIGPEN, C. H., and H. CLECKLEY. *The three faces of Eve*. New York: McGraw-Hill, 1957.

THOMAS, A., H. G. BIRCH, S. CHESS, M. E. HERTZIG, and S. KORN. *Behavior individuality in early childhood*. New York: New York University Press, 1963.

THOMSON, N., D. FRASER, and A. MCDOUGALL. The reinstatement of speech in near-mute chronic schizophrenics by instructions, imitative prompts and reinforcement. *Journal of Behavior Therapy and Experimental Psychiatry*, 1974, *5*, 83–89.

THORNE, F. C. The etiology of sociopathic reactions. *American Journal of Psychotherapy*, 1959, *13*, 319–330.

TINKLENBERG, J. R. A clinical view of the amphetamines. *American Family Physician*, 1971a, *4*(5), 82–86.

TINKLENBERG, J. R. Marihuana and crime (a consultant's report prepared for the National Commission on Marihuana and Drug Abuse), October 1971b.

TINKLENBERG, J. R. What a physician should know about marihuana.

Rational Drug Therapy (American Society for Pharmacology and Experimental Therapeutics), in press.

TINKLENBERG, J. R., and K. M. WOODROW. Drug use among youthful assaultive and sexual offenders. *The Association for Research in Nervous and Mental Disease: Aggression*, 1974, *52*, 209–224.

TIZARD, B. The personality of epileptics: A discussion of the evidence. *Psychological Bulletin*, 1962, *59*, 196–210.

TOBACCO: BASIC ANALYSIS. *Standard and Poor's Industry Surveys*, May 22, 1975, Section 2, pp. 105–120.

TORREY, E. F. Is schizophrenia universal? An open question. *Schizophrenia Bulletin*, 1973, *7*, 53–59.

TROTTER, S. Patuxent: "Therapeutic" prison faces test. *APA Monitor*, 1975, *6*(5), 1, 4, 12.

TRUAX, C. B. Reinforcement and nonreinforcement in Rogerian psychotherapy. *Journal of Abnormal Psychology*, 1966, *71*, 1–9.

TRUE, J. E., and C. E. YOUNG. Associate degree programs for human services workers. *Personnel and Guidance Journal*, 1974, *53*, 304–307.

TULKIN, S. R., and J. KAGAN. Mother-child interaction in the first year of life. *Child Development*, 1972, *43*, 31–41.

TURNER, W. J., and S. MERLIS. Clinical correlations between electroencephalography and antisocial behavior. *Medical Times*, 1962, *90*, 505–511.

U.S. DEPARTMENT OF HEALTH, EDUCATION, AND WELFARE. *Prevalence of selected chronic digestive conditions: United States, 1968*. Vital and Health Statistics, Series 10, No. 83, 1968.

U.S. DEPARTMENT OF HEALTH, EDUCATION, AND WELFARE. *Prevalence of selected chronic respiratory conditions*. Vital and Health Statistics, Series 10, No. 84, 1970.

U.S. DEPARTMENT OF HEALTH, EDUCATION, AND WELFARE. *Alcohol and health: Second special report to the U.S. Congress* (preprint edition). Washington, D.C.: U.S. Government Printing Office, 1974.

U.S. DEPARTMENT OF HEALTH, EDUCATION, AND WELFARE. *If you must smoke . . .* DHEW Publication No. (CDC) 75-8706. Washington, D.C.: U.S. Government Printing Office, 1974.

U.S. PUBLIC HEALTH SERVICE. *Smoking and health*, Report of the Advisory Committee to the Surgeon General of the Public Health Service. Washington, D.C.: Department of Health, Education, and Welfare, 1964.

U.S. PUBLIC HEALTH SERVICE. *XYY chromosome abnormality*. Publication No. 2103. Washington, D.C.: Government Printing Office, 1970.

VAN LOON, H. G. Protopathic instinctive phenomena in normal and pathologic Malay life. *British Journal of Medical Psychology*, 1928, *8*, 264–276.

VISCOTT, D. S. A musical idiot savant. *Psychiatry*, 1970, *33*(4), 494–515.

VOLPE, A., and R. KASTENBAUM. TLC. *American Journal of Nursing*, 1967, *67*, 100–103.

VONNEGUT, M. *The Eden Express*. New York: Praeger, 1975.

WAGGONER, R. W., and B. K. BAGCHI. Initial masking of organic brain changes by psychic symptoms. *American Journal of Psychiatry*, 1954, *110*, 904–910.

WALTER, W. G., V. J. ALDRIDGE, R. COOPER, G. O'GORMAN, C. MCCALLUM, and A. L. WINTER. Neurophysiological correlates of apparent defects of sensori-motor integration in autistic children. In D. W. Churchill, G. D. Alpern, and M. K. DeMyer, eds., *Infantile autism*. Springfield, Ill.: Charles C Thomas, 1971.

WALTON, D., and M. D. MATHER. The application of learning principles to the treatment of obsessive-compulsive states in the acute and chronic phases of illness. In H. J. Eysenck, ed., *Experiments in behavior therapy*. New York: Pergamon Press, 1964.

WATSON, J. B. Psychology as the behaviorist views it. *Psychological Review*, 1913, *20*, 158–177.

WATSON, J. B., and R. RAYNER. Conditioning emotional responses. *Journal of Experimental Psychology*, 1920, *3*, 1–14.

WECHSLER, D. *The measurement and appraisal of adult intelligence*, 4th ed. Baltimore, Md.: Williams and Wilkins, 1958.

WEISSMAN, M. M., and E. S. PAYKEL. *The depressed woman: A study of social relationships.* Chicago: University of Chicago Press, 1974.

WENAR, G., M. W. HANDLON, and A. M. GARNER. *Origins of psychosomatic and emotional disturbances: A study of mother-child relationships.* New York: Harper & Row, 1962.

WENDER, P. *Minimal brain dysfunction in children.* New York: Wiley-Interscience, 1971.

WERRY, J. S. Developmental hyperactivity. *Pediatric Clinics in North America*, 1968a, *15*, 581–599.

WERRY, J. S. Studies of the hyperactive child: IV. An empirical analysis of the minimal brain dysfunction syndrome. *Archives of General Psychiatry*, 1968b, *19*, 9–16.

WESSMAN, A., and D. F. RICKS. *Mood and personality.* New York: Holt, Rinehart and Winston, 1966.

WESSON, D. R., and D. E. SMITH. Barbiturate use as an intoxicant: A San Francisco perspective. Testimony to be presented to the subcommittee to investigate juvenile delinquency. December 15, 1971.

WHITE COLLAR CRIME: HUGE ECONOMIC AND MORAL DRAIN. *Congressional Quarterly*, May 7, 1971.

WHITE, R. W., and N. F. WATT. *The abnormal personality.* New York: The Ronald Press, 1973.

WHITMAN, T. L., V. CALONIGI, and J. MERCURIO. Reducing hyperactive behavior in a severely retarded child. *Mental Retardation*, 1971, *9*, 17–19.

WHYBROW, P. C., and J. MENDELS. Toward a biology of depression: Some suggestions from neurophysiology. *American Journal of Psychiatry*, 1969, *125*, 1491–1500.

WIELAND, I. H. Discussion of treatment approaches. In D. W. Churchill, G. D. Alpern, and M. K. DeMyer, eds., *Infantile autism.* Springfield, Ill.: Charles C Thomas, 1971.

WILLIAMS, E. An analysis of gaze in schizophrenics. *British Journal of Social and Clinical Psychology*, 1974, *13*, 1–8.

WILLIAMS, J. E. Management of the bereavement crisis. In G. A. Specter and W. L. Claiborn, eds., *Crisis intervention.* New York: Behavioral Publications, 1973.

WILLIAMS, R. L. Danger: Testing and dehumanizing black children. *Clinical Child Psychology Newsletter*, Spring 1970.

WILSON, G. T., and G. C. DAVISON. Behavior therapy and homosexuality: A critical perspective. *Behavior Therapy*, 1974, *5*, 16–28.

WING, L. The handicaps of autistic children: A comparative study. *Journal of Child Psychology and Psychiatry*, 1969, *10*, 1–40.

WING, L. *Autistic children: A guide for parents and professionals.* New York: Brunner/Mazel, 1972.

WITZIG, J. S. The group treatment of male exhibitionists. *American Journal of Psychiatry*, 1968, *25*, 75–81.

WOLF, M.M., T. RISLEY, and M. L. MEES. Application of operant conditioning procedures to the behavior problems of an autistic child. *Behavior Research and Therapy*, 1964, *1*, 305–313.

WOLF, S., and H. G. WOLFF. *Human gastric functions.* New York: Oxford University Press, 1947.

WOLLERSHEIM, J. P. Effectiveness of group therapy based on learning principles in the treatment of overweight women. *Journal of Abnormal Psychology*, 1970, *76*, 462–474.

WOLPE, J. *Psychotherapy by reciprocal inhibition.* Stanford, Calif.: Stanford University Press, 1958.

WOLPE, J. *The practice of behavior therapy.* New York: Pergamon Press, 1969.

WOLPE, J., and A. A. LAZARUS. *Behavior therapy techniques.* New York: Pergamon Press, 1966.

WOOD, H., and E. DUFFY. Psychological factors in alcoholic women. *American Journal of Psychiatry*, 1966, *123*(3), 341–345.

WOODWARD, K. L. The exorcism frenzy. *Newsweek*, February 11, 1974, pp. 60–66.

WRIGHT, H. T., JR. Prenatal factors in causation (viral). In R. Koch and J. C. Dobson, eds., *The mentally retarded child and his family.* New York: Brunner/Mazel, 1971.

YALOM, I. D., and M. A. LIEBERMAN. A study of encounter group casualties. *Archives of General Psychology*, 1971, *25*, 16–30.

YARNELL, P. R., and J. STEARS. Intracerebral hemorrhage and occult sepsis. *Neurology*, 1974, *24*, 870–873.

YESSLER, P. G., J. J. GIBBS, and H. A. BECKER. On the communication of suicidal ideas. *Archives of General Psychiatry*, 1961, *5*, 12–29.

ZASLOW, R. W., and L. BREGER. A theory and treatment of autism. In L. Breger, ed., *Clinical cognitive psychology.* Englewood Cliffs, N.J.: Prentice-Hall, 1969.

ZAX, M., and G. STRICKER. *Patterns of psychopathology: Case studies in behavioral dysfunction.* New York and London: Macmillan, 1963.

ZIGLER, E., and J. LEVINE. Premorbid adjustment and paranoid-nonparanoid status in schizophrenia: A further investigation. *Journal of Abnormal Psychology*, 1973, *82*(2), 189–199.

ZIGLER, E., and L. PHILLIPS. Psychiatric diagnosis and symptomatology. *Journal of Abnormal and Social Psychology*, 1961, *63*, 69–75.

ZILBOORG, G. *The medical man and the witch during the Renaissance.* New York: Cooper Square, 1935.

ZILBOORG, G., and G. W. HENRY. *A history of medical psychology.* New York: Norton, 1941.

on sexual inadequacy, 214–216
on suicide, 182
Behavior modification, 70–71, 201, 484–496. *See also* Behaviorism; Behaviorist perspective
and childhood psychosis, 342–343
operant conditioning, 488–492
pros and cons, 492–496
respondent conditioning and extinction, 485–488
social learning, 492
Belongingness needs, 83
Bender Visual-Motor Gestalt Test, 470
Beriberi, 371
Biochemical approach to schizophrenia, 325
Biochemical research on affective disorders, 175–177
Biofeedback, 151
Biogenic theory, vs. psychogenic, 18–21
Biological needs, 83
Biological perspective, 99–100
on affective disorders, 174–175
on alcoholism, 249
on childhood psychosis, 347–349
on dyssocial behavior, 204–205
on homosexuality, 232–233
on neuroses, 125–128
on psychophysiological disorders, 156
on schizophrenia, 321–326
Biological treatment
drugs, 504–505
electroconvulsive therapy, 506–507
pros and cons, 508
psychosurgery, 505–506
Blood alcohol level, 239
Borderline mental retardation, 380
Brain disorder. *See* Organic brain disorder
Brain trauma, 361, 363
Brain tumor, 366
Brainwashing, 118
Brain-waves and antisocial behavior, 205
Bromide psychosis, 375
Bromide schizophrenia, 375
Bulimia, 409

California F Scale, 469
Cannabis, 264
Carbon monoxide poisoning, 375
Castration anxiety, 40
Catalogic thinking and suicide, 179
Catastrophe, civilian, 119–120
Catastrophic reaction, 364
Catatonic schizophrenia, 295–296
Catatonic stupor, 289, 296
Catchment area, 513
Cathexis, 308
Cattell Scale, 383n
Cerebral arteriosclerosis, 370–371
Cerebral hemorrhage, 365
Cerebral evoked voltage (CEV), 349
Cerebral thrombosis, 364–365
Cerebrovascular accident, 364
Chemotherapy and schizophrenia, 326
Childhood developmental disorders
behaviorist perspective on, 421–424

classification systems, 405, 408
conduct disturbances, 417–420
habit disturbances, 409–413
humanistic-existential perspective on, 424
incidence, 404
interpersonal perspective on, 424–425
long-term consequences, 408–409
neurotic disturbances, 414–417
and normal vs. abnormal, 405
physiological perspective on, 426
psychodynamic perspective on, 420–421
Childhood psychosis
behaviorist perspective on, 342–344
biological perspective on, 347–349
classification, 330–333
defined, 329–330
cognitive perspective on, 346–347
humanistic-existential perspective on, 344–345
interpersonal perspective on, 345–346
psychodynamic perspective on, 337–342
Childhood schizophrenia, 336–337
vs. early infantile autism, 332–333
Children. *See* Childhood developmental disorders; Childhood psychosis
Children's Apperception Test (CAT), 464
Choreiform movement, 368
Chromosomal anomalies and mental retardation, 385
Chronic enuresis, 410
Clang association, 278
Classical conditioning. *See* Respondent conditioning
Classification and assessment, 454–455
Client-centered therapy, 82, 125, 496, 498
Clonic phase, grand mal, 377
Cocaine, 255
Coconscious personality, 111
Cognitive change and depression, 169–171
Cognitive perspective
on abnormal behavior, 95–97
on affective disorders, 174
on childhood psychosis, 344–345
Cognitive restructuring, 492
Coitus, 209
Collective unconscious, 44
Coma, epileptic, 377
Combat, 117–118
Community, mental retardation impact on, 390–393
Community mental health center, 513–515
Community Mental Health Centers Act (1963), 513
Compulsion, 112–113
Conceptualization and schizophrenia, 280–281
Concurrent validity, 457
Concussion, 361
Conditioned reflex, 56
Conditions of worth, 82
Conditioned reinforcer, 63
Conditioned response, 61

Conditioned stimulus, 61
Conduct disturbances, childhood, 417–420
Confabulation, 371
Congenital infections and mental retardation, 386
Congenital syphilis, 360
Conscience and superego, 33
Consciousness, levels of, 34
Consequenceless learning, 199
Consultation, community mental health center, 514–515
Contaminated thinking and suicide, 179
Contingency contracting, 492
Continuity hypothesis of depression, 165
Control
of behavior, 57
delusions of, 283–284
Control group, 305
Contusion of brain, 361
Conversion reaction, 108–110
Convert sensitization, 488
Countertransference, 482n
Creative values, 85
Cretinism, 372, 387
Crime
addiction related, 266, 268
juvenile delinquency, 195–196
organized, 196–197
white-collar, 197–198
scope of, 195
Criminal behavior. *See* Dyssocial behavior
Crisis intervention, mental health, 515–516
Crystallized intelligence, 432
Cultural deprivation, 388
Cultural model of abnormal behavior, 27
Cunnilingus, 229
Cushing's syndrome, 372

Day hospital, 514
Death instinct, 32
Debility and attitude change, 118
Defense mechanisms, 35
Degenerative brain disorders, 366–371
Delinquency, juvenile 195–196
Delinquent reaction, group, 419–420
Delirium, occupational vs. traumatic, 361
Delirium tremens, 243
Delusions, 160
and schizophrenia, 281–284
Dementia praecox, 275
Demonology
ancient, 5–6
Middle Ages, 8–13
Denial, 36
Dependency and attitude change, 118
Depressants, 250–255
Depression, 164–171
and aging, 446–447
and hopelessness, 96
overview, 159–161
Depressive neurosis, 161
Deprivation, cultural vs. environmental, 388–390
Dereflection, 498–499

Desensitization, systematic, 124, 269, 485–486
Determinism, 31
Detoxification, 249
Development and learning, 67–71
Deviance
defined, 4, 511
explanation of, 4
handling of, 4–5
Deviant label and abnormal behavior, 93
Diasthesis-stress theory, 99, 323, 348
Differential-association theory of crime, 204
Dildo, 229
Disaster syndrome, 119
Discrimination, 61
proprioceptive, 285
Dissociative reaction, 110
Disturbance, transient situational, 117–120
Donaldson v. *O'Connor*, 522
Double-bind communication, 319–320
Down's syndrome, 99, 384, 385
Draw-A-Person Test (DAP), 464
Dread and attitude change, 118–119
Dream interpretation, 121, 479–480
Drugs
in biological treatment, 504–505
dependence on, 236
depressants, 250–255
hallucinogens, 257, 259
marijuana and hashish, 259, 264–265
and mental retardation, 386
and organic brain disorders, 375
and personality, 266
psychoactive, 235
rehabilitation of addicts, 268–269
and society, 266–268
stimulants, 255–257
Durham v. *United States*, 206
Dysmenorrhea, 143, 146
Dyspareunia, 211
Dyssocial behavior, 193–195
behaviorist perspective on, 199–201
biological perspective on, 204–205
juvenile delinquency, 195–196
organized crime, 196–197
psychosocial perspective on, 204
and scope of crime, 195
white-collar crime, 197–198

Echolalia, 333
Economo's disease, 358
Eczema, 143
Education for mentally retarded, 393, 396–398
Effect, law of, 57
Ego, 32–33
Ego analysis, 483
Ego identity, 45
Egoistic suicide, 182
Ego psychology, 45
Ejaculation, premature, 211
Ejaculatory incompetence, 211
Electroconvulsive therapy, 506–507
Electroencephalogram, 205
Electromyograph, 472

Emergency services, community mental health center, 514
Emotional changes, depression, 165
Emotive imagery, 422, 486
Employment of mentally retarded, 393–394
Empty nest syndrome, 162
Encephalitis, 358
Encephalopathy, lead, 374
Encopresis, 411
Encounter groups, 501–502
Endocrine disorders, 371–372
Endocrine glands, 371
Enuresis, 410–411
Environment, and schizophrenia, 322–323
Environmental deprivation, 388–390
Environmental planning, 71–72
Epidemic encephalitis, 358
Epigastric aura, 376
Epilepsy, 375–376
Escape and avoidance, 64
Esteem needs, 83
Everything You Always Wanted to Know About Sex . . . But Were Afraid to Ask (Reuben), 211
Exhibitionism, 216, 219
Existentialism vs. humanism, 86
Existential perspective. *See* Humanistic-existential perspective
Existential psychology, 83–86
Existential therapy, 498–499
Exorcism, 6
and demonology, 8–10
Experiential values, 85
Experimental group, 305
Extinction, 64, 124
and respondent conditioning, 485–488

Factor analysis, 406
Family
and antisocial behavior, 202–203
and mental retardation, 388, 390–393
and psychophysiological disorders, 154, 156
and schizophrenia, 317–319
schizophrenogenic mother, 320
Family therapy, 45, 500–501
Fatigue syndrome, 113
Fears
childhood, 415–416
hierarchy of, 485
Fear Survey Schedule II, 469
Feeding disturbances, childhood, 409–410
Fetishism, 216, 217–218
The Fifty-Minute Hour (Lindner), 483
Fixation, 36
Fixed interval schedule, 65, 67
Fixed ratio schedule, 67
Flagellants, 8
Fluid intelligence, 432
Formication, 257
Free association, 21, 121, 479
Freedom and responsibility, 81
Freudian theory. *See* Psychodynamic theory
Frustration, existential, 86
Fugue, 111
Functional analysis, 474

Function lack, and aging, 435–438

Games People Play (Berne), 501
Gaze avoidance, schizophrenic, 289
Generalization, 61
Genetics
and behavior, 99–100
and childhood psychosis, 347–348
and schizophrenia, 321–325
Genital stage of psychosexual development, 40
Gestalt therapy, 499–500
Glove anesthesia, 20, 109
Grandeur, delusions of, 283
Grand mal, 376–377
Graves' disease, 372
Group delinquent reaction, 419–420
Group therapy, 45, 88–89, 500–504
Guilt and sin, delusions of, 284

Habit disturbances, childhood, 409–413
Habituation, 140
Halfway house, mental health, 515
Hallucinations, 160, 285–287
Hallucinogens, 257, 259
Halstead-Reitan Neuropsychological Battery, 470
Hashish, 259, 264–265
Heavy-metal toxins, 374–375
Hebephrenic schizophrenia, 293–295
Helplessness, learned, 173
Helplessness-hopelessness syndrome, 169
Hemiplegia, 365
Heroin, 252, 253
Hierarchy
of fears, 485
of needs, 83
Homosexuality
behaviorist perspective on, 231–232
biological perspective on, 232–233
humanistic-existential perspective on, 232
incidence of, 228–229
vs. lesbianism, 230–231
myths and realities, 229
psychodynamic perspective on, 231
Hopelessness and depression, 96
Hot line, mental health, 515–516
Human interaction, 483
Humanism vs. existentialism, 86
Humanistic-existential approach to assessment, 474–475
Humanistic-existential perspective, 79–80
on affective disorders, 173–174
on alcoholism, 248
on antisocial behavior, 201
assumptions, 80–81
vs. behaviorist perspective, 89
on childhood developmental disorders, 424
on childhood psychosis, 344–345
evaluating, 89–91
on homosexuality, 232
impact of, 88–89
on neurosis, 124–125
vs. psychodynamic perspective, 89
on psychophysiological disorders, 152